INTERNATIONAL TRADE AND BUSINESS:
LAW, POLICY AND ETHICS

Cavendish
Publishing
(Australia)
Pty Limited

Sydney • London

INTERNATIONAL TRADE AND BUSINESS: LAW, POLICY AND ETHICS

Professor Peter Gillies, MA, LLB, PhD
Landerer Professor of Business Law
School of Economics and Financial Studies
Macquarie University

Professor Gabriël Moens, JD, LLM, PhD
Professor of Law and Director
Australian Institute of Foreign and Comparative Law
TC Beirne School of Law
The University of Queensland

Cavendish
Publishing
(Australia)
Pty Limited

Sydney • London

First published in 1998 by Cavendish Publishing (Australia) Pty Limited,
43 Albert Road, Avalon, Sydney, New South Wales 2107

Telephone: (02) 9918 2199   Facsimile: (02) 9973 1223

Email: info@cavendish.aust.com

URL: http://www.cavendishpublishing.com

Australia Cataloguing in Publication Data

Gilles, Peter
International Trade and Business: Law, Policy and Ethics
1. Foreign trade regulation 2. International business enterprises – Law and legislation
I. Moens, Gabriel, 1948 II. Gilles, Peter, 1938
341.75

ISBN 1 876213 25 6

Printed and bound in Great Britain

CONTRIBUTORS

Chapter 1: The United Nations Convention on Contracts for the International Sale of Goods (**Professor Peter Gillies**)

Chapter 2: The UNIDROIT Principles of International Commercial Contracts (**Mr Julian David Wagner** with the assistance of **Professor Gabriël A Moens**)

Chapter 3: International Commercial Trade Terms – Incoterms 1990 (**Professor Peter Gillies**)

Chapter 4: Carriage of Goods by Sea (**Mr Howard Broderick**)

Chapter 5: Carriage of Goods by Land and Air (**Mr John Livermore**)

Chapter 6: Financing Exports: Letters of Credit (**Professor Gabriël A Moens** and **Mr Ted Tzovaras**)

Chapter 7: The General Agreement on Tariffs and Trade (GATT) and the World Trade Organisation (WTO) (**Mr Alexander Low**)

Chapter 8: Anti-dumping and Countervailing Laws in the United States, Australia and New Zealand (**Mr ANG Smith**)

Chapter 9: Trading Blocs: NAFTA (**Mr Simon Fisher**)

Chapter 10: Trading Blocs: the European Union (**Professor Gabriël A Moens**)

Chapter 11: International Commercial Arbitration (**Dr Suri Ratnapala** and **Ms Linda Haller**)

Chapter 12: Extraterritorial Control of Business (**Mr Alexander Bates**)

PREFACE

This book deals with the core topics of international trade, which include international sales contracts, international commercial terms, carriage of goods by sea, land and air, financing of exports, regulation of imports, international commercial arbitration, extraterritorial control of business, and trading blocs.

Every chapter offers a description and analysis of the relevant law, policies and, in some cases, relevant ethical issues, tutorial questions, and a short list of references. In addition, the most important international documents are reproduced in full or in part to facilitate the study of international commercial law.

International trade and business law courses are increasingly offered by most law and business schools. This increase is a response to repeated requests, by the legal and business communities, to provide courses for lawyers and business people to enable them to provide expert advice on international business practices and export trade law. In particular, *International Trade and Business: Law, Policy and Ethics* is aimed at students and practitioners, who are interested in international business transactions and want to gain familiarity with the law and practice of international trade law, policies and ethics. It is also hoped that this book will be used by academics as their teaching and research tool in international trade and business law courses. However, the book is not limited to law since it also aims to cover trade and business policies. In addition, the book also deals with relevant ethical issues.

We would like to thank the contributors to this volume. Without their dedication and commitment this book would not have been completed. The editorial process was greatly facilitated by the excellent work of Cavendish Publishing, London who ensured that the book met the highest editorial standards. The editors and contributors are also indebted to Jo Reddy, Managing Editor at Cavendish Publishing, London who decided to publish this book and provided us with moral support throughout this project.

Professor Peter Gillies
Professor Gabriël A Moens
March 1998

CONTENTS

Contributors   *v*

Preface   *vii*

Table of Cases   *xxi*

Table of Legislation   *xxxv*

**1   THE UN CONVENTION ON CONTRACTS
     FOR THE INTERNATIONAL SALE OF GOODS**   1
    INTRODUCTION   1
    SPHERE OF APPLICATION OF THE CONVENTION   3
        Overview   3
        The international element   3
        Goods – exclusions   7
        Aspects of the contract covered by the Convention – exclusions   8
        Convention does not apply to liability for death or personal injury   10
        Exclusion of the Convention by the parties   10
    GENERAL PROVISIONS OF THE CONVENTION   11
        Interpretation   11
        Determining intent and related matters   12
        Usages   13
        Requirement of writing; other requirements of form   13
    FORMATION OF THE CONTRACT   14
        Offer and acceptance   14
        Consideration   17
        Intention to create legal relations   18
    SALE OF GOODS   18
        General provisions   18
        Obligations of the seller   20
        Conformity of the goods and third party claims   22
        Remedies for breach of contract by the seller   24
        Obligations of the buyer   28
        Remedies for breach of contract by buyer   29
        Passing of risk   31
        Provisions common to the obligations of buyer and seller   33
    TUTORIAL QUESTIONS   41
    FURTHER READING   44
    UNITED NATIONS CONVENTION ON
        CONTRACTS FOR THE INTERNATIONAL SALE
        OF GOODS (VIENNA SALES CONVENTION)
        VIENNA – 11 APRIL 1980   46

United Nations Convention on Contracts for the
International Sale of Goods (Vienna, 1980)   47
Declarations and reservations   48
United Nations Convention on Contracts for the
International Sale of Goods (Vienna Sales Convention)   49
CONVENTION ON THE LAW APPLICABLE
TO CONTRACTS FOR THE INTERNATIONAL
SALE OF GOODS, THE HAGUE –
22 DECEMBER 1986   70
Convention on the Law Applicable to Contracts for the
International Sale of Goods   71

2   **THE UNIDROIT PRINCIPLES OF
INTERNATIONAL COMMERCIAL CONTRACTS**   79
INTRODUCTION   79
THE UNIDROIT PRINCIPLES   80
Overview   80
THE UNIDROIT PRINCIPLES AND CONTRACT LAW   82
PRE-CONTRACTUAL NEGOTIATIONS   84
FORMATION   85
VALIDITY   87
INTERPRETATION   88
CONTENT   89
PERFORMANCE   89
HARDSHIP AND *FORCE MAJEURE*   91
Hardship   91
Force majeure   92
NON-PERFORMANCE   93
REMEDIES   94
Right to performance   94
Termination and restitution   95
Damages   95
CONCLUSION   97
TUTORIAL QUESTIONS   98
FURTHER READING   99
UNIDROIT PRINCIPLES OF INTERNATIONAL
COMMERCIAL CONTRACTS, ROME, 1994   100
Introduction of the Governing Council of UNIDROIT,
Rome, 1994   100

UNIDROIT PRINCIPLES OF INTERNATIONAL
COMMERCIAL CONTRACTS   100
    Preamble – purpose of the principles   100

**3 INTERNATIONAL COMMERCIAL TRADE TERMS
– INCOTERMS 1990**   121
OVERVIEW   121
SOME PRELIMINARY MATTERS   122
    Incoterms – their functions   122
    Legal status of the Incoterms   123
    Incorporation of Incoterms   123
    Transport developments impacting upon Incoterms   123
    Use of intermediaries and related matters   124
    Electronic data transmission   124
THE INCOTERM CATEGORIES, STRUCTURE
OF EACH INCOTERM   126
THE E CATEGORY – 'EX–WORKS'   128
THE F CATEGORY – FCA, FAS, FOB   130
    Free carrier (FCA)   130
    Free alongside ship (FAS)   132
    Free on board (FOB)   134
THE C CATEGORY – CFR, CIF, CPT, CIP   137
    Cost and freight (CFR)/cost, insurance and freight (CIF)   137
    Cost and freight (CFR)   142
    Carriage paid to (CPT)/carriage and insurance paid to (CIP) 142
    Carriage and insurance paid to (CIP)   144
THE D CATEGORY – DAF, DES, DEQ, DDU, DDP   145
    Delivered at frontier (DAF)   145
    Delivered ex-ship (DES)   146
    Delivered ex-quay (duty paid) (DEQ)   148
    Delivery duty unpaid (DDU)   150
    Delivered duty paid (DDP)   151
TUTORIAL QUESTIONS   152
FURTHER READING   154
INCOTERMS 1990   155
    Ex-works (ExW)   155
    Free alongside ship (FAS)   157
    Free on board (FOB)   160
    Cost, insurance and freight (CIF)   162
    Carriage and insurance paid to (CIP)   164

Delivered at frontier (DAF)   167
Delivered duty unpaid (DDU)   170

4 CARRIAGE OF GOODS BY SEA   175
INTRODUCTION   175
COMPARISON OF HAGUE RULES, AMENDED
  HAGUE RULES AND HAMBURG RULES   179
    The *Vita Food* gap   181
    Application of rules   182
    Application of rules to third parties   184
    Non-contractual liability of the carrier   185
    Deck cargo   186
    Live animals   187
    Nautical fault and negligent management   188
    Fire   189
    When does carriage begin and end?   190
    Delay   191
    Time bars   193
    The package or unit definition   193
    Jurisdiction/arbitration   195
    Liability under the Hague and the Hamburg rules   196
    Limitation of liability   198
    Compatibility   200
ARGUMENTS AGAINST THE INTRODUCTION
  OF THE HAMBURG RULES   201
    The *status quo* argument   201
    The compatibility argument   202
    The uncertainty argument   204
TUTORIAL QUESTIONS   206
FURTHER READING   207
APPENDIX 1   210
    Details of cargo-carrying regimes of various nations
    (as at 25 March 1994)   210
INTERNATIONAL CONVENTION FOR THE
  UNIFICATION OF CERTAIN RULES OF LAW
  RELATING TO BILLS OF LADING
  (THE HAGUE RULES) BRUSSELS – 25 AUGUST 1924   216
    International Convention for the Unification of Certain
    Rules of Law Relating to Bills of Lading   218
    Protocol of signature   224

ANNEX   225
THE AMENDED HAGUE RULES   229
THE HAMBURG RULES   235

5   CARRIAGE OF GOODS BY LAND AND AIR   249
INTRODUCTION   249
CARRIAGE BY ROAD   250
    Background   250
    Common carriers   250
    Private carriers   251
    Carriage of passengers   255
FEDERAL ROAD TRANSPORT LEGISLATION
    AND REGULATION   257
    Freedom of interstate trade   257
    Trade Practices Act 1974 (Cth) and road transport   257
    Federal regulation of transport   257
    The Interstate Road Transport Act 1985   267
    The National Road Transport Commission   267
    Ministerial Council   268
    The Interstate Commission   268
    Road transport: State and Territory legislation   269
    State and Territory road transport legislation   269
CARRIAGE BY RAIL   284
    Commission's risk rate   287
    Owner's risk rate   288
INTERNATIONAL RAIL AND ROAD CARRIAGE
    CONVENTIONS   292
    International Carriage of Goods by Rail   292
    International Carriage of Goods by Road   295
CARRIAGE BY AIR   298
    Introduction   298
    International carriage, baggage and cargo   302
    Airlines and passenger liability   322
TUTORIAL QUESTIONS   327
FURTHER READING   330
CONVENTION FOR THE UNIFICATION OF
    CERTAIN RULES RELATING TO INTERNATIONAL
    CARRIAGE BY AIR (WARSAW
    CONVENTION) WARSAW, 1929   332

UNIFORM RULES CONCERNING THE
CONTRACT FOR INTERNATIONAL CARRIAGE
OF GOODS BY RAIL (CIM), 1980   339
CARRIAGE OF GOODS BY ROAD ACT 1965 –
SCHEDULE – CONVENTION ON THE CONTRACT
FOR THE INTERNATIONAL CARRIAGE OF
GOODS BY ROAD   371
IATA INTERCARRIER AGREEMENT ON
PASSENGER LIABILITY   384
INTERCARRIER AGREEMENT ON PASSENGER
LIABILITY   384
AGREEMENT ON MEASURES TO IMPLEMENT
THE IATA INTERCARRIER AGREEMENT   385

6 **FINANCING EXPORTS: LETTERS OF CREDIT**   387
   INTRODUCTION   387
   BASIC FORMS AND TYPES
      OF DOCUMENTARY CREDIT   390
      Basic forms of documentary credit   390
      Types of letters of credit   391
   FUNDAMENTAL PRINCIPLES   397
      The doctrine of strict compliance   397
   THE PRINCIPLE OF AUTONOMY OF THE
      LETTER OF CREDIT   409
      The principle   409
      The fraud exception   412
      The *Mareva* injunction   416
   CONCLUSION   417
   TUTORIAL QUESTIONS   418
   FURTHER READING   420
   ICC UNIFORM CUSTOMS AND PRACTICE FOR
      DOCUMENTARY CREDITS   421
      ICC arbitration   442

7 **THE GENERAL AGREEMENT
   ON TARIFFS AND TRADE (GATT) AND
   THE WORLD TRADE ORGANISATION (WTO)**   443
   INTRODUCTION   443
   THE GENERAL AGREEMENT
      ON TARIFFS AND TRADE   444
   THE GATT 1994   445
      The framework of GATT   446

THE LEGAL PRINCIPLES OF THE GATT	447
The most-favoured-nation principle	448
National treatment principle	449
The reciprocity principle	451
The legal framework of dispute settlement	452
Articles XXII and XXIII	452
The dispute settlement roles and procedures 1989	453
The panel system	454
The workings of a panel	455
Panel reports	455
The time lines involved with panels	455
PREFERENTIAL TREATMENT	456
Quantitative restriction: a protection for developing countries	459
The conditions to be observed by an applicant country	461
Protection for an infant industry	463
Part IV of the GATT	465
DUMPING	471
SUBSIDIES	471
THE WORLD TRADE ORGANISATION	473
Introduction	473
Significance of the WTO	474
The General Agreement on Trade in Services (GATS)	475
CONCLUDING COMMENTS	480
TUTORIAL QUESTIONS	480
FURTHER READING	481
AGREEMENT ESTABLISHING THE WORLD TRADE ORGANISATION	484
THE GENERAL AGREEMENT ON TARIFFS AND TRADE	490
UNDERSTANDING ON RULES AND PROCEDURES GOVERNING THE SETTLEMENT OF DISPUTES	544
GENERAL AGREEMENT ON TRADE IN SERVICES	565
8 ANTI-DUMPING AND COUNTERVAILING LAWS IN THE UNITED STATES, AUSTRALIA AND NEW ZEALAND	583
INTRODUCTION	583
DEFINITIONS	583
Anti-dumping	583
Countervailing	584
Prerequisites for imposition of anti-dumping or countervailing duties	584

A BACKGROUND TO THE
CURRENT INTERNATIONAL ANTI-DUMPING
AND COUNTERVAILING AGREEMENTS   585
A BRIEF HISTORY OF NATIONAL ANTI-DUMPING
AND COUNTERVAILING LAWS   585
   United States of America   585
   Australia   586
   New Zealand   586
LOCALISED TRADE AGREEMENTS   587
   The North American Free Trade Association   587
   Australia–New Zealand CER Trade Agreement   587
AUTHORITIES INVOLVED IN THE
ADMINISTRATION OF ANTI-DUMPING
AND COUNTERVAILING MEASURES   588
   United States of America   588
   Australia   589
   New Zealand   590
   Investigation procedures   590
THE GATT 1994 ANTI-DUMPING AGREEMENT   592
THE GATT 1994 AGREEMENT ON SUBSIDIES
AND COUNTERVAILING MEASURES   594
NATIONAL LEGISLATION IMPLEMENTING
THE GATT ANTI-DUMPING AGREEMENT   597
   United States of America   597
   Australia   598
   New Zealand   603
SAFEGUARDS – AS OPPOSED TO DUMPING
AND COUNTERVAILING ACTION   604
   United States of America   605
   Australia   605
   New Zealand   605
THE COURTS AND DUMPING/COUNTERVAILING   605
   United States of America   605
   Australia   607
   New Zealand   608
SUMMARY AND COMMENT   608
APPENDIX – A SUMMARY OF THE GATT 1994
AGREEMENT ON AGRICULTURE   609
TUTORIAL QUESTIONS   610

FURTHER READING — 612
Statutes — 613
ACKNOWLEDGMENTS — 613
AGREEMENT ON IMPLEMENTATION OF
ARTICLE VI OF THE GENERAL AGREEMENT
ON TARIFFS AND TRADE 1994 — 614
AGREEMENT ON SUBSIDIES AND
COUNTERVAILING MEASURES — 634

9 TRADING BLOCS: NAFTA — 669
INTRODUCTION — 669
NATIONAL TREATMENT
AND MARKET ACCESS FOR GOODS — 671
RULES OF ORIGIN — 673
ENERGY AND BASIC PETROCHEMICALS — 675
GOVERNMENT PROCUREMENT — 676
INVESTMENT — 681
CROSS-BORDER TRADE IN SERVICES — 688
TELECOMMUNICATIONS — 690
FINANCIAL SERVICES — 692
INTELLECTUAL PROPERTY — 695
PUBLICATION, NOTIFICATION
AND ADMINISTRATION OF LAWS — 698
INSTITUTIONAL ARRANGEMENTS
AND DISPUTE SETTLEMENT PROCEDURES — 699
EXCEPTIONS — 701
CONCLUSIONS — 702
TUTORIAL QUESTIONS — 702
FURTHER READING — 703

10 TRADING BLOC: THE EUROPEAN UNION — 705
INTRODUCTION — 705
THE THREE EUROPEAN COMMUNITIES
AND THE EUROPEAN UNION — 705
FUNDAMENTAL FREEDOMS OF THE EC TREATY — 706
CITIZENSHIP OF THE UNION — 707
THE COMMUNITY ORGANS — 707
DECLARATION ON APPROXIMATION — 708
ECONOMIC AND POLITICAL UNION — 709

CAPITAL AND PAYMENTS   710
MONETARY POLICY   710
EXCHANGE RATE POLICY   711
COMMUNITY LEGISLATION   711
    Article 189 of the EC Treaty   711
    Regulations   711
    Directives   712
    Decisions   713
    Recommendations and opinions   714
    Difference of nomenclature: EC and ECSC treaties   714
    Freedom of movement of goods   714
    Treaty provisions for the elimination of internal customs duties   715
    Common customs tariff   716
    Free circulation of goods in the Community   716
    Elimination of customs duties and establishment
       of the common customs tariff   716
    Article 30 of the EC Treaty   717
    Article 115 of the EC Treaty   718
    The rule of reason   719
    Rule of reason not an extension of Article 36   720
    The necessity and proportionality principles   721
    Application of the necessity principle   722
    The proposition of the rule of reason   723
    Harmonisation   723
    Mutual acceptance of goods   724
    Technical harmonisation and standards   724
    Directive on product safety   725
  APPENDIX – THE EC'S TREATY STRUCTURE   726
  TUTORIAL QUESTIONS   726
  FURTHER READING   728

11 INTERNATIONAL COMMERCIAL ARBITRATION   729
ARBITRATION AND INTERNATIONAL TRADE   729
TYPES OF ARBITRATION   730
    Arbitration   731
    Commercial arbitration   731
    International commercial arbitration   732
THE STATUTORY FRAMEWORK OF
  INTERNATIONAL COMMERCIAL

ARBITRATION IN AUSTRALIA	732
International arbitration agreements without opt-out clauses	733
International arbitration agreements with opt-out clauses	734
The requirement of written agreement	735
RECOGNITION AND ENFORCEMENT OF INTERNATIONAL ARBITRATION AGREEMENTS	735
Enforcement of agreement under the New York Convention	736
Enforcement of arbitration agreement under the Model Law	738
Null and void, inoperative or incapable of being performed	739
The question of severability	740
The applicable law	741
JUDICIAL REVIEW OF ARBITRAL AWARDS: THE BALANCE BETWEEN FINALITY AND LEGALITY	742
Judicial review under the Model Law – preliminary orders	742
Judicial review under the Model Law – final awards	743
Judicial review under the Commercial Arbitration Act 1984 (NSW)	746
ENFORCEMENT OF INTERNATIONAL ARBITRATION AWARDS	750
TUTORIAL QUESTIONS	752
FURTHER READING	753
UNCITRAL MODEL LAW ON INTERNATIONAL COMMERCIAL ARBITRATION	754
CONVENTION ON THE RECOGNITION AND ENFORCEMENT OF FOREIGN ARBITRAL AWARDS	764
12 EXTRATERRITORIAL CONTROL OF BUSINESS	769
INTRODUCTION	769
COMPETITION LAW OF THE EC	769
US COMPETITION LAW	773
OBJECTIVES OF EC COMPETITION RULES	773
AGREEMENT FOR THE COMPETITION RULES	774
Concerted practices	775
The object of the agreement	775
Effect on trade between Member States	776
The *Wood Pulp* case	776
Abuse of a dominant position	777
Derogation from free movement of goods	780

COMMERCIAL LAW OF THE EC   781
   Anti-dumping and subsidies   782
   Constructed value includes sales costs   785
   Constructed value includes profit   785
   Export price   786
   Calculation of the constructed export price   786
   Differences in exchange rate considered   786
   Dumping margin   787
   Subsidies   787
   Types of subsidy   787
   Injury   788
   Factors of injury   788
   Where dumping and injury have been established 789
   Threat of injury   790
   Community industry   790
   Division of market within the EC   791
   Community interest   791
   The investigation   791
   Termination of the investigation and the proceedings 792
   Undertakings accepted by the Commission   793
   Breach of undertaking   794
   Anti-dumping and countervailing duties   794
   Duty applied prospectively   794
   Definitive duty under Article 12   795
   Provisional duty   795
   Definitive duty   796
   Review of definitive duties   796
   The court in the review process   797
THE US APPLICATION OF ITS LAW   798
CONCLUSION   800
TUTORIAL QUESTIONS   801
FURTHER READING   803

Select Bibliography   805
Index   807

TABLE OF CASES

Abraham and Sons v Commissioner for Railways [1958] SR (NSW) 134 289

Abraham v Bullock (1902) 86 LT 796 251

Adamson v Western Australian Football league (1979) 143 CLR 190 774

AEG v Commission [1983] ECR 3151; [1984] 3 CMLR 325 774

AEG-Telefunken AG v Commission (Case 107/82) [1983] ECR 3151;
    [1984] 3 CMLR 325 775

AG v Mobil Oil New Zealand [1989] 2 NZLR 649 738

Ahlstrom Osakeyhito and Others v Commission (Wood Pulp case) (Cases 89/85,
    104/85, 116/85–117/85, 125/85–129/85) [1993] ECR 1307;
    [1993] 4 CMLR 407 . . . . .775, 776, 800

Airlines of New South Wales Pty Ltd v New South Wales (1964) 113 CLR 1 298

Airlines of New South Wales Pty Ltd v New South Wales (No 2) (1964) 113 CLR 54 299

Alan v El Nasr Import and Export [1972] 2 QB 189 419

Albacora SRL v Westcott and Lawrence Line [1966] 2 Lloyd's Rep 37 . . . . 196, 197

Alder Dickson [1955] 1 QB 158 184

Allied Corporation and Others v Commission [1984] ECR 1005 797

Amazonia, The [1989] 1 Lloyd's Rep 403 742

American Airlines v Ulen [1949] US Av R 338 310

American Banana Co v United Fruit Co 213 US 347 (1909) 798

American Spring Wire Corp v United States 590 F Supp 1273 (1984) 606

Amstelslot, The [1963] 2 Lloyd's Rep 223 196

Amsterdam Bulb BV v Hoofdproduktschap voor Siergewassen
    (Case 50/76) [1977] ECR 137 712

Anders Maersk, The [1986] 1 Lloyd's Rep 483 190

Angus v London, Tilbury and Southend Railway Co (1906) 22 TLR 222 (CA) 256

Anne Marty SA v Estée Lauder SA (Case 37/79) [1980] ECR 2481; [1981] 2 CMLR 143 781

Ansett Transport Industries (Operations) Pty Ltd v Commonwealth and Others
    (1978) 139 CLR 54 300

Antill Ranger and Co Pty Ltd v Commissioner for Motor Vehicle Transport
    (1956) 93 CLR 83 269

Arcweld Constructions Pty Ltd v Smith (1986) unreported
    (Victoria Supreme Court) 251

Aries Tanker Corp v Total Transport Ltd, The Aries [1977] 1 Lloyd's Rep 334 193

Artic Electronics Co (UK) Ltd v Mcgregor Sea and Air Services Ltd
    [1985] 1 Lloyd's Rep 510 297

Atlantic Sun, The [1972] 1 Lloyd's Rep 509 749

Auckland Harbour Board v Comptroller of Customs (1992) 3 NZLR 392 608

Australian National Airways Pty Ltd v The Commonwealth (1945) 71 CLR 39 300

Bamfield v Goole and Sheffield Transport Co [1910] 2 KB 94 265

Banque de l'Indochine et de Suez SA v JH Rayner (Mincing Lane) Ltd [1983] QB 711 . . . . . 404, 406

Barkway v South Wales Transport Co Ltd [1950] AC 185 256

Bart v British West Indian Airways Ltd [1967] 1 Lloyd's Rep 239 . . . . 307, 312

Barwick v English Joint Stock Bank (1867) LR 2 Ex 259 251

Basse and Selve v Bank of Australasia (1904) 90 LT 618 413

Belgische Radio en Televisie and Société Belge des Auteurs, Compositeurs et Editeurs v
    SV SABAM and NV Fonier (Case 127/73) [1974] ECR 51; [1974] 2 CMLR 238 . . . 770, 778, 781

Beswick v Beswick [1968] AC 58 750

BHP v Hapag-Lloyd A/G (1980) 2 NSWLR 572 253

Birtly v Windy Nook (No 2) [1960] 2 QB 1 750

Blackwell v Derby Corp (1911) 75 JP 129 736

Bock v Commission [1971] ECR 897 719

Bolivinter Oil SA v Chase Manhattan Bank NA and Others [1984] 1 WLR 392 . . . . 411, 413

Bonsignore v Oberstadtdirektor der Stadt Köln [1975] ECR 297 713

Boyd v Carah Coaches (1979) 27 ALR 161 257

Bradken Consolidation Ltd v BHP Pth Ltd (1979) 145 CLR 107 288

Bremer Vulkan Schiffbau und Maschinenfabrik v South India Shipping Corp
    [1981] 2 WLR 141 740

Briddon v GN Railway (1853) 28 LJ Ec 51 254

Brilawsky v Robertson and Cannell (1916) 10 QJPR 113 255

British Telecommunications, Re [1983] 1 CMLR 457 776

British Traders Ltd v Ubique Transport Ltd [1952] 2 Lloyd's Rep 236 254

Brookes v London Passenger Transport Board [1947] 1 All ER 506 256

Brooks Wharf and Bull Wharf Ltd v Goodman Bros [1937] 1 KB 934 253

Brother Industries Ltd and Others v Commission [1988] ECR 5655;
    [1990] 1 CMLR 792 . . . . 784, 789, 796

Brown-Boveri (Aust) Pty Ltd v Baltic Shipping Co Ltd (The Nadezhda Krupskaya)
    (1989) 1 NSWLR 448; [1989] 1 Lloyd's Rep 518 . . . . 176, 198

Buchanan (James) & Co Ltd v Babco Forwarding & Shipping (UK) Ltd [1978]
    AC 141 (HL) 294, 295, 297

Bunga Teratsai, The; Nisso Iwai Ltd v Malaysian International Shipping Corp
    (1989) 167 CLR 219 190

Butler Machine Tool Co Ltd v Ex-Cell-O Corporation (England) Ltd [1979] 1 WLR 401 87

Cadillon SA v Hoss Maschinenbau KG (Case 1/71) [1971] ECR 351; [1971] CMLR 420 776

Callimore v Moore (1867) 6 SCR (NSW) 388 255

Canada SS v The King [1952] AC 192 252

Canon Inc v Council [1988] ECR 5731; [1989] 1 CMLR 915 . . . . 785, 786, 789

Cape Asbestos Co v Lloyd's Bank [1921] WN 274 390

Captain Gregos [1990] Lloyd's Rep 310 . . . . 185, 186

Captain v Far East Steamship Co [1979] 1 Lloyd's Rep 595 190

Carlill v Carbolic Smoke Ball Co [1893] 1 QB 256. 15

Carlton United Breweries Ltd v Minister for Customs (C.P25/86) 590

Carrington Steamship v Commonwealth (1921) 29 CLR 596 736

Cashmore v Chief Commissioner for Railways and Tramways (NSW) (1915) 20 CLR 1 256

Cayrol v Giovanni Rivoira e Figli (Case 52/77) [1977] ECR 2261;
    [1978] 2 CMLR 253 719

Centrocoop Export-Import SA v Brit-European Transport Ltd
    [1984] 2 Lloyd's Rep 618 296

Channel Tunnel Group Ltd v Balfour Beatty Construction Ltd [1993] 2 WLR 262 736

Chapman v GW Railway and LNW Railway (1880) 5 QBD 278 253

Chellaram and Co (PS) v China Ocean Shipping Co [1989] 1 Lloyd's Rep 413 . . . . 193, 194

Chemidus Wavin Ltd v Société pour la Transformation et l'Exploitation des
    Résiners Industrielles SA [1987] 2 CMLR 387 770

China Ocean Shipping Co v PS Chellaram and Co (CA 762/88) unreported
    (New South Wales CA) 193

Christian Poucet v Générales de France (Cases 159/91 and 160/91) [1993] ECR I 637 774

Clark v Lelhberg [1969] Tas SR 190 (NC 11). 270

Cockle v Isaksen (1957) 99 CLR 155 741

Codelfa Construction Pty Ltd v State Rail Authority (NSW) (1982) 150
    CLR 29; (1992) 41 ALR 367 . . . . .93, 740

Collins v British Airways [1982] 1 All ER 302 313

Colombera v MacRobertson Miller Airlines Ltd [1972] WAR 68 324

Commercial Banking Co of Sydney Ltd v Jalsard Pty Ltd [1973] AC 279 . . . . 400, 405

Commission v Italian Republic (Case 39/72) [1973] ECR 101 712

Commission v Italy [1968] ECR 423 715

Commissioners for Railways (NSW) v Quinn (1946) 72 CLR 345 289

Commonwealth v Rian Financial Services and Developments Pty Ltd
    (1992) 36 FCR 101 750

Compagnie d'Armement Maritime SA v Compagnie Tunisienne de Navigation SA
    [1971] AC 572 744

Confédération Nationale des Producteurs de Fruits et Légumes v Council
    [1963] CMLR 160 . . . . .712, 713

Consten and Grundig v Commission (Joined Cases 56/64 and 58/64) [1966] ECR 299 776

Continentale Produkten-Gesellschaft Erhard-Renken GmbH und Co v
    Hauptzollamt München-West [1989] ECR 1151; [1991] 1 CMLR 761 . . . . .792, 794

Cöoperative Vereniging 'Suiker Unie' (CSM) v EC Commission (Joined Cases
    40/73–48/73, 50/73, 54/73–56/73, 111/73, 113/73–114/73) [1975]
    ECR 1663; [1976] 1 CMLR 295 777

Courtaulds North American Inc v North Carolina National Bank 528 F 2d 802
  (1975) (4th Circ) 404

Cowper v JG Goldner Pty Ltd (1986) 40 SASR 457. 250

Coxan v Great Western Railway Co (1860) LJ Ex 165. 287

Criel v Procureur de la République at the Tribunal de Grand Instance
  (Case 41/76) [1976] ECR 1921 719

Crows Transport Ltd v Phoenix Assurance Co Ltd [1965] 1 WLR 383 253

Daly v Commissioner of Railways (1906) 8 WALR 125 255

Data Card Corporation v Air Express International Corporation [1983] 2 All ER 639. 313

De Peijper [1976] ECR 613 722

Delco Australia Pty Ltd v Darlington Futures Ltd (1987) 43 SASR 519 252

Dillington Constructions v Downs (1969) 90 WN (Part 1) NSW 258 736

Directive on Animal Semen, Re EC Commission v Ireland (Case C236/91)
  [1993] 1 CMLR 320 713

Discount Records Ltd v Barclays Bank Ltd and another [1975] 1 WLR 315 . . . . 413, 416

Distillation of Table Wine, Re EC Commission v Germany (Case C217/88)
  [1993] ECR 137 712

Drei Glocken GmbH and Another v Unita Sanitaria [1988] ECR 4233; [1990] 1 CEC 540. 722

DST v Raknoc [1987] 2 All ER 769. 742

Dunbee Ltd v Gilmen & Co (Australia) Pty Ltd [1968] 2 Lloyd's Rep 394. 195

East Indian Railway Co v Kalidas Mukerjee [1901] AC 396. 256

Edward Owen Engineering Ltd v Barclays Bank International Ltd [1978] QB 159 . . . . 415, 416

Edwards v Newlands and Co [1952] 2 KB 532 253

EEC Seed Crushers' and Oil Processors' Federation (FEDIOL) v Commission
  [1983] ECR 2913 797

Electric Supply Stores v Gaywood (1909) 100 LT 855 255

Eleftheria, The [1969] 1 Lloyd's Rep 237 . . . . 195, 196

Elizabeth, The [1962] 1 Lloyd's Rep 172 736

EMI Records Ltd v CBS (UK) Ltd (Case 51/75) [1976] ECR 811;
  [1976] 2 CMLR 235 . . . . .717, 771, 776

Enichem Anic Srl v Anti-Dumping Authority (1992) 39 FCR 458 608

Epicheiriseon Metalleftikon Viomichanikon Kai Naftiliakon AE and Others v
  Council [1989] ECR 3919 . . . . .788, 792, 795

Equitable Trust Co of New York v Dawson Partners Ltd [1926] 27 Lloyd's Rep 49 . . . . 397, 405

Esso Australia Resources v Plowman (1995) 183 CLR 10 729

Establissement Esefka International Anstaff v Central Bank of Nigeria
  [1979] 1 Lloyd's Rep 455 416

Etrie Fans Ltd v NMB (UK) Ltd [1987] 2 Lloyd's Rep 565 735

Ets Perony v Ste Ethiopian Airlines (1975) 29 RFDA 395 (CA Paris, 30 May 1975) 312

European Asian Bank AG v Punjab and Sind Bank (No 2) [1983] 1 WLR 642 413

Europemballage Can Co Inc v Commission (Case 6/72) [1973] ECR 215 778

Extraordinary Customs Clearance, Re, EC Commission v Italy (Case 24/68)
    [1969] ECR 193; [1971] CMLR 611 715

Falconbridge Nickel Mines Ltd v Chimo Shipping Ltd [1969] 2 Lloyd's Rep 277 190

Ferris v Plaister (1994) 34 NSWLR 474 (CA) 740

Fire Insurance, Re [1985] 3 CMLR 246 776

Forder v Great Western Railway [1905] 2 KB 532 289

Francis Travel Marketing Pty Ltd v Virgin Atlantic Airways Ltd (1996) 39 NSWLR 160 737

Franco-Japanese Ballbearings Agreement, Re [1975] 1 CMLR D 8 774

Franklin Mint v TWA 525 F Supp 1288 (DC NY 1981); [1984] Lloyd's Rep 432 315

Freistaat Bayern v Eurim-Pharm GmbH [1993] 1 CMLR 616 717

Garnham Harris and Elton Ltd v Alfred E Ellis (Transport) Ltd [1967] 2 All ER 940 253

Gatewhite Ltd v Iberia Lineas Aereas de Espana SA [1989] 1 All ER 944 312

Gee v Metropolitan Railway Co (1873) LR 8 QB 161 256

General Motors Continental BV v Commission (Case 26/75) [1975] ECR 1367 778

Gestetner Holdings plc v Council and Commission [1990] 1 CMLR 820 . . . . 790, 798

Gian Singh and Co Ltd v Banque de l'Indochine [1974] 1 WLR 1234 400

Gibbons v Ogden 22 US (9 Wheat) 1, 7, 6 L Ed 23, 69 (1924) 773

Goldman v Thai Airways International Ltd [1983] 1 WLR 1186 310

Goldsborough v McCulloch (1868) 5 WW and A'B(L) 154 255

Golodetz (M) and Co Inc v Czarnikow-Rionda Co Inc, The Galatia [1980] 1 WLR 495 . . . . 402, 405

Grace Bros Pty Ltd v Rice (1976) 10 ALR 185 257

Grad v Finanzamt Traunstein [1971] CMLR 1 713

Grapham v Paterson (1950) 81 CLR 1 298

Greater Northern Railway v LEP Transport and Depository Ltd [1922] 2 KB 742 251

Greenwich Film Production v Société des Auteurs, Compositeurs et Editeurs de
    Musique (SCAEM) and Société des Editions Labrador (Case 22/79)
    [1979] ECR 3275; [1980] 1 CMLR 629 781

Gregory v Commonwealth Railway Commissioner (1941) 66 CLR 50 . . . . 255, 286

Grein v Imperial Airways Ltd [1937] 1 KB 50 303

Guaranteed Trust Co of New York v Hannay and Co [1918] 2 KB 623 413

Guiseppi Sachi (Case 155/73) [1974] ECR 409; [1974] 2 CMLR 177 773

GVL, Re [1982] 1 CMLR 221 776

Hadley v Baxendale (1854) 9 Ex 341 . . . . 35, 36, 96, 255

Hair and Skin Trading Co Ltd v Norman Air Freight Carriers and World
Transport Agencies Ltd [1974] 1 Lloyd's Rep 443 295

Hampson v Martin [1981] 2 NSWLR 782 270

Hamzeh Malas and Sons v British Imex Ltd [1958] 2 QB 127 . . . . 391, 410

Hansson v Hamel and Horley Ltd [1922] 2 AC 36 405

Harbottle (RD) (Mercantile) Ltd v National Westminster Bank Ltd [1978] QB 146 388

Harbour Assurance Co (UK) Ltd v Kansa General International Assurance Co Ltd
[1993] QB 701 740

Hardwick Game Farm v SAPPA [1966] 1 All ER 309 252

Hartford Fire Insurance Co v California 113 St Ct 2891, 125 L Ed 2d 612 (1993) 800

Hasselblad (GB) Ltd v Commission (Case 86/82) [1984] ECR 883;
[1984] 1 CMLR 559 775

Hayek, Re (1957) 19 ABC 1 751

Hayes v Brisbane City Council [1979] 5 QL 269 255

Hellenic Republic v Council [1989] ECR 3963 792

Heugh v L and NW Railway (1870) LR Ex 51 254

Heyman v Darwins Ltd [1942] AC 356 739

Hill (DH) & Co v Walter H Wright Pty Ltd [1971] VR 749 252

Hoffmann–La Roche and Co AG v Centrafarm Pharmazeutischer Erzeugnisse
GmbH (Case 102/77) [1978] ECR 1139; [1978] 3 CMLR 217 780

Hoffmann–La Roche and Co AG v Commission (Case 85/76) [1979] ECR 461;
[1979] 3 CMLR 211 778

Hofner and Elser v Macrotron (Case 41/90) [1991] ECR 179 774

Hollandia, The [1983] 1 AC 565 182

Holloway v Pilkington (1972) 46 ALJR 253 257

Hong King Fir Shipping Co Ltd v Kawasaki Kisen Kaisha Ltd [1962] 2 QB 265 19

Hong Kong and Shanghai Banking Corp v Kloeckner and Co AG
[1989] 2 Lloyd's Rep 323 388

Horabin v British Overseas Airways Corporation [1952] 2 All ER 1016 . . . . 309, 310

Horne v Midland Railway (1873) LR 8 CP 131 255

Hortico (Australia) Pty Ltd v Energy Equipment Co (Australia) Pty Ltd
[1985] 1 NSWLR 545 . . . . .416, 418

Hughes and Val Pty Ltd v New South Wales [1955] AC 241; (1955) 93 CLR 1 269

Hughes and Vale Pty Ltd v New South Wales (No 2) (1955) 93 CLR 127 . . . . 257, 269, 300

Hugin Kassaregister AB v Commission (Case 22/78) [1979] ECR 1869;
[1979] 3 CMLR 345 776

Hunt v Barber (1887) 3 VLR (L) 189 289

Hunt v Winterbotham (West of England) Ltd v BRS (Parcels) Ltd [1962] 1 QB 617 251

IBM Australia Ltd v National Distribution Services Ltd (1991) NSWLR 466 738

ICI v Commission (Case 48/69) [1972] ECR 619 . . . . 774, 775

ICI v MAT Transport [1987] 1 Lloyd's Rep 354 297

IFG Intercontinentale Fleischhandels GmbH and Co KG v Freistaat Bayern
    [1984] ECR 349; [1985] 1 CMLR 453 717

Import Ditoes on Gingerbread, Re, Commission v Grand Duchy of Luxemburg
    and Kingdom of Belgium [1963] CMLR 199 715

Imports of Animal Semen, Re, EC Commission v Ireland (Case 235/91) [1993]
    1 CMLR 325 717

Inflatable Toy Co Pty Ltd v State Bank of New South Wales (1994) 34 NSWLR 243 419

Inntrepreneur Estates Ltd v Mason [1993] 2 CMLR 293 . . . . 713, 770, 778

Instituto Chemioterapico Italiano SpA and Commercial Solvents
    Corporation v Commission (Joined Cases 6/73 and 7/73)
    [1974] ECR 223; [1974] 1 CMLR 309 773

Instituto Nacional de Comercialization Agricola v Continental Illinois Bank and
    Trust Co 858 F 2d 1264 (1988) 398

International Fruit Co v Produktschap voor Groenten en Fruit (No 2) [1971] ECR 1107. . . . 717, 719

Intraco Ltd v Notis Shipping Corp of Liberia (The Bhoja Trader)
    [1981] 2 Lloyd's Rep 256 . . . . .388, 416

ITT Schaub Lorenz v Birkart Johaan Internationale Spedition GmbH & Co Kg
    [1988] 1 Lloyd's Rep 487 297

IXL Timbers v AG for Tasmania (1963) 109 CLR 574 257

James v The Commonwealth (1936) 55 CLR 1 . . . . 257, 300

JI Case (Australia) Pty Ltd v Tasman Express Line Ltd (The Canterbury Express)
    (1990) 102 FLR 59 199

John Carter (Fine Worsteds) Ltd v Hanson Haulage (Leeds) Ltd [1965] 2 QB 495. . . . . . 251, 253, 256

Johnson v Midland Railway (1849) 4 Ex 367 250

Jones v Great Northern Railway Co (1918) 34 TLR 467 (Div Ct). 256

Joseph Travers and Sons Ltd v Cooper [1915] 1 KB 73. 251

Kali und Salz und Kali-Chemie v Commission (Joined Cases 19/74 and 20/74)
    [1975] ECR 499; [1975] 2 CMLR 154 779

Karberg, Arnold and Co v Blythe, Green Jourdain and Co [1915] 2 KB 379. 138

Kaufhof AG v Commission (Case 29/75) [1976] ECR 431 719

Keck and Mithouard [1995] 1 CMLR 101 723

Kelly v ASN Co (1885) 2 WN (NSW) 40 255

Kerry New Zealand Ltd v Comptroller of Customs (C.P1614/88) 590

Keskell v Continental Express Ltd [1950] 1 All ER 1033 255

Kilberg v North East Airlines Inc [1961] 2 Lloyd's Rep 406. 301

Kilners Ltd v John Dawson Investment Trust Ltd (1935) 35 SR (NSW) 274 . . . . 250, 255

King v Victorian Railway Commissioners (1892) 18 VLR 250 . . . . 255, 256

Kingsford Smith Air Services v Garrison (1938) 55 WN (NSW) 122 299

Koufos v Czarnikow Ltd (The Heron II) [1969] 1 AC 351. 255

Koyo Seiko Co Ltd v Council [1987] ECR 1899; [1989] 2 CMLR 76 794

Kruiddenier (H) (London) Ltd v Egyptian Navigation Co, The El Amria (No 2)
[1980] 2 Lloyd's Rep 166 739

Kunze v Vowles, ex p Vowles (1955) QSR 591 270

L'Oréal v De Nieuwe AMCK (Case 31/80) [1980] ECR 3775; [1981] 2 CMLR 235 778

Lee and Sons Pty Ltd v Abood (1968) 89 WN (NSW) (Pt 1) 430. 251

Life Savers (Australia) Ltd v Frigmobile Pty Ltd [1983] 1 NSWLR 431 252

Lisi v Alitalia-Linee Aeree Italiane SpA [1967] Lloyd's Rep 140; F 2d 508
(1966) (2nd Circ) affirmed [1968] 1 Lloyd's Rep 505; 390 US 455 (1968) 320

London and North Western Railway Co v Hellawell (1872) 26 LT 557 256

London, Tilbury and Southend Railway Co v Patterson (1913) 29 TLR 413 (HL) 256

Luddit v Ginger Coote Airways Ltd [1947] AC 233 301

Ludecke v Canadian Pacific Airlines Ltd (1979) 98 DLR (3d) 52; [1979] 2 Lloyd's Rep 260. 320

Lynch v Page (1940) 57 WN (NSW) 161 270

MacRobertson Millar Airlines Services v Commissioner of State Taxation of
State of Western Australia (1975) 133 CLR 125 320

Macrow v Great Western Railway Co (1871) LR 6 QB 612 256

Makedonia, The [1962] 1 Lloyd's Rep 316. 191

Maloney v Commissioner for Railways (NSW) (1978) 42 ALJR 292 255

Mannington Mills Inc v Congoleum Corporation 595 F 2d 1287 (1979) 799

Mannion v Pan American World Airways Inc 105 Misc 2d 927
(NY Sup Ct 1980) 319

Maple Leaf Fish Co v United States 762 F 2d 86 (1985) US Court of Appeals (Fed Cir) 606

Marchandise and Others, Re (Case C332/89) [1991] ECR 1027; [1992] 2 CEC 411 720

Mareva Compania Naviera SA v International Bulkcarriers SA
[1975] 2 Lloyd's Rep 509 . . . . .416, 417

Maurice O'Meara Co v National Park Bank of New York 239 NY 386, 146 NE 636 (1925). 410

Mayhew Foods v OCL [1984] 1 Lloyd's Rep 317 190

McKenna v Avion Pty Ltd [1981] WAR 255 324

Mertens v Flying Tiger Line Inc 341 F 2d 851 (1965) (2nd Circ) 319

Metalleftikon Viomichanikon Kai Naftiliakon and Others v Council [1989] ECR 3919 784

Metrotex Pty Ltd v Freight Investments Pty Ltd [1969] VR 9 252

Michael Galley Footwear Ltd v Dominic Iaboni [1982] 2 All ER 200 . . . . 293, 296

Middlemiss and Gould v Hartlepool Corp [1972] 1 WLR 1643. 751

Midland Bank Ltd v Seymour [1955] 2 Lloyd's Rep 147 401

Miller International Schallplatten GmbH v Commission (Case 19/77)
 [1978] ECR 131; [1978] 2 CMLR 334 776

Mineba Co Ltd v Council [1987] ECR 1975; [1989] 2 CMLR 76 . . . . 785, 786

Minister for Aboriginal Affairs v Peko Wallsend Ltd (1986) 162 CLR 24. 607

Minister for Justice for Western Australia, ex p Ansett Airlines v Australian
 National Airlines Commission and the Commonwealth (1977) 12 ALR 17 298

Mitsubushi Motors Corporation v Soler-Chrysler-Plymouth Inc 473 US 614 (1984) 738, 746

Modern Building Wales Ltd v Limmer and Trinidad [1975] 2 All ER 549. 740

Montreal Trust Co v Canadian Pacific Airlines Ltd (1976) 72 DLR (3d) 257. 320

Morris v CW Martin and Sons Ltd [1966] 1 QB 716 251

Moto-Vespa v MAT [1979] 1 Lloyd's Rep 175 297

Moukatoff v BOAC [1967] 1 Lloyd's Rep 396. 251

Muncaster Castle, The [1961] Lloyd's Rep 57 196

Murphy v Quaresmini, ex p Murphy [1978] Qd 210 275

Murray v The Charming Betsy 2 Cranch 64, 118 2 L Ed 208 (1804) 799

Musique Diffusion Francaise SA v Commission [1983] ECR 1825 718

Nachi Fujikoshi Corp v Council [1987] ECR 1861; [1989] 2 CMLR 76 . . . . 785, 786

Nashua Corporation v Council and Commission [1990] ECR 719; [1990] 2 CMLR 6 798

Natoli v Walker (1994) unreported 750

Nederlandsche Banden-industrie Michelin NV v Commission (Case 322/81)
 [1983] ECR 3461; [1985] 1 CMLR 282 778

Netherlands v Tankstation 't Heukske [1995] 3 CMLR 501. 723

New York Star, The [1981] WLR 138 184

New Zealand Cereal Foods Ltd v Minister for Customs (C.P423/87) 590

New Zealand Shipping Co Ltd v AM Satterthwaite and Co Ltd, The Eurymedon
 [1975] AC 154 184

Newberry v Simmonds [1961] 2 QB 345 270

Nippon Seiko KK v Council [1987] ECR 1923; [1989] 2 CMLR 76 . . . . 785, 786

Nippon Steel Corp and Others v United States and Others
 Consol Ct no 93-09-00555-INJ, 3 April 1995
 (US Court of International Trade) 606

Norske Atlas Insurance v London General Insurance [1927] 28 Lloyd's Rep 104. . . . . 741, 752

Northwest Airlines v South African Airways v Suzuki Pearl Shop (1979) Air Law
 227, 19 March 1972 (Supreme Court of Japan) 311

Nova (Jersey) Knit Ltd v Kammgarn Spinnerei GmbH [1977] 1 WLR 713. 411

NTN Toyo Bearing Co Ltd v Council [1987] ECR 1809; [1989] 2 CMLR 76 784

Nuss v Donaldson (1930) 31 SR (NSW) 63 271

Nysted and Anson v Wings Ltd [1942] 3 DLR 301

Officer van Justitie v Van Haaster (Case 190/73) [1974] ECR 1123;
[1974] 2 CMLR 521 717

Orlove v Philippine Airlines 257 F 2d 384 (2d Cir 1958) 316

Orsolina Leonesia v Ministry of Agriculture and Forestry of Italy (Case 93/71)
[1973] CMLR 343 712

Paczy v Haendler and Naterman [1981] 1 Lloyd's Rep 302 740

Pan American World Airways Inc v Fire and Accident Insurance Co Ltd (1965) 3 SA 150 312

Parsons and Whitmore Overseas Co v Société General de L'Industrie du Papier
508 F 2d 969 (2d Cir 1974) 746

Photo Productions Ltd v Securicor Transport Ltd [1980] AC 827 18

Pick v Lufthansa 9 AVI 18, 077 (1965) (New York City Court)...........................317

Pilkington (Australia) Ltd v The Anti-Dumping Authority (1995) unreported (Federal Court) ...607

Pilkington v Frank Hammond (1973) 2 ALR 563 257

Pioneer Shipping v BTP Tioxide, The Nema [1982] AC 724 ....749, 750

Power Curber International Ltd v National Bank of Kuwait SAK
[1981] 2 Lloyd's Rep 394; [1981] 1 WLR 1233 ....388, 411, 418

Price v Ramsay (Commissioner of Railways) (1882) 16 SASLR 95 255

Proctor v Jetway Aviation Pty Ltd [1984] 1 NSWLR 166 318

Procurer de Roi v Dassonville (Case 8/74) [1974] ECR 837; [1974] 1 CMLR 436 ....717, 723

Procureur de la République v Giry and Guerlain (Cases 253/78 and 1/79–3/79)
[1980] ECR 2327; [1981] 2 CMLR 99 772

Procureur du Roi v Dassonville [1974] ECR 837; [1974] 2 CMLR 436 ....718, 719

Promenade Investments Pty Ltd v State of New South Wales (1991) 26 NSWLR 203 749

Publico v Ratti (Case 148/78) [1971] CMLR 123 713

Purity Requirements for Beer, Re, EC Commission v Germany [1987]
ECR 1227; [1988] 1 CMLR 780 722

Purslow v Baily (1705) 2 Ld Raym 1039..750

Pyrene Co Ltd v Scindia Navigation Co Ltd [1954] 2 QB 402..........................134, 190

QH Tours Ltd v Ship Design and Management (Aust) Pty Ltd (1991) 33 FCR 227 738

Qantas Airways Ltd v SS Pharmaceutical Co Ltd [1989] 1 Lloyd's Rep 319..................310

R v Anderson, ex p IPEC Air Pty Ltd (1965) 39 ALJR 66 300

R v Burgess, ex p Henry (The Goya Henry Case) (1936) 55 CLR 605 299

R v Poole, ex p Henry (No 2) (1938) 61 CLR 634 299

R v Public Vehicle Licensing Appeal Tribunal of Tasmania, ex p Australian
National Airways Pty Ltd (1964) 113 CLR 207 298

R v Secretary of State for Transport, ex p Factortame Ltd (No 2) [1991] 1 AC 603.............712

Raphael v Pickford (1843) 5 Man and G 551 253

Rashap v American Airlines [1955] US Av R 593 (NY Southern District Court) 310

Rayner (SH) and Co v Hambros Bank Ltd [1943] 1 KB 37 398

Redpath v Railway Commissioners (1900) 17 NW (NSW) 47 256

Renton v Palmyra Trading Corp [1957] AC 149 191

Republic of Italy v Commission (Case 41/83) [1985] ECR 873; [1985] 2 CMLR 368 776

Republic of Italy v Council and Commission (Case 32/65) [1966] ECR 389;
    [1969] CMLR 39 773

Rewe-Zentral AG v Bundesmonopolverwalting für Branntwein
    (Cassis de Dijon Case) [1979] ECR 649; [1979] 3 CMLR 494 . . . . .719, 720, 723

Richardson v Mellish (1824) 2 Bing 228 746

Rick Cobby Haulage Ltd v Simsmetal Pty Ltd (1986) 43 SASR 533 252

Rio Sun, The [1982] 1 WLR 158 748

Ritts v American Overseas Airlines Inc [1949] US Av R 65 310

Rivendell Forest Products Ltd v Canadian Forest Products Ltd 810 F Supp 1116 (1993) 798

Riverstone Meat Co v Lancashire Shipping Co, The Muncaster Castle
    [1961] Lloyd's Rep 57 . . . . .175, 197

Robinson v Harman (1848) 1 Ex 850 . . . . 35, 96

Rolled Steel, Re [1980] 3 CMLR 193 775

Rothmans of Pall Mall (Overseas) Ltd v Saudi Arabian Airlines Corp [1981] QB 368 318

Royal Victorian Aero Club v Commonwealth (1954) 92 CLR 236 310

Russell v Walters (1957) 96 CLR 177 257

Rustenburg Platinum Mines Ltd and others v South African Airways and
    Pan American World Airways Inc [1977] 1 Lloyd's Rep 564 . . . . .310, 311

SACE SpA v Italian Ministry of Finance (Case 33/70) [1971] CMLR 123 713

SADAM v Comitato Interministeriale dei Prezzi [1976] ECR 323; [1977] 2 CMLR 183 718

Sandoz Prodotti Farmacceutici Spa v Commissioner (Case 277/87) [1990] ECR 45 775

Saycell v Bool [1948] 2 All ER 83 270

Schroder (I) KG v Oberdtaadtdirektor der Stadt Koln (Case 21/75) [1975] ECR 905 716

Schutzverband Gegen Unwesen ID Wirtschaft v Weinvertriebs GmbH [1983] ECR 1217 723

Scruttons v Midland Silicones [1962] AC 446 184

Secretary to the Department of Transport, ex p Aus Students Travel Pty
    Ltd (1978) 19 ALR 613 325

Securities (NZ) Ltd v Cadbury Schweppes Hudson Ltd [1988] 340
    (High Court of New Zealand) 250

Seth v BOAC 319 F 2d 303 (1964) (1st Circ) 319

Shamster Jute Mills Ltd v Sethia (London) Ltd [1987] 1 Lloyd's Rep 388 408

Sharp Corp v Council [1988] ECR 5813 785

Shipping Corp of India Ltd v Gamlen Chemical Co (Australasia) Pty Ltd
    (1980) 147 CLR 142 197

Shirt v Wyong Shire Council [1978] 1 NSWLR 631
  affirmed, Wyong Shire v Shirt (1980) 146 CLR 40 256

Sidarma Societa Italiana, etc v Holt Marine 515 F Supp 1362 (1981) 746

Silbert Ltd v Islander Trucking [1985] 2 Lloyd's Rep 243.............................295, 296

Silver Seiko Ltd v Council [1988] ECR 5927; [1989] 1 CMLR 249 ....785, 786, 789

Simmenthal v Administrazione delle Finanze dello Stato [1978] ECR 1453....................716

Sims v Midland Railway [1913] 1 KB 103 154

Sims v West (1961) 107 CLR 157..257

Skinner v Upshaw (1702) 2 Ld Raym 752 255

Smart v Allean [1963] 1 QB 291 270

Smith-Corona Group v United States 713 F 2d 1568 (1983) (Fed Cir) (US Court of Appeals) 606

Soames v British Empire Shipping Co (1880) 8 HL Cas 338..............................265

Soanes Bros v Meredith [1963] 2 Lloyd's Rep 293 253

Sociaal Fonds voor de Diamantarbeiders v SA Ch Brachfield and Sons
  (Joined Cases 2/69–3/69) [1969] CMLR 335 715

Société de Vente de Ciments et Bétons de l'Est SA v Kerpen and Kerpen
  (Case 319/82) [1983] ECR 4173; [1985] 1 CMLR 511 770

Société Technique Minière v Maschinenbau Ulm GmbH (Case 56/65)
  [1966] ECR 235; [1966] CMLR 357 ....770, 775

South Wales Switchgear Co Ltd [1978] 1 WLR 165 252

Spa Salgoil v Ministry of Foreign Trade of Italy (Case 13/68) [1969] CMLR 181 712

Springer v Great Western Railway [1921] 1 KB 257.....................................289

Sprinks and Cie v Air France 23 RFDA 405 (27 June 1969) (Paris CA) 308

SS Pharmaceutical Pty Ltd v Qantas Airways Ltd [1991] 1 Lloyd's Rep 288...........200, 313, 314

State Rail Authority (NSW) v Everson (1985) unreported (Supreme Court
  of New South Wales) 289

Stephenson v Hart (1828) 4 Bing 476 254

Stockdale v Lancashire and Yorkshire Railway Co (1863) 8 LT 289 256

Stoneham v Ryan's Removals Ltd (1979) 23 ALR 1 257

Suisse Atlantique Société d'Armement SA v NV Rotterdamsche Kolen Centrale
  [1967] 1 AC 361 18

Svenska Traktor Akt v Maritime Agencies (Southampton) [1953] 2 Lloyd's Rep 124 186

Swiss Bank v Brinks Mat [1986] 2 Lloyd's Rep 79 ....306, 307

Szteijn v J Henry Schroder Banking Corporation 31 NYS 2d 631
  (1941) (New York Supreme Court) 412, 413, 415

Tamar Timber Trading Co Pty Ltd v Pilkington (1968) 117 CLR 353 257

Tasman Pulp and Paper Co v Brambles JB O'Loghlen [1981] 2 NZLR 225 312

Tatton, William & Co Ltd v Ferrymasters [1974] 1 Lloyd's Rep 203 297

Taxi Services Pty Ltd, ex p, Re Commissioner for Road Transport and Tramways
(1937) 37 (NSW) 504; [1937] 54 WN 201 271

Taylor v GN Railway (1866) LR 1 CP 385 254

Technointorg v Council and Commission [1988] ECR 6077; [1989] 1 CMLR 281 . . . . 789, 796

Tepea BV v Commission (Case 28/77) [1978] ECR 1391; [1978] 3 CMLR 392 . . . . . . 771, 775, 776

Tetra Pak Rausing v Commission (Case T51/89) [1990] ECR II 309 778

Thermo Engineers Ltd v Ferrymasters Ltd [1981] 1 Lloyd's Rep 200 . . . . 295, 296

Thompson v Commissioner for Railways (1863) 2 SCR (NSW) 292 256

Timberlane Lumber Co v Bank of America 549 F 2d 597 (1976). 799

Timex Corporation v Council and Commission [1985] ECR 849;
[1985] 3 CMLR 550 . . . . .792, 797

TNT Pty Ltd v May and Baker (Australia) Pty Ltd (1966) 115 CLR 353 252

Tokyo Electric Co Ltd v Council [1988] ECR 5855; [1989] 1 CMLR 169. . . . . 785, 789

Tradesman, The, SA Hersent v United Towing Co Ltd [1961] 1 WLR 61 739

Trans World Airlines Inc v Franklin Mint Corporation [1952] 3 Lloyd's MCLQ 453 315

Trickett v Queensland Insurance [1936] AC 159 251

Tukan Timber Ltd v Barclays Bank plc [1987] 1 Lloyd's Rep 171 413

Turnleys Pty Ltd v Commissioner for Railways [1955] SR Qd 4 291

Tzoritz v Monarch Line AB [1968] 1 WLR 406. 752

Ulster Bank v Synott (1871) 5 IREq 595. 413

Ulster-Swift Ltd v Taunton Meat Haulage Ltd [1977] 1 Lloyd's Rep 346 294–97

Union Laitiere Normandie v French Dairy Farmers Ltd (Case 244/78) [1979] ECR 1629 712

United Brands Co and United Brands Continental BV v Commission
(Case 27/76) [1978] ECR 207; [1978] 1 CMLR 429 777–80

United City Merchants (Investments) Ltd v Royal Bank of Canada,
The American Accord [1985] 1 AC 168 . . . . .414, 415

United City Merchants (Investments) Ltd v Royal Bank of Canada [1982] QB 208 388

United International Stables Ltd v Pacific Western Airlines (1969)
5 DLR 367 (Supreme Court of British Columbia) 306

United States v Aluminium Co of America (ALCOA) 148 F 2d 416 (1945) 778, 798

Upperton v Union-Castle Mail Steamship Co Ltd (1902) 19 TLR 123 256

US Steel Products Co v GW Railway [1916] 1 AC 189 255

Van Duyn v Home Office [1974] ECR 1337 713

Verenigingter Bevordering van het Vlaamse Boekwezen (VBVB) and Vereniging
ter Bevordering van de Belangen des Boekhandels (VBBBV) v Commission
(Joined Cases 43/82 and 63/82) [1984] ECR 19; [1985] 1 CMLR 27; [1985] CMR 14 774

Vereniging van Cementhandelaren v Commission (Case 8/72)
[1972] ECR 977; [1973] CMLR 7 775

Victoria Laundry (Windsor Ltd) v Newman Industries Ltd [1949] 2 KB 528 255

Viho Europe BV v Commission (Case T102/92) [1995] ECR II 17 774

Vita Food Products Inc v Unus Shipping Co Ltd [1939] AC 277 182

Voest-Alpine International Corporation v Chase Manhattan Bank 707 F 2d 680 (1983) 387

Volk v Vervaecke (Case 5/69) [1969] ECR 295; [1969] CMLR 273. 776

Wallace v Major [1946] KB 473 270

Wallis v Downard Pickford (North Queensland) Pty Ltd (1992) unreported 257

Wattmaster Alco Pty Ltd v Button (1985) 8 FCR 471 608

Westminster Bank v Imperial Airways Ltd [1936] 2 All ER 890 307

Westpac Banking Corporation v South Carolina National Bank
    [1986] 1 Lloyd's Rep 311 403

Whitchurch v Commissioner for Railways (1901) 4 WALR 53 255

White v John Warwick & Co Ltd [1953] 1 WLR 1285 252

White v South Australian Railways Commissioner (1919) SALR 44 288

White v South Eastern Railway (1885) 1 TLR 391 (DC) 287

Wibau Maschinen Fabric Hartman SA v Mackinnon Mackenzie and Co
    [1989] 2 Lloyd's Rep 494 199

Wing Hang Bank Ltd v Japan Airlines 357 F Supp 94 DCNY (1973) 307

Wood Hall Ltd v Pipeline Authority (1979) 141 CLR 443. 410

Woods v Thiedemann (1862) 1 H and C 478 413

Worldwide Carriers v Ardtran [1983] 1 All ER 692 297

Young Jewel Manufacturing Co v Delta 414 NYS 2d 528 (1979) (App Div) 307

Z Ltd v A-Z and AA – LL [1982] 1 QB 558 417

Zenith Radio Corp v United States 437 US 443 (1978); 98 S Ct 2441, 2444,
    57 L Ed 2d 337 (1978) 589, 787

Zoni, Re [1988] ECR 4285; [1990] 1 CEC 570. 722

Züchner v Bayerische Vereinsbank AG (Case 172/80) [1981] ECR 2021;
    [1982] 1 CMLR 313 776

TABLE OF LEGISLATION

Australian Legislation

Acts Interpretation Act 1901 (Cth). 265

Administrative Decisions
  (Judicial Review) Act 1977 602
  s 5 . . . . .607, 608
  ss 5(1), (2), 6, 7, 9, 9(4) 602
  ss 11–14, 16, 19 602
  Sch 2 602

Air Navigation Act 1920 (Cth). . . 299, 325, 326
  s 19 301
  s 26 323

Air Navigation Act 1938 (NSW)–
  s 6 301

Air Navigation Act 1937 (Qld)–
  s 6 301

Air Navigation Act 1937 (SA)–
  s 7 301

Air Navigation Act 1937 (Tas)–
  s 6 301

Air Navigation Act 1958 (Vic)–
  s 6 301

Air Navigation Act 1937 (WA)–
  s 7 301

Air Navigation Regulations (Cth) 325
  Pt 33.1 301
  Pt XVI 323
  reg 106A(7) 325
  regs 120–20A 301
  regs 191–96, 211 325

Air Services Act 1995 326

Air Transport Act 1964 (NSW) 299

Airline Agreement Act 1981 (Cth). 324

Airline Agreement (Termination)
  Act 1990 (Cth)–
  s 3 324

Airline Equipment Act 1958 (Cth). 325

Airports (Business Concessions)
  Act 1959 (Cth)–
  ss 6–8 299

Anti-Dumping Authority Act 1988 598
  Pt I 598, 599
  s 3 599
  s 3A 587, 599

Pt II 598, 599
  ss 4, 5, 7, 7A, 7C, 8A(1), 8A(4) 599
  ss 8A(10), 10, 12 600
Pt III 598, 600
  ss 13–15 600
Pt IV 599, 600
  ss 22, 23, 23A, 24, 27 600
Pt V 599, 600
  ss 28, 29, 34 600

Australian National Airlines Act
  1945 (Cth) 325

Australian National Railways Act
  1917 (Cth) 284

Australian National Railways
  Commission Act 1983 (Cth) 284, 285
  ss 5, 6 285
  s 10 290
  s 49 286
  ss 72, 79 . . . . .286, 287
  s 200 286

Australian Airlines (Conversion to Public
  Company) Act 1988 (Cth)–
  ss 15, 16 324
  Sch 1 324

Carriage of Dangerous Goods by
  Road Act 1984 (Qld) 265, 289

Carriage of Goods by Land Act
  1967 (Qld) 257

Carriage of Goods by Land (Carrier's
  Liability) Act 1967 (Qld) 257

Carriage of Goods by Land (Carrier's
  Liability) Act Repeal Act 1993
  (Qld) (no 13 of 1993) 257

COGSA Carriage of Goods by
  Sea Act 1991 (Cth) 175, 177,
                                178, 182, 195
  Pt 3 177
  s 3 178
  s 3(a)–(c) 179
  s 8 182
  s 11 . . . . .195, 196, 738
  s 13 182
  s 31(1)(c) 200
  s 16 738
  Sch 2 177

Carriers Act 1891 (SA) 250
  s 13 286
Carriers Act 1920 (WA) 250
Carriers and Innkeepers Act 1958 (Vic) 250
Civil Aviation Act 1988 (Cth)–
  s 23(1), (3) 313
Civil Aviation (Carrier's Liability)
  Act 1959 (Cth) 298, 300,
                301, 318, 319,
                321, 323, 325
  Pts II, III 321
  Pt IIIA 321, 323
  Pts IIIB, IIIC 323, 324
  Pt IV 323, 324, 326
  Pt IVA 326
  ss 5, 8–10 302
  s 9 323
  s 10 318
  s 11(1) 302
  s 18 298
  s 19 318
  s 22 298
  s 25A 320, 323
  s 25B 321, 323
  s 25C 298
  s 26 300
  s 26(1) 323
  s 27, (1) 300, 323
  ss 28–33 324
  s 34 . . . . .318, 324
  s 42 301
  Sch 2 302
  Sch 2 Art 25 200
  Sch 3 320
Civil Aviation (Carrier's Liability)
  Act 1967 (NSW) 298
  s 4 300
Civil Aviation (Carrier's Liability)
  Act 1964 (Qld) .298
  s 4 300
Civil Aviation (Carrier's Liability)
Act 1962 (SA). 298
  s 5 300
Civil Aviation (Carrier's Liability)
  Act 1963 (Tas) .298
  s 4 300

Civil Aviation (Carrier's Liability)
  Act 1961 (Vic) .298
  s 4 300
Civil Aviation (Carrier's Liability)
  Act 1961 (WA) .298
  s 5 300
Civil Aviation (Carrier's Liability)
  Amendment Act 1982 (Cth) 314
Civil Aviation (Carrier's Liability)
  Amendment Act 1991 (Cth) 301, 302,
                315, 323, 324
  ss 7–8 323
  s 24A 302
  Schs 1–3 302
  Sch 1 319
  Sch 2 315
  Sch 2 Art 3(1), (1)(c), (2) 319
  Sch 2 Art 22 . . . . .313, 316
  Sch 2 Art 22(2)–(5) 313
  Sch 2 Art 22(2)(b), (4), (6) 316
  Sch 2 Art 25 316
  Sch 2 Arts 26(2)–(4), 28(1) 318
  Sch 2 Art 29(1) .318
  Sch 2 Arts 30, (3), 31, 31A 317
  Sch 2 Art 31(1) .318
  Sch 2 Art 31(2), (3) 317
  Sch 2 Arts 32, 35 318
Civil Aviation (Carrier's Liability)
  Amendment Bill 1991 315
  Art 35A 315
Civil Aviation Legislation
  Amendment Act 1995 326
Civil Aviation Regulations (Cth)
  (SR 1988 no 158) 301
Commercial Arbitration
  Act 1984 (NSW) 733, 746
  Pts II–V 733
  s 4(1) 729, 735
  s 22 731
  s 33 733
  s 33(1) 751
  ss 38–40 747
  s 38 . . . . .748, 749
  s 38(4)(b), (5)(b)(1)(ii) 750
  s 39 750
  s 40 748
  ss 42, 43 747

s 44 733
s 53 . . . . .733, 736
s 53(1) 740
ss 53(2), 73 741

Commercial Passenger (Road)
Transport Act 1991
(no 34 of 1991) .283
s 3 283
s 9(1) 283, 284
s 9(3) 283
ss 16–20, 22–27, 29–31 283
ss 34, 39, 40 284
s 47 283
ss 75, 77(2) 284

Commercial Passenger (Road)
Transport Act 1992 (no 29 of 1992) 283

Commercial Passenger (Road)
Transport Amendment
Act 1992 (no 29 of 1992) 283

Common Carriers' Act 1902 (NSW) . . 250, 290
s 9(c) 289

Common Carriers' Act 1874 (Tas) 250

Commonwealth Act 257

Commonwealth Constitution 1900 (Cth)–
s 51(1) 299
s 51(i) 257
s 51(vi), (xxix) 299
s 51(xxxiii), (xxxiv) 284
s 51(xxxvii) 286
s 51(xxxix) 299
s 52 299
s 92 . . . . .257, 269, 300
ss 122, 128 299

Commonwealth Powers (Air
Transport) Act 1952 (Tas) 298

Compensation to Relatives
Act 1897 (NSW) 318

Crimes (Aircraft) Act 1963 (Cth)–
s 18 301

Crimes (Aviation) Act 1991 326
Sch Pts 1–3 326

Customs Act 1901 (Cth) 601
Pt XV 599
Pt XVB 601, 602
Division 1 601

s 269TAA 601
s 269TAAA 587
s 269TAAC 601
ss 269TAB, 269TAC 585, 601
ss 269TACB, 269TACC 601
s 269TAE 585
Division 2 602
ss 269TD, 269TDA, 269TF 602
Division 3 602
s 269TG 602
s 269TH 601
ss 269TJ, 269TK 602
Divisions 4–7 602

Customs, Excise and Bounty Legislation
Amendment Act (no 85 of 1995) 601

Customs Legislation (World Trade
Organisation Amendments)
Act 1994 (Cth) .586

Customs Tariff (Anti-Dumping)
Act 1975 (Cth) 599, 500
s 7 601
s 8 . . . . .587, 601
s 8(1), (4), (5A), (5B), (7) 601
s 9 . . . . .587, 601
ss 9(1), 10(1), (3), 11 601

Dangerous Goods Act 1975 (NSW) . . . 265, 289

Dangerous Goods Act 1981 (NT) 289

Dangerous Goods Act 1987 (NT) 265

Dangerous Goods Act 1976 (Tas) 265, 289

Dangerous Goods Act 1985 (Vic) 265, 289

Dangerous Goods Act 1961 (WA) 289

Dangerous Goods Ordinance
1984 (Act) .265, 289

Dangerous Substances Act 1976 (SA) . . 265, 289

Evidence Act 1919 280

Explosive and Dangerous Goods
Act 1961 (WA) .265

Federal Airports Corporation
Act 1986 (Cth) .299
s 6 300

Government Railways Act 1904 (WA)–
s 22(2), (3) 292
s 25 . . . . .286, 292
s 28A 292

Government Railways Act 1912 (NSW)–
s 33 286

ICSID Implementation Act 1990 (Cth) 686

Industry Commission Act 1990 (Cth) 268
ss 19, 20, 24, 30(1), 48(2) 268

Insurance Contracts Act 1984 (Cth)–
s 43, (2) 738

International Arbitration Act 1974 (Cth) . . . 686
Pt II 732–35
Pt III 732–34
s 2C 738
s 3 . . . . .732, 735, 751
ss 3(1), (2)(a), 7 .735
s 7(2) 736, 739
s 7(5) 736
s 8 735
ss 8(1), (2), (5), (5)(f), 9 751
s 16 733
s 18 741
s 19 745
s 19(b) 744
s 20 734
s 21 733–35
s 22 734
s 32 686

International Air Services Commission
Act 1992 (Cth) 325

Interstate Commission Act 1975 (Cth). 268
s 9(i) 269

Interstate Road Transport Act
1985 (Cth) .250, 267
ss 3(1), 6, 25, 27 .267

Interstate Road Transport Charge
Act 1985 (Cth) 250, 267

Judicial Decisions (Administrative
Review) Act 1977 589

Judiciary Act 1903 (Cth) 302
s 28 318

Limitation Act 1969 (NSW)–
s 14 193

Limitation Act 1969 (NSW)–
s 14 193

Limitation Act 1981 (NT)–
s12 193

Limitation Act 1935–1978 (WA)–
s 38 193

Limitation of Actions Act 1974 (Qld)–
s 10 193

Limitation of Actions Act 1936–
1975 (SA)–
s 35 193

Limitation of Actions Act 1958 (Vic)–
s 5 193

Main Roads Acts 1920–59. 276

Melbourne Rail Loop Authority
Act 1970 273

Melbourne Tramways Act 1958. 273

Mercantile Law Ordinance 1962 (ACT)–
ss 17–32 255

Ministry of Transport Act 1958 273

Motor Traffic Act 1974–
s 4 282

Motor Traffic Act 1989–
Pt 8A 271

Motor Traffic Regulations 1993 282
s 2 271
Pts 10A, 11A 271
regs 126A–126C, 126G, 126N 271
regs 337–338 .271

Motor Vehicle Act 1959–
ss 5, 10–13, 19a, 72 277
ss 98(d)–(i), (pc), (1), (2) 277
ss 98(pd)(1), (2), (pf), (pg) 277
s 145 277

Motor Vehicle Act Regulations 1960–
Pt IV 277
regs 35a, 35b(1) 277
regs 49, 50(a)–(c), 54–55a 277
regs 56–57, 60, 66 277

Motor Vehicle Standards Act
1989 (Cth) 264, 266

Motor Vehicles Insurance Acts 1936–59 . . . 276

Motor Vehicle Taxation Act 1981 281
  s 3(1) 281
  Sch 1 281

Motor Vehicles Taxation Act 1988 270

Mutual Recognition Act 1992 (Cth) 690

Mutual Recognition (Australian Capital
  Territory) Act 1992 (Act) 690

Mutual Recognition (Northern
  Territory) Act 1992 (NT) 690

Mutual Recognition (New South
  Wales) Act 1992 (NSW) 690

Mutual Recognition (Queensland)
  Act 1992 (Qld) 690

Mutual Recognition (South Australia)
  Act 1993 (SA) 690

Mutual Recognition (Tasmania)
  Act 1993 (Tas) .690

Mutual Recognition (Victoria) Act
  1993 (Vic) 690

Mutual Recognition (Western Australia)
  Act 1995 (WA) .690

National Rail Corporation
  Agreement Act 1992 (Cth) 285
  Pt I 286
  s 5(3) 286, 287
  s 5(4) 286
  ss 7, 9, 17 285
  Pts III, VI, VII 286
  Pt VIII 286
  Sch 1 . . . . .285, 286
  Sch 2 . . . . .286, 287

National Railways Commission
  Amendment Act 1988
  (no 122 of 1988) 285

National Road Transport
  Commission Act 1991 (Cth)
  (no 8 of 1992) 250, 257–59,
                      264, 265, 267
  s 6 267
  ss 9, 10 268
  ss 12, 13, 46 267
  Sch 259, 267, 268
  Sch Recitals C, G 259

National Road Transport Commission
  Act 1992 (Cth) 260, 262, 268
  Sch 268

National Road Transport Commission
  Amendment Act 1992 (Cth)
  (no 149 of 1992) 259, 262
  Sch 2 Recitals C, E 259
  Sch 2 Recital F 260

Northern Territory Acceptance
  Act 1910 (Cth) 284

Passenger Movement Charge Act 1978 326

Passenger Movement Charge
  Amendment Act 1995 (Cth) 326

Passenger Movement Charge
  Collection Act 1978 326

Passenger Movement Charge Collection
  Amendment Act 1995 326

Passenger Transport Act 1990 271
  ss 3, 4 271

Passenger Transport Regulation
  Act 1990 272
  Pts 2–6 272
  regs 31C, 60 272

Public Transport Commission Act 1972 . . . 269

Qantas Empire Airways Act 1948 (Cth) 325

Qantas Sale Act 1992 (Cth) 325

Qantas Sale Amendment Act 1995
  (no 44 of 1995) .324

Queensland Act 1967 257
  s 6 257

Railway Management Act 1935 (Tas)–
  s 15 286

Railways Act 1912 (Qld)–
  ss 3, 108, 133 291
  Sch 2 291

Railways Act 1914 (Qld) 290
  ss 37, 95, (3), 100–108 291
  s 120 286

Railways Act 1958 (Vic) 273
  s 4 286

Railways Amendment Act 1985 (Qld)–
  s 17 291

Railways (South Australia) Act 1975 (SA) . . 284

Railways (Transfer to Commonwealth)
  Act 1975 (Tas) .284

Recreation Vehicles Act 1973 273

Road Traffic Act 1958 273

Road Traffic Act 1974 . . . . 277, 279
  ss 5, 16(2), 23, 23A, 24, 111 279
  Sch 1 279

Road Transport (Australian Capital
  Territory) Act 1993 (Cth) 250

Road Transport Charges (Australian
  Capital Territory) Act 1993
  (no 10 of 1993) .261
  ss 2–5 261

Road Transport Reform (Dangerous
  Goods) Act 1995 264

Road Transport Reform (Heavy Vehicle
  Standards) Regulations 1995 (no 42) 264

Road Transport Reform (Mass and
  Loading) Regulations 1995 (no 56) 264

Road Transport Reform (Oversize
  and Overmass Vehicles)
  Regulations 1995 (no 12) 264

Road Transport Reform (Vehicles
  and Traffic) Act 1993 (Cth) 250, 262–64
  s 2(1) 263
  ss 5(1), (2), 7(1), 8(2) 264
  ss 9(5), 13(2), 14(1), (2) 265
  s 15(1), (2) 265

Rules of the Supreme Court (Vic) 731

Rules Publication Act 1953 280
  s 24(1), (2) 280

Sale of Goods Act 1923 (NSW)–
  ss 35, 46–48 254

Sale of Goods (Vienna Convention)
  Act 1987 (ACT) .80

Sale of Goods (Vienna Convention)
  Act 1986 (Qld) 80

Sale of Goods (Vienna Convention)
  Act 1986 (NSW) .80

Sale of Goods (Vienna Convention)
  Act 1987 (NT) 80

Sale of Goods (Vienna Convention)
  Act 1986 (SA) 80

Sale of Goods (Vienna Convention)
  Act 1987 (Tas) 80

Sale of Goods (Vienna Convention)
  Act 1987 (Vic) 80

Sale of Goods (Vienna Convention)
  Act 1986 (WA) 80

Sea Carriage of Goods Act 1924 (Cth) 175
  s 6 . . . . .181, 182
  s 9 195,
                                                  196, 738

Seat of Government Act 1928 (Cth) 284

Service and Execution of Process
  Act 1901 (Cth) .751

State Air Navigation Act 1938 (NSW) 299

State Air Navigation Act 1937 (Qld) 299

State Air Navigation Act 1937 (SA) 299

State Air Navigation Act 1958 (Vic) 299

State Air Navigation Act 1937 (WA) 299

State Roads Act 1986 270

State Transport Act 1960 (Qld) . . 275, 276, 299

State Transport Act 1980–
  ss 5, 6 275

State Transport (Co-ordination)
  Act 1931 (NSW) 298

State Transport (Co-ordination)
  Act 1933 (WA) .299

State Transport (Co-ordination)
  Amendment Act 1954 269
  s 4 269

State Transport Co-ordination
  (Barring of Claims and Remedies)
  Act 1954 269

State Transport Regulations 1987
  (SR 30 of 1987) .275

Supreme Court Act 1935 (SA) 324
  s 65 731

Supreme Court Rules (NSW)–
  Pt 72 r 2 731

Supreme Court Rules (Qld)–
  r 1 731

Taxi-car Control Act 1985. 279

Tow Truck Act 1973 275

Tow Truck Act 1989 271

Tow Truck Regulations 1988 275

Tow Truck Regulations 1990 271

Trade Practices Act 1974 (Cth) 9, 80, 249,
257, 285, 288,
324, 712, 737
   s 2A 288
   s 4(1) 257
   ss 66ff 9
   s 66A 9, 80
   s 68 257
   ss 69–74 287
   s 74, (1) 257, 288
   s 74(2) 288
   s 74(3) 257

Trade Practices Act Amendment
Act 1992 712

Traffic Act 1909 . . . . 269, 270
   ss 2, 3 270

Traffic Act 1925 (Tas). 279, 280, 299
   s 2(15) 282
   s 3 270
   ss 5(1), (2), 6(1), 14AB(4) 280
   ss 14AB(5), 15(2)–(4), (6), (7) 281
   s 17(1)–(3) 282
   ss 19(2)–(3A), 20(1), 20A(1) 281
   s 20B(1), (2) 281
   ss 22(6B), (7), 26(6A), ...282
   ss 27B, 27(1B) .282
   s 29 . . . . .280, 281
   ss 30, 30B(1), (8), 33 282
   s 58(1) 279
   s 58(2), (3) 280

Traffic Act 1960 275

Traffic Act 1987 . . . . 282, 283
   ss 3, 6, 53, 55 283
   Sch 2 283

Traffic (General and Local) Regulations
1956 (SR 172 of 1956) 280

Traffic (Miscellaneous) Regulations
1968 (SR 143 of 1968) 280

Traffic (Monitoring Devices)
Exemption Order 1991 271

Traffic (Public Vehicles) Regulations
1967 (SR 213 of 1967) 280

Traffic Regulations (SR 19 of 1988)–
reg 3 283

Traffic (Speed Limiting Requirements)
Exemption Order 1991 271

Traffic (Vehicle Loads and Dimensions)
Regulations 1975 (SI 293 of 1975) 280

Transfer of Public Vehicles (Taxation)
Act 1969–
   Pt 2 272
   Divisions 1, 3 272
   s 7 272
   Pt 3 272
   ss 16, 17 272
   Pt 4 272
   Division 1 272
   ss 29–44, 54 272

Transport Act 1981 (Tas) 279, 280, 299
   s 27 280

Transport Act 1983 (Vic) 273, 291
   Pt II, Div 2 273
   Pt IIA 276
   s 24A 276
   Pt III 276
   Pt III, Div 3 . . . . .273, 274
   ss 13–16 273
   s 15(2) 276
   ss 17–18 274
   s 18 276
   ss 19–20 274
   s 21 276
   Pt IV 276
   ss 29, 30, 30(4) .276
   s 33 274
   Pt V 276
   s 37(10) 276
   ss 42–44 277
   s 49 . . . . .286, 291
   s 51 291
   s 56 274
   s 56(1) 291
   Pt VI, Divs 4, 5 .274
   ss 138–162 274
   Pt VI, Divs 6, 7 .274
   ss 163–170 274
   Pt VI, Div 8 275

ss 171–97 275
Pt VI, Div 10 275
ss 198–207 275
Sch 1 Pt II 273, 274

Transport Administration Act
1980 270
ss 45, 46 270

Transport Administration Act
1988 (NSW) 269, 270, 290
s 7 290
ss 22–23 269
ss 24(1), 25(3), 26(2) 270
ss 27(1), 28(1), (2), 29(1), (2) 270
ss 31(1)–(4), (6), 44(1) 270
ss 45, 46, 48, 49 270
s 85 290
s 91 . . . . .286, 289, 290

Transport Administration (Government
Bus and Ferry Services)
Regulation 1989 .272

Transport Administration (Traffic
Control-SRA and STA Land)
Regulation 1989 .272

Transport Administration (Transport
Districts) Regulation 1989 272

Transport Amendment Act 1986 280

Transport Amendment Act 1989 273

Transport (Amendment Act) 1992–
ss 1, 4, 14, 49 273

Transport (Amendment) Act 1993–
ss 8, 17, 25, 27, 32 274
ss 34–47, 54 275
s 166 274

Transport and Communications
Legislation Amendment Act
(no 2) 1993 (no 5 of 1994) 285

Transport Co-ordination Act 1966 . . . 277, 278
ss 3–5, 7–7B, 19–23, 25, 26 278
ss 28, 29, 31, 33, 34, 36 278
ss 37–39, 47Z–47ZG 279
s 60 . . . . .278, 279

Transport (Dangerous Goods)
Regulations 1983 (SR no
193 of 1984) 292

Transport (Delegation) Regulation 1989 . . . 272
Transport Infrastructure Amendment
(Rail) Act 1995 (Queensland)
(no 32 of 1995) .286

Transport Legislation Amendment
Act 1995 (no 95 of 1995) 285

Transport Legislation Amendment
Act (no 2) 1995 326

Transport Licensing Act 1931 271

Transport (Metropolitan Authority)
Regulation 1984 (SR no 196
of 1984) 291

Transport (Penalty Notices) Regulation
1989 272

Transport Regulation Act 1958 273

Transport (State Transport Authority)
Regulations 1984 (Vic) (SR no
193 of 1984)–
reg 3 291

Transport (Tow Truck) Regulations
1983 275

Uniform Road Transport Law 257

Warehousemen's Leins Act (WA) 255

Warehousemen's Leins Ordinance
1959 (NT) 255

Workplace Relations Act 1996 (Cth)–
ss 100(2), 104(1) .731

Canadian Legislation

Civil Code of Quebec 97
North American Free Trade
Implementation Act 1993 669

Dutch Legislation

Dutch Civil Code. 97

European Legislation

Berne Convention for the Protection
of Literary and Artistic Works 1971
(Berne Convention) 695

Chicago Convention (Convention on
International Civil Aviation) 325

CIM Convention on the Contract for
International Carriage of Goods
by Rail 339–371
Arts 1–3 339
Arts 4–5 340
Arts 6–8 341
Arts 9–11 342
Arts 12–13 343
Art 14 344
Art 15 . . . . .345, 345
Arts 16–18 347
Arts 19–20 348
Arts 21–22 349
Arts 23–24 350
Art 25 351
Art 26 352
Art 27 . . . . .191, 353, 354
Arts 28–29 355
Art 30 356
Art 31 357
Arts 32–33 358
Art 34 359
Arts 35–36 360
Arts 37–39 361
Arts 40–42 362
Arts 43–45 363
Arts 46–48 364
Arts 49–52 365
Arts 53–55 366
Arts 56–57 367
Art 58 368
Arts 59–60 369
Arts 61–63 370
Art 64 371

CMR Convention on the Contract
of International Carriage of Goods
by Road (Carriage of Goods
by Road Act 1965) 295–97,
371–83

Arts 1–2 371
Arts 1, 1(1), (2(1) 295
Arts 3–6 372
Art 3 296
Arts 4, 5(1), 6(1)(b), (c) 295
Art 6(1)(2) 295
Arts 7–8 373
Arts 9–12 374
Arts 10, 12(1) 296
Arts 13–14 375
Arts 13, 14(2) 296
Art 14(2)(c) 295
Arts 15–17 376
Art 16(3), (4) 296
Art 17 . . . . .191, 296
Art 17(1) 295
Art 17(2), (4) 296
Arts 18–20 296
Art 18 377
Art 18(3)–(5) 296
Arts 18–22 378
Arts 23–25 297
Arts 23–27 379
Arts 28–30 380
Arts 29, 30(3) 297
Arts 31–32 381
Art 32, (1) 297
Arts 33–37 382
Art 34 . . . . .295. 297
Art 37 297
Arts 38–41 383
Art 41(1) 297

CISG Convention on Contracts for
the International Sale of Goods
(Vienna Convention) 1980 . . . . . . .1–70, 72,
75, 79–81, 83,
85, 86, 88–90,
93–94, 97–99,
122, 123
Part I (Arts 1–13) 3, 18
Arts 1–5 50
Art 1 . . . . .3, 80, 83
Art 1(1) 3, 48, 67
Art 1(1)(a) 4, 6, 70
Art 1(1)(b) 5, 6, 48,
49, 68, 70
Art 1(2) 3
Art 1(3) 4

Arts 2, 3(1), (2) 7	Art 26 ....19, 34
Art 4 8–10	Art 27 ....19, 20
Art 4(a) 88	Art 28 ....20, 25, 29, 94
Art 4(b) 31, 41	Art 29 ....13, 24, 48, 49, 52
Art 5 10	Art 29(2) 20
Arts 6–11 51	Art 30 21
Arts 7ff 11	Arts 31–35 55
Art 7 ....2, 9, 11, 12	Arts 31ff 28
Art 7(1) 9, 12, 81	Art 31(1), (3) 21
Art 7(2) 12, 14, 81	Art 32(1) 21
Art 8 ....12, 88	Arts 33–44 22
Art 8(1)–(3) 12	Art 35 ....22, 23
Art 9 88	Art 35(1) 22
Art 9(1), (2) 13	Art 35(2), (3) 22, 23
Art 10 4	Art 35(3)(a)–(d) 22
Art 10(a) 5	Arts 36–39 56
Art 11 ....13, 48, 49, 52, 68	Art 36(1), (2) 23
Arts 12–18 52	Art 37 ....23, 27, 59, 93
Art 12 ....3, 10, 13,	Art 38 ....23, 24, 57, 65
48, 49, 51, 68	Art 38(1)–(3) 23
Part II (Arts 14–24) 8, 9, 14,	Art 39 ....24, 27, 57, 58
17, 48, 67–70	Art 39(1) 23, 24, 27, 27, 57
Art 14 ....14, 15, 18	Art 39(2) 24
Art 14(1) 14, 17, 85	Arts 40–44 57
Arts 15ff 18	Art 40 24
Art 15 85	Art 41 ....24, 57
Art 15(1), (2) 15, 85	Art 41(2) 28
Art 16 85	Art 42 ....24, 57
Art 16(1), (2) 15	Art 43 24
Art 17 ....15, 85	Art 43(1) 24, 57
Art 18 ....16, 85	Art 44 24
Art 18(1) 16	Arts 45–48 58
Art 18(2) 16, 17, 85	Arts 45–52 ....24, 29
Art 18(3) 16	Art 45 25
Arts 19–22 53	Art 45(1)(b) 35
Art 19 ....15, 16	Arts 46–50 ....27, 59
Art 19(1), (2) 86	Arts 46–52 ....25, 58
Art 19(3) 15, 86	Art 46(1) 25
Art 20 ....16, 86	Art 46(2) 25, 39
Art 21 86	Art 46(3) 25
Art 21(1), (2) 17	Art 46 20
Art 22 ....17, 86	Art 47 ....26, 30, 93
Arts 23–30 54	Art 47(1) 26, 27, 59
Art 23 17	Art 47(2) 26
Art 24 ....15, 17	Art 48 ....27, 59, 93
Part III (Arts 25–88) 8, 9, 18–20,	Art 48(1) 26, 27
67, 69, 70	Art 48(2)–(4) 26
Art 25 ....18, 19, 34, 95	Art 48(2) 27, 59

Arts 49–52 59
Art 49 . . . . .18, 26, 27,
30, 33, 38, 58
Art 49(1)(a) 26, 27
Art 49(1)(b) 26
Art 49(2) 27
Art 50 . . . . .24, 27, 57
Art 51 35
Art 51(1) 27
Art 52(1) 28, 29
Art 52(2) 28
Arts 53–59 60
Arts 53ff 17, 28
Art 53 . . . . .7, 28
Art 54 28
Art 55 . . . . .14, 18, 28, 89
Art 56 28
Art 57 89
Art 57(1), (2) 28
Art 58 . . . . .28, 89
Art 58(1)–(3) 28
Art 59 29
Arts 60–64 61
Arts 60–65 29
Art 61(1)(b) 35
Arts 62–65 . . . . .29, 61
Art 62 . . . . .20, 29, 30
Art 63 . . . . .26, 29, 30, 61, 62
Art 63(1), (2) 30
Art 64 . . . . .18, 30, 38
Art 64(1)(a), (b), (2) 30
Arts 65–69 62
Art 65(2) 30
Arts 66–70 31
Arts 66ff 38
Art 66 31
Arts 67–69 33
Art 67 . . . . .31, 33, 62, 63
Art 67(1), (2) 32
Art 68 . . . . .32, 33, 62, 63
Art 69 . . . . .33, 63
Art 69(1)–(3) 33
Arts 70–73 63
Arts 70–73 33
Art 71 34
Art 71(1) 33
Arts 71(3), 72, (1), (2) 34
Art 73 . . . . .34, 35

Art 73(1)–(3) 34
Arts 74–76 37
Arts 74–77 . . . . .25, 29, 35, 58, 61
Arts 74–79 64
Art 74 . . . . .35–37, 96
Arts 75, 76(2) 36
Art 77 . . . . .36, 37, 97
Art 78 . . . . .37, 96
Arts 79–80 37
Art 79 . . . . .37, 38, 91
Art 79(1)–(3) 37
Art 79(3), (4) 38
Art 79(5) 38, 93
Arts 80–83 65
Art 80 . . . . .38, 97
Arts 81–84 38
Arts 81ff 30, 34
Art 81 .26, 38, 39
Art 81(1), (2) 39
Arts 82(1), (2), (c), 83 39
Arts 84–88 66
Art 84(1) 39
Arts 85–88 40
Art 85 . . . . .29, 40
Arts 85(1), 86, (1), (2), 87 40
Art 88 . . . . .29, 41
Art 88(3) 40
Pt IV (Arts 89–101) 67
Arts 89–93 67
Art 90 . . . . .48, 49
Art 92 69
Art 92(1) 48, 49
Art 93 48
Arts 93(1), 94–97 .68
Art 94 69
Art 94(1), (2) 48
Art 95 .5, 6, 48, 83
Art 96 . . . . .13, 48, 49, 52
Arts 98–99 69
Art 99 1
Arts 100–101 70

COTIF Convention concerning
International Carriage by Rail 292, 293
Arts 1, 4(1), 11(5), 12(10) 292
Arts 13, 15(2)(d), 19(3) 293
Art 26(1), (2) 293
Art 30(4) 294
Arts 31, 34, 35(1), (2) 293

Arts 36(1)–(3), 37(2) 294
Art 38 293
Arts 40(1), (2), 44 294
Arts 45, 47(2), (3) 293
Arts 55(3), 57, 58 294
Convention on the Law Applicable
to Contracts for the International
Sale of Goods
(Hague Convention) 70–77, 83
Arts 5–5 71
Arts 6–8 72
Art 8(3) 75
Arts 7–12 73
Art 12 . . . . .72, 75
Arts 13–21 74
Art 21 77
Art 21(1)(b) 72
Art 21(1)(c) 73
Arts 22–25 75
Art 25 76
Arts 26–31 76
Arts 26, 30, 31 77
Convention on the Law Applicable
to the International Sale of Goods
(The Hague) 1955 76
Convention on the Limitation Period
in the International Sale of
Goods (New York) 1974 75
Convention on the Recognition and
Enforcement of Foreign Arbitral
Awards (New York Convention) . . .733–36,
739, 740,
742, 743,
746, 752,
764–68
Arts I–III 764
Art I(1), (3)(c) 732
Art II(1) 729, 732, 739
Arts IV–V 765
Arts VI–X 766
Arts XI–XV 767
Art XVI 768

Directive 64/221 713
Directive 70/50 (Free movement of
goods between Member States) 717, 724

Directive 79/623 (Harmonisation
of provisions relating to customs) 795
Directive 83/189 (Procedure for
the provision of information in
the field of technical standards
and regulations) .724
Directive 85/73 (Financing of
inspections and controls of
fresh meat and poultry meat) 717
Directive 85/374 (Laws regarding
manufacturers' liability for
defective products) 712
Directive 92/59 (General product
safety) 712, 725

Euratom (European Atomic
Energy) Treaty 705–07, 726
ECSC (European Coal and
Steel) Treaty 705–07, 726
Art 14 714
European Convention on Human
Rights (ECHR) .705
EC Treaty. 706–09, 714, 715
Art 3 . . . . .706, 716
Art 3(a) 706
Art 3(c) 706, 769
Art 3(e)–(h) 706
Art 3(g) 769, 770, 773, 778
Art 3a 706, 709
Art 4 707
Art 4A 710
Art 7a 708
Arts 8–8e 707
Arts 9–37 714
Arts 9, 10 716
Arts 12–17 715
Art 23(3) 716
Art 28 708
Arts 30–36 769
Art 30 . . . . .717, 718, 720,
721, 723, 724
Art 36 . . . . .717–20, 722, 780
Art 49 708
Art 57(2) 709
Art 59(2) 708

Arts 67–73 710
Art 70(1) 708
Arts 73(a)–(h), 73A 710
Art 84(2) 709
Arts 85–94 769
Art 85 . . . . .770–78, 780, 783
Art 85(1) 713, 770–78, 780
Art 85(2) 770
Art 85(3) 713, 771, 772, 778
Art 85(3)(a), (b) 771
Art 86 .770, 771,
                              774, 777–81, 783
Arts 87, 90 770
Art 99 709
Art 100 . . . . .709, 720
Art 100a 708
Art 100c(1), (3) 707
Art 103 718
Arts 105((1), (2), 105a, ...710
Art 106(1), (2) .710
Arts 106(3), 107 711
Art 109 .710, 711
Arts 109(1), (2), 109A(1), (2) 711
Arts 110–15 781
Art 110 716
Art 113 .716, 782
Art 115 .718, 719
Arts 138d, 138e 707
Art 164 797
Art 169 .713, 714
Art 170 714
Art 173 .777, 797
Art 177 723
Art 189 .711, 713
Art 189b 708
Art 228 781
EEC Treaty 1957 . . . . .705, 726
Art 1 705
EU Treaty on European Union
(Maastricht Treaty) 1993 . . . . .705, 710, 726
Art A 705
Art G(B)(4) 709
Art G(B)(7) 710
Art G(C) 707
Art G(D)(15) .710
Art G(D)(25) .711
Art G(E) 707

Art J 706
Art O 707

First Treaty of Accession 1972 726
Fourth Treaty of Accession 1995 726

GATS General Agreement on
   Trade in Services 563, 565, 689
   Art I 565, 574
   Art II   566, 570,
                                    572, 573, 580
   Art III 566
   Art IV 575
   Art V 567, 568
   Art VI 568, 569, 608
   Art VII .569, 570
   Art VIII 570
   Art IX .570, 580
   Art X 571
   Art XI .567, 571
   Art XII 567, 571, 572
   Art XIII 572
   Art XIV 567, 573
   Art XV 573
   Art XVI 572–576
   Art XVII 567, 572–77
   Arts XVIII, XIX, XX 575
   Art XXI 568, 570,
                                    571, 576, 577
   Arts XXII, XXIII 548, 577
   Art XXIV 577
   Art XXVII 578
   Art XXVIII 578–580
   Art XXIX 580
GATT 1994 Agreement on
   Agriculture 594, 609
   Art 1(f) 610
   Art 6 . . . . .609, 610
   Art 8 609
   Art 9 610
   Art 10 594
   Art 10.1 609
   Art 13, (a), (c) 610
   Art 15.2 609
   Arts 16, 17, 18(5) 610
   Annexes 1, 2 .610

GATT 1994 Agreement on
Subsidies and Countervailing
Measures .584, 585,
594, 634–67
Art 1 . . . . .584, 634
Art 2 . . . . .594, 634–35
Art 3 .584, 595, 635
Art 4 . . . . .635, 636
Arts 4.3–4.5, 4.9, 4.10 595
Arts 5–6 584
Art 5 636
Art 6 . . . . .637, 638
Art 7 . . . . .638, 639
Arts 7.3, 7.4, 7.7, 7.10 595
Art 8 .584, 640, 641
Art 8.2ff 595
Art 9 . . . . .641, 642
Art 10 642
Art 11 642–44
Arts 11.2, 11.4, 11.9 595
Art 12 644–46
Arts 12.1.1, 12.1.2, 12.4.1 595
Art 12.6 595
Art 13 646
Art 14 . . . . .959, 646, 647
Art 15 . . . . .647, 648
Art 15.1 596
Art 16 649
Art 16.1 595
Art 17 . . . . .649, 650
Art 17.1 596
Art 17.3 596
Art 18 . . . . .650, 651
Art 18.1 596
Art 19 651
Arts 19.1, 19.4 .596
Art 20 . . . . .651, 652
Art 21 . . . . .652, 653
Arts 21.1, 21.3 .596
Art 22 . . . . .653, 654
Arts 22.2, 22.3, 22.5 596
Art 23 . . . . .596, 602, 654
Art 24 . . . . .654, 655
Arts 24.1, 24.3 .595
Art 25 . . . . .655, 656
Art 26 656
Art 27 . . . . .596, 656–658
Art 28 658

Art 29 . . . . .658, 659
Arts 30, 31 659
Art 32 . . . . .659, 660
Annex I 595, 660, 661
Annex II 661, 662
Annex III 663
Annex IV .597, 664
Annex V 597, 664–66
Annex VI .959, 666
Annex VII 596, 667
GATT Anti-Dumping Agreement
(Agreement on the Implementation
of Article VI of GATT 1994) 583–667,
614–33
Art 1 614
Art 2 614–16
Art 2.1 583
Arts 2.4, 2.4.2, 2.5 593
Art 3 . . . . .584, 616–18
Arts 3.1, 3.5 592
Art 4 618
Art 5 618–20
Art 5.1 592
Art 5.4 . . . . .592, 595
Art 5.8 . . . . .593, 595, 599
Art 5.10 593
Art 6 620–22
Art 6.1 593
Art 6.1.1 595
Arts 6.1.2, 6.5.1 . . . . .592, 595
Art 6.7 . . . . .593, 595
Art 6.11 592
Art 7 623
Art 7.1(i) 593
Art 8 . . . . .623, 624
Arts 8.1, 8.2 593
Art 9 624–26
Art 9.3 593
Art 10 . . . . .626, 627
Art 11 . . . . .596, 627
Art 12 . . . . .596, 627, 628
Arts 12.1.1, 12.2.1, 12.2.2 593
Art 13 .590, 594,
596, 602, 629
Art 14 629
Arts 14.1, 14.2, 14.4 594
Art 15 . . . . .594, 629
Art 16 . . . . .594, 629, 630

Art 17 . . . . .630, 631
Art 18 631
Annex 1 .593, 632
Annex II .632, 633

GATT 1967 (Anti-Dumping
Agreement) 585

GATT 1947 (General Agreement
on Tariffs and Trade) 671
Art VI 585

GATT 1994 (General Agreement
on Tariffs and Trade) 443–581,
585, 597, 598,
602, 605, 782
Arts I–III 484
Art I .445, 448, 491
Art II 478, 497,
492, 493, 598
Art III 445, 448,
449, 451, 493,
494, 671, 672
Art IV 462, 477, 495
Art V 477, 495
Art VI 451, 471, 496,
497, 584, 783, 787
Art VII 452, 477, 497–499
Art VIII 452, 477, 485, 499
Art IX 477, 485,
486, 499, 500
Art X 446, 477,
478, 486–88, 500
Art XI 456, 488, 501,
673, 675, 676
Art XII 456, 457, 460,
478, 502–04
Art XIII 456, 462, 477,
478, 504–06
Art XIV 462, 478, 506, 714
Art XV 478, 489, 506, 507
Art XVI 471, 476,
478, 488, 508
Art XVII 476, 478, 508, 509
Art XVIII 456–64, 478, 509–15
Art XIX 477, 515, 516, 604
Art XX 450, 516
Art XXI 456, 517

Art XXII 452, 453, 476,
517, 545, 548, 596
Art XXIII 452, 453, 461,
472, 517, 518,
545, 548, 561, 596
Art XXIV 518–20
Art XXV 468, 521
Art XXVI 447, 466, 467, 521
Art XXVII 522
Art XXVIII 446, 451,
468, 522–24
Art XXIX 524
Arts XXX, XXXI 525
Art XXXII 447, 525
Art XXXIII 447, 468, 526
Art XXXIV 526
Art XXXV 474, 526
Art XXXVI 465–68,
470, 526, 527
Art XXXVII 465, 467–70, 527–29
Art XXXVIII 465, 468–70, 529
Annex A–C 530
Annex D–H 531
Annex I 532–44

Geneva Convention for the Protection
of Producers of Phonograms Against
Unauthorised Duplication of their
Phonograms 1971 (Geneva
Convention) 695

Guadalajara Convention 320, 321, 323
Art 1 320
Art 1(a) 321
Art 1(b) 320
Art 1(c) 317, 320, 321
Art 2 . . . . .320, 321
Art 3 .320, 321, 322
Art 3(2) 322
Arts 4, 5 321
Art 6 322
Art 7 . . . . .321, 322
Art 8 321
Arts 9(2) 322
Sch 3 302

Guatemala Protocol 1971 319

Hague Protocol 1955 (The amended
  Warsaw Convention) 302, 309,
                              311, 321–23, 385
  Arts 1, 3–9 302
  Art 11 314
  Arts 18, 34 302
  Sch 2 302
Hague Rules (International Convention
  for the Unification of Certain
  Rules of Law Relating to
  Bills of Lading) 1924 175–205,
                                    215–18
  Art 1 218
  Art 1(b) 182
  Art 1(c) 186
  Arts 2–3 219
  Arts 3–4 220
  Art 3 r 1 175
  Art 3 r 2 .186, 191
  Art 4 221
  Art 4 r 2(a), (b) 176
  Art 4 r 5 . . . . .176, 193, 198, 199
  Arts 5–7 222
  Art 6 182
  Arts 8–13 223
  Art 9 198
  Art 10 182
  Arts 14–16 224
  Art 30 r 1 177
Hague-Visby Rules
  (Amended Hague Rules
  of the International Convention
  for the Unification of Certain
  Rules of Law Relating to Bills of
  Lading) 1977 175–205,
                                    215, 229
  Arts 1–2 229
  Art 1(c) 186, 187
  Art 3 . . . . .196, 197, 230, 231
  Art 3 r 2 191
  Art 3 r 6 193
  Art 3 r 8 182
  Art 4 . . . . .184, 196, 231–34
  Art 4 r 1 .185, 202
  Art 4 r 2 196
  Art 4 r 2(a) 188
  Art 4 r 2(b) 189
  Art 4 r 5 193

Art 4 r 5(a) 198
Art 4 r 5(c) 193
Art 4 r 5(d) 198
Art 4 r 5(e) 199
Art 4 r 20 188
Art 5 . . . . .198, 234
Art 6 234
Art 6 r 1(a) 198
Art 6 r 2 194
Arts 7–10 235
Art 10 182
Hamburg Rules (United Nations
  Convention on the Carriage
  of Goods by Sea) 1978 177–205,
                                    215, 235
  Art 1 . . . . .235, 236
  Art 1(5) 187, 188
  Art 1 r 6 .180, 183
  Art 1(b) 182
  Art 2 236
  Art 2 rr 1, 3 183
  Arts 3–5 237
  Art 4 . . . . .189, 191, 197
  Art 4(a), (b) 189
  Art 4 r 1 .181, 190
  Art 4 r 2 181
  Art 4 r 5(c) 180
  Art 5 . . . . .191, 197
  Art 5 r 1 . . . . .189, 190, 197
  Art 5 r 3 192
  Art 5 r 4 . . . . .178, 189, 238
  Art 5 r 4(a) 190
  Art 6 . . . . .182, 187, 199, 238
  Art 6 r 1(b) 192
  Arts 7–9 239
  Art 7 r 1 .185, 186
  Art 7 r 2 185
  Art 8 r 1 199
  Art 9 187
  Arts 10–11 240
  Arts 12–14 241
  Arts 15–16 242
  Arts 16, 17 243
  Arts 18–20 244
  Art 20 r 1 193
  Art 21 . . . . .195, 245
  Art 21 r 1(d) 196
  Arts 22, 23 246

1

Arts 24, 25 247
Art 26 248
Havana Conference 1947. 443

Incoterms (International
Commercial Trade Terms) 1990 121–73
A1–A3 157
A1–A6 . . . . .160, 163
A1–A7 . . . . .168, 171
A1–A8 155
A1 .128–30, 132, 135,
                                    139, 143, 145,
                                    147, 149, 150, 164
A2–A7 165
A2 . . . . .128–32, 135,
                                    139, 143, 145, 147,
                                    148, 150, 152, 159
A3 . . . . .128, 132, 135,
                                    139, 140, 143–45,
                                    147, 149, 150, 167
A3(a) 130, 131
A3(b) 142
A4–B1 158
A4 . . . . .128, 130–36,
                                    139–41, 143–47,
                                    149–51, 156, 159,
                                    161, 164, 166, 167,
                                    169, 170, 172, 173
A5 . . . . .128, 129, 131, 133,
                                    135, 136, 140, 143,
                                    144, 146, 147, 149–51
A6 . . . . .128, 130, 131, 133,
                                    135, 136, 140, 141,
                                    143–47, 149, 150, 152
A7–A10 164
A7–B5 161
A7 . . . . .128, 132, 133,
                                    136, 139, 140, 143,
                                    146, 147, 149, 150
A8–B5 . . . . .166, 169, 172
A8 . . . . .128, 132, 133, 136,
                                    137, 140, 141, 143,
                                    144, 146, 147, 149,
                                    151, 159, 167, 170, 173
A9–B6 156
A9 . . . . .128–34, 136, 137, 140,
                                    141, 143, 144, 146–51

A10 . . . . .128, 130, 132–34,
                                    136, 137, 140–42,
                                    144, 146–49, 151,
                                    152, 160, 167, 173
B1 . . . . .128, 132, 133, 136,
                                    141, 146, 149, 151
B2–B9 159
B2 . . . . .128, 129, 132, 133,
                                    136, 141, 144, 146–52, 173
B3 . . . . .128, 129, 131–33,
                                    136, 141, 144, 149
B4 . . . . .128, 129, 132, 134,
                                    136, 137, 141, 143, 146,
                                    147, 149, 151, 163, 165
B5 . . . . .128, 129, 131–34,
                                    136, 137, 139–41, 143,
                                    144, 146–52, 160,
                                    163, 165, 168, 171
B6–B10 . . . . .162, 167, 170, 173
B6 . . . . .128, 130–37, 140,
                                    141, 143, 144, 146–52,
                                    158, 160, 163, 165, 171
B7–B10 157
B7 . . . . .128–31, 133, 136,
                                    141, 144, 146, 148,
                                    149, 151, 156, 166, 172
B8 . . . . .128, 137, 141, 144,
                                    146, 148, 149, 151
B9 .128, 130, 132,
                                    133, 137, 141, 144,
                                    146, 148, 149, 151
B10 .128, 130, 132,
                                    134, 137, 141,
                                    144, 146, 148,
                                    149, 151, 152, 160
International Convention for the
Protection of New Varieties of
Plants 1978 (UPOV Convention) 695
International Convention for the
Protection of New Varieties of
Plants 1991 (UPOV Convention) 695

Lomé Conventions. 782

Merger Treaty 1965 726
Montreal Agreement 1965 314

Montreal Agreement 1966 . . . . 319, 385

Montreal (No 3) Convention. 302

Montreal (No 4) Convention. 302

Montreal Protocol (No 3) 315, 316, 323

Montreal Protocol (No 4) 315–17, 323

Paris Convention 1919. 299

Paris Convention for the Protection
  of Industrial Property 1967
  (Paris Convention) 695

Regulation 17/62 (Enforcement
  Regulation) 713, 770–72

Regulation 459/68 (Anti-dumping
  Regulation) 782

Regulation 974/71 (Conjunctoral
  policy following the temporary
  widening of the margins allowed
  for the fluctuations of the currencies
  of some Member States) 718

Regulation 3017/79 (Investigation
  into anti-dumping) 792, 794,
                                          795, 797

Regulation 288/82 (Tariff and
  Trade) 782

Regulation 2176/84 (Anti-
  dumping) 788, 789, 792

Regulation 2641/84 (Anti-
  dumping) 782, 784, 786

Regulation 2658/87 (Tariff and
  statistical nomenclature and
  the common customs tariff) 716

Regulation 2423/88 (Current Anti-
  dumping Regulation) 782–96

Regulation 4151/88 (Provisions
  applicable to goods brought
  into the customs territory
  of the Community) 716

Second Treaty of Accession 1979. 726

Single European Act 1986 726

Statute of UNCITRAL–
  Art 8 79

Tokyo Round of Agreements 1979
  (Subsidies Code) 472,
                                          585, 586
  Art 2, (a)–(c) 473
  Arts 8, 9, 11(1), 14(3) 472

Third Treaty of Accession 1985 726

Treaty of Paris 1951 . . . . 706, 726

Treaty of Rome 1957. . . . . 706, 726, 769

UNCITRAL Model Law 732, 733,
                                      735, 738, 740–64
  Arts 1–2 754
  Art 1(2) 744
  Arts 3–7 755
  Art 5 742
  Art 7(1) 729
  Art 7(2) 735
  Art 1(2) 733
  Arts 8–11 756
  Art 8 . . . . .733, 739, 745
  Art 9 . . . . .733, 734
  Arts 12–15 757
  Arts 16–20 758
  Art 16 742
  Art 16(1), (3) 741, 742
  Arts 21–24 759
  Arts 25–29 760
  Arts 30–33 761
  Art 34 . . . . .743–45, 751, 762
  Art 34(1)–(4) 743
  Art 34(1), (2)(i), (ii) 744
  Art 34(2)(a)(iii) 744, 745
  Art 34(2)(a)(iv), (2)(b) 745
  Art 34(2)(b)(i) 745
  Art 34(2)(b)(ii) 744
  Art 35 . . . . .733, 734, 752, 763
  Art 36 . . . . .733, 734–45, 752, 763

UNCTAD I Conference 466, 469

Uniform Customs and Practice for
  Documentary Credits 1993
  (Revision, ICC publication
  no 500) 389, 393,
                                      399, 402, 405,
                                      417, 421–42
  Arts 1–5 421
  Art 1 . . . . .389, 394
  Art 2 389

Art 3 409
Art 4 . . . . .398, 410
Arts 6–9 422
Art 6(b), (c) 390
Art 7 400
Arts 7(a), 8(a) 390
Art 9(a)(iii)–(d)(ii) 423
Art 9(a)(iv) 392
Art 9(d)(i) 390
Arts 9(d)(iii), (iv), 10–11 424
Art 10(b)(ii) 392
Arts 12–13 425
Art 13(a) 399, 404
Art 13(b) 399
Art 14 426
Art 14(c) 403
Art 14(d)(i), (e) 399
Art 14(f) 406
Arts 15–19 427
Art 15 . . . . .400, 413
Arts 20–21 428
Art 22 400
Arts 22–23 429
Art 24 . . . . .430, 431
Art 25–26 432
Art 26(a)(ii)–(vii), (b) 433
Art 27 . . . . .433, 434
Art 28 434
Arts 29–31 435
Arts 43–34 436
Arts 37–37 437
Art 37(c) 404
Arts 39–42 438
Art 39(b) 402
Arts 43–46 439
Arts 47–48 440
Art 48 . . . . .394, 395
Art 48(b) 395
Art 48(g)–(j) 441
Art 49 . . . . .396, 442

Uniform Customs and Practice for
   Documentary Credits
   (UPC Revision 1973) 404

Uniform Customs and Practice for
   Documentary Credits
   (UPC Revision 1974) 403

Uniform Customs and Practice for
   Documentary Credits
   (UPC Revision 1983)–
   Art 7 400

UNIDROIT (Principles of
   International Commercial
   Contracts) 1994 79–119
   Arts 1.1–1.9 101
   Art 1.3 91
   Art 1.4 82
   Art 1.5 97
   Art 1.6 . . . . .82, 93, 98
   Art 1.6(1), (2) .82
   Art 1.7 . . . . .84, 97, 98
   Art 1.7(1), (2) .84
   Art 1.8 88
   Art 1.9 . . . . .87, 95
   Arts 1.10–2.6 .102
   Art 1.10 92
   Arts 2.1, 2.2 85
   Art 2.3 . . . . .85, 86
   Arts 2.3(1), (2), 2.4–2.6 85
   Arts 2.7–2.12 .103
   Art 2.7 85
   Arts 2.8–2.12 .86
   Arts 2.13–2.19 104
   Art 2.14(1), (2) 86
   Art 2.15, (1)–(3) 84
   Art 2.16 .84, 85
   Art 2.19(1), (2) 86
   Arts 2.20–3.5 .105
   Arts 2.20–2.22 86
   Art 2.22 87
   Art 3.1 88
   Art 3.2 85
   Art 3.3 88
   Arts 3.6–3.11 .106
   Art 3.8 . . . . .85, 87
   Arts 3.9–3.10 .87
   Arts 3.12–3.18 107
   Arts 3.12–3.17 87
   Art 3.13(2) 106
   Art 3.16 88
   Arts 3.19–4.7 .108
   Art 3.19 . . . . .87, 97
   Arts 4.1–4.5, 4.7–4.8 88
   Arts 4.8–5.6 109

Arts 4.8, 5.3–5.5 89
Arts 5.4, 5.5 95
Arts 5.7–6.1.4 .110
Art 5.7 . . . . .85, 89
Arts 6.1.1, 6.1.2 .89
Arts 6.1.5–6.1.9 .111
Art 6.1.6 . . . . .89, 90
Arts 6.1.7(1), 6.1.8(1), (2) 90
Art 6.1.9, (1)–(4) .90
Arts 6.1.10–6.1.16 112
Art 6.1.10 90
Art 6.1.11 89
Arts 6.1.12–6.1.17 90
Arts 6.1.17–7.1.1 113
Art 6.2.1–6.2.3 .91
Arts 6.2.2, 6.2.3 92
Art 7.1.1 . . . . .93, 95
Arts 7.1.2–7.1.5 114
Arts 7.1.2–7.1.3 94
Art 7.1.4, (2), (3), (5) 93
Art 7.1.5 . . . . .93, 116
Art 7.1.5(2) 93
Arts 7.1.6–7.2.4 115
Art 7.1.6 . . . . .94, 95
Art 7.1.7 . . . . .91–93, 95
Art 7.1.7(2) 92
Art 7.1.7(4) 93
Arts 7.2.1–7.2.3, 7.2.4(1), (4) 94
Arts 7.2.5–7.3.4 116
Arts 7.3.1–7.3.4 95
Arts 7.3.5–7.4.5 117
Arts 7.3.6, 7.4.1 95
Arts 7.4.2(1), (2), 7.4.3, (1), (2) 96
Arts 7.4.4–7.4.5 96
Arts 7.4.6–7.4.12 118
Art 7.4.6(1), (2) 96
Arts 7.4.7, 7.4.8 97
Arts 7.4.9, (1), (2), 7.4.10, 7.4.12 96
Art 7.4.13 . . . . .97, 119

Uniform Law on the Formation of
  Contracts for the International
  Sale of Goods (Hague Formation
  Convention) 1964 . . . . .1, 46, 69, 79

Uniform Law on the International
  Sale of Goods (Hague Sales
  Convention) 1964 . . . . .1, 46, 69, 70, 79

Uruguay Round of GATT
  Negotiations 585, 586, 597, 609

Warsaw Convention (Relating to
  the carriage of goods by air) 1929 200,
                                              249, 298,
                                         301–03, 313–15,
                                         318–22, 332–38,
                                              384, 385
Arts 1–5 332
Art 1(1)–(3) 302
Art 1(3) 303
Art 2 302
Art 4(1), (3), (4) 303
Arts 5–9 304
Arts 6–8 333
Arts 9–13 334
Art 10(2) 304
Art 11 307
Art 11(1) 304
Art 11(2) 305
Arts 12–14 312
Arts 12–15 305
Art 13(3) 306
Arts 14–18 335
Art 16(1), (2) .305
Art 17 . . . . .326, 384
Arts 18–19 306
Art 18 . . . . .308, 312
Art 18(1) 312
Art 18(2), (3) 308, 309
Arts 19–24 336
Art 19 . . . . .191, 311, 312
Arts 20–22 310
Art 20 311
Art 20(1) 312, 326, 327, 385
Art 21 311
Art 22 . . . . .307, 317, 322
Art 22(1) 326, 327, 384, 385
Art 22(2), (3) .304
Art 24(1) 306
Arts 25–30 337
Art 25 . . . . .309–11, 322
Art 26 321
Art 26(1) 305
Art 28 321
Art 29 193
Art 30(1), (3) .303
Arts 31–35 338
Art 31 309

World Trade Organisation
  Agreement (Marrakesh) 1994 443–45,
                    473–80,
                544–65, 603,
              670, 671, 695, 782
    Art 1 544
    Art 2 545
    Art 3 .545–47, 556
    Arts 4, 5 .547, 548
    Art 6 . . . . .547, 549
    Art 7 549
    Art 8 . . . . .549, 550
    Art 9 . . . . .550, 551
    Arts 10, 11 551
    Art 12 . . . . .547, 551–53, 556
    Art 13 . . . . .553, 565
    Arts 14–16 553
    Art 17 554–556
    Art 18 555
    Art 19 . . . . .555, 556
    Art 20 . . . . .553, 556
    Art 21 . . . . .556, 557, 559–61
    Art 22 557–61
    Art 23 . . . . .559, 560
    Arts 24, 25 560
    Art 26 561
    Art 27 562
    Annex 1A 604
    Annex 2 544
    Appendix 1 562
    Appendix 2 . . . . .562, 563
    Appendix 3 . . . . .563, 564
    Appendix 4 565

Mexican Legislation

Commercial Code of Mexico 97

New Zealand Legislation

Anti-Dumping and Countervailing
  Duties Act 1988–
    ss 3A, 3B, 4–11 603
    ss 13–15, 16(1)(b), 17, 18 604

Customs Act 1966–
    s 2 604

Dumping and Countervailing
  Duties Act 1988 588
    ss 3B, 10(10) 587

Judicature Act 1908 604
    Pt 1 . . . . .590, 604
    s 11 604

Temporary Safeguard Authorities
    Act 1987 605

North American Legislation (USA, Canada and the United Mexican States)

North American Free Trade Agreement
  1992 (NAFTA)–
    Arts 101, 102(1)(a)–(f) 669
    Art 103(1) 670
    Art 201 682
    Art 201(1) .671, 673
    Art 210 681
    Arts 300–318 671
    Art 301 676
    Art 301(1), (2) 672
    Art 302(1) .672, 673
    Arts 302(2), 303(1), (2) 672
    Arts 304(1), 305(1)(a) 672
    Arts 306, 307 673
    Arts 309, (1), (2), 310(1) 673
    Arts 314, 316 673
    Art 401 . . . . .674, 675
    Arts 402, (2), (3), 403–05 674
    Arts 405(1), (3)–(6), 406 674
    Arts 406(a), (b), 408–10 675
    Art 413 674
    Art 415 . . . . .674, 675
    Arts 501–08, 601(2), (3) 675
    Art 602 675
    Art 603 . . . . .675, 676
    Arts 604, 606(1), 607 676
    Arts 1001–25 676
    Arts 1001, 1002, 1003(1) 677
    Art 1003(2) 679
    Arts 1004, 1005(1) 677
    Arts 1005(2), 1006, 1007(1) 678
    Arts 1008–15 679
    Arts 1008–16 678

Arts 1010–13 679
Arts 1014(3), (4), 1016(2) 679
Art 1017 679
Arts 1018(1), (2), 1022(1), (2) 680
Art 1023 680
Art 1024 681
Art 1025(1) 678
Arts 1101–14 687
Arts 1101–39 681
Art 1101 682
Arts 1102–07 683
Art 1102(1)–(3) .682
Art 1102 684
Art 1103 . . . . .682, 684
Arts 1106–09 684
Art 1106 682
Arts 1109–10, 1112(1) 685
Art 1113(1) 686
Art 1113(1)(a) 678
Art 1114 682
Arts 1115–39 686
Arts 1116, (2), 1117, (1), (4) 687
Art 1118 687
Arts 1119, (a)–(d), 1120(1) 688
Arts 1121–38 688
Art 1139 . . . . .682, 684, 687
Art 1201(1) 688, 689
Arts 1201(2), 1202–05 689
Arts 1206–08, 1210(1), ...690
Art 1211(1) 690
Art 1213(2) 688, 689
Art 1301 . . . . .690, 691
Arts 1302(1)–(8), 1303(1) 691
Arts 1304, 1306 691
Art 1403 692
Art 1404 693
Art 1404(1) 692
Art 1405 693
Art 1406 . . . . .692, 693
Arts 1406(1), 1407, 1409–10 694
Arts 1411(1), (2), 1412–15 694
Art 1416 692
Arts 1592(3)(a), 1503(2) 687
Art 1701(1), (2) .695
Arts 1703(1), 1704 696
Arts 1705–10 695
Arts 1711–18 696

Arts 1715–16 697
Arts 1717–20, 1802–04 698
Art 1802(2) 694
Arts 1804, 2001–22 699
Art 2001(1), (2)(a)–(e) 669
Arts 2003, 2006–17 700
Arts 2018(1), 2020–22 700
Arts 2020(3), 2021, 22(1) 701
Arts 2102, 2103(1), (2) 701
Art 2104(2)–(4) .701
Art 2203 .669, 693
Annex 301.3 671
Annex 302.2 672
Annex 310.1 673
Annex 314 673
Annex 401 674
Annexes 602.3, 603.6, 605 676
Annexes 607, 608.2 676
Annex 1001.1(a)–(l) 680
Annex 1010.1 680
Annexes 1120.1, 1137.2 681
Annexes 1137.4, 1138.2 681
Annex 2001.2 699
North American Free Trade
    Association (NAFTA) 587, 589
    Art 1904 587

UK Legislation

Arbitration Act 1950 . . . . .747, 748
    s 4(1) 736, 740
    ss 21, 22 747

Common Law Procedure
    Act 1854 747

International Transport
    Conventions Act 1983 292

US Legislation

Anti-Dumping Act 1921 586
Anti-Dumping Authority Act 1988–
    s 3 586

Carriage of Goods by Sea Act 1936 175

Customs Act 1901 586

Customs Act 1966–
Pt VA 586

Customs Courts Act 1980 589

Customs Tariff (Anti-Dumping) Act
1975 (Anti-Dumping Act 1988) 586

Customs Tariff (Anti-Dumping)
(World Trade Organisation
Amendments) Act 1994 586

Dumping and Countervailing Duties
Act 1988 586

Emergency Tariff Act 1921 . . . . 585, 586

Foreign Trade Antitrust Improvements Act
1982 800

Harter Act 1892 . . . . 175, 204

North American Free Trade
Implementation Act 1993 669

Settlement of Investment Disputes
between States and Nationals of
Other States (ICSID Convention
1965 Washington) 686

Arts 25–63 686

Sherman Act 1890 . . . . 773, 778, 798

Tariff Act of 1897 (The Dingley Act). 585

Tariff Act 1930 . . . . 588, 597, 598
Title VII 586, 597
Title VII ss 701–07, 709 598
Title VII ss 731–38, 751(c)(1) 598
Title VII ss 771, 777(b) 598
s 303 585
s 332(g) 452

Trade Act 1974–
s 201 605

Trade Agreements Act 1979. . . . . 585, 586

Uniform Commercial Code. 121

Uruguay Round Agreement
Act 1994 . . . . .586, 598
Title II 586, 598

US Code–
Title 19 . . . . .597, 607
Title 19(IV) 597
Title 19 Art 1671 . . . . .597, 598
Title 19 Arts 1671a–f, h 598
Title 19 Arts 1673, a–g 598
Title 19 Arts 1675, 1677–77k 598

THE UN CONVENTION ON CONTRACTS FOR THE INTERNATIONAL SALE OF GOODS

INTRODUCTION

The United Nations Convention on Contracts for the International Sale of Goods (Vienna Convention) came into force on 1 January 1980.[1]

It continues to be open for ratification or accession. Four States signed it (it was open for signature until 30 September 1981) and as at May 1994 a further 38 had ratified it or acceded to it. These Contracting States include Australia, Canada, China, France, Germany, Italy, the Russian Federation, Spain and the USA. Notable omissions include Japan and the UK. The list of relevant States is set out at the end of this commentary, along with a statement of declarations and reservations made by certain States pursuant to provisions in the Convention.

The Convention was adopted by a conference of 62 States convened by the Secretary General of the United Nations. These States were representative in their legal system, their geographic spread and their trading profiles.

The Convention was intended to replace the Hague Uniform Laws on International Laws (ie The Uniform Law on International Sale of Goods of 1964, and the Uniform Law on the Formation of Contracts for the International Sale of Goods of 1964), which were adopted by the Hague Conference of 1964. The Hague Conventions were ratified by few States, being considered to be technically defective in certain aspects and Eurocentric in provenance, with, in the minds of some, an implicit bias in favour of the developed countries whose main trading interest was the export of industrial products.

The Convention, and the Hague Conventions which preceded it, were the result of decades of international discussions of, and studies on, the topic of a uniform international contracts of sale law. The Vienna Convention has been evolved under the aegis of the United Nations Commission on International Trade Law (UNCITRAL). The international sales contract, by its very nature, has long raised choice of law problems as well as difficult enforcement issues. The uniform international sales law movement has had as its goal a uniform law dealing with the international sale of goods transaction, a law which, necessarily, would be applied by the courts and tribunals of individual nations. The ultimate issues of enforcement would not be touched by such a law, which would be administered on a case-by-case municipal basis; but a uniform law would confer other benefits which could facilitate dispute resolution and, should it eventuate, litigation. The basic prospective benefit of a uniform sales law regime, of course, is that both parties can more readily know their legal rights and obligations

---

1   The requisite number of instruments of ratification or accession were deposited by the end of 1987, with the result that the Convention came into force on 1 January 1988, pursuant to Article 99.

arising from the contract, from a set of legal rules which, ideally, is expressed with comparative simplicity, is constructed without a bias towards any particular type of legal system or towards one party (buyer or seller) as opposed to another, and which is available in approved standard translations in the major languages.

The Convention's broad objectives are expressed in its preamble – the Convention is predicated upon recognition that 'the development of international trade on the basis of equality and mutual benefit is an important element in promoting friendly relations among States'; and more particularly the recognition that 'the adoption of uniform rules which govern contracts for the international sale of goods and take into account the different social, economic and legal systems would contribute to the removal of legal barriers in international trade and promote the development of international trade'. The ideal and logical outcome of the process which led to the adoption of the Vienna Convention would be the universal ratification of the Convention by all States, with the result that, in the normal course (assuming its non-exclusion by the parties themselves), a common legal code of rules dealing with international sales contracts would (within the limits of its scope) be applied to international sales contracts. Buyers and sellers on the international market therefore would have a relatively simple and common uniform regime governing their contracts and their performance. The alternative would be a potentially very complex lattice-work of individual State sales law regimes, resort to which was dictated by the rules of private international law applying in each jurisdiction. There would (in default of agreement upon an applicable law by the parties themselves) be uncertainty at two levels: which forum's law applies; and the requirements of this law. In the typical such case, one party would benefit from having his or her own jurisdiction's law applied, and the other party would be disadvantaged by the application of a foreign and possibly poorly understood law. The Convention has not been universally adopted of course, but to the extent that it is (and the number of countries acceding to it grows steadily), the benefits of a uniform sales law regime in international sales become more widespread.

The Convention was drafted in light of common law and civil law concepts and principles, but it is intended to be a self-contained body of law to be interpreted without resort to common law or civil law precepts. Only if this approach to interpretation fails and it cannot be interpreted according to the principles on which it is based, is resort to be made to the law which would otherwise be applicable by virtue of the rules of private international law (see Article 7). The result is that, although the Convention will be applied by the courts of a given State, the courts are not to construe it in light of their own law. This canon of construction is necessary, unless the Convention is, *de facto*, to become an extension of the forum's law. This risk is particularly obvious in the case of common law States, where the typical statute becomes encrusted with judicial precedents which are pivotal in resolving issues concerning the application of the statute. To the extent that the Convention was to be thus assimilated into the law of individual States, it would lose its currency as a uniform sales regime and, once again, choice of forum would be a critical issue in respect of determining the substantive rights and obligations of the parties in dispute. The question of interpreting the Convention will be returned to below.

In the following pages, the provisions of the Convention will be reviewed and commented on.

SPHERE OF APPLICATION OF THE CONVENTION

Overview

Chapter 1 of the Convention (headed 'Sphere of Application'), ie Articles 1–6, defines the scope of the Convention's application. A number of dimensions are important: the Convention itself must be identified by the applicable law as being applicable, or potentially so; and reference must then be made to the geography of the parties' business and the subject matter of the contract. A number of subsidiary matters must be taken into account. As well, the range of substantive issues addressed by the Convention is relatively limited. All in all, a number of tests must be satisfied before the Convention is applied. Notwithstanding this, the Convention can apply even though the parties did not contemplate this, and even in cases where neither knows of its existence. Put briefly, the Convention applies where:

(a) the contract is one for the sale of goods (certain exclusions apply);

(b) the parties have their places of business in different States;

(c) the States are Contracting States – or, in default of this, the rules of private international law lead to the application of the law of a Contracting State;

(d) the issue is one of the formation of the contract of sale and/or the rights and obligations of the parties (certain exclusions are expressed – *inter alia,* except as provided otherwise, the Convention does not deal with the validity of the contract or the effect the contract may have on the property in the goods sold);

(e) the issue is not one of the liability of the seller for death or personal injury caused by the goods to any person; and

(f) the parties have not excluded the application of the Convention in whole or in part (subject to Article 12), assuming that it is otherwise applicable.

The international element

The pivotal article in the Convention is Article 1. Article 1(1) states that:

1(1) This Convention applies to contracts of sale of goods between parties whose places of business are in different States:

(a) when the States are Contracting States; or

(b) when the rules of private international law lead to the application of the law of a Contracting State.

Article 1(2) provides that the fact that parties have their places of business in different States is to be disregarded whenever this fact does not appear from either the contract or from any dealings between, or from, information disclosed by the parties at any time before or at the conclusion of the contract. The effect of this is that a party in the usual case must become a willing party to an international contract for the Convention to apply.[2] This is quite different, however, from saying that the party must know of the Convention for it to apply – once the threshold tests are satisfied, the Convention applies whether or not the party had this knowledge.

Article 1(3) provides that neither the nationality of the parties nor the civil or commercial character of the parties or of the contract is to be taken into consideration in determining the application of the Convention.

Article 1(1)(a) deals with the paradigm case, where the parties to the contract have their places of business in different Contracting States – here the Convention applies. The pivotal international element attracting the Convention is that the places of business are located in different States. It follows that the nationality (or, in the case of company, place of incorporation/registration) of the parties is not the key to attracting the Convention under para (1)(a), nor is some other international element (such as the situation of the goods) sufficient.

So, for example, where a seller has its place of business in the USA, and contracts with a buyer with its place of business in the USA, knowing that the latter is to export the goods to a buyer in China, the contract between the first parties does not attract para (1)(a). Likewise, where a seller in the USA contracts with a buyer in the USA, and the subject matter of the contract is situated in China, the contract does not attract para (1)(a); such contract is subject to the Uniform Commercial Code (UCC). This is so whether the goods are to remain in China or be transported to a third country. A contract between a seller in the USA and a buyer in the USA, pursuant to which the seller is to deliver the goods to an address in China, does not attract para (1)(a). Such a contract will be subject to the UCC. The requirement that the international element consist in the fact that the parties have their places of business in different countries is a realistic one, because this is the case where the clear potential exists for choice of law problems and for the imposition of an unfamiliar sale of goods law on one of the parties.

The concept of 'place of business' is dealt with in Article 10. It is provided that:

(a) if a party has more than one place of business, the place of business is that which has the closest relationship to the contract and its performance, having regard to the circumstances known to or contemplated by the parties at any time before or at the conclusion of the contract; and

(b) if a party does not have a place of business, reference is to be made to that party's habitual residence.

It follows that, where a company has its headquarters in country X and a branch office in country Y, and the latter contracts, the company is deemed to have its place of business in Y.

What of the case of a transnational company which operates through subsidiary companies both in its own country of domicile and in other countries – does the subsidiary have an independent legal existence for the purposes of identifying the

---

2   Paragraph (2), *inter alia*, addresses the undisclosed foreign principal situation – see Honnold, J, *Uniform Law for International Sales under the 1980 United Nations Convention*, 2nd edn, 1991, p 76, Deventer, Boston: Kluwer.

contracting party when applying the Convention? The Convention is silent on the matter, but most problems in this regard should disappear having regard to Article 10(a). If company X has its head office in State X, and contracts through a subsidiary company whose place of business is in State Y, the contracting party's place of business will be in State Y, because this is where the place of business most closely connected to the contract is situated.[3]

As noted, where the parties do not have their places of business in different Contracting States, the Convention may in the alternative be attracted by the operation of Article 1(1)(b). This will be so where (again) the parties have their places of business in different States and the rules of private international law lead to the application of the law of a Contracting State.

The rules of private international law vary from State to State, being a part of domestic law, but a common formulation of them in relation to international contracts would be that the parties can nominate in their contract the law to be applied; failing this, the law to which the contract has the closest connection is applied.

If the law of the forum is thus, the parties can nominate the Convention, and the Convention will then apply to their contract and any litigation concerning it. The parties can nominate the Convention directly, or they can nominate it indirectly by nominating, as the applicable law, the law of a country which is a Contracting State and in which Article 1(1)(b) applies (ie it has not been the subject of a reservation under Article 95 (see below)). In this latter case, the parties may unwittingly become bound by the Convention, as where they nominate the law of an Australian State or of the USA.[4]

Alternatively, consistent with the formulation of the applicable private international law rules, above, the Convention may apply pursuant to para (1)(b) because the most closely connected law is that of a Contracting State, ie a State which has the Convention as part of its law. This application will be straightforward – the parties are parties to an international contract, in the terms defined by the Convention, and the Convention states that it applies to such contracts.

It will be noted that a contract having an international element, which attracts the law of a Contracting State pursuant to its rules of private international law but which does not answer all of the Convention tests governing the class of contracts to which it applies, will not attract the Convention. Rather, it will attract the domestic law of the forum. An instance might be a contract which is not between parties having their places of business in different States, or one which is for goods not within the Convention's definition of goods (see below).

As indicated above, a Contracting State has the option under Article 95 of declaring at a prescribed time that it will not be bound by sub-para (1)(b) of Article 1 of the Convention. A significant instance of such a reservation is that of the USA. Where the reservation is made, therefore, the domestic courts will apply the Convention in

---

3   See the discussion of this issue in Honnold, *ibid,* pp 76ff, 181; and in Roberts, J in Wilde, K and Islam, M (eds), *International Transactions – Trade and Investment, Law and Finance,* 1993, pp 33–34, Sydney: Law Book Co.

4   See the comment by Roberts in Wilde and Islam, *ibid,* p35.

litigation concerning the conforming contract pursuant to Article 1(1)(a), ie where the parties have their places of business in different Contracting States. Otherwise (eg where the facts are the same but one of the States is not a Contracting State), the rules of private international law will apply. In the case of a US court, for example, this may lead to the application of the Uniform Commercial Code in that country.

Why make the Article 95 reservation? The US position was summarised thus in 1983 in Appendix B to the Legal Analysis accompanying the Letter of Submittal from the Secretary of State to the President, in which the Secretary recommended to the President that the Vienna Convention be transmitted to the Senate for its advice and consent to ratification:

> This provision (ie Article 1(1)(b)) would displace our own domestic law more frequently than foreign law. By its terms sub-para (1)(b) would be relevant only in sales between parties in the USA (a Contracting State) and a non-Contracting State. (Transactions that run between the USA and other contracting State are subject to the Convention by virtue of sub-para (1)(a).) Under sub-para (1)(b), when private international law points to the law of a foreign non-Contracting State, the Convention will not displace that foreign law, since sub-para (1)(b) makes the Convention applicable only when 'the rules of private international law lead to the application of the law of a Contracting State'. Consequently, when those rules point to US law, sub-para (1)(b) would normally operate to displace US law (the Uniform Commercial Code) and would not displace the law of the foreign non-Contracting States.
>
> If US law were seriously unsuited to international transactions, there might be an advantage in displacing our law in favour of the uniform international rules provided by the Convention. However, the sales law provided by the Uniform Commercial Code is relatively modern and includes provisions that address the special problems that arise in international trade.[5]

From USA perspective above, policy considerations justify the reservation. The application of Article 1(1)(b) would not operate to displace the law of a foreign non-Contracting State (if chosen as the law applicable to the contract). It would, however, displace the UCC in circumstances where US law was chosen of the law applicable to the contract since the Convention would apply. Thus, foreign law would apply more frequently than would US law. This could be seen to be anomalous, in litigation in a US court. Most States have not made the reservation, however, seeing the enhanced prospects of the application of the Convention (ie under sub-para (1)(b) in default of the application of sub-para (1)(a)), as justifying the potential for the occurrence of this anomaly.

---

5   See the reproduction of the US documents in Kathrein, R and Magraw, D, *The Convention for the International Sale of Goods: A Handbook of Basic Materials*, 1987, Washington and Chicago: American Bar Association, Section of International Law and Practice (although the Appendices to the Legal Analysis are not included here); and likewise see Galston and Smit (eds), *International Sales: The United Nations Convention on Contracts for the International Sale of Goods*, 1984.

Goods – exclusions

The Convention does not define goods, but it is consistent with defining them as a common lawyer would define them, *viz*, as moveable tangibles (and thus not land, or fixtures attached to it and having the status of land, and intangibles). Scope for argument as to whether a given asset fits within the concept of goods remains of course – what, for instance, is the status of a fixture immediately after severance?

Where a contract which is a mix of goods and labour is concerned, Article 3(2) adopts an approach which is familiar to a common lawyer – in essence, contracts of this type which are predominantly for the supply of labour or other services, with the balance of the seller's obligation being to supply goods, are not contracts for the sale of goods for the purposes of the Convention. It may be supposed that a contract is predominantly one for services where the services element is more valuable than the goods element.

Article 3(1) states that contracts for the supply of goods to be manufactured or produced are to be considered sales unless the party who orders the goods undertakes to supply a substantial part of the materials necessary for such manufacture or production.

Certain things cannot be the subject of a sales contract for the purposes of the Convention. These exclusions are set out in Article 2. They are as follows:

(a) Sales of consumer goods (but note the precise definition). Consumer goods normally will not be the subject of an international sale; and in any event the consumer sale is, in many countries, regulated by extensive statutory provisions. For this reason in particular, the Convention was seen to be an inappropriate regime for their regulation.

(b) Sales by auction. These are often regulated by specific law within States, and are by their nature not negotiated sales.

(c) Sales on execution or otherwise by authority of law. These are not normal sales and could not sensibly be regulated by a typical sale of goods regime.

(d) Sales of stocks, shares, investment securities, negotiable instruments or money. Most of these are intangibles, and the sale of money in specie could not sensibly be regulated by a typical sale of goods regime.

(e) Sales of ships, hovercraft or aircraft. Special rules apply to these chattels (including those creating registration regimes) in municipal legal systems.

(f) Sales of electricity. Electricity is not a chattel, and a standard sale of goods regime could not sensibly be applied to a contract for its supply.

It is unclear whether the Convention applies to contracts of barter (known, *inter alia*, as counter-trade). The terms governing performance contemplate the standard transaction as being a sale for money (eg Article 53 referring to the buyer's obligation to pay the price for the goods), but they are not obviously inconsistent with a contract of barter (the 'price' can of course be in the equivalent of money).[6]

---

6   Honnold, *op cit*, p 103, is of the view that the convention does not exclude barter. See too the discussion by Maskow, D, 'Obligations of the Buyer' in Bianca, C and Bonell, M, *Commentary on the International Sales Law – the 1980 Vienna Sales Convention*, 1987, pp 386–87, Milan: Giuffrè.

Aspects of the contract covered by the Convention – exclusions

The Convention self-evidently is not a complete code of contract law, and therefore cannot apply to all contractual issues. For example, it does not say anything of the effect on the contract of the parties' rights or obligations because of the occurrence of a pre-contractual misrepresentation or duress, or undue influence.

Article 4 delineates the ambit of the substantive legal issues covered by it, and propounds a non-exhaustive list of matters not covered by it. According to Article 4, the Convention covers only the formation of the contract of sale (as to which see Part II of the Convention), and the rights and obligations of the seller and buyer arising from such a contract (as to which see Part III). Article 4 continues – in particular, except as otherwise expressly provided by this Convention, it is not concerned with (a) the validity of the contract or any of its provisions or of any usage; (b) the effect which the contract may have on the property in the goods sold.

It follows that many rules of the domestic law of a particular forum may apply to a contract's dispute which is otherwise covered by the Convention. It is possible, for example, that in a dispute concerning formation and undue influence, the Convention will apply side by side with the domestic rules of the forum, the law of which is invoked by the application of the rules of private international law.

The question of where matters relevant to the validity of a contract begin and end will depend on the domestic law of the applicable forum. For example, duress, undue influence, fraud, unconscionable dealings, mistake and misrepresentation may, in a particular case, render a contract voidable at the option of the 'innocent' party. In such a case, the complained of conduct may properly be viewed as raising an issue of validity. On the other hand, the domestic law may draw a distinction between the consequences of different sub-categories of conduct within a broader category of conduct, according to specified criteria. For instance, a distinction may be drawn between an innocent misrepresentation which does not involve a matter of substantial importance, and a fraudulent misrepresentation which does, with the law providing that the first type of misrepresentation does not render a contract voidable, while the second does.

Even if unlawful conduct by a party does not go to the validity of the contract, it may nonetheless lead to an alternative remedy outside of contract law. In a common law jurisdiction, for instance, a misrepresentation not amounting to validity may nonetheless ground a remedy in tort, or pursuant to a statute, such as one dealing with the consequences of misleading or deceptive conduct in commerce. Can the aggrieved party pursue this remedy in addition to, or in lieu of, any remedy it may have under the Convention? For example, consider a misrepresentation by the seller of goods which (a) does not make the contract voidable, but (b) does become embodied in the contract. As a result of the seller's misrepresentation, the plaintiff (buyer) is entitled to seek a Convention remedy for breach of contract; but, *prima facie*, this party can also seek a remedy in tort, or under a statutory provision in the domestic law of the forum. Does the plaintiff have a choice?

Ideally, legislation in the forum's law would attempt to regulate, in part at least, this interface between the Convention and domestic law, to resolve problems of application.[7]

In default of this (and such prescriptions could not very well cover all the problems which might arise), there will be a degree of uncertainty. How should these issues be resolved? The starting point is, of course, Article 4. Key words here are the reference to the Convention as being concerned with the formation of the agreement, and 'the rights and obligations of the seller and the buyer arising from such a contract'.[8] These words, taken with the scope of the substantive matters dealt with by the Convention (see Parts II and III) as noted, invite the conclusion that the Convention is concerned with relatively orthodox (conventional) issues arising between the parties. A threshold issue will be whether a contract, in the terms attracting the Convention, was formed. Thereafter, the Convention regulates, according to its terms and the terms of the agreement, matters of performance and the consequences of non-performance. If an issue is fairly within the scope of the Convention, then a domestic court should apply the Convention – to take a contrary approach would stultify it. Reference may also be made to Article 7 (considered below) dealing with the principles to be followed in interpreting the Convention.

However, even if this straightforward approach is adopted, the provisions of domestic law may be such that a question will occasionally arise as to whether the plaintiff has the option of pursuing a domestic law remedy. To repeat an example above, if a non-fundamental breach has become embodied in the agreement as a term, is the plaintiff confined to pursuing the Convention remedies for breach of contract, or can this party pursue domestic remedies which may also be grounded by such a misrepresentation? This is a problem on which the domestic law itself may waiver, dealing with a wholly domestic agreement – whether to confine the plaintiff to its contractual remedies or to allow a right of election. So, from the standpoint of the domestic court, the issue may not easily be resolved in a contest between the Convention and non-contractual domestic remedies. If the Convention is to be given full effect (again, the terms of Article 7(1) are significant here, taken together with the Article 4 injunction that the Convention is intended to regulate the rights and obligations of the parties arising from the contract), the Convention should be treated as the regime of first and only resort, in a conventional fact situation falling fairly and squarely within its scope, which does not generate an issue of validity. In this way, its goal of providing (within its terms) an exclusive, autonomous and uniform regime for the resolution of issues of formation and performance of international contracts, will more readily be fulfilled.

---

7   See, eg the Trade Practices Act (TPA) 1974 (Australia), ss 66ff, implying certain conditions and warranties into consumer transactions (with 'consumer' having the meaning ascribed by the TPA 1974). Section 66A provides that the Convention prevails over these provisions to the extent of any inconsistency.

8   See Khoo in Bianca and Bonell, *op cit*, p 46, stressing this phrase and concluding that it is 'surely a directive to the users of the Convention to look elsewhere for solutions to other questions, *viz*, concerning matters other than the rights and duties created by the terms of the agreement itself, as supplemented by the Convention'.

Given the scope and complexity of the typical State's municipal law dealing with the law relevant both directly and indirectly with contracts and related issues (such as property), it is unsurprising that the Convention is limited in the range of substantive issues comprehended by it. It would not have been feasible to create a universal and exclusive regime governing all matters, including those of validity, which might arise in the context of an international contract. To reiterate, the Convention is wisely targeted at relatively conventional issues of formation and performance. As well, the great variation in the treatment of the additional matters, including validity, by the municipal legal systems of the world, would have made it very difficult to arrive at an acceptable, global code dealing with a much wider range of contractual and related issues in the context of the international sale of goods.

It has been commented that the Convention is intended to be a self-contained, uniform code of law which is to be applied uniformly, notwithstanding its implantation in many domestic legal systems. This observation must be qualified, to the extent that the courts of the States, and domestic legislation, adopt different approaches to the very basic issue of where the Convention's sphere of application ends and that of the domestic law begins. At the edges, the Vienna Convention regime will, potentially, vary in scope from State to State.

Article 4, as noted, also provides that the Convention is not concerned with the effect which the contract may have on the property in the goods sold 'except as otherwise expressly provided in this Convention'. This, likewise, was a necessary reservation – the law of property will be immensely complex from State to State, and the terms of these different regimes will vary greatly. It was not practicable to annex to the Convention a comprehensive property law code.

The fact of the agreement, and the resolution of issues of formation and performance according to the Vienna regime, will naturally bear directly upon the treatment of property rights by the domestic law of the State concerned.

Convention does not apply to liability for death or personal injury

The Convention does not apply to the liability of the seller for death or personal injury caused by the goods to any person (Article 5). These are matters best regulated by domestic law.

Exclusion of the Convention by the parties

The parties may exclude the application of the Convention or, subject to Article 12, derogate from or vary the effect of any of its provisions.

Thus, in a case where the Convention would otherwise apply, the parties may, by a term in their agreement, exclude its application in part or in whole. There is no requirement that such an exclusion be express; logically, a clear, implied intention will suffice to do this. The right of exclusion is qualified by Article 12. (In essence, according to Article 12, a Contracting State may, notwithstanding the contrary provisions of the

Convention, preserve any rules in its domestic law imposing requirements that the contract or other aspects of it be in writing. Thus, if the law of the State is applicable in a given case, the requirement will apply and cannot be excluded by the parties.)

If the parties do exclude the otherwise applicable Convention in part or whole, their contract will be regulated in part or whole (depending upon the scope of the exclusions) by the law chosen by the rules of private international law. Thus, if these rules are in standard form, the parties will be permitted to choose the legal regime applicable, or the contract will be governed by the law having the closest connection with their contract.

The situation may be further complicated where the parties have agreed upon a regime of rules governing aspects of the contract's performance. In this case there will be an implied intention to exclude the Convention (and for that matter any applicable domestic law) to the extent of any inconsistency.

How is the Convention to be excluded? The obvious way is to exclude it expressly, in whole or in part. Another more oblique way of effecting exclusion is to nominate the law of a State as being the applicable law. If the State has not ratified the Convention, then this will manifest an intent to exclude it. If the State is a Contracting State, caution is needed. Simply to adopt the law of the given Contracting State will not exclude the Convention because, by virtue of ratification, this law includes the Convention. The safer course therefore is to adopt the domestic law of the Contracting State because this, clearly, excludes an adopted law like the Convention, which has its provenance in international law.[9]

GENERAL PROVISIONS OF THE CONVENTION

Articles 7ff set out provisions of general application.

Interpretation

The Convention is intended to be self-contained law. Thus, provision has been made in Article 7 for its principles to be followed in interpreting it. As mentioned, the issue of interpretation is a critical one because of the potential for the courts of each jurisdiction to give unique and potentially conflicting interpretations as to how one article or another is to be applied. This potential for differentiation is particularly evident in the case of common law jurisdictions, with their long-standing tradition of judicial interpretation. In these cases, decisions of the courts dealing with the meaning and application of statutory provisions become precedents which, over a long period, can come to be as significant as the original provisions themselves in delineating the law. There are numerous instances of brief, long-standing and frequently litigated provisions in statute law which have had grafted on to them countless words of judicial exegesis.

---

9   See the comments in Jones, G, 'Impact of the Vienna Convention in drafting International Sales Contracts' (1992) 20 *International Business Lawyer* 421 at 425–26; R Burnett, *The Law of International Business Transactions*, 1994, p 6, Sydney: Federation Press; Bonell in Bonell and Bianca, *op cit*, pp 56ff.

Recognising this problem, Article 7(1) provides that, in the interpretation of the Convention, regard is to be had to its international character and to the need to promote uniformity in its application and the observance of good faith in international trade. It follows that courts applying the Convention must not lose sight of the need to preserve its goals of a uniform code which is uniformly applied. The courts should be astute not to allow the principles and concepts of domestic law to condition their interpretations of the Convention, because to do this would be to assimilate it too thoroughly to domestic law and to defeat its role as a uniform international code. The interpretation should not be legalistic, and the terms of the Convention should not be treated as terms of art.

Where, notwithstanding that a given contract is governed by the Convention, a matter apparently within its general scope is not dealt with specifically by its provisions, Article 7(2) operates to maintain the status of the Convention as self-contained law and to minimise unduly hasty resort to domestic law. Article 7(2) provides that issues concerning matters governed by this Convention which are not expressly settled in it are to be settled in conformity with the general principles on which it is based; or, in the absence of such principles, in conformity with the law applicable by virtue of the rules of private international law. These 'general principles' include, of course, the status of the Convention as uniform law which is intended to achieve uniform application. They also include its more specific principles, as stated or implicit in its articles. Scope is allowed here for reasoning from analogy. If, however, the particular issue still cannot be resolved by the Convention, the applicable domestic law will apply. Clearly, such a resort is discouraged by Article 7, except in intractable cases.[10]

Extrinsic materials, no doubt, can be reviewed by courts in deciding issues of interpretation.[11]

Determining intent and related matters

Article 8 deals with the principles to be applied in determining the intention of the parties, and related matters. Article 8(1) approves a subjective approach to the question – statements made by, and other conduct of, a party are to be interpreted according to intent, where the other party knew or could not have been unaware what that intent was. Article 8(2) deals with cases where para (1) is not applicable, and its standpoint is one of objective assessment. Statements, etc are to be interpreted according to the understanding that a reasonable person of the same kind as the other party would have had in the same circumstances.

Article 8(3) defines what data may be reviewed in determining issues under paras (1) and (2) – due consideration is to be given to all relevant circumstances of the case including negotiations, any practices established by the parties between themselves, usages and any subsequent conduct of the parties. Nothing resembling the common law

---

10 On the principles of interpretation provided for in Article 7, see Nicholas, B, 'The Vienna Convention on International Sales Law' (1989) 105 LQR 201 at 210–11; Honnold *op cit*, pp 135ff; Roberts, *op cit*, pp 42ff.

11 See Honnold, *ibid*, pp 135ff.

parol evidence rule, then, applies to written contracts (unless the parties agree that the rule or some equivalent regime is to apply, as, for example, where they express their agreement to be wholly in writing).[12]

Usages

Article 9(1) provides that the parties are bound by any usage to which they have agreed and by any practice which they have established between themselves. This functions in a way analogous to the common law principle whereby terms may be implied into a contract by reference to their prior course of dealing.

Article 9(2) establishes a rebuttable presumption, that the parties have impliedly made applicable to their contract or its formation a usage of which they knew or ought reasonably to have known, and which in international trade is widely known to, and regularly observed by, parties to contracts of the type involved in the particular trade concerned. This term will assist to fill gaps in a contract in appropriate cases.

The parties can of course expressly agree upon a trade usage or analogous standardised practice in trade, such as where one or another of the International Chamber of Commerce's Incoterms is imported into the contract (see Chapter 2).

Requirement of writing, other requirements of form

No requirement of writing is imposed by the Convention, nor does it stipulate any other requirement of form (Article 11). A contract can be wholly or partially oral in form.

Many States, especially those belonging to the 'socialist' legal family, do impose a requirement or requirements of writing and of signature. The Convention permits a Contracting State to preserve a requirement in its domestic law that a contract be concluded in or evidenced in writing, by a declaration pursuant to Article 96. The effect of Article 12, taken with Article 96, is that the Contracting State may retain a writing/evidenced in writing requirement in relation to all or a selection of matters – the concluding of the contract itself, the variation or modification of a written contract, etc. Article 12 and Article 96 should be noted, in conjunction with Article 11 (providing generally that contracts need not be in writing or so evidenced), Article 29 (dealing with variation and modification, and again providing that a writing is not required, unless the contract is in writing; and containing a provision that variation, etc be in writing – although note the estoppel-type exception), and Part II (dealing with the formation of the contract).

Article 12 provides in effect that, where a Contracting State has made an Article 96 declaration, the parties cannot overcome the effect of this by contrary agreement among themselves. Thus, if, say, the domestic law of the Contracting State, which comes to be applicable to a particular contract, requires that it be concluded in writing or so evidenced, and signed by the party to be charged, this provision will be applied by a court adjudicating a dispute between the parties.

---

12 Even here, of course, the common law courts have inevitably needed to fashion exceptions to the parol evidence rule, pursuant to which extrinsic evidence is admissible.

FORMATION OF THE CONTRACT

Part II of the Convention (Articles 14–24) make provision for the formation of the contract. The concepts employed are analogous to common law concepts, although the common law authorities and concepts must not be resorted to in interpreting and applying Part II.

Offer and acceptance

Part II, broadly speaking, parallels the common law analysis of offer and acceptance in setting out a model which is to be employed in determining whether an agreement has been reached. The terms 'offer' and 'acceptance' are used (but to reiterate, they are not to be taken as being synonymous with the common law terms known by these names). In essence, for the purposes of the Convention, a contract is formed when an offer (as defined) meets with an acceptance (as defined). As it will be seen below, the Convention does not propound any other requisites for a binding contract, corresponding to the common law elements of consideration; but at least where the offer is concerned, it does refer to an intention to be bound – Article 14(1).

A given-fact situation may, upon examination, yield a contractual agreement but may not be readily amenable to the offer and acceptance analysis. Can it still be a contract for the purposes of the Convention? A reasoning from general principles (an approach permitted by the interpretation article, ie Article 7(2)), should satisfy the basic requirement of Part II, ie that an agreement has been formed. It would on occasions stultify the Convention to require a precise conformity with the offer-acceptance model.

Article 14 provides generally for the contractually significant offer. The offer must be sufficiently definite and indicate an intention to be bound in case of acceptance. It is sufficiently definite if it indicates the goods, and expressly or implicitly fixes or makes provision for determining the quantity and the price. This latter requirement might be thought to deviate from the common law – in the case of the common law, a failure to specify price, or a procedure for determining it, can be repaired by the implication of a term to pay a reasonable price. However, in such an event Article 55, on one view, comes to the rescue – where neither price nor a price-fixing procedure is agreed upon, and in the absence of any indication to the contrary, there is (what is in effect) an implied term that the parties have agreed that the price is the price generally charged at the time of the conclusion of the contract, for such goods sold under comparable circumstances in the trade concerned.[13]

---

13 Note the comment in Nicholas, *op cit*, at 213, on the drafting quirk evident in Article 55; if it was intended to cure the problem implicitly posited in Article 14(1), ie a failure to agree upon a price or a price-fixing procedure, which problem goes to formation. Why does Article 55 make the implication of the term in question depend upon the situation being one '[w]here a contract has been validly concluded ...'? Article 55 can only be allowed a full operation if the opening words in it are read as meaning 'where a contract has otherwise been validly concluded ...'.

Article 14 posits as the norm the making of an offer to one or more specific persons, and provides that a proposal, other than one so addressed, is to be considered merely as an invitation to make offers (ie in common law terms a communication falling within the concept of an invitation to treat), unless the contrary is clearly indicated by the person making the proposal. Thus, in appropriate cases an offer directed to the whole world (or at least those who will come forward), or to a class of persons, can be classed as an offer, and thus be capable of being accepted, where it was clearly the intent of the putative offeror. The result is in accordance with the common law's analysis in, for instance, one of its best known contracts decision.[14]

Article 15(1) speaks of the offer as becoming effective when it 'reaches' the offeree (see Article 24 on the concept of 'reaches'). This provision approximates the common law requirement that the offer must be communicated (but note the extended meaning of 'reaches', which is not synonymous with 'is communicated to').

By Article 15(2), an offer, even if it is irrevocable, may be withdrawn if the withdrawal reaches the offeree before or at the same time as the offer. The concept of an irrevocable offer is described in Article 16(2). In essence, an offer is irrevocable where the offeror indicates this, expressly or impliedly (as by stating a fixed time for acceptance), or it was reasonable for the offeree to so rely on it. There is no requirement that the offeree has given consideration for the offer to be irrevocable, so at this point a clear contrast with common law principle is evident; at common law consideration would be required (as in the case of an agreement conferring an option to purchase).

Until a contract is concluded, an offer (other than an irrevocable one) may be revoked if the revocation reaches the offeree before the latter dispatches an acceptance (Article 16(1)).

An offer, whether or not it is revocable, is terminated when the offeree rejects it (Article 17).

However, a counter-offer will not necessarily constitute a rejection and thus terminate the offer (contrast the common law, where a counter-offer terminates the offer, ie it has the same effect as a more emphatic rejection). This situation is dealt with by Article 19. Its terms should be noted, but in summary it provides than an acceptance which contains additions, limitations or other modifications, is a rejection of the offer and constitutes a counter-offer. However, if the purported acceptance does propose changes, but these changes do not materially alter the terms of the offer, then this reply constitutes an acceptance (and thus a contract is formed), unless the offeror, without undue delay, objects to the discrepancy. If he does not object, a contract is formed comprising his offer and the offeree's non-material changes. Article 19(3) enunciates, non-exhaustively, a list of material alterations of the offer; they include proposals relating

---

14 *Carlill v Carbolic Smoke Ball Co* [1893] 1 QB 256, where an offer made in a newspaper advertisement was determined to have contractual significance, with the result that it could be accepted by a reader unknown to the advertiser.

to price, payment, quality and quantity of goods. In aggregate, Article 19 provides for a regime quite different to that existing at common law. At common law, the offeree must accept the offer without qualification – a requirement that creates difficulties when enterprises purport to contract by an exchange of standard forms, drafted by each and differing in some of their terms. Article 19 would save purported contracts, but only where the points of difference concern non-material matters.

Acceptance is dealt with in Article 18. Article 18(1) states that a statement or other conduct by the offeree indicating assent to the offer is an acceptance. This parallels the common law concept. Article 18(1) does not require that the acceptance be in reliance on the offer, but this is implicit in the notion of 'assent'. As at common law, a contract cannot be unilaterally imposed upon an offeree – '[s]ilence or inactivity does not in itself amount to acceptance'. Thus, a party cannot deem another to be party to a contract, if the latter does not respond to the first party's offer by a fixed term.

The acceptance becomes effective (and thus the contract is formed) at the moment the indication of assent reaches the offeror (Article 18(2)). Again, note the definition of 'reaches' in Article 24 – *inter alia*, a contractual communication such as an acceptance 'reaches' a party when it is delivered to his place of business or mailing address. It follows that actual communication to the party is not necessarily required. A person, for instance, can become party to a contract some time before he learns of the communication of the acceptance (as where the acceptance is by letter – here it reaches him when it is deposited in his letter-box). The Convention does not replicate the common law's postal acceptance rule.

Article 18(2) also provides that an acceptance is not effective if the indication of assent does not reach the offeror within the time he has fixed, or, if no time is fixed, then within a reasonable time, due account being taken of the circumstances of the transaction, including the rapidity of the means of communication employed by the offeror. An oral offer must be accepted immediately unless the circumstances indicate otherwise.

At common law, the offeror can waive the need for communication of the acceptance as a basis for formation, and instead expressly or by implication stipulate that the doing of a given act shall be both an act of acceptance and of (partial or whole) performance, at one and the same time. This position is more or less replicated by Article 18(3), which postulates, as instances of its invocation, the dispatch of goods or payment of price without notice to the offeror. In such a case, acceptance is effective at the time the act (of acceptance-performance) is performed. This act must be performed within the period of time laid down by Article 18(2). The waiver of the need for communicating acceptance can be done in the offer, or be the result of practices established between the parties, or of usage.

Article 20 deals with an ancillary matter, ie the commencement of the period of time fixed by the offeror for acceptance; and the impact of official holidays or non-business days on the calculation of these periods.

An acceptance which reaches the offeror after the expiry of the offer period is by definition too late – the offer will have expired through the effluxion of time (see Article

18(2)). However, Article 21(1) provides, exceptionally, that a late acceptance is nevertheless effective as an acceptance if, without delay, the offeror so informs the offeree or dispatches a notice to that effect. Article 21(2) provides that, if a letter or other writing containing a late acceptance shows that it has been sent in such circumstances that, if its transmission had been normal, it would have reached the offeror in due time, the late acceptance is effective unless, without delay, the offeror orally informs the offeree that he considers his offer as having lapsed or dispatches a notice to that effect. This latter provision is, when examined, quite different to the postal acceptance rule at common law (which deems acceptance to have taken place as and when the letter of acceptance is posted, whether the letter arrives early, late or never). The rule in Article 18(2) is less likely to cause confusion than the postal acceptance rule.

An acceptance may be withdrawn if the withdrawal reaches the offeror before or at the same time that the acceptance would have become effective (Article 22). At common law, in a case comprehended by the postal acceptance rule, the acceptance would become effective and create a contract at the moment of its posting – thereafter there could not be a withdrawal of acceptance.

The time of contracting is defined by Article 23: the contract is concluded at the time when an acceptance of an offer becomes effective in accordance with the provisions of the Convention. The major such provision is Article 18(2), as noted above.

As noted, the concept of 'reaches' as applied to communications described in Part II is defined in Article 24. The concept includes communications of which, in particular circumstances, the addressee may not yet be cognisant (as where, for instance, an acceptance is delivered to the offeror's place of business; in this case it is deemed by Article 24 to have reached the offeror; and in the normal case, the contract will have been formed at this point in time – Articles 18(2), 23, 24, taken together).

If this outcome is potentially inconvenient or mischievous, the parties should agree upon an alternative regime of rules in their pre-contractual negotiations, concerning when they are to be taken to have formed a contract. The same comment may be made generally regarding the application of the formation rules. Such a variation is presumably permissible from the offeror's standpoint – by Article 14(1), the offer must, among other matters, sufficiently indicate 'the intention of the offeror to be bound in case of acceptance'. It is the offeror who is potentially most at risk, in problem cases which might be hypothesised about in light of a provision like Article 24.

Consideration

Unlike the common law, the Convention does not have, as one of its pivots of formation of contract, a requirement of consideration. To the extent that the Convention is about international sales, and necessarily refers to issues of price (see, eg Articles 14, 53ff), contracts comprehended by it will be supported, *de facto*, by consideration from both sides. But the concept of consideration does not otherwise figure in the Convention, so that there are no rules to be found in it corresponding to such common law rules as those dealing with legally insufficient consideration.

It is because consideration is not pivotal in the Convention that an offer can be irrevocable, without any requirement that the offeree have offered consideration for this benefit (see Article 15ff). As noted above, a contract can be formed although the parties have not fixed a price (see Articles 14, 55).

Intention to create legal relations

The common law requires that the parties manifest, on an objective view, an intent to create a legally binding agreement as an element of formation. The Convention imposes no such requirement. However, as noted, Article 14 does refer to the offer as being a proposal which, *inter alia*, indicates the intention of the offeror to be bound in case of acceptance. While it is perhaps of little practical significance, given that agreements alleged to be within the purview of the Convention will be entered into in a business context, no such parallel requirement is enunciated in respect of the party accepting the offer, thus forming a contract.

SALE OF GOODS

Part III of the Convention – the major section of it – deals with the performance of the contract, remedies for breach and related matters. Before reviewing its provisions, note needs to be made of Chapter I, headed 'General provisions'. These articles deal with concepts relevant to the interpretation and application of Part III.

General provisions

Fundamental breach

Article 25 defines what amounts to a fundamental breach of contract. A breach is fundamental if it results in such detriment to the other party as substantially to deprive him of what he is entitled to expect under the contract, unless the party in breach did not foresee, and a reasonable person of the same kind and in the same circumstances would not have foreseen, such a result. The consequences of such a breach are referred to later in Part III: see, for instance, Article 49, providing that the buyer may declare the contract avoided (ie in effect, rescinded) where the seller is responsible for a fundamental breach (note the limitations); and note the parallel article – Article 64 – vesting a parallel right in the seller.

The concept of avoiding or rescinding the contract for fundamental breach closely parallels the common law concept of rescinding a contract for breach of a condition. However, Article 25 does not replicate the common law. In particular, the usage of fundamental breach owes nothing to the concept which briefly attracted the attention of the English courts, in a development which has now been terminated.[15]

---

15   For a period the English courts propounded a doctrine of fundamental breach in the context of exclusion clauses, holding that no matter how broadly the clause was drafted, it could not exclude a so-called fundamental breach. The doctrine was disapproved by the House of Lords in *Suisse Atlantique Société d'Armement Maritime SA v NV Rotterdamsche Kolen Centrale* [1967] 1 AC 361, and finally repudiated by the House of Lords in *Photo Production Ltd v Securicor Transport Ltd* [1980] AC 827.

The common law in a number of jurisdictions seizes upon the concept of the condition as a basis for determining which breaches provide a basis for rescission, and the test for determining whether a term is a condition has, on one view, a partly subjective element.[16]

The focus of Article 25 is upon the nature of the breach itself rather than the term (although the more fundamental the term, in practice, the more readily will a party be able to prove that the breach is fundamental, as defined in Article 25). Also, the test is essentially objective in character (save for the exemption permitted the defendant – even here this party must fulfil the objective test of the foresight of the reasonable person). Article 25 does not define the time when the matter of fundamental breach is to be tested. At common law, the time for assessing whether a term is a condition is the time of formation.[17]

Given that Article 25 focuses on the breach, enquiry in a case where it is sought to be invoked cannot be confined to the circumstances at the time of formation, but must look as well at the circumstances as they stood at the time of breach, and at the consequences of breach. The Article 25 enquiry, therefore, cannot be tied down to the facts as they stood at any given moment; rather, it must, in the temporal sense, be potentially wide ranging.[18]

Notice of avoidance

Article 26 provides that a declaration of avoidance of the contract is effective only if made by notice to the other party. The circumstances where avoidance is permitted will be noted below (as seen above, *prima facie* avoidance is permitted for fundamental breach). Given that Article 26 is in non-prescriptive terms, this notice may, it would appear, be oral or written, direct or indirect.[19]

Miscarriage in communication

Article 27 provides in substance that the dispatch of any notice, request or other communication in accordance with Part III and by means appropriate to the circumstances, is (except where Part III expressly provides otherwise) sufficient. Thereafter, the person dispatching the communication can rely upon its having been duly made. This is so notwithstanding any delay or error in its transmission. The article

---

16 The condition is commonly described as a term going to the root of the contract, without which the party asserting its status as such would not have entered into the contract, with authority recognising that the plaintiff can depose as to his expectations.

17 Note, however, the famous judgment of Diplock LJ in *Hong Kong Fir Shipping Co Ltd v Kawasaki Kisen Kaisha Ltd* [1962] 2 QB 265 at 69, propounding the notion of an innominate term – a term which, given its broad nature, is not obviously classifiable as a warranty or condition – with the result that determination of whether its breach is sufficient to warrant rescission is dependent upon consideration of the seriousness of the breach, a matter which of course can only be determined by reference to the time of the breach (and of its consequences).

18 See the comments on the issue of time, in Nicholson, *op cit*, p 219.

19 See the comments on 'Notice of Avoidance' by Date-Bah, S, in Bianca and Bonell, *op cit*, pp 224–25.

avoids the need for evidence going beyond proof of dispatch. It is of course potentially productive of mischief, and in a case of importance the parties should expressly deal with the matter. To reiterate, Article 27 deals only with communications for the purposes of Part III (and not with those directed to formation of the contract).

Specific performance

Article 28 looks ahead to the provision of the specific performance remedy in later provisions (see, for example, Articles 46 and 62) and enacts a qualification on the remedy: assuming that a party is otherwise entitled to such an order, a court is not bound to enter such a judgment unless the court would do so under its own law in respect of similar contracts of sale not governed by the Convention.

The result is that, where the domestic law of the court is civil law derived, the court will more readily order specific performance; but where its law is common law derived, it is less likely to, because the bias of the common law (or more particularly its equitable strand) is that, *inter alia*, specific performance of contracts for the sale of goods ought not to be awarded where damages would constitute an adequate remedy. This bias tends to be replicated in statutory provisions in the common law countries. In most cases, of course, whether the court's domestic law be civil or common law derived, the plaintiff will prefer damages where substitute goods can readily be obtained.

The law of the court may not necessarily be the law of the contract (as where a court in State A has jurisdiction, but pursuant to the rules of private international law, is applying the law of State B).[20]

Modification or termination of the contract

Article 29(2), as noted above, provides that a contract may be modified or terminated by the mere agreement of the parties. The reference to 'mere' agreement emphasises that the common law concept of consideration is not to be resorted to in applying Article 29(2).[21]

Article 29(2) has also been reviewed earlier: it requires that the contract in writing which contains a provision requiring any modification or termination by agreement to be in writing, may not otherwise be modified or terminated by agreement – note the estoppel-type exception here.

Obligations of the seller

Part III Chapter II is headed 'Obligations of the seller'.

---

20 See Honnold, *op cit*, p 272.

21 Thus, a party who has (say) fully performed, can give a valid release to a party who has only partly performed, without any requirement of fresh consideration from the latter.

General obligations

Article 30 imposes a general obligation on the seller to deliver the goods, hand over any documents relating to them and to transfer the property in them, as required by the contract and the Convention.

The Convention, it has been seen, does not provide rules identifying when property is transferred – the property transfer rules are provided by the applicable domestic law. The parties, of course, may well make provision in their contract regarding this matter. Later provisions in the Convention deal with delivery, the handing over of documents, carriage and insurance, and the passing of risk, but they do not provide an exhaustive regime. The underlying premise is that the parties will have made specific provision regarding some of these matters, perhaps by using recognised trade terms such as the Incoterms 1990. Where these are used, they will prevail over contrary provisions in the Convention. The Convention in this area, particularly, will represent a fall-back regime. It would be surprising in a negotiated international sales contract were the parties not to make very specific provision regarding such matters as delivery, carriage, insurance, the passing of risk, incidental costs, etc.

Place of delivery

Article 31 deals with the situation where the seller is not bound to deliver the goods to any other particular place (ie where there is no agreement upon the matter). In this case, the obligation to deliver is as outlined in Article 31. For example, if the contract involves carriage of goods (it usually will), the seller must hand the goods over to the first carrier for transfer to the buyer. In cases not within this class, then, *inter alia*, where goods are to be manufactured or produced, they are to be placed at the buyer's disposal at the place of manufacture, provided that at the time of formation the parties knew that they were to be produced or manufactured at this place. In other cases, the goods are to be placed at the buyer's disposal at the place where the seller had his place of business at the time of contracting.

Needless to say, some of these fall-back provisions will impose inconvenience on the buyer so that specific contractual agreement on the mode of delivery is, in practice, important.

Carrier, insurance

Article 32 deals with aspects of carriage and insurance, but takes as its premise the concept that the parties have agreed upon some at least of the basic details in relation to these matters (eg by the use of an appropriate Incoterm). If the seller hands the goods over to a carrier, and the goods are not clearly identified to the contract by markings or documents, the seller must give notice to the buyer of the consignment specifying the goods (Article 32(1)). If the seller is bound to arrange for carriage, he must make the appropriate contracts according to the terms usual for such transportation (Article 31(2)). If the seller is not required to effect insurance regarding carriage, he must, at the buyer's request, provide him with the information necessary for the latter to do this (Article 31(3)).

Time for delivery

Article 33 in essence provides that the goods are to be delivered on or by the time specified, otherwise within a reasonable time after formation. The common law adopts a similar analysis.

Documents

Article 34 makes collateral provision regarding documents relating to the goods, and assumes that the contract makes provision for them. *Inter alia*, the seller can, in defined circumstances where he hands over the documents prior to the time required in the contract, cure any lack of conformity in them, although the buyer remains entitled to any damages which may be due.

Conformity of the goods and third party claims

Articles 35–44 deal with issues concerning conformity of the goods and third party claims.

Conformity of the goods – implied terms regarding quality, etc

Article 35 does not employ the usage of implied terms, but functions in a manner identical to the implied terms regime in the rules governing contracts for the sale of goods at common law and their statutory successors.

The requirements of the Convention in this regard are not identical to those of the common law's standard implied terms; in particular, no mention is made of merchantable quality, nor is there any term which (otherwise) requires that the goods supplied by a contract regulated by the Convention be at least of average quality.[22]

Article 35(1) requires that the goods be of the quantity, quality and description required by, and be contained or packaged in, the manner required by the contract.

Article 35(2) provides that, except where the parties have agreed otherwise, the goods do not conform to the contract unless they, in essence:

(a) are fit for the purposes for which goods of the same description would ordinarily be used;

(b) are fit for any particular purpose expressly or impliedly made known by the seller at the time of contracting (except where the buyer did not rely, or it was unreasonable for him to rely, on the seller's skill or judgment);

(c) possess the qualities which the seller has held out as a sample or model; and

(d) are contained or packaged in the manner usual for such goods, otherwise in a manner adequate to preserve and protect them.

By Article 35(3) the seller is not liable under sub-paras (a)–(d) in Article 35(2) for any lack of conformity where, at the time of formation, the buyer knew or could not have

---

22 Note the criticism in this latter regard by Bianca in Bianca and Bonell, *op cit*, pp 280–81.

been unaware of such lack of conformity. As the proviso to Article 35(2) recognises, the parties can agree that the requirements as to conformity delineated in Article 35 do not apply to their contract. Such agreement, presumably, may be express or implied. Can the implied term's regime in a domestic sale of goods code, including perhaps a prohibition on contracting out, be resorted to in the case of a contract governed by the Convention? If this code does not go to validity, then it should be inapplicable.[23]

The tests provided for in Article 35(3) are subjective. The phrase 'could not have been unaware' is, in context, ambiguous, but it is more demanding than the common standard objective test ('of which a reasonable person would not have been unaware').

Liability for non-conformity – time

The seller is liable for any non-conformity at the time the risk passes, although the buyer may only become aware of it at a later time (Article 36(1)). Further, the seller becomes liable for any non-conformity after risk passes when due to a breach of any of his obligations, including a breach of guarantee concerning, *inter alia*, that the goods will remain fit for their ordinary purpose, or that they will retain specified qualities (Article 36(2)).

Delivery before time due

By Article 37, the seller who delivers goods before the time due, can, up to that date, cure deficiencies in performance (as where there is a deficit in quantity or quality), provided that the buyer does not suffer unreasonable inconvenience or unreasonable expense. The buyer can still seek damages for loss.

Buyer – examination

Article 38 imposes (unusually by common law standards) a duty of examination of the goods, and regulates the time when this must occur. The goods must be examined as soon as it is practicable in the circumstances, although examination may be deferred until the goods have arrived at their destination (Article 38(1)–(2)). Article 38(3) allows examination to be deferred until the goods have reached their new destination, in a case of redirection in transit or redispatch by the buyer, provided that there was no reasonable earlier opportunity for examination and at the time of formation the seller knew or ought to have known of the possibility of such redirection or redispatch. The provision recognises that goods – especially manufactured goods – will frequently be packaged, perhaps in the form in which they will be delivered to the retailer; and shipped in containers. It recognises that goods may be resold while in transit.

Buyer: loss of right to rely on lack of conformity – time for notice

Article 39(1) requires the buyer to give notice to the seller of any lack of conformity of the goods, specifying its nature within a reasonable time after discovery or from when he should have discovered this; otherwise, the buyer loses the right to rely on this lack of

---

23   See generally the discussion of this issue in Honnold, *op cit*, pp 309ff.

conformity. By Article 39(2), the buyer in any event loses this right if this notice is not given within two years of the date on which the goods were actually handed over, unless this time limit is inconsistent with a contractual guarantee.

The relatively long period of two years is reasonable; eg the goods may have been packaged in the form in which they are to be retailed, in which case a non-conformity issue may arise quite late. On the other hand, it does permit a long period in which latent defects may emerge and be actionable; and the seller may wish to stipulate a shorter guarantee period (if one is to be stipulated at all).

Note that the seller cannot invoke Articles 38 or 39 where the non-conformity relates to facts of which he knew or could not have been unaware, and which he did not disclose to the buyer (Article 40).

See also Article 44 – notwithstanding Article 39(1), the buyer may reduce the price pursuant to Article 50 or claim damages, except for loss of profit, if he has a reasonable excuse for his failure to give notice.[24]

Freedom from right or claim of a third party – in general and those based on industrial or other intellectual property

The seller must deliver goods free of any third-party right or claim – Article 42 (which approximates the common law's implied warranties/conditions concerning good title). The situation is otherwise where the buyer has agreed to take the goods subject to such a qualification.

However, where such a right or claim is based on industrial property or other intellectual property, the situation is governed by Article 42, the terms of which should be noted. The buyer receives a parallel guarantee in this regard, but note the qualifications and ancillary provisions in Article 42.

Article 43 provides for qualifications on the application of Articles 41 and 42; and note the further qualification on the application of Article 43(1), effected by Article 44.

Remedies for breach of contract by the seller

Articles 45–52 (s III of Part III) provide for 'remedies for breach of contract by the seller'. The Convention propounds a range of possible remedies, some of them based on mandatory orders by a court after litigation while others are directed towards remedying disputes by means short of litigation. A number of them have no common law counterpart. It must also be remembered that the parties are free to negotiate their own solution to a problem, either by formal inclusion of terms in the contract or by an agreement post-contract, operating to modify the contract. (By Article 29, it will be recalled, the parties can modify the existing contract without any necessity for either one of them to supply what the common law would classify as new, legally sufficient

---

24 It will infrequently be the case that the buyer who has not given reasonable notice under Article 39(1) will have a reasonable excuse for this failure, for the purposes of Article 44: see the comments in Nicholas, *op cit*, pp 222–23; Bianca in Bianca and Bonell, *op cit*, p 238.

consideration.) Where the parties agree upon a regime for resolving a difference, this would, assuming that it has contractual force, override the remedial provisions in the Convention. (If the agreed upon regime fails to do this, then, *prima facie,* the Convention would apply once more, unless its remedial provisions have been permanently excluded and one of the parties opposes their revival, in which case the appropriate municipal law will come into play.)

It will often be in the parties' interests to attempt a negotiated resolution, given the difficulties and delays of litigation, especially litigation between parties who may be a great distance apart.

Buyer's options

Article 45 sets out the buyer's remedies in a case of breach by the seller – they are the rights in Articles 46–52, and the right to seek damages as provided in Articles 74–77. The buyer is still entitled to seek damages, even as he seeks other remedies. The court or arbitral tribunal may not grant a period of grace to the seller when the buyer seeks a remedy.

Specific performance and related remedies

By Article 46(1), the buyer may seek specific performance by the seller unless the buyer has resorted to an inconsistent remedy. The scope of the specific performance remedy has been limited by Article 28, as noted above (ie the court is not bound to order it unless it would do so pursuant to its own law). Specific performance would appear to have little role in relation to goods which are not unique and which can be readily sourced from another seller. Such an order of a court would be at the conclusion of litigation, meaning that much time would have passed since the default by the seller. In this period, the buyer ordinarily would be able to approach other suppliers. In practice, damages, if financial loss is suffered by going to another supplier, would seem to be the more obvious remedy in a case of refusal or inability on the part of the seller to supply.[25]

By Article 46(2), in a case of non-conformity between the contract and the goods amounting to a fundamental breach, the buyer may require the delivery of substitute goods (note the details). The result would, in the case of non-unique goods, approximate what would be obtained by specific performance. It is apt that the precondition for this remedy should be a fundamental breach to ensure that it is not invoked for a trivial non-conformity. The remedy is not paralleled in the common law.

If the goods do not conform to the contract, the buyer may require the seller to remedy the problem by repair, unless this is unreasonable in the circumstances (Article 46(3) – note the ancillary detail). The remedy, again, finds no counterpart in the common law. The reasonableness limitation is necessary, given that the seller may be at a vast distance from the buyer who has taken delivery. Distance alone, however, would not preclude its invocation, as where valuable machinery is supplied and the seller's technical expertise is not readily available in the buyer's country.

---

25   See Honnold, *op cit*, p 366.

Extra time for the seller to perform obligations

The buyer may give the seller an extra period of time of reasonable length for performance of the seller's obligations (Article 47(1)). The extra period is frequently referred to in commentaries as a *Nachfrist*.[26]

It will be noted that it is the buyer's option whether to grant this extra time. If, however, the buyer does do so, then unless he receives notice from the seller that the latter will not perform in this period, the buyer may not, during the period, resort to any remedy for breach of contract. He can, however, seek damages for delay in performance (Article 47(2)).

The Article 47 *Nachfrist* can, in terms, cover a variety of acts of default such as non-conformity, but its main practical application will be in cases of non-delivery. In this latter respect, note Article 49(1)(b), providing that, in the case of non-delivery, if the seller does not deliver within the period of the Article 47 period (or declare that he will not so deliver), the buyer may declare the contract avoided (ie at an end). The Article 47 procedure, then, can lay the foundation for avoidance.[27]

Seller – remedy after date of delivery

By Article 48(1), the seller may, even after the date for delivery, remedy shortcomings in his performance. Certain qualifications apply: *inter alia*, the buyer must not be subjected to unreasonable delay or inconvenience. This seller's right to cure is subject to Article 49, which deals with rescission. Among the provisions in Article 49 is that in Article 49(1)(a), which permits the buyer to avoid the contract because of a fundamental breach by the seller. The effect, according to one commentator, is that the parties need to know whether the seller is entitled to, and can indeed, cure pursuant to Article 48(1), before it can be established whether the breach is fundamental.[28]

The buyer can still seek damages, notwithstanding the seller's cure, where these are payable under the Convention (Article 48(1)). The procedure in Article 48(2), *inter alia*, permits a seller to seek the buyer's consent to a later delivery, and puts the onus on the buyer to reject any such proposal.[29] Note the ancillary provisions in Article 48(3) and (4). The notice referred to there can be oral or written.

Avoidance by buyer

Article 49 provides for avoidance of the contract by the buyer. (The effects of avoidance are set out in Article 81 – broadly, it brings the contract to an end, subject to any

---

26 German law recognises a similar concept, called the 'Nachfrist'. The concept of an extra period is found elsewhere in the Convention too, such as in Article 63, providing that the buyer may be given extra time by the seller to perform his obligations.

27 Note Honnold, *op cit*, pp 368–69, commenting that the Article 47 procedure only has teeth – courtesy of Article 49(1)(b) – in the case of non-delivery.

28 Honnold, *ibid*, p 376. See also Will in Bianca and Bonell, *op cit*, pp 349ff.

29 See Honnold, *ibid*, p 378, who also discusses Article 48(2) in respect of cases of proposals to cure by repair.

damages which may be due and subject to restitution being made, where this is practicable.) It is broadly comparable to the common law's termination of contract because of legally relevant fault on the part of the other party, but the details differ considerably.

As noted, the buyer may avoid because of a fundamental breach by the seller (Article 49(1)(a)); but the feasibility of a seller's cure under Article 48(1) must be considered in determining whether there has been a fundamental breach. The buyer may also avoid for non-delivery if the seller does not deliver the goods within any additional period of time fixed under Article 47(1), or declares that he will not deliver within this period.

Where goods are delivered, the buyer loses the right to avoid (ie for fundamental breach) unless he acts in conformity with the applicable requirements of Article 49(2). Where late delivery is concerned, the buyer must avoid within a reasonable time after becoming aware of non-delivery.

In respect of breaches other than late delivery (eg for a non-conformity of a fundamental nature), the buyer must avoid within a reasonable time after he knew, or ought to have known, of the breach. (Note, as well, the ancillary provisions concerning cases involving an Article 47(1) *Nachfrist*, and the Article 48(2) procedure – here again, the overriding requirement is for the buyer to act within a reasonable time.)

The essence of these limitations is that the buyer must avoid within a reasonable time, which will of course vary from case to case. (The complex common law rules revolving around the notion of the buyer's acceptance are not echoed in the Convention.)

Although it is not referred to in Article 49, the right of avoidance under it is clearly qualified by Article 39. This, as noted above, provides in para (1) that the buyer loses the right to rely on a lack of conformity of the goods if he does not give notice to the seller specifying this matter within a reasonable time after he has discovered it or ought to have discovered it. In any event, an over-arching two year period applies in which this notice must be given, after which the buyer cannot rely on the non-conformity (unless the contract contains an inconsistent period of guarantee): Article 39(2).[30]

Price reduction

Article 50 provides a remedy unknown at common law – the buyer's right to make a *pro rata* reduction in price where the goods do not conform. The right to reduce is qualified in cases where the seller remedies the problem under Articles 37 or 48, or if the buyer refuses to accept performance under these latter articles.

Part delivery only

Where the seller delivers part only of the goods, or part only of them conforms with the contract, Articles 46–50 apply to the missing or non-conforming part. So, for example, the contract may be avoided, in respect of this part, under Article 49: see Article 51(1).

---

30 Note the comment by Will in Bianca and Bonell, *op cit*, p 365, that 'Article 39 in this context is as important a filter as it is hidden'.

In such a case, avoidance of the entire contract is permissible only when the partial non-performance amounts to a fundamental breach (Article 41(2)).

Early delivery; excess delivery

The buyer may take or reject delivery where the goods are delivered early (Article 52(1)). The buyer has a comparable discretion in relation to the excess part of an excess delivery (although if the excess is accepted it must be paid for): Article 52(2).

The reservation of discretion in the buyer is reasonable; it may not be practicable to take an early or excess delivery.

Obligations of the buyer

Articles 53ff deal with the obligations of the buyer.

Article 53 provides compendiously that the buyer must pay and take delivery of the goods, as required by the contract and the Convention. The concept of delivery is not defined by the Convention, but a number of provisions deal with delivery – see Articles 31ff – on the place of delivery, time for delivery, and related matters.

Payment of the price

The buyer's obligation to pay the price includes ancillary matters such as complying with the laws governing the act of payment (see Article 54). Such obligations might run to, for example, payment of import duties, arrangement of foreign exchange approvals, and arranging letters of credit. The contract should deal with these matters (a shorthand way of dealing with certain of them would be resort to the appropriate Incoterms).

Where the price is not specified nor any procedure for fixing is agreed upon, then the parties are deemed to have agreed that the price shall be that generally charged at formation for such goods sold under comparable circumstances in the trade concerned (Article 55). If the price is fixed by weight, in cases of doubt the net weight is the decisive factor (Article 56).

The place of payment should be agreed in the contract, but in default of such an agreement, payment is to be made at the seller's place of business; or, if it is to be made against the handing over of the goods or documents, at the place of handing over (Article 57(1) and note para (2)).

If the time of payment is not specified in the agreement, it is governed by the detailed regime in Article 58. Broadly, in the absence of contrary agreement the buyer is to pay when the seller places the goods or documents controlling their disposition at the buyer's disposal; and the handing over of these can be made conditional on payment (Article 58(1)). (In a case of carriage, the handing over of the goods, etc can likewise be conditioned on payment (Article 58(2)).)

The buyer is not bound to pay until he has had an opportunity to examine them, unless the agreed upon procedures for delivery or payment are inconsistent with this (Article 58(3)). Given that contracting is often going to be at a great distance, the parties should agree in detail upon the procedures for verifying conformity, such as resort to a commercial inspection agency in the seller's country before dispatch.[31]

The buyer must pay the price without any need for request from the seller (Article 59).

Taking delivery

The buyer has a positive duty to take delivery (see Article 60). Thereby, the seller obtains a discharge from his primary obligation under the contract and avoids contingent liabilities, such as the safekeeping and retrieval of goods at a great distance. This obligation to accept delivery, of course, is qualified by other terms in the Convention where appropriate, such as where the goods are delivered too early (Article 52(1)).

Remedies for breach of contract by buyer

The seller's remedies for breach of contract by the buyer are set out in Articles 61–65. These provisions parallel those dealing with the remedies available to the buyer (Articles 45–52) although, inevitably, the seller's regime is less complex. In most cases, the seller's remedy is to be paid the price (less any amount secured by a sale in litigation), although given that goods in the international sale will usually be transported over a considerable distance, the seller typically will have a greater interest in the buyer taking delivery than might usually be the case in a domestic sale.

Article 61 sets out the scheme of remedies: the aggrieved seller confronted with a buyer's default has resort to the remedies in Articles 62–65, and to damages pursuant to Articles 74–77. The seller is not precluded from seeking damages, because he resorts to another remedy. No period of grace is to be granted to a buyer by a court or tribunal when the seller seeks a remedy.

Specific performance

The seller may require the buyer to pay the price, take delivery or perform his other obligations, unless the seller has resorted to an inconsistent remedy (Article 62). As it has been seen earlier, resort to specific performance is limited by the terms of Article 28 (providing that a court is not bound to order specific performance, unless the court would order this in respect of similar contracts of sale under its own law).

The fact that another remedy is resorted to does not necessarily mean that it is inconsistent with seeking specific performance – the alternative remedy may merely delay resort to Article 62. The giving of a *Nachfrist* under Article 63 (immediately below), perhaps, does no more than delay resort to Article 62, should the buyer perform in terms of the *Nachfrist*.

Articles 85 and 88 – providing for the preservation of the goods by the seller, in a case of the buyer's delay in taking delivery, coupled with their sale to a third party by the seller – illustrates a remedy which is inconsistent with seeking specific performance under Article 62.

---

31 See Honnold, *op cit*, p 423; and Jones, G, 'Impact of the Vienna Convention in Drafting International Sales Contracts' (1992) 20 *International Business Lawyer* 421 at 426.

For the reasons noted in respect of specific performance by the buyer under Article 46, specific performance under Article 62 often will not be a practical remedy.

Giving the buyer extra time

The seller may fix an extra period of time of reasonable length for performance by the seller – another example of a so-called *Nachfrist* (Article 63(1)). (Contrast the buyer's *Nachfrist* as provided for in the parallel Article 47.) The seller may not thereafter, during this period, resort to any remedy for breach of contract, unless the buyer gives him notice that the buyer will not perform during this period. The seller can nonetheless seek damages for delay in performance (Article 63(2)). The buyer's failure to perform within the *Nachfrist* period entitles the seller to avoid the contract under Article 64(1)(b), below.

Seller – avoiding the contract

The seller may avoid the contract pursuant to Article 64 (which parallels avoidance by the buyer under Article 49). The effects of avoidance are dealt with in Articles 81ff: essentially, the contract is terminated, subject to claims for damages and (if applicable) restitution.

The seller may avoid for fundamental breach by the buyer (Article 64(1)(a)); or avoid if the buyer does not perform within the period fixed by the Article 63 *Nachfrist* (above) (Article 64(1)(b)). The right to avoid is lost pursuant to Article 64(2) where the buyer has paid the price, unless the seller declares the contract avoided: (a) in respect of late performance; or (b) in respect of breaches other than late performance, then (in essence) within a reasonable time of becoming aware, actually or constructively, of the breach, or the expiry of the Article 63 *Nachfrist* period (note the details). These limitations set out in Article 64(2), it must be emphasised, apply only in the relatively unusual situation where the buyer has paid the price (which normally would make avoidance pointless), but the seller wishes to avoid anyhow. Such a situation might be one where the seller has found another buyer for the goods. In this case, a late and unexpected payment by the first buyer may be very inconvenient. Nonetheless, even in this case, the buyer's position merits some protection, hence the nullification of the seller's (not yet exercised) right to avoid where payment is received, albeit out of time, and the seller knows that this payment has been received.

Buyer's failure to supply specifications

The provision in Article 65 –that, where the buyer fails to supply relevant specifications for the goods, the seller may make these himself in accordance with any requirements of the buyer known to him, and thereafter perform – might be thought to be drastic and potentially productive of mischief (Article 65(2)). It is mitigated, however, by the provision in Article 65(2), that the seller who is minded to do this must inform the buyer of the details and fix a reasonable time for the buyer to specify differently (with a non-response by the buyer resulting in the seller's specification being deemed to be binding).

A more prudent response by the seller in the normal case would be to avoid the contract and seek damages.[32]

Passing of risk

Overview

Articles 66–70 deal with the passing of risk. The regime differs from the common law. At common law, *prima facie* the risk passes with the title, so that the buyer becomes burdened with the risk when he acquires a title. The Convention, of course, does not deal with the passing of title (see Article 4(b)), so that different rules with a different pivot point or points needed to be devised.

These provisions regarding risk apply only where the parties have not made contrary provision in their agreement. Commonly, of course, they will deal specifically with the matter, such as by the employment of Incoterms. Considerations which were relevant in settling the Convention rules in this regard include: the fact that international contracts for the sale of goods will frequently be transacted over great distances, with the buyer being in the best position, should damage occur, to assess the damage, claim on insurance and rectify the damage if this is possible; the use of containers and of multi-modal transport; the use of one or more carriers who are independent of either party; and the appropriateness of imposing responsibility for risk on the party who is better positioned to care for the goods and to insure them.[33]

The scheme of the provisions, generally, is to identify the risk with the person who has possession or control of the goods (and who is, therefore, best placed to preserve them), and to transfer this risk when the possession or control is transferred.[34] This general principle is not a formal pivot point in every one of the risk articles, however.

The provisions dealing with the allocation, and passing, of risk defer to the preliminary one in Article 66. This provides that loss of or damage to the goods after the risk has passed to the buyer does not discharge him from his obligation to pay the price. (The only exception is where the loss, etc is due to the act or omission of the seller.) This is realistic; the premise is that the buyer will have insurance in effect from (at least) the moment that risk passes, and the buyer taking delivery at the other end of the transit arrangements, is best placed to assess damage and to claim on his insurance.

Contracts involving carriage of goods – when risk passes

Article 67 is the most important provision in practice, dealing as it does with the contract which 'involves carriage' of the goods. Most international sales contracts will involve carriage. The terms make it clear that the arrangement is one where the seller uses a third party carrier (note the reference to the handing over to the 'first carrier').

---

32   See Nicholas, *op cit*, p 229.

33   See Honnold, *op cit*, p 473.

34   See Pryles, M, 'An Assessment of the Vienna Sales Convention', [1989] *AMPLA Yearbook* 342.

The first type of case dealt with in Article 67(1) is that where:

(a) the contract involves carriage; and

(b) the seller is not bound to hand the goods over at a particular place.

In such a case, the risk passes to the buyer when the goods are handed over to the first carrier for transmission, etc. The buyer should therefore have insurance in effect from this point (the assumption of risk should establish an insurable interest where the jurisdiction's insurance law requires this). At the other extreme, it could have been provided that risk passes only when the goods are handed over to the buyer by the (ultimate) carrier; but as one commentator notes, the balance of convenience in long distance transactions is with allocating risk for damage during carriage to the buyer, because the latter is better placed to assess the damage, salvage the goods (if practicable) and claim on the insurer.[35]

The risk could not conveniently pass at some point during carriage because of the difficulties of proof attending the issue of whether the damage occurred before or after the passing of risk (a problem compounded by the fact of containerisation).[36]

Article 67(1) provides alternatively, in the cases of contracts involving carriage, that, where the seller is bound to hand the goods over to a carrier at a particular place, the risk does not pass to the buyer until the goods are handed over to the carrier at that place. Again, in this class of case, the time when risk passes will be able to be established with certainty.

Article 67(2) provides that, notwithstanding the provisions of Article 67(1), the risk does not pass to the buyer until the goods are clearly identified to the contract, by markings on them, notice, etc. This requires the subject goods to be abstracted from the larger bulk. It is designed to preclude the seller from falsely and conveniently claiming, in a case where in fact abstraction and identification had not occurred and where part of the goods in the larger bulk were damaged or lost, that the latter were the buyer's and thus no longer the responsibility of the seller.

Goods sold in transit – when risk passes

The *prima facie* rule in Article 68 is that the risk in respect of goods sold in transit passes to the buyer from the conclusion of the contract. The assumption is that the buyer will organise insurance covering his interest from this point. In the absence of inspection at this time, there could be later problems of proof concerning when damage or loss occurred.

The *prima facie* rule is qualified: if the circumstances so indicate, the buyer assumes the risk from the time the goods were handed over to the carrier who issued the documents embodying the contract of carriage. Nevertheless, the risk remains with the seller in both cases, where he knew or ought to have known of the damage, etc at the time of contracting, and did not disclose this.

---

35 Honnold, *op cit*, p 367.

36 See Nicholas in Bianca and Bonell, *op cit*, p 494.

Catch-all provision – passing of risk in other cases

In cases not covered by Articles 67 and 68 (above) and not regulated by the contract, Article 69 regulates the passing of risk.

Article 69(1) enacts the primary rule: the risk in these residual cases passes to the buyer when he takes over the goods, or, if he does not do so in due time, from the time when the goods are placed at his disposal and he commits a breach of contract by failing to take delivery. The risk in this residual class of cases, logically, is put on the party who has possession or control of the goods.

Article 69(2) enacts a qualification on the primary rule: if the buyer is bound to take over the goods at a place other than the seller's place of business (such as a warehouse), the risk passes when delivery is due and the buyer is aware that the goods are placed at his disposal at that place.

Article 69(3) enacts a precautionary provision in respect of goods which have not yet been abstracted from a larger bulk: the goods are not considered to be placed at the buyer's disposal until they are identified to the contract.

Passing of risk and fundamental breach

If the seller has committed a fundamental breach of the contract, Articles 67–69 do not impair the remedies available to the buyer on account of this breach (Article 70). A primary remedy for fundamental breach is avoidance (Article 49). So, for example, *prima facie,* the buyer can avoid for a non-conformity amounting to fundamental breach, notwithstanding that the risk has passed to the buyer when he seeks to avoid.

Provisions common to the obligations of buyer and seller

Articles 71ff (Chapter V in Part III) impose obligations which (except where otherwise indicated) apply to both parties. These are cumulative upon the obligations specifically imposed upon each in the preceding articles (again, a specific provision may be to the contrary, in a particular case), or otherwise supplement these.

Anticipatory breach and instalment contracts

Articles 71–73 deal with cases of anticipatory breach and related matters. The doctrine of anticipatory breach is found at common law; while the details differ, the effect of the anticipatory breach provisions parallels the role of the common law doctrine.

Article 71(1) permits a party (ie a buyer or seller) to suspend the performance of his obligations under a concluded contract, if it becomes apparent that the other party will not perform a substantial part of his obligations, because, in essence, of the latter's inability or unwillingness to perform. Lack of credit-worthiness is an instance of inability. Where the seller, who is acting under para (1), has already dispatched the goods prior to the grounds for so acting becoming evident, he may prevent the handing over of the goods to the buyer (para (2)). The party suspending performance, before or after dispatch of the goods, must so notify the other party and must continue with the performance if the other party provides adequate assurance of his performance (Article

71(3)). Article 71 provides for a procedure which is less drastic than avoidance for anticipatory breach as provided for in Article 72 (below), but it could still be used with undue haste. Its invocation is limited by the requirements that the other party give the appearance that he will not perform a 'substantial' part of his obligations; and further, by the requirement that notice be given to the other party (Article 71(3)).

The more drastic remedy in this category of apprehended breach of obligation is that provided for in Article 72. Article 72(1) closely parallels the common law in providing that, if prior to the date for performance of the contract it is clear that one of the parties will commit a fundamental breach[37] of the contract, the other party may declare the contract avoided (ie terminated).[38]

If time permits, the party intending to so act must give reasonable notice to the other party in order to permit him to provide adequate assurance of his performance (Article 72(2)). Logically, if he can do this, the ground for avoidance under para (1) – anticipated fundamental breach – will not apply. Paragraph (2) is irrelevant, however, where the other party has declared that he will not perform his obligations.

Because Article 72 is more radical in its effect than Article 71, it is appropriate that the threshold for its application should be anticipated fundamental breach, as opposed to the less demanding test of an anticipated non-performance of a 'substantial' part of obligations in Article 71.[39]

Nonetheless, the anticipated non-performance of a substantial part of obligations will often constitute by itself, an anticipated fundamental breach. The para (2) requirement represents a brake on the para (1) remedy, one not found at common law.

An aggrieved party could invoke the Article 71 remedy if in doubt, and then, if this proves unproductive, invoke the Article 72 remedy. He could also invoke the two concurrently.[40]

Instalment contracts are dealt with by Article 73. Paragraph (1) provides that if a failure to perform by a party (buyer or seller) in respect of any one instalment constitutes a fundamental breach with respect to that instalment, the aggrieved party can avoid the contract with respect to that instalment. The premise is that this instalment is a readily severable part of the contract; and that to permit the avoiding of the contract with respect to all future instalments would be too harsh. Paragraph (2), however, permits avoidance of the contract with respect to all future instalments, where a party's failure to perform gives the other party grounds to conclude that a fundamental breach will occur with respect to future instalments. The latter must avoid within a reasonable time. By para (3), the party who avoids in respect of any delivery (ie under paras (1) or (2)), may, at the same time, declare it avoided in respect of prior or future deliveries if, by reason of their interdependence, those deliveries could not be used for the purposes contemplated

---

37 See Article 25.

38 See Articles 26, 81ff.

39 See the comment by Burnett, *op cit*, p 24.

40 See the comment by Bennett in Bianca and Bonell, *op cit*, p 529.

by the parties at the time of formation. In this latter case, the instalments will not be readily severable.

Article 51 should also be noted in respect of instalment contracts. It vests remedies in a buyer in respect of part-only deliveries or non-conformity in respect of a part of the goods delivered. It is not in terms confined to instalment contracts. Article 73 is, where instalment contracts are concerned, cumulative upon Article 51.

Damages

Articles 74–77 deal with the core aspects of damages: measurement and causation (or remoteness) issues. Damages will have been awarded by reference to other provisions (eg Articles 45(1)(b) and 61(1)(b)).

The primary provision is Article 74. It provides, firstly, that damages for breach of contract consist of a sum equal to the loss, including loss of profit, suffered in consequence of the breach. This measure of damages replicates the basic approach of the common law, ie that the plaintiff is to be put in the position he would have enjoyed had the contract been duly performed.[41]

The principle is compensation; punitive damages are not provided for. The specification that damages should include profit is precautionary.

Article 74 also provides, secondly, that the damages may not exceed the loss which the party in breach foresaw or ought to have foreseen at the time of the conclusion of the contract, in light of the facts and matters of which he then knew or ought to have known, as a possible consequence of the breach of contract.

In common law language, this provision deals with remoteness of causation: it specifies the ambit of the consequences of flowing from the breach, which are to be compensated – direct consequences are compensatable, but remote ones are not. The principle enunciated is broadly similar to that laid down in the leading common law decision of *Hadley v Baxendale*.[42]

There are, however, differences. *Hadley v Baxendale* broadly makes the defendant liable for those consequences of breach:

(a) which flow naturally, ie in the normal course of things, from the breach; or (in respect of less obvious consequences);

(b) which may reasonably be supposed to have been in the contemplation of both parties at the time of formation, as the probable result of such breach.

The Convention principle posits, fundamentally, an objective test (if the subjective one is not satisfied then the objective test comes into play). The loss is limited to that which was objectively predictable as a 'possible' consequence, by a reasonable person ('ought to have known' connotes reasonableness) possessed of the information which the defendant should reasonably have possessed, at the time of formation. One obvious departure from

---

41   *Robinson v Harman* (1848) 1 Ex 850 at 855.
42   *Hadley v Baxendale* (1854) 9 Ex 341 at 354.

the *Hadley v Baxendale* principle is the related test of eventuality governing the foresight test (the common law decision specifies foresight of probability, while Article 74 specifies foresight of possibility; clearly the latter is less demanding). It follows that the Convention will compensate more remote consequences than will *Hadley v Baxendale*. Nonetheless, these more remote consequences cannot, it is submitted, be freakishly remote, because the Convention test is build around the foresight of a hypothetical reasonable defendant.

The common law authority since *Hadley v Baxendale* has clarified a related matter – the reasonable person in the defendant's shoes must have foreseen the type of loss but need not have foreseen its extent, *viz*, the fact that the particular head of loss is greater in the quantum than the quantum contemplated is not a bar to full recovery. The Convention is silent on this point, but the key word is 'loss', which is unqualified and broad enough to yield an interpretation giving an outcome equivalent to the common law's on this issue. This approach is fortified by the reference of Article 74 to loss of profit as being compensatable – a prime issue in remoteness issues concerning contracts involving goods. Presumably, it would be enough that a loss of profit is foreseeable in terms of the remoteness test; it could not realistically be expected that the defendant seller or his hypothetical stand-in have been able to forecast the quantum of loss of profit owing to the late delivery of a machine, in order for the plaintiff buyer to recover this.

Articles 75 and 76 deal with cases where contracts are avoided by a party; and the consequential assessment of damages.

Article 75 states that, where a contract is avoided, and (within a reasonable time and in a reasonable manner) the buyer has bought replacement goods or the seller has resold the goods, the party claiming damages may recover the difference between the contract price and the price in the substitute transaction. As well, this party may claim any further damages (such as for storage expenses or loss of profit) recoverable under Article 74. The approach in Article 75 is logical; *prima facie*, the damages will approximate the difference in prices. To prevent abuse, the tests of reasonableness noted govern the plaintiff's conduct. If no direct loss results from the substitute transaction, then damages cannot be claimed under Article 75.

Article 76 provides a mechanism for assessing damages in an avoidance case by reference to a market price benchmark (termed 'current price' in Article 76 – see the definition in para (2)). Article 76 is not applicable where there is a substitute transaction pursuant to Article 75. Broadly, the innocent party can recover damages equal to the difference between the contract price and market price at the time of avoidance (or where the plaintiff has avoided the contract after taking over). He can also seek any further damages recoverable under Article 74. If a loss has not resulted under the Article 76 regime, damages logically cannot be recovered. Article 76 can lead to anomaly, as where the buyer in default has to pay more than the contract price because the 'current price' has gone up.

Article 77 enacts a standard mitigation principle paralleling that found in the common law. Broadly, the party seeking damages must take reasonable steps to minimise his loss; if he does not, a corresponding reduction will be applied in the assessment of damages. Article 77, therefore, qualifies the assessment of damages under Articles 74–76.

Interest

Article 78 provides that, if a party fails to pay the price or any other sum in arrears, the other party is entitled to interest without prejudice to a claim for damages under Article 74. The court is left to decide the interest rate.

Articles 79–80 enact certain exemptions from liability.

Frustration; force majeure; *impossibility*

Article 79 provides a qualified defence in cases where an impediment in prescribed terms comes into operation, impacting upon the party's ability to perform. The defence is broadly suggestive of the common law doctrine of frustration (or the overlapping concepts of impossibility, *force majeure*, etc), but many points of difference are apparent.

Frustration at common law deals with events which make the contract impossible to perform, or render its prospective performance something radically different to the parties' contemplation. The event is something which happens independently of the parties. It operates to terminate the contract with prospective effect.

The Article 79 defence is more limited. Paragraph (1) provides the defence: the party is not liable for a failure to perform any of his obligations where he proves that the failure was due to an impediment beyond his control and that he could not reasonably be expected to have taken it into account at the time of formation or to have avoided it or overcome it or its consequences.

Will a broader range of events trigger the Article 79(1) defence than will trigger the common law doctrine of frustration? Given that the consequences of the Article 79(1) doctrine (noted below) are much less drastic than the common law doctrine, this might be considered to be a reasonable conclusion. It must be stressed, however, that given that the Convention is self-contained law, the scope of Article 79(1) is not to be determined through the prism of common law principle. The very qualified nature of the defence, however, is nevertheless a factor which bears upon determining the ambit of the operative impediments.[43]

The reference to 'any one of his obligations' as opposed to 'obligations' suggests that the defence can be invoked to cover non-performance of a part of a contract, as in the case of an instalment contract, and that the defence is not an all or nothing affair.

Article 79(2) deals with the role of the defence where a party performs in whole or in part by way of a delegate.

The exemption provided by Article 79 applies only for the period during which the impediment exists (Article 79(3)). The defence, then, postpones performance, as noted; it does not terminate the contract.

---

43   *Cf* Nicholas, *op cit*, p 235, seeing Article 79 as dealing with cases of impossibility. On the other hand, see Sacks, P, 'Comment on an Assessment of the Vienna Convention' [1989] *Australian Mining and Petroleum Law Association Yearbook*, pp 376–77.

Paragraph (4) requires the party who fails to perform to give notice in prescribed terms to the other party – failure to comply with the notification requirements leads to liability for damages as specified.

Article 79(5) enacts a crucial limitation on the defence: nothing in the article prevents either party from exercising any right other than to claim damages under the Convention. The aggrieved party can, therefore, avoid the contract where ground for avoidance is made out under the Convention, although he could not sensibly be awarded specific performance of the contract during the period in which the defence is operative (this would defeat the role of Article 79). The postponement (para (3)) of the right to claim damages must be understood as making any eventual award of damages, subject to a deduction for damages which would otherwise accrue because of the delay sanctioned by Article 79. Article 79(5) cannot be read as having no more effect than postponing a claim for full damages, including losses caused by the permitted period of delay – such an interpretation would nullify Article 79.

Given the limited role of Article 79 and the uncertainties inherent in determining whether an event is a requisite 'impediment', the parties should (as per long-standing commercial practice) draft their own *force majeure* clauses.[44]

The contract should also deal with common impediments to performance, such as losses during carriage and related issues like insurance (in default of specific terms – Articles 66ff deal with the passing of risk).

Obstructing/facilitating other party's performance

Article 80 enacts a precautionary provision: a party must not rely on a failure of the other party to perform, to the extent that such a failure was caused by the first party's act or omission. This clause approximates the implication at common law of a term into a contract pursuant to which each party will do what is reasonably possible to facilitate the other's performance.[45]

Effects of avoidance

Articles 81–84 deal with the consequences of avoidance or, in common law terms, termination of the contract for a reason or reasons other than due performance by each party. A key issue which needed to be addressed was: should restitution be permitted? In the case of contracts for goods, especially, the possibility of restitution will more often be a live one than in some other classes of contract (such as contracts to erect a building, build a machine or supply services).

The avoidance provisions do not deal with the grounds for avoiding a contract. These are provided for elsewhere (see, in particular, Articles 49 and 64).

Avoidance does not preclude a party from seeking damages which may be due (see Article 81). Apart from this, the provisions aim at effecting an appropriate adjustment of the rights and obligations as between the parties, in a circumstance of termination.

---

44 See Sacks, *ibid,* p 366; Burnett, *op cit*, p 28; Jones, *op cit* at 426.

45 A negative implied term which overlaps in part is that each party will not take steps to make the other's performance difficult or impossible.

Avoidance releases the parties from their contractual obligations, subject to any damages due (Article 81(1)). Specified legal rights and obligations continue, however: those deriving from contractual provisions for the settlement of disputes; and those dealing with the consequences of avoidance (para (1)). A *prima facie* right to restitution is granted to the party who has performed in part or whole – this right vests in each and every party who has at least part-performed (Article 81(2)). It is not confined to the party who has avoided. A *prima facie* right to restitution is logical. As noted, contracts for the sale of goods, in particular, are typically by their nature amenable to restitution, with goods supplied/money paid being able to be readily returned. Subject to the availability of supplementary compensation in the form of damages, where applicable, a returning of the parties to their pre-contractual positions is the obvious and sensible outcome of avoidance.

Restitution may not be sensible in all cases, however, and in some it will be physically impossible. Article 82 deals with relevant cases of this type.

The buyer cannot avoid the contract or require the seller to deliver substitute goods (as to the latter power, see Article 46(2)) if it is impossible for the buyer to make restitution of the goods substantially in the condition received (Article 82(1)). The qualifier, 'substantially', is a sensible one; the right to avoid, etc should not be lost because of a minor change in the goods. This limitation of impossibility in para (1) does not apply, however, in cases delineated in para (2), including where the requisite impossibility is not due to the buyer's act or omission.

An apparently more controversial limitation is that enacted in Article 82(2)(c): the buyer is not precluded from avoiding the contract by the impossibility of substantial restitution if the goods have been sold in the normal course of business or have been consumed or transformed by the buyer in normal use before he discovered, or ought to have discovered, the lack of conformity (which entitles him to avoid). *Prima facie*, the buyer's remedy here would be damages – he clearly cannot avoid with a view to restitution, given that the goods have been consumed. One commentator sees the answer to this apparent problem as being that 'under Article 81 ... avoidance releases the buyer from his obligation to pay the price and entitles him to recover any payments on the price ...'.[46]

The buyer who loses the right to declare the contract avoided or to require the seller to deliver substitute goods (by virtue of Article 82) retains all other remedies under the contract and the Convention (Article 83). Damages will be the obvious such remedy.

The seller who is bound to refund the price, in an avoidance situation, must pay interest on it from the date of payment (Article 84(1)). (This does not preclude the seller from seeking other applicable remedies, such as damages.) The corollary is that the buyer must account to the seller for all benefits derived from the goods in whole or in part: (a) if he must make restitution of them in whole or in part; or (b) if it is impossible for him to do this substantially in the condition in which they were received, but he has nevertheless

---

46   Honnold, *op cit*, p 568 and note his further comments. See also the discussion by Tallon in Bianca and Bonell, *op cit*, p 609.

avoided the contract or required the delivery of substitute goods. (Again, this does not preclude the buyer from seeking other available remedies.)

Preservation of the goods

Articles 85–88 impose certain obligations upon a party to preserve the goods and, in the ultimate resort, create a power of sale. The obligation is not dependent upon fault being shown; the innocent party, where appropriate, must preserve the goods. The preservation regime aims to minimise the risk of damage to or loss of the goods, and hence to minimise the potential overall cost of a dispute between the parties concerning them. It has been enacted in recognition that, where many international sales contracts are concerned, the goods may be delivered at a vast distance from the supplier, and beyond the supplier's ready ability to preserve or salvage them in the event that the buyer is unable or unwilling to take delivery. It imposes the obligation of preservation on that party best able to preserve the goods, irrespective of their role in causing any contractual miscarriage, or miscarriage in transport arrangements, etc.

The preservation regime can be impinged upon by contrary agreement between the parties, and by their insurance arrangements.

The seller in possession or control of the goods must take reasonable steps to preserve the goods, where there is a delay on the part of the buyer in taking delivery or in making payment in cases where delivery and payment are to take place concurrently (Article 85). The seller can retain them until the buyer reimburses for reasonable expenses (eg storage or insurance) (Article 85). This obligation applies even as the risk or property (or both) in the goods may have passed to the buyer.

The buyer who has received the goods must take reasonable steps to preserve them where he intends to exercise any right to reject them. Again, he is entitled to reimbursement of reasonable expenses (Article 86(1)). Further, the buyer must take reasonable steps to preserve the goods where they have been placed at his disposal at their destination, notwithstanding that he exercises a right to reject them (Article 86(2)). His obligation to take them into possession applies only if he can do this without payment of the price. His para (2) obligation does not apply if the seller or agent is present at the destination. As part of fulfilling a duty of preservation, the party may deposit them in a third party's warehouse at the (reasonable) expense of the other party (Article 87).

The goods having been secured, the ultimate question arises: if the other party will not take them over, what is to be done with them? The issue can become progressively more urgent, given ongoing insurance and storage costs, to take two possible factors. Article 85 deals with this situation by providing qualified powers of sale. By Article 85(1), the party who has to preserve the goods under Article 85 or 86 may sell them by appropriate means where there has been an unreasonable delay by the other party in taking over the goods or paying the price or costs of preservation, although reasonable notice of intention to sell must be given. If the goods are subject to rapid deterioration, etc the party burdened under Articles 85 or 86 must take reasonable steps to sell them and give notice if possible (Article 88(2)). Where the goods are sold, the vendor can take reasonable expenses and must account to the other party for the balance (Article 88(3)).

The fact that a party is burdened with a duty of preservation, or that he ultimately exercises a power of sale, does not otherwise detract from the remedies which may be available to each party. Thus, a party may on the one hand have an obligation to account to the other for the balance of the price received on a sale under Article 88, but concurrently be entitled to offsetting damages.

The Convention does not deal with the passing of property in the goods (Article 4(b)). The vesting of a power of sale in a party by Article 88 will not necessarily vest title in this party for the purposes of vesting the third party purchaser with title; these are matters for the applicable domestic law. Given the recognition of the Convention by domestic law, however, it may be supposed that, in the usual case, the legal power of sale created by the Convention, and assimilated thereby into domestic law, would adequately answer a claim that the party exercising a power of sale was not competent to vest title in the third party purchaser.

TUTORIAL QUESTIONS

1   In what major way does the sale of goods regime provided for in the Convention differ from that provided by the domestic law of your jurisdiction? On balance, which regime is superior?

2   A company, B, is incorporated, and has its head office, in State X, which State has ratified the Convention. It runs a chain of bottling plants in several other States, some of which have adopted the Convention. These plants are run by subsidiary companies incorporated in these States. B approaches S, a company incorporated in State Y, which has not adopted the Convention. The approach is made to the S's sales office in State X, which is not incorporated. The terms of contracts for the supply of bottling machines are agreed upon between S and B, but contracts for the supply and installation of the machines are entered into between S and each subsidiary of B. The contracts are silent as to the applicable law. There is one exception, however – one of the contracts (entered into between S and a subsidiary in a non–Contracting State) makes the 'domestic law' of State X applicable to the contract. Does the Convention apply to all of these contracts, or only some of them; and in the latter case or cases, to which is it applicable?

3   Buyer B contracts with Seller S to buy 2,000 live sheep. S's State is drought affected and the costs of feeding stock are mounting. S faxes B, proposing that 1,000 sheep be delivered one month early. B does not respond. The sheep are fully delivered, one month early. B does not want to take delivery, not having the facilities, nor the need, for the sheep at this earlier time. Assuming that the Convention applies, what is the legal position of each party?

4   Buyer B and seller S enter into a contract to which the Convention applies. The goods to be supplied consist of frozen meat. B rejects the cargo tendered, contending that one separable part of the cargo (some 10%) has perished because of inadequate refrigeration. The contract is silent as to when risk passes. B claims that doubt must exist as to the whole cargo, and rejects it in toto. What is the legal position of each party?

What would the legal position be if the cargo was sound but B still rejected the cargo on the basis that his refrigerated premises burnt down a few days ago, and there is no alternative refrigerated space available in his small State?

5   A buyer B orders a large pump from S. The Convention applies to the contract. The contract specifies that the pump must pump at least x thousand litres *per* minute. The pump is delivered and installed, and it is then discovered that it pumps at only 80% of the nominated capacity. This will not do for B's purposes. B has the option: either replace the pump with another full-capacity pump (one has suddenly become available in B's own State); or buy a second smaller pump to make up the missing capacity. The second course of action would produce a higher aggregate expense than B contemplated when B entered into the contract. What are B's options at law?

6   Seller S ships goods to B, pursuant to a contract to which the Convention applies. The risk passes, after which time the goods suffer damage. When B takes delivery, he discovers the damage. He also discovers that, even apart from the damage, the goods do not conform to the contract and the non-conformity is such that, had B contemplated it, he would never have contracted. Examine the legal position as between the parties where (a) the goods can be repaired; and (b) they cannot be repaired.

7   Buyer B operates a theme park in State X. He contracts with S, who supplies hi-tech theme park rides to theme park operators. The contract is governed by the Convention. The machinery is very expensive, but in locations in other regions of State X previously supplied it has boosted patronage greatly, for several years. This happy outcome has boosted S's business significantly. The machinery is duly manufactured and installed. It is riddled with gremlins, and is closed for various intervals during a period of 18 months as these problems are rectified. B incurs much bad publicity and, *inter alia*, his business suffers. He incurs a heavy interest bill on the money borrowed to finance this acquisition. What is the legal position as between the parties?

8   The buyer, an Italian company, sent a purchase order form ordering goods from the seller in Brisbane. The buyer's form requested immediate shipment. The seller shipped the goods the next day and mailed an 'order confirmation form' to the buyer. The seller's order confirmation form contained the following language (in bold face type on the front of the form):

> The terms set forth on the reverse side are the only ones upon which we will accept orders. These terms supersede all prior written understandings, assurances and offers. Your attention is especially directed to the provisions concerning warranty and liability of supplier and claims procedures. Advise us immediately if anything in the acknowledgment is incorrect or is otherwise unacceptable.

The terms on the reverse of the form limited the seller's liability for breach of warranty to repair or replacement of the goods.

The delivered goods were non-conforming and the buyer is now threatening to sue. The seller claims that its liability for breach of warranty is limited by contract. Do the parties have a contract? If so, on what terms?

9   The plaintiff buyer had its place of business in Krefeld, Germany. On 18 September 1992, the buyer purchased from the defendant seller – whose place of business was located in Indiana, USA – a cutting machine to be installed in the veneer processing unit of a Russian furniture combine. After the machine had been put into operation, an accident occurred which led to the death of a worker and caused injuries to another. Subsequently, the Russian sub-purchaser demanded repair of the defective machine from the buyer, whereupon the buyer sued to recover the costs of repair from the seller. In its complaint, the buyer also moved for a declaratory judgment from the court establishing that the seller was required to indemnify the buyer against all damage claims raised by the Russian sub-purchaser and furniture combine with respect to the accident in dispute.

Identify and discuss all relevant issues pertaining to the United Nations Convention on Contracts for the International Sale of Goods, 1980 (Vienna Convention). Note that the Vienna Convention entered into force in Germany on 1 January 1991.

10 Mr Andrew Townsend is an American manufacturer of a computer software program called 'Anglialingua', which is designed to assist non-English speaking high school students in the learning of the English language. Ms Nicole Bitterand is a French distributor of educational materials with a head office in Paris, France. Townsend meets Bitterand at a party in Brisbane, Australia, during a conference on Teaching English as a Second Language. Townsend, in conversations with Bitterand, describes his computer software program (Anglialingua) in glowing terms and points out that it has already been successfully marketed in Germany.

Bitterand agrees orally to purchase 1,000 packages of 'Anglialingua' at $200 each. Townsend undertakes to ship the packages to Paris on his return to the USA. Bitterand agrees to pay for the packages by letter of credit upon the receipt of the appropriate shipping documents.

Upon her return to Paris, Bitterand decides to contact a German importer of 'Anglialingua' to ascertain the usefulness of the program. The German importer tells Bitterand that 'Anglialingua' has not been well received in Germany because the program does not work and is overpriced. Bitterand, who did not actually see 'Anglialingua' in operation, is now very worried and comes to realise that her purchase may turn out to be a bad investment. In particular, she is afraid that 'Anglialingua' may not actually be suitable for French high school students.

Bitterand has read in *Le Monde* that you have recently attended a series of lectures on international business law at the TC Beirne School of Law at The University of Queensland, Australia. As she is confident that you are an expert on transnational business deals, she seeks your advice as to her rights.

Answer the following questions:

(i)   Does the transaction have a sufficient connection with States that have ratified the United Nations Convention on Contracts for the International Sale of Goods (Vienna Convention) so that its provisions will govern the contract?

(ii) Has a valid contract for the international sale of goods been formed? Does it matter that the contract is not in writing?

(iii) If Bitterand does not wish the contract to be governed by the Vienna Convention, can she exclude some or all of its provisions?

(iv) Does the Vienna Convention govern all the issues that might arise in this transaction?

(v) If Bitterand refuses to accept the packages, is Townsend likely to receive specific performance? Should he request specific performance in a French court?

(vi) Assuming that a valid contract for the international sale of goods has been formed, under what circumstances would Bitterand be able to avoid the contract?

FURTHER READING

Anderson, R, 'Comment on an Assessment of the Vienna Sales Convention', [1989] *AMPLA Yearbook* 354.

Bianca, CM and Bonell, MJ (eds), *Commentary on the International Sales Law – The 1980 Vienna Sales Convention*, 1987, Milan: Giuffrè.

Burnett, R, *The Law of International Business Transactions*, 1994, Sydney: Federation Press, Chapter 1.

Corney, G, 'Obligations and Remedies under the 1980 Vienna Sales Convention', (1993) *Qld Law Society* 37.

Donner, 'Impact of the Vienna Sales Convention on Canada' (1992) 6 *Emory International Law R* 743.

Feltham, J, 'CIF and FOB Contracts and the Vienna Convention on Contracts for the Sale of Goods' (1991) *Journal of Business Law* 413.

Govey, I and Staker, C, 'Vienna Convention Takes Effect in Australia Next Year' (June 1988) *Australian Law News* 15.

Hill, A, 'A Comparative Study of the United Nations Convention on the Limitation Period in the International Sale of Goods and s 2–725 of the Uniform Commercial Code' (1990) *Texas International Law J* 1.

Honnold, J, *Uniform Law for International Sales Under the 1980 United Nations Convention*, 2nd edn, 1991, Deventer, Boston: Kluwer.

Honnold, J, 'Uniform Laws for International Trade: Early "Care and Feeding" for Uniform Growth' (1995) in *International Trade and Business Law Journal* 1.

Jones, G, 'Impact of the Vienna Convention in Drafting International Sales Contracts' (1992) 20 *International Business Lawyer* 421.

Kastley, A, 'The Right to Require Performance in International Sales: Towards an International Interpretation of the Vienna Convention' (1988) 63 *Washington Law R* 607.

Kathrein, R and Magraw, D (eds), *The Convention for the International Sale of Goods: a Handbook of Basic Materials*, 1987, Washington and Chicago: American Bar Association, Section of International Law and Practice.

Kritzer, A, *Guide to Practical Application of the United Nations Convention on Contracts for the International Sale of Goods*, 1990, Deventer, Boston: Kluwer.

Lavers, R, 'CSIG – to Use or Not to Use' (1993) 21 *International Business Lawyer* 10.

Lee, R, 'The UN Convention on Contracts for the International Sale of Goods – OK for the UK?' (1993) *Journal of Business Law* 131.

Lipstein, K, 'One Hundred Years of Hague Conferences on Private International Law' (1990) 42 *International and Comparative Law Qtly* 553 at 616–26.

Murphy, 'United Nations Convention on Contracts for the International Sale of Goods: Creating Uniformity in International Sales Law' (1989) 12 *Fordham International Law J* 727.

Ndulo, M, 'The Vienna Sales Convention 1980 and the Hague Uniform Laws on International Sale of Goods 1964: A Comparative Analysis' (1989) 38 *International and Comparative Law Qtly* 1.

Nicholas, B, 'The Vienna Convention on International Sales Law' (1989) 105 LQR 201.

Pryles, M, 'An Assessment of the Vienna Sales Convention' [1989] *Australian Mining and Petroleum Law Association Yearbook* 337.

Roberts, J, 'International Sale of Goods' in Wilde and Islam (eds), *International Transactions – Trade and Investment, Law and Finance*, 1993, Sydney: Law Book Co, Chapter 2.

Sacks, P, 'Comment on an Assessment of the Vienna Sales Convention' [1989] *Australian Mining and Petroleum Law Association Yearbook* 359.

Schlechtriem, P, *Uniform Sales Law – The UN Convention on Contracts for the International Sale of Goods*, 1986, Vienna: Manz.

Schmitthoff, C, *Export Trade – the Law and Practice of International Trade*, 9th edn, 1990, London: Stevens, Chapter 14.

Strub, M, 'The Convention on the International Sale of Goods: Anticipatory Repudiation Provisions and Developing Countries' (1989) 38 *International and Comparative Law Qtly* 475.

Winship, P, 'Formation of International Sales Contracts under the 1980 Vienna Convention' (1993) 17 *International Lawyer* 1.

Winship, P, 'Bibliography: International Sale of Goods (Symposium on International Sale of Goods Convention)' (1984) 18 *International Lawyer* 53.

UNITED NATIONS CONVENTION ON CONTRACTS FOR THE INTERNATIONAL SALE OF GOODS (VIENNA SALES CONVENTION) VIENNA – 11 APRIL 1980

The Convention entered into force on 1 January 1988 after the ratification of the USA. It culminated half a century of work to prepare uniform law for the international sales of goods.

This Convention replaces the Hague Convention Relating to a Uniform Law on the Formation of Contracts for the International Sale of Goods of 1964 and the Hague Convention Relating to a Uniform Law on the International Sale of Goods of 1964 which, because of defects, have not been widely accepted by the important trading States. The new Convention provides a balanced representation of all legal systems of the world.

United Nations Convention on Contracts for the International Sale of Goods (Vienna, 1980)

State	Signature	Ratification Accession Approval Acceptance Succession (*)	Entry into force
Argentina 1		19 Jul 1983	1 Jan 1988
Australia		17 Mar 1988	1 Apr 1989
Austria	11 Apr 1980	29 Dec 1987	1 Jan 1989
Belarus 1		9 Oct 1989	1 Nov 1990
Bosnia and Herzegovina		12 Jan 1994 ★	6 Mar 1992
Bulgaria		9 Jul 1990	1 Aug 1991
Canada 2		23 Apr 1991	1 May 1992
Chile 1	11 Apr 1980	7 Feb 1990	1 Mar 1991
China 3	30 Sep 1981	11 Dec 1986	1 Jan 1988
Cuba		2 Nov 1994	1 Dec 1995
Czech Republic a		30 Sep 1993 ★	1 Jan 1993
Denmark 4	26 May 1981	14 Feb 1989	1 Mar 1990
Ecuador		27 Jan 1992	1 Feb 1993
Estonia 1		20 Sep 1993	1 Oct 1994
Egypt		6 Dec 1982	1 Jan 1988
Finland 4	26 May 1981	15 Dec 1987	1 Jan 1989
France	27 Aug 1981	6 Aug 1982	1 Jan 1988
Georgia		16 Aug 1994	1 Sep 1995
Germany b 5	26 May 1981	21 Dec 1989	1 Jan 1991
Ghana	11 Apr 1980		
Guinea		23 Jan 1991	1 Feb 1992
Hungary 1 6	11 Apr 1980	16 Jun 1983	1 Jan 1988

Iraq		.5 Mar 1990	.1 Apr 1991
Italy	.30 Sep 1981	.11 Dec 1986	.1 Jan 1988
Lesotho	.18 Jun 1981	.18 Jun 1981	.1 Jan 1988
Lithuania 1		.18 Jan 1995	.1 Feb 1996
Moldova		.13 Oct 1994	.1 Nov 1995
Mexico		.29 Dec 1987	.1 Jan 1989
Netherlands	.29 May 1981	.13 Dec 1990	.1 Jan 1992
New Zealand 8		.22 Sep 1994	.1 Oct 1995
Norway 4	.26 May 1981	.20 Jul 1988	.1 Aug 1989
Poland	.28 Sep 1981		
Romania		.22 May 1991	.1 Jun 1992
Russian Federation c 1		.16 Aug 1990	.1 Sep 1991
Singapore 7	.11 Apr 1980	.16 Feb 1995	.1 Mar 1996
Slovak. Republic a		.28 May 1993 ★	.1 Jan 1993
Slovenia		.7 Jan 1994 ★	.25 Jun 1991
Spain		.24 Jul 1990	.1 Aug 1991
Sweden 4	.26 May 1981	.15 Dec 1987	.1 Jan 1989
Switzerland		.21 Feb 1990	.1 Mar 1991
Syrian Arab Republic		.19 Oct 1982	.1 Jan 1988
Uganda		.12 Feb 1992	.1 Mar 1993
Ukraine 1		.3 Jan 1990	.1 Feb 1991
USA 7	.31 Aug 1981	.11 Dec 1986	.1 Jan 1988
Venezuela	.28 Sep 1981		
Yugoslavia	.11 Apr 1980	.27 Mar 1985	.1 Jan 1988
Zambia		.6 Jun 1986	.1 Jan 1988

Signatures only: 3; ratifications, accessions, approval, acceptance and successions: 44.

(a) The Convention was signed by the former Czechoslovakia on 1 September 1981 and an instrument of ratification was deposited on 5 March 1990, with the Convention entering into force for the former Czechoslovakia on 1 April 1991. On 28 May 1993 the Slovak Republic, and on 30 September 1993 the Czech Republic, deposited instruments of succession with effect from 1 January 1993, the date of succession of States.

(b) The Convention was signed by the former German Democratic Republic on 13 August 1981, ratified on 23 February 1989 and entered into force on 1 March 1990.

(c) The Russian Federation continues, as from 24 December 1991, the membership of the former Union of Soviet Socialist Republics (USSR) in the United Nations and maintains, as from that date, full responsibility for all the rights and obligations of the USSR under the Charter of the United Nations and multilateral treaties deposited with the Secretary General.

Declarations and reservations

1   Upon adherence to the Convention the governments of Argentina, Belarus, Chile, Estonia, Hungary, Lithuania, Ukraine and USSR, in accordance with Articles 12 and 96 of the Convention, that any provision of Article 11, Article 29 or Part II of the Convention that allows a contract of sale or its modification or termination by agreement or any offer, acceptance or other indication of intention to be made in any form other than in writing, would not apply where any party had his place of business in their respective States.

2   Upon accession the government of Canada declared that, in accordance with Article 93 of the Convention, the Convention will extend to Alberta, British Columbia, Manitoba, New Brunswick, Newfoundland, Nova Scotia, Ontario, Prince Edward Island and the Northwest Territories. Upon accession the government of Canada declared that, in accordance with Article 95 of the Convention, with respect to British Columbia, it will not be bound by Article 1(1)(b) of the Convention. In a notification received on 31 July 1992, the government of Canada withdrew that declaration. In a declaration received on 9 April 1992 the government of Canada extended the application of the Convention to Quebec and Saskatchewan. In a notification received on 29 June 1992, Canada extended the application of the Convention to Yukon.

3   Upon approving the Convention the government of China declared that it did not consider itself bound by sub-para (b) of para 1 of Article 1 and Article 11 as well as the provisions in the Convention relating to the content of Article 11.

4   Upon ratifying the Convention, the governments of Denmark, Finland, Norway and Sweden declared in accordance with Article 92(1) that they would not be bound by Part II of the Convention (Formation of the Contract). Upon ratifying the Convention, the governments of Denmark, Finland, Norway and Sweden declared, pursuant to Article 94(1) and 94(2), that the Convention would not apply to contracts of sale where the parties have their places of business in Denmark, Finland, Sweden, Iceland or Norway.

5   Upon ratifying the Convention, the government of Germany declared that it would not apply Article 1(1)(b) in respect of any state that had made a declaration that that state would not apply Article 1(1)(b).

6   Upon ratifying the Convention, the government of Hungary declared that it considered the General Conditions of Delivery of Goods between Organisations of the Member Countries of the Council for Mutual Economic Assistance to be subject to the provisions of Article 90 of the Convention.

7   Upon ratifying the Convention, the governments of Czechoslovakia, Singapore and of the USA declared that they would not be bound by sub-para (1)(b) of Article 1.

8   Upon accession to the Convention, the government of New Zealand declared that this accession shall not extend to the Cook Islands, Niue or Tokelau.

The following States have deposited their declarations and reservations:

1   Upon signing the Convention, the governments of Denmark, Finland, Norway and Sweden declared in accordance with Article 92(1) that they would not he bound by Part II of the Convention (Formation of the Contract).

2   Upon ratifying the Convention, the government of Hungary declared that it considered the General Conditions of Delivery of Goods between Organisations of the Member Countries of the Council for Mutual Economic Assistance to be subject to the provisions of Article 90 of the Convention.

3   Upon ratifying the Convention, the governments of Argentina and Hungary stated, in accordance with Articles 12 and 96 of the Convention, that any provision of Article 11, Article 29 or Part II or the Convention that allowed a contract of sale or its modification or termination by agreement or any offer, acceptance or other indication of intention to be made in any form other than in writing, did not apply where any party had his place of business in their respective States.

4   Upon approving the Convention, the government of China declared that it did not consider itself bound by sub-para (b) of para 1 of Article 1 and Article 11 as well as the provisions in the Convention relating to the content of Article 11.

5   Upon ratifying the Convention, the government of the USA declared that it would not be bound by sub-para (1) (b) of Article 1.

See, United Nations General Assembly A/CN.9/325, 17 May 1989, pp 4–5; Honnold, J, *Uniform Law for International Sales – Under the 1980 United Nations Convention*, 1982, Deventer: Kluwer; Bianca, CM and Bonell, MJ, *Commentary on the International Sales Law – The 1980 Vienna Sales Convention*, 1987, Milan: Giuffrè.

United Nations Convention on Contracts for the International Sale of Goods (Vienna Sales Convention)

Vienna, 11 April 1980

The States Parties to this Convention,

Bearing in mind the broad objectives in the resolutions adopted by the sixth special session of the General Assembly of the United Nations on the establishment of a New International Economic Order,

Considering that the development of international trade on the basis of equality and mutual benefit is an important element in promoting friendly relations among States,

Being of the opinion that the adoption of uniform rules which govern contracts for the international sale of goods and take into account the different social, economic and legal systems would contribute to the-removal of legal barriers in international trade and promote the development of international trade,

Have agreed as follows:

PART I – SPHERE OF APPLICATION AND GENERAL PROVISIONS

CHAPTER I – SPHERE OF APPLICATION

Article 1

1   This Convention applies to contracts of sale of goods between parties whose places of business are in different States:

(a) when the States are Contracting States; or

(b) when the rules of private international law lead to the application of the law of a Contracting State.

2   The fact that the parties have their places of business in different States is to he disregarded whenever this fact does not appear either from the contract or from any dealings between, or from information disclosed by the parties at any time before or at the conclusion of the contract.

3   Neither the nationality of the parties nor the civil or commercial character of the parties or of the contract is to be taken into consideration in determining the application of this Convention.

Article 2

This Convention does not apply to sales:

(a) of goods bought for personal, family or household use, unless the seller, at any time before or at the conclusion of the contract, neither knew nor ought to have known that the goods were bought for any such use;

(b) by auction;

(c) on execution or otherwise by authority of law;

(d) of stocks, shares, investment securities, negotiable instruments or money;

(e) of ships, vessels, hovercraft or aircraft;

(f) of electricity.

Article 3

1   Contracts for the supply of goods to be manufactured or produced are to be considered sales unless the party who orders the goods undertakes to supply a substantial part of the materials necessary for such manufacture or production.

2   This Convention does not apply to contracts in which the preponderant part of the obligations of the party who furnishes the goods consists in the supply of labour or other services.

Article 4

This Convention governs only the formation of the contract of sale and the rights and obligations of the seller and the buyer arising from such a contract. In particular, except as otherwise expressly provided in this Convention, it is not concerned with:

(a) the validity of the contract or of any of its provisions or of any usage;

(b) the effect which the contract may have on the property in the goods sold.

Article 5

This Convention does not apply to the liability of the seller for death or personal injury caused by the goods to any person.

Article 6

The parties may exclude the application of this Convention or, subject to Article 12, derogate from or vary the effect of any of its provisions.

CHAPTER II – GENERAL PROVISIONS

Article 7

1   In the interpretation of this Convention, regard is to be had to its international character and to the need to promote uniformity in its application and the observance of good faith in international trade.

2   Questions concerning matters governed by this Convention which are not expressly settled in it are to be settled in conformity with the general principles on which it is based or, in the absence of such principles, in conformity with the law applicable by virtue of the rules of private international law.

Article 8

1   For the purposes of this Convention, statements made by and other conduct of a party are to be interpreted according to his intent where the other party knew or could not have been unaware what that intent was.

2   If the preceding paragraph is not applicable, statements made by and other conduct of a party are to be interpreted according to the understanding that a reasonable person of the same kind as the other party would have had in the same circumstances.

3   In determining the intent of a party or the understanding a reasonable person would have had, due consideration is to he given to all relevant circumstances of the case including the negotiations, any practices which the parties have established between themselves, usage's and any subsequent conduct of the parties.

Article 9

1   The parties are bound by any usage to which they have agreed and by any practices which they have established between themselves.

2   The parties are considered, unless otherwise agreed, to have impliedly made applicable to their contract or its formation a usage of which the parties knew or ought to have known and which in international trade is widely known to, and regularly observed by, parties to contracts of the type involved in the particular trade concerned.

Article 10

For the purpose of this Convention:

(a) if a party has more than one place of business, the place of business is that which has the closest relationship to the contract and its performance, having regard to the circumstances known to or contemplated by the parties at any time before or at the conclusion of the contract;

(b) if a party does not have a place of business, reference is to be made to his habitual residence.

Article 11

A contract of sale need not be concluded in or evidenced by writing and is not subject to any other requirement as to form. It may be proved by any means, including witnesses.

Article 12

Any provision of Article 11, Article 29 or Part II of this Convention that allows a contract of sale or its modification or termination by agreement or any offer, acceptance or other indication of intention to be made in any form other than in writing does not apply where any party has his place of business in a Contracting State which has made a declaration under Article 96 of this Convention. The parties may not derogate from or vary the effect of this article.

Article 13

For the purposes of this Convention, 'writing' includes telegram and telex.

PART II – FORMATION OF THE CONTRACT

Article 14

1   A proposal for concluding a contract addressed to one or more specific persons constitutes an offer if it is sufficiently definite and indicates the intention of the offeror to be bound in case of acceptance. A proposal is sufficiently definite if it indicates the goods and expressly or implicitly fixes or makes provision for determining the quantity and the price.

2   A proposal other than one addressed to one or more specific persons is to be considered merely as an invitation to make offers, unless the contrary is clearly indicated by the person malting the proposal.

Article 15

1   An offer becomes effective when it reaches the offeree.

2   An offer, even if it is irrevocable, may be withdrawn if the withdrawal reaches the offeree before or at the same time as the offer.

Article 16

1   Until a contract is concluded, an offer may be revoked if the revocation reaches the offeree before he has dispatched an acceptance.

2   However, an offer cannot be revoked:

    (a)   if it indicates, whether by stating a fixed time for acceptance or otherwise, that it is irrevocable; or

    (b)   if it was reasonable for the offeree to rely on the offer as being irrevocable and the offeree has acted in reliance on the offer.

Article 17

An offer, even if it is irrevocable, is terminated when a rejection reaches the offeror.

Article 18

1   A statement made by or other conduct of the offeree indicating assent to an offer is an acceptance. Silence or inactivity does not in itself amount to acceptance.

2   An acceptance of an offer becomes effective at the moment the indication of assent reaches the offeror. An acceptance is not effective if the indication of assent does not reach the offeror within the time he has fixed or if no time is fixed within a reasonable time, due account being taken of the circumstances of the transaction, including the rapidity of the means of communication employed by the offeror. An oral offer must be accepted immediately unless the circumstances indicate otherwise.

3   However, if, by virtue of the offer or as a result of practices which the parties have established between themselves or of usage, the offeree may indicate assent by performing an act, such as one relating to the dispatch of the goods or payment of the price, without notice to the offeror, the acceptance is effective at the moment the act is performed, provided that the act is performed within the period of time laid down in the preceding paragraph.

Article 19

1   A reply to an offer which purports to be an acceptance but contains additions, limitations or other modifications is a rejection of the offer and constitutes a counter-offer.

2   However, a reply to an offer which purports to be an acceptance but contains additional or different terms which do not materially alter the terms of the offer constitutes an acceptance, unless the offeror, without undue delay, objects orally to the discrepancy or dispatches a notice to that effect. If he does not so object, the terms of the contract are the terms of the offer with the modifications contained in the acceptance.

3   Additional or different terms relating, among other things, to the price, payment, quality and quantity of the goods, place and time of delivery, extent of one party's liability to the other or the settlement of disputes are considered to alter the terms of the offer materially.

Article 20

1   A period of time for acceptance fixed by the offeror in a telegram or a letter begins to run from the moment the telegram is handed in for dispatch or from the date shown on the letter or, if no such date is shown, from the date shown on the envelope. A period of time for acceptance fixed by the offeror by telephone, telex or other means of instantaneous communication, begins to run from the moment that the offer reaches the offeree.

2   Official holidays or non-business days occurring during the period for acceptance are included in calculating the period. However, if a notice of acceptance cannot be delivered at the address of the offeror on the last day of the period because that day falls on an official holiday or a non-business day at the place of business of the offeror, the period is extended until the first business day which follows.

Article 21

1   A late acceptance is nevertheless effective as an acceptance if without delay the offeror orally so informs the offeree or dispatches a notice to that effect.

2   If a letter or other writing containing a late acceptance shows that it has been sent in such circumstances that if its transmission had been normal it would have reached the offeror in due time, the late acceptance is effective as an acceptance unless, without delay, the offeror orally informs the offeree that he considers his offer as having lapsed or dispatches a notice to that effect.

Article 22

An acceptance may be withdrawn if the withdrawal reaches the offeror before or at the same time as time acceptance would have become effective.

Article 23

A contract is concluded at the moment when an acceptance of an offer becomes effective in accordance with the provisions of this Convention.

Article 24

For the purposes of this part of the Convention, an offer, declaration of acceptance or any other indication of intention 'reaches' the addressee when it is made orally to him or delivered by any other means to him personally, to his price of business or mailing address or, if he does not have a place of business or mailing address, to his habitual residence.

PART III – SALE OF GOODS

CHAPTER I – GENERAL PROVISIONS

Article 25

A breach of contract committed by one of the parties is fundamental if it results in such detriment to the other party as substantially to deprive him of what he is entitled to expect under the contract, unless the party in breach did not foresee and a reasonable person of the same kind in the same circumstances would not have foreseen such a result.

Article 26

A declaration of avoidance of the contract is effective only if made by notice to the other party.

Article 27

Unless otherwise expressly provided in this part of the Convention, if any notice, request or other communication is given or made by a party in accordance with this part and by means appropriate in the circumstances, a delay or error in the transmission of the communication or its failure to arrive does not deprive that party of the right to rely on the communication.

Article 28

If, in accordance with the provisions of this Convention, one party is entitled to require performance of ally obligation by the other party, a court is not bound to enter a judgment for specific performance unless the court would do so under its own law in respect of similar contracts of sale not governed by this Convention.

Article 29

1   A contract may be modified or terminated by the mere agreement of the parties.

2   A contract in writing which contains a provision requiring any modification or termination by agreement to be in writing may not be otherwise modified or terminated by agreement. However, a party may be precluded by his conduct from asserting such a provision to the extent that the other party has relied on that conduct.

CHAPTER II – OBLIGATIONS OF THE SELLER

Article 30

The seller must deliver the goods, hand over any documents relating to them and transfer the property in the goods, as required by the contract and this Convention.

Section I – Delivery of the goods and handing over of documents

Article 31

If the seller is not bound to deliver the goods at any other particular place, his obligation to deliver consists:

(a) if the contract of sale involves carriage of the goods – in handing the goods over to the first carrier for transmission to the buyer;

(b) if, in cases not within the preceding sub-paragraph, the contract relates to specific goods, or unidentified goods to be drawn from a specific stock; or to he manufactured or produced, and at the time of the conclusion of the contract the parties knew that the goods were at, or were to be manufactured or produced at, a particular place – in placing the goods at the buyer's disposal at that place;

(c) in other cases – in placing the goods at the buyer's disposal at the place where the seller had his place of business at the time of the conclusion of the contract.

Article 32

1   If the seller, in accordance with the contract or this Convention, hands the goods over to a carrier and if the goods are not clearly identified to the contract by markings on the goods, by shipping documents or otherwise, the seller must give the buyer notice of the consignment specifying the goods.

2   If the seller is bound to arrange for carriage of the goods, he must make such contracts as are necessary for carriage to the place fixed by means of transportation appropriate in the circumstances and according to the usual terms for such transportation.

3   If the seller is not bound to effect insurance in respect of the carriage of the goods, he must, at the buyer's request, provide him with all available information necessary to enable him to effect such insurance.

Article 33

The seller must deliver the goods:

(a) if a date is fixed by or determinable from the contract, on that date;

(b) if a period of time is fixed by or determinable from the contract, at any time within that period unless circumstances indicate that the buyer is to choose a date; or

(c) in any other case, within a reasonable time after the conclusion of the contract.

Article 34

If the seller is bound to hand over documents relating to the goods, he must hand them over at the time and place and in the form required by the contract. If the seller has handed over documents before that time, he may, up to that time, cure any lack of conformity in the documents, if the exercise of this right does not cause the buyer unreasonable inconvenience or unreasonable expense. However, the buyer retains any right to claim damages as provided for in this Convention.

Section II – Conformity of the goods and third party claims

Article 35

1   The seller must deliver goods which are of the quantity, quality and description required by the contract and which are contained or packaged in the manner required by the contract.

2   Except where the parties have agreed otherwise, the goods do not conform with the contract unless they:

(a)   are fit for the purposes for which goods of the same description would ordinarily he used;

(b)   are fit for any particular purpose expressly or impliedly made known to the seller at the time of the conclusion of the contract, except where the circumstances show that the buyer did not rely, or that it was unreasonable for him to rely, on the seller's skill and judgment;

(c)   possess the qualities of goods which the seller has held out to the buyer as a sample or model;

(d)   are contained or packaged in the manner usual for such goods or, where there is no such manner, in a manner adequate to preserve and protect the goods.

3   The seller is not liable under sub-paras (a) to (d) of the preceding paragraph for any lack of conformity of the goods if at the time of the conclusion of the contract the buyer knew or could not have been unaware of such lack of conformity.

Article 36

1   The seller is liable in accordance with the contract and this Convention for any lack of conformity which exists at the time when the risk passes to the buyer, even though the lack of conformity becomes apparent only after that time.

2   The seller is also liable for any lack of conformity which occurs after the time indicated in the preceding paragraph and which is due to a breach of any of his obligations, including a breach of any guarantee that for a period of time the goods will remain fit for their ordinary purpose or for some particular purpose or will retain specified qualities or characteristics.

Article 37

If the seller has delivered goods before the date for delivery, he may, up to that date, deliver any missing part or make up any deficiency in the quantity of the goods delivered, or deliver goods in replacement of any non-conforming goods delivered or remedy any lack of conformity in the goods delivered, provided that the exercise of this right does not cause the buyer unreasonable inconvenience or unreasonable expense. However, the buyer retains any right to claim damages as provided for in this Convention.

Article 38

1   The buyer must examine the goods, or cause them to he examined, within as short a period as is practicable in the circumstances.

2   If the contract involves carriage of the goods, examination may be deferred until after the goods have arrived at their destination.

3   If the goods are redirected in transit or redispatched by the buyer without a reasonable opportunity for examination by him and at the time of the conclusion of the contract the seller knew or ought to have known of the possibility, of such redirection or redispatch, examination may be deferred until after the goods have arrived at the new destination.

Article 39

1   The buyer loses the right to rely on a lack of conformity of the goods if he does not give notice to the seller specifying the nature of the lack of conformity within a reasonable time after he has discovered it or ought to have discovered it.

2   In any event, the buyer loses the right to rely on a lack of conformity of the goods if he does not give the seller notice thereof at the latest within a period of two years from the date on which the goods were actually handed over to the buyer, unless this time-limit is inconsistent with a contractual period of guarantee.

Article 40

The seller is not entitled to rely on the provisions of Articles 38 and 39 if the lack of conformity relates to facts of which he knew or could not have been unaware and which he did not disclose to the buyer.

Article 41

The seller must deliver goods which are free from any right or claim of a third party, unless the buyer agreed to take the goods subject to that right or claim. However, if such right or claim is based on industrial property or other intellectual property, the seller's obligation is governed by Article 42.

Article 42

1   The seller must deliver goods which are free from any right or claim of a third party based on industrial property or other intellectual property, of which at the time of the conclusion of the contract the seller knew or could not have been unaware, provided that the right or claim is based on industrial property or other intellectual property:

   (a) under the law of the State where the goods will be resold or otherwise used, if it was contemplated by the parties at the time of the conclusion of the contract that the goods would be resold or otherwise used in that State; or

   (b) in any other case, under the law of the State where the buyer has his place of business.

2   The obligation of the seller under the preceding paragraph does not extend to cases where:

   (a) at the time of the conclusion of the contract the buyer knew or could not have been unaware of the right or claim; or

   (b) the right or claim results from the seller's compliance with technical drawings, designs, formulae or other such specifications furnished by the buyer.

Article 43

1   The buyer loses the right to rely on the provisions of Article 41 or Article 42 if he does not give notice to the seller specifying the nature of the right or claim of the third party within a reasonable time after he has become aware or ought to have become aware of the right or claim.

2   The seller is not entitled to rely on the provisions of the preceding paragraph if he knew of the right or claim of the third party and the nature of it.

Article 44

Notwithstanding the provisions of para (1) of Article 39 and para (1) of Article 43, the buyer may reduce the price in accordance with Article 50 or claim damages, except for loss of profit, if he has a reasonable excuse for his failure to give the required notice.

Section III – Remedies for breach of contract by the seller

Article 45

1   If the seller fails to perform any of his obligations under the contract or this Convention, the buyer may:

    (a)   exercise the rights provided in Articles 46–52;

    (b)   claim damages as provided in Articles 74–77.

2   The buyer is not deprived of any right he may have to claim damages by exercising his right to other remedies.

3   No period of grace may he granted to the seller by a court of arbitral tribunal when the buyer resorts to a remedy for breach of contract.

Article 46

1   The buyer may require performance by the seller of his obligations unless the buyer has resorted to a remedy which is inconsistent with this requirement.

2   If the goods do not conform with the contract, the buyer may require delivery of substitute goods only if the lack of conformity constitutes a fundamental breach of contract and a request for substitute goods is made either in conjunction with notice given under Article 39 or within a reasonable time thereafter.

3   If the goods do not conform with the contract, the buyer may require the seller to remedy the lack of conformity by repair, unless this is unreasonable having regard to all the circumstances. A request for repair must be made either in conjunction with notice given under Article 39 or within a reasonable time thereafter.

Article 47

1   The buyer may fix an additional period of time of reasonable length for performance by the seller of his obligations.

2   Unless the buyer has received notice from the seller that he will not perform within the period so fixed, the buyer may not, during that period, resort to any remedy for breach of contracts. However, the buyer is not deprived thereby of any right he may have to claim damages for delay in performance.

Article 48

1   Subject to Article 49, the seller may, even after the date for delivery, remedy at his own expense any failure to perform his obligations, if he can do so without unreasonable delay and without causing the buyer unreasonable inconvenience or uncertainty of reimbursement by the seller of expenses advanced by the buyer. However, the buyer retains any right to claim damages as provided for in this Convention.

2   If the seller requests the buyer to make known whether he will accept performance and the buyer does not comply with the request within a reasonable time, the seller may perform within the time indicated in his request. The buyer may not, during that period of time, resort to any remedy which is inconsistent with performance by the seller.

3   A notice by the seller that he will perform within a specified period of time is assumed to include a request, under the preceding paragraph, that the buyer make known his decision.

4   A request or notice by the seller under para (2) or (3) of this article is not effective unless received by the buyer.

Article 49

1   The buyer may declare the contract avoided:

   (a) if the failure by the seller to perform any of his obligations under the contract or this Convention amounts to a fundamental breach of contract; or

   (b) in case of non-delivery, if the seller does not deliver the goods within the additional period of time fixed by the buyer in accordance with para (1) of Article 47 or declares that he will not deliver within the period so fixed.

2   However, in cases where the seller has delivered the goods, the buyer loses the right to declare the contract avoided unless he does so:

   (a) in respect of late delivery, within a reasonable time after he has become aware that delivery has been made;

   (b) in respect of any breach other than late delivery, within a reasonable time:

      (i)   after he knew or ought to have known of the breach;

      (ii) after the expiration of any additional period of time fixed by the buyer in accordance with para (1) of Article 47, or after the seller has declared that he will not perform his obligations within such an additional period; or

      (iii) after the expiration of any additional period of time indicated by the seller in accordance with para (2) of Article 48, or after the buyer has declared that he will not accept performance.

Article 50

If the goods do not conform with the contract and whether or not the price has already been paid, the buyer may reduce the price in the same proportion as the value that the goods actually delivered had at the time of the delivery bears to the value that conforming goods would have had at that time. However, if the seller remedies any failure to perform his obligation in accordance with Article 37 or Article 48 or if the buyer refuses to accept performance by the seller in accordance with those articles, the buyer may not reduce the price.

Article 51

1   If the seller delivers only a part of the goods or if only a part of the goods delivered is in conformity with the contract, Articles 46–50 apply in respect of the part which is missing or which does not conform.

2   The buyer may declare the contract avoided in its entirety only if the failure to make delivery completely or in conformity with the contract amounts to a fundamental breach of the contract.

Article 52

1   If the seller delivers the goods before the date fixed, the buyer may take delivery or refuse to take delivery.

2   If the seller delivers a quantity of goods greater than that provided for in the contract, the buyer may take delivery or refuse to take delivery of the excess quantity. If the buyer takes delivery of all or part of the excess quantity, he must pay for it at the contract rate.

CHAPTER III – OBLIGATIONS OF THE BUYER

Article 53

The buyer must pay the price for the goods and take delivery of them as required by the contract and this Convention.

Section I – Payment of the price

Article 54

The buyer's obligation to pay the price includes taking such steps and complying with such formalities as may be required under the contract or any laws and regulations to enable payment to be made.

Article 55

Where a contract has been validly concluded but does not expressly or implicitly fix or make provision for determining the price, the parties are considered, in the absence of any indication to the contrary, to have impliedly made reference to the price generally charged at the time of the conclusion of the contract for such goods sold under comparable circumstances in the trade concerned.

Article 56

If the price is fixed according to the weight of the goods, in case of doubt it is to be determined by the net weight.

Article 57

1   It the buyer is not bound to pay the price at any other particular place, he must pay it to the seller:

   (a)   at the seller's place of business; or

   (b)   if the payment is to be made against the handing over of the goods or of documents, at the place where the handing over takes place.

2   The seller must bear any increase in the expenses incidental to payment which is caused by a change in his place of business subsequent to the conclusion of the contract.

Article 58

1   If the buyer is not bound to pay the price at any other specific time, he must pay it when the seller places either the goods' or documents controlling their disposition at the buyer's disposal in accordance with the contract and this Convention. The seller may make such payment a condition for handing over the goods or documents.

2   If the contract involves carriage of the goods, the seller may dispatch the goods on terms whereby the goods, or documents controlling their disposition, will not be handed over to the buyer except against payment of the price.

3   The buyer is not bound to pay the price until he has had an opportunity to examine the goods, unless the procedures for delivery or payment agree upon by the parties are inconsistent with his having such an opportunity.

Article 59

The buyer must pay the price on the date fixed by or determinable from the contract and this Convention without the need for any request or compliance with any formality on the part of the seller.

Section II – Taking Delivery

Article 60

The buyer's obligation to take delivery consists:

(a) in doing all the acts which could reasonably be expected of him in order to enable the seller to make delivery; and

(b) in taking over the goods.

Section III – Remedies for breach of contract by the buyer

Article 61

1　If the buyer fails to perform any of his obligations under the contract or this Convention, the seller may:

(a) exercise the rights provided in Articles 62–65;

(b) claim damages as provided in Articles 74–77.

2　The seller is not deprived of any right he may have to claim damage by exercising his right to other remedies.

3　No period of grace may he granted to the buyer by a court or arbitral tribunal when the seller resorts to a remedy for breach of contract.

Article 62

The seller may require the buyer to pay the price, take delivery or perform his other obligations, unless the seller has resorted to a remedy which is inconsistent with this requirement.

Article 63

1　The seller may fix an additional period of time of reasonable length for performance by the buyer of his obligations.

2　Unless the seller has received notice from the buyer that he will not perform within the period so fixed, the seller may not, during that period, resort to any remedy for breach of contract. However, the seller is not deprived thereby of any right he may have to claim damages for delay in performance.

Article 64

1　The seller may declare the contract avoided:

(a) if the failure by the buyer to perform any of his obligations under the contract or this Convention amounts to a fundamental breach of contract; or

(b) if the buyer does not, within the additional period of time fixed by the seller in accordance with para (1) of Article 63, perform his obligation to pay the price or take delivery of the goods, or if he declares that he will not do so within the period so fixed.

2　However, in cases where the buyer has paid the price, the seller loses the right to declare the contract avoided unless he does so:

(a) in respect of late performance by the buyer, before the seller has become aware that performance has been rendered; or

(b) in respect of any breach other than late performance by the buyer, within a reasonable time:

(i) after the seller knew or ought to have known of the breach; or

(ii) after the expiration of any additional period of time fixed by the seller in accordance with para (1) of Article 63, or after the buyer has declared that he will not perform his obligations within such an additional period.

Article 65

1   If, under the contract, the buyer is to specify the form, measurement or other features of the goods and he fails to make such specification either on the date agreed upon or within a reasonable time after receipt of a request from the seller, the seller may, without prejudice to any other rights he may have, make the specification himself in accordance with the requirements of the buyer that may be known to him.

2   If the seller makes the specification himself, he must inform the buyer of the details thereof and must fix a reasonable time within which the buyer may make a different specification. If, after receipt of such a communication, the buyer fails to do so within the time so fixed, the specification made by the seller is binding.

CHAPTER IV – PASSING OF RISK

Article 66

Loss of or damage to the goods after the risk has passed to the buyer does not discharge him from his obligation to pay the price unless the loss or damage is due to an act or omission of the seller.

Article 67

1   If the contract of sale involves carriage of the goods and the seller is not bound to hand them over at a particular place, the risk passes to the buyer when the goods are handed over to the first carrier for transmission to the buyer in accordance with the contract of sale. If the seller is bound to hand the goods over to a carrier at a particular place, the risk does not pass to the buyer until the goods are handed over to the carrier at that place. The fact that the seller is authorised to retain documents controlling the disposition of the goods does not affect the passage of the risk.

2   Nevertheless, the risk does not pass to the buyer until the goods are clearly identified to the contract, whether by markings on the goods, by shipping documents, by notice given to the buyer or otherwise.

Article 68

The risk in respect of goods sold in transit passes to the buyer from the time of the conclusion of the contract. However, if the circumstances so indicate, the risk is assumed by the buyer from the time the goods were handed over to the carrier who issued the documents embodying the contract of carriage. Nevertheless, if at the time of the conclusion of the contract of sale the seller knew or ought to have known that the goods had been lost or damaged and did not disclose this to the buyer, the loss or damage is at the risk of the seller.

Article 69

1   In cases not within Articles 67 and 68, the risk passes to the buyer when he takes over the goods or, if he does not do so in due time, from the time when the goods are placed at his disposal and he commits a breach of contract by failing to take delivery.

2   However, if the buyer is bound to take over the goods at a place other than a place of business of the seller, the risk passes when delivery is due and the buyer is aware of the fact that the goods are placed at his disposal at that place.

3   If the contract relates to goods not then identified, the goods are considered not to be placed at the disposal of the buyer until they are clearly identified to the contract.

Article 70

If the seller had committed a fundamental breach of contract, Articles 67, 68 and 69 do not impair the remedies available to the buyer on account of the breach.

CHAPTER V – PROVISIONS COMMON TO THE OBLIGATIONS OF THE SELLER AND OF THE BUYER

Section I – Anticipatory breach and instalment contracts

Article 71

1   A party may suspend the performance of his obligations if, after the conclusion of the contract, it becomes apparent that the other party will not perform a substantial part of his obligations as a result of:

(a) a serious deficiency in his ability to perform or in his credit-worthiness; or

(b) his conduct in preparing to perform or in performing the contract.

2   If the seller has already dispatched the goods before the grounds described in the preceding paragraph become evident, he may prevent the handing over of the goods to the buyer even though the buyer holds a document which entitles him to obtain them. The present paragraph relates only to the rights in the goods as between the buyer and the seller.

3   A party suspending performance, whether before or after dispatch of the goods, must immediately give notice of the suspension to the other party and must continue with performance if the other party provides adequate assurance of his performance.

Article 72

1   If prior to the date for performance of the contract it is clear that one of the parties will commit a fundamental breach of contract, the other party may declare the contract avoided.

2   If time allows, the party intending to declare the contract avoided must give reasonable notice to the other party in order to permit him to provide adequate assurance of his performance.

3   The requirements of the preceding paragraph do not apply if the other party has declared that he will not perform his obligations.

Article 73

1   In the case of a contract for delivery of goods by instalments, if the failure of one party to perform any of his obligations in respect of any instalment constitutes a fundamental breach of contract with respect to that instalment, the other party may declare the contract avoided with respect to that instalment.

2   If one party's failure to perform any of his obligations in respect of any instalment gives the other party good grounds to conclude that a fundamental breach of contract will occur with respect to future instalments, he may declare the contract avoided for the future, provided that he does so within a reasonable time.

3   A buyer who declares the contract avoided in respect of any delivery may, at the same time, declare it avoided in respect of deliveries already made or of future deliveries if, by reason of their interdependence, those deliveries could not be used for the purpose contemplated by the parties at the time of the conclusion of the contract.

Section II – Damages

Article 74

Damages for breach of contract by one party consist of a sum equal to the loss, including loss of profit, suffered by the other party as a consequence of the breach. Such damages may not exceed the loss which the party in breach foresaw or ought to have foreseen at the time of the conclusion of the contract, in the light of the facts and matters of which he then knew or ought to have known, as a possible consequence of the breach of contract.

Article 75

If the contract is avoided and if, in a reasonable manner and within a reasonable time after avoidance, the buyer has bought goods in replacement or the seller has resold the goods, the party claiming damages may recover the difference between the contract price and the price in the substitute transaction as well as any further damages recoverable under Article 74.

Article 76

1   If the contract is avoided and there is a current price for the goods, the party claiming damages may, if he has not made a purchase or resale under Article 75, recover the differences between the price fixed by the contract and the current price at the time of avoidance as well as any further damages recoverable under Article 74. If, however, the party claiming damages has avoided the contract after taking over the goods, the current price at the time of such taking over shall be applied instead of the current price at the time of avoidance.

2   For the purpose of the preceding paragraph, the current price is the price prevailing at the place where delivery of the goods should have been made or, if there is no current price at that place, the price at such other place as serves as a reasonable substitute, making due allowance for differences in the cost of transporting the goods.

Article 77

A party who relies on a breach of contract must take such measures as are reasonable in the circumstances to mitigate the loss, including loss of profit resulting from the breach. If he fails to take such measures, the party in breach may claim a reduction in the damages in the amount by which the loss should have been mitigated.

Section III – Interest

Article 78

If a party fails to pay the price or any other sum that is in arrears, the other party is entitled to interest on it, without prejudice to any claim for damages recoverable under Article 74.

Section IV – Exemptions

Article 79

1   A party is not liable for a failure to perform any of his obligations it he proves that the failure was due to an impediment beyond his control and that he could not reasonably be expected to have taken the impediment into account at the time of the conclusion of the contract or to have avoided or overcome it or its consequences.

2   If the party's failure is due to the failure by a third person whom he has engaged to perform the whole or part of the contract, that party is exempt from liability only if:

(a) he is exempt under the preceding paragraph; and

(b) the person whom he has so engaged would be so exempt it the provisions of that paragraph were applied to him.

3   The exemption provided by this article has effect for the period during which the impediment exists.

4   The party who fails to perform must give notice to the other party of the impediment and its effects on his ability to perform. If the notice is not received by the other party within a reasonable time after the party who fails to perform knew or ought to have known of the impediment, he is liable for damages resulting from such non-receipt.

5   Nothing in this article prevents either party from exercising any right other than to claim damages under this Convention.

Article 80

A party may not rely on a failure of the other party in perform, to the extent that such failure was caused by the first party's act or omission.

Section V – Effects of avoidance

Article 81

1   Avoidance of the contract releases both parties from their obligations under it, subject to any damages which may be due. Avoidance does not affect any provision of the contract for the settlement of disputes or any other provision of the contract governing the rights and obligations of the parties consequent upon the avoidance of the contract.

2   A party who has performed the contract either wholly or in part may claim restitution from the other party of whatever the first party has supplied or paid under the contracts. If both parties are bound to make restitution, they must do so concurrently.

Article 82

1   The buyer loses the right to declare the contract avoided or to require the seller to deliver substitute goods if it is impossible for him to make restitution of the goods substantially in the condition in which he received them.

2   The preceding paragraph does not apply:

(a) if the impossibility of making restitution of the goods or of making restitution of the goods substantially in the condition in which the buyer received them is not due to his act or omission;

(b) if the goods or part of the goods have perished or deteriorated as a result of the examination provided for in Article 38; or

(c) if the goods or part of the goods have been sold in the normal course of business or have been consumed or transformed by the buyer in the course of normal use before he discovered or ought to have discovered the lack of conformity.

Article 83

A buyer who has lost the right to declare the contract avoided or to require the seller to deliver substitute goods in accordance with Article 82 retains all other remedies under the contract and this Convention.

Article 84

1   If the seller is bound to refund the price, he must also pay interest on it, from the date on which the price was paid.

2   The buyer must account to the seller for all benefits which he has derived from the goods or part of them:

(a)   if he must make restitution of the goods or part of them; or

(b)   if it is impossible for him to make restitution of all or part of the goods or to make restitution of all part of the goods substantially in the condition in which he received them, but he has nevertheless declared the contract avoided or required the seller to deliver substitute goods.

Section VI – Preservation of the goods

Article 85

If the buyer is in delay in taking delivery of the goods or, where payment of the price and delivery of the goods are to be made concurrently, if he fails to pay the price, and the seller is either in possession of the goods or otherwise able to control their disposition, the seller must take such steps as are reasonable in the circumstances to preserve them. He is entitled to retain them until he has been reimbursed his reasonable expenses by the buyer.

Article 86

1   If the buyer has received the goods and intends to exercise any right under the contract or this Convention to reject them, he must take such steps to preserve them as are reasonable in the circumstances. He is entitled to retain them until he has been reimbursed his reasonable expenses by the seller.

2   If goods dispatched to the buyer have been placed at his disposal at their destination and he exercises the right to reject them, he must take possession of them on behalf of the seller, provided that this can be done without payment of the price and without unreasonable inconvenience or unreasonable expense.

This provision does not apply if the seller or a person authorised to take charge of the goods on his behalf is present at the destination. If the buyer takes possession of the goods under this paragraph, his rights and obligations are governed by the preceding paragraph.

Article 87

A party who is bound to take steps to preserve the goods may deposit them in a warehouse of a third person at the expense of the other party provided that the expense incurred is not unreasonable.

Article 88

1   A party who is bound to preserve the goods in accordance with Article 85 or 86 may sell them by any appropriate means if there has been an unreasonable delay by the other party in taking possession of the goods or in taking them back or in paying the price or the cost of preservation, provided that reasonable notice of the intention to sell has been given to the other party.

2   If the goods are subject to rapid deterioration or their preservation would involve unreasonable expense, a party who is bound to preserve the goods in accordance with Article 85 or 86 must take reasonable measures to sell them, to the extent possible he must give notice to the other party of his intention to sell.

3   A party selling the goods has the right to retain out of the proceeds of sale an amount equal to the reasonable expenses of preserving the goods and of selling them. He must account to the other party for the balance.

PART IV – FINAL PROVISIONS

Article 89

The Secretary General of the United Nations is hereby designated as the depositary for this Convention.

Article 90

This Convention does not prevail over any international agreement which has already been or may be entered into and which contains provisions concerning the matters governed by this Convention, provided that the parties have their places of business in States parties to such agreement.

Article 91

1   This Convention is open for signature at the concluding meeting of the United Nations Conference on Contracts for the International Sale of Goods and will remain open for signature by all States at the headquarters of the United Nations, New York until 30 September 1981.

2   This Convention is subject to ratification, acceptance or approval by the signatory States.

3   This Convention is open for accession by all States which are not signatory States as from the date it is open for signature.

4   Instruments of ratification, acceptance, approval and accession are to he deposited with the Secretary General of the United Nations.

Article 92

1   A Contracting State may declare at the time of signature, ratification, acceptance, approval or accession that it will not be bound by Part II of this Convention or that it will not be bound by Part III of this Convention.

2   A Contracting State which makes it declaration in accordance with the preceding paragraph in respect of Part II or Part III of this Convention is not to be considered a Contracting State within para (1) of Article 1 of this Convention in respect of matters governed by the part to which the declaration applies.

Article 93

1   If a Contracting State has two or more territorial units in which, according to its constitution, different systems of law are applicable in relation to the matters dealt with in this Convention, it may, at the time of signature, ratification, acceptance, approval or accession, declare that this Convention is to extend to all its territorial units or only to one or more of them, and may amend its declaration by submitting another declaration at any time.

2   These declarations are to be notified to the depositary and are to state expressly the territorial units to which the Convention extends.

3   If, by virtue of a declaration under this article, this Convention extends to one or more but not all of the territorial units of a Contracting State, and if the place of business of a party is located in that State, this place of business, for the purposes of

this Convention, is considered not to be in a Contracting State, unless it is in a territorial unit to which the Convention extends.

4   If a Contracting State makes no declaration under para (1) of this article, the Convention is to extend to all territorial units of that State.

Article 94

1   Two or more Contracting States which have the same or closely related legal rules on matters governed by this Convention may at any time declare that the Convention is not to apply to contracts of sale or to their formation where the parties have their places of business in those States. Such declarations may be made jointly or by reciprocal unilateral declarations.

2   A Contracting State which has the same or closely related legal rules on matters governed by this Convention as one or more non-Contracting States may at any time declare that the Convention is not to apply to contracts of sale or to their formation where the parties have their places of business in those States.

3   If a State which is the object of a declaration under the preceding paragraph subsequently becomes a Contracting State, the declaration made will, as from the date on which the Convention enters into force in respect of the new Contracting State, have the effect of a declaration made under para (1), provided that the new Contracting State joins in such declaration or makes a reciprocal unilateral declaration.

Article 95

Any State may declare at the time of the deposit of its instrument of ratification, acceptance, approval or accession that it will not he bound by sub-para (1)(b) of Article 1 of this Convention.

Article 96

A Contracting State whose legislation requires contracts of sale to be concluded in or evidenced by writing may at any time make a declaration in accordance with Article 12 that any provision of Article 11, Article 29, or Part II of this Convention, that allows a contract of sale or its modification or termination by agreement or any offer, acceptance, or other indication of intention to be made in any form other than in writing, does not apply where any party has his place of business in that State.

Article 97

1   Declarations made under this Convention at the time of signature are subject to confirmation upon ratification, acceptance or approval.

2   Declarations and confirmations of declarations are to be in writing and be formally notified to the depositary.

3   A declaration takes effect simultaneously with the entry into force of this Convention in respect of the State concerned. However, a declaration of which the depositary receives formal notification after such entry into force takes effect on the first day of the month following the expiration of six months after the date of its receipt by the depositary. Reciprocal unilateral declarations under Article 94 take effect on the first day of the month following the expiration of six months after the receipt of the latest declaration by the depositary.

4   Any State which makes a declaration under this Convention may withdraw it at any time by a formal notification in writing addressed to the depositary. Such withdrawal

is to take effect on the first day of the month following the expiration of six months after the date of the receipt of the notification by the depositary.

5   A withdrawal of a declaration made under Article 94 renders inoperative, as from the date on which the withdrawal takes effect, any reciprocal declaration made by another State under that article.

Article 98

No reservations are permitted except those expressly authorised in this Convention.

Article 99

1   This Convention enters into force, subject to the provisions of para (a) of this article, on the first day of the month following the expiration of 12 months after the date of deposit of the tenth instrument of ratification, acceptance, approval or accession, including an instrument which contains a declaration made under Article 92.

2   When a State ratifies, accepts, approves or accedes to this Convention after the deposit of the 10th instrument of ratification, acceptance, approval or accession, this Convention, with the exception of the part excluded, enters into force in respect of that State, subject to the provisions of para (6) of this article, on the first day of the month following the expiration of 12 months after the date of the deposit of its instrument of ratification, acceptance, approval or accession.

3   A State which ratifies, accepts, approves or accedes to this Convention and is a party to either or both the Convention relating to a Uniform Law on the Formation of Contracts for the International Sale of Goods done at The Hague on 1 July 1964 (1964 Hague Formation Convention) and the Convention relating to a Uniform Law on the International Sale of Goods done at The Hague on 1 July 1964 (1964 Hague Sales Convention) shall at the same time denounce, as the case may be, either or both the 1964 Hague Sales Convention and the 1964 Hague Formation Convention by notifying the government of the Netherlands to that effect.

4   A State party to the 1964 Hague Sales Convention which ratifies, accepts, approves or accedes to the present Convention and declares or has declared under Article 93 that it will not be bound by Part II of this Convention shall at the time of ratification, acceptance, approval or accession denounce the 1964 Hague Sales Convention by notifying the government of the Netherlands to that effect.

5   A State party to the 1964 Hague Formation Convention which ratifies, accepts, approves or accedes to the present Convention and declares or has declared under Article 92 that it will not be bound by Part III of this Convention shall at the time of ratification, acceptance, approval or accession denounce the 1964 Hague Formation Convention by notifying the government of the Netherlands to that effect.

6   For the purpose of this article, ratifications, acceptances, approvals and accessions in respect of this Convention by States parties to the 1964 Hague Formation Convention or to the 1964 Hague Sales Convention shall not be effective until such denunciations as may be required on the part of those States in respect of the latter two conventions have themselves become effective. The depositary of this Convention shall consult with the government of the Netherlands, as the depositary of the 1964 conventions, so as to ensure necessary co-ordination in this respect.

Article 100

1   This Convention applies to the formation of a contract only when the proposal for concluding the contract is made on or after the date when the Convention enters into force in respect of the Contracting States referred to in sub-para (1)(a) or the Contracting State referred to in sub-para (1)(b) of Article 1.

2   This Convention applies only to contracts concluded on or after the date when the Convention enters into force in respect of the Contracting States referred to in sub-para (1)(a) or the Contracting State referred to in sub-para (1)(b) of Article 1.

Article 101

1   A Contracting State may denounce this Convention, or Part II or Part III of the Convention, by a formal notification in writing addressed to the depositary.

2   The denunciation takes effect on the first day of the month following the expiration of 12 months after the notification is received by the depositary. Where a longer period for the denunciation to take effect is specified in the notification, the denunciation takes effect upon the expiration of such longer period after the notification is received by the depositary.

Done at Vienna, this day of eleventh day of April, one thousand nine hundred and eighty, in a single original, of which the Arabic, Chinese, English, French, Russian and Spanish texts are equally authentic.

In witness whereof the undersigned plenipotentiaries, being duly authorised by their respective governments, have signed this Convention.

CONVENTION ON THE LAW APPLICABLE TO CONTRACTS FOR THE INTERNATIONAL SALE OF GOODS, THE HAGUE – 22 DECEMBER 1986

The Convention has not yet entered into force.

The Convention was intended to replace the Hague Convention on the law applicable to international sales of goods, concluded on 15 June 1955. The genesis of the effort to revise the 1955 Convention is due to the completion of the Vienna Convention drafted under the auspices of the UNCITRAL. Accordingly, pursuant to a decision made by the 14th session of the Hague Conference on Private International Law in 1980, all UNCITRAL Member States, not Members of the Hague Conference, were invited to participate in the preparatory work of the present Convention.

See, Pelichet, M, *Report on the Law Applicable to International Sales of Goods*, The Hague Conference on Private International Law, preliminary document no 1, September 1982; See also *Law Applicable to Contracts for the International Sale of Goods*, draft Convention adopted by the special commission and report, written by von Mehren, AT, preliminary document no 4, August 1984 for the attention of the diplomatic conference of October 1985.

Convention on the Law Applicable to Contracts for the International Sale of Goods

The States Parties to the Present Conventions,

Desiring to unify the choice of law rules relating to contracts for the international sale of goods,

Bearing in mind the United Nations Convention on Contracts for the International Sale of Goods, concluded at Vienna on 11 April 1980,

Have agreed upon the following provisions:

CHAPTER 1 – SCOPE OF THE CONVENTION

Article 1

This Convention determines the law applicable to contracts of sale of goods:

(a) between parties having their places of business in different States;

(b) in all other cases involving a choice between the laws of different States, unless such a choice arises solely from a stipulation by the parties as to the applicable law, even if accompanied by a choice of court or arbitration.

Article 2

The Convention does not apply to:

(a) sales by way of execution or otherwise by authority of law;

(b) sales of stocks, shares, investment securities, negotiable instruments or money; it does, however, apply to the sale of goods based on documents;

(c) sales of goods bought for personal, family or household use; it does, however, apply if the seller at the time of the conclusion of the contract neither knew nor ought to leave known that the goods were bought for any such use.

Article 3

For the purposes of the Convention, 'goods' includes:

(a) ships, vessels, boats, hovercraft and aircraft;

(b) electricity.

Article 4

1 Contracts for the supply of goods to be manufacturers or produced are to be considered contracts of sale unless the party who orders the goods undertakes to supply a substantial part of the materials necessary for such manufacture or production.

2 Contracts in which the preponderant part of the obligations of the party who furnishes goods consists of the supply of labour or other services are not to be considered contracts of sale.

Article 5

The Convention does not determine the law applicable to:

(a) the capacity of the parties or the consequences of nullity or invalidity of the contract resulting from the incapacity of a party;

(b) the question whether an agent is able to bind a principal, or an organ to bind a company or body corporate or unincorporate;

(c) the transfer of ownership; nevertheless, the issues specifically mentioned in Article 12 are governed by the law applicable to the contract under the Convention;

(d) the effect of the sale in respect of any person other than the parties;

(e) agreements on arbitration or on clerics of court, even if such an agreement is embodied in the contract of sale.

Article 6

The law determined under the Convention applies whether or not it is the law of a Contracting State.

CHAPTER 2 – APPLICABLE LAW

Section 1 – Determination of the applicable law

Article 7

1   A contract of sale is governed by the law chosen by the parties. The parties' agreement on this choice must express or be clearly demonstrated by the terms of the contract and the conduct of the parties, viewed in their entirety. Such a choice may be limited to a part of the contract.

2   The parties may at any time agree to subject the contract in whole or in part to a law other that which previously governed it, whether or not the law previously governing the contract was chosen by the parties. Any change by the parties of the applicable law made after the conclusion of the contract does not prejudice its formal validity or the rights of the third parties.

Article 8

1   To the extent that the law applicable to a contract of sale has not been chosen by the parties in accordance with Article 7, the contract is governed by the law of the State where the seller has his place of business at the time of conclusion of the contract.

2   However, the contract is governed by the law of the State where the buyer has his place of business at the time of conclusion of the contract, if:

(a) negotiations were conducted, and the contract concluded by and in the presence of the parties, in that State; or

(b) the contract provides expressly that the seller must perform his obligation to deliver the goods in that State; or

(c) the contract was concluded on terms determined mainly by the buyer and in response to an invitation directed by the buyer to persons invited to bid (a call for tenders).

3   By way of exception, where, in the light of the circumstances as a whole, for instance, any business relations between the parties, the contract is manifestly more closely connected with a law which is not the law which would otherwise be applicable to the contract under paras 1 or 2 of this article, the contract is governed by that other law.

4   Paragraph 3 does not apply if, at the time of the conclusion of the contract, the seller and the buyer have their places of business in States having made due reservation under Article 21, para 1, sub-para (b).

5   Paragraph 3 does not apply in respect of issues regulated in the United Nations Conventions on contracts for the International Sale of Goods (Vienna, 11 April 1980) where, at the time of the conclusion of the contract, the seller and the buyer

have their places of business in different States both of which are parties to that Convention.

Article 9

A sale by auction or on a commodity or other exchange is governed by the law chosen by the parties in accordance with Article 7 to the extent to which the law of the State where the auction takes place or the exchange is located does not prohibit such choice. Failing a choice by the parties or to the extent that such choice is prohibited, the law of the State where the auction takes place or the exchange is located shall apply.

Article 10

1   Issues concerning the existence and material validity of the consent of the parties as to the choice of the applicable law are determined where the choice satisfies the requirements of Article 7, by the law chosen. If under that law the choice is invalid the law governing the contract is determined under Article 8.

2   The existence and material validity of a contract of sale or of any term thereof are determined by the law which under the Convention would govern the contract or term if it were valid.

3   Nevertheless, to establish that he did not consent to the choice of law to the contract itself or to any term thereof, a party may rely on the law of the State where he has his place of business if in the circumstances it is not reasonable to determine that issue under the law specified in the preceding paragraphs.

Article 11

1   A contract of sale concluded between persons who are in the same State is formally valid if it satisfies the requirements either of the law which governs it under the Convention or of the law of the State where it is concluded.

2   A contract of sale concluded between persons who are in different States is formally valid if it satisfies the requirements either of the law which governs it under the Convention or of the law of one of those States.

3   Where the contract is concluded by an agent, the State in which the agent acts is the relevant State for the purposes of the preceding paragraphs.

4   An act intended to have legal effect relating to an existing or contemplated contract of sale is formally valid if it satisfies the requirements either of the law which under the Convention governs or would govern the contract or of the law of the State where the act was done.

5   The Convention does not apply to the formal validity of a contract of sale where one of the parties to the contract has, at the time of its conclusion, his place of business in a State which has made the reservation provided for in Article 21, para 1, sub-para (c).

Section 2 – Scope of the applicable law

Article 12

The law applicable to a contract of sale by virtue of Articles 7, 8 or 9 governs in particular:

(a) interpretation of the contract;

(b) the rights and obligations of the parties and performance of the contract;

(c) the time at which the buyer becomes entitled to the products, fruits and income deriving from the goods;

(d) the time from which the buyer bears the risk with respect to the goods;

(e) the validity and effect as between the parties of clauses reserving title to the goods;

(f) the consequences of non-performance of the contract, including the categories of loss for which compensation may be recovered, but without prejudice to the procedural law of the forum;

(g) the various ways of extinguishing obligations, as well as prescription and limitation of actions;

(h) the consequences of nullity or invalidity of the contract.

Article 13

In the absence of all express clauses to the contrary, the law of the State where inspection of the goods takes place applies to the modalities and procedural requirements for such inspection.

CHAPTER 3 – GENERAL PROVISIONS

Article 14

1   If a party has more than one place of business, the relevant place of business is that which has the closest relationship to the contract and its performance, having regard to the circumstances known to or contemplated by the parties at any time before or at the conclusion of the contract.

2   If a party does not have a place of business, reference is to be made to his habitual residence.

Article 15

In the Convention, 'law' means the law in force in a State other than its choice of law rules.

Article 16

In the interpretation of the Convention, regard is to be held to its international character and to the need to promote uniformity in its application.

Article 17

The Convention does not prevent the application of those provisions of the law of the forum that must be applied irrespective of the law that otherwise governs the contract.

Article 18

The application of a law determined by the Convention may be refused only where such application would be manifestly incompatible with public policy (*ordre public*).

Article 19

For the purpose of identifying the law applicable under the Convention, where a State comprises several territorial units each of which has its own system of law or its own rules of law in respect of contracts for the sale of goods, any reference to the law of that State is to be construed as referring to the law in force in the territorial unit in question.

Article 20

A State within which different territorial units have their own systems of law or their own rules of law in respect of contracts of sale is not bound to apply the Convention to conflicts between the laws in force in such units.

Article 21

1   Any State may, at the time of signature, ratification, acceptance, approval or accession make any of the following reservations:

(a) that it will not apply the Convention in the cases covered by sub-para (b) of Article 1;

(b) that it will not apply para 3 of Article 8, except where neither party to the contract has his place of business in a State which has made a reservation provided for under this sub-paragraph;

(c) that, for cases where its legislation requires contracts of sale to be concluded in or evidenced by writing, it will not apply the Convention to the formal validity of the contract, where any party has his place of business in its territory at the time of conclusion of the contract;

(d) that it will not apply sub-paragraph of Article 12 in so far as that sub-paragraph relates to prescription and limitation of actions.

2   No other reservation shall be permitted.

3   Any Contracting State may at any time withdraw a reservation which it has made; the reservation shall cease to have effect on the first day of the month following the expiration of three months after notification of the withdrawal.

Article 22

1   This Convention does not prevail over any Convention or other international agreement which has been or may be entered into and which contains provisions determining the law applicable to contracts of sale, provided that such instrument applies only if the seller and buyer have their places of business in States parties to that instrument.

2   This Convention does not prevail over any international Convention to which a Contracting State is, or becomes, a party, regulating the choice of law in regard to any particular category of contracts of sale within the scope of this Convention.

Article 23

This Convention does not prejudice the application:

(a) of the United Nations Conventions on Contracts for the International Sale of Goods (Vienna, 11 April 1980);

(b) of the Conventions on the Limitation Period in the International Sale of Goods (New York, 14 June 1974), or the Protocol amending that Convention (Vienna, 11 April 1980).

Article 24

The Convention applies in a Contracting State to contracts of sale concluded after its entry into force for that State.

CHAPTER 4 – FINAL CLAUSES

Article 25

1   The Convention is open for signature by all States.

2   The Convention is subject to ratification, acceptance or approval by the signatory States.

3   The Convention is open for accession by all States which are not signatory States as from the date it is open for signature.

4   Instruments of ratification, acceptance, approval and accession shall be deposited with the Ministry of Foreign Affairs of the Kingdom of the Netherlands, depositary of the Convention.

Article 26

1   If a State has two or more territorial units in which different systems of law are applicable in relation to matters dealt with in this Convention, it may at the time of signature, ratification, acceptance, approval or accession declare that this Convention shall extend to all its territorial units or only to one or more of them and may modify this declaration by submitting another declaration at any time.

2   Any such shall be notified to the depositary and shall state expressly the territorial units to which the Convention applies.

3   If a State makes no declaration under this Article, the Convention is to extend to all territorial units of that State.

Article 27

1   The Convention shall enter into force on the first day of the month following the expiration of three months after the deposit of the fifth instrument of ratification, acceptance, approval or accession referred to in Article 25.

2   Thereafter the Convention shall enter into force:

(a)   for each State ratifying, accepting, approving or acceding to it subsequently, on the first day of the month following the expiration of three months after the deposit of its instrument of ratification, acceptance, approval or accession; for a territorial unit to which the Convention has been extended in conformity with Article 26 on the first day of the month following the expiration of three months after the notification referred to in that article.

Article 28

For each State party to the Convention on the Law Applicable to International Sales of Goods, done at The Hague on 15 June 1955, which has consented to be bound by this Convention and for which this Convention is in force, this Convention shall replace the said Convention of 1955.

Article 29

Any State which becomes a party to this Convention after the entry into force of an instrument revising it shall be considered to be a party to the Convention as revised.

Article 30

1   A State party to this Convention may denounce it by a notification in writing addressed to the depositary.

2   The denunciation takes effect on the first day of the month following the expiration of three months after the notification is received by the depositary. Where a longer period for the denunciation to take effect is specified in the notification, the denunciation takes effect upon the expiration of such longer period after the notification is received by the depositary.

Article 31

The depositary shall notify the State Members of the League Conference on Private International Law and the States which have signed, ratified, accepted, approved or acceded in accordance with Article 25, of the following:

(a)   the signatures and ratifications, acceptances, approvals and accessions referred to in Article 25;

(b)   the date on which the Convention enters into force in accordance with Article 27;

(c) the declarations referred to in Article 26;

(d) the reservations and the withdrawals of reservations referred to in Article 21;

(e) the denunciations referred to in Article 30.

In witness whereof the undersigned, being duly authorised thereto, have signed this Convention.

Done at The Hague, on the twenty-second day of December 1986, in the English and French languages, both texts being equally authentic, in a single copy which shall be deposited in the archives of the government of the Kingdom of the Netherlands, and of which a certified copy shall be sent, through diplomatic channels, to each of the State Members of the Hague Conference on Private International Law as of the date of its extraordinary session of October 1985, and to each State which participated in that session.

CHAPTER 2

THE UNIDROIT PRINCIPLES OF INTERNATIONAL COMMERCIAL CONTRACTS

INTRODUCTION

As the world approaches the next millennium, it is astonishing to realise that only since the post World War II period has there been an increased impetus to unify and harmonise rules of international trade law.[1] This is particularly surprising when one realises that uniform international trade rules benefit countries and their citizens both economically and politically.[2] Perhaps the reason for the slow progress is that only in this century has there been a dramatic increase in transnational commerce[3] and a reduction in State protectionism.[4] Even though general principles of international trade law (known as the *lex mercatoria*) have been around since the middle ages,[5] it has only been as a result of the more recent work of international and inter-governmental organisations, such as Uncitral,[6] UNIDROIT,[7] the Hague Conference,[8] and various private trade associations such as the International Chamber of Commerce,[9] that any documented formulation of uniform international trade rules has evolved.

Perhaps the most significant achievement this century has been the United Nations Convention on Contracts for the International Sale of Goods (CISG) (1980)[10] to which

---

1   See Waincymer, J, 'The Internationalisation of Australia's Trade Law' [1995] 17 *Sydney Law Review* 298 at 299.

2   See Waincymer, *ibid* at 301.

3   See Ferrari, F, 'Defining the Sphere of the Application of the 1994 UNIDROIT Principles Of International Commercial Contracts' [1995] 69 *Tulane Law Review* 1225.

4   See Waincymer, *op cit* at 299.

5   See Pryles, M, Waincymer, J and Davies, M, *International Trade Law – Commentary and Materials*, 1996, p 41, Sydney: Law Book Company.

6   The United Nations Commission on International Trade Law which came into operation on 1 January 1968 and has the aim to further 'the progressive harmonisation and unification of the law of international trade'. See Article 8 of the Statute of Uncitral.

7   The International Institute for the Unification of Private International Law was originally established in 1926 and reorganised in 1940.

8   The Hague Conference on Private International Law was established in 1893. However conferences were not frequently held until after World War II. See generally, Lipstein, K, 'One Hundred Years of Hague Conferences on Private International Law' (1963) 42(3) *International and Comparative Law Qtly* 553.

9   That is, the International Chamber of Commerce.

10 Hereinafter referred to as the 'CISG'. The Hague Conventions of 1964, ie 'The Uniform Law for the International Sale of Goods' and 'The Uniform Law on the formation of Contracts for the International Sale of Goods' were significant achievements but only attracted a few accessions when they came into force in 1972.

Australia acceded on 1 April 1989.[11] In essence, the CISG provides some international uniform rules applicable to the sale of goods, where parties have places of business in States that are contracting States or when the rules of private international law lead to the application of the law of a contracting State which is a party to the Convention.[12] However, whilst the CISG is in force in nearly 40 countries, it nevertheless has a number of limitations. For example, it is confined to the international sale of goods as distinct to other international transactions and fails to deal with issues such as validity and transfer of property. This dilemma necessitates resort to the domestic law of a State chosen by the conflict of law rules of a given forum. This, in turn, can create inconvenience and uncertainty for international traders. For example, one party at least may be unfamiliar with the applicable law or such law, in itself, may be uncertain or impossible to interpret.

The UNIDROIT Principles of International Commercial Contracts, published by UNIDROIT in 1994 addresses a number of the limitations found in the CISG and, as will be seen, is a restatement of the principles of international trade law relevant to international commercial contracts. This chapter will initially provide a broad overview of the UNIDROIT Principles including their uses and how they are to be interpreted. Their status as an international restatement of legal principles will then be discussed followed by an examination of its most important provisions. Where relevant, the Principles will be compared with international conventions such as the CISG so as to emphasise their significance in international trade.

THE UNIDROIT PRINCIPLES

Overview

The UNIDROIT Principles of International Commercial Contracts[13] are the product of some 14 years of work by leading experts in the field of comparative law and international trade law from around the world.[14] The Principles set forth general rules governing 'international commercial contracts'[15] and, unlike the CISG, the Principles are not confined to the international sale of goods. On the contrary, the Comments to

---

11   See the Sale of Goods (Vienna Convention) Act 1986 (Qld); the Sale of Goods (Vienna Convention) Act 1986 (NSW); the Sale of Goods (Vienna Convention) Act 1986 (SA); the Sale of Goods (Vienna Convention) Act 1986 (WA); the Sale of Goods (Vienna Convention) Act 1987 (Tas); the Sale of Goods (Vienna Convention) Act 1987 (ACT); the Sale of Goods (Vienna Convention) Act 1987 (Vic); the Sale of Goods (Vienna Convention) Act 1987 (Vic); the Sale of Goods (Vienna Convention) Act 1987 (NT). Also note that section 66A of the Trade Practices Act 1974 (Cth) provides that the CISG takes precedence over provisions of the Trade Practices Act 1974 (Cth).

12   See Article 1 of the CISG.

13   Hereinafter referred to as 'the Principles'.

14   See Bonell, MJ, 'Unification of Law By Non-Legislative Means: The UNIDROIT Draft Principles For International Commercial Contracts' (1992) 40(3) *American Journal of Comparative Law* 617 at 619 and Furmston, MP, 'UNIDROIT General Principles For International Commercial Contracts' (1996) 10 *Journal of Contract Law* 11 at 19–20 as regards members of the 'working group'.

15   See the Preamble to the Principles.

the Preamble[16] suggest that the concept of 'commercial' contracts should be understood as broadly as possible and it has been suggested that the Principles are flexible enough to apply to international service, leasing and licensing agreements as well as finance, banking, insurance and other transactions.[17]

As with the CISG, the Principles only apply to international, as opposed to, domestic agreements.[18] Furthermore, the Principles are, generally speaking, the same as or similar to the relevant CISG provisions.[19] This similarity is due to the fact that the CISG was one of a number of instruments examined by UNIDROIT in drafting the Principles.[20] Because of its broad similarity to the CISG, the Principles may be used to interpret not only the CISG but also to supplement the deficiencies or gaps that appear in the CISG.[21]

Of particular significance to international traders and their lawyers, the UNIDROIT Principles may be incorporated into contracts as if they were the governing law or indeed the terms of the contract[22] subject to any exclusion or modification agreed to by the parties.[23] Furthermore, the Principles may be applied by judges and arbitrators[24] so as to provide a solution to an issue when it proves impossible to establish the relevant rule of the applicable law.[25] In this regard, it has been suggested that they 'probably represent the most accurate description to date of the emerging international consensus about the rules that are most suitable to international trade law'.[26] As will be seen, the Principles may also be applied by Arbitrators as the applicable law in adjudicating disputes and making awards. Lastly, as the Principles are in the nature

---

16 See Comment no 2 to the Preamble. The black letter text consisting of Articles is accompanied by Comments and Illustrations so as to assist in the interpretation of the Articles. See van Houtte, H, 'The UNIDROIT Principles of International Commercial Contracts' (1996) *International Trade and Business Annual* 1 at 2 and Bonell, *op cit* at 620 as to the use of the Comments and the Illustrations.

17 See Bonell, MJ, *An International Restatement of Contract Law*, 1994, Irvington, New York: Transnational Juries, p 36.

18 See Bonell, *ibid*, p 32–33.

19 Albeit with some exceptions. See Bonell, *ibid*, p 47; Perillo, JM, 'UNIDROIT Principles of International Commercial Contracts: the black letter text and a review' [1994] 63 *Fordham Law Review* 281 at 282; Garro, AM, 'The Gap-Filling Role of the UNIDROIT Principles in International Sales Law: some comments of the interplay between the Principles and the CISG' [1995] 69 *Tulane Law Review* 1149 at 1189.

20 See Bonell, *op cit*, p 43.

21 See Article 7(1) and 7(2) of the CISG and explanations of such roles in Bonell, *ibid*, p 110–13 and Garro, *op cit* at 1189. As regards gap filling in codes of law generally, see Kritzer, AH, *International Contract Manual – ICM Guide to UN Conventions*, Deventer, Boston: Kluwer Law and Taxation (looseleaf) Vol 1 at 83–84.

22 See the Preamble to the Principles.

23 Note, however, that once the Principles are incorporated, some provisions cannot be excluded or modified. See Article 1.5 of the Principles.

24 Though see the discussion below as regards the non-obligatory law status of the Principles.

25 See the Preamble.

26 See Hyland, R, 'On setting forth the law of contract: a foreword' (1992) 40 *American Journal of Comparative Law* 541 at 550.

of a restatement of the commercial law of the world,[27] they may additionally serve as a model for national and international legislators.[28]

Before considering the various 120 articles in the Principles, it is apt to note that the Principles cover numerous issues concerning international commercial contracts such as pre-contractual negotiation, formation, validity, interpretation, various aspects of performance, including hardship and *force majeure*, termination and remedial provisions. The Principles basically reflect concepts of contract law to be found in nearly all legal systems of the world.[29]

In interpreting the Principles, Article 1.6(1) stipulates that 'regard is to be had to their international character and to their purposes including the need to promote uniformity in their application'. Accordingly, the various articles must be interpreted in the context of themselves without cognisance or regard to any domestic law meaning or preconceived notions. As further emphasised by Comment 3 to Article 1.6, the articles must not be interpreted in a literal or strict sense but in light of the purposes of the Principles as well as the rationale(s) behind the individual articles. As evident from the Introduction to the UNIDROIT Principles, one purpose is to establish a balanced set of rules for worldwide use 'irrespective of the legal traditions and the economic and political conditions of the countries in which they are to be applied'. Other examples are the various purposes outlined in the Preamble.

In a similar vein, Article 1.6(2) stipulates that issues within the scope of the Principles but not expressly settled are, as far as possible, to be settled in accordance with their underlying general principles. Thus, gaps in the Principles which would ordinarily be addressed by rules on international commercial contracts should be *prima facie* resolved by drawing an analogy with specific articles of the Principles and their rationales.

THE UNIDROIT PRINCIPLES AND CONTRACT LAW

Whilst drafted in the style of European Codes and potentially furnishing a valuable source of the *lex mercatoria*,[30] it must, at the outset, be appreciated that the Principles do not have any multinational legislative force even if the Comments to the Preamble state that they 'represent a system of rules of contract law'.[31]

As stated by Article 1.4 of the Principles: 'Nothing in these Principles shall restrict the application of mandatory rules, whether of national, international or supranational origin, which are applicable in accordance with the relevant rules of private international law.' Hence, the proper law that strictly speaking governs an international commercial contract will be determined by the rules of private international law of a particular forum

---

27 See Perillo, *op cit*, p 283.

28 See the Preamble to the Principles.

29 See Bonell, *op cit*, p 42.

30 See Pryles, Waincymer and Davies, *op cit*, p 41. Also see Mustill, MJ, 'The New *Lex Mercatoria*: The First 25 Years' (1988) 4 *Arbitration International* 86 where the concept of *lex mercatoria* is examined.

31 See the Comment to Preamble 4a.

or in the case of sale of goods, the Hague Convention of the Law Applicable to Contracts for the International Sale of Goods (1985).[32] Generally speaking, the rules of private international law of most countries enable application of the domestic law of a State expressly or inferentially chosen by the parties[33] or the system of law with which the transaction has its closest and most real connection.[34] Alternatively, an international convention such as the CISG may be directly or indirectly applicable to the contract if it concerns the international sale of goods and other threshold requirements are satisfied.[35]

Whilst the courts of some forums have given limited recognition to general principles of international trade law,[36] it will normally be the case that judges are obliged to apply the proper law as determined by rules of private international law or an applicable convention even if parties have expressly agreed that the Principles are to govern their contract.[37] However, as suggested by the Preamble to the Principles, judges could use the Principles to assist in the interpretation of international uniform law instruments and also use the principles to provide a solution to an issue raised when it proves impossible to establish the relevant rule of the applicable law where, for example, the law of a given State is obscure, underdeveloped or simply difficult to ascertain.[38]

Because of the increased use of arbitration and the fact that in most countries arbitrators are able to apply general principles of international commercial law,[39] the Principles will be of great benefit to parties who stipulate in their agreement that any dispute or claim arising out of or in connection with the contract shall be referred to arbitration and that the Principles shall be incorporated in and govern the contract, its interpretation and performance.[40] Arbitration is generally more attractive to international traders than court forums because it is usually less expensive than litigation and provides a speedier resolution of the conflict with confidentiality being maintained. Arbitrators may find the Principles to be a highly attractive choice of law and therefore

---

32 Note, however, that Australia has not as yet adopted the Hague Convention.

33 As is the case, generally speaking, in Australia provided the selection of law is *bona fide* see: *Golden Acres Ltd v Qld States Pty Ltd* [1969] Qd R 378 and *Vita Food Products Inc v Unus Ship Co Ltd* [1937] AC 277 at 290–92.

34 As is the position generally in Australia under rules of private international law: see *Mendelson – Zeller Co Inc v TC Providores Pty Ltd* [1981] 1 NSWLR 566.

35 See Article 1 of the CISG and note Article 95 as to the applicability of the CISG.

36 At least in upholding the validity of arbitration awards based on the *lex mercatoria* see Ferrari, *op cit* at 1231. Also see Kirby, P in *Brown Boveri (Australia) Pty Ltd v Baltic Shipping Co (T Andezhba Krupskaya)* [1989] 1 Lloyd's Rep 518 where principles of international trade law concerning transport rules were used to assist in interpretation.

37 See Luiz, OB, 'The UNIDROIT Principles for International Commercial Law Project: Aspects of International Private Law' [1995] 69 *Tulane Law Review* 1209 at 1220.

38 See Perillo, *op cit* at 281.

39 See Furmston, MP, 'UNIDROIT General Principles for international commercial contracts' (1996) 10 *Journal of Contract Law* 11 at 12. Also see *Channel Tunnel Group Ltd v Balfour Beatty Construction Ltd* [1992] 1 QB 656; [1993] AC 334.

40 See the recommended model clause as proposed by Brazil, P, 'UNIDROIT Principles of international commercial contracts in the context of international commercial arbitration', October 1994, paper presented at the 25th Biennial Conference of the International Bar Association, Melbourne, as extracted in Bonell, *op cit*, p 124. As regards organisations available to do arbitration and model arbitration rules, see generally Waincymer, *op cit* at 315–16.

use them in making awards because they provide an equitable solution to nearly all issues that could possibly arise in international commercial contracts.[41]

PRE-CONTRACTUAL NEGOTIATIONS

The requirement of Article 1.7 that each party must act in accordance with 'good faith and fair dealing in international trade'[42] not only applies during the life of a contract but also during pre-contractual negotiations. Such requirements in conducting negotiations generally reflect the civil law.[43] They can be contrasted with Australian or English law in that the common law does not require that negotiations be conducted in good faith where no lawyers are involved.[44]

Whilst Article 2.15(1) provides that a party is free to negotiate and is not liable for failure to reach an agreement, Article 2.15(2) nevertheless makes a party liable for losses caused to another party where the first party negotiates or breaks off negotiations in bad faith. It is bad faith, in particular, for a party to enter into or to continue negotiations when intending not to reach an agreement.[45] The Principles, therefore, censure a party who negotiates without ever intending to reach an agreement or who initially acts *bona fide* but subsequently continues negotiations without an intention to reach an agreement. It would appear, however, that the Principles do not apply to parallel negotiations where a party also engages in negotiations with a third party where only one agreement can result.[46]

A party in breach of Article 2.15(2) is liable for 'losses caused' to the other party though liability does not extend to lost profit which could have been made if the negotiations had not been aborted.[47] Liability would extend to expenses such as legal fees, travel expenses, translation costs and other costs arising out of the negotiations.[48] Indeed, it also has been suggested that liability may extend to the innocent party's loss of an opportunity to conclude another contract with a third party as a result of the bad faith negotiations.[49] The Principles also impose a duty not to disclose confidential information or use it improperly for a party's own purposes when such is obtained in the course of negotiations regardless of whether a contract is subsequently concluded.[50]

---

41 Arbitrators generally consider the most relevant law to be that which affords a fair or equitable solution. See Baptista, *op cit* at 1223.

42 See Article 1.7(1). Also see Article 1.7(2).

43 See van Houtte, *op cit* at 4 and Bonell, *op cit*, p 80.

44 See Lord Acker in *Walfort v Miles* [1979] 2 WLR 174 and van Houtte, *op cit* at 4.

45 See Article 2.15(3).

46 See van Houtte, *op cit* at 5 and *Mine v Guinea* (1989) Yb Conn Arb, 82–87, as an example of the application of French law concerning bad faith in negotiations.

47 See Article 2.15, Comment 2.

48 See van Houtte, *op cit* at 6.

49 See van Houtte, *op cit* at 6.

50 See Article 2.16.

Compensation for breach of confidentiality may include compensation reflecting the benefit received by the other party.[51] Compensation may also include compensation for the loss suffered by the breach or for the benefit received by disclosing information to third parties.[52]

Lastly, it should be noted that even if a contract is concluded, it may be avoided where a fraudulent representation or non-disclosure occurred during the negotiation phase.[53]

FORMATION

The Principles generally reflect the CISG provisions concerning the formation of a contract[54] and both documents embody the concept of *favor contractus* in that they both have the aim of preserving a contract wherever possible. The Principles, however, go further than the CISG by providing in Article 2.1 that a contract may be concluded not only by the acceptance of an offer but also by the conduct of parties 'that is sufficient to show agreement'. Comment 2 to Article 2.1 explains that the sufficiency of conduct basis of formation reflects commercial practice in that contracts are often concluded after prolonged negotiations without an identifiable sequence of offer and acceptance particularly in the case of complex transactions.

The Principles, by Article 3.2, provide, *inter alia*, that a contract is concluded by the mere agreement of the parties. Hence, unlike the common law, consideration is not an essential element.[55] An offer is effectively defined as a sufficiently definite proposal before concluding a contract which indicates the offeror's intention to be bound in the case of acceptance.[56]

The Principles provide comprehensive rules similar to the CISG as to the withdrawal of an offer;[57] revocation and irrevocability of a fixed term offer;[58] rejection of an offer;[59] methods of acceptance;[60] time for acceptance;[61] calculation of time for

---

51 See Article 2.16.

52 See Comment 3 to Article 2.16 and van Houtte, *op cit* at 6.

53 See Article 3.8.

54 For example, compare Article 14(1) CISG and Article 2.2 of the Principles as to the definition of offer; also see Article 3.2 of the principles; Article 15(1) CISG and Article 2.3(1) of the Principles as to effective offers; Article 15(2) CISG and Article 2.3(2) as to withdrawal of offer; Article 16 CISG and Article 2.4 as to revocation of offer; Article 17 CISG and Article 2.5 as to rejection of offer; Article 18 CISG and Article 2.6 as to the mode of acceptance.

55 Article 3.2 appears in Chapter 3 concerning validity however, it is appropriate to mention the Article at this juncture. Also see Article 5.7 as to determination of price.

56 See Article 2.2 of the Principles.

57 See Article 2.3 which reflects Article 15 CISG.

58 See Article 2.4 which reflects Article 16 CISG.

59 See Article 2.5 which is similar to Article 17 CISG.

60 See Article 2.6 which, in substance, reflects Article 18 CISG.

61 See Article 2.7 which is similar to Article 18(2) CISG.

acceptance;[62] late acceptance and unavoidable delay in acceptance;[63] withdrawal of acceptance[64] and modified acceptance.[65]

The Principles, unlike the CISG, also provide for the situation where one party, after the conclusion of a contract, sends the other a writing which purportedly confirms the contract but in reality contains additional or different terms. In such a situation, Article 2.12 provides that such terms become part of the contract unless they materially alter the contract or the recipient of the writing, without undue delay, objects to the discrepancy.

Article 2.3 provides that no contract is concluded where, during negotiations, one party insists that the contract is not concluded until there is agreement on specific matters or in a specific form. On the other hand, a contract will result where parties intend to conclude a contract but intentionally leave a term to be agreed upon in further negotiations or to be determined by a third party.[66] The contract remains unaffected where no subsequent agreement on the term or no third party determination results, provided there is an alternative reasonable means of rendering the term in question definite having regard to the intention of the parties.[67]

The 'battle of the forms' dilemma, where either or both the parties use pre-printed standard business forms, receives innovative and sound treatment in the Principles.[68] Article 2.19(2) defines standard terms as 'provisions which are prepared in advance for general and repeated use by one party and which are actually used without negotiation with the other party'. Article 2.19(1) provides the general rule that where one party or both parties use standard terms in concluding a contract, the general rules of formation apply, subject to Articles 2.20–2.22.

Article 2.20(1) addresses 'surprising terms' and provides that no term contained in standard terms which is of such a character that the other party could not reasonably have expected it is effective unless it has been expressly accepted by that party. By Article 2.20(2), regard is to be had to the content of a term, language and presentation in determining whether the term is a 'surprising term'. Article 2.21 however, provides that, in a case of conflict between a standard term and a term which is not a standard term, the latter prevails.

Probably the most significant rule is the Article 2.22 'knockout rule' which provides that if both parties use standard terms and reach agreement except on those terms, a contract is concluded on the basis of the agreed terms and any standard terms which are common in substance, unless one party clearly indicates in advance, or later and without undue delay informs the other party, that it does not intend to be bound by such a

---

62 See Article 2.8 which reflects Article 20 CISG.
63 See Article 2.9 which reflects Article 21 CISG.
64 See Article 2.10 which reflects Article 22 CISG.
65 See Article 2.11 which generally reflects Article 19(1), 19(2) though not 19(3) of the CISG.
66 See Article 2.14(1).
67 See Article 2.14(2).
68 See Perillo, *op cit* at 288. Also note that no such provisions appear in the CISG.

contract. As indicated by Comment 3 to Article 2.22, a party's assertion in advance of formation not to be bound by such standard terms should be made in a document separate to any standard term form.

Article 2.22 departs from the typical common law starting point of analysing the battle of the forms dilemma by using the 'offer-counter-offer-acceptance approach'.[69] Article 2.22 possibly provides a better approach because as explained in Comment 3 to Article 2.22, parties often exchange pre-printed standard term forms where the terms are on the reverse side and the parties pay no attention to the terms.[70]

VALIDITY

Chapter 3 of the Principles deals with validity addresses, mistake of fact or law,[71] fraud,[72] duress[73] and gross disparity.[74] The provisions in this chapter are mandatory except in so far as they relate to the binding force of a mere agreement, initial impossibility or mistake.[75]

An innocent party may avoid a contract if grounds of invalidity exist by giving notification of avoidance[76] in accordance with the notice provision[77] within the specified time periods.[78] Avoidance takes effect retroactively[79] and upon avoidance either party may claim restitution.[80] Because the Principles embody the *favor contractus* concept, the right to avoid may be lost or limited in specified circumstances.

Avoidance of the contract is excluded where a party entitled to avoid the contract expressly or impliedly confirms the contracts after the period of time for giving notice of avoidance has begun to run.[81] The right to avoid on the grounds of mistake may be automatically lost if the other party declares itself willing to perform, or performs the contract as it was understood by the party entitled to avoid.[82] A ground of avoidance applicable only to individual terms of a contract only enables a party to exercise the right

---

69　See, for example, *Butler Machine Tool Co Ltd v Ex-Cell-O Corporation (England) Ltd* [1979] 1 WLR 401 where a standard order form sent in response to the seller's standard order form but containing significantly different terms was construed as a counter offer which was then accepted by the seller's subsequent response.

70　Also see Bonell, *op cit*, p 72.

71　See Articles 3.14–3.17.

72　See Article 3.8.

73　See Article 3.9.

74　See Article 3.10. Gross disparity is akin to the common law doctrines of unconscionable conduct.

75　See Article 3.19.

76　See Article 3.14.

77　See Article 1.9.

78　See Article 3.15.

79　Without the need for any court declaration. See Garro, *op cit* at 1176.

80　See Article 3.17.

81　See Article 3.12.

82　See Article 3.13.

of avoidance in relation to those terms unless it is unreasonable to uphold the remaining contract.[83]

By Article 3.3, invalidity does not arise by the mere fact that at the time of the conclusion of the contract, performance was impossible or that the party was not entitled to dispose of the assets to which the contract relates. It should be noted, however, that irrespective of whether or not the contract has been avoided, the party who knew or ought to have known of the ground for avoidance is liable for damages.

Unfortunately, the Principles do not address invalidity arising from lack of capacity, authority or issues of immorality or illegality.[84] However, the Principles otherwise outshine the CISG because the CISG avoids validity issues completely.[85] Obviously, the failure of the CISG to address validity makes the Principles attractive to courts or perhaps more particularly international arbitrators,[86] as they may be used to fill in the gaps in the CISG.

INTERPRETATION

Chapter 4 of the Principles also outshines the CISG in that it provides comprehensive rules concerning the interpretation of contracts.[87] The rules concerning interpretation are based on the concept of good faith and fair dealing and attempt to strike a neutral balance of fairness between the parties.[88]

Article 4.1 of the Principles provides the general rule that a contract shall be interpreted according to the common intention of the parties. If such an intention cannot be established, then it shall be interpreted according to the meaning that reasonable persons would give to it in the same circumstances. The subjective and reasonable persons approaches are also applied in the interpretation of a statement and the party's conduct.[89] In applying the general rules in Articles 4.1 and 4.2, Article 4.3 enables consideration to be given to preliminary negotiations, common trade meanings and usages.[90]

The *contra proferentem* rule, which requires an interpretation of unclear contract terms against the party who supplied them, appears in Chapter 4[91] and a special rule concerning linguistic discrepancies is also provided.[92] Lastly, Article 4.8 enables an omitted term to be supplied where such a term is important for a determination of the

---

83   See Article 3.16.

84   See Article 3.1.

85   See Article 4(a) of the CISG. Also see Garro, *op cit* at 1173 who criticises the CISG in this regard.

86   See the previous discussion as to the non-binding effect of the Principles.

87   The issue of interpretation is only dealt with in Article 8 and 9 of the CISG.

88   See Bonell, *op cit* at 84.

89   See Article 4.2.

90   Also note Article 1.8 which provides that parties are generally bound by their own usages or trade usages.

91   See Article 4.6 and also Articles 4.4 to 4.5 and Bonell, *op cit* at 94.

92   See Article 4.7.

party's rights and duties and the parties have not agreed with respect to the term.[93] None of these latter provisions appear in the CISG.

CONTENT

Chapter 5 on Content deals with express and implied obligations, duties in performing such obligations, co operation between the parties, quality of performance, price determination and contracts for an indefinite period.

Of particular note are the criteria in Articles 5.4 and 5.5 which help determine the extent to which a party's obligation simply involves a duty to exert its best efforts in performance of an activity, or a duty to achieve a specific result. The best efforts phenomenon, as opposed to the specific result approach, is of French origin and it has been suggested that the UNIDROIT working group thought that the adoption of such a concept would help judges and arbitrators determine liability for breach of contract.[94] As a general rule, it should be noted that Article 5.3 states that each party shall cooperate with the other party when such cooperation may reasonably be expected for the performance of that party's obligation.

Of particular importance is Article 5.7 which provides criteria as to the determination of price where an agreement is an open price contract.[95] Whilst Article 55 of the CISG provides one basis for price determination, the Principles by Article 5.7 provide a further four bases for price determination. The first rule in Article 5.7, reflecting Article 55 of the CISG, provides that parties are taken to have impliedly made reference to the price generally charged at the time of the conclusion of the contract (ie formation) for such goods sold under comparable circumstances in the trade concerned, in the absence of any indication to the contrary.

PERFORMANCE

Chapter 6 concerning performance is sectionalised into 'performance in general' and 'hardship'.[96] The section on performance commences with rules concerning the time of performance[97] and then addresses issues such as partial performance, order of performance, earlier performance and place of performance. As a general rule, each party bears the costs of performance of its obligations.[98]

Article 6.1.6 provides that a party is to perform a monetary obligation at the obligee's place of business. In this regard, it is analogous to Article 57 of the CISG which

---

93 See Article 4.8.

94 See Garro, *op cit* at 117 and Perillo, *op cit* at 296.

95 It is not uncommon in international commercial contracts for price to be left undetermined by the parties. See Garro, *op cit* at 1179.

96 Hardship together with *force majeure* are discussed below, 'Hardship and *Force Majeure*'.

97 See Article 6.1.1 and 6.1.2 which are consistent with Articles 33 and 34 (seller's obligations) and Articles 57 and 58 (buyer's obligations) in the CISG.

98 See Article 6.1.11.

requires a buyer to pay at the seller's place of business unless the contract indicates otherwise.

Article 6.1.7(1) enables payment to be made in any form used in the ordinary course of business at the place of payment and Article 6.1.8(1) reflects commercial reality by enabling payment to be made by a transfer of funds to any of the financial institutions in which the obligee has made it known it has an account, unless the obligee has indicated a particular account. The obligor is discharged once a transfer becomes effective.[99] No similar provisions appear in the CISG.

Unlike the CISG, the Principles also address currency of payment issues;[100] the imputation of payments where an obligor has several debts owing to an obligee;[101] the imputation of non-monetary obligations;[102] duties of a party in obtaining public permissions such as export licences and impossibility of performance and validity issues that may arise where permission is refused.[103]

The currency of payment provisions make a significant contribution to the resolutions of problems such as the fluctuation of currencies, the non-convertibility of some currencies and the failure of parties to adequately address such issues in a contract. For example, where currency is not expressed, payment must be made in the currency of the place where payment is to be made.[104] As noted above, this will be at the seller or obligee's place of business when the contract does not expressly or impliedly address place of payment.[105]

Where, however, currency is expressed but not as the currency of the place for payment, the monetary obligations may nevertheless still be paid in the currency of the place for payment, unless that currency is not freely convertible or the parties have agreed that payment should be made only in the currency in which the monetary obligations is expressed.[106] However, if it is impossible to make such payment in the expressed currency due, for example, to exchange regulations, then an obligee may require payment in the currency of the place for payment.[107]

Of particular note, Article 6.1.9(3) provides that payment in the currency of the place for payment is to be made according to the applicable rate of exchange prevailing when payment is due. If, however, payment is not made when due, an obligee may require payment according to the applicable rate of exchange prevailing either when payment is due or at the time of actual payment.[108] In such a situation, an obligee could

---

99   See Article 6.1.8(2).

100 See Articles 6.1.9 and 6.1.10.

101 See Article 6.1.12 and Perillo at 298.

102 See Article 6.1.13.

103 See Articles 6.1.14–6.1.17. Also see Bonell, *op cit* at 53–54 and, in particular, 118 as regards draft clauses concerning public permission issues.

104 See Article 6.1.10.

105 See Article 6.1.6.

106 See Article 6.1.9(1).

107 See Article 6.1.9(2).

108 See Article 6.1.9(4).

quite legitimately choose the time that yields a more favourable monetary rate of exchange.

HARDSHIP AND *FORCE MAJEURE*

The concept of *favor contractus*, reflected expressly[109] and implicitly in the Principles,[110] is again instanced by the hardship provisions[110] and the force majeure (impossibility) provision.[112] For example, Article 6.2.1 (the first of the three provisions addressing hardship) stipulates that; 'Where the performance of a contract becomes more onerous for one of the parties, that party is nevertheless bound to perform its obligations subject to the following provisions on hardship.'

Whilst hardship and *force majeure* appear in different chapters, it is appropriate to consider them together as they are related concepts in that *force majeure* applies when performance becomes impossible and hardship occurs when performance becomes much more burdensome albeit not impossible.[113]

Hardship

Hardship, by definition,[114] arises where the occurrence of events fundamentally alters the equilibrium of the contract either because the costs of a party's performance have increased or because the value of the performance a party receives has diminished and:

(a) the events occur or become known to the disadvantaged party after the conclusion (ie formation) of the contract;

(b) the events could not reasonably have been taken into account by the disadvantaged party at the time of the formation of the contract;

(c) the events are beyond the control of the disadvantaged party; and

(d) the risk of the events was not assumed by the disadvantaged party.

What amounts to a fundamental alteration of the contractual equilibrium is not defined in the black letter rules.

Comment number 2 to Article 6.2.2 initially states: 'Whether an alteration is 'fundamental' in a given case will of course depend upon the circumstances.' Fortunately, Comment number 2 goes on to state that: 'If, however, the performances are capable of precise measurement in monetary terms, an alteration amounting to 50% or more of the cost or the value of the performance is likely to amount to a "fundamental" alteration.'

---

109 See Article 1.3 which reflects the maxim *'pacta sunt servanda'*.

110 See Bonell, *op cit* at 65–79.

111 See Article 6.2.1–6.2.3.

112 See Article 7.1.7 and compare Article 79 of the CISG.

113 See Garro, *op cit* at 1183–184.

114 See Article 6.2.2.

It is further indicated in the Comment that the cost of a party's performance may increase because of a dramatic rise in the price of raw materials or as a result of the introduction of new safety regulations necessitating more expensive production procedures. The value of the performance received by a party may diminish where the market conditions have drastically changed.[115]

Article 6.2.3 provides that, in the case of hardship, the disadvantaged party is entitled to request renegotiation provided the request is made without undue delay and the hardship grounds are indicated. Where renegotiation is unsuccessful, a court or an arbitral tribunal[116] may, if reasonable, terminate the contract at a date and on terms to be fixed or adapt the contract with a view to restoring the equilibrium. As shortly explained, a renegotiation clause combined with a hardship clause should be included in international trade agreements.[117]

The ability to adapt the contract is discretionary and the courts in a given forum may refuse to modify the contract. For example, English and Belgium courts are more likely to refuse adaptation than other legal systems such as Japanese, German and Dutch forums.[118] Arbitrators may be less reluctant than judges to modify a contract whereby it would be wise to have an arbitration clause in any agreement so as to ensure a dispute goes to arbitration.[119] However, arbitrators are nevertheless inclined not to intervene in hardship situations where parties have not specifically included a hardship clause in their contract. This is especially the case where a contract is speculative and the risk of a change in circumstances is higher.[120] The last condition in the definition of hardship, namely that the risk of events must not have been assumed by the disadvantaged party, may be more easy satisfied if a hardship clause specifies what risks are or are not assumed by the parties.

Force majeure

Under the *force majeure* provision,[121] a party's non-performance is excused if the party 'proves that the non-performance was due to an impediment beyond its control and that it could not reasonably be expected to have taken the impediment into account at the time of the conclusion of the contract or to have avoided or overcome it or its consequences'.

The requisite 'impediment' may be temporary[122] and the party seeking invocation of the provision must give notice to the other party of the impediment and the effect on its ability to perform within a reasonable time, otherwise damages liability may arise

---

115 See Article 6.2.2, Comment 2.

116 See Article 1.10 definition of 'court' which includes an arbitral tribunal.

117 See Bonell, *op cit*, p 75, fn 120 and Perillo, *op cit* at 301.

118 See van Houtte, *op cit* at 17–18.

119 See van Houtte, *op cit* at 18.

120 See van Houtte, *op cit* at 16.

121 See Article 7.1.7 and compare Article 79 of the CISG.

122 See Article 7.1.7(2) and van Houtte, *op cit* at 18, as to temporary *vis à vis* definite impossibility.

from non-receipt. Nothing in Article 7.1.7, however, prevents a party from exercising a right to terminate the contract or to withhold performance or request interest on money due.[123]

The *force majeure* provision is reminiscent of the common law doctrine of frustration which, broadly speaking, enables termination when there has been a fundamental or radical change in the surrounding circumstances and in the significance of contractual obligations.[124] However, the Principles are not to be interpreted in accordance with the common law or, for that matter, other notions of law.[125] The *force majeure* provision is in fact much more limited than the common law, whereby parties should include a *force majeure* clause in their contract such as the '*force majeure* (exemption) clause' prepared by the International Chamber of Commerce[126] which contains a list of specific events which normally qualify as grounds for relief.[127] A party who cannot satisfy the *force majeure* provision may nevertheless be able to satisfy the less demanding hardship provisions. In this regard, the Principles again outshine the CISG because the CISG does not address hardship.[128]

NON-PERFORMANCE

Non-performance is defined as a failure to perform any of a party's obligations under a contract, including defective performance or late performance.[129] As with the CISG, the Principles strive to preserve a contract wherever possible. Thus, a non-performing party is given an opportunity to cure non-performance[130] and additional time for performance may be granted by an aggrieved party,[131] albeit an aggrieved party in either situation may still claim damages.[132] All other remedies, however, including right of termination are suspended during the operation period of these provisions.[133]

---

123 See Article 7.1.7(4). The provision is clearer than Article 79(5) of the CISG. See Bonell *op cit*, p 112, fn 21.

124 See *Codelfa Construction Pty Ltd v State Rail Authority of NSW* (1992) 41 ALR 367.

125 See Article 1.6.

126 See publication no 421.

127 See Bonell, *op cit*, p 119.

128 By way of illustration, assume that the Suez Canal is closed again and the closure is a post-contract event not reasonably contemplated nor a risk assumed by a carrier. The carrier takes a deviation around the Cape of Good Hope which not only results in late performance (which by Article 7.1.1 is 'non-performance') but also causes the costs of performance to increase in excess of 50% of the initial cost of performance. The *force majeure* provision would not temporarily excuse the carrier because an increase in cost or price appears to be insufficient to constitute *force majeure*. The hardship provisions would, however, arguably apply as *prima facie* the equilibrium of the contract has been fundamentally altered due to the substantial increase in costs of performance.

129 See Article 7.1.1.

130 See Article 7.1.4 which is similar to Article 37 and 48 of the CISG.

131 See Article 7.1.5 and compare Article 47 of the CISG, which also embodies the German *Nachfrist* concept of setting a deadline for performance by notice.

132 See Articles 7.1.4(5) and 7.1.5(2) respectively.

133 See Article 7.1.4(2) and (3) and also Article 7.1.5(2) respectively.

Section 1 of Chapter 7, also addresses non-performance due to interference by a third party[134] and the withholding of performance where performance is simultaneous or consecutive.[135] The Principles prohibit the invocation of exemption clauses by a party who seeks to limit or exclude liability for non-performance or sanction a substantially different performance,[136] where to do so would be grossly unfair having regard to the purpose of the contract.[137] This latter provision reflects the underlying principle of good faith and fair dealing which is common to most of the articles in the Principles.

REMEDIES

The Principles, generally speaking, provide remedies found in most legal systems and in the CISG where a breach of contract (referred to as non-performance) occurs and is not excused by the Principles. The remedial provisions are addressed in the last three sections of Chapter 7.

Right to performance

Section 2 of Chapter 7 provides for specific performance[138] as a remedy for non-performance of monetary and non-monetary obligations.[139] The right to performance includes, where appropriate, the right to require repair, replacement or other cure of defective performance.[140]

In contrast to the CISG[141] and equitable principles of non-civil law countries, a court has no discretion in decreeing performance. By Article 7.2.4(1), a Court does, however, have a discretion to impose a default penalty for non-compliance with a performance order. Such a penalty, which does not exclude any claim for damages, must be paid to the aggrieved party unless mandatory provisions of the law of the given forum provide otherwise.[142]

The right to performance in relation to non-monetary obligations is not available in the extensive list of circumstances outlined in Article 7.2.2 which range from where performance is impossible in law or in fact to where the aggrieved party has been dilatory in requesting performance. The circumstances would ordinarily be viewed by a court or an arbitrator as making specific performance inappropriate or otherwise unfair in any event.[143]

---

134 See Article 7.1.2 and Perillo, *op cit* at 302.

135 See Article 7.1.3.

136 See Article 7.1.6.

137 For further discussion, see Bonell, *op cit*, p 96–98.

138 Termed a right to performance.

139 See Articles 7.2.1 and 7.2.2 and compare Article 46 of the CISG.

140 See Article 7.2.3.

141 See Article 28 of the CISG.

142 See Article 7.2.4(2).

143 Also Garro, *op cit* at 1186.

Termination and restitution

Section 3 of Chapter 7 addresses termination for actual or anticipated non-performance. Restitution upon termination is also addressed.

The most important prerequisite enabling termination is that the failure to perform an obligation amounts to a 'fundamental' non-performance.[144] Unlike the CISG,[145] Article 7.3.1(2) provides a non-exclusive list of factors to help determine whether a failure amounts to a fundamental non-performance. Factors range from the substantial deprivation of expected entitlement to a consideration of whether the non-performing party will suffer disproportionate loss if the contract is terminated. In this regard, it can be seen that the provision attempts to strike a fair balance in addressing both party's interests.

A party may also terminate for a clear anticipated fundamental non-performance[146] or where the innocent party reasonably believes that there will be a fundamental non-performance and despite demand no adequate assurance of performance is forthcoming within a reasonable period of time.[147]

The right to terminate must be exercised by notice[148] and a party may lose the right to terminate if notification is not given within a reasonable period of time.[149]

Termination releases both parties from their obligations but does not preclude a claim for damages for non-performance or affect any contract condition which addresses settlement of disputes or any other post-termination matter. Accordingly, an arbitration clause would be one such condition that remains unaffected. Lastly, either party may claim restitution upon termination in accordance with Article 7.3.6.[150]

Damages

Any non-performance,[151] regardless of fault,[152] entitles the aggrieved party to damages either exclusively or in conjunction with any other remedy, unless non-performance has been excused under the Principles.[153]

---

144 See Article 7.3.1.

145 See Article 25.

146 See Article 7.3.3.

147 See Article 7.3.4.

148 See Article 7.3.2 and Article 1.9 concerning 'notice'.

149 See Article 7.3.2.

150 As to restitution, see Article 7.3.6, Comment 2 as to restitution in kind and or money where reasonable. Also see Bonell, *op cit*, p 27.

151 Defined in Article 7.1.1 as a failure by a party to perform any of its obligations under the contract, including defective or late performance.

152 Contrast the requirement of fault in civil law systems (see Perillo, *op cit* at 308) though the burden of proving non-performance may depend upon whether the obligation is one of best efforts or an obligation to achieve a specific result (see Article 7.4.1, Comment 1 and Articles 5.4 and 5.5. Also see Garro, *op cit* at 1187).

153 Non-performance may be excused, for example, where an exemption clause not offending Article 7.1.6 exists or where *force majeure* arises under Article 7.1.7. See Garro, *op cit* at 1186.

The aggrieved party is entitled to full compensation for harm sustained as a result of the non-performance[154] provided harm is established with a reasonable degree of certainty.[155] Compensation may be awarded for lost opportunity[156] and, in either case, damages may be assessed in the court's discretion even if damages cannot be established with a sufficient degree of certainty[157] It can be seen, therefore, that whilst the Principles make every effort to ensure a contract is performed, they also ensure that some avenue of assessment of damages is available in the event of non-performance.[158]

The type of harm compensatable includes any loss suffered or deprivation of gain,[159] as well as non-pecuniary harm, for instance, physical suffering or emotional distress.[160] However, the non-performing party is liable only for harm which it foresaw or could reasonably have foreseen at the time of the conclusion (ie formation) of the contract as being likely to result from its non-performance.[161]

Where the aggrieved party has terminated the contract and has made a replacement contract, the aggrieved party may recover the difference in price between the respective contracts[162] as well as damages for future harm. Where termination occurs but no replacement contract is formed, the aggrieved party may recover the difference between the contract price and the price current at the time of termination as well as damages for any further harm.[163]

Damages are to be paid in a lump sum or, where appropriate, in instalments that may be indexed.[164] Furthermore, damages are to be assessed either in the currency in which the monetary obligation was expressed or in the currency in which the harm was suffered, whichever is more appropriate.[165] By Article 7.4.10, interest on damages for non-performance of non-monetary obligations accrues as from the time of the non-performance.

A non-performance by way of a failure to pay money by the due time entitles the aggrieved to interest[166] on that sum whether or not the non-payment is excused together with additional damages if the non-payment caused greater harm.[167]

---

154 See Article 7.4.2(1) which reflects Article 74 of the CISG. Those Articles reflect the common law position, ie the plaintiff is to be put in a position as if the contract had been performed. See *Robinson v Harman* (1848) 1 Ex 850 at 855 *per* Parke B.

155 See Article 7.4.3(1).

156 See Article 7.4.3(2).

157 See Article 7.4.3.

158 Article 7.4.3 may supplement Article 74 of the CISG. See Garro, *op cit* at 1188.

159 See Article 7.4.2(1).

160 See Article 7.4.2(2).

161 See Article 7.4.4 which broadly reflects the common law rule in *Hadley v Baxendale* (1854) 9 Ex 341 at 354.

162 See Article 7.4.5 provided the replacement contract is made within a reasonable time and in a reasonable manner.

163 See Article 7.4.6(1) and Article 7.4.6(2) which define 'current price'.

164 See Article 7.4.10.

165 See Article 7.4.12.

166 See Article 7.4.9(1) and Article 7.4.9(2) as to interest rates. Contrast Article 78 of the CISG.

167 See Article 7.4.9 generally.

Mitigation is addressed in terms familiar to all jurisdictions.[168] Unfamiliar to the common law,[169] however, is a concept of contributive harm on the part of the aggrieved party which is incorporated by Article 7.4.7.[170] According to the contributive harm principle, damages shall be reduced to reflect the extent to which an aggrieved party's act or omission or an event for which the aggrieved party bears the risk has contributed to the overall harm.[171]

Also unique to common law concepts but reflective of the civil law is Article 7.4.13, which upholds penalty clauses and enables a penalty sum to be reduced to a reasonable amount, where it is 'grossly excessive' in comparison to the harm resulting from the non-performance and to other circumstances.[172]

CONCLUSION

The UNIDROIT Principles are a most impressive multinational promulgation of rules for international commercial contracts which have many uses. Because the Principles are not legally binding, they are easily capable of modification in the future to reflect changes in international trade practice. As already noted, Article 1.5 allows parties to exclude or derogate from or vary the Principles except where they are mandatory. For example, the duty of good faith and fair dealing[173] and some aspects of validity[174] cannot be excluded or limited.

In their capacity as a model for national legislators, the Principles have already influenced the drafting of recent national codifications such as the Civil Code of Quebec, the Commercial Code of Mexico and the Dutch Civil Code.[175] Indeed, countries closer to Australian shores such as Indonesia and Vietnam may derive significant use from the Principles in drafting basic contract law particularly given the fact that the Principles are free from any political or particular jurisprudential persuasion.[176] This can only benefit Australian ties with such Asian countries particularly given the growing economic need for trade with Asian countries.

On an international level, the Principles may play a major role in supplementing deficiencies in conventions such as the CISG. In time, they may themselves be embodied in an internationally binding convention or at least be a significant source of reference for drafting international conventions.

Because the Principles have no mandatory force of law, they will ordinarily not be recognised by court forums as the applicable law. Therefore, parties who contractually

---

168 See Article 7.4.8 and compare Article 77 of the CISG.

169 See Perillo, *op cit* at 310.

170 Compare Article 80 of the CISG.

171 See the Illustrations to Article 7.4.7 and Perillo, *op cit* at 310.

172 See Perillo, *op cit* at 313–14.

173 See Article 1.7.

174 See Article 3.19.

175 See Bonell, *op cit* at 107.

176 See the letter of the Commonwealth Attorney General's Department (Australia) to the Secretary-General of UNIDROIT of 19 November 1993, as extracted in Bonell, *op cit*, p 108–09.

incorporate the Principles as the governing law and/or the terms of their contract, should always include an arbitration clause so as to ensure that any dispute goes to arbitration. As previously discussed, Arbitrators are generally not obliged to apply a particular domestic law or convention whereby the UNIDROIT Principles should be applied as the party's choice of law in Arbitration Tribunals.

In the event of gaps in the Principles, it is submitted that a choice of law clause resembling the suggested draft in Comment 4 to Article 1.6 should be included as a matter of prudence.[177] One notable gap in the Principles, which is actually addressed in Chapter IV of the CISG, is the passing of risk in relation to the international sale of goods.

Only time will tell as to whether the Principles will be universally accepted by the international trade community. They are, however, certainly worthy of consideration and are capable of universal application in all facets of their potential uses.

TUTORIAL QUESTIONS

1   Professor Ulrich Magnus has argued that, in his opinion, the Principles are 'to be considered as additional general principles in the context of the CISG. The most important reason for this is that they vastly correspond both to the respective provisions of the CISG as well as to the general principles which have been derived from the CISG' (Magnus, 'General Principles of UN-Sales Law', 3 *International Trade and Business Law Annual* 34 at 54). Do you agree with his statement? Give reasons for your point of view.

2   Why are parties who wish to adopt the Principles well advised to combine their reference to the Principles with an arbitration agreement?

3   Discuss the obligations imposed on each party by Article 1.7 to act in accordance with 'good faith and fair dealing'. Does this obligation apply to pre-contractual negotiations? Compare Article 1.7 with your own civil law or common law system.

4   What are the differences, if any, between 'hardship' and '*force majeure*'?

5   In September 1989, Mr Müller, a dealer in furniture located in the former German Democratic Republic, buys stocks from Mr Volkov, situated in Bulgaria, also a former socialist country. The goods are to be delivered by Mr Volkov in December 1990. In November 1990, Mr Müller informs Mr Volkov that the goods are no longer of any use to him, claiming that after the unification of the German Democratic Republic and the Federal Republic of Germany there is no longer any market for such goods imported from Bulgaria. Is Mr Müller entitled to invoke hardship under the UNIDROIT Principles? (question is based on UNIDROIT, *Principles of International Commercial Contracts*, Rome 1994 at 147).

---

177 One suggested clause in Comment 4 to Article 1.6 is 'the contract is governed by the UNIDROIT Principles supplemented by the law of country x'.

6   Discuss, compare and assess the interrelationship between the United Nations Convention on Contracts for the International Sale of Goods (CISG, 1980) and the UNIDROIT Principles of International Commercial Contracts.

FURTHER READING

Baptista, LO, 'The UNIDROIT Principles for International Commercial Law Project: Aspects of International Private Law' [1995] 69 *Tulane Law Review* 1209.

Bonell, MJ, *An International Restatement of Contract Law – the UNIDROIT Principles of International Commercial Contracts*, 1994, Irvington, New York: Transnational Juris.

Bonell, MJ, 'Unification of Law by Non-Legislative Means: The UNIDROIT Draft Principles for International Commercial Contracts' [1992] 40 *American Journal of Comparative Law* 617.

Ferrari, F, 'Defining the Sphere of Application of the 1994 UNIDROIT Principles of International Commercial Contracts' [1995] 69 *Tulane Law Review* 1225.

Furmston, MP, 'UNIDROIT General Principles for International Commercial Contracts' (1996) 10 *Journal of Contract Law* 11.

Garro, AM, 'The Gap-Filling Role of the UNIDROIT Principles in International Sales Law: Some Comments on the Interplay between the Principles and the CISG' [1995] 69 *Tulane Law Review* 1149.

Honnold, JO, *Uniform Law for International Sales Under the 1980 United Nations Convention*, 2nd edn, 1991, Deventer: Kluwer Law and Taxation Publishers.

Pryles, JM, Waincymer, J and Davies, M, *International Trade Law, Commentary and Materials*, 1996, Sydney: Law Book Company.

van Houtte, H, 'The UNIDROIT Principles of International Commercial Contracts' (1996) *International Trade and Business Law Annual* 1.

Waincymer, J, 'The Internationalisation of Australia's Trade Laws' [1995] 17 *Sydney Law Review* 298.

UNIDROIT PRINCIPLES OF INTERNATIONAL COMMERCIAL CONTRACTS, ROME, 1994[178]

... The objective of the UNIDROIT Principles is to establish a balanced set of rules designed for use throughout the world irrespective of the legal traditions and the economic and political conditions of the countries in which they are to be applied.

... In offering the UNIDROIT Principles to the international legal and business communities, the Governing Council is fully conscious of the fact that the principles, which do not involve the endorsement of governments, are not a binding instrument and that in consequence their acceptance will depend upon their persuasive authority. There are a number of significant ways in which the UNIDROIT Principles may find practical application, the most important of which are amply explained in the Preamble.

Introduction of the Governing Council of UNIDROIT, Rome, 1994

Reproduced from the UNIDROIT Principles of Intentional Commercial Contracts, published by the International Institute for the Unification of Private Law (UNIDROIT), Rome, Italy, Copyright UNIDROIT 1994, by permission of UNIDROIT. Readers are reminded that the official version of the UNIDROIT Principles of International Commercial Contracts also includes the Commentary thereto. The integral edition of the English French German, Italian and Spanish versions may be ordered directly from UNIDROIT Publications, Via Panisperna 28, 00184 Italy (fax +39-6 69 94 13 94). The English version may also be ordered from Transnational Juris Publications, One Bridge Street, Irvington-on-Hudson, NY 10533 (fax: +1 (914) 591-2688).

UNIDROIT PRINCIPLES OF INTERNATIONAL COMMERCIAL CONTRACTS

Preamble – purpose of the principles

These Principles set forth general rules for international commercial contracts.

They shall be applied when the parties have agreed that their contract be governed by them.

They may be applied when the parties have agreed that their contracts be governed by general principles of law, the *lex mercatoria* or the like.

They may provide a solution to an issue raised when it proves impossible to establish the relevant rule of applicable law.

They may be used to interpret or supplement international uniform law instruments.

They may serve as a model for national and international legislators.

---

178 Courtesy of UNIDROIT Principles of International Commercial Contracts, Rome, 1994 UNIDROIT.

CHAPTER 1 – GENERAL PROVISIONS

Article 1.1 – Freedom of contract

The parties are free to enter into a contract and to determine its content.

Article 1.2 – No form required

Nothing in these Principles requires a contract to be concluded in or evidenced by writing. It may be proved by any means, including witnesses.

Article 1.3 – Binding character of contract

A contract validly entered into is binding upon the parties. It can only be modified or terminated in accordance with its terms or by agreement or as otherwise provided in these Principles.

Article 1.4 – Mandatory rules

Nothing in these Principles shall restrict the application of mandatory rules, whether of national, international or supranational origin, which are applicable in accordance with the relevant rules of private international law.

Article 1.5 – Exclusion or modification by the parties

The parties may exclude the application of these Principles or derogate from or vary the effect of any of their provisions, except as otherwise provided in the Principles.

Article 1.6 – Interpretation and supplementation of the Principles

1   In the interpretation of these Principles, regard is to be had to their international character and to their purposes including the need to promote uniformity in their application.

2   Issues within the scope of these Principles but not expressly settled by them are as far as possible to be settled in accordance with their underlying general principles.

Article 1.7 – Good faith and fair dealing

1   Each party must act in accordance with good faith and fair dealing in international trade.

2   The parties may not exclude or limit this duty.

Article 1.8 – Usages and practices

1   The parties are bound by any usage to which they have agreed and by any practices which they have established between themselves.

2   The parties are bound by a usage that is widely known to and regularly observed in international trade by parties in the particular trade concerned except where the application of such usage would be unreasonable.

Article 1.9 – Notice

1   Where notice is required it may be given by any means appropriate to the circumstances.

2   A notice is effective when it reaches the person to whom it is given.

3   For the purpose of para 2, a notice 'reaches' a person when given to that person orally or delivered at that person's place of business or mailing address.

4   For the purpose of this article, 'notice' includes a declaration, demand, request or any other communication of intention.

Article 1.10 – Definitions

In these Principles:

- 'court' includes an arbitral tribunal;

- where a party has more than one place of business the relevant 'place of business' is that which has the closest relationship to the contract and its performance, having regard to the circumstances knows to or contemplated by the parties at any time before or at the conclusion of the contract;

- 'obliger' refers to the party who is to perform an obligation and 'obligee' refers to the party who is entitled to performance of that obligation;

- 'writing' means any mode of communication that preserves a record of the information contained therein and is capable of being reproduced in tangible form.

CHAPTER 2 – FORMATION

Article 2.1 – Manner of formation

A contract may be concluded either by the acceptance of an offer or by conduct of the parties that is sufficient to show agreement.

Article 2.2 – Definition of offer

A proposal for concluding a contract constitutes an offer if it is sufficiently definite and indicates the intention of the offeror to be bound in case of acceptance.

Article 2.3 – Withdrawal of offer

1 An offer becomes effective when it reaches the offeree.

2 An offer, even if it is irrevocable, may be withdrawn if the withdrawal reaches the offeree before or at the same time as the offer.

Article 2.4 – Revocation of offer

1 Until a contract is concluded, an offer may be revoked if the revocation reaches the offeree before it has dispatched an acceptance.

2 However, an offer cannot be revoked:

(a) if it indicates, whether by stating a fixed time for acceptance or otherwise, that it is irrevocable; or

(b) if it was reasonable for the offered to rely on the offer as being irrevocable and the offeree has acted in reliance of the offer.

Article 2.5 – Rejection of offer

An offer is terminated when a rejection reaches the offeror.

Article 2.6 – Mode of acceptance

1 A statement made by or other conduct of the offered assent to an offer is an acceptance. Silence or inactivity does not in itself amount to acceptance.

2 An acceptance of an offer becomes effective when the indication of assent reaches the offeror.

3 However, if, by virtue of the offer or as a result of practices which the parties have established between themselves or of usage, the offeree may indicate assent by performing an act without notice to the offeror, the acceptance is effective when the act is performed.

Article 2.7 – Time of acceptance

An offer must be accepted within the time the offeror has fixed or, if no time is fixed, within a reasonable time having regard to the circumstances, including the rapidity of the means of communication employed by the offeror. An oral offer must be accepted immediately unless the circumstances indicate otherwise.

Article 2.8 – Acceptance within a fixed period of time

1   A period of time for acceptance fixed by the offeror in a telegram or a letter begins to run from the moment the telegram is handed in for dispatch or from the date shown on the letter or, if no such date is shown, from the date shown on the envelope. A period of time for acceptance fixed by the offeror by means of instantaneous communication begins to run from the moment that offer reaches the offeree.

2   Official holidays or non-business days occurring during the period for acceptance are included in calculating the period. However, if a notice of acceptance cannot be delivered at the address of the offeror on the last day of the period because that day falls on an official holiday or a non-business day at the place of business of the offeror, the period is extended until the first business day which follows.

Article 2.9 – Late acceptance. Delay in transmission

1   A late acceptance is nevertheless effective as an acceptance if without undue delay the offeror so informs the offeree or gives notice to that effect.

2   If a letter or other writing containing a late acceptance shows that it has been sent in such circumstances that if its transmission had been normal it would have reached the offeror in due time, the late acceptance is effective as an acceptance unless without undue delay, the offeror informs the offeree that it considers the offer as having lapsed.

Article 2.10 – Withdrawal of acceptance

An acceptance may be withdraws if the withdrawal reaches the offeror before or at the same time as the acceptance would have become effective.

Article 2.11 – Modified acceptance

1   A reply to an offer which purports to be an acceptance but contains additions, limitations or other modifications is a rejection of the offer and constitutes a counter-offer.

2   However, a reply to an offer which purports to be an acceptance but contains additional or different terms which do not materially alter the terms of the offer constitutes an acceptance, unless the offeror without undue delay, objects to the discrepancy. If the offeror does not object, the terms of the contract are the terms of the offer with the modifications contained in the acceptance.

Article 2.12 – Writings in confirmation

If a writing which is sent within a reasonable time after the conclusion of the contract and which purports to be a confirmation of the contract contains additional or different terms, such terms become part of the contract, unless they materially alter the contract or the recipient, without undue delay, objects to the discrepancy.

Article 2.13 – Conclusion of contract dependent on agreement on specific matters or in a specific form

Where in the course of negotiations one of the parties insists that the contract is not concluded until there is agreement on specific matters or in a specific form, no contract is concluded before agreement is reached on those matters or in that form.

Article 2.14 – Contract with terms deliberately left open

1 If the parties intend to conclude a contract, the fact that they intentionally leave a term to be agreed upon in further negotiations or to be determined by a third person does not prevent a contract from coming into existence.

2 The existence of the contract is not affected by the fact that subsequently:

(a) the parties reach no agreement on the terms; or

(b) the third person does not determine the term, provided that there is an alternative means of rendering the term definite that is reasonable in the circumstances, having regard to the intention of the parties.

Article 2.15 – Negotiations in bad faith

1 A party is free to negotiate and is not liable for failure to reach an agreement.

2 However, a party who negotiates or breaks off negotiations in bad faith is liable for the losses caused to the other party.

3 It is bad faith, in particular, for a party to enter into or continue negotiations when intending not to reach an agreement with the other parts.

Article 2.16 – Duty of confidentiality

Where information is given as confidential by one party in the course of negotiations, the other party is under a duty not to disclose that information or to use it improperly for its own purposes, whether or not a contract is subsequently concluded. Where appropriate, the remedy for breach of that duty may include compensation based on the benefit received by the other party.

Article 2.17 – Merger clause

A contract in writing which contains a clause indicating that the writing completely embodies the terms on which the parties have agreed cannot be contradicted or supplemented by evidence of prior statements or agreements. However, such statements or agreements may be used to interpret the writing.

Article 2.18 – Written modification clause

A contract in writing which contains a clause requiring any modification or termination by agreement to be in writing may not be otherwise modified or terminated. However, a party may be precluded by its conduct from asserting such a clause to the extent that the other party has acted in reliance on that conduct.

Article 2.19 – Contracting under standard terms

1 Where one party or both parties use standard terms in concluding a contract, the general rules of formation apply, subject to Articles 2.20–2.22.

2 Standard terms are provisions which are prepared in advance for general and repeated use by one party and which are actually used without negotiation with the other party.

Article 2.20 – Surprising terms

1   No term contained in standard terms which is of such a character that the other party could not reasonably have expected it, is effective unless it has been expressly accepted by that party.

2   In determining whether a term is of such a character, regard is to be had to its content, language and presentation.

Article 2.21 – Conflict between standard terms and non-standard terms

In case of conflict between a standard term which is not a standard term, the latter prevails.

Article 2.22 – Battle of forms

Where both parties use standard terms and reach agreement except on those terms, a contract is concluded on the basis of the agreed terms and of any standard terms which are common in substance unless one party clearly indicates in advance, or later and without undue delay informs the other party that it does not intend to be bound by such a contract.

CHAPTER 3 – VALIDITY

Article 3.1 – Matters not covered

These Principles do not deal with invalidity arising from:

(a) lack of capacity;

(b) lack of authority;

(c) immorality or illegality.

Article 3.2 – Validity of mere agreement

A contract is concluded, modified or terminated by the mere agreement of the parties, without any further requirements.

Article 3.3 – Initial impossibility

1   The mere fact that at the time of the conclusion of the contract the performance of the obligation assumed was impossible does not affect the validity of the contract.

2   The mere fact that at the time of the conclusion of the contract a party was not entitled to dispose of the assets to which the contract relates does not affect the validity of the contract.

Article 3.4 – Definition of mistake

Mistake is an erroneous assumption relating to facts or to law existing when the contract was concluded.

Article 3.5 – Relevant mistake

1   A party may only avoid the contract for mistake if, when the contract was concluded, the mistake was of such importance that a reasonable person in the same situation as the party would not have concluded it at all if the true state of affairs had been known, and:

   (a) the other party made the same mistake, or caused the mistake, or knew or ought to have known of the mistake and it was contrary to reasonable commercial standards of fair dealing to leave the mistaken party in error; or

   (b) the other party had not at the time of avoidance acted in reliance on the contract.

2   However, a party may not avoid the contract if:

    (a) it was grossly negligent in committing the mistake; or

    (b) the mistake relates to a matter in regard to which the risk of mistake was assumed or, having regard to the circumstances, should be borne by the mistaken party.

Article 3.6 – Error in expression or transmission

An error occurring in the expression or transmission of a declaration is considered to be a mistake of the person from whom the declaration emanated.

Article 3.7 – Remedies for non-performance

A party is not entitled to avoid the contract on the ground of mistake if the circumstances on which that party relies afford, or could have afforded, a remedy for non-performance.

Article 3.8 – Fraud

A party may avoid the contract when it has been led to conclude the contract by the other partakes fraudulent representation, including language or practices, or fraudulent non-disclosure of circumstances which, according to reasonable commercial standards of fair dealing, the latter party should have disclosed.

Article 3.9 – Threat

A party may avoid the contract when it has been led to conclude the contract by the other party's unjustified threat which, having regard to the circumstances, is so imminent and serious as to leave the first party no reasonable alternative in particular, a threat is unjustified if the act or omission with which a party has been threatened is wrongful in itself, or is wrong to use it as a means to obtain the conclusion of the contract.

Article 3.10 – Gross disparity

1   A party may avoid the contract or an individual term of it if, at the time of the conclusion of the contract, the contract term unjustifiably gave the other party an excessive advantage. Regard is to be had among other factors, to:

    (a) the fact that the other party has taken unfair advantage of the first part's dependence, economic distress or urgent needs, or of its improvidence, ignorance, inexperience or lack of bargaining skill; and

    (b) the nature and purpose of the contract.

2   Upon the request of the party entitled to avoidance, a court may adapt the contract or term in order to make it accord with reasonable commercial standards of fair dealing.

3   A court may also adapt the contract or term upon the request of the party receiving notice of avoidance, provided that that party informs the other party of its request promptly after receiving such notice and before the other party has acted in reliance on it. The provisions of Article 3.13(2) apply accordingly.

Article 3.11 – Third persons

1   Where fraud, threat, gross disparity or a part's mistake is imputable to, or is known or ought to be known by, a third person for whose acts the other party is responsible, the contract may be avoided under the same conditions as if the behaviour or knowledge had been that of the party itself.

2   Where fraud, threat or gross disparity is imputable to a third person for whose acts the other party is not responsible, the contract may be avoided if that party knew or ought to have known of the fraud, threat or disparity, or has not at the time of avoidance acted in reliance on the contract.

Article 3.12 – Confirmation

If the party entitled to avoid the contract expressly or impliedly confirms the contract after the period of time for giving notice of avoidance has begun to run, avoidance of contract is excluded.

Article 3.13 – Loss of right to avoid

1   If a party is entitled to avoid the contract for mistake but the other party declares itself willing to perform or performs the contract as it was understood by the party entitled to avoidance, the contract is considered to have been concluded as the latter party understood it. The other party must make such a declaration or render such performance promptly after having been informed of the manner in which the party entitled to avoidance had understood the contract and before that party has acted in reliance on a notice of avoidance.

2   After such a declaration or performance, the right to avoidance is lost and any earlier notice of avoidance is ineffective.

Article 3.14 – Notice of avoidance

The right of a party to avoid the contract is exercised by notice to the other party.

Article 3.15 – Time limits

1   Notice of avoidance shall be given within a reasonable time, having regard to the circumstances, after the avoiding party knew or could not have been unaware of the relevant facts or became capable of acting freely.

2   Where an individual term of the contract may be avoided by a party under Article 3.10, the period of time for giving notice of avoidance begins to run when that term is asserted by the other party.

Article 3.16 – Partial avoidance

Where a ground of avoidance affects only individual terms of the contract, the effect of avoidance is limited to those terms unless, having regard to the circumstances, it is unreasonable to uphold the remaining contract.

Article 3.17 – Retroactive effect of avoidance

1   Avoidance takes effect retroactively.

2   On avoidance either party may claim restitution of whatever is supplied under the contract or the part of it avoided, provided that it concurrently makes restitution of whatever it has received under the contract or the part of it avoided or, if it cannot make restitution in kind, it makes an allowance for what it has received.

Article 3.18 – Damages

Irrespective of whether or not the contract has been avoided, the party who knew or ought to have known of the ground for avoidance is liable for damages so as to put the other party in the same position in which it would have been if it had not concluded the contract.

Article 3.19 – Mandatory character of the provision

The provisions of this chapter are mandatory, except in so far as they relate to the binding force of mere agreement, initial impossibility or mistake.

Article 3.20 – Unilateral declarations

The provisions of this chapter apply with appropriate adaptations to any communication of intention addressed by one party to the other.

CHAPTER 4 – INTERPRETATION

Article 4.1 – Intention of the parties

1   A contract shall be interpreted according to the common intention of the parties.

2   If such an intention cannot be established, the contract shall be interpreted according to the meaning that reasonable persons of the same kind as the parties would give to it in the same circumstances.

Article 4.2 – Interpretation of statements and other conduct

1   The statements and other conduct of a party shall be interpreted according to that part's intention if the other party knew or could not have been unaware of that intention.

2   If the preceding paragraph is not applicable, such statements and other conduct shall be interpreted according to the meaning that a reasonable person of the same kind as the other party would give to it in the same circumstances.

Article 4.3 – Relevant circumstances

In applying Articles 4.1 and 4.2, regard shall be had to all the circumstances, including:

(a)   preliminary negotiations between the parties;

(b)   practices which the parties have established between themselves;

(c)   the conduct of the parties subsequent to the conclusion of the contract;

(d)   the nature and purpose of the contract;

(e)   the meaning commonly given to terms and expressions in the trade concerned;

(f)   usages.

Article 4.4 – Reference to contract or statement as a whole

Terms and expressions shall be interpreted in the light of the whole contract or statement in which they appear.

Article 4.5 – All terms to be given effect

Contract terms shall be interpreted so as to give effect to all the terms rather than to deprive some of them of effect.

Article 4.6 – Contra proferentem *rule*

If contract terms supplied by one party are unclear, an interpretation against that party is preferred.

Article 4.7 – Linguistic discrepancies

Where a contract is drawn up in two or more language versions which are equally authoritative there is, in case of discrepancy between the versions, a preference for the interpretation according to a version in which the contract was originally drawn up.

Article 4.8 – Supplying an omitted term

1   Where the parties to a contract have not agreed with respect to a term which is important for a determination of their rights and duties, a term which is appropriate in the circumstances shall be supplied.

2   In determining what is an appropriate term regard shall be had, among other factors, to:

(a)   the intention of the parties;

(b)   the nature and purpose of the contract;

(c)   good faith and fair dealing;

(d)   reasonableness.

CHAPTER 5 – CONTENT

Article 5.1 – Express and implied obligations

The contractual obligations of the parties may be express or implied.

Article 5.2 – Implied obligations

Implied obligations stem from:

(a)   the nature and purpose of the contract;

(b)   practices established between the parties and usages;

(c)   good faith and fair dealing;

(d)   reasonableness.

Article 5.3 – Cooperation between the parties

Each party shall cooperate with the other party when such co-operation may reasonably be expected for the performance of that party's obligations.

Article 5.4 – Duty to achieve a specific result. Duty of best efforts

1   To the extent that an obligation of a party involves a duty to achieve a specific result, that party is bound to achieve that result.

2   To the extent that an obligation of a party involves a duty of best efforts in the performance of an activity, that party is bound to make such efforts as would be made by a reasonable person of the same kind in the same circumstances.

Article 5.5 – Determination of kind of duty involved

In determining the extent to which an obligation of a party involves a duty of best efforts in the performance of an activity or duty to achieve a specific result, regard shall be had, among other factors, to:

(a)   the way in which the obligation is expressed in the contract;

(b)   the contractual price and other terms of the contract;

(c)   the degree of risk normally involved in achieving the expected result;

(d)   the ability of the other party to influence the performance of the obligation.

Article 5.6 – Determination of quality of performance

Where the quality of performance is neither fixed by, nor determinable from, the contract a party is bound to render a performance of a quality that is reasonable and not less than average in the circumstances.

Article 5.7 – Price determination

1 Where a contract does not fix or make provision for determining the price, the parties are considered, in the absence of any indication to the contrary, to have made reference to the price generally charged at the time of the conclusion of the contract for such performance in comparable circumstances in the trade concerned or, if no such price is available, to a reasonable price.

2 Where the price is to be determined by one party and that determination is manifestly unreasonable, a reasonable price shall be substituted notwithstanding any contract term to the contrary.

3 Where the price is to be fixed by a third person, and that person cannot or will not do so, the price shall be a reasonable price.

4 Where the price is to be fixed by reference to factors which do not exist or have ceased to exist or to be accessible, the nearest equivalent factor shall be treated as a substitute.

Article 5.8 – Contract for an indefinite period

A contract for an indefinite period may be ended by either party by giving notice a reasonable time in advance.

CHAPTER 6 – PERFORMANCE

Section 1 – Performance in general

Article 6.1.1 – Time of performance

A party must perform its obligations:

(a) if a time is fixed by or determinable from the contract, at that time;

(b) if a period of time is fixed by or determinable from the contract, at any time within that period unless circumstances indicate that the other party is to choose a time;

(c) in any other case, within a reasonable time after the conclusion of the contract.

Article 6.1.2 – Performance at one time or in instalments

In cases under Article 6.1(b) or (c), a party must perform its obligations at one time if that performance can be rendered at one time ad the circumstances do not indicate otherwise.

Article 6.1.3 – Partial performance

1 The obligee may reject an offer to perform in part at the time performance is due, whether or not such offer is coupled with an assurance as to the balance of the performance, unless the obligee has no legitimate interest in so doing.

2 Additional expenses caused to the obligor by partial performance are to be borne by the obligor without prejudice to any other remedy.

Article 6.1.4 – Order of performance

1 To the extent that the performances of the parties can be rendered simultaneously, the parties are bound to render them simultaneously unless the circumstances indicate otherwise.

2 To the extent that the performance of only one party requires a period of time, that party is bound to render its performance first, unless the circumstances indicate otherwise.

Article 6.1.5 – Earlier performance

1   The obligee may reject an earlier performance unless it has no legitimate interest in so doing.

2   Acceptability by a party of an earlier performance does not affect the time for the performance of its own obligations if that time has been fixed irrespective of the performance of the other Party's obligations.

3   Additional expenses caused to the obligee by earlier performance are to be borne by the obligor, without prejudice to any other remedy.

Article 6.1.6 – Place of performance

1   If the place of performance is neither fixed by, nor determinable from the contract, a party is to perform:

(a)   a monetary obligation, at the obligates place of business;

(b)   any other obligation, at its own place of business.

2   A party must bear any increase in the expenses incidental to performance which is caused by a change in its place of business subsequent to the conclusion of the contract.

Article 6.1.7 – Payment by cheque or other instrument

1   Payment may be made in any form used in the ordinary course of business at the place for payment.

2   However, an obligee who accepts, either by virtue of para 1 or voluntarily, a cheque, any other order to pay or a promise to pay, is presumed to do so only on condition that it will be honoured.

Article 6.1.8 – Payment by funds transfer

1   Unless the obligee has indicated a particular account, payment may be made by a transfer to any of the financial institutions in which the obligee has made it known that it has an account.

2   In case of payment by a transfer the obligation of the obligor is discharged when the transfer to the obligee's financial institution becomes effective.

Article 6.1.9 – Currency of payment

1   If a monetary obligation is expressed in a currency other than that of the place of payment, it may be paid by the obligor in the currency of the place for payment unless:

(a)   the currency is freely convertible; or

(b)   the parties have agreed that payment should be made only in the currency in which the monetary obligation is expressed.

2   If it is impossible for the obligor to make payment in the currency in which the monetary obligation is expressed, the obligee may require payment in the currency of the place for payment, even in the case referred to in para 1(b).

3   Payment in the currency of the place for payment is to be made according to the applicable rate of exchange prevailing there when payment is due.

4   However, if the obligor has not paid at the time when payment is due, the obligee may require payment according to the applicable rate of exchange prevailing either when payment is due or at the time of actual payment.

Article 6.1.10 – Currency not expressed

Where a monetary obligation is not expressed in a particular currency, payment must be made in the currency of the place where payment is to be made.

Article 6.1.11 – Costs of performance

Each party shall bear the costs of performance of its obligations.

Article 6.1.12 – Imputation of payments

1   An obligor owing several monetary obligations to the same obligee may specify at the time of payment the debt to which it intends the payment to be applied. However, the payment discharges first any expenses, then interest due and finally the principal.

2   If the obligor makes no such specification, the obligee may, within a reasonable time after payment, declare to the obligor the obligation to which it imputes the payment, provided that the obligation is due and undisputed.

3   In the absence of imputation under paras 1 or 2, payment is imputed to that obligation which satisfies one of the following criteria and in the order indicated:

  (a) an obligation which is due or which is the first to fall due;

  (b) the obligation for which the obligee has least security;

  (c) the obligation which is the most burdensome for the obligor;

  (d) the obligation which has arisen first.

If none of the preceding criteria applies, payment is imputed to all the obligations proportionally.

Article 6.1.13 – Imputation of non-monetary obligations

Article 6.1.12 applies with appropriate adaptations to the imputation of performance of non-monetary obligations.

Article 6.1.14 – Application for public permission

Where the law of a State requires a public permission affecting the validity of the contract or its performance and neither that law nor the circumstances indicate otherwise:

(a) if only one partly has its place of business in that State, that party shall take the measures necessary to obtain the permission;

(b) in any other case the party whose performance requires permission shall take the necessary measures.

Article 6.1.15 – Procedure in applying for permission

1   The party required to take the measures necessary to obtain the permission shall do so without undue delay and shall bear any expenses incurred.

2   That party shall whenever appropriate give the other party notice of the grant or refusal of such permission without undue delay.

Article 6.1.16 – Permission neither granted nor refused

1   If, notwithstanding the fact that the party responsible has taken all measures required, permission is neither granted nor refused within an agreed period or, where no period has been agreed, within a reasonable time from the conclusion of the contract, either party is entitled to terminate the contract.

2   Where the permission affects some terms only, para 1 does not apply if, having regard to the circumstances, it is reasonable to uphold the remaining contract even if the permission is refused.

Article 6.1.17 – Permission refused

1   The refusal of a permission affecting the validity of the contract renders the contract void. If the refusal affects the validity of some terms only, only such terms are void if, having regard to the circumstances, it is reasonable to uphold the remaining contract.

2   Where the refusal of a permission renders the performance of the contract impossible in whole or in part, the rules on non-performance apply.

Section 2 – Hardship

Article 6.2.1 – Contract to be observed

Where the performance of a contract becomes more onerous for one of the parties, that party is nevertheless bound to perform its obligations subject to the following provisions on hardship.

Article 6.2.2 – Definition of hardship

There is hardship where the occurrence of events fundamentally alters the equilibrium of the contract either because the cost of a party's performance has increased or because the value of the performance a party receives has diminished, and:

(a)   the events occur or become known to the disadvantaged party after the conclusion of the contract;

(b)   the events could not reasonably have been taken into account by the disadvantaged party at the time of the conclusion of the contract;

(c)   the events are beyond the control of the disadvantaged party; and

(d)   the risk of the events was not assumed by the disadvantaged party.

Article 6.2.3 – Effects of hardship

1   In case of hardship the disadvantaged party is entitled to request renegotiations. The request shall be made without undue delay and shall indicate the grounds on which it is based.

2   The request for renegotiation does not itself entitle the disadvantaged party to withhold performance.

3   Upon failure to reach agreement within a reasonable time either party may resort to the court.

4   If the court finds hardship it may, if reasonable:

(a)   terminate the contract at a date and on terms to be fixed; or

(b)   adapt the contract with a view to restoring its equilibrium.

CHAPTER 7 – NON-PERFORMANCE

Section 1 – Non-performance in general

Article 7.1.1 – Non-performance defined

Non-performance is failure by a party to perform any of its obligations under the contract, including defective performance or late performance.

Article 7.1.2 – Interference by the other party

A party may not rely on the non-performance of the other party to the extent that such non-performance was caused by the first party's act or omission or by another event as to which the first party bears the risk.

Article 7.1.3 – Withholding performance

1   Where the parties are to perform simultaneously, either party may withhold performance until the other party tenders performance.

2   Where the parties are to perform consecutively, the party that is to perform later may withhold its performance until the first party has performed.

Article 7.1.4 – Cure by non-performing party

1   The non-performing party may, at its own expense, cure any non-performance, provided that:

   (a)   without undue delay, it gives notice indicating the proposed manner and timing of the cure;

   (b)   cure is appropriate in the circumstances;

   (c)   the aggrieved party has no legitimate interest in refusing cure; and

   (d)   cure is effected promptly.

2   The right to cure is not precluded by notice of termination.

3   Upon effective notice of cure, rights of the aggrieved party that are inconsistent with the non-performing Party's performances are suspended until the time for cure has expired.

4   The aggrieved party may withhold performance pending cure.

5   Notwithstanding cure, the aggrieved party retains the right to claim damages for delay as well as for any harm caused or not prevented by the cure.

Article 7.1.5 – Additional period for performance

1   In a case of non-performance, the aggrieved party may by notice to the other party allow an additional period of time for performance.

2   During the additional period, the aggrieved party may withhold performance of its oval reciprocal obligations and may claim damages but may not resort to any other remedy. If it receives notice from the other party that the latter will not perform within that period, or if upon expiry of that period due performance has not been made, the aggrieved party may resort to any of the remedies that may be available under this chapter.

3   Where in a case of delay in performance which is not fundamental the aggrieved parts has given notice allowing an additional period of time of reasonable length, it may terminate the contract at the end of that period. If the additional period allowed is not of reasonable length, it shall be extended to a reasonable length. The aggrieved party may in its notice provide that if the other party fails to perform within the period allowed by the notice the contract shall automatically terminate.

4   Paragraph 3 does not apply where the obligation which has not been performed is only a minor part of the contractual obligation of the non-performing party.

Article 7.1.6 – Exemption clauses

A clause which limits or excludes one party's liability for non-performance or which permits one party to tender performance substantially different from what the other party reasonably expected may not be invoked if it would be grossly unfair to do so, having regard to the purpose of the contract.

Article 7.1.7 – Force majeure

1   Non-performance by a party is excused if that party proves that the non-performance was due to an impediment beyond its control and that it could not reasonably be expected to have taken the impediment into account at the time of the conclusion of the contract or to have avoided or overcome it or its consequences.

2   When the impediment is only temporary, the excuse shall have effect for such period as is reasonable having regard to the effect of the impediment on performance of the contract.

3   The party who fails to perform must give notice to the other party of the impediment and its effect on its ability to perform. If the notice is not received by the other party within a reasonable time after the party who fails to perform knew or ought to have known of the impediment, it is liable for damages resulting from such non-receipt.

4   Nothing in this article prevents a party from exercising a right to terminate the contract or to withhold performance or request interest on money due.

Section 2 – Right to performance

Article 7.2.1 – Performance of monetary obligation

Where a party who is obliged to pay money does not do so, the other may require payment.

Article 7.2.2 – Performance of non-monetary obligation

Where a party who owes an obligation other than one to pay money does not perform, the other party may require performance, unless:

(a)   performance is impossible in law or fact;

(b)   performance or, where relevant, enforcement is unreasonably burdensome or expensive;

(c)   the parts entitled to performance may reasonably obtain performance from another source;

(d)   performance is of an exclusively personal character; or

(e)   the party entitled to performance does not require performance within a reasonable time after it has, or ought to have, become aware of the non-performance.

Article 7.2.3 – Repair and replacement of defective performance

The right to performance includes in appropriate cases the right to require repair, replacement, or other cure of defective performance. The provisions of Articles 7.2.1 and 7.2.2 apply accordingly.

Article 7.2.4 – Judicial penalty

1   Where the court orders a party to perform, it may also direct that this party pay a penalty if it does not comply with the order.

2   The penalty shall be paid to the aggrieved party unless mandatory provisions of the law of the forum provide otherwise. Payment of the penalty to the aggrieved party does not exclude any claim for damages.

Article 7.2.5 – Change of remedy

1   An aggrieved party who has required performance of a non-monetary obligation and who has not received performance within a period fixed or otherwise within a reasonable period of time may invoke any other remedy.

2   Where the decision of a court for performance of a non-monetary obligation cannot be enforced, the aggrieved party may invoke any other remedy.

Section 3 – Termination

Article 7.3.1 – Right to terminate the contract

1   A Party may terminate the contract where the failure of the other party to perform an obligation under the contract amounts to a fundamental performance.

2   In determining whether a failure to perform an obligation amounts to a fundamental non-performance, regard shall be had, in particular, to whether:

(a)   the non-performance substantially deprives the aggrieved party of what it was entitled to expect under the contract unless the other party did not foresee and could not reasonably have foreseen such result;

(b)   strict compliance with the obligation which has not been performed is of essence under the contract;

(c)   the non-performance is intentional or reckless;

(d)   the non-performance gives the aggrieved party reason to believe that it cannot rely on the other party's future performance;

(e)   the non-performing party will suffer disproportionate loss as a result of the preparation or performance if the contract is terminated.

3   In the case of delay, the aggrieved party may also terminate the contract if the other party fails to perform before the time allowed under Article 7.1.5 has expired.

Article 7.3.2 – Notice of termination

1   The right of a party to terminate the contract is exercised by notice to the other party.

2   If performance has been offered late or otherwise does not conform to the contract the aggrieved party will lose its right to terminate the contract unless it gives notice to the other party within a reasonable time after it has or ought to have become aware of the non-conforming performance.

Article 7.3.3 – Anticipatory non-performance

Where prior to the date for performance by one of the parties it is clear that there will be a fundamental non-performance by that party, the other party may terminate the contract.

Article 7.3.4 – Adequate assurance of due performance

A party who reasonably believes that there will be a fundamental non-performance by the other party may demand adequate assurance of due performance and may meanwhile withhold its own performance. Where this assurance is not provided within a reasonable time the party demanding it may terminate the contract.

Article 7.3.5 – Effects of termination in general

1　Termination of the contract releases both parties from their obligation to effect and to receive future performance.

2　Termination does not preclude a claim for damages for non-performance.

3　Termination does not affect any provision in the contract for the settlement of disputes or any other term of the contract which is to operate even after termination.

Article 7.3.6 – Restitution

1　On termination of contract either party may claim restitution of whatever it has supplied, provided that such party concurrently makes restitution of whatever it has received. If restitution in kind is not possible or appropriate allowance should be made in money whenever reasonable.

2　However, if performance of the contract has extended over a period of time and the contract is divisible, such restitution can only be claimed for the period after termination has taken effect.

Section 4 – Damages

Article 7.4.1 – Right to damages

Any non-performance gives the aggrieved party a right to damages either exclusively or in conjunction with any other remedies except where the non-performance is excused under these Principles.

Article 7.4.2 – Full compensation

1　The aggrieved party is entitled to full compensation for harm sustained as a result of the non-performance. Such harm includes both any loss which it suffered and any gain of which it was deprived, taking into account any gain to the aggrieved party resulting from its avoidance of cost or harm.

2　Such harm may be non-pecuniary and includes, for instance, physical suffering or emotional distress.

Article 7.4.3 – Certainty of harm

1　Compensation is due only for harm, including future harm, that is established with a reasonable degree of certainty.

2　Compensation may be due for the loss of a chance in proportion to the stability of its occurrence.

3　Where the amount of damages cannot be established with a sufficient degree of certainty, the assessment is at the discretion of the court.

Article 7.4.4 – Foreseeability of harm

The non-performing party is liable only for harm which it foresaw or could reasonably have foreseen at the time of the conclusion of the contract as being likely to result from its non-performance.

Article 7.4.5 – Proof of harm in case of replacement transaction

Where the aggrieved party has terminated the contract and has made a replacement transaction within a reasonable time and in a reasonable manner, it may recover the difference between the contract price and the price of the replacement transaction as well as damages for any further harm.

Article 7.4.6 – Proof of harm by current price

1   Where the aggrieved party has terminated the contract and has not made a replacement transaction but there is a current price for the performance contracted for, it may recover the difference between the contract price and the price current at the time the contract is terminated as well as damages for any further harm.

2   Current price is the price generally charged for goods delivered or services rendered in comparable circumstances at the place where the contract should have been performed or, if there is no current price at that place, the current price at such other place that appears reasonable to take as a reference.

Article 7.4.7 – Harm due in part to aggrieved party

Where the harm is due in part to an act or omission of the aggrieved party or to another event as to which that party bears the risk, the amount of damages shall be reduced to the extent that these factors have contributed to the harm, having regard to the conduct of the parties.

Article 7.4.8 – Mitigation of harm

1   The non-performing party is not liable for harm suffered by the aggrieved party to the extent that the harm could have been reduced by the latter party's taking reasonable steps.

2   The aggrieved party is entitled to recover any expenses reasonably incurred in attempting to reduce the harm.

Article 7.4.9 – Interest for failure to pay money

1   If a party does not pay a sum of money when it falls due, the aggrieved party is entitled to interest upon that sum from the time when payment is due to the time of payment whether or not the non-payment is excused.

2   The rate of interest shall be the average bank short term lending rate to prime borrowers prevailing for the currency of payment at the place for payment, or where no such rate exists at that place, then the same rate in the State of the currency of payment. In the absence of such a rate at either place the rate of interest shall be the appropriate rate fixed by the law of the State of the currency of payment.

3   The aggrieved party is entitled to additional damages if the non-payment caused it a greater harm.

Article 7.4.10 – Interest on damages

Unless otherwise agreed, interest on damages for non-performance of non-monetary obligations accrues as from the time of non-performance.

Article 7.4.11 – Manner of monetary redress

1   Damages are to be paid in a lump sum. However, they may be payable in instalments where the nature of the harm makes this appropriate.

2   Damages to be paid in instalments may be indexed.

Article 7.4.12 – Currency in which to access damages

Damages are to be assessed either in the currency in which the monetary obligation was expressed or in the currency in which the haven was suffered, whichever is more appropriate.

Article 7.4.13 – Agreed payment for non-performance

1   Where the contract provides that a party who does not perform is to pay a specified sum to the aggrieved party for such non-performance, the aggrieved party is entitled to that sum irrespective of its actual harm.

2   However, notwithstanding any agreement to the contrary, the specified sum may be reduced to a reasonable amount where it is grossly excessive in relation to the harm resulting from the non-performance and to the other circumstances.

CHAPTER 3

INTERNATIONAL COMMERCIAL TRADE TERMS
– INCOTERMS 1990

OVERVIEW

The law in many jurisdictions recognises standardised usages in contracts for the sale of goods in international dealings: 'CIF' and 'FOB' are among the best known of these usages. The usages, and the distinctive types of sale transaction they represent, were in a number of cases evolved by the practices of merchants, following which they were adopted and formalised in various municipal legal systems such as in case law (in the common law jurisdictions) or in legislation (eg the US Uniform Commercial Code). These usages represent a shorthand way of incorporating, in a sales contract, a precise regime covering aspects of contractual obligations and performance. They focus particularly on the delivery of the goods, and collateral matters such as the issues of when risk passes, which party is responsible for the carriage and its costs, which party is responsible for insuring the goods and the costs of this, etc. They do not provide a general contracts law regime – this must still be sought for in the applicable law of contract.

The International Chamber of Commerce (based in Paris) has, since 1936, formulated and published its so-called Incoterms – an abbreviation of 'international commercial terms' – and which are known officially as the 'International Rules for the Interpretation of Trade Terms'. The rules are periodically revised; changes were made in 1953, 1967, 1976, 1980 and 1990. The current Incoterms are the 1990 terms, and are referred to by the shorthand usage of 'Incoterms 1990'. The Incoterms were devised in recognition of the fact that the so-called standard trade usages of CIF, FOB, etc were not altogether uniform, with their meaning varying from one municipal legal system to the next, in matters of detail and, in some cases, at a more fundamental level. If the parties to the sales contract incorporate a particular Incoterm in their contract, the Incoterm Code – which contains a detailed statement of what each trade usage means – can be referred to for a detailed interpretation of the rights and obligations created as between these parties, by their use of the given term. Thereby, uncertainty as to the precise incidents of a given term is more readily avoided. In default of this, the meaning to be attributed to a given trade term would depend upon the interpretation given to it (if one is given at all) by the applicable municipal law. The use of Incoterms (as does the use of other standard trade usages outside the Incoterm regime) also makes the process of drafting a contract more straightforward, the shorthand usage functioning as it does to incorporate a more detailed code of rights and obligations as between the parties.

The Incoterms are intended to reflect current international practice in respect of the matters covered by them, hence the periodical revision of the Incoterms. Practice evolves over time because of the impact of various factors, such as the use of containers in shipping cargo, the growing use of air carriers in moving goods, and the growing use of electronic data interchange (EDI) between parties with respect to the contract and its performance.

In this chapter, the Incoterms 1990 will be reviewed. First, some preliminary matters will be noted.

SOME PRELIMINARY MATTERS

Incoterms – their functions

As reflected above, the Incoterms identify standard trade usages (which in turn reflect standardised trade practices or customs) and provide a detailed statement of what each term requires the parties to do. According to the Introduction to the Incoterms 1990:

> The purpose of 'Incoterms' is to provide a set of international rules for the interpretation of the most common trade terms in foreign trade. Thus, the uncertainties of different interpretations of such terms in different countries can be avoided or at least reduced to a considerable degree.[1]

As mentioned, the Incoterms, like other standard trade terms, facilitate contracting by giving the parties the option of incorporating detailed regimes of rights and obligations, by the simple use of a shorthand expression.

The Incoterms are limited in their scope, dealing as they do with nominated aspects of the delivery of goods pursuant to the international sales contract, and collateral matters – a compass expressed as being concerned with the 'carriage of goods from seller to buyer', 'export and import clearance' and 'the division of costs and risks between the parties'.[2]

Many matters are not dealt with by the Incoterms; they do not provide a general regime for the regulation of the contract. They do not, for example, regulate the passing of property in the goods, nor do they specify the consequences of a breach of contract. The rules dealing with these broader matters must be sought for in the other terms of the contract, and the law of the contract (ie the applicable municipal law, which will in the normal case be the law agreed upon by the parties).[3] Further, the Incoterms have no bearing upon the interpretation of any contract of carriage which may be entered into by a party to the sales contract.[4]

When the parties adopt as the law of their contract (directly or indirectly) the Vienna Convention on Contracts for the International Sale of Goods, and use an

---

1   International Chamber of Commerce, *Incoterms 1990*, 1990, p 6, Paris: ICC Publishing SA, (known hereafter as ICC – *Incoterms 1990*). Fundamentally, the Incoterms regime provides rules of interpretation for selected trade usages.

2   Ramberg, J, *Guide to Incoterms 1990*, 1991, p 8, Paris: ICC Publishing SA. This document is the leading commentary on the Incoterms 1990.

3   The parties may also agree directly that the Vienna Sales Convention (see Ch 1) should, within its compass, govern their contract; or this may come to be applied indirectly where they agree that the law of a State which has adopted the convention should be the applicable law.

4   See ICC – *Incoterms 1990*, p 18, noting that the Incoterms (self-evidently, in referring to the buyer and seller) relate only to terms used in contracts of sale, and thus do not deal with terms used in contracts of carriage, including charterparties.

appropriate Incoterm, they achieve a relatively greater degree of certainty as to the regime of rules, contractual and ex-contractual, which govern the performance of their transaction. Both the Convention and the Incoterms represent standardised, internationally well-recognised codes.

Legal status of the Incoterms

The Incoterms do not possess the status of law. Unlike the Vienna Convention on Contracts for the International Sale of Goods, they have not been assimilated into the municipal law of any State. Such a process of adoption would be potentially counterproductive. The intent of the International Chamber of Commerce is to revise the Incoterms periodically (such as every decade) with a view to their amendment to reflect changing practices in the international trade of goods. Rather, they are a standardised, published and widely known code which is available for incorporation in foreign goods contracts at the option of the parties.

Incorporation of Incoterms

A preferred Incoterm will be incorporated into a contract by unambiguous reference to it: eg 'CIF (... named place) (Incoterms 1990)' or 'Cost, insurance and freight (named place) (Incoterms 1990)'. Another comparable reference may be used, but given that numerous of the well-known trade usages are found in domestic case law or legislation in municipal legal systems, the parties should refer specifically to the Incoterms.

Such a reference requires the parties (and directs a court trying a case involving the contract) to refer to the Incoterms in order to determine the rights and obligations created by the reference.

The chosen Incoterm can be modified or amplified by provision in the contract. Exceptionally, the details of a contract may be such as to negate the Incoterm chosen, as where a term requiring the seller to deliver the goods is used, but the specific provisions of the contract impose the obligation of carriage, and its ancillary incidents, upon the buyer.

Transport developments impacting upon Incoterms

The traditional trade usages were focused on marine transport (sea and inland waterway). Over the years the range of transport options has widened: the most recent major development in this respect has been of course the increasing resort to air transportation of cargo. Parallel with this development has been the use of multi-modal transportation, where different modes of transport are employed to carry the goods from seller to buyer. These developments have been reflected in the Incoterms, in their progressive revisions. Some of them, for instance, are still intended for purely marine transport (such as FAS, FOB and CIF), but there are also terms for air transport (FCA), for rail (likewise FCA) and a number for any mode of transport, including multi-modal operations (such as ExW, CPT and CIP).

The advent of containerisation (and other forms of unitisation) coupled with new methods of loading (such as roll-on/roll-off, or ro-ro loading using trucks, etc) has had implications for international trade and in turn the Incoterms. In particular, the identification of the ship's rail as the place where the costs and risks are to be divided (with the buyer assuming responsibility at the moment the cargo passes over the rail) – a feature of such traditional marine terms as CIF and FOB – has had to be supplemented with new and alternative pivot points in other trade terms for the division of risk and costs. Containerised goods, including those intended for sea transport, tend to pass out of the hands of the seller and into the (first) carrier's hands at an earlier point, such as where the goods are delivered to a freight forwarder at a freight-forwarding depot, container terminal, etc for shipping, either in the original container or after removal and re-packing. Further, the ship's rail is irrelevant in the so-called 'arrival' terms where the seller undertakes to deliver the goods to the buyer at a point in the buyer's State. These latter arrangements, imposing more comprehensive obligations on sellers, are increasingly common.

Use of intermediaries and related matters

The Incoterms (in common with the different standardised practices they represent) must take account of the use of a variety of intermediaries involved in transacting the delivery, such as a succession of carriers in multi-modal transport arrangements, freight forwarders (who may act as customs brokers), stevedores, commercial inspection agents, and insurers. They must as well reflect the different types of cargo, such as general cargo (which, where sea transport is concerned, will usually be carried by the so-called liner trade, ie ships following regular schedules) and bulk cargo commodities which will often be carried by a ship chartered by either the seller or (more commonly) the buyer.

Electronic data transmission

As mentioned, the Incoterms 1990 recognise that a range of documents relevant to the performance of the contract are in practice being replaced to an increasing degree by so-called electronic data interchange, ie the computer-to-computer transmission of electronic messages. This electronic data interchange, or EDI, simplifies processes and reduces costs. Accordingly, the Incoterms 1990 provide, where applicable (and in some cases subject to agreement), that an equivalent electronic message may replace such documents as commercial invoices, documents required for customs clearance (import or export), transport documents, and (where agreed) documents which are to be tendered in proof of delivery.[5]

The bill of lading has represented a problem for the application of electronic messages in this context. The bill of lading is of course a traditional fixture in the transport of goods by sea. The bill is issued by the ship's master to the party dispatching

---

5   On EDI, in this context, see Ramberg, *Guide to Incoterms 1990, op cit*, pp 8–9, 31, 80–81, 144ff; Burnett, R, *The Law of International Business Transactions*, 1994, pp 29–30, 84ff, Sydney: Federation Press.

the cargo. It constitutes proof that the goods were delivered on board; evidences the contract to transport the goods; and functions in certain respects as a document of title. In its latter role, it is traditionally and concisely described as being the equivalent of the goods – 'the documents are the goods'. In its latter role, the bill enables the buyer to obtain delivery from the carrier at destination (upon presentation of the original[6] bill, which is sent ahead); and it also permits the buyer to sell the goods to a third party while they are in transit. (Dependent upon the contract between buyer and seller, the bill may be made non-negotiable so as to preclude this last facility, of resale in transit.)

The bill is not an unqualified document of title. The transferee acquires no better a title than the transferor. The bill, that is, represents a right to possession, and thus establishes possessory title, but it does not *per se* establish legal title.

The bill of lading can be dispensed with in the maritime context, when the resale in transit facility is not required and the parties do not see any need for the delivery of the goods at destination by the carrier, to be contingent upon production of the original of the document issued by the carrier upon receipt at the place of shipment. The situation is explained thus, in the Introduction to the ICC *Incoterms 1990*:

> In recent years, a considerable simplification of documentary practices has been achieved. Bills of lading are frequently replaced by non-negotiable documents similar to those which are used in other modes of transport than carriage by sea. These documents are called 'sea waybills', 'liner waybills', 'freight receipts' or variants of such expressions. These non-negotiable documents are quite satisfactory to use except when the buyer wishes to sell the goods in transit by surrendering a paper document to the new buyer. In order to make this possible, the obligation of the seller to provide a bill of lading under CFR and CIF must necessarily be retained. However, when the contracting parties know that the buyer does not contemplate selling the goods in transit, they may specifically agree to relieve the seller from the obligation to provide a bill of lading, or alternatively they may use CPT and CIF where there is no obligation to provide a bill of lading.[7]

Given that the originals of these documents do not have the significance which the originals have for the bill of lading, they are more readily replaced by EDI.

Even in the case of the bill of lading, however, progress has been made towards replacing it with EDI. Provision is made for electronic bills of lading by the regime laid down in the Rules for Electronic Bills of Lading adopted in 1990 by the Comité Maritime International (CMI).[8]

The CMI scheme preserves the security of communications by resort to the so-called (electronic) Private Key system (in substance, the private key is a unique identification number). The CMI scheme will only be used where both seller and buyer have agreed to this.

---

6   Or original where multiple originals are issued.

7   ICC *Incoterms 1990*, p15.

8   The text is set out in the Annexes to the *Guide to the Incoterms 1990, op cit,* pp 144–45; and see the commentaries in the *Guide to the Incoterms 1990,* pp 8–9, 31, 80–81, 144ff; and in Burnett, *op cit,* pp 84ff.

The electronic messages in this context may be sent in conformity with the international systems developed under the aegis of the United Nations known as EDIFACT (Electronic Date Interchange for Administration, Commerce and Transport) and UNCID (Uniform Rules of Conduct for Interchange of Trade Date by Teletransmission).[9]

THE INCOTERM CATEGORIES, STRUCTURE OF EACH INCOTERM

There are 13 Incoterms, and they are grouped into four categories. There are several principles underpinning this system of classification, and the subdivisions within each category (ie in the individual terms themselves). Broadly, the terms are grouped according to the extent to which the seller on the one hand, or the buyer on the other, are each responsible for the delivery of the goods, and related aspects of this. More specifically, they regulate the extent of each party's responsibility (if any) for such matters as arranging for export and import clearance; arranging and paying for carriage (the main carriage, and pre- and on-carriage); and arranging and paying for insurance; and they also regulate the passing of risk. At one extreme, the EXW term imposes the minimum responsibility on the seller and a corresponding maximum liability on the buyer (the seller's delivery obligations are ended when he makes the goods available to the buyer at his premises). At the other extreme the D terms impose the maximum obligation on the seller with a corresponding diminution of responsibility on the part of the buyer, because these terms oblige the seller to deliver the goods to an agreed destination in the buyer's country. (The term which is most onerous of all where the seller is concerned is the DDP term.) The intermediate terms in categories F and C impose intermediate levels of obligation on each party; C is more onerous where the seller is concerned than is F (see below).

The Incoterms may be tabulated as shown in Figure 1.

The E category is named thus because the sole term in this category commences with 'E', ie ex-works. As noted, this is the term which is most beneficial to the seller.

The F terms are so named because the seller hands the goods over to the carrier free of expense and risk to the buyer. Once, however, the carrier has them, the buyer assumes the risk and expense including the expense of carriage. These contracts are known as 'shipment' contracts, with the seller fulfilling his delivery obligation in his own country. (D-class contracts, in contrast, are 'arrival' contracts.) After the EXW term, the F terms are the most beneficial to the seller.

The C terms are so designated because the seller bears specified *costs*, even after delivery, at which point the general risks and costs pass to the buyer. Under C terms (and unlike the F terms), the seller is responsible for organising the main carriage. These contracts are also known as 'shipment' contracts (again, in contrast to the D, or 'arrival' contracts). The risk passes to the buyer upon this delivery to the carrier, but unlike the

---

9   *Guide to the Incoterms 1990, ibid*, p 8.

Group E Departure	EXW	Ex-works
Group F Main carriage unpaid	FCA	Free carrier
	FAS	Free alongside ship
	FOB	Free on board
Group C Main carriage paid	CFR	Cost and freight
	CIF	Cost, insurance and freight
	CPT	Carriage paid to
	CIP	Carriage and insurance paid to
Group D Arrival	DAF	Delivered at frontier
	DES	Delivered ex-ship
	DEQ	Delivered ex-quay
	DDU	Delivered duty unpaid
	DDP	Delivered duty paid

Figure 1. Incoterms 1990

case in respect of the F terms, the seller is liable for the costs of carriage and (in certain cases) insurance up until the arrival of the goods at the agreed destination in the buyer's country. Nonetheless, the seller is not at risk during the main carriage; if the goods are lost or damaged during this phase, this is the buyer's burden. Because of the obligations concerning aspects of the main carriage, the C terms are relatively more burdensome for the seller than F terms. Notwithstanding that the seller has these extra obligations, his delivery obligation is, as in the case of the F, fulfilled in his own country.

The D terms are so named because the seller contracts to deliver the goods at an agreed *destination* (normally) in the buyer's country. It follows that the seller's delivery obligation is fulfilled, not at an earlier time in his own country (a characteristic of the E, F and C categories), but at the later time in the buyer's country. The D terms (known also as 'delivered' terms) are the most onerous from the seller's viewpoint. He must arrange the main carriage to the agreed destination and bear the costs and risks pertaining to and during this carriage. If the goods are lost in transit, this is the seller's problem.

D terms are becoming relatively more popular. Sellers of goods who can undertake delivery in the buyer's country are more likely to get orders for these goods.

Some of the Incoterms are designed for certain modes of transport while others are flexible. The following are for use with any mode of transport (or for multi-modal systems): EXW, FCA, CPT, CIP, DAF, DDU and DDP. FCA is to be used for air transport or rail transport; and the following are for sea or inland waterway transport – FAS, FOB, CFR, CIF, DES and DEQ.

The text of each Incoterm has been structured in a standardised format, with the seller's obligations being stated under 10 headings; and with the buyer's most closely corresponding obligations being likewise grouped under 10 headings. The obligations on each side broadly mirror those on the other side (the details of course differ). Thereby, a check list of obligations imposed upon each party is generated. In some cases, a particular heading will be inapplicable, having regard to the particular term; in this case, the text under the heading reads 'no obligation'. Because this standard table of obligations has been used not only as between the parties, but also from one term to the next, it is relatively easy to determine the differences between each Incoterm, especially in those cases where two terms are largely identical but differ on some pivotal point.

The standard heads in each term are as shown in Figure 2.

The individual Incoterms are reviewed in the following pages.

THE E CATEGORY – 'EX–WORKS'

Seller's responsibility		Buyer's responsibility	
A1	Provision of goods in conformity with the contract	B1	Payment of the price
A2	Licences, authorisation and formalities	B2	Licences, authorisations and formalities
A3	Contract of carriage and insurance	B3	Contract of carriage
A4	Delivery	B4	Taking delivery
A5	Transfer of risks	B5	Transfer of risks
A6	Division of costs	B6	Division of costs
A7	Notice to the buyer	B7	Notice to the seller
A8	Proof of delivery, transport document or equivalent electronic message	B8	Proof of delivery, transport document or equivalent electronic message
A9	Checking/packaging/marking	B9	Inspection of goods
A10	Other obligations	B10	Other obligations

Figure 2. The division of responsibilities

As noted, the E category of Incoterms has only one term – ex-works (... named place) or ExW (... named place). This term requires that the seller make the goods available at the seller's premises (as agreed upon and identified). These premises will be his works, factory, warehouse, etc. The core obligations of the seller are stated in A1 of the seller's obligations (provision of goods in conformity with the contract), and in A4, headed 'Delivery'. The seller must:

> Place the goods at the disposal of the buyer at the named place of delivery on the date or within the period stipulated or, if no such place or time is stipulated, at the usual place and time for the delivery of such goods.

The seller has no delivery obligation beyond this point. It has been commented that the ex-works sale:

> ... is the most favourable arrangement which can be obtained by a seller desirous of conducting an export transaction as closely as possible on the lines of an ordinary sale of goods in the home market.[10]

The contract should specify, where appropriate, which party is responsible for loading the goods onto any vehicle sent by the buyer. The goods will, where applicable, need to be identified to the contract before they can be so delivered, ie where the contract is, at formation, one for the sale of unascertained goods.

A5 provides that (subject to B5) the seller bears all risks of loss of or damages to the goods until such time as they have been placed at the buyer's disposal in accordance with A4. The provision follows the standard Incoterms scheme, ie that risk normally passes from seller to buyer when the seller has performed his required act of delivery – replicating the approach of the Vienna Convention on Contracts for the International Sale of Goods.[11]

It follows that, *prima facie*, the seller has no liability for damage to or loss of the goods post-delivery. The seller will only be liable in the case where, independently of this provision in A5, or parallel provisions in the contract or the applicable law, the seller can be made legally liable for loss or damage. Such might be the case, for instance, where any required packaging (see A9) is inadequate and such a deficiency in performance amounts to breach of contract, and this breach causes damage or loss (see A9). Also, the fact that the risk passes cannot excuse the seller from liability for a non-conformity as between goods and contract (which, *inter alia*, would be a breach of A1).[12]

As A5 recognises, B5 – the parallel provision dealing with risk in the table of buyer's obligations – may operate to pass risk to the buyer prior to the seller delivering them to the buyer. This will happen where the buyer is entitled to determine the time within a stipulated period and/or the place of delivery, and he does not, as required by B7, give sufficient notice to the seller. In such a case, a failure to give notice will have the effect that the risk passes pre-delivery, ie from the agreed date or the expiry date of any period fixed for taking delivery (provided that the goods have been appropriated to the contract) (see B5). The buyer, that is, cannot delay performing his obligations by refusing to give the required notice. If he does so delay, he is liable for the risks and costs pertaining to the goods.

The seller must assist the buyer to obtain export or import clearance (but at the buyer's expense) (A2); but consistently with the ExW scheme, the buyer must obtain at his own risk and expense any export licence, etc (B2). The arrangement of carriage from the seller's premises is of course a burden on the buyer (B3). The buyer must take delivery (B4).

---

10 Schmitthoff, C, *Export Trade – the Law and Practice of International Trade*, 9th edn, 1990, p 11, London: Stevens.

11 See *Guide to Incoterms 1990, op cit*, p 44.

12 See the discussion in *ibid*, p 44.

The seller bears the costs, up until the time they are placed at the buyer's disposal, after which time the buyer has this burden (A6, B6). As in the case of the risks, delivery is the pivotal point for dividing costs. The buyer must pay additional costs generated by his failure to take delivery when it is duly made, or his failure to give any notice required under B7 (see B6). An obvious instance of additional costs would be storage costs.

The buyer is to give the seller a receipt upon taking delivery (see B8). The buyer is responsible for any pre-shipment inspection of the goods including inspection mandated by the authorities of the country of exportation (B9). On the other hand, the seller is responsible for the routine checking operations (eg checking quality and weighing) which are necessary for the purpose of delivering the goods to the buyer (A9).

Note, A10 and B10, concerning the obtaining of documents (or EDI equivalents) for the export/import clearance of the goods, and their intermediate transit through third countries. These are the buyer's responsibility, but the seller is to give every assistance and is entitled to be reimbursed for any expenses incurred. Likewise, under A10 the seller is to give the buyer any necessary information, if requested, for procuring insurance.

THE F CATEGORY – FCA, FAS, FOB

As noted, an F term constitutes a contract for the international sale of goods, a shipment contract (as distinct from an arrival or D class contract). They are so designated because the seller delivers the goods to the carrier *free* of expense and risk to the buyer, whereupon the buyer assumes the risks and costs including the cost of carriage (which will have been organised by the buyer). The seller therefore fulfils his delivery obligations in his own country. These terms are the next most beneficial to the seller after the EXW term.

Free carrier (FCA)

The free carrier (... named place) term is abbreviated FCA (... named place). FCA requires that the seller deliver the goods to the carrier nominated by the buyer, at the specified place, after having cleared them for export. Once delivery has been effected, the seller has fulfilled his delivery obligations. The term is suitable for all forms of transport and for multi-modal operations.

The seller's core obligations are set out in A1 (provision of goods in conformity with the contract); A2 (requiring him at his own risk and expense to obtain any export licence, etc for the exportation of the goods); and A4, obliging him to deliver the goods to the nominated carrier of the buyer, at the nominated place. It is the A2 (clear for export) and A4 (deliver to carrier) terms which distinguish the FCA usage.

A4 – the delivery term – is a lengthy stipulation. It requires the seller to deliver the goods into the custody of the carrier or another person (eg a freight forwarder) named by the buyer, or chosen by the seller in accordance with A3(a), at the named place or point (eg transport terminal or other receiving point), on the date or within the period agreed for delivery and in the manner agreed or customary at such point. (Note the ancillary detail.) The reference to A3(a) is to the situation where (notwithstanding that the seller has no obligation to arrange the contract of carriage), the seller accedes to the buyer's request to arrange carriage, or arranges it pursuant to commercial practice. In such a case, the buyer is still liable for the risks and costs of carriage. The balance of the A4 term deals with the precise details of when delivery is completed, from one transport mode to the next (eg in the case of air transport, delivery is completed when the goods have been handed over to the air carrier or to another person acting on his behalf). More detailed stipulations may be needed in a particular case regarding the mechanics of transfer to the carrier – eg account will need to be taken of the issue of containerisation and the issue of who unloads delivery vehicles.

The concepts of 'carrier', 'transport terminal' and 'container' are defined in the preamble to the statement of obligations in FCA. The delivery by the seller of the goods to a freight forwarder will satisfy his obligation under A4, when the buyer instructs him to so deliver.

The seller must arrange and pay for carriage to the place of delivery to the carrier (ie he is responsible for what might be termed the pre-carriage transit). Thereafter, the buyer is responsible. B3 requires that the buyer contract at his own expense for the carriage of the goods from the named place, except as provided for in A3(a). (Pursuant to A3(a), the seller can upon the request of the buyer or in accordance with commercial practice, contract for usual carriage at the buyer's risk and expense, but he is never obliged to do so.)

Risk is divided between the parties when the goods are delivered into the custody of the carrier in accordance with A4 – see A5 on the transfer of risks. This is a standard provision in the Incoterms – risk passes when control passes upon delivery to the relevant person (here, the carrier). The parallel provision in B5 reflects this stipulation. Therefore, the buyer and not the seller is liable for damage to or loss of the goods (including of course during the main carriage). The seller may incur liability, however, for loss or damage occurring, or manifesting itself, after risk is transferred, where the damage, etc is caused by conduct of the seller for which he is independently liable. An instance would be inadequate packaging of the goods which amounts to a breach of contract (note the packaging obligation in A9).

The division of costs is also effected at the point of delivery (A6). Pursuant to his obligation to obtain export clearance (see A2), the seller remains liable for any costs incurred, or to be incurred, in securing this. B6 reflects this principle of division. Thus, the buyer is liable for the costs of the main carriage, including the costs of insurance – see B3.

Although the risks and costs are normally divided at the point of delivery, B5 (transfer of risks) and B6 (division of costs) provide exceptionally that the risks and costs can be imposed upon the buyer at an earlier point, where he fails to give any notice required under B7. B7 requires the buyer to give notice of the name of the carrier and, where necessary, the mode of transport and date of period for delivering the goods to him and the precise point where the goods are to be delivered, in cases where the contract has given the buyer options in respect of one or more of these matters. This pre-delivery passing of risks and costs cannot happen, however, unless (again where necessary) the goods have been appropriated to the contract by the seller (ie where the contract is for the sale of unascertained goods). The risks, etc will also pass pre-delivery, in a case where the carrier nominated by the buyer fails to take the goods into charge (B5, B6).

The seller's other obligations include giving notice to the buyer that the goods have been delivered to the carrier (A7); provision of specified transport documents or the EDI equivalent (A8); performing routine checking, packaging and marking operations pre-delivery (A9); and rendering the buyer, at the latter's request, risk and expense, every assistance in obtaining any documents (or EDI equivalent) for the importation of the goods into the buyer's country, and providing necessary information, if requested, for the procuring of insurance (A10).

The buyer's other obligations include payment for the goods (B1); organising and paying for import clearance into his own country (and where applicable, transit through a third country) (B2); contracting at his own expense for the carriage after the buyer has fulfilled his delivery obligations – viz, in effect, taking responsibility for the main carriage and any post-carriage transport (eg from a container terminal at his end to his premises) (B3); taking delivery (B4); paying pre-shipment inspection except[13] when mandated by the authorities in the country of export (B9); and paying the costs incurred in the buyer's obtaining of the documents or EDI equivalents pursuant to A10 (B10).

Free alongside ship (FAS)

The Free alongside ship (... named place) term is abbreviated FAS (... named place). FAS requires the seller to deliver the goods alongside the ship, ie on the wharf or in one or more lighters. Thereupon, the risks and costs are divided. In principle, the transaction, from the seller's viewpoint, is little different from a domestic sale where he delivers goods to the premises of a domestic buyer. The buyer is responsible for export clearance and the main contract of carriage. By its nature, FAS is to be used only for sea and inland waterway transport.

The seller has the standard duty to supply goods in conformity with the contract (A1). He has no obligations in respect of export clearance (other than assisting the buyer to obtain, at the latter's risk and expense, the export clearance – A2); nor does he have any obligations to arrange the main carriage, or insurance for the time after delivery alongside the ship (note A3). (He will have organised and paid for pre-delivery carriage.)

His delivery obligation is succinctly stated in A4:

Deliver the goods alongside the named vessel at the loading place named by the buyer at the named port of shipment on the date or within the period stipulated and in the manner customary at the port.

---

13 This inspection would go beyond the routine checking required of the seller prior to delivery, by A9. Note that the mandatory inspection required by the authorities is not an expense for the buyer, consistent with the seller being responsible for export clearance. Cf the situation with EXW, where this inspection is to the account of the buyer, consistently with the EXW principle that the seller's obligations are very limited – delivery to the buyer at the seller's own premises.

As noted, this requires delivery on the appropriate wharf, but it is also satisfied by loading onto lighters where this is more apt. Where the ship is not alongside a wharf, the seller will have to load the goods onto lighters so that it may be transported alongside the ship. In this case the seller is liable for the costs of the lighters and of loading them, up until the time the lighter is alongside the ship. (He is not thereafter liable for the costs of loading from the lighters onto the ship – his duty is to deliver the goods alongside the ship.) The responsibility of the seller for damage and loss runs until the lighters are alongside the ship, unless the parties agree that the delivery is to be made 'free on lighter', signifying that the seller's responsibility ends once the goods pass the lighter's rail.[14]

The seller's risks end and the buyer's begin once the goods have been delivered in accordance with A4, ie once they have been placed alongside the ship (A5). The seller would need to insure the goods up to this point. Costs are likewise divided at the point of delivery (A6). The division of risks and costs at the point of delivery is standard in the Incoterms. Although the seller is not liable for the costs of obtaining export clearance; dock dues and similar charges are the seller's responsibility.[15]

The seller is to give sufficient notice to the buyer that the goods have been delivered alongside the ship (A7); provide the buyer at the seller's expense with the usual document evidencing delivery; and, if this document is not the transport document, assist the buyer to obtain the transport document (such as a bill of lading, non-negotiable sea waybill or EDI equivalent) (A8); perform routine checking obligations necessary for delivery, pack the goods as appropriate, and mark them as appropriate (A9); and assist the buyer at the latter's request, risk and expense to obtain any documents or equivalent EDI messages required for exportation or importation, or transit through a third country (A10). The seller is also to supply the buyer with the necessary information for obtaining insurance (A10).

The buyer must pay the price provided in the contract (B1). The buyer, as noted, is responsible for obtaining export clearance (B2) (and of course import clearance); for organising and paying for main carriage (ie transport after delivery) (B3); and for taking delivery in accordance (A4, B4). The buyer, that is, must organise the loading of the goods onto the vessel after they have been placed alongside the vessel by the seller.

B5 (dealing with the transfer of risks) and B6 (on the division of costs) mirror A5 and A6, in providing that the risks and costs are transferred to the buyer upon delivery by the seller alongside the ship. Both B5 and B6 provide, however, that where the buyer fails to obtain export clearance as required by B2, he will bear all additional risks of loss or damage which are incurred thereby. B5 and B6 also provide for a pre-delivery passing of risk, where the buyer fails to give the seller sufficient notice of the vessel name, loading place and required delivery time, as required by B7 (it is assumed that one or more of these matters is not specified in the contract, or that the buyer is given a

---

14 Schmitthoff, *op cit*, p 13, discussing the use of lighters.

15 See the discussion by Schmitthoff, *ibid*, p 15, noting that in certain cases it may be advisable to deal specifically in the contract with the issue of port rates.

discretion – eg to nominate delivery within a specified period – see A4 and B4). The costs and risks will pass upon the day determined to be the day by which the notice should have been given, or such other date as it identifiable by reference to the contract. Pursuant to B5 and B6, risks and costs also pass where the nominated carrier fails to arrive on time, or to take the goods. The goods must have been identified to the contract in order for there to be a pre-delivery passing of risk.

The buyer must pay the costs of pre-shipment (including that mandated by the authorities of the export country) (B9) (these do not include the routine checking operations referred to in A9). The buyer is to pay the costs of obtaining the documents or their EDI equivalents, mentioned in A10, and to reimburse the seller any expenses he incurred in this regard (B10).

Free on board (FOB)

Under free on board (... named port of shipment), or FOB (... named port of shipment), the seller's delivery obligation is concluded the instant the cargo passes over the ship's rail. The passing over the rail is the point when the risks and costs are divided, with the buyer thereupon assuming both burdens. The FOB term also imposes on the seller the obligation to clear the goods for export.

The FOB is a long-standing term in mercantile usage and domestic legal systems. Its meaning varies from jurisdiction to jurisdiction in some respects, and in the common law countries it has attracted a wealth of judicial exegesis. It is a traditional marine-transport term, and can only be used for sea and inland waterway transport. Its preoccupation with the ship's rail is based upon the recognition that this is equivalent to the frontier – to the line dividing the countries of export and import – of the seller's and buyer's countries respectively. Taking the ship's rail as the pivot point for the division of risks and costs is somewhat arbitrary (and potentially productive of anomaly), as reflected in the well-known comment by Devlin J in an English decision dealing with the FOB term at common law:

> Only the most enthusiastic lawyer could watch with satisfaction the spectacle of liabilities shifting uneasily as the cargo sways at the end of a derrick across a notional perpendicular projecting from the ship's rail.[16]

A trade term like FOB, which pivots on the ship's rail, may be appropriate for general cargo delivered over the rail (including bulk cargo), as where a commodity is loaded *via* a conveyer belt or a chute. It is less appropriate for the roll-on/roll-off loading operation or for containerised cargo (which will be delivered at an earlier point, such as to a container terminal); in such cases FCA is more apt.[17]

FOB differs from FAS; the latter, as seen above, provides for the fulfilment of the seller's delivery obligation at an earlier time (when the goods are delivered alongside the ship), and does not impose the obligation to secure export clearance upon the seller. The

---

16   *Pyrene Co Ltd v Scindia Navigation Co Ltd* [1954] 2 QB 402 at 419.
17   So observed in *Guide to Incoterms 1990, op cit*, p 69.

FOB term progresses a stage further towards the truly international sales contract model, in requiring the seller to obtain export clearance (in recognition that he is delivering at the notional 'frontier' of the ship's rail).

The seller has the standard duty in A1 of providing goods in conformity with the contract. A distinguishing feature of FOB, ie the seller's obligation to obtain export clearance at his own risk and expense, is provided for in A2.

As his delivery obligation is fulfilled at the ship's rail, he does not have to arrange the contract of (main) carriage, ie from port, nor does he have any obligation to insure the goods (although he may wish to insure them up until his risk passes, ie upon loading) (A3). He will have to organise pre-delivery carriage and pay for this. While arranging the main contract of carriage is technically the buyer's responsibility, in practice it may be convenient for the seller to do this. The price of the goods can be adjusted to take account of this.[18]

In such a case the seller still completes his delivery once the goods pass over the rail, and costs (less the cost of carriage, if this has been dealt with specifically in the contract and allocated to the seller) and risks still divide at this point. Thus, even as the seller may have organised and paid for main carriage, he is not liable for the damage to, or loss of, the goods during this phase. Of course, if the parties additionally impose the risks upon the seller during main carriage, by a specific provision in the contract, the contract is not a true FOB contract, and one of the D (arrival) terms should be used instead.

The seller's delivery obligation is stated in A4:

Deliver the goods on board the vessel named by the buyer at the named port of shipment on the date or within the period stipulated and in the manner customary at the port.

A5 and A6, in referring to the passing of the ship's rail as the key point of division for risks and costs, emphasise that delivery is effected pursuant to A4 the moment the goods pass the rail. (A contrary interpretation is that the A4 stipulation does indeed move beyond the ship's rail as the defining moment for completion of the delivery obligation, and require delivery on board.[19] Nonetheless, A5 and A6, in dividing risks and costs at the ship's rail, are in conformity with the traditional common law concept of FOB.)[20]

The risks of loss of, or damage to, the goods are expressly transferred from seller to buyer at the time the goods pass the ship's rail at the named port of shipment (A5). The seller is not liable, therefore, for mishaps to the goods after this point; although he retains liability for any deficiency in the goods resulting from non-conformity with the contract, or inadequate packaging by him amounting to a breach of contract, etc.

The costs of delivery are also divided at the ship's rail. A6 provides that (subject to B6) the seller is to pay all costs relating to the goods until this time. It also provides that the seller (consistent with his obligation under A2) is to bear the costs of obtaining

---

18   See Burnett, *op cit*, pp 40–41.

19   Burnett, *ibid*, pp 42–43.

20   Burnett, *ibid*, p 39, notes that given the premise that A4 requires delivery on board, the FOB Incoterm 'separates risk and delivery' (by virtue of A5). In *Guide to Incoterms 1990* it is assumed that the division of risks and costs is at the ship's rail, which is equated to delivery – *op cit*, p 70–71.

export clearance, including the costs of customs formalities, duties, taxes and other official charges incident to this. The task of dividing the costs of loading could be difficult, given that the one party (such as a stevedore) will be responsible for the pre- and post-rail operations.[21] This is usually not necessary. As explained in *Guide to Incoterms 1990*:

> The reference in FOB A4 to 'the manner customary at the port' highlights the problem of using the passing of the ship's rail as the guiding factor in practice. The parties in these circumstances will have to follow the custom of the port regarding the actual measures to be taken in delivering the goods on board. Usually the task is performed by stevedoring companies, and the practical problem normally lies in deciding who should bear the costs of their services.[22]

Normally, the risks (A5) and the costs (A6) are divided when the goods pass over the rail. Both A5 and A6 are expressly qualified by B5 and B6, respectively, which relate of course to the buyer's obligations. These are noted below.

The seller must give the buyer sufficient notice that the goods have been delivered on board (A7). The seller must supply to the buyer the usual document (or equivalent EDI) in proof of delivery at the seller's own expense. If this document is not the transport document, the seller must assist the buyer at the latter's request, risk and expense, to obtain a transport document (or equivalent EDI) for the contract of carriage, such as a negotiable bill of lading or a non-negotiable sea waybill (A8). The seller has the standard routine pre-delivery checking obligation, and packaging and marking obligations (A9), and must assist the buyer if required, at the latter's expense, to obtain any documents or EDI equivalents to permit the import of the goods, and (if applicable) their intermediate transit through another country (A10).

The buyer must pay the contract price (B1); obtain at his own risk and expense import clearance (and satisfy formalities for their transit through another country) (B2); organise the contract of carriage (B3) after taking delivery (and for that matter, any post-carriage contracts of transportation); and take delivery of the goods in accordance with A4 (B4).

B5 and B6 parallel A5 and A6 in recognising that the risks and costs, relating to the goods respectively, pass from seller to buyer at the time they pass the ship's rail. Accordingly, the buyer may wish to insure the goods from this point. However, the risks and costs can, pursuant to B5 and B6, be transferred earlier, ie prior to delivery across the ship's rail. This will happen where the buyer, when required, fails to give the seller sufficient notice of the vessel name, loading point and required delivery time (see B7, on notice to the seller). The notice may be required having regard to the terms of the contract, as where one or more of these matters is left open – see A4, in particular, which envisages that the delivery may (by agreement) be either on a nominated date, or within the period stipulated. The risks and costs would be transferred, in a case where notice is not given, upon the date agreed for delivery, or at the end of the period during

---

21 Note the comment in Burnett, *ibid*, p 43.
22 *Guide to Incoterms 1990, op cit*, p 70.

which notice is to be given. The buyer cannot delay his obligation to take delivery (B4) by declining to give notice. If the vessel cannot take the goods by the agreed date, risks and costs are likewise divided at the agreed date, pre-delivery. This earlier division cannot, however, operate unless and until the goods, if originally unascertained, have been identified to the contract (B5 and B6).

The buyer must accept proof of delivery in accordance with A8 (B8); pay the costs of pre-shipment inspection except where mandated by the authorities of the country of export (B9) (any such costs would not include the costs of pre-delivery checking by the seller under A9); and pay costs and charges incurred in obtaining the documents or EDI equivalents mentioned in A10 (B10).

THE C CATEGORY – CFR, CIF, CPT, CIP

As noted, the C terms are so designated because the seller bears specified *costs* even after delivery, at which point the general costs and risks have passed to the buyer. Under C terms (and contrary to the situation under the F terms), the seller is responsible for organising the contract of (main) carriage. C contracts are often referred to as shipment contracts (in contrast to the D contracts, which are known as arrival contracts – see below).

Cost and freight (CFR)/cost, insurance and freight (CIF)

The twin Incoterms, cost and freight (... named port of destination) or CFR (... named port of destination), and cost, insurance and freight (... named port of destination) or CIF (... named port of destination), are identical with one exception – CIF additionally imposes upon the seller the obligation to insure the goods during their main carriage. Given that CIF is more commonly employed, the focus of review will be on it; after which CFR will be briefly commented upon. All comments regarding CIF apply to CFR, with this one exception.

Cost, insurance and freight (CIF)

CIF is another term which, like FOB, requires the seller to deliver the goods over the ship's rail, whereupon his delivery obligation is discharged. However, the CIF seller has additional obligations (compared to the FOB seller): he must organise the main contract of carriage and effect insurance for the risks of the voyage.

The CIF seller's obligations, then, are: obtain and pay for export clearance; and transport the goods to the ship and deliver them on board, with the risks and costs being transferred to the buyer at the moment when the goods pass over the ship's rail. This division of risks and costs is qualified, however, by the two requirements:

(a) that the seller organise and pay for the main contract of carriage; and

(b) that he procure insurance to cover the risk of damage to or loss of the goods during main carriage.

Notwithstanding these qualifications, it is still appropriate to speak of his delivery obligation as being concluded at the moment the goods pass the ship's rail. The qualifications on the passing of costs are limited – the seller must pay for the main carriage, and export clearance. The qualification where the passing of risks is concerned is not a true exception – certainly the CIF seller must organise insurance to cover the voyage, but he is not thereby left at risk during (or after) this phase. If there is a mishap involving the goods for which the seller has no independent liability (ie independent of the CIF term), the buyer will need to claim on the policy, or pursue some other party.

As it was observed in relation to FOB, the 'ship's rail' class of Incoterm (like CIF) may well be appropriate for general cargo delivered over the rail (especially bulk cargo such as that delivered via a chute or conveyer belt), but it is less appropriate for the roll-on/roll-off loading operation, for containerised cargo which will be delivered at an earlier point, such as to a container terminal. In such a case FCA is more apt.[23]

CIF (and CFR) are by their nature for use only where carriage is by sea or inland waterway.

CIF is a long-standing term in mercantile usage and domestic legal systems, and can vary in its meaning from jurisdiction to jurisdiction. The Incoterm CIF is one version of it. The rationale of CIF class trade terms has been explained thus: the exporter is typically an expert in organising export clearance and carriage, and:

> ... often in a position to make favourable arrangements as regards freight and insurance. In particular, they will often secure reductions in these charges when engaged in substantial or regular trade with the buyer's country, or they may be able to group several consignments to the same consignee or a number of consignments to different consignees in order to make the best use of the available shipping space; in these cases the CIF clause offers them distinct advantages.[24]

The CIF clause enables the bundling of the main carriage and insurance obligations, and their allocation to the exporter (export managers, confirming houses, manufacturers, etc). All things being equal, the cost of insurance and freight will be built into the price but at a potential saving to the buyer in time and expense.

It has often been remarked of the CIF contract at common law that, where it is concerned, 'the documents are the goods'; *viz*, the seller's obligation is to ship the goods from a port in his own country, with the result that the contract is a shipment and not an arrival (delivery at destination) class of contract. Where the destination is concerned, he undertakes only to tender a bill of lading. This feature is reflected in the statement by Scrutton J in an English case:

> It is not a contract that goods shall arrive, but a contract to ship goods complying with the contract of sale, to obtain, unless the contract otherwise provides, the ordinary contract of carriage to the place of destination, and the ordinary contract of insurance on that voyage, and to tender these documents against payment of the contract price.[25]

---

23   *Guide to Incoterms 1990, op cit*, p 69.

24   Schmitthoff, *op cit*, p 35.

25   *Arnold Karberg and Co v Blythe, Green Jourdain and Co* [1915] 2 KB 379 at 388. See the comments in Schmitthoff, *ibid*, pp 34ff.

Accordingly, in the normal case the seller is still entitled to be paid upon tender of the insurance policy and the bill of lading, even if the goods are damaged or lost during main carriage.

These shipping documents – the bill of lading and the insurance policy – are the hallmarks of the traditional CIF contract. This is reflected in the following comment. The parties, although they may adapt and modify what purports to be a CIF contract, must:

> ... take care that these amendments and variations do not destroy the essential characteristics of the CIF stipulation, which are that, as the result of the transfer of the shipping documents, a direct relationship is established between the buyer on the one hand and the carrier and insurer on the other, so as to enable the buyer to make direct claims against these persons in the case of loss of, or damage to, the goods. If the parties vary this quality of the shipping documents, eg by providing that the seller shall be at liberty to tender, instead of a bill of lading, a delivery order on his agent in the port of destination or the goods themselves, the contract ceases to be a true CIF contract in the legal sense.[26]

This comment is directed to the CIF contract (or term) in its common law incidents. The use of the shorthand CIF (Incoterm 1990) imports the rules of interpretation there appended, and, as it will be seen, the negotiable bill of lading (or electronic equivalent) is optional – non-negotiable sea waybills, etc may also be tendered (A7). In this respect, the Incoterm CIF may or may not (depending upon the precise agreement of the parties) be synonymous with the traditional CIF contract. A bill of lading will still be used where the parties contemplate that the goods may be sold (to a third party) during transit.

Under CIF, the seller must provide goods in conformity with the contract (A1). He must (a key obligation) obtain export clearance at his own risk and expense (A2). He must organise and pay for the carriage of the goods to the named destination; and he must obtain at his own expense cargo insurance (A3). These are also key obligations.

The insurance must be effected on terms permitting the buyer, or other person having an insurable interest, to claim directly on the policy. The insurance is to be with an insurer of good repute, and (unless agreed otherwise) it is to be in accordance with minimum cover of the Institute Cargo Clauses (Institute of London Underwriters) or any similar set of clauses. The minimum insurance is to cover the contract price plus 10%, in the currency of the contract. The insurance is to be from the time risks are transferred to the buyer (ie as provided for in B5, once the goods have passed over the ship's rail), until they arrive at the named port of destination. The buyer may wish to stipulate for more than minimum cover by express provision in the contract.[27]

The delivery obligation is: 'Deliver the goods on board the vessel at the port of shipment on the date or within the period stipulated' (A4). The seller, then, delivers the

---

26   Schmitthoff, *ibid*, p 36.

27   See *Guide to Incoterms 1990, op cit*, p 88, commenting that minimum cover is only suitable for bulk cargoes which usually do not suffer loss or damage in transit unless something happens to the ship as well as the cargo.

cargo to the port from which the main carriage commences. He will have arranged and paid for this main carriage (and, by definition, pre-delivery carriage will be entirely his own responsibility). Unless the contract provides otherwise, he has a discretion as to port of shipment and choice of carrier (although note that A3 lays down some broad parameters, including that the normal route be taken). It has been commented that the CIF contract should not specify a (latest) date of delivery at the destination, because this could, on one view, be read as converting what should be a delivery contract into an arrival contract.[28] If the latter is intended, a D term should be used.

Although A4 posits the conclusion of delivery at the moment the goods are delivered 'on board', A5 and A6 make it clear that the precise moment when the delivery is effected is that moment when the goods pass over the ship's rail.

A5 specifies that, subject to the provisions of B5, the seller bears the risks of loss or damage until the goods have passed the ship's rail at the point of shipment. The seller, that is, is not liable for damage, etc after this time, including during the voyage. An exception will be where he is independently liable for damage, etc occurring after this time, as where the goods are later found to be non-conforming, or suffer damage because of inadequate packaging amounting to a breach of contract (see A9).

A6 divides the costs at the ship's rail (subject to B6). As noted, there are certain exceptions: the seller has to pay the costs of freight and other costs associated with organising the contract of main carriage, including the costs of loading the goods on board and any costs of unloading at the port of discharge which may be changed by regular shipping lines when contracting for carriage (see A6). The seller must also pay for export clearance (including any taxes). The seller also, as noted, pays the costs of insuring the cargo during carriage.

The seller must give notice to the buyer of delivery of the goods on board the vessel (A7).

The seller must at his own expense provide the buyer with the usual transport document for the agreed port of destination (A8). This may be a bill of lading – necessary if the parties contemplate the possible resale of the cargo while afloat; but A8 also recognises that something short of a bill, such as a non-negotiable sea waybill, may be employed (the parties will have to stipulate in their contract what form of documentation is to be tendered). The documents used must, at the least, permit the buyer to claim the goods from the carrier. EDI equivalents to the transport documents may be used, by agreement.[29]

The seller must carry out routine pre-delivery checking operations, pack the goods adequately, if applicable, and mark any such packaging (A9). He must assist the buyer, if requested, and at the latter's risk and expense, obtain any documents or EDI equivalents required for importation or transit through another country (A10).

---

28 *Guide to Incoterms 1990, ibid*, p 79.

29 See above.

The buyer must pay the contract price (B1); obtain import clearance – the CIF contract is not an arrival contract (see B2); but he has no obligation concerning the main carriage (B3 – although he must arrange carriage from the port of destination).

The buyer must accept delivery when delivered in accordance with A4, and receive them from the carrier at the named port of destination (B4). Taking delivery over the ship's rail has the consequences earlier noted – the risks of the goods, and (with certain exception) the costs, are thereupon transferred to him. The requirement that the buyer receive them from the carrier at destination, has the consequence that, if costs additional to normal freight are generated because of an undue delay in unloading, these are to the buyer's account.[30]

The seller, pursuant to A6, bears any charges for unloading at the port of destination which may be levied by regular shipping lines when contracting for carriage (as part of the seller's obligation to organise and pay for the main carriage). Otherwise, in default of contrary agreement, the buyer will pay the costs of unloading.

The risks are transferred to the buyer when the goods pass over the ship's rail (B5). The costs are likewise divided at the ship's rail (B6 – except, as noted, the seller must pay for the main carriage and export clearance; and it is the buyer's responsibility to pay for import clearance). In both cases – the division of risks and costs – the transfer of responsibility from seller to buyer can happen before delivery over the rail. This can occur when the buyer fails to give notice under B7. B7 requires the buyer, whenever he is entitled to determine the time for shipping the goods and/or the port of destination, to give the seller sufficient notice thereof. Whether he is so entitled will depend upon the contract. This is recognised in A4, which obliges the seller to deliver the goods on board the vessel at the port of shipment on the date or within the period specified (B4 imposes on the buyer the mirror obligation to take delivery thus). Naturally, there can be no such delivery unless a port of destination is specified or notified. A failure to notify a relevant matter under B7 will mean that the risks of loss/damage pass from the agreed date or the expiry date of the period fixed for shipment (B5). Responsibility for costs is likewise transferred – the buyer must pay the additional costs incurred from a failure to give a B7 notice, from the agreed date or the expiry date of the period fixed for shipment. In both cases, the earlier passing of responsibility cannot occur unless the goods have (if originally unascertained) been appropriated to the contract.

The buyer must accept the transport documents or EDI equivalent, in accordance with A8, if in conformity with the contract (B8); pay, unless otherwise agreed, the costs of pre-shipment inspection except where mandated by the authorities of the country of inspection (B9) (this does not include the costs of routine pre-delivery checking by the seller, as per A9); and pay the costs of obtaining the documents or EDI equivalents mentioned in A10 (B10).

---

30 The parties may need to agree specifically on aspects of the unloading, and distribution of costs, in the charterparty case – see the comment in *Guide to Incoterms 1990, op cit,* p 83.

Cost and freight (CFR)

As noted, the CFR term is identical to the CIF term in the Incoterm regime, with one crucial exception. This is, that in a CFR contract the seller is not responsible for procuring insurance to cover the main carriage (see A3(b)). If he desires to be insured, the buyer must effect this. The seller must provide the buyer, upon request, with the necessary information for procuring insurance (A10).

It has been commented that the CFR term is not popular among exporters (unless their country requires insurance to be effected at home), because it 'leads to an artificial separation of the arrangements for insurance and freight, whereas the CIF stipulation, like the FOB clause, provides a natural division of responsibilities between the export merchant and the overseas buyer'.[31]

Carriage paid to (CPT)/carriage and insurance paid to (CIP)

The twin Incoterms, carriage paid to (... named place of destination) or CPT (... named place of destination), and carriage and insurance paid to (... named place of destination) or CIP (... named place of destination), are identical with one exception: CIP imposes upon the seller, the obligation to insure the goods against loss or damage during their carriage to the named destination, while CPT does not. CPT will be reviewed in some detail, following which CIP will be briefly commented upon.

The two terms, CPT and CIP, parallel the Incoterms CFR and CIF respectively. The difference between the two sets of terms is that CPT and CIP are for use with any mode of transport, and for contracts where multi-modal transport is to be employed (or for that matter several successive main carriers). On the other hand, CFR and CIP, it has been seen, are confined to marine carriers (sea or inland waterway). Accordingly, while CFR and CIF provide that delivery is completed when the goods are placed on board (with risks and costs being divided when the goods pass the ship's rail), the multi-modal terms CPT and CIP provide that delivery is completed when the goods are delivered into the custody of the carrier (or first carrier, where more than one carrier is to be used to get the goods to the named place of destination). This delivery might be at a port, where a ship is used as the carrier/first carrier, but equally it can be to an inland point. Also, the terms CPT and CIP should be used when, even as the transport is to be by sea or inland waterway, the cargo cannot sensibly be viewed as being handed over the ship's rail, as in the case of containerised cargo, or cargo loaded by roll-on/roll-off means.[32] In such cases, delivery to the carrier will be at an earlier point, than at the ship's rail.

CPT and CIP are (like CFR and CIF) shipment contracts, where the seller undertakes not to deliver the goods to their agreed destination (which would be an arrival, or D-term, contract), but to ship them (by sea, air, etc) to this destination; ie his delivery obligations are completed at this earlier point.

---

31 Schmittoff, *op cit*, p 55 (referring to the 'c' and 'f' clause).
32 *Guide to Incoterms 1990, op cit*, p 92.

Carriage paid to (CPT)

The carriage paid to (CPT) term requires the seller to organise and pay for carriage to the agreed destination named in the contract; to deliver the goods to the carrier (or first carrier, if there is more than one); and to obtain export clearance. The risks and costs divide at the point of delivery to the carrier.

The primary seller's obligations are: to provide the goods in conformity with the contract (A1); to obtain, at his own expense and risk, export clearance; (A2); to contract on usual terms, at his own expense, for the carriage of the goods to the agreed point at the named place of destination (A3) (if more than one carrier is involved, he will be obliged to organise and pay for these further transport sectors – in practice he might deal with only one party, such as a freight forwarder); and delivery. The delivery obligation is defined in A4:

> Deliver the goods into the custody of the carrier or, if there are subsequent carriers, to the first carrier, for transportation to the named place of destination on the date or within the period stipulated.

Delivery will take place at the place identified by the contract, eg a container terminal.

The risks (subject to B5) are transferred from seller to buyer when the goods are delivered to the carrier (A5). Thus, the seller has no responsibility for the loss of or damage to the goods during carriage; this is the seller's problem and must be pursued by the seller. Accordingly, the seller would ordinarily organise insurance from the point of delivery. The seller may be liable, exceptionally for post-delivery loss or damage where he has an independent legal liability for this, eg because of a failure to pack the goods adequately, which failure causes loss or damage (see A9); and obviously the seller will still be liable for any non-conformity as between the goods and the contract, where this amounts to a breach.

The costs are also divided at the point of delivery to the carrier (A6). Certain qualifications apply: as noted, the seller will have had to pay for export clearance and for carriage to the agreed destination. The costs of carriage include any charges for unloading at the place of destination which may be included in the freight or incurred by the seller when contracting for carriage. This division of costs is subject to B6.

The seller must give notice of delivery pursuant to A4, to the buyer (A7). He must provide the buyer at his own expense, if customary, with the usual transport documents (or, where agreed, equivalent electronic message) (A8). This document may, for example, be a negotiable bill of lading, a non-negotiable sea waybill, an air waybill or a multi-modal transport document. If the transport is by sea and the parties contemplate a resale during transit, a negotiable bill of lading will be stipulated.

The seller must pay the costs of routine pre-delivery checking operations; if appropriate, pack the goods in an adequate way; and mark any packaging (A9). He is to assist the buyer at the latter's expense to obtain any documents (or EDI equivalents) needed for import clearance and transit through another country.

The buyer has the familiar C-term obligations. He must pay the contract price (B1) and take delivery when the seller has effected it under A4 (B4) (ie when the goods have been delivered to the carrier). He has no obligation to arrange the main carriage (or, where there are several carriers, the contracts of main carriage) (B3) – this is the responsibility of the seller. While the seller, it has been seen, is responsible for export clearance, the buyer is responsible for import clearance and for any formalities governing transit through another country (B2).

Consistent with A5 and A6, the parallel B5 and B6 recognise that risks and costs are transferred at the point when the seller delivers the goods into the custody of the carrier (or first carrier). The buyer should have insurance running from this point. His obligation to bear costs does not include, of course, those covered by the seller's contract or those incurred in obtaining export clearance of carriage. Otherwise, he must pay costs incurred in transit for unloading at the place of destination, and beyond (see B6).

While normally the risks and costs are allocated upon delivery, exceptionally these may be transferred to the buyer pre-delivery. This will happen (pursuant to B5 and B6) where he does not give notice to the seller under B7 if required to do so. B7 provides that he must give sufficient notice to the seller whenever he is entitled to determine the time for dispatching the goods and/or the destination. (These options may be provided for in the contract, as reflected in A4.) If he fails to give notice under B7, he bears the risks of the goods from the agreed date or the expiry date of the period fixed for delivery (B5). Likewise, a failure to give notice means that he bears the additional costs resulting from the agreed date, etc (B6). In both cases, the earlier passing of responsibility is conditional upon the goods (if originally unascertained) being identified to the contract.

The buyer must accept the transport document in accordance with A8, if in conformity with the contract (B8); pay, unless there is a contrary agreement, the costs of pre-shipment inspection except where mandated by the authorities in the export country (B9) (the buyer does not have to pay for the seller's routine pre-delivery checking – see A9); and pay any costs incurred in obtaining the documents mentioned in A10 (B10).

Carriage and insurance paid to (CIP)

This term, it has been noted, is identical to CPT (above) with one critical exception: CIP (unlike CPT) obliges the seller to effect insurance of the cargo, on a minimum cover basis, against the risks of the carriage from the point of delivery into the custody of the carrier (or first carrier), until arrival at the agreed point at the named place of destination (A3). The insurance obligation is similar to that imposed on the seller by A3 in the CIF term (see discussion above).[33]

Accordingly, B10 requires the buyer to provide the seller, upon request, with the necessary information for procuring insurance.

---

33 See above.

THE D CATEGORY – DAF, DES, DEQ, DDU, DDP

The D terms, it has been seen, are so designated because the seller contracts to deliver the goods at an agreed *destination* (normally, in the buyer's country). Therefore, the seller's delivery obligation is not fulfilled at an earlier time in his own country (a feature of the E, F and C categories) but at a later time after the conclusion of the main carriage. The D terms (also known as 'delivered' terms) are the most demanding, from the seller's viewpoint. He must arrange the main carriage to the agreed destination and bear the costs and risks during this carriage. If the goods are lost in transit, this is to the seller's account rather than the buyer's (although the seller may have recourse against a third party, such as the carrier). D terms are increasingly used, as exporters who can deliver in the buyer's country are, all things being equal, more likely to get an order for their goods.

Delivered at frontier (DAF)

Delivered at frontier (... named place) (abbreviated as DAF (... named place)) can be used for any transport mode (or for multi-modal transport), but in practice it is used for road and rail deliveries and is frequently used in continental Europe trade.[34]

It imposes on the seller the obligation to deliver the goods to a named place at the specified frontier, but before the customs border of the adjacent country. In practice the precise place may be some distance from the frontier. The frontier can be that of any country, including the exporter's country. The seller arranges and pays for export clearance, and the buyer is responsible for import clearance.

The seller must provide conforming goods (A1); and organise and pay for export clearance, and likewise clearance to travel through other countries if required for delivery (A2). The seller is to organise and pay for carriage to the agreed place of delivery at the frontier (or the specified equivalent place), an obligation including paying the costs of transit, if necessary, through another country or countries (A3). If the precise delivery point is not agreed, or settled by practice, the seller may select one.

His delivery obligation is delineated in A4: 'Place the goods at the disposal of the buyer at the named place of delivery at the frontier on the date or within the period stipulated.' He will be responsible for unloading, if applicable (see A6 – this may in any event be included in the cost of freight). A comment in *Guide to Incoterms* may be noted:

> DAF may be used irrespective of the intended mode of transport, though it is more frequently used for rail carriage. The rail carriage usually continues past the border without any discharge of the goods from the railway wagon and re-loading on another one. Consequently, there will be no real 'placing of the goods at the disposal of the buyer'. Instead, the seller, on the buyer's request, will provide the buyer with a through railway consignment note to the place of final destination in the country of importation ...[35]

---

34 Schmitthoff, *op cit*, p 59.
35 *Guide to Incoterms 1990, op cit*, p 105.

The risks are transferred from seller to buyer upon delivery in accordance with A4 (see A5). The buyer should, therefore, consider insuring the goods from this point. The seller will be liable for loss or damage after this time only when an independent contractual or other liability may be established against him (eg a loss caused by inadequate packaging).

Costs are likewise divided upon delivery (A6). A6 emphasises that the seller is liable for the expenses of discharge operations if applicable (as an incident of his having responsibility for carriage), and export clearance. The buyer will of course pay the costs of post-delivery carriage.

The seller is to give notice to the buyer of the dispatch of the goods to the named place at the frontier, as well as any other notice required to allow the buyer to take measures normally necessary for taking the goods (A7). The seller must provide the buyer with the usual documents (or EDI equivalents) or other evidence of delivery at the named place; provide the buyer at the latter's request, risk and expense, with a through document of transport (or, if agreed, EDI equivalent) (A8); provide pre-delivery checking operations at his own expense, and, if applicable, packaging which is appropriately marked (A9); and assist the buyer at the latter's expense to obtain the documents or EDI equivalents needed for import, etc (A10).

The buyer must pay the contract price (B1); obtain and pay for import clearance at the named point, and for any subsequent transport sector (B2); and take delivery at the named point (B4).

B5 and B6 mirror A5 and A6 in recognising the transfer of risks and division of costs upon delivery under A4. Both B5 and B6 recognise that the allocation of risks and costs can happen prior to delivery, in consequence of the buyer's failure to take delivery or to give notice to the seller under B7, if required to do so. (B7 provides that, wherever he is entitled to determine the time within a stipulated period and/or the place of taking delivery, the buyer must give the seller sufficient notice thereof.) A failure to give this notice means that he bears all risks of loss, etc from the agreed date or expiry date of the period stipulated for delivery, and in any event he is at risk from the moment of a delivery in terms of A4 (B5). If he fails to give notice under B7, or if he fails to take delivery, he bears any additional costs resulting thereby (B6). In both cases, the transfer of responsibility is conditional upon the goods having been appropriated to the contract.

The buyer is to accept the transport documents and other evidence of delivery if it is in order (B8); pay the costs of pre-shipment inspection except when mandated by the authorities in the export country (B9) (he is not liable for the seller's pre-delivery checking under A9, however); and pay the costs and charges incurred in obtaining the A10 documents or their electronic equivalents (B10).

Delivered ex-ship (DES)

Delivered ex-ship (... named port of destination) or DES (... named port of destination) is confined to contracts involving carriage by sea or inland waterway. It requires the seller to deliver the goods to the agreed port (which usually will be in the buyer's country). The goods are to be placed by the seller at the disposal of the buyer (on the ship). The seller completes his delivery obligation at the port; thus, he must contract for (main) carriage. He must also clear the goods for export; but the buyer has responsibility for import clearance. The DES term places the seller at risk during the voyage (unlike the C class terms, such as CIF, where delivery is earlier).

The seller must provide the goods in conformity with the contract (A1); organise and pay for export clearance (and if necessary carry out customs formalities for transit through another country) (A2); and organise and pay for carriage to the agreed port of destination (A3). He has a discretion here – he can ship *via* the usual route and in a customary manner to the agreed point. If a point is not agreed or determined by practice, he may select the point which best suits his purpose. Within these parameters, he will not incur liability for breach of contract (contrast the situation where he selects an unusual, and circuitous route, thereby causing economic loss to the buyer).

He delivers the goods when he places them at the disposal of the buyer on board the vessel at the usual unloading point in the named port uncleared for import on the date or within the period stipulated, in such a way as to enable them to be removed from the vessel by unloading equipment appropriate to the situation (A4). The buyer, then, is responsible for unloading the goods.

Risks are (subject to B5) transferred to the buyer upon delivery (A5). The seller, then, is at risk during the carriage. In appropriate cases he should effect insurance. The buyer should consider insuring the goods from the time of delivery. The seller may be liable for loss of or damage to the goods post-delivery where there is an independent head of liability, as where damage is caused by his failure to package the goods adequately in breach of his obligation in A9.

Costs are divided upon delivery (subject to the operation of B6) (A6). Thereafter the buyer is liable. As it has been noted, the seller is liable for the costs of the carriage and export clearance (and customs clearances required for other countries, if applicable). The buyer is responsible for unloading (see B6) and for post-delivery costs. The buyer is responsible for costs incurred by his delay in unloading once the goods are at his disposal on the ship.

The seller's other obligations include giving notice to the buyer of the estimated time of arrival, etc (A7). He is to provide the buyer (at the seller's expense) with the delivery order and/or the usual transport document (eg a negotiable bill of lading – necessary if resale while afloat is contemplated as a possibility – or non-negotiable sea waybill, or their EDI equivalent) to allow the buyer to take delivery from the carrier (A8). He is to pay the costs of routine pre-delivery checking operations, package the goods adequately, where appropriate, and mark the packaging (A9). He is to assist the buyer (at the buyer's expense) to obtain the documents or EDI equivalents which the buyer might require for import clearance, and provide the buyer, if requested, with information relevant to procuring insurance (A10).

The buyer must pay the contract price (A1); obtain and pay for import clearance (B2); and take delivery when the goods have been placed at his disposal in accordance with A4 (B4). He is not obliged to take delivery earlier than any agreed time.

The risks of loss of, or damage to, the goods are transferred to the buyer when the goods have been duly delivered (B5). Costs are divided at the same time; thus, the buyer must pay for unloading (B6). In both cases, ie risks and costs, the transfer of responsibility to the buyer can happen pre-delivery. B7 requires him to give notice to the seller when he is entitled to determine the time within a stipulated period and/or the place of delivery. Accordingly, he bears the risks from the time the goods are placed at his disposal (such as where he delays unloading); and should he fail to give any required B7 notice, he bears the risks from the agreed date or the expiry date of the period stipulated for delivery (B5). Similarly, he must pay costs from the time of delivery (and thus is responsible for costs flowing from a failure to unload), and he is likewise liable for additional costs flowing from a failure to give any required B7 notice (B6). In both cases, the earlier division of risks and costs cannot occur until the goods have been identified to the contract, where originally unascertained.

The buyer must accept the A8 documents if they are in order (B8); pay (unless otherwise agreed) the costs of any pre-shipment inspection except when mandated by the authorities of the country of export (B9) (as noted, the seller is liable for the costs of pre-delivery checking pursuant to A9); and pay the costs of obtaining the documents or EDI equivalents mentioned in A10 (B10).

Delivered ex-quay (duty paid) (DEQ)

The delivered ex-quay (duty paid) (... named port of destination) or DEQ (... named port of destination) term is only for use where the main carriage is to be by ship or inland waterway. DEQ parallels DES (which has just been reviewed) but it has two points of distinction – it imposes additional obligations upon the seller, ie:

1   the seller must make the goods available on the quay (or wharf) at the named port of destination (ie he must unload from the ship); and

2   the seller must organise and pay for import clearance. The buyer's obligation to take delivery arises when the goods are duly delivered on the quay.

In summary, then, the seller must deliver the goods to the quay at the named port of destination (which will usually be in the buyer's country). He must therefore organise and pay for carriage. He is at risk during this carriage. He must organise and pay both for export clearance and import clearance (and satisfy at his own expense any customs formalities arising in another country).

The review of seller's and buyer's obligations concerning DES (immediately above) may be consulted regarding their obligations under DEQ, given the parallel nature of these terms. The qualifications on this review, to cover the distinctive features of DEQ, are as noted below.

To begin, the seller must obtain and pay for both export and import clearance, and satisfy customs formalities required by any third country (or countries) (A2). These include taxes, so if the parties desire to contract on the basis that the buyer will be responsible for any import duties or similar taxes, the term should be amended in the contract, eg to read 'DEQ VAT unpaid'.[36]

The carriage obligation on the seller is to carry the goods to the quay at the named port of destination (A3). The seller has no insurance obligation (ie it is optional for him to insure against risks during carriage). His delivery obligation is to place the goods at the disposal of the buyer on the quay or wharf at the agreed port of destination and on the date or within the period stipulated (A4). He must therefore organise and pay for their unloading (including the use of lighters if necessary).

The division of risks and costs clauses (A5 and A6) in DEQ parallel those applying in the case of DES. The A7 terms are identical. The comments on the DES terms, above, should be noted. Applying the DEQ regime in context, the risks and costs pass at the slightly later point, ie when the goods are made available to the buyer on the quay. Exceptionally, the division may be effected prior to delivery (ie in the circumstances set out in B5 and B6 below).

The A1, A8, A9 and A10 obligations in DEQ are as for DES, with appropriate modifications to take account of the facts that the DEQ seller must deliver on the quay and organise import clearance.

The buyer's obligations in DEQ parallel those in DES, again with the modifications needed to take account of the fact that the buyer takes delivery at the later point when the goods are on the quay, and that he is not responsible for import clearance. In particular, the B5 and B6 obligations in DEQ parallel those in DES (above), subject to the same two qualifications: the buyer takes delivery on the quay; and is not responsible for import clearance. Once again, the risks and costs are divided and transferred to the buyer when the goods are placed at his disposal (in a DEQ contract – on the quay). Thereafter, he is liable for any loss/damage to the goods, or continuing costs, and thus should take them into custody promptly. The risks and costs will also be transferred, at a pre-delivery point, where the buyer fails to give a B7 notice when required to do so (see B5 and B6). The rules are as for DES.

The other buyer terms (B1, B3, B4, B8 and B9) parallel those for DES. Unlike DES, B2 requires only that the buyer assist the seller, at the latter's expense, to obtain import clearance; and B10 requires the buyer to assist the seller, at the latter's expense, to obtain any documents or EDI equivalents needed to deliver the goods in the country of importation.

The preamble to the DEQ provisions notes that DEQ should not be used if the seller cannot obtain the import licence; and that if the parties want the buyer to do this, the words 'duty unpaid' and not 'duty paid' should follow the usage DEQ.

---

36   *Guide to Incoterms 1990, op cit,* p 120, noting that, if a right to deduct these duties for tax purposes is available only to residents, it might be lost. Clearly such a tax would ordinarily be factored into the contract price, so shifting its formal incidence will not be pivotal to the underlying bargain between the parties.

Delivery duty unpaid (DDU)

Delivered duty unpaid (... named place of destination) or DDU (... named place of destination) can be used for any mode of transport (or for multi-modal transport). It is the second most demanding Incoterm from the seller's viewpoint, being eclipsed in the regard only by the term delivered duty paid (DDP). DDU and DDP are identical with the one exception: the latter requires the seller to perform all of the DDU obligations plus an additional one, ie to clear the goods for import. Below, the DDU obligations will be reviewed, following which the DDP term will be briefly reviewed.

DDU imposes on the seller the obligation to clear the goods for export, and to organise and pay for their carriage to the named destination in the country of delivery (which will be the buyer's country, or country of delivery nominated by him). The delivery is effected in the country of importation when the goods are placed at the buyer's disposal at the specified place. The buyer must organise and pay for import clearance.

The seller's obligations include providing goods in conformity with the contract (A1); obtaining, at his own expense, export clearance and satisfying customs formalities for transit through another country during carriage (A2); and organising and paying for (main) carriage of the goods to the place of destination (A3). He has some discretion in selecting the route for carriage (note the details in A3). He has no insurance obligations, but should consider insuring the goods up until the point of delivery (he is at risk until this time).

His delivery obligation is to place the goods at the disposal of the buyer (ie at the named place of destination) on the date or within the period stipulated (A4). The parties should agree upon a precise point or delivery; in default of this the seller may select the point at the named destination which best suits his purpose (see A3).

The risks are (subject to B5) transferred from seller to buyer upon delivery (A5). The buyer should consider having insurance from this point. This term does not negate any liability which the seller may have, independently of A5, for loss or damage, such as where it is caused by inadequate packaging or marking in breach of his packaging obligations under A9.

The costs are (subject to B6) also divided upon delivery (A6). Thus, from this point on, the buyer is liable for any costs (including those resulting from his failure to take them into custody). The buyer is responsible for the costs of import clearance (see B2). The buyer, of course, is liable for post-delivery carriage.

The seller is to give notice to the buyer of the dispatch of the goods as well as any other notice required to allow him to take the goods (A7). The seller is to provide at his own expense the delivery order and/or the usual transport document (eg a negotiable bill of lading, a non-negotiable sea waybill, etc) which the buyer may require to take delivery. If agreed, an EDI equivalent may be used. A negotiable bill of lading will be used where carriage is by sea, and the parties contemplate an in-transit resale. The seller is to pay for any routine checking operations required for delivery, to package the goods appropriately (if applicable) and to mark any such packaging (A9). He is to assist the buyer, at the latter's expense, to obtain any documents or EDI equivalents needed for the import of the goods; and to provide the buyer with any information needed to effect insurance (a matter which becomes a critical issue for the buyer upon the moment of delivery) (A10).

The buyer must of course pay the contract price (B1). He must organise import clearance and pay for this (B2). He must take delivery where this is duly tendered in accord with A4 (B4). B5 mirrors A5 in recognising that the risks of the goods are transferred to the buyer upon delivery. He should therefore consider insuring the goods from this point. Thus, if he delays taking the goods into custody, once they have been duly placed at his disposal in conformity with A4 and loss/damage results, this is to his account. Likewise, if he fails to obtain import clearance by the agreed time of delivery, he is at risk from this point (assuming the goods have been placed at his disposal). The risks will transfer to him prior to delivery where he fails to give notice, if required, under B7. B7 states that the buyer must, whenever he is entitled to determine the time within a stipulated period and/or the place of taking delivery, give the seller sufficient notice thereof. If he fails to give this notice, he must bear the risks from the agreed date or the expiry date of the period stipulated for delivery, provided the goods have been appropriated to the contract (if originally unascertained) (B5). He cannot, that is, delay taking delivery with legal impunity by failing to give a B7 notice.

The costs are likewise divided from the time the goods are placed at the buyer's disposal in accordance with A4 (B6). If he fails to obtain import clearance as required by B2 (with the result that the goods cannot be delivered); fails to take delivery when they have been placed at his disposal, in accordance with A4; or fails to give any B7 notice required (see above) – all additional costs thereby incurred are to his account, provided that the goods (if required) have been appropriated to the contract. He is, as noted, liable for all the costs of importation.

He must accept the delivery order or transport document in accordance with A8 (B8); pay, unless otherwise agreed, the costs of pre-shipment inspection except when mandated by the export country (B9) (it will be recalled that the seller has the expense of any routine pre-delivery checking – A9); and pay for the documents or EDI equivalents mentioned in A10 (B10).

The parties can of course amend the standard DDU provisions, such as where the parties want the seller to bear some of the costs of importation, by appropriate wording – an instance given in the DDU preamble is 'delivered duty unpaid, VAT paid (... named place of destination)'.

Delivered duty paid (DDP)

The Incoterm delivered duty paid (... named place of destination) or DDP (... named place of destination) is, from the seller's viewpoint, the most demanding of all of the Incoterms. As noted in the discussion of DDU above, the DDP term is identical to DDU with one exception: the seller must, additionally, procure import clearance and pay for it (the corollary is that this obligation has been dropped from the buyer's obligations). The term is apt if the seller can readily obtain import clearance; otherwise, if the buyer can more readily effect this, the DDU should be used. Also, DDU may be preferred if clearing the goods for import involves the payment of a VAT or equivalent tax which can only be deducted for tax purposes by a resident of the country of importation.[37]

The preamble to DDP notes that DDP should not be used if the seller cannot obtain, directly or indirectly, the import licence.

The seller's DDP obligations then, broadly, are to deliver the goods at the point specified in the named place of destination in the import country. He must arrange both export and import clearance and pay for these, and likewise organise and pay for the fulfilment of any customs formalities where carriage is to be through a third country or countries. He has to organise and pay for main carriage. He is at risk until the goods are delivered, and must bear the costs until this point. The buyer's main obligations are to pay the contract price and to take delivery.

The DDP provisions relating to seller's and buyer's obligations are more or less the same as those for DDU, with modifications being necessary only to take account of the transfer of responsibility for import clearance to the seller in the case of DDP. Accordingly, the commentary on the DDU term (above) may be applied to the DDP provisions, subject to this qualification. DDP obligations which have been amended to take account of the transfer of the import obligation are: A2 (requiring the seller to organise and pay for both export and import clearances); A6 (a consequential change, again identifying the cost of import clearance as being to the seller's account); A10 (again, to take account of the transfer of the import obligation); B2 (confining the buyer's obligation to render the seller, at the latter's expense, assistance in obtaining import clearance); B5 and B6 (recognising that import clearance is no longer the buyer's responsibility); and B10 (imposing on the buyer the obligation to assist the seller, at the seller's expense, to obtain any documents or EDI equivalents needed for import clearance).

TUTORIAL QUESTIONS

(In some instances reference may need to be made to the applicable law of the contract. It may be convenient to assume application of the Vienna Convention, in which case Chapter 1 should also be read.)

1 What is the major, consistent principle governing the division of risks and costs in the Incoterms? Nominate some common situations where – pursuant to numerous of the Incoterms – this principle of allocation is displaced.

2 What are the general differences between each of the two classes of 'shipment' terms and the 'arrival' terms?

3 What terms are particularly apt for containerised cargo?

4 What terms are particularly apt for bulk cargo?

---

37 See the comment in *Guide to Incoterms 1990, ibid*, p 136.

5 In the case of the FOB and CIF Incoterms, does the buyer have the right to inspect the goods before making payment? If so, can the buyer reject the goods for non-conformity with the contract after they have arrived at the port to which they are to be shipped?

6 What terms impose liability on the seller for loss in transit?

7 Goods are sold on a CIF basis. They are lost in transit. Does the buyer nonetheless have to pay for the goods?

8 Goods are shipped on a CIF basis by a buyer in State X to a seller in State Y. While they are in transit, State Y bans the importation of goods of this class. Is the buyer still obliged to pay?

9 Goods are sold on a CIF basis. The contract provides for payment on presentation of the transport documents on arrival, or in any event no later than one month of the date on the bill of lading. The ship is delayed because of an event which is independent of any fault on the part of the seller. The goods arrive three months late and well beyond the month specified. Can the buyer reject the goods because the documents are presented at a very late date?

10 Goods are sold on a FOB basis, with the buyer being required to nominate a vessel within 30 days of contract. The buyer does not nominate a vessel within this period. What is the legal position as between the parties?

11 Goods are sold on an FOB basis. By agreement between the parties, the goods are to be loaded by a stevedore at the seller's expense. They are damaged during loading once they have passed the ship's rail. Who is liable for this damage, as between the buyer and the seller?

12 What term(s) should the parties use if it is desired that the seller organise and pay for the main carriage and insure against the risks of this journey? If, where such a term is used, the goods are damaged and the insurer is unable or unwilling to pay, is the seller liable to the buyer for this damage?

13 Goods are sold on a DAF basis. The seller does not, as required by the contract, give sufficient notice to the buyer of the dispatch of the goods to the nominated place at the frontier. What are the consequences of this failure?

14 The goods are sold on a DAF basis and dispatched by the seller. The buyer does not take delivery of the goods when they have been placed at his disposal. What are the legal consequences?

15 Goods are sold on a DDU basis. What is the legal position as between the parties where the buyer purports to reject the goods for non-conformity with the contract when they are placed at his disposal at the named destination?

16 Goods are sold on an FCA basis. The seller experiences delays in obtaining export clearance. The buyer is unaware of this but neglects to notify the seller of the name of the carriers, as required by the contract. The contractual deadlines pass for both the obtaining of export clearance and the giving of the buyer's notice. Finally, the seller obtains clearance. Can the buyer reject the goods?

FURTHER READING

Burnett, R, *The Law of International Business Transactions*, 1994, Sydney: Federation Press, Chapter 1, pp 29–64.

Evans, P, 'FOB and CIF Contracts' (1993) 67 *Australian Law Journal* at 844–58.

International Chamber of Commerce, *Incoterms 1990*, 1990, Paris: ICC Publishing SA.

Murray, D, 'Risk of Loss of Goods in Transit; a Comparison of the 1990 Incoterms with Terms from Other Voices' (1991) 23 *University of Miami Inter-American Law Review* 1 at 93–131.

Ramberg, J, *Guide to Incoterms 1990*, 1991, Paris: ICC Publishing SA.

Sassoon, D, 'The Origin of FOB and CIF Terms and the Factors Influencing their Choice' (1967) *Journal of Business Law* at 32.

Sassoon, D and Merren, M, *CIF and FOB Contracts*, 1984, Vol 5, 3rd edn, London: Stevens, British Shipping Laws series.

Schmitthoff, C, *Export Trade – the Law and Practice of International Trade*, 9th edn, 1990, London: Stevens, Chapter 2.

Sriro, 'Incoterms – A Quick Reference Guide' (1993) *East Asian Executive Reports* 9 at 21.

INCOTERMS 1990

Ex-works (ExW)

(… named place)

'Ex-works' means that the seller fulfils his obligation to deliver when he has made the goods available at his premises (ie works, factory, warehouse, etc) to the buyer. In particular, he is not responsible for loading the goods on the vehicle provided by the buyer or for clearing the goods for export, unless otherwise agreed. The buyer bears all costs and risks involved in taking the goods from the seller's premises to the desired destination. This term thus represents the minimum obligation for the seller. This term should not be used when the buyer cannot carry out directly or indirectly the export formalities. In such circumstances, the FCA term should be used.

A   The seller must

A.1   *Provision of goods in conformity with the contract*

Provide the goods and the commercial invoice, or its equivalent electronic message, in conformity with the contract of sale and any other evidence of conformity which may be required by the contract.

A.2   *Licences, authorisations and formalities*

Render the buyer, at the latter's request, risk and expense, every assistance in obtaining any export licence or other official authorisation necessary for the exportation of the goods.

A.3   *Contract of carriage and insurance*

(a)   Contract of carriage

No obligation.

(b)   Contract of insurance

No obligation.

A.4   *Delivery*

Place the goods at the disposal of the buyer at the named place of delivery on the date or within the period stipulated or, if no such place or time is stipulated, at the usual place and time for delivery of such goods.

A.5   *Transfer of risks*

Subject to the provisions of B.5, bear all risks of loss of or damage to the goods until such time as they have been placed at the disposal of the buyer in accordance with A.4.

A.6   *Division of costs*

Subject to the provisions of B.6, pay all costs relating to the goods until such time as they have been placed at the disposal of the buyer in accordance with A.4.

A.7   *Notice to the buyer*

Give the buyer sufficient notice as to when and where the goods will be placed at his disposal.

A.8   *Proof of delivery, transport document or equivalent electronic message*

No obligation.

A.9   *Checking – packaging – marking*

Pay the costs of those checking operations (such as checking quality, measuring, weighing, counting) which are necessary for the purpose of placing the goods at the disposal of the buyer.

Provide at his own expense packaging (unless it is usual for the particular trade to make the goods of the contract description available unpacked) which is required for the transport of the goods, to the extent that the circumstances relating to the transport (eg modalities, destination) are made known to the seller before the contract of sale is concluded. Packaging is to be marked appropriately.

A.10   *Other obligations*

Render the buyer at the latter's request, risk and expense, every assistance in obtaining any documents or equivalent electronic messages issued or transmitted in the country of delivery and/or of origin which the buyer may require for the exportation and/or importation of the goods and, where necessary, for their transit through another country.

Provide the buyer, upon request, with the necessary information for procuring insurance.

B   The buyer must

B.1   *Payment of the price*

Pay the price as provided in the contract of sale.

B.2   *Licences, authorisations and formalities*

Obtain at his own risk and expense any export and import licence or other official authorisation and carry out all customs formalities for the exportation and importation of the goods and, where necessary, for their transit through another country.

B.3   *Contract of carriage*

No obligation.

B.4   *Taking delivery*

Take delivery of the goods as soon as they have been placed at his disposal in accordance with A.4.

B.5   *Transfer of risks*

Bear all risks of loss of or damage to the goods from the time they have been placed at his disposal in accordance with A.4. Should he fail to give notice in accordance with B.7, bear all risks of loss of or damage to the goods from the agreed date or the expiry date of any period fixed for taking delivery provided, however, that the goods have been duly appropriated to the contract, that is to say clearly set aside or otherwise identified as the contract goods.

B.6   *Division of costs*

Pay all costs relating to the goods from the time they have been placed at his disposal in accordance with A.4.

Pay any additional costs incurred by failing either to take delivery of the goods when they have been placed at his disposal, or to give appropriate notice in accordance with B.7, provided, however, that the goods have been duly appropriated to the contract, that is to say clearly set aside or otherwise identified as the contract goods.

Pay all duties, taxes and other official charges as well as the costs of carrying out customs formalities payable upon exportation and importation of the goods and, where necessary, for their transit through another country.

Reimburse all costs and charges incurred by the seller in rendering assistance in accordance with A.2.

B.7 *Notice to the seller*

Whenever he is entitled to determine the time within a stipulated period, and/or the place of taking delivery, give the seller sufficient notice thereof.

B.8 *Proof of delivery, transport document or equivalent electronic message*

Provide the seller with appropriate evidence of having taken delivery.

B.9 *Inspection of goods*

Pay, unless otherwise agreed, the costs of pre-shipment inspection (including inspection mandated by the authorities of the country of exportation).

B.10 *Other obligations*

Pay all costs and charges incurred in obtaining the documents or equivalent electronic messages mentioned in A.10 and reimburse those incurred by the seller in rendering his assistance in accordance therewith.

Free alongside ship (FAS)

(... named port of shipment)

'Free alongside ship' means that the seller fulfils his obligation to deliver when the goods have been placed alongside the vessel on the quay or in lighters at the named port of shipment. This means that the buyer has to bear all costs and risks of loss of or damage to the goods from that moment.

The FAS term requires the buyer to clear the goods for export. It should not be used when the buyer cannot carry out directly or indirectly the export formalities.

This term can only be used for sea or inland waterway transport.

A   The seller must

A.1 *Provision of goods in conformity with the contract*

Provide the goods and the commercial invoice, or its equivalent electronic message, in conformity with the contract of sale and any other evidence of conformity which may be required by the contract.

A.2 *Licences, authorisations and formalities*

Render the buyer, at the latter's request, risk and expense, every assistance in obtaining any export licence or other official authorisation necessary for the exportation of the goods.

A.3 *Contract of carriage and insurance*

(a)   Contract of carriage

No obligation.

(b)   Contract of insurance

No obligation.

A.4   *Delivery*

Deliver the goods alongside the named vessel at the loading place named by the buyer at the named port of shipment on the date or within the period stipulated and in the manner customary at the port.

A.5   *Transfer of risks*

Subject to the provisions of B.5, bear all risks of loss of or damage to the goods until such time as they have been delivered in accordance with A.4.

A.6   *Division of costs*

Subject to the provisions of B.6, pay all costs relating to the goods until such time as they have been delivered in accordance with A.4.

A.7   *Notice to the buyer*

Give the buyer sufficient notice that the goods have been delivered alongside the named vessel.

A.8   *Proof of delivery, transport document or equivalent electronic message*

Provide the buyer at the seller's expense with the usual document in proof of delivery of the goods in accordance with A.4.

Unless the document referred to in the preceding paragraph is the transport document, render the buyer at the latter's request, risk and expense, every assistance in obtaining a transport document (for example, a negotiable bill of lading, a non-negotiable sea waybill, an inland waterway document).

When the seller and the buyer have agreed to communicate electronically, the document referred to in the preceding paragraphs may be replaced by an equivalent electronic data interchange (EDI) message.

A.9   *Checking – packaging – marking*

Pay the costs of those checking operations (such as checking quality, measuring, weighing, counting) which are necessary for the purpose of placing the goods at the disposal of the buyer. Provide at his own expense packaging (unless it is usual for the particular trade to ship the goods of the contract description unpacked) which is required for the transport of the goods, to the extent that the circumstances relating to the transport (eg modalities, destination) are made known to the seller before the contract of sale is concluded. Packaging is to be marked appropriately.

A.10   *Other obligations*

Render the buyer at the latter's request, risk and expense, every assistance in obtaining any documents or equivalent electronic messages (other than those mentioned in A.8) issued or transmitted in the country of shipment and/or of origin which the buyer may require for the exportation and/or importation of the goods and, where necessary, for their transit through another country.

Provide the buyer, upon request, with the necessary information for procuring insurance.

B   **The buyer must**

B.1   *Payment of the price*

Pay the price as provided in the contract of sale.

B.2   *Licences, authorisations and formalities*

Obtain at his own risk and expense any export and import licence or other official authorisation and carry out all customs formalities for the exportation and importation of the goods and, where necessary, for their transit through another country.

B.3   *Contract of carriage*

Contract at his own expense for the carriage of the goods from the named port of shipment.

B.4   *Taking delivery*

Take delivery of the goods in accordance with A.4.

B.5   *Transfer of risks*

Bear all risks of loss of or damage to the goods from the time they have been delivered in accordance with A.4.

Should he fail to fulfil his obligations in accordance with B.2, bear all additional risks of loss of or damage to the goods incurred thereby and should he fail to give notice in accordance with B.7, or should the vessel named by him fail to arrive on time, or be unable to take the goods, or close for cargo earlier than the stipulated time, bear all risks of loss of or damage to the goods from the agreed date or the expiry date of the period stipulated for delivery provided, however, that the goods have been duly appropriated to the contract, that is to say, clearly set aside or otherwise identified as the contract goods.

B.6   *Division of costs*

Pay all costs relating to the goods from the time they have been delivered in accordance with A.4.

Pay any additional costs incurred, either because the vessel named by him has failed to arrive on time, or will be unable to take the goods, or will close for cargo earlier than the stipulated time or because the buyer has failed to fulfil his obligations in accordance with B.2, or to give appropriate notice in accordance with B.7, provided, however, that the goods have been duly appropriated to the contract, that is to say, clearly set aside or otherwise identified as the contract goods.

Pay all duties, taxes and other official charges as well as the costs of carrying out customs formalities payable upon exportation and importation of the goods and, where necessary, for their transit through another country.

Pay all costs and charges incurred by the seller in rendering assistance in accordance with A.2.

B.7   *Notice to the seller*

Give the seller sufficient notice of the vessel name, loading place and required delivery time.

B.8   *Proof of delivery, transport document or equivalent electronic message*

Accept the proof of delivery in accordance with A.8.

B.9   *Inspection of goods*

Pay unless otherwise agreed, the costs of pre-shipment inspection (including inspection mandated by the authorities of the country of exportation).

B.10 Other obligations

Pay all costs and charges incurred in obtaining the documents or equivalent electronic messages mentioned in A.10 and reimburse those incurred by the seller in rendering his assistance in accordance therewith.

Free on board (FOB)

(... named port of shipment)

'Free on board' means that the seller fulfils his obligation to deliver when the goods have passed over the ship's rail at the named port of shipment. This means that the buyer has to bear all costs and risks of loss of or damage to the goods from that point.

The FOB term requires the seller to clear the goods for export.

This term can only be used for sea or inland waterway transport. When the ship's rail serves no practical purpose, such as in the case of roll-on/roll-off or container traffic, the FCA term is more appropriate to use.

A   The seller must

A.1   Provision of goods in conformity with the contract

Provide the goods and the commercial invoice or its equivalent electronic message, in conformity with the contract of sale and any other evidence of conformity which may be required by the contract.

A.2   Licences, authorisations and formalities

Obtain at his own risk and expense any export licence or other official authorisation and carry out all customs formalities necessary for the exportation of the goods.

A.3   Contract of carriage and insurance

(a)   Contract of carriage.

No obligation.

(b)   Contract of insurance.

No obligation.

A.4   Delivery

Deliver the goods on board the vessel named by the buyer at the named port of shipment on the date or within the period stipulated and in the manner customary at the port.

A.5   Transfer of risks

Subject to the provisions of B.5, bear all risks of loss of or damage to the goods until such time as they have passed the ship s rail at the named port of shipment.

A.6   Division of costs

Subject to the provisions of B.6:

- pay all costs relating to the goods until such time as they have passed the ship's rail at the named port of shipment;

- pay the costs of customs formalities necessary for exportation as well as all duties, taxes and other official charges payable upon exportation.

A.7   Notice to the buyer

Give the buyer sufficient notice that the goods have been delivered on board.

A.8   Proof of delivery, transport document or equivalent electronic message

Provide the buyer at the seller's expense with the usual document in proof of delivery in accordance with A.4.

Unless the document referred to in the preceding paragraph is the transport document, render the buyer, at the latter's request, risk and expense, every assistance in obtaining a transport document for the contract of carriage (eg, a negotiable bill of lading, a non-negotiable sea waybill, an inland waterway document, or a multi-modal transport document).

Where the seller and the buyer have agreed to communicate electronically, the document referred to in the preceding paragraph may be replaced by an equivalent electronic data interchange (EDI) message.

A.9   Checking – packaging – marking

Pay the costs of those checking operations (such as checking quality, measuring, weighing, counting) which are necessary for the purpose of delivering the goods in accordance with A.4.

Provide at his own expense packaging (unless it is usual for the particular trade to ship the goods of the contract description unpacked) which is required for the transport of the goods, to the extent that the circumstances relating to the transport (eg modalities, destination) are made known to the seller before the contract of sale is concluded. Packaging is to be marked appropriately.

A.10   Other obligations

Render the buyer at the latter's request, risk and expense, every assistance in obtaining any documents or equivalent electronic messages (other than those mentioned in A.8) issued or transmitted in the country of shipment and/or of origin which the buyer may require for the importation of the goods and, where necessary, for their transit through another country. Provide the buyer, upon request, with the necessary information for procuring insurance.

B   The buyer must

B.1   Payment of the price

Pay the price as provided in the contract of sale.

B.2   Licences, authorisations and formalities

Obtain at his own risk and expense any import licence or other official authorisation and carry out all customs formalities for the importation of the goods and, where necessary, for their transit through another country.

B.3   Contract of carriage

Contract at his own expense for the carriage of the goods from the named port of shipment.

B.4   Taking delivery

Take delivery of the goods in accordance with A.4.

B.5   Transfer of risks

Bear all risks of loss of or damage to the goods from the time they have passed the ship's rail at the named port of shipment.

Should he fail to give notice in accordance with B.7, or should the vessel named by him fail to arrive on time or be unable to take the goods, or close for cargo earlier than the stipulated time, bear all risks of loss of or damage to the goods from the agreed date or the expiry date of the period stipulated for delivery provided, however, that the goods have been duly appropriated to the contract, that is to say, clearly set aside or otherwise identified as the contract goods.

B.6   *Division of costs*

Pay all costs relating to the goods from the time they have passed the ship's rail at the named port of shipment.

Pay any additional costs incurred, either because the vessel named by him has failed to arrive on time, or is unable to take the goods, or will close for cargo earlier than the stipulated date, or because the buyer has failed to give appropriate notice in accordance with B.7, provided, however, that the goods have been duly appropriated to the contract, that is to say, clearly set aside or otherwise identified as the contract goods.

Pay all duties, taxes and other official charges as well as the costs of carrying out customs formalities payable upon importation of the goods and, where necessary, for their transit through another country.

B.7   *Notice to the seller*

Give the seller sufficient notice of the vessel name, loading point and required delivery time.

B.8   *Proof of delivery, transport document or equivalent electronic message*

Accept the proof of delivery in accordance with A.8.

B.9   *Inspection of goods*

Pay unless otherwise agreed, the costs of pre-shipment inspection except when mandated by the authorities of the country of export.

B.10   *Other obligations*

Pay all costs and charges incurred in obtaining the documents or equivalent electronic messages mentioned in A.10 and reimburse those incurred by the seller in rendering his assistance in accordance therewith.

Cost, insurance and freight (CIF)

(… named port of destination)

'Cost, insurance and freight' means that the seller has the same obligations as under CFR but with the addition that he has to procure marine insurance against the buyer's risk of loss of or damage to the goods during the carriage. The seller contracts for insurance and pays the insurance premium.

The buyer should note that under the CIF term the seller is only required to obtain insurance on minimum coverage. The CIF term requires the seller to clear the goods for export.

This term can only be used for sea and inland waterway transport. When the ship's rail serves no practical purposes such as in the case of roll-on/roll-off or container traffic, the CIP term is more appropriate to use.

A   The seller must

A.1   Provision of goods in conformity with the contract

Provide the goods and the commercial invoice, or its equivalent electronic message, in conformity with the contract of sale and any other evidence of conformity which may be required by the contract.

A.2   Licences, authorisations and formalities

Obtain at his own risk and expense any export licence or other official authorisation and carry out all customs formalities necessary for the exportation of the goods

A.3   Contract of carriage and insurance

(a)   Contract of carriage

Contract on usual terms at his own expense for the carriage of the goods to the named port of destination by the usual route in a seagoing vessel (or inland waterway vessel as appropriate) of the type normally used for the transport of goods of the contract description

(b)   Contract of insurance

Obtain at his own expense cargo insurance as agreed in the contract, that the buyer, or any other person having an insurable interest in the goods, shall be entitled to claim directly from the insurer and provide the buyer with the insurance policy or other evidence of insurance cover

The insurance shall be contracted with underwriters or an insurance company of good repute and, failing express agreement to the contrary, be in accordance with minimum cover of the Institute Cargo Clauses (Institute of London Underwriters) or any similar set of clauses The duration of insurance cover shall be in accordance with B.5 and B.4. When required by the buyer, the seller shall provide at the buyer's expense war, strikes, riots and civil commotion risk insurances if procurable. The minimum insurance shall cover the price provided in the contract plus 10% (ie 110 %) and shall be provided in the currency of the contract.

A.4   Delivery

Deliver the goods on board the vessel at the port of shipment on the date or within the period stipulated.

A.5   Transfer of risks

Subject to the provisions of B.5, bear all risks of loss of or damage to the goods until such time as they have passed the ship's rail at the port of shipment.

A.6   Division of costs

Subject to the provisions of B.6:

- pay all costs relating to the goods until they have been delivered in accordance with A.4 as well as the freight and all other costs resulting from A.3, including costs of loading the goods on board and any charges for unloading at the port of discharge which may be levied by regular shipping lines when contracting for carriage;

- pay the costs of customs formalities necessary for exportation as well as all duties, taxes and other official charges payable upon exportation.

A.7   Notice to the buyer

Give the buyer sufficient notice that the goods have been delivered on board the vessel as well as any other notice required in order to allow the buyer to take measures which are normally necessary to enable him to take the goods.

A.8   Proof of delivery, transport document or equivalent electronic message

Unless otherwise agreed, at his own expense provide the buyer without delay with the usual transport document for the agreed port of destination.

This document (eg, a negotiable bill of lading, a non-negotiable sea waybill or an inland waterway document) must cover the contract goods. be dated within the period agreed for shipment, enable the buyer to claim the goods from the carrier at destination and, unless otherwise agreed, enable the buyer to sell the goods in transit by the transfer of the document to a subsequent buyer (the negotiable bill of lading) or by notification to the carrier.

When such a transport document is issued in several originals, a full set of originals must be presented to the buyer. If the transport document contains a reference to a charter party, the seller must also provide a copy of this latter document.

Where the seller and the buyer have agreed to communicate electronically, the document referred to in the preceding paragraphs may be replaced by an equivalent electronic data Interchange (EDI) message.

A.9   Checking – packaging – marking

Pay the costs of those checking operations (such as checking quality, measuring, weighing, counting) which are necessary for the purpose of delivering the goods in accordance with A.4.

Provide at his own expense packaging (unless it is usual for the particular trade to ship the goods of the contract description unpacked) which is required for the transport of the goods arranged by him. Packaging is to be marked appropriately.

A.10   Other obligations

Render the buyer at the latter's request, risk and expense, every assistance in obtaining any documents or equivalent electronic messages (other than those mentioned in A.8) issued or transmitted in the country of shipment and/or of origin which the buyer may require for the importation of the goods and, where necessary, for their transit through another country.

Carriage and insurance paid to (CIP)

(... named place of destination)

'Carriage and insurance paid to...' means that the seller has the same obligations as under CPT but with the addition that the seller has to procure cargo insurance against the buyer's risk of loss of or damage to the goods during the carriage. The seller contracts for insurance and pays the Insurance premium.

A   The seller must

A.1   Provision of goods in conformity with the contract

Provide the goods and the commercial invoice, or its equivalent electronic message, in conformity with the contract of sale and any other evidence of conformity which may be required by the contract.

A.2   Licences, authorisations and formalities

Obtain at his own risk and expense any export licence or other official authorisation and carry out all customs formalities necessary for the exportation of the goods

A.3   Contract of carriage and insurance

(a)   Contract of carriage

Contract on usual terms at his own expense for the carriage of the goods to the agreed point at the named place of destination by a usual route and in a customary manner. If a point is not agreed or is not determined by practice, the seller may select the point at the named place of destination which best suits his purpose.

(b)   Contract of insurance

Obtain at his own expense cargo insurance as agreed in the contract, that the buyer, or any other person having an insurable interest in the goods, shall be entitled to claim directly from the insurer and provide the buyer with the insurance policy or other evidence of insurance cover.

The insurance shall be contracted with underwriters or an insurance company of good repute and, failing express agreement to the contrary. be in accordance with minimum cover of the Institute Cargo Clauses (Institute of London Underwriters) or any similar set of clauses. The duration of insurance cover shall be in accordance with B.5 and B.4. When required by the buyer, the seller shall provide at the buyers expense war, strikes, riots and civil commotion risk insurances if procurable. The minimum insurance shall cover the price provided in the contract plus 10% (ie 110 %) and shall be provided in the currency of the contract.

A.4   Delivery

Deliver the goods into the custody of the carrier or, if there are subsequent carriers, to the first carrier, for transportation to the named place of destination on the date or within the period stipulated

A.5   Transfer of risks

Subject to the provisions of B.5, bear all risks of loss of or damage to the goods until such time as they have been delivered in accordance with A.4.

A.6   Division of costs

Subject to the provisions of B.6:

- pay all costs relating to the goods until they have been delivered in accordance with A.4 as well as the freight and all other costs resulting from A.3, including costs of loading the goods and any charges for unloading at the place of destination which may be included in the freight or incurred by the seller when contracting for carriage;

- pay the costs of customs formalities necessary for exportation as well as all duties, taxes or other official charges payable upon exportation.

A 7   Notice to the buyer

Give the buyer sufficient notice that the goods have been delivered in accordance with A.4 as well as any other notice required in order to allow the buyer to take measures which are normally necessary to enable him to take the goods.

A 8   *Proof of delivery, transport document or equivalent electronic message*

Provide the buyer at the seller's expense, if customary, with the usual transport document (eg a negotiable bill of lading, a non-negotiable sea waybill, an inland waterway document, an air waybill, a railway consignment note, a road consignment note or a multi-modal transport document).

Where the seller and the buyer have agreed to communicate electronically, the document referred to in the preceding paragraph may be replaced by an equivalent electronic data Interchange (EDI) message.

A 9   *Checking – packaging – marking*

Pay the costs of those checking operations (such as checking quality, measuring, weighing, counting) which are necessary for the purpose of delivering the goods In accordance with A.4.

Provide at his own expense packaging (unless it is usual for the particular trade to send the goods of the contract description unpacked) which is required for the transport of the goods arranged by him. Packaging is to be marked appropriately

A.10   *Other obligations*

Render the buyer at the latter's request, risk and expense, every assistance in obtaining any documents or equivalent electronic messages (other than those mentioned in A.8) issued or transmitted in the country of dispatch and/or of origin, which the buyer may require for the importation of the goods and where necessary, for their transit through another country

B   **The buyer must**

B.1   *Payment of the price*

Pay the price as provided in the contract of sale.

B.2   *Licences, authorisations and formalities*

Obtain at his own risk and expense any import licence or other official authorisation and carry out all customs formalities for the importation of the goods and, where necessary, for their transit through another country.

B.3   *Contract of carriage*

No obligation

B.4   *Taking delivery*

Accept delivery of the goods when they have been delivered in accordance with A.4 and receive them from the carrier at the named port of destination.

B.5   *Transfer of risks*

Bear all risks of loss of or damage to the goods from the time they have passed the ship's rail at the port of shipment.

Should he fail to give notice in accordance with B.7, bear all risks of loss of or damage to the goods from the agreed date or the expiry date of the period fixed for shipment provided, however. that the goods have been duly appropriated to the contract, that is to say, clearly set aside or otherwise identified as the contract goods.

B 6   Division of costs

Subject to the provisions of A.3, pay all costs relating to the goods from the time they have been delivered in accordance with A.4 and, unless such costs and charges have been levied by regular shipping lines when contracting for carriage, pay all costs and charges relating to the goods whilst in transit until their arrival at the port of destination, as well as unloading costs including lighterage and wharfage charges.

Should he fail to give notice in accordance with B.7, pay the additional costs thereby incurred for the goods from the agreed date or the expiry date of the period fixed for shipment provided, however, that the goods have been duly appropriated to the contract, that is to say, clearly set aside or otherwise identified as the contract goods.

Pay all duties, taxes and other official charges as well as the costs of carrying out customs formalities payable upon importation of the goods and, where necessary, for their transit through another country.

B.7   Notice to the seller

Whenever he is entitled to determine the time for shipping the goods and/or the port of destination, give the seller sufficient notice thereof.

B.8   Proof of delivery, transport document or equivalent electronic message

Accept the transport document in accordance with A.8 if it is in conformity with the contract.

B.9   Inspection of goods

Pay, unless otherwise agreed, the costs of pre-shipment inspection except when mandated by the authorities of the country of exportation.

B.10   Other obligations

Pay all costs and charges incurred in obtaining the documents or equivalent electronic messages mentioned in A.10 and reimburse those incurred by the seller in rendering his assistance in accordance therewith.

Provide the seller, upon request, with the necessary information for procuring insurance.

Delivered at frontier (DAF)

(… named place)

'Delivered at frontier' means that the seller fulfils his obligation to deliver when the goods have been made available, cleared for export, at the named point and place at the frontier, but before the customs border of the adjoining country. The term 'frontier', may be used for any frontier including that of the country of export. Therefore, it is of vital importance that the frontier in question be defined precisely by always naming the point and place in the term. The term is primarily intended to be used when goods are to be carried by rail or road, but it may be used for any mode of transport.

A   The seller must

A.1   Provision of goods in conformity with the contract

Provide the goods and the commercial invoice, or its equivalent electronic message, in conformity with the contract of sale and any other evidence of conformity which may be required by the contract.

A.2   Licences, authorisations and formalities

Obtain at his own risk and expense any export licence or other official authorisation or other document necessary for placing the goods at the buyer's disposal. Carry out all customs formalities for the exportation of the goods to the named place of delivery at the frontier and, where necessary, for their prior transit through another country.

A.3   Contract of carriage and insurance

(a)   Contract of carriage

Contract at his own expense for the carriage of the goods by a usual route and in a customary manner to the named point at the place of delivery at the frontier (including, if necessary, for their transit through another country).

If a point at the named place of delivery at the frontier is not agreed or is not determined by practice, the seller may select the point at the named place of delivery which best suits his purpose.

(b)   Contract of insurance

No obligation.

A.4   Delivery

Place the goods at the disposal of the buyer at the named place of delivery at the frontier on the date or within the period stipulated.

A.5   Transfer of risks

Subject to the provisions of B.5, bear all risks of loss of or damage to the goods until such time as they have been delivered in accordance with A.4.

A.6   Division of costs

Subject to the provisions of B.6:

•   pay all costs of the goods until they have been delivered in accordance with A.4 as well as, in addition to costs resulting from A.3(a), the expenses of discharge operations (including lighterage and handling charges), if it is necessary or customary for the goods to be discharged on their arrival at the named place of delivery at the frontier, in order to place them at the buyer's disposal;

•   pay the costs of customs formalities necessary for exportation as well as all duties, taxes or other official charges payable upon exportation and, where necessary, for their transit through another country prior to delivery in accordance with A.4.

A.7   Notice to the buyer

Give the buyer sufficient notice of the dispatch of the goods to the named place at the frontier as well as any other notice required in order to allow the buyer to take measures which are normally necessary to enable him to take the goods.

A.8 *Proof of delivery, transport document or equivalent electronic message*

Provide the buyer at the seller's expense with the usual document or other evidence of the delivery of the goods at the named place at the frontier.

Provide the buyer at the latter's request, risk and expense, with a through document of transport normally obtained in the country of dispatch covering on usual terms the transport of the goods from the point of dispatch in that country to the place of final destination in the country of importation named by the buyer.

Where the seller and the buyer have agreed to communicate electronically, the document referred to in the preceding paragraph may be replaced by an equivalent electronic data interchange (EDI) message.

A.9 *Checking – packaging – marking*

Pay the costs of those checking operations (such as checking quality, measuring, weighing, counting) which are necessary for the purpose of delivering the goods in accordance with A.4.

Provide at his own expense packaging (unless it is usual for the particular trade to deliver the goods of the contract description unpacked) which is required for the delivery of the goods at the frontier and for the subsequent transport to the extent that the circumstances (eg modalities, destination) are made known to the seller before the contract of sale is concluded. Packaging is to be marked appropriately.

A.10 *Other obligations*

Render the buyer at the latter's request, risk and expense, every assistance in obtaining any documents or equivalent electronic messages (other than those mentioned in A.8) issued or transmitted in the country of dispatch and/or origin which the buyer may require for the importation of the goods and, where necessary, for their transit through another country. Provide the buyer, upon request, with the necessary information for procuring insurance.

B **The buyer must**

B.1 *Payment of the price*

Pay the price as provided in the contract of sale.

B.2 *Licences, authorisations and formalities*

Obtain at his own risk and expense any import licence or other official authorisation and carry out all customs formalities at the named point of delivery at the frontier or elsewhere for the importation of the goods and where necessary, for their subsequent transport.

B.3 *Contract of carriage*

No obligation.

B.4 *Taking delivery*

Take delivery of the goods as soon as they have been placed at his disposal in accordance with A.4.

B.5 *Transfer of risks*

Bear all risks of loss of or damage to the goods from the time they have been placed at his disposal in accordance with A.4.

Should he fail to give notice in accordance with B.7, bear all risks of loss of or damage to the goods from the agreed date or the expiry date of the period stipulated for delivery provided, however, that the goods have been duly appropriated to the contract, that is to say, clearly set aside or otherwise identified as the contract goods.

B.6   *Division of costs*

Pay all costs relating to the goods from the time they have been placed at his disposal in accordance with A.4.

Should he fail to take delivery of the goods when they have been placed at his disposal in accordance with A.4, or to give notice in accordance with B.7, bear all additional costs incurred thereby provided, however, that the goods have been appropriated to the contract, that is to say, clearly set aside or otherwise identified as the contract goods.

Pay all duties, taxes and other official charges as well as the costs of carrying out customs formalities payable upon importation of the goods and, where necessary, for their subsequent transport.

B.7   *Notice to the seller*

Whenever he is entitled to determine the time within a stipulated period and/or the place of taking delivery, give the seller sufficient notice thereof.

B.8   *Proof of delivery, transport document or equivalent electronic message*

Accept the transport document and/or other evidence of delivery in accordance with A.8.

B.9   *Inspection of goods*

Pay, unless otherwise agreed, the costs of pre-shipment inspection except when mandated by the authorities of the country of exportation.

B.10   *Other obligations*

Pay all costs and charges incurred in obtaining the documents or equivalent electronic messages mentioned in A.10 and reimburse those incurred by the seller in rendering his assistance in accordance therewith.

If necessary, provide the seller at his request and the buyer's risk and expense with exchange control authorisation, permits, other documents or codified copies thereof, or with the address of the final destination of the goods in the country of importation for the purpose of obtaining the through document of transport or any other document contemplated in A.8.

Delivered duty unpaid (DDU)

(... named place of destination)

'Delivered duty unpaid' means that the seller fulfils his obligation to deliver when the goods have been made available at the named place in the country of importation. The seller has to bear the costs and risks involved in bringing the goods thereto (excluding duties, taxes and other official charges payable upon importation) as well as the costs and risks of carrying out customs formalities. The buyer has to pay any additional costs and to bear any risks caused by his failure to clear the goods for import in time.

If the parties wish to include in the seller's obligations some of the costs payable upon importation of the goods (such as value added tax (VAT)), this should be made clear by adding words to this effect: 'Delivered duty unpaid, VAT paid, (… named place of destination).'

This term may be used irrespective of the mode of transport.

A   The seller must

A.1   Provision of the goods in conformity with the contract

Provide the goods and the commercial invoice, or its equivalent electronic message, in conformity with the contract of sale and any other evidence of conformity which may be required by the contract.

A.2   Licences, authorisations and formalities

Obtain at his own risk and expense any export licence and other official authorisation and carry out all customs formalities for the exportation of the goods and, where necessary, for their transit through another country.

A.3   Contract of carriage and insurance

(a)   Contract of carriage

Contract on usual terms at his own expense for the carriage of the goods by a usual route and in the customary manner to the agreed point at the named place of destination. If a point is not agreed or is not determined by practice, the seller may select the point at the named place of destination which best suits his purpose.

(b)   Contract of insurance

No obligation.

A.4   Delivery

Place the goods at the disposal of the buyer in accordance with A.3, on the date or within the period stipulated. If the parties wish the seller to carry out customs formalities and bear the costs and risks resulting therefrom, this has to be made clear by adding words to this effect.

A.5   Transfer of risks

Subject to the provisions of B.5, bear all risks of loss of or damage to the goods until such time as they have been delivered in accordance with A.4.

A.6   Division of costs

Subject to the provisions of B.6:

•   in addition to costs resulting from A.3(a), pay all costs relating to the goods until such time as they have been delivered in accordance with A.4;

•   pay the costs of customs formalities necessary for exportation as well as all duties, taxes and other official charges payable upon exportation and, where necessary, for their transit through another country prior to delivery in accordance with A.4.

A.7   Notice to the buyer

Give the buyer sufficient notice of the dispatch of the goods as well as any other notice required in order to allow the buyer to take measures which are normally necessary to enable him to take the goods.

A.8   Proof of delivery, transport document or equivalent electronic message

Provide at his own expense the delivery order and/or the usual transport document (eg, a negotiable bill of lading, a non-negotiable sea waybill, an inland waterway document, an air waybill, a railway consignment note, a road consignment note, or a multi-modal transport document) which the buyer may require to take delivery of the goods.

Where the seller and the buyer have agreed to communicate electronically, the document referred to in the preceding paragraph may be replaced by an equivalent electronic data interchange (EDI) message.

A.9   Checking – packaging – marking

Pay the costs of those checking operations (such as checking quality, measuring, weighing, counting) which are necessary for the purpose of delivering the goods in accordance with A.4.

Provide at his own expense packaging (unless it is usual for the particular trade to deliver the goods of the contract description unpacked) which is required for the delivery of the goods. Packaging is to be marked appropriately.

A.10   Other obligations

Render the buyer at the latter's request, risk and expense, every assistance in obtaining any documents or equivalent electronic messages other than those mentioned in A.8, issued or transmitted in the country of dispatch and/or of origin which the buyer may require for the importation of the goods.

Provide the buyer, upon request, with the necessary information for procuring insurance.

B   The buyer must

B.1   Payment of the price

Pay the price as provided in the contract of sale.

B.2   Licences, authorisations and formalities

Obtain at his own risk and expense any import licence or other official authorisation and carry out all customs formalities necessary for the importation of the goods.

B.3   Contract of carriage

No obligation.

B.4   Taking delivery

Take delivery of the goods as soon as they have been placed at his disposal in accordance with A.4.

B.5   Transfer of risks

Bear all risks of loss of or damage to the goods from the time they have been placed at his disposal in accordance with A.4. Should he fail to fulfil his obligations in accordance with B.2, bear all additional risks of loss of or damage to the goods incurred thereby and should he fail to give notice in accordance with B.7, bear all risks of loss of or damage to the goods from the agreed date or the expiry date of the period stipulated for delivery provided, however, that the goods have been duly appropriated to the contract, that is to say, clearly set aside or otherwise identified as the contract goods.

B.6   *Division of costs*

Pay all costs relating to the goods from the time they have been placed at his disposal at the named point of destination in accordance with A.4.

Should he fail to fulfil his obligations in accordance with B.2, or to take delivery of the goods when they have been placed at his disposal in accordance with A.4, or to give notice in accordance with B.7, bear all additional costs incurred thereby provided, however, that the goods have been duly appropriated to the contract, that is to say, clearly set aside or otherwise identified as the contract goods.

Pay all duties, taxes and other official charges as well as the costs of carrying out customs formalities payable upon importation of the goods.

B.7   *Notice to the seller*

Whenever he is entitled to determine the time within a stipulated period and/or the place of taking delivery, give the seller sufficient notice thereof.

B.8   *Proof of delivery, transport document or equivalent electronic message*

Accept the appropriate delivery order or transport document in accordance with A.8.

B.9   *Inspection of goods*

Pay, unless otherwise agreed, the costs of pre-shipment inspection except when mandated by the authorities of the country of exportation.

B.10   *Other obligations*

Pay all costs and charges incurred in obtaining the documents or equivalent electronic messages mentioned in A.10 and reimburse those incurred by the seller in rendering his assistance in accordance therewith.

CHAPTER 4

CARRIAGE OF GOODS BY SEA

INTRODUCTION

When carriers became powerful in the 19th century they included limitation of liability rules in their bills of lading. These rules resulted in hardship for shippers. In the USA this problem led to the adoption by Congress of the Harter Act of 1892 which sets out the liability of carriers for the care of their cargoes and imposed restrictions on the use of limitation of liability clauses in bills of lading. The Harter Act 1892 was used in 1924 as a model for the drafting of the International Convention for the Unification of Certain Rules of Law Relating to Bills of Lading which is popularly known as the Hague Rules. These rules describe the liability of ocean carriers for damage to, or loss of, goods on the seas. In the USA, the Convention was implemented by the Carriage of Goods by Sea Act of 1936. In 1924, the Australian Parliament enacted the Sea Carriage of Goods Act which introduced the Hague Rules into Australian law.[1] For the next 67 years[2] these Rules governed international sea carriage of goods from Australia to overseas destinations.[3] Even today such carriage is governed by a variant of those rules, known as the Hague-Visby Rules or Amended Hague Rules.

The Hague Rules were a compromise between the shipper and the sea carrier,[4] the three main elements of which were as follows:

1 the carriers agreed to exercise due diligence before and at the beginning of the voyage to make the ship seaworthy (replacing the common law obligation of absolute seaworthiness);[5]

2 the carrier agreed to a duty of care to load properly and carefully and to handle, stow, carry, keep, care for and discharge the goods carried;[6] and

3 the shipper agreed that, if the carrier was liable, then the carrier could limit its liability to £100 per package or unit.

The Hague Rules have been very successful and today over 80 nations are signatories to those rules or the Amended Hague Rules.[7]

---

1   As from 1 January 1925.

2   Until 31 October 1991 when the Carriage of Goods by Sea Act 1991 (COGSA) was assented to.

3   Carriage of goods from overseas countries into Australia is usually governed by the laws in that overseas country – often this is also the Hague or Hague-Visby Rules.

4   See McNair, Sir WL, Mocatta, Sir AA and Mustill, MJ, in *Scrutton on Charterparties*, 17th edn, 1971, pp 402–09, London: Sweet & Maxwell, for summary of the background to the Hague Rules. See also Astle, WE, *The Hamburg Rules*, 1981, London: Fairplay Publications.

5   *Riverstone Meat Co v Lancashire Shipping Co (The Muncaster Castle)* [1961] Lloyd's Rep 57; Article 3, Rule 1.

6   This duty was subject to the exceptions set out in Article 4, rule 2.

7   See Appendix 1 to this chapter.

Seventy years is a long time in the world of shipping. Navigation has been revolutionised by satellite technology. Communication advances are such that a vessel is now almost continuously in touch with its owner. Vessels themselves are better constructed, faster and more economical to run – steam and sail have long since given way to today's engine technology. Perhaps most importantly, cargo handling has been revolutionised with bulk handling and containerisation accounting for the vast majority of tonnage carried.[8]

Despite these major advances, the Hague Rules and the Amended Hague Rules continued to govern carriage of goods by sea from Australia unchanged[9] as they did throughout much of the world. The rules were not perfect but, with over half a century of development behind them, they offered 'a comforting patina of certainty and stability so vital to maritime affairs'.[10] Everybody – the shipper, carrier and their respective insurers – knew the rules and where their respective responsibilities lay.

A key provision of the Hague Rules is Article IV, rule 5, which provides that:

> Neither the carrier nor the ship shall in any event be or become liable for any loss or damage to or in connection with goods in an amount exceeding £100 sterling per package or unit or the equivalent of that sum in other currency unless the nature and value of such goods have been declared by the shipper before shipment and inserted in the bill of lading.

While £100 sterling was a very significant sum in 1924 and was intended to be so,[11] it has, in today's currency, a much reduced value.[12] Effluxion of time and inflation have tilted the 1924 balance between the carrier and the shipper in the carrier's favour; as the value of the cargo carried increased, the liability limit of the carrier in real terms decreased. As a result, the amount of risk held by the shipper or the shipper's insurer has steadily increased.

Not only do the Hague Rules allow the carrier to limit its liability to this increasingly favourable limitation amount but, in some instances, the carrier may escape liability altogether if it can bring itself under one of the exemptions from liability in the rules.[13] While most of these exemptions are unexceptional in that they, in effect, exempt the carrier where the loss or damage occurs through no fault of the carrier, its servants or agents (ie no negligence on the carrier's behalf), Article 4, rule 2(a) and (b) exempt the carrier from liability if it establishes that the loss or damage occurred as a result of:

---

8   See generally Kendall, LC, *The Business of Shipping*, 2nd edn, 1986, London: Chapman and Hall.

9   Until 31 October 1991.

10   Shah, MJ, 'The Revision of the Hague Rules on Bills of Lading within the UN System – Key Issues', in Mankabady, S (ed), *The Hamburg Rules on the Carriage of Goods by Sea*, 1978, p 415, Leyden/Boston: AW Sijthoff.

11   Diamond, A, 'Responsibility for Loss of, or Damage to, Cargo on a Sea Transit: the Hague or Hamburg Conventions', in Koh Soan Kwong, P, *Carriage of Goods by Sea*, 1986, p 111, Singapore: Butterworths.

12   See *Brown-Boveri (Aust) Pty Ltd v Baltic Shipping Co Ltd* (1989) 1 NSWLR 448 where the real value of this sum in 1988 Australian dollars was canvassed.

13   Article 4, rule 2.

(a) Act, neglect or default of the master, mariner, pilot, or the servants of the carrier in the navigation or in the management of the ship;[14]

(b) Fire, unless caused by the actual fault or privity of the carrier.

A person outside the shipping industry may well find it surprising that a carrier should escape liability either because its master or servant was negligent in navigating or managing the ship or because its servant caused a fire on board the ship. It runs counter to the general principles of negligence and bailment. It is not difficult to imagine a shipper new to the export trade being somewhat bemused by the fact that, while its cargo has been damaged or lost owing to the vessel's crew's negligence, it is unable to recover the loss because that same negligence is a defence to any recovery action.

In Australia, as with many other cargo owning nations (as opposed to shipowning nations), there is a view held by shippers and certain sections of government that the existing Hague Rules (and more recently, the Amended Hague Rules) are not in the best interests of the shippers in cargo owning nations and therefore not in the best interests of the nation.[15] However, almost all other elements of the shipping industry are opposed to the introduction of the Hamburg Rules.[16]

On 31 October 1991, the required number of States[17] ratified the Hamburg Rules and, by operation of Article 30(1) of the rules, they came into force on 1 November 1992.

In 1991 the Australian government enacted the Carriage of Goods by Sea Act 1991[18] which took effect on 31 October, 1991. This Act:

1   amended the Hague Rules[19] by adding two protocols known as the Visby Protocol and the SDR Protocol;[20] and

2   provided that Part 3 and Schedule 2 of the Act would come into force at the expiration of three years unless Parliament resolved either to repeal those provisions or to reconsider them after a further period of three years.

Thus, this second strand of the Act could, after 31 October 1994 have delivered Australia into a new sea carriage regime – the so-called 'Hamburg Rules'[21] which form Schedule 2 to the Act. However, the Australian government resolved[22] to defer the introduction of the Hamburg Rules for a further period of three years.

---

14   The so-called 'nautical fault' and 'negligent management' exemptions.

15   For a detailed exposition of these views, see Levingstones (ed), *Commentary on the Arguments For and Against Adoption of the Hamburg Rules: A Collection of Papers*, 1994, Sydney: Levingstones.

16   For the background to introduction of the Hamburg Rules, see Astle, WE, *The Hamburg Rules*, 1981, London: Fairplay Publications.

17   Article 30, rule 1: 'This convention enters into force on the first day of the month following the expiration of one year from the date of deposit of the 20th instrument of ratification, acceptance, approval or accession.' See above for names of ratifying nations.

18   Abbreviated throughout this chapter to COGSA.

19   From 31 October 1991.

20   Referred to in this chapter as the Amended Hague Rules.

21   The United Nations Convention on the Carriage of Goods by Sea done at Hamburg on 31 March 1978.

22   On 17 October 1994 and 18 October 1994 for the House of Representatives and the Senate respectively

Like the Hague Rules, the Hamburg Rules limit the carrier's liability, but there are important differences, such as:

1   the abolition of the negligent navigation and negligent management defences;

2   the abolition of the fire defence where the fire is caused by the negligence of the carrier's servants;[23]

3   the period of loading and discharge of the goods is covered as well as the actual carriage;

4   the Hamburg Rules apply to all contracts of carriage by sea except for charterparties and not just to bills of lading (as with the Hague Rules); and

5   the Hamburg Rules impose higher liability limits.

The ratifying nations for the Hamburg Rules were: Barbados, Botswana, Burkina Faso, Chile, Egypt, Guinea, Hungary, Kenya, Lebanon, Lesotho, Malawi, Morocco, Nigeria, Romania, Senegal, Sierra Leone, Tunisia, Uganda, Tanzania and Zambia. These nations are far from being Australia's major trading partners, accounting for considerably less than 1% of Australia's trade.

Australia's major trading partners are Japan, USA and the European Union.[24] Currently, Japan is operating under the Hague-Visby Rules and the USA under the Hague Rules; the countries comprising the EEC also operate under Hague or Hague-Visby Rules although some of them may be leaning towards adopting the Hamburg Rules.[25] So why the need for change? No other country with which Australia has a significant trade relationship seems to be really rushing towards the implementation of the Hamburg Rules. What is the government's intention?

The Australian government's objects behind the ultimate introduction of the Hamburg Rules into Australian law are:

> to introduce a regime of marine cargo liability that:
>
> (a) is up to date, equitable and efficient; and
>
> (b) is compatible with arrangements existing in countries that are major trading partners of Australia; and
>
> (c) takes into account developments within the United Nations in relation to marine-cargo liability arrangements.[26]

As the deadline for giving effect to the Hamburg Rules edged closer, there was considerable debate by the parties involved in sea carriage of goods as to whether or not COGSA 1991 and the Hamburg Rules met the above objects, or indeed whether those objects are desirable.[27]

---

23 But the onus of proof is on the shipper to demonstrate that the fire was so caused – Article 5 rule 4, Hamburg Rules.

24 See Makins, B, 'The Hamburg Rules: A Casualty' (January–February 1994) *Maritime Studies* 16 at 18–19 where statistical information from Department of Foreign Affairs and Trade is set out.

25 See Appendix 1.

26 Section 3 of the COGSA 1991.

27 Many of the positions of the various parties are set out in a series of papers collated in a useful publication entitled *Commentary on the Arguments for and against the Hamburg Rules: A Collection of Papers*, 1984, Sydney: Levingstones.

Essentially there are two positions:

1 that of the shippers and some P&I[28] insurers, who strongly support the introduction of the Hamburg Rules; and

2 that of the carriers, some P&I insurers, the cargo insurers and virtually everybody else, who believe that the Hamburg Rules should either never be introduced or should be delayed.

It comes as no surprise that the shippers support the Hamburg Rules while carrier interests favour the Amended Hague Rules. Interestingly, cargo insurance interests also favour the carrier's point of view,[29] whereas some P&I insurance interests favour the Hamburg Rules. This may be a function of the cargo insurer anticipating a reduced premium income under the Hamburg Rules and the P&I insurer anticipating a commensurate increase.

Supporters of the Amended Hague Rules argue that, while there may be problems with the Amended Hague Rules, the existing system works well and the 'Hamburg Rules cure' would set sea carriage backwards rather than forwards. Hamburg Rules proponents acknowledge that there are possible problems with the Hamburg Rules but believe that the existing Amended Hague Rules discriminate against their interests, and that even no rules at all may be better than the Hague or Amended Hague Rules.

The Hamburg Rules are a product of UNCTAD[30] and UNCITRAL,[31] which have been actively campaigning for their introduction. Thus the Hamburg Rules would appear to meet the requirements of sub-s 3(c) of COGSA 1991 that the marine cargo liability regime should take into account United Nations developments in this area. However, whether the rules also meet the objectives expressed in sub-s 3(a) and (b) is somewhat more problematic.

This chapter, in comparing the Hague Rules and Amended Hague Rules with the Hamburg Rules, examines whether the introduction of the Hamburg Rules satisfies the objectives in sub-s 3(a) and (b) of COGSA 1991, namely whether they are:

(a) up to date, equitable and efficient; and

(b) compatible with arrangements existing in countries which are major trading partners of Australia.

---

28 Protection and Indemnity (P&I) insurers are the insurers of the vessel for the shipowner; cargo insurers insure a vessel's cargo for the shipper.

29 For example, see Hill, MA, 'Hamburg Rules: an Exercise in Risk Management' in *Commentary on the Arguments for and Against Adoption of the Hamburg Rules*, May 1984, p 203 *et seq*, *op cit*.

30 United Nations Conference on Trade and Development.

31 United Nations Commission on International Trade Law.

COMPARISON OF HAGUE RULES, AMENDED HAGUE RULES AND HAMBURG RULES

As has already been mentioned, one of the objects of the proposed introduction of the Hamburg Rules was to introduce a cargo regime which is 'up to date, equitable and efficient'. The baseline for assessing this must be as compared to the existing predominant carriage regimes – the Hague Rules and the Amended Hague Rules.

Are the Hamburg Rules 'up to date'? Comparing chronologically, the Hague Rules were made at Brussels on 25 August 1924 and took effect from 1 January 1925. The Visby Protocol, which amended the Hague Rules so as to produce the Hague-Visby Rules,[32] was made on 23 February 1968. The SDR Protocol, which amended the Hague Rules as amended by the Visby Protocol, was made on 21 December 1979. This Protocol did not make any substantial amendment to the Hague Rules – it merely substituted a limitation amount in Special Drawing Rights.

The Hamburg Rules were finalised on 31 March 1978. Given that the SDR Protocol did not make substantial amendments to the Amended Hague Rules, it is clear that, at least on a chronological basis, the Hamburg Rules are the most 'up to date'. However, a chronological comparison alone is not determinative of whether the rules are up to date. It is also necessary to examine whether the rules take into account modern shipping and trading practices, such as containerisation and freight forwarding.

While consolidation of cargo has been around for a long time, containerisation as we know it today originated in America in the mid-1950s, and in 1968, when the Visby Protocol was being finalised, it was still a developing concept.[33] However, by 1978, when the Hamburg Rules were being finalised, it had grown into a well developed and widely used method of cargo carrying. While the Hague Rules do not consider containerisation at all, both the Visby Protocol and the Hamburg Rules take some account of containerisation. They both address the vexing problem of the package or unit limitation as it applies to consolidated cargoes and try to give some certainty to the problems caused by consolidation by providing, for example, in the Visby Protocol:

> (c) Where a container, pallet or similar article of transport is used to consolidate goods, the number of packages or units enumerated in the bill of lading as packed in such article of transport shall be deemed the number of packages or units for the purpose of this paragraph as far as these packages or units are concerned. Except as aforesaid such article of transport shall be considered the package or unit.[34]

The Hamburg Rules deal with this issue in a similar manner. In addition the Hamburg Rules consider other elements of modern export trade such as the burgeoning concept of multi-modalism. Article 1 rule 6, which defines a 'contract of carriage by sea', excludes coverage by the Hamburg Rules (where the contract has a non-sea leg of

---

32 Called the Amended Hague Rules in this chapter.

33 Kendall, *The Business of Shipping, op cit.*

34 Article 4, rule 5(c).

carriage) of that non-sea leg of carriage. Unfortunately there is no change to the body of the Hamburg Rules which gives any indication as to how the rules are to operate in detail where multi-modal transport is involved. It is not clear whether the Hamburg Rules apply when the carrier takes possession of the goods from the shipper at some point prior to the goods being delivered to the port of loading or when the carrier continues to have responsibility for the goods and for their delivery to the ultimate destination after the goods have been discharged from the vessel at the port of discharge.[35]

Accordingly, although the drafters of the Hamburg Rules wished to have the rules dovetail with emerging multi-modal practices, what the result will be in practice is far from clear. Nevertheless, at least the Hamburg Rules have made a start in endeavouring to take into account current transport practices.

As to just how equitable and efficient the Hamburg Rules are, or may be as compared to the existing carriage regimes, while the issue is not clear cut it does seem that the Hamburg Rules will tend on balance to favour the cargo owner.

There are significant differences between the Hague Rules and the Amended Hague Rules on the one hand, and the Hamburg Rules on the other. One way to examine the differences is to look at the existing situation under the Hague Rules, to identify problems which have occurred with those rules and to examine how they have been addressed by the Hamburg Rules.

The *Vita Food* gap

One notable difference between the Hague Rules and the Amended Hague Rules is in the legislative technique for giving effect to them. The Hague Rules were incorporated into any bill of lading by way of a legislative requirement that any such bill must contain a clause[36] providing that the bill has effect subject to the provisions of the Hague Rules; ie they were given the status of contractual terms, not legal enactments having the force of law.[37] The Hague Rules were accordingly interpreted by courts as they would interpret any other term of a contract.

This method of incorporation by way of a clause paramount gave rise to the so-called *Vita Food* gap. It potentially enables the Hague Rules to be avoided by using a 'choice of law' clause providing for the contract of carriage to be governed by the law of a jurisdiction which either had not adopted the rules at all or did not apply them to that

---

35 While Article 4, rule 1 provides that 'the responsibility of the carrier for the goods under this convention covers the period during which the carrier is in charge of the goods at the port of loading, during the carriage and at the port of discharge'; Article 4, rule 2 provides that the carrier is deemed to be in charge of the goods from the time it has taken over the goods from the shipper. If the carrier takes possession prior to the goods arriving at the port, the carrier is clearly in charge of the goods, but do the rules apply to this period? It seems not, but the question appears to be open to interpretation.

36 This clause became known as the 'clause paramount'.

37 Section 6 of the Sea Carriage of Goods Act 1924. 'Every bill of lading or similar document of title issued in the Commonwealth which contains or is evidence of any contract to which the rules apply shall contain an express statement that it is to have effect subject to the provisions of the rules as applied by this Act.'

voyage.[38] In essence, if the clause paramount was omitted from the bill of lading for shipment out of a Hague Rules country, and if the choice-of-law clause elected the jurisdiction of a country which either did not apply the Hague Rules or did not apply them to that voyage, then the Hague Rules would not apply.[39]

COGSA 1991 closed this gap[40] by providing that the Amended Hague Rules and (possibly after 31 October 1997) the Hamburg Rules 'have the force of law in Australia'.[41]

Clearly, giving the Amended Hague Rules and the Hamburg Rules the force of law in Australia is an improvement over the 'clause paramount' method of incorporating the original Hague Rules.

Application of rules

The Hague Rules and Amended Hague Rules only apply to outbound cargo[42] or other cargo where the carriage documentation provides for the rules to apply,[43] provided that the cargo is carried under bills of lading or 'any similar document of title'.[44] Cargo carried under non-negotiable documents of carriage[45] is not subject to the rules.

So cargo from countries which are not signatories to the rules and cargo carried under a consignment note, a non-negotiable receipt, a sea waybill and such like are outside the ambit of those rules, unless the Hague Rules or the Amended Hague Rules are contractually incorporated into them.

---

38 The *Vita Food* gap took its name from *Vita Food Products Inc v Unus Shipping Co Ltd* [1939] AC 277. The bills of lading were issued in Newfoundland. Although the law of that country provided that all bills of lading must contain an express statement that the bill is subject to the Hague Rules, the bills issued without such a statement. The bills also stated that they were subject to English law. The cargo was damaged and the question before the court was whether the carrier could rely upon the exemption from liability clauses in the bill of lading. The action was taken in the courts in Nova Scotia. The Privy Council *per* Lord Wright found that the carrier could rely on the exemption clause. It found that if the bill had been governed by Newfoundland law, then the Hague Rules would have applied; but as they were not, the bills were not subject to the Hague Rules; and were not illegal under Newfoundland law or any other relevant law; the bills were enforceable in accordance with their terms. Even if the bills were illegal in Newfoundland, they were still enforceable in Nova Scotia.

39 Of course, this may breach s 6 of the Sea Carriage of Goods Act 1924, s 6, but it will not affect the validity of the contract of carriage.

40 See s 8 of the COGSA 1991, for Amended Hague Rules and s 13 for Hamburg Rules.

41 An example of how the *Vita Food* gap closes by giving the rules the force of law can be seen in *The Hollandia* [1983] 1 AC 565. It involved a shipment from Scotland in a Dutch vessel with the bill of lading being governed by Dutch law. At that time, the UK had the Hague-Visby Rules while the Dutch had the Hague Rules. The liability limits are lower in the Hague Rules. The English court found that, if they gave effect to the jurisdiction clause, it would introduce lower carriers liability limits than those available under the Hague-Visby rules which had the force of law. Accordingly, the jurisdiction clause was a clause reducing carriers liability as defined by Article III, rule 8 of the Hague-Visby Rules and as such it was invalid. As the jurisdiction clause was invalid, the appropriate jurisdiction was looked at on a *forum conveniens* basis and England was found to be the appropriate forum.

42 Inbound cargo may be covered where it is carried from a country where the rules also apply.

43 Article 10.

44 Article 1(b).

45 Article 1(b) and Article 6.

In practice, where the bargaining power of the carrier is significantly greater than that of the shipper, as it usually is with liner shipping, the carrier controls the carriage documentation and can, and does, contractually exclude liability for loss or damage to the cargo in any situation where the rules do not apply. In addition, particularly on short haul routes, for the convenience of both carrier and shipper, non-negotiable documents have come into common use. These also circumvent the Hague Rules and Amended Hague Rules and, once again, the carrier is in a position to exempt itself completely from liability for loss or damage to cargo.[46]

In contrast, the Hamburg Rules apply to all contracts of carriage by sea between two different States if:

(a) the port of loading, as provided for in the contract of carriage by sea, is located in a Contracting State;

(b) the port of discharge, as provided for in the contract of carriage by sea, is located in a Contracting State;

(c) one of the optional ports of discharge in the contract of carriage by sea is the actual port of discharge, and such part is located in a Contracting State;

(d) the bill of lading or other document evidencing the contract of carriage by sea is issued in a Contracting State; or

(e) the bill of lading or other document evidencing the contract of carriage by sea provides that the convention or the legislation of any State giving effect to the convention are to govern the contract.[47]

So, unlike the Hague and Amended Hague Rules, the Hamburg Rules apply to contracts of carriage by sea for both inward and outward cargo. From the shipper's point of view, this is a distinct advantage as the shipper knows that the same rules apply to all cargoes, both inward and outward.

Under the Hamburg Rules there is no distinction between negotiable and non-negotiable contracts of carriage. The rules cover all sea cargo carriage whether under bills of lading or not, except gratuitous carriage and charterparties.[48] A contract of carriage by sea is defined under the rules as:

> Any contract whereby the carrier undertakes against payment of freight to carry goods by sea from one part to another; however, a contract which involves carriage by sea and also carriage by some other means is deemed to be a contract of carriage by sea for the purposes of this convention only in so far as it relates to the carriage by sea.[49]

Unlike the Hague and Amended Hague Rules, the Hamburg Rules apply to nearly all contracts of carriage by sea,[50] whether negotiable or not and whether the cargo is

---

46 By way of example, much Trans-Tasman cargo is carried under non-negotiable documentation. For an example, see the TNT All-Trans Trans-Tasman consignment note.

47 Article 2, rule 1.

48 Article 2, rule 3.

49 Article 1, rule 6.

50 Article 1(6).

inbound or outbound; they are more difficult to circumvent and apply uniformly to nearly all contracts for carriage. From the Australian shipper's point of view, there is no need for it to concern itself with whether the cargo is an import or an export cargo, or whether it is carried under a bill of lading or a sea waybill – the same rules will always apply. This uniformity of treatment of cargo seems to be a considerable advance over the existing situation, where a shipper's rights can vary according to where inbound cargo is shipped from and whether the shipping documents are negotiable or not.

Application of rules to third parties

A further problem with the Hague Rules arose with their application to third parties, as highlighted by *Scruttons v Midland Silicones*,[51] where the court held that stevedores were not parties to the contract of carriage and could not rely upon the limitations of liability in the Hague Rules; ie the rules only dealt with contractual liability and not tortious or other liability of third parties.[52] This case made it clear that the Hague Rules, being contract based, only related to contractual liability, and a shipper could circumvent the Hague Rules and obtain full recovery for its loss if negligence could be established against a third party such as a stevedore or a negligent crew member sued in tort. The shipowners responded to the *Scruttons* decision with the creation of the so-called 'Himalaya' clause. This was a clause inserted in a bill of lading which originally provided[53] that the carrier's employees and agents could also rely on the limitations of liability under the Hague Rules available to the carrier. After the *Scruttons* decision, the Himalaya clause was broadened to provide the same umbrella of protection to subcontractors; over the years this drafting technique has been very successful[54] and it is now adopted almost universally by carriers.

Even though the technique has been so successful, the Visby Protocol incorporated amendments into the Amended Hague Rules which also addressed this issue. Article 4 *bis* provides that:

1 The defences and limits of liability provided for in this convention shall apply in any action against the carrier in respect of loss or damage to goods covered by a contract of carriage whether the action be founded in contract or in tort.

2 If such an action is brought against a servant or agent of the carrier (such servant or agent not being an independent contractor), such servant or agent shall be entitled to avail himself of the defences and limits of liability which the carrier is entitled to invoke under this convention.

While these amendments have the force of law (unlike the contractual force of the Himalaya clause), however, they only protect servants or agents of the carrier. The

---

51 [1962] AC 446.

52 This case followed an earlier case of *Adler v Dickson* [1955] 1 QB 158 where a passenger was able successfully to sue the captain and bosun of the vessel *Himalaya* as a result of an accident involving the operation of the ship's gangway.

53 After *Adler v Dickson, ibid.*

54 *New Zealand Shipping Co Ltd v AM Satterthwaite and Co Ltd 'The Eurymedon'* [1975] AC 154; *The New York Star* [1981] WLR 138.

Himalaya clause must still be used to protect the independent contractor as the Amended Hague Rules do not give the carrier any greater protection than the carrier already obtains through appropriate wording on the bill of lading.

The Hamburg Rules contain similar provisions to those in the Amended Hague Rules. Article 7, rules 1 and 2 of the Hamburg Rules provide that:

1   The defences and limits of liability provided for in this convention apply in any action against the carrier in respect of loss or damage to the goods covered by the contract of carriage by sea, as well as of delay in delivery whether the action is founded in contract, in tort or otherwise.

2   If such an action is brought against a servant or agent of the carrier, such servant or agent, if he proves that he acted within the scope of his employment, is entitled to avail himself of the defences and limits of liability which the carrier is entitled to invoke under this convention.

As with the Amended Hague Rules, there is no mention of independent contractors, so a Himalaya clause is clearly required to cover them. However, under the Hamburg Rules, the carrier is responsible for the goods during the loading and unloading phases, unlike the Amended Hague Rules and Hague Rules where the carrier can exclude liability for that phase. Accordingly, it must be an open question whether the carrier and its insurers would wish to continue the existing practice of extending protection to independent contractors under the Himalaya clause since the carrier will be liable in any event for damage to cargo caused by the stevedore. If the carrier no longer extends protection under the Himalaya clause to the stevedore, that may work to the advantage of Australian shippers as a right of recovery may again open up against stevedores.

Non-contractual liability of the carrier

The Hague Rules deal only with contractual liability. The Amended Hague Rules[55] provide that:

The defences and limits of liability provided for in these rules shall apply in any action against the carrier in respect of loss of or damage to the goods covered by a contract of carriage whether the action be founded in contract or in tort.

The intention presumably is that this rule will apply to limit liability in tort, even where there is no corresponding contractual right available – eg where a shipper contracts with a carrier or freight forwarder and then seeks to sue the actual carrier.[56]

However, the *Captain Gregos*[57] seems to indicate that, notwithstanding the apparent intention of this rule, it may only apply to limit liability in tort if the carrier could be sued either in contract or in tort in respect of the loss, and tort was elected. If, on the other hand, there is no contractual liability, then there will be no limitation on tortious liability.[58]

---

55   Article 4 *bis*, rule 1.

56   This was the view of Anthony Diamond QC in 'The Hague Visby Rules' [1987] *Lloyd's MCLQ* 225.

57   [1990] Lloyd's Rep 310.

58   This is the view in the above case and also that taken by Professor Treitel in [1984] *Lloyd's MCLQ* 304.

The Hamburg Rules provide that:

The defences and limits of liability provided for in this convention apply in any action against the carrier in respect of loss or damage to the goods covered by the contract of carriage by sea, as well as of delay in delivery whether the action is founded in contract, in tort or otherwise.[59]

This rule is very similar in wording to the Amended Hague Rules, and it may well be that the *Captain Gregos* could be cited as authority for the fact that there is still potential for the limitation provisions to be circumvented in certain situations where it is possible for the shipper to proceed in tort against someone other than the carrier.

Deck cargo

Neither the Hague Rules nor the Amended Hague Rules apply to deck cargo[60] unless:

(a) the parties agree that the goods will be carried on deck under these rules; and

(b) the goods are actually carried on deck.

As a result, the way is open for the carrier to exclude liability absolutely where goods are carried as deck cargo, and this, in fact, is what happens in practice. The carrier also commonly inserts a provision in the bill of lading under which the carrier is given liberty to stow the cargo above or below deck at the carrier's discretion, the 'liberty' clause.

If the parties agree to carry the goods on deck, then no liability will accrue to the carrier. However, where the goods are carried on deck without the express agreement of the shipper, then the question arises as to whether the liberty clause commonly found in a bill of lading would give the carrier a right to carry the goods on deck and then to claim an exemption from liability.

There are a number of possible reasons why the carrier may wish to carry the goods on deck:

(a) where the carrier moves the goods to the deck to ensure the safety of the cargo[61] when there seems no doubt that the liberty clause would be valid and the carrier exempt from liability;

(b) where the cargo is carried on the deck purely for the convenience of the carrier and not out of any necessity. Here it seems that the liberty clause may not amount to a statement that the goods were to be carried as deck cargo and the goods will continue to be covered by the Hague Rules;[62]

(c) if the goods are carried on deck because they cannot otherwise be carried by the vessel (eg if too big to be carried below decks or if some legislative requirement mandates that they be carried above deck), then the liberty clause may well be valid.[63]

---

59 Article 7, rule 1.

60 See definition of 'goods' in Article 1(c) of the rules which excludes deck cargo: 'cargo which, by the contract of carriage, is stated as being carried on deck and is so carried'.

61 Here the carrier would be carrying out its duty under Article 3 rule 2 to care properly for the cargo.

62 *Svenska Traktor Akt v Maritime Agencies (Southampton)* [1953] 2 Lloyd's Rep 124.

63 The carrier would be complying with its duty under Article 3 rule 2.

The difficulty with the Hague Rules is that, even where goods are customarily carried on deck, a statement that the goods are to be carried on deck is still required; if not and if the carrier cannot fall back on the liberty clause then carrying the cargo as deck cargo may be a deviation outside the terms of the carriage contract, in which case the carrier could become liable for the full value of the cargo as the carrier will not be able to limit its liability under the Hague Rules.

The Hamburg Rules (which were formulated after containerisation became commonplace) apply to all cargo, whether carried on or below deck.[64] However, while the carrier cannot exclude liability for deck cargo under the Hamburg Rules, as a trade-off the carrier is given an express right to carry cargo on deck if:

(a) the shipper agrees;

(b) it is the usage of the trade; or

(c) it is required by law.[65]

An important provision in the Hamburg Rules is whether or not carriage of the goods on deck is a usage of the particular trade. In particular, container cargo is often carried on deck; is this 'usage of the particular trade'? It may well be. If so, then the carrier can limit its liability in accordance with the limitation provisions set out in Article 6 of the Hamburg Rules.

With the advent of containerisation, very large numbers of containers are carried as deck cargo and, even though deck cargo does involve special risks, in view of the volume of container cargo now carried this way it does not seem unreasonable that some steps should be taken to provide a shipper with some redress where cargo is carried on deck.

There were very good reasons for the exclusion of deck cargo at the turn of the century when the Hague Rules were being formulated, but the changes to shipping practices which have occurred since then do tend to indicate that the carrier should bear some responsibility for loss or damage to deck cargo, and the Hamburg Rules would appear to be a definite improvement over the Amended Hague Rules in this regard.

Live animals

Carriage of live animals is outside the coverage of both the Hague Rules and the Amended Hague Rules[66] and carriers can and do insert exclusion clauses in the contract of carriage denying liability completely in respect of such carriage.

Australia has in recent years developed a considerable trade in the export of live animals. Advances in technology and in shipping practice mean that carriage of live animals does not present the same level of substantial risk that existed half a century ago. As with deck cargo, it would seem that the time has come when it is not unreasonable for the carrier to shoulder some of the risk associated with carriage of live animals.

---

64   Article 1(5) and the Hamburg Rules.

65   Article 9.

66   See definition of 'goods' in Article 1(c).

The Hamburg Rules potentially have an advantage over both the Hague Rules and the Amended Hague Rules in that the definition of goods in the Hamburg Rules specifically provides[67] that goods include 'live animals', so a shipper gets the benefit of some recovery where loss or damage is suffered.

Nautical fault and negligent management

Both the Hague Rules and the Amended Hague Rules contain[68] a very lengthy list of excepted perils. Most of these exceptions are based on the principle that the carrier should be exempt from liability because the loss occurred without any fault or negligence on its part. However, Article 4 rule 2(a) sets out the so-called 'nautical fault' and 'negligent management' defences. It provides that:

> Neither the carrier nor the ship shall be responsible for loss or damage arising or resulting from:
>
> (a) act, neglect or default of the master, mariner, pilot, or the servants of the carrier in the navigation or the management of the ship.

This rule turns the usual duty of care in negligence on its head. The original rationale for this exemption appears to be that, at the turn of the century, vessels were sailing into uncharted or poorly charted areas and maritime adventures were potentially very hazardous. The master of the vessel was out of contact for long periods and, in effect, the shipowner was risking his ship and cargo owners their cargo. The master was out of the effective control of the shipowner as he was out of contact for long periods. This is not the situation today. While sea carriage today still presents risks, the carriage of goods is considerably less hazardous than it was.

Accordingly, there do seem to be grounds for the termination of this exemption on at least three grounds:

1 the background to the creation of this special exemption no longer exists;

2 the exemption is contrary to the general principles of negligence;

3 the exemption is unique to sea carriage and is not found in other carriage regimes and hence detracts from uniformity.

As Anthony Diamond QC stated:[69]

> Much ingenuity has been devoted to trying to justify these exceptions but, it is submitted, there has not been any argument which really gets off the ground. It is difficult to see why negligence in navigating a ship should have different legal consequences than any other kind of negligence. As to negligence in the management of the ship, this exception requires the court to ascertain whether the negligent management occurred before or after the voyage began. If it occurred before the beginning of the voyage, the shipowner is liable for failing to exercise due diligence. If afterwards, it is necessary to decide whether the negligence was in managing the ship or

---

67 Article 1(5).

68 Article 4, rule 20.

69 Diamond, 'Responsibility for Loss of, or Damage to, Cargo on a Sea Transit', *op cit*, p 111.

in looking after the cargo. ... The exceptions of negligent navigation and negligent management of the ship are distinctly out of place in a regime based on a duty of care.

The Hamburg Rules make such a change. Article 5, rule 1 provides that:

> The carrier is liable for loss resulting from loss of or damage to the goods, as well as from delay in delivery, if the occurrence which caused the loss, damage or delay took place while the goods were in his charge as defined in Article 4, unless the carrier proves that he, his servants or agents took all measures that could reasonably be required to avoid the occurrence and its consequences.

This rule effectively does away with the nautical fault and negligent management defence, as a carrier could not demonstrate in those situations that all reasonably required measures were taken by the carrier's servant or agent.

The Hamburg Rules are an improvement over the Hague Rules and the Amended Hague Rules in this area from the viewpoints of equity and uniformity. However, there are policy considerations to consider with this exemption, as their implementation would see a substantial shift in the amount of risk assumed by the carrier and the cargo owner.[70]

Fire

The fire exemption is another provision unique to the Hague and Amended Hague Rules. Article 4, rule 2(b) provides that:

> Neither the carrier nor the ship shall be responsible for loss or damage arising or resulting from:
>
> (b) fire, unless caused by the actual fault or privity of the carrier.

As with the nautical fault exception, it seems a curious anomaly in today's world to have a defence based on fire caused by the negligence of the carrier's servants or agents, and the tide of opinion may be turning against maintaining such special case exemptions.

The Hamburg Rules do away with this exemption. They provide that:

4(a) The carrier is liable:

(i) for loss of or damage to the goods or delay in delivery caused by fire, if the claimant proves that the fire arose from fault or neglect on the part of the carrier, his servants or agents;

(ii) for such loss, damage or delay in delivery which is proved by the claimant to have resulted from the fault or neglect of the carrier, his servants or agents, in taking all measures that could reasonably be required to put out the fire and avoid or mitigate its consequences.

(b) In case of fire on board the ship affecting the goods, if the claimant or the carrier so desires, a survey in accordance with shipping practices must be held into the cause and circumstances of the fire, and a copy of the surveyor's report shall be made available on demand to the carrier and the claimant.[71]

---

70   See Makins, B, 'Sea Carriage of Goods Liability: Which Route for Australia? The case for the Hague-Visby Rules and SDR Protocol', 14th International Trade Law Conference, Canberra, 16 October 1987, Australian Government Publishing Service, 1988.

71   Article 5, rule 4.

While the Hamburg Rules remove the fire defence, they place the onus of proof of the negligence on the shipper,[72] unlike the general formulation of liability set out in Article 5, rule 1, where the onus is placed on the carrier to show that it took all measures reasonably required to avoid the occurrence and its consequences.

When does carriage begin and end?

With both the Hague Rules and the Amended Hague Rules there has been a problem in establishing just when the rules commence and cease to have application; ie whether they cover loading and unloading. The general rule in Australia (following the UK approach) is that the rules apply from tackle to tackle; ie from when the tackle is hooked on to the goods until the tackle is removed from the goods on delivery.[73]

However, the application of these rules could be extended by agreement between the parties.[74] So, under the Hague Rules, the cargo could be covered by the rules while on the dock or while being transferred to another vessel during the original voyage.[75]

Notwithstanding that the application of the Hague Rules can, in some instances, be extended by agreement or custom, it is generally the case that carriers operating under the Hague or Amended Hague Rules provide 'tackle to tackle' coverage, ie they exclude liability for any period which the goods are being loaded or off-loaded.[76]

The Hamburg Rules attempt to extend the scope of this coverage. Article 4 rule 1 provides that:

> The responsibility of the carrier for the goods under this convention covers the period during which the carrier is in charge of the goods at the port of loading, during the carriage and at the port of discharge.

So, instead of 'tackle to tackle' coverage, the Hamburg Rules cover from 'port to port'; ie they include the loading and unloading phases which are the times when damage to goods is most likely to occur.[77] As loading and unloading is usually performed by a stevedoring company – usually an independent entity to the carrier although sometimes with close links – is it reasonable for a carrier to be responsible for the actions of an independent contractor? The answer would appear to be 'yes'. The shipper engages the carrier to move the goods from one place to another, leaving all arrangements including

---

72 Article 5, rule 4(a).

73 *Pyrene v Scindia* [1954] 2 QB 402.

74 *Pyrene v Scindia* [1954] 2 QB 402; *Falconbridge Nickel Mines Ltd v Chimo Shipping Ltd* [1969] 2 Lloyd's Rep 277.

75 But see *Captain v Far East Steamship Co* [1979] 1 Lloyd's Rep 595, 602 where it was held that the Hague Rules did not apply where two bills of lading issued for two voyages and the goods were stored on the dock for a lengthy period during which the damage occurred while awaiting transhipment by water. This case was distinguished in *Mayhew Foods v OCL* [1984] 1 Lloyd's Rep 317 where only one bill of lading issued for the voyage and the cargo owner was not made aware of the transhipment the court held that the goods were covered by the Amended Hague Rules for the whole voyage including transfers. See also *The Anders Maersk* [1986] 1 Lloyd's Rep 483.

76 *The Bunga Teratsai; Nissho Iwai Ltd v Malaysian International Shipping Corp* (1989) 167 CLR 219.

77 See submission by NSW Shippers Association to the Australian Department of Transport entitled 'Implementation of Hamburg Rules', March 1994.

loading and unloading and subcontracting of the carriage up to the carrier or the freight forwarder. It does not seem unreasonable for the carrier to be responsible for the loss or damage to the cargo during this period. The carrier, of course, will have its own remedies against the third party who caused the loss or damage to the cargo.

What happens at present with the Hague and Amended Hague Rules is that the carrier contracts out of liability at this stage and, by the use of a Himalaya clause, it also contracts out of liability on behalf of the stevedoring company. The result is that, when the goods are on the docks before loading or after unloading, at the times when loss or damage is most likely to occur, both the carrier and the stevedore will often have no responsibility to the shipper. This, surely, is inequitable, and the Hamburg Rules approach has to be considered to be more fair and more in keeping with modern shipping practice than the Hague Rules in this regard.

Delay

As neither the Hague Rules nor the Amended Hague Rules deal with delay, the common law imposes a duty on the carrier to deliver the goods within a reasonable time if that is within the reasonable contemplation of the parties.[78] As the common law can be overridden by contractual provisions to the contrary, the carrier is free to deny liability for any economic loss caused by delay in the contract of carriage, and it is common to see clauses in bills of lading doing this. Where the delay causes physical damage to the goods, the Hague Rules and Amended Hague Rules will usually cover the situation as Article 3, rule 2 imposes a duty of care on the carrier in the handling of the cargo.

Perhaps it is somewhat anomalous that a shipper can be denied recompense for loss or damage arising out of delay when the shipper does receive some recompense for loss or damage to the goods. On the other hand, under the Hague Rules, if the carrier does not exclude liability for delay in the conditions of carriage, then the carrier may be fully responsible for all losses caused by delay, whereas it could limit its liability if the goods were lost or damaged. There is a lack of uniformity in the application of the Hague Rules. Most other conventions relating to carriage deal with this issue[79] and permit recovery of damages for delay. Surely some uniformity of approach with sea carriage would be appropriate.

The Hamburg Rules do address this issue and, in general, give the shipper rights against the carrier in respect of delay. Article 5 provides that:

1   The carrier is liable for loss resulting from loss of or damage to the goods, as well as from delay in delivery, if the occurrence which caused the loss, damage or delay took place while the goods were in his charge as defined in Article 4, unless the carrier proves that he, his servants or agents took all measures that could reasonably be required to avoid the occurrence and its consequences.

---

78   *Renton v Palmyra Trading Corp* [1957] AC 149; *The Makedonia* [1962] 1 Lloyd's Rep 316.

79   Article 19 of the Warsaw Convention (air), Article 27 of the CIM Convention (rail) and Article 17 of the CMR Convention (road).

2   Delay in delivery occurs when the goods have not been delivered at the port of discharge provided for in the contract of carriage by sea within the time expressly agreed upon or, in the absence of such agreement, within the time which it would be reasonable to require of a diligent carrier, having regard to the circumstances of the case.

However, the rules impose a special limit on recoverable damages, where delay is concerned, of 'two and a half times the freight payable for the goods delayed, but not exceeding the total freight payable under the contract of carriage of goods by sea'.[80] This limit applies unless the delay period exceeds 60 days, in which case the shipper may treat the goods as lost.[81]

While this may give a shipper some benefits (as opposed to a contractual denial of liability for loss from delay under the Hague and Amended Hague Rules) it also raises some difficulties. First, it is difficult to understand the reasoning behind the differing method of calculating the limitation of liability for delay. From the shipper's point of view, a loss is a loss – whether it is caused by loss of or damage to the goods or by delay. So why not the same limitation amount?

Secondly, can the carrier specify in the contract of carriage that the delivery period will be 12 months (or some other excessively long period) and thereby avoid any liability for delay until that date is reached? If so, does this mean the shipper cannot claim for loss of the goods until 60 days after the long transport period? Does the delivery time stop running for strikes by the carrier's employees?

Thirdly, given that the Hamburg Rules are supposed to take into account multi-modal transport, how will this provision apply where multi-modal transport is involved? Does delay in another mode of carriage have to be taken into account?

Another difficulty of interpretation posed by the Hamburg Rules is in respect to the application of the 60 day period in Article 5, rule 3.[82] Does the consignee have to abandon the goods to claim them as lost? If so, who owns the goods? If the carriage document is a bill of lading, then how can the bill of lading remain a negotiable document?

These questions await interpretation by the courts. The provisions are very complex to interpret and it is difficult to predict whether they will ultimately be of benefit to the carrier or whether, indeed, they will be any improvement on the existing situation under the Amended Hague Rules which is also unsatisfactory. So, while the Hamburg Rules deal with delay, the way in which they have dealt with delay is unfortunate.

---

80   Article 6, rule 1(b).

81   Under Article 5, rule 3.

82   The period appears to have been taken from the 60 day period in the CMR Convention of 1956.

Time bars

Under the Hague Rules and the Amended Hague Rules, the time bar for taking action against the carrier is one year.[83] However, the usual time limit applies if the carrier takes action against the shipper for freight.[84] A classic example of this is the case of *The Aries*,[85] where the carrier was able to claim successfully against the shipper for freight, and the shipper's claims against the carrier was time-barred.

There are two criticisms of this time bar:

1 the one year time bar is short and tends to favour the carrier; and

2 it is not even-handed, in that the carrier is under no such constraint in any action the carrier takes against the shipper for, say, freight where the usual limitation periods apply.

The Hamburg Rules provide for a longer time bar period which applies equally to both parties. Article 20, rule 1 provides that:

> Any action relating to carriage of goods under this convention is time-barred if judicial or arbitral proceedings have not been instituted within a period of two years.

Under this rule, the time bar applies to all actions, whether by the carrier or by the shipper, so that both are treated equally. The time bar here is equivalent to the time bar provided for in the Warsaw Convention,[86] which has the added benefit of providing some uniformity between both the regimes of carriage applicable to Australia.[87]

The package or unit definition

One area which has caused considerable confusion is the meaning of the words 'package or unit' in both the Hague Rules and the Amended Hague Rules.[88] The courts in different countries have given differing interpretations to this phrase. The only Australian authority in this area is *PS Chellaram and Co v China Ocean Shipping Co*,[89] a case on the original Hague Rules where Carruthers J adopted the 'functional package' test: that the package or unit is determined by reference to the physical nature of the packaging of the goods, particularly the unit in which the shipper packaged the goods.[90]

In the Amended Hague Rules, the Visby Protocol introduced Article 4, rule 5(c), which provides that:

---

83 Article 3, rule 6.

84 This is usually six years under the limitation acts in force in Australia. Section 10 of the Limitation of Actions Act 1974 (Qld); s 14 of the Limitation Act 1969 (NSW); s 5 of the Limitation of Actions Act 1958 (Vic); s 4 of the Limitation Act 1974 (Tas); s 35 of the Limitation of Actions Act 1936–75 (SA); s 38 of the Limitation Act 1935–78 (WA); s 12 of the Limitation Act 1981 (NT) s 12.

85 *Aries Tanker Corp v Total Transport Ltd* [1977] 1 Lloyd's Rep 334.

86 Article 29.

87 However, the CMR Convention relating to international road carriage imposes a one year limit.

88 Article 4, rule 5.

89 [1989] 1 Lloyd's Rep 413.

90 NB: the decision of Carruthers J was reversed by the NSW Court of Appeal but on other grounds – *China Ocean Shipping Co v PS Chellaram and Co*, unreported, Court of Appeal NSW, no CA762/88.

> When a container, pallet or similar article of transport is used to consolidate goods, the number of packages or units enumerated in the bill of lading as packed in such article of transport shall be deemed the number of packages or units for the purpose of this paragraph as far as these packages or units are concerned. Except as aforesaid such article of transport shall be considered the package or unit.

The Amended Hague Rules look at the description of the goods on the bill of lading rather than the physical nature of the packaging of the goods, so if the bill of lading, for example, specifies on its face that it is 'one container containing 20 cartons of ...' then the carton is the unit. However, if it says 'one container of ...', then the container itself becomes the unit. This seems to rule out the 'functional package' test favoured by the court in *China Ocean Shipping Co v PS Chellaram and Co*.[91]

The Hamburg Rules have adopted a similar formula to the Amended Hague Rules. Article 6 rule 2 provides that:

> For the purpose of calculating which amount is the higher in accordance with para 1(a) of this article, the following rules apply:
>
> (a) Where a container, pallet or similar article of transport is used to consolidate goods, the package or other shipping units enumerated in the bill of lading, if issued, or otherwise in any other document evidencing the contract of carriage by sea, as packed in such article of transport, are deemed packages or shipping units. Except as aforesaid, the goods in such article of transport are deemed one shipping unit.
>
> (b) In cases where the article of transport itself has been lost or damaged, that article of transport, if not owned or otherwise supplied by the carrier, is considered one separate shipping unit.

The Hamburg Rules seems to allow for three possibilities:

(a) if the bill of lading does not detail the contents of the container, the container is one shipping unit;

(b) if it specifies the contents individually, then each of the specified packages is a unit; and

(c) if it specifies certain packages plus general cargo in the container, then each package is a unit and the general cargo is another unit.

The Hamburg Rules follow the Amended Hague Rules; ie the wording on the face of the bill of lading or other document of carriage will be examined and will be determinative of the package or shipping unit.

So, while there is a problem with the Hague Rules in determining what is a package or unit, the Amended Hague Rules addressed this, and their method of determining a package or unit has also been adopted by the Hamburg Rules. This method removes the uncertainty of the original Hague Rule formulation. However, there is still some ambiguity where an entry in a bill of lading reads 'said to contain'. For example, if an entry reads 'one container said to contain 50 electric motors', what then is the appropriate shipping unit? It could be arguably either the container or the 50 electric motors.

---

91   *Ibid.*

Jurisdiction/arbitration

The Hague Rules and the Amended Hague Rules are silent on jurisdiction and arbitration. As documents of carriage are habitually prepared by the carrier, the carrier generally is given the advantage of choosing a forum for arbitration or litigation which is convenient to itself. That forum is often inconvenient to the shipper which may find itself having to take action in an unfamiliar jurisdiction to seek redress, even though the rules themselves are uniform. The burden of proof and the interpretation of the rules can differ from country to country. The carrier can forum shop to have its bill of lading interpreted by courts of a country giving the most favourable interpretations.

While the Hague Rules and the Amended Hague Rules do not deal with jurisdiction, in Australia, s 9 of the Sea Carriage of Goods Act 1924[92] provided that:

1   All parties to any bill of lading or document relating to the carriage of goods from any place in Australia to any place outside Australia shall be deemed to have intended to contract according to the laws in force at the place of shipment, and any stipulation or agreement to the contrary, or purporting to oust or lessen the jurisdiction of the courts of the Commonwealth or of a State in respect of the bill of lading or document, shall be illegal, null and void, and of no effect.

2   Any stipulation or agreement, whether made in the Commonwealth or elsewhere, purporting to oust or lessen the jurisdiction of the courts of the Commonwealth or of a State in respect of any bill of lading or document relating to the carriage of goods from any place outside Australia to any place in Australia, shall be illegal, null and void, and of no effect.

Section 11 of COGSA 1991 makes similar provisions in respect of the Amended Hague Rules. So, even though there was no jurisdiction clause in the rules, the problems this caused in overseas jurisdictions[93] were not apparent here because the jurisdiction of the Australian courts could not be ousted. However, in respect of cargo inbound to Australia, the Australian courts may have to interpret the contract of carriage subject to the governing law of another jurisdiction.[94]

The Hamburg Rules specifically deal with jurisdiction. Article 21 provides that a plaintiff (who apparently can be either the carrier or the shipper) can bring an action in the courts of:

1   the place of the defendant's business (or, if none, habitual residence);

2   the place where the contract was made;

3   the port of loading;

4   the port of discharge;

5   the agreed place in the contract; or

6   the place where the vessel has been arrested.

---

92   This is the Act which gave effect to the Hague Rules. It was repealed by COGSA 1991.

93   *The Eleftheria* [1969] 1 Lloyd's Rep 237.

94   *Dunbee Ltd v Gilmen and Co (Australia) Pty Ltd* [1968] 2 Lloyd's Rep 394 – if the law of a particular country was the proper law of the contract, this did not mean there had been a submission to the law of that country.

There is some doubt as to whether the insertion of these provisions on jurisdiction is an improvement over the Hague and Amended Hague Rules. As can be seen from *The Eleftheria*,[95] the courts were able to formulate a satisfactory solution to the jurisdiction problem. In Australia, the courts have always been given the benefit of a statutory jurisdiction provision,[96] so the Hamburg Rules provisions on jurisdiction make no significant improvement in the Australian context.

Indeed, the Hamburg Rules may be a backward step. There is some ambiguity in terms such as 'agency' and 'residence'. It is also difficult to see why rule 5 has been inserted – it apparently covers the same ground as Article 21, rule 1(d). The Hamburg Rules may once again muddy the waters which had been cleared up by judicial interpretation of the Hague Rules.

Liability under the Hague and the Hamburg Rules

The carrier's duties under the Hague Rules and the Amended Hague Rules are set out in Article 3, which provides that:

1   The carrier shall be bound before and at the beginning of the voyage to exercise due diligence to:

   (a)   make the ship seaworthy;

   (b)   properly man, equip and supply the ship; and

   (c)   make the holds, refrigerating and cool chambers, and all other parts of the ship in which goods are carried, fit and safe for their reception, carriage and preservation.

2   Subject to the provisions of Article 4, the carrier shall properly and carefully load, handle, stow, carry, keep, care for and discharge the goods carried.

There are two duties here:

1   a duty at the commencement of the voyage to provide a seaworthy vessel – this duty is non-delegable[97] and is not subject to the carrier's defences in Article 4, rule 2, ie if the carrier fails to provide a seaworthy vessel at the commencement of the voyage, then it cannot rely on the usual defences in the event of loss or damage to the cargo; and

2   a duty to care for the cargo properly, subject to the defences in Article 4, rule 2.

The duty of seaworthiness imposed by the Hague, and Amended Hague Rules is something greater than the tortious duty of care.[98] However, the duty to care for the cargo is closer to the tortious duty (except the nautical fault and fire exemptions in Article 4, rule 2), but there have been problems interpreting the word 'properly'[99] in

---

95   [1969] 1 Lloyd's Rep 237.

96   Section 9 of the Sea Carriage of Goods Act 1924, and s 11 of the COGSA 1991.

97   *The Muncaster Castle* [1961] Lloyd's Rep 57; *The Amstelslot* [1963] 2 Lloyd's Rep 223.

98   *Ibid.*

99   *Albacora SRL v Westcott and Lawrence Line* [1966] 2 Lloyd's Rep 37.

'properly man, equip and supply the ship', and it may be that the obligation is something more than a duty to take reasonable care.[100]

The Hague Rules liability provisions create some anomalies. Firstly, a ship can be seaworthy for the purpose of carriage of certain types of cargo but not for others. As a result, the owner of one cargo for which the vessel was unseaworthy could obtain full recovery, whereas another cargo owner may not as the vessel was seaworthy for that cargo. Secondly, the carrier's duty is only to exercise due diligence to make the vessel seaworthy at the commencement of the voyage defined on the bill of lading. A ship will commonly stop at a number of ports *en route*. If the ship is seaworthy (or if due diligence has been exercised) at the time of loading of the first shipper's cargo, but it is no longer seaworthy at a port *en route* where a second shippers' cargo is loaded, then when both cargoes are unloaded at the destination port, only the second shipper will be able to recover.

The Hamburg Rules, in Article 5, make a significant change to the basis of liability. Article 5, rule 1 provides that:

> The carrier is liable for loss resulting from loss of or damage to the goods, as well as from delay in delivery, if the occurrence which caused the loss, damage or delay took place while the goods were in his charge as defined in Article 4, unless the carrier proves that he, his servants or agents took all measures that could reasonably be required to avoid the occurrence and its consequences.

Under the Hamburg Rules, the same duty applies to both the carrier's vessel and the cargo; ie to take 'all measures that could reasonably be required to avoid the occurrence and its consequences'. This places a continuing duty on the carrier to maintain the vessel in a seaworthy state throughout the voyage rather than just at the commencement of the voyage. The nautical fault and fire exemptions in relation to the cargo are effectively removed by the Hamburg Rules as in these situations the shipowner could not demonstrate that all reasonable measures were taken to avoid the occurrence. It also places the onus of proof on the carrier to establish that it exercised due diligence, unlike the Hague Rules and Amended Hague Rules where the onus was on the shipper to establish that there had been a breach of Article 3 of those rules. The rationale behind this reversal of the onus of proof is that the shipper is in a very difficult position in being able to prove a want of due diligence, whereas the carrier should be in a better position to establish, positively, due diligence.

While the duty on the carrier under the Hamburg Rules has the merit of being uniform, a question which remains unanswered is just what is the standard of care; is it the 'negligence' standard or something more, as it is under the Hague and Amended Hague Rules?[101]

The Hamburg Rules apparently impose a significantly greater level of liability on the carrier. However, whether the duty of care imposed is any greater than the usual negligence standard remains to be seen. At least the standard is uniform in its application

---

100 *Shipping Corp of India Ltd v Gamlen Chemical Co (Australasia) Pty Ltd* (1980) 147 CLR 142 at 150.

101 *The Muncaster Castle* [1961] Lloyd's Rep 57; *Albacora SRL v Westcott and Lawrence Line* [1966] 2 Lloyd's Rep 37.

to the ship and to the cargo, and all shippers are treated equally regardless of the port of loading.

Limitation of liability

Under the Hague Rules, Article 4, rule 5 provides that the carrier's liability is limited to '£100 per package or unit'. Article 9 provides that 'the monetary units mentioned in these rules are to be taken to be gold value'. Until recently in Australia this was taken to be a package or unit limitation of $200 in today's currency. This significantly limits the carrier's liability as inflationary pressures have made $200 (£100) significantly less in real terms then it was in 1924.

However, the New South Wales Court of Appeal in *Brown Boveri (Aust) Pty Ltd v Baltic Shipping Co Ltd*[102] found that the Hague Rules limit is the market value today of the amount of gold contained in 100 gold sovereigns in the year 1924.[103]

The Amended Hague Rules incorporate the SDR Protocol, which provides that:

Unless the nature and value of such goods have been declared by the shipper before shipment and inserted in the bill of lading, neither the carrier nor the ship shall in any event be or become liable for any loss or damage to or in connection with the goods in an amount exceeding 666.67 units of account per package or unit or two units of account per kilogram weight of the goods lost or damaged, whichever is the higher.[104]

The unit of account under the Amended Hague Rules is the Special Drawing Right (SDR) as defined by the International Monetary Fund.[105] The effect of the introduction of the Amended Hague Rules has been to reduce by about 98% the liability limit under the Hague Rules (as defined by the NSW Court of Appeal in *Brown Boveri*). So, from the shipper's point of view, the introduction of the Amended Hague Rules has meant a very significant potential diminution in the amount which could be recovered by the shipper.

Under the Hamburg Rules, the liability limits are increased by about 20% over the limits set down in the Amended Hague Rules. Article 6, rule 1(a) provides that:

The liability of the carrier for loss resulting from loss of or damage to goods according to the provisions of Article 5 is limited to an amount equivalent to 835 units of account per package or other shipping unit or 2.5 units of account per kilogramme gross weight of the goods lost or damaged, whichever is the higher.

So, while the package or unit limitation has been significantly lifted, it is still much less than the limitation amount under the Hague Rules (after *Brown Boveri*).

The rationale behind the introduction of limitation of liability was to encourage investment in shipping.[106] The rationale now for retaining the limitation is that it enables the carrier to calculate risks, to establish uniform and cheaper freight rates and to

---

102 (*The Nadezhda Krupskaya*) (1989) 15 *NSWLR* 448; [1989] 1 Lloyd's Rep 518.

103 In 1989 when *Brown Boveri* was decided that value was in excess of $11,000.

104 Article 4, rule 5(a).

105 Article 5, rule 5(d).

106 Wilson, JF, 'Basic Carrier Liability and the Right of Limitation' in Mankabady, S (ed), *The Hamburg Rules On The Carriage of Goods by Sea*, 1978, pp 137, 146, Leyden/Boston: AW Sijthoff.

protect itself from risks associated with the carriage of undisclosed, high value cargo. On the other hand, from the shipper's point of view, the liability limitations should be set high enough to give the carrier sufficient incentive to care properly for the cargo. The old $200 limit per package a unit was plainly insufficient for this purpose. The Hamburg limits are more realistic.

Unlimited liability

Although the Hague Rules have no specific provision dealing with the circumstances in which a carrier may be deprived of its right to limit its liability under the rules, the courts have deprived carriers of the right to limit its liability in some circumstances. In particular, a deviation from the agreed course of the contract may deprive a carrier of its right to limit its liability under those rules.[107]

In Australia, in *JI Case (Australia) Pty Ltd v Tasman Express Line Ltd (The Canterbury Express)*,[108] Carruthers J found that a carrier was not entitled to the benefit of contractual exclusion clauses in a bill of lading as it had deviated from the agreed course of the contract by interfering with the goods during their discharge from the ship. The reasoning behind this is that, at common law, a carrier impliedly promises that the carriage will be performed without unjustified deviation and where such a deviation occurs, the shipper can treat the contract as at an end and take action against the carrier outside the contract.[109]

Unlike the Hague Rules, the Amended Hague Rules have the force of law, and it seems unlikely that an unjustified deviation under the Amended Hague Rules would have the effect of depriving the carrier of exclusions and limitations imposed by force of law. However, the Amended Hague Rules in Article 4, rule 5(e) provide that:

> Neither the carrier nor the ship shall be entitled to the benefit of the limitation of liability provided for in this paragraph if it is proved that the damage resulted from an act or omission of the carrier done with intent to cause damage, or recklessly and with knowledge that damage would probably result.

So the Visby Protocol amends the Hague Rules by inserting a specific provision depriving the carrier of the right to limit liability if the carrier's conduct falls within this reckless or wilful conduct exemption. This provision in the Amended Hague Rules is carried through in similar form in the Hamburg Rules. Article 8, rule 1 provides that:

> The carrier is not entitled to the benefit of the limitation of liability provided for in Article 6 if it is proved that the loss, damage or delay in delivery resulted from an act or omission of the carrier done with the intent to cause such loss, damage or delay, or recklessly and with knowledge that such loss, damage or delay would probably result.

---

107 *Wibau Maschinen Fabric Hartman SA v Mackinnon Mackenzie and Co* [1989] 2 Lloyd's Rep 494 where Hirst J found that a carrier who deviated from the agreed course of the contract by carrying on deck containers which were supposed to be carried under deck was unable to rely upon the protection of Article 4, rule 5 of the Hague Rules.

108 (1990)102 FLR 59.

109 *Ibid* at 74.

There is some uncertainty in what test the court should adopt in interpreting the phrase 'recklessly and with knowledge that damage would probably result'. Should the court adopt an objective test or a subjective test?

The New South Wales Court of Appeal considered a very similar provision in the Warsaw Convention (a convention relating to the carriage of goods by air enacted under the Civil Aviation (Carrier's Liability) Act 1959) as amended by the Hague Protocol.[110] In that case – *SS Pharmaceutical Pty Ltd v Qantas Airways Ltd*[111] the Court of Appeal adopted a subjective approach (as did Rogers CJ at first instance). It is likely this reasoning would be persuasive.

Compatibility

Carriers contend that the Hamburg Rules are not 'compatible' with the Hague and Hague-Visby Rules. As no other major trading partner of Australia is an adherent of the Hamburg Rules, if Australia were to adopt those rules there would be problems because of the incompatibility of the Hamburg Rules with the Hague Rules and Amended Hague Rules. It is certainly true that the Hamburg Rules differ from the Hague-Visby Rules, but are they 'incompatible'? If so, of course, they would not meet the object laid down by the legislation in s 31(1)(c) of COGSA 1991.

The *Macquarie Dictionary* defines 'compatible' as:

1   capable of existing together in harmony; and

2   capable of orderly, efficient integration with other elements in a system.

An analysis by James L Roberts[112] shows that 50% of the Hamburg Rules are common to the Hague Rules or Amended Hague Rules. The Hamburg Rules have also borrowed from the Warsaw Convention, which is a convention which has been in use now in many countries for many years. Surely then, there is sufficient compatibility between the Hamburg Rules and the Amended Hague Rules to mean that the trade between the nations will not be unduly hindered. Trade is, after all, possible between countries which use the Amended Hague Rules and countries which have no rules or different rules; why then should the Hamburg Rules be incompatible.

It is suggested that the Hamburg Rules, in the broader sense of the word, are 'compatible with arrangements existing in countries that are major trading partners of Australia', in that the Hamburg Rules:

• have about half their content in common with the Amended Hague Rules;

• have part of their content based on conventions dealing with air and/or road carriage with which Australia's major trading partners are familiar; and

• will not make it impossible or unduly difficult for trade to take place between Australia (under the Hamburg Rules) and other countries which adhere to the Hague Rules or the Amended Hague Rules.

---

110 Article 25 in Schedule 2 of that Act.

111 [1991] 1 Lloyd's Rep 288 – on appeal. Case at first instance before Rogers CJ (SCNSW) *SS Pharmaceutical Pty Ltd v Qantas Airways Ltd* (1989) 92 FLR 244.

112 Wilde, KCM (ed), to *International Transactions – Trade and Investment Law and Finance*, 1993, Appendix 19, North Ryde: Law Book Co.

ARGUMENTS AGAINST THE INTRODUCTION OF THE HAMBURG RULES

Since the possible implementation of the Hamburg Rules was signalled, the Australian carriers have summoned a formidable array of arguments against their introduction. The major arguments against adoption of the Hamburg Rules seem to be:

1   the existing system works well, has been in force for over 70 years and the rules and the positions of each party are well understood (the *status quo* argument);

2   the Hamburg Rules are not compatible with the rules in force in the countries which are Australia's major trading partners (the compatibility argument); and

3   introduction of a new carriage regime will mean substantial litigation because of the uncertainty of the rules (the uncertainty argument).

The *status quo* argument

As to the *status quo* argument, it is certainly true that, thanks to some 70 years of litigation, the Hague Rules have come to be well understood. However, there continue to be problems with those rules and with the Amended Hague Rules.[113] Certainly, from the point of view of the carrier, there appear to be considerable advantages continuing to operate under the existing rules. But there appear to be substantial problems with the Amended Hague Rules from the point of view of the shipper.[114]

The carriers argue that the interests of the shipper are covered by insurance and that, therefore, it is of little importance to increase the liability of the carrier or to change the carriage regime, as any problems in the existing system are adequately addressed by cargo insurance. This view is supported by cargo insurance interests.[115]

The shipper argues that its primary requirement is that the goods be delivered on time to the consignee in good condition. This is how the shipper builds up and maintains the trading links between itself and its customer. The shipper's most important consideration is to preserve that trading link. Having the goods arrive late or not at all, or to arrive in a damaged condition, will not improve the consignor's trading relationship with the consignee, no matter that the consignee is compensated by insurance – it was the goods the consignee really wanted, not the fall-back of insurance.

Regardless of insurance cover, loss or damage which occurs during this transportation period has a potentially significant impact on the shipper's trade relationship with the consignee, and there appears to be little incentive for the carrier or its subcontractors to improve their cargo-handling procedures during this period. Any remedy in tort the shipper may have because of a breach of the duty of care by the

---

113   See also Diamond, A, 'The Hague-Visby Rules' [1978] *Lloyd's MCLQ* 225.

114   See Beaufort, F, 'Marine Cargo Liability: Hamburg Rules v the Rest – the Shipper's Viewpoint', 3 February 1994 in Levingstones (ed), *Commentary on the Arguments for or against adoption of the Hamburg Rules – a Collection of Papers*, May 1994, Sydney: Levingstones.

115   Hill, MA, 'Shipowners Liability for Loss or Damage to Cargo – Economic Implications of Hague-Visby and Hamburg Rules', 1992, Bern Conference of International Union of Marine Insurance, September.

stevedore or agent of the carrier will usually come within the ambit of the carrier's Himalaya clause. Remedies against the carrier are, of course, limited by the bill of lading and the Amended Hague Rules.

Even when the shipper has remedies against the carrier, there is a significant degree of unevenness in the potential for recovery by the shipper. The shipper must first identify where the loss occurred and then see if he comes within the Hague Rules or whether the loss occurred during the period the rules did not apply.

Conversely, with the Hamburg Rules, the rules are defined in such a way that they have considerably wider application. They will, in many cases, include deck cargo. They will include live animals. They apply to virtually all contracts of carriage by sea.[116]

Under the Hamburg Rules it does not matter whether the goods are transported by way of a negotiable or a non-negotiable instrument – either attracts the same rules and is dealt with the same way. The rules cover a longer period – so-called 'port to port' coverage. So, if the loss occurs during the period in 'which the carrier is in charge of the goods at the port of loading, during the carriage and at the port of discharge', then the shipper will have rights of recovery not presently available under the Amended Hague Rules.[117]

The Hamburg Rules, on their face, appear to treat cargo owning interests more equitably, on balance, than either the Hague Rules or the Amended Hague Rules. The shipper (and for that matter, the shipper's insurer) know that once cargo has been delivered into the hands of the carrier at the port of discharge, the same rules will apply to all those goods until the carrier delivers those goods at the port of discharge. The coverage of the Hamburg Rules – in the scope of goods covered by the rules, the types of instruments of carriage covered by the rules and period of time during which the goods are covered by the rules – all seem more equitable than the existing Hague Rules or the Amended Hague Rules.

The shipper interests clearly believe that, in the current regime, there is insufficient 'encouragement' for the carrier to perform its contractual obligations and that increased liability, together with making the carrier responsible for the loading and unloading operations, will result in the carrier 'lifting its game'.[118]

Whether, with the introduction of the Hamburg Rules, these hopes of the shipper will be fulfilled, is another story, but the mere fact that the shippers are so united in the push for the introduction of the Hamburg Rules shows that there is a big problem with the Amended Hague Rules as far as their interests are concerned.

The compatability argument

Another argument of the proponents of the *status quo* is that the Hamburg Rules will never be accepted anywhere else in the world and that Australia would certainly be

---

116 Except for gratuitous carriage.

117 Article 4, rule 1.

118 New South Wales Shippers submission, *op cit*. Beaufort, *op cit*.

foolish to go it alone. There is force in this argument as it would certainly be unfortunate if Australia were the only country, or one of only a handful, to ever operate under the Hamburg Rules, as uniformity of rules is desirable. Would it be in Australia's best interests, as a comparatively small nation, to introduce a set of rules which are utilised by only a handful of nations, none of whom are major trading partners of Australia? If the Hamburg Rules never come into force with any of Australia's trading partners, then this would not promote uniform trade rules and that would mean Australia would then have to give consideration to moving back into the mainstream. But it would not be a disaster – Australia as a Hamburg Rule country could trade with Hague Rule or Amended Hague Rule countries.

However, there is a real possibility that the Hamburg Rules will eventually find favour and there are potential advantages to Australia of being 'first kid on the block', for shippers, carriers and insurers. From the carrier's point of view, they would obtain first-hand experience of how the regime would operate in an industrialised Western country. Because the size of the Australian shipping market is relatively small in world terms, it gives carriers an opportunity to experiment with the systems required to comply with the rules. The lessons learned by the carriers could then be scaled up into larger markets should they subsequently adopt the Hamburg Rules. This may be preferable to a carrier rather than the alternative of having a very large market, such as the EU or the USA, suddenly adopt the Hamburg Rules. Similarly, the international insurance market would benefit by having the advantage of experience in the 'test' Australian market, which may be useful in formulating risk management strategies in larger countries if Europe and America should decide to adopt the Hamburg Rules.

There may even be benefits for lawyers. There are ambiguities in the Hamburg Rules which would fall to the Australian Courts to interpret. Australian courts are well respected and their decisions would receive serious consideration when the rules come into play in other countries. There is the potential for Australian lawyers, and the shipping industry generally, establishing a repository of knowledge on the operation of the Hamburg Rules which may tend to attract arbitration or litigation on the Hamburg Rules to this country as a focal point for the region and facilitate an academic build-up of knowledge in this area.

If no other country adopts the Hamburg Rules, this is not necessarily a disaster for Australia. Although the Hague Rules and Amended Hague Rules are currently pre-eminent for international carriage of goods by sea, there are many countries that operate on variations of those rules or different carriage regimes entirely. If it were an enormous disadvantage for these countries not to operate under a Hague Rule regime, they would have already joined the Hague Rules club. They have not done so.

Accordingly, if Australia did become the odd man out in adopting the Hamburg Rules, it seems unlikely that it would spell the end of trade as we know it. It may be that freight rates would be higher, which may affect marginal exports, but such marginal exports are also affected by any number of other factors such as exchange rate risks.

There are a number of advantages, in an equitable sense, in adopting the Hamburg Rules:

- they presage a more evenly balanced sharing of responsibility between the carrier and the shipper;
- they are more compatible with the move towards multi-modalism; and
- they are to be more in line with the generally accepted principles of common law liability.

It is worth bearing in mind that, when the Hague Rules were being formulated, they were the first of their kind. When the rules were being drafted there were no other equivalent conventions on carriage of goods that the drafters of the Hague Rules could have regard to – the Hague Rules were the fore runner of all subsequent carriage conventions.

In contrast, the drafters of the Hamburg Rules were in a position to examine, not only the Hague Rules, but also other carriage of goods regimes in other modes of transport. They could refer to not only the state of the law relating to sea carriage of goods, but also (although not directly comparable) the carriage regimes in respect of carriage by air, carriage by road and carriage by rail. It is appropriate that these conventions should be considered, as, after all, in these days of emergent multi-modalism, cargo will often travel by road, rail and/or sea in reaching its destination.

The Hague Rules have been in existence since 1924.[119] They or the Amended Hague Rules have been adopted by over 80 countries. During the 70 years since their introduction, a very considerable body of case law has evolved to give a good deal of certainty to most of the rules within each country. This certainty makes for efficient administration.

The uncertainty argument

A strong argument in favour of retention of the Hague Rules is that, with the introduction of the Hamburg Rules, many points on carrier's liability will need re-deciding. Much of the work of the courts in giving clarity to the existing rules would be thrown away, as the Hamburg Rules do not just build on established principles, as occurred with the introduction of the Visby Protocol, but rather introduce new concepts, discussed earlier.[120]

The drawback to this certainty argument is that some of those decisions, allied with some unfortunate drafting of the Hague Rules, have moved the law into what have been perceived as undesirable directions. In addition, different countries have interpreted the same rule in different ways (eg the package or unit limitation).

It is a perceived disadvantage of the Hamburg Rules that, in many areas, they have not been drafted with sufficient clarity. As a result, they may not accomplish what they set out to do, ie to remove outstanding technical uncertainties in the Hague Rules and to alter the Hague Rules where it has been perceived they were moving in an

---

119 Indeed, they are based on the USA Harter Act 1893.
120 Tetley, W, 'The Hamburg Rules – a Commentary' [1979] *Lloyd's MCLQ* 1.

undesirable direction.[121] If the Hamburg Rules were to be introduced, this would mean, for both carrier and shipper alike, a new period of uncertainty in the short-to-medium term as all parties grapple with their application.

It may be many decades before the law relating to carriage of goods by sea conducted under the Hamburg Rules would again have the certainty it has today under the Amended Hague Rules. Lord Diplock noted this in a seminar in 1976.[122]

> So, while there has been no real criticism of the Hague Rules, there has been I think a consensus of criticism of the changes suggested in the UNCTAD/UNCITRAL draft; criticisms because basically these changes will increase the number of recourse actions and also because of the vagueness of the phrases used leading to great uncertainty and doubt as to what the subjective position of the judge will be in the various jurisdictions. They will render useless all that expensive jurisprudence accumulated over 50 years upon the meanings of the phrases in the Hague Rules, and for many years after a new and vague criterion has been set down there will be all the expense incurred again while the uncertainty continues to exist.

If certainty were to be the sole criteria of efficiency, then the Hamburg Rules fall short of providing it in the short term and, possibly, the medium term. The question must be asked whether it is more desirable to stay with the Hague-Visby Rules, with their acknowledged problems, or to go with the Hamburg Rules, which create their own set of new problems but which, on the face of it, move the laws relating to carriage of goods by sea into a more desirable direction having regard to modern shipping practice.

It must always be remembered that it is the shipper who creates international trade – it is the carrier who services it. It is universally acknowledged that trade is of vital importance to the Australian economy. The shipper's position does have merit. While there are legitimate concerns in adopting a new set of rules and while the consequences may be far-reaching, if Australia adopted the Hamburg Rules this would not be the end of trade or a disaster for Australia. For Australia, the perceived advantages of the adoption of the Hamburg Rules would appear to outweigh the disadvantages.

---

121 Tetley, *op cit.*

122 In Reynolds, F, 'The Hague Rules, the Hague-Visby Rules and the Hamburg Rules' (1990) 7 *Marine Lawyers Association of Australia and New Zealand Journal* 16, 32.

TUTORIAL QUESTIONS

1   Should Australia and the USA adopt the Hamburg Rules? Give reasons for your view.

2   Printing Press Ltd, an American manufacturer of printing presses located in New York, enters into a contract with L'Awful Printing Pty Ltd, a Sydney based company in Australia, for the international sale of a printing press.

The contract of sale calls for a documentary sale, CIF Sydney. The printing press is shipped at New York for delivery at Sydney, under a bill of lading which incorporates the Amended Hague Rules. The bill of lading is issued on 15 July 1992 on which date the printing press is shipped on board the 'Joyride' in a container. Americaline Ltd (owned by Antwerp Bulk Carriers NV) issues a bill of lading to 'seller or order' stating that 'one container, containing one printing press', has been received on board as container cargo for shipment from New York to Sydney.

The bill of lading was a port to port bill and contained a Himalaya clause, extending the benefit of defences and immunities conferred by the bill of lading upon the carrier to independent contractors employed by the carrier.

On 14 August 1992, the printing press was in the custody and control of stevedores employed by the carrier. While the printing press was being conveyed on a low bed trailer, the printing press fell from the trailer and was damaged beyond economic repair. The buyer alleged that the sole cause of the damage was the negligence of the servants and agents of the carrier.

The buyer decides to initiate legal proceedings against the carrier in a Sydney court. The buyer has heard that you have, recently, successfully completed a course in international business law and, confident that you are an expert on trade law, hires you to represent their interests.

Advise the buyer on all legal aspects of this case. Refer to, and discuss, relevant statutory provisions and relevant cases. In particular, give advice regarding whether the buyer can recover damages from the carrier.

3   A load of chicken feet was shipped from Brisbane to New York, CIF New York. Before the cargo was shipped or the bill of lading issued, the ship's agent promised the shipper orally that the cargo would arrive in New York by June 30, 1995. On shipment a bill of lading which incorporated the Amended Hague Rules was issued by the carrier to the shipper.

Scenario one: *en route* to New York the vessel called in at a number of ports as the carrier found cargo for the vessel and it did not arrive in New York until August 15, 1995.

Due to a recent amendment to the relevant American Customs law, import duty had become payable on the chicken feet from August 1, 1995 and the market for chicken feet had deteriorated substantially.

Advise the shipper.

Scenario two: A few weeks before the vessel arrived in New York, the American government had prohibited the importation of chicken feet due to the outbreak of a disease affecting the bones of chicken feet. Hence, upon arrival in New York, the chicken feet were confiscated and destroyed by the American customs authorities.

Advise the holder of the bill of lading.

FURTHER READING

Articles

Bauer, RB, 'Conflicting Liability Regimes: Hague-Visby v Hamburg Rules – a Case by Case Analysis' (1993) 24 *J Maritime L* 53.

Beatson, J and Cooper, JJ, 'Rights of Suit in Respect of Carriage of Goods by Sea' [1991] *Lloyd's MCLQ* 196.

Berlingieri, F, 'Uniformity in Maritime Law and Implementation of International Conventions' (1987) 18 *J Maritime L* 317.

Berlingieri, F, 'Uniformity of the Law of Carriage of Goods by Sea: the 1990s', 1990, Paris: CMI, II, 110–77.

Carr, IM, 'The Scope of Application of Hamburg Rules and Hague Visby Rules: a Comparison' [1992] 6 ICCLR.

Chandler, GF, 'A comparison of COGSA, the Hague-Visby Rules and the Hamburg Rules' (1984) 15 *J Maritime L* 233.

Cooper, R, 'The Hamburg Rules and the Carriage of Goods by Sea' – dissertation for LLM, 1981, University of Queensland.

Davies, M, 'Carriage of Goods by Sea' (1991) ABusLR 57.

Diplock, Lord, 'Conventions and Morals – Limitation Clauses in International Maritime Conventions' (1970) 1 *J Maritime L* 525.

Goldie, CWH, 'Effect of the Hamburg Rules on Shipowners' Liability Insurance' (1993) *J Maritime L* 111.

Hannah, F, 'Which Rules for Australian Maritime Trade? The Controversy Continues', 1993, Proceedings of MLAANZ 20th Annual Conference, Melbourne, 6–11 November.

Hetherington, S, 'Bills of Lading: Do They Have a Future? Freight Forwarders Bills of Lading', 1993, paper presented by University of Sydney Faculty of Law, 17 August.

Honnold, J, 'Ocean Carriers and Cargo: Clarity and Fairness – Hague or Hamburg' (1993) 24 *J Maritime L* 75.

Kimball, JD, 'Owner's Liability and the Proposed Reunion of the Hague Rules' (1975) *J Maritime L* 217.

Kindred, HM, 'From Hague to Hamburg: International Regulation of Carriage of Goods by Sea' (1984) 7 *Dalhousie LJ* 585.

Mendelsohn, AI, 'Why the US Did Not Ratify the Visby Amendments' (1992) 23 *J Maritime L* 29.

Mustill, Lord, 'Ships are different – or are they' [1993] *Lloyd's MCLQ* 433.

Myburgh, P, 'Bits, Bytes and Bills of Lading: EDI and New Zealand Maritime Law' [1993] NZLJ 324.

New Zealand Department of Transport, *Maritime Discussion Paper*, 1992, January.

O'Hare, CW, 'Shipping Documentation for the Carriage of Goods and the Hamburg Rules' (1978) 52 ALJ 415.

Ramberg, J, 'Freedom of Contract: Maritime Law' [1992] *Lloyd's MCLQ* 178.

Ramberg, J, 'Freedom of Contract in Maritime Law' [1993] *Lloyd's MCLQ* 145.

Reynolds, F, 'The Hague Rules, the Hague-Visby Rules and the Hamburg Rules' (1990) 7 *Marine Lawyers Association of Australia and New Zealand Journal* 16.

Sturley, JF, 'Changing Liability Rules and Marine Insurance: Conflicting Empirical Evidence Arguments About Hague, Visby and Hamburg in a Vacuum of Empirical Evidence' (1993) 24 *J Maritime L* 119.

Sweeney, JC, 'UNCITRAL and the Hamburg Rules' (1991) 22 *J Maritime L* 511.

Sweeney, JC, The UNCITRAL Draft Convention on Carriage of Goods by Sea Parts 1–5 (1975) 7 *J Maritime L* 69–125, 327–50; (1977) 8 *J Maritime L* 167–94.

Tetley, W, 'The Hamburg Rules – a Commentary' [1979] *Lloyd's MCLQ* 1.

'COGSA, Hague-Visby and Hamburg' (1984) 15 *J Maritime L* 233.

Thompson, SM, 'The Hamburg Rules: Should they be Implemented in Australia and New Zealand' (1992) 4 *Bond LR* 168.

Yancey, BW, 'The Carriage of Goods: Hague, COGSA, Visby and Hamburg' (1983) 57 *Tulane Law Review* 1238.

Books

Department of Transport and Communication, *Australian Marine Cargo Liability: a Discussion Paper*, September 1987 (1988) 159 Parliamentary Debates (H of R) 980.

Astle, WE, *The Hamburg Rules*, 1981, London: Fairway Publications.

Luddeke, CF and Johnson, A, *A Guide to the Hamburg Rules: from Hague to Hamburg via Visby*, 1991, London: Lloyds.

Department of Transport and Communication, *Carriage of Goods by Sea Act 1991: Possible Implementation of the Hamburg Rules*, 1993, Issues Paper, December.

Attorney General's Department in conjunction with Department of Transport and Communications, *Discussion Paper: Proposals for Reform of Australian Bills of Lading Legislation*, 1993, August.

Butler, DA and Duncan, WD, *Maritime Law in Australia*, 1991, Sydney: Legal Books.

Koh Soan Kwong, P, *Carriage of Goods by Sea*, 1986, Singapore: Butterworths.

UNCTAD, *The Economic and Commercial Implications of the Entry into Force of the Hamburg Rules and the Multi-modal Convention*, 1991, New York: United Nations.

Wilde, DM and Wilde, KC, *International Transactions*, 1993, Sydney: The Law Book Co.

European Institute of Maritime and Transport Law, *The Hamburg Rules: A Choice for the EEC?*, 1993, International Colloquium, 18–19 November.

APPENDIX 1

Details of cargo carrying regimes of various nations (as at 25 March 1994)

Country	Limitation	Hague	Hague-Visby	Hamburg	SDR
Algeria		★			
Angola		★			
Antigua and Barbuda			★		
Anguilla					
Argentina	400 pesos gold				3
Australia			★	★	3
Austria					4
Bahamas		★			
Bangladesh					★
Barbados		★			★
Belgium			★	2	
Belize		★			
Bermuda			★		
Bolivia		★			
Botswana					★
Brazil	Commercial Code 1850 applies, Article 102, 103				4
Burkina Faso				★	
Cameroon United Rep				★	
Canada			★		3
Cape Verde Islands				★	
Chile					★
China (PRC)	Maritime Code			7	7
Colombia	Not signatory: Commercial Code applies parts of Hague Rules				
Croatia		★			
Cuba		★			
Cyprus		★			
Denmark			★	2	4
Dominican Rep		★			4
Ecuador			★		4
Egypt, Arab Rep of					★
Estonia		★			

Country	Limitation	Hague	Hague-Visby	Hamburg	SDR
Fiji	Gold value	★			
Finland			★	2	4
France			★	2	3
Gambia		★			
Germany			★		4
Ghana		★			4
Gibraltar				2	
Goa		★			
Greece	8,000 Drachmas (National law equivalent)			★	★
Grenada		★			
Guinea		★			★
Guyana		★			★
Holy See			★	★	4
Hong Kong				2	
Hungary		★			★
India	Gold value				
Indonesia	Commercial Code 6				
Iran		★			
Ireland	100	★			
Isle of Man					
Israel	pgf.	★			
Italy			★	2	
Ivory Coast		★			
Jamaica		★			
Japan	1 June 1993		★	★	5
Kenya		★			★
Kingdom of Serbia			★		
Kiribati		★			
Korea	Commercial Code			8	
Kuwait		★			
Lebanon			★		★
Lesotho					★
Liberia	Maritime law			★	
Luxemburg			★	★	

Country	Limitation	Hague	Hague-Visby	Hamburg	SDR
Malagasy Rep		★			
Madagascar		★		★	4
Malay, Fed States of	★				
Malay, Non-Fed State of		★			
Malaysia	Gold value except Sabah, Sarawak R850				4
Malawi					★
Mauritius		★			
Mauritania			★		
Mexico	Contractual limitation				4
Monaco		★			
Morocco					★
Mozambique		★			
Naura		★			
Netherlands	pgf.		★	★	
New Zealand	NZ$200				3
Nigeria	Gold value	★			★
North Borneo		★			
Norway			★	2	4
Palestine		★			
Pakistan	Gold value				4
Panama					4
Papua New Guinea	★				
Paraguay			★		
Peru	Gold value	★			
Philippines	USA COGSA Limit US$500		★		4
Poland			★	2	
Portugal	Esc12,000	★		★	4
Romania		★			★
Saint Lucia		★			
Sao Tome and Principe		★			
Sarawak		★			
Senegal		★			★
Seychelles		★			

Country	Limitation	Hague	Hague-Visby	Hamburg	SDR
Sierra Leone		★			★
Singapore	S$1,563.65p/4.69kg		★	★	4
Slovakia					4
Solomon Islands		★			
Somalia		★			
South Africa	pgf				
Spain	161 pesetas			★	1
Sri Lanka			★		
St Christopher and Nevis			★		
St Vincent and the Grenadines			★		
Sweden			★	★	4
Switzerland	1pgf = 0.27095 francs			★	1
Syria, Arab Rep of				★	★
Taiwan	NT$9,000(Applies USA COGSA)				
Tanzania					★
Tanganyika		★			
Thailand	Not signatory				
Timor					
Timores		★			
Togo					
Tonga			★		
Trinidad and Tobago		★			
Tunisia					★
Turkey		★			
Tuvalu		★			
Uganda					★
United Kingdom			★	2	
Uruguay			★		
USA	$500	★			4
USSR	R250				
Venezuela	Contractual limit				4
Yugoslavia	D40,000	★			
Zaire			★		4
Zambia					★

Notes

★   Denotes adoption.

1   SDR Protocol applies national currency.

2   Applies a limitation of 666.67 SDRs per package or 2 SDRs per kg.

3   These nations have made legislative provision, or are believed to be considering a provision which will trigger adoption of the Hamburg Rules in the future.

4   These nations have signed but have not yet ratified or acceded to the Hamburg Rules.

5   Under the Japanese COGSA 1994, a carrier's liability shall be limited by a bigger amount calculated by the following two methods of calculation:

   (a)   666.67 SDR as per the package or unit;

   (b)   2 x SDR per kg.

From the above (a) and (b), until the weight of 333.335 kg (666.67/2 = 333.335) a fixed figure of (a) 666.67 SDR shall be applied, but from the weight in excess of 333.335, (b) shall be applied as in the following list:

Kg	SDR
333.335	666.67
400	800
500	1,000
600	1,200
700	1,400
800	1,600
900	1,800
1,000	2,000
2,000	4,000
3,000	6,000
4,000	8,000
5,000	10,000
10,000	20,000

6   Indonesian commercial code applies the Hague Rules unless specific agreement provides for the Hague-Visby Rules.

7   On 1 July 1993, the new Chinese Maritime Code came into effect. This Code, whilst adopting some Hamburg Rules principles, has substantially adopted Hague-Visby Rules principles. Effectively adopts SDR.

8   On 1 July 1993, Korea's Revised Commercial Code came into effect. The Code substantially adopts the Hague-Visby Rules.

Hague Rules

The full name of this Convention is International Convention for the Unification of Certain Rules of Law Relating to Bills of Lading, Brussels, 25 August 1924.

Some nations have adopted these rules into their national law, but with variations to the rules.

Some nations which originally ratified or acceded to the Hague Rules have renounced the Hague Rules and adopted either Hague-Visby, or Hague-Visby with the SDR Protocol.

Hague-Visby Rules

The 1968 Visby amendments to the Hague Rules came into force in 1977.

The full name of this Convention is Protocol to Amend the International Convention for the Unification of Certain Rules of Law Relating to Bills of Lading , Brussels, 23 February 1968.

Hamburg Rules

This is the United Nations Convention on the Carriage of Goods by Sea, Hamburg, 1978. The Convention achieved 20 ratifications and accessions on 31 October 1991.

SDR Protocol

This Protocol came into effect on 4 February 1984.

The full name of this Convention is Protocol Amending the International Convention for the Unification of Certain Rules of Law Relating to Bills of Lading (25 August 1924, as amended by the Protocol of 23 February 1968, Brussels, 21 December 1979).

The main effect of this Protocol is to substitute SDRs for poincare gold francs (pgf).

10,000 pgf became 666.67 SDRs per package or 2 SDRs per kg. But some nations have specified a currency conversion rate which applies instead.

Gold value

This has now been established by a number of courts to be today's value of the quantity of gold contained in 100 gold sovereigns specified in the Hague Rules.

PGF

These are poincare gold French francs per kilo.

INTERNATIONAL CONVENTION FOR THE UNIFICATION OF CERTAIN RULES OF LAW RELATING TO BILLS OF LADING (THE HAGUE RULES) BRUSSELS – 25 AUGUST 1924

The Convention entered into force on 2 June 1931.

The government of Belgium reports that the following ratifications (r), accessions (a) or notifications of succession (s) have been deposited with it:[123]

Algeria	(a)	13 April 1964
Angola	(a)	2 February 1952
Antigua and Barbuda	(a)	2 December 1930
Argentina	(a)	19 April 1961
Australia	(a)	4 July 1955
Bahamas	(a)	2 December 1930
Barbados	(a)	2 December 1930
Belgium	(r)	2 June 1930
Belize	(a)	December 1930
Bolivia	(a)	28 May 1982
Cameroon	(a)	2 December 1930
Cape Verde	(a)	2 February 1952
Cuba	(a)	25 July 1977
Cyprus	(a)	2 December 1930
Denmark	(a)	1 July 1938
Dominican Republic	(a)	2 December 1930
Egypt	(a)	29 November 1933
Ecuador	(a)	23 March 1977
Fiji	(a)	10 October 1970
Finland	(a)	1 July 1939
France	(r)	4 January 1937
Gambia	(a)	2 December 1930
Germany, Federal Republic of	(r)	1 July 1939
Ghana	(a)	2 December 1930
Grenada	(a)	2 December 1930
Guinea-Bissau	(a)	2 February 1952
Guyana	(a)	2 December 1930

123 List taken from a publication of the Ministry of Foreign Affairs and Foreign Trade of Belgium dated 13 January 1987.

Hungary ....(r) ....2 June 1930

Iran ....(a) ....26 April 1966

Ireland ....(a) ....30 January 1962

Israel ....(a) ....5 September 1959

Italy ....(r) ....7 October 193S

Ivory Coast ....(a) ....15 December 1961

Jamaica ....(a) ....2 December 1930

Japan ....(r) ....2 July 1957

Kenya ....(a) ....2 December 1930

Kiribati ....(a) ....2 December 1930

Kuwait ....(a) ....25 July 1969

Lebanon ....(a) ....19 July 1975

Madagascar ....(a) ....13 July 1965

Malaysia ....(a) ....2 December 1930

Mauritius ....(a) ....24 August 1970

Monaco ....(a) ....15 May 1931

Mozambique ....(a) ....2 February 1952

Nauru ....(a) ....4 July 1955

Netherlands ....(a) ....18 August 1956

Nigeria ....(a) ....2 December 1930

Norway ....(a) ....1 July 1938

Palestine ....(a) ....2 December 1930

Papua New Guinea ....(a) ....4 July 1955

Paraguay ....(a) ....22 November 1967

Peru ....(a) ....29 October 1964

Poland ....(r) ....26 October 1936

Portugal ....(a) ....24 December 1931

Macao ....(a) ....2 February 1952

Romania ....(r) ....4 August 1937

Sabah, North Borneo ....(a) ....2 December 1930

Solomon Islands ....(a) ....2 December 1930

Sao Tome and Principe ....(a) ....2 February 1952

Sarawak ....(a) ....3 November 1931

Senegal ....(a) ....14 February 1978

Seychelles ....(a) ....2 December 1930

Sierra Leone ....(a) ....2 December 1930

Singapore . . . .(a) . . . . . . .2 December 1930

Somalia . . . .(a) . . . . . . .2 December 1930

Spain . . . .(r) . . . . . . .2 June 1930

Sri Lanka . . . .(a) . . . . . . .2 December 1930

St Christopher-Nevis . . . .(a) . . . . . . .2 December 1930

St Lucia . . . .(a) . . . . . . .2 December 1930

St Vincent . . . .(a) . . . . . . .2 December 1930

Sweden . . . .(a) . . . . . . .1 July 1938

Switzerland . . . .(a) . . . . . . .28 May 1954

Syrian Arab Republic . . . .(a) . . . . . . .1 August 1974

Timor . . . .(a) . . . . . . .2 December 1952

Tonga . . . .(a) . . . . . . .2 December 1930

Trinidad and Tobago . . . .(a) . . . . . . .2 December 1930

Turkey . . . .(a) . . . . . . .4 July 1955

Tuvalu . . . .(a) . . . . . . .2 December 1930

United Kingdom of Great Britain and
Northern Ireland including Jersey,
Guernsey and Isle of Man . . . .(r) . . . . . . .2 June 1930

British oversee territories: Bermuda, ...(a) . . . . . . .2 December 1930
Falkland Islands and Dependencies,
Gibraltar, Hong Kong, Turk and Caicos
Islands and Cayman Islands, British
Virgin Islands, Monserrat, British
Antarctic Territories, Anguilla

Ascension, St Helena . . . .(a) . . . . . . .November 1931

United Republic of Tanzania . . . .(a) . . . . . . .3 December 1962

United States of America . . . .(r) . . . . . . .29 June 1937

Yugoslavia . . . .(r) . . . . . . .17 April 1959

Zaire . . . .(a) . . . . . . .17 July 1967

International Convention for the Unification of Certain Rules of Law Relating to Bills of Lading

Signed at Brussels, 25 August 1924

Article 1

In this Convention the following words are employed with the meanings set out below:

(a) 'Carrier' includes the owner of the vessel or the charterer who enters into a contract of carriage with a shipper.

(b) 'Contract of carriage' applies only to contracts of carriage covered by a bill of lading or any similar document of title, in so far as such document relates to the carriage of goods by sea; it also applies to any bill of lading or any similar document as aforesaid issued under or pursuant to a charterparty from the moment at which such instrument regulates the relations between a carrier and a holder of the same.

(c) 'Goods' includes goods, wares, merchandise, and articles of every kind whatsoever except live animals and cargo which by the contract of carriage is stated as being carried on deck and is so carried.

(d) 'Ship' means any vessel used for the carriage of goods by sea.

(e) 'Carriage of goods' covers the period from the time when the goods are loaded on to the time they are discharged from the ship.

Article 2

Subject to the provisions of Article 6, under every contract of carriage of goods by sea the carrier, in relation to the loading, handling, stowage, carriage, custody, care, and discharge of such goods shall be subject to the responsibilities and liabilities, and entitled to the rights and immunities hereinafter set forth.

Article 3

1 The carrier shall be bound before and at the beginning of the voyage to exercise due diligence to:

(a) make the ship seaworthy;

(b) properly man, equip, and supply the ship;

(c) make the holds, refrigerating and cool chambers, and all other parts of the ship in which goods are carried, fit and safe for their reception, carriage, and preservation.

2 Subject to the provisions of Article 4, the carrier shall properly and care fully load, handle, stow, carry, keep, care for, anti discharge the goods carried.

3 After receiving the goods into his charge, the carrier or the master or agent of the carrier shall, on demand of the shipper, issue to the shipper a bill of lading showing among other things:

(a) the leading marks necessary for identification of the goods as the same are furnished in writing by the shipper before the loading of such goods starts, provided such marks are stamped or otherwise shown clearly upon the goods if uncovered, or on the eases or coverings in which such goods are contained, in such a manner as should ordinarily remain legible until the end of the voyage;

(b) either the number of packages or pieces, or the quantity, or weight, as the case may be, as furnished in writing by the shipper;

(c) the apparent order and condition of the goods.

Provided that no carrier, master, or agent of the carrier shall be bound to state or show in the bill of lading any marks, number, quantity, or weight which he has reasonable grounds for suspecting not accurately to represent the goods actually received or which he has had no reasonable means of checking.

4 Such a bill of lading shall be *prima facie* evidence of the receipt by the carrier of the goods as therein described in accordance with para 3(a), (b) and (c).

5   The shipper shall be deemed to have guaranteed to the carrier the accuracy at the time of shipment of the marks, number, quantity, and weight, as furnished by him, and the shipper shall indemnify the carrier against all loss, damages, and expenses arising or resulting from inaccuracies in such particulars. The right of the carrier to such indemnity shall in no way limit his responsibility and liability under the contract of carriage to any person other than the shipper.

6   Unless notice of loss or damage and the general nature of such loss or damage be given in writing to the carrier or his agent at the port of discharge before or at the time of the removal of the goods into the custody of the person entitled to delivery thereof under the contract of carriage, such removal shall be *prima facie* evidence of the delivery by the carrier of the goods as described in the bill of lading.

If the loss or damage is not apparent, the notice must be given within three days of the delivery.

The notice in writing need not be giver it the state of the goods has at the time of their receipt been the subject of joint survey or inspection.

In any event, the carrier and the ship shall be discharged from all liability in respect of loss or damage unless suit is brought within one year after delivery of the goods or the date when the goods should have been delivered.

In the ease of any actual or apprehended loss or damage the carrier and the receiver shall give all reasonable facilities to each other for inspecting and tallying the goods.

7   After the goods are loaded, the bill of lading to be issued by the carrier master, or agent of the carrier to the shipper shall, if the shipper so demands, be a 'shipped' bill of lading, provided that if the shipper shall have previously taken up any document of title to such goods, he shall surrender the same as against the issue of the 'shipped' bill of lading. At the option of the carrier such document of title may be noted at the port of shipment by the carrier, master, or agent with the name or names of the ship or ships upon which the goods have been shipped and the date or dates of shipment, and when so noted, if it shows the particulars mentioned in para 3 of Article 3, it shall for the purpose of this article be deemed to constitute a 'shipped' bill of lading.

8   Any clause, covenant, or agreement in a contract of carriage relieving the carrier or the ship from liability for loss or damage to or in connection with goods arising from negligence, fault, or failure in the duties and obligations provided in this article, or lessening such liability otherwise than as provided in this convention, shall be null and void and of no effect. A benefit of insurance in favour of the carrier or similar clause shall be deemed to be a clause relieving the carrier from liability.

Article 4

1   Neither the carrier nor the ship shall be liable for loss or damage arising or resulting from unseaworthiness unless caused by want of due diligence on the part of the carrier to make the ship seaworthy and to secure that the ship is properly manned, equipped, and supplied and to make the holds, refrigerating and cool chambers, and all other parts of the ship in which goods are carried fit and safe for their reception, carriage, and preservation in accordance with the provisions of para 1 of Article 3. Whenever loss or damage has resulted from unseaworthiness, the burden of proving the exercise of due diligence shall be on the carrier or other person claiming exemption under this article.

2 Neither the carrier nor the ship shall be responsible for loss or damage arising or resulting from:

(a) Act, neglect, or default of the master, mariner, pilot, or the servants of the carrier in the navigation or in the management of the ship.

(b) Fire, unless caused by the actual fault or privity of the carrier.

(c) Perils, dangers, and accidents of the sea or other navigable water.

(d) Act of God.

(e) Act of war.

(f) Act of public enemies.

(g) Arrest or restraint of princes, rulers, or people or seizure under legal process.

(h) Quarantine restrictions.

(I) Act or omission of the shipper or owner of the goods, his agent, or representative.

(j) Strikes or lockouts or stoppage or restraint of labour from whatever cause, whether partial or general.

(k) Riots and civil commotions.

(l) Saving or attempting to save life or property at sea.

(m) Wastage in hulk or weight or any other loss or damage arising from inherent defect, quality, or vice of the goods.

(n) Insufficiency of packing.

(o) Insufficiency or inadequacy of marks.

(p) Latent defects not discoverable by due diligence.

(q) Any other cause arising without the actual fault or privity of the carrier, or without the fault or neglect of the agents or servants of the carrier, but the burden of proof shall be on the person claiming the benefit of this exception to show that neither the actual fault or privity of the carrier nor the fault or neglect of the agents or servants of the carrier contributed to the loss or damage.

3 The shipper shall not be responsible for loss or damage sustained by the carrier or the ship arising or resulting from any cause without the act, fault, or neglect of the shipper, his agents, or his servants.

4 Any deviation in saving or attempting to save life or property at sea or any reasonable deviation shall not be deemed to be an infringement or breach of this convention or of the contract of carriage, and the carrier shall not be liable for any loss or damage resulting therefrom.

5 Neither the carrier nor the ship shall in any event be or become liable for any loss or damage to or in connection with goods in an amount exceeding £100 sterling per package or unit or the equivalent of that sum in other currency unless the nature and value of such goods have been declared by the shipper before shipment and inserted in the bill of lading.

This declaration if embodied in the bill of lading shall be *prima facie* evidence but shall not be binding or conclusive on the carrier.

By agreement between the carrier, master, or agent of the carrier and the shipper another maximum amount than that mentioned in this paragraph may be fixed, provided that such maximum shall not be less than the figure above named.

Neither the carrier nor the ship shall be responsible in any event for loss or damage to, or in connection with, goods if the nature or value thereof has been knowingly misstated by the shipper in the bill of lading.

6   Goods of an inflammable, explosive, or dangerous nature to the shipment whereof the carrier, master, or agent of the carrier has not consented with knowledge of their nature and character may at any time before discharge be landed at any place or destroyed or rendered innocuous by the carrier without compensation, and the shipper of such goods shall be liable for all damages and expenses directly or indirectly arising out of or resulting from such shipment. If any such goods shipped with such knowledge and consent shall become a danger to the ship or cargo, they may in like manner be landed at any place or destroyed or rendered innocuous by the carrier without liability on the part of the carrier except to general average, if any.

Article 5

A carrier shall be at liberty to surrender in whole or in part all or any of this rights and immunities, or to increase any of his responsibilities and liabilities under this convention provided such surrender or increase shall be embodied in the bill of lading issued to the shipper.

The provisions of this convention shall not be applicable to charter parties, but if bills of lading are issued in the case of a ship under a charter party they shall comply with the terms of this convention. Nothing in these rules shall be held to prevent the insertion in a bill of lading of any lawful provision regarding general average.

Article 6

Notwithstanding the provisions of the preceding articles, a carrier, master, or agent of the carrier and a shipper shall in regard to any particular goods be at liberty to enter into any agreement in any terms as to the responsibility and liability of the carrier for such goods, and as to the rights and immunities of the carrier in respect of such goods, or concerning his obligation as to seaworthiness so far as this stipulation is not contrary to public policy, or concerning the care or diligence of his servants or agents in regard to the loading, handling, stowage, carriage, custody, care, and discharge of the goods carried by sea, provided that in this case no bill of lading has been or shall be issued and that the terms agreed shall be embodied in a receipt which shall be a non-negotiable document and shall be marked as such.

Any agreement so entered into shall have full legal effect:

Provided that this article shall not apply to ordinary commercial shipments made in the ordinary course of trade, but only to other shipments where the character or condition of the property to be carried or the circumstances, terms, and conditions under which the carriage is to be performed are such as reasonably to justify a special agreement.

Article 7

Nothing herein contained shall prevent a carrier or a shipper from entering into any agreement stipulation, condition, reservation, or exemption as to the responsibility and liability of the carrier or the ship for the loss or damage to, or in connection with, the custody and care and handling of goods prior to the loading on, and subsequent to the discharge from, the ship on which the goods are carried by sea.

Article 8

The provision of this convention shall not affect the rights and obligations of the carrier under any statute for the time being in force relating to the limitation of the liability of owners of seagoing vessels.

Article 9

The monetary units mentioned in this convention are to be taken to be gold value.

Those Contracting States in which the pound sterling is not a monetary unit reserve to themselves the right of translating the sums indicated in this convention in terms of pound sterling into terms of their own monetary system in round figures.

The national laws may reserve to the debtor the right of discharging his debt in national currency according to the rate of exchange prevailing on the day of the arrival of the ship at the port of discharge of the goods concerned.

Article 10

The provisions of this convention shall apply to all bills of lading issued in any of the Contracting States.

Article 11

After an interval of not more than two years from the day on which the convention is signed, the Belgian government shall place itself in communication with the governments of the high contracting parties which have declared themselves prepared to ratify the convention, with a view to deciding whether it shall be put into force. The ratifications shall be deposited at Brussels at a date to be fixed by agreement among the said governments. The first deposit of ratifications shall be recorded in a *procès-verbal* signed by the representatives of the powers which take part therein and by the Belgian Minister for Foreign Affairs.

The subsequent deposits of ratifications shall be made by means of a written notification, addressed to the Belgian government and accompanied by the instrument of ratification.

A duly certified copy of the *procès-verbal* relating to the first deposit of ratifications, of the notifications referred to in the previous paragraph, and also of the instruments of ratification accompanying them, shall he immediately sent by the Belgian government through the diplomatic channel to the powers who have signed this convention or who have acceded to it. In the cases contemplated in the preceding paragraph, the said government shall inform them at the same time of the date on which it received the notification.

Article 12

Non-signatory States may accede to the present convention whether or not they have been represented at the international conference at Brussels.

A State which desires to accede shall notify its intention in writing to the Belgian government, forwarding to it the document of accession, which shall be deposited in the archive of the said government.

The Belgian government shall immediately forward to all the States which have signed or acceded to the convention a duly certified copy of the notification and of the act of accession, mentioning the date on which it received the notification.

Article 13

The high contracting parties may at the time of signature, ratification, or accession declare that their acceptance of the present convention does not include any or all of the self-governing dominions, or of the colonies, overseas possessions, protectorates, or territories under their sovereignty or authority, and they may subsequently accede separately on behalf of any self-governing dominion, colony, overseas possession, protectorate, or territory excluded in their declaration. They may also denounce the convention separately in accordance with its provisions in respect of any self-governing dominion, or any colony, overseas possession, protectorate, or territory under their sovereignty or authority.

Article 14

The present convention shall take effect, in the case of the States which have taken part in the first deposit of ratifications, one year after the date of the *procès-verbal* recording such deposit. As respects the States which ratify subsequently or which accede, and also in cases in which the convention is subsequently put into effect in accordance with Article 13, it shall take effect six months after the notifications specified in para 2 of Article 11, and para 2 of Article 12, have been received by the Belgian government.

Article 15

In the event of one of the Contracting States wishing to denounce the present convention, the denunciation shall be notified in writing to the Belgian government, which shall immediately communicate a duly certified cony of the notification to all the other States informing them of the date on which it was received.

The denunciation shall only operate in respect of the State which made the notification, and on the expiry of one year after the notification has reached the Belgian government.

Article 16

Any one of the Contracting States shall have the right to call for a fresh conference with a view to considering possible amendments.

A State which would exercise this right should notify its intention to the other States through the Belgian government. which would make arrangements for convening the conference.

Done at Brussels, in a single copy, 25 August 1924.

Protocol of signature

In proceeding to the signature of the international convention for the unification of certain rules in regard to bills of lading, the undersigned plenipotentiaries have agreed on the present Protocol which shall have the same force and the same scope as if these provisions were inserted in the text of the convention to which they relate.

The high contracting parties may give effect to this convention either by giving it the force of law or by including in their national legislation in a form appropriate to that legislation, the rules adopted under this convention.

They may reserve the right:

1   To prescribe that in the cases referred to in para 2(c)–(p) of Article 4, the holder of a bill of lading shall be entitled to establish responsibility for loss or damage arising from the personal fault of the carrier or the fault of his servants which are not covered by para (a).

2   To apply Article 6 in so far as the national coasting trade is concerned to all classes of goods without taking account of the restriction set out in the last paragraph of that article.

Done at Brussels, in a single copy, 25 August 1924.

ANNEX

Reservations and declarations

Australia

... Now therefore, I, Sir William Joseph Slim, the Governor General in and over the Commonwealth of Australia acting with the advice of the Federal Executive Council and in the exercise of all powers me thereunto enabling do by these presents accede in the name and on behalf of Her Majesty in respect of the Commonwealth of Australia and the Territories of Papua and Norfolk Island and the Trust Territories of New Guinea and Nauru to the convention aforesaid subject to the following reservations, namely:

(a) The Commonwealth of Australia reserves the right to exclude from the operation of legislation passed to give effect to the convention the carriage of goods by sea which is not carriage in the course of trade or commerce with other countries or among the States of Australia.

(b) The Commonwealth of Australia reserves the right to apply Article 6 of the convention in so far as the national coasting trade is concerned to all classes of goods without taking account of the restriction set out in the last paragraph of that article.

Belgium

In proceeding to the deposit of the ratifications of His Majesty the King of the Belgians, the Belgian Minister for Foreign Affairs declared, in accordance with the provisions of Article 13 of the convention, that these ratifications extend only to Belgium and do not apply to the Belgian Congo and Ruanda–Urundi, Territories under mandate.

Denmark

This accession is subject to the proviso that the other Contracting States do not object to the application of the provisions of the convention being limited in the following manner with regard to Denmark:

1   Under the Danish Navigation Law of 7 May 1937, bills of lading and similar documents may continue to be made out, for national coasting trade, in accordance with the provisions of that Law without the provisions of the convention being applied to them or to the legal relationship which is thereby established between the carrier and the holder of the document.

2   Maritime carriage between Denmark and other Nordic States, whose navigation laws contain similar provisions, shall be considered as equivalent to national coasting trade for the purposes mentioned in para 1 – if a provision to that effect is decreed pursuant to the last paragraph of Article 122 of the Danish Navigation Law.

3   The provisions of the International Conventions on the Transport of Passengers and Baggage by Rail and on the Traffic of Goods by Rail, signed at Rome on 23 November 1933, shall not be affected by this convention.

Egypt

We have resolved hereby to accede to the said convention and undertake to cooperate in its application.

Egypt is, however, of the opinion that the convention does not in any part apply to national coasting trade. Consequently, it reserves to itself the right freely to regulate the national coasting trade by its own law.

In witness whereof ...

France

... In proceeding to this deposit, the Ambassador of France at Brussels declares, in accordance with Article 13 of the above-mentioned convention, that the French government's acceptance of the convention does not include any of the colonies, overseas possessions, protectorates or territories under its sovereignty or authority.

Ireland

... subject to the following declarations and reservations:

1   In relation to the carriage of goods by sea in ships carrying goods from any port in Ireland to any other port in Ireland or to a port in the UK, Ireland will apply Article 6 of the convention as though the Article referred to goods of any class instead of to particular goods, and as though the proviso in the third paragraph of the said article were omitted;

2   Ireland does not accept the provisions of the first paragraph of Article 9 of the convention.

Ivory Coast

The government of the Republic of the Ivory Coast, in acceding to the said convention, specifies that:

1   For the application of Article 9 of the convention, concerning the value of the monetary units used, the limit of liability shall be equal to the exchange value in CFA francs, one gold pound being equal to two pounds sterling in notes, at the rate of exchange prevailing at the arrival of the ship at the port of discharge.

2   It reserves the right to regulate, by specific provisions of national law, the system of limitation of liability to be applied to maritime carriage between two ports in the Republic of the Ivory Coast.

Japan

(at time of signature)

Subject to the reservations formulated in the note relative to this treaty and appended to my letter dated 25 August 1925 to HE the Minister for Foreign Affairs of Belgium.

At the moment of proceeding to the signature of the International Convention for the Unification of Certain Rules Relating to Bills of Lading, the undersigned, plenipotentiary of Japan, makes the following reservations:

(a) To Article 4:

Japan reserves to itself until further notice the acceptance of the provisions in (a) of para 2 of Article 4.

(b) Japan is of the opinion that the convention does not in any part apply to national coasting trade: consequently there should be no occasion to make it the object of provisions in the Protocol. However, if it be not so, Japan reserves to itself the right freely to regulate the national coasting trade by its own law.

(at time of ratification)

... The government of Japan declares:

1   that it reserves to itself the application of the first paragraph of Article 9 of the convention

2   that it maintains reservation (b) formulated in the note annexed to the letter of the Ambassador of Japan to the Minister for Foreign Affairs of Belgium, of 25 August 1925, concerning the right freely to regulate the national coasting trade by its own law; and

3   that it withdraws reservation (a) in the above-mentioned note, concerning the provisions in (a) of para 2 of Article 4 of the convention.

Kuwait

… subject to the following reservation: the maximum amount for liability for any loss or damage to or in connection with goods referred to in Article 4, para 5, to be raised to £250 instead of £100.

This reservation was rejected by France and Norway.

In a note of 30 March 1971, received by the Belgian government on 30 April 1971, the government of Kuwait declares that the amount of '£250' should be replaced by '250 Kuwait Dinars'.[124]

Netherlands

… Desiring to exercise the option of accession reserved to non-signatory States under Article 12 of the International Convention for the Unification of Certain Rules Relating to Bills of Lading, with protocol of signature, concluded at Brussels on 25 August 1924, we have resolved hereby definitively to accede, in respect of the Kingdom in Europe, to the said convention, with protocol of signature, and undertake co operate in its application, while reserving the right by legal enactment:

1   to prescribe that in the cases referred to in para 2(c)–(p) of Article 4 of the convention, the holder of a bill of lading shall be entitled to establish responsibility for loss or damage arising from the personal fault of the carrier or the fault of his servants which are not covered by para (a).

2   To apply Article 6 in so far as the national coasting trade is concerned to all classes of goods without taking account of the restriction set out in the last paragraph of that article; and subject to the following:

    1   accession to the convention is subject to the exclusion of the first paragraph of Article 9 of the convention;

    2   Netherlands law may limit the possibilities of furnishing evidence to the contrary against the bill of lading.

In witness whereof …

Norway

… The accession of Norway to the International Convention for the Unification of Certain Rules Relating to Bills of Lading, signed at Brussels on 25 August 1924, and to the protocol of signature annexed thereto, is subject to the proviso that the other Contracting States do not object to the application of the provisions of the convention being limited in the following manner with regard to Norway:

1   Under the Norwegian Navigation Law of 7 May 1937, bills of lading and similar documents may continue to be made out, for national coasting trade, in accordance with the provisions of that law without the provisions of the convention being

---

124 The reservation made by Kuwait has been rejected by France and Norway.

applied to them or to the legal relationship which is thereby established between the carrier and the holder of the document.

2 Maritime carriage between Norway and other Nordic States, whose navigation laws contain similar provisions, shall be considered as equivalent to national coasting trade for the purpose mentioned in para 1 – if a provision to that effect is decreed pursuant to the last paragraph of Article 122 of the Norwegian Navigation Law.

3 The provisions of the International Conventions on the Transport of Passengers and Baggage by Rail and on the Traffic of Goods by Rail, signed at Rome on 23 November 1933, shall not be affected by this convention.

Switzerland

… In accordance with the second paragraph of the protocol of signature, the federal authorities reserve the right to give effect to this international act by including in Swiss legislation, in a form appropriate to that legislation, the rides adopted under this convention.

United Kingdom of Great Britain and Northern Ireland

(*at time of signature*)

… I declare that His Britannic Majesty's government adopt the last reservation in the additional Protocol of the Bills of Lading Convention. I further declare that my signature applies only to Great Britain and Northern Ireland. I reserve the right of each of the British Dominions, Colonies, Overseas Possessions and Protectorates, and of each of the territories over which His Britannic Majesty exercises a mandate to accede to this convention under Article 13.

(*at time of ratification*)

… In accordance with Article 13 of the above-named convention, I declare that the acceptance of the convention given by His Britannic Majesty in the instrument of ratification deposited this day extends only to the United Kingdom of Great Britain and Northern Ireland and does not apply to any of His Majesty's Colonies or Protectorates, or territories under suzerainty or mandate.

United Republic of Tanzania

The government of the Republic of Tanganyika has requested the government of Belgium to circulate the following remarks concerning Tanganyika's relation to the International Convention for the unification of certain rules of Law relating to Bills of Lading, done at Brussels, 25 August 1924.

Tanganyika acceded to the convention by instrument dated 16 November 1962. As the convention had been applied to the territory of Tanganyika prior to its independence, Tanganyika was given the opportunity to declare that it considered the convention in force as to its territory from the date of independence, rather than having to wait the normal six month period provided for in Article 11 of the convention. While Tanganyika availed itself of this opportunity of having the convention in force from the day of its independence, by virtue of the instrument of 16 November 1962, this in no way should be considered as indicating that Tanganyika considered itself bound by the UK accession to the convention which had applied to the territory of Tanganyika prior to independence. It is the position of Tanganyika that it has adhered to the convention of its own volition and did not inherit, or consider itself in any way bound, by the obligations of the government of the UK vis à vis the convention.

United States of America

... and whereas, the Senate of the USA by their resolution of 1 April (legislative day 13 March), 1935 (two thirds of the Senators present concurring therein), did advise and consent to the ratification of the said convention and protocol of signature thereto, 'with the understanding, to be made part of such ratification, that, notwithstanding the provisions of Article 4, s 5, and the first paragraph of Article 9 of the convention, neither the carrier nor the ship shall in any event be or become liable within the jurisdiction of the USA for any loss or damage to or in connection with goods in an amount exceeding $500.00, lawful money of the USA, per package or unit unless the nature and value of such goods have been declared by the shipper before shipment and inserted in the bill of lading'.

And whereas, the Senate of the USA by their resolution of 6 May 1937 (two thirds of the Senators present concurring therein), did add to and make a part of their aforesaid resolution of 1 April 1935, the following understanding:

That should any conflict arise between the provisions of the convention and the provision of the Act of 16 April 1936, known as the 'Carriage of Goods by Sea Act', the provisions of said Act shall prevail.

Now, therefore, be it known that I, Franklin D Roosevelt, President of the USA, having seen and considered the said convention and protocol of signature, do hereby in pursuance of the aforesaid advice and consent of the Senate, ratify and confirm the same and every article and clause thereof, subject to the two understandings herein above recited and made part of this ratification.

THE AMENDED HAGUE RULES

Article 1

In this convention the following words are employed, with the meanings set out below:

(a) 'Carrier' includes the owner or the charterer who enters into a contract of carriage with a shipper.

(b) 'Contract of carriage' applies only to contracts of carriage covered by a bill of lading or any similar document of title, in so far as such document relates to the carriage of goods by sea, including any bill of lading or any similar document as aforesaid issued under or pursuant to a charter party from the moment at which such bill of lading or similar document of title regulates the relations between a carrier and a holder of the same.

(c) 'Goods' includes goods, wares, merchandise, and articles of every kind whatsoever except live animals and cargo which by the contract of carriage is stated as being carried on deck and is so carried.

(d) 'Ship' means any vessel used for the carriage of goods by sea.

(e) 'Carriage of goods' covers the period from the time when the goods are loaded on to the time they are discharged from the ship.

Article 2

Subject to the provisions of Article 6, under every contract of carriage of goods by sea the carrier, in relation to the loading, handling, stowage, carriage, custody, care and discharge of such goods, shall be subject to the responsibilities and liabilities, and entitled to the rights and immunities hereinafter set forth.

Article 3

1   The carrier shall be bound before and at the beginning of the voyage to exercise due diligence to:

   (a) Make the ship seaworthy.

   (b) Properly man, equip and supply the ship.

   (c) Make the holds, refrigerating and cool chambers, and all other parts of the ship in which goods are carried, fit and safe for their reception, carriage and preservation.

2   Subject to the provisions of Article 4, the carrier shall properly and carefully load, handle, stow, carry, keep, care for, and discharge the goods carried.

3   After receiving the goods into his charge the carrier or the master or agent of the carrier shall, on demand of the shipper, issue to the shipper a bill of lading showing among other things:

   (a) The leading marks necessary for identification of the goods as the same are furnished in writing by the shipper before the loading of such goods starts, provided such marks are stamped or otherwise shown clearly upon the goods if uncovered, or on the cases or coverings in which such goods are contained, in such a manner as should ordinarily remain legible until the end of the voyage.

   (b) Either the number of packages or pieces, or the quantity, or weight, as the case may be, as furnished in writing by the shipper.

   (c) The apparent order and condition of the goods.

   Provided that no carrier, master or agent of the carrier shall be bound to state or show in the bill of lading any marks, number, quantity, or weight which he has reasonable ground for suspecting not accurately to represent the goods actually received, or which he has had no reasonable means of checking.

4   Such a bill of lading shall be *prima facie* evidence of the receipt by the carrier of the goods as therein described in accordance with para 3(a), (b) and (c). However, proof to the contrary shall not be admissible when the bill of lading has been transferred to a third party acting in good faith.

5   The shipper shall be deemed to have guaranteed to the carrier the accuracy at the time of shipment of the marks, number, quantity and weight, as furnished by him, and the shipper shall indemnify the carrier against all loss, damages and expenses arising or resulting from inaccuracies in such particulars. The right of the carrier to such indemnity shall in no way limit his responsibility and liability under the contract of carriage to any person other than the shipper.

6   Unless notice of loss or damage and the general nature of such loss or damage be given in writing to the carrier or his agent at the port of discharge before or at the time of the removal of the goods into the custody of the person entitled to delivery thereof under the contract of carriage, or, if the loss or damage be not apparent, within three days, such removal shall be *prima facie* evidence of the delivery by the carrier of the goods as described in the bill of lading.

   The notice in writing need not be given if the state of the goods has, at the time of their receipt, been the subject of joint survey or inspection.

   Subject to para 6 *bis* the carrier and the ship shall in any event be discharged from all liability whatsoever in respect of the goods, unless suit is brought within one year of their delivery or of the date when they should have been delivered. This period may, however, be extended if the parties so agree after the cause of action has arisen.

In the case of any actual or apprehended loss or damage the carrier and the receiver shall give all reasonable facilities to each other for inspecting and tallying the goods.

6 *bis* An action for indemnity against a third person may be brought even after the expiration of the year provided for in the preceding paragraph if brought within the time allowed by the law of the court seized of the case. However, the time allowed shall be not less than three months, commencing from the day when the person bringing such action for indemnity has settled the claim or has been served with process in the action against himself.

7 After the goods are loaded the bill of lading to be issued by the carrier, master, or agent of the carrier, to the shipper shall, if the shipper so demands, be a 'shipped' bill of lading, provided that if the shipper shall have previously taken up any document of title to such goods, he shall surrender the same as against the issue of the 'shipped' bill of lading, but at the option of the carrier such document of title may be noted at the port of shipment by the carrier, master, or agent with the name or names of the ship or ships upon which the goods have been shipped and the date or dates of shipment, and when so noted, if it shows the particulars mentioned in para 3 of Article 3, shall for the purpose of this article be deemed to constitute a 'shipped' bill of lading.

8 Any clause, covenant, or agreement in a contract of carriage relieving the carrier or the ship from liability for loss or damage to, or in connection with, goods arising from negligence, fault, or failure in the duties and obligations provided in this article or lessening such liability otherwise than as provided in this convention, shall be null and void and of no effect. A benefit of insurance in favour of the carrier or similar clause shall be deemed to be a clause relieving the carrier from liability.

Article 4

1 Neither the carrier nor the ship shall be liable for loss or damage arising or resulting from unseaworthiness unless caused by want of due diligence on the part of the carrier to make the ship seaworthy, and to secure that the ship is properly manned, equipped and supplied, and to make the holds, refrigerating and coot chambers and all other parts of the ship in which goods are carried fit and safe for their reception carriage and preservation in accordance with the provisions of para 1 of Article 3. Whenever loss or damage has resulted from unseaworthiness the burden of proving the exercise of due diligence shall be on the carrier or other person claiming exemption under this article.

2 Neither the carrier nor the ship shall be responsible for loss or damage arising or resulting from:

(a) Act, neglect or default of the master, mariner, pilot, or the servants of the carrier in the navigation or in the management of the ship.

(b) Fire, unless caused by the actual fault or privity of the carrier.

(c) Perils, dangers and accidents of the sea or other navigable waters.

(d) Act of God.

(e) Act of war.

(f) Act of public enemies.

(g) Arrest or restraint of princes, rulers or people, or seizure under legal process.

(h) Quarantine restrictions.

(i) Act or omission of the shipper or owner of the goods, his agent or representative.

(j) Strikes or lock outs or stoppage or restraint of labour from whatever cause, whether partial or general.

(k) Riots and civil commotions.

(l) Saving or attempting to save life or property at sea.

(m) Wastage in bulk or weight or any other loss or damage arising from inherent defect, quality or vice of the goods.

(n) Insufficiency of packing.

(o) Insufficiency or inadequacy of marks.

(p) Latent defects not discoverable by due diligence.

(q) Any other cause arising without the actual fault or privity of the carrier, or without the fault or neglect of the agents or servants of the carrier, but the burden of proof shall be on the person claiming the benefit of this exception to show that neither the actual fault or privity of the carrier nor the fault or neglect of the agents or servants of the carrier contributed to the loss or damage.

3   The shipper shall not be responsible for loss or damage sustained by the carrier or the ship arising or resulting from any cause without the act, fault or neglect of the shipper, his agents or his servants.

4   Any deviation in saving or attempting to save life or property at sea or any reasonable deviation shall not be deemed to be an infringement or breach of this convention or of the contract of carriage, and the carrier shall not be liable for any loss or damage resulting therefrom.

5   (a) Unless the nature and value of such goods have been declared by the shipper before shipment and inserted in the bill of lading, neither the carrier nor the ship shall in any event be or become liable for any loss or damage to or in connection with the goods in an amount exceeding 666.67 units of account per package or unit or two units of account per kg of gross weight of the goods lost or damaged, whichever is the higher.

(b) The total amount recoverable shall be calculated by reference to the value of such goods at the place and time at which the goods are discharged from the ship in accordance with the contract or should have been so discharged.

The value of the goods shall be fixed according to the commodity exchange price, or, if there be no such price, according to the current market price, or, if there be no commodity exchange price or current market price, by reference to the normal value of goods of the same kind and quality.

(c) Where a container, pallet or similar article of transport is used to consolidate goods, the number of packages or units enumerated in the bill of lading as packed in such article of transport shall be deemed the number of packages or units for the purpose of this paragraph as far as these packages or units are concerned. Except as aforesaid such article of transport shall be considered the package or unit.

(d) The unit of account mentioned in this article is the Special Drawing Right as defined by the International Monetary Fund. The amounts mentioned in sub-para (a) of this paragraph shall be converted into national currency on the basis of the value of that currency on a date to be determined by the law of the court seized of the case.

The value of the national currency, in terms of the Special Drawing Right, of a State which is a member of the International Monetary Fund, shall be calculated in accordance with the method of valuation applied by the International Monetary Fund in effect at the date in question for its operations and transactions. The value of the national currency, in terms of the Special Drawing Right, of a State which is not a member of the International Monetary Fund, shall be calculated in a manner determined by that State.

Nevertheless, a State which is not a member of the International Monetary Fund and whose law does not permit the application of the provisions of the preceding sentences may, at the time of ratification of the protocol of 1979 or accession thereto or at any time thereafter, declare that the limits of liability provided for in this convention to be applied in its territory shall be fixed as follows:

(i) in respect of the amount of 666.67 units of account mentioned in sub-para (a) of para 5 of this article, 10,000 monetary units;

(ii) in respect of the amount of 2 units of account mentioned in sub-para (a) of para 5 of this article, 30 monetary units.

The monetary unit referred to in the preceding sentence corresponds to 65.5 mg of gold of millesimal fineness 900. The conversion of the amounts specified in that sentence into the national currency shall be made according to the law of the State concerned.

The calculation and the conversion mentioned in the preceding sentences shall be made in such a manner as to express in the national currency of the State as far as possible the same real value for the amounts in sub-para (a) of para 5 of this article as is expressed there in units of account.

States shall communicate to the depositary the manner of calculation or the result of the conversion as the case may be, when depositing an instrument of ratification of the protocol of 1979 or of accession thereto and whenever there is a change in either.

(e) Neither the carrier nor the ship shall be entitled to the benefit of the limitation of liability provided for in this paragraph if it is proved that the damage resulted from an act or omission of the carrier done with intent to cause damage, or recklessly and with knowledge that damage would probably result.

(f) The declaration mentioned in sub-para (a) of this paragraph, embodied in the bill of lading, shall be *prima facie* evidence, but shall not be binding or conclusive on the carrier.

(g) By agreement between the carrier, master or agent of the carrier and the shipper other maximum amounts than those mentioned in sub-para (a) of this paragraph may be fixed, provided that no maximum amount so fixed shall be less than the appropriate maximum mentioned in that sub-paragraph.

(h) Neither the carrier nor the ship shall be responsible in any event for loss or damage to, or in connection with, goods if the nature or value thereof has been knowingly misstated by the shipper in the bill of lading.

6   Goods of an inflammable, explosive or dangerous nature to the shipment whereof the carrier, master or agent of the carrier has not consented with knowledge of their nature and character, may at any time before discharge be landed at any place, or destroyed or rendered innocuous by the carrier without compensation and the shipper of such goods shall be liable for all damages and expenses directly or indirectly arising out of or resulting from such shipment. If any such goods shipped with such knowledge and consent shall become a danger to the ship or cargo, they may in like manner be landed at any place, or destroyed or rendered innocuous by the carrier without liability on the part of the carrier except to general average, if any.

Article 4 bis

1   The defences and limits of liability provided for in this convention shall apply in any action against the carrier in respect of loss or damage to goods covered by a contract of carriage whether the action be founded in contract or in tort.

2   If such an action is brought against a servant or agent of the carrier (such servant or agent not being an independent contractor) such servant or agent shall be entitled to avail himself of the defences and limits of liability which the carrier is entitled to invoke under this convention.

3   The aggregate of the amounts recoverable from the carrier, and such servants and agents, shall in no case exceed the limit provided for in this convention.

4   Nevertheless, a servant or agent of the carrier shall not be entitled to avail himself of the provisions of this article, if it is proved that the damage resulted from an act or omission of the servant or agent done with intent to cause damage or recklessly and with knowledge that damage would probably result.

Article 5

A carrier shall be at liberty to surrender in whole or in part all or any of his rights and immunities or to increase any of his responsibilities and obligations under this convention, provided such surrender or increase shall be embodied in the bill of lading issued to the shipper. The provisions of this convention shall not be applicable to charterparties, but if bills of lading are issued in the case of a ship under a charterparty they shall comply with the terms of this convention. Nothing in these rules shall be held to prevent the insertion in a bill of lading of any lawful provision regarding general average.

Article 6

Notwithstanding the provisions of the preceding articles, a carrier master or agent of the carrier and a shipper shall in regard to any particular goods be at liberty to enter into any agreement in any terms as to the responsibility and liability of the carrier for such goods, and as to the rights and immunities of the carrier in respect of such goods, or his obligation as to seaworthiness, so far as this stipulation is not contrary to public policy, or the care or diligence of his servants or agents in regard to the loading, handling, stowage, carriage, custody, care and discharge of the goods carried by sea, provided that in this ease no bill of lading has been or shall be issued and that the terms agreed shall be embodied in a receipt which shall be a non-negotiable document and shall be marked as such.

Any agreement so entered into shall have full legal effect.

Provided that this article shall not apply to ordinary commercial shipments made in the ordinary course of trade, but only to other shipments where the character or condition of the property to be carried or the circumstances, terms and conditions under which the carriage is to be performed are such as reasonably to justify a special agreement.

Article 7

Nothing herein contained shall prevent a carrier or a shipper from entering into any agreement, stipulation, condition, reservation or exemption as to the responsibility and liability of the carrier or the ship for the loss or damage to, or in connection with, the custody and care and handling of goods prior to the loading on, and subsequent to the discharge from the ship on which the goods are carried by sea.

Article 8

The provisions of this convention shall not affect the rights and obligations of the carrier under any statute for the time being in force relating to the limitation of the liability of owners of sea going vessels.

Article 9

This convention shall not affect the provisions of any international convention or national law governing liability for nuclear damage.

Article 10

The provisions of this convention shall apply to every bill of lading relating to the carriage of goods between ports in two different States if:

(a)   the bill of lading is issued in a Contracting State; or

(b)   the carriage is from a port in a Contracting State; or

(c)   the contract contained in or evidenced by the bill of lading provides that the rules of this convention or legislation of any State giving effect to them are to govern the contract whatever may be the nationality of the ship, the carrier, the shipper, the consignee, or any other interested person.

Each Contracting State shall apply the provisions of this convention to the Bills of Lading mentioned above.

This article shall not prevent a Contracting State from applying the rules of this convention to bills of lading not included in the preceding paragraphs.

THE HAMBURG RULES

PART I – GENERAL PROVISIONS

Article 1 – Definitions In this convention

1   'Carrier' means any person by whom or in whose name a contract of carriage of goods by sea has been concluded with a shipper.

2   'Actual carrier' means any person to whom the performance of the carriage of the goods, or of part of the carriage, has been entrusted by the carrier, and includes any other person to whom such performance has been entrusted.

3   'Shipper' means any person by whom or in whose name or on whose behalf a contract of carriage of goods by sea has been concluded with a carrier, or any person by whom or in whose name or on whose behalf the goods are actually delivered to the carrier in relation to the contract of carriage by sea.

4   'Consignee' means the person entitled to take delivery of the goods.

5   'Goods' includes live animals; where the goods are consolidated in a container, pallet or similar article of transport or where they are packed, 'goods' includes such article of transport or packaging if supplied by the shipper.

6   'Contract of carriage by sea' means any contract whereby the carrier undertakes against payment of freight to carry goods by sea from one port to another, however, a contract which involves carriage by sea and also carriage by some other means is deemed to be a contract of carriage by sea for the purposes of this convention only in so far as it relates to the carriage by sea.

7   'Bill of lading' means a document which evidences a contract of carriage by sea and the taking over or loading of the goods by the carrier, and by which the carrier undertakes to deliver the goods against surrender of the document. A provision in the document that the goods are to be delivered to the order of a named person, or to order, or to bearer, constitutes such an undertaking.

8   'Writing' includes, *inter alia*, telegram and telex.

Article 2 – Scope of application

1   The provisions of this convention are applicable to all contracts of carriage by sea between two different States, if:

   (a)   the port of loading as provided for in the contract of carriage by sea is located in a Contracting State; or

   (b)   the port of discharge as provided for in the contract of carriage by sea is located in a Contracting State; or

   (c)   one of the optional ports of discharge provided for in the contract of carriage by sea is the actual port of discharge and such port is located in a Contracting State,; or

   (d)   the bill of lading or other document evidencing the contract of carriage by sea is issued in a Contracting State; or

   (e)   the bill of lading or other document evidencing the contract of carriage by sea provides that the provisions of this convention or the legislation of any State giving effect to them are to govern the contract.

2   The provisions of this convention are applicable without regard to the nationality of the ship, the carrier, the actual carrier, the shipper, the consignee or any other interested person.

3   The provisions of this convention are not applicable to charterparties. However, where a bill of lading is issued pursuant to a charterparty, the provisions of the convention apply to such a bill of lading if it governs the relation between the carrier and the holder of the bill of lading, not being the charterer.

4   If a contract provides for future carriage of goods in a series of shipments during an agreed period, the provisions of this convention apply to each shipment. However, where a shipment is made under a charterparty, the provisions of para 3 of this article apply.

Article 3 – Interpretation of the convention

In the interpretation and application of the provisions of this convention regard shall be had to its international character and to the need to promote uniformity.

PART II – LIABILITY OF THE CARRIER

Article 4 – Period of responsibility

1   The responsibility of the carrier for the goods under this convention covers the period during which the carrier is he charge of the goods at the port of loading, during the carriage and at the port of discharge.

2   For the purpose of para 1 of this article, the carrier is deemed to be in charge of the goods:

    (a) from the time he has taken over the goods from:

        (i)   the shipper, or a person acting on his behalf; or

        (ii) an authority or other third party to whom, pursuant to law or regulations applicable at the port of loading, the goods must be handed over for shipment;

    (b) until the time he has delivered the goods:

        (i)   by handing over the goods to the consignee; or

        (ii) in cases where the consignee does not receive the goods from the carrier, by placing them at the disposal of the consignee in accordance with the contract or with the law or with the usage of the particular trade, applicable at the port of discharge; or

        (iii) by handing over the goods to an authority or other third party to whom, pursuant to law or regulations applicable at the port of discharge, the goods must be handed over.

3   In paras 1 and 2 of this article, reference to the carrier or to the consignee means, in addition to the carrier or the consignee, the servants or agents, respectively of the carrier or the consignee.

Article 5 – Basis of liability

1   The carrier is liable for loss resulting from loss of or damage to the goods, as well as from delay in delivery, if the occurrence which caused the loss, damage or delay took place while the goods were in his charge as defined in Article 4, unless the carrier proves that he, his servants or agents took all measures that could reasonably be required to avoid the occurrence and its consequences.

2   Delay in delivery occurs when the goods have not been delivered at the port of discharge provided for in the contract of carriage by sea within the time expressly agreed upon or, in the absence of such agreement, within the time which it would be reasonable to require of a diligent carrier, having regard to the circumstances of the case.

3   The person entitled to make a claim for the loss of goods may treat the goods as lost if they have not been delivered as required by Article 4 within 60 consecutive days following the expiry of the time for delivery according to para 2 of this article.

4   (a) The carrier is liable:

       (i) for loss of or damage to the goods or delay in delivery caused by fire, if the claimant proves that the fire arose from fault or neglect on the part of the carrier, his servants or agents;

      (ii) for such loss, damage or delay in delivery which is proved by the claimant to have resulted from the fault or neglect of the carrier, his servants or agents, in taking all measures that could reasonably be required to put out the fire and avoid or mitigate its consequences.

    (b) In ease of fire on board the ship affecting the goods if the claimant or the carrier so desires, a survey in accordance with stripping practices must be held into the cause and circumstances of the fire, and a copy of the surveyor's report shall be made available on demand to the carrier and the claimant.

5   With respect to live animals, the carrier is not liable for loss damage or delay in delivery resulting from any special risks inherent in that kind of carriage. If the carrier proves that he has complied with any special instructions given to him by the shipper respecting the animals and that, in the circumstances of the case, the loss, damage or delay in delivery could be attributed to such risks, it is presumed that the loss, damage or delay in delivery was so caused, unless there is proof that all or a part of the loss, damage or delay in delivery resulted from fault or neglect on the part of the carrier, his servants or agents.

6   The carrier is not liable, except in general average, where loss damage or delay in delivery resulted from measures to save life or from reasonable measures to save property at sea.

7   Where fault or neglect on the part of the carrier, his servants or agents combines with another cause to produce loss, damage or delay in delivery, the carrier is liable only to the extent that the loss, damage or delay in delivery is attributable to such fault or neglect, provided that the carrier proves the amount of the loss, damage or delay in delivery not attributable thereto.

Article 6 – Limits of liability

1   (a) The liability of the carrier for loss resulting from loss of or damage to goods according to the provisions of Article 5 is limited to an amount equivalent to 835 units of account per package or other shipping unit or 2.5 units of account per kg of gross weight of the goods lost or damaged, whichever is the higher.

    (b) The liability of the carrier for delay in delivery according to the provisions of Article 5 is limited to an amount equivalent to two and a half times the freight payable for the goods delayed, but not exceeding the total freight payable under the contract of carriage of goods by sea.

    (c) In no case shall the aggregate liability of the carrier under both sub–paras (a) and (b) of this paragraph, exceed the limitation which would be established under sub–para (a) of this paragraph for total loss of the goods with respect to which such liability was incurred.

2   For the purpose of calculating which amount is the higher in accordance with para 1(a) of this article, the following rules apply:

    (a) Where a container, pallet or similar article of transport is used to consolidate goods, the package or other shipping units enumerated in the bill of lading, if issued, or otherwise in any other document evidencing the contract of carriage by sea, as packed in such article of transport are deemed packages or shipping units. Except as aforesaid the goods in such article of transport are deemed one shipping unit.

(b) In cases where the article of transport itself has been lost or damaged, that article of transport, if not owned or otherwise supplied by the carrier, is considered one separate shipping unit.

3   Unit of account means the unit of account mentioned in Article 26.

4   By agreement between the carrier and the shipper, limits of liability exceeding those provided for in para 1 may be fixed.

Article 7 – Application to non-contractual claims

1   The defences and limits of liability provided for in this convention apply in any action against the carrier in respect of loss or damage to the goods covered by the contract of carriage by sea, as well as of delay in delivery whether the action is founded in contract, in tort or otherwise.

2   If such an action is brought against a servant or agent of the carrier, such servant or agent, if he proves that he acted within the scope of his employment, is entitled to avail himself of the defences and limits of liability which the carrier is entitled to invoke under this convention.

3   Except as provided in Article 8, the aggregate of the amounts recoverable from the carrier and from any persons referred to in para 2 of this article shall not exceed the limits of liability provided for in this convention.

Article 8 – Loss of right to limit responsibility

1   The carrier is not entitled to the benefit of the limitation of liability provided for in Article 6 if it is proved that the loss, damage or delay in delivery resulted from an act or omission of the carrier, done with the intent to cause such loss, damage or delay, or recklessly and with knowledge that such loss, damage or delay would probably result.

2   Notwithstanding the provisions of para 2 of Article 7, a servant or agent of the carrier is not entitled to the benefit of the limitation of liability provided for in Article 6, if it is proved that the loss, damage or delay in delivery resulted from an act or omission of such servant or agent, done with the intent to cause such loss, damage or delay, or recklessly and with knowledge that such loss, damage or delay would probably result.

Article 9 – Deck cargo

1   The carrier is entitled to carry the goods on deck only if such carriage is in accordance with an agreement with the shipper or with the usage of the particular trade or is required by statutory rules or regulations.

2   If the carrier and the shipper have agreed that the goods shall or may be carried on deck, the carrier must insert in the bill of lading or other document evidencing the contract of carriage by sea a statement to that effect. In the absence of such a statement, the carrier has the burden of proving that an agreement for carriage on deck has been entered into; however, the carrier is not entitled to invoke such an agreement against a third party, including a consignee, who has acquired the bill of lading in good faith.

3   Where the goods have been carried on deck contrary to the provisions of para 1 of this article or where the carrier may not under para 2 of this article invoke an agreement for carriage on deck, the carrier, notwithstanding the provisions of para 1 of Article 5, is liable for loss of or damage to the goods, as well as for delay in delivery, resulting solely from the carriage on deck, and the extent of his liability is to be determined in accordance with the provisions of Article 6 or Article 8 of this Convention, as the case may be.

4   Carriage of goods on deck contrary to express agreement for carriage under deck is deemed to be an act or omission of the carrier within the meaning of Article 8.

Article 10 – Liability of the carrier and actual carrier

1   Where the performance of the carriage or part thereof has been entrusted to an actual carrier, whether or not in pursuance of a liberty under the contract of carriage by sea to do so, the carrier nevertheless remains responsible for the entire carriage according to the provisions of this convention. The carrier is responsible, in relation to the carriage performed by the actual carrier, for the acts and omissions of the actual carrier and of his servants and agents acting within the scope of their employment.

2   All the provisions of this convention governing the responsibility of the carrier also apply to the responsibility of the actual carrier for the carriage performed by him. The provisions of paras 2 and 3 of Article 7 and of para 2 of Article 8 apply if an action is brought against a servant or agent of the actual carrier.

3   Any special agreement under which the carrier assumes obligations not imposed by this convention or waives rights conferred by this convention affects the actual carrier only if agreed to by him expressly and in writing. Whether or not the actual carrier has so agreed, the carrier nevertheless remains bound by the obligations or waivers resulting from such special agreement.

4   Where and to the extent that both the carrier and the actual carrier are liable, their liability is joint and several.

5   The aggregate of the amounts recoverable from the carrier, the actual carrier and their servants and agents shall not exceed the limits of liability provided for in this convention.

6   Nothing in this article shall prejudice any right of recourse as between the carrier and the actual carrier.

Article 11 – Through carriage

1   Notwithstanding the provisions of para 1 of Article 10, where a contract of carriage by sea provides explicitly that a specified part of the carriage covered by the said contract is to be performed by a named person other than the carrier, the contract may also provide that the carrier is not liable for loss, damage or delay in delivery caused by an occurrence which takes place while the goods are in the charge of the actual carrier during such part of the carriage. Nevertheless, any stipulation limiting or excluding such liability is without effect if no judicial proceedings can be instituted against the actual carrier in a court competent under para 1 or 2 of Article 21. The burden of proving that any loss, damage or delay in delivery has been caused by such an occurrence rests upon the carrier.

2   The actual carrier is responsible in accordance with the provisions of para 2 of Article 10 for loss, damage or delay in delivery caused by an occurrence which takes place while the goods are in his charge.

PART III – LIABILITY OF THE SHIPPER

Article 12 – General rule

The shipper is not liable for loss sustained by the carrier or the actual carrier, or for damage sustained by the ship, unless such loss or damage was caused by the fault or neglect of the shipper, his servants or agents. Nor is any servant or agent of the shipper liable for such loss or damage unless the loss or damage was caused by fault or neglect on his part.

Article 13 – Special rules on dangerous goods

1   The shipper must mark or label in a suitable manner dangerous goods as dangerous.

2   Where the shipper hands over dangerous goods to the carrier or an actual carrier, as the case may be, the shipper must inform him of the dangerous character of the goods and, if necessary, of the precautions to be taken. If the shipper fails to do so and such carrier or actual carrier does not otherwise have knowledge of their dangerous character:

   (a)   the shipper is liable to the carrier and any actual carrier for the loss resulting from the shipment of such goods; and

   (b)   the goods may at any time be unloaded, destroyed or rendered innocuous, as the circumstances may require, without payment of compensation.

3   The provisions of para 2 of this article may not be invoked by any person if during the carriage he has taken the goods in his charge with knowledge of their dangerous character.

4   If, in cases where the provisions of para 2, sub-para (b) of this article do not apply or may not be invoked, dangerous goods become an actual danger to life or property, they may be unloaded, destroyed or rendered innocuous, as the circumstances may require, without payment of compensation except where there is an obligation to contribute in general average or where the carrier is liable accordance with the provisions of Article 5.

PART IV – TRANSPORT DOCUMENTS

Article 14 – Issue of bill of lading

1   When the carrier or the actual carrier takes the goods in his charge, the carrier must, on demand of the shipper, issue to the shipper a bill of lading.

2   The bill of lading may be signed by a person having authority from the carrier. A bill of lading signed by the master of the ship carrying the goods is deemed to have been signed on behalf of the carrier.

3   The signature on the bill of lading may be in handwriting printed in facsimile, perforated, stamped, in symbols, or made by any other mechanical or electronic means, if not inconsistent with the law of the country where the bill of lading is issued.

Article 15 – Contents of bill of lading

1   The bill of lading must include, *inter alia*, the following particulars:

   (a)   the general nature of the goods, the leading marks necessary for identification of the goods, an express statement, if applicable, as to the dangerous character of the goods, the number of packages or pieces, and the weight of the goods or their quantity otherwise expressed, all such particulars as furnished by the shipper;

   (b)   the apparent condition of the goods;

   (c)   the name and principal place of business of the carrier;

   (d)   the name of the shipper;

   (e)   the consignee if named by the shipper;

   (f)   the port of loading under the contract of carriage by sea and the date on which the goods were taken over by the carrier at the port of loading;

   (g)   the port of discharge under the contract of carriage by sea;

   (h)   the number of originals of the bill of lading, if more than one;

   (i)   the place of issuance of the bill of lading;

   (j)   the signature of the carrier or a person acting on his behalf;

   (k)   the freight to the extent payable by the consignee or other indication that freight is payable by him;

   (l)   the statement referred to in para 3 of Article 23;

   (m) the statement, if applicable, that the goods shall or may be carried on deck;

   (n)   the date or the period of delivery of the goods at the port of discharge if expressly agreed upon between the parties; and

   (o)   any increased limit or limits of liability where agreed in accordance with para 4 of Article 6.

2   After the goods have been loaded on board, if the shipper so demands, the carrier must issue to the shipper a 'shipped' bill of lading which, in addition to the particulars required under para 1 of this article, must state that the goods are on board a named ship or ships, and the date or dates of loading. If the carrier has previously issued to the shipper a bill of lading or other document of title with respect to any of such goods, on request of the carrier, the shipper must surrender such document in exchange for a 'shipped' bill of lading. The carrier may amend any previously issued document in order to meet the shipper's demand for a 'shipped' bill of lading if, as amended, such document includes all the information required to be contained in a 'shipped' bill of lading.

3   The absence in the bill of lading of one or more particulars referred to in this article does not affect the legal character of the document as a bill of lading provided that it nevertheless meets the requirements set out in para 7 of Article 1.

Article 16 – Bills of lading: reservations and evidentiary effect

1   If the bill of lading contains particulars concerning the general nature, leading marks, number of packages or pieces, weight or quantity of the goods which the carrier or other person issuing the bill of lading on his behalf knows or has reasonable grounds to suspect do not accurately represent the goods actually taken over or, where a

'shipped' bill of lading is issued, loaded, or if he had no reasonable means of checking such particulars, the carrier or such other person must insert in the bill of lading a reservation specifying these inaccuracies, grounds of suspicion or the absence of reasonable means of checking.

2   If the carrier or other person issuing the bill of lading on his behalf fails to note on the bill of lading the apparent condition of the goods, he is deemed to have noted on the bill of lading that the goods were in apparent good condition.

3   Except for particulars in respect of which and to the extent to which a reservation permitted under para 1 of this article has been entered:

   (a) the bill of lading is *prima facie* evidence of the taking over or, where a 'shipped' bill of lading is issued, loading, by the carrier of the goods as described in the bill of lading; and

   (b) proof to the contrary by the carrier is not admissible if the bill of lading has been transferred to a third party, including a consignee, who in good faith has acted in reliance on the description of the goods therein.

4   A bill of lading which does not, as provided in para 1, sub-para (k) of Article 15, set forth the freight or otherwise indicate that freight is payable by the consignee or does not set forth demurrage incurred at the port of loading payable by the consignee, is *prima facie* evidence that no freight or such demurrage is payable by him. However, proof to the contrary by the carrier is not admissible when the bill of lading has been transferred to a third party, including a consignee, who in good faith has acted in reliance on the absence in the bill of lading of any such indication.

Article 17 – Guarantees by the shipper

1   The shipper is deemed to have guaranteed to the carrier the accuracy of particulars relating to the general nature of the goods, their marks, number, weight and quantity as furnished by him for insertion in the bill of lading. The shipper must indemnify the carrier against the loss resulting from inaccuracies in such particulars. The shipper remains liable even if the bill of lading has been transferred by him. The right of the carrier to such indemnity in no way limits his liability under the contract of carriage by sea to any person other than the shipper.

2   Any letter of guarantee or agreement by which the shipper undertakes to indemnify the carrier against loss resulting from the issuance of the bill of lading by the carrier, or by a person acting on his behalf, without entering a reservation relating to particulars furnished by the shipper for insertion in the bill of lading, or to the apparent condition of the goods, is void and of no effect as against any third party, including a consignee, to whom the bill of lading has been transferred.

3   Such letter of guarantee or agreement is valid as against the shipper unless the carrier or the person acting on his behalf, by omitting the reservation referred to in para 2 of this article, intends to defraud a third party, including a consignee, who acts in reliance on the description of the goods in the bill of lading. In the latter case, if the reservation omitted relates to particulars furnished by the shipper for insertion in the bill of lading, the carrier has no right of indemnity from the shipper pursuant to para 1 of this article.

4   In the case of intended fraud referred to in para 3 of this article, the carrier is liable, without the benefit of the limitation of liability provided for in this convention, for

the loss incurred by a third party, including a consignee, because he has acted in reliance on the description of the goods in the bill of lading.

Article 18 – Documents other than bills of lading

Where a carrier issues a document other than a bill of lading to evidence the receipt of the goods to be carried, such a document is *prima facie* evidence of the conclusion of the contract of carriage by sea and the taking over by the carrier of the goods as therein described.

PART V – CLAIMS AND ACTIONS

Article 19 – Notice of loss, damage or delay

1   Unless notice of loss or damage, specifying the general nature of such loss or damage, is given in writing by the consignee to the carrier not later than the working day after the day when the goods were handed over to the consignee, such handing over is *prima facie* evidence of the delivery by the carrier of the goods as described in the document of transport or, if no such document has been issued, in good condition.

2   Where the loss or damage is not apparent, the provisions of para 1 of this article apply correspondingly if notice in writing is not given within 15 consecutive days after the day when the goods were handed over to the consignee.

3   If the state of the goods at the time they were handed over to the consignee has been the subject of a joint survey or inspection by the parties, notice in writing need not be given of loss or damage ascertained during such survey or inspection.

4   In the case of any actual or apprehended loss or damage the carrier and the consignee must give all reasonable facilities to each other for inspecting and tallying the goods.

5   No compensation shall be payable for loss resulting from delay in delivery unless a notice has been given in writing to the carrier within 60 consecutive days after the day when the goods were handed over to the consignee.

6   If the goods have been delivered by an actual carrier, any notice given under this article to him shall have the same effect as if it had been given to the carrier, and any notice given to the carrier shall have effect as if given to such actual carrier.

7   Unless notice of loss or damage, specifying the general nature of the loss or damage, is given in writing by the carrier or actual carrier to the shipper not later than 90 consecutive days after the occurrence of such loss or damage or after the delivery of the goods in accordance with para 2 of Article 4, whichever is later, the failure to give such notice is *prima facie* evidence that the carrier or the actual carrier has sustained no loss or damage due to the fault or neglect of the shipper, his servants or agents.

8   For the purpose of this article, notice given to a person acting on the carrier's or the actual carrier's behalf, including the master or the officer in charge of the ship, or to a person acting on the shipper's behalf is deemed to have been given to the carrier, to the actual carrier or to the shipper, respectively.

Article 20 – Limitation of actions

1   Any action relating to carriage of goods under this convention is time-barred if judicial or arbitral proceedings have not been instituted within a period of two years.

2   The limitation period commences on the day on which the carrier has delivered the goods or part thereof or, in cases where no goods have been delivered, on the last day on which the goods should have been delivered.

3 The day on which the limitation period commences is not included in the period.

4 The person against whom a claim is made may at any time during the running of the limitation period extend that period by a declaration in writing to the claimant. This period may be further extended by another declaration or declarations.

5 An action for indemnity by a person held liable may be instituted even after the expiration of the limitation period provided for in the preceding paragraphs if instituted within the time allowed by the law of the State where proceedings are instituted. However, the time allowed shall not be less than 90 days commencing from the day when the person instituting such action for indemnity has settled the claim or has been served with process in the action against himself.

Article 21 – Jurisdiction

1 In judicial proceedings relating to carriage of goods under this convention, the plaintiff, at his option, may institute an action in a court which, according to the law of the State where the court is situated, is competent and within the jurisdiction of which is situated one of the following places:

(a) the principal place of business or, in the absence thereof, the habitual residence of the defendant; or

(b) the place where the contract was made provided that the defendant has there a place of business, branch or agency through which the contract was made; or

(c) the port of loading or the port of discharge; or

(d) any additional place designated for that purpose in the contract of carriage by sea.

2 (a) Notwithstanding the preceding provisions of this article, an action may be instituted in the courts of any port or place in a Contracting State at which the carrying vessel or any other vessel of the same ownership may have been arrested in accordance with applicable rules of the law of that State and of international law. However, in such a case, at the petition of the defendant, the claimant must remove the action, at his choice, to one of the jurisdictions referred to in para 1 of this article for the determination of the claim, but before such removal the defendant must furnish security sufficient to ensure payment of any judgment that may subsequently be awarded to the claimant in the action.

(b) All questions relating to the sufficiency or otherwise of the security shall be determined by the court of the port or place of the arrest.

3 No judicial proceedings relating to carriage of goods under this convention may be instituted in a place not specified in para 1 or 2 of this article. The provisions of this paragraph do not constitute an obstacle to the jurisdiction of the Contracting States for provisional or protective measures.

4 (a) Where an action has been instituted in a court competent under para 1 or 2 of this article or where judgment has been delivered by such no new action may be started between the same parties on the same grounds unless the judgment of the court before which the first action was instituted is not enforceable in the country in which the new proceedings are instituted;

(b) for the purpose of this article the institution of measures with a view to obtaining enforcement of a judgment is not to be considered as the starting of a new action;

(e) for the purpose of this article, the removal of an action to a different court within the same country, or to a court in another country, in accordance with para 2(a) of this article, is not to be considered as the starting of a new action.

5   Notwithstanding the provisions of the preceding paragraphs, an agreement made by the parties, after a claim under the contract of carriage by sea has arisen, which designates the place where the claimant may institute an action, is effective.

Article 22 – Arbitration

1   Subject to the provisions of this article, parties may provide by agreement evidenced in writing that any dispute that may arise relating to carriage of goods under this convention shall be referred to arbitration.

2   Where a charterparty contains a provision that disputes arising thereunder shall be referred to arbitration and a bill of lading issued pursuant to the charterparty does not contain a special annotation providing that such provision shall be binding upon the holder of the bill of lading, the carrier may not invoke such provision as against a holder having acquired the bill of lading in good faith.

3   The arbitration proceedings shall, at the option of the claimant be instituted at one of the following places:

(a) a place in a State within whose territory is situated:

(i) the principal place of business of the defendant or, in the absence thereof, the habitual residence of the defendant; or

(ii) the place where the contract was made, provided that the defendant has there a place of business, branch or agency through which the contract was made; or

(iii) the port of loading or the port of discharge; or

(b) any place designated for that purpose in the arbitration clause or agreement.

4   The arbitrator or arbitration tribunal shall apply the rules of this convention.

5   The provisions of paras 3 and 4 of this article are deemed to be part of every arbitration clause or agreement, and any term of such clause or agreement which is inconsistent therewith is null and void.

6   Nothing in this article affects the validity of an agreement relating to arbitration made by the parties after the claim under the contract of carriage by sea has arisen.

PART VI – SUPPLEMENTARY PROVISIONS

Article 23 – Contractual stipulations

1   Any stipulation in a contract of carriage by sea, in a bill of lading, or in any other document evidencing the contract of carriage by sea is null and void to the extent that it derogates, directly or indirectly, from the provisions of this convention. The nullity of such a stipulation does not affect the validity of the other provisions of the contract or document of which it forms a part. A clause assigning benefit of insurance of the goods in favour of the carrier, or any similar clause, is null and void.

2   Notwithstanding the provisions of para 1 of this article, a carrier may increase his responsibilities and obligations under this convention.

3   Where a bill of lading or any other document evidencing the contract of carriage by sea is issued, it must contain a statement that the carriage is subject to the provisions

of this convention which nullify any stipulation derogating therefrom to the detriment of the shipper or the consignee.

4   Where the claimant in respect of the goods has incurred loss as a result of a stipulation which is null and void by virtue of the present article, or as a result of the omission of the statement referred to in para 3 of this article, the carrier must pay compensation to the extent required in order to give the claimant compensation in accordance with the provisions of this convention for any loss of or damage to the goods as well as for the delay in delivery. The carrier must, in addition, pay compensation for costs incurred by the claimant for the purpose of exercising his right, provided that costs incurred in the action where the foregoing provision is invoked are to be determined in accordance with the law of the State where proceedings are instituted.

Article 24 – General average

1   Nothing in this convention shall prevent the application of provisions in the contract of carriage by sea or national law regarding the adjustment of general average.

2   With the exception of Article 20, the provisions of this convention relating to the liability of the carrier for loss of or damage to the goods also determine whether the consignee may refuse contribution in general average and the liability of the carrier to indemnify the consignee in respect of any such contribution made or any salvage paid.

Article 25 – Other conventions

1   This convention does not modify the rights or duties of the carrier, the actual carrier and their servants and agents, provided for in international conventions or national law relating to the limitation of liability of owners of seagoing ships.

2   The provisions of Articles 21 and 22 of this convention do not prevent the application of the mandatory provisions of any other multilateral convention already in force at the date of this convention relating to matters dealt with in the said articles, provided that the dispute arises exclusively between parties having their principal place of business in States members of such other convention. However, this paragraph does not affect the application of para 4 of Article 22 of this convention.

3   No liability shall arise under the provisions of this convention for damage caused by a nuclear incident if the operator of a nuclear installation is liable for such damage:

   (a) under either the Paris Convention of 29 July 1960 on Third Party Liability in the Field of Nuclear Energy as amended by the Additional Protocol of 28 January 1964 or the Vienna Convention of 21 May 1963 on Civil Liability for Nuclear Damage; or

   (b) by virtue of national law governing the liability for such damage, provided that such law is in all respects as favourable to persons who may suffer damage as either the Paris or Vienna Conventions.

4   No liability shall arise under the provisions of this convention for any loss of or damage to or delay in delivery of luggage for which the carrier is responsible under any international convention or national law relating to the carriage of passengers and their baggage by sea.

5   Nothing contained in this convention prevents a Contracting State from applying any other international convention which is already in force at the date of this convention and which applies mandatorily to contracts of carriage of goods primarily by a mode of transport other than transport by sea. This provision also applies to any subsequent revision or amendment of such international convention.

Article 26 – Unit of account

1   The unit of account referred to in Article 6 of this convention is the Special Drawing Right as defined by the International Monetary Fund. The amounts mentioned in Article 6 are to be converted into the national currency of a State according to the value of such currency at the date of judgment or the date agreed upon by the parties. The value of a national currency, in terms of the Special Drawing Right, of a Contracting State which is a member of the International Monetary Fund is to be calculated in accordance with the method of valuation applied by the International Monetary Fund in effect at the date in question for its operations and transactions. The value of a national currency in terms of the Special Drawing Right of a Contracting State which is not a member of the International Monetary Fund is to be calculated in a manner determined by that State.

2   Nevertheless, those States which are not members of the International Monetary Fund and whose law does not permit the application of the provisions of para 1 of this article may, at the time of signature, or at the time of ratification, acceptance, approval or accession or at any time thereafter, declare that the limits of liability provided for in this convention to be applied in their territories shall be fixed as: 12,500 monetary units per package or other shipping unit or 37.5 monetary units per kg of gross weight of the goods.

3   The monetary unit referred to in para 2 of this article corresponds to 65.5 mg of gold of millesimal fineness 900. The conversion of the amounts referred to in para 2 into the national currency is to be made according to the law of the State concerned.

4   The calculation mentioned in the last sentence of para 1 and the conversion mentioned in para 3 of this article is to be made in such a manner as to express in the national currency of the Contracting State as far as possible the same real value for the amounts in Article 6 as is expressed there in units of account. Contracting States must communicate to the depositary the manner of calculation pursuant to para 1 of this article, or the result of the conversion mentioned in para 3 of this article, as the case may be, at the time of signature or when depositing their instruments of ratification, acceptance, approval or accession, or when availing themselves of the option provided for in para 2 of this article and whenever there is a change in the manner of such calculation or in the result of such conversion.

CHAPTER 5

CARRIAGE OF GOODS BY LAND AND AIR

INTRODUCTION

The modern law of carriage has evolved from a long historical past, in which the position of the common carrier was crucial.[1] Although the common carrier has ceased to exist, for all practical purposes, in the regimes of land and air transport the distinction between common and private carriers has moulded the law significantly.

The modern law of carriage is regulated by standard form contracts between the parties and, increasingly, by Federal legislation and enacted international conventions. Air carriage, while still in its technological infancy, was subjected to an early attempt to secure uniformity of international law in the shape of the Warsaw Convention of 1929.

Modern standard form contracts provide a detailed framework for the law of carriage and the rules governing such contracts are those that apply to standard form contacts and exemption clauses. The general position is that once the courts accept a document as contractual in nature and its terms clearly protect the carrier from a range of liabilities then the consignor will normally bear the risks of carriage. However, statute has made inroads into this principle, particularly in relation to consumer protection under the Trade Practices Act 1974 (Cth).

The Commonwealth government has actively legislated in the field of road carriage law. It has created, by cooperative agreement with the States and Territories, the National Road Transport Commission to develop uniformity in road transport law. The Commonwealth government has similarly established the National Rail Corporation as a separate company to achieve co-ordinated development of a national rail system. The International Air Services Commission has also been set up by the Commonwealth to allocate international aviation capacity and route entitlement among Australian international carriers.

These developments have occurred against a background of transport deregulation, including that of the domestic airline system, the rise of international airline megacarriers and national micro-economic reform in general. The Commonwealth government have accordingly amended the statutory provisions governing Australian international air carrier's liability and legislated for the sale and restructuring of Qantas and Australian Airlines. These changes underline the active role of the Commonwealth government in attempting to update the complex matrix of State, Territory, Commonwealth enactments in order to secure a more rational framework for those that operate and regulate transport services and their multifarious users.

---

1   See Kahn-Freund, O, *The Law of Contract by Inland Transport*, 1965, London: Stevens, p 194. This chapter is based on material published under the *Laws of Australia 34: Transport*, titled 'Carriage', Sydney: Law Book Co. I gratefully acknowledge permission granted by the publishers to draw upon that publication. The section on 'rail' in this chapter is similarly based, and I also acknowledge the permission granted by the author of the majority of that section, Ms Patricia Lane, University of Sydney, to use that material.

CARRIAGE BY ROAD

Background

The impact of Federal legislation on road transport in recent years has been significant and this area is dealt with in detail, with particular reference to the Interstate Road Transport Act 1985 (Cth), the Interstate Road Transport Charge Act 1985 (Cth), the National Road Transport Commission Act 1991 (Cth), the Road Transport (Australian Capital Territory) Act 1993 (Cth) and the Road Transport Reform (Vehicles and Traffic) Act 1993. The development of the Uniform Road Transport Law on a cooperative basis between the Federal, State and Territory governments is accordingly set out.

An outline of State and Territory motor vehicle licensing law is provided so far as it relates to commercial freight and passenger services.

The principles that govern the carriage of goods by road, like the rules applying to carriage generally, are based upon wide historical foundations. The duty of the common carrier to carry and deliver goods entrusted to them safely, and to answer for any loss or damage to those goods, developed as part of the law of bailment well before greater stress was laid upon the contractual element. The duty of a carrier to safeguard the goods is considered at common law to exist apart from contract and is laid upon them not as a consequence of the contract of carriage but because they have been put in possession of another's goods. One of the consequences of this is that the owner of goods may successfully sue a carrier for loss or damage to goods even though no contract of carriage can be proved.[2] Despite the virtual extinction of the common carrier for the purposes of Australian law; principally by the effect of disclaimers in standard form contracts of carriage, the present law can be made comprehensible only by understanding the distinction between common and private carriers.

Common carriers

A common carrier is one who undertakes for reward to transport passengers and the goods of any who wish to employ their services. Even though a carrier limits the kind of goods they are prepared to carry and/or the rate at which they are carried, the carrier may still remain a common carrier. Similarly, the status is not lost if they hold themselves ready to carry goods between two fixed or variable termini.[3] State legislation, based on the Carrier's Act 1830 (UK), regulates the position of the common carrier.[4]

---

2   See Palmer, NE, *Bailment*, 2nd edn, 1979, Sydney: Law Book Co, p 14; Paton, GW, *Bailment*, 1962, London: Stevens.

3   *Johnson v Midland Railway* (1849) 4 Ex 367 at 373. Common carriers are only liable for injuries to persons and are not insurers in regard to persons; see *Johnson v Midland Railway* (1849) 4 Ex 367 at 373. Whether a common carrier has modified what is generally a contract of carriage or whether the contract is a special contract of carriage has to be determined specially in each case; see *Kilners Ltd v John Dawson Investment Trust Ltd* (1935) 35 SR (NSW) 274 at 279; Paton, *Bailment*, p 230. See *Cowper v JG Goldner Pty Ltd* (1986) 40 SASR 457 where the fact that the defendant carriers could not carry horses at the time requested was held decisive against them being common carriers; see also *Securities (NZ) Ltd v Cadbury Schweppes Hudson Ltd* [1988] 340 (High Court of New Zealand).

4   See the Common Carrier's Act 1902 (NSW); the Carriers and Innkeepers Act 1958 (Vic); the Common Carriers Act 1874 (Tas); the Carriers Act 1891 (SA); the Carriers Act 1920 (WA). For a general discussion of the definition and position of the common carrier by road, see Palmer, *Bailment, op cit*, pp 969–84.

Private carriers

The majority of carriers by road are, almost without exception, not common carriers but private carriers. A private carrier is under no obligation to carry goods offered for carriage.[5]

Liability for negligence

Unlike the common carrier, the private carrier is only liable for negligence.[6]

The onus is on the carrier to show that their servants exercised reasonable care in relation to the consignor's property. If the goods are lost or damaged in transit, it is for the carrier to show that either they or their servants were not negligent or that such negligence did not contribute to the loss.[7]

The breach by the carrier of any statutory provisions relating to the fitness of the vehicle for carriage raises a strong presumption of negligence.[8]

The private carrier will be liable if his servant, having been entrusted with the goods, steals or commits any intentional or negligent harm, whether the servant is acting for the carrier's benefit or not.[9]

The carrier and their servants are under a duty to ensure that goods entrusted to them for carriage are saved in the event of fire, breakage or theft, whether or not caused by the negligence of either the carrier or their servants. A carrier will be liable to pay the owner of the goods damages if they do not do all they can to mitigate damage to such goods.[10]

Contracting out

The obligations outlined above can be varied or modified and abrogated by contractual agreement. Commonly, standard form agreements of private carriers exclude their sole liability, that of negligence. However, an exemption clause will not be construed as

---

5   The distinction, however, between common and private carriers, is no longer relevant. Note the judicial tendency in the UK courts not to attach the liability of common carriers to carriers by road. Palmer notes that 'the species is not entirely extinct' (971) citing *Hunt v Winterbotham (West of England) Ltd v BRS (Parcels) Ltd* [1962] 1 QB 617 and *Greater Northern Railway v LEP Transport and Depository Ltd* [1922] 2 KB 742.

6   *John Carter (Fine Worsteds) Ltd v Hanson Haulage (Leeds) Ltd* [1965] 2 QB 495; or, of course, for the breach of any express or implied contractual term.

7   See *Joseph Travers and Sons Ltd v Cooper* [1915] 1 KB 73.

8   See *Arcweld Constructions Pty Ltd v Smith* (1986) Unreported, Victorian Supreme Court; *Lee and Sons Pty Ltd v Abood* (1968) 89 WN (NSW) (Pt 1) 430. There is no absolute warranty of roadworthiness akin to the common law warranty of seaworthiness imposed on a shipowner; see the refusal of the Privy Council to assimilate the position of a ship at sea to that of a motor car on land in *Trickett v Queensland Insurance* [1936] AC 159 at 165 onwards.

9   See *Barwick v English Joint Stock Bank* (1867) LR 2 Ex 259; *Morris v CW Martin and Sons Ltd* [1966] 1 QB 716; *Moukatoff v BOAC* [1967] 1 Lloyd's Rep 396.

10 *Abraham v Bullock* (1902) 86 LT 796.

relieving a private carrier from negligence unless it does so expressly.[11] Such an exemption will not exclude liability as a consequence of wilful negligence or misconduct on the part of servants or agents, unless that is also expressly excluded.[12]

Total loss of goods carried was held to be covered by an exemption clause in a contract of carriage in *Metrotex Pty Ltd v Freight Investments Pty Ltd*.[13] The defendant agreed to carry three parcels of goods of the plaintiff's from Sydney to Melbourne. The goods were delivered to the defendant in Sydney but did not arrive in Melbourne and could not subsequently be found and their disappearance was unexplained. An exemption clause in the contract of carriage purporting to exempt the carrier for damage, loss, injury or delay was held by the Supreme Court of Victoria to exempt the carrier for damages for the loss. This would have been so even if the loss had been due to theft by the carrier's servants (unless such action could be treated as that of the carrier himself).

The High Court has held that where there is a breach of an implied term in a contract of carriage by the carrier the contract will be construed to ascertain if this breach prevents reliance by the carrier on the exempting terms. In *TNT Pty Ltd v May and Baker (Australia) Pty Ltd*,[14] the appellant regularly employed a driver to pick up goods in Melbourne and take them to its central depot in the city for interstate transmission. On a number of occasions previously, because the driver was late in reaching the depot when it closed in the afternoon, they were directed by two-way radio to take the goods they had collected to their residence. The respondent's goods were collected and because the driver was too late to reach the depot they took the loaded truck home and put it in an unsecured garage which did not contain a fire extinguisher. The load was damaged by fire overnight. The contract of carriage contained exempting terms which set out to absolve the carrier from any loss or damage to the goods when in the carrier's custody. The High Court held that the carriers were in breach of an implied term of the contract that the respondent's goods would be taken to the depot by the driver and that the contract, on its construction, did not permit the storage of goods in the driver's garage.

What amounts to notice of terms and conditions of carriage is a matter of fact.[15]

A carrier, whose servant or agent converts the goods entrusted to the carrier, is liable to the owner of the goods, unless an exemption clause in the contract of carriage precludes liability.[16]

---

11   See *White v John Warwick and Co Ltd* [1953] 1 WLR 1285; *Canada SS v The King* [1952] AC 192; *South Wales Switchgear Co Ltd* [1978] 1 WLR 165. On the construction of exemption clauses, see Livermore, J, *Exemption Clauses and Implied Obligations in Contracts*, 1986, Sydney: Law Book Co, pp 19–25.

12   *Metrotex Pty Ltd v Freight Investments Pty Ltd* [1969] VR 9.

13   [1969] VR 9.

14   (1966) 115 CLR 353.

15   See *DH Hill and Co v Walter H Wright Pty Ltd* [1971] VR 749 (full court); distinguishing *Hardwick Game Farm v SAPPA* [1966] 1 All ER 309.

16   See *Rick Cobby Haulage Ltd v Simsmetal Pty Ltd* (1986) 43 SASR 533; following *Delco Australia Pty Ltd v Darlington Futures Ltd* (1987) 43 SASR 519, distinguishing *Life Savers (Australia) Ltd v Frigmobile Pty Ltd* [1983] 1 NSWLR 431.

Subcontractors

The right to subcontract is almost an invariable term in the contract of carriage. In the absence of such an express term, the contract might be performed by the employment of a subcontractor unless the carrier had undertaken expressly or impliedly to perform it themselves.[17]

Standard form contracts of carriage usually expressly authorise the carrier to employ another carrier to perform the contract and give such another carrier similar powers to subcontract. These conditions also require the subcontractor to indemnify the carrier against liability arising where the goods are in transit and that of any failure by the subcontractor to collect the goods within a reasonable time.[18]

Liability of the carrier as a warehouse person

A carrier's liability lasts only for the period of carriage; where they hold goods before or after their carriage, these are held as a warehouse person and not a carrier.[19] The liability of a warehouseman is that of a bailee and, as such, the carrier is only liable for their negligence.[20]

Unless the carrier holds the goods expressly and impliedly as a warehouse person before carriage commences, transit begins, and the goods are possessed as a carrier when they are delivered to the carrier or to actual or ostensibly authorised agents or employees.[21]

Delay

Unless protected by an express term in the contract (which will usually be the case), the carrier is under a duty to use all reasonable care to deliver goods within a reasonable time.[22] For a carrier to be liable in damages for delay the plaintiff must show failure to

---

17   *John Carter (Fine Worsteds) Ltd v Hanson Haulage (Leeds) Ltd* [1965] 2 QB 495 at 523; *Garnham Harris and Elton Ltd v Alfred E Ellis (Transport) Ltd* [1967] 2 All ER 940 at 942. Where the nature of the goods to be carried requires particular skill and handling, or where the goods are valuable and attractive to thieves the implication is that the carrier shall not subcontract without express authority; see *Edwards v Newlands and Co* [1952] 2 KB 532; *Garnham Harris and Elton Ltd v Alfred E Ellis (Transport) Ltd* [1967] 2 All ER 940 at 942.

18   A carrier may subcontract their duties expressly and by so doing transfer indemnity to a third party; see *BHP v Hapag-Lloyd A/G* (1980) 2 NSWLR 572 (a sea carrier entitled to subcontract his duties and transfer an indemnity to a land carrier; land carrier entitled to recover from the sea carrier on claim against the land carrier by the cargo owners, the sea carrier being entitled to be indemnified by the cargo owners under the terms of the bill of lading).

19   *Chapman v GW Railway and LNW Railway* (1880) 5 QBD 278 at 281. See Palmer, *Bailment, op cit,* pp 983–84.

20   The carrier is not liable fire or theft or destruction of the goods in the carrier's warehouse where the transit is at an end and the carrier has not been negligent; see *Brooks Wharf and Bull Wharf Ltd v Goodman Bros* [1937] 1 KB 934. See the position where the carrier, having no proper storage, denies responsibility for damage arising from this fact; see Palmer, *Bailment, op cit,* p 984 and Chapter 13.

21   *Soanes Bros v Meredith* [1963] 2 Lloyd's Rep 293 at 307. Acceptance of goods by a third party or employee without the express or implied authority of the carrier is not regarded as delivery to the carrier; see *Crows Transport Ltd v Phoenix Assurance Co Ltd* [1965] 1 WLR 383.

22   *Raphael v Pickford* (1843) 5 Man and G 551.

deliver within a reasonable time and negligence on the part of the carrier or their employees.[23]

Deviation

At common law no carrier, private or common, is permitted to deviate from their usual or agreed route.[24] A private road carrier will be liable in such circumstances where no special contract exists. This situation will be exceptional since a private road carrier is normally protected in a contract of carriage by an exemption clause which is subject to the canons of construction laid down by the courts.[25]

Misdelivery

Where a carrier delivers the goods to any other person than the consignee they are liable for breach of contract and conversion on the basis of misdelivery.[26] However, if the carrier obeys the consignor's instructions and the goods are delivered to a person who commits a fraud on a consignor, the carrier will not be liable for misdelivery.[27]

Transit and stoppage in transit

Standard contracts of carriage by road usually provide that transit begins when the consignment is handed in at the carrier's place of business or point of collection and ends when the consignment is tendered at the usual place of delivery at the consignee's address within the usual delivery hours of the area. Transit will end where the consignment cannot be delivered or is held by the carrier 'to await order' or 'to be kept until called for' and such instructions are not given or the consignment is not called for and removed within a reasonable time.[28]

---

23 *Taylor v GN Railway* (1866) LR 1 CP 385; a carrier will not be liable for delay beyond their reasonable foreseeability and control; see *Briddon v GN Railway* (1853) 28 LJ Ex 51; *Sims v Midland Railway* [1913] 1 KB 103.

24 *Taylor v GN Railway* (1866) LR 1 CP 385.

25 See fn 11 above.

26 *Stephenson v Hart* (1828) 4 Bing 476.

27 *British Traders Ltd v Ubique Transport Ltd* [1952] 2 Lloyd's Rep 236 delivery to the consignee's address is due performance by the carrier even if the person taking delivery is not authorised to do so by the consignee, unless the circumstances should have made the carrier suspicious; see *Heugh v L and NW Railway* (1870) LR Ex 51; *Stephenson v Hart* (1828) 4 Bing 476.

28 Delivery to the carrier is deemed to be delivery to the buyer subject to any contrary agreement made by the parties to the contract of sale; see s 35 of the Sale of Goods Act 1923 (NSW); for the position respecting an insolvent seller and stoppage in transit see ss 46–48 of the Sale of Goods Act 1923 (NSW).

The carrier's lien

A common carrier has a right at common law to hold goods against payment of freight.[29] Carriers who are not common carriers do not have a specific lien on the goods they carry unless there is a particular agreement to that effect.[30]

A general lien cannot be exercised until the goods reach their destination or the unpaid seller stops them in transit. This right of the unpaid seller has priority over the carrier's general, but not their particular lien.[31]

Measure of damages

A carrier who is responsible for loss or injury to goods arising naturally from their default, where no agreement to the contrary exists, must compensate their owner.[32] The measure of damages as a general rule is the difference in the market value of the goods at the time and place at which they were due to be delivered and when they were delivered.[33]

Carriage of passengers

A private carrier for reward is under a duty to exercise reasonable care in the carriage of its passengers, independent of any contract.[34] However, a private carrier must exercise reasonable care to carry them safely, including any person lawfully on the carrier's vehicle.[35] Such a duty may be excluded or modified by the terms of any contract.[36]

---

29 *Skinner v Upshaw* (1702) 2 Ld Raym 752; *Goldsbrough v McCulloch* (1868) 5 WW and A'B(L) 154; *Callimore v Moore* (1867) 6 SCR (NSW) 388; *Kilners Ltd v John Dawson Investment Trust Ltd* (1935) 35 SR (NSW) 274; *Brilawsky v Robertson and Cannell* (1916) 10 QJPR 113.

30 *Electric Supply Stores v Gaywood* (1909) 100 LT 855.

31 *US Steel Products Co v GW Railway* [1916] 1 AC 189. The carrier's right to exercise liens under their function as warehouseperson is regulated by statute; see Warehousemen's Leins Act (WA); Warehousemen's Liens Ordinance 1959 (NT); ss 17–32 of the Mercantile Law Ordinance 1962 (ACT).

32 *Hadley v Baxendale* (1854) 9 Ex ch 341 at 345–55; *Victoria Laundry (Windsor Ltd) v Newman Industries Ltd* [1949] 2 KB 528.

33 *Koufos v Czarnikow Ltd (The Heron II)* [1969] 1 AC 351. A carrier is not liable for indirect or consequential damages or loss of a particular market unless there is a special contract to this effect. A carrier is not liable for the inability of an owner of goods to effect a sale; *Heskell v Continental Express Ltd* [1950] 1 All ER 1033 at 1048. Similarly a carrier is only liable for loss of exceptional profits if it can be proved that the carrier was aware of the facts that would result in such a loss if the carrier were guilty of delay in carriage of the goods; see *Horne v Midland Railway* (1873) LR 8 CP 131.

34 *Maloney v Commissioner for Railways (NSW)* (1978) 52 ALJR 292; *Hayes v Brisbane City Council* [1979] 5 QL 269; *Price v Ramsay (Commissioner of Railways)* (1882) 16 SASLR 95. With reference to the carriage of passengers by private carriers, see Halsbury 121,079–151; for common carrier's liability regarding the carriage of passengers and luggage see 121,150 and 121,152. As a common carrier would appear to be under the same standard of care as a private carrier with respect to the carriage of passengers their position is not considered separately here.

35 *Gregory v Commonwealth Railways Commission* (1941) 66 CLR 50; *Kelly v ASN Co* (1885) 2 WN (NSW) 40; *King v Victorian Railway Commissioners* (1892) 18 VLR 250; *Whitchurch v Commissioner for Railways* (1901) 4 WALR 53; *Daly v Commissioner of Railways* (1906) 8 WALR 125.

36 *Gregory v Commonwealth Railways Commission* (1941) 66 CLR 50.

A carrier of passengers does not warrant that its vehicles are sound or that they will be fit for the purpose of carriage.[37] A passenger would not appear to acquire a right of action to damages for breach of statutory duty only because the carrier fails to comply with regulations as to the construction and use of motor vehicles.[38]

Duties and liabilities of a carrier by road to passengers alighting from or entering a carrying vehicle are based on principles equally applicable to the carriage of passengers by rail. In each case whether or not the carrier is negligent is a question of fact.[39] A carrier of passengers must take reasonable care that the carrying vehicle does not start while passengers are in the process of entering or alighting.[40]

The carrier does not relinquish its obligation to take reasonable care to carry passengers safely if the passenger, in alighting, is put in a position of clear danger, without the passenger being warned or the carrier not providing them with an opportunity to avoid the risk.[41]

Failure by an employee of the carrier to secure a carrying vehicle's doors before it moves off may be evidence of negligence.[42] A notice posted in a carrying vehicle or carriage requesting passengers not to put their heads or arms out of windows does not become a condition of the contract of carriage, even where it can be proved to have been drawn to the actual notice of passengers.[43]

A carrier of passengers is under a duty to provide reasonable accommodation for the passengers.[44] Damages may be claimable for loss or injury directly caused by overcrowding.[45]

A carrier is negligent if permitting a passenger to take with them onto the carrying vehicle any article or object likely to injure other passengers.[46] The degree of care to be exercised in an emergency by a carrier will depend on the circumstances of each case.[47]

In the absence of a contract, private carriers are under no duty to accept passenger's luggage for carriage.[48] A carrier must provide reasonable facilities for the carrying of passenger's luggage.[49]

---

37 John Carter (Fine Worsteds) Ltd v Hanson Haulage (Leeds) Ltd [1965] 2 QB 495.

38 Barkway v South Wales Transport Co Ltd [1950] AC 185.

39 Shirt v Wyong Shire Council [1978] 1 NSWLR 631 at 648 (affirmed Wyong Shire v Shirt (1980) 146 CLR 40).

40 London and North Western Railway Co v Hellawell (1872) 26 LT 557; Stockdale v Lancashire and Yorkshire Railway Co (1863) 8 LT 289; Angus v London, Tilbury and Southend Railway Co (1906) 22 TLR 222 (CA).

41 Thompson v Commissioner for Railways (1863) 2 SCR (NSW) 292.

42 Gee v Metropolitan Railway Co (1873) LR 8 QB 161; Brookes v London Passenger Transport Board [1947] 1 All ER 506.

43 Cashmore v Chief Commissioner for Railways and Tramways (NSW) (1915) 20 CLR 1; King v Victorian Railways Commissioners (1892) 18 VLR 250.

44 Jones v Great Northern Railway Co (1918) 34 TLR 467 (Div Ct).

45 Redpath v Railway Commissioners (1900) 17 WN (NSW) 47.

46 East Indian Railway Co v Kalidas Mukerjee [1901] AC 396.

47 See London, Tilbury and Southend Railway Co v Patterson (1913) 29 TLR 413 (HL).

48 A duty to accept such luggage will normally be the case and an implication on the part of a carrier may be made; Macrow v Great Western Railway Co (1871) LR 6 QB 612.

49 Upperton v Union-Castle Mail Steamship Co Ltd (1902) 19 TLR 123.

FEDERAL ROAD TRANSPORT LEGISLATION AND REGULATION

Freedom of interstate trade

The Commonwealth has power to legislate with respect to trade and commerce among the States under s 51(i) of the Constitution, but this power can only be used subject to the restriction of s 92[50] which provides that trade and commerce between the States shall be absolutely free. The phrase trade and commerce including the business of carrying goods and passengers for reward means that although the Commonwealth can regulate interstate transport it cannot restrict or prevent it. The requirement of interstate road traffic to pay more than a reasonable sum for the uses of roads infringes s 92.[51] The balance between reasonable regulation and prohibition of interstate trade has been extensively explored by the courts as has the issue of what constitutes part of interstate road transport.[52]

Trade Practices Act 1974 (Cth) and road transport

Section 4(1) of the Trade Practices Act 1974 (Cth) by its wide definition of services covers transportation of goods, including storage and warehousing. Accordingly, where goods are carried under a contract between a consumer and a corporation the services must be rendered with due care and skill (s 74(l)). This does not apply to contracts for the storage or transportation of goods for commercial purposes (s 74(3)).[53]

Federal regulation of transport

Interstate road transport is increasingly regulated by Federal legislation which is exemplified in the National Road Transport Commission Act 1991 (Cth) and related legislation intended to form the basis of the new Uniform Road Transport Law.[54]

---

50   *James v The Commonwealth* (1936) 55 CLR 1.

51   *Hughes and Vale Pty Ltd v New South Wales (No 2)* (1955) 93 CLR 127.

52   *Russell v Walters* (1957) 96 CLR 177; *Sims v West* (1961) 107 CLR 157; *IXL Timbers v AG for Tasmania* (1963) 109 CLR 574; *Tamar Timber Trading Co Pty Ltd v Pilkington* (1968) 117 CLR 353; *Holloway v Pilkington* (1972) 46 ALJR 253; *Pilkington v Frank Hammond* (1973) 2 ALR 563; see also *Boyd v Carah Coaches* (1979) 27 ALR 161; *Stoneham v Simkin* [1977] VR 357; *Stoneham v Ryan's Removals Ltd* (1979) 23 ALR 1. On the issue of 'border hopping' see Brazil, P, 'Border Hopping and Section 92 of the Constitution' (1960) 34 ALJ 77.

53   On the interrelationship of the Trade Practices Act 1974 (Cth) and State transport legislation, see *Grace Bros Pty Ltd v Rice* (1976) 10 ALR 185 where the district court held that the Carriage of Goods by Land Act 1967 (Qld) was intended to be a code in respect of contract of carriage by land in the State of Queensland, finding that s 6 of the Queensland Act 1967 was inconsistent with ss 68 and 74 of the Trade Practices Act 1974 (Cth). In *Wallis v Downard Pickford (North Queensland) Pty Ltd*, 1992, unreported, full court of the Supreme Court of Queensland, 30 October, the full court held that the provisions of the Carriage of Goods by Land (Carrier's Liabilities) Act 1967 (Qld) did not amount to a term of a contract restricting the effect of s 74 of the Trade Practices Act 1974 (Cth) and that there was no inconsistency between the Queensland Act and the Commonwealth Act. The Carriage of Goods by Land (Carrier's Liabilities) Act 1967 (Qld) was repealed by the Carriage of Goods by Land (Carrier's Liabilities) Act Repeal Act 1993 (Qld) (no 13 of 1993).

54   See Pollard, M, 'Road Transport Reform – the Legislative Challenge', 1993, Chartered Institute of Transport National Conference, Perth, 13–16 September, p 265. I gratefully acknowledge the assistance of Mr Martin Pollard, Director, Legislation, National Road Transport Commission for assistance with material in relation to the new uniform road transport law.

Since Federation and the advent of commercial road vehicles legislative regulation of road transport has been, until recently, the province of the States and Territories. As a result, by the early 1980s, Australia had eight substantial bodies of legislation governing motor vehicles and traffic, one for each State and Territory. By the beginning of the 1990s, there were more than one 100 separate Acts and regulations within the nation dealing with road transport. Differing laws between the jurisdictions had produced economic disadvantages and these were identified as a cause of inefficiency at a time when improvement of industrial efficiency and international market competitiveness were key elements of Federal government policy. Accordingly, the heads of the Commonwealth, State and Territory governments became increasingly determined that uniformity in road transport law was a desirable and mutual goal.

The heads of the State, Territory and Commonwealth governments signed an agreement (subsequently referred to as the Agreement) on 30 July 1991 which adopted, and committed their respective governments to, the objectives of improving both road safety and transport efficiency and reductions in the costs of administration of road transport, together with a scheme to bring these objectives to realisation. The scheme envisaged the enactment of Commonwealth legislation establishing a National Road Transport Commission which would have the task of initiating and co-ordinating the development of uniform or consistent road transport law.

The Agreement also set out to establish a Ministerial Council for Road Transport to perform the following functions:

(a) to consider and where appropriate disallow legislative proposals made by the Commission within two months;

(b) to allow Application and Emergency Orders (exemptions for certain jurisdictions from particular aspects of the road transport package);

(c) to make decisions as to budget and funding; and

(d) to oversee the administration of the legislation by the States and Territories.

Under the Agreement, the Commonwealth Parliament enacted the National Road Transport Commission Act 1991. The Act set up the National Road Transport Commission, defined its legal status and set out its functions and relationship to the Ministerial Council the Act and the Agreement together set out the respective roles of the Commission and the Council in the development of the national legislative scheme.

The scheme was be to implemented through national template legislation. The scheme envisaged legislation enacted by the Commonwealth for the Australian Capital Territory would be adopted by the States and the Northern Territory and applied as their own law and amended from time to time.

Under the Agreement (and the Heavy and Light Vehicle Agreements) the States and the Northern Territory are required to seek passage of legislation which provides for:

(a) automatic repeal, amendment or modification of existing legislation to the extent necessary to avoid conflict with the new legislation;

(b) automatic adoption of amendments to the new law(including any regulations) approved by the Ministerial Council and enacted (or made) by the Commonwealth;

(c) a Minister to make application and emergency orders to the Ministerial Council; and

(d) the conferral on the Commission and the Ministerial Council of the same powers as are conferred by the National Road Transport Commission Act 1991.

Heavy Vehicles Agreement

The Heavy Vehicles Agreement which is contained in the National Road Transport Commission Act 1991 (Cth) (no 8 of 1992)[55] provides in the Recitals to the Agreement that the heads of government endorse the principles that there should be improvements to both road safety and transport efficiency and reductions in the costs of administration of transport.[56] The heads of government agreed that these principles required uniform or consistent road transport legislation throughout Australia.[57] The essential element of the scheme is an agreement between the Commonwealth, the States, the Northern Territory and the Australian Capital Territory to provide for and bring into force of legislation, establishment of a Ministerial Council and a National Road Transport Commission (referred to subsequently as the Commission).

The Heavy Vehicles Agreement requires the Commission to recommend changes to charging principles, subject to the disapproval powers of the Ministerial Council. Until these principles are changed, the Agreement requires adherence to the principles in the definitions in the definitions 'road charge', 'access charge', 'mass–distance charge' and 'paygo'.[58]

Light Vehicles Agreement

The Light Vehicles Agreement made on 11 May 1992 is contained in the National Road Transport Commission Amendment Act 1992 (no 149 of 1992) follows identical objectives[59] to those outlined in the Heavy Vehicles Agreement. This encompasses uniform or consistent road transport legislation, capable of effective administration and specifically applies the principles of the Heavy Vehicle Agreement to proposed light vehicle legislation.

The essential element of the cooperative scheme, between the Commonwealth, New South Wales, Victoria, Queensland, South Australia and the Northern Territory and the Australian Capital Territory, to set up the light vehicle legislation is an agreement between the respective governments.[60]

---

55 See Schedule to Act.

56 Schedule, Recital C.

57 Schedule, Recital G.

58 Schedule, Recital G. As to road charges see Schedule, clauses 20(3), (4), (5); charging principles, see Schedule, Part 1, clause 2. On the definition of 'zone' in relation to road charge, see Schedule, para 20(2)(c).

59 Schedule 2, Recital C.

60 Schedule 2, Recital E.

There is also a conferring of powers on the National Road Transport Commission in respect of the parties referred to above[61] (see provisions of the Light Vehicle Agreement (a)–(c)).

There are three significant differences between the Light Vehicle and Heavy Vehicle Agreements. These are:

(a) the fixing of registration charges for light vehicles is specifically excluded from the Light Vehicle Agreement where it is a key part of the Heavy Vehicles Agreement;

(b) the Heavy Vehicle Agreement involves a firm commitment to develop a package of road transport legislation on the matters to be set out in that Agreement – in contrast, the Light Vehicle Agreement specifies certain matters that are to be proceeded with only if there are shown to be significant net benefits;

(c) the Light Vehicle Agreement is not limited to matters concerning road vehicles, but extends to all road users including pedestrians.

Under the Agreements, the National Road Transport Commission set up by the National Road Transport Commission Act 1992 (Cth) is directed to develop policy, and submit recommended legislation to the Ministerial Council on the following matters:

(a) Heavy vehicles – design, construction and use; registration; driver licensing; traffic rules relating to heavy vehicles; and charging principles and road charges.

(b) Light vehicles – vehicle standards; driver standards; traffic rules for all users; and transport of dangerous goods.

(c) Light vehicles (if significant net benefits are shown) – procedures for dealing with unroadworthy vehicles; vehicle registration and driver and operation licensing; and other matters referred to the Commission by the Ministerial Council.

The Ministerial Council decided at its meeting in October 1992 to separate the task of creating a national uniform road transport law into the following five elements or modules:

(a) heavy vehicle charges;

(b) vehicle operations;

(c) vehicle registration system;

(d) driver licensing system; and

(e) compliance and enforcement.

With the exception of the road charges module which cannot be extended to light vehicles, legislation covering light vehicles will be incorporated into the modules as these are developed, as far as possible. The final road transport law package as envisaged by the Agreements is intended to fill any gaps in the modules and be the means by which any remaining modules will be enacted.

---

61   Schedule 2, Recital F.

Operation of the Agreement

The Agreement is stated to come into force when executed by the Commonwealth and a majority of the States, of the Northern Territory and of the Australian Capital Territory (s 4(1)). The Agreement may, after coming into force, be amended only by the unanimous decision of participating parties and the Australian Capital Territory. (s 4(2)).

The Heavy Vehicle Agreement envisaged development of legislation in all area of its program simultaneously. This would involve an enactment of a single Act of the Commonwealth Parliament together with one adopting Act in each State and Territory.

As an alternative to this, the Commission proposed to the Ministerial Council in 1992 an alternative strategy. This was to divide the legislative task into a number of stand alone modules, each dealing with a specific subject matter.

Accordingly, work on each module has proceeded on the basis that legislation covering light vehicles would be incorporated, as far as possible, into the modules as they are developed. The Commission has regarded the final integrated road transport law as filling any gaps in the modules and providing the means by which any remaining subjects could be included in the national legislation.

The Heavy Vehicle Agreement required the Commission to recommend national charges for heavy vehicles based on defined charging principles. These national charges were approved by the Ministerial Council in 1992 and are enshrined in the Road Transport Charges (Australian Capital Territory) Act 1993 (no 10 of 1993). Under the Heavy Vehicle Agreement the States and the Northern Territory are obliged to enact adopting legislation to cause this Act to apply as part of the law of those other jurisdictions.

The Road Transport Charges (Australian Capital Territory) Act obliges the government of the Australian Capital Territory to determine annual registration charges for vehicles charges.[62] The Australian Capital Territory government is similarly obliged to determine charges for the grant of a permit to operate a vehicle, or combination of vehicles.[63]

The government of the Australian Capital Territory is empowered to charge fees, make rebates, refunds or charge other administrative fees in respect of vehicles.[64]

---

62 The Road Transport Charges (ACT) Act 1993 came into effect on 1 July 1995 in respect of vehicles referred to in Part 2 of the Schedule to the Act in accordance with charges applicable under that Schedule (s 2(a)). The Road Transport Charges (ACT) Regulations 1995 (no 42) were Gazetted on 14 March 1995 but as the Road Transport Charges (ACT) Act 1993 only requires the charges to be applied from 1 July 1995 that is the date on which the Regulations come into practical effect.

63 See Schedule, Part 3; these are vehicles, or a combination of vehicles with a loaded mass exceeding 125 tonnes, and carrying a load that can without considerable effort, expense or risk or damage be divided into two or more smaller loads for transport on public roads (s 2(b)).

64 Section 3. Regulations may be made by the Governor General (s 5) which may alter the amounts specified in the Schedule in relation to a year, but this must not increase or decrease the amounts applicable to the previous year by more than 5% (s 4).

Nothing in the Schedule applies any vehicle with an MRC (mass rating for charging) of less or equal to 4.5 tonnes.[65]

Part 1 contains key definitions.[66]

Part 2 lists a table (in four divisions) of the registration charges applicable to the vehicles affected. If a vehicle falls into two or more categories in the table the registration charge for the vehicle is the higher of the highest charges that can apply to the vehicle.

Part 3 provides that the charge for the grant of a permit to operate a vehicle, or a combination of vehicles with a loaded mass exceeding 125 tonnes and carrying an indivisible load is worked out on a formula.[67]

The Heavy Vehicle Agreement was amended by the National Road Transport Commission Amendment Act 1992 (Cth).[68] The amended provisions in the Heavy Vehicle Agreement regarding funding of the National Commission now state that the funds for the establishment and functioning of the Commission will be provided after 30 June 1993 by the Commonwealth States and the Territories in shares to be unanimously decided by the Ministerial Council.[69]

Vehicle operations module
(the Road Transport Reform (Vehicles and Traffic) Act 1993)

During the development of uniform road charges by the National Road Transport Commission, substantial progress was made with the States and Territories, the road transport industry and with the assistance of Austroads, in the development of uniform standards for heavy motor vehicles and trailers including road trains and B-doubles. These standards, which were essentially related to design and construction, were initially published as discussion papers and drafted in the form of codes.[70]

---

65   See Schedule, Part 1.

66   'MRC', 'operating mass', 'truck' (type 1 and 2), 'prime mover', 'long combination prime mover' (type 1 and 2), 'medium combination prime mover', 'long combination truck', 'medium combination truck', 'semi trailer', 'bus' (type 1 and 2), 'special purpose vehicle', 'compliance plate', 'indivisible load', 'load carrying vehicle', 'loaded mass'.

67   The formula being K x 4 cents; where K is the number of kilometres involved in the journey, and N is the number ascertained in accordance with the regulation.

68   Schedule 2, Part XVII, clause 32(1), (2), (3). National Road Transport Commission Act 1992 (Cth), Schedule, Part XII, clause 31.

69   However, if the Ministerial Council agree unanimously after the road transport legislation commences, any State or Territory not a party to the Heavy Vehicle Agreement may cease to pay funds for the operation of the Commission; amending the Heavy Vehicle Agreement, Schedule, Part XVII, clause 31. The Heavy Vehicle Agreement provides that a State or the Northern Territory will not submit legislation or take action to make regulations which, in force, would conflict with the Commonwealth road transport legislation. An amendment now adds the proviso that no proposed State or Northern Territory legislation concerning interstate trade or commerce in relation to road transport should proceed without first consulting the National Commission; see Schedule, Part XVII, clause 31.

70   See 'Integration of the Road Transport Law', discussion paper, June 1995, National Road Transport Commission, Chapter 2. See Pollard, M, 'Road Transport Reform – the Legislative Challenge', 1993, Chartered Institute of Transport National Conference, Perth, 13–16 September, p 270.

The National Road Transport Commission set up a Legislation Advisory Committee made up of legal and technical representatives of the jurisdictions concerned to advise on the implementation of technical and policy decisions, including the codes. The decision was made to promulgate matters of a mandatory nature in the regulations rather than in external documents.[71]

It was agreed that a bill (the 'Peg Bill') be prepared to provide the necessary regulation making powers and to deal with matters such as offences and penalties which are more would be more appropriately dealt with in the primary legislation. The subsequent legislation, the Road Transport Reform (Vehicles and Traffic) Act 1993 (Cth) was given the Royal Assent in January 1994.[72] The Act states in the preamble that its intent is to assist in the adoption of nationally uniform or consistent road transport laws and that it forms part of a scheme to create uniform road transport legislation, as envisaged by the agreements scheduled to the National Road Transport Commission Act 1991 (Cth) (the Heavy Vehicle and Light Vehicle Agreements) (s 2(1)).

The Road Transport Reform (Vehicles and Traffic)Act 1993 incorporates a range of heavy vehicle design, construction and operation issues. These cover:

(a) vehicle construction standards;

(b) mass and loading requirements;

(c) vehicle roadworthiness;

(d) access restrictions for oversize and overmass vehicles (such as B-doubles and road trains);[73]

(e) network access for other restricted access vehicles; and

(f) driving hours.

Also included are light vehicle matters having priority under the Light Vehicles Agreement; these include:

(a)   uniform traffic rules; and

(b)   light vehicle standards.

The scheme under the Road Transport Reform (Vehicles and Traffic) Act 1993 is designed to improve the safety and efficiency of transport on roads and other areas that are open to and used by the public; and reduce the costs of administration of that transport.

---

71 The reason for this decision was that there exists a community concern about delegated legislation in general and the availability of legislative instruments that are not published as formal legislation; see report of the Administrative Review Council on *Rule Making by Commonwealth Agencies,* May 1992 and *Operation of the Subordinate Legislation Act 1962,* 1993, discussion paper, Scrutiny of Acts and Regulations Committee of the Victorian Parliament, March.

72 See Minister of Transport's second reading speech, Senate, 18 August 1993; House of Representatives, 5 October 1993.

73 Regulations covering oversize and overmass vehicle operations were approved by the Ministerial Council in April 1995.

Light vehicle standards and roadworthiness will be accommodated by amending the Heavy Vehicle Standards Regulations to become the Vehicle Standards Regulations.[74] The Road Transport Reform (Vehicles and Traffic) Act 1993 ceases to be in force[75] when the National Road Transport Commission Act 1991 (Cth) ceases to be in force (s 5(1)). Even if the Act ceases to be in force, regulations continue as if they were laws made by the Legislative Assembly of the Australian Capital Territory, which may be amended or repealed by the Legislative Assembly (s 5(2)).

The Commission found no significant net benefit in extending the registration laws to light vehicles.[76]

Compliance and enforcement module

The development of a compliance strategy and legislative framework as part of the uniform road transport legislation is intended to allow regulators to adopt a flexible response to non-complying conduct in the road transport industry.[77]

Compliance and enforcement provisions include:

(a) offences and penalties;

(b) appointment of officers and their powers;

(c) evidentiary provisions;

(d) procedural matters; and

(e) review and appeals.

Under Part 2 of the Road Transport Reform (Vehicles and Traffic) Act 1993 (Cth) the Governor General is empowered to make regulations to apply as laws for the Australian Capital Territory and the Jervis Bay Territory (s 7(1)).

Regulations may provide for a matter by applying, adopting or incorporating national standards under the Motor Vehicle Standards Act 1989 (Cth) as in force at the time (s 8(2)).

Dangerous goods module

There currently exists a substantial measure of uniformity in the existing State and Territory regarding the carriage of dangerous goods by road as a result of the adoption by these jurisdictions of the Uniform Code for the Carriage of Dangerous Goods by Road and Rail. However, there are significant differences from jurisdiction to jurisdiction on matters such as penalty levels and enforcement procedures. The Road Transport Reform (Dangerous Goods) Act 1995 was passed by the Commonwealth

---

74 These amendments were submitted to the Ministerial Council in April 1995. Regulations for managing bus driver working hours were approved by the Ministerial Council in October 1994. Austroads – a draft set of uniform road rules are likely to be submitted in late 1998. See National Road Transport Commission website at http://www.pubserv.com.au/nrtc/reform 01.html.

75 Other than s 5(2).

76 The Road Transport Reform (Heavy Vehicle Standards) Regulations 1995 (no 42), the Road Transport Reform (Mass and Loading) Regulations 1995 (no 56) and the Road Transport Reform (Oversize and Overmass Vehicles) Regulations 1995 (no 12) came into operation in 1996.

77 Op cit, fn 70.

Parliament in March 1995. It establishes an integrated framework for the regulation of road transport of dangerous goods, containing provisions relating to enforcement, compliance and administration.[78]

Under common law, the consignor is liable to a carrier for all damages caused by dangerous goods that have been delivered to the carrier by the consignor, unless the nature of the goods has been declared to the carrier on delivery for carriage and accepted by the carrier in full knowledge of their dangerous attributes.[79] A common carrier is not obliged to carry dangerous goods.[80]

Provisions applying to National Road Transport Laws

It is intended that Part 3, Division 2 and the regulations in force from time to time will form part of the law of each jurisdiction of Australia.[81]

Division 2 provides for the Minister to declare, by notice in the government Gazette,[82] that the operation of the regulations, or specified parts:

(a) is suspended for a specified period; or

(b) is varied in a manner specified by the Minister (s 15(1)).[83]

Scope of the uniform road transport legislation

Neither the National Road Transport Commission Act 1991(Cth) nor the Agreements expressly sets out the scope concerning subject matter or effect of national legislation to be recommended by the Commission. The question has been posed as to whether the legislation is to be broadly framed to cover all aspects of road transport legislation or be only recommended where it comes within a narrow view of the objectives in the Agreements.[84]

The Commission recommends the broad view on the basis of the discussions prior to the Agreements, the impracticability of developing certain elements of legislation on

---

78 Accompanying regulations are being developed; these are due to be submitted to the Ministerial Council in December 1995. For State and Territory legislation, see the Dangerous Goods Act 1975 (NSW); 1985 (Vic); 1987 (NT); 1976 (Tas); the Dangerous Substances Act 1976 (SA); the Carriage of Dangerous Goods by Road Act 1984 (Qld); the Explosives and Dangerous Goods Act 1961 (WA); the Dangerous Goods Ordinance 1984 (Act).

79 Soames v British Empire Shipping Co (1880) 8 HL Cas 338.

80 Bamfield v Goole and Sheffield Transport Co [1910] 2 KB 94. See above for the general position of common carriers.

81 That is (a) the ACT and Jervis Bay Territory and (when they are adopted), (b) of each State and the Northern Territory (s 13). The provisions dealing with regulations for fees do not apply in the case of (b); see s 13(2) (see s 9(5) above).

82 Reference to the Minister and the government Gazette is to that of the jurisdiction concerned (s 14(2)). The Acts Interpretation Act 1901 (Cth) applies to the interpretation of Division 2 and the regulations when they are adopted by each State and the Northern Territory (s 14(1)).

83 Such a declaration must be consistent with the provisions relating to application and emergency orders in agreements scheduled to the National Road Transport Commission Act 1991 (s 15(2)).

84 See 'Integration of the Road Transport Law', 1995, discussion paper, National Road Transport Commission, June, p 11.

any other basis, and the wording of the Agreements themselves. In the Commission's view, its powers are those that the Agreements provide for it to have.

The Heavy Vehicle Agreement requires legislation, the Commission argues, that covers the field in relation to all aspects of heavy vehicle regulation, with the exception of 'economic regulation' defined in the Agreements. A similar broad obligation is placed on the Commission by the Light Vehicle Agreement.[85]

The Commission concludes that that the Agreements require it to develop the legislative framework of Uniform Road Transport Law as one which will accommodate both light and heavy vehicles.

In respect of the Uniform Road Transport Law as adopted by the States and the Northern Territory being intended to cover the field the Commission regards itself as bound to resolve the issue by reference to the wording of the Agreements.[86] By stating that the legislation recommended by the Commission is to apply in place of existing legislation, the Agreements strongly suggest an intention to cover the field.[87] The Commission concludes that in order to reconcile the Agreements with their stated objectives, the national law is intended to replace all existing substantive law relating to road transport and light vehicle transport and to cover the field.[88]

The Commission's position is that it is:

(a) required to recommend national legislation to replace State and Territory legislation dealing with all aspects of heavy vehicle construction and use, except economic regulation;

(b) required to similarly recommend national legislation dealing with all aspects of light vehicle construction and use, except economic regulation, charges and items subject to significant net benefit where this is not demonstrated; and

(c) at liberty to recommend a national legislative framework to accommodate significant net benefit items. Such legislation would not be implemented until and unless significant net benefit is shown.[89]

The Commission's views stated above have implications for existing Commonwealth legislation governing road transport.[90] While it is clear that the Motor Vehicle Standards Act 1989 (Cth) continues to govern new vehicle standards, in each Agreement the Commonwealth undertakes to amend that Act in accordance with a recommendation of the Commission not approved by the Ministerial Council. The Agreements are silent on

---

85 Except light vehicle charges are excluded and where the Commission is only able to recommend legislation if it is able to demonstrate 'significant net benefits' – the scope of this term not being clear in relation to charges.

86 See s 8(1) of the Agreement.

87 Discussion paper, p 18.

88 Subject to the effect of the clause 17(2)(c) exceptions in the Agreements, this conclusion, it is argued, is consistent with the intentions lying behind the Agreements; discussion paper, p 19.

89 See discussion paper, p 20. For the alternative approach see discussion paper pp 20–21.

90 See discussion paper, p 21.

the relationship with the Interstate Road Transport Act 1985 (Cth).[91] The implication is that it will be replaced by the new legislative scheme.

The Interstate Road Transport Act 1985

The Interstate Road Transport Act 1985 (Cth) together with the Interstate Road Transport Charge Act 1985 (Cth) came into effect on 1 January 1987. The Interstate Road Transport Act 1985 (Cth) is incorporated with the Interstate Road Transport Charge Act 1985 (Cth) and is read as one with the latter (s 3(1)).

Part II of the Interstate Road Transport Act 1985 Act (Cth) deals with registration of interstate motor vehicles.

Under Part V of the Act, operators are not permitted to carry on long distance interstate road transport business unless that person is either a holder of a Federal operator's licence or a State operator's licence (s 25).[92]

The Interstate Road Transport Charge Act 1985 (Cth) provides for the imposition of a charge by way of a tax in respect of registration of a motor vehicle or trailer under the Interstate Road Transport Act 1985 (Cth).[93]

The National Road Transport Commission

The National Road Transport Commission Act 1991 (Cth) which came into effect on 15 January 1992 set up the National Road Transport Commission.[94] This Agreement established the Ministerial Council for Road Transport.

The Commission has similar responsibilities regarding policy development to the light vehicle legislation in the case of the Heavy Vehicle Agreement and the road transport legislation.[95]

These cover:

(a) the proposed road transport legislation;

(b) proposed road charges, and a road use charge relating to vehicles operating within or across the boundary of a zone;

(c) charging principles;

(d) uniform reporting and audit regime;[96]

---

91 See below.

92 A court, on application from the licensing authority, may make an order disqualifying a person from taking part in the long distance interstate road transport business (s 27).

93 The amount of the charge in respect of the registration of a motor vehicle or trailer is the actual distance amount which the owner may nominate under the Interstate Road Transport Act 1985 (Cth). For the basis for the amount, see s 5; for provision for indexation of the charge, see s 6.

94 See Schedule 1 of the Act. For membership of the Commission, see s 6; for terms of appointment and duration, see ss 12 and 13. The Act ceases to be in force six years after its commencement (s 46).

95 National Road Transport Commission Act 1992 (Cth), Part IX, clause 20(1).

96 See Schedule, clause 30 (4).

(e) guidelines for the preparation of regulatory impact statements concerning proposed road transport legislation;

(f) recommending allowing the expiry of the road transport legislation, re-enactment for a further six years or less, or re-enactment in its existing or modified form;[97] and

(g) recommending application orders and emergency orders to the participating parties and the Australian Capital Territory.[98]

The Commission is charged with the responsibility for preparing regulatory impact statements accompanying the proposed Commonwealth road transport legislation submitted to the Ministerial Council.[99]

The Commission is obliged to report and provide advice to the Ministerial Council on the latter's direction (s 9). In carrying out its functions the Commission must, where appropriate and practicable, consult with government and government bodies, industry representatives, including the road transport industry and representatives of people living in rural or remote areas of Australia, and other interested people, bodies or organisations (s 10).

Ministerial Council

The Ministerial Council, under the National Road Transport Commission Act 1992 (Cth),[100] consists of Commonwealth, State, Northern Territory and the Australian Capital Territory Ministers and is known as the Ministerial Council for Road Transport[101] (clause 10) (subsequently referred to as the Council). The Council is made up of members representing each Party to the Heavy Vehicle Agreement, up to the date of the Commonwealth road transport legislation coming into force. After that date, membership of the Council is constituted by a Minister appointed by each participating party and the Australian Capital Territory (clause 11(1)). A member of the Council may appoint a delegate to attend a meeting of the Council in their place (clause 11(2)).

The Interstate Commission

The functions of the Interstate Commission have been absorbed into the Industrial Commission, the Interstate Commission Act 1975 (Cth) having been repealed.[102] The Minister under the Act is empowered to direct the Commission to investigate any

---

97 See Schedule, clause 38 (1).

98 For the powers of the Commission in relation to zones, see Schedule, Part IX, clause 20(2). To assist the Commission in the discharge of its duties under (a)–(g), it is required to consult interested persons and appoint committees; see Schedule, Part IX, clause 20(6).

99 Schedule, Part IX, clause 20(7) and (8).

100 Schedule, Part VI.

101 The functions of the Ministerial Council include consideration of policy questions relating to the uniform road transport legislation and approval of guidelines for the preparation of the regulatory impact statements produced by the National Commission; see Schedule, Part VII, clause 12, Part IX, clause 20(1)(e).

102 See Industry Commission Act 1990 (Cth), Part 7, s 48(2) (other than Part II, ss 19, 20, 24, 30(1)).

matter or matters relating to interstate transport (s 9(i)). These may include whether the terms and conditions of a service either of, or related to, interstate transport service is just or reasonable, whether any undue or unreasonable preference is given to any person, State, locality or class or type of transport, or in relation to a railway.

Road transport: State and Territory legislation

As previously outlined, State and Territory legislation governing road transport will be changed within the next two years to bring it into line with the uniform road transport law. Therefore, the existing State and Territory statutes and regulations dealing with road transport law are given here in outline and only with particular reference to commercial road freight and public passenger vehicles.

State and Territory road transport legislation

New South Wales

The principal Act governing regulation of road transport in the jurisdiction is the Traffic Act 1909.[103] Specific New South Wales road transport legislation has, in the past, been subject to invalidation by the High Court.[104]

State Transit Authority

The Transport Administration Act 1988 came into force on 16 January 1989 and replaced and repealed the Public Transport Commission Act 1972. The 1988 Act recast the State Rail Authority and the Urban Transit Authority under the name of the State Transit Authority (STA).

The general duties of the STA include the operation of bus and ferry services, including establishment of new services and discontinuance of existing services (ss 22–23). The STA is obliged to operate such services safely and efficiently and in accordance with sound commercial practice (s 23(1)). This provision does not, as a result, impose on the STA a duty that is enforceable by court proceedings or limit any other duty imposed on the STA by or under the Act (s 23(2)). The STA, without limiting any other functions conferred or imposed on it, may:

---

103 On uniform road transport law in New South Wales generally, see Britts, MMG, *Traffic Law (NSW)*, 4th edn, 1994, Sydney: Butterworths.

104 The State Transport (Co-ordination) Amendment Act 1954 and the State Transport Co-ordination (Barring of Claims and Remedies) Act 1954 was passed in response to the decision of the Judicial Committee of the Privy Council in *Hughes and Val Pty Ltd v New South Wales* [1955] AC 241; (1955) 93 CLR 1. Section 4 of the State Transport (Coordination) Amendment Act 1954 and the Third Schedule applied to persons operating or intending to operate a public motor vehicle in the course of and for the purpose of interstate trade. These provisions were declared invalid under s 92 of the Constitution by the High Court in *Hughes and Vale Pty Ltd v New South Wales (No 2)* (1956) 93 CLR 127. The State Transport Co-ordination (Barring of Claims and Remedies) Act 1954 was declared similarly invalid by the High Court in *Antill Ranger and Co Pty Ltd v Commissioner for Motor Vehicle Transport* (1956) 93 CLR 83; affirmed by the Privy Council [1956] AC 527; (1956) 94 CLR 177. See Britts, MMG, *Traffic Law (NSW)*, 4th edn, 1994, Sydney: Butterworths, para 8.430.

(a) conduct any business, whether or not related to the operation of its bus or ferry services, and for that purpose use any property or services of any staff of the authority;

(b) acquire and develop land;

(c) acquire or build, and maintain or dispose of, any vehicles, vessels, wharves, plant, machinery or equipment;

(d) maker and enter into contracts or arrangements for the carrying out of works or the performance of services for the supply of goods or materials;

(e) make and enter into contracts or arrangements with any person for the operation by that person, on such terms as may be agreed upon, of any of the Authority's bus or ferry services or any of the Authority's businesses; and

(f) appoint agents, and act as agent for other persons (s 24(1)).[105]

State Transit Co-ordination Advisory Council

The Transport Administration Act 1980 establishes a State Transit Co-ordination Advisory Council.[106]

The function of the Council is to advise the Minister and the Secretary of the Ministry of Transport on any matter relating to the development, co-ordination or regulation of passenger services in New South Wales (s 45).

Roads and Traffic Authority

The Roads and Traffic Authority has functions under the Transport Administration Act 1980, the State Roads Act 1986, the Traffic Act 1909, the Motor Vehicles Taxation Act 1988 and any other Act. It is a statutory body representing the Crown (s 46).[107]

The Traffic Act 1909 defines a number of key terms (s 2).[108]

Part 3 of the Traffic Act 1909 deals with offences under the Act[109] and Part 3A of the Traffic Act 1909 regulates the monitoring of heavy vehicles and vehicles carrying dangerous loads.

---

105 The Transport Administration Act 1988 set up a State Transit Authority Board; for composition, see s 25(3); for functions see s 26(2); for Chief Executive, see ss 27(1), 28(1), (2); for Ministerial direction, see s 29(1), (2); for corporate plan, see s 31(1), (2), (3), (4), (6).

106 For composition of the Council see s 44(1).

107 For appointment, functions and direction of the Chief Executive, see ss 48, 49. For functions of the Council, see Division 2 of the Transport administration Act 1980.

108 These include 'Authority', 'driver' 'coach', 'vehicle', 'motor vehicle'. A person steering a towed vehicle is not the driver of that vehicle; *Wallace v Major* [1946] KB 473; *Hampson v Martin* [1981] 2 NSWLR 782. However, a person steering a motor vehicle with the engine off downhill is driving it; *Saycell v Bool* [1948] 2 All ER 83. The driver of a vehicle to which a trailer is attached is also the driver of that trailer; *Lynch v Page* (1940) 57 WN (NSW) 161. Even if the motor vehicle is at rest on a public street or not being a motor vehicle within the definition and under reg 93 of the Motor Vehicle Regulations under the Traffic Act 1909 a car may be a 'motor vehicle' although it is impossible to drive it because of its condition; *Kunze v Vowles: ex parte Vowles* (1955) QSR 591. If the vehicle is temporarily without is engine, it is still within the definition of a 'motor vehicle'; *Newberry v Simmonds* [1961] 2 QB 345. This will not be so if the removal of the engine is permanent; *Smart v Allean* [1963] 1 QB 291. A bulldozer was held by the Supreme Court of Tasmania to be 'motor vehicle' for the purposes s 3 of the Traffic Act 1925 (Tas); *Clark v Felhberg* [1969] Tas SR 190 (NC 11). A boring plant attached to a motor car is a trailer; *Lynch v Page* (1940) 57 WN (NSW) 161.

109 See Motor Traffic Regulations 1935 made under s 3 of the Traffic Act 1909. See Britts, MMG, *Traffic Law (NSW)*, 4th edn, 1992, Sydney: Butterworths, pp 16–117.

Exemptions may be granted by order published in the *Gazette* or in a newspaper circulating in New South Wales or by notice in writing signed by the Chief Executive of the Authority or a person authorised by the Authority and served on the person whose vehicle is, or is to be, exempted.[110]

Driving hours of heavy motor vehicles and coaches are dealt with in Part 11A of the Regulations. Part 11A regulates driving and rest period requirements, the issue of, and requirement to carry, log books the keeping and production of records and offences.[111]

Part 8A of the Motor Traffic Act 1989 applies to road trains.[112]

Tow trucks as such are regulated by the Tow Truck Act 1989 and the Tow Truck Regulations 1990.

Passenger Transport Act 1990

The Passenger Transport Act 1990 commenced on 14 July 1990 and regulates the licensing of operators and drivers of public passenger vehicles, including buses, taxis and ferries. The Act contains key definitions (s 3).[113]

Public passenger vehicles generally

The Act, by s 4, requires:

(a) the accreditation by the Director General of the operators and drivers involved in public passenger services;

(b) dispensing with the licensing of ferries and buses used provide a public passenger service, providing instead for:

(i) ferry and bus services to be operated under fixed term contracts entered into between the Director General and operators;

(ii) deregulation of long distance and tourist services; and

(iii) regulation of government and non-government buses and ferries on a more equal basis;

(c) encourage the provision of school bus services on a more commercial basis, without disregarding the reasonable expectations of traditional service operators; and

(d) to consolidate and re-enact (with modifications) the provisions of the Transport Licensing Act 1931 relating to the regulation of taxi-cabs and private hire

---

110 See reg 126N. For vehicles exempted from the Traffic (Monitoring Devices) Exemption Order 1991, see Britts, MMG, regs 337–38. See application of Part 10A of the Motor Traffic Regulations by reg 123B. For categories of vehicles exempted from Part 10A of the Regulations, see Traffic (Speed Limiting Requirements) Exemption Order 1991, para 4; see Britts, *Traffice Law (NSW)*, *op cit*, p 339.

111 See Part IIA, reg 126A; reg 126B, C; reg 126G.

112 Defined in s 2 of the Motor Traffic Regulations.

113 These definitions include 'bus', 'ferry', 'long distance service', 'private hire vehicle' 'taxi-cab', 'tourist service', 'public passenger service', 'public passenger vehicle', and 'regular passenger service'. A taxi-cab is a public motor vehicle; see *ex p Taxi Services Pty Ltd; Re Commissioner for Road Transport and Tramways* (1937) 37 (NSW) 504; 54 WN 201. In relation to 'plying for hire', see *Nuss v Donaldson* (1930) 31 SR (NSW) 63. See Britts, *op cit*, para 8.1060.

vehicles and (without substantial revision) the provisions of the Transfer of Public Vehicles (Taxation) Act 1969.

Part 2 of the Act deals with the credentials of operators and drivers.[114]

Part 3 deals with Regular Passenger Services.

Service contracts

Part 3 provides for the entry into a service contract with the Director General by the operator or driver in connection with any regular passenger service within New South Wales (s 16).[115]

Part 3 distinguishes between commercial and non-commercial service contracts (s 18). Under a commercial contract, the holder's enumeration is to be derived from revenue generated by passenger's fares. Under a non-commercial contract, the holder's renumeration is to be derived from revenue generated by passenger's fares. Under a non-commercial contract, the holder's remuneration is to be a contract price, or remuneration fixed at an agreed rate, payable by the Crown to the holder in the manner provided by the contract.

Taxi-cabs and hire vehicles

Part 4 of the Act governs the regulation of taxi-cabs and private hire vehicles. Division 1 deals principally with licensing requirements (ss 29–39), stand-by taxi-cabs (s 40), authority required for the operation of taxi-service radio communication network (s 41), operation of taxi-cab meters (s 54) and inspection of vehicles (s 42).

Passenger Transport Regulation Act 1990

The Passenger Transport Regulation Act 1990[116] covers operators and drivers of public passenger vehicles (Part 2), public passenger services (Part 3), rights and obligations of passengers and drivers (Part 4), special provisions relating to ferries (Part 5) and similar provisions relating to taxi-cabs and private hire vehicles (Part 6).

---

114 See Division 1; s 7, Accreditation; Division 3, Fees.

115 As to the terms and provisions of such service contracts, see s 17.

116 SR 832 (Part 2) 1990; commenced 14 July 1990. For limits on passengers to be carried by a bus driver, see reg 31C; for assistance to be rendered by a taxi driver in relation to loading of passenger's luggage and the care to be taken by the taxi driver in removal, loading and conveyance of goods or luggage, see reg 60. See also the Transport Administration (Government Bus and Ferry Services) Regulation 1989; the Transport Administration (Transport Districts) Regulation 1989; the Transport (Delegation) Regulation 1989; the Transport (Penalty Notices) Regulation 1989 and the Transport Administration (Traffic Control-SRA and STA Land) Regulation 1989.

Victoria

Introduction

The Transport Act 1983 repealed the Road Traffic Act 1958[117] and set up the State Transport Authority, the Metropolitan Transit Authority, the Road Construction Authority and the Road Traffic Authority. The Public Transport Corporation and the Roads Corporation were established by the Transport Amendment Act 1989 replacing the previous organisations.[118]

Public Transport Corporation

The Public Transport Corporation was set up by the Transport (Amendment Act) 1992,[119] which came into effect on 24 November 1992 and established new management and accountability arrangements.[120]

The function of the Public Transport Corporation is to efficiently manage and provide a safe and reliable public transport system in Victoria that has due recognition for the needs and interests of the users of that system and the tax payers of Victoria (s 14).

Functions of the Public Transport Corporation

The functions of the Public Transport Corporation are outlined in Part III of the Transport Act 1983.[121] These include provision for the management and operation of transport services and facilities for passengers and freight. It arranges transport operators for the provision of transport facilities and services, operates as an employing authority for all officers engaged in the provision of railway and ancillary services in Victoria, and controls, maintains and co-ordinates all such services in Victoria. The Public Transport Corporation also is empowered to provide, manage and operate tourist and recreational facilities. The functions of the corporation[122] include the provision and management of operation of transport services and facilities for passengers and freight.

The Public Transport Corporation is not a common carrier (s 49).[123]

---

117 Re-enacting the relevant parts of the Road Traffic Act 1958 and related legislation in the Transport Act 1983. The latter are the Melbourne Tramways Act 1958; the Ministry of Transport Act 1958; the Railways Act 1958; the Transport Regulation Act 1958; the Melbourne Rail Loop Authority Act 1970 and the Recreation Vehicles Act 1973. The bodies replaced by the new organisations were the Victorian Railways Board, the Melbourne and Metropolitan Tramways Board, the Country Roads Board, the Road Safety and Traffic Authority, the Transport Regulation Board, the Railway Construction and Property Board and the Melbourne Underground Rail Loop Authority. For a general reference to road transport law in Victoria, see Vickery, NA, *Motor and Traffic Law (Victoria)* Sydney: Butterworths (looseleaf).

118 The two new bodies were formed by the merging of the State Transport Authority, the Metropolitan Transit Authority, the Road Construction Authority and the Road Traffic Authority respectively.

119 Section 4, repealing Division 2, Part II of the Transport Act 1983, replacing the Victorian Transport Directorate.

120 See s 1 of the Transport (Amendment) Act 1992.

121 Part III, Division 3, ss 13–15. Part II of Schedule 1 of the Act applies to the State Transport Authority; s 13(3). The Public Transport Corporation includes the functions of the former State Transport Authority and the Metropolitan Transit Authority.

122 Part III, Division 3, ss 15–16. Part II of Schedule 1 applies to the Metropolitan Transit Authority; s 15(3); see now the Public Transport Corporation.

123 The State Transport Authority and the Metropolitan Transit Authority had a similar status.

Functions of the Roads Corporation

The Roads Corporation includes the functions of the former Road Construction Authority and the Road Traffic Authority.[124]

These functions include provision of registration and licensing procedures, development and implementation of traffic management strategies and practice.[125]

Regulation of traffic, registration and licensing of vehicles

Part VI of the Transport Act 1983 regulates traffic and the registration and licensing of vehicles. Part VI covers recreational vehicles, commercial passenger vehicles, buses, tow trucks, commercial goods vehicles and passenger ferry services.

Commercial passenger vehicles

Part VI, Division 5 governs the regulation of commercial passenger vehicles.[126]

The Road Transport Licensing Tribunal has been abolished by the Transport (Amendment) Act 1993 (s 8)[127] and in the case of refusal, suspension or cancellation a commercial passenger vehicle licence an applicant or holder may apply to the Administrative Appeals Tribunal for a review of the particular decision by the Roads Corporation (ss 143C and 146C).

A goods vehicle used as a passenger vehicle must be licensed for that purpose.[128]

Buses

Part VI, Divisions 6 and 7 of the Transport Act 1983 govern the operation of private buses and hire drive buses.[129] As with commercial passenger vehicle licences, application for a private bus licence has to be made to the Roads Corporation in the form and manner approved by that Corporation.[130] The Transport Act 1983 contains provisions for regulations concerning private buses.[131]

---

124 Part III, Division 3, ss 17–18. Part II of Schedule 1 applies to the Road Construction Authority; s 17(3). These functions include maintenance, upgrading and extension of the State's road network and the determination of load and speed limits.

125 Part III, Division 3, ss 19–20. Part II of Schedule 1 applies to the Road Traffic Authority; s 19(2); see now Roads Corporation. On the power of the Governor to make regulations, see s 56 of the Transport Act 1983. See Vickery, *op cit*, paras 2711–13.

126 Sections 138–162 of the Transport Act 1983. In granting and refusing a commercial vehicle licence, the Roads Corporation is directed by s 143 of the Transport Act 1983 to take into account specified matters.

127 The Act came wholly into effect on 30 May 1994; repealing Part VI, Division 4 of the Transport Act 1983. For the powers of the Roads Corporation to suspend a licence see ss 143A(11) and 147A(3); to cancel a licence see ss 143A(11), 144B(1B), 146(1) and 147A(3); to alter licence conditions or route or area for which it is granted see ss 146(1) and 146B of the Transport Act 1983 as amended by s 17 of the Transport (Amendment) Act 1993. See also s 25 of the Transport (Amendment) Act 1993 regarding cancellation in respect of a licensed vehicle. Section 148 of the Transport Act 1983 dealing with renewal of commercial passenger vehicle licences is repealed by s 27 of the Transport (Amendment) Act 1993.

128 Section 155(1) of the Transport Act 1983, as amended by s 27 of the Transport (Amendment) Act 1993.

129 Sections 163–70.

130 Section 164(1) and (2)Transport Act 1983, as amended by s 32 of the Transport (Amendment) Act 1993.

131 See s 166 of the Transport (Amendment) Act 1993. Section 33 repeals s 166(1) paras (c) and (d).

Tow trucks

Tow trucks are regulated by Part VI, Division 8.[132] An applicant may apply to the Administrative Appeals Tribunal for a review of a decision by the Roads Corporation to refuse to grant an application for a tow truck licence or its cancellation.[133]

Commercial Goods Vehicles

Commercial Goods Vehicles are regulated by Part VI, Division 9.[134] Commercial goods vehicles are no longer required to be licensed.[135]

Interstate commercial goods vehicles do not require a permit.[136]

Ferries

Part VI, Division 10 regulates ferries.[137] A ferry is required to be licensed and an application must include, amongst other matters, the routes on which it is intended to operate and the maximum number of passengers and vehicles it is to carry.[138] The Authority may approve, refuse or vary an application for a licence.[139]

The Authority may cancel a ferry licence after notifying the owner where it is satisfied that the licensed ferry is no longer fit or suitable for the purpose for which the ferry is licensed.[140]

Queensland

The principal Acts governing road transport regulation in Queensland are the State Transport Act 1960 and the Traffic Act 1960. Commercial vehicle operations in Queensland are regulated by the State Transport Act 1960.[141] The Traffic Act 1949 governs general regulation concerning traffic operations. The State Transport Act 1960

---

132 Sections 171–85 of the Transport Act 1983 as amended by the Transport (Amendment) Act 1993, ss 34–46. With respect to regulations, see s 185(1) of the Transport Act 1983, amended by s 46 of the Transport (Amendment) Act 1993. See Transport (Tow Truck) Regulations 1983 (SR 344 of 1983).

133 Section 36 of the Transport (Amendment) Act 1993, inserting new ss 173A, AB after ss 173, 174A of the Transport Act 1983.

134 Transport Act 1983, ss 186–97. For regulations for commercial goods vehicles, see s 197 of the Transport Act 1983, as amended by s 54 of the Transport (Amendment) Act 1993.

135 Section 47 of the Transport (Amendment) Act 1993, repealing ss 186 and 187 of the Transport Act 1983.

136 Section 51 of the Transport (Amendment) Act 1993, repealing s 191 of the Transport Act 1983.

137 Sections 198–207 of the Transport Act 1983. For definition of 'passenger ferry' and 'Victorian waters', see s 198.

138 Section 203.

139 Section 203.

140 Section 206.

141 See generally, Martin, P and Morley, S, *Motor Vehicle Law* (Queensland), Sydney: Butterworths (looseleaf). The State Transport Act 1960 came into operation on 27 February 1961. See also the State Transport Regulation 1987 (SR 30 of 1987); see Martin and Morley, para 3501. Tow trucks are regulated by the Tow truck Act 1973 and the Tow Truck Regulation 1988 and are not discussed here; see Martin and Morley, paras 6011, 6201. For definition of 'motor car', 'motor truck', 'motor vehicle' and 'passenger service licence', see s 6 of the State Transport Act 1980. 'Passenger' is defined in s 5 of the Act as a person being carried or about to be carried under a hiring; see in relation to a taxi hiring *Murphy v Quaresmini ex p Murphy* [1978] Qd 210.

provisions which will be noted are the for administration of the Transport Act, hire vehicles and road passenger services.

Vehicles for hire

Part III of the Transport Act governs the hire of vehicles, including trailers that are:

(a) kept or let for hire (other than under a hire purchase agreement) without the services of a driver;

(b) used for the carriage of passengers or goods, or both passengers and goods, for hire;

(c) plying or standing for hire for the carriage of passengers or goods, or both passengers and goods (s 15(2)).[142]

Part IIA of the Transport Act specifically deals with rented vehicles.[143]

Road passenger services

Part IV of the Transport Act deals with road passenger services. The passenger service licensee shall carry on the authorised service in compliance with its conditions unless otherwise permitted or directed by the Director General. The service authorised by the license may not be sold or disposed of without the Director General's consent or contrary to any terms and conditions in his consent (s 29).

Transfer of a license may be made subject terms and conditions determined by the Director General.[144] The Director General may, at his discretion, refuse to transfer any passenger service licence and shall refuse such a transfer if he considers it to be contrary to, or not desirable in, the public interest (s 30).[145]

Permits for passenger service and goods vehicles

Part V of the Transport Act regulates the issue of permits by the Director General for the carrying of goods or passengers on any road or in district (s 37). An applicant must satisfy the Director General that every vehicle to which the application relates is appropriately insured.[146]

---

142 The Director General may offer any new licence for sale by public tender at a price fixed by him or her (s 18). For prohibition of words such as 'cab', 'licensed cab', 'for hire' or 'vacant' on unlicensed vehicles, see s 21.

143 A rental vehicle operator's licence is in force for seven years unless cancelled suspended or surrendered; the licence may not be assigned transferred, leased or encumbered, see s 24A.

144 In considering an application for transfer, the Director General shall have regard to the following: (a) the experience and character of the transferee and his financial capacity to carry on the service; (b) the amount which the transferee is paying for the service, and the value at the time of application of the vehicles and other property used in such business which are acquired by the transferee; (c) any other factors the Director General considers relevant.

145 An application may be made for transfer of part of a passenger service; see s 30(4).

146 In accordance with the provisions of the Motor Vehicles Insurance Acts 1936–59 and the Main Roads Acts 1920–59 (s 37(10)).

The Director General may require any holder of a passenger service license to make a approved passenger carrying vehicle available for an authorised and licensed service (s 42).[147]

South Australia

The Motor Vehicles Act 1959–82 includes the regulation and registration of motor vehicles, driver's licences and third party motor insurance.[148]

Classes of licences

Part IV of The Motor Vehicle Act Regulations 1960–81 includes provision for classes of driver licences under the Act (s 72).[149] The prescribed classifications are set out in Part IV.[150]

Licence conditions, exemptions, cancellations, licence transfer and surrender

The Regulations provide for the imposition of a condition on a licence or learner's permit (reg 49a). Provisions are made for exemption from holding a class or licence (reg 50(a)–(c)). Prescribed licence fees are set out in Part VII of the regulations.[151]

Tow trucks

Part IIIc of the Act regulates the certification of tow-trucks. Provisions are made for the requirement of tow truck drivers to hold certificates, application for certificates, entitlement, renewal, conditions of such certificates and their surrender and suspension.[152]

Western Australia

The Transport Co-ordination Act 1966 includes provisions regulating the licensing of public vehicles. General traffic regulation is covered by the Road Traffic Act 1974. The Transport Co-ordination Act 1966, provides for the co-ordination, planning and

---

147 The Director General may require any holder of a passenger service licence to make an approved passenger carrying vehicle available for an authorised and licensed service. For powers of the Director General to cancel or suspend permits in the public interest or for breach of the Act or permit conditions, see s 43. Regarding permit fees payment and as a condition of a permit for the carriage of both passengers and goods, see s 44.

148 For a definition of 'motor vehicle', 'interstate licence' and 'Tribunal' (Tow Truck Tribunal), see s 5. For exemptions of vehicles, see ss 10–13, 19a. The Governor is empowered to make regulations for administration and carrying out the objects of the Act; see s 145.

149 Regulations, reg 35a.

150 Regulations, Schedule, col 1. Transitional provisions are set out for licences in force before 3 June 1991 or issued three months after that date; reg 35b(1).

151 Regulations, Schedule, col 1. Transitional provisions are set out for licences in force before 3 June 1991 or issued three months after that date; reg 35b(1). For cancellation of registration, see Part III of the Regulations, regs 54–55a, 60; for transfer of registration, see regs 56–57; for surrender of a licence, see reg 66.

152 Part (ii)(c), ss 98(d)–(i). For the composition of the Tribunal, see s 98(pc)(1), (2); for its powers, see s 98(pd)(1), (2) and s 98(pf). For application to the Tribunal by an aggrieved person for a review of the decision or order by the Registrar under the accident towing roster scheme, see s 98(pc), no liability attaches to the Registrar of Motor Vehicles, a member of the consultative committee or a member of the Tow truck Tribunal for an act or omission in good faith in performance or discharge of a power, function or duty under the Motor Vehicles Act 1959; see s 98(pg).

advancement of all forms of transport in Western Australia and the review, control of licensing of transport services.[153]

The Transport Co-ordination Act 1966 is to be construed subject to the Commonwealth Constitution Act so as not to exceed the legislative power of Western Australia (s 5).

Administration

The Minister administering the Transport Co-ordination Act 1966 is for that purpose a body corporate.[154] The Minister is also empowered to set up Transport Strategy Committees to advise the Minister on transport policy. The members of such a committee may be appointed and removed at the Minister's discretion (s 7B).

Buses

Part III, Division 1 of the Act deals with public vehicle licensing.[155] Under Division 2 every application for a bus licence has to set out:

(a) the routes in the area intended the bus is to operate;

(b) a description of the vehicle;

(c) the maximum number of passengers to be carried at any one time by the vehicle;

(d) the service proposed to be provided;

(e) the fares proposed to be charged; and

(f) other particulars that may be prescribed (s 25).

Commercial goods vehicles

Commercial goods vehicle licensing is dealt with under Part III, Division 3.[156]

In granting or refusing a licence, the Minister may take into account the same factors as for bus licences (s 36).

---

153 Sections 19–23 of the Transport Co-ordination Act 1966. The objects of the Transport Co-ordination Act 1966 are to co-ordinate transport resources in Western Australia; provide reliable, efficient and economic transport services by rationalisation and control if necessary and by reduction or elimination of controls under the Act where practicable (s 3). The Transport Co-ordination Act 1966 defines commercial goods vehicle, omnibus and transport service (s 4).

154 The Minister is empowered to join with any body, including a corporation, to carry out research or studies to improve transport or transport safety within the Commonwealth (ss 7 and 7A). For the power of the Governor to make regulations for the purposes of the Transport Co-ordination Act 1966, see s 60.

155 In granting or refusing a licence the Mister may consider one or more of the following factors; the necessity of the service proposed and public convenience; the adequacy of the present service; the condition of the roads in the proposed route or area; the interests of the persons requiring the proposed service and of the community generally (s 26). Each bus licence is subject to the implied condition of fitness and serviceability of the vehicle (s 28). The Minister may attach conditions to a bus licence including route and area of operation (s 29) and a permit may be granted to the operator permitting deviation from the licensed route or operation on a route not specified in the licence (s 31).

156 No commercial goods vehicle licence is required for a vehicle specified in the First Schedule to the Transport Co-ordination Act 1966 (s 33(4)). For distance limitations on commercial goods vehicle licences see, ss 33 and 34.

The Minister may grant or refuse an application for a licence (s 37) and attach conditions to a licence concerning operation on or in specified routes or areas (s 39).[157]

Ferries

Division 4A regulates the licensing and operation of ferries.

Taxi-cars

Part IIIB regulates the licensing of taxi-cars in country districts. A taxi-car is defined as a vehicle that is used for the purpose of standing or plying for hire or otherwise for the carrying of passengers for reward.[158] Taxi-cars generally are regulated by the Taxi-car Control Act 1985.[159]

Traffic regulation

The Road Traffic Act 1974 deals generally with traffic regulation.[160]

Vehicle licensing

Part III of the Act governs vehicle licensing.[161] Licences for vehicles issued by another State or Territory are not regarded as a licence granted for the purposes of the Act (s 16(2)).[162] The Traffic Board may refuse to grant a licence under Part III if the vehicle does not meet the prescribed standards or requirements or the vehicle is unfit for the purpose of the licence (s 23).[163]

Tasmania

Tasmanian road transport legislation is principally made up of two major enactments, the Traffic Act 1925 and the Transport Act 1981. Those aspects of both statutes dealt with here relate to the general powers and duties of the Transport Commission and the regulation of public transport.

The Transport Commission

(a) General powers and duties of the Commission

The general powers and duties of the Transport Commission are laid down in Part VI, s 58(1) of the Traffic Act 1925. These include considering and determining licence applications; fares, freights and charges and traffic areas.

---

157 It is an implied condition of every licence that the vehicle is maintained in a fit and serviceable condition, the provisions of the Road Traffic Act 1974 are complied with, the limitation of driving hours and relevant award conditions are complied with and that the vehicle does not carry a load over that required by the licence (s 38).

158 See ss 47Z–47ZG.

159 Without limiting the power under s 60 of the Transport Co-ordination Act 1966.

160 See definitions of 'motor vehicle', 'omnibus', 'passenger vehicle' (s 5).

161 Vehicle classes are set out in the First Schedule to the Road Traffic Act 1974.

162 For a definition of a 'commercial vehicle' see the description in the First Schedule to the Act.

163 For cancellation and transfer of vehicle licences, see ss 23A and 24. For the power of the Governor to make regulations required by the Act, see Part IX (s 111).

The Commission has powers which include the regulation and control of all or any means of transport by road, water, or air and the co-ordination of transport services, and the improvement of the means and facilities for transport within Tasmania.

The Commission also has powers to operate shipping services between Tasmania and interstate as well as within Tasmania (s 5(2)).[164]

(b) Functions

In the exercise of its functions under the Traffic Act 1925, the Commission is required to have particular regard to criteria which include the suitability of the routes on which a service may be provided under a licence; whether the proposed service is necessary or desirable in the public interest and the co-ordination of all forms of transport, including transport by rail (s 58(2)).[165]

The functions of the Commission under the Transport Act 1981 include facilitation of measures for the co-ordination, improvement, and economic operation, of the means of, and facilities for, transport in Tasmania and the administration of the Traffic Act 1925 (s 6(1)).

(c) By laws and regulations

The Commission may make bylaws in respect of the Commission, or branch, officers or employees. Such bylaws are not statutory rules for the purposes of the Rules Publication Act 1953 (Tasmania) (s 24(1) and (2)).[166]

Part III of the Traffic Act 1925 deals with the licensing and operation of public vehicles, Part IIIA governs appeals from the Commission's decisions to the Public Vehicles Licensing Appeal Tribunal and Part VI deals with the general powers and duties of the Commission. The Traffic Act 1925 covers both private and public motor vehicles and aircraft (s 14AB(4)).[167]

---

164 The Commission also has power to enter into contracts with any person for the carrying on, and maintenance of, transport services; carry on as a commercial undertaking the manufacture, maintenance and repair, and sale of light engineering products; grant exemptions from payments or obligations (s 5(1)); contract with other persons to maintain transport services in an emergency (s 6(1)); collect statistics required under regulations (s 5); contract for professional, consulting and technical services (Transport Amendment Act 1986);

165 The Commission is also required by s 58(2) to consider the suitability of routes, the extent of existing adequate service, the conditions of the roads involved; the traffic needs of the district, traffic area or locality; elimination of unnecessary services; the suitability of the applicant to hold the licence applied for. The Commission may, with Ministerial consent, hold public inquiries into the above or any matters relating to transport (s 58(3)). The Commission, for the purpose of a public inquiry, has all the powers and authority conferred on a Commission appointed by the Governor, Evidence Act 1919 (Tasmania), Division II, Part II. For critical comment, amongst other matters, on the reform of the public vehicle licensing system in Tasmania, see Livermore, J, *Public Inquiry into the Modal Split of Bulk Traffic between Road and Rail in Tasmania*, Department of Transport and Works, Hobart, November 1992; see also Joy, S, *Review of Tasmania's Public Vehicle Licensing System*, 1988, Hobart: Transport Tasmania.

166 See the Traffic (Vehicle Loads and Dimensions) Regulations 1975 (SR 293 of 1975); Traffic (Public Vehicles) Regulations 1967 (SR 213 of 1967); Traffic (General and Local) Regulations 1956 (SR 172 of 1956); Traffic (Miscellaneous) Regulations 1968 (SR 143 of 1968). For the power of the Governor to make regulations for the purposes of the Transport Act 1981, see s 27.

167 Part III does not apply to any vehicle, driver, conductor of the Metropolitan Transport Trust (s 29).

Public vehicle licensing

A public vehicle, for the purposes of the Act, includes any vehicle or aircraft used as a public vehicle (s 14AB(4)), (s 14AB(5)).

Classification of vehicles

The Motor Vehicle Taxation Act 1981 provides for the classification of vehicles.[168]

Public vehicle classification

Under Part III of the Traffic Act 1925, referred to as the Act, the Commission may issue public vehicle licences (s 15(2)).

(i) Coach licences

A coach licence authorises the use of a vehicle a public vehicle for the carriage of passengers and goods between places on such routes as specified in the licence (s 15(3)).

(ii) Bus and cab licences

A bus licence similarly authorises the use of a vehicle for the carriage of passengers between places within the area in respect of which it is issued (s 15(3)).

A cab licence authorises a vehicle to ply or stand for hire in any public street in the area in respect of which the licence is issued for the carriage of passengers in that area (s 15(3)).[169]

(iii) Hire car licences

A hire car licence authorises the use of the vehicle for the carriage of passengers (other than on any part of excluded roads in the area of the licence) between any places within Tasmania and also authorises the vehicle to ply or stand for hire as in the case of a taxi licence (s 15(3)).

(iv) Carrier licences

A carrier licence authorises the use of a vehicle for the carriage of goods between places in respect of which it is issued, but does not authorise that vehicle to be used in the carrying on of a goods transport service between two extreme points (s 15(3)).[170]

Public vehicle licences; transfer, exemptions and charges, conditions

A licence holder may apply to the Commission to have the licence transferred to a person nominated in the application[171] and the Commission may grant exemptions.[172]

---

168 Motor Vehicle Taxation Act 1981, Schedule 1; for definition of 'commercial goods vehicle', 'omnibus' and 'articulated vehicle', see s 3(1) of the Act.

169 A bus licence may only be issued for vehicle capable of carrying more than eight adults, excluding the driver, s 15(6); a cab licence may only be similarly issued where not more than eight adults are carried (s 15(7)).

170 For ancillary licences, see s 15(3); a licence for the carriage of passengers also authorises the use of that vehicle for passenger's luggage (s 15(4)).

171 For transfer of a licence for its unexpired term, see s 19(2), (3) and (3A).

172 See Traffic Act 1925, ss 20(1), 20A(1), 20B(1) and 20B(2).

The Commission, when issuing a licence, may impose any conditions and restrictions it thinks necessary or desirable (s 17(1)).[173]

The Public Vehicles Appeals Tribunal may cancel or suspend a public vehicle licence on complaint of the Commission.[174]

Appeals to the Public Vehicles Appeals Tribunal

A holder of a public vehicle licence may appeal to the Public Vehicle Appeals Tribunal against the refusal of the Commission to renew a licence, or its imposition of any restriction or condition on a licence or refusal by the Commission to transfer a licence (s 30B(1)).[175]

Australian Capital Territory

The road traffic law of the Australian Capital Territory governs general driving laws and only peripherally deals with the regulation of buses and freight vehicles.[176]

Private hire cars and taxi licences

Transferable taxi licences are defined and limitations placed on the grant and transfer of taxi licences (s 27(1B). Limitation is also placed on the number of taxi licences the Registrar of Motor Vehicles may grant (s 27B).[177]

Bus service licences

The Registrar is empowered to grant a motor bus service licence to an applicant who must apply in writing stating certain matters.[178]

Licensed goods vehicles

The Registrar may grant a licence for any motor vehicle to ply for hire for the carriage of goods (s 2(15)).

Exemptions

Certain vehicles are exempted from the licensing provisions of the Act.

---

173 See also ss 17(2) and (3).

174 For other grounds of cancellation or suspension by the Tribunal, see ss 26(6A), 22(6B) and 22(7).

175 The Tribunal may make any order it thinks just and reasonable in the circumstances (unless it dismisses the appeal) and the Commission has to comply with such an order; see s 30B(8).

176 For definitions of 'B-double', 'light truck' and 'motor omnibus', see s 4 of the Motor Traffic Act 1974. Part II of the Act deals with the registration and licensing of vehicles; Part III governs licences for public motor vehicles for a review of a decision made by the Minister by the Australian Capital Territory Tribunal, see 217C. The Executive is empowered to make regulations consistent with the Act; see Motor Traffic Regulations 1993.

177 For licensing of private hire cars and taxis for tourist purposes, see s 28. For the powers of the Registrar to suspend private car hire or taxi licences see, s 30.

178 See s 33.

Northern Territory

Road transport regulation in the Northern Territory is effectively embodied in the Traffic Act 1987,[179] the Traffic Regulations 1988,[180] and the Commercial Passenger (Road) Transport Act 1991.

Administration of the Traffic Act is governed by Part II. The Minister is given authority to appoint a Director and Deputy Director of Transport (s 6).[181]

The Commercial Passenger (Road) Transport Act 1991 (no 34 of 1991)[182] regulates the carrying of passengers in motor vehicles for hire or reward within the Northern Territory.

A commercial passenger vehicle is defined as a taxi, private hire car, motor omnibus, tourist vehicle or special passenger vehicle.[183]

Accreditation

An operator of a commercial passenger vehicle is required to be accredited. The Director may refuse, accept or allow an applicant to amend an application for accreditation, or accept it as amended (s 9(1)).[184]

Taxi licences

The Minister may declare an area a taxi area by notice in the *Gazette* and determine the number of taxi licences which may be granted by the Director or held in the taxi area (s 16).[185]

Private hire cars

A person proposing to operate a private hire car must hold a private hire car licence prior to operation.

---

179 Commenced 20 June 1988. For definitions of motor vehicle and trailer, see s 3 of the Traffic Act 1987; 'articulated vehicle', 'goods vehicle' and 'road train' are defined by reg 3 of the Traffic Regulations.

180 (SR 19 of 1988.)

181 The Administrator of the Northern Territory is empowered to make regulations under the Act; see s 53. Schedule 2 to the Traffic Act 1987 lists the Acts repealed; see s 55.

182 As amended by the Commercial Passenger (Road) Transport Act 1992 (no 29 of 1992) and the Commercial Passenger (Road) Transport Amendment Act 1992 (no 59 of 1992). The Commercial Passenger (Road) Transport Act 1991 came into force on 27 October 1992.

183 See s 3, defining 'motor omnibus', 'private hire car', 'route service', 'special passenger vehicle', 'substitute taxi' (see s 29),' supplementary taxi' (see s 31), 'taxi', 'tourist vehicle' and 'urban service area' (see s 47).

184 For ground of such refusal, see s 9(3).

185 For number of licences in taxi area, see s 17; offering of licences by tender or auction, see ss 18 and 19; residency or business location requirement for issue, see s 20; endorsement of registration number, see s 22; granting licence subject to conditions, see s 23; limitation of carrying of passengers to designated taxi area, see s 24; period of licence, see s 25; transfer of licence, see s 26; licence as security for loan or liability, see s 27; grant of a substitute licence, see ss 29 and 30; grant of supplementary taxi licences, see s 31.

Motor omnibuses

A person proposing to operate a motor omnibus licence is required to hold a motor omnibus licence before commencing the operation (s 39).[186]

Pioneer routes

The Director is empowered to declare certain routes to be pioneer routes.

Urban service areas

The Director may, by notice in the *Gazette*, declare an area specified in the notice, being an area wholly or partly urban, to be a motor omnibus urban route service area.

Tourist vehicles

A person who proposes to operate a motor vehicle as a tourist vehicle must hold a tourist vehicle licence before commencing the operation.

Special passenger vehicles

A person who proposes to operate a special passenger vehicle has to hold a special passenger vehicle licence before commencing operation.

Powers of the Director, and other matters

The Director has power to cancel or suspend accreditation or a licence (s 75). There is no appeal against suspension by the Director of accreditation or a licence (s 77(2)).

A person aggrieved by a decision of the Director may appeal to the local court against the decision of the Director.[187]

CARRIAGE BY RAIL

The responsibility for the operation of railways under the Commonwealth once vested in the Australian National Railways Commission is now under the National Rail Corporation. The responsibilities of the Commission and operation of the Federal rail network (interstate system) had been governed by the Australian National Railways Commission Act 1983–88.[188] While the Commonwealth government has no direct constitutional power over railways (except for military purposes) it does have power to acquire or construct railways in a State either by agreement or with the consent of that State.[189] Both Tasmania and South Australia have legislated to pass control of their separate railways to the Commonwealth.[190]

---

186 The Director has the same discretion in relation to such a licence as under s 9(1) (s 40). Conditions applicable by the Director to such a licence are similar to those under s 34.

187 A person aggrieved by the decision of the Director in refusing an application, revoking an approval or cancelling or suspending any accreditation or licence may appeal to the local court against that decision; see s 77.

188 The National Railways Commission Act 1983 (Cth) continued the existence of the Commission established by the Australian National Railways Act 1917 (Cth). This chapter is largely based on Lane, P, *Bailment*, 2nd edn, 1991, Chapter 16; and I gratefully acknowledge the permission granted to draw upon that chapter.

189 Section 51(xxxiii) and (xxxiv) of the Constitution Act 1900 (Cth).

190 The Railways (Transfer to Commonwealth) Act 1975 (Tas); the Railways (South Australia) Act 1975 (SA). See also the Seat of Government Act 1928 (Cth) and the Northern Territory Acceptance Act 1910 (Cth).

The main function of the Australian National Railways Commission under the Australian National Railways Commission Act 1983 (Cth) was to provide railway services for the carriage of passengers and goods over railways acquired or constructed in the States under the constitutional powers.[191] The Commission was empowered to provide services for carrying passengers and goods other than by rail.[192] The Commission was under a duty to carry out its operations in a safe and efficient manner.

The National Rail Corporation Agreement Act 1992 (Cth) approves and gives effect to the Agreement made on 30 July 1991 between the Commonwealth, New South Wales, Victoria, Queensland and Western Australia.[193] The Act set up the National Rail Corporation (the Company) which has taken over the Commonwealth rail freight assets, that is, the assets of the Australian National Railways Commission, assets of the Commonwealth and other assets required or authorised to be transferred to, or acquired by the Company under the 1991 Agreement. The Commonwealth is empowered to acquire, hold, dispose of, or deal with shares in the Company in accordance with the Agreement (s 7).[194]

The National Rail Corporation Agreement is expressly intended to achieve micro-economic reform in the Australian rail industry.[195] The Commonwealth and State and Territory governments agree that the National Rail Corporation be set up for conducting rail freight operations (amongst other matters) in Australia on a commercial basis in accordance with agreed principles.[196] These are:

(i)   operation of the Company on a strictly commercial basis, with a viable corporate plan and subject to the Trade Practices Act 1974 (Cth);

(ii) access by the Company to assets including track infrastructure necessary to achieve commercial viability;

(iii) operation of the Company under labour arrangements in an enterprise award reflecting best practice in productivity;[197]

(iv) the Company to have capacity to contract out activities where that is the most efficient approach;

(v) the Company to provide access on a commercial basis to the national Rail Corporation network and terminal facilities for private and public sector operators;

---

191 Sections 5 and 6. See the National Railways Commission Amendment Act 1988 (no 122 of 1988); s 6 of the Transport and Communications Legislation Amendment Act (no 2) 1993 (no 5 of 1994); the Transport Legislation Amendment Act 1995 (no 95 of 1995).

192 Section 5.

193 The Agreement is contained in the Schedule to the Act.

194 For vesting of specified rail assets in the Company by Ministerial direction, see s 9; the Governor General is empowered to make regulations required under the Act; see s 17.

195 See Schedule, Part A.

196 See Schedule, Part B. These principles are those compatible with the Heads of Government Agreement on the National Rail Freight Corporation of 31 October 1990.

197 In line with those arrangements identified by the National Rail Freight Initiative Task Force, see Attachment 1, Report of 21 March 1991, Canberra: Australian Government Publishing Service.

(vi) the Company to have capacity to provide services to governments, charging on a strictly commercial basis;

(vii) the Company not to be responsible for redundancies arising in rail authorities resulting from the Company's formation and transfer of assets to it.[198]

The Commonwealth and the States (including Queensland) undertake to enact legislation to make provision for the implementation of the National Rail Agreement (Part III).[199] Provision is made for contracts to be entered into, at the request of the Company, by the respective rail authorities, for the provision of rail services.[200]

Both the Australian National Railways Commission (now the National Rail Corporation) and all the rail authorities in the States have ceased to be common carriers.[201] The Australian National Railways Commission does, however, undertake common carrier liabilities when goods are carried at the Commission's risk.[202]

The interstate system (or inter-system) raises questions of special liability. Conditions of carriage by rail between the States, or between a State and a Territory are regulated by the Inter-system Conditions of Carriage. This Inter-system traffic operates under an agreement between the Commission and other State rail carriers. The conditions on which goods are carried on the Inter-system are those contained in the respective rates

---

198 Part I includes the following key interpretations; 'interstate rail freight' means interstate rail freight carried on the National Rail Corporation network, 'NRC network' means the rail network connecting mainland State capitals and Alice Springs as specified in the corporate Plan, 'Railways of Australia Agreement' means the interstate rail freight revenue sharing arrangements determined by rules contained in the Railways of Australia Commissioners conference minute 7248 as these arrangements stand at the date of the commencement of the National Rail Corporation's operations.

199 This includes legislation to refer to the Commonwealth, under s 51(xxxvii) of the Constitution the matter of the Commonwealth holding shares in the Company when the Company engages in intrastate rail transport services in the States; providing for means of transferring or vesting assets in the Company owned or leased by the Commonwealth or States and their rail authorities in contracts where this has been agreed under the Agreement; authorising the making of legislation. See 8 *Australian Current Law Digest* (1995) 425; see Transport Infrastructure Amendment (Rail) Act 1995 (Queensland) (no 32 of 1995).

200 See s 5(3) in relation to interstate freight. See s 5(4) in respect of special arrangements for Western Australia. Part VI deals with funding of the company, Part VII with resolution of disputes between the Company, the Commonwealth and States, Part VIII deals with the variation of the agreement, Schedule I contains the memorandum of incorporation of the Company; Schedule 2 deals with the major interstate rail freight functions of the Company.

201 Section 72 of the Australian National Railways Commission Act (Cth); s 49 of the Transport Act 1983 (Vic) (repealing s 4 of the Railways Act 1958–72 (Vic)) stating that neither the State Transit Authority, nor the Metropolitan Transit Authority is a common carrier; s 91 of the Transport Administration Act 1988 (NSW) stating that the rail authority is not a common carrier (see previously s 33 of the Government Railways Act 1912 (NSW)); s 120 of the Railways Act 1914–82 (Qld); s 25 of the Government Railways Act 1904–82 (WA); s 13 of the Carriers Act 1891 (SA). Section 15 of the Railway Management Act 1935 (Tas) declares the Commissioner to be a common carrier. That function in respect of railways is now effectively altered by the application s 49 of the Australian National Railways Commission Act (Cth). For the earlier position of the Commonwealth Railway Commissioner, see *Gregory v Commonwealth Railway Commissioner* (1941) 66 CLR 50. On the general position of the Australian National Railways Commission and State railway authorities, see Palmer, NE, *Bailment,* 2nd edn, 1991, Sydney: Law Book Co, Chapter 16.

202 The Federal Minister for Transport has to approve the principles on which the Commission's rates are based; see s 200. The Commission is authorised to make regulations for the carriage of passengers and goods; see s 79.

books, Railway Acts and bylaws in force on each system to which carriage will extend in respect of carriage on that system.[203]

The Inter-system raises questions of liability of the operators of different railway systems which have been considered by the English courts. In *White v South Eastern Railway*,[204] it was held that where one person books goods through by one railway authority for a journey over more than one railway line, they may, in the case of damage to the goods on any part of the journey, sue the railway authority that booked the goods. Additionally, that person may also sue the other railway authority concerned if the damage occurs on their line and due to their negligence, but not otherwise. The difficulty will be proving that goods were in the custody of one or other of the carriers when lost.

The Australian National Railway Commission General Conditions for the Carriage of Goods lays down two rates for acceptance of goods by the Commission:[205]

(1) the Commission's risk rate, where the Commission is liable as a common carrier, subject to certain exceptions; and

(2) the owner's risk rate, where the consignor, in return for a lower freight rate, agrees to limitation of the Commission's liability except for wilful misconduct by the Commission or subject to the statutory warranties under ss 69–74 of the Trade Practices Act 1974 (Cth).

Commission's risk rate

Although the Commission is no longer a common carrier,[206] the Commission accepts the liability of a common carrier under the Commission's risk. The exceptions to this liability are as follows:

(a) loss or delivery of any goods improperly or insufficiently addressed, marked, directed or described;

(b) loss or damage to goods consisting of a variety of articles in the same package liable by breakage to damage each other or other articles;

(c) loss or damage arising from leakage due to bad vessels or bad cooperage or fermentation;

(d) damage to perishable goods arising from the perishable nature of such goods or from the same not being taken away forthwith on arrival at the destination station;

(e) loss arising from delay in the delivery of goods which may have been occasioned by flood, storm, tempest, strikes, industrial disputes or other unforeseen cause;

---

203 Condition 108 of the Australian National Goods Rates Book. See now, s 5(3) of the National Rail Corporation Agreement Act 1992 (Cth) and Schedule 2 (National Rail Corporation Ltd major interstate rail freight functions).

204 (1885) 1 TLR 391 (DC); *Coxan v Great Western Railway Co* (1860) LJ Ex 165.

205 See the Australian National Goods Rates Book: General Conditions for the Carriage of Goods, under s 79 of the Australia National Railways Commission Act 1983 (Cth).

206 Section 72 of the Australian National Railways Act 1983 (Cth).

(f) any loss of market or any indirect or consequential damages in respect of goods lost, damaged, or delayed;

(g) loss of or injury to any articles or goods put into wrapped boxes, packages, cases or baskets and consigned as 'empties' unless arising from:

(i) wilful misconduct by the Commission; or

(ii) the breach by the Commission of a warranty implied by the Trade Practices Act 1974 (Cth).[207]

Owner's risk rate

Where the goods are accepted by the Commission at owner's risk rates, the consignor agrees that the Commission will have no liability for loss, detention, injury, delay or damage occurring before, during or after carriage, during storage except where this arose from the wilful misconduct of the Commission.[208]

The Commission is also liable under the Trade Practices Act (Cth) s 74(1), (2) which imply a warranty into contracts of supply of goods and services by a corporation to a consumer that services will be rendered with due care and skill. Since April 1989, however, Australian National Railways do not accept for carriage consignments of less than car load quantities. As a result, s 74(1) and (2) are unlikely to apply to contracts for the carriage of goods but will probably apply to the storage or transport of passenger's luggage and the carriage of parcels.

While the provisions of the Trade Practices Act 1974 (Cth) do apply to Commonwealth statutory corporations, such as Australian National Railways, it has been held that these provisions do not apply to State Railway Commissions or similar authorities.[209]

Australian National Railways Commission: rights and liabilities

Misconduct

Liability for misconduct was considered in *White v South Australian Railways Commissioner.*[210] In that case, goods were delivered to the defendant to be consigned to the plaintiff's 'care AH Landseer, Morgan'. Landseer had a river steamship which traded to Morgan. The clerk of the defendants in making out the consignment note omitted the above words. Because of this omission, the goods, on arrival at Morgan, were handed to a steamship belonging to a different owner. The vessel sunk and part of the goods were lost. The goods were carried at owner's risk, which relieved the defendant

---

207 See s 74.

208 See condition 103. For cases, see Palmer, *Bailment, op cit,* p 1021 onwards.

209 See s 2A of the Trade Practices Act 1974 (Cth); see *Bradken Consolidated Ltd v BHP Pty Ltd* (1979) 145 CLR 107. However, under the Hilmer report proposals, State instrumentalities, including railway authorities (such as Commissions and Commissioners), would be subject to State legislation mirroring the Trade Practices Act 1974, including s 74.

210 (1919) SALR 44.

from liability unless the loss arose through wilful misconduct. The Supreme Court of South Australia held that the defendant's clerk made an unintentional slip and there was no evidence of conscious wrongdoing.[211]

Right to sell goods

If freight or other charges are not paid, the Commission is entitled to detain and sell any goods or other property belonging to the person liable for the charges in order to recover those charges.[212]

Dangerous goods

Carriage of dangerous goods is expressly covered by conditions in the goods rates books incorporating the Railways of Australia Code of Practices and Conditions for the Carriage of Dangerous Goods. This Code has effect subject to the various provisions made under the legislation of the States and Territories.[213]

The General Conditions entitle the Commission to refuse to accept goods for carriage it considers dangerous, offensive or unsafe or unfit. Provision is made for the removal of dangerous goods by the owner at any time during carriage.

Time limit for claims

Any claims against the Commission for loss of, or damage to, goods must be lodged in writing and must be made in the case of total loss of goods within 60 days after the day of consignment, in the case of partial loss within 14 days of delivery of the goods.[214]

It is well established that delivery of the goods entitles the railway authority to payment.[215]

Subcontracting

The Australian National Railways Commission can make arrangements with any person for the carriage of passengers and goods between a place or places in Australia or outside

---

211 Murray, CJ, applying *Forder v G W Ry* [1905] 2 KB 532. See also *Abraham and Sons v Commissioner for Railways* [1958] SR (NSW) 134.

212 General Conditions, condition 121. For power to sell unclaimed goods including perishables, see General Conditions, condition 126.1. The Commission also has the common law power to sell goods under agency of necessity which will arise where there is a necessity for saving goods and communication with the owner is not possible; see *Springer v Great Western Railway* [1921] 1 KB 257. See, Palmer, *Bailment, op cit*, pp 720–21. This will be unlikely to arise in modern conditions of mobile phones and faxes.

213 See the Dangerous Goods Act 1975 (NSW); the Dangerous Goods Act 1985 (Vic); the Carriage of Dangerous Goods by Road Act 1984 (Qld); the Dangerous Substances Act 1979 (SA); the Dangerous Goods Act 1961 (WA); the Dangerous Goods Act 1976 (Tas); the Dangerous Goods Ordinance 1984 (ACT); the Dangerous Goods Act 1981(NT).

214 See *Commissioner for Railways (NSW) v Quinn* (1946) 72 CLR 345, particularly at 376–77; discussed in *Bailment, op cit*, pp 1081–82. See also *State Rail Authority (NSW) v Everson* (unreported, Supreme Court of New South Wales, 27 May 1985) in which, following *Quinn's* case, it was held in relation to the conditions governing passenger's luggage, that the special contract entered into by the common carrier must also be signed by the consignor as required by s 9(c) of the Common Carrier's Act 1902 (NSW). Note that the new South Wales State Rail Authority is no longer a common carrier; see s 91 of the Transport Administration Act 1988 (NWS). See above.

215 *Hunt v Barber* (1887) 3 VLR (L) 189.

Australia.[216] The Commission can also connect with, and operate over, railway owned by another person (ie a State rail authority) and appoint agents.

Liability for passenger's luggage and parcels

Liability of the Commission for loss or damage to passenger's luggage is limited to $300 unless the prescribed surcharge for Commission's risk is paid. Parcels are also carried under the owner's risk and Commissioner's risk conditions. Under the inter-system conditions the maximum liability for loss or damage to parcels is $1,000. However, a greater liability may be accepted by special arrangement.

State rail authorities

The duties and liabilities of particular State railway authorities are governed under the relevant and specific legislation and are now of less relevance with the development of the national rail system and the creation of the National Rail Corporation. Only a brief note is given here and reference should be made to specialist works.[217]

New South Wales

The New South Wales State Rail Authority is required to run its rail and other transport operations safely and efficiently and in accordance with sound commercial practice.[218] The Authority is no longer a common carrier by statute;[219] however, where the Authority accepts the risk and liability of a common carrier under a contract for the carriage of passengers and goods the provisions of the Common Carrier's Act 1902 (New South Wales) apply.

The current conditions of carriage of goods, passengers and luggage are continued in force under the Transport Administration Act 1988 as are conditions of freight.[220]

Goods may be carried by the authority partly or entirely by road on terms identical to those applying exclusively to rail carriage.[221]

The Authority under the Authority's risk rate is liable for loss in the case of negligence,[222] in contrast to the Australian National Railways Commission (now Corporation) being liable only in the case of wilful misconduct.

Queensland

In Queensland, under the Railways Act 1914 (Qld) a Commissioner of Railways is appointed as a corporation sole with power to construct and provide services over

---

216 Section 10 of the Australian National Railways Commission Act 1983 (Cth).

217 See Laws of Australia: 34 Transport (Carriage by Rail). See Palmer, *Bailment, op cit*, pp 1079–92.

218 Section 7 of the Transport Administration Act 1988 (NSW). This obligation is not in limitation of other obligations of the Authority under the Act nor is it enforceable in a court of law.

219 See s 91 of the Transport Administration Act 1988 (NSW).

220 Charges, terms and conditions for the carriage of passengers and freight may be fixed by way of order; see s 85 of the Transport administration Act 1988 (NSW).

221 Freight Conditions, condition 43.

222 Freight Conditions, condition 3.

railways.[223] The Commissioner is not a common carrier[224] and contracts entered into by the Commissioner are subject to the Act and bylaws unless excluded or modified.[225] The Commissioner is authorised to make special contracts under which the Commissioner's power may be limited.[226] The Commissioner is empowered to fix charges other than those prescribed for the carriage of goods[227] and to make bylaws.[228] Where the Commissioner is an insurer, the Commissioner does not accept liability for loss or misdelivery or damage to goods occurring in situations similar to those laid down in the Australian National Railways Conditions.

Goods classed solely at carriage by owner's risk will be carried on the basis that the Commissioner is exempt from liability for negligence.[229]

The conditions in Queensland, unlike those of Australian National Railways, do not have any reference whatsoever to misconduct or negligence on the part of the Commissioner. This has the effect of total exclusion of liability in any of the listed conditions.[230]

Victoria

The State Transport Authority of Victoria (the Authority) established under the Transport Act 1983 (Victoria) is not a common carrier.[231] The Authority is empowered to fix charges for the passenger and goods services it operates.[232] The Transport (State Transport Authority) Regulations 1984 (Victoria)[233] sets out the terms and conditions for the carriage of goods.

The Authority is excluded from liability in terms essentially identical to those in the Australian National Railway Conditions. There is no express liability imposed on the Authority for its misconduct or default.

The carriage of dangerous goods is subject to both the provisions of the Australian Code for the Transport of Dangerous Goods by Road and Rail and the Transport

---

223 Sections 37, 95 and 100 of the Railways Act 1914 (Qld).

224 Section 17 of the Railways Amendment Act 1985 (Qld).

225 Section 95(3) of the Railways Act 1914 (Qld).

226 *Ibid*, ss 101 and 108.

227 Section 108 of the Railways Act 1912 (Qld). 'Goods' include animals and things of every kind conveyed by railway; s 3.

228 *Ibid*, s 108. These powers include incorporation of and handbook issued by the Commissioner and any code of practice for the transport of dangerous goods (s 133); regulation of the carriage of goods by road by the Commissioner; prescribing of fares, charges, terms and conditions for the carriage of passengers and goods the carriage of corpses or diseased or drunken persons and the disposal of unclaimed goods; 2nd Schedule of the Railways Act 1912 (Qld).

229 See *Turnleys Pty Ltd v Commissioner for Railways* [1955] SR Qd 4.

230 Cl 9.

231 Section 49 of the Transport Act 1983 (Vic). See also the terms and conditions of carriage of passengers and freight by the Metropolitan Transport Authority in the Melbourne Metropolitan area, Transport (Metropolitan Authority) Regulation 1984 (SR no 196 of 1984).

232 Section 51 of the Transport Act 1983 (Vic).

233 SR no 193 of 1984 made under s 56 (1) of the Transport Act 1983 (Vic). Goods are defined under the regulation as including any article, package, item of luggage or thing, merchandise or chattels of every description and animals alive or dead (reg 3).

(Dangerous Goods) Regulations 1983.[234] The provisions of the Regulations apply in the event of inconsistency between these and the Dangerous Goods Code.

Western Australia

Carriage by rail in Western Australia is governed by the Government Railways Act 1904 (Western Australia) (The Act) which established the Western Australian government Railway Commission. The Commission is not a common carrier under the Act.[235]

The Commission is empowered by the Act to fix charges for the carriage of goods and passengers. It is expressly authorised to fix special charges for the carriage of specific goods and merchandise, or risk in respect of goods over a certain value, or those likely to be injured or cause injury.[236] The Commission may carry goods over road or rail.[237]

Goods are accepted at Commission's risk where these are tendered in good order and condition and packed to the Commission's satisfaction,[238] checked by the Commission's employees and the appropriate charges paid for the goods. The list of excepted perils is similar to the Australian National Railway Conditions, with the difference that strikes or industrial disputes are not included and an infirmity or defect in the goods consigned, or insufficient packing are additional grounds for the Commission to deny liability. The Commission is liable for negligence, and not only for wilful misconduct, in relation to the listed exceptions.[239]

INTERNATIONAL RAIL AND ROAD CARRIAGE CONVENTIONS

International Carriage of Goods by Rail

The Convention concerning International Carriage by Rail (COTIF) is given force of law in the United Kingdom by the International Transport Conventions Act 1983.[240]

The COTIF Convention applies to passengers and their luggage under international transport documents made out for a journey over territories of at least two member states. Application of COTIF is limited to carriage which takes place exclusively over railway lines registered under the Convention.[241]

---

234 SR no 193 of 1984 made under s 56(1).of the Transport Act 1983 (Vic).

235 Section 25 of the Government Railway Act 1904–82 (WA).

236 Section 22(2) and (3).

237 Section 28A.

238 See General Conditions, clause 41.

239 General Conditions, clause 2(4).

240 See Palmer, *Bailment, op cit*, pp 1044–1068 for a detailed commentary on COTIF. For text of COTIF see Appendices.The Convention has not been adopted in Australia.

241 See Article 1 of the Convention.

The Convention obliges the railway to carry passengers and their luggage except in certain specified circumstances.[242] Failure by the railway to comply with this obligation gives the passenger a right to sue for damages.[243]

Passengers are liable for the care of hand luggage and animals and the railway is not liable for loss or damage to them unless the loss or damage was caused by its fault.[244] The railway is liable for such loss or damage if the passenger is the victim of an accident which arises from the operation of the railway.[245] The railway will not be responsible if the accident has not been caused by the operation of the railway, or occurred despite the care taken by the railway, or consequences the railway was unable to prevent.[246]

The railway has a limitation of liability, in addition to the above defences, of 700 Units of Account[247] per passenger for loss of or damage to hand luggage and animals.

The railway is liable for registered luggage for delay in its delivery or total or partial loss or damage.[248] The defences available to the railway are a fault on the part of a passenger, an order given by the passenger other than as a result of fault on the part of the railway, inherent vice of the registered luggage and circumstances which the railway could not avoid and the consequences of which it could not prevent.[249]

The railway is liable 'for its servants and for any other persons whom it employs to perform the carriage' unless, at the passenger's request, these persons render services the railway is under no obligation to do.[250] In respect of registered luggage if the plaintiff can prove the extent of their loss or damage they can recover up to 34 Units of Account per kg of weight missing or 500 Units of Account per item of luggage. If not the damages are fixed at 10 Units of Account per kg of weight missing or 150 Units of Account per item of luggage.[251]

The Convention provides that each successive railway taking over the passenger's luggage becomes a party to the contract of carriage.[252]

The consignor is obliged to present a consignment note to the railway,[253] which travels with the goods, this note being a memorandum of the contract.[254] The consignment note must specify the weight of the goods or similar information.[255]

---

242 See Article 4(1)

243 See Article 15(2)(d).

244 See Article 47(2), 47(3).

245 See Article 26(1)

246 See Article 26(2).

247 See Article 31. Units of Account are Special Drawing Rights as defined by the International Monetary Fund.

248 See Article 35(1)

249 See 35(2). On the last defence see *Michael Galley Footwear Ltd v Dominic Iaboni* [1982] 2 All ER 200.

250 See Article 45.

251 See Article 38.

252 See Article 34.

253 See Article 12(10).

254 See Articles 11(5), 13.

255 Article 13. In respect of defective packing see Article 19(3).

The consignor is given the right in specified circumstances to radically alter the contract of carriage, including withdrawal of the goods from the forwarding station, stopping them in transit, order delivery to a person other than the consignee and sending on the goods to a destination other than shown in the consignment note.[256]

The railway is liable for loss or damage resulting from total or partial loss of, or damage to the goods between the time of acceptance for carriage and the time of delivery and for the loss or damage resulting from the transit period being exceeded.[257]

The railway is relieved of liability if it can prove that the damage or delay was caused by a fault on the part of the person entitled to the goods, by their order, inherent vice of the goods (eg decay, wastage) or by circumstances which the railway could not avoid and the consequences of which it could not prevent.[258] The railway can also avoid liability if the loss, damage or delay arose from 'the special risks' listed in the Convention.[259] This will not be available as a defence to the railway where an abnormally large quantity or a package has been lost.[260]

Compensation to be paid by the railway is not to exceed 17 Units of Account per kg of weight lost.[261] In the event of total or partial loss of goods the railway must pay, to the exclusion of all other damages, compensation calculated according to the commodity exchange quotation, or the normal value of such goods where this quotation is not available.[262]

The consignor will lose the benefit of these limitations, and full compensation will be payable, where the consignor has made a special declaration in the consignment note, where there has been gross negligence on the part of the railway and where it has been guilty of wilful misconduct.[263]

The railway initially accepting the goods is primarily liable, with the consignor able to bring an action against the railway unless the consignee has accepted the goods.[264] Action against the railway is extinguished where the goods are accepted by the person entitled to them unless the plaintiff proves wilful misconduct or gross negligence on the part of the railway.[265]

---

256 See Article 30. For cessation of the consignor's right to modify the contract see Article 30(4).

257 See Article 36(1).

258 See Article 36(2)

259 See Article 36(3).

260 See Article 37(2).For the interpretation of similar provisions in CMR see *Ulster Swift Ltd v Taunton Meat Haulage Ltd* [1977] 1 Lloyd's Rep 346.

261 See Article 40(2).

262 See Article 40(1). For interpretation of similar provisions in the CMR see *James Buchanan & Co Ltd v Babco Forwarding & Shipping (UK) Ltd* [1978] AC 141 (HL).

263 See Article 44.

264 See Article 55(3).

265 See Article 57.There is a one year limitation period for actions against the railway; see Article 58.

International Carriage of Goods by Road

The Convention on the Contract of International Carriage of Goods by Road (CMR) has been adopted by European countries including the United Kingdom.[266]

The Convention applies to the contracts of carriage of goods by road where the place for taking the goods and the place for their delivery are in different countries.[267] The Convention only has force of law so far as it relates to the rights and liabilities of 'persons concerned'. These are the sender, the consignee, any carrier party to the contract and any person for whom the carrier is responsible.[268]

If a freight forwarder acts as an agent to bring about a contract between their principal and carrier, the Convention will not apply to the freight forwarder. If the freight forwarder contracts to carry cargo they may then be a carrier for the purposes of the Convention.[269] The consignment note has to set out the identities of the sender and receiver respectively.[270]

Where goods are sent by a vehicle over part of a journey by sea, rail, inland waterways or air and the goods are not unloaded, the Convention applies to the whole of the carriage.[271]

If it can be proved that any loss, damage or delay was not caused by any act or omission of the road carrier but in the course of or reason of other form of transport then the Convention will not apply.[272]

The consignment note is made in three parts, the first to the consignor, the second to the carrier and the third to accompany the goods.[273] The sender is responsible for all expenses, loss and damage sustained by the carrier by reason of the inaccuracy or required particulars required by the Convention. The consignment functions as a carrier's receipt for the goods.

The carrier is strictly liable for any loss of, or damage to, the goods occurring between the time when the carrier takes over the goods and the time of delivery.[274] The

---

266 For a detailed commentary on the CMR see Clarke, MA, *International Carriage by Road: CMR*, 1982, London: Stevens; and Palmer, *Bailment, op cit*, pp 1114–56. On the issue of the decisions of foreign courts in respect of the Convention not being followed by English courts see *Ulster-Swift v Taunton Meat Haulage Ltd* [1977] 1 Lloyd's Rep 346 and *Buchanan v Babco* [1978] AC 141; discussed at Palmer, *op cit*, pp 1117–19. See also *Silbert Ltd v Islander Trucking* [1985] 2 Lloyd's Rep 243.

267 See Article 1.

268 Article 1(1). The third and fourth categories are qualified by Article 34.

269 See *Ulster-Swift Ltd v Taunton Meat Haulage Ltd* [1977] 1 Lloyd's Rep 346. see Article 14(2)(c). See also *Hair and Skin Trading Co Ltd v Norman Air Freight Carriers and World Transport Agencies Ltd* [1974] 1 Lloyd's Rep 443.

270 Article 6(1)(b), (c).

271 Article 2(1).

272 For application of Article 2(1) see *Thermo Engineers Ltd v Ferrymasters Ltd* [1981] 1 Lloyd's Rep 200.

273 Articles 4, 5(1). Article 6(1)(2) details the required contents of the consignment note.

274 Article 17(1).

carrier is also liable for delay in delivery. The carrier is liable for the acts or omissions of subcontractors, servants or agents whose services he uses to perform the carriage.[275]

The carrier may use the following defences, with the burden of proving them on the carrier, to the liability above if the loss, damage or delay was caused by:

(a) the wrongful act or neglect of the claimant; or

(b) the instructions of the claimant given other than as a result of a wrongful act or neglect on the part of the carrier; or

(c) the inherent vice of the goods; or

(d) through consequences which the carrier could not avoid and was unable to prevent.[276]

the carrier is also relieved of liability when the loss or damage arises from the 'special risks inherent' in specified cases, including the nature of certain types of goods.[277]

The consignor has the right to dispose of the goods while they are in the carrier's control by requesting the carrier to stop them in transit, change delivery or substitute another consignee.[278]

Delay is regarded as occurring when the goods are not delivered in an agreed time limit, or within a reasonable time if time limit is agreed.[279] The sender is liable to the carrier for damage to persons, equipment or other goods, and for any expenses due to the defective packing of the goods, unless the defect was apparent or known to the carrier at the time they took the goods and no reservations were made by the carrier in the consignment note.[280]

The carrier is entitled to sell the goods without waiting for instructions from the person entitled to dispose of them, if the goods are perishable or their condition requires sale or storage costs are disproportionate to the value of the goods, if the carrier has not received contrary instructions after a reasonable time from the person entitled to dispose of the goods.[281]

The value of goods, for compensation purposes, is fixed to the commodity exchange price, failing which on the current market price, otherwise by the normal value of such

---

275 Article 3.

276 Article 17(2); see *Ulster-Swift v Taunton Meat Haulage* [1977] 1 Lloyd's Rep 346; *Thermo Engineers v Ferrymasters Ltd* [1981] 1 Lloyd's Rep 200; *Michael Galley Footwear Ltd v Dominic Iaboni* [1982] 2 All ER 200; *Silbert v Islander Trucking* [1985] 2 Lloyd's Rep 243

277 Article 17(4) subject to the provisions of Article 18(3)–(5).For consideration of carrier's liability under Articles 17 and 18 see *Ulster-Swift Ltd v Taunton Meat Haulage* [1977] 1 Lloyd's Rep 346 and *Centrocoop Export-Import SA v Brit-European Transport Ltd* [1984] 2 Lloyd's Rep 618. As to whether deviation has an effect on a road carrier's liability in the context of the Convention see Clarke, *op cit*, p 31 and Palmer, *op cit*, pp 1134–35.

278 Article 12(1).

279 Article 19; see also Articles 13 and 20.

280 Article 10.

281 Article 16(3), (4) and see Article 14(2) for the position where the carrier is unable to obtain instructions from the person entitled to the goods.

goods. Compensation shall not exceed 8.33 Units of Account per kg of gross weight.[282] Compensation is fixed at the amount that the goods have diminished in value but may not exceed, in the case of total damage, the amount payable for total loss; in the case of partial damage, the amount payable for part loss.[283] The carrier's liability may be increased if the sender pays an agreed surcharge to the carrier and makes a declaration in the consignment note that the goods are of a value over the Convention's limits.[284]

Where loss, damage or delay has been caused by the wilful misconduct of the carrier or of the agents, servants or other persons employed by the carrier to perform the carriage, the carrier will not be able to use the defences or the liability limits in the Convention.[285]

If the carriage is governed by a single contract performed by successive road carriers, each of them is responsible for the performance of the whole operation, the second carrier and each successive carrier becoming a party to the whole contract, under the terms of the consignment note, by reason of their acceptance of the goods and the consignment note.[286] Although the first carrier, and all successive carriers, are each liable to the sender for the entire carriage for loss, damage and delay, legal proceedings may only be brought against the first carrier, the last carrier or the carrier carrying the goods when the loss, damage or delay occurred.[287]

A carrier who has paid compensation under the Convention may recover it, together with all costs and expenses arising out of the claim, from the carrier responsible for the loss or damage.[288]

Parties are not entitled to contract out of the provisions of the Convention and any contractual term purporting to do so is void to the extent it is repugnant to Convention's provisions.[289]

---

282 Article 23. For cases on Article 23 see *James Buchanan & Co Ltd v Babco Forwarding and Shipping (UK) Ltd* [1978] AC 141; *William Tatton & Co Ltd v Ferrymasters* [1974] 1 Lloyd's Rep 203 and *ICI v MAT Transport* [1987] 1 Lloyd's Rep 354.

283 Article 25; see *William Tatton & Co Ltd v Ferrymasters* [1974] 1 Lloyd's Rep 203 and *Worldwide Carriers v Ardtran* [1983] 1 All ER 692.

284 Article 24.

285 Article 29.

286 Article 34. See *Ulster-Swift v Taunton Meat Haulage* [1977] 1 Lloyd's Rep 346. To be successive carriers for the purpose of Article 34 carriers must only perform carriage 'governed by a single contract' but also carry under a single consignment note; sse *Arctic Electronics Co (UK) Ltd v Mcgregor Sea and Air Services Ltd* [1985] 1 Lloyd's Rep 510.

287 See *Arctic v McGregor Sea and Air Services Ltd* [1985] 1 Lloyd's Rep 510; except in the case of counterclaim or setoff. For time limits for claims for delay see Article 30(3); for other time limits see Article 32(1). For cases on Article 32 see *Moto-Vespa v MAT* [1979] 1 Lloyd's Rep 175; *Worldwide Carriers v Ardtran* [1983] 1 All ER 692.

288 Article 37; see *ITT Schaub Lorenz v Birkart Johann Internationale Spedition GmbH & Co Kg* [1988] 1 Lloyd's Rep 487; *Ulster-Swift Ltd v Taunton Meat Haulage Ltd* [1977] 1 Lloyd's Rep 346.

289 Article 41(1).

CARRIAGE BY AIR

Introduction

Claims arising in carriage of goods by air are determined, depending on the circumstances of the carriage, under common law, Commonwealth or State legislation, or international convention given force of law by statute. This regime does not cover claims based on non-performance of carriage; there, the general law of contract applies.[290]

The Civil Aviation (Carriers' Liability) Act 1959–91 (Cth) gives force of law in Australia to three international agreements to which Australia is a party concerning international carriage by air of passengers and goods: the Warsaw Convention, the Hague Protocol and the Guadalajara Convention. In Part IV, the Act also sets out substantive rules applying, in broad terms, to international carriage of passengers by air falling outside the scope of those conventions,[291] to interstate carriage of passengers, and to carriage of passengers to, from and within the Territories.[292]

Intrastate carriage of passengers by air by holders of airline or charter licences in the course of commercial transport operations under a contract of carriage is controlled by State legislation.[293] The State Acts which apply to such carriage adopt the Commonwealth provisions applying to interstate carriage of passengers, so that a uniform scheme applies to interstate and intrastate carriage of passengers by air under Commonwealth and State legislation.

The right of the Commonwealth to exercise general control over civil air carriage was firmly established in *Airlines of New South Wales Pty Ltd v New South Wales*.[294] In 1963, Airlines of New South Wales Pty Ltd (a subsidiary of Ansett Transport Industries Ltd) challenged the validity of the State Transport (Co-ordination) Act 1931 (NSW) in relation to the provisions governing State licensing of aircraft engaging in intrastate air

---

290 See Shawcross and Beaumont, *Air Law*, 4th edn, 1982, London: Butterworths, Vol 1, para VII (referred to subsequently as Shawcross and Beaumont). See *Laws of Australia: 34 Transport*; '34.2 Aviation'.

291 The texts of conventions and the protocol are given force in Australia by the Civil Aviation (Carrier's Liability) Act 1959–91 (Cth).

292 The Minister administering the Act may publish notices in the Commonwealth *Gazette* giving information about the States which are parties to the conventions (ss 18, 22, 25C).

293 For the reference of air transport in a State to the Commonwealth, see the Commonwealth Powers (Air Transport) Act 1952 (Tas) considered in relation to licensing of intrastate carriage in *R v Public Vehicle Licensing Appeal Tribunal of Tasmania; ex p Australian National Airways Pty Ltd* (1964) 113 CLR 207 applied in *Minister for Justice for Western Australia (ex p Ansett Airlines) v Australian National Airlines Commission and the Commonwealth* (1977) 12 ALR 17. See also the Commonwealth Powers (Air Transport) Act 1952 (Qld); 1921 (SA); see *Graham v Paterson* (1950) 81 CLR 1. See the Civil Aviation (Carrier's Liability) Act 1967 (NSW); the Civil Aviation (Carrier's Liability) Act 1964 (Qld); the Civil Aviation (Carrier's Liability) Act 1962 (SA); the Civil Aviation (Carrier's Liability) Act 1963 (Tas); the Civil Aviation (Carrier's Liability) Act 1961 (Vic); the Civil Aviation (Carrier's Liability) Act 1961 (WA).

294 (1964) 113 CLR 1.

flights.[295] The High Court held that the provisions of the State Act were not inconsistent with the Federal law and that Airlines of New South Wales Pty Ltd were not entitled to use aircraft within New South Wales without a licence under the State Act.[296]

The right of the Commonwealth to make navigational laws applicable to all flying operations in Australia has been clearly established by the High Court in *Airlines of New South Wales Pty Ltd v New South Wales (No 2)* (1964–65) 113 CLR 54.[297]

The Commonwealth can support its ownership, maintenance, and control of airports by relying on the interstate and overseas and commerce powers including those it owns in State capital cities, and any traffic.[298]

Under the Airports (Business Concessions) Act 1959 (Cth), which binds the Crown in right of a State, the Minister of Civil Aviation is empowered to grant leases and licences for business purposes in respect of land within an airport on such terms and conditions as they think fit and a person may not trade within an airport without authority of the Minister.[299]

The Federal Airports Corporation Act 1986 (Cth) set up the Federal Airports Corporation which is empowered to operate Federal airports in Australia. It is also charged with providing the Commonwealth, governments, local government bodies

---

295 The first Commonwealth aviation statute, the Air Navigation Act 1920 (Cth), empowered the Governor General to make regulations to give effect to the Paris Convention of 1919 and further, to make regulations providing for the control of air navigation throughout the Commonwealth and Territories. The Act was passed on the assumption that the Commonwealth Parliament possessed three main sources of primary power; (a) interstate and overseas trade and commerce power under s 51(1) of the Constitution; (b) the external affairs power in s 51(xxix); and (c) the power to make regulations to give effect to the Paris Convention of 1919 and further, to make regulations providing for the control of air navigation throughout the Commonwealth and Territories. The Act was passed on the assumption that the Commonwealth Parliament possessed three main sources of primary power; (a) interstate and overseas trade and commerce power under s 51(1) of the Constitution; (b) the external affairs power in s 51(xxix); and (c) the power to make laws for the Territories under s 122.

In *R v Burgess; ex p Henry* (1936) 55 CLR 605, the High Court held that; (i) the Commonwealth could not exercise control over civil aviation in the Commonwealth, including intrastate legislation; and (ii) in respect of the Air Navigation Act (Cth) empowering the Governor General to make regulations for the carrying out of the Paris Convention, it was a valid exercise of the external affairs power. Subsequent to this case, the Commonwealth withdrew from attempted regulation of intrastate air navigation and the new Air Navigation Act (Cth) as redrafted was upheld in *R v Poole; ex p Henry (No 2)* (1938) 61 CLR 634. An attempt by the Commonwealth in 1937 to add 'air navigation and aircraft' to the powers in s 51 of the Constitution was defeated in a referendum under s 128 of the Constitution. See Lane, PH, 'The Airlines Case' (1965–66) 39 ALJ 17.

296 Under the State Air Navigation Acts 1938 (NSW); 1937–47 (Qld); 1937 (SA); 1958 (Vic); 1937 (WA) the Regulations provide for Federal licensing of intrastate commercial services; most States, however, in addition to Federal licences require State issued licences to conduct intrastate air operations; the Air Transport Act 1964 (NSW); the State Transport Act 1960 (Qld); the State Transport Co-ordination Act 1933 (WA); the Traffic Act 1925 (Tas); the Transport Act 1981 (Tas). No State administered licensing system exists in South Australia.

297 See also *R v Burgess; ex p Henry (The Goya Henry Case)* (1936) 55 CLR 608. See Armstrong, G, 'Note on *Airlines of New South Wales Pty Ltd v New South Wales (No 2)*' (1964–65) 1 Fed LR 348–58.

298 Other powers are the defence power (s 51(vi) of the Constitution), territories power (s 122 of the Constitution) and the incidental power (s 51(xxxix) of the Constitution). Power is also provided under s 52 of the Constitution; see *Kingsford Smith Air Services v Garrison* (1938) 55 WN (NSW) 122.

299 Section 6 and ss 7–8.

and others who operate or propose to operate airports or related facilities with consultancy and management services.[300]

Section 92 of the Constitution is not infringed by refusal of the Director General of Civil Aviation to grant permission for the importation of aircraft so that a potential interstate operator may not be able to obtain aircraft with which to operate a service.[301]

Imposition of air navigation charges upon aircraft engaged in interstate commerce raises the question whether s 92 applies as it does in respect of charges made for the use of roads by interstate commercial road transport vehicles.[302] Charges imposed by a State for the use of a wharf or a government aerodrome indispensable to interstate air or sea navigation may be within s 92 so that the charges should be no more than a reasonable cover for the use of facilities.[303]

The conventions and the State and Commonwealth legislation will not apply in some situations, the most important being:

(1) Carriage by air of goods (other than passengers' baggage) within Australia, since the Commonwealth and State legislation mentioned above applies only to carriage of passengers.[304]

(2) Carriage of cargo outside the scope of the conventions. The conventions adopted by the Civil Aviation (Carriers' Liability) Act 1959 (Cth) do not apply to gratuitous carriage not performed by an air transport undertaking[305] or to carriage without origin or destination in the territory of a party to the relevant convention.

(3) Non-commercial carriage within Australia. Where carriage not covered by the conventions is concerned, the provisions of Commonwealth and State legislation limiting air carriers' liability are restricted to carriage of passengers in aircraft being operated by the holder of an airline licence or a charter licence in the course of 'commercial transport operations', under an arrangement for carriage between the relevant places.[306]

---

300 Section 6 of the Federal Airports Corporation Act 1986 (Cth). The reorganisation of the airports currently controlled by the Federal Airports Corporations, the changes to the Civil Aviation Authority and the deregulation of domestic and international airlines, see below at p 295.

301 *R v Anderson; ex p IPEC Air Pty Ltd* (1965) 39 ALJR 66. See also *Ansett Transport Industries (Operations) Pty Ltd v Commonwealth and Others* (1978) 139 CLR 54 at 62 (an agreement by the Commonwealth under the Two Airline Agreement (see below) not to grant permits under the Customs (Prohibited Imports) Regulations held by the High Court not to breach s 92 of the Constitution as importation precedes interstate trade and so does not form part of that trade). See Livermore, J, 'The legal status of the two airline agreement' (1983) 8 *Air Law* 210 at 211–13. See also *Australian National Airways Pty Ltd v The Commonwealth* (1945) 71 CLR 39 (elimination of a private airline from interstate operations held by the High Court to be unconstitutional as interfering with freedom of interstate trade, and so breaching s 92) applying *James v The Commonwealth* (1936) 55 CLR 1. See *Laws of Australia: 34 Transport;* '34.2 Aviation', Chapter 4, paras 161–63.

302 See *Hughes and Vale Pty Ltd v New South Wales (no 2)* (1955) 93 CLR 127.

303 See Richardson, J, 'Aviation Law in Australia' (1964–65) 1 Fed LR 242.

304 The Civil Aviation (Carriers' Liability) Act 1959 (Cth) s 27(1); (NSW); (Qld); (Tas); (Vic) s 4; (WA); (SA) s 5.

305 'Air transport undertaking' is not defined in the conventions; Shawcross and Beaumont, 4th edn, Vol 1, para VII (103), London: Butterworths, suggests it means a person, firm or company part of whose regular business is the carriage of passengers or goods by air for reward.

306 (Cth) s 26, 27; (NSW), (Vic), (Tas), (Qld) s 4; (SA), (WA), s 5.

In these situations, the matters dealt with in the conventions and the Act, carriers' liability in particular, will be determined under general law concerning carriers. In determining these issues, 'it seems likely that the courts will proceed by analogy from cases relating to the operation of the various forms of land and water transport'.[307]

The liability of the carrier may be excluded or limited by contract in such cases, subject to general law on exemption clauses: carriers by air usually specify in the contracts of carriage they make with their customers that they are not common carriers, and this will exclude the special liabilities of a common carrier at common law.

The requirements for the consigning of dangerous goods for transport by air are contained in Part 33.1 of the Air Navigation Regulations (Cth). It is also an offence under s 18 of the Crimes (Aircraft) Act 1963 (Cth) to carry dangerous goods on board certain aircraft (broadly, those used for international or interstate flight).[308]

Cases of stowaways are covered by the liability limits available under the Warsaw Convention, the Hague Protocol or s 42 of the Civil Aviation (Carrier's Liability) Act 1959 (Cth).[309]

---

307 *Halsbury*, 4th edn, Vol 2, para 1369. See generally Shawcross and Beaumont, 4th edn, Vol 1, para VII (75) on the application of common law principles to carriage by air. The view has been taken that carriers by air may be regarded as common carriers; see *Luddit v Ginger Coote Airways Ltd* [1947] AC 233 where the case was disposed of on a narrow ground. In *Nysted and Anson v Wings Ltd* [1942] 3 DLR, the King's Bench Court of Manitoba held that the defendant was a common carrier, the law governing carriers by air being the same as that governing carriers by land or sea. It asserted that the position is similar in the USA, citing *Kilberg v North East Airlines Inc* [1961] 2 Lloyd's Rep 406 at 407; McNair, *The Law of the Air*, 3rd edn, London: Stevens, p 139: 'If air carriers have invariably chosen to employ written notices and contracts limiting their liability, this surely shows, if anything, that they are concerned to escape the duties which might otherwise be imposed upon them as common carriers. It is certainly not indicative of the conclusion that they cannot be so regarded. And while it is true that the strict liability of the common carrier and inkeeper is not found today in the case of other bailees for reward, this does not advance the argument materially. It may be answered that the air carrier who otherwise fulfils the necessary requirements of a common carrier, does not represent a completely new genus of bailee for reward. He is rather a species belonging to the genus common carrier.'

308 The carriage of firearms, munitions and dangerous goods without Commonwealth government permission is prohibited by s 19 of the Air Navigation Act 1920 (Cth), and regs 120–120A of the Air Navigation Regulations (Cth). The operation of Air Navigation Orders made under these Regulations (now substantially replaced by the Civil Aviation Regulations) is continued by reg 311 of the Civil Aviation Regulations (Cth), (SR 1988, no 158). The Regulations are applied to intrastate aviation by the Air Navigation Act 1938 (NSW); the Air Navigation Acts 1937–47 (Qld); the Air Navigation Act 1937 (SA); the Air Navigation Act 1937 (Tas); the Air Navigation Act 1958 (Vic); the Air Navigation Act 1937 (WA).

309 Applied to intrastate carriage by Air Navigation Acts (NSW), (Qld), (Tas) (Vic), s 6; (WA), (SA), s 7; the principal Act is now amended by the Civil Aviation (Carrier's Liability) Amendment Act 1991 (Cth).

International carriage, baggage and cargo

International carriage: the Amended Warsaw Convention

Introduction

The Civil Aviation (Carriers' Liability) Amendment Act 1991 (Cth)[310] sets out the Warsaw Convention,[311] the Warsaw Convention as amended by the Hague Protocol of 1955 (the amended Convention)[312] the Guadalajara Convention[313] and the Montreal nos 3 and 4 Conventions.[314]

Under Article 18 of the amended Convention, this only applies to international carriage as defined in Article 1 of the Convention, but only where the places of departure and destination are either in the Territories of two parties to the Hague Protocol, or in the Territory of one party to the protocol with an agreed stopping place in the territory of another State.[315]

Of the numerous amendments made by the protocol, the most important relates to the contents of the air waybill, the carrier's liability and the passenger ticket. References are to the Warsaw Convention as amended by the Hague Protocol unless otherwise indicated.

The Warsaw Convention 1929 on international carriage by air is given force of law in Australia by s 11(1) of the Civil Aviation (Carriers' Liability) Act 1959 (Cth). Australia has ratified amendments made to the convention by the Hague Protocol 1955, but not all countries that were parties to the convention have done the same. Because these amendments apply only to carriage involving the territory of parties which have ratified the protocol, the original convention without the protocol amendments continues to govern transport involving the territory of some States. The USA, for example, has not ratified the amendments made by the Hague Protocol.

The Convention applies under the basic application provision, Article 1(1), to all 'international carriage', as defined, of persons, baggage or cargo by aircraft performed for reward, or performed gratuitously by an air transport undertaking (including carriage by a State), or by a legally constituted public body, but not including carriage under an international postal convention (Article 2). 'International carriage' is defined in Articles 1(2) and (3) as carriage in which, according to the agreement between the parties, the

---

310 Amending s 5 of the Civil Aviation (Carrier's Liability) Act 1959 (Cth), repealing ss 8, 9, 10 and Schedule 2. Section 24A of the Civil Aviation (Carriers' Liability) Amendment Act 1991 (Cth) preserves the jurisdiction of State courts in respect of an action brought under the amended Warsaw Convention for the purposes s 38 of the Judiciary Act 1903 (Cth).

311 Schedule 1.

312 Schedule 2.

313 Schedule 3.

314 Schedule 3.

315 The scope of the amended convention is altered slightly by the repeal and replacement of Article 34 (convention not to apply to experimental or extraordinary carriage). Under the new Article 34 the provisions of Articles 3–9 relating to documents of carriage do not apply in the case of carriage performed in extraordinary circumstances outside the scope of an air carrier's business. See Schedule 1, Ch V of the Civil Aviation (Carrier's Liability) Amendment Act 1991 (Cth).

place of departure and the place of destination are within the territory of two parties to the Convention, or within the territory of one such party, if there is an agreed stopping place in the territory of another country (whether that country is a party to the Convention or not).[316] The Convention thus applies only to transport involving States which are parties to the Convention.

Successive carriers

Where the first carrier and the passenger or consignor agree that carriage is to be performed by several successive air carriers, and regard the carriage as a single operation, the carriage is deemed to be one undivided carriage for the purposes of the Convention (Article 1(3)). In such cases, each carrier who accepts baggage or cargo is subject to the rules of the Convention, and is deemed to be one of the parties to the contract of carriage in so far as the contract deals with the part of the carriage which is performed under its supervision (Article 30(1)). The passenger or consignor has a right of action against the last carrier, and each may take action against the carrier which performed the carriage during which destruction, loss, damage or delay took place (these carriers being jointly and severally liable to the passenger or the consignor and consignee) (Article 30(3)).

Baggage check

The carrier must deliver a baggage check for the carriage of baggage other than small personal items of which the passenger takes charge (Article 4(1)). The baggage check must contain specified information about the baggage and the carriage, and a statement that the carriage is subject to the rules relating to liability established by the Convention (Article 4(3)).

Absence, irregularity or loss of the baggage check does not affect the existence or validity of the contract of carriage, or the application to it of the Convention (Article 4(4)).[317] However, the carrier loses the benefit of exclusions and limitations of liability under the convention if it accepts baggage without a baggage check having been issued, or if the baggage check does not contain the number of the passenger ticket, the number and weight of the packages, or the statement that the carriage is subject to the convention's liability rules (Article 4(4)).

---

316 Despite the difficulties that may arise in deciding whether or not a contract of carriage by air is one of international carriage, an important factor in determining this may be the common practice of travelling on a return ticket. In *Grein v Imperial Airways Ltd* [1937] 1 KB 50, Mr Grein took a return ticket from London to Antwerp, with an agreed stopping place at Brussels. On the return flight the plane crashed due to the pilot's negligence and Mr Grein was killed. The English Court of Appeal (Greer J, dissenting) took the view that the carriage was international although Belgium, having signed but not yet ratified the Warsaw Convention, was not regarded as a high contracting party – the court treating the contract as being in respect of one carriage only, namely, London-Antwerp and return. Thus, the damages to the plaintiff were limited to the amount laid down by the Carriage by Air Act 1932 (UK). On the liability of the carrier under the Warsaw Convention see Miller, G, *Liability in International Air Transport*, 1977, The Hague: Kluwer; see also Goldhirsh, LB, *The Warsaw Convention Annotated: A Legal Handbook*, 1988, The Hague: Martinus Nijhoff.

317 On the adequacy of the baggage check, see Shawcross and Beaumont, *op cit*, 4th edn, Vol 1, para VII (168).

Air waybill

A carrier of cargo has the right to require the consignor to make out and hand over an air waybill under Article 5 of the convention, and a consignor has the right to require the carrier to accept the air waybill. Further requirements for the completion and signature of the air waybill are found in Articles 6 and 7. Article 8 sets out 17 separate particulars which are to be included in the air waybill, concerning the carriage, the cargo, and the documentation itself. The air waybill is *prima facie* evidence of the conclusion of the contract, the receipt of the cargo, and the conditions of carriage (Article 11(1)).

As with the baggage check, absence, irregularity or loss of the air waybill does not affect the existence or validity of the contract of carriage, or the application to it of the convention (Article 5(2). The carrier loses the benefit of exclusions and limitations of liability under the convention if they accept cargo without an air waybill having been made out, or if the air waybill omits certain of the particulars required by Articles 8 and 9.

These are:

(a) the place and date of its execution;

(b) the place of departure and destination;

(c) the agreed stopping places (which can be altered by the carrier in necessity);

(d) the name and address of the consignor;

(e) the name and address of the first carrier;

(f) the name and address of the consignee if the circumstances require it;

(g) the nature of the goods;

(h) the number of the packages, the method of packing and the particular marks or numbers on them;

(I) the weight, quantity and volume or dimensions of the goods;

(j) the apparent condition of the goods and of the packing;

(k) the freight, if it has been agreed upon, the date and place of payment, and the person who is to pay for it;

(l) the price of the goods if they are sent for payment on delivery, and the amount of the expenses incurred if the circumstances require it;

(m) the amount of the value declared under Article 22(2) and (3);

(n) the number of parts of the air waybill;

(o) the documents handed to the carrier to accompany the air waybill;

(p) the time fixed for the completion of the carriage and a brief note of the route to be followed, if these matters have been agreed upon;

(q) a statement that the carriage is subject to the rules relating to liability established by the Convention.[318]

---

318 The consignor is liable for damage suffered by any person by reason of irregularity, incorrectness or incompleteness of the particulars and statements concerning the cargo which the consignor inserts in the air waybill (Article 10(2)).

Statements in the air waybill relating to the weight, dimensions and packing of the cargo, and the number of packages, are evidence of the facts stated. Those relating to the quantity, volume and condition of the cargo are not evidence against the carrier unless they relate to apparent condition of the cargo or have been, and are stated in the air waybill to have been, checked by the carrier in the presence of the consignor (Article 11(2)).

Information and documents necessary to meet formalities of customs and police must be provided by the consignor before the cargo can be delivered to the consignee, and the documents must be attached to the air waybill (Article 16(1)). The consignor is liable to the consignee for damage occasioned by absence, insufficiency or irregularity of such information or documents, unless the damage is due to the fault of the carrier or its servants or agents, and the carrier is under no obligation to inquire into their correctness or sufficiency (Article 16(1) and (2)).

The consignee is entitled, on arrival of the cargo at its destination, to require the carrier to hand over to them the air waybill and the cargo, on payment of charges due and compliance with the conditions of carriage set out in the air waybill (Article 13(1)). The carrier must notify the consignee as soon as the cargo arrives at its destination (Article 13(2)).

The consignor has a right under Article 12 to dispose of the cargo by withdrawing it at departure or destination, stopping it on the journey, requiring it to be delivered at destination or on the journey to someone other than the consignee named in the air waybill, or requiring it to be returned to the place of departure. This right of the consignor ends when the right of the consignee to require delivery begins under Article 13, but revives if the consignee refuses delivery or cannot be communicated with (Article 12(4)). The consignor's right is also subject to obligations not to prejudice the carrier or other consignors, and to pay expenses (Article 12(1)).

The provisions of Articles 12, 13 and 14 can be varied by express provision in the air waybill, but only by such provision (Article 15(2)).

Receipt by the person entitled to delivery of baggage or cargo without complaint is evidence that the baggage or cargo has been delivered in good condition and in accordance with the document of carriage (Article 26(1)). If the carrier admits the loss of the cargo, or if the cargo has not arrived seven days after it ought to have arrived, the consignee is entitled to put into force against the carrier the rights which flow from the contract of carriage (Article 13(3)). Provided they carry out their obligations under the contract of carriage, the consignor and the consignee can enforce their respective rights under Article 12 and 13 in their own respective names, whether they are acting in their own interests or in the interests of others (Article 14).

The relations of consignor and consignee with each other, or the relations of third parties claiming through them are not effected by Articles 12–14 (Article 15).

Liability for destruction, damage or loss

Liability is imposed on the carrier for damage sustained in the event of the destruction or loss or, or damage to, cargo and registered baggage, if the occurrence which caused the damage took place during the carriage by air (Article 18).[319] For this purpose, the carriage comprises the period during which the baggage or cargo is in charge of the carrier (Article 18).[320] The carrier is also liable for damage occasioned by delay in the carriage by air of baggage and cargo (Article 19). In cases covered by Articles 18 and 19, an action for damages, however founded, can only be brought subject to the conditions and limits in the convention (Article 24(1)).

Article 18(2) and (3) define 'air transportation' as the period during which the baggage or goods are in the control of the carrier in an airport or on board an aircraft. In the case of landing outside an airport the carriers' liability for the goods is extended to 'any place whatsoever'.

Article 18 requires that the goods be shown to have been damaged while in the carrier's charge in an airport or on board. If there is a loss while the goods are not on board or were outside an airport, then Article 18(3) determines that the carrier is not responsible under the convention for damage.

Generally, when the carrier has physical possession of the goods in an airport or on board it is 'in charge' of them. This may not be the case where cargo is placed at the disposition of the consignee while still on board the aircraft. Similarly, the carrier may be considered to be 'in charge' of the goods without having physical possession where these are with a handling agent.

In *United International Stables Ltd v Pacific Western Airlines*,[321] a horse being carried with others broke loose from its stall aboard the aircraft. The captain had to kill the horse to avoid endangering the aircraft. In an action for the loss of the animal, the carrier claimed that as the shipper had supplied handlers to accompany and look after the horses the carrier could not be held responsible for being 'in charge'. The Supreme Court of British Columbia, however, held that even where the cargo was being looked after by another the carrier was still 'in charge' as Article 18 was intended to define when the carrier's liability began and ended.

The term 'in charge' was considered in *Swiss Bank v Brinks Mat*.[322] Three consignments of banknotes were stolen when armed robbers broke into a warehouse at Heathrow airport when goods were being weighed and checked. The Swiss Bank brought an action (amongst others) against Brinks Mat (the road carrier), KLM (from whose warehouse the goods were stolen) and Swiss Air (the air carrier). It was necessary to decide whether or not the air carrier was 'in charge' of the goods at the moment they

---

319 Articles 18 and 19 do not say to whom the liability is owed. It will generally be owed to the owner of the goods, and the consignor or consignee may also claim in some cases provided for specifically by the convention: Shawcross and Beaumont, *op cit*, 4th edn, Vol 1, para VII (188), (190). On 'damage', see *Fothergill v Monarch Airlines Ltd* [1981] AC 251.

320 Carriage by land, sea or river performed outside an aerodrome is excluded from the period of carriage by air, but where such carriage takes place for loading, delivery or trans-shipment in the performance of a contract for carriage by air, damage is presumed to have occurred during the carriage by air (Article 13(3)).

321 (1969) 5 DLR 367 (Supreme Court of British Columbia).

322 [1986] 2 Lloyd's Rep 79.

were stolen, so entitling the air carrier to limit its liability under Article 22. Although the goods were within the airline's warehouse, the warehouse staff had no control over them until the goods had been checked and weighed. Bingham J in the Commercial Court of Queens' Bench therefore concluded that the two consignments which had already been checked and weighed were no longer in the custody of Brinks Mat, but passed into the control of Swiss Air. The last consignment remained in charge of Brinks Mat.

The carrier is 'in charge' of the goods in an airport from the time the goods are delivered to it in the legal sense (which the *Swiss Bank* case usefully illustrates), until the carrier transfers the custody of the goods to the consignee. The carrier accepts the goods, in respect to cargo, when it issues an air waybill, this being evidence of receipt of the goods by the carrier under Article 11. Where goods are damaged while being stored on the carrier's premises the carrier is liable.[323] The carrier will also be liable if goods are damaged when the cargo is being brought out to the aircraft by an airport truck or trailer.[324]

In *Bart v British West Indian Airways Ltd*,[325] the plaintiff claimed damages from the airline on the basis of delay in delivering what was a winning football coupon sent them by the plaintiff's agent in Georgetown, to the UK from Guyana. By a majority the Guyana Court of Appeal, allowing an appeal by the air carrier, held that the plaintiff was not a party to the contract and so not entitled to damages. Bollers CJ argued (at 275) that in the absence of a fixed time there would be an implied agreement between the shipper and carrier that the goods would be conveyed by air within a reasonable time but that under the air consignment note issued by the defendants, it was agreed that no time was fixed for completion of the carriage and no obligation was assumed by the carrier to carry the goods by any specific aircraft or over any particular route or to make any connection at any point according to any particular schedule. Further, Bollers CJ observed that under the general conditions of carriage for cargo no time was fixed for the commencement or completion of the carriage; time tables were to be regarded as approximate only, were not guaranteed and formed no part of the contract of carriage:

> ... it would be surprising to me to find an airline company willing to bind itself to deliver goods within a fixed time when weather conditions, aircraft worthiness and expected or unexpected eventualities may intervene to render futile their most earnest intention.

It is clear that the carrier will not stop being in charge of the goods when, in order for the contract of carriage to be performed, the goods are put in the actual custody of another carrier. In *Wing Hang Bank Ltd v Japan Airlines*,[326] the plaintiff, a Hong Kong Bank, Had shipped a package containing $US250,000 in banknotes, consigned to a New York bank. The package was carried by Japan Air Lines to New York. At the time, the air carrier did not have adequate facilities at the airport in New York. At the time, the air carrier did not have adequate facilities at the airport in New York. Under

---

323 *Westminster Bank v Imperial Airways Ltd* [1936] 2 All ER 890.

324 *Young Jewel Manufacturing Co v Delta* 414 NYS 2d 528 (App Div 1979).

325 [1967] 1 Lloyd's Rep 239.

326 357 F Supp 94 (DCNY 1973).

an agreement with Japan Air Lines, American Airlines took on the obligation of storing and processing through customs all terminating freight received from Japan Air Lines. The package of banknotes was stored by American Airlines in its valuable cargo area at the Airport. Just before the consignee was due to take delivery of the packages, armed robbers broke into the valuable cargo area and stole the bank's packages. Although it was acknowledged that American Airlines exercised physical control over the goods and not Japan Air Lines, there was no argument that the robbery had occurred during the 'carriage by air' under Article 18(2).

Numerous cases arise under Article 18 where the goods reach the destination airport but do not reach the consignee. The carrier does not cease to be legally in charge of the goods merely because the goods leave the carrier's actual control. It is important to know when that legal control ends.

The air carrier is regarded as being in charge of the goods until delivery to the consignee or their agent takes place. In *Sprinks and Cie v Air France*,[327] an ice cream confectionery machine was purchased in England and carried by Air France to Orly airport, clearing the machine through customs. From customs, an Air France employee took it from the customs warehouse, and carried it to where it could be placed on the consignee's truck. During this last part of the handling, the machine was seriously damaged. Air France argued that at the time when the accident occurred its duties as an air carrier had ended. The French court found that the custody of the machine had not transferred to the consignee and, as a result, Air France were held liable for the damage to the machine. The court stated that the damage occurred 'during a surface transportation executed in view of delivery' and so, under Article 18(3), the damage was presumed to have happened in the performance of the contract of carriage by air.

The carrier, therefore, does not stop being legally in charge of the goods simply because these leave the carrier's actual control. The common law cases do not give an indication of when a carrier ceases to be in charge of the goods. There are however, general common law rules governing carriage which determine when transit ends. These rules are consistent with the existing cases dealing with 'carriage by air' and additionally may account for the absence of particular difficulties in cases of carriage by air dealt with by common law courts. The general rule at common law is that the carrier's duties end when the goods are tendered to the consignee, whether accepted by him or not. Carriage will usually end by the handing over of the goods to the consignee. When the consignee refuses to accept the goods, the carriage may end without the handing over of the goods to the consignee. Where goods are not to be delivered at the consignee's premises, the common law principles are that transit ends when a reasonable time has passed after the arrival of the goods at the place of destination.

Article 18(3) provides that the period of carriage by air does not extend to any carriage by land, by sea or river. Where loading, delivery or trans–shipment in carrying out the contract of carriage by air is performed outside an airport, there is a presumption that any damage occurring took place during the carriage by air. This is consistent with

---

327 23 RFDA 405 (CA Paris, 27 June 1969).

Article 31, which provides that in the case of combined carriage performed partly by air and partly by any other carriage mode, the provisions of the convention apply only to carriage by air.

Before the presumption in Article 18(3) can apply, the surface transport must be shown to be incidental to air carriage. Aside from that, in a combined carriage situation the plaintiff will have to establish that the damage occurred during the carriage by air if he wishes to sue the air carrier.

In *Cie UTA v Ste Electro-Enterprise*,[328] equipment had been sent from Le Bourget airport in Paris to Lome airport in Togo in West Africa. Since Lome airport was not able to take the jet aircraft used by the carrier, the equipment was flown to Cotonou airport in the neighbouring State of Benin. From there it was taken by truck to Lome airport. The cargo was damaged on arrival and the consignee brought an action against the air carrier. The French court held that the air carrier was liable on the basis of Article 18(3) as, for his own convenience, he had flown the cargo to Cotonou and from there by road to Lome.

Article 18(3) has been used chiefly where the meaning of carriage by air defined by Article 18(2) was in doubt, the plaintiff then attempting to use the presumption in Article 18(3) to extend the concept of carriage to include the occurrence of the damage. In *Dabrai v Air India*,[329] the plaintiff sought to extend the period of carriage by air in order to include the time when the goods were awaiting delivery to the consignee. The issue of incidental carriage did not arise; the plaintiff simply was attempting to avoid the result of a very narrow definition of carriage by air favoured by the court.

Wilful misconduct and the cargo carrier

Article 25 of the convention, in its original form, prohibited the carrier from relying on any clauses limiting or excluding liability for damage to goods or baggage if either it or its agents were guilty of wilful misconduct. The term 'wilful misconduct'[330] gave rise to a number of problems of interpretation and resultant criticism. The Hague Protocol of 1955 amended Article 25 so that it must now be shown that the act or omission causing

---

328 (1977) RFDA (CA Paris, 6 May 1976).

329 (1955) 42 AIR, NUC 18 (High Court of Bombay, 1952).

330 In *Horabin v British Overseas Airways Corporation* [1952] 2 All ER 1016, 'wilful misconduct' was held to be a term that might include even a comparatively minor breach of safety regulations or a minor lapse from comparative standards of safety. However, the mere fact that an act was done contrary to a plan or to instructions, or even to the standards of safe flying, to the knowledge of the person doing it, does not establish wilful misconduct on his part, unless it is shown that he know that he was doing something contrary to the best interests of the passengers and of his employers or involving them in a greater risk than if he had not done it. A grave error of judgment, particular one apparent as such in the light of after events, is not wilful misconduct if the person responsible thought he was acting in the best interests of the passengers and of the aircraft. Per Barry J at 1019: 'Wilful misconduct [is that] to which the will is a party; and it is wholly different in kind from mere negligence or carelessness, however gross that negligence or carelessness may be. The will must be a party to the misconduct, and not merely a party to the conduct of which the complaint is made. As an example, if the pilot of an aircraft knowingly does something which subsequently a jury find amounted to misconduct, that fact alone does not show that he was guilty of wilful misconduct. To establish wilful misconduct on the part of this imaginary pilot, it must be shown, not only that he knowingly (and in that sense wilfully) did the wrongful act, but also that, when he did it, he was aware that it was a wrongful act, ie that he ...

damage was done 'with intent to cause damage or recklessly and with knowledge that damage would result'. It defined 'wilful misconduct' in terms of a person's actions and not in terms of a legal concept. Although Article 25 penalised the carrier by prohibiting it from using limitations under Article 22 of the convention other defences were still open to the carrier, such as Article 20 (all necessary measures) or Article 21 (contributory negligence). The amended Article 25 has produced as many problems of interpretation as its predecessor.

Article 25 gives the court to which the case is submitted the right to apply its own law. The court has to determine first, if the act complained of is considered 'wilful misconduct'; secondly, whether there is a casual connection between the act and the damage; thirdly, the amount of proof required to establish knowledge on the part of the alleged wrongdoer; and, fourthly, damages.

In *Goldman v Thai Airways International Ltd*,[331] the English Court of Appeal held in the context of a passenger injury claim that the word 'recklessly' could not be separated from 'and with knowledge that damage would probably result'. Therefore the test under Article 25 must be regarded as subjective.

In *Qantas Airways Ltd v SS Pharmaceutical Co Ltd*,[332] the defendant airline left a consignment of pharmaceutical products in the open during trans-shipment even though there has been a thunderstorm forecast and there were indications on the goods themselves that these were likely to be damaged if exposed to water. Qantas admitted liability and even wrote a letter to the plaintiffs apologising for what they described as 'deplorably bad handling'. However, this did not prevent Qantas from seeking limitation of liability under Article 22. In the lower court, the judge found against Qantas and awarded full compensation to the plaintiffs.

In the New South Wales Court of Appeal, Goldman was cited with approval. It was not disputed that the test for the existence of knowledge' for the purposes of Article 25 was subjective rather than objective. Qantas, while conceding that the damage resulted from acts or omissions of its servants or agents, called no evidence to explain what happened to the cargo or to account for the way in which it was handled. It therefore had to be established whether or not this failure to give evidence, together with the admission of fault and the proved facts, were enough to bring the case within Article 25.

---

330 ...was aware that he was committing misconduct.' The view of wilful misconduct was applied by Webb J in *Royal Victorian Aero Club v Commonwealth* (1954) 92 CLR 236. *Horabin's* case was considered in *Rustenburg Platinum Mines Ltd and others v South African Airways and Pan American World Airways Inc* [1977] 1 Lloyd's Rep 564. See also *American Airlines v Ulen* [1949] US Av R 338; *Ritts v American Overseas Airlines Inc* [1949] US Av R 65, 68; *Rashap v American Airlines* [1955] US Av R 593 (NY Southern District Court).

331 [1983] 1 WLR 1186.

332 [1989] 1 Lloyd's Rep 319; see, however, the strong dissenting judgment of Kirby P. He argued that, even though there should be a natural sympathy for claimants, especially in personal injury cases such as *Goldman*, the concept of 'recklessness' should be kept within very strict limits and regard should be given to the overall aims of the convention. After examining in detail the standard practice adopted by Qantas in relation to loading cargo, the rainfall evidence and the failure of Qantas to give evidence, Kirby P concluded that it had not been shown that Qantas or their servants and agents had acted recklessly with full knowledge that damage would probably result.

By a majority, the Court of Appeal held that Article 25 was applicable and the plaintiffs were entitled to compensation for their entire loss.

In *Rustenburg Platinum Mines v South African Airways*,[333] it was decided by the English Court of Appeal that the theft of a box of platinum at Heathrow airport, presumably by a Pan Am loader, was within the scope of his employment and that there was no wilful misconduct by any other servant except for that theft. Judgment was given for the plaintiffs as it was held that Pan Am had not taken all measures to avoid damage to them. Pan Am could have instructed their loaders not to leave an aircraft hold with valuable cargo when, due a security emergency at the airport, there were few security guards available. There is some authority in the USA's cases that theft by an employee does not constitute wilful misconduct since the act is not within his or her employment. The better rule is that of the English, Dutch and Japanese cases, holding the reverse view.[334]

The carrier can avoid their liability by Article 20 as follows:

(i) if they prove that they and their agents have taken all necessary measures to avoid the damage, or that it was impossible for him or them to take such measures;[285]

(ii) if, in the case of the carriage of goods or luggage, they prove that the damage was caused by negligent pilotage or negligence in the handling of the aircraft or in navigation, and that, in all other respects, they and their agents have taken all necessary measures to avoid the damage.[336]

Liability for cargo loss and damage due to delay

The air carrier is liable for damage caused by delay to passengers, baggage and goods under Article 19 of the convention. The carrier is presumed to be liable once the plaintiff shows that damage arose due to delay. The plaintiff must prove delay and damage and show delay as the proximate cause of the damage. Claims have to be made against the carrier in writing within 14 days under the convention and 21 days under the Hague Protocol. The majority of air carriers, that is, those using IATA General Conditions of Carriage, provide in their waybills that they are not bound by any indication of time that they have given for the completion of the carriage. The object of such clauses is to deny to the shipper of the goods the right to expect the performance of the carriage at a particular time.

The carrier can only be relieved of liability for delay if he proves that all necessary measures were taken by him to avoid the delay or that it was impossible for him to take

---

333 [1977] 1 Lloyd's Rep 564.

334 See *Northwest Airlines v South African Airways v Suzuki Pearl Shop* (1979) *Air Law* 227 (Supreme Court of Japan, 19 March 1972).

335 If the carrier had literally taken all necessary measures to avoid the damage, the damage would not have occurred. 'Necessary' thus means 'reasonably necessary'. See Shawcross and Beaumont, *op cit*, 4th edn, Vol 1, para VII (116).

336 The carrier may in appropriate cases raise the defence of contributory negligence against the person whose goods were damaged (Article 21).

such measures under Article 20(1). In *Ets Perony v Ste Ethiopian Airlines*,[337] the Paris Court of Appeal ruled void a clause that, except as the convention or other particular law provided rendered the carrier not liable to the shipper or any other person for any damage, delay or loss of whatsoever nature arising out of the carriage of the goods, unless such damage was caused by the negligence or wilful default of the carrier. The court also stated that such a clause should be severed from the contract, since, by moving the burden of proof, it had the tendency to clear the carrier of liability put on him by Articles 18(1) and 19.

In *Bart v West Indian Airways Ltd*,[338] the plaintiff sent a winning combination entry worth over 20,000 to Sherman's pools in England through a Guyana based agent. Due to series of delays, the package missed its scheduled flight from Guyana and arrived in London too late to be included in the pool prize allocation.

In *Bart's* case, Article 18 was applied to the issue of delay; carriage by air was held not to commence as soon as the cargo is received at the airline's terminal office. It would seem then if delay occurs because the carrier is late in transporting the goods from the terminal office to the airport, this is not delay within the meaning of the convention. Article 14, in relation to who can sue the carrier, provides that the consignor and consignee can each enforce all the rights they have under Articles 12 and 13. In *Bart's* case, the court ruled, applying Article 14 is that only the consignor or consignee could sue the carrier, thus ruling out the plaintiff whose winning coupon had missed the draw.

The position has been confirmed in *Tasman Pulp and Paper Co v Brambles JB O'Loghlen*,[339] where Prichard J held that any attempt to deprive the owner of their common law right to sue the carrier for loss or damage occurring while in the carrier's custody should be clearly expressed in the carriage contract. Article 14 should be construed as giving the consignor and consignee rights which they would not normally have, not being owner of the goods; not removing the rights of the owner.

The position was supported in *Gatewhite Ltd v Iberia Lineas Aereas de Espana SA*,[340] where a consignment of chrysanthemums arrived at Heathrow some four days late and in a damaged condition. These flowers belonged to the first plaintiff (ownership having passed from the grower on delivery to the carrier). The defendant airline argued that the plaintiff was precluded from suing. In the Commercial Court, Gatehouse J was led to conclude that the convention did not intend to exclude the right of the owner of goods to bring an action.[341]

In most cases, the consignee will usually be the forwarding agent or freight forwarder or the buyer's bank, and it would appear undesirable that the buyer's remedy

---

337 (1975) 29 RFDA 395 (CA Paris, 30 May 1975).

338 [1967] 1 Lloyd's Rep 239.

339 [1981] 2 NZLR 225.

340 [1989] 1 All ER 944.

341 On the basis of Pritchard J's comments in the *Tasman Pulp* case, Sir Keith Stoby's dissenting judgment in *Bart's* case and that of Steyn CJ in *Pan American World Airways Inc v Fire and Accident Insurance Co Ltd* 1965 (3) SA 150 taken with the silence of the convention on the issue.

should have to rely on the ability and preparedness of the actual consignee to bring an action against the carrier.

The position under the Convention of persons other than the consignor, consignee or owner suffering damage as a result of delay or loss or damage to the goods is not clear. On a common law basis, an action for delay alone brought against the carrier as bailee of goods is likely to depend on the terms of the contract between the carrier and the consignor, ie those contained in the consignment note and air waybill.

Hazardous Goods

Those national legal systems that have implemented the ICAO Technical Instructions respecting dangerous goods incorporate a standard list of what constitute dangerous goods. In Australia, s 23(3) of the Civil Aviation Act 1988 (Cth) by defines dangerous goods to include explosive substances, things likely to endanger the safety of aircraft or persons on board and items which the Regulations issued under the Act declare to be dangerous goods, primarily in the Dangerous Goods List contained in the ICAO Technical Instructions. Dangerous goods must not be carried on aircraft except in accordance with the Regulations or with the written permission of the Civil Aviation Authority and in accordance with any conditions specified in the permission (s 23(1)).

Limitations of carrier's liability

The carrier's liability is limited in the carriage of cargo and registered baggage to 17 SDR per kg of the weight of the lost or damaged package.[342] This is so unless the consignor has made, at the time when the package was handed to the carrier, a special declaration of the value at delivery, and has paid a supplementary sum if the case so required (Article 22(2)).[343] The carrier's liability is then limited to the declared amount, unless the carrier proves that the declared amount is greater than the actual value to the consignor at delivery (Article 22(2)(b)). As regards objects of which the passenger takes charge, the carrier's liability is limited to 300 SDR Article 22(3).[344]

When the Warsaw Convention was being drafted, the delegates to the 1925 Paris conference avoided using local currency for compensation to measure the carrier's liability. Instead, a gold standard was used in order to avoid the effects of devaluation which might result if the limits of liability were expressed in local currencies. The limitation provided in Article 22 was originally expressed as the French gold franc, the 'poincare' franc.

---

342 Civil Aviation (Carriers' Liability) Amendment Act 1991 (Cth) Schedule 2, Article 22(2)(b). The baggage limitation is expressed as 250 francs per kg (Article 22(2)(b)). These are poincare francs defined in Article 22(4), consisting of 65.5 mg of gold of millesimal fineness 900, Schedule 2, Article 22(5). See Kirby, M, 'Civil Aviation Liabilities: Australian Developments in a Global Context' (1992) 17(2) *Annals of Air and Space Laws* 255; *International Air Carriers Liability*, discussion paper, Department of Transport and Communications, 1993, Canberra (mimeo).

343 See *Data Card Corporation v Air Express International Corporation* [1983] 2 All ER 639; for comment on this case, see Bentil, JK, (1984) 128 Sol J 525. On the right of a carrier to limit liability under Article 22(2), on issue of an incomplete baggage check, see *Collins v British Airways* [1982] 1 All ER 302.

344 Australian, English and American authority suggests costs and interest are included in these limits: Shawcross and Beaumont, *op cit*, 4th edn, Vol 1, para VII (124) n 5 (125); see *SS Pharmaceutical Co Ltd v Qantas Airways Ltd* [1989] 1 NSWLR 319.

Passenger levels of compensation for some time had been regarded as too low and in 1955 the Hague Protocol by Article 11 doubled the passenger limits and reference to the French gold franc was removed, reference being made simply to a 'currency unit'. However, the US government regarded the Hague limits as too low and never ratified the protocol. In 1965, the USA threatened to denounce the Warsaw Convention unless airlines agreed to raise their passenger limits to $75,000. As a result, the Montreal Agreement 1965 came into being, which governs flights to and from the USA. In 1975 the high contracting parties agreed to adopt the four Montreal Protocols, so abandoning the conversion based on a gold standard, replacing this with the SDR (Special Drawing Right).

A major problem is the inconsistency in the methods of conversion adopted by different countries. A local (ie national court) can use either:

(a) the official price of gold, or where there is none the latest 'official' price;

(b) the free market price of gold;

(c) SDR's as under the Montreal (an Guatemala) Protocols;

(d) the current value of the French gold franc;

(e) some other countries' currency.

In *SS Pharmaceutical v Qantas Airlines*,[345] Rogers CJ in the Supreme Court of New South Wales outlined the difficulties facing courts in arriving at a suitable conversion for the limitation of liability. His Honour noted that in 1982 on the reading of the Bill which subsequently was enacted as the Civil Aviation (Carrier's Liability) Amendment Act 1982 (Cth) the then Australian Minister for Transport expressed the concern of the Federal government at the inadequacy of the domestic passenger aviation liability levels. He observed that the value of gold had fluctuated considerably over time and that the government was examining the interim arrangements regarding limits on airline liability for international carriage came into effect.

He stated that it was the self-evident intention of the nations signing the Warsaw Convention that there should be means open to air carriers to limit their liability, a provision of international operation. In such circumstances his Honour regarded it as the duty of a court to find means to sustain such a provision and not permit it to be set aside because of changed circumstances. He also cited two reasons, persuasive of the majority of the US Supreme Court. First, unless there was a clear expression by the legislature to abrogate an international treaty, courts were bound to give effect to it. Secondly, the Convention provided for six months' notice by a signatory to be no longer bound.

---

345 [1989] 1 NSWLR 319.

Rogers CJ agreed with Stephens J in the US Supreme Court in *Franklin Mint v TWA*,[346] that if the limitation was unworkable the remedy was to amend the convention. What was required was an amendment in the form of ratification of Montreal Protocol no 4. Rogers CJ regarded this statement as being of particular application in Australia. Those nations which have adopted Montreal Protocol no 4 had applied the SDR alternative. This his Honour regarded as the most satisfactory choice in the conversion dilemma.

However, Rogers CJ found that the SDR solution was not open to him due to the pronouncement of the Australian Federal Minister of Transport in 1982. It was not open for a judge sitting at first instance or for a court to take over the role of Parliament or interpose its views and interpretation.

The next alternative open to the court considered by his Honour was the last official price of gold, the standard accepted by the US Supreme Court. This was viewed by Rogers CJ as neither satisfying the intention of the framers of the Convention nor paying sufficient regard to the changed circumstances. The last official price for gold fixed in Australia was done with little regard for world prices. The only advantage the last official price for gold had, on the basis of the CAB limit in the USA was that, as distinct from the market rate, it avoided the wide swings characteristic of the gold market in the last decade.

Conversion from the current French franc, the fourth alternative, was ruled out by Rogers CJ, as being totally against what was decided at the Warsaw Convention in 1929. Finally, his Honour ruled in favour of the fourth action the current market price of gold.

The Civil Aviation (Carrier's Liability) Amendment Act 1991 (Cth) which came into effect on 27 November 1991 enables the ratification of Montreal Protocols nos 3 and 4.[347] However, at the time of writing, these protocols had not received the

---

346 525 F Supp 1288 (DC NY 1981); [1984] Lloyd's Rep 432. In *Trans World Airlines Inc v Franklin Mint Corporation,* the US Supreme Court, overruling the US Court of Appeals, held that the 1978 repeal of legislation setting an official price for gold in the USA and the erosion of the international gold standard could not be construed as terminating or repudiating the USA's duty to abide by the convention's cargo liability limit; the limit remained enforceable in the US. On the problems of recovery for cargo loss under the 1929 Convention, see Solomon, SH and Goldman, SE, 'Recovery under the Warsaw Convention for the loss of valuable air cargo' [1952] 3 *Lloyd's MCLQ* 453.

347 Schedule 2 of the Civil Aviation (Carriers' Liability) Amendment Act 1991 (Cth). See below and see first reading of the Civil Aviation (Carriers' Liability) Amendment Bill 1991, House of Representatives, Snowdon, MHR, *Weekly Hansard* (1991) no 17, 1991, 17 October, p 2201. The Australian government is currently examining policy options obtainable to give international airline passengers access to compensation higher than the airlines' liability limits, without increasing them. This includes a study of the feasibility of establishing a supplemental scheme under Article 35A. A number of airlines, including Qantas and Japan Airlines have voluntarily accepted the 100,000 SDR passenger limit of Montreal Protocol 3. Some, such as British Airways, are required by statute to observe this limit. Altogether, some 14 national airlines operating on Australian routes have accepted this passenger limit. For a comment on the problems concerning convention limitations, see Pengilley, W and McPhee, J, *Law for Aviators*, 1994, Sydney: Legal Books, pp 244–45, 247. See below under 'New developments'.

necessary number of ratifications.[348] The Montreal Protocol no 3 applies a 100,000 SDR limit to the carrier's liability limit applying to the international carriage of passengers by air. The Montreal Protocol no 4 covers all international carriage of persons baggage or cargo by air for reward and specifically limits the carrier's liability for the carriage of cargo to 17 SDR's per kg (Article 22(2)(b)).

The limits under Article 22 do not prevent a court form additionally awarding the whole or part of the court costs and of the other expenses incurred in the litigation. This will not apply if the amount of damages awarded excluding court costs and other litigation expenses does not exceed the sum the carrier has offered in writing to the plaintiff within a period of six months from the date the occurrence causing the damage, or before commencement of the action, if that is later (s 22(4)).[349]

Special declarations

Article 25 of the Convention gives carriers, shippers and passengers the right to enter into a special agreement to increase the carrier's liability limits.

In the case of cargo, the shipper can make a special declaration of the higher value of the goods before carriage. This gives the carrier notice that the shipment contains items of higher value. But the mere knowledge by the carrier of the higher value of a shipment may not give effect to a higher limitation liability for the shipper. It is necessary to declare the higher value of the cargo on the air waybill.

In *Orlove v Philippine Airlines*,[350] the plaintiff had made special declarations of value on the 'phone and by letter to the contracting air carrier. However, the contracting carrier delivered to a substitute carrier who performed the initial stage of carriage. The two carriers had an interline agreement which included a provision requiring documents disclosing a shipment's value should be requested from a prior carrier. Recovery by the plaintiff from the substitute carrier was limited under the convention as it failed to make a special declaration against that carrier. The plaintiff sued the contracting carrier that the special declaration had been made to, and the carrier then sought indemnity from the substitute carrier under the interline agreement. The court held that the plaintiff could obtain unlimited damages from the contracting carrier to whom he made the special declaration. This was so because the contracting carrier failed to instruct the plaintiff to make another 'special declaration' to the substitute carrier's negligence, would not do so in this case. However, under the interline agreement, the contracting carrier could obtain indemnity from the substitute carrier as a result of the provision requiring the substitute carrier to request documents disclosing a special value.

---

348 As at February 1996, 21 States had ratified Protocol 3 and 25 had ratified Protocol 4. The required number of signatories required for the protocols to come into force is 30. Even after this number is reached, the Federal government would need to enact domestic legislation to bring the protocols into effect in Australia. It would seem unlikely that the protocols will be in force before 1998.

349 Conversion of the SDRs into national currencies shall, in the case of judicial proceedings, be made according to the value of such currencies in terms of the SDR at the date of judgment. The value of a national currency of a High Contracting Party (such as Australia) in terms of the SDR which is a member of the International Monetary Fund (IMF) is to be calculated in accord with the IMF's method of valuation, in effect at the date of the judgment, for its operations and transactions. (Article 22 (6)).

350 257 F 2d 384 (2d Cir 1958).

The above case indicates that the failure to note the 'special declaration' on the air waybill may only protect the carrier if it has no knowledge of the value; actual notice may not be presumed from customs declarations.

Recourse between successive carriers

Where more than one carrier is involved the situation is governed by Article 30 (successive carriers) and Article 31 (combined carriage) in determining which carriers are liable. Successive carriage has been defined as a factual, chronological partition of a single service as contemplated by the contracting parties. Successive carriage is expressly excluded from the scope of the Guadalajara Convention (Article 1(c) (see below)). Therefore, it is vital to distinguish between a successive carrier and an actual carrier.

A successive carrier may be held fully liable for damage occurring during the carriage performed by another successive carrier. However, an actual carrier cannot be liable in excess of the limits laid down by Article 22 of the Warsaw Convention for the acts and omissions of the contracting carrier.

Although Article 30 designates the carrier who is answerable to the passenger, consignor or consignee, it does not determine which carrier will ultimately be liable for financial damages. Article 30A, however (inserted in the convention by Montreal Protocol no 4 of 1975), provides that nothing in the Convention shall prejudice the right of recourse against another person.

Article 30(3) gives a right of action against the first carrier to the passenger or consignor and against the last carrier to the passenger or consignee entitled to delivery.

Article 31 deals with combined carriage. Article 31(2) permits the parties to put in the air waybill conditions regulating transport modes other than air carriage, as long as the provisions of the convention are followed in respect of the carriage by air. So the parties can apply the conditions similar to the Convention, but do so through conditions in the air waybill.

In *Pick v Lufthansa*,[351] a truck carrying a shipment of furs to an airport was hijacked. The shipper claimed that the carriage by air had not begun, but since the truck driver was employed by the air carrier, it was liable for the full value of the goods. The carrier claimed that air carriage had begun at the time of the theft and so Article 22 afforded protection, or, alternatively, that the contract contained a limitation similar to that imposed by the treaty, covering all transport modes required to carry goods to their final destination. As a result, on either ground, the air carrier's liability was limited, even though the treaty did not apply to ground losses occurring before arrival of the goods at the airport. The court held that the Warsaw Convention, operating as a treaty, did not limit the value of the shipper's recovery below its actual proved value because the damage did not occur during air carriage. Even so, the convention limits applied as contractual limits as the parties had followed Article 31(3) and inserted in the air waybill conditions of carriage covering the whole transport, including that by road to the airport. It is worth noting that had Lufthansa not been the truck driver's principal, the airline would have been liable for the theft of the furs.

---

351 9 AVI 18, 077 (NY City Ct 1965).

Limitation on time for claim on carrier

Unless complaint is dispatched to the carrier in writing within prescribed time limits, no action lies against the carrier except in the case of fraud by the carrier: Article 26(3) and (4). The person entitled to delivery must complain, at the latest, within three days[352] from the date of receipt in the case of damage to baggage, seven days from the receipt in the case of damage to cargo, and, in the case of delay, within 14 days from the date on which the baggage or cargo has been placed at that person's disposal (Article 26(2)). The right to damages is extinguished if an action is not brought within two years from the date of arrival at the destination, or from the date on which the aircraft ought to have arrived, or from the date on which the carriage stopped (Article 29(1)); s 34 of the Civil Aviation (Carriers' Liability) Act 1959 (Cth).[353]

Action for damages

An action for damages must be brought in the territory of a party to the convention. At the option of the plaintiff, the action may be brought before the court having jurisdiction:

(i)   where the carrier is ordinarily resident, or has its principal place of business, or has an establishment at which the contract has been made; or

(ii) at the place of destination: Article 28(1).[354]

Section 19 of the Civil Aviation (Carriers' Liability) Act 1959 (Cth) (read with the definition of 'convention' in s 10) deems an action under the convention as amended by the Hague Protocol not to be an action arising directly under a treaty for the purposes of s 28 of the Judiciary Act 1903 (Cth). Although there is no corresponding provision for claims under the unamended convention, it is to be assumed that the same conclusion would follow.

In the case of combined carriage partly by air within the scope of the convention and partly by other modes of carriage, the convention applies only to the carriage by air: Article 31(1).

Contractual clauses and special agreements purporting to infringe the rules laid down in the convention by deciding the law to be applied or altering the rules as to jurisdiction are null and void, although arbitration clauses are allowed for the carriage of cargo if the place of arbitration agrees with the rules as to jurisdiction in Article 28(1) (Article 32).

---

352 'Days' in the Convention means current, not working days (Article 35).

353 Time begins to run on the latest of these dates, if they are different: Shawcross and Beaumont, *op cit*, 4th edn, Vol 1, para VII (144). In *Proctor v Jetway Aviation Pty Ltd* [1984] 1 NSWLR 166, the New South Wales Supreme Court held that it had the power to amend a statement of claim in an action under the Compensation to Relatives Act 1897 (NSW) by adding a claim under the Civil Aviation (Carriers' Liability) Act 1959 (Cth) notwithstanding the expiration of the two year period.

354 As to the meaning of these expressions, see Shawcross and Beaumont, *op cit*, Vol 1, para VII (137) ff and *Rothmans of Pall Mall (Overseas) Ltd v Saudi Arabian Airlines Corp* [1981] QB 368.

Passenger ticket

The passenger ticket constitutes evidence of the conclusion and the conditions of the contract of carriage (Article 3(2)). The ticket must be delivered before the passenger embarks for the relevant flight.[355] The absence, irregularity or loss of the passenger ticket does not affect the validity of the contract of carriage which will be subject to the rules of the convention. However, if the carrier accepts a passenger without a passenger ticket having been delivered, they will not be entitled to protection of the convention provisions excluding or limiting the carrier's liability (Article 3(2)).[356]

The purpose of the provision in Article 3(1)(c) that the passenger ticket must contain the prescribed notice of the possible application of the Warsaw Convention has been cited as giving the passenger fair warning of the carrier's limited liability[357] in order to take measures such as buying insurance to obtain protection against the limitation of liability.[358] On such an assumption, the following propositions[359] have been advanced by courts in the USA:

(i) the ticket must be delivered to the passenger or a close associate (spouse or parent);

(ii) the ticket must be delivered in time for the passenger to take out insurance;

(iii) a ticket not designed to bring the necessary information clearly to the passengers' attention may be regarded as so defective that it does not meet the requirements of the convention.

In addition to the notice required by Article 3, most passenger tickets now contain a further notice headed: 'Advice to international passengers on limitation of liability.' This is required by the Montreal Agreement 1966[360] in relation to carriage falling within the terms of the agreement; international carriage within either the amended or unamended Warsaw Convention where a point in the USA is a point of origin, point of destination or agreed stopping place. The Agreement requires the printing of the advice to conform to prescribed specifications as to size of type, colour and location. A failure to print the advice or to comply with the format specifications can have no effect on the passengers' rights: the Agreement is essentially a contract between the air carriers which have become a party to it. Although the Agreement prescribes the terms of conditions of

---

355 See *Mannion v Pan American World Airways Inc* 105 Misc 2d 927 (NY Sup Ct 1980): a passenger who was travelling New York-Rome-Beirut-Saudi Arabia was injured during a terrorist attack during the Rome-Beirut flight; the failure by the carrier to deliver a ticket before embarkation in New York was held to be immaterial, the omission having been rectified before embarkation in Rome. The case was governed by the unamended Warsaw Convention which requires delivery of the ticket 'before the carrier accepts a passenger' as opposed 'embarkation' under the amended convention. A different result might be reached by a common law court outside the US on the wording of the amended convention; see Shawcross and Beaumont, *op cit*, Vol 1, para VII (150). Express provision is made in the Guatemala Protocol 1971 (amending Article 3(1) by Article (2) for collective tickets).

356 Schedule 1, Chapter 2.

357 *Seth v BOAC* 329 F2d 303 (1st Circ, 1964).

358 *Mertens v Flying Tiger Line Inc* 341 F 2d 851 (2nd Circ, 1965).

359 There is no express support of these propositions in the Civil Aviation (Carriers' Liability) Act 1959 (Cth).

360 CAB 18900: see Gilchrist, N, 'Notice in the passenger ticket' [1982] 3 *Lloyd's MCLQ* 444.

carriage to be adopted by signatory carriers, these do not include a reference to the advice.[361]

Guadalajara Convention

The Warsaw Convention clearly applies to a carrier making an agreement with a passenger or consignor for carriage within the scope of the convention, and also to any successive carrier. However, it is uncertain whether the convention applies to any other carriers performing carriage contemplated in the agreement. This uncertainty is addressed by the Guadalajara Convention, which is given force of law in Australia by s 25A of the Civil Aviation (Carriers' Liability) Act 1959 (Cth).[362]

Under the Guadalajara convention, the rules of the Warsaw Convention apply to both the 'contracting carrier' and any 'actual carrier' performing all or part of carriage contemplated in an agreement for carriage governed by the Warsaw Convention (Articles 1 and 2 of the Guadalajara Convention). The 'contracting carrier' is the person who, as a principal, makes an agreement for carriage governed by the Warsaw Convention with a passenger or consignor or with a person acting on behalf of the passenger or consignor (Articles 1(b) of the Guadalajara Convention). An 'actual carrier' is a carrier, other than the contracting carrier, who performs all or part of the carriage contemplated in the agreement under authority from the contracting carrier, and is not a successive carrier for the relevant carriage (Articles 1(c) of the Guadalajara

---

361 See *Montreal Trust Co v Canadian Pacific Airlines Ltd* (1976) 72 DLR (3d) 257. In *Lisi v Alitalia-Linee Aeree Italiane SpA* [1967] Lloyd's Rep 140; 370 F 2d 508 (2nd Circ 1966) [affirmed [1968] 1 Lloyd's Rep 505; 390 US 455 (1968)] the US Court of Appeal held that a carrier that issued a ticket under the 1966 Montreal Agreement giving the notice 'Advice to International Passengers on Limitation of Liability' in eight and a half point rather than 10 point type was in the same position as if they had not complied with Article 3. The court held that although the Agreement was essentially a contract between carriers the plaintiff in the case was a third party beneficiary to enforce the agreement. (This is stated by Shawcross and Beaumont, *op cit*, 4th edn, Vol 1, para VII (151) not to be the position in English law; it would also appear to be the Australian position.) This approach has been expressly rejected by the Supreme Court of Canada; in *Ludecke v Canadian Pacific Airlines Ltd* (1979) 98 DLR (3d) 52; [1979] 2 Lloyd's Rep 260 approving *Montreal Trust Co v Canadian Pacific Airlines Ltd* (1976) 72 DLR (3d) 257; [1977] 2 Lloyd's Rep 80, the Supreme Court of Canada expressly rejected the *Lisi* judgment, holding that Article 3 of the unamended Warsaw Convention was plain and admitted of no misunderstanding; that the benefit on limitation of liability was lost only if no ticket was delivered. Shawcross and Beaumont, *op cit*, 4th edn, Vol 1, para VII (151) submit that the '*Lisi* principle' cannot be reconciled with the words of the Convention and should not be followed. For a High Court of Australia decision in which the contractual status of an airline ticket was discussed as distinct from the position under the Convention, see *MacRobertson Miller Airlines Services v Commissioner of State Taxation of State of Western Australia* (1975) 133 CLR 125. The High Court there held that the ticket at date of issue was only a written offer open for acceptance by the passenger when they had a reasonable opportunity of accepting or rejecting the conditions which the carrier by the ticket sought to impose. See Pengilley, W and McPhee, J, *Law for Aviators*, 1994, Sydney: Legal Books, for a discussion of the 'ticket cases' in the aviation context, pp 78–81.

362 The text of the Guadalajara Convention is contained in Schedule 3 of the Civil Aviation (Carriers' Liability) Act 1959 (Cth).

Convention).[363] Authority from the contracting carrier is presumed in the absence of proof to the contrary (Article 1(c) of the Guadalajara Convention).

Article 1(a) of the Guadalajara Convention and s 25B of the Civil Aviation (Carriers' Liability) Act 1959 (Cth) have the effect of applying the unamended Warsaw Convention, the amended Warsaw Convention or the supplementary provisions in the Civil Aviation (Carriers' Liability) Act 1959 (Cth) to carriage under the Guadalajara Convention according to whichever rules apply to the carriage by the contracting carrier independently of the Guadalajara Convention.[364]

Where the contracting carrier makes an agreement with a passenger or consignor for carriage governed by the Warsaw Convention (with or without the Hague Protocol) which is performed by another carrier (the actual carrier) in whole or part, both the contracting carrier and the actual carrier are subject to the Warsaw Convention (and the Hague Protocol, if applicable), the contracting carrier for the whole of the carriage the actual carrier for the part they perform (Article 2).

The acts and omissions of one carrier are deemed to be those of the other (Article 3). The plaintiff has an option whether to sue the contracting carrier, or actual carrier who performed the relevant part of the carriage, or both, either together or separately and either carrier, if sued alone can require that the other be made a party to the proceedings (Article 7). However, an action must be brought either in a court where the contracting carrier may be sued in accordance with Article 28 of the Warsaw Convention or before a court having jurisdiction at the place where the actual carrier is ordinarily resident or has his principal place of business (Article 8). Before any action for damage to baggage or goods is commenced the consignor is required by the Warsaw Convention (Article 26) to make a complaint in writing within the specified time limit and by the Guadalajara Convention such complaints can be made either to the contracting carrier or actual carrier (Article 4).

The contracting carrier and the actual carrier are each vicariously liable in certain circumstances for the acts and omissions of the servants and agents of the other (Article 3). Such liability can arise only when the servant or agent is acting within the scope of their employment and when the act or omission relates to the carriage performed by the actual carrier. Subject to these limitations, both the contracting carrier and the actual carrier incur liability, apart from the provision that each servant or agent can avail themselves of the limits or liability applicable to their employer unless they acted in such a way so as to deprive themselves of this right (Article 5). If the actual carrier is liable on the ground of vicarious liability solely their liability never exceeds the limits laid down in

---

363 A contract for international carriage may be, however, partly performed by an actual carrier, who is not a 'successive carrier', or performed wholly by carriers or a carrier other than the contracting carrier; eg where the contracting carrier charters aircraft from another operator to perform all of the flight. In such circumstances, opinion is divided as to whether the contracting carrier is 'the carrier' for the purposes of the Warsaw Convention, or in respect of such part of the carriage as he performs. The better view would appear to be that 'carrier' refers to the contracting carrier, but English courts would be ready to hold that an implied contract arises, in the absence of an express contract, between the passenger (or, perhaps, consignor) and the actual carrier, and that the carriage is performed on the terms of the original contact made with the contracting carrier. McNair, *op cit*, p 229.

364 See Parts II, III and IIIA of the Civil Aviation (Carrier's Liability) Act 1959 (Cth).

Article 22 of the Warsaw Convention. But where the damage is caused by a servant or agent of the actual carrier and the circumstances are such that the limited liability provisions do not apply, both the liability of the actual carrier and contractual carrier is unlimited Article 3(2).[365]

The possibility of proceedings against one or more defendants is provided for in the Guadalajara Convention (Article 6).

If a servant or agent of either carrier is liable for the damage and is not entitled to limit their liability[366] because at the material time they were acting outside the scope of his employment, their unlimited liability does not increase the limit of liability under Article 7 as is regulated by the maximum liability or either the actual carrier or the contracting carrier.

Airlines and passenger liability

Liability for passenger injury and death

The problem of compensation of victims of international air disasters has become one of extreme legal complexity exemplified in resultant litigation and claims. The issues raised in such claims are covered elsewhere but important aspects need briefly noting.[367]

Limitation of liability may arise as litigated issue where plaintiffs claim that the carrier is not protected by the limitation provided by the unamended or amended Warsaw Convention due to alleged failure by the carrier to adhere to the requirements of statement or notice of liability limitation.[368]

---

365 Article 3 further provides that any special agreement whereby the contracting carrier has assumed additional obligations or waived any of the carrier's rights under the Warsaw Convention does not affect the actual carrier unless they agree to this assumption or waiver. Even if the responsibility lay with a servant or agent of the actual carrier, it appears that the actual carrier would incur no liability to the consignor, and the contracting carrier would be solely responsible to the consignor. See McNair, *op cit*, p 232.

366 Under Article 25 of the Warsaw Convention (as amended by the Hague Protocol) which provides that the aggregate of amounts recoverable from the carrier and their servants shall not, in such circumstances, exceed the limits laid down in Article 22 of the Warsaw Convention. Article 9 of Guadalajara Convention precludes attempts to relieve the liabilities of the contracting and actual carrier or avoid the application of the convention but the actual carrier is given the right to exclude liability for loss or damage resulting from inherent defect, quality or vice of the cargo carried (Article 9(2)).

367 See Shawcross and Beaumont, *op cit*, 4th edn, Vol 1, para VII (152)–(163); Hannappel, PPC, 'The right to sue in death cases under the Warsaw Convention' (1981) 6(2) *Air Law* 66; Maulawicz, A, 'The Liability Regime of the International Air Carrier' (1979) 4 *Annals of Air and Space Law* 122–31. See the arrangement of 10 Japanese airlines, putting into effect on 20 November 1992 a regime of unlimited liability in respect passenger death and injury claims; see Sakamoto, T, 'The Fate of Passenger Liability Limit Under the Warsaw Convention' and Okabe, S, 'Aviation Personal Injury Claim Settlement in Japan' both given at the International Conference on Air Transport and Space Application in a New World, June 1993, Tokyo. See Cheng, B, 'Air carrier's Liability for Passenger Injury and Death: the Japanese Initiative and Response to the Recent EC Consultation Paper' (1993) 18 *Air and Space Law* 109; for a concise note on the Japanese initiative, see Pengilley and McPhee, *op cit*, pp 290–93, 263.

368 Edwards, LR, 'The Liability of Air Carriers for Death and Personal Injury to Passengers' (1982) 56 ALJ 108; Gold (a response) (1982) 56 ALJ 558; Camarda, G, 'Liability for carriers for damages of passengers on charter flights' (1977) 11(2) *Air Law* 62.

Legal claims arising from an air accident may also raise important questions concerning the appropriate legal forum in which the claims are to be adjudicated.[369]

Air accidents are subject to standard enquiry procedures.[370] Issues of negligent navigation and pilot error may raise issues of negligence on the part of the carrier themselves including those relating to flight information and pilot briefing.[371]

Main provisions of the Carrier's Liability Act

The Civil Aviation (Carriers' Liability) Act 1959 (Cth) has been modified by the Civil Aviation (Carriers' Liability) Amendment Act 1991 (Cth). Part IV of the Civil Aviation (Carriers' Liability) Act 1959 (Cth) applies to carriage of a passenger where the passenger is or is to be carried in an aircraft being operated by the holder of an airline licence or a charter licence (as defined) in the course of commercial transport operations, or in an aircraft being operated in the course of trade and commerce between Australia and another country, under an arrangement for the carriage of the passenger:

(a) between a place in a State and a place in another State;

(b) between a place in a Territory and a place in Australia outside that Territory;

(c) between a place in a Territory and another place in that Territory; or

(d) between a place in Australia and a place outside Australia (ss 26(1) and 27(1).

The Civil Aviation (Carriers' Liability) Amendment Act 1991 (Cth) modifies and amends the Civil Aviation (Carriers' Liability) Act 1959 (Cth). The 1991 Act inserts two new parts IIIB and IIIC into the 1959 Act covering carriage to which Montreal Protocols no 3 and no 4 apply.[372] These parts become law on dates no earlier than the entry into force of the protocols.[373]

The carrier is liable under Part IV of the Civil Aviation (Carriers' Liability) Act 1959 (Cth) where it applies to the carriage of a passenger and not otherwise, for damage sustained in the event of the destruction or loss of, or injury to, the passenger's baggage,

---

369 See Levy, SJ, 'The Rights of International Airline Passengers' (1976) (1) *Air Law* 275, where the 1974 Turkish Airlines DC-10 crash at Ermonville near Paris is used as an instance of the complexity of issues that can arise.

370 See Air Navigation Regulations (Cth) Part XVI made under s 26 of the Air Navigation Act 1920 (Cth). For inquiry procedures see Laws of Australia: 34 Transport; 34.2, Part E, paras 75–88.

371 These issues were dramatically raised in the aftermath of 1979 Mt Erebus DC-10 crash of an Air New Zealand flight; see 'Aircraft Accident Report no 79–139', Ministry of Transport, Wellington, 1979; 'Report of the Royal Commission to Enquire into the Crash on Mount Erebus Antarctica, of a DC-10 Aircraft operated by Air New Zealand Limited, Wellington' (1981); see Vennel, MA, 'Report of the Royal Commission to Enquire into the Crash on Mt Erebus, Antarctica of a DC-10 Aircraft operated by Air New Zealand Limited' (1981) 6(4) *Air Law* 254; 'The Erebus Inquiry' (1981) 8 NZLJ 189; 'Judges and Royal Commissions' (1982) 2 NZLJ 37; Mahon, P, 'The Mount Erebus Royal Commission – some Lessons About Investigation and Interpretation of Evidence' (1982) 12 *Queensland Law Society Journal* 287.

372 Sections 7–8 of the Civil Aviation (Carriers' Liability) Amendment Act 1991 (Cth) amending ss 25A, 25B of the Principal Act, Parts IIIB and IIIC referring to Montreal Protocols nos 3 and 4 are inserted after Part IIIA, s 9 of the Principal Act.

373 See s 7–8 of the Civil Aviation (Carriers' Liability) Amendment Act 1991 (Cth). Section II provides for amendment of s 27 of the Principal Act by adding the Montreal Protocols nos 3 and 4 after the Hague Protocol and before the Guadalajara Convention respectively.

if the occurrence which causes the destruction, loss or injury takes place during the period of the carriage by air (s 29(1)). The carrier's liability is excluded if they prove that they and their servants and agents took all necessary measures to avoid the destruction, loss or injury, or that it was impossible for them to take such measures (s 29(1)).

Further provisions in ss 29–30 define the period of carriage, set time limits for the making of complaints, and deal with other matters incidental to liability.

Carriers' liability in general terms, is limited by s 31. These limits have now been changed by the Parts IIIB and IIIC under the Civil Aviation (Carriers' Liability) Amendment Act 1991 (Cth). It has been held that these limits do not of themselves limit awards of cost or interest.[374]

Exclusions and limitation clauses are nullified as inconsistent with the Act (s 32(1)) while s 32(2) permits such clauses with respect to loss or damage resulting from the inherent vice, quality or defect of goods carried. Servants and agents of the carrier may claim the benefit of liability limits under s 33. The right to damages under Part IV is extinguished if an action is not brought within two years of the carriage in question, in general terms (s 34). The passenger's contributory negligence may reduce damages under s 39.

Domestic airline deregulation

The deregulation of domestic airlines commenced on 31 October 1990 with the ending of the 'Two Airline Agreement'.[375] After that date, the operation of domestic airlines has been subject to the Trade Practices Act 1974 (Cth).[376] It should be noted that the States are still entitled to exercise the right to require an air transport operator wishing to engage in intrastate carriage to hold both State and Federal licences.

The Airlines Agreement Act 1981 (Cth) has been repealed by the Airlines Agreement (Termination) Act 1990 (Cth) s 3, and the 1981 Airlines Agreement between the Commonwealth and the two major domestic airlines has been terminated. The Commonwealth in 1990 withdrew from the application of passenger capacity

---

374 In *Colombera v MacRobertson Miller Airlines Ltd* [1972] WAR 68, it was held that provision limiting liability did not prevent an order being made for costs; in *Saunders v Ansett Industries*, under s 31 of the 1959 Act (1975) 10 SASR 579, ss 28 and 31 of the 1959 Act were held to limit the liability of a carrier only as to the damage caused by the carrier. The limitation did not extend to an award of interest on the judgement under the Supreme Court Act 1935–74 (SA). In *McKenna v Avion Pty Ltd* [1981] WAR 255, damages recoverable under s 28 by a member of a deceased's family were held not to include any amount by way of compensation for grief or suffering.

375 This is a collective term applied to a series of agreements, the most recent being that of 1981; see Livermore, J, 'The legal status of the two airline agreement' (1983) 8 (2), (4) *Air Law* 90, 221. The deregulation of the industry followed the recommendations of the *Independent Review of Economic Regulation of Domestic Aviation*, 1986 (the May Report), Australian Government Publishing Service. Canberra. For note on the 'two airline policy '(incorporating material from the Livermore article) and an extract of a travel industry review article critical of the lease system operating at FAC controlled airports at the time of the entry of the Compass airline, see Pengilley and McPhee, *op cit*, pp 230–37. See Harbison, P, 'Legal and Administrative Problems of Airline Deregulation: Australia' *Australian Law and Legal Thinking in the 1990s*, 1994, Sydney: Faculty of Law, University of Sydney, pp 299–324.

376 See ss 15 and 16 and Schedule 1 of the Australian Airlines (Conversion to Public Company) Act 1988 (Cth); see Qantas Sale Amendment Act 1995 (no 44 of 1995).

provisions in the Airline Equipment Acts 1958-81 (Cth). Also in 1990 the Commonwealth announced the privatisation of Australian Airlines[377] and control of domestic air fares through the Independent Air Fares Committee was abandoned with the abolition of the Commission. Qantas and Australian Airlines were merged on 14 September 1992 with the provisions for the sale of part of Qantas being provided by the Qantas Sale Act 1992 (Cth).[378]

Bilateral airline agreements

The international framework for the operation of international commercial air services is administered by multilaterally agreed rules established by the convention on International Civil Aviation, termed the Chicago Convention, by the International Air Transport Association (IATA) and by principles governing bilateral air services agreements.[379] Australia's approval of the Chicago Convention is made under the Air Navigation Act 1920 (Cth) (as amended). An international airline other than Australian may only operate scheduled international air services over or into Australian territory in accordance with an international airline licence issued by the Secretary to the Department of Transport and Communications under the Air Navigation Regulations.[380] The International Air Services Commission set up under the International Air Services Commission Act 1992 (Cth) is an independent body with the duty of allocating international aviation capacity and route entitlements among Australian international carriers.

The international commercial aviation market has to be seen in the context of globalisation which involves the integration of the commercial aviation market world wide with the gradual deregulation of international commercial air services.[381]

---

377 Qantas had transferred to it share certificates by the Commonwealth and five nominated shareholders of the original TAA (Australian Airlines). Qantas appearing as owner of the shares on the ACT share registry.

378 Superseding Qantas Empire Airways Act 1948 (Cth) which the 1992 Act repealed together with the Australian National Airlines Act 1945 (Cth). See Laws of Australia: 34 Transport, para 176. On 1 Nov 1993, Qantas and Australian Airlines operationally merged to become Qantas, the Australian Airline. Qantas and British Airways lodged an application with the then Trade Practices Commission on 10 August 1994 for authorisation of a wide ranging and open ended agreement, which the Commission subsequently approved in May 1995, subject to conditions; see Application A90565 and determination of 12 May (file no CA 94/95).

379 See Singh, P, 'Some Aspects of Australia's bilateral air services agreements' (1984) 9(3)(4), *Air Law* 149, 235. See Shawcross and Beaumont, *op cit,* Vol 1, para IV (25–41). See *Laws of Australia: 34 Transport*, Chapter 4, Part C, paras 206–07, 221–22.

380 Civil Aviation Regulations 211 provides for the granting of a charter operator's licence; regs 191–6 requires approval of the Secretary to the Department of Transport and Communications for the operation of all international non-scheduled flights to and from Australia. See *Secretary to the Department of Transport ex p Aus Students Travel Pty Ltd* (1978) 19 ALR 613 (breach of reg 106A(7)) requiring carriage under approved travel resulted in Secretary refusing permission to operation of charter flights by the Malaysian Airline System (MAS).

381 See Wassenbergh, H, 'The Globalisation of International Air Transport', in *The Highways of Air and Outer Space over Asia*, 1992, The Hague: Martinus Nijhoff; Ward, J, 'Globalisation, Concentration and Ownership – Aviation Issues and Australia's National Interests' in De Mellow (ed), *Australian Transport in the 1990s: Policies for Change in Land and Air Transport*, 1991, Sydney: Institute of Transport Studies, Graduate School of Business, University of Sydney.

New developments

The Air Services Act 1995 sets up Airservices Australia (AA) which has taken over the role and functions of the Civil Aviation Authority (CAA). The Civil Aviation Legislation Amendment Act 1995 transfers CAA assets, liabilities and staff to the AA after 30 November 1995.[382]

The Transport Legislation Amendment Act (no 2) 1995 contains amendments to the Air Navigation Act 1920, the Civil Aviation (Carrier's Liability) Act 1959 and the Crimes (Aviation) Act 1991 concerning air passenger and baggage screening and security measures at airports and on aircraft.[383]

In October 1995 the IATA annual general meeting unanimously adopted the IATA Intercarrier Agreement of Passenger Liability (IIA) signed by seven airlines.[384] Airlines participating in this agreement agreed to take measures to waive the limits in international agreements for damages in the case of personal injury and death. In 1996 IATA adopted a supplemental agreement, the Agreement on Measures to Implement the IATA Intercarrier Agreement (MIA). The MIA provides that participating carriers shall incorporate the following provisions in their conditions of carriage and tariffs where necessary:

1   (The carrier) shall not invoke the limitation of liability in Article 22(1) of the (Warsaw) Convention as to any claim for recoverable compensatory damages arising under Article 17 of the Convention.

2   (The carrier) shall not avail itself of any defence under Article 20(1) of the Convention with respect to that portion of such claim which does not exceed 100,000 SDR.

3   Except as otherwise provided in paragraphs 1 and 2 (the Carrier) reserves all defences available under the Convention to any such claim. With respect to third parties, the carrier also reserves all rights of recourse against any other person, including without limitation, rights of contribution and indemnity.

The MIA also provides that at the option of the carrier the following provisions may be included in the conditions of carriage:

1   (The carrier) agrees that subject to applicable law, recoverable compensatory damages for such claims may be determined by reference to the law of the domicile or permanent residence of the passenger.

---

382   Both Acts came into effect on this date.

383   The Act came into force on 20 July 1995. See Schedule, Part 1; Part 2; Part 3. Part 2 requires carriers to produce evidence of current insurance against liability to passengers for death or personal injury (s 41C). The amount so insured must not be less than $500,000 in respect of domestic carriage to which Part IV of Civil Aviation (Carrier's Liability) Act 1959 applies and 260,000 SDRs for any other carriage (ie international) (s 41c(3)); Part 2 inserting Part IVA after Part IV of the 1959 Act. The Passenger Movement Charge Act 1978 and the Passenger Movement Charge Collection Act 1978 are amended respectively by the Passenger Movement Charge Amendment Act 1995 (Cth) and the Passenger Movement Charge Collection Amendment Act 1995 (Cth).

384   See Appendices for a copy of the Intercarrier Agreement. Qantas is a signatory to the agreement.

2   (The carrier) shall not avail itself of any defence under Article 20(1) of the Convention with respect to that portion of such claims which do not exceed 100,000 SDR, except that such waiver is limited to the amounts shown below for the routes indicated, as may be authorised by governments concerned with the transportation involved.[385]

3   Neither the waiver of limits nor the waiver of defences shall be applicable in respect of claims made by public social insurance or similar bodies however asserted. Such claims shall be subject to the limit in Article 22(1) of the Convention. The Carrier will compensate the passenger or his dependents for recoverable compensatory damages in excess of payments received from any public social insurance or similar body.

TUTORIAL QUESTIONS

1   What are the main provisions in the Constitution that impact on the regulation of land and air transport in Australia and to what extent have these provisions been used by the Federal Parliament to successfully regulate transport in Australia?

2   The Advisory Committee on Trade and National Economic Management suggested various changes to the Constitution to assist the Commonwealth in the co-ordination and regulation of a national transport system. What were these recommendations and are they justified? (see report of the Trade and National Economic Committee 1987, particularly p 53 onwards).

3   Obtain a carriage document (road, rail or air) used by a transport or distribution operation (either one it issues or is issued to it by a carrying firm). Read through it carefully and identify the clauses that set out the following:

(a) limit the liability of the carrier (that is, for negligence, damage);

(b) extend protection from liability to subcontractors;

(c) set time limit for claims for loss of, or damage to goods.

4   Express Carriers Pty Ltd agree to carry cartons of cigarettes for Supermarket Supplies Pty from Burnie to Hobart. The deal is made on the phone and on arrival the Express Carriers driver obtains a signature from an employee of Supermarket Supplies on a consignment note issued by Express Carriers.

After the load of cigarettes has been delivered the number of cartons is rechecked and found to be 100 cartons short of the consigned load. In fact, these have been stolen from the lorry while it was left unattended at Oatlands on the Midland Highway while the driver went to buy a sandwich at a local cafe.

Two days after the loss was discovered Supermarkets Pty Ltd receive the standard form of conditions of carriage by post from Express Carrier's Burnie office. This document contains terms similar to the consignment note signed by the employee of Supermarkets Pty Ltd in Hobart. The following statement is included in both documents:

---

385 The MIA provides for the amounts and routes to be inserted.

The carrier accepts no responsibility for any damage, including injury, delay or loss of any nature arising out of or incidental to the carriage or any services ancillary thereto or which may occur at any time after the goods have been delivered to the consignee whether due or alleged to be due to misconduct on the part of the carrier or not and whether the cause of the damage is known or unknown to the carrier.

Supermarkets Pty Ltd claim against Express Carriers Pty Ltd for the loss of the cartons on the basis of the negligence of Express Carrier's driver, claiming that the consignment note was evidence of receipt only and not a contractual document. Supermarkets Pty Ltd also deny that the clause quoted in the carriage document sent by post exempts Express Carriers Pty Ltd from liability as it was sent after the carriage of the goods was completed and that Express Carriers Pty Ltd and Supermarkets Supplies Pty Ltd had only once before, three years ago, had any dealings with each other using the same form of carriage document.

Advise Express Carriers Pty Ltd.

5   Outline the development of the uniform road transport law and indicate the main issues that have arisen regarding its scope and implementation.

6   What are the differences between the Commission's risk rate and the owner's risk rate offered by the National Rail Corporation?

7   Hi-tech Industries of Geelong consign computer software in packages to Ansett in Melbourne. These are to be sent from Tullamarine International Airport and flown by Singapore airlines to London. The packages are labelled 'heat and moisture sensitive' and 'keep dry' with umbrella signs on the packages. The packages are sent to Melbourne by road from Geelong and due to delays in flight schedules are left outside on the tarmac at Tullamarine, despite 30° heat and the forecast of a heavy thunderstorm in the afternoon.

In a heavy downpour the packages are soaked and, on arrival in London, the software is found to be substantially damaged.

Is Singapore airlines liable for misconduct, and, if so, on what basis?

8   Abalone consigned to Kaisha Imports (Yokohama) to be sent to Japan on a Nippon Airways flight are taken by road by Expresslines Ltd from Clayton to Tullamarine International Airport and warehoused there in premises controlled by Qantas. Before the abalone is sent by Nippon Airlines to Ykohama, thieves break into the warehouse and steal the abalone.

Can Kaisha Imports (Yokohama) sue Expresslines, Qantas or Nippon Airlines, and on what grounds?

9   Ticket cases of former times were concerned with railways, steamships and cloakrooms where booking clerks issued tickets to customers who took them away without reading them. In those cases, the issue of the ticket was regarded as an offer by the company. If the customer took it and retained it without objection, his act was regarded as an acceptance of the offer based on the theory that the customer, on being handed the ticket, could refuse it and decline to enter into a contact on those terms. (Lord Denning MR in *Thornton v Shoe Lane Parking Ltd* [1971] 2 QB 163 at 169.)

Lord Denning in this case added that such an analysis was a fiction and inappropriate to modern conditions.

Apply this critical view to the issue of a standard airline ticket and examine the legal position of both the carrier (or its agent) and the passenger (see the Australian High Court judgment in *MacRobertson Miller Airline Services v Commissioner for State Taxation (Western Australia)* and Powell, M, 'Acceptance by Silence in the Law of Contract' (1977) 6 ABusLR 260 at 264–68.

10 What are the main provisions of the IATA Intercarrier Agreement 1995 and what effect do these have on the limitation of liability of the airlines subject to the 1995 IATA Agreement for passenger injury and death?

FURTHER READING

Armstrong, G, 'Notes on *Airlines of New South Wales v New South Wales (No 2)*' 1 (1964–5) 1 Fed LR 348–58.

Bartsch, RIC, *Aviation Law in Australia*, 1996, Sydney: LBC Information Services.

Camard, G, 'Liability for Carriers for Damages of Passengers on Charter Flights' (1977) 11(2) *Air Law* 82.

Cheng, B, 'Air Carrier's Liability for Passengers Injury and Death: the Japanese Initiative and Response to the Recent EC Consultation Paper (1993), 18 *Air and Space Law* 109

Department of Transport and Communications (Aust), International Air Carriers Liability, discussion paper, 1993, Canberra (mimeo).

Edwards, LR, 'The Liability of Air Carriers for Death and Personal Injury to Passengers' (1982) 56 ALJ 108.

Gilchrist, N, 'Notice in the Passenger Ticket' [1982] 3 *Lloyd's MCLQ* 444.

Goldhirsch, LB, *The Warsaw Convention Annotated: A Legal Handbook*, 1988, The Hague: Martinus Nijhoff.

Goldman, 'Recovery under the Warsaw Convention for the Loss of Valuable Air Cargo' [1982] 3 *Lloyd's MCLQ* 453.

Hannapel, PPC, 'The Right to Sue in Death Cases Under the Warsaw Convention' (1981) 6(2) *Air Law* 66.

Joy, S, Review of Tasmania's Public Vehicle Licensing System, *Transport Tasmania*, 1988, Hobart.

Kahn-Freund, O, *The Law of Carriage by Inland Transport*, 1965, London: Stevens.

Kirby, M, 'Civil Aviation Liabilities: Australian Developments in a Global Context' (1992) 17 *Annals of Air and Space Laws* 255.

Lane, PH, 'The Airlines Case' (1965–66) ALJ 17.

Levy, SJ, 'The Rights of International Airline Passengers' (1976) (1) *Air Law* 275.

Livermore, J (ed), *Laws of Australia: 34 Transport,* Sydney: Law Book Co.

Livermore, J, *Exemption Clauses and Implied Obligations in Contracts*, 1986, Sydney: Law Book Co.

Livermore, J, Public Enquiry into the Modal Split of Bulk Traffic Between Road and Rail in Tasmania, Department of Transport and Works, Hobart, November 1992.

McNair, *The Law of the Air*, 3rd edn, 1964, London: Stevens.

Mahon, P, 'The Mount Erebus Royal Commission – some Lessons about Investigation and Interpretation of Evidence' (1982) 12 *Queensland Law Society Journal* 287.

Maulawicz, A, 'The Liability Regime of the International Air Carrier' (1979) 4 *Annals of Air and Space Law* 122–31.

Miller, G, *Liability in International Air Transport*, 1977, The Hague: Kluwer.

Ministry of Transport (NZ), Aircraft Accident Report no 79–139, Wellington, 1979.

National Road Transport Commission (Aust), 'Integration of the road transport law', 1995, discussion paper, June, Chapter 2.

Okabe, S, 'Aviation Personal Injury Claim Settlement in Japan', paper given at the International Conference on Air Transport and Space Application in a New World, June 1993, Tokyo.

Palmer, NE, *Bailment*, 2nd edn, 1991, Sydney: Law Book Co.

Pengilley, W and McPhee, J, *Law for Aviators*, 1994, Sydney: Legal Books.

Pollard, M, 'Road Transport Reform – the Legislative Challenge', 1993, Chartered Institute of Transport National Conference, Perth, 13–16 September, 265.

'Report of the Royal Commission to Enquire into the Crash on Mount Erebus of a DC-10 Aircraft Operated by Air New Zealand Ltd', 1981, Wellington.

Richardson, J, 'Aviation Law in Australia' (1964–65) 1 Fed LR 247.

Sakamoto, T, 'The Fate of Passenger Liability Limit under the Warsaw Convention', 1993, paper given at the International Conference on Air Transport and Space Application in a New World, June, Tokyo.

Shawcross and Beaumont, *Air Law*, 4th edn, 1982, London: Butterworths.

Singh, P, 'Some Aspects of Australia's Bilateral Air Service Agreements' (1984) 9(3)(4) *Air Law* 149, 235.

Solomon and Goldman 'Recovery under the Warsaw Convention for the Loss of Valuable Air Cargo' [1982] 3 *Lloyd's MCLQ* 453.

Ward, J in De Mellow (ed), *Globalisation, Concentration and Ownership – Aviation Issues and Australia's National Interests, Australian Transport in the 1990s: Policies for Change in Land and Air Transport*, 1991, Institute of Transport Studies, Graduate School of Business, University of Sydney.

Wassenbergh, H, 'The Globalisation of International Air Transport' in *The Highways of Air and Outer Space Over Asia*, 1992, The Hague: Martinus Nijhoff.

CONVENTION FOR THE UNIFICATION OF CERTAIN RULES RELATING TO INTERNATIONAL CARRIAGE BY AIR (WARSAW CONVENTION) WARSAW, 1929

CHAPTER I – SCOPE AND DEFINITIONS

Article 1

1   This Convention applies to all international carriage of persons, luggage or goods performed by aircraft for reward. It applies equally to gratuitous carriage by aircraft performed by an air transport undertaking.

2   For the purpose of this Convention the expression 'international carriage' means any carriage in which, according to the contract made by the parties, the place of departure and the place of destination, whether or not there be a break in the carriage or a trans-shipment, are situated either within the territories of two high contracting parties, or within the territory of a single high contracting party, if there is an agreed stopping place within a territory subject to the sovereignty, suzerainty, mandate or authority of another power, even though that power is not a party to this Convention. A carriage without such an agreed stopping place between territories subject to the sovereignty, suzerainty, mandate or authority of the same high contracting party is not deemed to be international for the purposes of this Convention.

3   A carriage to be performed by several successive air carriers is deemed, for the purposes of this Convention, to be one undivided carriage, if it has been regarded by the parties as a single operation, whether it had been agreed upon under the form of a single contract or of a series of contracts, and it does not lose its international character merely because one contract or a series of contracts is to be performed entirely within a territory subject to the sovereignty, suzerainty, mandate or authority of the same high contracting party.

Article 2

1   This convention applies to carriage performed by the State or by legally constituted public bodies provided it falls within the conditions laid down in Article 1.

2   This convention does not apply to carriage performed under the terms of any international postal convention.

CHAPTER II – DOCUMENTS OF CARRIAGE

Section 1— Passenger ticket

Article 3 [omitted]

Section 2 — Luggage ticket

Article 4 [omitted]

Section 3 — Air consignment note

Article 5

1   Every carrier of goods has the right to require the consignor to make out and over to him a document called an 'air consignment note'; every consignor has the right to require the carrier to accept this document.

2   The absence, irregularity or loss of this document does not affect the existence or the validity of the contract of carriage which shall, subject to the provisions of Article 9, be none the less governed by the rules of this Convention.

Article 6

1   The air consignment note shall be made out by the consignor in three original parts and be handed over with the goods.

2   The first part shall be marked 'for the carrier', and shall be signed by the consignor. The second part shall be marked 'for the consignee', it shall be signed by the consignor and by the carrier and shall accompany the goods. The third part shall be signed by the carrier and handed by him to the consignor after the goods have been accepted.

3   The carrier shall sign on acceptance of the goods.

4   The signature of the carrier may be stamped; that of the consignor may be printed or stamped.

5   If, at the request of the consignor, the carrier makes out the air consignment note, he shall be deemed, subject to proof to the contrary, to have done so on behalf of the consignor.

Article 7

The carrier of goods has the right to require the consignor to make out separate consignment notes when there is more than one package.

Article 8

The air consignment note shall contain the following particulars:

(a)   The place and date of its execution;

(b)   The place of departure and of destination;

(c)   The agreed stopping places, provided the carrier may reserve the right to alter the stopping places in case of necessity, and that if he exercises that right the alteration shall not have the affect of depriving the carriage of its international character;

(d)   The name and address of the consignor;

(e)   The name and address of the first carrier;

(f)   The name and address of the consignee, if the case so requires;

(g)   The nature of the goods;

(h)   The number of the packages, the method of packing and the particular marks or numbers upon them;

(i)   The weight, the quantity and the volume or dimensions of the goods;

(j)   The apparent condition of the goods and of the packing;

(k)   The freight, if it has been agreed upon, the date and place of payment, and the person who is to pay it;

(l)   If the goods are sent for payment on delivery, the price of the goods, and, if the case so requires, the amount of the expenses incurred;

(m)   The amount of the value declared in accordance with Article 22(2);

(n)   The number of parts of the air consignment note;

(o)   The document handed to the carrier to accompany the air consignment note;

(p)   The time fixed for the completion of the carriage and a brief note of the route to be followed, if these matters have been agreed upon;

(q)   A statement that the carriage is subject to the rules relating to liability established by this Convention.

Article 9

If the carrier accepts goods without an air consignment note having been made out, or if the air consignment note does not contain all the particulars set out in Article 8(a) to (i) inclusive and (q), the carrier shall not be entitled to avail himself of the provisions of this Convention which exclude or limit his liability.

Article 10

1   The consignor is responsible for the correctness of the particulars and statements relating to the goods which he inserts in the air consignment note.

2   The consignor will be liable for all damage suffered by the carrier or any other person by reason of the irregularity, incorrectness or incompleteness of the said particulars and statements.

Article 11

1   The air consignment note is *prima facie* evidence of the conclusion of the contract, of the receipt of the goods and of the conditions of carriage.

2   The statements in the air consignment note relating to the weight, dimensions and packing of the goods, as well as those relating to the number of packages, are *prima facie* evidence of the facts stated; those relating to the quantity, volume and condition of the goods do not constitute evidence against the carrier except so far as they both have been, and are stated in the air consignment note to have been, checked by him in the presence of the consignor, or relate to the apparent condition of the goods.

Article 12

1   Subject to his liability to carry out all his obligations under the contract of carriage, the consignor has the right to dispose of the goods by withdrawing them at the aerodrome of departure or destination, or by stopping them in the course of the journey on any landing, or by calling for them to be delivered at the place of destination or in the course of the journey to a person other than the consignee named in the air consignment note, or by requiring them to be returned to the aerodrome of departure. He must not exercise this right of disposition in such a way as to prejudice the carrier or other consignors and he must repay any expenses occasioned by the exercise of this right.

2   If it is impossible to carry out the orders of the consignor the carrier must so inform him forthwith.

3   If the carrier obeys the orders of the consignor for the disposition of the goods without requiring the production of the part of the air consignment note delivered to the latter, he will be liable, without prejudice to his right of recovery from the consignor, for any damage which may be caused thereby to any person who is lawfully in possession of that part of the air consignment note.

4   The right conferred on the consignor ceases at the moment when that of the consignee begins in accordance with Article 13. Nevertheless, if the consignee declines to accept the consignment note or the goods, or if he cannot be communicated with, the consignor resumes his right of disposition.

Article 13

1   Except in the circumstances set out in the preceding article, the consignee is entitled, on arrival of the goods at the place of destination, to require the carrier to hand over to him the air consignment note and to deliver the goods to him, on payment of the

charges due and on complying with the conditions of carriage set out in the air consignment note.

2   Unless it is otherwise agreed, it is the duty of the carrier to give notice to the consignee as soon as the goods arrive.

3   If the carrier admits the loss of the goods have not arrived at the expiration of seven days after date on which they ought to have arrived, the consignee is entitled to put into force against the carrier the rights which flow from the contract of carriage.

Article 14

The consignor and the consignee can respectively enforce all the rights given them by Articles 12 and 13, each in his own name, whether he is acting in his own interest or in the interest of another, provided that he carries out the obligations imposed by the contract.

Article 15

1   Articles 12, 13 and 14 do not affect either the relations of the consignor or the consignee with each other or the mutual relations of third parties whose rights are derived either from the consignor or from the consignee.

2   The provisions of Articles 12, 13 and 14 can only be varied by express provision in the air consignment note.

Article 16

1   The consignor must furnish such information and attach to the air consignment note such documents as are necessary to meet the formalities of Customs, *Octroi* or police before the goods can be delivered to the consignee. The consignor is liable to the carrier for any damage occasioned by the absence, insufficiency or irregularity of any such information or documents, unless the damage is due to the fault of the carrier or his agents.

2   The carrier is under no obligation to enquire into the correctness or sufficiency of such information or documents.

Chapter III – Liability of the carrier

Article 17

The carrier is liable for damage sustained in the event of the death or wounding of a passenger or any other bodily injury suffered by a passenger, if the accident which caused the damage so sustained took place on board the aircraft or in the course of any of the operations of embarking or disembarking.

Article 18

1   The carrier is liable for damage sustained in the event of the destruction or loss of, or of damage to, any registered luggage or any goods, if the occurrence which caused the damage so sustained took place during the carriage by air.

2   The carriage by air within the meaning for the preceding paragraph comprises the period during which the luggage or goods are in charge of the carrier, whether in an aerodrome or on board an aircraft, or, in the case of a landing outside an aerodrome, in any place whatsoever.

3   The period of the carriage by air does not extend to any carriage by land, by sea or by river performed outside an aerodrome. If, however, such a carriage takes place in the performance of a contract for carriage by air, for the purpose of loading, delivery

or trans-shipment, any damage is presumed, subject to proof to the contrary, to have been the result of an event which took place during the carriage by air.

Article 19

The carrier is liable for damage occasioned by delay in the carriage by air of passengers, luggage or goods.

Article 20

1   The carrier is not liable if he proves that he and his agents have taken all necessary measures to avoid the damage or that it was impossible for him or them to take such measures.

2   In the carriage of goods and luggage, the carrier is not liable if he proves that the damage was occasioned by negligent pilotage or negligence in the handling of the aircraft or in navigation and that, in all other respects, he and his agents have taken all necessary measures to avoid the damage.

Article 21

If the carrier proves that the damage was caused by or contributed to by the negligence of the injured person, the court may, in accordance with the provisions of its own law, exonerate the carrier wholly or partly from his liability.

Article 22

1   In the carriage of passengers, the liability of the carrier for each passenger is limited to the sum of 125,000 francs. Where, in accordance with the law of the court seised of the case, damages may be awarded in the form of periodical payments, the equivalent capital value of the said payment shall not exceed 125,000 francs. Nevertheless, by special contract, the carrier and the passenger may agree to a higher limit of liability.

2   In the carriage of registered luggage and of goods, the liability of the carrier is limited to a sum of 250 francs per kg, unless the consignor has made, at the time when the package was handed over to the carrier, a special declaration of the value at delivery and has paid a supplementary sum if the case so requires. In that case, the carrier will be liable to pay a sum not exceeding the declared sum, unless he proves that the sum is greater than the actual value to the consignor at delivery.

3   As regards objects of which the passenger takes charge himself the liability of the carrier is limited to 5000 francs per passenger.

4   The sums mentioned above shall be deemed to refer to the French franc consisting of 65.5 mg gold of millesimal fineness 900. These sums may be converted into any national currency in round figures.

Article 23

Any provision tending to relieve the carrier of liability or to fix a lower limit than that which is laid down in this Convention shall be null and void, but the nullity of any such provision does not involve the nullity of the whole contract, which shall remain subject to the provisions of this Convention.

Article 24

1   In the cases covered by Articles 18 and 19, any action for damages, however founded, can only be brought subject to the conditions and limits set out in this Convention.

2   In the cases covered by Article 17, the provisions of the preceding paragraph also apply, without prejudice to the questions as to who are the persons who have the right to bring suit and what are their respective rights.

Article 25

1   The carrier shall not be entitled to avail himself of the provisions of this Convention which exclude or limit his liability, if the damage is caused by his wilful misconduct or by such default on his part as, in accordance with the law of the court seised of the case, is considered to be equivalent to wilful misconduct.

2   Similarly, the carrier shall not be entitled to avail himself of the said provisions, if the damage is caused as aforesaid by any agent of the carrier acting within the scope of his employment.

Article 26

1   Receipt by the person entitled to delivery of luggage or goods without complaint is *prima facie* evidence that the same have been delivered in good condition and in accordance with the document of carriage.

2   In the case of damage, the person entitled to delivery must complain to the carrier forthwith after the discovery of the damage, and, at the latest, within three days from the date of receipt in the case of luggage and seven days from the date of receipt in the case of goods. In the case of delay, the complaint must be made at the latest within 14 days from the date on which the luggage or goods have been placed at his disposal.

3   Every complaint must be made in writing upon the document of carriage or by separate notice in writing dispatched within the times aforesaid.

4   Failing complaint within the times aforesaid, no action shall lie against the carrier, save in the case of fraud on his part.

Article 27

In the case of the death of the person liable, an action for damages lies in accordance with the terms of this Convention against those legally representing his estate.

Article 28

1   An action for damages must be brought, at the option of the plaintiff, in the territory of one of the high contracting parties, either before the court having jurisdiction where the carrier is ordinarily resident, or has his principal place of business, or has an establishment by which the contract has been made or before the court having jurisdiction at the place of destination.

2   Questions of procedure shall be governed by the law of the court seised of the case.

Article 29

1   The right to damages shall be extinguished if an action is not brought within two years, reckoned from the date of arrival at the destination, or from the date on which the aircraft ought to have arrived, or from the date on which the carriage stopped.

2   The method of calculating the period of limitation shall be determined by the law of the court seised of the case.

Article 30

1   In the case of carriage to be performed by various successive carriers and falling within the definition set out in the third paragraph of Article 1, each carrier who

accepts passengers, luggage or goods is subjected to the rules set out in this Convention, and is deemed to be one of the contracting parties to the contract of carriage in so far as the contract deals with that part of the carriage which is performed under his supervision.

2   In the case of carriage of this nature, the passenger or his representative can take action only against the carrier who performed the carriage during which the accident or the delay occurred, save in the case where, by express agreement, the first carrier has assumed liability for the whole journey.

3   As regards luggage or goods, the passenger or consignor will have a right of action against the first carrier, and the passenger or consignee who is entitled to delivery will have a right of action against the last carrier, and further, each may take action against the carrier who performed the carriage during which the destruction, loss, damage or delay took place. These carriers will be jointly and severally liable to the passenger or to the consignor or consignee.

Chapter IV – Provisions to combined carriage

Article 31

1   In the case of combined carriage performed partly by air and partly by any other mode of carriage, the provisions of the Convention apply only to the carriage by air, provided that the carriage by air falls within the terms of Article 1.

2   Nothing in this convention shall prevent the parties in the case of combined carriage from inserting in the document of air carriage conditions relating to other modes of carriage, provided that the provisions of this Convention are observed as regards the carriage by air.

Chapter V – General and final provisions

Article 32

Any clause contained in the contract and all special agreements entered into before the damage occurred by which the parties purport to infringe the rules laid down by this Convention, whether by deciding the law to be applied, or by altering the rules as to jurisdiction, shall be null and void. Nevertheless, for the carriage of goods arbitration clauses are allowed, subject to this convention, if the arbitration is to take place within one of the jurisdictions referred to in the first paragraph of Article 28.

Article 33

Nothing contained in this Convention shall prevent the carrier either from refusing to enter into any contract of carriage, or from making regulations which do not conflict with the provisions of this Convention.

Article 34

This Convention does not apply to international carriage by air performed by way of experimental trial by air navigation undertakings with the view to the establishment of a regular line of air navigation, nor does it apply to carriage performed in extraordinary circumstances outside the normal scope of an air carrier's business.

Article 35

The expression 'days' when used in this convention means current days not working days.

Articles 36–41 [omitted]

UNIFORM RULES CONCERNING THE CONTRACT FOR INTERNATIONAL CARRIAGE OF GOODS BY RAIL (CIM) 1980

TITLE 1 – GENERAL PROVISIONS

Article 1 – Scope

1   Subject to the exceptions provided for in Article 2, the Uniform Rules shall apply to all consignments of goods for carriage under a through consignment note made out for a route over the territories of at least two States and exclusively over lines or services included in the list provided for in Articles 3 and 10 of the Convention.

2   In the Uniform Rules the expression 'station' covers: railway stations, ports used by shipping services and all other establishments of transport undertakings, open to the public for the execution of the contract of carriage.

Article 2 – Exceptions from scope

1   Consignments between sending and destination stations situated in the territory of the same State, which pass through the territory of another State only in transit, shall not be subject to the Uniform Rules:

   (a) if the lines or services over which the transit occurs are exclusively operated by a railway of the State of departure; or

   (b) if the States or the railways concerned have agreed not to regard such consignments as international.

2   Consignments between stations in two adjacent States and between stations in two states in transit through the territory of a third State shall, if the lines over which the consignments are carried are exclusively operated by a railway of one of those three States, be subject to the internal traffic regulations applicable to that railway if the sender, by using the appropriate consignment note, so elects and where there is nothing to the contrary in the laws and regulation of any of the States concerned.

Article 3 – Obligation to carry

1   The railway shall be bound to undertake all carriage of any goods in complete wagon-loads, subject to the terms of the Uniform Rules, provided that:

   (a) the sender complies with the Uniform Rules, the supplementary provisions and the tariffs;

   (b) carriage can be undertaken by the normal staff and transport resources which suffice to meet usual traffic requirements;

   (c) carriage is not prevented by circumstances which the railway cannot avoid and which it is not in a position to remedy.

2   The railway shall not be obliged to accept goods of which the loading, trans-shipment or unloading requires the use of special facilities unless the stations concerned have such facilities at their disposal.

3   The railway shall only be obliged to accept goods the carriage of which can take place without delay; the provisions in force at the forwarding station shall determine the circumstances in which goods not complying with that condition must be temporarily stored.

4   When the competent authority decides that:

(a) a service shall be discontinued or suspended totally or partially,

(b) certain consignments shall be refused or accepted only subject to conditions,

these measures shall, without delay, be brought to the notice of the public and the railways; the latter shall inform the railways of the other States with a view to their publication.

5   The railways may, by joint agreement, concentrate goods traffic between certain places on specified frontier points and transit countries. These measures shall be notified to the central office. They shall be entered by the railways in special lists, published in the manner laid down for international tariffs, and shall come into force one month after the date of notification to the central office.

6   Any contravention of this article by the railway may constitute a cause of action for compensation for loss or damage caused.

Article 4 – Articles not acceptable for carriage

The following shall not be accepted for carriage:

(a) articles the carriage of which is prohibited in any one of the territories in which the articles would be carried;

(b) articles the carriage of which is a monopoly of the postal authorities in any one of he territories in which the articles would be carried;

(c) articles which, by reason of their dimensions, their mass, or their packaging, are not suitable for the carriage proposed, having regard to the installations or rolling stock of any one of the railways which would be used;

(d) substances and articles which are not acceptable for carriage under the regulations concerning the international carriage of dangerous goods by rail (RID), Annex 1 to the Uniform Rules, subject to the exceptions provided for in Articles 5, §2.

Article 5 – Articles acceptable for carriage subject to conditions

1   The following shall be acceptable for carriage subject to conditions:

(a) substances and articles acceptable for carriage subject to the conditions laid down in the RID or in the agreements and tariff clauses provided for in §2.

(b) funeral consignments, railway rolling stock running on its own wheels, live animals and consignments the carriage of which presents special difficulties by reason of their dimensions, their mass or their packaging: subject to the conditions laid down in the supplementary provision; these may derogate from the Uniform Rules.

Live animals must be accompanied by an attendant provided by the consignor. Nevertheless, an attendant shall not be required when the international tariffs permit or when the railways participating in the carriage so permit at the consignor's request; in such cases, unless there is an agreement to the contrary, the railway shall not be liable for any loss or damage resulting from any risk which the attendant was intended to avert.

2   Two or more States, by agreement, or two or more railways, by tariff clauses, may jointly determine the conditions with which certain substances or articles not acceptable for carriage under the RID must comply if they are nevertheless to be

accepted. States or railways may, in the same manner, make the conditions for acceptance laid down in the RID less rigorous. Such agreements and tariff clauses must be published and notified to the central office which will bring them to the notice of the States.

Article 6 – Tariffs, private agreements [omitted]

Article 7 – Unit of account. Rate of exchange or of acceptance of foreign currency

1   The unit of account referred to in the Uniform Rules shall be the Special Drawing Right as defined by the International Monetary Fund.

The value in Special Drawing Right of the national currency of a State which is a Member of the International Monetary fund shall be calculated in accordance with the method of valuation applied by the International Monetary Fund for its own operations and transactions.

2   The value in Special Drawing Right of the national currency of a State which is not a member of the International Monetary Fund shall be calculated by the method determined by that State.

The calculation must express in the national currency a real value approximating as closely to that which would result from the application of §1.

3   In the case of a State which is not a member of the International Monetary Fund and whose legislation does not permit the application of §1 or §2 above, the unit of account referred to in the Uniform Rules shall be deemed to be equal to three gold francs.

The gold franc is defined as 10/31 of a gram of gold of millesimal fineness 900.

The conversion of the gold franc must express in the national currency a real value approximating as closely to that which would result from the application of §1.

4   Within three months after the entry into force of the Convention and each time that a change occurs in their method of calculation or in the value of their national currency in relation to the unit of account, States shall notify the central office of their method of calculation in accordance with §2, or the results of the conversion in accordance with §3.

The central office shall notify the States of this information.

5   The railway shall publish the rates at which:

(a)   it converts sums expressed in foreign currencies but payable in domestic currency (rates of conversion);

(b)   It accepts payment in foreign currencies (rates of acceptance).

Article 8 – Special provisions for certain types of transport

1   In the case of the haulage of privately owned wagons, special provisions are laid down in the regulations concerning the international haulage of private owners' wagons by rail (RIP), Annex II to the Uniform Rules.

2   In the case of the carriage of containers, special provisions are laid down in the regulations concerning the international carriage of containers by rail (RICo), Annex III to the Uniform Rules.

3   In the case of express parcels traffic, railways may, by tariff clauses, agree on special provisions in accordance with the regulations concerning the international carriage of express parcels by rail (RIEx), Annex IV to the Uniform Rules.

4   Two or more States, by special agreement, or two or more railways by supplementary provisions or by tariff clauses, may agree on terms derogating from the Uniform Rules for the following types of consignments:

(a) consignments under cover of a negotiable document;

(b) consignments to be delivered only against return of the duplicate of the consignment note;

(c) consignments of newspapers;

(d) consignment intended for fairs or exhibitions;

(e) consignment of loading tackle and of equipment for protection of goods in transit against heat or cold;

(f) consignments over all or part of the route under cover of consignment notes which are not used for charging and billing;

(g) consignments sent under cover of an instrument suitable for automatic data transmission.

Article 9 – Supplementary provision

1   Two or more States or two or more railways may make supplementary provisions for the execution of the Uniform Rules. They may not derogate from the Uniform Rules unless the latter expressly so provide.

2   The supplementary provisions shall be put into force and published in the manner required by the laws and regulations of each State. The central office shall be notified of the supplementary provisions and of their coming into force.

Article 10 – National law

1   In the absence of provisions in the Uniform Rules, supplementary provisions or international tariffs, national law shall apply.

2   'National law' means the law of the State in which the person entitled asserts his rights, including the rules relating to conflict of laws.

TITLE II – MAKING AND EXECUTION OF THE CONTRACT OF CARRIAGE

Article 11 – Making of the contract of carriage

1   The contract of carriage shall come into existence as soon as the forwarding railway has accepted the goods for carriage together with the consignment note. Acceptance is established by the application to the consignment note and, where appropriate, to each additional sheet, of the stamp of the forwarding station, or accounting machine entry, showing the date of acceptance.

2   The procedure laid done in §1 must be carried out immediately after all the goods to which the consignment note relates have been handed over for carriage and – where the provisions in force at the forwarding station so require – such charges as the consignor has undertaken to pay have been paid or a security deposited in accordance with Article 15, §7. The procedure shall be carried out in the presence of the consignor if he so requests.

3   When the stamp has been affixed or the accounting machine entry has been made, the consignment note shall be evidence of the making and content of the contract.

4 Nevertheless, when the loading of the goods is the duty of the consignor in accordance with tariffs or agreements existing between him and the railway, and provided that such agreements are authorised at the forwarding station, the particulars in the consignment note relating to the mass of the goods or to the number of packages shall only be evidence against the railway when that weight or number of packages has been verified by the railway and certified in the consignment note. If necessary these particulars may be proved by other means.

If it is obvious that there is no actual deficiency corresponding to the discrepancy between the mass or number of packages and the particulars in the consignment note, the latter shall not be evidence against the railway. This shall apply in particular when the wagon is handed over to the consignee with the original seals intact.

5 The railway shall certify receipt of the goods and the date of acceptance for carriage by affixing the date stamp to or making the accounting machine entry on the duplicate of the consignment note before returning the duplicate to the consignor. The duplicate shall not have effect as the consignment note accompanying the goods, nor as a bill of lading.

Article 12 – Consignment note

1 The consignor shall present a consignment note duly completed. A separate consignment note shall be made out for each consignment. One and the same consignment note may not relate to more than a single wagon load. The supplementary provisions may derogate from these rules.

2 The railways shall prescribe, for both *petite vitesse* and *grande vitesse* traffic, a standard form of consignment note, which must include a duplicate for the consignor. The choice of consignment note by the consignor shall indicate whether the goods are to be carried by *petite vitesse* or by *grande vitesse*. A request for *grande vitesse* over one part of the route and *petite vitesse* over the remainder will not be allowed except by agreement between all the railways concerned.

In the case of certain traffic, notably between adjacent countries, the railways may prescribe, in the tariffs, the use of a simplified form of consignment note.

3 The consignment note must be printed in two or where necessary in three languages, at least one of which shall be one of the working languages of the organisation.

International tariffs may determine the language in which the particulars to be filled in by the consignor in the consignment note shall be entered. In the absence of such provisions, they must be entered in one of the official languages of the State of departure and a translation in one of the working languages of the organisation must be added unless the particulars have been entered in one of those languages. The particulars entered by the consignor in the consignment note shall be in Roman lettering, save where the supplementary provisions or international tariffs otherwise provide.

Article 13 – Wording of the consignment note

1 The consignment note must contain:

(a) the name of the destination station;

(b) the name and address of the consignee; only one individual or legal person shall be shown as consignee;

(c) the description of the goods;

(d) the mass, or failing that, comparable information in accordance with the provisions in force at the forwarding station;

(e) the number of packages and a description of the packing in the case of consignments in less than wagon loads, and in the case of complete wagon loads comprising one or more packages, forwarded by rail-sea and requiring to be trans-shipped;

(f) the number of the wagon and also, for privately owned wagons, the tare, in the case of goods where the loading is the duty of the consignor,

(g) a detailed list of the documents which are required by Customs or other administrative authorities and are attached to the consignment note or shown as held at the disposal of the railway at a named station or at an office of the Customs or of any other authority;

(h) the name and address of the consignor; only one individual or legal person shall be shown as the consignor; if the provisions in force at the forwarding station so require, the consignor shall add to his name and address his written, printed or stamped signature.

The provisions in force at the forwarding station shall determine the meanings of the terms 'wagon load' and 'less than wagon load' for the whole of the route.

2   The consignment note must, where appropriate, contain all the other particulars provided for in the Uniform Rules. It shall not contain other particulars unless they are required or allowed by the laws and regulations of a State, the supplementary provisions or the tariffs, and are not contrary to the Uniform Rules.

3   Nevertheless, the consignor may insert in the consignment note in the space set apart for the purpose, but as information for the consignee, remarks relating to the consignment, without involving the railway in any obligation or liability.

4   The consignment note shall not be replaced by other documents or supplemented by documents other than those prescribed or allowed by the Uniform Rules, the supplementary provisions or the tariffs.

Article 14 – Route and tariffs applicable

1   The consignor may stipulate in the consignment note the route to be followed, indicating it by reference to frontier points or frontier stations and where appropriate, to transit stations between railways. He may only stipulate frontier points and frontier stations which are open to traffic between the forwarding and destination places concerned.

2   The following shall be regarded as routing instructions:

(a) designation of stations where formalities required by Customs or other administrative authorities are to be carried out, and of stations where special care is to be given to the goods (attention to animals, re-icing, etc);

(b) designation of the tariffs to be applied, if this is sufficient to determine the stations between which the tariffs requested are to be applied;

(c) instructions as to the payment of the whole or a part of the charges up to X (X indicating by name the point at which the tariffs of adjacent countries are applied).

3   Except in the cases specified in Article 3 §§4 and 5, and Article 33 §1, the railway may not carry the goods by a route other than that stipulated by the consignor unless both:

(a) the formalities required by Customs or other administrative authorities, as well as the special care to be given to the goods, will in any event be carried out at the stations indicated by the consignor; and

(b) the charges and the transit periods will not be greater than the charges and transit periods calculated according to the route stipulated by the consignor.

Sub-para (a) shall not apply to consignments in less than wagon loads if one of the participating railways is unable to adhere to the route chosen by the consignor by virtue of the routing instructions arising from its arrangements for the international carriage of consignments in less than wagon loads.

4   Subject to the provisions of §3, the charges and transit periods shall be calculated according to the route stipulated by the consignor or, in the absence of any such indication, according to the route chosen by the railway.

5   The consignor may stipulate in the consignment note which tariffs are to be applied. The railway must apply such tariffs if the conditions laid down for their application have been fulfilled.

6   If the instructions given by the consignor are not sufficient to indicate the route or tariffs to be applied, or if any of those instructions are inconsistent with one another, the railway shall choose the route or tariffs which appear to it to be the most advantageous to the consignor.

7   The railway shall not be liable for any loss or damage suffered as a result of the choice made in accordance with §6, except in the case of wilful misconduct or gross negligence.

8   If an international tariff exists from the forwarding to the destination station and if, in the absence of adequate instructions from the consignor, the railway has applied that tariff, the railway shall, at the request of the person entitled, refund him the difference between the carriage charges thus applied and those which the application of other tariffs would have produced over the same route, when such difference exceeds four units of account per consignment note.

The same shall apply if, in the absence of adequate instructions from the consignor, the railway has applied consecutive tariffs, even though there is an international tariff offering a more advantageous charge, all other conditions being the same.

Article 15 – Payment of charges

1   The charges (carriage charges, supplementary charges, Customs duties and other charges incurred from the time of acceptance for carriage to the time of delivery) shall be paid by the consignor or the consignee in accordance with the following provisions.

In applying these provisions, charges which, according to the applicable tariff, must be added to the standard rates or special rates when calculating the carriage charges, shall be deemed to be carriage charges.

2   A consignor who undertakes to pay a part or all of the charges shall indicate this on the consignment note by using one of the following phrases:

(a) (i) 'carriage charges paid', if he undertakes to pay carriage charges only;

(ii) 'carriage charges paid including ...', if he undertakes to pay charges additional to those for carriage; he shall give an exact description of those charges; additional indications, which may relate only to the supplementary charges or other charges incurred from the time of acceptance for carriage until the time of delivery as well as to sums collected either by Customs or other administrative authorities shall not result in any division of the total amount of any one category of charges (eg the total amount of Customs duties and of other amounts payable to Customs, value added tax being regarded as a separate category);

(iii) 'carriage charges paid to X' (X indicating by name the point at which the tariffs of adjacent countries are applied), if he undertakes to pay carriage charges to X;

(iv) 'carriage chargers paid to X including ...' (X indicating by name the point at which the tariffs of adjacent countries are applied), if he undertakes to pay charges additional to those for carriage to X, but excluding all charges relating to the subsequent country or railway; the provisions of (ii) shall apply analogously;

(b) 'all charges paid', if he undertakes to pay all charges (carriage charges, supplementary charges, Customs duties and other charges);

(c) 'charges paid not exceeding ...', if he undertakes to pay a fixed sum; save where the tariffs otherwise provide, this sum shall be expressed in the currency of the country of departure.

Supplementary and other charges which, according to the provisions in force at the forwarding station, are to be calculated for the whole of the route concerned, and the charge for interest in delivery laid down in Article 16, §2, shall always be paid in full by the consignor in the case of payment of the charges in accordance with (a)(iv).

3   The international tariffs may, as regards payment of charges, prescribe the exclusive use of certain phrases set out in §2 of this article or the use of other phrases.

4   The charges which the consignor has not undertaken to pay shall be deemed to be payable by the consignee. Nevertheless, such charges shall be payable by the consignor if the consignee has not taken possession of the consignment note nor asserted his rights under Article 28, §4, nor modified the contract of carriage in accordance with Article 31.

5   Supplementary charges, such as charges for demurrage and standage, warehousing and weighing, which arise from an act attributable to the consignee or from a request which he has made, shall always be paid by him.

6   The forwarding railway may require the consignor to prepay the charges in the case of goods which in its opinion are liable to undergo rapid deterioration or which, by reason of their low value or their nature, do not provide sufficient cover for such charges.

7   If the amount of the charges which the consignor undertakes to pay cannot be ascertained exactly at the time the goods are handed over for carriage, such charges shall be entered in a charges note and a settlement of accounts shall be made with the consignor not later than 30 days after the expiry of the transit period. The railway may require as security a deposit approximating to the amount of such charges, for

which a receipt shall be given. A detailed account of charges drawn up from the particulars in the charges note shall be delivered to the consignor in return for the receipt.

8   The forwarding station shall specify, in the consignment note and in the duplicate, the charges which have been prepaid, unless the provisions in force at the forwarding station provide that those charges are only to be specified in the duplicate. In the case provided for in §7 of this article, these charges are not to be specified either in the consignment note or in the duplicate.

Article 16 – Interest in delivery

1   Any consignment may be the subject of a declaration of interest in delivery. The amount declared shall be shown in figures in the consignment note in the currency of the country of departure, in another currency determined by the tariffs or in units of account.

2   The charge for interest in delivery shall be calculated for the whole of the route concerned, in accordance with the tariffs of the forwarding railway.

Article 17 – Cash on delivery and disbursements

1   The consignor may make the goods subject to a cash on delivery payment not exceeding their value at the time of acceptance at the forwarding station. The amount of such cash on delivery payment shall be expressed in the currency of the country of departure; the tariffs may provide for exceptions.

2   The railway shall not be obliged to pay over any amount representing a cash on delivery payment unless the amount in question has been paid by the consignee. That amount shall be placed at the consignor's disposal within 30 days of payment by the consignee; interest at 5% per annum shall be payable from the date of the expiry of that period.

3   If the goods have been delivered, wholly or in part, to the consignee without prior collection of the amount of the cash on delivery payment, the railway shall pay the consignor the amount of any loss or damage sustained up to the total amount of the cash on delivery payment without prejudice to any right of recovery from the consignee.

4   Cash on delivery consignment shall be subject to a collection fee laid down in the tariffs; such fee shall be payable notwithstanding cancellation or reduction of the amount of the cash on delivery payment by modification of the contract of carriage in accordance with Article 30, §1.

5   Disbursements shall only be allowed if made in accordance with the provisions in force in force at the forwarding station.

6   The amounts of the cash on delivery payment and of disbursements shall be entered in figures on the consignment note.

Article 18 – Responsibility for particulars furnished in the consignment note

The consignor shall be responsible for the correctness of the particulars inserted by, or for, him, in the consignment note. He shall bear all the consequences in the event of those particulars being irregular, incorrect, incomplete, or not entered in the allotted space. If that space is insufficient, the consignor shall indicate therein the place in the consignment note where the rest of the particulars are to be found.

Article 19 – Condition, packing and marking of goods

1   When the railway accepts for carriage goods showing obvious signs of damage, it may require the condition of such goods to be indicated in the consignment note.

2   When the nature of the goods is such as to require packing, the consignor shall pack them in such a way as to protect them from total or partial loss and from damage in transit and to avoid risk of injury or damage to persons, equipment or other goods.

Moreover the packing shall comply with the provisions in force at the forwarding station.

3   If the consignor has not complied with the provisions of §2, the railway may either refuse the goods or require the sender to acknowledge in the consignment note the absence of packing or the defective condition of the packing, with an exact description thereof.

4   The consignor shall be liable for all the consequences of the absence of packing or defective condition of packing and shall in particular make good any loss or damage suffered by the railway from this cause. In the absence of any particulars in the consignment note, the burden of proof of such absence of packing or defective condition of the packing shall rest upon the railway.

5   Save where the tariffs otherwise provide, the consignor of a consignment amounting to less than a wagon load shall indicate on each package or on a label approved by the railway in a clear and indelible manner which will avoid confusion and correspond exactly with the particulars in the consignment note:

(a)   the name and address of the consignee;

(b)   the destination station.

The details required under (a) and (b) above shall also be shown on each article or package comprised in a wagon load forwarded by rail/sea and requiring to be trans-shipped.

Old markings or labels shall be obliterated or removed by the consignor.

6   Save where the supplementary provisions or the tariffs otherwise provide, goods which are fragile or may become scattered in wagons and goods which may taint or damage other goods shall be carried only in complete wagon loads, unless packed or fastened together in such a manner that they cannot become broken or lost, or taint or damage other goods.

Article 20 – Handing over of goods for carriage and loading of goods

1   The handing over of goods for carriage shall be governed by the provisions in force at the forwarding station.

2   Loading shall be the duty of the railway or the consignor according to the provisions in force at the forwarding station, unless otherwise provided in the Uniform Rules or unless the consignment note includes a reference to a special agreement between the consignor and the railway.

When the loading is the responsibility of the consignor, he shall comply with the load limit. If different load limits are in force on the lines traversed, the lowest load limit shall be applicable to the whole route. The provisions laying down load limit shall be applicable to the whole route. The provisions laying down load limits shall be published in the same manner as tariffs. If the consignor so requests, the railway shall inform him of the permitted load limit.

3 The consignor shall be liable for all the consequences of defective loading carried out by him and shall, in particular, make good any loss or damage suffered by the railway through this cause. Nevertheless, Article 15 shall apply to the payment of costs arising from the reloading of goods in the event of defective loading. The burden of proof of defective loading shall rest upon the railway.

4 Unless otherwise provided in the Uniform Rules, goods shall be carried in covered wagons, open wagons, sheeted open wagons or specially equipped wagons according to the international tariffs. If there are no international tariffs, or if they do not contain any provisions on the subject, the provisions in force at the forwarding station shall apply throughout the whole of the route.

5 The affixing of seals to wagons shall be governed by the provisions in force at the forwarding station.

The consignor shall indicate in the consignment note the number and description of the seals affixed to the wagons by him.

Article 21 – Verification

1 The railway shall always have the right to verify that the consignment corresponds with the particulars furnished in the consignment note by the consignor and that the provisions relating to the carriage of goods accepted subject to conditions have been complied with.

2 If the contents of the consignment are examined for this purpose, the consignor or the consignee, according to whether the verification takes place at the forwarding station or the destination station, shall be invited to be present. Should the interested party not attend, or should the verification take place in transit, it shall be carried out in the presence of two witnesses not connected with the railway, unless the laws or regulations of the State where the verification takes place provide otherwise. The railway may not, however, carry out the verification in transit unless compelled to do so by operational necessities or by the requirements of the Customs or of other administrative authorities.

3 The result of the verification of the particulars in the consignment note shall be entered therein. If verification takes place at the forwarding station, the result shall also be recorded in the duplicate of the consignment note if it is held by the railway.

If the consignment does not correspond with the particulars in the consignment note or if the provisions relating to the carriage of goods accepted subject to conditions have not been complied with, the costs of the verification shall be charged against the goods, unless paid at the time.

Article 22 – Ascertainment of weight and number of packages

1 The provisions in force in each state shall determine the circumstances in which the railway must ascertain the mass of the goods or the number of packages and the actual tare of the wagons.

The railway shall enter in the consignment note the results ascertained.

2 If weighing by the railway, after the contract of carriage has been made, reveals a difference, the mass ascertained by the forwarding station or, failing that, the mass declared by the consignor, shall still be the basis for calculating the carriage charges:

(a) if the difference is manifestly due to the nature of the goods or to atmospheric conditions; or

(b) the weighing takes place on a weighbridge and does not reveal a difference exceeding 2% of the mass ascertained by the forwarding station or, failing that, of that declared by the consignor.

Article 23 – Overloading

1   When overloading of a wagon is established by the forwarding station or by an intermediate station, the excess load may be removed from the wagon even if no surcharge is payable. Where necessary the consignor or, if the contract of carriage has been modified in accordance with Article 31, the consignee shall be asked without delay to give instructions concerning the excess load.

2   Without prejudice to the payment of surcharges under Article 24, the excess load shall be charged for the distance covered in accordance with the carriage charges applicable to the main load. If the excess load is unloaded, the charge for unloading shall be determined by the tariffs of the railway which carries out the unloading.

If the person entitled directs that the excess load be forwarded to the same destination station as the main load or to another destination station, or directs that it be returned to the forwarding station, the excess load shall be treated as a separate consignment.

Article 24 – Surcharges

1   Without prejudice to the railway's entitlement to the difference in carriage charges and to compensation for any possible loss or damage, the railway may impose:

(a) a surcharge equal to one unit of account per kg of gross mass of the whole package;

   (i) in the case of irregular, incorrect or incomplete description of substances and articles not acceptable for carriage under the RID;

   (ii) in the case of irregular, incorrect or incomplete description of substances and articles which under the RID are acceptable for carriage subject to conditions, or in the case of failure to observe such conditions;

(b) a surcharge equal to five units of account per 100 kg of mass in excess of the load limit, where the wagon has been loaded by the consignor;

(c) a surcharge equal to twice the difference;

   (i) between the carriage charge which should have been payable from the forwarding station to the destination station and that which had been charged, in the case of irregular, incorrect or incomplete description of goods other than those referred to in (a), or in general where the description of the consignment would enable it to be carried at a lower tariff than the one that is actually applicable;

   (ii) between the carriage charge for the mass declared and that for the ascertained mass, where the mass declared is less than the real mass.

When a consignment is composed of goods charged at different rates and their mass can be separately determined without difficulty, the surcharge shall be calculated on the basis of the rates respectively applicable to such goods if this method of calculation results in a lower surcharge.

2   Should there be both an underdeclaration of mass and overloading in respect of one and the same wagon, the surcharges payable in respect thereof shall be cumulative.

3   The surcharges shall be charged against the goods irrespective of the place where the facts giving rise to the surcharges were established.

4   The amount of the surcharges and the reason for imposing them must be entered in the consignment note.

5   No surcharge shall be due in the case of:

(a)   an incorrect declaration of mass, if the railway is bound to weigh the goods under the provisions in force at the forwarding station;

(b)   an incorrect declaration of mass, or overloading, if the consignor has requested in the consignment note that the railway should weigh the goods;

(c)   overloading arising in the course of carriage from atmospheric conditions if it is proved that the load on the wagon did not exceed the load limit when it was consigned;

(d)   an increase in mass during carriage, without overloading, if it is proved that the increase was due to atmospheric conditions;

(e)   an incorrect declaration of mass, without overloading, if the difference between the mass indicated in the consignment note and the ascertained mass does not exceed 3% of the declared mass;

(f)   overloading of a wagon when the railway has neither published nor informed the consignor of the load limit in a way which would enable him to observe it.

Article 25 – Documents for completion of administrative formalities, custom seals

1   The consignor must attach to the consignment note the documents necessary for the completion of formalities required by Customs or other administrative authorities before delivery of the goods. Such documents shall relate only to goods which are the subject of one and the same consignment note, unless otherwise provided by the requirements of Customs or of other administrative authorities or by the tariffs.

However, when these documents are not attached to the consignment note or if they are to be provided by the consignee, the consignor shall indicate in the consignment note the station, the Customs office or the office of any other authority where the respective documents will be made available to the railway and where the formalities must be completed. If the consignor will himself be present or be represented by an agent when the formalities required by Customs or other administrative authorities are carried out, it will suffice for the documents to be produced at the time when those formalities are carried out.

2   The railway shall not be obliged to check whether the documents furnished are sufficient and correct.

3   The consignor shall be liable to the railway for any loss or damage resulting from the absence or insufficiency of or any irregularity in such documents, save in the case of fault by the railway. The railway shall, where it is at fault, be liable for any consequences arising from the loss, non-use or misuse of the documents referred to in the consignment note and accompanying it or deposited with the railway; nevertheless, any compensation shall not exceed that payable in the event of loss of the goods.

4   The consignor must comply with the requirements of Customs or of other administrative authorities with respect to the packing and sheeting of the goods. If the consignor has not packed or sheeted the goods in accordance with those

requirements the railway shall be entitled to do so; the resulting costs shall be charged against the goods.

5   The railway may refuse consignments when the seals affixed by Customs or other administrative authorities are damaged or defective.

Article 26 – Completion of administrative formalities

1   In transit, the formalities required by Customs or other administrative authorities shall be completed by the railway. The railway may, however, delegate that duty to an agent.

2   In completing such formalities, the railway shall be liable for any fault committed by itself or by its agent; nevertheless, any compensation shall not exceed that payable in the event of loss of the goods.

3   The consignor, by so indicating in the consignment note, or the consignee by giving orders as provided for in Article 31, may ask:

(a)   to be present himself or to be represented by an agent when such formalities are carried out, for the purpose of furnishing any information or explanations required;

(b)   to complete such formalities himself or to have them completed by an agent, in so far as the laws and regulations of the State in which they are to be carried out so permit;

(c)   to pay Customs duties and other charges, when he or his agent is present at or completes such formalities, in so far as the laws and regulations of the State in which they carried out permit such payment.

Neither the consignor, nor the consignee who has the right of disposal, nor the agent of either may take possession of the goods.

4   If, for the completion of the formalities, the consignor designated a station where the provision in force do not permit of their completion, or if he has stipulated for the purpose any other procedure which cannot be followed, the railway shall act in the manner which appears to it to be the most favourable to the interests of the person entitled and shall inform the consignor of the measures taken.

If the consignor, by an entry in the consignment note, has undertaken to pay charges including Customs duty, the railway shall have the choice of completing Customs formalities either in transit or at the destination station.

5   Subject to the exception provided for in the second sub-para §4, the consignee may complete Customs formalities at the destination station if that station has a Customs office and the consignment note requests Customs clearance on arrival, or, in the absence of such request, if the goods arrive under Customs control. The consignee may also complete these formalities at a destination station that has no Customs officer if the national laws and regulations so permit or it the prior authority of the railway and the Customs authorities has been obtained. If the consignee exercises any of these rights, he shall pay in advance the amounts chargeable against the goods.

Nevertheless, the railway may proceed in accordance with §4 if the consignee has not taken possession of the consignment note within the period fixed by the provisions in force at the destination station.

Article 27 – Transit periods

1   The transit periods shall be specified either by agreement between the railways participating in the carriage, or by the international tariffs applicable from the forwarding station to the destination station. For certain special types of traffic and on certain routes, these periods may also be established on the basis of transport plans applicable between the railways concerned; in that case they must be included in international tariffs or special agreements which, where appropriate, may provide for derogations from §§3 to 9 below.

Such periods shall not in any case exceed those which would result from the application of the following paragraphs.

2   In the absence of any indication in regard to the transit periods as provided for in §1, and subject to the following paras, the transit periods shall be as follows:

(a) for wagon load consignments:

(i) by *grande vitesse*: period for despatch – 12 hours; period for carriage, for each 400 km or fraction thereof – 24 hours;

(ii) by *petite vitesse*: period for despatch – 24 hours; period for carriage, for each 300 km or fraction thereof – 24 hours;

(b) for less than wagon load consignments:

(i) by *grande vitesse*: period for despatch – 12 hours; period for carriage, for each 300 km or fraction thereof – 24 hours;

(ii) by *petite vitesse*: period for despatch – 24 hours; period for carriage, for each 200 km or fraction thereof – 24 hours;

All these distances shall relate to the kilometric distances contained in the tariffs.

3   The period for carriage shall be calculated on the total distance between the forwarding station and the destination station. The period for despatch shall be counted only one, irrespective of the number of systems traversed.

4   The railway may fix additional transit periods of specified duration in the following cases:

(a) consignments handed in for carriage, or to be delivered, at places other than stations;

(b) consignments to be carried:

(i) by a line or system not equipped to deal rapidly with consignments;

(ii) by a junction line connecting two lines of the same system or of different systems;

(iii) by a second line;

(iv) by lines of different gauge;

(v) by sea or inland navigable waterway;

(vi) by road if there is no rail link;

(c) consignments charged at reduced rates in accordance with special or exceptional internal tariffs;

(d) exceptional circumstances causing an exceptional increase in traffic or exceptional operating difficulties.

5   The additional transit period provided for in §4 (a) to (c) shall be shown in the tariffs or in the provisions duly published in each State.

Those provided for in §4 (d) must be published and may not come into force before their publication.

6   The transit period shall run from midnight next following acceptance of the goods for carriage. In the case, however, of traffic consigned *grande vitesse* the period shall start 24 hours later if the day which follows the day of acceptance for carriage is a Sunday or a statutory holiday and if the forwarding station is not open for *grande vitesse* traffic on that Sunday or statutory holiday.

7   Except in the case of any fault by the railway, the transit period shall be extended by the duration of the period necessitated by:

(a)   verification or ascertainment in accordance with Article 21 and Article 22, §1, which reveals differences from the particulars shown in the consignment note;

(b)   completion of the formalities required by Customs or other administrative authorities;

(c)   modification of the contract of carriage under Article 30 or 31;

(d)   special care to be given to the goods;

(e)   the trans-shipment or reloading of any goods loaded defectively by the consignor;

(f)   any interruption of traffic temporarily preventing the commencement or continuation of carriage.

The reason for and the duration of such extensions shall be entered in the consignment note. If necessary proof may be furnished by other means.

8   The transit period shall be suspended for:

(a)   *petite vitesse*, on Sundays and statutory holidays;

(b)   *grande vitesse*, on Sundays and certain statutory holidays when the provisions in force in any State provide for the suspension of domestic railway transit periods on those days;

(c)   *grande vitesse* and *petite vitesse*, on Saturdays when the provisions in force in any State provide for the suspension of domestic railway transit periods on those days.

9   When the transit period ends after the time at which the destination station closes, the period shall be extended until two hours after the time at which the station next opens.

In addition, in the case of *grande vitesse* consignments, if the transit period ends on a Sunday or a holiday as defined in 8(b) the period shall be extended until the same time on the next working day.

10   The transit period is observed if, before its expiry:

(a)   in cases where consignments are to be delivered at a station and notice of arrival must be given, such notice is given and the goods are held at the disposal of the consignee;

(b)   in cases where consignments are to be delivered at a station and notice of arrival need not be given, the goods are held at the disposal of the consignee;

(c) in the case of consignments which are to be delivered at places other than stations, the goods are placed at the disposal of the consignee.

Article 28 – Delivery

1 The railway shall hand over the consignment note and deliver the goods to the consignee at the destination station against a receipt and payment of the amounts chargeable to the consignee by the railway.

Acceptance of the consignment note obliges the consignee to pay to the railway the amounts chargeable to him.

2 It shall be equivalent to delivery to the consignee if, in accordance with the provisions in force at the destination station:

(a) the goods have been handed over to Customs or *Octroi* authorities at their premises or warehouses, when these are not subject to railway supervision;

(b) the goods have been deposited for storage with the railway, with a forwarding agent or in a public warehouse.

3 The provisions in force at the destination station or the terms of any agreements with the consignee shall determine whether the railway is entitled or obliged to hand over the goods to the consignee elsewhere than at the destination station, whether in a private siding, at his domicile or in a railway depot. If the railway hands over the goods, or arranges for them to be handed over in a private siding, at his domicile or in a depot, delivery shall be deemed to have been effected at the time when they are so handed over. Save where the railway and the user of a private siding have agreed otherwise, operations carried out by the railway on behalf of and under the instructions of that user shall not be covered by the contract of carriage.

4 After the arrival of the goods at the destination station, the consignee may require the railway to hand over the consignment note and deliver the goods to him.

If the loss of the goods is established or if the goods have not arrived on the expiry of the period provided for in Article 39, §1, the consignee may assert, in his own name, any rights against the railway which he may have acquired by reason of the contract of carriage.

5 The person entitled may refuse to accept the goods, even when he has received the consignment note and paid the charges, so long as an examination for which he has asked in order to establish alleged loss or damage has not been made.

6 In all other respects, delivery of goods shall be carried out in accordance with the provisions in force at the destination station.

Article 29 – Correction of charges

1 In case of incorrect application of a tariff or of error in the calculation or collection of charges, overcharges shall be repaid by the railway and undercharges paid to the railway only if they exceed four units of account per consignment note. The repayment shall be made as a matter of course.

2 If the consignee has not taken possession of the consignment note, the consignor shall be obliged to pay to the railway any amounts undercharged. When the consignment note has been accepted by the consignee or the contract of carriage modified in accordance with Article 31, the consignor shall be obliged to pay any undercharge only to the extent that it relates to the costs which he has undertaken to pay by an entry in the consignment note. Any balance of the undercharge shall be paid by the consignee.

3   Sums due under this Article shall bear interest at 5% per annum from the day of receipt of the demand for payment or from the day of the claim referred to in Article 53 or, if there has been no such demand or claim, from the day on which legal proceedings are instituted.

If, within a reasonable period allotted to him, the person entitled does not submit to the railway the supporting documents required for the amount of the claim to be finally settled, no interest shall accrue between the expiry of the period laid down and the actual submission of such documents.

TITLE III – MODIFICATION OF THE CONTRACT OF CARRIAGE

Article 30 – Modification by the consignor

1   The consignor may modify the contract of carriage by giving subsequent orders:

(a) for the goods to be withdrawn at the forwarding station;

(b) for the goods to be stopped in transit;

(c) for delivery of the goods to be delayed;

(d) for the goods to be delivered to a person other than the consignee shown in the consignment note;

(e) for the goods to be delivered at a station other than the destination station shown in the consignment note;

(f) for the goods to be returned to the forwarding station;

(g) for the consignment to be made subject to a cash on delivery payment;

(h) for a cash on delivery payment to be increased, reduced or cancelled;

(i) for charges relating to a consignment which has not been prepaid to be debited to him, or for charges which he has undertaken to pay in accordance with Article 15, §2 to be increased.

The tariffs of the forwarding railway may provide that orders specified in (g) to (i) are not acceptable.

The supplementary provisions or the international tariffs in force between the railways participating in the carriage may provide for the acceptance of orders other than those listed above.

Orders must not in any event have the effect of splitting the consignment.

2   Such orders shall be given to the forwarding station by means of a written declaration in the form laid down and published by the railway. The declaration shall be reproduced and signed by the consignor in the duplicate of the consignment note which shall be presented to the railway at the same time. The forwarding station shall certify that the order has been received by affixing its date stamp on the duplicate note below the declaration made by the consignor and the duplicate shall then be returned to him.

If the consignor asks for a cash on delivery payment to be increased, reduced or cancelled, he shall produce the document which was delivered to him. Where the cash on delivery payment is to be increased or reduced, such document shall be returned to the consignor after correction; in the event of cancellation it shall not be returned. Any order given in a form other than that prescribed shall be null and void.

3   If the railway complies with the consignor's orders without requiring the production of the duplicate, where this has been sent to the consignee, the railway shall be liable to the consignee for any loss or damage caused thereby. Nevertheless, any compensation shall not exceed that payable in the event of loss of the goods.

4   The consignor's right to modify the contract of carriage shall, notwithstanding that he is in possession of the duplicate of the consignment note, be extinguished in cases where the consignee:

(a) has taken possession of the consignment note;

(b) has accepted the goods;

(c) has asserted his rights in accordance with Article 28, §4;

(d) is entitled, in accordance with Article 31, to give orders as soon as the consignment had entered the Customs territory of the country of destination.

From that time onwards, the railway shall comply with the orders and instructions of the consignee.

Article 31 – Modification by the consignee

1   When the consignor has not undertaken to pay the charges relating to carriage in the country of destination, and has not inserted in the consignment note the words 'Consignee not authorised to give subsequent orders', the consignee may modify the contact of carriage by giving subsequent orders:

(a) for the goods to be stopped in transit;

(b) for delivery of the goods to be delayed;

(c) for the goods to be delivered in the country of destination to a person other than the consignee shown in the consignment note;

(d) for the goods to be delivered in the country of destination at a station other than the destination station shown in the consignment note, subject to contrary provisions in international tariffs;

(e) for formalities required by Customs or other administrative authorities to be carried out in accordance with Article 26, §3.

The supplementary provisions or the international tariffs in force between the railways participating in the carriage may provide for the acceptance of orders other than those listed above.

Orders must not in any case have the effect of splitting the consignment. The consignee's orders shall only be effective after the consignment has entered the Customs territory of the country of destination.

2   Such orders shall be given either to the destination station or to the station of entry into the country of destination, by means of a written declaration in the form laid down and published by the railway.

Any order given in a form other than that prescribed shall be null and void.

3   The consignee's right to modify the contract of carriage shall be extinguished in cases where he has:

(a) taken possession of the consignment note;

(b) accepted the goods;

(c) asserted his rights in accordance with Article 28, §4;

(d) designated a person in accordance with §1(c) and that person has taken possession of the consignment note or asserted his rights in accordance with Article 28, §4.

4 If the consignee has given instructions for delivery of the goods to another person, that person shall not be entitled to modify the contract of carriage.

Article 32 – Execution of subsequent orders

1 The railway may not refuse to execute orders given under Articles 30 or 31 or delay doing so save where:

(a) it is no longer possible to execute the orders by the time they reach the station responsible for doing so;

(b) compliance with the orders would interfere with normal railway operations;

(c) a change of destination station would contravene the laws and regulations of a State, and in particular the requirements of the Customs or of other administrative authorities;

(d) in the case of a change of destination station, the value of the goods will not, in the railway's view, cover all the charges which would be payable on the goods on arrival at the new destination, unless the amount of such charges is paid or guaranteed immediately.

The person who has given the orders shall be informed as soon as possible of any circumstances which prevent their execution.

If the railway is not in a position to foresee such circumstances, the person who has given the orders shall be liable for all the consequences of starting to execute them.

2 The charges arising from the execution of an order, except those arising from any fault by the railway, shall be paid in accordance with Article 15.

3 Subject to §1, the railway shall, in the case of any fault on its part, be liable for the consequences of failure to execute an order or failure to execute it properly. Nevertheless, any compensation shall not exceed that payable in the event of loss of the goods.

Article 33 – Circumstances preventing carriage

1 When circumstances prevent the carriage of goods, the railway shall decide whether it is preferable to carry the goods as a matter of course by modifying the route or whether it is advisable in the consignor's interest to ask him for instructions and at the same time give him any relevant information available to the railway.

Save fault on its part, the railway may recover the carriage charges applicable to the route followed and shall be allowed the transit periods applicable to such route.

2 If it is impossible to continue carrying the goods, the railway shall ask the consignor for instructions. It shall not be obliged to do so in the event of carriage being temporarily prevented as a result of measures taken in accordance with Article 3, §4.

3 The consignor may enter in the consignment note instructions to cover the event of circumstances preventing carriage. If the railway considers that such instructions cannot be executed, it shall ask for fresh instructions.

4 The consignor, on being notified of circumstances preventing carriage, may give his instructions either to the forwarding station or to the station where the goods are being held. If those instructions change the consignee or the destination station or

are given to the station where the goods are being held, the consignor must enter them in the duplicate of the consignment note and present this to the railway.

5   If the railway complies with the consignor's instructions without requiring the production of the duplicate, when this has been sent to the consignee, the railway shall be liable to the consignee for any loss or damage caused thereby. Nevertheless, any compensation shall not exceed that payable in the event of loss of the goods.

6   If the consignor, on being notified of a circumstance preventing carriage, fails to give within a reasonable time instructions which can be executed, the railway shall take action in accordance with the provisions relating to circumstances preventing delivery, in force at the place where the goods have been held up. If the goods have been sold, the proceeds of sale, less any amounts chargeable against the goods, shall be held at the disposal of the consignor. If the proceeds are less than those costs, the consignor shall pay the difference.

7   When the circumstances preventing carriage cease to obtain before the arrival of instructions from the consignor, the goods shall be forwarded to their destination without waiting for such instructions; the consignor shall be notified to that effect as soon as possible.

8   When the circumstances preventing carriage arise after the consignee has modified the contract of carriage in accordance with Article 31, the railway shall notify the consignee. §§2, 6, 7 and 9 shall apply analogously.

9   Save fault on its part, the railway may raise demurrage or standage charges if circumstances prevent carriage.

10   Article 32 shall apply to carriage undertaken in accordance with Article 33.

Article 34 – Circumstances preventing delivery

1   When circumstances prevent delivery of the goods, the destination station shall without delay notify the consignor through the forwarding station, and ask for his instructions. The consignor shall be notified direct, either in writing, by telegram or by teleprinter, if he has so requested in the consignment note; the costs of such notification shall be charged against the goods.

2   If the circumstances preventing delivery cease to obtain before the arrival at the destination station of instructions from the consignor the goods shall be delivered to the consignee. The consignor shall be notified without delay be registered letter; the costs of such notification shall be charged against the goods.

3   If the consignee refuses the goods, the consignor shall be entitled to give instructions even if he is unable to produce the duplicate of the consignment note.

4   The consignor may also request, by an entry in the consignment note, that the goods be returned to him as a matter of course in the event of circumstances preventing delivery. Unless such request is made, his express consent is required.

5   Unless the tariffs otherwise provide, the consignor's instructions shall be given through the forwarding station.

6   Except as otherwise provided for above, the railway responsible for delivery shall proceed in accordance with the provisions in force at the place of delivery. If the goods have been sold, the proceeds of sale, less any costs chargeable against the goods, shall be held at the disposal of the consignor. If such proceeds are less than those costs, the consignor shall pay the difference.

7   When the circumstances preventing delivery arise after the consignee has modified the contract of carriage in accordance with Article 31, the railway shall notify the consignee. §§ 1, 2 and 6 shall apply analogously.

8   Article 32 shall apply to carriage undertaken in accordance with Article 34.

TITLE IV – LIABILITY

Article 35 – Collective responsibility of railways

1   The railway which has accepted goods for carriage with the consignment note shall be responsible for the carriage over the entire route up to delivery.

2   Each succeeding railway, by the very act of taking over the goods with the consignment note, shall become a party to the contract of carriage in accordance with the terms of that document and shall assume the obligations arising therefrom, without prejudice to the provisions of Article 55, §3, relating to the railway of destination.

Article 36 – Extent of liability

1   The railway shall be liable for loss or damage resulting from the total or partial loss of, or damage to, the goods between the time of acceptance for carriage and the time of delivery and for the loss or damage resulting from the transit period being exceeded.

2   The railway shall be relieved of such liability if the loss or damage or the exceeding of the transit period was caused by a fault on the part of the person entitled, by an order given by the person entitled other than as a result of a fault on the part of the railway, by inherent vice of the goods (decay, wastage, etc) or by circumstances which the railway could not avoid and the consequences of which it was unable to prevent.

3   The railways shall be relieved of such liability when the loss or damage arises from the special risks inherent in one or more of the following circumstances:

(a) carriage in open wagons under the conditions applicable thereto or under an agreement made between the consignor and the railway and referred to in the consignment note;

(b) absence or inadequacy of packing in the case of goods which by their nature are liable to loss or damage when not packed or when not properly packed;

(c) loading operations carried out by the consignor or unloading operations carried out by the consignee under the provisions applicable thereto or under an agreement made between the consignor and the railway and referred to in the consignment note, or under an agreement between the consignee and the railway;

(d) defective loading, when loading has been carried out by the consignor under the provisions applicable thereto or under an agreement made between the consignor and the railway and referred to in the consignment note;

(e) completion by the consignor, the consignee or an agent of either, of the formalities required by Customs or other administrative authorities;

(f) the nature of certain goods which renders them inherently liable to total or partial loss or damage, especially through breakage, rust, interior and spontaneous decay, desiccation or wastage;

(g) irregular, incorrect or incomplete description of articles not acceptable for carriage or acceptable subject to conditions, or failure on the part of the consignor to observe the prescribed precautions in respect of articles acceptable subject to conditions;

(h) carriage of live animals;

(i) carriage which, under the provisions applicable or under an agreement made between the consignor and the railway and referred to in the consignment note, must be accompanied by an attendant, if the loss or damage results from any risk which the attendant was intended to avert.

Article 37 – Burden of proof

1 The burden of proving that the loss, the damage or the exceeding of the transit period was due to one of the causes specified in Article 36, §2 shall rest upon the railway.

2 When the railway establishes that, having regard to the circumstances of a particular case, the loss or damage could have arisen from one or more of the special risks referred to in Article 36, §3, it shall be presumed that it did so arise. The person entitled shall, however, have the right to prove that the loss or damage was not attributable either wholly or partly to one of those risks.

This presumption shall not apply in the case referred to in Article 36, §3(a) if an abnormally large quantity has been lost or if a package has been lost.

Article 38 – Presumption in case of reconsignment

1 When a consignment dispatched in accordance with the Uniform Rules has been reconsigned subject to the same rules and partial loss or damage has been ascertained after the reconsignment, it shall be presumed that it occurred during the latest contract of carriage if the consignment remained in the care of the railway and was reconsigned in the same condition as it arrived at the station from which it was reconsigned.

2 This presumption shall also apply when the contract of carriage prior to the reconsignment was not subject to the Uniform Rules, if the rules would have applied in the case of a through consignment from the original forwarding station to the final destination station.

Article 39 – Presumption of loss of goods

1 The person entitled may, without being required to furnish further proof, consider the goods lost when they have not been delivered to the consignee or are not being held at his disposal within 30 days after the expiry of the transit periods.

2 The person entitled may, on compensation for the lost goods, make a written request to be notified without delay should the goods be recovered within one year after the payment of compensation. The railway shall give a written acknowledgement of such request.

3 Within 30 days after receipt of such notification, the person entitled may require the goods to be delivered to him at any station on the route. In that case, he shall pay the charges in respect of carriage from the forwarding station to the station where delivery is effected and shall refund the compensation received, less any costs which may have been included therein. Nevertheless, he shall retain his rights to claim compensation for exceeding the transit period provided for in Articles 43 and 46.

4   In the absence of the request mentioned in §2 or of any instructions given within the period specified in §3, or if the goods are recovered more than one year after the payment of compensation, the railway shall dispose of them in accordance with the laws and regulations of the State having jurisdiction over the railway.

Article 40 – Compensation for loss

1   In the event of total or partial loss of the goods, the railway must pay, to the exclusion of all other damages, compensation calculated according to the commodity exchange quotation or, if there is no such quotation, according to the current market price, or if there is neither such quotation nor such price, according to the normal value of goods of the same kind and quality at the time and place at which the goods were accepted for carriage.

2   Compensation shall not exceed 17 units of account per kg of gross mass short, subject to the limit provided for in Article 45.

3   The railway shall in addition refund carriage charges, Customs duties and other amounts incurred in connection with carriage of the lost goods.

4   When the calculation of compensation requires the conversion of amounts expressed in foreign currencies, conversion shall be at the rate of exchange applicable at the time and place of payment of compensation.

Article 41 – Liability for wastage in transit

1   In respect of goods which, by reason of their nature, are generally subject to wastage in transit by the sole fact of carriage, the railway shall only be liable to the extent that the wastage exceeds the following allowances, whatever the length of the route:

(a)   Two per cent of the mass for liquid goods or goods consigned in a moist condition, and also for the following goods:

Bark; leather; whole or ground bones; liquorice root; coal and coke; fresh mushrooms; grated or ground dye-woods; peat and turf; fats; putty or mastic; fresh fish; dried roots; fresh, dried or cooked fruit; salt; furs; animal sinews; hide cuttings; soap and solidified oils; hides; cut tobacco; hog bristles; fresh tobacco leaves; hops; fresh vegetables; horns and hooves; wool; horsehair.

(b)   One per cent of the weight for all other dry goods.

2   The limitation of liability provided for in §1 may not be invoked if, having regard to the circumstances of a particular case, it is proved that the loss was not due to cause which would justify an allowance.

3   Where several packages are carried under a single consignment note, the wastage in transit shall be calculated separately for each package if its mass on despatch is shown separately in the consignment note or can otherwise be ascertained.

4   In the event of total loss of the goods, no deduction for wastage in transit shall be made in calculating the compensation payable.

5   This Article shall not derogate from Articles 36 and 37.

Article 42 – compensation for damage

1   In case of damage to goods, the railway must pay compensation equivalent to the loss in value of the goods, to the exclusion of all other damages. The amount shall be calculated by applying to the value of the goods as defined in Article 40 the percentage of loss in value noted at the place of destination.

2   The compensation may not exceed:

(a) if the whole consignment has lost value through damage, the amount which would have been payable in case of total loss;

(b) if only part of the consignment has lost value through damage, the amount which would have been payable had that part been lost.

3   The railway shall in addition refund the amounts provided for in Article 40, §3, in the proportion set out in §1.

Article 43 – compensation for exceeding the transit period

1   If loss or damage has resulted from the transit period being exceeded, the railway shall pay compensation not exceeding three times the carriage charger.

2   In case of total loss of the goods, the compensation provided for in §1 shall not be payable in addition to that provided for in Article 40.

3   In case of partial loss of the goods, the compensation provided for in §1 shall not exceed three times the carriage charges in respect of that part of the consignment which has not been lost.

4   In case of damage to the goods, not resulting from the transit period being exceeded, the compensation provided for in §1 shall, where appropriate, be payable in addition to that provided for in Article 42.

5   In no case shall the total of compensation payable under §1 together with that payable under Articles 40 and 42 exceed the compensation which would be payable in the event of total loss of the goods.

6   The railway may provide, in international tariffs or in special agreements for other forms of compensation than those provided for in §1 when, in accordance with Article 27, §1, the transit period has been established on the basis of transport plans.

If, in this case, the transit periods provided for in Article 27, §2 are exceeded, the person entitled may demand either the compensation provided for in §1 above or that determined by the international tariff or the special agreement applied.

Article 44 – Compensation in case of wilful misconduct or gross negligence

When the loss, damage or exceeding of the transit period, or the failure to perform or failure to perform properly the railway's additional services provided for in the Uniform Rules, has been caused by wilful misconduct or gross negligence on the part of the railway, full compensation for the loss or damage proved shall be paid to the person entitled by the railway.

In case of gross negligence, liability shall, however, be limited to twice the maxima specified in Articles 25, 26, 30, 32, 33, 40, 42, 43, 45 and 46.

Article 45 – Limitation of compensation under certain tariffs

When the railway agrees to special conditions of carriage through special or exceptional tariffs, involving a reduction in the carriage charge calculated on the basis of the general tariffs, it may limit the amount of compensation payable to the person entitled in the event of loss, damage or exceeding of the transit period, provided that such limit is indicated in the tariff.

When the special conditions of carriage apply only to part of the route, the limit may only be invoked if the event giving rise to the compensation occurred on that part of the route.

Article 46 – Compensation in case of interest in delivery

In case of a declaration of interest in delivery, further compensation for loss or damage proved may be claimed, in addition to the compensation provided for in Articles 40, 42, 43 and 45, up to the amount declared.

Article 47 – Interest on compensation

1   The person entitled may claim interest on compensation payable, calculated at 5% per annum, from the date of the claim referred to in Article 53 or, if no such claim has been made, from the day on which legal proceedings are instituted.

2   Interest shall only be payable if the compensation exceeds four units of account per consignment note.

3   If, within a reasonable period allotted to him, the person entitled does not submit to the railway the supporting documents required for the amount of the claim to be finally settled, no interest shall accrue between the expiry of the period laid down and the actual submission of such documents.

Article 48 – Liability in respect of rail-sea traffic

1   In rail-sea transport by the services referred to in Article 2, §2 of the convention each State may, by requesting that a suitable note be included in the list of lines or services to which the Uniform Rules apply, indicate that the following grounds for exemption from liability will apply in their entirety in addition to those provided for in Article 36.

The carrier may only avail himself to these grounds for exemption if he proves that the loss, damage or exceeding of the transit period occurred in the course of the sea journey between the time when the goods were loaded on board the ship and the time when they were discharged from the ship.

The grounds for exemption are as follows:

(a)   act, neglect or default on the part of the master, a mariner, pilot or the carrier's servants in the navigation or management of the ship;

(b)   unseaworthiness of the ship, if the carrier proves that the unseaworthiness is not attributable to lack of due diligence on his part to make the ship seaworthy, to ensure that it is properly manned, equipped and supplied or to make all parts of the ship in which the goods are loaded fit and safe for their reception, carriage and protection;

(c)   fire, if the carrier proves that it was not caused by his act or fault, or that of the master, a mariner, pilot or the carrier's servants;

(d)   perils, dangers and accidents of the sea or the navigable waters;

(e)   saving or attempting to save life or property at sea;

(f)   the loading of goods on the deck of the ship, if they are so loaded with the consent of the consignor given in the consignment note and are not in wagons.

The above grounds for exemption in no way affect the general obligations of the carrier and, in particular, his obligation to exercise due diligence to make the ship seaworthy, to ensure that it is properly manned, equipped and supplied and to make all parts of the ship in which the goods are loaded fit and safe for their reception, carriage and protection.

Even when the carrier can rely on the foregoing grounds for exemption, he shall nevertheless remain liable if the person entitled proves that the loss, damage or exceeding of the transit period is due to a fault of the carrier, the master, a mariner, pilot or the carrier's servants, fault other than provided for under (a).

2   Where one and the same sea route is served by several undertakings included in the list referred to in Articles 3 and 10 of the convention, the regime of liability applicable to that route shall be the same for all those undertakings.

In addition, where such undertakings have been included in the list at the request of several States, the adoption of this regime shall be the subject of prior agreement between those States.

3   The measures taken under this Article shall be notified to the central office. They shall come into force at the earliest at the expiry of a period of 30 days from the date of the letter by which the central office notifies them to the other States.

Consignments already in transit shall not be affected by such measures.

Article 49 – Liability in case of nuclear incidents

The railway shall be relieved of liability under the Uniform Rules for less or damage caused by a nuclear incident when the operator of a nuclear installation or another person who is substituted for him is liable for the loss or damage pursuant to a State's laws and regulations governing liability in the field of nuclear energy.

Article 50 – Liability of the railway for its servants

The railway shall be liable for its servants and for any other persons whom it employs to perform the carriage. If, however, such servants and other persons, at the request of an interested party, make out consignment notes, make translations or render other services which the railway itself is under no obligation to render, they shall be deemed to be acting on behalf of the person to whom the services are rendered.

Article 51 – Other actions

In all cases to which the Uniform Rules apply, any action in respect of liability on any grounds whatsoever may be brought against the railway only subject to the conditions and limitations laid down in the rules. The same shall apply to any action brought against those servants and other persons for whom the railway is liable under Article 50.

TITLE V – ASSERTION OF RIGHTS

Article 52 – Ascertainment of partial loss or damage

1   When partial loss of, or damage to, goods is discovered or presumed by the railway or alleged by the person entitled, the railway must without delay, and if possible in the presence of the person entitled, draw up a report stating, according to the nature of the loss or damage, the condition of the goods, their mass and, as far as possible, the extent of the loss or damage, its cause and the time of its occurrence.

A copy of the report must be supplied free of charge to the person entitled.

2   Should the person entitled not accept the findings in the report, he may request that the condition and mass of the goods and the cause and amount of the loss or damage be ascertained by an expert appointed either by the parties or by a court. The procedure to be followed shall be governed by the laws and regulations in the State in which such ascertainment takes place.

Article 53 – Claims

1 Claims relating to the contract of carriage shall be made in writing to the railway specified in Article 55.

2 A claim may be made by persons who have the right to bring an action against the railway under Article 54.

3 To make the claim, the consignor must produce the duplicate of the consignment note. Failing this, he must produce an authorisation from the consignee or furnish proof that the consignee has refused to accept the consignment. To make the claim, the consignee must produce the consignment note if it has been handed over to him.

4 The consignment note, the duplicate and any other documents which the person entitled thinks fit to submit with the claim shall be produced either in the original or as copies, the copies to be duly authenticated if the railway so requires. On settlement of the claim, the railway may require the production, in the original form, of the consignment note, the duplicate or the cash on delivery voucher so that they may be endorsed to the effect that settlement has been made.

Article 54 – Persons who may bring an action against the railway

1 An action for the recovery of a sum paid under the contract of carriage may only be brought by the person who made the payment.

2 An action in respect of the cash on delivery payments provided for in Article 17 may only be brought by the consignor.

3 Other actions arising from the contract of carriage may be brought:

   (a) by the consignor, until such time as the consignee has:

      (i) taken possession of the consignment note;

      (ii) accepted the goods; or

      (iii) asserted his rights under Article 28, §4 or Article 31;

   (b) by the consignee, from the time when he has:

      (i) taken possession of the consignment note;

      (ii) accepted the goods;

      (iii) asserted his rights under Article 28, §4; or

      (iv) asserted his rights under Article 31 provided that the right of action shall be extinguished from the time when the person designated by the consignee in accordance with Article 31, §1(c) has taken possession of the consignment note, accepted the goods, or asserted his rights under Article 28, §4.

4 In order to bring an action, the consignor must produce the duplicate of the consignment note. Failing this, in order to bring an action under §3(a) he must produce an authorisation from the consignee or furnish proof that the consignee has refused to accept the consignment. In order to bring an action, the consignee shall produce the consignment note if it has been handed over to him.

Article 55 – Railways against which an action may be brought

1 An action for the recovery of a sum paid under the contract of carriage may be brought against the railway which has collected that sum or against the railway on whose behalf it was collected.

2 An action in respect of the cash on delivery payments provided for in Article 17 may only be brought against the forwarding railway.

3 Other actions arising from the contact of carriage may be brought against the forwarding railway, the railway of destination or the railway on which the event giving rise to the proceedings occurred. Such actions may be brought against the railway of destination even if it has received neither the goods nor the consignment note.

4 If the plaintiff can choose between several railways, his right to choose shall be extinguished as soon as he brings an action against any one of them.

5 An action may be brought against a railway other than those specified in §§1, 2 and 3 when instituted by way of counterclaim or by way of exception to the principal claim based on the same contract of carriage.

Article 56 – Competence

Actions brought under the Uniform Rules may only be instituted in the competent court of the State having jurisdiction over the defendant railway, unless otherwise provided in agreements between States or in acts of concession. When a railway operates independent railway systems in different States, each system shall be regarded as a separate railway for the purposes of this article.

Article 57 – Extinction of right of action against the railway

1 Acceptance of the goods by the person entitled shall extinguish all rights of action against the railway arising from the contract in case of partial loss, damage or exceeding of the transit period.

2 Nevertheless, the right of action shall not be extinguished:

(a) in the case of partial loss or of damage, if:

(i) the loss or damage was ascertained before the acceptance of the goods in accordance with Article 52 by the person entitled;

(ii) the ascertainment which should have been carried out under Article 52 was omitted solely through the fault of the railway;

(b) in the case of loss or damage which is not apparent and is not ascertained until after acceptance of the goods by the person entitled, provided that he:

(i) asks for ascertainment in accordance with Article 52 immediately after discovery of the loss or damage and not later than seven days after the acceptance of the goods;

(ii) and, in addition, proves that the loss or damage occurred between the time of acceptance for carriage and the time of delivery;

(c) in cases where the transit period has been exceeded, if the person entitled has, within 60 days, asserted his rights against one of the railways referred to in Article 55, §3;

(d) if the person entitled furnishes proof that the loss or damage was caused by wilful misconduct or gross negligence on the part of the railway.

3 If the goods have been reconsigned in accordance with Article 38, §1 rights of action in case of partial loss or of damage, arising from one of the previous contracts of carriage, shall be extinguished as if there had been only one contract of carriage.

Article 58 – Limitation of action

1   The period of limitation for an action arising from the contract of carriage shall be one year. Nevertheless, the period of limitation shall be two years in the case of an action:

   (a) to recover a cash on delivery payment collected by the railway from the consignee;

   (b) to recover the proceeds of a sale affected by the railway;

   (c) for loss or damage caused by wilful misconduct;

   (d) for fraud;

   (e) arising from one of the contracts of carriage prior to the reconsignment in the case provided for in Article 38, §1.

2   The period of limitation shall run:

   (a) in actions for compensation for total loss, from the thirtieth day after the expiry of the transit period;

   (b) in actions for compensation for partial loss, for damage or for exceeding the transit period, from the day when delivery took place;

   (c) in actions for payment or refund of carriage charges, supplementary charges, other charges or surcharges, or for correction of charges in case of a tariff being wrongly applied or of an error in calculation or collection:

      (i)   if payment has been made, from the day of payment;

      (ii) if payment has not been made, from the day when the goods were accepted for carriage if payment is due from the consignor, or from the day when the consignee took possession of the consignment note if payment is due from him;

      (iii) in the case of sums to be paid under a charge note, from the day on which the railway submits to the consignor the account of charges provided for in Article 15, §7; if no such account has been submitted, the period in respect of sums due to the railway shall run from the 30th day following the expiry of the transit period;

   (d) in an action by the railway for recovery of a sum which has been paid by the consignee instead of by the consignor or *vice versa* and which the railway is required to refund to the person entitled, from the day of the claim for a refund;

   (e) in actions relating to cash on delivery as provided for in Article 17, from the 30th day following the expiry of the transit period;

   (f) in actions to recover the proceeds of a sale, from the day of the sale;

   (g) in actions to recover additional duty demanded by Customs or other administrative authorities, from the day of the demand made by such authorities;

   (h) in all other cases, from the day when the right of action arises.

      The day indicated for the commencement of the period of limitation shall not be included in the period.

3   When a claim is presented to a railway in accordance with Article 53 together with the necessary supporting documents, the period of limitation shall be suspended until the day that the railway rejects the claim by notification in writing and returns the

documents. If part of the claim is admitted, the period of limitation shall recommence in respect of that part of the claim still in dispute. The burden of proof of receipt of the claim or of the reply and of the return of the documents shall rest on the party who relies on those facts.

The period of limitation shall not be suspended by further claims having the same object.

4   A right of action which has become time-barred may not be exercised by way of counter claim or relied upon by way of exception.

5   Subject to the foregoing provisions, the suspension and interruption of periods of limitation shall be governed by national law.

TITLE VI – RELATIONS BETWEEN RAILWAYS

Article 59 – Settlement of accounts between railways

1   Any railway which has collected, either at the time of forwarding or on arrival, charges or other sums due under the contract of carriage must pay to the railways concerned their respective shares.

The methods of payment shall be settled by agreements between railways.

2   Subject to its rights of recovery against the consignor, the forwarding railway shall be liable for carriage and other charges which it has failed to collect when the consignor has undertaken to pay them in accordance with Article 15.

3   Should the railway of destination deliver the goods without collecting charges or other sums due under the contract of carriage, it shall be liable for them to the railways which have taken part in the carriage and to the other parties concerned.

4   Should one railway default in payment and such default be confirmed by the central office at the request of one of the creditor railways, the consequences thereof shall be borne by all the other railways which have taken part in the carriage in proportion to their shares of the carriage charges.

The right of recovery against the defaulting railway shall not be affected.

Article 60 – Recourse in case of loss or damage

1   A railway which has paid compensation in accordance with the Uniform Rules, for total or partial loss or for damage, has a right of recourse against the other railways which have taken part in the carriage in accordance with the following provision:

(a)   the railway which has caused the loss or damage shall be solely liable for it;

(b)   when the loss or damage has been caused by more than one railway, each shall be liable for the loss or damage it has caused; if such distinction cannot be made, the compensation shall be apportioned between those railways in accordance with (c);

(c)   if it cannot be proved that the loss or damage has been caused by one or more railways in particular, the compensation shall be apportioned between all the railways which have taken part in the carriage, except those which can prove that the loss or damage was not caused on their lines; such apportionment shall be in proportion to the kilometric distances contained in the tariffs.

2   In the case of the insolvency of any one of the railways, the unpaid share due from it shall be apportioned among all the other railways which have taken part in the carriage, in proportion to the kilometric distances contained in the tariffs.

Article 61 – Recourse in case of exceeding the transit period

1   Article 60 shall apply where compensation is paid for exceeding the transit period. If this has been caused by more than one railway, the compensation shall be apportioned between such railways in proportion to the length of the delay occurring on their respective lines.

2   The transit periods specified in Article 27 shall be apportioned in the following manner:

(a)   where two railways have taken part in the carriage;

(i)   the period for despatch shall be divided equally;

(ii)   the period for transport shall be divided in proportion to the kilometric distances contained in the tariffs;

(b)   where three or more railways have taken part in the carriage;

(i)   the period for despatch shall be divided equally between the forwarding railway and the railway of destination;

(ii)   the period for transport shall be divided between all the railways: one-third in equal shares, the remaining two-thirds in proportion to the kilometric distances contained in the tariffs.

3   Any additional periods to which a railway may be entitled shall be allocated to that railway.

4   The interval between the time when the goods are handed over to the railway and commencement of the period for despatch shall be allocated exclusively to the forwarding railway.

5   Such apportionment shall only apply if the total transit period has been exceeded.

Article 62 – Procedure for recourse

1   The validity of the payment made by the railway exercising one of the rights of recourse under Articles 60 and 61 may not be disputed by the railway against which the right of recourse is exercised, when compensation has been determined by a court and when the latter railway duly served with notice, has been afforded an opportunity to intervene in the proceedings. The court seised of the main proceedings shall determine what time shall be allowed for such notification and for intervention in the proceedings.

2   A railway exercising its right of recourse must take proceedings by one and the same action against all the railways concerned with which it has not reached a settlement, failing which it shall lose its right of recourse in the case of those against which it has not taken proceedings.

3   The court shall give its decision in one and the same judgment on all recourse claims brought before it.

4   The railways against which such action has been brought shall have no further right of recourse.

5   Recourse proceedings may not be joined with proceedings for compensation taken by the person entitled on the basis of the contract of carriage.

Article 63 – Competence for recourse

1   The courts of the country in which the railway against which the recourse claim has been made, has its headquarters shall have exclusive competence for all recourse claims.

2   When the action is to be brought against several railways, the plaintiff railway shall be entitled to choose the court in which it will bring the proceedings from among those having competence under §1.

Article 64 – Agreements concerning recourse

By agreement, railways may derogate from the provisions concerning reciprocal rights of recourse set out in Title VI, apart from that contained in Article 62, §5.

Articles 65–66 [omitted]

CARRIAGE OF GOODS BY ROAD ACT 1965

SCHEDULE

CONVENTION ON THE CONTRACT FOR THE INTERNATIONAL CARRIAGE OF GOODS BY ROAD

CHAPTER I – SCOPE OF APPLICATION

Section 1

Article 1

1   This Convention shall apply to every contract for the carriage of goods by road in vehicles for reward, when the place of taking over of the goods and the place designated for delivery, as specified in the contract, are situated in two different countries, of which at least one is a contracting country, irrespective of the place of residence and the nationality of the parties.

2   For the purposes of this Convention, 'vehicles' means motor vehicles, articulated vehicles, trailers and semi-trailers as defined in Article 4 of the Convention on Road Traffic dated 19th September 1949.

3   This Convention shall apply also where carriage coming within its scope is carried out by States or by governmental institutions or organisations.

4   This Convention shall not apply:

    (a)   to carriage performed under the terms of any international postal convention:

    (b)   to funeral consignments;

    (c)   to furniture removal.

5   The contracting parties agree not to vary any of the provisions of this Convention by special agreements between two or more of them, except to make it inapplicable to their frontier traffic or to authorise the use in transport operations entirely confined to their territory of consignment notes representing a title to the goods.

Article 2

1   Where the vehicle containing the goods is carried over part of the journey by sea, rail, inland waterways or air, and, except where the provisions of article 14 are applicable, the goods are not unloaded from the vehicle, this Convention shall nevertheless apply to the whole of the carriage. Provided that to the extent that it is proved that any loss, damage or delay in delivery of the goods which occurs during the carriage by the other means of transport was not caused by an act or omission of the carrier by road, but by some event which could only have occurred in the course

of and by reason of the carriage by that other means of transport, the liability of the carrier by road shall be determined not by this Convention but in the manner in which the liability of the carrier by the other means of transport would have been determined if a contract for the carriage of the goods alone had been made by the sender with the carrier by the other means of transport in accordance with the conditions prescribed by law for the carriage of goods by that means of transport. If, however, there are no such prescribed conditions, the liability of the carrier by road shall be determined by this Convention.

2   If the carrier by road is also himself the carrier by the other means of transport, his liability shall also be determined in accordance with the provisions of para 1 of this article, but as if, in his capacities as carrier by road and as carrier by the other means of transport, he were two separate persons.

CHAPTER II – PERSONS FOR WHOM THE CARRIER IS RESPONSIBLE

Article 3

For the purposes of this Convention the carrier shall be responsible for the acts and omissions of his agents and servants and of any other persons of whose services he makes use for the performance of the carriage, when such agents, servants or other persons are acting within the scope of their employment, as if such acts or omissions were his own.

CHAPTER III – CONCLUSION AND PERFORMANCE OF THE CONTRACT OF CARRIAGE

Article 4

The contract of carriage shall be confirmed by the making out of a consignment note. The absence, irregularity or loss of the consignment note shall not affect the existence or the validity of the contract of carriage which shall remain subject to the provisions of this Convention.

Article 5

1   The consignment note shall be made out in three original copies signed by the sender and by the carrier. These signatures may be printed or replaced by the stamps of the sender and the carrier if the law of the country in which the consignment note has been made out so permits. The first copy shall be handed to the sender, the second shall accompany the goods and the third shall be retained by the carrier.

2   When the goods which are to be carried have to be loaded in different vehicles, or are of different kinds or arc divided into different lots, the sender or the carrier shall have the right to require a separate consignment note to be made out for each vehicle used, or for each kind or lot of goods.

Article 6

1   The consignment note shall contain the following particulars:

   (a)   the date of the consignment note and the place at which it is made out;

   (b)   the name and address of the sender;

   (c)   the name and address of the carrier;

   (d)   the place and the date of taking over of the goods and the place designated for delivery;

   (e)   the name and address of the consignee;

   (f)   the description in common use of the nature of the goods and the method of packing, and, in the case of dangerous goods, their generally recognised description;

(g) the number of packages and their special marks and numbers;

(h) the gross weight of the goods or their quantity otherwise expressed;

(i) charges relating to the carriage (carriage charges, supplementary charges, customs duties and other charges incurred from the making of the contract to the time of delivery);

(j) the requisite instructions for Customs and other formalities;

(k) a statement that the carriage is subject, notwithstanding any clause to the contrary, to the provisions of this Convention.

2   Where applicable, the consignment note shall also contain the following particulars:

(a) a statement that trans-shipment is not allowed;

(b) the charges which the sender undertakes to pay;

(c) the amount of 'cash on delivery' charges;

(d) a declaration of the value of the goods and the amount representing special interest in delivery;

(e) the sender's instructions to the carrier regarding insurance of the goods;

(f) the agreed time limit within which the carriage is to be carried out;

(g) a list of the documents handed to the carrier.

3   The parties may enter in the consignment note any other particulars which they may deem useful.

Article 7

1   The sender shall be responsible for all expenses, loss and damage sustained by the carrier by reason of the inaccuracy or inadequacy of:

(a) the particulars specified in Article 6, para 1, (b), (d), (e), (f), (g), (h) and (j):

(b) the particulars specified in Article 6, para 2;

(c) any other particulars or instructions given by him to enable the consignment note to be made out or for the purpose of their being entered therein .

2   If, at the request of the sender, the carrier enters in the consignment note the particulars referred to in para 1 of this article, he shall be deemed, unless the contrary is proved, to have done so on behalf of the sender.

3   If the consignment note does not contain the statement specified in Article 6, para 1(k) the carrier shall be liable for all expenses, loss and damage sustained through such omission by the person entitled to dispose of the goods.

Article 8

1   On taking over the goods, the carrier shall check:

(a) the accuracy of the statements in the consignment note as to the number of packages and their marks and numbers, and

(b) the apparent condition of the goods and their packaging.

2   Where the carrier has no reasonable means of checking the accuracy of the statements referred to in para 1(a) of this article, he shall enter his reservations in the consignment note together with the grounds on which they are based. He shall likewise specify the grounds for any reservations which he makes with regard to the

apparent condition of the goods and their packaging. Such reservations shall not bind the sender unless he has expressly agreed to be bound by them in the consignment note.

3   The sender shall be entitled to require the carrier to check the gross weight of the goods or their quantity otherwise expressed. He may also require the contents of the packages to be checked. The carrier shall be entitled to claim the cost of such checking. The result of the checks shall be entered in the consignment note.

Article 9

1   The consignment note shall be *prima facie* evidence of the making of the contract of carriage, the conditions of the contract and the receipt of the goods by the carrier.

2   If the consignment note contains no specific reservations by the carrier, it shall be presumed, unless the contrary is proved, that the goods and their packaging appeared to be in good condition when the carrier took them over and that the number of packages. their marks and numbers corresponded with the statements in the consignment note.

Article 10

The sender shall be liable to the carrier for damage to persons, equipment or other goods, and for any expenses due to defective packing of the goods, unless the defect was apparent or known to the carrier at the time when he took over the goods and he made no reservations concerning it.

Article 11

1   For the purposes of the Customs or other formalities which have to be completed before delivery of the goods, the sender shall attach the necessary documents to the consignment note or place them at the disposal of the carrier and shall furnish him with all the information which he requires.

2   The carrier shall not be under any duty to enquire into either the accuracy or the adequacy of such documents and information. The sender shall be liable to the carrier for any damage caused by the absence, inadequacy or irregularity of such documents and information, except in the case of some wrongful act or neglect on the part of the carrier.

3   The liability of the carrier for the consequences arising from the loss or incorrect use of the documents specified in and accompanying the consignment note or deposited with the carrier shall be that of an agent, provided that the compensation payable by the carrier shall not exceed that payable in the event of loss of the goods.

Article 12

1   The sender has the right to dispose of the goods, in particular by asking the carrier to stop the goods in transit, to change the place at which delivery is to take place or to deliver the goods to a consignee other than the consignee indicated in the consignment note.

2   This right shall cease to exist when the second copy of the consignment note is handed to the consignee or when the consignee exercises his right under Article 13, para 1; from that time onwards the carrier shall obey the orders of the consignee.

3   The consignee shall, however, have the right of disposal from the time when the consignment note is drawn up, if the sender makes an entry to that effect in the consignment note.

4 If, in exercising his right of disposal, the consignee has ordered the delivery of the goods to another person, that other person shall not be entitled to name other consignees.

5 The exercise of the right of disposal shall be subject to the following conditions:

(a) that the sender or, in the case referred to in para 3 of this article, the consignee who wishes to exercise the right produces the first copy of the consignment note on which the new instructions to the carrier have been entered and indemnifies the carrier against all expenses, loss and damage involved in carrying out such instructions;

(b) that the carrying out of such instructions is possible at the time when the instructions reach the person who is to carry them out and does not either interfere with the normal working of the carrier's undertaking or prejudice the senders or consignees of other consignments;

(c) that the instructions do not result in a division of the consignment.

6 When, by reason of the provisions of para 5(b) of this article, the carrier cannot carry out the instructions which he receives, he shall immediately notify the person who gave him such instructions.

7 A carrier who has not carried out the instructions given under the conditions provided for in this article, or who has carried them out without requiring the first copy of the consignment note to be produced, shall be liable to the person entitled to make a claim for any loss or damage caused thereby.

Article 13

1 After arrival of the goods at the place designated for delivery, the consignee shall be entitled to require the carrier to deliver to him, against a receipt, the second copy of the consignment note and the goods. If the loss of the goods is established or if the goods have not arrived after the expiry of the period provided for in Article 19, the consignee shall be entitled to enforce in his own name against the carrier any rights arising from the contract of carriage.

2 The consignee who avails himself of the rights granted to him under para 1 of this article shall pay the charges shown to be due on the consignment note, but in the event of dispute on this matter the carrier shall not be required to deliver the goods unless security has been furnished by the consignee.

Article 14

1 If for any reason it is or becomes impossible to carry out the contract in accordance with the terms laid down in the consignment note before the goods reach the place designated for delivery, the carrier shall ask for instructions from the person entitled to dispose of the goods in accordance with the provisions of Article 12.

2 Nevertheless, if circumstances are such as to allow the carriage to be carried out under conditions differing from those laid down in the consignment note and if the carrier has been unable to obtain instructions in reasonable time from the person entitled to dispose of the goods in accordance with the provisions of Article 12, he shall take such steps as seem to him to be in the best interests of the person entitled to dispose of the goods.

Article 15

1   Where circumstances prevent delivery of the goods after their arrival at the place designated for delivery, the carrier shall ask the sender for his instructions. If the consignee refuses the goods the sender shall be entitled to dispose of them without being obliged to produce the first copy of the consignment note.

2   Even if he has refused the goods, the consignee may nevertheless require delivery so long as the carrier has not received instructions to the contrary from the sender.

3   When circumstances preventing delivery of the goods arise after the consignee, in exercise of his rights under Article 12, para 3, has given an order for the goods to be delivered to another person, paras 1 and 2 of this article shall apply as if the consignee were the sender and that other person were the consignee.

Article 16

1   The carrier shall be entitled to recover the cost of his request for instructions and any expenses entailed in carrying out such instructions, unless such expenses were caused by the wrongful act or neglect of the carrier.

2   In the cases referred to in Article 11, para 1, and in Article 15, the carrier may immediately unload the goods for account of the person entitled to dispose of them and thereupon the carriage shall be deemed to be at an end. The carrier shall then hold the goods on behalf of the person so entitled. He may however entrust them to a third party, and in that case he shall not be under any liability except for the exercise of reasonable care in the choice of such third party. The charges due under the consignment note and all other expenses shall remain chargeable against the goods.

3   The carrier may sell the goods, without awaiting instructions from the person entitled to dispose of them. if the goods are perishable or their condition warrants such a course, or when the storage expenses would be out of proportion to the value of the goods. He may also proceed to the sale of the goods in other cases if after the expiry of a reasonable period he has not received from the person entitled to dispose of the goods instructions to the contrary which he may reasonably be required to carry out.

4   If the goods have been sold pursuant to this article, the proceeds of sale, after deduction of the expenses chargeable against the goods, shall be placed at the disposal of the person entitled to dispose of the goods. If these charges exceed the proceeds of sale, the carrier shall be entitled to the difference.

5   The procedure in the case of sale shall be determined by the law or custom of the place where the goods are situated.

CHAPTER IV – LIABILITY OF THE CARRIER

Article 17

1   The carrier shall be liable for the total or partial loss of the goods and for damage thereto occurring between the time when he takes over the goods and the time of delivery, as well as for any delay in delivery.

2   The carrier shall however be relieved of liability if the loss, damage or delay was caused by the wrongful act or neglect of the claimant, by the instructions of the claimant given otherwise than as the result of a wrongful act or neglect on the part of the carrier, by inherent vice of the goods or through circumstances which the carrier could not avoid and the consequences of which he was unable to prevent.

3   The carrier shall not be relieved of liability by reason of the defective condition of the vehicle used by him in order to perform the carriage, or by reason of the wrongful act or neglect of the person from whom he may have hired the vehicle or of the agents or servants of the latter.

4   Subject to Article 18, paras 2 to 5, the carrier shall be relieved of liability when the loss or damage arises from the special risks inherent in one or more of the following circumstances:

(a) use of open unsheeted vehicles, when their use has been expressly agreed and specified in the consignment note;

(b) the lack of, or defective condition of packing in the case of goods which, by their nature, are liable to wastage or to be damaged when not packed or when not properly packed;

(c) handling, loading, stowage or unloading of the goods by the sender, the consignee or persons acting on behalf of the sender or the consignee;

(d) the nature of certain kinds of goods which particularly exposes them to total or partial loss or to damage, especially through breakage, rust, decay, desiccation, leakage, normal wastage, or the action of moth or vermin;

(e) insufficiency or inadequacy of marks or numbers on the packages;

(f) the carriage of livestock.

5   Where under this article the carrier is not under any liability in respect of some of the factors causing the loss, damage or delay, he shall only be liable to the extent that those factors for which he is liable under this article have contributed to the loss, damage or delay.

Article 18

1   The burden of proving that loss, damage or delay was due to one of the causes specified in Article 17, para 2, shall rest upon the carrier.

2   When the carrier establishes that in the circumstances of the case, the loss or damage could be attributed to one or more of the special risks referred to in Article 17, para 4, it shall be presumed that it was so caused. The claimant shall however be entitled to prove that the loss or damage was not, in fact, attributable either wholly or partly to one of these risks.

3   This presumption shall not apply in the circumstances set out in Article 17, para 4(a), if there has been an abnormal shortage, or a loss of any package .

4   If the carriage is performed in vehicles specially equipped to protect the goods from the effects of heat, cold, variations in temperature or the humidity of the air. the carrier shall not be entitled to claim the benefit of Article 17 para 4(d), unless he proves that all steps incumbent on him in the circumstances with respect to the choice, maintenance and use of such equipment were taken and that he complied with any special instructions issued to him.

5   The carrier shall not be entitled to claim the benefit of Article 17 para 4(f), unless he proves that all steps normally incumbent on him in the circumstances were taken and that he complied with any special instructions issued to him.

Article 19

Delay in delivery shall be said to occur when the goods have not been delivered within the agreed time limit or when? failing an agreed time limit, the actual duration of the carriage having regard to the circumstances of the case, and in particular, in the case of partial loads, the time required for making up a complete load in the normal way, exceeds the time it would be reasonable to allow a diligent carrier.

Article 20

1   The fact that goods have not been delivered within thirty days following the expiry of the agreed time limit, or, if there is no agreed time limit, within 60 days from the time when the carrier took over the goods, shall be conclusive evidence of the loss of the goods, and the person entitled to make a claim may thereupon treat them as lost.

2   The person so entitled may, on receipt of compensation for the missing goods, request in writing that he shall be notified immediately should the goods be recovered in the course of the year following the payment of compensation. He shall be given a written acknowledgment of such request.

3   Within the 30 days following receipt of such notification, the person entitled as aforesaid may require the goods to be delivered to him against payment of the charges shown to be due on the consignment note and also against refund of the compensation he received less any charges included therein but without prejudice to any claims to compensation for delay in delivery under Article 23 and, where applicable, Article 26.

4   In the absence of the request mentioned in para 2 or of any instructions given within the period of 30 days specified in para 3, or if the goods are not recovered until more than one year after the payment of compensation, the carrier shall be entitled to deal with them in accordance with the law of the place where the goods are situated.

Article 21

Should the goods have been delivered to the consignee without collection of the cash on delivery charge, which should have been collected by the carrier under the terms of the contract of carriage, the carrier shall be liable to the sender for compensation not exceeding the amount of such charge without prejudice to his right of action against the consignee.

Article 22

1   When the sender hands goods of a dangerous nature to the carrier, he shall inform the carrier of the exact nature of the danger and indicate, if necessary, the precautions to be taken. If this information has not been entered in the consignment note, the burden of proving, by some other means, that the carrier knew the exact nature of the danger constituted by the carriage of the said goods shall rest upon the sender or the consignee.

2   Goods of a dangerous nature which, in the circumstances referred to in para 1 of this article, the carrier did not know were dangerous, may, at any time or place, be unloaded, destroyed or rendered harmless by the carrier without compensation; further, the sender shall be liable for all expenses, loss or damage arising out of their handing over for carriage or of their carriage.

Article 23

1   When, under the provisions of this Convention, a carrier is liable for compensation in respect of total or partial loss of goods, such compensation shall be calculated by reference to the value of the goods at the place and time at which they were accepted for carriage.

2   The value of the goods shall be fixed according to the commodity exchange price or, if there is no such price, according to the current market price or, if there is no commodity exchange price or current market price, by reference to the normal value of goods of the same kind and quality.

3   Compensation shall not, however, exceed 25 francs per kg of gross weight short. 'Franc' means the gold franc weighing 10/31 of a gramme and being of millesimal fineness 900.

4   In addition, the carriage charges, Customs duties and other charges incurred in respect of the carriage of the goods shall be refunded in full in case of total loss and in proportion to the loss sustained in case of partial loss, but no further damages shall be payable.

5   In the case of delay, if the claimant proves that damage has resulted therefrom the carrier shall pay compensation for such damage not exceeding the carriage charges.

6   Higher compensation may only be claimed where the value of the goods or a special interest in delivery has been declared in accordance with Articles 24 and 26.

Article 24

The sender may, against payment of a surcharge to be agreed upon, declare in the consignment note a value for the goods exceeding the limit laid down in Article 23, para 3, and in that case the amount of the declared value shall be substituted for that limit.

Article 25

1   In case of damage, the carrier shall be liable for the amount by which the goods have diminished in value, calculated by reference to the value of the goods fixed in accordance with Article 23, paras 1, 2 and 4.

2   The compensation may not, however, exceed:

(a) if the whole consignment has been damaged the amount payable in the case of total loss;

(b) if part only of the consignment has been damaged, the amount payable in the case of loss of the part affected.

Article 26

1   The sender may, against payment of a surcharge to be agreed upon. fix the amount of a special interest in delivery in the case of loss or damage or of the agreed time-limit being exceeded, by entering such amount in the consignment note .

2   If a declaration of a special interest in delivery has been made, compensation for the additional loss or damage proved may be claimed, up to the total amount of the interest declared, independently of the compensation provided for in Articles 23, 24 and 25.

Article 27

1   The claimant shall be entitled to claim interest on compensation payable. Such interest, calculated at 5% per annum, shall accrue from the date on which the claim

was sent in writing to the carrier or, if no such claim has been made, from the date on which legal proceedings were instituted.

2   When the amounts on which the calculation of the compensation is based are not expressed in the currency of the country in which payment is claimed, conversion shall be at the rate of exchange applicable on the day and at the place of payment of compensation.

Article 28

1   In cases where, under the law applicable, loss, damage or delay arising out of carriage under this Convention gives rise to an extra-contractual claim, the carrier may avail himself of the provisions of this Convention which exclude his liability or which fix or limit the compensation due.

2   In cases where the extra-contractual liability for loss. damage or delay of one of the persons for whom the carrier is responsible under the terms of Article 3 is in issue, such person may also avail himself of the provisions of this Convention which exclude the liability of the carrier or which fix or limit the compensation due.

Article 29

1   The carrier shall not be entitled to avail himself of the provisions of this chapter which exclude or limit his liability or which shift the burden of proof if the damage was caused by his wilful misconduct or by such default on his part as, in accordance with the law of the court or tribunal seised of the case, is considered as equivalent to wilful misconduct.

2   The same provision shall apply if the wilful misconduct or default is committed by the agents or servants of the carrier or by any other persons of whose services he makes use for the performance of the carriage, when such agents, servants or other persons are acting within the scope of their employment. Furthermore, in such a case such agents, servants or other persons shall not be entitled to avail themselves, with regard to their personal liability, of the provisions of this chapter referred to in para 1.

CHAPTER V – CLAIMS AND ACTIONS

Article 30

1   If the consignee takes delivery of the goods without duly checking their condition with the carrier or without sending him reservations giving a general indication of the loss or damage, not later than the time of delivery in the case of apparent loss or damage and within seven days of delivery, Sundays and public holidays excepted, in the case of loss or damage which is not apparent, the fact of his taking delivery shall be *prima facie* evidence that he has received the goods in the condition described in the consignment note. In the case of loss or damage which is not apparent the reservations referred to shall be made in writing.

2   When the condition of the goods has been duly checked by the consignee and the carrier, evidence contradicting the result of this checking shall only be admissible in the case of loss or damage which is not apparent and provided that the consignee has duly sent reservations in writing to the carrier within seven days, Sundays and public holidays excepted, from the date of checking.

3   No compensation shall be payable for delay in delivery unless a reservation has been sent in writing to the carrier, within 21 days from the time that the goods were placed at the disposal of the consignee.

4　In calculating the time limits provided for in this Article the date of delivery, or the date of checking, or the date when the goods were placed at the disposal of the consignee, as the case may be, shall not be included.

5　The carrier and the consignee shall give each other every reasonable facility for making the requisite investigations and checks.

Article 31

1　In legal proceedings arising out of carriage under this Convention, the plaintiff may bring an action in any court or tribunal of a contracting country designated by agreement between the parties and, in addition, in the courts or tribunals of a country within whose territory

(a)　the defendant is ordinarily resident, or has his principal place of business, or the branch or agency through which the contract of carriage was made,

(b)　the place where the goods were taken over by the carrier or the place designated for delivery is situated,

and in no other courts or tribunals.

2　Where in respect of a claim referred to in para 1 of this article an action is pending before a court or tribunal competent under that paragraph, or where in respect of such a claim a judgment has been entered by such a court or tribunal no new action shall be started between the same parties on the same grounds unless the judgment of the court or tribunal before which the first action was brought is not enforceable in the country in which the fresh proceedings are brought.

3　When a judgment entered by a court or tribunal of a contracting country in any such action as is referred to in para 1 of this article has become enforceable in that country, it shall also become enforceable in each of the other contracting States, as soon as the formalities required in the country concerned have been complied with. The formalities shall not permit the merits of the case to be re-opened.

4　The provisions of para 3 of this article shall apply to judgments after trial, judgments by default and settlements confirmed by an order of the court, but shall not apply to interim judgments or to awards of damages, in addition to costs against a plaintiff who wholly or partly fails in his action.

5　Security for costs shall not be required in proceedings arising out of carriage under this Convention from nationals of contracting countries resident or having their place of business in one of those countries.

Article 32

1　The period of limitation for an action arising out of carriage under this Convention shall be one year. Nevertheless, in the case of wilful misconduct, or such default as in accordance with the law of the court or tribunal seised of the case, is considered as equivalent to wilful misconduct, the period of limitation shall be three years. The period of limitation shall begin to run:

(a)　in the case of partial loss, damage or delay in delivery, from the date of delivery;

(b)　in the case of total loss, from the 30th day after the expiry of the agreed time limit or where there is no agreed time limit from the 60th day from the date on which the goods were taken over by the carrier;

(c)　in all other cases, on the expiry of a period of three months after the making of the contract of carriage.

The day on which the period of limitation begins to run shall not be included in the period.

2   A written claim shall suspend the period of limitation until such date as the carrier rejects the claim by notification in writing and returns the documents attached thereto. If a part of the claim is admitted the period of limitation shall start to run again only in respect of that part of the claim still in dispute. The burden of proof of the receipt of the claim, or of the reply and of the return of the documents, shall rest with the party relying upon these facts. The running of the period of limitation shall not be suspended by further claims having the same object.

3   Subject to the provisions of para 2 above, the extension of the period of limitation shall be governed by the law of the court or tribunal seised of the case. That law shall also govern the fresh accrual of rights of action.

4   A right of action which has become barred by lapse of time may not be exercised by way of counterclaim or set off.

Article 33

The contract of carriage may contain a clause conferring competence on an arbitration tribunal if the clause conferring competence on the tribunal provides that the tribunal shall apply this Convention.

CHAPTER VI – PROVISIONS RELATING TO CARRIAGE PERFORMED BY SUCCESSIVE CARRIERS

Article 34

If carriage governed by a single contract is performed by successive road carriers, each of them shall be responsible for the performance of the whole operation, the second carrier and each succeeding carrier becoming a party to the contract of carriage, under the terms of the consignment note, by reason of his acceptance of the goods and the consignment note.

Article 35

1   A carrier accepting the goods from a previous carrier shall give the latter a dated and signed receipt. He shall enter his name and address on the second copy of the consignment note. Where applicable, he shall enter on the second copy of the consignment note and on the receipt reservations of the kind provided for in Article 8, para 2.

2   The provisions of Article 9 shall apply to the relations between successive carriers .

Article 36

Except in the case of a counterclaim or a set off raised in an action concerning a claim based on the same contract of carriage, legal proceedings in respect of liability for loss, damage or delay may only be brought against the first carrier, the last carrier or the carrier who was performing that portion of the carriage during which the event causing the loss, damage or delay occurred; an action may be brought at the same time against several of these carriers.

Article 37

A carrier who has paid compensation in compliance with the provisions of this Convention, shall be entitled to recover such compensation, together with interest thereon and all costs and expenses incurred by reason of the claim, from the other carriers who have taken part in the carriage, subject to the following provisions:

(a) the carrier responsible for the loss or damage shall be solely liable for the compensation whether paid by himself or by another carrier;

(b) when the loss or damage has been caused by the action of two or more carriers, each of them shall pay an amount proportionate to his share of liability; should it be impossible to apportion the liability, each carrier shall be liable in proportion to the share of the payment for the carriage which is due to him;

(c) if it cannot be ascertained to which carriers liability is attributable for the loss or damage, the amount of the compensation shall be apportioned

Article 38

If one of the carriers is insolvent, the share of the compensation due from him and unpaid by him shall be divided among the other carriers in proportion to the share of the payment for the carriage due to them.

Article 39

1   No carrier against whom a claim is made under Articles 37 and 38 shall be entitled to dispute the validity of the payment made by the carrier making the claim if the amount of the compensation was determined by judicial authority after the first mentioned carrier had been given due notice of the proceedings and afforded an opportunity of entering an appearance.

2   A carrier wishing to take proceedings to enforce his right of recovery may make his claim before the competent court or tribunal of the country in which one of the carriers concerned is ordinarily resident, or has his principal place of business or the branch or agency through which the contract of carriage was made. All the carriers concerned may be made defendants in the same action.

3   The provisions of Article 31, paras 3 and 4, shall apply to judgments entered in the proceedings referred to in Articles 37 and 38.

4   The provisions of Article 32 shall apply to claims between carriers. The period of limitation shall, however, begin to run either on the date of the final judicial decision fixing the amount of compensation payable under the provisions of this Convention, or, if there is no such judicial decision, from the actual date of payment.

Article 40

Carriers shall be free to agree among themselves on provisions other than those laid down in Articles 37 and 38.

CHAPTER VII – NULLITY OF STIPULATIONS CONTRARY TO THE CONVENTION

Article 41

1   Subject to the provisions of Article 40, any stipulation which would directly or indirectly derogate from the provisions of this Convention shall be null and void. The nullity of such a stipulation shall not involve the nullity of the other provisions of the contract.

2   In particular, a benefit of insurance in favour of the carrier or any other similar clause, or any clause shifting the burden of proof shall be null and void.

[Chapter VIII of the Convention is not reproduced. This deals with the coming into force of the Convention, the settlement of disputes between the high contracting parties and related matters.]

1   This Convention shall not apply to traffic between the United Kingdom of Great Britain and Northern Ireland and the Republic of Ireland.

IATA INTERCARRIER AGREEMENT ON PASSENGER LIABILITY

Whereas: The Warsaw Convention system is of great benefit to international air transportation; and

Noting that: The Convention's limits of liability, which have not been amended since 1955, are now grossly inadequate in most countries and that international airlines have previously acted together to increase them to the benefit of passengers;

The undersigned carriers agree

1   To take action to waive the limitation of liability on recoverable compensatory damages in Article 22 para 1 of the Warsaw Convention as to claims for death, wounding or other bodily injury of a passenger within the meaning of Article 17 of the Convention, so that recoverable compensatory damages may be determined and awarded by reference to the law of the domicile of the passenger.

2   To reserve all available defences pursuant to the provisions of the Convention; nevertheless, any carrier may waive any defence, including the waiver of any defence up to a specified monetary amount of recoverable compensatory damages, as circumstances may warrant.

3   To reserve their rights of recourse against any other person, including rights of contribution or indemnity, with respect to any sums paid by the carrier.

4   To encourage other airlines involved in the international carriage of passengers to apply the terms of this Agreement to such carriage.

5   To implement the provisions of this Agreement no later than 1 November 1996 or upon receipt of requisite government approvals, whichever is later.

6   That nothing in this Agreement shall affect the rights of the passenger or the claimant otherwise available under the Convention.

7   That this Agreement may be signed in any number of counterparts, all of which shall constitute one Agreement. Any carrier may become a party to this Agreement by signing a counterpart hereof and depositing it with the Director General of the International Air Transport Association (IATA).

8   That any carrier party hereto may withdraw from this Agreement by giving twelve (12) months' written notice of withdrawal to the Director General of IATA and to the other carriers parties to the Agreement.

Signed this   day of   199

INTERCARRIER AGREEMENT ON PASSENGER LIABILITY

EXPLANATORY NOTE

The Intercarrier Agreement is an 'umbrella accord'; the precise legal rights and responsibilities of the signatory carriers with respect to passengers will be spelled out in the applicable Conditions of Carriage and tariff filings.

The carriers signatory to the Agreement undertake to waive such limitations of liability as are set out in the Warsaw Convention (1929), The Hague Protocol (1955), the Montreal Agreement of 1966, and/or limits they may have previously agreed to implement or were required by Governments to implement.

Such waiver by a carrier may be made conditional on the law of the domicile of the passenger governing the calculation of the recoverable compensatory damages under the Intercarrier Agreement. But this is an option. Should a carrier wish to waive the limits of liability but not insist on the law of the domicile of the passenger governing the calculation of the recoverable compensatory damages, or not be so required by a governmental authority, it may rely on the law of the court to which the case is submitted.

The Warsaw Convention system defences will remain available, in whole or in part, to the carriers signatory to the Agreement, unless a carrier decides to waive them or is so required by a governmental authority.

AGREEMENT ON MEASURES TO IMPLEMENT THE IATA INTERCARRIER AGREEMENT

I Pursuant to the IATA Intercarrier Agreement of 31 October 1995, the undersigned carriers agree to implement said Agreement by incorporating in their conditions of carriage and tariffs, where necessary, the following:

1 [CARRIER] shall not invoke the limitation of liability in Article 22(1) of the Convention as to any claim for recoverable compensatory damages arising under Article 17 of the Convention.

2 [CARRIER] shall not avail itself of any defence under Article 20(1) of the Convention with respect to that portion of such claim which does not exceed 100,000 SDRs [unless option II(2) is used].

3 Except as otherwise provided in paras 1 and 2 hereof, [CARRIER] reserves all defences available under the Convention to any such claim. With respect to third parties, the carrier also reserves all rights of recourse against any other person, including without limitation, rights of contribution and indemnity.

II At the option of the carrier, its conditions of carriage and tariffs also may include the following provisions:

1 [CARRIER] agrees that subject to applicable law, recoverable compensatory damages for such claim may be determined by reference to the law of the domicile or permanent residence of the passenger.

2 [CARRIER] shall not avail itself of any defence under Article 20(1) of the Convention with respect to that portion of such claims which does not exceed 100,000 SDRs, except that such waiver is limited to the amounts shown below for the routes indicated, as may be authorised by governments concerned with the transportation involved.

[Amounts and routes to be inserted]

3 Neither the waiver of limits nor the waiver of defences shall be applicable in respect of claims made by public social insurance or similar bodies however asserted. Such claims shall be subject to the limit in Article 22(1) and to the defences under Article 20(1) of the Convention. The carrier will compensate

the passenger or his dependents for recoverable compensatory damages in excess of payments received from any public social insurance or similar body.

III Furthermore, at the option of a carrier, additional provisions may be included in its conditions of carriage and tariffs, provided they are not inconsistent with this Agreement and are in accordance with applicable law.

IV Should any provision of this Agreement or a provision incorporated in a condition of carriage or tariff pursuant to this Agreement be determined to be invalid. illegal or unenforceable by a court of competent jurisdiction, all other provisions shall nevertheless remain valid, binding and effective.

V

1 This Agreement may be signed in any number of counterparts, all of which shall constitute one Agreement. Any carrier may become party to this Agreement by signing a counterpart hereof and depositing it with the Director General of the International Air Transport Association (IATA).

2 Any carrier party hereto may withdraw from this Agreement by giving twelve (12) months' written notice of withdrawal to the Director General of IATA and to the other carriers Parties to the Agreement.

3 The Director General of IATA shall declare this Agreement effective on 1 November 1996, or such later date as all requisite Government approvals have been obtained for this Agreement and the IATA Intercarrier Agreement of 31 October 1995.

Signed this   day of

CHAPTER 6

FINANCING EXPORTS: LETTERS OF CREDIT

INTRODUCTION

The expressions 'documentary credit' and 'letter of credit' are used interchangeably to refer to the most frequent and most secure facility for financing international trade. The security aspect of a documentary credit rests upon the fact that it represents an undertaking by the bank issuing the documentary credit at the request of its customer (usually the buyer of goods), to pay the beneficiary (usually the seller of goods), a specified amount on condition that the beneficiary presents to the bank stipulated documents. These documents evidence, among other things, the shipment of goods within a prescribed period of time. The bank thus acts as an intermediary between the buyer and the seller, satisfying the competing interests between them, and removes the risk of each party to the commercial transaction. While the bank guarantees payment to the seller for the goods, it protects the buyer by ensuring that no payment is made to the seller until the latter has shipped the goods, delivered the relevant documents, and otherwise complied with the prescribed conditions.

Hence, a letter of credit is a conditional promise issued by the issuing bank, to pay a specified amount in the stated currency, within the prescribed time limit and against stipulated documents. These documents are specified to the bank by its customer, namely the buyer who applies for the issuing of a letter of credit. Letters of credit are popular instruments in international trade because they substitute the financial standing of a bank for that of an individual or firm. The popularity of letters of credit derives from the fact that a seller can be confident that, provided he can meet the requirements stipulated in the letter, he will receive prompt payment. Also, a buyer who is able to offer the security of payment by a letter of credit is usually in a better bargaining position than a buyer offering an alternative method of payment. A letter of credit is described in *Voest-Alpine International Corporation v Chase Manhattan Bank*[1] as follows:

> A typical letter of credit transaction ... involves three separate and independent relationships – an underlying sale of goods contract between buyer and seller, an agreement between a bank and its customer (buyer) in which the bank undertakes to issue a letter of credit, and the bank's resulting engagement to pay the beneficiary (seller) providing that certain documents presented to the bank conform with the terms and conditions of the credit issued on its customer's behalf. Significantly, the bank's payment obligation to the beneficiary is primary, direct and completely independent of any claims which may arise in the underlying sale of goods transaction.

A letter of credit is the most frequently used method of financing international trade because of its autonomy. As appears from the above quotation, a documentary credit transaction is separate from and independent of the underlying contract for the sale of

---

1   707 F 2d 680, 682 (1983).

goods or other relevant transaction which it is financing. The bank is obliged to make payment to the seller under the letter of credit upon delivery by the seller of the stipulated documents, provided these documents comply with the terms and conditions contained in the letter of credit. The bank is not concerned with the underlying contract and whether the terms thereof have been complied with. This autonomous character of the letter of credit has made it 'the lifeblood of commerce', because the mercantile practice is to treat rights under it 'as being equivalent to cash in hand'.[2]

Typically, the buyer accepts the seller's offer in respect of the sale of goods including the requirement that payment be made under a letter of credit. The buyer then instructs his bank, namely the issuing bank, to issue a letter of credit in favour of the seller as beneficiary. Next, the issuing bank in accordance with the buyer's instructions issues a letter of credit to the beneficiary and for such purpose instructs a correspondent bank (located in the seller's country) to act as an advising bank. In turn, the advising bank informs the seller/beneficiary that a letter of credit is opened in his favour and that payment will be made conditional upon the presentation of the stipulated documents by the seller to the advising bank (or another bank nominated for payment purposes) by a specified date. Finally, the beneficiary presents the documents to that bank and thereupon receives payment. Thus, a request for the issue of a letter of credit is made by the buyer, while settlement usually takes place in the seller's country.

Often the seller may require as an additional term of payment that the documentary credit be confirmed, that is guaranteed, by the advising bank located in his country. In such case, the advising bank will also be acting as a confirming bank. A request to confirm a letter of credit will usually be made by the beneficiary (seller) if he doubts the credit worthiness of the issuing bank or if that bank is located in a country subject to political or economic turmoil. A confirmed letter of credit provides the seller with increased security because the confirming bank would be obliged to make the specified payment if the issuing bank is prevented from honouring the letter of credit. For example, the issuing bank would be prevented from making payment if the government of the country in which that bank is located imposes currency restrictions between the time of the issuing of the letter of credit and the time the documents are delivered to the bank by the beneficiary. Thus, it is often good commercial practice for the seller to require the buyer to arrange for the confirmation of the letter of credit by a bank located in the beneficiary's country.

There are, therefore, usually four parties to the documentary credit transaction, namely:

(i)   the applicant of the letter of credit (buyer/importer);

(ii) the issuing bank in the applicant's country;

---

2   *Intraco Ltd v Notis Shipping Corp of Liberia (The Bhoja Trader)* [1981] 2 Lloyd's Rep 256 at 257 (Donaldson LJ). A similar reference to 'the lifeblood of commerce' has been made by Kerr LJ in *RD Harbottle (Mercantile) Ltd v National Westminster Bank Ltd* [1978] QB 146 at 155; Griffiths LJ in *Power Curber International Ltd v National Bank of Kuwait SAK* [1981] 2 Lloyd's Rep 394 at 400; Stevenson LJ in *United City Merchants (Investments) Ltd v Royal Bank of Canada* [1982] QB 208 at 222; and Hirst J in *Hong Kong and Shanghai Banking Corp v Kloeckner and Co AG* [1989] 2 Lloyd's Rep 323, 330.

(iii) the correspondent bank in the seller's country acting as advising and/or confirming bank; and

(iv) the beneficiary of the documentary credit (seller/exporter).

The universal use of commercial credit has resulted in the standardisation of the banking practice relating to documentary credit by the establishment and publication of the *Uniform Customs and Practice for Documentary Credits* (commonly referred to as the UCP) by the International Chamber of Commerce (ICC). The current version of the UCP is contained in ICC publication no 500 which entered into force on 1 January 1994. The UCP 500 sets out the rules by which banks will process letter of credit transactions. It also defines the rights and responsibilities of all parties to the credit. The UCP 500 is used by most banks throughout the world. Its use has resulted in documentary credits achieving the highest degree of uniformity. Article 2 defines a documentary credit as follows:

> For the purposes of these articles, the expressions 'documentary credit(s)' and 'standby letter(s) of credit' (hereinafter referred to as 'credit(s)'), mean any arrangement, however named or described, whereby a bank (the 'issuing bank') acting at the request and on the instruction of a customer (the 'applicant') or on its own behalf:
>
> (i)   is to make a payment to or to the order of a third party (the 'beneficiary'), or is to accept and pay bills of exchange (draft(s)) drawn by the beneficiary; or
>
> (ii) authorises another bank to effect such payment, or to accept and pay such bills of exchange (draft(s)); or
>
> (iii) authorises another bank to negotiate,
>
> against stipulated document(s), provided that the terms and conditions of the credit are complied with.

For the purposes of these articles, branches of a bank in different countries are considered another bank.

This definition envisages three forms which the issuing bank's obligation to make payment may take. First, the bank may undertake to pay cash against the tender of documents. This type of 'cash credit' is frequently used in continental Europe and South America. Secondly, the bank may undertake to accept (ie to guarantee) a bill of exchange for the amount to be drawn on it by the seller and to be accompanied by the stipulated documents. This form of documentary credit is commonly used in the UK, Australia and most other Commonwealth countries, and in the USA. Thirdly, the bank may undertake to negotiate (that is to give value for) a bill of exchange for the amount to be drawn on it by the seller on the buyer and to be accompanied by the stipulated documents. This type of documentary credit is frequently used in South East Asia.

In accordance with Article 1, the UCP provisions have no application to a documentary credit unless they are expressly incorporated into the text of such credit. These provisions are, however, usually incorporated by banks in their standard forms of instructions and in their letters of credit. Consequently, the UCP provisions are practically universally imposed upon customers of banks and upon the beneficiaries of letters of credit. For this reason, it is essential when dealing with letters of credit to have a thorough understanding and knowledge of the UCP provisions and judicial decisions dealing with them.

BASIC FORMS AND TYPES OF DOCUMENTARY CREDIT

Basic forms of documentary credit

There are two basic forms of documentary credit, namely irrevocable credit and revocable credit. The quality of a documentary credit being 'irrevocable' or 'revocable' refers to the obligation of the issuing bank to the beneficiary. The quality of the credit being confirmed or unconfirmed, on the other hand, refers to the obligation of the advising bank to the beneficiary. Pursuant to Article 6(b) of the UCP 500 the letter of credit 'should clearly indicate whether it is revocable or irrevocable'. In cases governed by the UCP, a letter of credit is deemed to be irrevocable unless the issuing bank clearly indicates that it is revocable (Article 6(c)).

Revocable and unconfirmed credits

A revocable credit can be amended or cancelled by the issuing bank at any time without prior notice to the beneficiary (Article 8(a)). A bank will thus not be liable to the beneficiary (exporter) for revocation of the revocable credit before the transaction is completed. The standard form of instructions by the buyer to the issuing bank in respect of a revocable letter of credit usually contains an express provision to the effect that the bank may revoke the credit at any time during its currency. Because of its revocable nature such credit cannot be confirmed by a correspondent or advising bank which will usually advise that the notification 'is merely an advice of opening of the (subject credit) and is not a confirmation of the same'[3] and that therefore the credit is subject to cancellation or modification at any time without notice. As such, the revocable credit fails to provide adequate security for the beneficiary exporter.

Irrevocable and unconfirmed credits

An irrevocable credit constitutes a legally binding undertaking by the issuing bank to make payment. It cannot be amended or cancelled with the consent of the beneficiary or the issuing bank (Article 9(d)(i)). Thus, if the seller wishes to amend any of the provisions of the credit, he must request the buyer to instruct the issuing bank to that effect.

Being an unconfirmed irrevocable credit, the correspondent bank acts merely as an advising bank when notifying the beneficiary that the credit has been opened. It does not itself undertake to make payment under the credit and is therefore under no obligation to honour documents presented by the beneficiary (Article 7(a)). The only recourse open to the beneficiary is against the buyer's bank acting as the issuing bank. Because the issuing bank is usually a foreign bank, located in the country of the buyer, an unconfirmed irrevocable credit is inappropriate where the buyer's country is politically unstable or where there are in that country restrictions on foreign exchange or other transfer risks.

---

3   *Cape Asbestos Co v Lloyd's Bank* [1921] WN 274.

Confirmed irrevocable credit

A confirmed irrevocable credit gives the beneficiary the highest degree of assurance that he will be paid for his goods. It provides him with the greatest security, particularly where the confirming bank to the irrevocable credit is the seller's own bank. By adding its confirmation to the credit, the correspondent, advising bank, thereby undertakes to honour the documents which conform with the terms and conditions of the credit and are presented within the prescribed time limit. In this case, the beneficiary has recourse not only against the issuing bank in respect of its undertaking, but also separate and independent recourse against the confirming bank in respect of its independent promise of payment under the documentary credit. With a confirmed irrevocable credit, the exporter removes any political and transfer risks which may prevail in the buyer's country. The confirmed irrevocable credit imposes on the confirming bank an absolute obligation to pay and provides the seller with an absolute assurance of payment. In the words of Jenkins LJ in *Hamzeh Malas and Sons v British Imex Ltd*:[4]

> It seems to me plain enough that the opening of a confirmed letter of credit constitutes a bargain between the banker and the vendor of the goods, which imposes upon the banker an absolute obligation to pay, irrespective of any dispute there may be between the parties as to whether the goods are up to the contract or not ... A vendor of goods selling against a confirmed letter of goods is selling under the assurance that nothing will prevent him from receiving the price. That is no mean advantage when goods manufactured in one country are being sold in another.

Types of letters of credit

Documentary credits are classified into various types depending on the way in which the credit is made available to the beneficiary. The different types of credit include sight credit, deferred payment credit, acceptance credit, red clause credit, revolving credit, negotiation credit, standby letter of credit, transferable credit, and back-to-back credit.

Sight credit

Sight credit is the most commonly used type of credit. It provides for payment to be made to the beneficiary immediately after presentation of the stipulated documents and on condition that the submitted documents comply with the terms and conditions of the credit. Following presentation of the documents, the issuing bank (or its correspondent bank) will carefully examine the documents to ensure that these comply strictly with the terms and conditions contained in the letter of credit. Following satisfactory examination of the documents, the bank then pays to the beneficiary the proceeds of the credit. It is simply a process of payment against documents.

Deferred payment credit

Under a deferred payment credit, provision is made in the letter of credit itself for payment to be made by the bank at a future, determinable time, eg 90 days after the

---

4   [1958] 2 QB 127.

issuing of the bill of lading. In effect, this type of credit enables the buyer (importer) to make payment for the goods after obtaining the prescribed documents. The time given to the buyer to make payment could be used by him to resell the goods and use the proceeds of any such sale to provide for payment under the deferred payment credit by the due date.

Acceptance credit

In the case of an acceptance credit, the beneficiary (seller) draws a bill of exchange either on the issuing bank, confirming bank, or on the buyer, or even sometimes on another bank depending on the terms of the credit. An acceptance credit provides for payment on the date on which the bill of exchange matures. Following the tendering of conforming documents in accordance with the terms and conditions of the credit, the bill of exchange is accepted by the bank.

The purpose of an acceptance credit is to give the buyer (importer) time to make payment. Thus, if the buyer can resell the goods before payment falls due, he can use the proceeds to meet the bill of exchange and thereby avoid the necessity of borrowing funds to finance the transaction. However, if the exporter as beneficiary of the bill requires payment before the maturity date, he may negotiate the accepted bill to his own bank to be discounted. The readiness of the exporter's bank to discount the bill will depend on the standing of the accepting bank.

Negotiation credit

A negotiation credit empowers the beneficiary to draw a bill of exchange on the issuing bank, or on any other drawee stipulated in the credit. However, Article 9(a)(iv) of the UCP 500 states that a letter of credit 'should not be issued available by draft(s) on the applicant'. The beneficiary may then present the bill to a bank for negotiation, together with the original letter of credit and the documents stipulated therein. Usually a negotiation credit permits negotiation by any bank, although the negotiation may be limited to specified banks. The bill of exchange may either be a sight or a time draft. The main advantage of a negotiation credit lies in the fact that the beneficiary is not limited to receive payment of the credit from the advising bank, but may obtain payment from any bank of his choice by drawing a bill of exchange which is guaranteed by the issuing bank. Thus, negotiation involves the 'giving of value for draft(s) and/or document(s) by the bank authorised to negotiate' (Article 10(b)(ii)).

Red clause credit

Under a 'red clause' credit the seller is able to obtain an advance from the correspondent/advising bank prior to the presentation of the prescribed documents by the seller. The red clause, which derives its name from the fact that it was formerly written in red ink, authorises the advising bank to advance a part of the credit amount to the seller for the delivery of the merchandise. Such advance which will be delivered under the documentary credit, is frequently intended to finance the manufacture or purchase of the goods by the seller. On receiving the advance, the beneficiary (seller) must give a receipt (eg a warehouse receipt) and an undertaking to present the prescribed documents within the period of validity of the credit. This type of credit is used very often in the Australian wool trade. The clause may simply read for example: 'red clause A$50,000 permitted'. Such clause means that, with the issuing bank assuming liability for the transaction, the advising bank is authorised to advance the beneficiary A$50,000 prior to the presentation of the documents.

Although the advance is paid out by the advising bank, it is the issuing bank that assumes liability. If the seller fails to present the prescribed documents in time and fails to refund the advance, the advising bank will debit the issuing bank with the amount of the advance, together with interest thereon. The issuing bank, in turn, will have recourse against the buyer (importer), who therefore bears the ultimate risk for the advance and the interest thereon.

Revolving credit

A revolving credit is used commonly where the buyer (importer) is a regular customer of the seller (exporter), or where the buyer receives goods from the exporter in instalments at specified intervals. In such cases, provisions may be made under a revolving credit to cover the value of each instalment as it is delivered. For example, a revolving credit may contain a clause which reads: 'credit amount A$100,000, revolving 11 times up to a total amount of A$1,200,000'. After utilisation of the first A$100,000, the next portion becomes automatically available, up to the total of A$1,200,000. Frequently, a revolving clause will also stipulate the dates of individual instalments in which case it may, for example, read:

> Credit amount A$100,000, revolving every month for the same amount for the first time in January 1996, for the last time in November 1996, maximum amount payable under this credit A$1,200,000.

A revolving credit may be cumulative or non-cumulative. As the expressions suggest, in the case of cumulative revolving credit, amounts from unused or incompletely used portions may be carried forward and utilised in a subsequent period. In the case of a non-cumulative revolving credit, non-utilised instalments or balances may not be added to later instalments.

The main advantage of a revolving credit is that it avoids banking charges and clerical costs to the importer which would otherwise be incurred if a separate letter of credit were issued in respect of each transaction in a series of similar, or instalment, transactions.

A revolving credit should not be confused with an 'evergreen clause' in a letter of credit. An 'evergreen clause', if incorporated in the letter, has the effect of automatically extending the credit for another fixed period from the expiration date, unless the bank notifies the beneficiary by registered mail that it has elected not to renew the credit.

Standby credit

Standby letters of credit are in effect bank guarantees which because of their documentary character, unlike ordinary bank guarantees, are governed by the UCP. They are principally used in the USA, where they take the place of guarantees, which, under most state laws, may not be issued by banks. However, the use of this type of credit is increasing in continental Europe, England, and Australia. Standby credit may be used to guarantee performance of services as well as payment by a party. For example, a standby credit may guarantee the payment of bills payable after sight, the repayment of a bank advance, the payment for goods delivered, the delivery of goods in accordance with a contract, and the fulfilment of contracts for work and materials.

The principal difference between the standby letter of credit and an ordinary letter of credit is that in the case of the latter, but not the former, the documents which the beneficiary has to tender normally relate to an underlying sales transaction. In the case of a standby letter of credit, the required documents may be of any description. For example, the prescribed document may merely be a demand for payment by the beneficiary; or it may be a statement or a certification by the beneficiary to the effect that the other party is in default. It is for this reason that a standby letter of credit is often equated to a bank guarantee or, because of the documents required thereunder, a documentary bank guarantee.

By virtue of Article 1, the UCP applies to standby letters of credit.

Transferable credit

The transferable credit is used mainly to enable the beneficiary (known in Article 48 as the 'first beneficiary') to transfer the whole or part of the credit to his supplier ('second beneficiary') of goods or raw materials. Indeed, the seller (beneficiary) may only be able to sell goods to the buyer (importer) which have previously been manufactured or produced by the beneficiary. The manufacture of goods requires the beneficiary to obtain components or raw materials from his supplier. Thus, in effect, the beneficiary becomes a 'middleman' in that he owes money to his supplier, but is himself owed money by the buyer (importer) who applies for the issuing of a letter of credit. A transferable credit enables the beneficiary who receives payment from his own buyer under a documentary credit to transfer the whole or part of his claim under that credit to his own supplier. In this manner, the beneficiary can carry out transactions with only a limited outlay of his own funds or capital.

Typically, the procedure would be as follows. The beneficiary requires as a term of his contract with his own buyer (importer or applicant for the credit), that the buyer provide an irrevocable transferable credit in his favour. Upon the beneficiary receiving confirmation of the issuing of the transferable credit, he may then instruct the bank to transfer the credit to his own supplier as second beneficiary. The transfer takes the form of the issuing of a fresh, or second, credit separate from the original (transferable) credit. In other words, the original (transferable) credit itself is not, in fact, physically transferred to the transferee.

Following notification of such transfer (that is, of the issuing of the second credit), the supplier will dispatch the goods to his own buyer (first beneficiary), and upon presentation of the prescribed documents, he will receive the agreed payment from the confirming or advising bank. The documents are then forwarded to the transferee bank upon receipt of which it will debit the beneficiary's account. The beneficiary then delivers to the transferring bank his own invoice made out to the buyer, receives in exchange the invoice of his supplier, and is credited with the amount of his own invoice. Finally, the transferring bank forwards to the issuing bank all the prescribed documents including the beneficiary's invoice. The difference between the amount debited and the amount credited to the beneficiary's account represents his profit. To ensure that the identity of the supplier does not become known to the buyer, the middleman will require of his supplier that none of the prescribed documents (other than the invoice which will be substituted with the beneficiary's own invoice) contain any indication of the supplier's identity. Similarly, to prevent the buyer's identity from becoming known to the supplier, the beneficiary will ensure that the transferable letter of credit does not stipulate any documents that contain the buyer's name.

In order to meet the objective of the transferable credit, it is essential that the terms and conditions of the transferred credit be identical to those of the original credit except for the following:

(i)   the amount of the credit and the unit price may be reduced;

(ii) the expiry date may be brought forward;

(iii) the period of shipment may be shortened provided that the original credit does not specify a particular date for shipment;

(iv) the first beneficiary may require additional documents which remain in his keeping; and

(v)   the first beneficiary has the right to substitute his own invoice for that of the supplier/second beneficiary.

Thus, the beneficiary is not only able to trade with a limited outlay of his own funds, but is able to do so while preventing the buyer and supplier from knowing each other's identity and from receiving knowledge of his profit margin.

To make credit transferable, it is essential that the issuing bank expressly designates the credit to have such quality. It may be so expressed by the use of the word 'transferable'. Terms such as 'divisible', 'fractionable', 'assignable', and 'transmissible' do not render the credit transferable (Article 48(b)). Without an expressed quality of transferability, the advising bank is not authorised to extend the cover provided by the credit by making finance available thereunder to any person satisfying the conditions of the credit; it is bound to make payment under the credit on tender of the stipulated documents to the named beneficiary only. This is because, unlike a bill of exchange, a letter of credit is not a negotiable instrument and therefore may not be transferred unless the parties thereto (the issuing bank and the applicant) have so agreed.

Comprehensive provisions for the regulation of transferable credits is made under Article 48 of the UCP 500 which, pertinently, states:

(a)   A transferable credit is a credit under which the beneficiary (first beneficiary) may request the bank authorised to pay, incur a deferred payment undertaking, accept or negotiate (the 'transferring bank'), or in the case of a freely negotiable credit, the bank specifically authorised in the credit as a transferring bank, to make the credit available in whole or in part to one or more other beneficiary(ies) (second beneficiary(ies)).

(b) A credit can be transferred only if it is expressly designated as 'transferable' by the issuing bank. Terms such as 'divisible', 'fractionable', 'assignable', and 'transmissible' do not render the credit transferable. If such terms are used they shall be disregarded.

(c) The transferring bank shall be under no obligation to effect such transfer except to the extent and in the manner expressly consented to by such bank.

Paragraph (f) deals with bank charges. Paragraph (g) provides that a transferable credit can be transferred only once, but 'a retransfer to the first beneficiary does not constitute a prohibited transfer'. Paragraph (g) also makes provision for fractions of a transferable credit the aggregate of which will be considered as constituting only one transfer of the credit. Paragraph (i) gives the first beneficiary the right to substitute his own invoices in exchange for those of the second beneficiary. Finally, para (j) entitles the first beneficiary of a transferable credit to request that the credit be transferred to a second beneficiary in the same country or in another country.

Back-to-back credit

In the case of a back-to-back credit, a confirmed letter of credit opened by the buyer (applicant for the credit) in favour of the beneficiary, known as 'overriding credit', is used by the latter as security for the opening by him of a second credit in favour of his own supplier. This arrangement may be repeated where the same goods are sold or resold by several sellers (middlemen) as in the case of string contracts. In such case, each seller will use the credit in his favour as security for the credit which he needs to open in favour of his own seller, right through the chain of contracts until the first buyer in the chain opens a credit in favour of the original supplier. The back-to-back arrangement may involve different banks for each of the parties concerned, although it is preferable to have the whole operation conducted by one bank. It is essential that, save in relation to prices, the terms of each of the credits in a chain of back-to-back credits be identical.

Assignment of proceeds under a documentary credit

If a documentary credit is not transferable and the beneficiary is unable to obtain a back-to-back credit, he may nonetheless finance his own purchase in order to effect a sale of goods by assigning to his supplier the proceeds of the credit issued by his buyer (applicant for the credit) in his favour. In such case, the bank acting on the instructions of the beneficiary of the credit transmits to the assignee (the supplier) a declaration in which it undertakes to pay him a specified sum out of funds that have become available under the documentary credit.

Article 49 of the UCP 500 provides that the fact that a credit is not stated to be transferable shall not affect the beneficiary's right to assign any proceeds thereunder 'in accordance with the provisions of the applicable law'. The applicable law in Australia, as in England, is that dealing with the assignment of choses in action. As a letter of credit is a chose in action, it is capable to be assigned without the consent of either the buyer or the issuing bank. In this context, all the beneficiary needs to do is to satisfy the legal requirement relating to the assignment of choses in action or debts. In respect of the requirements of the credit itself, it is necessary that the condition relating to the tendering of documents as stipulated in the letter of credit be complied with. Such condition, being an obligation, is incapable of assignment and therefore can only be discharged by the beneficiary of the letter of credit, and not by the supplier/assignee. The latter's dependence on the beneficiary for the satisfaction of the condition relating to the tendering of documents constitutes a risk to which a supplier is exposed under an assignment of credit, and which renders the credit of limited security worth. The supplier does not receive payment until after the credit has been honoured and, yet, has no assurance that the beneficiary will present the documents in time and in conformity with the provisions of the credit.

FUNDAMENTAL PRINCIPLES

There are two fundamental principles governing letters of credit, namely:

(1) the doctrine of strict compliance; and

(2) the autonomy of the credit.

Pursuant to the autonomy principle, a letter of credit is a separate and independent transaction from the contract of sale or other transaction on which it is based. According to the doctrine of strict compliance a bank is entitled to reject documents which do not strictly conform with the terms and conditions of the credit. These two principles will be discussed under separate headings below.

The doctrine of strict compliance

The doctrine of strict compliance requires that the prescribed documents which are tendered by the beneficiary strictly conform with the terms and conditions of the credit. There is no obligation on the bank to honour non-conforming documents. In the words of Lord Sumner in *Equitable Trust Co of New York v Dawson Partners Ltd*: 'There is no room for documents which are almost the same, or which will do just as well. Business could not proceed securely on any other lines.'[5]

In that case the defendants bought vanilla beans from a seller in Batavia (Jakarta) in respect of which they instructed the plaintiff bank to open a confirmed letter of credit in favour of the seller. The documents required to be tendered under the letter of credit included a certificate of quality to be issued 'by experts who are sworn brokers'. The advising bank incorrectly informed the seller that the requisite certificate was to be issued 'by expert who is sworn broker'. The error occurred because of an incorrect decoding of the message sent by private and secret telegraphic code of the advising bank which used the same symbols for both the singular and plural of words. The seller fraudulently shipped rubbish (with only 1% of vanilla beans) and managed to extract a certificate from a sworn broker. The plaintiff bank, having accepted the tender of documents and having honoured the letter of credit, sought to be reimbursed by the buyer who refused to accept the documents. The plaintiff bank was successful at first

---

5   [1926] 27 Lloyd's Rep 49 at 52.

instance but lost on appeal in the Court of Appeal, and in the House of Lords where it was held that the plaintiff bank was not entitled to be reimbursed by the buyer because, in making available finance on the certificate of one expert instead of at least two experts, the plaintiff bank had acted contrary to the instructions of its customer. Lord Sumner reasoned as follows:[6]

> The bank's branch abroad, which knows nothing officially of the details of the transaction thus financed, cannot take upon itself to decide what will do well enough and what will not. If it does as it is told, it is safe; if it declines to do anything else, it is safe; if it departs from the conditions laid down, it acts at its own risk. The documents tendered were not exactly the documents which the defendants had promised to take up, and *prima facie* they were right in refusing to take them.

In determining whether the documents conform strictly with the terms of the credit, the bank is only concerned with what appears on the face of the documents. It does not need to look behind the documents. It is not concerned with the underlying transaction. This is made clear by Article 4 of the UCP 500 which states that: 'In credit operations all parties concerned deal with documents, and not with goods, services and/or other performances to which the documents may relate.' In *Instituto Nacional de Comercializacion Agricola v Continental Illinois National Bank and Trust Co*,[7] the court decided that a buyer had no cause of action for negligent misrepresentation against the confirming bank which negligently confirmed that documents submitted by the beneficiary of the credit complied with its terms and conditions. The court decided that a letter of credit transaction is not even amenable to the tort of negligent misrepresentation and that, in any event, the confirming bank has no duty of care to the customer, but only to the issuing bank.

The strictness of the doctrine of strict compliance is well illustrated in *SH Rayner and Co v Hambros Bank Ltd*.[8] There, a bank received instructions from a customer/buyer to open a confirmed credit in favour of the plaintiff seller in respect of a cargo of 'coromandel groundnuts'. The bank opened the credit and notified the plaintiff that it was available against invoice and bills of lading of 'coromandel groundnuts'. The plaintiff presented bills of lading for 'machine-shelled groundnut kernels' accompanied by an invoice for 'coromandel groundnuts'. The bank refused payment on the ground of non-compliance and the plaintiff sued the bank on the credit. At the trial, there was evidence that 'machine-shelled groundnut kernels' were universally understood in the trade to be identical with 'coromandel groundnuts'. In these circumstances, the trial judge gave judgment for the plaintiff. On appeal, the Court of Appeal reversed the trial judge's decision. In rejecting the central submission for the seller that the bank ought to be affected with the knowledge prevailing in the relevant trade that the two expressions referred to the same thing, MacKinnon LJ stated that 'it is quite impossible to suggest that a banker is to be affected with knowledge of the customs

---

6   *Ibid* at 52.

7   858 F 2d 1264 (1988).

8   [1943] 1 KB 37.

and customary terms of every one of the thousands of trades for whose dealings he may issue letters of credit'.[9]

Goddard LJ took it a step further, so that even if the bank had knowledge of the customary term, it was bound to comply strictly and literally with the terms of its mandate. He stated:[10]

> It does not matter whether the terms imposed by the person who requires the bank to open the credit seem reasonable or unreasonable. The bank is not concerned with that. If it accepts the mandate to open the credit, it must do exactly what its customer requires it to do. If the customer says: 'I require a bill of lading "for coromandel groundnuts",' the bank is not justified, in my judgment, in paying against a bill of lading for anything except coromandel groundnuts, and it is no answer to say: 'You know perfectly well that "machine-shelled groundnut" kernels are the same as "coromandel groundnuts".' For all the bank knows, its customer may have a particular reason for wanting 'coromandel groundnuts' in the bill of lading.

Time for accepting/rejecting tender of documents

Both at common law and under Article 13(a) of the UCP the bank has an obligation to examine the documents with reasonable care to ascertain whether they appear on their face to be in accordance with the terms and conditions of the credit. Pursuant to Article 13(b), 'The issuing bank, the confirming bank, if any, or a nominated bank acting on their behalf, shall each have a reasonable time, not to exceed seven banking days following the day of receipt of the documents, to examine the documents and determine whether to take up or refuse the documents and to inform the party from which it received the documents accordingly'. Although the bank has a maximum of seven banking days in which to examine the document, the bank has an obligation to proceed with such examination with reasonable promptness. If it decides to refuse the documents, it must give notice to that effect without delay to the remitting bank or the beneficiary as the case may be (Article 14(d)(i)). If it delays in deciding whether to refuse the documents, it will be precluded from claiming that the documents are not in accordance with the terms and conditions of the credit (Article 14(e)).

Appearance and not substance of documents is critical

The bank is only concerned with ascertaining that the documents appear on their face to conform with the terms and conditions of the credit. It is entitled to treat as non-conforming documents which appear on their face to be ambiguous or inconsistent with one another (Article 13(a)). The situation is the same at common law. Hence, the position of the bank and the extent of the application of the doctrine of strict compliance remain unchanged even where the provisions of the UCP 500 are not incorporated in a documentary credit. This is clear from a judgment of the Privy Council on appeal from the Court of Appeal in Singapore in *Gian Singh and Co Ltd v*

---

9   *Ibid* at 41.

10   *Ibid* at 42–43.

Banque de l'Indochine.[11] The judgment of their Lordships was delivered by Lord Diplock who stated:[12]

> The duty of the issuing bank, which it may perform either by itself, or by its agent, the notifying bank, is to examine documents with reasonable care to ascertain that they appear on their face to be in accordance with the terms and conditions of the credit. The express provision to this effect in Article 7 of the Uniform Customs and Practice for Documentary Credits [being Article 15 of the UCP 1983 Revision] does no more than re-state the duty of the bank at common law. In business transactions financed by documentary credits, banks must be able to act promptly on presentation of the documents. In the ordinary case visual inspection of the actual documents presented is all that is called for. The bank is under no duty to take any further steps to investigate the genuineness of a signature which, on the face of it, purports to be the signature of the person named or described in the letter of credit.

The principle that the bank is only concerned with the appearance of the tendered documents and not with their substance is further reinforced by Article 15 of the UCP 500 which provides as follows:

> Banks assume no liability or responsibility for the form, sufficiency, accuracy, genuineness, falsification or legal effect of any document(s), or for the general and/or particular conditions stipulated in the document(s) or superimposed thereon; nor do they assume any liability or responsibility for the description, quantity, weight, quality, condition, packing, delivery, value or existence of the goods represented by any document(s), or for the good faith of acts and/or omissions, solvency, performance or standing of the consignors, the carriers, the forwarders, the consignees or the insurers of the goods, or any other person whomsoever.

In accordance with Article 22 of the UCP 500, banks will usually accept a document bearing a date of issuance prior to that of the credit, subject to such document being presented within the time limits set out in the credit.

Ambiguous terms interpreted by bank

It is clear that, if the bank is confronted with an ambiguity when examining the tendered documents, it is entitled to reject the tender and refuse to make payment under the letter of credit. The bank may, however, give an interpretation to the ambiguous term which will render the documents in conformity with the terms and conditions of the credit. Assuming that in such case the bank were wrong in its interpretation and that, therefore, on a proper interpretation of the ambiguous term, the documents do not comply with the terms and conditions of the credit, the question would then arise whether the bank is in breach of its obligations or whether it is entitled to be reimbursed in respect of the payment made under the credit.

This question is answered by the Privy Council in an appeal from the Supreme Court of New South Wales in *Commercial Banking Co of Sydney Ltd v Jalsard Pty Ltd.*[13] In that case, the buyer (the respondent) contracted to purchase a quantity of battery-

---

11 [1974] 1 WLR 1234.

12 *Ibid* at 1238–39.

13 [1973] AC 279.

operated Christmas lights from a seller in Taiwan to be shipped to Sydney in two consignments. The buyer requested the bank (the appellant) to issue a letter of credit to authorise the seller to draw upon the bank's correspondent in Taiwan for a sum to cover invoice, costs FOB of the two shipments. The documents required to be tendered under the credit included a packing list certifying the quantity of the goods exported. Later, in accordance with the buyer's instructions, the bank amended the letter of credit by adding to the documents required a 'certificate of inspection'.

In due course, the documents were tendered by the seller and handed over by the bank to the buyer against reimbursement of the purchase price of the goods. The documents included 'certificates of inspection' in relation to the two shipments, issued by two firms of surveyors in Taiwan each certifying that the surveyors had supervised the packing of the boxes for checking the quantity and condition of the contents. On arrival in Sydney, the goods were found to be of defective quality and substantially unsaleable. The defects were not discoverable by visual inspection but only by physical testing. The buyer brought an action against the bank claiming damages for breach of contract for accepting tendered documents, namely the certificates of inspection, which did not comply with the terms of the letter of credit. The buyer contended that 'certificate of inspection' meant a document certifying the condition and quality of the goods inspected and not merely the condition and quantity of such goods. The buyer succeeded in his action in the Supreme Court of New South Wales.

In reversing the judgment of the Supreme Court, the Judicial Committee held that the minimum requirement implicit in the ordinary meaning of the words 'certificate of inspection' was 'that the goods the subject matter of the inspection have been inspected, at any rate visually, by the person issuing the certificate'. If it is intended that a particular method of inspection should be adopted or that particular information as to the result of the inspection should be recorded, this, in their Lordship's view, would not be implicit in the words 'certificate of inspection' by themselves, but would need to be expressly stated.[14] His Lordship then went on to deal specifically with the question posed earlier:[15]

> It is a well established principle in relation to commercial credits that if the instructions given by the customer to the issuing banker as to the documents to be tendered by the beneficiary are ambiguous or are capable of covering more than one kind of document, the banker is not in default if he acts upon a reasonable meaning of the ambiguous expression or accepts any kind of document which fairly falls within the wide description used: See *Midland Bank Ltd v Seymour* [1955] 2 Lloyd's Rep 147. There is good reason for this. By issuing the credit, the banker does not only enter into a contractual obligation to his own customer, the buyer, to honour the seller's drafts if they are accompanied by the specified documents. By confirming the credit to the seller through his correspondent at the place of shipment he assumes a contractual obligation to the seller that his drafts on tender to the correspondent bank will be accepted if accompanied by the specified documents, and a contractual obligation to his correspondent bank to reimburse it for accepting the seller's drafts. The banker is not concerned as to whether the documents

for which the buyer has stipulated serve any useful commercial purpose or as to why the customer called for tender of a document of a particular description. Both the issuing banker and his correspondent bank have to make quick decisions as to whether a document which has been tendered by the seller complies with the requirements of a credit at the risk of incurring liability to one or other of the parties to the transaction if the decision is wrong. Delay in deciding may in itself result in a breach of his contractual obligations to the buyer or to the seller. This is the reason for the rule that where the banker's instructions from his customer are ambiguous or unclear he commits no breach of his contract with the buyer if he has construed in a reasonable sense, even though upon the closer consideration which can be given to questions of construction in a court of law, it is possible to say that some other meaning is to be preferred.

Irrelevant discrepancies

Not all discrepancies would entitle a bank to reject the tender of documents. Slight discrepancies must be disregarded if the instructions in the tendered documents, notwithstanding such irregularity, make sense and have the same meaning as the related documents. Indeed, the UCP 500 itself makes allowance for irrelevant or immaterial irregularities. For example, Article 39(b) permits under-shipment or over-shipment within a tolerance of 5% provided there is no contrary stipulation in the credit. It is impossible to provide any guidelines which will assist in determining what discrepancies are and are not relevant. It is a matter of applying good commercial sense in each case. In the words of Schmitthoff:[16]

> If the tendered documents are ambiguous, the tender is, in principle, a bad tender. But the bank, when examining the tendered documents, should not insist on the rigid and meticulous fulfilment of the precise wording in all cases. If, 'properly read and understood', the words in the instructions and in the tendered documents have the same meaning, if they correspond though not being identical, the bank should not reject the documents. ... But the margin allowed to the bank in interpreting the documents is very narrow and the bank will be at risk if it does not insist on strict compliance.

An illustration of an irrelevant discrepancy is provided in *M Golodetz and Co Inc v Czarnikow-Rionda Co Inc, The Galatia*.[17] There, buyers of sugar in India opened a letter of credit in favour of their supplier in respect of goods to be shipped in *The Galatia* which was to load in Kandla, India. When the vessel was partly loaded, fire broke out and a large quantity of the sugar already on board was damaged by the fire as well as by the water used to extinguish the fire. The damaged sugar was discharged and a note was typed on the bill of lading stating '[c]argo covered by this bill of lading has been discharged Kandla view damaged by fire and/or water used to extinguish for which general average declared'.[18] The confirming bank refused to take up the bill of lading on the ground that the note typed on the bill made it a claused bill. Such view accorded with the commercial view that every bill which contains a notation or clausing is automatically to be regarded as a claused bill. The Court of Appeal preferred the legal

16 Schmitthoff, CM, *The Law and Practice of International Trade*, 9th edn, 1990, p 411, London: Stevens.
17 [1980] 1 WLR 495.
18 *Ibid* at 498.

view and held that the bill was a clean bill because the note on it referred to an event which had occurred after the goods were loaded in good order and condition.

Another illustration of an irrelevant discrepancy which also related to a bill of lading is found in *Westpac Banking Corporation v South Carolina National Bank*[19] which was decided by the Privy Council on appeal from the Court of Appeal in New South Wales. In that case, Commonwealth Steel Co Ltd (CSC) agreed to sell 400 truck side frames and 200 truck bolsters to National Railway Utilisation Corporation of Charlestown, South Carolina. The buyers requested South Carolina National Bank (SCNB) to open an irrevocable letter of credit in favour of the seller. The credit was available on presentation of 'shipped' bills of lading. Except as otherwise expressly stated, the letter of credit incorporated the UCP (1974 Revision). The credit was advised to the seller by Westpac Banking Corporation (Westpac). The bills tendered by the seller to Westpac were in the form 'received for shipment'. On the face of each of the bills were the words 'shipped on board' and 'freight pre-paid' and the intended vessel was stated to be *Columbus America*. The advising bank, Westpac, accepted the bills of lading and negotiated an accompanying bill of exchange drawn on SCNB. However, the latter, as the issuing bank, rejected the bills of lading. In the New South Wales Court of Appeal and in the Privy Council, SCNB relied on the contention that the bills were internally inconsistent in that on their face they stated to be in the nature of both 'shipped on board' and 'received for shipment'. The argument was accepted by the Court of Appeal but rejected by the Privy Council. The judgment of their Lordships was delivered by Lord Goff who stated:[20]

> Their Lordships approached the matter as follows. First, they are unable to accept the proposition that the words 'shipped on board' make the bill internally inconsistent. True, it is that the bill is on a 'received for shipment' form and for that reason refers to *Columbus America* as the intended vessel; but there is nothing inconsistent in a document which states that the specified goods have been received for shipment on board a named vessel and have in fact been shipped on board that vessel ... True, this bill of lading was, in form, a 'received for shipment' bill; but with the words 'shipped on board' forming part of the stencilled wording inserted in the bill and present at the time of its signature and issue, it was plain on the face of the bill that it stated that the goods had at that time been shipped on board the intended ship, *Columbus America*, at the intended port of loading, Melbourne, and it followed that the set of bills presented to SCNB was a set of on board ocean bills of lading as required by the letter of credit.

Thus, mere technical or irrelevant discrepancies as distinct from discrepancies which go to the substance of the documents may not be relied upon to reject tendered documents.

Pursuant to Article 14(c) of the UCP 500, 'If the issuing bank determines that the documents appear on their face not to be in compliance with the terms and conditions of the credit, it may in its sole judgment approach the applicant for a waiver of the discrepancy(ies).' The bank's decision to seek a waiver from its customer (applicant for

---

19 [1986] 1 Lloyd's Rep 311.
20 *Ibid* at 315–16.

the credit) does not, however, extend the maximum period of seven banking days available to the bank to examine the submitted documents.

The requirement of linkage of documents

Article 37(c) of the UCP 500 stipulates that 'The description of the goods in the commercial invoice must correspond with the description in the credit. In all other documents, the goods may be described in general terms not inconsistent with the description of the goods in the credit'. Thus, although the goods must be described in the commercial invoice in the same way in which they are described in the letter of credit, their description in other documents, for example, the transport and insurance documents, need not correspond with the description in the credit. An example of the application of this rule is provided by *Courtaulds North America Inc v North Carolina National Bank*[21] which was decided under the UCP (1973 Revision). In this case, the bank issued an irrevocable letter of credit on behalf of its customer, Adastra Knitting Mills. It undertook to pay orders to pay for up to US$135,000 covering shipments of '100% acrylic yarn'. Courtaulds' commercial invoice described the goods as 'imported acrylic yarn', but the packing lists attached to the invoices described the goods as '100% acrylic yarn'. The bank refused to pay because it found a discrepancy between the letter of credit and the commercial invoice. The bank's refusal was condoned by the Court of Appeal for the 4th Circuit. Courtaulds also argued unsuccessfully that the packing lists, which were stapled to the invoice, were part of the invoice and that, therefore, the description of the goods in the invoice corresponded with the description of the goods in the letter of credit. On this issue, the court ruled that packing lists, even if attached to the commercial invoice, are not part of the invoice.

The issue of the description of the goods in documents and its consistency with the description of the goods in the credit is, however, different from the requirement of linkage of documents. A genuine discrepancy of documents will exist where the documents cannot be properly linked together and, therefore, may not relate to the same goods. The linkage requirement is expressly provided by Article 13(a) of the UCP 500 which in part states that 'documents which appear on their face to be inconsistent with one another will be considered as not appearing on their face to be in accordance with the terms and conditions of the credit'.

What is required is that all documents tendered to the bank clearly and unequivocally relate to the same goods. It is not necessary that, as in the case of the commercial invoice, each document comprehensively describes the goods but that each unambiguously makes reference to the same goods. It is in this manner that the documents to be tendered are said to be linked together. A case in point is *Banque de l'Indochine et de Suez SA v JH Rayner (Mincing Lane) Ltd*.[22] In that case, a bank in Djibouti, acting as issuing bank, opened an irrevocable credit which was advised and confirmed by the plaintiff bank. The credit related to the sale of sugar by the defendants

---

21 528 F 2d 802 (1975) (4th Circ).

22 [1983] QB 711. The judgment of Parker J, the first instance judge, which was affirmed by the Court of Appeal, is reported at 713–22; and the judgments of the Court of Appeal are reported at 726–34.

to the buyers on whose instructions the credit was opened in favour of the defendants. The defendants tendered the documents under the credit and requested payment of the amount due thereunder, approximately one million dollars. After examining the documents, the plaintiff bank considered that the tender was defective because of discrepancies between the documents. The defendants disputed that the tender was defective. Following discussions between the parties, the plaintiff bank proceeded to pay, advising that such payment was 'effected under reserve due to the discrepancies' which the plaintiff bank went on to list. The last of the listed discrepancies was directed to an alleged absence of linkage stating that: '(4) Certificates of weight, quality, packing and certificates of origin and EUR1 certificates cannot be related to remaining documents or to letter of credit.'

The issuing bank having refused to accept the documents, the plaintiff bank sought to recover from the defendants the payment it had made 'under reserve'. In dealing with the issue of linkage, Parker J stated:[23]

> I have no doubt that as long as the documents can be plainly seen to be linked with each other, are not inconsistent with each other or with the terms of the credit, do not call for enquiry and between them state all that is required in the credit, the beneficiary is entitled to be paid.

His Honour then went on to consider the specific discrepancies in the documents which gave rise to inconsistencies and, therefore, lack of linkage both between the documents themselves and between the documents and the credit. For this and other reasons, his Honour considered that the tender was bad and found for the plaintiff bank.

In respect to linkage, Parker J's reasoning and decision were affirmed by the Court of Appeal. In particular, Sir John Donaldson MR stated:

> I approach this aspect of the appeal [that is the linking of documents] on the same basis as did the judge, namely that the banker is not concerned with why the buyer has called for particular documents (*Commercial Banking Co of Sydney Ltd v Jalsard Pty Ltd* [1973] AC 279), that there is no room for documents which are almost the same, or which will do just as well, as those specified, *Equitable Trust Co of New York v Dawson Partners Ltd* (1926) 27 Lloyd's Rep 49, that whilst the bank is entitled to put a reasonable construction upon any ambiguity in its mandate, if the mandate is clear there must be strict compliance with that mandate (*Jalsard's* case [1973] AC 279), that documents have to be taken up or rejected promptly and without opportunity for prolonged enquiry (*Hansson v Hamel and Horley Ltd* [1922] 2 AC 36) and that a tender of documents which properly read and understood call for further enquiry or are such as to invite litigation are a bad tender (*M Golodetz and Co Inc v Czarnikow-Rionda Co Inc* [1980] 1 WLR 495).

His Lordship then dealt with the subject documents and found that the inconsistencies were such that the documents were not on their face linked to each other and to the commercial invoice. Interestingly, he also considered that the reference in the certificate of origin to 'nv Markhor or substitute' was inconsistent with the reference appearing in the other documents to 'nv Markhor' and considered that the words 'or substitute' could be referring to a different vessel and, therefore, the reference could be to a

---

23 *Ibid* at 72.

different parcel of sugar which was the subject of the sale. This aspect of the judgment has been criticised by Schmitthoff[24] who considers that the requirement of linkage in this respect was applied by the court too strictly.

Payment under reserve

If a bank finds the tendered documents to be clearly defective, it will reject the documents. Where, however, the position is not clear, the bank may still wish to accommodate the beneficiary and accept them subject to certain protective measures. In such a case, the bank may make 'payment under reserve', that is, on condition that if the documents are rejected by any subsequent recipient, for instance, by the issuing bank or the buyer, the bank will be entitled to reimbursement by the beneficiary of the amount paid by the bank under reserve. Provision for payment under reserve is made by Article 14(f) of the UCP 500 as follows:

> If the remitting bank draws the attention of the issuing bank and/or confirming bank, if any, to any discrepancy(ies) in the document(s) or advises such banks that it has paid, incurred a deferred payment undertaking, accepted draft(s) or negotiated under reserve or against an indemnity in respect of such discrepancy(ies), the issuing bank and/or confirming bank, if any, shall not be thereby relieved from any of their obligations under any provision of this article. Such reserve or indemnity concerns only the relations between the remitting bank and the party towards whom the reserve was made, or from whom, or on whose behalf, the indemnity was obtained.

The UCP provisions do not, however, define the expression 'payment under reserve'. Nor has any such expression been judicially defined in any complete or absolute manner. The meaning of such expression may for that reason vary from case to case depending on the meaning which the parties intended to give to such expression, having regard to all the facts and circumstances surrounding the subject transaction and, in particular, giving rise to the making of the payment 'under reserve'. It will be recalled that payment under reserve was made by the plaintiff bank in *Banque de l'Indochine et de Suez SA v JH Rayner (Mincing Lane) Ltd*[25] discussed above in the context of the linkage of documents requirement. In that case the court of first instance and the Court of Appeal, having reached the view that certain discrepancies alleged by the plaintiff bank were valid grounds for rejecting the tendered documents, then examined the meaning of the expression 'under reserve'. Parker J considered that in the absence of any established custom, the meaning of such expression had to be determined in the light of the surrounding circumstances or as it is also called 'the factual matrix' namely:

(i) that the remitting bank genuinely believed that there were one or more discrepancies justifying non-payment;

(ii) that the beneficiary believed that the bank was wrong and that it was entitled to payment under the credit; and

---

24   Schmitthoff, *op cit* fn 16, pp 415–16.

25   [1983] QB 711.

(iii) that both parties hoped that, notwithstanding the alleged discrepancies which were disputed by the beneficiary, the issuing bank would take up the documents and reimburse the remitting bank.

Other relevant facts were that the confirming bank proceeded to effect payment in order to resolve the beneficiary's cash flow problems, and that the beneficiary was considered by the confirming bank to be a reputable, valued and credit-worthy customer.

In the Court of Appeal, Kerr LJ dealt with the 'commercial reality of the situation'.[26] The reality was that, while holding opposite views, both the confirming bank and the beneficiary hoped that, whichever of them was right, neither the issuing bank nor the buyer would raise any objection to the documents. It was with this hope, uppermost in its mind, that the confirming bank agreed to pay but only 'under reserve'. But, in so agreeing, the bank could not, in his Lordship's view, be taken to have agreed to become involved in legal proceedings, if the documents were rejected, by having to sue the beneficiary to recover the money, and establishing the defect of the tendered documents, or by suing the issuing bank on the ground that the tender was in fact good. In his Lordship's view the proper approach was as follows:[27]

> What the parties meant, I think, was that payment was to be made under reserve in the sense that the beneficiary would be bound to repay the money on demand if the issuing bank should reject the documents, whether on its own initiative or on the buyer's instructions. I would regard this as a binding agreement made between the confirming bank and the beneficiary by way of a compromise to resolve the impasse created by the uncertainty of their respective legal obligations and rights.

A commercial view of the meaning of the expression 'under reserve' was also adopted by Sir John Donaldson MR who expounded his reasoning by imputing a dialogue between the parties as follows:[28]

Merchant: These documents are sufficient to satisfy the terms of the letter of credit and certainly will be accepted by my buyer. I am entitled to the money and need it.

Bank: If we thought that the documents satisfied the terms of the letter of credit, we would pay you at once. However, we do not think that they do and we cannot risk paying you and not being paid ourselves. We are not sure that your buyer will authorise payment, but we can of course ask.

Merchant: But we will take time and meanwhile we will have a cash flow problem.

Bank: Well the alternative is for you to sue us and that will take time.

Merchant: What about you paying us without prejudice to whether we are entitled to payment and then you seeing what is the reaction of your correspondent bank and our buyer?

Bank: That is all right, but if we are told that we should not have paid, how do we get our money back?

Merchant: You sue us.

---

26 *Ibid* at 733.
27 *Ibid.*
28 *Ibid* at 727–28.

Bank: Oh no, that would leave us out of our money for a substantial time. Further, it will involve us in facing in two directions. We should not only have to sue you, but also to sue the issuing bank in order to cover the possibility that you might be right. We cannot afford to pay on those terms.

Merchant: All right. I am quite confident that the issuing bank and my buyer will be content that you should pay, particularly since the documents are in fact in order. You pay me and if the issuing bank refuses to reimburse you for the same reason that you are unwilling to pay, we will repay you on demand and then sue you. But we do not think that this will happen.

Bank: We agree. Here is the money under reserve.

This dialogue gives rise to the agreement, referred to by Kerr LJ in his judgment (and quoted above), made between the plaintiff bank and the beneficiary. In this agreement, they made a commitment to resolve their dispute as to the compliance, or otherwise, of intended documents.

Seller's right of recovery against the buyer in case of non-conforming documents

It will be recalled that in accordance with the principle of autonomy, the credit is separate and independent from the underlying contract of sale. Assume that a seller has been refused payment by a bank under a documentary credit on the ground that the documents tendered by the seller failed to comply with the terms and conditions of the credit. The question for consideration is whether the seller, in those circumstances, is entitled to claim payment against the buyer personally under the separate contract of sale in respect of which the documentary credit was issued.

This question came for consideration before Bingham J in the English Commercial Court in *Shamster Jute Mills Ltd v Sethia (London) Ltd*.[29] In that case, pursuant to a contract, the plaintiff seller sold to the defendant buyer 200 tonnes of Jute yarn for a specified price. Payment was to be by irrevocable and confirmed letter of credit at sight. The buyer opened letters of credit to cover four monthly shipments under the contract. The credit was to be available by the seller's drafts drawn on the buyer, accompanied by specified documents. A number of consignments were shipped for which documents were presented and payment made under the relevant letter of credit. Subsequently, Oriental Credit Ltd of London (Oriental) opened a further irrevocable letter of credit in favour of the seller which did not appear in this case to be confirmed. The sellers submitted the documents to their own bank, namely Sonali Bank (Sonali) in Dhaka asking that the documents be negotiated and paid. Although Sonali agreed to negotiate the documents it did so 'under reserve' as there were a number of specified discrepancies which were not acceptable to Sonali. The documents were then transmitted to Sonali's London branch with instructions to present to Oriental. Oriental, having been presented with the documents, informed the buyer of the discrepancies. The buyer refused to accept the documents and as a result the seller brought an action against the buyer to recover the contract price or damages for non-acceptance. Justice Bingham

---

29   [1987] 1 Lloyd's Rep 388.

held that the sellers, having failed to comply with the terms of the credit, could not recover against the buyers personally. His Honour approached the matter as follows:[30]

> The parties are right to agree in the present case that the letter of credit is, on Lord Denning's classification in *Alan*, conditional payment. The sellers never agreed that they would only look to Oriental Credit for payment whatever happened. Nor is the credit to be regarded as no payment at all but only a means by which payment may be obtained, a form of collateral security. But to speak of a letter of credit as conditional payment of the price does not perhaps make very clear what the condition is or how it works. If the buyer establishes a credit which conforms or is to be treated as conforming with the sale price, he has performed his part of the bargain so far. If the credit is honoured according to its terms, the buyer is discharged even though the credit terms differ from the contract terms: that was the *Alan* case. If the credit is not honoured according to its terms because the bank fails to pay, the buyer is not discharged because the condition has not been fulfilled. That was the *Nigerian Sweets* case. This makes good sense: 'for the buyers promised *to pay* by letter of credit, not to provide by a letter of credit a source of payment which did *not* pay [as Stephenson LJ put it in the *Alan* case at 329 and 220G].'

> If the seller fails to obtain payment because he does not and cannot present the documents which under the terms of the credit, supplementing the terms of the contract, are required, the buyer is discharged: that was the *Ficom* case. In the ordinary case, therefore, of which the present is an example, the due establishment of the letter of credit fulfils the buyer's payment obligations unless the bank which opens the credit fails for any reason to make payment in accordance with the credit terms against documents duly presented. I know of no case where a seller who has failed to obtain payment under a credit because of failure on his part to comply with its terms has succeeded in recovering against the buyer personally. If this were an available road to recover, many of the familiar arguments about discrepancies in documents would be unnecessary. Bearing in mind the likelihood that buyers will (as here) sell unto sub-buyers such a result would, I think, throw the course of international trade into some confusion. It must in my view follow that the sellers here, not having complied with the credit terms, cannot recover against the buyers personally.

Although dismissing the seller's claim, his Honour noted the harshness of the result because the seller who appeared to have set out to perform the contract in an honest, efficient and businesslike way, had parted with the goods and had received no payment from anyone.

THE PRINCIPLE OF AUTONOMY OF THE LETTER OF CREDIT

The principle

The essential feature of a documentary credit is its independence of any underlying transactions, such as the contract of sale, and the contract between the issuing bank and the buyer as applicant of the credit. This fundamental principle is given expression in Article 3 of the UCP 500 which reads as follows:

---

30   *Ibid* at 392, col 2.

(a) Credits, by their nature, are separate transactions from the sales or other contract(s) on which they may be based and banks are in no way concerned with or bound by such contract(s), even if any reference whatsoever to such contract(s) is included in the credit. Consequently, the undertaking of a bank to pay, accept and pay draft(s) or negotiate and/or to fulfil any other obligation under the credit, is not subject to claims or defences by the applicant resulting from his relationships with the issuing bank or the beneficiary.

(b) A beneficiary can in no case avail himself of the contractual relationships existing between the banks or between the applicant and the issuing bank.

The autonomy principle is supported by the maxim, incorporated in Article 4, that the bank deals in documents and not in goods. The absoluteness of the bank's undertaking, in the form of a credit issued in favour of the seller as beneficiary, has been firmly upheld by the courts. These have frequently refused to interfere with such undertaking by making restraining orders that would prevent compliance. The leading Australian case is *Wood Hall Ltd v Pipeline Authority*[31] in which Stephen J indicated that the autonomy principle is necessary to ensure that letters of credit remain as good as cash. The obligation of the issuing bank is described well in *Maurice O'Meara Co v National Park Bank of New York*.[32] In this case, the issuing bank refused to pay on a letter of credit which covered a shipment of newsprint paper. Its refusal was based on the ground that there was a reasonable doubt regarding the quality of the newspaper print. The court, in holding for the plaintiff, restated the autonomy principle when it decided that the bank 'was absolutely bound to make the payment under the letter of credit, irrespective of whether it knew, or had reason to believe, that the paper was not of the tensile strength contracted for'. In *Hamzeh Malas and Sons v British Imex Industries Ltd*,[33] where the Court of Appeal refused to grant an injunction, Lord Jenkins stated:[34]

> It seems to be plain enough that the opening of a confirmed letter of credit constitutes a bargain between the banker and the vendor of the goods, which imposes upon the banker an absolute obligation to pay, irrespective of any dispute there may be between the parties as to whether the goods are up to contract or not. ...

There is this to be remembered, too. A vendor of goods selling against a confirmed letter of credit is selling under the assurance that nothing will prevent him from receiving the price. That is of no mean advantage when goods manufactured in one country are being sold in another.

The quality of autonomy of the documentary credit provides it with attributes similar to those of a bill of exchange. In each case, the instrument is separate from and independent to the underlying transaction. The parties to the instrument are not concerned with any dispute arising out of the underlying transaction. The obligation under the instrument is absolute and is not capable of any defence (save in the case of fraud which will be discussed below) and entitles the beneficiary thereunder to obtain

---

31   (1979) 141 CLR 443 at 457.
32   239 NY 386, 146 NE 636, 639 (1925).
33   [1958] 2 QB 127.
34   *Ibid* at 129.

summary judgment. An application for summary judgment (save in the case of fraud) cannot be resisted by any defence or cross-claim. The analogy with the bill of exchange was noted by Lord Denning MR in *Power Curber International Ltd v National Bank of Kuwait SAK*:[35]

> It is vital that every bank which issues a letter of credit should honour its obligations. The bank is in no way concerned with any dispute that the buyer may have with the seller. The buyer may say that the goods are not up to contract. Nevertheless the bank must honour its obligations. The buyer may say that he has a cross-claim in a large amount. Still the bank must honour its obligations. A letter of credit is like a bill of exchange given for the price of goods. It ranks as cash and must be honoured. No set off or counterclaim is allowed to detract from it: see *Nova (Jersey) Knit Ltd v Kammgarn Spinnerei GmbH*.[36] All the more so with a letter of credit. Whereas a bill of exchange is given by buyer to seller, a letter of credit is given by a bank to the seller with the very intention of avoiding anything in the nature of a set off or counterclaim.

That case concerned an action brought by an American seller (Power Curber) against the National Bank of Kuwait (NBK), claiming under an irrevocable letter of credit issued by NBK. Power Curber had sold to a Kuwaiti distributor machinery which was duly delivered to the Kuwaiti buyer. However, the latter apparently on the basis of a large counterclaim against Power Curber obtained from a court in Kuwait a provisional attachment order against NBK which prevented NBK from paying under the credit notwithstanding its willingness to do so. NBK operated a branch in London, hence Power Curber's decision to commence proceedings in England. The matter came at first instance before Parker J who gave summary judgment against NBK but imposed a stay upon the execution of the judgment. Power Curber appealed against the stay and NBK cross-appealed against the judgment. The Court of Appeal dismissed the cross-appeal and allowed the appeal. In upholding the bank's obligation to pay under the irrevocable letter of credit, the court held that such obligation was not affected by the Kuwaiti court's provisional attachment order. In this context, Lord Denning MR observed that the order for 'provisional attachment' operated against NBK's head office in Kuwait but not against its branch office in London. That branch was subject to the orders of the English courts.[37]

Thus, in the absence of fraud, summary judgment will be granted in respect of claims made under letters of credit. Similarly, in the absence of fraud no injunction would be granted to restrain a bank from honouring its obligations under a letter of credit. In *Bolivinter Oil SA v Chase Manhattan Bank NA and others*,[38] an application was made for an injunction restraining the defendant bank from making payment pursuant to an irrevocable letter of credit. The application was based on disputes between the parties over the performance of the underlying contract. The judge at first instance

---

35 [1981] 1 WLR 1233 at 1241.

36 [1977] 1 WLR 713, where summary judgment was given to a plaintiff as holder in due course of bills of exchange.

37 [1981] 1 WLR 1233 at 1241.

38 [1984] 1 WLR 392.

refused to grant the injunction and an appeal against such refusal was dismissed. In his judgment, Sir John Donaldson MR stated:[39]

> Judges who are asked, often at short notice and *ex parte*, to issue an injunction restraining payment by a bank under an irrevocable letter of credit or performance bond or guarantee should ask whether there is any challenge to the validity of the letter, bond or guarantee itself. If there is not or if the challenge is not substantial, *prima facie* no injunction should be granted and the bank should be left free to honour its contractual obligation, although restrictions may well be imposed upon the freedom of the beneficiary to deal with the money after he has received it. The wholly exceptional case where an injunction may be granted is where it is proved that the bank knows that any demand for payment already made or which may thereafter be made will clearly be fraudulent. But the evidence must be clear, both as to the fact of fraud and as to the bank's knowledge. It would certainly not normally be sufficient that this rests upon the uncorroborated statement of the customer, for irreparable damage can be done to a bank's credit in the relatively brief time which must elapse between the granting of such an injunction and an application by the bank to have it discharged.

The fraud exception will now be considered in detail in the next section of this chapter.

The fraud exception

Fraud is the only exception to the absolute obligation of a bank to pay under a letter of credit; this obligation is founded on the principle of autonomy of letters of credit. Not surprisingly, a mere allegation of fraud is insufficient to affect the bank's obligation to make payment under a credit. Indeed, although an allegation of fraud made by a buyer may be based on a genuine belief or suspicion, such belief or suspicion may itself be ill-founded. It is clear that something more than an allegation of fraud is required. However, it is far from clear what degree of evidence of fraud is required, and what knowledge of such fraud the beneficiary and/or the bank must have for the fraud exception to be available.

The fraud exception can be traced back to the American case of *Szteijn v J Henry Schroder Banking Corporation*.[40] In that case, the issuing bank opened an irrevocable credit covering a shipment of bristles. The seller shipped crates containing rubbish, but managed to procure and tender documents which were regular on their face. The buyer, having discovered the fraud, made an application for an injunction restraining the issuing bank from accepting the documents and making payment under the credit. The bank made an application to strike out the action on the ground that it did not disclose a cause of action. The strike out application was dismissed by Shientag J who held that:[41]

> ... where the seller's fraud has been called to the bank's attention before the drafts and documents have been presented for payment, the principle of the independence of the bank's obligation under the letter of credit should not be extended to protect the unscrupulous seller.

---

39   *Ibid* at 393.
40   31 NYS 2d 631 (NY Sup Ct, 1941).
41   *Ibid* at 634.

Szteijn was distinguished by Megarry J in *Discount Records Ltd v Barclays Bank Ltd and Another.*[42] That case was concerned with an application for an injunction restraining the defendant bank from paying a draft pursuant to an irrevocable credit opened at the plaintiff's request to enable the purchase of certain goods. The plaintiff's evidence was that on arrival the cartons containing the goods were found to be empty or half empty, or filled with rubbish or containing, mostly, goods not ordered. Megarry J dismissed the application for an injunction holding that the evidence of the alleged fraud had yet to be established and the draft might be in the hands of a holder in due course. In this context he stated that 'I would be slow to interfere with bankers' irrevocable credits, and not least in the sphere of international banking, unless a sufficiently grave cause is shown.'[43]

If a bank has no knowledge of the fraud at the time when it makes payment or negotiates the letter of credit, assuming the relevant tendered documents appear regular on their face, it will not be liable to its principal if it is later discovered that the documents were forged. Such liability is precluded by Article 15 of the UCP 500 which provides, in its relevant part, that 'banks assume no liability or responsibility for the form, sufficiency, accuracy, genuineness, falsification or legal effect of any document(s)'. Even if the provisions of the UCP are not incorporated in the letter of credit, the position at common law is the same and the bank would not be liable.[44]

The relevant time for considering the bank's state of knowledge in relation to any forgery or other relevant fraud is when payment falls due and is refused by the bank.[45] If the party claiming payment has negotiated the documents in good faith with the remitting bank, the issuing bank cannot excuse refusal to honour the credit on the ground that at some earlier time the remitting bank was a mere agent for collection on the part of the seller and allege against the beneficiary fraud or forgery.[46]

It will be recalled that in *Bolivinter Oil SA v Chase Manhattan Bank NA and Others,*[47] Sir John Donaldson MR stated that the evidence of fraud must be clear, both as to the fact of fraud and as to the bank's knowledge.[48] The evidentiary requirement was further elaborated by Hirst J in *Tukan Timber Ltd v Barclays Bank plc*[49] where his Honour stated:[50]

> We would expect the court to require strong corroborative evidence of the allegation, usually in the form of contemporaneous documents, particularly those emanating from the seller. In general, for the evidence of fraud to be clear, we would also expect the seller

---

42   [1975] 1 WLR 315.

43   *Ibid* at 320.

44   *Woods v Thiedemann* (1862) 1 H and C 478; *Ulster Bank v Synott* (1871) 5 IREq 595; *Basse and Selve v Bank of Australasia* (1904) 90 LT 618; *Guaranteed Trust Co of New York v Hannay and Co* [1918] 2 KB 623.

45   *European Asian Bank AG v Punjab and Sind Bank (No 2)* [1983] 1 WLR 642.

46   *Ibid* at 658.

47   [1984] 1 WLR 392.

48   *Ibid* at 393.

49   [1987] 1 Lloyd's Rep 171.

50   *Ibid* at 175.

to have been given an opportunity to answer the allegation and to have failed to provide
any, or any adequate answer in circumstances where one could properly be expected.

If, therefore, the bank has received corroborative evidence of fraud which includes some
contemporaneous documents emanating from the buyer, and the seller has not given a
satisfactory answer to the allegations, the bank will be entitled (and probably ought) to
refuse payment under the credit.

What if the bank is furnished with such strong corroborative evidence, but there is
no evidence showing that the beneficiary (seller) knew of the fraud? Although one
would have thought that in such a hypothetical situation the fraud exception would
apply, the House of Lords took an opposite view in *United City Merchants (Investments)
Ltd v Royal Bank of Canada (The American Accord)*.[51] In that case, a Peruvian company
('the buyers') agreed to buy from English sellers ('the sellers') a plant for the manufacture
of glass fibres ('the goods') at a specified price FOB London for shipment to Callao.
Payment was to be in London by confirmed irrevocable transferable credit on
presentation of specified documents. The buyers' bank which acted as the issuing bank
appointed Royal Bank of Canada ('the confirming bank') to advise and confirm the
credit to the sellers. This was duly done. The credit was expressed to be subject to the
UCP and to be available by sight drafts on the issuing bank against delivery, *inter alia*, of
a full set 'on board' bills of lading evidencing receipt for shipment of the goods from
London to Callao on or before a specified date which was subsequently extended to 15
December 1976.

It was intended by the loading brokers acting on behalf of the carriers that the goods
be shipped on a vessel belonging to the carriers namely the *American Legend* which was
due to arrive at an agreed substituted destination on 10 December 1976. The arrival of
American Legend at such destination was cancelled and another vessel, *American Accord*,
was substituted by the loading brokers even though its date of arrival was scheduled for
16 December 1976, ie one day after the latest date of shipment required by the
documentary credit. The goods were in fact loaded on board *American Accord* on 16
December 1976 but the loading brokers who issued bills of lading as agents for the
carriers, issued in the first instance a set of 'received for shipment' bills of lading dated 15
December 1976 which they handed over to the sellers in return for payment of the
freight.

On presentation of the shipping documents to the confirming bank on 17
December, that bank raised various objections including the fact that the bills of lading
did not bear any dated 'on board' notations. The bills of lading were returned to the
brokers who then issued a fresh set bearing the notation which was untrue: 'these goods
are actually on board 15 December 1976. EH Munday and Co (Freight Agents) Ltd as
agents.' The amended bills of lading and all other relevant documents were presented to
the confirming bank on 22 December 1976. The confirming bank again refused
payment, this time on the ground that they had information in their possession which
suggested that shipment was not effected as it appeared on the bills of lading. At the trial,

---

51 [1983] 1 AC 168.

it was found that an employee of the loading brokers had acted fraudulently in issuing the bills of lading bearing a false date. The trial judge also found that the sellers (and their transferee) were not privy to any fraud and had acted in good faith without knowledge of the false date which appeared on the bills of lading when tendering the documents to the confirming bank.

The leading judgment was delivered by Lord Diplock with whom the other Law Lords agreed. Having referred to the general principle governing the contractual obligations of the confirming bank and the seller, his Lordship went on as follows:[52]

> To this general statement of principle ... there is one established exception: that is, where the seller, for the purpose of drawing on the credit, fraudulently presents to the confirming bank documents that contain, expressly or by implication, material representations of fact that to his knowledge are untrue. Although there does not appear among the English authorities any case in which this exception has been applied, it is well established in the American cases of which the leading or 'landmark' case is *Szteijn v J Henry Schroder Banking Corp* (1941) 31 NYS 2d 631. This judgment of the New York Court of Appeals was referred to with approval by the English Court of Appeal in *Edward Owen Engineering Ltd v Barclays Bank International Ltd* [1978] QB 159, though this was actually a case about a performance bond ... The exception for fraud on the part of the beneficiary seeking to avail himself of the credit is a clear application of the maxim *ex turpi causa non oritur actio* or if plain English is to be preferred 'fraud unravels all'. The courts will not allow their process to be used by a dishonest person to carry out a fraud.

The instant case, however, does not fall within the fraud exception. Mocatta J found the sellers to have been unaware of the inaccuracy of Mr Baker's notation of the date at which the goods were actually on board *American Accord*. What rational ground can there be for drawing any distinction between apparently conforming documents that, unknown to the seller, in fact contain a statement of fact that is inaccurate where the inaccuracy was due to inadvertence by the maker of the document, and the like documents where the same inaccuracy had been inserted by the maker of the documents with intent to deceive, among others, the seller/beneficiary himself? *Ex hypothesi*, we are dealing only with a case in which the seller/beneficiary claiming under the credit *has* been deceived, for if he presented documents to the confirming bank with knowledge that this apparent conformity with the terms and conditions of the credit was due to the fact that the documents told a lie, the seller/beneficiary would himself be a party to the misrepresentation made to the confirming bank by the lie in the documents and the case would come within the fraud exception.

In summary, the House of Lords held that the fraud exception which entitles a banker to refuse to pay under a letter of credit does not extend to fraud to which a seller or beneficiary under the credit was not a party.

There is no Australian judicial authority which deals comprehensively with the fraud exception. However, it appears from one case, namely *Hortico (Australia) Pty Ltd v Energy*

---

52   *Ibid* at 183.

Equipment Co (Australia) Pty Ltd[53] that the fraud exception may be more extensively applied. Although that case was concerned with an instrument, the true character of which was a performance bond, Young J made reference to and applied the principles governing letters of credit.[54] In dealing with a submission on fraud in respect of the exercise of the power, Young J stated:[55]

> [I]t is probably true to say that there is a wide general principle of equity that whenever a person unconscionably makes use of a statutory or contractual power for an improper purpose, that equity may step in and restrain the exercise of that power ... However, equity intervenes in such a case in the exercise of its discretion. As I have said, with commercial transactions such as the present, the courts have consistently taken a 'hands-off' approach and it does not seem to me that anything short of actual fraud would warrant this court in intervening, though it may be that in some cases ... the unconscionable conduct may be so gross as to lead to exercise of the discretionary power.

From the passage quoted above, it would seem that, at least in the State of New South Wales, there is a second basis or exception to the principle of autonomy of letters of credit, namely, that of unconscionable conduct. If that is correct, the quality of letters of credit being equivalent to cash would be exposed to a substantial risk of erosion which will adversely affect the standing of banks and ultimately international trade in Australia. For, unlike the fraud exception which is rarely capable of being established, unconscionable conduct provides very fertile ground for successful applications for injunctions restraining banks from making payment under letters of credit.

The *Mareva* injunction

Apart from the fraud exception, a buyer against whose account the payment of a letter of credit may be debited could prevent the bank making payment by obtaining a *Mareva* injunction[56] against the seller/beneficiary which would have the effect of freezing the funds held by the bank for the benefit of, and payable to, the beneficiary. The principles relating to the grant of the *Mareva* injunction affecting the payment under a letter of credit were discussed by the Court of Appeal in *Etablissement Esefka International Anstaff v Central Bank of Nigeria*.[57] The fundamental principle relating to the grant of a *Mareva* injunction remains that it is to be granted only where there is a danger of the money being taken out of the jurisdiction so that, if the plaintiff succeeded, he was not likely to get his money.[58] That a *Mareva* injunction may be imposed upon the fruits of the letter of credit was made authoritatively clear by the Court of Appeal in *Intraco Ltd v Notis Shipping Corp*[59] where Donaldson LJ stated:[60]

---

53 [1985] 1 NSWLR 545.

54 For instance his Honour followed *Discount Records Ltd v Barclays Bank Ltd* [1975] 1 WLR 315; and *Edward Owen Engineering Ltd v Barclays Bank International Ltd* [1978] QB 159.

55 *Ibid* at 554.

56 So named after *Mareva Compania Naviera SA v International Bulkcarriers SA* [1975] 2 Lloyd's Rep 509.

57 [1979] 1 Lloyd's Rep 455.

58 *Ibid* at 448, col 2; 449, cols 1 and 2.

59 [1981] 2 Lloyd's Rep 256.

60 *Ibid* at 258.

The learned judge went on to say that this did not prevent the court, in an appropriate case, from imposing a *Mareva* injunction upon the fruits of the letter of credit or guarantee. Again we agree. It is a natural corollary of the proposition that a letter of credit or bank guarantee is to be treated as cash that when the bank pays and cash is received by the beneficiary, it should be subject to the same restraints as any other of his cash assets.

Similarly, in *Z Ltd v A-Z and AA – LL*[61] the Court of Appeal held that the *Mareva* injunction was an established feature of English law which should be granted where it appeared likely that the plaintiff would recover judgment against the defendant for a certain or approximate sum, and there were reasons to believe that the defendant had assets within the jurisdiction to meet the judgment, wholly or in part, but might deal with them so that they were not available or traceable when judgment was given against him. It was further held that a *Mareva* injunction operated *in rem* and took effect from the moment it was pronounced on every asset of the defendant which it covered. If such assets included the defendant's bank account, upon the relevant bank receiving notice of the *Mareva* injunction, the defendant's instructions to the bank as its customer regarding that account were automatically revoked and the injunction made it unlawful for the bank to honour the defendant's cheques. Confirming the availability of a *Mareva* injunction to prevent payment under a letter of credit, Lord Denning said that: 'The injunction does not prevent payment under a letter of credit or under a bank guarantee, but it may apply to the proceeds as and when received by the defendant.'[62]

Nonetheless, it is thought that the courts will normally refuse to issue a *Mareva* injunction against a bank restraining it from making payment under a letter of credit unless, of course, the fraud exception is established.

CONCLUSION

Documentary credit is by far the most universally used method of payment in foreign trade transactions. Through the bank acting as an intermediary between the buyer and the seller, the competing interests between these two parties are balanced. The exporter achieves security of payment before parting with the goods and delivering the prescribed documents. Also, if a credit is confirmed, the exporter never needs to sue outside his own jurisdiction. He may also use the security of the credit to raise money from his own bank. The overseas buyer also has his interest secured: the negotiating bank ensures that the documents of title representing the goods and other related documents tendered by the seller comply strictly with the requirements of the purchaser before making payment under the credit to the seller. Furthermore, the importer may benefit from a letter of credit transaction in cases where the issuing bank provides liquidity without requiring immediate reimbursement.

Appropriately, the legal principles governing letters of credit as well as the provisions of the UCP 500 have maintained a balance between the respective rights and obligations

---

61   [1982] 1 QB 558.
62   *Ibid* at 574.

of the exporter and the overseas buyer, while promoting and protecting the interests of the issuing, advising and confirming banks.

Further, the courts have continuously promoted the sanctity of the principle of autonomy of letters of credit by admitting one only exception to such principle, namely the fraud exception. Even then, the courts have not been prepared to allow the operation of the fraud exception unless there was clear evidence of fraud which required not only the knowledge of the bank at the time a claim for payment was made, but also that the beneficiary had been privy to such fraud.

Erosion of the principle of autonomy, either by allowing a broader application of the fraud exception or by introducing other exceptions, for example, one based on unconscionable conduct which was referred to by Young J in *Hortico (Australia) Pty Ltd v Energy Equipment Co (Australia) Pty Ltd*[63] may adversely affect international trade in Australia and its traditional trading partners. In this respect, it is apt to quote Lord Denning LR in the *Power Curber International Ltd v National Bank of Kuwait SAK*:[64]

> If the court of any of the countries should interfere with the obligations of one of its banks (by ordering it not to pay under a letter of credit) it would strike at the very heart of that country's international trade. No foreign seller would supply goods to that country on letters of credit – because he could no longer be confident of being paid. No trader would accept a letter of credit issued by a bank of that country if it might be ordered by its courts not to pay.

TUTORIAL QUESTIONS

1 The Deflatable Toy Co, located in South Bend, Indiana (buyer) was the purchaser of a consignment of deflatable plastic toys, manufactured by Toyworld, Brisbane, Australia (seller). Payment for each shipment of toys was made by a confirmed irrevocable letter of credit (LC) issued in favour of Toyworld. In the final shipment to be made under the LC, Toyworld sent a draft to the confirming bank accompanied by a bill of lading showing the various goods shipped, including deflatable Pineapple Men. The confirming bank paid Toyworld, as the documentation conformed with that required by the LC.

In fact the bill of lading was inaccurate. Because of a manufacturing fault the deflatable Pineapple Men had been removed from the container after the manufacturer's customs broker had made up the shipping documents. According to the seller, it was too late to amend the shipping documents. It advised the purchaser of the change in the shipment and contended that the purchaser was fully aware that the bill of lading did not accurately reflect the contents of the container.

When the issuing bank advised Deflatable Toy Co that it had received the documents, the buyer informed the bank that it regarded the bill of lading as fraudulent and it requested that the LC should not be honoured. When the issuing

---

63 [1985] 1 NSWLR 545.
64 [1981] 1 WLR 1233 at 1241.

bank refused the buyer's request, the buyer applied for a court order to prevent payment under the LC.

Give judgment. Under what circumstances are banks entitled to refuse payment under the LC?

(Consult *Inflatable Toy Co Pty Ltd v State Bank of New South Wales* (1994) 34 NSWLR 243.)

2   An exporter of goods and the purchaser of those goods may adopt the letter of credit as the method of payment.

Discuss (i) the nature of this method of payment; (ii) the circumstances in which this method would be appropriately used; (iii) the manner in which this method of payment addresses an exporter's concerns in relation to (a) obtaining maximum security of payment for the goods supplied, and (b) minimising delay in payment for the goods supplied. Refer in your answer to relevant provisions of the ICC Uniform Customs and Practice for Documentary Credits and relevant case law.

3   The Forgan Smith Bank Ltd, an Australian bank, received a cable from an English company, Better Living Ltd, requesting that an irrevocable letter of credit be opened in favour of Furniture Unlimited and Co which have their Head Office in Brisbane, Queensland. Better Living Ltd instructed the Forgan Smith Bank that the letter of credit be for 'A$25,000 against commercial invoice, certificate of inspection, clean shipped bill of lading covering 500 computer desks made from Tasmanian oak'. The bill of lading presented to the Forgan Smith Bank by Furniture Unlimited referred to '500 Tasmanian desks'. The Forgan Smith Bank refused to pay on this letter of credit. Furniture Unlimited and Co sued the Forgan Smith Bank for failing to honour its letter of credit.

Was the bank correct in denying payment on this letter of credit? Discuss the scope of the doctrine of strict compliance. Refer in your answer to relevant cases.

4   Assume that a letter of credit opened by the buyer does not conform with the underlying contract. In what circumstances will such letter of credit bind the buyer and seller? Consult *Alan v El Nasr Import and Export* [1972] 2 QB 189.

FURTHER READING

Burnett, R, *The Law of International Business Transactions*, 1994, Annandale: The Federation Press, pp 132–87.

Roberts, JL, 'International Payments' in Wilde, KCDM and Islam, MR, *International Transactions: Trade and Investment, Law and Finance*, 1993, North Ryde: The Law Book Co, pp 74–84.

Schaffer, R, Earle, B and Agusti, F, *International Business Law and Its Environment*, 2nd edn, 1993, St Paul, Minneapolis: West Publishing Co, pp 182–209

Schmitthoff, CM, *The Law and Practice of International Trade*, 9th edn, 1990, London: Stevens, pp 379–452.

Van Houtte, H, *The Law of International Trade*, 1995, London: Sweet & Maxwell, pp 257–311.

ICC UNIFORM CUSTOMS AND PRACTICE FOR DOCUMENTARY CREDITS

1993 Revision in force as of 1 January 1994.

A   General provisions and definitions

Article 1 – Application of UCP

The Uniform Customs and Practice for Documentary Credits, 1993 Revision, ICC publication no 500, shall apply to all documentary credits (including to the extent to which they may be applicable, standby letter(s) of credit) where they are incorporated into the text of the credit. They are binding on all parties thereto, unless otherwise expressly stipulated in the credit.

Article 2 – Meaning of credit

For the purposes of these articles, the expressions 'documentary credit(s)' and 'standby letter(s) of credit' (hereinafter referred to as 'credit(s)'), mean any arrangement, however named or described, whereby a bank (the 'issuing bank') acting at the request and on the instructions of a customer (the 'applicant') or on its own behalf:

(i)   is to make a payment to or to the order of a third party (the 'beneficiary'), or is to accept and pay bills of exchange (draft(s)) drawn by the beneficiary; or

(ii)   authorises another bank to effect such payment, or to accept and pay such bills of exchange (draft(s)); or

(iii) authorises another bank to negotiate;

against stipulated document(s), provided that the terms and conditions of the credit are complied with.

For the purposes of these articles, branches of a bank in different countries are considered another bank.

Article 3 – Credits v contracts

(a)   Credits, by their nature, are separate transactions from the sales or other contract(s) on which they may be based and banks are in no way concerned with or bound by such contract(s), even if any reference whatsoever to such contract(s) is included in the credit. Consequently, the undertaking of a bank to pay, accept and pay draft(s) or negotiate and/or to fulfil any other obligation under the credit, is not subject to claims or defences by the applicant resulting from his relationships with the issuing bank or the beneficiary.

(b)   A beneficiary can in no case avail himself of the contractual relationships existing between the banks or between the applicant and the issuing bank.

Article 4 – Documents v goods/services/performances

In credit operations all parties concerned deal with documents, and not with goods, services and/or other performances to which the documents may relate.

Article 5 – Instructions to issue/amend credits

(a)   Instructions for the issuance of a credit, the credit itself, instructions for an amendment thereto, and the amendment itself, must be complete and precise.

In order to guard against confusion and misunderstanding, banks should discourage any attempt:

(i)   to include excessive detail in the credit or in any amendment thereto;

(ii) to give instructions to issue, advise or confirm a credit by reference to a credit previously issued (similar credit) where such previous credit has been subject to accepted amendment(s), and/or unaccepted amendment(s).

(b) All instructions for the issuance of a credit and the credit itself and, where applicable, all instructions for an amendment thereto and the amendment itself, must state precisely the document(s) against which payment, acceptance or negotiation is to be made.

B   Form and notification of credits

Article 6 – Revocable v irrevocable credits

(a) A credit may be either (i) revocable or (ii) irrevocable.

(b) The credit, therefore, should clearly indicate whether it is revocable or irrevocable.

(c) In the absence of such indication the credit shall be deemed to be irrevocable.

Article 7 – Advising bank's liability

(a) A credit may be advised to a beneficiary through another bank (the 'advising bank') without engagement on the part of the advising bank, but that bank, if it elects to advise the credit, shall take reasonable care to check the apparent authenticity of the credit which it advises. If the bank elects not to advise the credit, it must so inform the issuing bank without delay.

(b) If the advising bank cannot establish such apparent authenticity it must inform, without delay, the bank from which the instructions appear to have been received that it has been unable to establish the authenticity of the credit and if it elects nonetheless to advise the credit it must inform the beneficiary that it has not been able to establish the authenticity of the credit.

Article 8 – Revocation of a credit

(a) A revocable credit may be amended or cancelled by the issuing bank at any moment and without prior notice to the beneficiary.

(b) However, the issuing bank must:

(i)   reimburse another bank with which a revocable credit has been made available for sight payment, acceptance or negotiation – for any payment, acceptance or negotiation made by such bank – prior to receipt by it of notice of amendment or cancellation, against documents which appear on their face to be in compliance with the terms and conditions of the credit;

(ii) reimburse another bank with which a revocable credit has been made available for deferred payment, if such a bank has, prior to receipt by it of notice of amendment or cancellation, taken up documents which appear on their face to be in compliance with the terms and conditions of the credit.

Article 9 – Liability of issuing and confirming banks

(a) An irrevocable credit constitutes a definite undertaking of the issuing bank, provided that the stipulated documents are presented to the nominated bank or to the issuing bank and that the terms and conditions of the credit are complied with:

(i)   if the credit provides for sight payment – to pay at sight;

(ii) if the credit provides for deferred payment – to pay on the maturity date(s) determinable in accordance with the stipulations of the credit;

    (iii) if the credit provides for acceptance:

        (a) by the issuing bank – to accept draft(s) drawn by the beneficiary on the issuing bank and pay them at maturity; or

        (b) by another drawee bank – to accept and pay at maturity draft(s) drawn by the beneficiary on the issuing bank in the event the drawee bank stipulated in the credit does not accept draft(s) drawn on it, or to pay draft(s) accepted but not paid by such drawee bank at maturity;

    (iv) if the credit provides for negotiation – to pay without recourse to drawers and/or *bona fide* holders, draft(s) drawn by the beneficiary and/or document(s) presented under the credit. A credit should not be issued available by draft(s) on the applicant. If the credit nevertheless calls for draft(s) on the applicant, banks will consider such draft(s) as an additional document(s).

(b) A confirmation of an irrevocable credit by another bank ('the confirming bank') upon the authorisation or request of the issuing bank, constitutes a definite undertaking of the confirming bank, in addition to that of the issuing bank, provided that the stipulated documents are presented to the confirming bank or to any other nominated bank and that the terms and conditions of the credit are complied with:

    (i) if the credit provides for sight payment – to pay at sight;

    (ii) if the credit provides for deferred payment – to pay on the maturity date(s) determinable in accordance with the stipulations of the credit;

    (iii) if the credit provides for acceptance:

        (a) by the confirming bank – to accept draft(s) drawn by the beneficiary on the confirming bank and pay them at maturity; or

        (b) by another drawee bank – to accept and pay at maturity draft(s) drawn by the beneficiary on the confirming bank, in the event the drawee bank stipulated in the credit does not accept draft(s) drawn on it, or to pay draft(s) accepted but not paid by such drawee bank at maturity;

    (iv) if the credit provides for negotiation – to negotiate without recourse to drawers and/or *bona fide* holders, draft(s) drawn by the beneficiary and/or document(s) presented under the credit. A credit should not be issued available by draft(s) on the applicant. If the credit nevertheless calls for draft(s) on the applicant, banks will consider such draft(s) as an additional document(s).

(c) (i) If another bank is authorised or requested by the issuing bank to add its confirmation to the credit but is not prepared to do so, it must so inform the issuing bank without delay.

    (ii) Unless the issuing bank specifies otherwise in its authorisation or request to add confirmation, the advising bank may advise the credit to the beneficiary without adding its confirmation.

(d) (i) Except as otherwise provided by Article 48, an irrevocable credit can neither be amended nor cancelled without the agreement of the issuing bank, the confirming bank, if any, and the beneficiary.

    (ii) The issuing bank shall be irrevocably bound by an amendment(s) issued by it from the time of the issuance of such amendment(s). A confirming bank may, however, choose to advise an amendment to the beneficiary without extending its confirmation and if so must inform the issuing bank and the beneficiary without delay.

(iii) The terms of the original credit (or a credit incorporating previously accepted amendment(s)) will remain in force for the beneficiary until the beneficiary communicates his acceptance of the amendment to the bank that advised such amendment. The beneficiary should give notification of acceptance or rejection of amendment(s). If the beneficiary fails to give such notification, the tender of documents to the nominated bank or issuing bank, that conform to the credit and to not yet accepted amendment(s), will be deemed to be notification of acceptance by the beneficiary of such amendment(s) and as of that moment the credit will be amended.

(iv) Partial acceptance of amendments contained in one and the same advice of amendment is not allowed and consequently will not be given any effect.

Article 10 – Types of credit

(a) All credits must clearly indicate whether they are available by sight payment, by deferred payment, by acceptance or by negotiation.

(b) (i) Unless the credit stipulates that it is available only with the issuing bank, all credits must nominate the bank (the 'nominated bank') which is authorised to pay, to incur a deferred payment undertaking, to accept draft(s) or to negotiate. In a freely negotiable credit, any bank is a nominated bank.

Presentation of documents must be made to the issuing bank or the confirming bank, if any, or any other nominated bank.

(ii) Negotiation means the giving of value for draft(s) and/or document(s) by the bank authorised to negotiate. Mere examination of the documents without giving of value does not constitute a negotiation.

(c) Unless the nominated bank is the confirming bank, nomination by the issuing bank does not constitute any undertaking by the nominated bank to pay, to incur a deferred payment undertaking, to accept draft(s), or to negotiate. Except where expressly agreed to by the nominated bank and so communicated to the beneficiary, the nominated bank's receipt of and/or examination and/or forwarding of the documents does not make that bank liable to pay, to incur a deferred payment undertaking, to accept draft(s), or to negotiate.

(d) By nominating another bank, or by allowing for negotiation by any bank, or by authorising or requesting another bank to add its confirmation, the issuing bank authorises such bank to pay, accept draft(s) or negotiate as the case may be, against documents which appear on their face to be in compliance with the terms and conditions of the credit and undertakes to reimburse such bank in accordance with the provisions of these articles.

Article 11 – Teletransmitted and pre-advised credits

(a) (i) When an issuing bank instructs an advising bank by an authenticated teletransmission to advise a credit or an amendment to a credit, the teletransmission will be deemed to be the operative credit instrument or the operative amendment, and no mail confirmation should be sent. Should a mail confirmation nevertheless be sent, it will have no effect and the advising bank will have no obligation to check such mail confirmation against the operative credit instrument or the operative amendment received by teletransmission.

(ii) If the teletransmission states 'full details to follow' (or words of similar effect) or states that the mail confirmation is to be the operative credit instrument or the operative amendment, then the teletransmission will not be deemed to be the operative credit instrument or the operative amendment. The issuing bank must forward the operative credit instrument or the operative amendment to such advising bank without delay.

(b) If a bank uses the services of an advising bank to have the credit advised to the beneficiary, it must also use the services of the same bank for advising an amendment(s).

(c) A preliminary advice of the issuance or amendment of an irrevocable credit (pre-advice), shall only be given by an issuing bank if such bank is prepared to issue the operative credit instrument or the operative amendment thereto. Unless otherwise stated in such preliminary advice by the issuing bank, an issuing bank having given such pre-advice shall be irrevocably committed to issue or amend the credit, in terms not inconsistent with the pre-advice, without delay.

Article 12 – Incomplete or unclear instructions

If incomplete or unclear instructions are received to advise, confirm or amend a credit, the bank requested to act on such instructions may give preliminary notification to the beneficiary for information only and without responsibility. This preliminary notification should state clearly that the notification is provided for information only and without the responsibility of the advising bank. In any event, the advising bank must inform the issuing bank of the action taken and request it to provide the necessary information.

The issuing bank must provide the necessary information without delay. The credit will be advised, confirmed or amended, only when complete and clear instructions have been received and if the advising bank is then prepared to act on the instructions.

C   Liabilities and responsibilities

Article 13 – Standard for examination of documents

(a) Banks must examine all documents stipulated in the credit with reasonable care, to ascertain whether or not they appear, on their face, to be in compliance with the terms and conditions of the credit. Compliance of the stipulated documents on their face with the terms and conditions of the credit, shall be determined by international standard banking practice as reflected in these articles. Documents which appear on their face to be inconsistent with one another will be considered as not appearing on their face to be in compliance with the terms and conditions of the credit.

Documents not stipulated in the credit will not be examined by banks. If they receive such documents, they shall return them to the presenter or pass them on without responsibility.

(b) The issuing bank, the confirming bank, if any, or a nominated bank acting on their behalf, shall each have a reasonable time, not to exceed seven banking days following the day of receipt of the documents, to examine the documents and determine whether to take up or refuse the documents and to inform the party from which it received the documents accordingly.

(c) If a credit contains conditions without stating the document(s) to be presented in compliance therewith, banks will deem such conditions as not stated and will disregard them.

Article 14 – Discrepant documents and notice

(a) When the issuing bank authorises another bank to pay, incur a deferred payment undertaking, accept draft(s), or negotiate against documents which appear on their face to be in compliance with the terms and conditions of the credit, the issuing bank and the confirming bank, if any, are bound:

    (i) to reimburse the nominated bank which has paid, incurred a deferred payment undertaking, accepted draft(s), or negotiated,

    (ii) to take up the documents.

(b) Upon receipt of the documents the issuing bank and/or confirming bank, if any, or a nominated bank acting on their behalf, must determine on the basis of the documents alone whether or not they appear on their face to be in compliance with the terms and conditions of the credit. If the documents appear on their face not to be in compliance with the terms and conditions of the credit, such banks may refuse to take up the documents.

(c) If the issuing bank determines that the documents appear on their face not to be in compliance with the terms and conditions of the credit, it may in its sole judgment approach the applicant for a waiver of the discrepancy(ies). This does not, however, extend the period mentioned in sub-Article 13(b).

(d) (i) If the issuing bank and/or confirming bank, if any, or a nominated bank acting on their behalf, decides to refuse the documents, it must give notice to that effect by telecommunication or, if that is not possible, by other expeditious means, without delay but no later than the close of the seventh banking day following the day of receipt of the documents. Such notice shall be given to the bank from which it received the documents, or to the beneficiary, if it received the documents directly from him.

    (ii) Such notice must state all discrepancies in respect of which the bank refuses the documents and must also state whether it is holding the documents at the disposal of, or is returning them to, the presenter.

    (iii) The issuing bank and/or confirming bank, if any, shall then be entitled to claim from the remitting bank refund, with interest, of any reimbursement which has been made to that bank.

(e) If the issuing bank and/or confirming bank, if any, fails to act in accordance with the provisions of this article and/or fails to hold the documents at the disposal of, or return them to the presenter, the issuing bank and/or confirming bank, if any, shall be precluded from claiming that the documents are not in compliance with the terms and conditions of the credit.

(f) If the remitting bank draws the attention of the issuing bank and/or confirming bank, if any, to any discrepancy(ies) in the document(s) or advises such banks that it has paid, incurred a deferred payment undertaking, accepted draft(s) or negotiated under reserve or against an indemnity in respect of such discrepancy(ies), the issuing bank and/or confirming bank, if any, shall not be thereby relieved from any of their obligations under any provision of this article. Such reserve or indemnity concerns only the relations between the remitting bank and the party towards whom the reserve was made, or from whom, or on whose behalf, the indemnity was obtained.

Article 15 – Disclaimer on effectiveness of documents

Banks assume no liability or responsibility for the form, sufficiency, accuracy, genuineness, falsification or legal effect of any document(s), or for the general and/or particular conditions stipulated in the document(s) or superimposed thereon; nor do they assume any liability or responsibility for the description, quantity, weight, quality, condition, packing, delivery, value or existence of the goods represented by any document(s), or for the good faith or acts and/or omissions, solvency, performance or standing of the consignors, the carriers, the forwarders, the consignees or the insurers of the goods, or any other person whomsoever.

Article 16 – Disclaimer on the transmission of messages

Banks assume no liability or responsibility for the consequences arising out of delay and/or loss in transit of any message(s), letter(s) or document(s), or for delay, mutilation or other error(s) arising in the transmission of any telecommunication. Banks assume no liability or responsibility for errors in translation and/or interpretation of technical terms, and reserve the right to transmit credit terms without translating them.

Article 17 – Force majeure

Banks assume no liability or responsibility for the consequences arising out of the interruption of their business by Acts of God, riots, civil commotions, insurrections, wars or any other causes beyond their control, or by any strikes or lockouts. Unless specifically authorised, banks will not, upon resumption of their business, pay, incur a deferred payment undertaking, accept draft(s) or negotiate under credits which expired during such interruption of their business.

Article 18 – Disclaimer for acts of an instructed party

(a) Banks utilising the services of another bank or other banks for the purpose of giving effect to the instructions of the applicant do so for the account and at the risk of such applicant.

(b) Banks assume no liability or responsibility should the instructions they transmit not be carried out, even if they have themselves taken the initiative in the choice of such other bank(s).

(c) (i) A party instructing another party to perform services is liable for any charges, including commissions, fees, costs or expenses incurred by the instructed party in connection with its instructions.

    (ii) Where a credit stipulates that such charges are for the account of a party other than the instructing party, and charges cannot be collected, the instructing party remains ultimately liable for the payment thereof.

(d) The applicant shall be bound by and liable to indemnify the banks against all obligations and responsibilities imposed by foreign laws and usages.

Article 19 – Bank-to-bank reimbursement arrangements

(a) If an issuing bank intends that the reimbursement to which a paying, accepting or negotiating bank is entitled, shall be obtained by such bank (the 'claiming bank'), claiming on another party (the 'reimbursing bank'), it shall provide such reimbursing bank in good time with the proper instructions or authorisation to honour such reimbursement claims.

(b) Issuing banks shall not require a claiming bank to supply a certificate of compliance with the terms and conditions of the credit to the reimbursing bank.

(c) An issuing bank shall not be relieved from any of its obligations to provide reimbursement if and when reimbursement is not received by the claiming bank from the reimbursing bank.

(d) The issuing bank shall be responsible to the claiming bank for any loss of interest if reimbursement is not provided by the reimbursing bank on first demand, or as otherwise specified in the credit, or mutually agreed, as the case may be.

(e) The reimbursing bank's charges should be for the account of the issuing bank. However, in cases where the charges are for the account of another party, it is the responsibility of the issuing bank to so indicate in the original credit and in the reimbursement authorisation. In cases where the reimbursing bank's charges are for the account of another party they shall be collected from the claiming bank when the credit is drawn under. In cases where the credit is not drawn under, the reimbursing bank's charges remain the obligation of the issuing bank.

D Documents

Article 20 – Ambiguity as to the issuers of documents

(a) Terms such as 'first class', 'well-known', 'qualified', 'independent', 'official', 'competent', 'local' and the like, shall not be used to describe the issuers of any document(s) to be presented under a credit. If such terms are incorporated in the credit, banks will accept the relative document(s) as presented, provided that it appears on its face to be in compliance with the other terms and conditions of the credit and not to have been issued by the beneficiary.

(b) Unless otherwise stipulated in the credit, banks will also accept as an original document(s), a document(s) produced or appearing to have been produced:

(i)   by reprographic, automated or computerised systems;

(ii) as carbon copies;

provided that it is marked as original and, where necessary, appears to be signed.

A document may be signed by handwriting, by facsimile signature, by perforated signature, by stamp, by symbol, or by any other mechanical or electronic method of authentication.

(c) (i)   Unless otherwise stipulated in the credit, banks will accept as a copy(ies), a document(s) either labelled copy or not marked as an original – a copy(ies) need not be signed.

(ii) Credits that require multiple document(s) such as 'duplicate', 'two-fold', 'two copies' and the like, will be satisfied by the presentation of one original and the remaining number in copies except where the document itself indicates otherwise.

(d) Unless otherwise stipulated in the credit, a condition under a credit calling for a document to be authenticated, validated, legalised, visaed, certified or indicating a similar requirement, will be satisfied by any signature, mark, stamp or label on such document that on its face appears to satisfy the above condition.

Article 21 – Unspecified issuers or contents of documents

When documents other than transport documents, insurance documents and commercial invoices are called for, the credit should stipulate by whom such documents are to be issued and their wording or data content. If the credit does not so stipulate, banks will accept such documents as presented, provided that their data content is not inconsistent with any other stipulated document presented.

Article 22 – Issuance date of documents v credit date

Unless otherwise stipulated in the credit, banks will accept a document bearing a date of issuance prior to that of the credit, subject to such document being presented within the time limits set out in the credit and in these articles.

Article 23 – Marine/ocean bill of lading

(a) If a credit calls for a bill of lading covering a port to port shipment, banks will, unless otherwise stipulated in the credit, accept a document, however named, which:

  (i) appears on its face to indicate the name of the carrier and to have been signed or otherwise authenticated by:

  • the carrier or a named agent for or on behalf of the carrier; or

  • the master or a named agent for or on behalf of the master.

  Any signature or authentication of the carrier or master must be identified as carrier or master, as the case may be. An agent signing or authenticating for the carrier or master must also indicate the name and the capacity of the party, ie carrier or master, on whose behalf that agent is acting; and

  (ii) indicates that the goods have been loaded on board, or shipped on a named vessel.

  Loading on board or shipment on a named vessel may be indicated by pre-printed wording on the bill of lading that the goods have been loaded on board a named vessel or shipped on a named vessel, in which case the date of issuance on, the bill of lading will be deemed to be the date of loading on board and the date of shipment.

  In all other cases loading on board a named vessel must be evidenced by a notation on the bill of lading which gives the date on which the goods have been loaded on board, in which case the date of the on board notation will be deemed to be the date of shipment.

  If the bill of lading contains the indication 'intended vessel', or similar qualification in relation to the vessel, loading on board a named vessel must be evidenced by an on board notation on the bill of lading which, in addition to the date on which the goods have been loaded on board, also includes the name of the vessel on which the goods have been loaded, even if they have been loaded on the vessel named as the 'intended vessel'.

  If the bill of lading indicates a place of receipt or taking in charge different from the port of loading, the on board notation must also include the port of loading stipulated in the credit and the name of the vessel on which the goods have been loaded, even if they have been loaded on the vessel named in the bill of lading. This provision also applies whenever loading on board the vessel is indicated by pre-printed wording on the bill of lading; and

  (iii) indicates the port of loading and the port of discharge stipulated in the credit, notwithstanding that it:

  • indicates a place of taking in charge different from the port of loading, and/or a place of final destination different from the port of discharge; and/or

- contains the indication 'intended' or similar qualification in relation to the port of loading and/or port of discharge, as long as the document also states the ports of loading and/or discharge stipulated in the credit; and

(iv) consists of a sole original bill of lading or, if issued in more than one original, the full set as so issued; and

(v) appears to contain all of the terms and conditions of carriage, or some of such terms and conditions by reference to a source or document other than the bill of lading (short form/blank back bill of lading); banks will not examine the contents of such terms and conditions; and

(vi) contains no indication that it is subject to a charterparty and/or no indication that the carrying vessel is propelled by sail only; and

(vii) in all other respects meets the stipulations of the credit.

(b) For the purpose of this article, trans-shipment means unloading and reloading from one vessel to another vessel during the course of ocean carriage from the port of loading to the port of discharge stipulated in the credit.

(c) Unless trans-shipment is prohibited by the terms of the credit, banks will accept a bill of lading which indicates that the goods will be trans-shipped, provided that the entire ocean carriage is covered by one and the same bill of lading.

(d) Even if the credit prohibits trans-shipment, banks will accept a bill of lading which:

- indicates that trans-shipment will take place as long as the relevant cargo is shipped in container(s), trailer(s) and/or 'Lash' barge(s) as evidenced by the bill of lading, provided that the entire ocean carriage is covered by one and the same bill of lading; and/or

- incorporates clauses stating that the carrier reserves the right to trans-ship.

Article 24 – Non-negotiable sea waybill

(a) If a credit calls for a non-negotiable sea waybill covering a port to port shipment, banks will, unless otherwise stipulated in the credit, accept a document, however named, which:

(i) appears on its face to indicate the name of the carrier and to have been signed or otherwise authenticated by:

- the carrier or a named agent for or on behalf of the carrier; or

- the master or a named agent for or on behalf of the master;

Any signature or authentication of the carrier or master must be identified as carrier or master, as the case may be. An agent signing or authenticating for the carrier or master must also indicate the name and the capacity of the party, ie carrier or master, on whose behalf that agent is acting, and

(ii) indicates that the goods have been loaded on board, or shipped on a named vessel.

Loading on board or shipment on a named vessel may be indicated by pre-printed wording on the non-negotiable sea waybill that the goods have been loaded on board a named vessel or shipped on a named vessel, in which case the date of issuance of the non-negotiable sea waybill will be deemed to be the date of loading on board and the date of shipment.

In all other cases loading on board a named vessel must be evidenced by a notation on the non-negotiable sea waybill which gives the date on which the goods have been loaded on board, in which case the date of the on board notation will be deemed to be the date of shipment.

If the non-negotiable sea waybill contains the indication 'intended vessel', or similar qualification in relation to the vessel, loading on board a named vessel must be evidenced by an on board notation on the non-negotiable sea waybill which, in addition to the date on which the goods have been loaded on board, includes the name of the vessel on which the goods have been loaded, even if they have been loaded on the vessel named as the 'intended vessel'.

If the non-negotiable sea waybill indicates a place of receipt or taking in charge different from the port of loading, the on board notation must also include the port of loading stipulated in the credit and the name of the vessel on which the goods have been loaded, even if they have been loaded on a vessel named in the non-negotiable sea waybill. This provision also applies whenever loading on board the vessel is indicated by pre-printed wording on the non-negotiable sea waybill; and

(iii) indicates the port of loading and the port of discharge stipulated in the credit, notwithstanding that it:

- indicates a place of taking charge different from the port of loading, and/or a place of final destination different from the port of discharge; and/or

- contains the indication 'intended' or similar qualification in relation to the port of loading and/or port of discharge, as long as the document also states the ports of loading and/or discharge stipulated in the credit; and

(iv) consists of a sole original non-negotiable sea waybill, or if issued in more than one original, the full set as so issued; and

(v) appears to contain all of the terms and conditions of carriage, or some of such terms and conditions by reference to a source or document other than the non-negotiable sea waybill (short form/blank back non-negotiable sea waybill); banks will not examine the contents of such terms and conditions; and

(vi) contains no indication that it is subject to a charter party and/or no indication that the carrying vessel is propelled by sail only; and

(vii) in all other respects meets the stipulations of the credit.

(b) For the purpose of this article, trans-shipment means unloading and reloading from one vessel to another vessel during the course of ocean carriage from the port of loading to the port of discharge stipulated in the credit.

(c) Unless trans-shipment is prohibited by the terms of the credit, banks will accept a non-negotiable sea waybill which indicates that the goods will be trans-shipped, provided that the entire ocean carriage is covered by one and the same non-negotiable sea waybill.

(d) Even if the credit prohibits trans-shipment, banks will accept a non-negotiable sea waybill which:

(i) indicates that trans-shipment will take place as long as the relevant cargo is shipped in container(s), trailer(s) and/or 'Lash' barge(s) as evidenced by the non-negotiable sea waybill, provided that the entire ocean carriage is covered by one and the same non-negotiable sea waybill; and/or

(ii) incorporates clauses stating that the carrier reserves the right to trans-ship.

Article 25 – Charterparty bill of lading

(a) If a credit calls for or permits a charterparty bill of lading, banks will, unless otherwise stipulated in the credit, accept a document, however named, which:

    (i) contains any indication that it is subject to a charterparty; and

    (ii) appears on its face to have been signed or otherwise authenticated by:

        • the master or a named agent for or on behalf of the master; or

        • the owner or a named agent for or on behalf of the owner.

    Any signature or authentication of the master or owner must be identified as master or owner as the case may be. An agent signing or authenticating for the master or owner must also indicate the name and the capacity of the party, ie master or owner, on whose behalf that agent is acting; and

    (iii) does or does not indicate the name of the carrier; and

    (iv) indicates that the goods have been loaded on board or shipped on a named vessel.

    Loading on board or shipment on a named vessel may be indicated by pre-printed wording on the bill of lading that the goods have been loaded on board a named vessel or shipped on a named vessel, in which case the date of issuance of the bill of lading will be deemed to be the date of loading on board and the date of shipment.

    In all other cases loading on board a named vessel must be evidenced by a notation on the bill of lading which gives the date on which the goods have been loaded on board, in which case the date of the on board notation will be deemed to be the date of shipment; and

    (v) indicates the port of loading and the port of discharge stipulated in the credit; and

    (vi) consists of a sole original bill of lading or, if issued in more than one original, the full set as so issued; and

    (vii) contains no indication that the carrying vessel is propelled by sail only; and

    (viii) in all other respects meets the stipulations of the credit.

(b) Even if the credit requires the presentation of a charterparty contract in connection with a charterparty bill of lading, banks will not examine such charterparty contract, but will pass it on without responsibility on their part.

Article 26 – Multi-modal transport document

(a) If a credit calls for a transport document covering at least two different modes of transport (multi-modal transport), banks will, unless otherwise stipulated in the credit, accept a document, however named, which:

    (i) appears on its face to indicate the name of the carrier or multi-modal transport operator and to have been signed or otherwise authenticated by:

        • the carrier or multi-modal transport operator or a named agent for or on behalf of the carrier or multi-modal transport operator; or

        • the master or a named agent for or on behalf of the master.

    Any signature or authentication of the carrier, multi-modal transport operator or master must be identified as carrier, multi-modal transport operator or master, as the case may be. An agent signing or authenticating for the carrier, multi-modal transport operator or master must also indicate the name and the capacity of the party, ie carrier, multi-modal transport operator or master, on whose behalf that agent is acting; and

(ii) indicates that the goods have been dispatched, taken in charge or loaded on board.

Dispatch, taking in charge or loading on board may be indicated by wording to that effect on the multi-modal transport document and the date of issuance will be deemed to be the date of dispatch, taking in charge or loading on board and the date of shipment. However, if the document indicates, by stamp or otherwise, a date of dispatch, taking in charge or loading on board, such date will be deemed to be the date of shipment; and

(iii) • indicates the place of taking in charge stipulated in the credit which may be different from the port, airport or place of loading, and the place of final destination stipulated in the credit which may be different from the port, airport or place of discharge; and/or

• contains the indication 'intended' or similar qualification in relation to the vessel and/or port of loading and/or port of discharge; and

(iv) consists of a sole original multi-modal transport document or, if issued in more than one original, the full set as so issued; and

(v) appears to contain all of the terms and conditions of carriage, or some of such terms and conditions by reference to a source or document other than the multi-modal transport document (short form/blank back multi-modal transport document); banks will not examine the contents of such terms and conditions; and

(vi) contains no indication that it is subject to a charterparty and/or no indication that the carrying vessel is propelled by sail only; and

(vii) in all other respects meets the stipulations of the credit.

(b) Even if the credit prohibits trans-shipment, banks will accept a multi-modal transport document which indicates that trans-shipment will or may take place, provided that the entire carriage is covered by one and the same multi-modal transport document.

Article 27 – Air transport document

(a) If a credit calls for an air transport document, banks will, unless otherwise stipulated in the credit, accept a document, however named, which:

(i) appears on its face to indicate the name of the carrier and to have been signed or otherwise authenticated by:

• the carrier; or

• a named agent for or on behalf of the carrier.

Any signature or authentication of the carrier must be identified as carrier. An agent signing or authenticating for the carrier must also indicate the name and the capacity of the party, ie carrier, on whose behalf that agent is acting; and

(ii) indicates that the goods have been accepted for carriage; and

(iii) where the credit calls for an actual date of dispatch, indicates a specific notation of such date, the date of dispatch so indicated on the air transport document will be deemed to be the date of shipment.

For the purpose of this article, the information appearing in the box on the air transport document (marked 'For Carrier Use Only' or similar expression) relative to the flight number and date will not be considered as a specific notation of such date of dispatch.

In all other cases, the date of issuance of the air transport document will be deemed to be the date of shipment; and

(iv) indicates the airport of departure and the airport of destination stipulated in the credit; and

(v) appears to be the original for consignor/shipper even if the credit stipulates a full set of originals, or similar expressions; and

(vi) appears to contain all of the terms and conditions of carriage, or some of such terms and conditions, by reference to a source or document other than the air transport document; banks will not examine the contents of such terms and conditions; and

(vii) in all other respects meets the stipulations of the credit.

(b) For the purpose of this article, trans-shipment means unloading and reloading from one aircraft to another aircraft during the course of carriage from the airport of departure to the airport of destination stipulated in the credit.

(c) Even if the credit prohibits trans-shipment, banks will accept an air transport document which indicates that trans-shipment will or may take place, provided that the entire carriage is covered by one and the same air transport document.

Article 28 – Road, rail or inland waterway transport documents

(a) If a credit calls for a road, rail, or inland waterway transport document, banks will, unless otherwise stipulated in the credit, accept a document of the type called for, however named, which:

(i) appears on its face to indicate the name of the carrier and to have been signed or otherwise authenticated by the carrier or a named agent for or on behalf of the carrier and/or to bear a reception stamp or other indication of receipt by the carrier or a named agent for or on behalf of the carrier.

Any signature, authentication, reception stamp or other indication of receipt of the carrier, must be identified on its face as that of the carrier. An agent signing or authenticating for the carrier, must also indicate the name and the capacity of the party, ie carrier, on whose behalf that agent is acting; and

(ii) indicates that the goods have been received for shipment, dispatch or carriage or wording to this effect. The date of issuance will be deemed to be the date of shipment unless the transport document contains a reception stamp, in which case the date of the reception stamp will be deemed to be the date of shipment; and

(iii) indicates the place of shipment and the place of destination stipulated in the credit; and

(iv) in all other respects meets the stipulations of the credit.

(b) In the absence of any indication on the transport document as to the numbers issued, banks will accept the transport document(s) presented as constituting a full set. banks will accept as original(s) the transport document(s) whether marked as original(s) or not.

(c) For the purpose of this article, trans-shipment means unloading and reloading from one means of conveyance to another means of conveyance, in different modes of transport, during the course of carriage from the place of shipment to the place of destination stipulated in the credit.

(d) Even if the credit prohibits trans-shipment, banks will accept a road, rail, or inland waterway transport document which indicates that trans-shipment will or may take place, provided that the entire carriage is covered by one and the same transport document and within the same mode of transport.

Article 29 – Courier and post receipts

(a) If a credit calls for a post receipt or certificate of posting, banks will, unless otherwise stipulated in the credit, accept a post receipt or certificate of posting which:

  (i) appears on its face to have been stamped or otherwise authenticated and dated in the place from which the credit stipulates the goods are to be shipped or dispatched and such date will be deemed to be the date of shipment or dispatch; and

  (ii) in all other respects meets the stipulations of the credit.

(b) If a credit calls for a document issued by a courier or expedited delivery service evidencing receipt of the goods for delivery, banks will, unless otherwise stipulated in the credit, accept a document, however named, which:

  (i) appears on its face to indicate the name of the courier/service, and to have been stamped, signed or otherwise authenticated by such named courier/service (unless the credit specifically calls for a document issued by a named courier/service, banks will accept a document issued by any courier/service); and

  (ii) indicates a date of pick-up or of receipt or wording to this effect, such date being deemed to be the date of shipment or dispatch; and

  (iii) in all other respects meets the stipulations of the credit.

Article 30 – Transport documents issued by freight forwarders

Unless otherwise authorised in the credit, banks will only accept a transport document issued by a freight forwarder if it appears on its face to indicate:

(i) the name of the freight forwarder as a carrier or multi-modal transport operator and to have been signed or otherwise authenticated by the freight forwarder as carrier or multi-modal transport operator; or

(ii) the name of the carrier or multi-modal transport operator and to have been signed or otherwise authenticated by the freight forwarder as a named agent for or on behalf of the carrier or multi-modal transport operator.

Article 31 – 'On deck', 'shipper's load and count', name of consignor

Unless otherwise stipulated in the credit, banks will accept a transport document which:

(i) does not indicate, in the case of carriage by sea or by more than one means of conveyance including carriage by sea, that the goods are or will be loaded on deck. Nevertheless, banks will accept a transport document which contains a provision that the goods may be carried on deck, provided that it does not specifically state that they are or will be loaded on deck; and/or

(ii) bears a clause on the face thereof such as 'shipper's load and count' or 'said by shipper to contain' or words of similar effect; and/or

(iii) indicates as the consignor of the goods a party other than the beneficiary of the credit.

Article 32 – Clean transport documents

(a) A clean transport document is one which bears no clause or notation which expressly declares a defective condition of the goods and/or the packaging.

(b) Banks will not accept transport documents bearing such clauses or notations unless the credit expressly stipulates the clauses or notations which may be accepted.

(c) Banks will regard a requirement in a credit for a transport document to bear the clause 'clean on board' as complied with if such transport document meets the requirements of this article and of Articles 23, 24, 25, 26, 27, 28 or 30.

Article 33 – Freight payable/prepaid transport documents

(a) Unless otherwise stipulated in the credit, or inconsistent with any of the documents presented under the credit, banks will accept transport documents stating that freight or transportation charges (hereafter referred to as 'freight') have still to be paid.

(b) If a credit stipulates that the transport document has to indicate that freight has been paid or prepaid, banks will accept a transport document on which words clearly indicating payment or prepayment of freight appear by stamp or otherwise, or on which payment or prepayment of freight is indicated by other means. If the credit requires courier charges to be paid or prepaid banks will also accept a transport document issued by a courier or expedited delivery service evidencing that courier charges are for the account of a party other than the consignee.

(c) The words 'freight prepayable' or 'freight to be prepaid' or words of similar effect, if appearing on transport documents, will not be accepted as constituting evidence of the payment of freight.

(d) Banks will accept transport documents bearing reference by stamp or otherwise to costs additional to the freight, such as costs of, or disbursements incurred in connection with, loading, unloading or similar operations, unless the conditions of the credit specifically prohibit such reference.

Article 34 – Insurance documents

(a) Insurance documents must appear on their face to be issued and signed by insurance companies or underwriters or their agents.

(b) If the insurance document indicates that it has been issued in more than one original, all the originals must be presented unless otherwise authorised in the credit.

(c) Cover notes issued by brokers will not be accepted, unless specifically authorised in the credit.

(d) Unless otherwise stipulated in the credit, banks will accept an insurance certificate or a declaration under an open cover pre-signed by insurance companies or underwriters or their agents. If a credit specifically calls for an insurance certificate or a declaration under an open cover, banks will accept, in lieu thereof, an insurance policy.

(e) Unless otherwise stipulated in the credit, or unless it appears from the insurance document that the cover is effective at the latest from the date of loading on board or dispatch or taking in charge of the goods, banks will not accept an insurance document which bears a date of issuance later than the date of loading on board or dispatch or taking in charge as indicated in such transport document.

(f) (i) Unless otherwise stipulated in the credit, the insurance document must be expressed in the same currency as the credit.

(ii) Unless otherwise stipulated in the credit, the minimum amount for which the insurance document must indicate the insurance cover to have been effected is the CIF (cost, insurance and freight (… 'named port of destination')) or CIP (carriage and insurance paid to (… 'named place of destination')) value of the goods, as the case may be, plus 10%, but only when the CIF or CIP value can be determined from the documents on their face. Otherwise, banks will accept as such minimum amount 110% of the amount for which payment, acceptance or negotiation is requested under the credit, or 110% of the gross amount of the invoice, whichever is the greater.

Article 35 – Type of insurance cover

(a) Credits should stipulate the type of insurance required and, if any, the additional risks which are to be covered. Imprecise terms such as 'usual risks' or 'customary risks' shall not be used; if they are used, banks will accept insurance documents as presented, without responsibility for any risks not being covered.

(b) Failing specific stipulations in the credit, banks will accept insurance documents as presented, without responsibility for any risks not being covered.

(c) Unless otherwise stipulated in the credit, banks will accept an insurance document which indicates that the cover is subject to a franchise or an excess (deductible).

Article 36 – All risks insurance cover

Where a credit stipulates 'insurance against all risks', banks will accept an insurance document which contains any 'all risks' notation or clause, whether or not bearing the heading 'all risks', even if the insurance document indicates that certain risks are excluded, without responsibility for any risk(s) not being covered.

Article 37 – Commercial invoices

(a) Unless otherwise stipulated in the credit, commercial invoices;

(i) must appear on their face to be issued by the beneficiary named in the credit (except as provided in Article 48); and

(ii) must be made out in the name of the applicant (except as provided in sub-Article 48(h)); and

(iii) need not be signed.

(b) Unless otherwise stipulated in the credit, banks may refuse commercial invoices issued for amounts in excess of the amount permitted by the credit. Nevertheless, if a bank authorised to pay, incur a deferred payment undertaking, accept draft(s), or negotiate under a credit accepts such invoices, its decision will be binding upon all parties, provided that such bank has not paid, incurred a deferred payment undertaking, accepted draft(s) or negotiated for an amount in excess of that permitted by the credit.

(c) The description of the goods in the commercial invoice must correspond with the description in the credit. In all other documents, the goods may be described in general terms not inconsistent with the description of the goods in the credit.

Article 38 – Other documents

If a credit calls for an attestation or certification of weight in the case of transport other than by sea, banks will accept a weight stamp or declaration of weight which appears to have been superimposed on the transport document by the carrier or his agent unless the credit specifically stipulates that the attestation or certification of weight must be by means of a separate document.

E   Miscellaneous provisions

Article 39 – Allowances in credit amount, quantity and unit price

(a) The words 'about', 'approximately', 'circa' or similar expressions used in connection with the amount of the credit or the quantity or the unit price stated in the credit are to be construed as allowing a difference not to exceed 10% more or 10% less than the amount or the quantity or the unit price to which they refer.

(b) Unless a credit stipulates that the quantity of the goods specified must not be exceeded or reduced, a tolerance of 5% more or 5% less will be permissible, always provided that the amount of the drawings does not exceed the amount of the credit. This tolerance does not apply when the credit stipulates the quantity in terms of a stated number of packing units or individual items.

(c) Unless a credit which prohibits partial shipments stipulates otherwise, or unless sub-Article (b) above is applicable, a tolerance of 5% less in the amount of the drawing will be permissible, provided that if the credit stipulates the quantity of the goods, such quantity of goods is shipped in full, and if the credit stipulates a unit price, such price is not reduced. This provision does not apply when expressions referred to in sub-Article (a) above are used in the credit.

Article 40 – Partial shipments / drawings

(a) Partial drawings and/or shipments are allowed, unless the credit stipulates otherwise.

(b) Transport documents which appear on their face to indicate that shipment has been made on the same means of conveyance and for the same journey, provided they indicate the same destination, will not be regarded as covering partial shipments, even if the transport documents indicate different dates of shipment and/or different ports of loading, places of taking in charge, or dispatch.

(c) Shipments made by post or by courier will not be regarded as partial shipments if the post receipts or certificates of posting or courier's receipts or dispatch notes appear to have been stamped, signed or otherwise authenticated in the place from which the credit stipulates the goods are to be dispatched, and on the same date.

Article 41 – Instalment shipments / drawings

If drawings and/or shipments by instalments within given periods are stipulated in the credit and any instalment is not drawn and/or shipped within the period allowed for that instalment, the credit ceases to be available for that and any subsequent instalments, unless otherwise stipulated in the credit.

Article 42 – Expiry date and place for presentation of documents

(a) All credits must stipulate an expiry date and a place for presentation of documents for payment, acceptance, or with the exception of freely negotiable credits, a place for presentation of documents for negotiation. An expiry date stipulated for payment, acceptance or negotiation will be construed to express an expiry date for presentation of documents.

(b) Except as provided in sub-Article 44(a), documents must be presented on or before such expiry date.

(c) If an issuing bank states that the credit is to be available 'for one month', 'for six months', or the like, but does not specify the date from which the time is to run, the date of issuance of the credit by the issuing bank will be deemed to be the first day from which such time is to run. Banks should discourage indication of the expiry date of the credit in this manner.

Article 43 – Limitation on the expiry date

(a) In addition to stipulating an expiry date for presentation of documents, every credit which calls for a transport document(s) should also stipulate a specified period of time after the date of shipment during which presentation must be made in compliance with the terms and conditions of the credit. If no such period of time is stipulated, banks will not accept documents presented to them later than 21 days after the date of shipment. In any event, documents must be presented not later than the expiry date of the credit.

(b) In cases in which sub-Article 40(b) applies, the date of shipment will be considered to be the latest shipment date on any of the transport documents presented.

Article 44 – Extension of expiry date

(a) If the expiry date of the credit and/or the last day of the period of time for presentation of documents stipulated by the credit or applicable by virtue of Article 43 falls on a day on which the bank to which presentation has to be made is closed for reasons other than those referred to in Article 17, the stipulated expiry date and/or the last day of the period of time after the date of shipment for presentation of documents, as the case may be, shall be extended to the first following day on which such bank is open.

(b) The latest date for shipment shall not be extended by reason of the extension of the expiry date and/or the period of time after the date of shipment for presentation of documents in accordance with sub-Article (a) above. If no such latest date for shipment is stipulated in the credit or amendments thereto, banks will not accept transport documents indicating a date of shipment later than the expiry date stipulated in the credit or amendments thereto.

(c) The bank to which presentation is made on such first following business day must provide a statement that the documents were presented within the time limits extended in accordance with sub-Article 44(a) of the Uniform Customs and Practice for Documentary Credits, 1993 Revision, ICC publication no 500.

Article 45 – Hours of presentation

Banks are under no obligation to accept presentation of documents outside their banking hours.

Article 46 – General expressions as to dates for shipment

(a) Unless otherwise stipulated in the credit, the expression 'shipment' used in stipulating an earliest and/or a latest date for shipment will be understood to include expressions such as, 'loading on board', 'dispatch', 'accepted for carriage', 'date of post receipt', 'date of pick-up', and the like, and in the case of a credit calling for a multi-modal transport document the expression 'taking in charge'.

(b) Expressions such as 'prompt', 'immediately', 'as soon as possible', and the like should not be used. If they are used, banks will disregard them.

(c) If the expression 'on or about' or similar expressions are used, banks will interpret them as a stipulation that shipment is to be made during the period from five days before to five days after the specified date, both end days included.

Article 47 – Date terminology for periods of shipment

(a) The words 'to', 'until', 'till', 'from' and words of similar import applying to any date or period in the credit referring to shipment will be understood to include the date mentioned.

(b) The word 'after' will be understood to exclude the date mentioned.

(c) The terms 'first half', 'second half' of a month shall be construed respectively as the 1st to the 15th, and the 16th to the last day of such month, all dates inclusive.

(d) The terms 'beginning', 'middle', or 'end' of a month shall be construed respectively as the 1st to the 10th, the 11th to the 20th, and the 21st to the last day of such month, all dates inclusive.

F   Transferable credit

Article 48 – Transferable credit

(a) A transferable credit is a credit under which the beneficiary (first beneficiary) may request the bank authorised to pay, incur a deferred payment undertaking, accept or negotiate (the 'transferring bank'), or in the case of a freely negotiable credit, the bank specifically authorised in the credit as a transferring bank, to make the credit available in whole or in part to one or more other beneficiary(ies) ('second beneficiary(ies)).

(b) A credit can be transferred only if it is expressly designated as 'transferable' by the issuing bank. Terms such as 'divisible', 'fractionable', 'assignable', and 'transmissible' do not render the credit transferable. If such terms are used they shall be disregarded.

(c) The transferring bank shall be under no obligation to effect such transfer except to the extent and in the manner expressly consented to by such bank.

(d) At the time of making a request for transfer and prior to transfer of the credit, the first beneficiary must irrevocably instruct the transferring bank whether or not he retains the right to refuse to allow the transferring bank to advise amendments to the second beneficiary(ies). If the transferring bank consents to the transfer under these conditions, it must, at the time of transfer, advise the second beneficiary(ies) of the first beneficiary's instructions regarding amendments.

(e) If a credit is transferred to more than one second beneficiary(ies), refusal of an amendment by one or more second beneficiary(ies) does not invalidate the acceptance(s) by the other second beneficiary(ies) with respect to whom the credit will be amended accordingly. With respect to the second beneficiary(ies) who rejected the amendment, the credit will remain unamended.

(f) Transferring bank charges in respect of transfers including commissions, fees, costs or expenses are payable by the first beneficiary, unless otherwise agreed. If the transferring bank agrees to transfer the credit it shall be under no obligation to effect the transfer until such charges are paid.

(g) Unless otherwise stated in the credit, a transferable credit can be transferred once only. Consequently, the credit cannot be transferred at the request of the second beneficiary to any subsequent third beneficiary. For the purpose of this article, a re-transfer to the first beneficiary does not constitute a prohibited transfer.

Fractions of a transferable credit (not exceeding in the aggregate the amount of the credit) can be transferred separately, provided partial shipments/drawings are not prohibited, and the aggregate of such transfers will be considered as constituting only one transfer of the credit.

(h) The credit can be transferred only on the terms and conditions specified in the original credit, with the exception of:

- the amount of the credit;
- any unit price stated therein;
- the expiry date;
- the last date for presentation of documents in accordance with Article 43;
- the period for shipment.

any or all of which may be reduced or curtailed.

The percentage for which insurance cover must be effected may be increased in such a way as to provide the amount of cover stipulated in the original credit, or these articles.

In addition, the name of the first beneficiary can be substituted for that of the applicant, but if the name of the applicant is specifically required by the original credit to appear in any document(s) other than the invoice, such requirement must be fulfilled.

(i) The first beneficiary has the right to substitute his own invoice(s) (and draft(s)) for those of the second beneficiary(ies), for amounts not in excess of the original amount stipulated in the credit and for the original unit prices if stipulated in the credit, and upon such substitution of invoice(s) (and draft(s)) the first beneficiary can draw under the credit for the difference, if any, between his invoice(s) and the second beneficiary's(ies') invoice(s).

When a credit has been transferred and the first beneficiary is to supply his own invoice(s) (and draft(s)) in exchange for the second beneficiary's(ies') invoice(s) (and draft(s)) but fails to do so on first demand, the transferring bank has the right to deliver to the issuing bank the documents received under the transferred credit, including the second beneficiary's(ies') invoice(s) (and draft(s)) without further responsibility to the first beneficiary.

(j) The first beneficiary may request that payment or negotiation be effected to the second beneficiary(ies) at the place to which the credit has been transferred up to and including the expiry date of the credit, unless the original credit expressly states that it may not be made available for payment or negotiation at a place other than that stipulated in the credit. This is without prejudice to the first beneficiary's right to substitute subsequently his own invoice(s) (and draft(s)) for those of the second beneficiary(ies) and to claim any difference due to him.

G   Assignment of proceeds

Article 49 – Assignment of proceeds

The fact that a credit is not stated to be transferable shall not affect the beneficiary's right to assign any proceeds to which he may be, or may become, entitled under such credit, in accordance with the provisions of the applicable law. This article relates only to the assignment of proceeds and not to the assignment of the right to perform under the credit itself.

ICC arbitration

Contracting parties that wish to have the possibility of resorting to ICC Arbitration in the event of a dispute with their contracting partner should specifically and clearly agree upon ICC Arbitration in their contract or, in the event no single contractual document exists, in the exchange of correspondence which constitutes the agreement between them. The fact of issuing a letter of credit subject to the UCP 500 does NOT by itself constitute an agreement to have resort to ICC Arbitration. The following standard arbitration clause is recommended by the ICC:

All disputes arising in connection with the present contract shall be finally settled under the Rules of Conciliation and Arbitration of the International Chamber of Commerce by one or more arbitrators appointed in accordance with the said rules.

THE GENERAL AGREEMENT ON TARIFFS AND TRADE (GATT) AND THE WORLD TRADE ORGANISATION (WTO)

INTRODUCTION

Even before the Second World War had drawn to a close, trade leaders in the Allied countries had come to realise the significant contribution that trade tensions had made in leading to its outbreak. A consensus was emerging that there was a critical need for international cooperation in establishing disciplines within economic relations in order to prevent a recurrence.[1]

It can be said that the seeds for GATT were planted back in 1946 at the February meeting of the United Nations Economic and Social Council (ECOSOC) where a resolution was passed to prepare a convention to establish a world organisation whereby signatory countries would join in an effort to establish ground rules for trade among them. This effort was to be embodied in the International Trade Organisation (ITO).

Resulting from this resolution the Havana Conference was held between November 1947 and March 1948. Hence the charter for the ITO (The Havana Charter) was drafted which would have established a governing body consisting of representation from all member countries. This was the first attempt by an international body to set out fair and uniform guidelines for international trade at both private and international levels.

However, the ITO did not become a reality. When the high ideals of the charter were taken to their own electorates by the member countries, the detailed debates that ensued raised substantial obstacles. It became clear by the late 1940s that many countries could not agree with the terms of the charter and others looked to the larger countries like the USA for guidance. In the USA, the ITO was submitted to a congress that had become increasingly protectionist in response to the diminution of international co-operation following the Second World War. After meeting stiff resistance and delay that foreshadowed defeat, in December 1950 its president withdrew the charter from further consideration. This sounded the death knell for the ITO.

Fortunately, at earlier meetings of the Havana Conference held in Geneva from April to October 1947, multilateral tariff negotiations were being conducted and with unusual foresight the General Agreement on Tariffs and Trade (GATT) had been drafted concurrently with the ITO Charter. The GATT incorporated the agreed tariff reductions along with a code of conduct aimed at preserving the trade benefits flowing from tariff reductions. This code aimed to restrict certain government practices that

---

1   For detailed discussions of the history of GATT, see Jackson, JH, *World Trade and the Law of GATT*, 1969, Chapters 3 and 4, Virginia, USA: The Bobbs-Merrill Co Inc. For a discussion of the various issues, see Wang, G, *International Trade Order*, 1988, Chapters 1 and 3, Beijing: Publishing House of Law; Wang, G, *International Monetary and Financial Law* (hereinafter *Financial Law*), 1993, Chapter 1, Hong Kong: Wide Angle Press.

would operate to circumvent the tariff commitments. As the code of conduct was itself a part of the anticipated ITO Charter, it was never formally implemented. It was, however, brought into force by means of a Provisional Protocol, signed on 30 October 1946, and effective from 1 January 1948, under which the signatory countries[2] agreed to apply the provisions of the GATT until the ITO could take over supervision of its operation upon ratification through the appropriate domestic mechanisms of each of the countries.

With the collapse of ITO, the GATT Agreement[3] became the centrepiece for the ordering of the international trade relationships of its signatories.

There has been a series of eight periods of negotiations, called multilateral trade negotiations or rounds since the GATT was established, the most recent being the Uruguay Round, ending in 1994. The first five of these rounds focused on the reduction of tariffs. The sixth, the Kennedy Round, saw the inclusion of some negotiation on non-tariff barriers with this being the primary focus of the Tokyo and Uruguay Rounds. The latest round, the Uruguay Round, successfully saw the establishment of the new World Trade Organisation (WTO), similar to the original ITO, which has become an umbrella organisation with responsibility for the GATT and its side codes as well as a greatly expanded scope of coverage, including services, under the General Agreement on Trade in Services (GATS), and intellectual property, under the Agreement on Trade-Related Aspects of Intellectual Property Rights (TRIPS).

THE GENERAL AGREEMENT ON TARIFFS AND TRADE

It is a basic premise of customary international law that under the concept of sovereignty, a country is relatively free to conduct or regulate trade across or within its borders on any terms it sees fit. The actual mechanisms of trade regulation are usually, but not always, those of domestic law through which a State controls activity over which it has jurisdiction, for instance goods and people crossing its borders. However, such controls may not necessarily be exercised through law or legal institutions but may be encountered in the form of unspecified administrative discretion. This is related to the discussion on 'transparency' below.

The GATT and the WTO Agreements are essentially the multilateral acceptance of disciplines upon the exercise of sovereignty whereby signatory nations agree to limits upon what they will and will not do in respect of trade regulation, for instance in the

---

2   In 1934, Congress empowered the President to negotiate and implement reciprocal tariff reduction agreements. It was under this power that the USA participated in the negotiations resulting in the GATT. This authority has been renewed periodically, usually for three year periods, and during the Tokyo and Uruguay Rounds became associated with 'fast track' authority. The fact that this authority was due to expire in mid 1948, prior to the expected ratification of the ITO Charter, gave extra incentive for a timely signing of the protocol. The eight original signatories were Australia, Belgium, Canada, France, Luxemburg, The Netherlands, the UK and the USA.

3   Twenty three countries signed what was called a Final Act authenticating the text of the GATT (55 UNTS 194; TIAS 1700. See Jackson, *op cit*, Chapter 2).

setting of tariffs and other barriers to trade in goods and services and investment. This is not usually viewed as a surrender or loss of sovereignty as countries still maintain the power to act, for instance through domestic regulation, in contravention of their international obligations.

THE GATT 1994

In addition to agreeing to maximum tariff levels, negotiated separately for each country, each GATT/WTO member is bound to the obligations and principles concerning:

(i) non-discrimination, comprised of both most-favoured-nation (MFN) and national treatment;

(ii) disciplines on non-tariff barriers;

(iii) transparency; and

(iv) dispute resolution.

Breach of these obligations places in jeopardy the expectations that a country has in regard to the reciprocal performance of obligations by other member countries.

If any member country acts in a manner inconsistent with its obligations, it will be potentially subject to retaliatory action by other member countries provided that any applicable dispute resolution procedures are followed. Some responsive mechanisms are self-enforcing, which allow a country to respond to certain practices without the employment of the WTO dispute settlement mechanism; for instance by the imposition of anti-dumping and countervailing duties. A specific objective of Uruguay Round, changes in the dispute resolution process, was to ensure that except for those responses that are based on these self-enforcing provisions, any country seeking to impose trade sanctions in response to an alleged breach of obligations must avail themselves of the WTO dispute resolution process and there establish their claim. There are, however, many exceptions within the GATT that may provide a defence to a claim of breach of its obligations.

The obligations of a GATT contracting party (which also serve as the rights of other contracting parties) include most-favoured-nation (MFN) treatment, national treatment, tariff concessions, and restrictions in respect of non-tariff measures.

One of the requirements of GATT is that a contracting party must grant other contracting parties equal tariff treatment or MFN trading status automatically;[4] and domestic policy must also be non-discriminatory. This requires that internal taxes and other charges, laws, regulations and other requirements affecting business transactions be applied to domestic entities and foreign concerns on an equal basis.[5]

GATT contracting parties must also look to the elimination and reduction of non-tariff barriers such as subsidies, dumping and quantitative restrictions. These rules

---

4   Article 1 of the General Agreement on Tariffs and Trade.

5   *Ibid*, Article III.

set out a mechanism for the contracting parties to file their complaints and for the determination of damages.

Every GATT Protocol has its own tariffs schedules that bind the applicant to a duty to limit tariffs imposed on imports from other GATT contracting parties. GATT contracting parties also have an obligation not to impose any non-tariff measures on imports from other contracting parties.

Transparency of the laws and regulations in respect of trade is another requirement of the GATT. Under Article X, the contracting parties must make known, among other things, their trade policies and law, import and export systems and domestic regulations in respect of trade.

Last but not least, on assuming the role of a contracting party, a country may not raise its tariffs for a period of three years.[6] After this period, any move to modify or raise tariffs must be discussed with the other contracting parties. Should a country increase its tariff rates in one category of products, it may be required to reduce the rates in another category or categories.[7]

The framework of GATT

The organs of GATT are as follows:[8]

1   The contracting parties

2   The Council of Representatives

3   Committees, consisting of :

- Committee on Balance of Payments Restrictions

- Committee on Tariff Concession

- Committee on the Budget

- Committee on Trade and Development

- Committee on Trade Negotiations (not permanent)

4   Working parties

5   Panels of experts

6   The Consultative Group of 18

---

6   Article XXVIII of the GATT, para 2 with regard to negotiations of tariffs, provides: 'In such negotiations and agreement, which may include provision for compensatory adjustment with respect to other products, the contracting parties concerned shall endeavour to maintain a general level of reciprocal and mutually advantageous concessions not less favourable to trade than that provided for in this agreement prior to such negotiations.'

7   Since the institutions of GATT in 1947, the average tariff rates on finished products imposed by industrialised countries have been reduced from 40% to a mere 5%. This has been considered as one of the main factors for the development of world trade. See the Department of International Liaison of the Ministry of Foreign Economic Relations and Trade of China (eds), *GATT: A Handbook*, 1992, p 2, Beijing: Economic Administration Press.

8   Long, O, *Law and Its Limitation in the GATT Multilateral Trade System*, pp 45–54, 1985, The Hague: Martinus Nijhoff.

7   The Director General

8   The Secretariat

The meaning of contracting parties

Article XXXII states that contracting parties are countries which apply the provisions of the GATT *via* Article XXVI or Article XXXIII or under a Protocol of Provisional Application.

Membership

In GATT we find the following membership classes:[9]

1   In Article XXVI(2) and (4) provision is made for acceptance of GATT by a country. This is in practice rare and only two countries, Haiti and Liberia, who subsequently withdrew, have sought admission this way.

2   Being a party to the Protocol of Provisional Application. This has been the method adopted by Western countries and European countries. Australia gained her admission this way. This method simply means a country agrees to apply provisionally GATT, except where there is inconsistency of domestic legislation.

3   Protocol of Accession. This is dealt with in Article XXXIII and allows a country to join GATT by negotiating a list of concessions with the contracting parties who then decide on allowing entry by a two thirds majority. GATT practice is to allow countries who have provisionally agreed to accession to have non-observer or non-voting participation rights in relevant matters at meetings.

4   Being a prior dependent territory: this is provided for in Article XXVI and in particular, sub-Article 5(c). This applies in a situation where a country had previously accepted GATT and now part of that country becomes an independent territory. However, the new independent territory must satisfy the requirements of Article XXVI(2) requiring initial provisional application as set out above.

THE LEGAL PRINCIPLES OF THE GATT

The aims of the GATT are equality of treatment for both imported and exported goods and the creation of a world wide open trading system.

The essential GATT principle is that of non-discrimination from which three other principles are derived:

1   The most-favoured-nation principle

2   The national treatment principle

3   The reciprocity principle

---

9   Jackson, *op cit*, p 87ff.

The most-favoured-nation principle

The most-favoured-nation (MFN) principle is found in Article 1 of the GATT and is the corner stone of the GATT.

Article I(1) provides:

With respect to customs duties and charges of any kind imposed on or in connection with importation or exportation or imposed on the international transfer of payments for imports or exports, and with respect to the method of levying such duties and charges, and with respect to all rules and formalities in connection with importation and exportation and with respect to all matters referred to in para 2 and 4 of Article III, any advantage, favour, privilege or immunity granted by any contracting party to any product originating in or destined for any other country shall be accorded immediately and unconditionally to the like product originating in or destined for the territories of all other contracting parties.

This article specifies four categories of exchange concession agreements:

1 Those relating to an obligation to pay customs duties and charges of any kind imposed on the export and import of goods or imposed on the international transfer of payments for import and export purposes.

2 Those relating to the methods of levying such duties and charges.

3 Those relating to the rules and formalities of import and export.

4 Those relating to all matters referred to in para 2 and 4 of Article III regarding internal taxation.

These obligations are imposed on exporters and importers when their product enters other States and involve various types of obligations, formalities and procedures. The aim of the GATT is to achieve a compromise between national and international interest in international trade through tariff and non-tariff negotiations.

Trade negotiations involve the exchange of concessions among the principal suppliers and it consists of the grant of advantages, favours, privileges and immunities.[10] These concessions may be given to a product originating in or destined for a particular country.

According to the most-favoured-nation principle all other contracting parties may automatically take advantage of any concession exchange. The most-favoured-nation principle set out in the GATT is unconditional. It applies automatically and immediately to third parties without any need for the grant of any compensation or concession to the negotiators. Tariffs which have been negotiated based on the most-favoured-nation principle are included in the Tariffs Schedules of the GATT and are put on the agenda of the contracting parties. As a result all contracting parties may benefit from any such negotiations. Even developing countries not involved in the tariff negotiations may benefit from these, although the GATT Rounds seem to have been more beneficial to the developed countries than for developing countries.

---

10 Article I(1) of the GATT.

It can be observed that trade concessions have been typically between importing countries and their principal suppliers about particular items, and the principal suppliers have usually been the developed countries.

National treatment principle

The national treatment principle is contained in Article III of the GATT. According to Schwarzenberger: 'This standard provides for inland parity, that is to say equality of treatment between nationals and foreigners.'[11]

Herman Mosler[12] refers with approval to the definition of national treatment contained in the agreement between the Federal Republic of Germany and the USA in 1954 as follows:

National treatment is defined as a treatment accorded within the territory of a Party upon terms no less favourable than treatment accorded therein in like situations to nationals, companies, products, ship and other objects as the case may be of such a party.

From the above definition, the elements of national treatment seem to be:

1 There is an interest concerning more than one country;

2 The interest is located in the territory or jurisdiction of one country;

3 The host country gives equal treatment to both nationals and national products of the other country;

4 Equality and the non-disadvantageous treatment of the other countries' nationals.

Mosler sees the national treatment principle only as a part of national law, not international customary law.

National treatment appears to be a liberal economic concept which in the view of many developing countries, is difficult to implement because in their view it can impede the fulfilment of national development policy. This is an important element in GATT.

Article III, whilst laying the national treatment principle, prohibits discrimination between imported and like domestic products. GATT does not define 'like products' and it is left to the GATT panels to decide what constitutes a like product.

The overall purpose of Article III is to ensure that the determination of like product is not made in such a way that it infringes the regulatory authority and domestic policy options of contracting parties.[13] In so doing, the panels also consider the following criteria:

1 tariff classification;

2 nature of the product;

3 intended use;

---

11 Schwarzenberger, G, *The Frontiers of International Law*, 1962, p 220, London: Stevens.

12 Mosler, H, *The International Society as a Legal Community*, 1980, p 255, Germantown, MD: Sijtihoff, Nordhoff.

13 GATT document DS 23/R, p 95.

4 commercial value; and

5 price and substitutability.

In the legal framework of the GATT, the principle of national treatment supplements the 'most-favoured-nation treatment' (MFN) principle which gives third parties the opportunity to benefit from concessions already negotiated.

But there are certain exceptions. Thus, Article XX of the GATT, *inter alia*, exempts measures:

> relating to the conservation of exhaustible natural resources if such measures are made effective in conjunction with restrictions on domestic production or consumption.

and excludes measures:

> involving restriction on export of domestic materials necessary to ensure essential quantities of such materials to a domestic processing industry during periods when the domestic price of such materials is held below the world price as part of a governmental stabilisation plan; provided that such restrictions shall not operate to increase the export of or the protection afforded to such domestic industry, and shall not depart from the provisions of this agreement relating to non-discrimination.

The standards for imposing trade measures usually reflect the values of the commodities in the importing countries. Obviously, value preferences are not strictly based on purely empirical scientific judgments and, as such, it may be difficult to invoke this exception.

This is a particular problem for developed countries for, with the greening of these nations, a government is under pressure from environmental lobbies to take trade-restricting measures on the basis of value preference.

An example is the ancillary harvesting of dolphins in a fish catch, a particular problem that arose between the USA and Mexico, where the USA argued that Mexico should require certain standards of its fishermen whilst harvesting fish. The GATT panel stated that:

> If the broad interpretation given by the USA were accepted, each contracting party could unilaterally determine the life or health protection policies from which other contracting parties could not deviate without jeopardising their rights under the General Agreement.[14]

This poses a real threat to international trade, and there appears to be two solutions:

1 Compensation for trade rights which have been affected. However, there is a strong counter-argument that trade compensation payments would undermine the very basis of GATT, which is to encourage the growth of trade and increased economic growth of that country. On the other side of the coin, a country may not be in a financial position to make such payments, and therefore it leads to the view that if a country has economic power it is also morally superior.

---

14 GATT document DS 21/R, para 5.27.

2   To engage and negotiate international cooperation between the countries involved. This is obviously the preferred solution but it is time consuming, yet does satisfy the GATT ideal that countries must exhaust all options reasonably available to it before resorting to other measures. Yet green groups may not give their governments the time necessary to negotiate such agreements as negotiations would be complex and moral values would rate highly in any case submission.

The reciprocity principle

One of the objectives of the GATT is to give a mutual advantage to all contracting parties. The preamble of the GATT describes the contracting parties as:

> Being desirous of contributing to these objectives by entering into reciprocal and mutually advantageous arrangements directed to the substantial reduction on tariffs and other barriers to trade and to the elimination of discriminatory treatment in international commerce.

GATT encourages negotiations based on the reciprocity principle. Article XXVIII *bis* 1 provides:

> The contracting parties recognise that customs duties often constitute serious obstacles to trade; thus negotiations on reciprocal and mutually advantageous basis, directed to the substantial reduction of the general level of tariffs and other charges on imports and exports and in particular to the reduction of such high tariffs as discourage the importation even of minimum quantities, and conducted with due regard to the objectives of this agreement and the varying needs of individual contracting parties, are of great importance to the expansion of international trade. The contracting parties may therefore sponsor such negotiations from time to time.

The reciprocity principle and its implementation may be found in the following articles:

1   Article III which regulates internal tax, in order that imported goods shall not be subject to the discriminatory charges.[15]

2   Article VI which condemns dumping if it causes or threatens material injury.[16] This article permits the levying of anti–dumping duties to offset dumping.

---

15   Article III(1) provides, *inter alia*: 'The contracting parties recognise that internal taxes and other internal charges, and laws, regulations and requirements affecting the internal sale, offering for sale, purchase, transportation, distribution or use of products, and internal quantitative regulations requiring the mixture, processing or use of products in special amounts or proportions, should not be applied to imported or domestic products so as to afford protection to domestic production.'

16   Article VI(1) provides, *inter alia*: 'The contracting parties recognise that dumping, by which products of one country are introduced into the commerce of another country at less than the normal value of the products, is to be condemned if it causes or threatens materials injury to an established industry in the territory of a contracting party or materially retards the establishment of a domestic industry. For the purposes of this article, a product is to be considered as being introduced into the commerce of an importing country at less than its normal value, if the price of the product exported from one country to another.'

3   Article VII which establishes general principles of valuation and Article VIII which provides that fees and charges must not represent an indirect protection.[17]

The reciprocity principle under the GATT regulation has these consequences:

1   A concession which is given to another country must be carried out on an equitable basis.

2   All contracting parties will gain an advantage from every negotiated concession by the negotiator and that advantage would be given reciprocally through the most-favoured-nation principle.

3   Every imported goods must be treated equally to, and as promptly and adequately as domestic products.

The strict application of the reciprocity principle in relations between developed and developing countries could be to the latter's disadvantage, for developing countries wish to build up what are described as 'infant industries'. Developing countries frequently promote their infant industries with the idea of raising the general standard of living of its people. It is therefore difficult for some developing countries to implement direct reciprocity between developed countries and developing countries, if they wish to continue to protect infant industries.

The legal framework of dispute settlement[18]

The procedure for dispute settlement is found in:

1   Articles XXII and XXIII.

2   The Understanding on Dispute Settlement reached at the Tokyo Round in 1979 and the Dispute Settlement Rules and Procedures adopted at the Uruguay Round in 1989.

Articles XXII and XXIII

These articles govern dispute resolution.

Article XXII(I) states:

Each contracting party shall accord sympathetic consideration to, and shall afford adequate opportunity for consultation regarding, such representations as may be made by

---

17   Article VII(1) provides, *inter alia*: 'The contracting parties recognise the validity of the general principles of valuation set forth in the following paragraphs of this article, and they undertake to give effect to such principles, in respect of all products subject to duties other charges or restrictions on importation and exportation based upon or regulated in any manner by value. Moreover, they shall, upon a request by another contracting party review the operation of any of their laws or regulations relating to value for customs purposes in the light of these principles. The contracting parties may request from contracting parties reports on steps taken by them in pursuance of the provisions of this article.'

18   For a review of the history of dispute resolution under the GATT, see US International Trade Commission, *Review of the Effectiveness of Trade Dispute Settlement under the GATT and the Tokyo Round Agreements*, Report to the Committee on Finance, US Senate, on Investigation no 332-212, under s 332(g) of the US Tariff Act of 1930 (US International Trade Commission (USITC) Publication 1793, December 1985).

another contracting party with respect to any matter affecting the operation of this agreement.

It can be seen that the emphasis is on consultation and if this fails one of the parties may seek multilateral consultation with the contracting parties as a whole under Article XXII:2.

This consultative process outlined in Article XXII becomes a more formal process of dispute settlement in Article XXIII where consultation is provided for in specific instances. This list is not limited to breaches of GATT but also includes claims that do not conflict with GATT, but lead to the total or partial stoppage of benefits that may accrue under GATT ('non-violation nullification or impairment').

If agreement cannot be reached, then Article XXIII provides a procedure for investigation and, recommending or the possible authorisation of suspension of concessions or other obligations by the complaining contracting party.

Normal procedure is to have a panel system of 3–5 experts who are assigned to settle a dispute. The settlement process has the following six steps:

1   bilateral consultations and negotiations;

2   request for the appointment of a panel by the complaining party;

3   establishment of a panel by the Council;

4   receipt by the Panel of Oral Submissions, followed by deliberations, consideration of a report drafted by the GATT Secretariat, and issuance of the proposed report;

5   submission of the report to the GATT Council;

6   adoption of the report by the Council.

A dispute can be settled by adopting the panel report or a negotiated settlement resulting from the report. If this does not occur there are other types of solutions that may result:

1   removal of the offending measure;

2   compensation to the complainant;

3   retaliation by reciprocal suspension or withdrawal of GATT concessions or obligations. This is rare and has happened only once.[19]

The dispute settlement roles and procedures 1989

This was a most important result of the Uruguay Round. This document was an attempt at codifying all procedures and developing a set of rules.

A new Dispute Settlement Body (DSB) was created to be the administrative support body for the panels. More importantly, there was established an appellate body of seven members, elected for a four year term, serving in rotation at three year intervals and were to be representatives of the GATT membership.

---

19   The Netherlands was authorised in 1952 to suspend obligations to the USA on grounds of injury suffered as the result of restrictions on imports of dairy products imposed by the USA. It was also authorised to impose a quantitative restriction on imports of wheat-flour from the USA. Netherlands Measures of Suspension of Obligations to the USA, BISD, 1st Supp 32 (1953).

There was also provision for limited arbitration relating to specific matters like damages and compensation amounts. Thus, the features of the system are the DSB, the panels including the appellate body, with an arbitration arm. Following an appeal to the appellate body, the adoption of its report is automatic and final.

The understanding also redefined a number of general principles:

1   Dispute settlement is a central element in providing security and predictability in the multilateral trading system.

2   Dispute settlement cannot add to or diminish the rights and obligations provided in the GATT.

3   The maintenance of a proper balance between the rights and obligations of members. This is in reality conciliation.

4   Panels should adopt a positive approach to any dispute.

5   A solution mutually acceptable to the parties is preferred. This is once again a reversion to conciliation.

6   To secure the withdrawal of the measure concerned, and compensation should be resorted to only if immediate withdrawal of the measure is impracticable.

In summary, everything points to conciliation and not arbitration by a third party, although there is a clear will to strengthen mechanisms such as adoption of panel reports.

The panel system

Each panel is given a term of reference thus: 'to examine taking into account the relevant GATT provisions and the complaint is formulated to allow panels to make such findings and recommendations as it sees fit.'

Panels are usually made up of three members and five member panels are rare. The underlying reason for this appears to be the desire for mutual understanding and consensus.

The GATT secretariat provides the panel secretary and as the secretary generally will have been involved in handling discussions between the contracting parties, this means he or she is conversant with the problem at hand.

A legal representative is also provided and he or she has the job of advising on points of law and assisting in the drafting of the panel's findings and recommendations.

Panel members are generally drawn from countries other than the USA, the European Community and Japan. This simply happens because there is a rule that the country involved in the dispute is debarred from having a panel member. Most disputes concern these three countries. It is the Director General of GATT who proposes panel members. This once again reinforces the conciliation approach for in an arbitration situation, each party nominates its own arbitrators. This selection method also gives each panel member a sense of independence given to them by a mandate of the GATT community.

The workings of a panel

Two rounds of written submissions, each following an oral hearing are allowed. Third parties can only be involved if they have declared their interest when the panel was constituted. Hearings are informal and progress depends very much on the chairperson.

The first round of submissions allows the parties to set out to the panel the arguments which are being put. The parties can then direct their second submissions to the issues identified as being decisive.

Panel reports

These are of persuasive value only and are not decisions in the sense of a judgment. The idea of a report is not to direct issues but to avoid controversy and present arguments as being logical and leading to an obvious result. This means the choice of language and argument is generally understated. Legal principles also do not play a significant part and often facts dominate. This approach contrasts dramatically with a judgment where conflicts are seized upon and the judge decides this conflict using legal argument.

As panel members change, it is obvious that it is difficult to get a consistent approach and it would appear stability or conformity is provided by the legal representative of GATT. It would appear the legal representative then would be relied upon heavily by the panel members and perhaps in the long run a consistency in approach and presentation of reports would result. This would in the course of time result in a body of uniform application of legal principles and if not principles, at the least, a legal approach to the problem.

This means panel reports are directly effective in a substantive way, for they provide arguments which can be turned into legal principle or approach at a GATT level. For example, following upon from a panel report, a contracting country may institute procedures against dumping or unfair trade practices. This could well result in a source of trade law, deriving from a practical application by GATT countries.

The time lines involved with panels

A request for a panel is received in writing by the GATT Secretariat. The usual procedure is to appoint a three member panel, but if the parties agree then within 10 days of the establishment of the panel it may be increased to five members. Terms of reference are agreed upon within 20 days from the date of setting up of the panel. A report is generally issued by the panel three months following completion of the hearing, but in any case, not more than six months after the hearing. The report is then given to the contracting parties and after 30 days it is adopted by the Director General of GATT or his or her representative.

A contracting party may object to the panel report by circulating written reasons at least 10 days prior to the GATT adoption meeting.

The objecting parties then can present further argument at this meeting and a decision upon the report's adoption must be given by the Director General or his or her representative not more than 15 months later. At this adoption meeting, the decision is a consensus decision and without prejudice to the GATT provisions on decision making.

The understanding also sought to prevent delays, stating that a panel be established at a Council meeting following that at which the request first appeared as an agenda item on the Council agenda.

PREFERENTIAL TREATMENT

Preferential treatment is provided for under Article XVIII and Part IV of the GATT.

The prohibition on quantitative restrictions contained in Article XI[20] of the GATT is subject to an exception regarding measures imposed for balance-of-payments purposes.

This exception is set out in Article XII[21] with special provision for developing countries being made in Article XVIII B of the GATT.

Under these, any country may restrict the quantity or value of imports in order:

1   to safeguard its external financial position; and

2   either to protect its balance of payments or to ensure a level of reserves adequate for the implementation of its programme of economic development.[22]

Restrictions must not exceed those necessary:[23]

1   to forestall the imminent threat of, or to stop, a serious decline in monetary reserves; or

2   if such reserves are very low, to achieve a reasonable rate of increase (Article XVIII does not use the word imminent, and refers to reserves which are 'inadequate' rather than very low). Due regard must be paid to special factors which may affect

---

20   Article XI of the GATT provides, *inter alia*: 'No prohibitions or restrictions other than duties, taxes or other charges, whether made effective through quotas, import or export licences or other measures, shall be instituted or maintained by any contracting party on the importation of any product of the territory of any other contracting party or on the exportation or sale for export of any product destined for the territory of any other contracting party.'

21   Article XXI(1) of the GATT provides, *inter alia*: 'Notwithstanding the provisions of para 1 of Article XI, any contracting party, in order to safeguard its external financial position and its balance of payments may restrict the quantity or value of merchandise permitted to be imported, subject to the provisions paragraphs of this article.'

22   Article XVIII(9) provides, *inter alia*: 'In order to safeguard its external financial position and to ensure a level of reserves adequate for implementation of its programme of economic development, a contracting party coming within the scope of para 4(a) of this article may, subject to the provisions of paras 10–12, control the general level of its imports by restricting the quantity or value of merchandise permitted to be imported; provided that the import restrictions instituted, maintained or intensified shall not exceed those necessary.'

23   McGovern, E, *op cit*, p 285.

reserves[24] or the need for reserves. As conditions improve the restrictions must be progressively relaxed.[25]

Article XVIII gives developing countries special rights in regards to balance-of-payments measures and safeguards action for development. Under this, a developing country is permitted to apply a discriminatory quantitative restriction to assist in its development and the improvement of its economy.

Article XVIII allows a developing country to modify or withdraw tariff concessions[26] or to take other measures affecting imports[27] in order to promote the establishment of a particular industry.

In order to safeguard their external financial position and to ensure an adequate level of reserves for their economic development, developing contracting parties are allowed to control the general level of their imports as necessary to forestall or stop a serious decline in monetary reserves, or to achieve a reasonable rate of increase in reserves. In applying such import restrictions, a developing contracting party may differentiate between products so as to give priority to the importation of products which are essential for its economic development. The justification for these measures must remain essentially to protect monetary reserves, and not to protect a particular domestic industry or agricultural sector.[28]

However, before a country adopts quantitative restriction, the following must be satisfied.

---

24 Article XII(1) and Article XVIII(9) of the GATT.

25 Article XII(2) of the GATT provides: (a) Import restrictions instituted, maintained or intensified by a contracting party under this article shall not exceed those necessary; (i) to forestall the imminent threat of, or to stop, a serious decline in its monetary reserves; or (ii) in the case of a contracting party with very low monetary reserves, to achieve a reasonable rate of increase in its reserves. Due regard shall be paid in either case to any special factors which may be affecting the reserves of such contracting party or its need for reserves, including, where special external credits or other resources are available to it, the need to provide for the appropriate use of such credits or resources. (b) Contracting parties applying restrictions under sub-para (a) of this paragraph shall progressively relax them as such conditions improve, maintaining them only to the extent that the conditions specified in that sub-paragraph still just justify their application. They shall eliminate the restrictions when conditions would no longer justify their institution or maintenance under that sub-paragraph.

Article XVIII(11) of the GATT provides: 'In carrying out its domestic policies, the contracting parties concerned shall pay due regard to the need for restoring equilibrium in its balance of payments on a sound and lasting basis and to the desirability of assuring an economic employment of productive resources. It shall progressively relax any restrictions applied under this section as conditions improve, maintaining them only to the extent necessary under the terms of para 9 of this article and shall eliminate them when conditions no longer justify such maintenance; Provided that no contracting party shall be required to withdraw or modify restrictions on the ground that a change in its development policy would render unnecessary the restrictions which it is applying under this section.'

26 Article XVIII, s A of the GATT.

27 Article XVIII, s C of the GATT.

28 Article XVIII, s B of the GATT.

First, the contracting party must be one which can only support a low standard of living and is in the early stage of development.[29] Further, it must be undergoing a process of industrialisation to correct an excessive dependence on primary production.[30]

Second, the measures must be intended to protect an infant industry.[31] An infant industry involves not only the establishment of a new industry, but also the establishment of a new branch of production in an existing industry, the substantial transformation of an existing industry and the substantial expansion of an existing industry, supplying a relatively small proportion of domestic demand. It may also cover the reconstruction of an industry destroyed or substantially damaged as a result of hostilities or natural disasters.[32]

The GATT also conceives of circumstances where, for example, it is appropriate to permit the government to assist in solving problems in cases where special circumstances could not be achieved by the facilities under the GATT.[33]

The facilities are provided in Article XVIII, para 4(a) and (b). Furthermore Article XVIII para 2 provides as follows:

They agree, therefore, that those contracting parties should enjoy additional facilities to enable them:

(a) to maintain sufficient flexibility in their tariff structure to be able to grant the tariff protection required for the establishment of a particular industry; and

(b) to apply quantitative restrictions for balance of payments purposes in a manner which takes full account of the continued high level of demand for imports likely to be generated by their programmes of economic development'.

Article XVIII provides for special treatment and is set out in sections A to D; sections A to C apply to a country which has a low standard of living and is in the early stages of development.

The terms 'low standards of living' and 'early stages of development' under this article are obscure. Section A to C may be applied by countries which fulfil the following criteria:[34]

• the country should be underdeveloped in the sense that there are resources which have not yet been tapped;

• it should have a low standard of living.

Thus, a country which has a low standard of living, but does not have resources which can be exploited, may not use the facility provided by sections A to C.

---

29 Article XVIII(1) of the GATT.

30 Annex I and Article XVIII(2) paras 1 and 4 of the GATT.

31 Article XVIII(2) of the GATT.

32 Annex I ad Article XVIII paras 2, 3, 7, 13 and 22 of the GATT.

33 Article XVIII(3) paras 2, 3, 7, 13 and 22 of the GATT provides, *inter alia*: 'They agree, however, that there may be circumstances where no measure inconsistent with those provisions is practicable to permit a contracting party in the process of economic development to grant the governmental assistance required to promote to grant the establishment of particular industries with a view to raising the general standard of living of its people.'

34 Gupta, KR, *A Study of General Agreement on Tariffs and Trade*, 1967, p 149, Delhi: S Chand and Co.

Similarly, a country which has resources which have been exploited may also not use these facilities. The GATT does not set out the level of per capita income below which a country can only support low standards of living nor does it provide criteria for determining when a country is in the early stages of development.

Article XVIII permits underdeveloped countries access to additional facilities referred to in para 2 of Article XVIII through the provision of sections A to D of the article.

Sections A to D prescribe details of the facilities for those contracting parties subject to low standards of living and in the early stages of development. A contracting party whose economic development does not come within the scope of Article XVIII para 4(a) may submit an application to the contracting parties under section D. Both sections C and D make provision for government assistance to promote the establishment of a particular industry.

While Article XVIII is important for developing countries, in practice its use is limited for the following reasons:

First, the limited bargaining position of developing countries in the GATT Round makes them unable to offer exchanges of concessions of interest to developed countries.

Secondly, the practice of GATT Rounds being negotiated by the principal economic powers means that developing countries have been effectively excluded from the negotiating process.

Thirdly, because developing countries lack substantial expertise in international trade law, they are unable to enjoy the advantage of having highly skilled representation in the negotiations and so have not been adequately represented.

Quantitative restriction: a protection for developing countries

Developing countries which 'can only support a low standard of living' and 'are at an early stage of development' typically face balance of payments difficulties and instability in their trade performance. Frequently they will attempt to protect their markets from foreign exporters. The purpose of this is to safeguard the country's external position and to protect its economic programme.

Article XVIII, para 4(a) (b) provides that:

(a) Consequently, a contracting party the economy of which can only support low standards of living and is in the early stages of development shall be free to deviate temporarily from the provisions of the other articles of this agreement, as provided in sections A, B, and C of this article.

(b) A contracting party the economy of which is in the process of development, but which does not come within the scope of sub-para (a) above, may submit applications to the contracting parties under section D of this article.

To prevent misuse of the facilities, the article provides:[35]

---

35   Article XVIII B, para 9.

provided that the import restrictions instituted, maintained or intensified shall not exceed those necessary:

(a) to forestall the threat of, or to stop, a serious decline in its monetary reserves; or

(b) in the case of a contracting party with inadequate monetary reserves, to achieve a reasonable rate of increase in its reserves.

In applying these restrictions, the contracting party may determine their incidence on imports of different products or classes of products in such a way as to give priority to the importation of those products which are more essential in the light of its policy of economic development. But, this is subject to the following provisions:[36]

(a) the restrictions are so applied as to avoid unnecessary damage to the commercial or economic interests of any other contracting party and not to prevent unreasonably the importation of any description of goods in minimum commercial quantitative the exclusion of which would impair regular channels of trade;

(b) further that the restrictions are not so applied as to prevent the importation of commercial samples or to prevent compliance with patent, trade mark, copyright or similar procedures.

Furthermore, Article XVIII (11) of the GATT provides, *inter alia* :

In carrying out its domestic policies, the contracting party concerned shall pay due regard to the need for restoring equilibrium in its balance of payments on a sound and lasting basis and to the desirability of assuring an economic employment of productive resources.

Three safeguard measures were adopted as a result of the Tokyo Round:[37]

Declaration on trade measures for balance of payment purposes

The contracting parties decided in 1979 that all restrictive import measures taken for balance-of-payments purposes should be subject to the same rules and procedures. Three additional conditions were established: (a) parties must abide by GATT disciplines and give preference to those measures which have the least disruptive effect on trade; (b) they should avoid the simultaneous application of more than one type of trade measures; and (c) whenever practicable they should publicly announce a time schedule for the removal of the measures.[38] The contracting parties also decided that all import restriction measures undertaken by developed countries based on Article XII and developing countries based on Article XVIII, section B should be carried out in consultation with 'Balance of Payments Restriction Committees'. In this declaration, GATT's members expressed their conviction that restrictive trade measures are in general an inefficient means to maintain or restore balance of payments equilibrium and they recognise that developed contracting parties should avoid the imposition of

---

36 Article XVIII B, para 10.

37 McGovern, *op cit*, p 9. The other text is Decision on Differential and More Favourable Treatment and Reciprocity and Fuller Participation of Developing Countries (known as the 'Enabling Clause').

38 *Ibid*, p 286.

restrictive trade measures for balance of payments purposes to the maximum extent possible.[39]

Decision on safeguard action for development purposes

The article gives the notion of establishment a wide meaning, and a decision of the contracting parties in 1979 brought within its scope '... the development of new or the modification or extension of existing production structures with a view to achieving fuller and more efficient use of resources in accordance with the priorities of their economic development.' Furthermore, the contracting parties recognised that there may be unusual circumstances where delay in the application of the measures may give rise to difficulties and they agreed that in such circumstances the developing countries may deviate from the rules to the extent necessary for introducing the measures on a provisional basis immediately after the notification. Thus, the 1979 decision permits emergency action to be taken pending consultation.[40]

Understanding regarding notification, consultation, dispute settlement and surveillance

This draws attention to the notification requirements found both in the General Agreement and in decisions made under it, linking them with the notion of surveillance of national measures by the GATT. It is related to dispute settlement is so far as it provides opportunities for aggrieved parties to raise issues when they would be reluctant to invoke the more formal procedures of Article XXIII.[41]

The conditions to be observed by an applicant country

Article XVIII, para 12(a) provides that:

> Any contracting party applying new restrictions or raising the general level of its existing restrictions by a substantial intensification of the measures applied under this section, shall immediately after instituting or intensifying such restriction (or in circumstances in which prior consultation is practicable, before doing so) consult with the contracting parties as to the nature of its balance of payments difficulties, alternative corrective measures which may be available, and the possible effect of the restrictions on the economies of other contracting parties.

Hence, full consultation with the contracting parties is required immediately after or prior to the application of quantitative restrictions.

Article XVIII, section B, para 12(b) provides that:

> On a date to be determined by them, the contracting parties shall review all restriction still applied under this section on that date. Beginning two years after that date, contracting parties applying restrictions under this section shall enter into consultations of the type provided for in sub-para (a) above with the contracting parties at intervals of approximately, but not less than, two years according to a programme to be drawn up

---

39 *Focus*, GATT Newsletter, no 11, February 1982, p 3.

40 McGovern, *op cit*, pp 295–96.

41 *Ibid*, p 33.

each year by the contracting parties; provided that no consultation under this sub-paragraph shall take place within two years after the conclusion of a consultation of a general nature under any other provisions of this paragraph.

Since 1972, a more simplified procedure than full consultation is permitted under Article XVIII B.[42]

The purpose of the simplification is to minimise the burden of the administrative procedures and to encourage transparency in quantitative restriction imposed by developing countries. If consultation before imposing new, or increasing the general level of quantitative restriction is impracticable, such consultation should take place immediately afterwards.

Where full consultation is undertaken, the relevant contracting parties, as well as the GATT Secretariat and the International Monetary Fund (IMF) are required to provide documentary input. The IMF is required to comment on whether in its view the relevant consulting country's policy stance for correcting its balance of payments problems and reliance on import restrictions is appropriate.

In a simplified consultation, the documentary requirements are slight, and the IMF does not participate actively in proceedings. All the committee can do is to formulate a recommendation as to whether a full consultation would be warranted, whereas in a full consultation, the committee is required to reach conclusions and, in language that is not always very direct, formulate recommendations.[43]

If the contracting parties deem that the quantitative restrictions applied by relevant contracting party are inconsistent with Article XVIII (subject to the stipulation under Article XIV),[44] the contracting parties shall indicate the nature of the inconsistency and may advise that the restrictions suitably modified.

If the result of the consultation is that the quantitative restrictions are held inconsistent with Article XIII (and Article IV) and have impeded the international trade of other contracting parties the relevant contracting parties will be informed and appropriate recommendations made for securing conformity with GATT provisions within a specified period.

If agreement is not reached between the applying country and the partner country, the decision will be handed over to the contracting parties which may take one of three possible courses of action:

First, if in the course of consultation with a contracting party it is found that the restrictions are not consistent with the provisions of section B of Article XVIII or with those of Article XIII (subject to the provisions of Article XIV), they shall indicate the nature of the inconsistency and may advise that the restrictions be suitably modified.[45]

---

42 Whalley, J, *The Uruguay Round and Beyond*: The Final Report from the Ford Foundation Supported Project, 1989, Houndmills, Basingstoke: Macmillan.

43 *Ibid*, p 118.

44 Which regulate the implementation of allocation of quantitative restriction, import licensing, or other non discrimination import licences.

45 Article XVIII, para 12(c)(i) of the GATT.

Secondly, if as a result of the consultations with the contracting parties no agreement is reached and they determine that the restrictions are being applied inconsistently with such provisions, and that damage to the trade of the contracting party initiating the procedure is caused or threatened thereby, they shall recommend the withdrawal or modification of the restrictions. If the restrictions are not withdrawn or modified within such time as the contracting parties may prescribe, they may release the contracting party initiating the procedure from such obligations under the agreement towards the contracting party applying such restriction as they determine to be appropriate in the circumstances.[46]

Thirdly, if a contracting party against which action has been taken finds that the release of obligations authorised by the contracting parties affects the operation of its programme and policy of economic development, it shall be free, not later than 60 days after such action is taken, to give written notice to the Executive Secretary to the contracting parties of its intention to withdraw from this agreement. Such withdrawal shall take effect on the 60th day following the day on which the notice is received.[47]

Protection for an infant industry

The GATT makes provision for the concept of an infant industry and for its protection under Article XVIII.

Developing countries whose economy can only support low standards of living and are in the early stages of development enjoy additional facilities to allow them to grant tariff protection required for the establishment of a particular industry. A country which can only support a low standard of living and is in the early stages of development may require government assistance to promote the establishment of a particular industry. Where the contracting party decides that whilst inconsistent with other provisions of this agreement, and it is practicable to achieve the objective, it may have recourse to the procedures under section C, para 13 of Article XVIII.

Where protection measures are proposed for an infant industry, the contracting parties must be informed about the measures that will be carried out. The policy must comply with the appropriate time limit determined by Article XVIII, para 14 and approval may be given by the contracting parties after discussion.

Gilbert P Verbit observes that:[48]

> Article XVIII has been interpreted liberally, too liberally for some commentators have characterised it as a 'rubber clause' and many developing countries have taken advantage of it to impose quantitative import restrictions.

Article XVIII is an important article for developing countries. This article allows a developing country to apply non-discriminatory quantitative restrictions to assist the development and restructuring of its economy. But this exception is limited by the

---

46   Article XVIII s B, para 12(d) of the GATT.

47   Article XVIII s B, para 12(e) of the GATT.

48   Gilbert, VP, *Trade Agreements for Developing Countries*, 1969, p 57, New York and London: Columbia University Press.

obligation to seek a prior request from the contracting parties and includes a time limit for the proposed quantitative restriction. There is also an obligation to provide periodical reports.

The provisions of Article XVIII have been considerably relaxed in recent years to a degree that most advocates of liberal trade policy would find excessive. According to Robert Hudec:[49]

> This article allows developing countries to set aside tariff bindings and the prohibition of quantitative import restriction with little or no compensation, with little or no control as to the purpose of measures taken and with only a power to disapprove of such measures after they are taken, a power that looks as though it could easily be blocked by the developing country majority in the GATT, but the procedure still provides the developed countries with the opportunity to interrogate developing countries about economic necessity and this provide an occasion for bullying and other kinds of ad hoc pressures. If the procedure stimulates developed country interest in stopping a measure, the legal loopholes of Article XVIII will not necessarily prevent them from doing so.

Furthermore he comments that:[50]

> There is probably no solution that does not require some degree of trust. If nothing were to be gained, there would be no reason to ask the governments of developing countries to take such a risk. But, if the observations which have been made earlier about the difficulty of controlling interventionist policies are correct, then GATT obligations do offer a positive gain for any government pursuing an interventionist some judgment about where to intervene. Such government can acquire substantially greater control over policy, and thus substantially greater welfare gains from it, with the aid of the restraints created by the type of procedure established by XVIII. Far from diminishing sovereignty, such legal restraints would increase it.

Criticisms has been directed at GATT's balance of payments provisions.[51]

> First, there is no provision for an adequate examination of the justification for trade measures to protect the level of reserves. In any event, the GATT is powerless to address the root causes of balance of payments problems, so it cannot take a sufficiently strong position on what should be done.

> Second, specific quantitative restrictions cannot affect the trade balance in anything but the very short term. Increased international capital mobility has weakened the case for using quantitative restrictions for these purposes. Exchange rate adjustments supported by appropriate macro economic policies are the way to deal with balance of payments disequilibria.

Developed countries have also criticised the article.[52] First, not all countries will respect their notification obligations and it is not always possible to identify the GATT justification for import restrictions. Secondly, background documentation is sometimes less than explicit as to the nature and coverage of measures being applied. Thirdly, the GATT Balance of Payments Committee's examination of consulting countries is

---

49   Hudec, R, *Developing Countries in the GATT Legal System*, 1987, London: Gower.

50   Hudec, *ibid*.

51   Whalley, *op cit*, p 120–21.

52   *Ibid*, p 121.

considered by some to be perfunctory and pro forma and the simplified consultations have become so frequent as to almost represent the norm.

On the other hand, some argue the article does not go far enough:[53]

What the paragraph did not do and still does not do is consider the necessity for positive assistance to exports as distinct from protection against imports. While the section recognises that country which can only support low standards of living and which are in the early stages of development have special problems, the solution proposed by the article do not seem to have been adequate to meet the problems in the eyes of developed countries who have thus far shown their opinion of the article by studiously ignoring it.

Part IV of the GATT

In February 1965, Part IV consisting of Articles XXXVI, XXXVII, XXXVIII was added to the General Agreement, committing industrialised countries to assist developing countries in their development programmes.

This Part provides for freedom from the obligations to offer reciprocal concessions when negotiations for tariff reductions is being held. The developed countries agreed that, except when compelling reasons made it impossible, they will refrain from increasing barriers to the exports of primary and other products of special interest to developing countries. High priority was accorded to the reduction and elimination of the existing barriers by developed countries to developing countries and elimination of existing barriers to the products of particular export interest of developing countries.[54]

This provision demonstrates that the GATT is sympathetic to the concerns of developing countries. It was an attempt to codify in some way the discussions that had gone on in GATT over the previous 15 years.[55]

John H Jackson is of the view that the articles are really a statement of the ideal goals rather than a measured technical statement of obligations with legal implications. However, more substantive legal and procedural obligations are set out in para 1(b) and (c).[56]

Article XXXVI generally, recognises the development needs of developing countries, the importance to them of improved market access, commodity price stability, the diversification of economic structures and the advantages of general cooperation.

Article XXXVI, para 8 of the GATT provides that:

The developed contracting parties do not expect reciprocity for commitments made by them in trade negotiations to reduce or remove tariffs and other barriers to the trade of less developed contracting parties.

This paragraph is of great importance for developing countries.

---

53 Gupta, KR, *A Study of the General Agreement on Tariffs and Trade*, 1967, Delhi: S Chand and Co.

54 Das, DK, *International Trade Policy: a Developing Country Perspective*, London: Macmillan, p 43.

55 Whalley, *op cit*, p 114.

56 Jackson, JH, *Legal Problems of International Economic Relations*, 1977, p 1015, St Paul, Minnesota: West Publishing Co.

The need for such an exemption from the Reciprocity principle was first advanced by the UNCTAD I conference which recommend the principles to govern international relations and trade policies conducive to development.

Under the General Principles, no 8 of the Final Act of UNCTAD it is stated as follows:

> International trade should be conducted to mutual advantage on the basis of the most favoured nation treatment and should be free from measures detrimental to the trading interest of either countries. However, developed countries should grant concessions to all developing countries and extend to developing countries all concession they grant to one another and should not, in granting these or other concessions, require any concession in return from developing countries. New preferential concessions, both tariffs and non-tariffs, should be made to developing countries as a whole and such preferences should not be extended to developed countries. ... Special preferences at present enjoyed by certain developing countries and developed countries should be regarded as transitional and subject to progressive reduction. They should be eliminated as and when effective international measures guaranteeing as least equivalent advantages of the countries concerned come into operation.[57]

The new preferential concession was intended to be a temporary measure. The non-reciprocity principle is founded on the basic objectives of the GATT laid down in Article XXXVI and also in the Preamble of the GATT. It will be recalled that the main objectives of the GATT are:[58]

1   to ensure that their relationships in the field of trade and economic endeavour be conducted with a view to raising standards of living;

2   ensuring full employment and a large and steadily growing volume of real income and effective demand;

3   developing the full use of the resources of the world and expanding the production and exchange of goods.

In attaining those objectives, the contracting parties are described as:[59]

> Being desirous of contributing to these objectives by entering into reciprocal and mutually advantageous arrangements directed to the substantial reduction of tariffs and other barriers to trade and to the elimination of discriminatory treatment in international commerce.

Following the emergence of developing countries, particularly when they united and formed UNCTAD, they have been able to obtain some recognition on their particular needs. Thus, the contracting parties are described as:[60]

> Recalling that the basic objectives of this agreement include the raising of standards of living and the progressive development of the economies of all contracting parties, and considering that the attainment of these objectives is particularly urgent for less developed contracting parties.

---

57   Kirdar, U, *The Structure of United Nations Economic Aid to Underdeveloped Countries*, 1966, pp 247–46, The Hague: Martinus Nijhoff.

58   Preamble of the GATT.

59   Preamble of the GATT.

60   Article XXVI, para 1(a) of the GATT.

Further, it is noted:[61]

> that export earnings of the less developed contracting parties can play a vital part in their economic development and that the extent of this contribution depends on the prices paid by the less developed contracting parties for essential imports, the volume of their exports, and the prices received for these exports.

Thus, the concept of equality has changed into a concept of inequality. It means that equality for developing countries will not be achieved through the giving of the same opportunities, reciprocity and equality before the law. It is hoped it will be achieved through the provision of different opportunities, protection, preferential rights relationship which is not based on reciprocity.

This change of conception can be seen from the following statement:[62]

> It is understood that the phrase 'do not expect reciprocity' means, in accordance with the objectives set forth in this article, that the less developed contracting parties should not be expected, in the course of trade negotiations, to make contributions which are inconsistent with their individual development, financial and trade needs, taking into consideration past trade developments.

The process of trade liberalisation was originally based on the traditional principle that all parties were bargaining from an equal position. This new non-reciprocity principle constitutes a recognition of the present interest of developing countries. The change of concepts is still within the context of trade liberalisation, and this new principle is only temporary. The implementation of the non-reciprocity principle for developing countries, however, is difficult to realise in international trade.

Articles XXXVII contains a 'best endeavours' commitment relating to prioritisation of products of interest to developing countries in any trade liberalisation exercise, including tariff escalation. It contains a form of 'standstill' commitment, and refers also to fiscal or internal taxes. These commitments are all of a 'best endeavours' nature, carrying no obligation for action on anybody's part.[63]

This article may more appropriate be deemed as a 'standstill principle'. The meaning of standstill is:[64]

> The developed contracting parties shall to the fullest extent possible – ie except when compelling reasons, which may include legal reasons, make it impossible – give effect to the following provisions:
>
> (a) accord high priority to the reduction and elimination of barriers to products currently or potentially of particular export interest to less developed contracting parties, including customs duties and other restrictions which differentiate unreasonably between such products in their primary and in their processed forms;

---

61 Article XXVI, para 1(b) of the GATT.
62 Annex I of ad Article XXXVI, para 8 of the GATT.
63 Whalley, *op cit*, p 114.
64 Article XXXVII, para 1 of the GATT.

(b) refrain from introducing, or increasing the incidence of, customs duties or non–tariff import barriers on products currently or potentially of particular export interest to less developed contracting parties; ...

The standstill principle gives rise to an expectation that developed countries will give a first priority to the reduction and elimination of restrictions against potential products or particular products exported by developing countries. These restrictions include not only customs duties but also others which differentiate unreasonably between such products in both their primary and processed forms.

These considerations are relevant in negotiations for the reduction and elimination of tariffs based on Article XXVIII, XXVIII *bis*, Article XXXIII.[65]

The priority and standstill principles assume developed countries will refrain from any action that would hinder increasing the consumption of primary products, as either raw materials or processed goods, wholly or mainly produced in the territories of less developed contracting parties.

The standstill principle has had a limited influence in any further negotiations, because developed countries have insisted that it should be dealt with in the context of multilateral negotiations within the GATT framework.

In developed countries whenever it is considered that effect is not being given to any of the provisions of Article XXXVI, para 1(a), (b) or (c), the matter shall be reported to the contracting parties either by the contracting party not so giving effect to the relevant provisions or by any other interested contracting party.[66]

If contracting parties are requested so to do by any interested contracting party, and without prejudice to any bilateral consultations that may be undertaken, they are to consult with the contracting party concerned and all interested contracting parties with respect to the matter with a view to reaching solutions satisfactory to all contracting parties concerned in order to further the objectives set forth in Article XXXVI. In the course of these consultations, the reasons given in cases where effect was not being given to the provisions of Article XXXVII para 1 (a), (b) or (c) shall be examined.[67]

In the realisation of Article XXXVIII para (c), the consultations by the contracting parties might also, in appropriate cases, be directed towards agreement on joint action designed to further the objectives of this agreement as envisaged in para 1 of Article XXV.[68]

Developing countries argue that in connection with trade between them, they agree to take appropriate action in the implementation of articles under Part IV for the benefit of trade in other developing countries. In so far that action is consistent with their individual present and future development, financial and trade needs past trade

---

65 Annex I of ad Article XXXVII of the GATT.

66 Article XXXVII, para 2(a) of the GATT.

67 Article XXXVII, para 2(b)(i) of the GATT.

68 Article XXXVII, para 2(b)(iii) of the GATT.

developments as well as the trade interest of developing contracting parties as a whole are taken into account.[69]

Article XXXVIII provides for joint action within the framework of this agreement, where appropriate, to take action through international arrangement to:

1   provide improved and acceptable conditions of access to world markets for primary products of particular interest to developing countries,

2   devise measures designed to attain stable, equitable and remunerative prices for exports of such products,[70]

3   seek appropriate collaboration in matters of trade and development policy with the United Nations and its organs and agency, including any institutions that may be created on the basis of recommendations by the UNCTAD,[71]

4   study the export potential of developing countries to facilitate access to export markets for the products of the industries thus developed

5   seek appropriate collaboration with governments and international organisations.[72]

Part IV is important for developing countries. But, this Part only contains guidelines for developed countries which wish to expand their assistance to developing countries in the field of export promotion. It does not give explicit commitments to developing countries. As Gupta observes:[73]

> The actual realisation of the hopes of the developing countries will depend upon the attitude which the developed countries may take in this regards. The proviso cited in this chapter leaves enough scope for a developed country, if it so desires, for not abiding by the commitments. Ultimately, whatever may be the institutional machinery devised, if the required political will is lacking, the objectives sought cannot be realised.

Part IV does not provide any exception for developing countries from Article I. It does, however, contain the first formal statement in the GATT legal text on the principle of non-reciprocity.[74]

The Committee on Trade and Development is charged with overseeing the implementation of Part IV. Each year it reviews action taken by developed countries in favour of developing countries, in particular in the context of the Generalised System of Preferences (GSP) as well as trade measures establishing or intensifying barriers to the trade of developing counties.

Since March 1980, it has been assisted by the Sub-Committee on Protective Measures. This was established after developing countries called for closer supervision of the operation of the standstill clause in the light of renewed protectionism, and also in response to Resolution 131 of the Fifth United Nations Conference on Trade and

---

69   Article XXXVII, para 4 of the GATT.

70   Article XXXVIII, para 2(a) of the GATT

71   Article XXXVIII, para 2(c) of the GATT.

72   Article XXXVIII, para 2(c) of the GATT.

73   Gupta, *op cit*, p 189.

74   Whalley, *op cit*, p 114.

Development in 1979. This resolution invited GATT to examine protective measures affecting export of developing countries.[75]

Because of problems encountered by developing countries in their trade, a call was made at the Tokyo Round on 28 November 1979, for 'differential and more favourable treatment, reciprocity and fuller participation of developing countries'.[76] This became known as the Enabling Clause.

The Enabling Clause provide a permanent legal basis for the granting of preferences to developing countries which was considerably expanded in 1970s particularly through the GSP developed countries. If difficulties arise in connection with the establishment, modification or withdrawal of such preferential treatment, the parties concerned must consult. In addition, the Enabling Clause reaffirms[77] the concept of non reciprocity. It includes a clause stipulating that less developed contracting parties expect that their capacity to make contributions or negotiated concessions would improve with the progressive development of their economies and improvement in their trade situation, and would accordingly expect to participate more fully in the framework of rights and obligations under the General Agreement.

This is referred to as the 'graduation provision'.[78] The 'concept of graduation' has assumed a prominent place in the debate on special and differential treatment.

The Ministerial declaration established more detailed and concrete procedures for the review of the implementation of Part IV. These took the form of individual and collective consultation. The Committee on Trade and Development makes arrangements for consultations, and agrees on a tentative time table for them. Discussions include assessment as to how the economic and trade policies of countries consulted have responded to their commitments under Article XXXVI, XXXVII, and the joint action requirements embodied in Article XXXVIII.

Each consulting country will be invited to supply information on all these point covering a period of at least three years. That information will be supplemented by material prepared by the GATT secretariat on developments in trade and commercial policies. The Sub-Committee on Protective Measures will under Part IV also continue to examine any new measures not yet considered in the consultations. Because of the relationship between Part IV commitments and the Enabling Clause, the Committee on Trade and Development will at the same time look at how both are being put into effect. The committee thus reviews the operation of the enabling clause with a view to its more effective implementation, *inter alia*, with respect to objectivity and transparency of modifications to GSP schemes and the operation of consultative provisions relating to differential and more favourable treatment for developing countries.[79]

---

75 *Focus*, GATT Newsletter no 21, April–May 1983, p 3.

76 *Ibid.*

77 *Ibid.*

78 *Ibid.*

79 *Focus, op cit*, pp 3–4.

If we look closer at the role of the developing countries in the GATT system, it can be seen that the developing countries did not have a meaningful role in drafting the GATT system; it was, therefore, not dominated by development considerations.

Presently, a number of developing countries, accounting for the bulk of developing countries trade, are contracting parties of the GATT. For a long time, the stance taken by developing countries in the GATT has been that in terms of economic strength, trade volumes and market sizes, the contracting parties of the GATT are highly unequal. Therefore, in the international trading system, unequals should not be treated as equals.

Premised on this belief, they sought and obtained a variety of special and differential treatment measures for their products, notably through relief from certain GATT obligation and the GSP. It is debatable how valuable these special and differential measures had been for some developing countries.

DUMPING

Anti–dumping and countervailing measures are dealt with in Article VI of GATT. This is dealt with in detail in Chapter 8

SUBSIDIES

Article XVI of GATT has two sections dealing with subsidies.

Section A deals with subsidies that 'operate directly or indirectly to increase exports of any product from, or to reduce imports of any product into, its territory ...'. If a State grants this type of subsidy, that state is obligated to notify the other contracting parties. Furthermore, if it is determined that this subsidy may prejudice the interest of another contracting party then the subsidising state is obliged to enter into negotiations to limit this subsidy at the request of an affected party.

Section B sets out additional provisions which recognise that the granting of a subsidy can cause harm to another contracting party and upset the equilibrium of normal commercial interest.

Therefore, the use of subsidies should be avoided as far as possible but if a subsidy must be applied then it should not result in that contracting party gaining more than an equitable share of world exports in that product, taking into account the contracting parties' share of that trade in a prior representative period.

The section goes on in para 4 to provide that 'from 1 January 1958 or the earliest practicable date thereafter, contracting parties shall cease to grant either directly or indirectly any form of subsidy on the export of any product other than a primary product ...'.

Primary product means any product of farm, forest or fishery, or any mineral, in its natural form or which has undergone such processing as is customarily required to prepare it for marketing in a substantial volume in international trade.[80]

---

80   GATT explanatory note.

It is significant to note that developing countries are not signatories to this section. Whilst they can use subsidies, this may be offset by other countries using countervailing duties under Article VI against them.

Whilst the GATT articles only provided general principles, a Subsidies Code introduced in the Tokyo Round of 1979 attempted to give meaning to the term subsidies without defining it.

Specifically the code:

1 Forbids subsidies upon non-primary products.

2 Minerals are not included although export subsidies on minerals/manufactured goods causing adverse effects are prohibited (Article 9).

3 Permits the use of domestic subsidies and acknowledges the role they play in the development of the economy.

Article II(1) goes on to say:

> Signatories recognise that subsidies other than export subsidies are widely used as important instruments for the promotion of social and economic policy objectives and do not intend to restrict the right of signatories to use subsidies to achieve these and other important policy objectives which they consider desirable.[81]

4 Export subsidies must not cause serious injury to the trade or production of another contracting party.[82] This means that if an industry is injured by a subsidy, then that country can impose a countervailing duty and may also be subject to Article XXIII, the general dispute resolution article if it involves an export subsidy.

5 Compensation is allowed in response to any one of three effects as set out in Article 8:

   (a) injury to the domestic industry of another GATT member;

   (b) nullification or impairment of any benefits set out in GATT;

   (c) serious prejudice to the interests of another member;

   (d) serious prejudice in the domestic market of either the complaining member, the subsidising country or a third country.

However, the Subsidies Code was administratively difficult. Terminology was ill-defined and not all countries were signatories, although developed countries did become signatories. Very few signatories reflect the fact that there were uncertainties.

The Uruguay Round attempted to further refine the word 'subsidy'. The resultant 1994 Agreement on Subsidies and Countervailing Measures sought to rectify these problems:

1 The agreement defined subsidy by stating that a government must contribute financially, directly or through another public body or mechanism, or provide income or price support.

---

81 Article 11(1), 31 UST at 632, 1186 UNTS at 224.
82 Article 14(3), 31 UST at 524, 1186 UNTS at 228.

Article 1 also recognised that government aid can be financial assistance *via* direct grants, taxation benefits, provision of goods or services or provision of assets. The only proviso being that it benefited the recipient.

2 The assistance must be limited to an industry or a company (Article 2).

Subsidies benefiting domestic industries, such as public investment in infrastructure, roads, electricity grids, and the like, are non-specific and therefore outside the reach of the agreement. A subsidy is specific where the 'granting authority ... explicitly limits access to a subsidy to certain enterprise' (Article 2(a)). If 'objective criteria or conditions governing the eligibility' for the subsidy exist, it is considered non-specific (Article 2(b)).

However, 'notwithstanding any appearance of non-specificity ... other factors may be considered', such as provision of a subsidy to a limited number of enterprises, predominant use by a limited number of enterprises, disproportionately large amounts to certain enterprises, or the discretion exercised by the granting authority in providing the subsidy (Article 2(c)).

THE WORLD TRADE ORGANISATION

Introduction

The then Director General of GATT, Arthur Dunkle in 1991 was responsible for the preparation of what became known as the 'Dunkle Text' covering the Uruguay Round negotiations to date and a projection as to what the round proposed to achieve.

The Text contained a charter for a Multilateral Trade Organisation (MTO) with the aim of providing an institutional framework within which the results of the Uruguay Round could operate. Within the MTO was set up a new dispute settlement mechanism and a Trade Policy Review Mechanism (TPRM). In addition, the framework provided annexes of the more important areas such as The General Agreement on Trade in Services (GATS) and The Agreement on Trade Related Intellectual property (TRIPS). Virtually all contracting parties to GATT favoured the new MTO, although at the insistence of the USA it was renamed the World Trade Organisation (WTO).

The WTO Constitution and Charter provided:

1 All GATT contracting parties become members.

2 A conference of Ministers. This peak organisation was to meet at least every two years.

3 Councils were set up to overlook the obligations in goods, services and intellectual property, these being the key areas of trade and investment. Sub-constitutions were drawn up for each of these councils, although it was recognised that these constitutions would change and require amendment as a result of subsequent practice.

4 A series of annexes setting out treaty rights and obligations of contracting parties.

5   Dispute resolution was highlighted. Besides the general dispute settlement mechanism and the TPRM, specific dispute resolution mechanisms are found in annexes where it was felt warranted. For example, in GATS and TRIPS.

6   Grandfather rights was a big problem in GATT. No such problem exists with WTO for there are no longer provisional applications only, so henceforth there will only be definite applications of WTO structure.

7   The vexing opt out clause (Article XXXV) of GATT was no longer applicable, except for smaller countries and only at the time of their initial entry to WTO.

8   WTO recognised concern for the environment, thus recognising that depending on a country's level of development, its reaction to environment matters may differ, thus recognising the special position of less developed countries.

9   The dispute resolution procedures are detailed. It aimed to ensure that any decision is made by 'consensus'. Consensus is arrived at if no member present at the meeting when the decision is taken, formally objects to the proposed decision, no vote of contracting parties is required. If a solution cannot be found in a mediation, consultation or conciliation a complaints panel comprising trade experts who report in accordance with a time line to a committee of the contracting parties. Appeals are allowed only on legal issues to a body of legal experts. If the defending party does not conform, then the Dispute Settlement Body (DSB) comprising WTO members by consensus, can sanction the complainant to withdraw benefits.

Significance of the WTO

WTO in time will become a formidable arm of the international trade system together with the IMF and the World Bank. WTO will provide a high profile and prestigious organisation properly accredited by national governments. The new international structure is aimed at creating better understanding, co-ordination between WTO, a trade organisation and monetary organisations like IMF and the World Bank and hopefully provide a cross pollination of ideas helpful to all organisations.

A key to the new framework is the dispute settlement mechanism. The lessons learned positively from GATT was that to take a case approach to resolving problems required a structure within which a case could be examined and resolved. The resultant mechanism in WTO is a regime to solve disputes, a regime that is open for all the world to see and hopefully will assist in ensuring that contracting parties will follow set procedures and thus making the system appear and in reality produce a credible, easily recognised and respected result effective in implementing a contracting party's treaty obligations.

Another important feature of the institutional framework is the setting up of the Trade Policy Review Mechanism (TPRM). The TPRM looks overall at a contracting party's trading policies whilst the dispute mechanism as mentioned earlier, concentrates on specific obligations under the WTO charter. The idea of the TPRM is to look at general trade policies of contracting parties to see if they have or potentially will have any adverse effects on member countries, even though these trade policies at the moment do not have any adverse effects or are inconsistent with trading policies of any contracting countries.

In time we can see TPRM playing a very important role in raising potential problems before they actually affect the trading world. This could be put in place to stop the brush fire from fanning into a destructive bush fire.

The General Agreement on Trade in Services (GATS)

The world is becoming service orientated and GATS is of obvious importance. Banking, management consultancies, law, engineering, advertising, telecommunications and many other professions and trades are all based on service. The installation of computers and the accompanying software is a good example of where both the service industry and the goods themselves depend upon each other; yet goods and services can be distinguished for trade purposes:

1   Services generally are intangible processes between producers and consumers, involving rights and obligations.

2   They involve supply from one country to another country.

3   They are generally subject to government regulations.

4   They are generally not portable from one place to another.

5   On a cost benefit basis, services vary from one country to another, depending upon their state of economic development.

GATS consists of:

1   A definition of the obligations of members.

2   Annexes dealing with such matters as movement of personnel, the service provided and the industry involved.

3   Schedules setting out commitments of member countries in the service sector.

4   Ministerial decisions as attachments to GATS, eg terms of reference for future negotiations on service in the maritime industry.

Important general aspects of the GATS are dealt with in Part I, Article 1 which defines the meaning of supply in a model way:

1   Supply of a service from the territory of one member into the territory of any other member (cross-border sense), eg international shipping or telecommunications.

2   Supply of a service in the territory of one member to the service consumer of any other member (movement of consumers to the location of the supplier), eg tourism, ship repairs.

3   Supply of a service through the presence of service supplying entities of one member in the territory of any other member (service by establishing a presence in the other country), eg establishing a foreign banking subsidiary or a joint venture.

4   'Supply of a service by natural persons of one Member in the territory of any other Member' (service requiring personnel being moved into the other country), eg consultants or supply of foreign experts.

Article 1 defines any 'measures of Members' to mean any measure made, given or taken by central, regional or a local government or authority and includes measures by non-governmental bodies in the exercise of such delegated powers.

The core obligation of GATS is set out in Article II. GATS members commit themselves to treat services and service providers from a member country in the same way as they treat service and service providers from any other country. However, note that a country could ban all providers – and this is consistent with the MFN principle.

An annex to Article II allows an exception to the MFN principle provided the exception complies with the requirements of the annexure. This allows for specific or temporary exemptions. The annex provides:

1   An exemption is only granted if it refers to an existing measure that was in existence at the completion of the Uruguay Round in December 1993.

2   An exemption must not be given for more than 10 years.

3   The Council for Trade in Services must review all exemptions granted for over five years. The review considers whether the enabling condition for the exemption still exists and if so, to set a date for the next review.

In dealing with the MFN principle, we need also to consider Article XVI and Article XXII.

Article XVI(i) deals with market access commitments under which:

... each member shall accord services and service suppliers of any other Member treatment no less favourable than that provided for under the terms, limitations and conditions agreed and specified in its Schedule.

Sub-Article (2) lists types of quantitative restrictions including:

... types of legal entity or joint venture through which a service supplier may provide a service, and limitations on the participation of foreign capital.

This means putting a limit on members of foreign suppliers in a specific market, a quota on the monetary value of service transactions or assets or the number of services and the number of employees in a certain service industry or even the type of legal entity used in providing the service. This provides a control over the amount of foreign capital in a service industry.

Article XVII states:

Each member shall accord to services and service suppliers of any other member, in respect of all measures affecting the supply of services, treatment no less favourable than that it accords to its own like services and service suppliers.

It further states:

Formally, identical or formally different treatment shall be considered to be less favourable if it modifies the conditions of competition in favour of services or service suppliers of the member compared to like services or services suppliers of any member.

Article XVII protects foreign suppliers from being discriminated against by a country's taxation laws. This is of importance when one considers that services are establishment based and for developing countries the transfer of skill and know-how leads to the hiring and training of local workers.

The article is of great importance in situations of *de jure* co-existence with domestic competitors, paralleled by *de facto* inequality, eg where a country's trade practices legislation gives the government power to control monopolistic mergers that may have the effect of determining foreign investment, yet effectively acts as a protectionist device.

National treatment commitments thus prevent both *de jure* and *de facto* types of discrimination.

Article III is the transparency requirement which means that all relevant laws, regulations and administrative guidelines pertaining to trade in services are to be published. There is also a duty to notify the Council for Trade in Services of anything new or changes in national standards which affect commitments set out in Part III of GATS dealing with market access and national treatment.

Article IV facilitates the inclusion of developing countries to GATS. This accords with the idea that there is a need to recognise developing country participants in services. It is important to allow developing countries some control over access to their markets to sustain that government's policy ideals which may vary from protection for infant industries to the acquiring of know-how, depending on the state of that country's economic development.

In looking at Article IV, it is relevant also to consider Article XIX which covers the situation of negotiations being carried out over a sector of differing services at the same time. This clearly benefits developing countries for they may give a concession in one sector and limit them in another.

Article V provides for the prevention of discrimination among the parties.

The next article of importance is Article XI which sets a request to be reasonable, objective and important and to provide a quick review of an administrative decision of domestic law. This is arrived at providing due process of law to a member, including access to courts and tribunals so far as exists for a domestic dispute.

Article VII encourages international recognition of licences certificates and authorisation in services. Presumably this is to ensure an easily recognisable and attainable standard among GATS members.

Article XIII and IX can be looked at together. Article VIII ensures that monopolies and exclusive service suppliers do not overstep the mark and proceed in a way that is inconsistent with GATS.

Article IX is a requirement to consult with the aim of eliminating restrictive business practices if such practices restrict competition. Article X is an exception based on the principle of non-discrimination and is of no consequence.

It can be seen that Article VIII is aimed at government activity, whilst Article IX is aimed at the private sector. The question of dumping is important here for services allow the adoption of an aggressive pricing system in a particular market to increase market share or to enter a new market. This is simply done by subsidising incentives given at the market place to a level where the cost of the service provided is less than the subsidy in many cases.

As mentioned earlier under the section on dumping, one has to prove material injury and in the case of services it may be a difficult task.

Articles X to XV deal generally with matters at a national level. Exceptions are provided for emergency safeguard measures based on the principle of non-discrimination (Article X); for non-discriminatory, temporary restrictions to safeguard the balance of payments (Article XII); for government procurement (Article XIII); and certain public policy measures (Articles XIV, XIV *bis*). Similar to the commitments to negotiate additional multilateral disciplines for emergency safeguards measures (*cf* Article X) and for government procurement in services (*cf* Article XIII), Article XV provides for 'negotiations with a view to developing the necessary multilateral disciplines to avoid ... trade-distortive effects' of subsidies and to 'address the appropriateness of countervailing procedures'. Finally, any 'member which considers that it is adversely affected by a subsidy of another member may request consultations with that member on such matters' (Article XV(2)).

It can be seen that GATS does not stop discriminatory subsidies or anti-dumping yet such measures will be inconsistent with GATS obligations unless they are dealt with as exemptions under Article II.

Part III of GATS deals with specific commitments (Article XVI) national treatment (Article XVII) and additional commitments (Article XVIII).

Article XVI provides members give market access to service providers subject to 'the terms limitations and conditions agreed and specified' by each Member State in its national schedule. The mandate, does not apply to services for which a Member State did not make a market access commitment in its national schedule. However, market access is not defined. Instead, it provides for six limiting elements that unless specified in a member's schedule are in principle prohibited. The limiting elements are:

1   members of service suppliers allowed;

2   the value of transactions or assets;

3   quantity of service allowed;

4   numbers of employees;

5   the type of legal entity used by a service supplier;

6   maximum amount of foreign participation allowed.

There is also recognition that national treatment does not mean identical treatment to domestic services, rather that the treatment does not place the foreign service at a competitive disadvantage.

Finally, there is allowance for commitments to be made on measures going beyond the provisions of the current GATS.

Part IV dealing with progressive liberalisation of GATS provides that future rounds be directed 'towards increasing the general level of specific commitments undertaken by members under this agreement'. Essentially, it is arrived at liberalising trade over time and by so doing it will lead in the future to an incentive to export overseas and business at home will benefit either by a wider range of choice or a lowering of prices.

Part IX sets out specific commitments on market access and national treatment by a list of scheduled service sections, sub-sections or activities and the schedule is subject to conditions, qualifications and limitations either across all types of services supplied on a specific type of service.

This means there is a commitment schedule of services and service sectors allowed by a member. Parallel with this schedule is another that sets out services that do not conform. This means that commitments made in these schedules are binding and a member cannot impose new restrictions that affect market access or national treatment without compensating an affected member.

The annexes and the Ministerial decisions flesh out GATS. They can be categorised as either exceptions to the principles of MFN or movement of staff; sector specific services; or those dealing with ongoing negotiations of the aforementioned.

The annexes provide for exemptions to the general principles enshrined in GATS.

1   We have looked earlier at the annex on Article II exemptions in the context of the Council for Trade in Services.

2   The annex on Movement of National Persons Supplying Services states that members can agree on criteria to allow temporary entry of all categorises of natural persons. However, it does not apply to persons seeking employment, citizenship, residence or employment on a permanent basis. It simply allows natural persons who supply services or are employees of such to provide services according to the terms of specific commitments agreed for such persons.

This annex is of greatest effect to the developing countries who have a comparative advantage in labour intensive industries. A ministerial decision was also adopted for negotiations to continue after the Uruguay Round to attempt to achieve higher levels of commitment by members, for most developed countries did not include in their schedules categories that were of a labour intensive nature.

3   The annex on financial services lists activities classified as financial services. It also is restrictive in its application to control binding and domestic regulation of financial services. However, at least it did provide a forum whereby members could rely on the annex as a base to achieve greater liberalisation. A ministerial decision provided that regulations be extended for a further six months after the birth of WTO by which the members could improve, modify or withdraw total or part of their commitment to the annex without compensation.

4   The annex on telecommunications attempts to ensure that a service provider is given access and use of public telecommunications and other basic services on reasonable and non-discriminatory terms to supply services listed in its schedule.

5   The annex on negotiations on basic telecommunications deals with market accessibility and commitment at a national level of this service. A ministerial decision dealing with the same subject gives members until April 1996 to negotiate with each other upon this service. Members have agreed until negotiations are complete not to apply for any MFN exemptions even though it may have been referred to as an exemption under Article II. Important issues being considered are licensing,

standardisation of equipment, safeguards against monopoly supplies and the ownership and operations of telecommunication networks.

6   The annex on air transport services attempts to spell out all air traffic rights and ancillary activities that may be subject of future MFN negotiations in air traffic agreements. However, it does not apply to aircraft repair, maintenance, reservations or marketing. The annex recognises that the air transport industry is fluid and dynamic and so is subject to review five years hence.

7   The annex on maritime transport services is a blueprint for the liberalisation of international shipping and canalling services, access and use of port facilities and commercial practices applicable to the sector. The accompanying ministerial decisions on negotiations allows until June 1996 to negotiate an acceptable parcel. Until the deadline members can improve change and withdraw proposals without any fear of compensation and MFN will not be an issue during the transition period.

8   A ministerial decision on professional services establishes a working party to examine licensing and accreditation for professional services. This is basic to trade and investment between members and will facilitate cooperation between members. The accountancy problem is an area of prime importance and is regarded as essential to business development for uniformity of standards is necessary if trade is to develop.

CONCLUDING COMMENTS

On one side of the coin it may be said that GATS is a set of legally binding rules, transparent to allow and encourage trade and investment liberalisation of services. It represents a first attempt to resolve policy conflicts between members in a peaceful way. Allied benefits flow to the member countries in the form of more efficient allocation of domestic resources and access to technology available in a member country, leading to export opportunities.

On the other side of the coin, GATS is in effect a loose document based on broad non-specific obligations, allowing far too many exemptions and wobbly annexes and ministerial decisions.

Effectively it allows members to draft sectors and schedules which are beneficial to the member alone. This approach is not liberalising for support of other members in each sector is necessary for long term international trade liberalisation.

GATS as it is, relies far too much on the political goodwill of individual members to agree on a schedule of commitments in all the main sectors.

TUTORIAL QUESTIONS

1   Article II is pivotal to the GATT. Why?

2   Describe the most-favoured-nation principle of the GATT.

3   A central feature of the GATT is the non-discrimination principle. Discuss.

4   Outline the national treatment obligation in the GATT.

5   Outline the meaning of 'subsidies' and 'countervailing' duties.

6   Article XVII of GATT refers to state trading. What does this mean? Consider the position of market economies as against socialist economies.

7   'GATT is full of exceptions'. Discuss.

8   Outline the escape clause of Article XIX.

9   Discuss the use of quotas in the GATT.

10 What is a customs union and the meaning of free trade areas under the GATT?

11 National health, safety and security concerns allow a country to abuse the GATT. Discuss.

12 Which clause of the GATT provides for amending procedure? What is this procedure? What happens when new circumstances arise and GATT does not cover the situation?

13 Outline the GATT dispute settlement mechanism.

14 What are the weaknesses in the GATT dispute settlement mechanism?

15 Discuss and evaluate the new panel system of dispute resolution in the GATT.

16 Outline the waiver provisions of Article XXI.

17 Is Article XXIII adequate insurance to a member who has suffered harm as a result of a waiver?

18 How does a country become a contracting party to the GATT?

19 Why is the Uruguay Round of GATT considered so important?

20 What is the World Trade Organisation?

21 Discuss the General Agreement on Trade in Services.

22 What are the basic principles of the agreement on trade related aspects of intellectual property rights?

FURTHER READING

Articles

Arup, CJ, 'The Prospective GATT Agreement for Intellectual Property Protection' (1993) 4 *Australian Intellectual Property Journal* 181–208.

Bagchi, S, 'The Integration of the Textile Trade into GATT' (1994) 28 *Journal of World Trade* 31–42.

Castel, JG, 'The Uruguay Round and the Improvements to the GATT Dispute Settlement Rules and Procedures' (1989) 38 *International and Comparative Law Quarterly* 835–49.

Ching, MM, 'Evaluating the Effectiveness of the GATT Dispute Settlement System for Developing Countries' (1992–93) 16 *World Competition* 81–112.

Dharjee, R and Boisson de Chazournes, L, 'Trade Related Aspects of Intellectual Property Rights (TRIPS): Objectives, Approaches and Basic Principles of the GATT and of Intellectual property Conventions' (1990) 24 *Journal of World Trade* 5–15.

Evans, GE, 'Intellectual Property as a Trade Issue' (1994–95) 18 *World Competition* 137–180.

Feaver, D and Wilson, K, 'An Evaluation of Australia's Anti-Dumping and Countervailing Law and Policy' (1995) 29 *Journal of World Trade* 207–37.

Finger, JM, 'That Old GATT Magic No More Casts its Spell' (1991) 25 *Journal of World Trade* 19–22.

Gibbs, JM, 'The Uruguay Round and the International Trade System' (1987) 21 *Journal of World Trade* 5–12.

Horlick, GN and Shea, EC, 'The World Trade Organisation Anti-Dumping Agreement' (1994) 29 *Journal of World Trade* 5–31.

Knobl, PF, 'GATT Application: The Grandfather is Still Alive' (1991) 25 *Journal of World Trade* 101–18.

Kohona, PTB, 'Dispute Resolution under the World Trade Organisation' (1994) 28 *Journal of World Trade* 23–47.

Komuro, N, 'The WTO Dispute Settlement Mechanism' (1995) 29 *Journal of World Trade* 5–95.

Lukas, M, 'The Role of Private Parties in the Enforcement of the Uruguay Round Agreements' (1995) 29 *Journal of World Trade* 181–205.

Lutz, JM, 'GATT Reform or Regime Maintenance: Differing Solutions to World Trade Problems' (1991) 25 *Journal of World Trade* 107–122.

Marceau, G, 'Transition from GATT to WTO' (1995) 29 *Journal of World Trade* 147–163.

Nordgren, I, 'The GATT Panels During the Uruguay Round' (1991) 25 *Journal of World Trade* 57–72.

Pangratis, A and Vermulst, E, 'Injury in Anti-Dumping Proceedings' (1994) 28 *Journal of World Trade* 61–96.

Qureski, AH, 'The New GATT Trade Policy Review Mechanism: An Exercise in Transparency or Enforcement?' (1990) 24 *Journal of World Trade* 147–60.

Roessler, F, 'The Competence of GATT' (1987) 21 *Journal of World Trade* 73–83.

Rom, M, 'Some Early Reflections on the Uruguay Round Agreement as Seen from the Viewpoint of a Developing Country' (1994) 28 *Journal of World Trade* 5–30.

Sauve, P, 'Assessing the General Agreement on Trade in Services' (1995) 29 *Journal of World Trade* 125–45.

See also 'Various Issues of Focus', *GATT Newsletter* and *Inside US Trade*.

Smeets, M, 'Main Features of the Uruguay Round Agreement on Textiles and Clothing, and Implications for the Grading System' (1995) 29 *Journal of World Trade* 97–109.

Smeets, M, 'Tariff Issues in the Uruguay Round' (1995) 29 *Journal of World Trade* 91–105.

Vernon, R, 'The World Trade Organisation: A New Stage in International Trade and Development' (1995) 36 *Harvard International Law Journal* 329–40.

Waincymer, JM, 'Revitalising GATT Article XXIII Issues in the Context of the Uruguay Round' (1988–89) 12 *World Competition* 5–47.

Books

Burnett, R, *The Law of International Business Transactions*, 1994, Sydney: Federation Press.

Cheng, CJ (ed), *Basic Documents on International Trade Law*, Dordrecht: Martinus Nijhoff.

Das, DK, *International Trade Policy: a Developing Country Perspective*, 1990, London: Macmillan.

Department of Foreign Affairs and Trade, Canberra, Australia. *Uruguay Round Outcomes*: *Agriculture*, July 1994; *Services*, September 1994; *Industrials*, September 1994; *Intellectual Property*, September 1994.

Department of International Liaison of the Ministry of Foreign Economic Relations and Trade of China (eds), *GATT: a Handbook*, 1992, Beijing: Economic Administration Press.

Gupta, KR, *A Study of the General Agreement on Tariffs and Trade*, 1967, Delhi: S Chand and Co, p 149.

Henkin, L, Pugh, RC, Schachter, O and Smit, H, *International Law: Cases and Materials*, 3rd edn, 1992, St Paul, Minnesota: West Publishing.

Hudec, R, *Developing Countries in the GATT Legal System*, 1987, Gower.

Jackson, JH, *World Trade and the Law of GATT*, 1969, Bobbs Mervill.

Jackson, JH, *Legal Problems of International Economic Relations*, 1977, St Paul, Minnesota: West Publishing Co.

Kirdar, U, *The Structure of United Nations Economic Aid to Underdeveloped Countries*, 1966, The Hague: Martinus Nijhoff.

Long, O, *Law and its Limitations in the GATT Multilateral Trade System*, 1985, The Hague: Martinus Nijhoff.

McGovern, E, *International Trade Regulations*, 2nd edn, 1986, Exeter: Globefield Press.

Mosler, H, *The International Society as a Legal Community*, 1980, Sijtihoff, Nordhoff, USA, p 255.

Raworth, P and Reif, LC, *The Law of the WTO*, 1995, New York: Oceana Publications.

Schmitthoff, CM, *The Law and Practice of International Trade*, 9th edn, 1990, London: Stevens.

Schwarzenberger, G, *The Frontiers of International Law*, 1962, London: Stevens, p 220.

Simmonds, KR and Hill, BHW, *Law Practice under the GATT*, 1994, New York: Oceana Publications.

Synder, F and Slinn, P (eds) *International Law of Development: Corporate Perspectives*, 1987, Abingdon: Professional Books.

US *International Trade Commission Review of the Effectiveness of Trade Dispute Settlement under the GATT*, 1985, US International Trade Commission (USITC) Publication 1793, December.

Verbit, PG, *Trade Agreements for Developing Countries*, 1969, New York and London: Columbia University Press, p 57.

Whalley, J, *The Uruguay Round and Beyond*, 1989, London: Macmillan.

Wilde, KCDM and Islam MR (eds), *International Transactions, Trade and Investment, Law and Finance*, 1993, Sydney: The Law Book Co.

AGREEMENT ESTABLISHING THE WORLD TRADE ORGANISATION

Article I – Establishment of the organisation

The World Trade Organisation (hereinafter referred to as 'the WTO') is hereby established.

Article II – Scope of the WTO

1 The WTO shall provide the common institutional framework for the conduct of trade relations among its Members in matters related to the agreements and associated legal instruments included in the Annexes to this agreement.

2 The agreements and associated legal instruments included in Annexes 1, 2 and 3 (hereinafter referred to as 'Multilateral Trade Agreements') are integral parts of this agreement, binding on all Members.

3 The agreements and associated legal instruments included in Annex 4 (hereinafter referred to as 'Plurilateral Trade Agreements') are also part of this agreement for those Members that have accepted them, and are binding on those Members. The Plurilateral Trade Agreements do not create either obligations or rights for Members that have not accepted them.

4 The General Agreement on Tariffs and Trade 1994 as specified in Annex 1A (hereinafter referred to as 'GATT 1994') is legally distinct from the General Agreement on Tariffs and Trade, dated 30 October 1947, annexed to the Final Act Adopted at the Conclusion of the Second Session of the Preparatory Committee of the United Nations Conference on Trade and Employment, as subsequently rectified, amended or modified (hereinafter referred to as 'GATT 1947').

Article III – Functions of the WTO

1 The WTO shall facilitate the implementation, administration and operation and further the objectives, of this agreement and of the Multilateral Trade Agreements, and shall also provide the framework for the implementation administration and operation of the Plurilateral Trade Agreements.

2 The WTO shall provide the forum for negotiations among its Members concerning their multilateral trade relations in matters dealt with under the agreements in the

Annexes to this agreement. The WTO may also provide a forum for further negotiations among its Members concerning their multilateral trade relations, and a framework for the implementation of the results of such negotiations, as may be decided by the Ministerial Conference.

3   The WTO shall administer the Understanding on Rules and Procedures Governing the Settlement of Disputes (hereinafter referred to as the 'Dispute Settlement Understanding' or 'DSU') in Annex 2 to this agreement.

4   The WTO shall administer the Trade Policy Review Mechanism (hereinafter referred to as the 'TPRM') provided for in Annex 3 to this agreement.

5   With a view to achieving greater coherence in global economic policy making the WTO shall cooperate, as appropriate, with the International Monetary Fund and with the International Bank for Reconstruction and Development and its affiliated agencies.

Article VIII – Status of the WTO

1   The WTO shall have legal personality, and shall be accorded by each of its Members such legal capacity as may be necessary for the exercise of its functions.

2   The WTO shall be accorded by each of its Members such privileges and immunities as are necessary for the exercise of its functions.

3   The officials of the WTO and the representatives of the Members shall similarly be accorded by each of its Members such privileges and immunities as are necessary for the independent exercise of their functions in connection with the WTO.

4   The privileges and immunities to be accorded by a Member to the WTO, its officials, and the representatives of its Members shall be similar to the privileges and immunities stipulated in the Convention on the Privileges and Immunities of the Specialised Agencies, approved by the General Assembly of the United Nations on 21 November 1947.

5   The WTO may conclude a headquarters agreement.

Article IX – Decision making

1   The WTO shall continue the practice of decision-making by consensus followed under GATT 1947.[1] Except as otherwise provided, where a decision cannot be arrived at by consensus, the matter at issue shall be decided by voting. At meetings of the Ministerial Conference and the General Council, each Member of the WTO shall have one vote. Where the European Communities exercise their right to vote, they shall have a number of votes equal to the number of their member States[2] which are Members of the WTO. Decisions of the Ministerial Conference and the General Council shall be taken by a majority of the votes cast, unless otherwise provided in this agreement or in the relevant Multilateral Trade Agreement.[3]

2   The Ministerial Conference and the General Council shall have the exclusive authority to adopt interpretations of this agreement and of the Multilateral Trade

---

1   The body concerned shall be deemed to have decided by consensus on a matter submitted for its consideration, if no Member, present at the meeting when the decision is taken, formally objects to the proposed decision.

2   The number of votes of the European Communities and their member States shall in no case exceed the number of the Member States of the European Communities.

3   Decisions by the General Council when convened as the Dispute Settlement Body shall be taken only in accordance with the provisions of para 4 of Article 2 of the Dispute Settlement Understanding.

Agreements. In the case of an interpretation of a Multilateral Trade Agreement in Annex 1, they shall exercise their authority on the basis of a recommendation by the Council overseeing the functioning of that agreement. The decision to adopt an interpretation shall be taken by a three fourths majority of the Members. This paragraph shall not be used in a manner that would undermine the amendment provisions in Article X.

3   In exceptional circumstances, the Ministerial Conference may decide to waive an obligation imposed on a Member by this agreement or any of the Multilateral Trade Agreements, provided that any such decision shall be taken by three fourths of the Members unless otherwise provided for in this paragraph.

(a)   A request for a waiver concerning this agreement shall be submitted to the Ministerial Conference for consideration pursuant to the practice of decision making by consensus. The Ministerial Conference shall establish a time period, which shall not exceed 90 days, to consider the request. If consensus is not reached during the time period, any decision to grant a waiver shall be taken by three fourths of the Members.

(b)   A request for a waiver concerning the Multilateral Trade Agreements in Annexes IA or IB or IC and their annexes shall be submitted initially to the Council for Trade in Goods, the Council for Trade in Services or the Council for TRIPS, respectively, for consideration during a time period which shall not exceed 90 days. At the end of the time period, the relevant Council shall submit a report to the Ministerial Conference.

4   A decision to a grant a waiver in respect of any obligation subject to a transition period or a period for staged implementation that the requesting Member has not performed by the end of the relevant period shall be taken only by consensus.

5   A decision by the Ministerial Conference granting a waiver shall state the exceptional circumstances justifying the decision, the terms and conditions governing the application of the waiver, and the date on which the waiver shall terminate. Any waiver granted for a period of more than one year shall be reviewed by the Ministerial Conference not later than one year after it is granted, and thereafter annually until the waiver terminates. In each review, the Ministerial Conference shall examine whether the exceptional circumstances justifying the waiver still exist and whether the terms and conditions attached to the waiver have been met. The Ministerial Conference, on the basis of the annual review, may extend, modify or terminate the waiver.

6   Decisions under a Plurilateral Trade Agreement, including any decisions on interpretations and waivers, shall be governed by the provisions of that agreement.

Article X – Amendments

1   Any Member of the WTO may initiate a proposal to amend the provisions of this agreement or the Multilateral Trade Agreements in Annex 1 by submitting such proposal to the Ministerial Conference. The Councils listed in para 5 of Article IV may also submit to the Ministerial Conference proposals to amend the provisions of the corresponding Multilateral Trade Agreements in Annex 1 the functioning of which they oversee. Unless the Ministerial Conference decides on a longer period, for a period of 90 days after the proposal has been tabled formally at the Ministerial Conference any decision by the Ministerial Conference to submit the proposed

amendment to the Members for acceptance shall be taken by consensus. Unless the provisions of paras 2, 5 or 6 apply, that decision shall specify whether the provisions of paras 3 or 4 shall apply. If consensus is reached, the Ministerial Conference shall forthwith submit the proposed amendment to the Members for acceptance. If consensus is not reached at a meeting of the Ministerial Conference within the established period, the Ministerial Conference shall decide by a two thirds majority of the Members whether to submit the proposed amendment to the Members for acceptance. Except as provided in paras 2, 5 and 6, the provisions of para 3 shall apply to the proposed amendment, unless the Ministerial Conference decides by a three fourths majority of the Members that the provisions of para 4 shall apply.

2 Amendments to the provisions of this article and to the provisions of the following articles shall take effect only upon acceptance by all Members:

Article IX of this agreement;

Articles I and II of GATT 1994;

Article II(1) of GATTS;

Article 4 of the Agreement on TRIPS.

3 Amendments to provisions of this agreement, or of the Multilateral Trade Agreements in Annexes 1A and 1C, other than those listed in paras 2 and 6 of a nature that would alter the rights and obligations of the Members, shall take effect for the Members that have accepted them upon acceptance by two thirds of the Members and thereafter for each other Member upon acceptance by it. The Ministerial Conference may decide by a three fourths majority of the Members that any amendment made effective under this paragraph is of such a nature that any Member which has not accepted it within a period specified by the Ministerial Conference in each case shall be free to withdraw from the WTO or to remain a Member with the consent of the Ministerial Conference.

4 Amendments to provisions of this agreement or of the Multilateral Trade Agreements in Annexes 1A and 1C, other than those listed in paras 2 and 6, of a nature that would not alter the rights and obligations of the Members, shall take effect for all Members upon acceptance by two thirds of the Members.

5 Except as provided in para 2 above, amendments to Parts I, II and III of GATS and the respective annexes shall take effect for the Members that have accepted them upon acceptance by two thirds of the Members and thereafter for each Member upon acceptance by it. The Ministerial Conference may decide by a three fourths majority of the Members that any amendment made effective under the preceding provision is of such a nature that any Member which has not accepted it within a period specified by the Ministerial Conference in each case shall be free to withdraw from the WTO or to remain a Member with the consent of the Ministerial Conference. Amendments to Parts IV, V and VI of GATS and the respective annexes shall take effect for all Members upon acceptance by two thirds of the Members.

6 Notwithstanding the other provisions of this article, amendments to the Agreement on TRIPS meeting the requirements of para 2 of Article 71 thereof may be adopted by the Ministerial Conference without further formal acceptance process.

7 Any Member accepting an amendment to this agreement or to a Multilateral Trade Agreement in Annex I shall deposit an instrument of acceptance with the Director

General of the WTO within the period of acceptance specified by the Ministerial Conference.

8   Any Member of the WTO may initiate a proposal to amend the provisions of the Multilateral Trade Agreements in Annexes 2 and 3 by submitting such proposal to the Ministerial Conference. The decision to approve amendments to the Multilateral Trade Agreement in Annex 2 shall be made by consensus and these amendments shall take effect for all Members upon approval by the Ministerial Conference. Decisions to approve amendments to the Multilateral Trade Agreement in Annex 3 shall take effect for all Members upon approval by the Ministerial Conference.

9   The Ministerial Conference, upon the request of the Members parties to a trade agreement, may decide exclusively by consensus to add that agreement to Annex 4. The Ministerial Conference, upon the request of the Members parties to a Plurilateral Trade Agreement, may decide to delete that agreement from Annex 4.

10   Amendments to a Plurilateral Trade Agreement shall be governed by the provisions of that agreement.

Article XI – Original membership

1   The contracting parties to GATT 1947 as of the date of entry into force of this agreement, and the European Communities, which accept this agreement and the Multilateral Trade Agreements and for which Schedules of Concessions and Commitments are annexed to GATT 1994 and for which Schedules of Specific Commitments are annexed to GATS shall become original Members of the WTO.

2   A Member which accepts this agreement after its entry into force shall implement those concessions and obligations in the Multilateral Trade Agreements that are to be implemented over a period of time starting with the entry into force of this agreement as if it had accepted this agreement on the date of its entry into force.

3   Until the entry into force of this agreement, the text of this agreement and the Multilateral Trade Agreements shall be deposited with the Director General to the contracting parties to GATT 1947. The Director General shall promptly furnish a certified true copy of this agreement and the Multilateral Trade Agreements, and a notification of each acceptance thereof, to each government and the European Communities having accepted this agreement. This agreement and the Multilateral Trade Agreements, and any amendments thereto, shall, upon the entry into force of this agreement, be deposited with the Director General of the WTO.

4   The acceptance and entry into force of a Plurilateral Trade Agreement shall be governed by the provisions of that agreement. Such agreements shall be deposited with the Director General to the contracting parties to GATT 1947. Upon the entry into force of this agreement, such agreements shall be deposited with the Director General of the WTO.

Article XVI – Withdrawal

1   Any Member may withdraw from this agreement. Such withdrawal shall apply both to this agreement and the Multilateral Trade Agreements and shall take effect upon the expiration of six months from the date on which written notice of withdrawal is received by the Director General of the WTO.

2   Withdrawal from a Plurilateral Trade Agreement shall be governed by the provisions of that agreement.

Article XV – Miscellaneous provisions

1   Except as otherwise provided under this agreement or the Multilateral Trade Agreements, the WTO shall be guided by the decisions, procedures and customary practices followed by the contracting parties to GATT 1947 and the bodies established in the framework of GATT 1947.

2   To the extent practicable, the Secretariat of GATT 1947 shall become the Secretariat of the WTO, and the Director General to the contracting parties to GATT 1947, until such time as the Ministerial Conference has appointed a Director General in accordance with para 2 of Article VI of this agreement, shall serve as Director General of the WTO.

3   In the event of a conflict between the provision of this agreement and a provision of any of the Multilateral Trade Agreements, the provision of this agreement shall prevail to the extent of the conflict.

4   Each Member shall ensure the conformity of its laws, regulations and administrative procedures with its obligations as provided in the annexed agreements.

5   No reservations may be made in respect of any provision of this agreement. Reservations in respect of any of the provisions of the Multilateral Trade Agreements may only be made to the extent provided for in those agreements. Reservations in respect of a provision of a Plurilateral Trade Agreement shall be governed by the provisions of that agreement.

6   This agreement shall be registered in accordance with the provisions of Article 102 of the Charter of the United Nations.

Done at Marrakesh this fifteenth day of April one thousand nine hundred and ninety-four, in a single copy, in the English, French and Spanish languages, each text being authentic.

Explanatory notes

The terms 'country' or 'countries' as used in this agreement and the Multilateral Trade Agreements are to be understood to include any separate customs territory Member of the WTO.

In the case of a separate customs territory Member of the WTO, where an expression in this agreement and the Multilateral Trade Agreements is qualified by the term 'national', such expression shall be read as pertaining to that customs territory, unless otherwise specified.

List of annexes
Annex 1

Annex 1A

   Multilateral Agreements on Trade in Goods

   General Agreement on Tariffs and Trade 1994

   Agreement on Agriculture

   Agreement on the Application of Sanitary and Phytosanitary Measures

   Agreement on Textiles and Clothing

   Agreement on Technical Barriers to Trade

   Agreement on Trade Related Investment Measures

Agreement on Implementation of Article VI of the General Agreement on Tariffs and Trade 1994

Agreement on Implementation of Article VII of the General Agreement on Tariffs and Trade 1994

Agreement on Preshipment Inspection Agreement on Rules of Origin

Agreement on Import Licensing Procedures

Agreement on Subsidies and Countervailing Measures Agreement on Safeguards.

Annex 1B

General Agreement on Trade in Services and Annexes

Annex 1C

Agreement on Trade-Related Aspects of Intellectual Property Rights.

Annex 2

Understanding on Rules and Procedures Governing the Settlement of Disputes

Annex 3

Trade Policy Review Mechanism

Annex 4

Plurilateral Trade Agreements

Agreement on Trade in Civil Aircraft

Agreement on government Procurement

International Dairy Agreement

International Bovine Meat Agreement

THE GENERAL AGREEMENT ON TARIFFS AND TRADE

The governments of the Commonwealth of Australia, the Kingdom of Belgium, the United States of Brazil, Burma, Canada, Ceylon, the Republic of Chile, the Republic of China, the Republic of Cuba, the Czechoslovak Republic, the French Republic, India, Lebanon, the Grand-Duchy of Luxemburg, the Kingdom of The Netherlands, New Zealand, the Kingdom of Norway, Pakistan, Southern Rhodesia, Syria, the Union of South Africa, the United Kingdom of Great Britain and Northern Ireland, and the United States of America:

Recognising that their relations in the field of trade and economic endeavour should be conducted with a view to raising standards of living, ensuring full employment and a large and steadily growing volume of real income and effective demand, developing the full use of the resources of the world and expanding the production and exchange of goods,

Being desirous of contributing to these objectives by entering into reciprocal and mutually advantageous arrangements directed to the substantial reduction of tariffs and other barriers to trade and to the elimination of discriminatory treatment in international commerce,

Have through their Representatives agreed as follows:

PART I

Article I – General most-favoured-nation treatment

1   With respect to customs duties and charges of any kind imposed on or in connection with importation or exportation or imposed on the international transfer of payments for imports or exports, and with respect to the method of levying such duties and charges, and with respect to all rules and formalities in connection with importation and exportation, and with respect to all matters referred to in paras 2 and 4 of Article III, any advantage, favour, privilege or immunity granted by any contracting party to any product originating in or destined for any other country shall be accorded immediately and unconditionally to the like product originating in or destined for the territories of all other contracting parties.

2   The provisions of para 1 of this article shall not require the elimination of any preferences in respect of import duties or charges which do not exceed the levels provided for in para 4 of this article and which fall within the following descriptions:

(a)   preferences in force exclusively between two or more of the territories listed in Annex A, subject to the conditions set forth therein:

(b)   preferences in force exclusively between two or more territories which on 1 July 1939, were connected by common sovereignty or relations of protection or suzerainty and which are listed in Annexes B, C and D, subject to the conditions set forth therein;

(c)   preferences in force exclusively between the USA and the Republic of Cuba;

(d)   preferences in force exclusively between neighbouring countries listed in Annexes E and F.

3   The provisions of para 1 shall not apply to preferences between the countries formerly a part of the Ottoman Empire and detached from it on 24 July 1923, provided such preferences are approved under para 5 of Article XXV, which shall be applied in this respect in the light of para 1 of Article XXIX.

4   The margin of preference on any product in respect of which a preference is permitted under para 2 of this article but is not specifically set forth as a maximum margin of preference in the appropriate Schedule annexed to this agreement shall not exceed:

(a)   in respect of duties or charges on any product described in such Schedule, the difference between the most-favoured-nation and preferential rates provided for therein; if no preferential rate is provided for, the preferential rate shall for the purposes of this paragraph be taken to be that in force on 10 April 1947, and, if no most-favoured-nation rate is provided for, the margin shall not exceed the difference between the most-favoured-nation and preferential rates existing on 10 April 1947;

(b)   in respect of duties or charges on any product not described in the appropriate Schedule, the difference between the most-favoured-nation and preferential rates existing on 10 April 1947.

In the case of the contracting parties named in Annex G. the date of 10 April 1947, referred to in sub-paras (a) and (b) of this para shall be replaced by the respective dates set forth in that Annex.

Article II – Schedules of concessions

1   (a)   Each contracting party shall accord to the commerce of the other contracting parties treatment no less favourable than that provided for in the appropriate Part of the appropriate Schedule annexed to this agreement.

   (b)   The products described in Part I of the Schedule relating to any contracting party, which are the products of territories of other contracting parties, shall on their importation into the territory to which the Schedule relates, and subject to the terms, conditions or qualifications set forth in that Schedule, be exempt from ordinary customs duties in excess of those set forth and provided for therein. Such products shall also be exempt from all other duties or charges of any kind imposed on or in connection with importation in excess of those imposed on the date of this agreement or those directly and mandatorily required to be imposed thereafter by legislation in force in the importing territory on that date.

   (c)   The products, described in Part II of the Schedule relating to any contracting party which are the products of territories entitled under Article I to receive preferential treatment upon importation into the territory to which the Schedule relates shall, on their importation into such territory, and subject to the terms, conditions or qualifications set forth in that Schedule, be exempt from ordinary customs duties in excess of those set forth and provided for in Part II of that Schedule. Such products shall also be exempt from all other duties or charges of any kind imposed on or in connection with importation in excess of those imposed on the date of this agreement or those directly and mandatorily required to be imposed thereafter by legislation in force in the importing territory on that date. Nothing in this article shall prevent any contracting party from maintaining its requirements existing on the date of this agreement as to the eligibility of goods for entry at preferential rates of duty.

2   Nothing in this article shall prevent any contracting party from imposing at any time on the importation of any product:

   (a)   a charge equivalent to an internal tax imposed consistently with the provisions of para 2 of Article III in respect of the like domestic product or in respect of an article from which the imported product has been manufactured or produced in whole or in part;

   (b)   any anti-dumping or countervailing duty applied consistently with the provisions of Article VI;

   (c)   fees or other charges commensurate with the cost of services rendered.

3   No contracting party shall alter its method of determining dutiable value or of converting currencies so as to impair the value of any of the concessions provided for in the appropriate Schedule annexed to this agreement.

4   If any contracting party establishes, maintains or authorises, formally or in effect, a monopoly of the importation of any product described in the appropriate Schedule annexed to this agreement, such monopoly shall not, except as provided for in that Schedule or as otherwise agreed between the parties which initially negotiated the concession, operate so as to afford protection on the average in excess of the amount of protection provided for in that Schedule. The provisions of this paragraph shall not limit the use by contracting parties of any form of assistance to domestic producers permitted by other provisions of this agreement.

5   If any contracting party considers that a product is not receiving from another contracting party the treatment which the first contracting party believes to have been contemplated by a concession provided for in the appropriate Schedule annexed to this agreement, it shall bring the matter directly to the attention of the other contracting party. If the latter agrees that the treatment contemplated was that claimed by the first contracting party, but declares that such treatment cannot be accorded because a court or other proper authority has ruled to the effect that the product involved cannot be classified under the tariff laws of such contracting party so as to permit the treatment contemplated in this agreement, the two contracting parties, together with any other contracting parties substantially interested, shall enter promptly into further negotiations with a view to a compensatory adjustment of the matter.

6   (a)   The specific duties and charges included in the Schedules relating to contracting parties members of the International Monetary Fund, and margins of preference in specific duties and charges maintained by such contracting parties, are expressed in the appropriate currency at the par value accepted or provisionally recognised by the Fund at the date of this agreement. Accordingly, in case this par value is reduced consistently with the Articles of Agreement of the International Monetary Fund by more than 20%, such specific duties and charges and margins of preference may be adjusted to take account of such reduction; provided that the contracting, parties (ie the contracting parties acting jointly as provided for in Article XXV) concur that such adjustments will not impair the value of the concessions provided for in the appropriate Schedule or elsewhere in this agreement, due account being taken of all factors which may influence the need for, or urgency of such adjustments.

    (b)   Similar provisions shall apply to any contracting party not a member of the Fund, as from the date on which such contracting party becomes a member of the Fund or enters into a special exchange agreement in pursuance of Article XV.

7   The Schedules annexed to this agreement are hereby made an integral part of Part I of this agreement.

PART II

Article III – National treatment on internal taxation and regulation

1   The contracting parties recognise that internal taxes and other internal charges, and laws, regulations and requirements affecting the internal sale, offering for sale, purchase, transportation, distribution or use of products, and internal quantitative regulations requiring the mixture, processing or use of products in specified amounts or proportions, should not be applied to imported or domestic products so as to afford protection to domestic production.

2   The products of the territory of any contracting party imported into the territory of any other contracting party shall not be subject, directly or indirectly, to internal taxes or other internal charges of any kind in excess of those applied, directly or indirectly, to like domestic products. Moreover, no contracting party shall otherwise apply internal taxes or other internal charges to imported or domestic products in a manner contrary to the principles set forth in para 1.

3   With respect to any existing internal tax which is inconsistent with the provisions of para 2, but which is specifically authorised under a trade agreement, in force on 10

April 1947, in which the import duty on the taxed product is bound against increase, the contracting party imposing the tax shall be free to postpone the application of the provisions of para 2 try such tax until such time as it can obtain release from the obligations of such trade agreement in order to permit the increase of such duty to the extent necessary to compensate for the elimination of the protective element of the tax.

4   The products of the territory of any contracting party imported into the territory of any other contracting party shall be accorded treatment no less favourable than that accorded to like products of national origin in respect of all laws, regulations and requirements affecting their internal sale, offering for sale, purchase, transportation, distribution or use. The provisions of this paragraph shall not prevent the application of differential internal transportation charges which are based exclusively on the economic operation of the means of transport and not on the nationality of the product.

5   No contracting party shall establish or maintain any internal quantitative regulation relating to the mixture, processing or use of products in specified amounts or proportions which requires, directly or indirectly, that any specified amount or proportion of any product which is the subject of the regulation must be supplied from domestic sources. Moreover, no contracting party shall otherwise apply internal quantitative regulations in a manner contrary to the principles set forth in para 1.

6   The provisions of para 5 shall not apply to any internal quantitative regulation in force in the territory of any contracting party on 1 July 1939, 10 April 1947 or 24 March 1948, at the option of that contracting party; Provided that any such regulation which is contrary to the provisions of para 5 shall not be modified to the detriment of imports and shall be treated as a customs duty for the purpose of negotiation.

7   No internal quantitative regulation relating to the mixture, processing or use of products in specified amounts or proportions shall be applied in such a manner as to allocate any such amount or proportion among external sources of supply.

8   (a)   The provisions of this article shall not apply to laws, regulations or requirements governing the procurement by governmental agencies of products purchased for governmental purposes and not with a view to commercial resale or with a view to use in the production of goods for commercial sale.

    (b)   The provisions of this article shall not prevent the payment of subsidies exclusively to domestic producers, including payments to domestic producers derived from the proceeds of internal taxes or charges applied consistently with the provisions of this article and subsidies effected through governmental purchases of domestic products.

9   The contracting parties recognise that internal maximum price control measures, even though conforming to the other provisions of this article, can have effects prejudicial to the interests of contracting parties supplying imported products. Accordingly, contracting parties applying such measures shall take account of the interests of exporting contracting parties with a view to avoiding to the fullest practicable extent such prejudicial effects.

10   The provisions of this article shall not prevent any contracting party from establishing or maintaining internal quantitative regulations relating to exposed cinematograph films and meeting the requirements of Article IV.

Article IV – Special provisions relating to cinematograph films

If any contracting party establishes or maintains internal quantitative regulations relating to exposed cinematograph films, such regulations shall take the form of screen quotas which shall conform to the following requirements:

(a) screen quotas may require the exhibition of cinematograph films of national origin during a specified minimum proportion of the total screen time actually utilised, over a specified period of not less than one year, in the commercial exhibition of all films of whatever origin, and shall be computed on the basis of screen time per theatre per year or the equivalent thereof;

(b) with the exception of screen time reserved for films of national origin under a screen quota, screen time including that released by administrative action from screen time reserved for films of national origin, shall not be allocated formally or in effect among sources of supply;

(c) notwithstanding the provisions of sub-para (b) of this article, any contracting party may maintain screen quotas conforming to the requirements of sub-para (a) of this article which reserve a minimum proportion of screen time for films of a specified origin other than that of the contracting party imposing such screen quotas; provided that no such minimum proportion of screen time shall be increased above the level in effect on 10 April 1947;

(d) screen quotas shall be subject to negotiation for their limitation, liberalisation or elimination.

Article V – Freedom of transit

1   Goods (including baggage), and also vessels and other means of transport, shall be deemed to be in transit across the territory of a contracting party when the passage across such territory, with or without trans-shipment,. warehousing, breaking bulk, or change in the mode of transport, is only a portion of a complete journey beginning and terminating beyond the frontier of the contracting party across whose territory the traffic passes. Traffic of this nature is termed in this article 'traffic in transit'.

2   There shall be freedom of transit through the territory of each contracting party, via the routes most convenient for international transit, for traffic in transit to or from the territory of other contracting parties. No distinction shall be made which is based on the flag of vessels, the place of origin, departure, entry, exit or destination. or on any circumstances relating to the ownership of goods, of vessels or of other means of transport.

3   Any contracting party may require that traffic in transit through its territory be entered at the proper custom house, but, except in cases of failure to comply with applicable customs laws and regulations, such traffic coming from or going to the territory of other contracting parties shall not be subject to any unnecessary delays or restrictions and shall be exempt from customs duties and from all transit duties or other charges imposed in respect of transit, except charges for transportation or those commensurate with administrative expenses entailed by transit or with the cost of services rendered.

4   All charges and regulations imposed by contracting parties on traffic in transit to or from the territories of other contracting parties shall be reasonable, having regard to the conditions of the traffic.

5   With respect to all charges, regulations and formalities in connection with transit, each contracting party shall accord to traffic in transit to or from the territory of any other contracting party treatment no less favourable than the treatment accorded to traffic in transit to or from any third country.

6   Each contracting party shall accord to products which have been in transit through the territory of any other contracting party treatment no less favourable than that which would have been accorded to such products had they been transported from their place of origin to their destination without going through the territory of such other contracting party. Any contracting party shall, however, be free to maintain its requirements of direct consignment existing on the date of this agreement, in respect of any goods in regard to which such direct consignment is a requisite condition of eligibility for entry of the goods at preferential rates of duty or has relation to the contracting party's prescribed method of valuation for duty purposes.

7   The provisions of this article shall not apply to the operation of aircraft in transit, but shall apply to air transit of goods (including baggage).

Article VI – anti-dumping and countervailing duties

1   The contracting parties recognise that dumping, by which products of one country are introduced into the commerce of another country at less than the normal value of the products, is to be condemned if it causes or threatens material injury to an established industry in the territory of a contracting party or materially retards the establishment of a domestic industry. For the purposes of this article, a product is to be considered as being introduced into the commerce of an importing country at less than its normal value, if the price of the product exported from one country to another:

(a)   is less than the comparable price, in the ordinary course of trade, for the like product when destined for consumption in the exporting country; or

(b)   in the absence of such domestic price, is less than either:

(i)   the highest comparable price for the like product for export to any third country in the ordinary course of trade; or

(ii)   the cost of production of the product in the country of origin plus a reasonable addition for selling cost and profit.

Due allowance shall be made in each case for differences in conditions and terms of sale, for differences in taxation, and for other differences affecting price comparability.

2   In order to offset or prevent dumping, a contracting party may levy on any dumped product an anti-dumping duty not greater in amount than the margin of dumping in respect of such product. For the purposes of this article, the margin of dumping is the price difference determined in accordance with the provisions of para 1.

3   No countervailing duty shall be levied on any product of the territory of any contracting party imported into the territory of another contracting party in excess of an amount equal to the estimated bounty or subsidy determined to have been granted, directly or indirectly, on the manufacture, production or export of such product in the country of origin or exportation, including any special subsidy to the transportation of a particular product. The term 'countervailing duty' shall be understood to mean a special duty levied for the purpose of offsetting any bounty or subsidy bestowed, directly or indirectly, upon the manufacture, production or export of any merchandise.

4   No product of the territory of any contracting party imported into the territory of any other contracting party shall he subject to anti-dumping or countervailing duty by reason of the exemption of such product from duties or taxes borne by the like product when destined for consumption in the country of origin or exportation, or by reason of the refund of such duties or taxes.

5   No product of the territory of any contracting party imported into the territory of any other contracting party shall be subject to both anti-dumping and countervailing duties to compensate for the same situation of dumping or export subsidisation.

6   (a) No contracting party shall levy any anti-dumping or countervailing duty on the importation of any product of the territory of another contracting party unless it determines that the effect of the dumping or subsidisation, as the case may be, is such as to cause or threaten material injury to an established domestic industry, or is such as to retard materially the establishment of a domestic industry.

   (b) The contracting parties may waive the requirement of sub-para (a) of this paragraph so as to permit a contracting party to levy an anti-dumping or countervailing duty on the importation of any product for the purpose of offsetting dumping or subsidisation which causes or threatens material injury to an industry in the territory of another contracting party exporting the product concerned to the territory of the importing contracting party. The contracting parties shall waive the requirements of sub-para (a) of this paragraph, so as to permit the levying of a countervailing duty, in cases in which they find that a subsidy is causing or threatening material injury to an industry in the territory of another contracting party exporting the product concerned to the territory of the importing contracting party.

   (c) In exceptional circumstances, however, where delay might cause damage which would be difficult to repair, a contracting party may levy a countervailing duty for the purpose referred to in sub-para (b) of this paragraph without the prior approval of the contracting parties; provided that such action shall be reported immediately to the contracting parties and that the countervailing duty shall be withdrawn promptly if the contracting parties disapprove.

7   A system for the stabilisation of the domestic price or of the return to domestic producers of a primary commodity, independently of the movements of export prices, which results at times in the sale of the commodity for export at a price lower than the comparable price charged for the like commodity to buyers in the domestic market, shall be presumed not to result in material injury within the meaning of para 6 if it is determined by consultation among the contracting parties substantially interested in the commodity concerned that:

   (a) the system has also resulted in the sale of the commodity for export at a price higher than the comparable price charged for the like commodity to buyers in the domestic market, and

   (b) the system is so operated, either because of the effective regulation of production, or otherwise, as not to stimulate exports unduly or otherwise seriously prejudice the interests of other contracting parties.

Article VII – Valuation for customs purposes

1   The contracting parties recognise the validity of the general principles of valuation set forth in the following paragraphs of this article, and they undertake to give effect

to such principles, in respect of all products subject to duties or other charges or restrictions on importation and exportation based upon or regulated in any manner by value. Moreover, they shall, upon a request by another contracting party, review the operation of any of their laws or regulations relating to value for customs purposes in the light of these principles. The contracting parties may request from contracting parties reports on steps taken by them in pursuance of the provisions of this article.

2 (a) The value for customs purposes of imported merchandise should be based on the actual value of the imported merchandise on which duty is assessed, or of like merchandise, and should not be based on the value of merchandise of national origin or on arbitrary or fictitious values.

 (b) 'Actual value' should be the price at which, at a time and place determined by the legislation of the country of importation such or like merchandise is sold or offered for sale in the ordinary course of trade under fully competitive conditions. To the extent to which the price of such or like merchandise is governed by the quantity in a particular transaction, the price to be considered should uniformly be related to either (i) comparable quantities, or (ii) quantities, not less favourable to importers than those in which the greater volume of the merchandise is sold in the trade between the countries of exportation and importation.

 (c) When the actual value is not ascertainable in accordance with sub-para (b) of this paragraph, the value for customs purposes should be based on the nearest ascertainable equivalent of such value.

3 The value for customs purposes of any imported product should not include the amount of any internal tax, applicable within the country of origin or export, from which the imported product has been exempted or has been or will be relieved by means of refund.

4 (a) Except as otherwise provided for in this paragraph, where it is necessary for the purposes of para 2 of this article for a contracting party to convert into its own currency a price expressed in the currency of another country, the conversion rate of exchange to be used shall be based, for each currency involved, on the par value as established pursuant to the Articles of Agreement of the International Monetary Fund or on the rate of exchange recognised by the Fund. or on the par value established in accordance with a special exchange agreement entered into pursuant to Article XV of this agreement.

 (b) Where no such established par value and no such recognised rate of exchange exist, the conversion rate shall reflect effectively the current value of such currency in commercial transactions.

 (c) The contracting parties, in agreement with the International Monetary Fund, shall formulate rules governing the conversion by contracting parties of any foreign currency in respect of which multiple rates of exchange are maintained consistently with the Articles of Agreement of the International Monetary Fund. Any contracting party may apply such rules in respect of such foreign currencies for the purposes of para 2 of this article as an alternative to the use of par values. Until such rules are adopted by the contracting parties, any contracting party may employ, in respect of any such foreign currency, rules of conversion for the purposes of para 2 of this article which are designed to reflect effectively the value of such foreign currency in commercial transactions.

(d) Nothing in this paragraph shall be construed to require any contracting party to alter the method of converting currencies for customs purposes which is applicable in its territory on the date of this agreement, if such alteration would have the effect of increasing generally the amounts of duty payable.

5   The bases and methods for determining the value of products subject to duties or other charges or restrictions based upon or regulated in any manner by value should be stable and should be given sufficient publicity to enable traders to estimate, with a reasonable degree of certainty, the value for customs purposes.

Article VIII – Fees and formalities connected with importation and exportation

1   (a) All fees and charges of whatever character (other than import and export duties and other than taxes within the purview of Article III) imposed by contracting parties on or in connection with importation or exportation shall be limited in amount to the approximate cost of services rendered and shall not represent an indirect protection to domestic products or a taxation of imports or exports for fiscal purposes.

(b) The contracting parties recognise the need for reducing the number and diversity of fees and charges referred to in sub-para (a).

(c) The contracting parties also recognise the need for minimising the incidence and complexity of import and export formalities and for decreasing and simplifying import and export documentation requirements.

2   A contracting party shall, upon request by another contracting party or by the contracting parties, review the operation of its laws and regulations in the light of the provisions of this article.

3   No contracting party shall impose substantial penalties for minor breaches of customs regulations or procedural requirements. In particular, no penalty in respect of any omission or mistake in customs documentation which is easily rectifiable and obviously made without fraudulent intent or gross negligence shall be greater than necessary to serve merely as a warning.

4   The provisions of this article shall extend to fees, charges, formalities and requirements imposed by governmental authorities in connection with importation and exportation, including those relating to: (a) consular transactions, such as consular invoices and certificates; (b) quantitative restrictions; (c) licensing; (d) exchange control; (e) statistical services; (f) documents, documentation and certification; (g) analysis and inspection; and (h) quarantine, sanitation and fumigation.

Article IX – Marks of origin

1   Each contracting party shall accord to the products of the territories of other contracting parties treatment with regard to marking requirements no less favourable than the treatment accorded to like products of any third country.

2   The contracting parties recognise that, in adopting and enforcing laws and regulations relating to marks of origin, the difficulties and inconveniences which such measures may cause to the commerce and industry of exporting countries should be reduced to a minimum, due regard being had to the necessity of protecting consumers against fraudulent or misleading indications.

3   Whenever it is administratively practicable to do so, contracting parties should permit required marks of origin to be affixed at the time of importation.

4   The laws and regulations of contracting parties relating to the marking of imported products shall be such as to permit compliance without seriously damaging the products, or materially reducing their value, or unreasonably increasing their cost.

5   As a general rule, no special duty or penalty should be imposed by any contracting party for failure to comply with marking requirements prior to importation unless corrective marking is unreasonably delayed or deceptive marks have been affixed or the required marking has been intentionally omitted.

6   The contracting parties shall cooperate with each other with a view to preventing the use of trade names in such manner as to misrepresent the true origin of a product, to the detriment of such distinctive regional or geographical names of products of the territory of a contracting party as are protected by its legislation. Each contracting party shall accord full and sympathetic consideration to such requests or representations as may be made by any other contracting party regarding the application of the undertaking set forth in the preceding sentence to names of products which have been communicated to it by the other contracting party.

Article X – Publication and administration of trade regulations

1   Laws, regulations, judicial decisions and administrative rulings of general application, made effective by any contracting party, pertaining to the classification or the valuation of products for customs purposes, or to rates of duty, taxes or other charges, or to requirements, restrictions or prohibitions on imports or exports or on the transfer of payments therefore, or affecting their sale, distribution, transportation, insurance, warehousing, inspection, exhibition, processing, mixing or other use, shall be published promptly in such a manner as to enable governments and traders to become acquainted with them. Agreements affecting international trade policy which are in force between the government or a governmental agency of any contracting party and the government or governmental agency of any other contracting party shall also be published. The provisions of this paragraph shall not require any contracting party to disclose confidential information which would impede law enforcement or otherwise be contrary to the public interest or would prejudice the legitimate commercial interests of particular enterprises, public or private.

2   No measure of general application taken by any contracting party effecting an advance in a rate of duty or other charge on imports under an established and uniform practice, or imposing a new or more burdensome requirement, restriction or prohibition on imports, or on the transfer of payments, therefore, shall be enforced before such measure has been officially published.

3   (a) Each contracting party shall administer in a uniform, impartial and reasonable manner all its laws, regulations, decisions and rulings of the kind described in para 1 of this article.

    (b) Each contracting party shall maintain, or institute as soon as practicable, judicial, arbitral or administrative tribunals or procedures for the purpose, *inter alia*, of the prompt review and correction of administrative action relating to customs matters. Such tribunals or procedures shall be independent of the agencies entrusted with administrative enforcement and their decisions shall be implemented by, and shall govern the practice of, such agencies unless an appeal is lodged with a court or tribunal of superior jurisdiction within the time prescribed for appeals to be lodged by importers; provided that the central administration of such agency may take steps to obtain a review of the matter in another proceeding if there is good cause to believe that the decision is inconsistent with established principles of law or the actual facts.

(c) The provisions of sub-para (b) of this paragraph shall not require the elimination or substitution of procedures in force in the territory of a contracting party on the date of this agreement which in fact provide for an objective and impartial review of administrative action even though such procedures are not fully or formally independent of the agencies entrusted with administrative enforcement. Any contracting party employing such procedures shall, upon request, furnish the contracting parties with full information thereon in order that they may determine whether such procedures conform to the requirements of this sub-paragraph.

Article XI – General elimination of quantitative restrictions

1   No prohibitions or restrictions other than duties, taxes or other charges whether made effective through quotas, import or export licences or other measures, shall be instituted or maintained by any contracting party on the importation of any product of the territory of any other contracting party or on the exportation or sale for export of any product destined for the territory of any other contracting party.

2   The provisions of para 1 of this article shall not extend to the following:

(a) export prohibitions or restrictions temporarily applied to prevent or relieve critical shortages of foodstuffs or other products essential to the exporting contracting party;

(b) import and export prohibitions or restrictions necessary to the application of standards or regulations for the classification, grading or marketing of commodities in international trade;

(c) Import restrictions on any agricultural or fisheries product. imported in any form, necessary to the enforcement of governmental measures which operate:

(i) to restrict the quantities of the like domestic product permitted to be marketed or produced, or, if there is no substantial domestic production of the like product, of a domestic product for which the imported product can be directly substituted; or

(ii) to remove a temporary surplus of the like domestic product, or, if there is no substantial domestic production of the like product, of a domestic product for which the imported product can be directly substituted, by making the surplus available to certain groups of domestic consumers free of charge or at prices below the current market level; or

(iii) to restrict the quantities permitted to be produced of any animal product the production of which is directly dependent, wholly or mainly, on the imported commodity, if the domestic production of that commodity is relatively negligible.

Any contracting party applying restrictions on the importation of any product pursuant to sub-para (c) of this paragraph shall give public notice of the total quantity or value of the product permitted to be imported during a specified future period and of any change in such quantity or value. Moreover, any restrictions applied under (i) above shall not be such as will reduce the total of imports relative to the total of domestic production, as compared with the proportion which might reasonably be expected to rule between the two in the absence of restrictions. In determining this proportion, the contracting party shall pay due regard to the proportion prevailing during a previous representative period and to any special factors. which may have affected or may be affecting the trade in the product concerned.

Article XII – Restrictions to safeguard the balance of payments

1   Notwithstanding the provisions of para 1 of Article XI, any contracting party, in order to safeguard its external financial position and its balance of payments, may restrict the quantity or value of merchandise permitted to be imported, subject to the provisions of the following paragraphs of this article.

2   (a) Import restrictions instituted, maintained or intensified by a contracting party under this article shall not exceed those necessary:

       (i)   to forestall the imminent threat of, or to stop, a serious decline in its monetary reserves; or

       (ii) in the case of a contracting party with very low monetary reserves, to achieve a reasonable rate of increase in its reserves.

     Due regard shall be paid in either case to any special factors which may be affecting the reserves of such contracting party or its need for reserves, including, where special external credits or other resources are available to it, the need to provide for the appropriate use of such credits or resources.

    (b) contracting parties applying restrictions under sub-para (a) of this paragraph shall progressively relax them as such conditions improve, maintaining them only to the extent that the conditions specified in that sub-paragraph still justify their application. They shall eliminate the restrictions when conditions would no longer justify their institution or maintenance under that sub-paragraph.

3   (a) Contracting parties undertake, in carrying out their domestic policies, to pay due regard to the need for maintaining or restoring equilibrium in their balance of payments on a sound and lasting basis and to the desirability of avoiding an uneconomic employment of productive resources. They recognise that, in order to achieve these ends, it is desirable so far as possible to adopt measures which expand rather than contract international trade.

    (b) contracting parties applying restrictions under this article may determine the incidence of the restrictions on imports of different products or classes of products in such a way as to give priority to the importation of those products which are more essential.

    (c) contracting parties applying restrictions under this article undertake:

       (i)   to avoid unnecessary damage to the commercial or economic interests of any other contracting party;

       (ii) not to apply restrictions so as to prevent unreasonably the importation of any description of goods in minimum commercial quantities the exclusion of which would impair regular channels of trade; and

       (iii) not to apply restrictions which would prevent the importation of commercial samples or prevent compliance with patent, trade mark, copyright, or similar procedures.

(d) The contracting parties recognise that, as a result of domestic policies directed towards the achievement and maintenance of full and productive employment or towards the development of economic resources, a contracting party may experience a high level of demand for imports involving a threat to its monetary reserves of the sort referred to in para 2(a) of this article. Accordingly, a contracting party otherwise complying with the provisions of this article shall not be required to withdraw or modify restrictions on the ground that a change in those policies would render unnecessary restrictions which it is applying under this article.

4 (a) Any contracting party applying new restrictions or raising the general level of its existing restrictions by a substantial intensification of the measures applied under this article shall immediately, after instituting or intensifying such restrictions (or, in circumstances in which prior consultation is practicable, before doing so) consult with the contracting parties as to the nature of its balance of payments difficulties, alternative corrective measures which may be available, and the possible effect of the restrictions on the economies of other contracting parties.

(b) On a date to be determined by them, the contracting parties shall review all restrictions still applied under this article on that date. Beginning one year after that date, contracting parties applying import restrictions under this article shall enter into consultations of the type provided for in sub-para (a) of this paragraph with the contracting parties annually.

(c) (i) If, in the course of consultations with a contracting party under sub-para (a) or (b) above, the contracting parties find that the restrictions are not consistent with the provisions of this article or with those of Article XIII (subject to the provisions of Article XIV), they shall indicate the nature of the inconsistency and may advise that the restrictions be suitably modified.

(ii) If, however, as a result of the consultations, the contracting parties determine that the restrictions are being applied in a manner involving an inconsistency of a serious nature with the provisions of this article or with those of Article XIII (subject to the provisions of Article XIV) and that damage to the trade of any contracting party is caused or threatened thereby, they shall so inform the contracting party applying the restrictions and shall make appropriate recommendations for securing conformity with such provisions within a specified period of time. If such contracting party does not comply with these recommendations within the specified period, the contracting parties may release any contracting party the trade of which is adversely affected by the restrictions from such obligations under this agreement towards the contracting party applying the restrictions as they determine to be appropriate in the circumstances.

(d) The contracting parties shall invite any contracting party which is applying restrictions under this article to enter into consultations with them at the request of any contracting party which can establish a *prima facie* case that the restrictions are inconsistent with the provisions of this article or with those of Article XIII (subject to the provisions of Article XIV) and that its trade is adversely affected thereby. However, no such invitation shall be issued unless the contracting parties have ascertained that direct discussions between the contracting parties concerned have not been successful. If, as a result of the consultations with the contracting parties, no agreement is reached and they determine that the restrictions are being applied inconsistently with such provisions, and that damage to the trade of the contracting party initiating the procedure is caused or threatened thereby, they shall recommend the withdrawal or modification of the restrictions. If the restrictions are not withdrawn or modified within such time as the contracting parties may prescribe, they may release the contracting party initiating the procedure from such obligations under this agreement towards the contracting party applying the restrictions as they determine to be appropriate in the circumstances.

(e) In proceeding under this paragraph, the contracting parties shall have due regard to any special external factors adversely affecting the export trade of the contracting party applying restrictions.

(f) Determinations under this paragraph shall be rendered expeditiously and, if possible, within 60 days of the initiation of the consultations.

5   If there is a persistent and widespread application of import restrictions under this article, indicating the existence of a general disequilibrium which is restricting international trade, the contracting parties shall initiate discussions to consider whether other measures might be taken, either by those contracting parties the balances of payments of which are under pressure or by those the balances of payments of which are tending to be exceptionally favourable, or by any appropriate intergovernmental organisation, to remove the underlying causes of the disequilibrium. On the invitation of the contracting parties, contracting parties shall participate in such discussions.

Article XIII – Non-discriminatory administration of quantitative restrictions

1   No prohibition or restriction shall be applied by any contracting party on the importation of any product of the territory of any other contracting party or on the exportation of any product destined for the territory of any other contracting party, unless the importation of the like product of all third countries or the exportation of the like product of all third countries is similarly prohibited or restricted.

2   In applying import restrictions to any product, contracting parties shall aim at a distribution of trade in such product approaching as closely as possible the shares which the various contracting parties might be expected to obtain in the absence of such restrictions, and to this end shall observe the following provisions:

(a) Wherever practicable, quotas representing the total amount of permitted imports (whether allocated among supplying countries or not) shall be fixed, and notice given of their amount in accordance with para 3(b) of this article.

(b) In cases in which quotas are not practicable, the restrictions may be applied by means of import licences or permits without a quota.

(c) Contracting parties shall not, except for purposes of operating quotas allocated in accordance with sub-para (d) of this paragraph, require that import licences or permits be utilised for the importation of the product concerned from a particular country or source.

(d) In cases in which a quota is allocated among supplying countries, the contracting party applying the restrictions may seek agreement with respect to the allocation of shares in the quota with all other contracting parties having a substantial interest in supplying the product concerned. In cases in which this method is not reasonably practicable, the contracting party concerned shall allot to contracting parties having a substantial interest in supplying the product shares based upon the proportions, supplied by such contracting parties during a previous representative period, of the total quantity or value of imports of the product, due account being taken of any special factors which may have affected or may be affecting the trade in the product. No conditions or formalities shall be imposed which would prevent any contracting party from utilising fully the share of any such total quantity or value which has been allotted to it, subject to importation being made within any prescribed period to which the quota may relate.

3   (a)   In cases in which import licences are issued in connection with import restrictions, the contracting party applying the restrictions shall provide, upon the request of any contracting party having an interest in the trade in the product concerned, all relevant information concerning the administration of the restrictions, the import licences granted over a recent period and the distribution of such licences among supplying countries; provided that there shall be no obligation to supply information as to the names of importing or supplying enterprises.

    (b)   In the case of import restrictions involving the fixing of quotas, the contracting party applying the restrictions shall give public notice of the total quantity or value of the product or products which will be permitted to be imported during a specified future period and of any change in such quantity or value. Any supplies of the product in question which were *en route* at the time at which public notice was given shall not be excluded from entry: provided that they may be counted so far as practicable, against the quantity permitted to be imported in the period in question, and also, where necessary, against the quantities permitted to be imported in the next following period or periods; and provided further that if any contracting party customarily exempts from such restrictions products entered for consumption or withdrawn from warehouse for consumption during a period of 30 days after the day of such public notice, such practice shall be considered full compliance with this sub-paragraph.

    (c)   In the case of quotas allocated among supplying countries, the contracting party applying the restrictions shall promptly inform all other contracting parties having an interest in supplying the product concerned of the shares in the quota currently allocated, by quantity or value, to the various supplying countries and shall give public notice thereof.

With regard to restrictions applied in accordance with para 2(d) of this article or under para 2(c) of Article XI, the selection of a representative period for any product and the appraisal of any special factors affecting the trade in the product shall be made initially by the contracting party applying the restriction; provided that such contracting party shall, upon the request of any other contracting party having a substantial interest in supplying that product or upon the request of the contracting parties, consult promptly with the other contracting party or the contracting parties regarding the need for an adjustment of the proportion determined or of the base period selected. or for the reappraisal of the special factors involved, or for the elimination of conditions, formalities or any other provisions established unilaterally relating to the allocation of an adequate quota or its unrestricted utilisation.

5   The provisions of this article shall apply to any tariff quota instituted or maintained by any contracting party, and, in so far as applicable, the principles of this article shall also extend to export restrictions.

Article XIV – exceptions to the rule of non-discrimination

1   A contracting party which applies restrictions under Article XII or under section B of Article XVIII may, in the application of such restrictions, deviate from the provisions of Article XIII in a manner having equivalent effect to restrictions on payments and transfers for current international transactions which that contracting party may at that time apply under Article VIII or XIV of the Articles of Agreement of the International Monetary Fund, or under analogous provisions of a special exchange agreement entered into pursuant to para 6 of Article XV.

2   A contracting party which is applying import restrictions under Article XII or under section B of Article XVIII may, with the consent of the contracting parties, temporarily deviate from the provisions of Article XIII in respect of a small part of its external trade where the benefits to the contracting party or contracting parties concerned substantially outweigh any injury which may result to the trade of other contracting parties.

3   The provisions of Article XIII shall not preclude a group of territories having a common quota in the International Monetary Fund from applying against imports from other countries, but not among themselves, restrictions in accordance with the provisions of Article XII or of section B of Article XVIII on condition that such restrictions are in all other respects consistent with the provisions of Article XIII.

4   A contracting party applying import restrictions under Article XII or under section B of Article XVIII shall not be precluded by Articles XI to XV or section B of Article XVIII of this agreement from applying measures to direct its exports in such a manner as to increase its earnings of currencies which it can use without deviation from the provisions of Article XIII.

5   A contracting party shall not be precluded by Articles XI to XV, inclusive, or by section B of Article XVIII, of this agreement from applying quantitative restrictions:

   (a)   having equivalent effect or exchange restrictions authorised under section 3 (b) of Article VII of the Articles of Agreement of the International Monetary Fund; or

   (b)   under the preferential arrangements provided for in Annex A of this Agreement, pending the outcome of the negotiations referred to therein.

Article XV – Exchange arrangements

1   The contracting parties shall seek co-operation with the International Monetary Fund to the end that the contracting parties and the Fund may pursue a co-ordinated policy with regard to exchange questions within the jurisdiction of the Fund and questions of quantitative restrictions and other trade measures within the jurisdiction of the contracting parties.

2   In all cases in which the contracting parties are called upon to consider or deal with problems concerning monetary reserves, balances of payments or foreign exchange arrangements, they shall consult fully with the International Monetary Fund. In such consultations, the contracting parties shall accept all findings of statistical and other facts presented by the Fund relating to foreign exchange, monetary reserves and balances of payments, and shall accept the determination of the Fund as to whether

action by a contracting party in exchange matters is in accordance with the Articles of Agreement of the International Monetary Fund, or with the terms of a special exchange agreement between that contracting party and the contracting parties. The contracting parties, in reaching their final decision in cases involving the criteria set forth in para 2(a) of Article XII or in para 9 of Article XVIII, shall accept the determination of the Fund as to what constitutes a serious decline in the contracting party's monetary reserves, a very low level of its monetary reserves or a reasonable rate of increase in its monetary reserves, and as to the financial aspects of other matters covered in consultation in such cases.

3   The contracting parties shall seek agreement with the Fund regarding procedures for consultation under para 2 of this article.

4   Contracting parties shall not, by exchange action frustrate the intent of the provisions of this agreement, nor, by trade action, the intent of the provisions of the Articles of Agreement of the International Monetary Fund.

5   If the contracting parties consider, at any time, that exchange restrictions on payments and transfers in connection with imports are being applied by a contracting party in a manner inconsistent with the exceptions provided for in this agreement for quantitative restrictions, they shall report thereon to the Fund.

6   Any contracting party which is not a member of the Fund shall. within a time to be determined by the contracting parties after consultation with the Fund, become a member of the Fund, or, failing that, enter into a special exchange agreement with the contracting parties. A contracting party which ceases to be a member of the Fund shall forthwith enter into a special exchange agreement with the contracting parties. Any special exchange agreement entered into by a contracting party under this paragraph shall thereupon become part of its obligations under this agreement.

7   (a) A special exchange agreement between a contracting party and the contracting parties under para 6 of this article shall provide to the satisfaction of the contracting parties that the objectives of this agreement will not be frustrated as a result of action in exchange matters by the contracting party in question.

     (b) The terms of any such agreement shall not impose obligations on the contracting party in exchange matters generally more restrictive than those imposed by the Articles of Agreement of the International Monetary Fund on members of the Fund.

8   A contracting party which is not a member of the Fund shall furnish such information within the general scope of section 5 of Article VIII of the Articles of Agreement of the International Monetary Fund as the contracting parties may require in order to carry out their functions under this agreement.

9   Nothing in this agreement shall preclude:

     (a) the use by a contracting party of exchange controls or exchange restrictions in accordance with the Articles of Agreement of the International Monetary Fund or with that contracting party's special exchange agreement with the contracting parties; or

     (b) the use by a contracting party of restrictions or controls on imports or exports the sole effect of which, additional to the effects permitted under Articles XI XII, XIII and XIV, is to make effective such exchange controls or exchange restrictions.

Article XVI – Subsidies

Section A – Subsidies in general

1   If any contracting party grants or maintains any subsidy, including any form of income or price support, which operates directly or indirectly to increase exports of any product from, or to reduce imports of any product into, its territory, it shall notify the contracting parties in writing of the extent and nature of the subsidisation, of the estimated effect of the subsidisation on the quantity of the affected product or products imported into or exported from its territory and of the circumstances making the subsidisation necessary. In any case in which it is determined that serious prejudice to the interests of any other contracting party is caused or threatened by any such subsidisation, the contracting party granting the subsidy shall, upon request, discuss with the other contracting party or parties concerned, or with the contracting parties, the possibility of limiting the subsidisation.

Section B – Additional provisions on export subsidies

2   The contracting parties recognise that the granting by a contracting party of a subsidy on the export of any product may have harmful effects for other contracting parties, both importing and exporting, may cause undue disturbance to their normal commercial interests, and may hinder the achievement of the objectives of this Agreement.

3   Accordingly, contracting parties should seek to avoid the use of subsidies on the export of primary products. If, however, a contracting party grants directly or indirectly any form of subsidy which operates to increase the export of any primary product from its territory, such subsidy shall not be applied in a manner which results in that contracting party having more than an equitable share of world export trade in that product, account being taken of the shares of the contracting parties in such trade in the product during a previous representative period, and any special factors which may have affected or may be affecting such trade in the product.

4   Further, as from 1 January 1958 or the earliest practicable date thereafter, contracting parties shall cease to grant either directly or indirectly any form of subsidy on the export of any product other than a primary product which subsidy results in the sale of such product for export at a price lower than the comparable price charged for the like product to buyers in the domestic market. Until 31 December 1957, no contracting party shall extend the scope of any such subsidisation beyond that existing on 1 January 1955 by the introduction of new, or the extension of existing, subsidies.

5   The contracting parties shall review the operation of the provisions of this article from time to time with a view to examining its effectiveness, in the light of actual experience, in promoting the objectives of this Agreement and avoiding subsidisation seriously prejudicial to the trade or interests of contracting parties.

Article XVII – State trading enterprises

1   (a)   Each contracting party undertakes that if it establishes or maintains a State enterprise, wherever located, or grants to any enterprise, formally or in effect, exclusive or special privileges, such enterprise shall, in its purchases or sales involving either imports or exports, act in a manner consistent with the general principles of non-discriminatory treatment prescribed in this Agreement for governmental measures affecting imports or exports by private traders.

(b) The provisions of sub-para (a) of this paragraph shall be understood to require that such enterprises shall, having due regard to the other provisions of this agreement, make any such purchases or sales solely in accordance with commercial considerations, including price, quality, availability, marketability transportation and other conditions of purchase or sale, and shall afford the enterprises of the other contracting parties adequate opportunity, in accordance with customary business practice, to compete for participation in such purchases or sales.

(c) No contracting party shall prevent any enterprise (whether or not an enterprise described in sub-para (a) of this paragraph) under its jurisdiction from acting in accordance with the principles of sub-paras (a) and (b) of this paragraph.

2   The provisions of para 1 of this article shall not apply to imports of products for immediate or ultimate consumption in governmental use and not otherwise for resale or use in the production of goods for sale. With respect to such imports, each contracting party shall accord to the trade of the other contracting parties fair and equitable treatment.

3   The contracting parties recognise that enterprises of the kind described in para 1(a) of this article might be operated so as to create serious obstacles to trade; thus negotiations on a reciprocal and mutually advantageous basis designed to limit or reduce such obstacles are of importance to the expansion of international trade.

4   (a) Contracting parties shall notify the contracting parties of the products which are imported into or exported from their territories by enterprises of the kind described in para 1(a) of this article.

(b) A contracting party establishing, maintaining or authorising an import monopoly of a product, which is not the subject of a concession under Article II shall, on the request of another contracting party having a substantial trade in the product concerned, inform the contracting parties of the import mark-up on the product during a recent representative period, or, when it is not possible to do so, of the price charged on the resale of the product.

(c) The contracting parties may, at the request of a contracting party which has reason to believe that its interests under this agreement are being adversely affected by the operations of an enterprise of the kind described in para 1(a), request the contracting party establishing, maintaining or authorising such enterprise to supply information about its operations related to the carrying out of the provisions of this agreement.

(d) The provisions of this paragraph shall not require any contracting party to disclose confidential information which would impede law enforcement or otherwise be contrary to the public interest or would prejudice the legitimate commercial interests of particular enterprises.

Article XVIII – Governmental assistance to economic development

1   The contracting parties recognise that the attainment of the objectives of this agreement will be facilitated by the progressive development of their economies, particularly of those contracting parties the economies of which can only support low standards of living and are in the early stages of development.

2   The contracting parties recognise further that it may be necessary for those contracting parties, in order to implement programmes and policies of economic

development designed to raise the general standard of living of their people, to take protective or other measures affecting imports, and that such measures are justified in so far as they facilitate the attainment of the objectives of this agreement. They agree, therefore, that those contracting parties should enjoy additional facilities to enable them:

(a) to maintain sufficient flexibility in their tariff structure to be able to grant the tariff protection required for the establishment of a particular industry; and

(b) to apply quantitative restrictions for balance of payments purposes in a manner which takes full account of the continued high level of demand for imports likely to be generated by their programmes of economic development.

3   The contracting parties recognise finally that, with those additional facilities which are provided for in sections A and B of this article, the provisions of this agreement would normally be sufficient to enable contracting parties to meet the requirements of their economic development. They agree, however, that there may be circumstances where no measure consistent with those provisions is practicable to permit a contracting party in the process of economic development to grant the governmental assistance required to promote the establishment of particular industries with a view to raising the general standard of living of its people. Special procedures are laid down in sections C and D of this article to deal with those cases.

4   (a)   Consequently, a contracting party the economy of which can only support low standards of living and is in the early stages of development shall be free to deviate temporarily from the provisions of the other articles of this agreement, as provided in sections A, B and C of this article.

(b)   A contracting party the economy of which is in the process of development but which does not come within the scope of sub-para (a) above, may submit applications to the contracting parties under section D of this article.

5   The contracting parties recognise that the export earnings of contracting parties, the economies of which are of the type described in para 4(a) and (b) above and which depend on exports of a small number of primary commodities, may be seriously reduced by a decline in the sale of such commodities. Accordingly, when the exports of primary commodities by such a contracting party are seriously affected by measures taken by another contracting party, it may have resort to the consultation provisions of Article XXII of this agreement.

6   The contracting parties shall review annually all measures applied pursuant to the provisions of sections C and D of this article.

Section A

7   (a)   If a contracting party coming within the scope of para 4(a) of this article considers it desirable, in order to promote the establishment of a particular industry with a view to raising the general standard of living of its people, to modify or withdraw a concession included in the appropriate Schedule annexed to this agreement, it shall notify the contracting parties to this effect and enter into negotiations with any contracting party with which such concession was initially negotiated, and with any other contracting party determined by the contracting parties to have a substantial interest therein. If agreement is reached between such contracting parties concerned, they shall be free to modify or withdraw concessions under the appropriate Schedules to this agreement in

order to give effect to such agreement, including any compensatory adjustments involved.

(b) If agreement is not reached within 60 days after the notification provided for in sub-para (a) above, the contracting party which proposes to modify or withdraw the concession may refer the matter to the contracting parties, which shall promptly examine it. If they find that the contracting party which proposes to modify or withdraw the concession has made every effort to reach an agreement and that the compensatory adjustment offered by it is adequate, that contracting party shall be free to modify or withdraw the concession if, at the same time, it gives effect to the compensatory adjustment. If the contracting parties do not find that the compensation offered by a contracting party proposing to modify or withdraw the concession is adequate, but find that it has made every reasonable effort to offer adequate compensation, that contracting party shall be free to proceed with such modification or withdrawal. If such action is taken, any other contracting party referred to in sub-para (a) above shall be free to modify or withdraw substantially equivalent concessions initially negotiated with the contracting party which has taken the action.

Section B

8 The contracting parties recognise that contracting parties coming within the scope of para 4(a) of this article tend, when they are in rapid process of development, to experience balance of payments difficulties arising mainly from efforts to expand their internal markets as well as from the instability in their terms of trade.

9 In order to safeguard its external financial position and to ensure a level of reserves adequate for the implementation of its programme of economic development, a contracting party coming within the scope of para 4(a) of this article may, subject to the provisions of paras 10–12, control the general level of its imports by restricting the quantity or value of merchandise permitted to be imported; provided that the import restrictions instituted, maintained or intensified shall not exceed those necessary:

(a) to forestall the threat of, or to stop, a serious decline in its monetary reserves; or

(b) in the case of a contracting party with inadequate monetary reserves, to achieve a reasonable rate of increase in its reserves.

Due regard shall he paid in either case to any special factors which may be affecting the reserves of the contracting party or its need for reserves, including, where special external credits or other resources are available to it, the need to provide for the appropriate use of such credits or resources.

10 In applying these restrictions, the contracting party may determine their incidence on imports of different products or classes of products in such a way as to give priority to the importation of those products which are more essential in the light of its policy of economic development; provided that the restrictions are so applied as to avoid unnecessary damage to the commercial or economic interests of any other contracting party and not to prevent unreasonably the importation of any description of goods in minimum commercial quantities the exclusion of which would impair regular channels of trade; and provided further that the restrictions are not so applied as to prevent the importation of commercial samples or to prevent compliance with patent, trade mark, copyright or similar procedures.

11 In carrying out its domestic policies, the contracting party concerned shall pay due regard to the need for restoring equilibrium in its balance of payments on a sound and lasting basis and to the desirability of assuring an economic employment of productive resources. It shall progressively relax any restrictions applied under this section as conditions improve maintaining them only to the extent necessary under the terms of para 9 of this article and shall eliminate them when conditions no longer justify such maintenance; provided that no contracting party shall be required to withdraw or modify restrictions on the ground that a change in its development policy would render unnecessary the restrictions which it is applying under this section.

12 (a) Any contracting party applying new restrictions or raising the general level of its existing restrictions by a substantial intensification of the measures applied under this section, shall immediately after instituting or intensifying such restrictions (or, in circumstances in which prior consultation is practicable, before doing so) consult with the contracting parties as to the nature of its balance of payments difficulties, alternative corrective measures which may be available, and the possible effect of the restrictions on the economies of other contracting parties.

    (b) On a date to be determined by them, the contracting parties shall review all restrictions still applied under this section on that date. Beginning two years after that date, contracting parties applying restrictions under this section shall enter into consultations of the type provided for in sub-para (a) above with the contracting parties at intervals of approximately, but not less than, two years according to a programme to be drawn up each year by the contracting parties; provided that no consultation under this sub-paragraph shall take place within two years after the conclusion of a consultation of a general nature under any other provision of this paragraph.

    (c) (i) If, in the course of consultations with a contracting party under sub-para (a) or (b) of this paragraph, the contracting parties find that the restrictions are not consistent with the provisions of this section or with those of Article XIII (subject to the provisions of Article XIV), they shall indicate the nature of the inconsistency and may advise that the restrictions be suitably modified.

         (ii) If, however, as a result of the consultations, the contracting parties determine that the restrictions are being applied in a manner involving an inconsistency of a serious nature with the provisions of this section or with those of Article XIII (subject to the provisions of Article XIV) and that damage to the trade of any contracting party is caused or threatened thereby, they shall so inform the contracting party applying the restrictions anti shall make appropriate recommendations for securing conformity with such provisions within a specified period. If such contracting party does not comply with these recommendations within the specified period, the contracting parties may release any contracting party the trade of which is adversely affected by the restrictions from such obligations under this agreement towards the contracting party applying the restrictions as they determine to be appropriate in the circumstances.

    (d) The contracting parties shall invite any contracting party which is applying restrictions under this section to enter into consultations with them at the request of any contracting party which can establish a *prima facie* case that the restrictions are inconsistent with the provisions of this section or with those of Article XIII (subject to the provisions of Article XIV) and that its trade is adversely affected thereby. However, no such invitation shall be issued unless the contracting parties have ascertained that direct discussions between the contracting parties concerned have not been successful. If, as a result of the consultations with the contracting parties no agreement is reached and they determine that the restrictions are being applied inconsistently with such provisions, and that damage to the trade of the contracting party initiating the procedure is caused or threatened thereby, they shall recommend the withdrawal or modification of the restrictions. If the restrictions are not withdrawn or modified within such time as the contracting parties may prescribe, they may release the contracting party initiating the procedure from such obligations under this agreement towards the contracting party applying the restrictions as they determine to be appropriate in the circumstances.

(e) If a contracting party against which action has been taken in accordance with the last sentence of sub-para (c)(ii) or (d) of this paragraph, finds that the release of obligations authorised by the contracting parties adversely affects the operation of its programme and policy of economic development, it shall be free, not later than 60 days after such action is taken, to give written notice to the Executive Secretary to the contracting parties of its intention to withdraw from this agreement and such withdrawal shall take effect on the 60th day following the day on which the notice is received by him.

(f) In proceeding under this paragraph the contracting parties shall have due regard to the factors referred to in para 2 of this article. Determinations under this paragraph shall be rendered expeditiously and, if possible within 60 days of the initiation of the consultations.

Section C

13 If a contracting party coming within the scope of para 4(a) of this article finds that governmental assistance is required to promote the establishment of a particular industry with a view to raising the general standard of living of its people, but that no measure consistent with the other provisions of this agreement is practicable to achieve that objective, it may have recourse to the provisions and procedures set out in this section.

14 The contracting party concerned shall notify the contracting parties of the special difficulties which it meets in the achievement of the objective outlined in para 13 of this article and shall indicate the specific measure affecting imports which it proposes to introduce in order to remedy these difficulties. It shall not introduce that measure before the expiration of the time limit laid down in para 15 or 17, as the case may be, or if the measure affects imports of a product which is the subject of a concession included in the appropriate Schedule annexed to this agreement, unless it has secured the concurrence of the contracting parties in accordance with the provisions of paragraph; provided that, if the industry receiving assistance has already started production, the contracting party may, after informing the contracting parties, take such measures as may be necessary to prevent, during that period, imports of the product or products concerned from increasing substantially above a normal level.

15 If, within 30 days of the notification of the measure, the contracting parties do not request the contracting party concerned to consult with them, that contracting party shall be free to deviate from the relevant provisions of the other articles of this agreement to the extent necessary to apply the proposed measure.

16 If it is requested by the contracting parties to to so, the contracting party shall consult with them as to the purpose of the proposed measure, as to alternative measures which may be available under this agreement, and as to the possible effect of the measure proposed on the commercial and economic interests of other contracting parties. If, as a result of such consultation, the contracting parties agree that there is no measure consistent with the other provisions of this agreement which is practicable in order to achieve the objective outlined in para 13 of this article, and concur in the proposed measure, the contracting party concerned shall be released from its obligations under the relevant provisions of the other articles of this agreement to the extent necessary to apply that measure.

17 If, within 90 days after the date of the notification of the proposed measure under para 14 of this article, the contracting parties have not concurred in such measure. the contracting party concerned may introduce the measure proposed after informing the contracting parties.

18 If the proposed measure affects a product which is the subject of a concession included in the appropriate Schedule annexed to this agreement, the contracting party concerned shall enter into consultations with any other contracting party with which the concession was initially negotiated, and with any other contracting party determined by the contracting parties to have a substantial interest therein. The contracting parties shall concur in the measure if they agree that there is no measure consistent with the other provisions of this agreement which is practicable in order to achieve the objective set forth in para 13 of this article, and if they are satisfied:

(a) that agreement has been reached with such other contracting parties as a result of the consultations referred to above; or

(b) if no such agreement has been reached within 60 days after the notification provided for in para 14 has been received by the contracting parties that the contracting party having recourse to this section has made all reasonable efforts to reach an agreement and that the interests of other contracting parties are adequately safeguarded.

The contracting party having recourse to this section shall thereupon be released from its obligations under the relevant provisions of the other articles of this agreement to the extent necessary to permit it to apply the measure.

19 If a proposed measure of the type described in para 13 of this article concerns an industry the establishment of which has in the initial period been facilitated by incidental protection afforded by restrictions imposed by the contracting party concerned for balance of payments purposes under the relevant provisions of this agreement, that contracting party may resort to the provisions and procedures of this section; provided that it shall not apply the proposed measure without the concurrence of the contracting parties.

20 Nothing in the preceding paragraphs of this section shall authorise any deviation from the provisions of Articles I, II and XIII of this agreement. The provisos to para 10 of this article shall also be applicable to any restriction under this section.

21 At any time while a measure is being applied under para 17 of this article any contracting party substantially affected by it may suspend the application to the trade of the contracting party having recourse to this section of such substantially equivalent concessions or other obligations under this agreement the suspension of which the contracting parties do not disapprove, provided that 60 days notice of such suspension is given to the contracting parties not later than six months after the measure has been introduced or changed substantially to the detriment of the contracting party affected. Any such contracting party shall afford adequate opportunity for consultation in accordance with the provisions of Article XXII of this agreement.

Section D

22 A contracting party coming within the scope of sub-para 4(b) of this article desiring, in the interest of the development of its economy, to introduce a measure of the type described in para 13 of this article in respect of the establishment of a particular industry may apply to the contracting parties for approval of such measure. The contracting parties shall promptly consult with such contracting party and shall, in making their decision, be guided by the considerations set out in para 16. If the contracting parties concur in the proposed measure the contracting party concerned shall be released from its obligations under the relevant provisions of the other articles of this agreement to the extent necessary to permit it to apply the measure. If the proposed measure affects a product which is the subject of a concession included in the appropriate Schedule annexed to this agreement, the provisions of para 18 shall apply.

23 Any measure applied under this section shall comply with the provisions of para 20 of this article.

Article XIX – Emergency action on imports of particular products

1 (a) If, as a result of unforeseen developments and of the effect of the obligations incurred by a contracting party under this agreement, including tariff concessions, any product is being imported into the territory of that contracting party in such increased quantities and under such conditions as to cause or threaten serious injury to domestic producers in that territory of like or directly competitive products, the contracting party shall be free, in respect of such product, and to the extent and for such time as may be necessary to prevent or remedy such injury, to suspend the obligation in whole or in part or to withdraw or modify the concession.

(b) If any product, which is the subject of a concession with respect to a preference, is being imported into the territory of a contracting party in the circumstances set forth in sub-para (a) of this paragraph, so as to cause or threaten serious injury to domestic producers of like or directly competitive products in the territory of a contracting party which receives or received such preference, the importing contracting party shall be free, if that other contracting party so requests, to suspend the relevant obligation in whole or in part or to withdraw or modify the concession in respect of the product, to the extent and for such time as may be necessary to prevent or remedy such injury.

2 Before any contracting party shall take action pursuant to the provisions of para 1 of this article, it shall give notice in writing to the contracting parties as far in advance as may be practicable and shall afford the contracting parties and those contracting

parties having a substantial interest as exporters of the product concerned an opportunity to consult with it in respect of the proposed action. When such notice is given in relation to a concession with respect to a preference, the notice shall name the contracting party which has requested the action. In critical circumstances, where delay would cause damage which it would be difficult to repair, action under para 1 of this article may be taken provisionally without prior consultation, on the condition that consultation shall be effected immediately after taking such action.

3   (a) If agreement among the interested contracting parties with respect to the action is not reached, the contracting party which proposes to take or continue the action shall, nevertheless, be free to do so, and if such action is taken or continued, the affected contracting parties shall then be free, not later than 90 days after such action is taken, to suspend, upon the expiration of 30 days from the day on which written notice of such suspension is received by the contracting parties, the application to the trade of the contracting party taking such action, or, in the case envisaged in para 1(b) of this article, to the trade of the contracting party requesting such action, of such substantially equivalent concessions or other obligations under this agreement the suspension of which the contracting parties do not disapprove.

   (b) Notwithstanding the provisions of sub-para (a) of this paragraph, where action is taken under para 2 of this article without prior consultation and causes or threatens serious injury in the territory of a contracting party to the domestic producers of products affected by the action, that contracting party shall, where delay would cause damage difficult to repair, be free to suspend, upon the taking of the action and throughout the period of consultation, such concessions or other obligations as may be necessary to prevent or remedy the injury.

Article XX – General exceptions

Subject to the requirement that such measures are not applied in a manner which would constitute a means of arbitrary or unjustifiable discrimination between countries where the same conditions prevail, or a disguised restriction on international trade, nothing in this agreement shall be construed to prevent the adoption or enforcement by any contracting party of measures:

(a) necessary to protect public morals;

(b) necessary to protect human, animal or plant life or health;

(c) relating to the importation or exportation of gold or silver;

(d) necessary to secure compliance with laws or regulations which are not inconsistent with the provisions of this agreement, including those relating to customs enforcement, the enforcement of monopolies operated under para 4 of Article II and Article XVII, the protection of patents, trade marks and copyrights, and the prevention of deceptive practices;

(e) relating to the products of prison labour;

(f) imposed for the protection of national treasures of artistic, historic or archeological value;

(g) relating to the conservation of exhaustible natural resources if such measures are made effective in conjunction with restrictions on domestic production or consumption;

(h) undertaken in pursuance of obligations under any intergovernmental commodity agreement which conforms to criteria submitted to the contracting parties and not disapproved by them or which is itself so submitted and not so disapproved;

(i) involving restrictions on exports of domestic materials necessary to ensure essential quantities of such materials to a domestic processing industry during periods when the domestic price of such materials is held below the world price as part of a governmental stabilisation plan; provided that such restrictions shall not operate to increase the exports of or the protection afforded to such domestic industry, and shall not depart from the provisions of this agreement relating to non-discrimination;

(j) essential to the acquisition or distribution of products in general or local short supply; provided that any such measures shall be consistent with the principle that all contracting parties are entitled to an equitable share of the international supply of such products, and that any such measures, which are inconsistent with the other provisions of this agreement, shall be discontinued as soon as the conditions giving rise to them have ceased to exist. The contracting parties shall review the need for this sub-paragraph not later than 30 June 1960.

Article XXI – Security exceptions

Nothing in this agreement shall be construed:

(a) to require any contracting party to furnish any information the disclosure of which it considers contrary to its essential security interests; or

(b) to prevent any contracting party from taking any action which it considers necessary for the protection of its essential security interests:

    (i) relating to fissionable materials or the materials from which they are derived;

    (ii) relating to the traffic in arms, ammunition and implements of war and to such traffic in other goods and materials as is carried on directly or indirectly for the purpose of supplying a military establishment;

    (iii) taken in time of war or other emergency in international relations; or

(c) to prevent any contracting party from taking any action in pursuance of its obligations under the United Nations Charter for the maintenance of international peace and security.

Article XXII – Consultation

1 Each contracting party shall accord sympathetic consideration to, and shall afford adequate opportunity for consultation regarding, such representations as may be made by another contracting party with respect to any matter affecting the operation of this agreement.

2 The contracting parties may, at the request of a contracting party consult with any contracting party or parties in respect of any matter for which it has not been possible to find a satisfactory solution through consultation under para 1.

Article XXIII – Nullification or impairment

1 If any contracting party should consider that any benefit accruing to it directly or indirectly under this agreement is being nullified or impaired or that the attainment of any objective of the agreement is being impeded as the result of:

    (a) the failure of another contracting party to carry out its obligations under this agreement; or

(b) the application by another contracting party of any measure, whether or not it conflicts with the provisions of this agreement; or

(c) the existence of any other situation,

the contracting party may, with a view to the satisfactory adjustment of the matter, make written representations or proposals to the other contracting party or parties which it considers to be concerned. Any contracting party thus approached shall give sympathetic consideration to the representations or proposals made to it.

2　If no satisfactory adjustment is effected between the contracting parties concerned within a reasonable time, or if the difficulty is of the type described in para 1(c) of this article, the matter may be referred to the contracting parties. The contracting parties shall promptly investigate any matter so referred to them and shall make appropriate recommendations to the contracting parties which they consider to be concerned, or give a ruling on the matter, as appropriate. The contracting parties may consult with contracting parties, with the Economic and Social Council of the United Nations and with any appropriate intergovernmental organisation in cases where they consider such consultation necessary. If the contracting parties consider that the circumstances are serious enough to justify such action, they may authorise a contracting party or parties to suspend the application to any other contracting party or parties of such concessions or other obligations under this agreement as they determine to be appropriate in the circumstances. If the application to any contracting party of any concession or other obligation is in fact suspended, that contracting party shall then be free, not later than 60 days after such action is taken, to give written notice to the Executive Secretary to the contracting parties of its intention to withdraw from this agreement and such withdrawal shall take effect upon the 60th day following the day on which such notice is received by him.

PART III

Article XXIV – Territorial application, frontier traffic, customs unions and free-trade areas

1　The provisions of this agreement shall apply to the metropolitan customs territories of the contracting parties and to any other customs territories in respect of which this agreement has been accepted under Article XXVI or is being applied under Article XXXIII or pursuant to the Protocol of Provisional Application. Each such customs territory shall, exclusively for the purposes of the territorial application of this agreement, be treated as though it were a contracting party; provided that the provisions of this paragraph shall not be construed to create any rights or obligations as between two or more customs territories in respect of which this agreement has been accepted under Article XXVI or is being applied under Article XXXIII or pursuant to the Protocol of Provisional Application by a single contracting party.

2　For the purposes of this agreement a customs territory shall be understood to mean any territory with respect to which separate tariffs or other regulations of commerce are maintained for a substantial part of the trade of such territory with other territories.

3　The provisions of this agreement shall not be construed to prevent:

(a) advantages accorded by any contracting party to adjacent countries in order to facilitate frontier traffic;

(b) advantages accorded to the trade with the Free Territory of Trieste by countries contiguous to that territory, provided that such advantages are not in conflict with the Treaties of Peace arising out of the Second World War.

4 The contracting parties recognise the desirability of increasing freedom of trade by the development, through voluntary agreements, of closer integration between the economies of the countries parties to such agreements. They also recognise that the purpose of a customs union or of a free-trade area should be to facilitate trade between the constituent territories and not to raise barriers to the trade of other contracting parties with such territories.

5 Accordingly, the provisions of this agreement shall not prevent, as between the territories of contracting parties, the formation of a customs union or of a free-trade area or the adoption of an interim agreement necessary for the formation of a customs union or of a free-trade area; provided that:

(a) with respect to a customs union, or an interim agreement leading to the formation of a customs union, the duties and other regulations of commerce imposed at the institution of any such union or inter-union agreement in respect of trade with contracting parties not parties to such union or agreement shall not on the whole be higher or more restrictive than the general incidence of the duties and regulations of commerce applicable in the constituent territories prior to the formation of such union or the adoption of such interim agreement, as the case may be;

(b) with respect to a free-trade area, or an interim agreement leading to the formation of a free-trade area, the duties and other regulations of commerce maintained in each of the constituent territories and applicable at the formation of such free-trade area or the adoption of such interim agreement to the trade of contracting parties not included in such area or not parties to such agreement shall not be higher or more restrictive than the corresponding duties and other regulations of commerce existing in the same constituent territories prior to the formation of the free-trade area, or interim agreement, as the case may be; and

(c) any interim agreement referred to in sub-paras (a) and (b) shall include a plan and schedule for the formation of such a customs union or of such a free-trade area within a reasonable length of time.

6 If, in fulfilling the requirements of sub-para 5(a), a contracting party proposes to increase any rate of duty inconsistently with the provisions of Article II, the procedure set forth in Article XXVIII shall apply. In providing for compensatory adjustment, due account shall be taken of the compensation already afforded by the reductions brought about in the corresponding duty of the other constituents of the union.

7 (a) Any contracting party deciding to enter into a customs union or free-trade area, or an interim agreement leading to the formation of such a union or area, shall promptly notify the contracting parties and shall make available to them such information regarding the proposed union or area as will enable them to make such reports and recommendations to contracting parties as they may deem appropriate.

(b) If, after having studied the plan and schedule included in an interim agreement referred to in para 5 in consultation with the parties to that agreement and taking due account of the information made available in accordance with the provisions of sub-para (a), the contracting parties find that such agreement is not likely to result in the formation of a customs union or of a free-trade area within the period contemplated by the parties to the agreement or that such period is not a reasonable one, the contracting parties shall make recommendations to the parties to the agreement. The parties shall not maintain or put into force, as the case may be, such agreement if they are not prepared to modify it in accordance with these recommendations.

(c) Any substantial change in the plan or schedule referred to in para 5(c) shall be communicated to the contracting parties, which may request the contracting parties concerned to consult with them if the change seems likely to jeopardise or delay untruly the formation of the customs union or of the free-trade area.

8   For the purposes of this agreement:

(a) A customs union shall be understood to mean the substitution of a single customs territory for two or more customs territories, so that:

  (i) duties and other restrictive regulations of commerce (except, where necessary, those permitted under Articles XI, XII, XIII, XIV, XV and XX) are eliminated with respect to substantially all the trade between the constituent territories of the union or at least with respect to substantially all the trade in products originating in such territories; and

  (ii) subject to the provisions of para 9, substantially the same duties and other regulations of commerce are applied by each of the members of the union to the trade of territories not included in the union.

(b) A free-trade area shall be understood to mean a group of two or more customs territories in which the duties and other restrictive regulations of commerce (except, where necessary, those permitted under Articles XI, XII, XIII XIV, XV and XX) are eliminated on substantially all the trade between the constituent territories in products originating in such territories.

9   The preferences referred to in para 2 of Article I shall not be affected by the formation of a customs union or of a free-trade area but may be eliminated or adjusted by means of negotiations with contracting parties affected. This procedure of negotiations with affected contracting parties shall, in particular, apply to the elimination of preferences required to conform with the provisions of para 8(a)(i) and para 8(b).

10   The contracting may, by a two thirds majority, approve proposals which do not fully comply with the requirements of paras 5–9 inclusive, provided that such proposals lead to the formation of a customs union or a free-trade area in the sense of this article.

11   Taking into account the exceptional circumstances arising out of the establishment of India and Pakistan as independent States and recognising the fact that they have long constituted an economic unit, the contracting parties agree that the provisions of this agreement shall not prevent the two countries from entering into special arrangements with respect to the trade between them, pending the establishment of their mutual trade relations on a definitive basis.

12   Each contracting party shall take such reasonable measures as may be available to it to ensure observance of the provisions of this agreement by the regional and local governments and authorities within its territory.

Article XXV – Joint action by the contracting parties

1   Representatives of the contracting parties shall meet from time to time for the purpose of giving effect to those provisions of this agreement which involve joint action and generally, with a view to facilitating the operation and furthering the objectives of this agreement. Wherever reference is made in this agreement to the contracting parties acting jointly they are designated as the contracting parties.

2   The Secretary General of the UN is requested to convene the first meeting of the contracting parties, which shall take place not later than 1 March 1948.

3   Each contracting party shall be entitled to have one vote at all meetings of the contracting parties.

4   Except as otherwise provided for in this agreement, decisions of the contracting parties shall be taken by a majority of the votes cast.

5   In exceptional circumstances not elsewhere provided for in this agreement, the contracting parties may waive an obligation imposed upon a contracting party by this agreement; provided that any such decision shall be approved by a two thirds majority of the votes cast and that such majority shall comprise more than half of the contracting parties. The contracting parties may also by such a vote:

(i)   define certain categories of exceptional circumstances to which other voting requirements shall apply for the waiver of obligations; and

(ii)   prescribe such criteria as may be necessary for the application of this paragraph.

Article XXVI – Acceptance, entry into force and registration

1   The date of this agreement shall be 30 October 1947.

2   This agreement shall be open for acceptance by any contracting party which, on 1 March 1955, was a contracting party or was negotiating with a view to accession to this agreement.

3   This agreement, done in a single English original and in a single French original, both texts authentic, shall be deposited with the Secretary General of the United Nations, who shall furnish certified copies thereof to all interested governments.

4   Each government accepting this agreement shall deposit an instrument of acceptance with the Executive Secretary to the contracting parties, who will inform all interested governments of the date of deposit of each instrument of acceptance and of the day on which this agreement enters into force under para 6 of this article.

5   (a)   Each government accepting this agreement does so in respect of its metropolitan territory and of the other territories for which it has international responsibility, except such separate customs territories as it shall notify to the Executive Secretary to the contracting parties at the time of its own acceptance.

(b)   Any government, which has so notified the Executive Secretary under the exceptions in sub-para (a) of this paragraph, may at any time give notice to the Executive Secretary' that its acceptance shall be effective in respect of any separate customs territory or territories so excepted and such notice shall take effect on the 30th day following the day on which it is received by the Executive Secretary.

(c)   If any of the customs territories, in respect of which a contracting party has accepted this agreement, possesses or acquires full autonomy in the conduct of its external commercial relations and of the other matters provided for in this agreement, such territory shall, upon sponsorship through a declaration by the responsible contracting party establishing the above-mentioned fact, be deemed to be a contracting party.

6   This agreement shall enter into force, as among the governments which have accepted it, on the 30th day following the day on which instruments of acceptance have been deposited with the Executive Secretary to the contracting parties on behalf of governments named in Annex H the territories of which account for 85% of the total external trade of the territories of such governments, computed in accordance with the applicable column of percentages set forth therein. The instrument of acceptance of each other government shall take effect on the 30th day following the day on which such instrument has been deposited.

7   The United Nations is authorised to effect registration of this agreement as soon as it enters into force.

Article XXVII – Withholding or withdrawal of concessions

Any contracting party shall at any time be free to withhold or to withdraw in whole or in part any concession, provided for in the appropriate Schedule annexed to this agreement, in respect of which such contracting party determines that it was initially negotiated with a government which has not become, or has ceased to be, a contracting party. A contracting party taking such action shall notify the contracting parties and, upon request, consult with contracting parties which have a substantial interest in the product concerned.

Article XXVIII – Modification of schedules

1   On the first day of each three year period, the first period beginning on 1 January 1958 (or on the first day of any other period that may be specified by the contracting parties by two thirds of the votes cast) a contracting party (hereafter in this article referred to as the 'applicant contracting party') may, by negotiation and agreement with any contracting party with which such concession was initially negotiated and with any other contracting party determined by the contracting parties to have a principal supplying interest (which two preceding categories of contracting parties, together with the applicant contracting party, are in this article hereinafter referred to as the 'contracting parties primarily concerned'), and subject to consultation with any other contracting party determined by the contracting parties to have a substantial interest in such concession, modify or withdraw a concession' included in the appropriate Schedule annexed to this agreement.

2   In such negotiations and agreement, which may include provision for compensatory adjustment with respect to other products, the contracting parties concerned shall endeavour to maintain a general level of reciprocal and mutually advantageous concessions not less favourable to trade than that provided for in this agreement prior to such negotiations.

3   (a) If agreement between the contracting parties primarily concerned cannot be reached before I January 1958 or before the expiration of a period envisaged in para 1 of this article, the contracting party which proposes to modify or withdraw the concession shall, nevertheless, be free to do so and if such action is taken any contracting party with which such concession was initially negotiated, any contracting party determined under para 1 to have a principal supplying interest and any contracting party determined under para 1 to have a substantial interest shall then be free not later than six months after such action is taken, to

withdraw, upon the expiration of 30 days from the day on which written notice of such withdrawal is received by the contracting parties, substantially equivalent concessions initially negotiated with the applicant contracting party.

(b) If agreement between the contracting parties primarily concerned is reached but any other contracting party determined under para 1 of this article to have a substantial interest is not satisfied, such other contracting party shall be free, not later than six months after action under such agreement is taken, to withdraw, upon the expiration of 30 days from the day on which written notice of such withdrawal is received by the contracting parties, substantially equivalent concessions initially negotiated with the applicant contracting party.

4   The contracting parties may, at any time, in special circumstances, authorise a contracting party to enter into negotiations for modification or withdrawal of a concession included in the appropriate Schedule annexed to this agreement subject to the following procedures and conditions:

(a) Such negotiations and any related consultations shall be conducted in accordance with the provisions of paras 1 and 2 of this article.

(b) If agreement between the contracting parties primarily concerned is reached in the negotiations, the provisions of para 3(b) of this article shall apply.

(c) If agreement between the contracting parties primarily concerned is not reached within a period of 60 days after negotiations have been authorised, or within such longer period as the contracting parties may have prescribed, the applicant contracting party may refer the matter to the contracting parties.

(d) Upon such reference, the contracting parties shall promptly examine the matter and submit their views to the contracting parties primarily concerned with the aim of achieving a settlement. If a settlement is reached the provisions of para 3(b) shall apply as if agreement between the contracting parties primarily concerned had been reached. If no settlement is reached between the contracting parties primarily concerned, the applicant contracting party shall be free to modify or withdraw the concession, unless the contracting parties determine that the applicant contracting party has unreasonably failed to offer adequate compensation. If such action is taken, any contracting party with which the concession was initially negotiated, any contracting party determined under para 4(a) to have a principal supplying interest and any contracting party determined under para 4(a) to have a substantial interest, shall be free. not later than six months after such action is taken, to modify or withdraw, upon the expiration of 30 days from the day on which written notice of such withdrawal is received by the contracting parties substantially equivalent concessions initially negotiated with the applicant contracting party.

5   Before I January 1958 and before the end of any period envisaged in para 1 a contracting party may elect by notifying the contracting parties to reserve the right, for the duration of the next period, to modify the appropriate Schedule in accordance with the procedures of paras 1–3. If a contracting party so elects, other contracting parties shall have the right, during the same period, to modify or withdraw, in accordance with the same procedures, concessions initially negotiated with that contracting party.

Article XXVIII bis – Tariff negotiations

1   The contracting parties recognise that customs duties often constitute serious obstacles to trade; thus negotiations on a reciprocal and mutually advantageous basis, directed to the substantial reduction of the general level of tariffs and other charges on imports and exports and in particular to the reduction of such high tariffs as discourage the importation even of minimum quantities, and conducted with due regard to the objectives of this agreement and the varying needs of individual contracting parties, are of great importance to the expansion of international trade. The contracting parties may therefore sponsor such negotiations from time to time.

2   (a)   Negotiations under this article may be carried out on a selective product-by-product basis or by the application of such multilateral procedures as may be accepted by the contracting parties concerned. Such negotiations may be directed towards the reduction of duties, the binding of duties at then existing levels or undertakings that individual duties or the average duties on specified categories of products shall not exceed specified levels. The binding against increase of low duties or of duty free treatment shall, in principle, be recognised as a concession equivalent in value to the reduction of high duties.

(b)   The contracting parties recognise that in general the success of multilateral negotiations would depend on the participation of all contracting parties which conduct a substantial proportion of their external trade with one another.

3   Negotiations shall be conducted on a basis which affords adequate opportunity to take into account:

(a)   the needs of individual contracting parties and individual industries

(b)   the needs of less developed countries for a more flexible use of tariff protection to assist their economic development and the special needs of these countries to maintain tariffs for revenue purposes; and

(c)   all other relevant circumstances, including the fiscal, developmental, strategic and other needs of the contracting parties concerned.

Article XXIX – The relation of this agreement to the Havana Charter

1   The contracting parties undertake to observe to the fullest extent of their executive authority the general principles of Chapters I to VI inclusive and of Chapter IX of the Havana Charter pending their acceptance of it in accordance with their constitutional procedures.

2   Part II of this agreement shall be suspended on the day on which the Havana Charter enters into force.

3   If by 30 September 1949, the Havana Charter has not entered into force, the contracting parties shall meet before 31 December 1949 to agree whether this agreement shall be amended, supplemented or maintained.

4   If at any time the Havana Charter should cease to be in force, the contracting parties shall meet as soon as practicable thereafter to agree whether this agreement shall be supplemented, amended or maintained. Pending such agreement, Part II of this agreement shall again enter into force; provided that the provisions of Part II other than Article XXIII shall be replaced, *mutatis mutandis*, in the form in which they then appeared in the Havana Charter; and provided further that no contracting party shall be bound by any provisions which did not bind it at the time when the Havana Charter ceased to be in force.

5   If any contracting party has not accepted the Havana Charter by the date upon which it enters into force, the contracting parties shall confer to agree whether, and if so in what way, this agreement in so far as it affects relations between such contracting party and other contracting parties, shall be supplemented or amended. Pending such agreement the provisions of Part II of this agreement shall, notwithstanding the provisions of para 2 of this article, continue to apply as between such contracting party and other contracting parties.

6   Contracting parties which are members of the International Trade Organisation shall not invoke the provisions of this agreement so as to prevent the operation of any provision of the Havana Charter. The application of the principle underlying this paragraph to any contracting party which is not a member of the International Trade Organisation shall be the subject of an agreement pursuant to para 5 of this article.

Article XXX – Amendments

1   Except where provision for modification is made elsewhere in this agreement, amendments to the provisions of Part I of this agreement or to the provisions of Article XXIX or of this agreement shall become effective upon acceptance by all the contracting parties, and other amendments to this agreement shall become effective, in respect of those contracting parties which accept them, upon acceptance by two thirds of the contracting parties and thereafter for each other contracting party upon acceptance by it.

2   Any contracting party accepting an amendment to this agreement shall deposit an instrument of acceptance with the Secretary General of the United Nations within such period as the contracting parties may specify. The contracting parties may decide that any amendment made effective under this article is of such a nature that any contracting party which has not accepted it within a period specified by the contracting parties shall be free to withdraw from.this agreement, or to remain a contracting party with the consent of the contracting parties.

Article XXXI – Withdrawal

Without prejudice to the provisions of para 12 of Article XVIII, of Article XXIII or of para 2 of Article XXX, any contracting party may withdraw from this agreement, or may separately withdraw on behalf of any of the separate customs territories for which it has international responsibility and which at the time possesses full autonomy in the conduct of its external commercial relations and of the other matters provided for in this agreement. The withdrawal shall take effect upon the expiration of six months from the day on which written notice of withdrawal is received by the Secretary General of the United Nations.

Article XXXII – Contracting parties

1   The contracting parties to this agreement shall be understood to mean those governments which are applying the provisions of this agreement under Articles XXVI or XXXIII or pursuant to the Protocol of Provisional Application.

2   At any time after the entry into force of this agreement pursuant to para 6 of Article XXVI those contracting parties which have accepted this agreement pursuant to para 4 of Article XXVI may decide that any contracting party which has not so accepted it shall cease to be a contracting party.

Article XXXIII – Accession

A government not party to this agreement. or a government acting on behalf of a separate customs territory possessing full autonomy in the conduct of its external commercial relations and of the other matters provided for in this agreement, may accede to this agreement, on its own behalf or on behalf of that territory, on terms to be agreed between such government and the contracting parties. Decisions of the contracting parties under this paragraph shall be taken by a two thirds majority.

Article XXXIV – Annexes

The annexes to this agreement are hereby made an integral part of this agreement.

Article XXXV – Non-application of the agreement between particular contracting parties

1   This agreement, or alternatively Article II of this agreement, shall not apply as between any contracting party and any other contracting party if:

   (a) the two contracting parties have not entered into tariff negotiations with each other, and

   (b) either of the contracting parties, at the time either becomes a contracting party, does not consent to such application.

2   The contracting parties may review the operation of this article in particular cases at the request of any contracting party and make appropriate recommendations.

PART IV – TRADE AND DEVELOPMENT

Article XXXVI – Principles and objectives

1   The contracting parties:

   (a) recalling that the basic objectives of this agreement include the raising of standards of living and the progressive development of the economies of all contracting parties, and considering that the attainment of these objectives is particularly urgent for less developed contracting parties;

   (b) considering that export earnings of the less developed contracting parties can play a vital part in their economic development and that the extent of this contribution depends on the prices paid by the less developed contracting parties for essential imports, the volume of their exports, and the prices received for these exports;

   (c) noting, that there is a wide gap between standards of living in less developed countries and in other countries;

   (d) recognising that individual and joint action is essential to further the development of the economies of less developed contracting parties and to bring about a rapid advance in the standards of living in these countries;

   (e) recognising that international trade as a means of achieving economic and social advancement should be governed by such rules and procedures – and measures in conformity with such rules and procedures – as are consistent with the objectives set forth in this article;

   (f) noting that the contracting parties may enable less developed contracting parties to use special measures to promote their trade and development;

   agree as follows.

2   There is need for a rapid and sustained expansion of the export earnings of the less developed contracting parties.

3   There is need for positive efforts designed to ensure that less developed contracting parties secure a share in the growth in international trade commensurate with the needs of their economic development.

4   Given the continued dependence of many less developed contracting parties on the exportation of a limited range of primary products, there is need to provide in the largest possible measure more favourable and acceptable conditions of access to world markets for these products, and wherever appropriate to devise measures designed to stabilise and improve conditions of world markets in these products, including in particular measures designed to attain stable, equitable and remunerative prices, thus permitting an expansion of world trade and demand and a dynamic and steady growth of the real export earnings of these countries so as to provide them with expanding resources for their economic development.

5   The rapid expansion of the economies of the less developed contracting parties will be facilitated by a diversification of the structure of their economies and the avoidance of an excessive dependence on the export of primary products. There is, therefore, need for increased access in the largest possible measure to markets under favourable conditions for processed and manufactured products currently or potentially of particular export interest to less developed contracting parties.

6   Because of the chronic deficiency in the export proceeds and other foreign exchange earnings of less developed contracting parties, there are important inter-relationships between trade and financial assistance to development. There is, therefore, need for close and continuing collaboration between the contracting parties and the international lending agencies so that they can contribute most effectively to alleviating the burdens these less developed contracting parties assume in the interest of their economic development.

7   There is need for appropriate collaboration between the contracting parties, other intergovernmental bodies and the organs and agencies of the United Nations system, whose activities relate to the trade and economic development of less developed countries.

8   The developed contracting parties do not expect reciprocity for commitments made by them in trade negotiations to reduce or remove tariffs and other barriers to the trade of less developed contracting parties.

9   The adoption of measures to give effect to these principles and objectives shall be a matter of conscious and purposeful effort on the part of the contracting parties both individually and jointly.

Article XXXVII – Commitments

1   The developed contracting parties shall to the fullest extent possible – ie except when compelling reasons, which may include legal reasons, make it impossible – give effect to the following provisions:

(a)   accord high priority to the reduction and elimination of barriers to products currently or potentially of particular export interest to less developed contracting parties, including customs duties and other restrictions which differentiate unreasonably between such products in their primary and in their processed forms;

(b) refrain from introducing, or increasing the incidence of, customs duties or non-tariff import barriers on products currently or potentially of particular export interest to less developed contracting parties; and

(c) (i) refrain from imposing new fiscal measures, and

    (ii) in any adjustments of fiscal policy accord high priority to the reduction and elimination of fiscal measures,

which would hamper, or which hamper, significantly the growth of consumption of primary products, in raw or processed form, wholly or mainly produced in the territories of less developed contracting parties, and which are applied specifically to those products.

2 (a) Whenever it is considered that effect is not being given to any of the provisions of sub-para (a), (b) or (c) of para 1, the matter shall be reported to the contracting parties either by the contracting party not so giving effect to the relevant provisions or by any other interested contracting party.

(b) (i) The contracting parties shall, if requested so to do by any interested contracting party, and without prejudice to any bilateral consultations that may be undertaken, consult with the contracting party concerned and all interested contracting parties with respect to the matter with a view to reaching solutions satisfactory to all contracting parties concerned in order to further the objectives set forth in Article XXXVI. In the course of these consultations, the reasons given in cases where effect was not being given to the provisions of sub-para (a), (b) or (c) of para 1 shall be examined.

    (ii) As the implementation of the provisions of sub-para (a), (b) or (c) of para 1 by individual contracting parties may in some cases be more readily achieved where action is taken jointly with other developed contracting parties, such consultation might, where appropriate, be directed towards this end.

    (iii) The consultations by the contracting parties might also, in appropriate cases, be directed towards agreement on joint action designed to further the objectives of this agreement as envisaged in para 1 of Article XXV.

3 The developed contracting parties shall:

(a) make every effort, in cases where a government directly or indirectly determines the resale price of products wholly or mainly produced in the territories of less developed contracting parties, to maintain trade margins at equitable levels;

(b) give active consideration to the adoption of other measures designed to provide greater scope for the development of imports from less developed contracting parties and collaborate in appropriate international action to this end;

(c) have special regard to the trade interests of less developed contracting parties when considering the application of other measures permitted under this agreement to meet particular problems and explore all possibilities of constructive remedies before applying such measures where they would affect essential interests of those contracting parties.

4 Less developed contracting parties agree to take appropriate action in implementation of the provisions of Part IV for the benefit of the trade of other less developed contracting parties, in so far as such action is consistent with their

individual present and future development, financial and trade needs taking into account past trade developments as well as the trade interests of less developed contracting parties as a whole.

5　In the implementation of the commitments set forth in paras 1–4 each contracting party shall afford to any other interested contracting party or contracting parties full and prompt opportunity for consultations under the normal procedures of this agreement with respect to any matter or difficulty which may arise.

Article XXXVIII – Joint action

1　The contracting parties shall collaborate jointly, within the framework of this agreement and elsewhere, as appropriate, to further the objectives set forth in Article XXXVI.

2　In particular, the contracting parties shall:

(a) where appropriate, take action, including action through international arrangements, to provide improved and acceptable conditions of access to world markets for primary products of particular interest to less developed contracting parties and to devise measures designed to stabilise and improve conditions of world markets in these products including measures designed to attain stable, equitable and remunerative prices for exports of such products;

(b) seek appropriate collaboration in matters of trade and development policy with the United Nations and its organs and agencies, including any institutions that may be created on the basis of recommendations by the United Nations Conference on Trade and Development;

(c) collaborate in analysing the development plans and policies of individual less developed contracting parties and in examining trade and aid relationships with a view to devising concrete measures to promote the development of export potential and to facilitate access to export markets for the products of the industries thus developed and, in this connection, seek appropriate collaboration with governments and international organisations, and in particular with organisations having competence in relation to financial assistance for economic development, in systematic studies of trade and aid relationships in individual less developed contracting parties aimed at obtaining a clear analysis of export potential, market prospects and any further action that may be required;

(d) keep under continuous review the development of world trade with special reference to the rate of growth of the trade of less developed contracting parties and make such recommendations to contracting parties as may, in the circumstances, be deemed appropriate;

(e) collaborate in seeking feasible methods to expand trade for the purpose of economic development, through international harmonisation and adjustment of national policies and regulations, through technical and commercial standards affecting production, transportation and marketing, and through export promotion by the establishment of facilities for the increased flow of trade information and the development of market research; and

(f) establish such institutional arrangements as may be necessary to further the objectives set forth in Article XXXVI and to give effect to the provisions of this Part.

Annex A – List of territories referred to in para 2(a) of Article I

United Kingdom of Great Britain and Northern Ireland; Dependent territories of the United Kingdom of Great Britain and Northern; Ireland; Canada; Commonwealth of Australia; Dependent territories of the Commonwealth of Australia; New Zealand; Dependent territories of New Zealand; Union of South Africa including South West Africa; India (as on 10 April 1947); Newfoundland; Southern Rhodesia; Burma; Ceylon.

Certain of the territories listed above have two or more preferential rates in force for certain products. Any such territory may, by agreement with the other contracting parties which are principal suppliers of such products at the most-favoured-nation rate, substitute for such preferential rates a single preferential rate which shall not on the whole be less favourable to suppliers at the most-favoured-nation rate than the preferences in force prior to such substitution.

The imposition of an equivalent margin of tariff preference to replace a margin of preference in an internal tax existing on 10 April 1947 exclusively between two or more of the territories listed in this Annex or to replace the preferential quantitative arrangements described in the following paragraph, shall not be deemed to constitute an increase in a margin of tariff preference.

The preferential arrangements referred to in para 5(h) of Article XIV are those existing in the UK on 10 April 1947, under contractual agreements with the governments of Canada, Australia and New Zealand, in respect of chilled and frozen beef and veal, frozen mutton and lamb, chilled and frozen pork, and bacon. It is the intention, without prejudice to any action taken under sub-para (h) of Article XX, that these arrangements shall be eliminated or replaced by tariff preferences, and that negotiations to this end shall take place as soon as practicable among the countries substantially concerned or involved.

The film hire tax in force in New Zealand on 10 April 1947, shall, for the purposes of this agreement, be treated as a customs duty under Article I. The renters film quota in force in New Zealand on 10 April 1947, shall, for the purposes of this agreement, be treated as a screen quota under Article IV.

The Dominions of India and Pakistan have not been mentioned separately in the above list since they had not come into existence as such on the base date of 10 April 1947.

Annex B

List of territories of the French union referred to in para 2(b) of Article I

France; French Equatorial Africa (Treaty Basin of the Congo and other territories); French West Africa; Cameroons under French Trusteeship; French Somali Coast and Dependencies; French Establishments in Oceania; French Establishments in the Condominium of the New Hebrides; Indo-China; Madagascar and Dependencies; Morocco (French zone); New Caledonia and Dependencies; Saint-Pierre and Miquelon; Togo under French Trusteeship; Tunisia.

Annex C

List of territories referred to in para 2(h) of Article I as respects the customs union of Belgium, Luxemburg and The Netherlands

The Economic Union of Belgium and Luxemburg; Belgian Congo; Ruanda Urundi; The Netherlands; New Guinea; Surinam; Netherlands Antilles; Republic of Indonesia.

For imports into the territories constituting the Customs Union only.

Annex D

List of territories referred to in para 2(h) of Article I as respects the USA

USA (customs territory); Dependent territories of the USA; Republic of the Philippines.

The imposition of an equivalent margin of tariff preference to replace a margin of preference in an internal tax existing on 10 April 1947, exclusively between two or more of the territories listed in this Annex shall not be deemed to constitute an increase in a margin of tariff preference.

Annex E

List of territories covered by preferential arrangements between Chile and neighbouring countries referred to in para 2(d) of Article I

Preferences in force exclusively between Chile on the one hand and (i) Argentina, (ii) Bolivia and (iii) Peru, on the other hand.

Annex F

List of territories covered by preferential arrangements between Lebanon and Syria and neighbouring countries referred to in para 2(d) of Article I

Preferences in force exclusively between the Lebanon-Syrian Customs Union, on the one hand, and (i) Palestine, (ii) Transjordan, on the other hand.

Annex G

Dates establishing maximum margins of preference referred to para 4 of Article I

Australia	15 October 1946
Canada	1 July 1939
France	1 January 1939
Lebanon-Syrian Customs Union	30 November 1938
Union of South Africa	1 July 1938
Southern Rhodesia	1 May 1941

Annex H

Percentage shares of total external trade to be used for the purpose of making the determination referred to in Article XXVI (based on the average of 1949–53)

If, prior to the accession of the government of Japan to the General Agreement, the present agreement has been accepted by contracting parties the external trade of which under column I accounts for the percentage of such trade specified in para 6 of Article XXVI, column I shall be applicable for the purposes of that paragraph. If the present agreement has not been so accepted prior to the accession of the government of Japan. column II shall be applicable for the purposes of that paragraph.

	Column I (contracting parties on 1/3/55)	Column II (contracting parties on 1/3/55 and Japan)
Australia	3.1	3.0
Austria	0.9	0.8
Belgium-Luxemburg	4.3	4.2
Brazil	2.5	2.4

	Column I (contracting parties on 1/3/55)	Column II (contracting parties on 1/3/55 and Japan)
Burma	0.3	0.3
Canada	6.7	6.5
Ceylon	0.5	0.5
Chile	0.6	0.6
Cuba	1.1	1.1
Czechoslovakia	1.4	1.4
Denmark	1.4	1.4
Dominican Republic	0.1	0.1
Finland	1.0	1.0
France	8.7	8.5
Germany, Federal Republic of	5.3	5.2
Greece	0.4	0.4
Haiti	0.1	0.1
India	2.4	2.4
Indonesia	1.3	1.3
Italy	2.9	2.8
Netherlands, Kingdom of the	4.7	4.6
New Zealand	1.0	1.0
Nicaragua	0.1	0.1
Norway	1.1	1.1
Pakistan	0.9	0.8
Peru	0.4	0.4
Rhodesia and Nyasaland	0.6	0.6
Sweden	2.5	2.4
Turkey	0.6	0.6
Union of South Africa	1.8	1.8
UK	20.3	19.8
USA	20.6	20.1
Uruguay	0.4	0.4
Japan	-	2.3
	100.0	100.0

Note: These percentages have been computed taking into account the trade of all territories in respect of which the General Agreement on Tariffs and Trade is applied.

Annex I

Notes and supplementary provisions

Ad *Article I*

Paragraph 1

The obligations incorporated in para 1 of Article I by reference to paras 2 and 4 of Article III and those incorporated in para 2(b) of Article II by reference to Article VI shall be considered as falling within Part II for the purposes of the Protocol of Provisional Application.

The cross-references, in the paragraph immediately above and in para 1 of Article I, to paras 2 and 4 of Article III shall only apply after Article III has been modified by the entry into force of the amendment provided for in the protocol modifying Part II and Article XXVI of the General Agreement on Tariffs and Trade, dated 14 September 1948.

Paragraph 4

The term 'margin of preference' means the absolute difference between the most-favoured-nation rate of duty and the preferential rate of duty for the like product, and not the proportionate relation between those rates. As examples:

(1) If the most-favoured-nation rate were 36% *ad valorem* and the preferential rate were 24% *ad valorem*, the margin of preference would be 12% *ad valorem*, and not one third of the most-favoured-nation rate;

(2) If the most-favoured-nation rate were 36% *ad valorem* and the preferential rate were expressed as two thirds of the most-favoured-nation rate, the margin of preference would be 12% *ad valorem*;

(3) If the most-favoured-nation rate were 2 francs per kilogramme and the preferential rate were 1.50 francs per kg, the margin of preference would be 0.50 franc per kg.

The following kinds of customs action, taken in accordance with established uniform procedures, would not be contrary to a general binding of margins of preference:

(i) The re-application to an imported product of a tariff classification or rate of duty, properly applicable to such product, in cases in which the application of such classification or rate to such product was temporarily suspended or inoperative on 10 April 1947; and

(ii) The classification of a particular product under a tariff item other than that under which importations of that product were classified on 10 April 1947, in cases in which the tariff law clearly contemplates that such product may be classified under more than one tariff item.

This protocol entered into force on 14 December 1948.

Ad *Article II*

Paragraph 2(a)

The cross-reference, in para 2(a) of Article II, to para 2 of Article III shall only apply after Article III has been modified by the entry into force of the amendment provided for in the Protocol Modifying Part II and Article XXVI of the General Agreement on Tariffs and Trade, dated 14 September 1948.

Paragraph 2(b)

See the note relating to para 1 of Article I.

Paragraph 4

Except where otherwise specifically agreed between the contracting parties which initially negotiated the concession, the provisions of this paragraph will be applied in the light of the provisions of Article 31 of the Havana Charter.

Ad *Article III*

Any internal tax or other internal charge, or any law, regulation or requirement of the kind referred to in para 1 which applies to an imported product and to the like domestic product and is collected or enforced in the case of the imported product at the time or point of importation, is nevertheless to be regarded as an internal tax or other internal charge, or a law, regulation or requirement of the kind referred to in para 1, and is accordingly subject to the provisions of Article III.

Paragraph 1

The application of para 1 to internal taxes imposed by local governments and authorities within the territory of a contracting party is subject to the provisions of the final paragraph of Article XXIV. The term 'reasonable measures' in the last-mentioned paragraph would not require, for example, the repeal of existing national legislation authorising local governments to impose internal taxes which, although technically inconsistent with the letter of Article III, are not in fact inconsistent with its spirit, if such repeal would result in a serious financial hardship for the local governments or authorities concerned. With regard to taxation by local governments or authorities which is inconsistent with both the letter and spirit of Article III, the term 'reasonable measures' would permit a contracting party to eliminate the inconsistent taxation gradually over a transition period, if abrupt action would create serious administrative and financial difficulties.

Paragraph 2

A tax conforming to the requirements of the first sentence of para 2 would be considered to be inconsistent with the provisions of the second sentence only in cases where competition was involved between, on the one hand, the taxed product and, on the other hand, a directly competitive or substitutable product which was not similarly taxed.

Paragraph 5

Regulations consistent with the provisions of the first sentence of para 5 shall not be considered to be contrary to the provisions of the second sentence in any case in which all of the products subject to the regulations are produced domestically in substantial quantities. A regulation cannot be justified as being consistent with the provisions of the second sentence on the ground that the proportion or amount allocated to each of the products which are the subject of the regulation constitutes an equitable relationship between imported and domestic products.

Ad *Article V*

Paragraph 5

With regard to transportation charges, the principle laid down in para 5 refers to like products being transported on the same route under like conditions.

Ad *Article VI*

Paragraph 1

1 Hidden dumping by associated houses (ie the sale by an importer at a price below that corresponding to the price invoiced by an exporter with whom the importer is associated, and also below the price in the exporting country) constitutes a form of price dumping with respect to which the margin of dumping may be calculated on the basis of the price at which the goods are resold by the importer.

2 It is recognised that, in the case of imports from a country which has a complete or substantially complete monopoly of its trade and where all domestic prices are fixed by the State, special difficulties may exist in determining price comparability for the purposes of para 1, and in such cases importing contracting parties may find it necessary to take into account the possibility that a strict comparison with domestic prices in such a country may not always be appropriate.

Paragraphs 2 and 3

1   As in many other cases in customs administration, a contracting party may require reasonable security (bond or cash deposit) for the payment of anti-dumping or countervailing duty pending final determination on the facts in any case of suspected dumping or subsidisation.

2   Multiple currency practices can in certain circumstances constitute a subsidy to exports which may be met by countervailing duties under para 3 or can constitute a form of dumping by means of a partial depreciation of a country's currency which may be met by action under para 2. By 'multiple currency practices' is meant practices by governments or sanctioned by governments.

Paragraph 6(b)

Waivers under the provisions of this sub-paragraph shall be granted only on application by the contracting party proposing to levy an anti-dumping or countervailing duty, as the case may be.

Ad *Article VII*

Paragraph 1

The expression 'or other charges' is not to be regarded as including internal taxes or equivalent charges imposed on or in connection with imported products.

Paragraph 2

1   It would be in conformity with Article VII to presume that 'actual value' may be represented by the invoice price, plus any non-included charges for legitimate costs which are proper elements of 'actual value' and plus any abnormal discount or other reduction from the ordinary competitive price.

2   It would be in conformity with Article VII, para 2(b), for a contracting party to construe the phrase 'in the ordinary course of trade ... under fully competitive conditions', as excluding any transaction wherein the buyer and seller are not independent of each other and price is not the sole consideration.

3   The standard of 'fully competitive conditions' permits a contracting party to exclude from consideration prices involving special discounts limited to exclusive agents.

4   The wording of sub-paras (a) and (b) permits a contracting party to determine the value for customs purposes uniformly either (1) on the basis of a particular exporter's prices of the imported merchandise, or (2) on the basis of the general price level of like merchandise.

Ad *Article VIII*

1   While Article VIII does not cover the use of multiple rates of exchange as such, paras 1 and 4 condemn the use of exchange taxes or fees as a device for implementing multiple currency practices; if, however, a contracting party is using multiple currency exchange fees for balance of payments reasons with the approval of the International Monetary Fund, the provisions of para 9(a) of Article XV fully safeguard its position.

2   It would be consistent with para 1 if, on the importation of products from the territory of a contracting party into the territory of another contracting party, the production of certificates of origin should only be required to the extent that is strictly indispensable.

Ad *Articles XI, XII, XIII, XIV and XVIII*

Throughout Articles XI, XII, XIII, XIV and XVIII, the terms 'import restrictions' or 'export restrictions' include restrictions made effective through State-trading operations.

Ad *Article XI*

Paragraph 2(c)

The term 'in any form' in this paragraph covers the same products when in an early stage of processing and still perishable, which compete directly with the fresh product and if freely imported would tend to make the restriction on the fresh product ineffective.

Paragraph 2, last sub-paragraph

The term 'special factors' includes changes in relative productive efficiency as between domestic and foreign producers, or as between different foreign producers, but not changes artificially brought about by means not permitted under the agreement.

Ad *Article XII*

The contracting parties shall make provision for the utmost secrecy in the conduct of any consultation under the provisions of this article.

Paragraph 3(c)(i)

Contracting parties applying restrictions shall endeavour to avoid causing serious prejudice to exports of a commodity on which the economy of a contracting party is largely dependent.

Paragraph 4(b)

It is agreed that the date shall be within 90 days after the entry into force of the amendments of this article effected by the Protocol Amending the Preamble and Parts II and III of this agreement. However, should the contracting parties find that conditions were not suitable for the application of the provisions of this sub-paragraph at the time envisaged, they may determine a later date; provided that such date is not more than thirty days after such time as the obligations of Article VIII, sections 2, 3 and 4, of the Articles of Agreement of the International Monetary Fund become applicable to contracting parties, members of the Fund, the combined foreign trade of which constitutes at least 50% of the aggregate foreign trade of all contracting parties.

Paragraph 4(e)

It is agreed that para 4(e) does not add any new criteria for the imposition or maintenance of quantitative restrictions for balance of payments reasons. It is solely intended to ensure that all external factors such as changes in the terms of trade, quantitative restrictions, excessive tariffs and subsidies, which may be contributing to the balance of payments difficulties of the contracting party applying restrictions, will be fully taken into account.

Ad *Article XIII*

Paragraph 2(d)

No mention was made of 'commercial considerations' as a rule for the allocation of quotas because it was considered that its application by governmental authorities might not always be practicable. Moreover, in cases where it is practicable, a contracting party could apply these considerations in the process of seeking agreement, consistently with the general rule laid down in the opening sentence of para 2.

Paragraph 4

See note relating to 'special factors' in connection with the last sub-paragraph of para 2 of Article XI.

Ad *Article XIV*

Paragraph 1

The provisions of this paragraph shall not be so construed as to preclude full consideration by the contracting parties, in the consultations provided for in para 4 of Article XII and in para 12 of Article XVIII, of the nature, effects and reasons for discrimination in the field of import restrictions.

Paragraph 2

One of the situations contemplated in para 2 is that of a contracting party holding balances acquired as a result of current transactions which it finds itself unable to use without a measure of discrimination.

Ad *Article XV*

Paragraph 4

The word 'frustrate' is intended to indicate, for example, that infringements of the letter of any article of this agreement by exchange action shall not be regarded as a violation of that article if, in practice, there is no appreciable departure from the intent of the article. Thus, a contracting party which, as part of its exchange control operated in accordance with the Articles of Agreement of the International Monetary Fund, requires payment to be received for its exports in its own currency or in the currency of one or more members of the International Monetary Fund will not thereby be deemed to contravene Article XI or Article XIII. Another example would be that of a contracting party which specifies on an import licence the country from which the goods may be imported, for the purpose not of introducing any additional element of discrimination in its import licensing system of enforcing permissible exchange controls.

Ad *Article XVI*

The exemption of an exported product from duties or taxes borne by the like product when destined for domestic consumption, or the remission of such duties or taxes in amounts not in excess of those which have accrued, shall not be deemed to be a subsidy.

Section B

1   Nothing in section B shall preclude the use by a contracting party of multiple rates of exchange in accordance with the Articles of Agreement of the International Monetary Fund.

2   For the purposes of section B, a 'primary product' is understood to be any product of farm, forest or fishery, or any mineral, in its natural form or which has undergone such processing as is customarily required to prepare it for marketing in substantial volume in international trade.

Paragraph 3

1   The fact that a contracting party has not exported the product in question during the previous representative period would not in itself preclude that contracting party from establishing its right to obtain a share of the trade in the product concerned.

2   A system for the stabilisation of the domestic price or of the return to domestic producers of a primary product independently of the movements of export prices, which results at times in the sale of the product for export at a price lower than the comparable price charged for the like product to buyers in the domestic market, shall be considered not to involve a subsidy on exports within the meaning of para 3 if the contracting parties determine that:

(a) the system has also resulted, or is so designed as to result, in the sale of the product for export at a price higher than the comparable price charged for the like product to buyers in the domestic market, and

(b) the system is so operated, or is designed so to operate, either because of the effective regulation of production or otherwise, as not to stimulate exports unduly or otherwise seriously to prejudice the interests of other contracting parties.

Notwithstanding such determination by the contracting parties, operations under such a system shall be subject to the provisions of para 3 where they are wholly or partly financed out of government funds in addition to the funds collected from producers in respect of the product concerned.

Paragraph 4

The intention of para 4 is that the contracting parties should seek before the end of 1957 to reach agreement to abolish all remaining subsidies as from 1 January 1958; or, failing this, to reach agreement to extend the application of the standstill until the earliest date thereafter by which they can expect to reach such agreement.

Ad *Article XVII*

Paragraph 1

The operations of Marketing Boards, which are established by contracting parties and are engaged in purchasing or selling, are subject to the provisions of sub-paras (a) and (b).

The activities of Marketing Boards which are established by contracting parties and which do not purchase or sell but lay down regulations covering private trade are governed by the relevant articles of this agreement.

The charging by a state enterprise of different prices for its sales of a product in different markets is not precluded by the provisions of this article, provided that such different prices are charged for commercial reasons, to meet conditions of supply and demand in export markets.

Paragraph 1(a)

Governmental measures imposed to ensure standards of quality and efficiency in the operation of external trade, or privileges granted for the exploitation of national natural resources but which do not empower the government to exercise control over the trading activities of the enterprise in question, do not constitute 'exclusive or special privileges'.

Paragraph 1(b)

A country receiving a 'tied loan' is free to take this loan into account as a 'commercial consideration' when purchasing requirements abroad.

Paragraph 2

The term 'goods' is limited to products as understood in commercial practice, and is not intended to include the purchase or sale of services.

Paragraph 3

Negotiations which contracting parties agree to conduct under this paragraph may be directed towards the reduction of duties and other charges on imports and exports or towards the conclusion of any other mutually satisfactory arrangement consistent with the provisions of this agreement. (See para 4 of Article II and the note to that paragraph.)

Paragraph 4(b)

The term 'import mark-up' in this paragraph shall represent the margin by which the price charged by the import monopoly for the imported product (exclusive of internal taxes within the purview of Article III, transportation, distribution, and other expenses incident to the purchase, sale or further processing, and a reasonable margin of profit) exceeds the landed cost.

Ad *Article XVIII*

The contracting parties and the contracting parties concerned shall preserve the utmost secrecy in respect of matters arising under this article.

Paragraphs 1 and 4

1   When they consider whether the economy of a contracting party 'can only support low standards of living', the contracting parties shall take into consideration the normal position of that economy and shall not base their determination on exceptional circumstances such as those which may result from the temporary existence of exceptionally favourable conditions for the staple export product or products of such contracting party.

2   The phrase 'in the early stages of development' is not meant to apply only to contracting parties which have just started their economic development, but also to contracting parties the economies of which are undergoing a process of industrialisation to correct an excessive dependence on primary production.

Paragraphs 2, 3, 7, 13 and 22

The reference to the establishment of particular industries shall apply not only to the establishment of a new industry, but also to the establishment of a new branch of production in an existing industry and to the substantial transformation of an existing industry, and to the substantial expansion of an existing industry supplying a relatively small proportion of the domestic demand. It shall also cover the reconstruction of an industry destroyed or substantially damaged as a result of hostilities or natural disasters.

Paragraph 7(b)

A modification or withdrawal, pursuant to para 7(b), by a contracting party, other than the applicant contracting party, referred to in para 7(a), shall be made within six months of the day on which the action is taken by the applicant contracting party, and shall become effective on the 30th day following the day on which such modification or withdrawal has been notified to the contracting parties.

Paragraph 11

The second sentence in para 11 shall not be interpreted to mean that a contracting party is required to relax or remove restrictions if such relaxation or removal would thereupon produce conditions justifying the intensification or institution, respectively, of restrictions under para 9 of Article XVIII.

Paragraph 12(b)

The date referred to in para 12(b) shall be the date determined by the contracting parties in accordance with the provisions of para 4(b) of Article XII of this agreement.

Paragraphs 13 and 14

It is recognised that, before deciding on the introduction of a measure and notifying the contracting parties in accordance with para 14, a contracting party may need a reasonable period of time to assess the competitive position of the industry concerned.

Paragraphs 15 and 16

It is understood that the contracting parties shall invite a contracting party proposing to apply a measure under section C to consult with them pursuant to para 16 if they are requested to do so by a contracting party the trade of which would be appreciably affected by the measure in question.

Paragraphs 16, 18, 19 and 22

1 It is understood that the contracting parties may concur in a proposed measure subject to specific conditions or limitations. If the measure as applied does not conform to the terms of the concurrence, it will to that extent be deemed a measure in which the contracting parties have not concurred. In cases in which the contracting parties have concurred in a measure for a specified period, the contracting party concerned, if it finds that the maintenance of the measure for a further period of time is required to achieve the objective for which the measure was originally taken, may apply to the contracting parties for an extension of that period in accordance with the provisions and procedures of section C or D, as the case may be.

2 It is expected that the contracting parties will, as a rule, refrain from concurring in a measure which is likely to cause serious prejudice to exports of a commodity on which the economy of a contracting party is largely dependent.

Paragraphs 18 and 22

The phrase 'that the interests of other contracting parties are adequately safeguarded' is meant to provide latitude sufficient to permit consideration in each case of the most appropriate method of safeguarding those interests. The appropriate method may, for instance, take the form of an additional concession to be applied by the contracting party having recourse to section C or D during such time as the deviation from the other articles of the agreement would remain in force or of the temporary suspension by any other contracting party referred to in para 18 of a concession substantially equivalent to the impairment due to the introduction of the measure in question. Such contracting party would have the right to safeguard its interests through such a temporary suspension of a concession; provided that this right will not be exercised when, in the case of a measure imposed by a contracting party coming within the scope of para 4(a), the contracting parties have determined that the extent of the compensatory concession proposed was adequate.

Paragraph 19

The provisions of para 19 are intended to cover the cases where an industry has been in existence beyond the 'reasonable period of time' referred to in the note to paras 13 and 14, and should not be so construed as to deprive a contracting party coming within the scope of para 4(a) of Article XVIII, of its right to resort to the other provisions of section C, including para 17, with regard to a newly established industry even though it has benefited from incidental protection afforded by balance of payments import restrictions.

Paragraph 21

Any measure taken pursuant to the provisions of para 21 shall be withdrawn forthwith if the action taken in accordance with para 17 is withdrawn or if the contracting parties concur in the measure proposed after the expiration of the 90 day time limit specified in para 17.

Ad *Article XX*

Sub-paragraph (h)

The exception provided for in this sub-paragraph extends to any commodity agreement which conforms to the principles approved by the Economic and Social Council in its resolution (IV) of 28 March 1947.

Ad Article XXIV

Paragraph 9

It is understood that the provisions of Article I would require that, when a product which has been imported into the territory of a member of a customs union or free-trade area at a preferential rate of duty is re-exported to the territory of another member of such union or area, the latter member should collect a duty equal to the difference between the duty already paid and any higher duty that would be payable if the product were being imported directly into its territory.

Paragraph 11

Measures adopted by India and Pakistan in order to carry out definitive trade arrangements between them, once they have been agreed upon, might depart from particular provisions of this agreement, but these measures would general be consistent with the objectives of the agreement.

Ad Article XXVIII

The contracting parties and each contracting party concerned should arrange to conduct the negotiations and consultations with the greatest possible secrecy in order to avoid premature disclosure of details of prospective tariff changes. The contracting parties shall be informed immediately of all changes in national tariffs resulting from recourse to this article.

Paragraph 1

1   If the contracting parties specify a period other than a three year period a contracting party may act pursuant to para 1 or para 3 of Article XXVIII on the first day following the expiration of such other period and, unless the contracting parties have again specified another period, subsequent periods will be three-year periods following the expiration of such specified period.

2   The provision that on 1 January 1958, and on other days determined pursuant to para 1, a contracting party 'may ... modify or withdraw a concession means that on such day, and on the first day after the end of each period, the legal obligation of such contracting party under Article II is altered; it does not mean that the changes in its customs tariff should necessarily be made effective on that day. If a tariff change resulting from negotiations undertaken pursuant to this article is delayed, the entry into force of any compensatory concessions may be similarly delayed.

3   Not earlier than six months, nor later than three months, prior to 1 January 1958, or to the termination date of any subsequent period, a contracting party wishing to modify or withdraw any concession embodied in the appropriate Schedule, should notify the contracting parties to this effect. The contracting parties shall then determine, the contracting party or contracting parties with which the negotiations or consultations referred to in para 1 shall take place. Any contracting party so determined shall participate in such negotiations or consultations with the applicant contracting party with the aim of reaching agreement before the end of the period.

Any extension of the assured life of the Schedules shall relate to the Schedules as modified after such negotiations, in accordance with paras 1, 2 and 3 of Article XXVIII. If the contracting parties are arranging for multilateral tariff negotiations to take place within the period of six months before 1 January 1958, or before any other day determined pursuant to para 1, they shall include in the arrangements for such negotiations suitable procedures for carrying out the negotiations referred to in this para.

4   The object of providing for the participation in the negotiations of any contracting party with a principal supplying interest, in addition to any contracting party with which the concession was initially negotiated, is to ensure that a contracting party with a larger share in the trade affected by the concession than a contracting party with which the concession was initially negotiated shall have an effective opportunity to protect the contractual right which it enjoys under this agreement. On the other hand, it is not intended that the scope of the negotiations should be such as to make negotiations and agreement under Article XXVIII unduly difficult nor to create complications in the application of this article in the future to concessions which result from negotiations thereunder. Accordingly, the contracting parties should only determine that a contracting party has a principal supplying interest if that contracting party has had, over a reasonable period of time prior to the negotiations, a larger share in the market of the applicant contracting party than a contracting party with which the concession was initially negotiated or would, in the judgment of the contracting parties, have had such a share in the absence of discriminatory quantitative restrictions maintained by the applicant contracting party. It would therefore not be appropriate for the contracting parties to determine that more than one contracting party, or in those exceptional cases where there is near equality more than two contracting parties, had a principal supplying interest.

5   Notwithstanding the definition of a principal supplying interest in note 4 to para 1, the contracting parties may exceptionally determine that a contracting party has a principal supplying interest if the concession in question affects trade which constitutes a major part of the total exports of such contracting party.

6   It is not intended that provision for participation in the negotiations of any contracting party with a principal supplying interest, and for consultation with any contracting party having a substantial interest in the concession which the applicant contracting party is seeking to modify or withdraw, should have the effect that it should have to pay compensation or suffer retaliation greater than the withdrawal or modification sought, judged in the light of the conditions of trade at the time of the proposed withdrawal or modification. making allowance for any discriminatory quantitative restrictions maintained by the applicant contracting party.

7   The expression 'substantial interest' is not capable of a precise definition and accordingly may present difficulties for the contracting parties. It is, however, intended to be construed to cover only those contracting parties which have, or in the absence of discriminatory quantitative restrictions affecting their exports could reasonably be expected to have, a significant share in the market of the contracting party seeking to modify or withdraw the concession.

Paragraph 4

1   Any request for authorisation to enter into negotiations shall be accompanied by all relevant statistical and other data. A decision on such request shall be made within 30 days of its submission.

2   It is recognised that to permit certain contracting parties, depending in large measure on a relatively small number of primary commodities and relying on the tariff as an important aid for furthering diversification of their economies or as an important source of revenue, normally to negotiate for the modification or withdrawal of concessions only under para 1 of Article XXVIII, might cause them at such a time to make modifications or withdrawals which in the long run would prove unnecessary. To avoid such a situation the contracting parties shall authorise any such contracting party, under para 4, to enter into negotiations unless they consider this would result in, or contribute substantially towards, such an increase in tariff levels as to threaten the stability of the Schedules to this agreement or lead to undue disturbance of international trade.

3   It is expected that negotiations authorised under para 4 for modification or withdrawal of a single item, or a very small group of items, could normally be brought to a conclusion in 60 days. It is recognised, however, that such a period will be inadequate for cases involving negotiations for the modification or withdrawal of a larger number of items and in such cases, therefore, it would be appropriate for the contracting parties to prescribe a longer period.

4   The determination referred to in para 4(d) shall be made by the contracting parties within 30 days of the submission of the matter to them unless the applicant contracting party agrees to a longer period.

5   In determining under para 4(d) whether an applicant contracting party has unreasonably failed to offer adequate compensation, it is understood that the contracting parties will take due account of the special position of a contracting party which has bound a high proportion of its tariffs at very low rates of duty and to this extent has less scope than other contracting parties to make compensatory adjustment.

Ad *Article XXVIII* bis

Paragraph 3

It is understood that the reference to fiscal needs would include the revenue aspect of duties and particularly duties imposed primarily for revenue purpose, or duties imposed on products which can be substituted for products subject to revenue duties to prevent the avoidance of such duties.

Ad *Article XXIX*

Paragraph 1

Chapters VII and VIII of the Havana Charter have been excluded from para 1 because they generally deal with the organisation, functions and procedures of the International Trade Organisation.

Ad *Part IV*

The words 'developed contracting parties' and the words 'less developed contracting parties' as used in Part IV are to be understood to refer to developed and less developed countries which are parties to the General Agreement on Tariffs and Trade.

Ad *Article XXXVI*

Paragraph 1

This article is based upon the objectives set forth in Article I as it will be amended by section A of para 1 of the protocol amending Part I and Articles XXIX and XXX when that protocol enters into force.

Paragraph 4

The term 'primary products' includes agricultural products, *vide* para 2 of the note ad Article XVI, section B.

Paragraph 5

A diversification programme would generally include the intensification of activities for the processing of primary products and the development of manufacturing industries, taking into account the situation of the particular contracting party and the world outlook for production and consumption of different commodities.

Paragraph 8

It is understood that the phrase 'do not expect reciprocity' means, in accordance with the objectives set forth in this article, that the less developed contracting parties should not be expected, in the course of trade negotiations, to make contributions which are inconsistent with their individual development, financial and trade needs, taking into consideration past trade developments.

This paragraph would apply in the event of action under section A of Article XVIII, Article XXVIII, Article XXVIII *bis* (Article XXIX after the amendment set forth in section A of para 1 of the protocol amending Part I and Articles XXIX and XXX shall have become effective), Article XXXIII, or any other procedure under this agreement.

Ad *Article XXXVII*

Paragraph 1(a)

This paragraph would apply in the event of negotiations for reduction or elimination of tariffs or other restrictive regulations of commerce under Articles XXVIII, XXVIII *bis* (XXIX after the amendment set forth in section A of para 1 of the protocol amending Part I and Articles XXIX and XXX shall have become effective), and Article XXXIII, as well as in connection with other action to effect such reduction or elimination which contracting parties may be able to undertake.

Paragraph 3(b)

The other measures referred to in this paragraph might include steps to promote domestic structural changes, to encourage the consumption of particular products, or to introduce measures of trade promotion.

UNDERSTANDING ON RULES AND PROCEDURES GOVERNING THE SETTLEMENT OF DISPUTES

Annex 2 to the WTO Agreement

Members hereby agree as follows:

Article 1 – Coverage and application

1   The rules and procedures of this understanding shall apply to disputes brought pursuant to the consultation and dispute settlement provisions of the agreements listed m Appendix 1 to this understanding (referred to in this understanding as the 'covered agreements'). The rules and procedures of this understanding shall also apply to consultations and the settlement of disputes between Members concerning their rights and obligations under the provisions of the Agreement Establishing the World Trade Organisation (referred to in this understanding as the 'WTO

Agreement') and of this understanding taken in isolation or in combination with any other covered agreement.

2   The rules and procedures of this understanding shall apply subject to such special or additional rules and procedures on dispute settlement contained in the covered agreements as are identified in Appendix 2 to this understanding. To the extent that there is a difference between the rules and procedures of this understanding and the special or additional rules and procedures set forth in Appendix 2, the special or additional rules and procedures in Appendix 2 shall prevail. In disputes involving rules and procedures under more than one covered agreement, If there is a conflict between special or additional rules and procedures or such agreements under review, and where the parties to the dispute cannot agree on rules and procedures within 20 days of the establishment of the panel, the Chairman of the Dispute Settlement Body provided for in para 1 of Article 2 (referred to in this understanding as the 'DSB'), in consultation with the parties to the dispute, shall determine the rules and procedures to be followed within 10 days after a request by either Member. The Chairman shall be guided by the principle that special or additional rules and procedures should be used where possible, and the rules and procedures set out in this understanding should be used to the extent necessary to avoid conflict.

Article 2 – Administration

1   The Dispute Settlement Body is hereby established to administer these rules and procedures and, except as otherwise provided in a covered agreement, the consultation and dispute settlement provisions of the covered agreements. Accordingly, the DSB shall have the authority to establish panels, adopt panel and Appellate Body reports, maintain surveillance of implementation of rulings and recommendations, and authorise suspension of concessions and other obligations under the covered agreements. With respect to disputes arising under a covered agreement which is a Plurilateral Trade Agreement, the term 'Member' as used herein shall refer only to those Members that are parties to the relevant Plurilateral Trade Agreement. Where the DSB administers the dispute settlement provisions of a Plurilateral Trade Agreement, only those Members that are parties to that agreement may participate in decisions or actions taken by the DSB with respect to that dispute.

2   The DSB shall inform the relevant WTO Councils and Committees of any developments in disputes related to provisions of the respective covered agreements.

3   The DSB shall meet as often as necessary to carry out its functions within the time frames provided in this understanding.

4   Where the rules and procedures of this understanding provide for the DSB to take a decision, it shall do so by consensus.

Article 3 – General provisions

1   Members affirm their adherence to the principles for the management of disputes heretofore applied under Articles XXII and XXIII of GATT 1947, and the rules and procedures as further elaborated and modified herein.

2   The dispute settlement system of the WTO is a central element in providing security and predictability to the multilateral trading system. The Members recognise that it serves to preserve the rights and obligations of Members under the covered agreements, and to clarify the existing provisions of those agreements in accordance with customary rules of interpretation of public international law.

Recommendations and rulings of the DSB cannot add to or diminish the rights and obligations provided in the covered agreements.

3   The prompt settlement of situations in which a Member considers that any benefits accruing to it directly or indirectly under the covered agreements are being impaired by measures taken by another is essential to the effective functioning of the WTO and the maintenance of a proper balance between the rights and obligations of Members.

4   Recommendations or rulings made by the DSB shall be aimed at achieving a satisfactory settlement of the matter in accordance with the rights and obligations under this understanding and under the covered agreements.

5   All solutions to matters formally raised under the consultation and dispute settlement provisions of the covered agreements, including arbitration awards, shall be consistent with those agreements and shall not nullify or impair benefits accruing to any Member under those agreements, nor impede the attainment of any objective of those agreements.

6   Mutually agreed solutions to matters formally raised under the consultation and dispute settlement provisions of the covered agreements shall be notified to the DSB and the relevant Councils and Committees, where any Member may raise any point relating thereto.

7   Before bringing a case, a Member shall exercise its judgment as to whether action under these procedures would be fruitful. The aim of the dispute settlement mechanism is to secure a positive solution to a dispute. A solution mutually acceptable to the parties to a dispute and consistent with the covered agreements is clearly to be preferred. In the absence of a mutually agreed solution, the first objective of the dispute settlement mechanism is usually to secure the withdrawal of the measures concerned if these are found to be inconsistent with the provisions of any of the covered agreements. The provision of compensation should be resorted to only if the immediate withdrawal of the measure is impracticable and as a temporary measure pending the withdrawal of the measure which is inconsistent with a covered agreement. The last resort which this understanding provides to the Member invoking the dispute settlement procedures is the possibility of suspending the application of concessions or other obligations under the covered agreements on a discriminatory basis vis à vis the other Member, subject to authorisation by the DSB of such measures.

8   In cases where there is an infringement of the obligations assumed under a covered agreement, the action is considered *prima facie* to constitute a case of nullification or impairment. This means that there is normally a presumption that a breach of the rules has an adverse impact on other Members parties to that covered agreement, and in such cases, it shall be up to the Member against whom the complaint has been brought to rebut the charge.

9   The provisions of this understanding are without prejudice to the rights of Members to seek authoritative interpretation of provisions of a covered agreement through decision-making under the WTO Agreement or a covered agreement which is a Plurilateral Trade Agreement.

10 It is understood that requests for conciliation and the use of the dispute settlement procedures should not be intended or considered as contentious acts and that, if a

dispute arises, all Members will engage in these procedures in good faith in an effort to resolve the dispute. It is also understood that complaints and counter-complaints in regard to distinct matters should not be linked.

11 This understanding shall be applied only with respect to new requests for consultations under the consultation provisions of the covered agreements made on or after the date of entry into force of the WTO Agreement. With respect to disputes for which the request for consultations was made under GATT 1947 or under any other predecessor agreement to the covered agreements before the date of entry into force of the WTO Agreement, the relevant dispute settlement rules and procedures in effect immediately prior to the date of entry into force of the WTO Agreement shall continue to apply.

12 Notwithstanding para 11, if a complaint based on any of the covered agreements is brought by a developing country Member against a developed country Member, the complaining party shall have the right to invoke, as an alternative to the provisions contained in Articles 4, 5, 6 and 12 of this understanding, the corresponding provisions of the decision of 5 April 1966 (BISD 14S/18), except that where the panel considers that the time frame provided for in para 7 of that decision is insufficient to provide its report and with the agreement of the complaining party, that time frame may be extended. To the extent that there is a difference between the rules and procedures of Articles 4, 5, 6 and 12 and the corresponding rules and procedures of the decision, the latter shall prevail.

Article 4 – Consultations

1 Members affirm their resolve to strengthen and improve the effectiveness of the consultation procedures employed by Members.

2 Each Member undertakes to accord sympathetic consideration to and afford adequate opportunity for consultation regarding any representations made by another Member concerning measures affecting the operation of any covered agreement taken within the territory of the former.

3 If a request for consultations is made pursuant to a covered agreement, the Member to which the request is made shall, unless otherwise mutually agreed, reply to the request within 10 days after the date of its receipt and shall enter into consultations in good faith within a period of no more than 30 days after the date of receipt of the request, with a view to reaching a mutually satisfactory solution. If the Member does not respond within 10 days after the date of receipt of the request, or does not enter into consultations within a period of no more than 30 days, or a period otherwise mutually agreed, after the date of receipt of the request, then the Member that requested the holding of consultations may proceed directly to request the establishment of a panel.

4 All such requests for consultations shall be notified to the DSB and the relevant Councils and Committees by the Member which requests consultations. Any request for consultations shall be submitted in writing and shall give the reasons for the request, including identification of the measures at issue and an indication of the legal basis for the complaint.

5 In the course of consultations in accordance with the provisions of a covered agreement, before resorting to further action under this understanding, Members should attempt to obtain satisfactory adjustment of the matter.

6   Consultations shall be confidential, and without prejudice to the rights of any Member in any further proceedings.

7   If the consultations fail to settle a dispute within 60 days after the date of receipt of the request for consultations, the complaining party may request the establishment of a panel. The complaining party may request a panel during the 60 day period if the consulting parties jointly consider that consultations have failed to settle the dispute.

8   In cases or urgency, including those watch concern perishable goods, Members shall enter into consultations within a period of no more than 10 days after the date of receipt of the request. If the consultations have failed to settle the dispute within a period of 20 days after the date of receipt of the request, the complaining party may request the establishment of a panel.

9   In cases of urgency, including those which concern perishable goods, the parties to the dispute, panels and the Appellate Body shall make every effort to accelerate the proceedings to the greatest extent possible.

10 During consultations Members should give special attention to the particular problems and interests of developing country Members.

11 Whenever a Member other than the consulting Members considers that it has a substantial trade interest in consultations being held pursuant to para 1 of Article XXII of GATT 1994, para 1 of Article XXII of GATS, or the corresponding provisions in other covered agreements, such Member may notify the consulting Members and the DSB, within 10 days after the date of the circulation of the request for consultations under said article, of its desire to be joined in the consultations. Such Member shall be joined in the consultations, provided that the Member to which the request for consultations was addressed agrees that the claim of substantial interest is well founded. In that event they shall so inform the DSB. If the request to be joined in the consultations is not accepted, the applicant Member shall be free to request consultations under para 1 of Article XXII or para 1 of Article XXIII of GATT 1994, para 1 of Article XXII or para 1 of Article XXIII of GATS, or the corresponding provisions in other covered agreements.

Article 5 – Good offices, conciliation and mediation

1   Good offices, conciliation and mediation are procedures that are undertaken voluntarily if the parties to the dispute so agree.

2   Proceedings involving good offices, conciliation and mediation, and in particular positions taken by the parties to the dispute during these proceedings shall be confidential, and without prejudice to the rights of either party in any further proceedings under these procedures.

3   Good offices, conciliation or mediation may be requested at any time by any party to a dispute. They may begin at any time and be terminated at any time. Once procedures for good offices, conciliation or mediation are terminated, a complaining party may then proceed with a request for the establishment of a panel.

4   When good of offices, conciliation or mediation are entered into within 60 days after the date of receipt of a request for consultations, the complaining party must allow a period of 60 days after the date of receipt of the request for consultations before requesting the establishment of a panel. The complaining party may request the establishment of a panel during the 60 day period if the parties to the dispute

jointly consider that the good offices, conciliation or mediation process has failed to settle the dispute.

5   If the parties to a dispute agree, procedures for good offices, conciliation or mediation may continue while the panel process proceeds.

6   The Director General may, acting in an *ex officio* capacity, offer good offices, conciliation or mediation with the view to assisting Members to settle a dispute.

Article 6 – Establishment of panels

1   If the complaining party so requests, a panel shall be established at the latest at the DSB meeting following that at which the request first appears as an item on the DSB's agenda, unless at that meeting the DSB decides by consensus not to establish a panel.

2   The request for the establishment of a panel shall be made in writing. It shall indicate whether consultations were held, identify the specific measures at issue and provide a brief summary of the legal basis of the complaint sufficient to present the problem clearly. In case the applicant requests the establishment of a panel with other than standard terms of reference, the written request shall include the proposed text of special terms of reference.

Article 7 – Terms of reference of panels

1   Panels shall have the following terms of reference unless the parties to the dispute agree otherwise within 20 days from the establishment of the panel:

> To examine, in the light of the relevant provisions in (name of the covered agreement(s) cited by the parties to the dispute), the matter referred to the DSB by (name of party) in document ... and to make such findings as will assist the DSB in making the recommendations or in giving the rulings provided for in that/those agreement(s).

2   Panels shall address the relevant provisions in any covered agreement or agreements cited by the parties to the dispute.

3   In establishing a panel, the DSB may authorise its Chairman to draw up the terms of reference of the panel in consultation with the parties to the dispute, subject to the provisions of para 1. The terms of reference thus drawn up shall be circulated to all Members. If other than standard terms of reference are agreed upon, any Member may raise any point relating thereto in the DSB.

Article 8 – Composition of panels

1   Panels shall be composed of well qualified governmental and/or non-governmental individuals, including persons who have served on or presented a case to a panel, served as a representative of a Member or of a contracting party to GATT 1947 or as a representative to the Council or Committee of any covered agreement or its predecessor agreement, or in the Secretariat, taught or published on international trade law or policy, or served as a senior trade policy official of a Member.

2   Panel members should be selected with a view to ensuring the independence of the members, a sufficiently diverse background and a wide spectrum of experience.

3   Citizens of Members whose governments are parties to the dispute or third parties as defined in para 2 of Article 10 shall not serve on a panel concerned with that dispute, unless the parties to the dispute agree otherwise.

4   To assist in the selection of panelists, the Secretariat shall maintain an indicative list of governmental and non-governmental individuals possessing the qualifications outlined in para 1, from which panelists may be drawn as appropriate. That list shall include the roster of non-governmental panelists established on 30 November 1984 (BISD 31S/9), and other rosters and indicative lists established under any of the covered agreements, and shall retain the names of persons on those rosters and indicative lists at the time of entry into force of the WTO Agreement. Members may periodically suggest names of governmental and non-governmental individuals for inclusion on the indicative list, providing relevant information on their knowledge of international trade and of the sectors or subject matter of the covered agreements, and those names shall be added to the list upon approval by the DSB. For each of the individuals on the list, the list shall indicate specific areas of experience or expertise of the individuals in the sectors or subject matter of the covered agreements.

5   Panels shall be composed of three panelists unless the parties to the dispute agree, within 10 days from the establishment of the panel, to a panel composed of five panelists. Members shall be informed promptly of the composition of the panel.

6   The Secretariat shall propose nominations for the panel to the parties to the dispute. The parties to the dispute shall not oppose nominations except for compelling reasons.

7   If there is no agreement on the panelists within 20 days after the date of the establishment of a panel, at the request of either party, the Director General, in consultation with the Chairman of the DSB and the Chairman of the relevant Council or Committee, shall determine the composition of the panel by appointing the panelists whom the Director General considers most appropriate in accordance with any relevant special or additional rules or procedures of the covered agreement or covered agreements which are at issue in the dispute, after consulting with the parties to the dispute. The Chairman of the DSB shall inform the Members of the composition of the panel thus formed no later than 10 days after the date the Chairman receives such a request.

8   Members shall undertake, as a general rule, to permit their officials to serve as panelists.

9   Panelists shall serve in their individual capacities and not as government representatives, nor as representatives of any organisation. Members shall therefore not give them instructions nor seek to influence them as individuals with regard to matters before a panel.

10   When a dispute is between a developing country Member and a developed country Member the panel shall, if the developing country Member so requests, include at least one panelist from a developing country Member.

11   Panelists' expenses, including travel and subsistence allowance, shall be met from the WTO budget in accordance with criteria to be adopted by the General Council, based on recommendations of the Committee on Budget, Finance and Administration.

Article 9 – Procedures for multiple complainants

1   Where more than one Member requests the establishment of a panel related to the same matter, a single panel may be established to examine these complaints taking

into account the rights of all Members concerned. A single panel should be established to examine such complaints whenever feasible.

2   The single panel shall organise its examination and present its findings to the DSB in such a manner that the rights which the parties to the dispute would have enjoyed had separate panels examined the complaints are in no way impaired. If one of the parties to the dispute so requests, the panel shall submit separate reports on the dispute concerned. The written submissions by each of the complainants shall be made available to the other complainants, and each complainant shall have the right to be present when any one of the other complainants presents its views to the panel.

3   If more than one panel is established to examine the complaints related to the same matter, to the greatest extent possible the same persons shall serve as panelists on each of the separate panels and the timetable for the panel process in such disputes shall be harmonised.

Article 10 – Third parties

1   The interests of the parties to a dispute and those of other Members under a covered agreement at issue in the dispute shall be fully taken into account during the panel process.

2   Any Member having a substantial interest in a matter before a panel and having notified its interest to the DSB (referred to in this understanding as a 'third party') shall have an opportunity to be heard by the panel and to make written submissions to the panel. These submissions shall also be given to the parties to the dispute and shall be reflected in the panel report.

3   Third parties shall receive the submissions of the parties to the dispute to the first meeting of the panel.

4   If a third party considers that a measure already the subject of a panel proceeding nullifies or impairs benefits accruing to it under any covered agreement, that Member may have recourse to normal dispute settlement procedures under this understanding. Such a dispute shall be referred to the original panel wherever possible.

Article 11 – Function of panels

The function of panels is to assist the DSB in discharging its responsibilities under this understanding and the covered agreements. Accordingly, a panel should make an objective assessment of the matter before it, including an objective assessment of the facts of the case and the applicability of and conformity with the relevant covered agreements, and make such other findings as will assist the DSB in making the recommendations or in giving the rulings provided for in the covered agreements. Panels should consult regularly with the parties to the dispute and give them adequate opportunity to develop a mutually satisfactory solution.

Article 12 – Panel procedures

1   Panels shall follow the working procedures in Appendix 3 unless the panel decides otherwise after consulting the parties to the dispute.

2   Panel procedures should provide sufficient flexibility so as to ensure high quality panel reports, while not unduly delaying the panel process.

3   After consulting the parties to the dispute, the panelists shall, as soon as practicable and whenever possible within one week after the composition and terms of

reference of the panel have been agreed upon, fix the timetable for the panel process, taking into account the provisions of para 9 of Article 4, if relevant.

4   In determining the timetable for the panel process, the panel shall provide sufficient time for the parties to the dispute to prepare their submissions.

5   Panels should set precise deadlines for written submissions by the parties and the parties should respect those deadlines.

6   Each party to the dispute shall deposit its written submissions with the Secretariat for immediate transmission to the panel and to the other party or parties to the dispute. The complaining party shall submit its first submission in advance of the responding party's first submission unless the panel decides, in fixing the timetable referred to in para 3 and after consultations with the parties to the dispute, that the parties should submit their first submissions simultaneously. When there are sequential arrangements for the deposit of first submissions, the panel shall establish a firm time period for receipt of the responding party's submission. Any subsequent written submissions shall be submitted simultaneously.

7   Where the parties to the dispute have failed to develop a mutually satisfactory solution, the panel shall submit its findings in the form of a written report to the DSB. In such cases, the report of a panel shall set out the findings of fact, the applicability of relevant provisions and the basic rationale behind any findings and recommendations that it makes. Where a settlement of the matter among the parties to the dispute has been found, the report of the panel shall be confined to a brief description of the case and to reporting that a solution has been reached.

8   In order to make the procedures more efficient, the period in which the panel shall conduct its examination, from the date that the composition and terms of reference of the panel have been agreed upon until the date the final report is issued to the parties to the dispute, shall, as a general rule, not exceed six months. In cases of urgency, including those relating to perishable goods, the panel shall aim to issue report to the parties to the dispute within three months.

9   When the panel considers that it cannot issue its report within six months, or within three months in cases of urgency, it shall inform the DSB in writing of the reasons for the delay together with an estimate of the period within which it will issue its report. In no case should the period from the establishment of the panel to the circulation of the report to the Members exceed nine months.

10   In the context of consultations involving a measure taken by a developing country Member, the parties may agree to extend the periods established in paras 7 and 8 of Article 4. If, after the relevant period has elapsed, the consulting parties cannot agree that the consultations have concluded, the Chairman of the DSB shall decide, after consultation with the parties, whether to extend the relevant period and, If so, for how long. In addition, in examining a complaint against a developing country Member, the pane! shall accord sufficient time for the developing country Member to prepare and present its argumentation. The provisions of para 1 of Article 20 and para 4 of Article 21 are not affected by any action pursuant to this paragraph.

11   Where one or more of the parties is a developing country Member, the panel's report shall explicitly indicate the form in which account has been taken of relevant provisions on differential and more-favourable treatment for developing country Members that form part of the covered agreements which have been raised by the developing country Member in the course of the dispute settlement procedures.

12   The panel may suspend its work at any time at the request of the complaining party for a period not to exceed 12 months. In the event of such a suspension, the time frames set out in paras 8 and 9 of this Article, para 1 of Article 20, and para 4 of Article 21 shall be extended by the amount of time that the work was suspended. If the work of the panel has been suspended for more than 12 months, the authority for establishment of the panel shall lapse.

Article 13 – Right to seek information

1   Each panel shall have the right to seek information and technical advice from any individual or body which it deems appropriate. However, before a panel seeks such information or advice from any individual or body within the jurisdiction of a Member it shall inform the authorities of that Member. A Member should respond promptly and fully to any request by a panel for such information as the panel considers necessary and appropriate. Confidential information which is provided shall not be revealed without formal authorisation from the individual, body, or authorities of the Member providing the information.

2   Panels may seek information from any relevant source and may consult experts to obtain their opinion on certain aspects of the matter. With respect to a factual issue concerning a scientific or other technical matter raised by a party to a dispute, a panel may request an advisory report in writing from an expert review group. Rules for the establishment of such a group and its procedures are set forth in Appendix 4.

Article 14 – Confidentiality

1   Panel deliberations shall be confidential.

2   The reports of panels shall be drafted without the presence of the parties to the dispute in the light of the information provided and the statements made.

3   Opinions expressed in the panel report by individual panelists shall be anonymous.

Article 15 – Interim review stage

1   Following the consideration of rebuttal submissions and oral arguments, the panel shall issue the descriptive (factual and argument) sections of its draft report to the parties to the dispute. Within a period of time set by the panel, the parties shall submit their comments in writing.

2   Following the expiration of the set period of time for receipt of comments from the parties to the dispute, the panel shall issue an interim report to the parties, including both the descriptive sections and the panel's findings and conclusions. Within a period of time set by the panel, a party may submit a written request for the panel to review precise aspects of the interim report prior to circulation of the final report to the Members. At the request of a party, the panel shall hold a further meeting with the parties on the issues identified in the written comments. If no comments are received from any party within the comment period, the interim report shall be considered the final panel report and circulated promptly to the Members.

3   The findings of the final panel report shall include a discussion of the arguments made at the interim review stage. The interim review stage shall be conducted within the time period set out in para 8 of Article 12.

Article 16 – Adoption of panel reports

1   In order to provide sufficient time for the Members to consider panel reports the reports shall not be considered for adoption by the DSB until 20 days after the date they have been circulated to the Members.

2   Members having objections to a panel report shall give written reasons to explain their objections for circulation at least 10 days prior to the DSB meeting at which the panel report will be considered.

3   The parties to a dispute shall have the right to participate fully in the consideration of the panel report by the DSB, and their views shall be fully recorded.

4   Within 60 days after the date of circulation of a panel report to the Members the report shall be adopted at a DSB meetings unless a party to the dispute formally notifies the DSB of its decision to appeal or the DSB decides by consensus not to adopt the report. If a party has notified its decision to appeal, the report by the panel shall not be considered for adoption by the DSB until after completion of the appeal. This adoption procedure is without prejudice to the right of Members to express their views on a panel report.

7   If a meeting of the DSB is not scheduled within this period at a time that enables the requirements of paras 1 and 4 of Article 16 to be met, a meeting of the DSB shall be held for this purpose.

Article 17 – Appellate review

Standing Appellate Body

1   A Standing Appellate Body shall be established by the DSB. The Appellate Body shall hear appeals from panel cases. It shall be composed of seven persons three of whom shall serve on any one case. Persons serving on the Appellate Body shall serve in rotation. Such rotation shall be determined in the working procedures of the Appellate Body.

2   The DSB shall appoint persons to serve on the Appellate Body for a four year term, and each person may be reappointed once. However, the terms of three of the seven persons appointed immediately after the entry into force of the WTO Agreement shall expire at the end of two years, to be determined by lot. Vacancies shall be filled as they arise. A person appointed to replace a person whose term of office has not expired shall hold office for the remainder of the predecessor's term.

3   The Appellate Body shall comprise persons of recognised authority, with demonstrated expertise in law, international trade and the subject matter of the covered agreements generally. They shall be unaffiliated with any government. The Appellate Body membership shall be broadly representative of membership in the WTO. All persons serving on the Appellate Body shall be available at all times and on short notice, and shall stay abreast of dispute settlement activities and other relevant activities of the WTO. They shall not participate in the consideration of any disputes that would create a direct or indirect conflict of interest.

4   Only parties to the dispute, not third parties, may appeal a panel report. Third parties which have notified the DSB of a substantial interest in the matter pursuant to para 2 of Article 10 may make written submissions to, and be given an opportunity to be heard by the Appellate Body.

5   As a general rule, the proceedings shall not exceed 60 days from the date a party to the dispute formally notifies its decision to appeal to the date the Appellate Body circulates its report. In fixing its timetable the Appellate Body shall take into account the provisions of para 9 of Article 4, if relevant. When the Appellate Body considers that it cannot provide its report within 60 days, it shall inform the DSB in writing of

the reasons for the delay together with an estimate of the period within which it will submit its report. In no case shall the proceedings exceed 90 days.

6   An appeal shall be limited to issues of law covered in the panel report and legal interpretations developed by the panel.

7   The Appellate Body shall be provided with appropriate administrative and legal support as it requires.

8   The expenses of persons serving on the Appellate Body, including travel and subsistence allowance, shall be met from the WTO budget in accordance with criteria to be adopted by the General Council, based on recommendations of the Committee on Budget, Finance and Administration.

Procedures for appellate review

9   Working procedures shall be drawn up by the Appellate Body in consultation with the Chairman of the DSB and the Director General, and communicated to the Members for their information.

10   The proceedings of the Appellate Body shall be confidential. The reports of the Appellate Body shall be drafted without the presence of the parties to the dispute and in the light of the information provided and the statements made.

11   Opinions expressed in the Appellate Body report by individuals serving on the Appellate Body shall be anonymous.

12   The Appellate Body shall address each of the issues raised in accordance with para 6 during the appellate proceeding.

13   The Appellate Body may uphold, modify or reverse the legal findings and conclusions of the panel.

Adoption of appellate body reports

14   An Appellate Body report shall be adopted by the DSB and unconditionally accepted by the parties to the dispute unless the DSB decides by consensus not to adopt the Appellate Body report within 30 days following its circulation to the Members. This adoption procedure is without prejudice to the right of Members to express their views on an Appellate Body report.

Article 18 – Communications with the panel or Appellate Body

1   There shall be no *ex parte* communications with the panel or Appellate Body concerning matters under consideration by the panel or Appellate Body.

2   Written submissions to the panel or the Appellate Body shall be treated as confidential, but shall be made available to the parties to the dispute. Nothing in this understanding shall preclude a party to a dispute from disclosing statements of its own positions to the public. Members shall treat as confidential information submitted by another Member to the panel or the Appellate Body which that Member has designated as confidential. A party to a dispute shall also, upon request of a Member, provide a non-confidential summary of the information contained in its written submissions that could be disclosed to the public.

Article 19 – Panel and appellate body recommendations

1   Where a panel or the Appellate Body concludes that a measure is inconsistent with a covered agreement, it shall recommend that the Member concerned bring the measure into conformity with that agreement. In addition to its recommendations,

the panel or Appellate Body may suggest ways in which the Member concerned could implement the recommendations.

2   In accordance with para 2 of Article 3, in their findings and recommendations, the panel and Appellate Body cannot add to or diminish the rights and obligations provided in the covered agreements.

Article 20 – Time frame for DSB decisions

Unless otherwise agreed to by the parties to the dispute, the period from the date of establishment of the panel by the DSB until the date the DSB considers the panel or appellate report for adoption shall as a general rule not exceed nine months where the panel report is not appealed or 12 months where the report is appealed. Where either the panel or the Appellate Body has acted, pursuant to para 9 of Article 12 or para 5 of Article 17, to extend the time for providing its report, the additional time taken shall be added to the above periods.

Article 21 – Surveillance of implementation of recommendations and rulings

1   Prompt compliance with recommendations or rulings of the DSB is essential at order to ensure effective resolution of disputes to the benefit of all Members.

2   Particular attention should be paid to matters affecting the interest of developing country Members with respect to measures which have been subject to dispute settlement.

3   At a DSB meeting held within 30 days after the date of adoption of the panel or Appellate Body report, the Member concerned shall inform the DSB of its intentions in respect of implementation of the recommendations and rulings of the DSB. If it is impracticable to comply immediately with the recommendations and rulings the Member concerned shall have a reasonable period of time in which to do so. The reasonable period of time shall be:

(a)   the period of time proposed by the Member concerned, provided that such period is approved by the DSB; or, in the absence of such approval;

(b)   a period of time mutually agreed by the parties to the dispute within 45 days after the date of adoption of the recommendations and rulings; or, in the absence of such agreement;

(c)   a period of time determined through binding arbitration within 90 days after the date of adoption of the recommendations and rulings. In such arbitration, a guideline for the arbitrator should be that the reasonable period of time to implement panel or Appellate Body recommendations should not exceed 15 months from the date of adoption of a panel or Appellate Body report. However, that time may be shorter or longer, depending upon the particular circumstances.

4   Except where the panel or the Appellate Body has extended, pursuant to para 9 of Article 12 or para 5 of Article 17, the time of providing its report, the period from the date of establishment of the panel by the DSB until the date of determination of the reasonable period of time shall not exceed 15 months unless the parties to the dispute agree otherwise. Where either the panel or the Appellate Body has acted to extend the time of providing its report, the additional time taken shall be added to the 15-month period; provided that unless the parties to the dispute agree that there are exceptional circumstances, the total time shall not exceed 18 months.

5   Where there is disagreement as to the existence or consistency with a covered agreement of measures taken to comply with the recommendations and rulings such dispute shall be decided through recourse to these dispute settlement procedures, including wherever possible resort to the original panel. The panel shall circulate its report within 90 days after the date of referral of the matter to it. When the panel considers that it cannot provide its report within this time frame, it shall inform the DSB in writing of the reasons for the delay together with an estimate of the period within which it will submit its report.

6   The DSB shall keep under surveillance the implementation of adopted recommendations or rulings. The issue of implementation of the recommendations or rulings may be raised at the DSB by any Member at any time following their adoption. Unless the DSB decides otherwise, the issue of implementation of the recommendations or rulings shall be placed on the agenda of the DSB meeting after six months following the date of establishment of the reasonable period of time pursuant to para 3 and shall remain on the DSB's agenda until the issue is resolved. At least 10 days prior to each such DSB meeting, the Member concerned shall provide the DSB with a status report in writing of its progress in the implementation of the recommendations or rulings.

7   If the matter is one which has been raised by a developing country Member, the DSB shall consider what further action it might take which would be appropriate to the circumstances.

8   If the case is one brought by a developing country Member, in considering what appropriate action might be taken, the DSB shall take into account not only the trade coverage of measures complained of, but also their impact on the economy of developing country Members concerned.

Article 22 – Compensation and the suspension of concessions

1   Compensation and the suspension of concessions or other obligations are temporary measures available in the event that the recommendations and rulings are not Implemented within a reasonable period of time. However, neither compensation nor the suspension of concessions or other obligations is preferred to full implementation of a recommendation to bring a measure into conformity with the covered agreements. Compensation is voluntary and, if granted, shall be consistent with the covered agreements.

2   If the Member concerned fails to bring the measure found to be inconsistent with a covered agreement into compliance therewith or otherwise comply with the recommendations and rulings within the reasonable period of time determined pursuant to para 3 of Article 21, such Member shall, if so requested, and no later than the expiry of the reasonable period of time, enter into negotiations with any party having invoked the dispute settlement procedures, with a view to developing mutually acceptable compensation. If no satisfactory compensation has been agreed within 20 days after the date of expiry of the reasonable period of time any party having invoked the dispute settlement procedures may request authorisation from the DSB to suspend the application to the Member concerned of concessions or other obligations under the covered agreements.

3   In considering what concessions or other obligations to suspend, the complaining party shall apply the following principles and procedures:

(a) the general principle is that the complaining party should first seek to suspend concessions or other obligations with respect to the same sector(s) as that in which the panel or Appellate Body has found a violation or other nullification or impairment;

(b) if that party considers that it is not practicable or effective to suspend concessions or other obligations with respect to the same sector(s), it may seek to suspend concessions or other obligations in other sectors under the same agreement;

(c) if that party considers that it is not practicable or effective to suspend concessions or other obligations with respect to other sectors under the same agreement, and that the circumstances are serious enough, it may seek to suspend concessions or other obligations under another covered agreement;

(d) in applying the above principles, that party shall take into account:

    (i) the trade in the sector or under the agreement under which the panel or Appellate Body has found a violation or other nullification or impairment, and the importance of such trade to that party;

    (ii) the broader economic elements related to the nullification or impairment and the broader economic consequences of the suspension of concessions or other obligations;

(c) if that party decides to request authorisation to suspend concessions or other obligations pursuant to sub-paras (b) or (c), it shall state the reasons therefore In its request. At the same time as the request is forwarded to the DSB, it also shall be forwarded to the relevant Councils and also, in the case of a request pursuant to sub-para (b), the relevant sectoral bodies;

(f) for purposes of this paragraph, 'sector' means:

    (i) with respect to goods, all goods;

    (ii) with respect to services, a principal sector as identified in the current 'Services Sectoral Classification List' which identifies such sectors;

    (iii) with respect to trade-related intellectual property rights, each of the categories of intellectual property rights covered in sections 1–7 of Part II, or the obligations under Part III, or Part IV of the Agreement on TRIPS;

(g) for purposes of this para, 'agreement' means:

    (i) with respect to goods, the agreements listed in Annex IA of the WTO Agreement, taken as a whole as well as the Plurilateral Trade Agreements in so far as the relevant parties to the dispute are parries to these agreements;

    (ii) with respect to services, the GATS;

    (iii) with respect to intellectual property rights, the Agreement on TRIPS.

4   The level of the suspension of concessions or other obligations authorised by the DSB shall be equivalent to the level of the nullification or impairment.

5   The DSB shall not authorise suspension of concessions or other obligations if a covered agreement prohibits such suspension.

6   When the situation described in para 2 occurs, the DSB, upon request, shall grant authorisation to suspend concessions or other obligations within 30 days of the expiry of the reasonable period of time unless the DSB decides by consensus to reject the request. However, if the Member concerned objects to the level of suspension

proposed, or claims that the principles and procedures set forth in para 3 have not been followed where a complaining party has requested authorisation to suspend concessions or other obligations pursuant to para 3(b) or (c), the matter shall be referred to arbitration. Such arbitration shall be carried out by the original panel, if members are available, or by an arbitrators appointed by the Director General and shall be completed within 60 days after the date of expiry of the reasonable period of time. Concessions or other obligations shall not be suspended during the course of the arbitration.

7   The arbitrators acting pursuant to para 6 shall not examine the nature of the concessions or other obligations to be suspended but shall determine whether the level of such suspension is equivalent to the level of nullification or impairment. The arbitrator may also determine if the proposed suspension of concessions or other obligations is allowed under the covered agreement. However, if the matter referred to arbitration includes a claim that the principles and procedures set forth in para 3 have not been followed, the arbitrator shall examine that claim. In the event the arbitrator determines that those principles and procedures have not been followed, the complaining party shall apply them consistent with para 3. The parties shall accept the arbitrator's decision as final and the parties concerned shall not seek a second arbitration. The DSB shall be informed promptly of the decision of the arbitrator and shall upon request, grant authorisation to suspend concessions or other obligations where the request is consistent with the decision of the arbitrator, unless the DSB decides by consensus, to reject the request.

8   The suspension of concessions or other obligations shall be temporary and shall only be applied until such time as the measure found to be inconsistent with a covered agreement has been removed, or the Member that must implement recommendations or rulings provides a solution to the nullification or impairment of benefits, or a mutually satisfactory solution is reached. In accordance with para 6 of Article 21, the DSB shall continue to keep under surveillance the implementation adopted recommendations or rulings including those cases where compensation has been provided or concessions or other obligations have been suspended but the recommendations to bring a measure into conformity with the covered agreements have not been implemented.

9   The dispute settlement provisions of the covered agreements may be invoked m respect of measures affecting their observance taken by regional or local governments or authorities within the territory of a Member. When the DSB has ruled that a provision of a covered agreement has not been observed, the responsible Member shall take such reasonable measures as may be available to it to ensure its observance. The provisions of the covered agreements and this understanding relating to compensation and suspension of concessions or other obligations apply in cases where it has not been possible to secure such observance.

Article 23 – Strengthening of the multilateral system

1   When Members seek the redress of a violation of obligations or other nullification or impairment of benefits under the covered agreements or an impediment to the attainment of any objective of the covered agreements, they shall have recourse to, and abide by, the rules and procedures of this understanding.

2   In such cases, Members shall:

(a) not make a determination to the effect that a violation has occurred, that benefits have been nullified or impaired or that the attainment of any objective of the covered agreements has been impeded, except through recourse to dispute settlement in accordance with the rules and procedures of this understanding, and shall make any such determination consistent with the findings contained in the panel or Appellate Body report adopted by the DSB or an arbitration award rendered under this understanding;

(b) follow the procedures set forth in Article 21 to determine the reasonable period of time for the Member concerned to implement the recommendations and rulings; and

(c) follow the procedures set forth in Article 22 to determine the level of suspension of concessions or other obligations and obtain DSB authorisation in accordance with those procedures before suspending concessions or other obligations under the covered agreements in response to the failure of the Member concerned to implement the recommendations and rulings within that reasonable period of time.

Article 24 – Special procedures involving least-developed country members

1   At all stages of the determination of the causes of a dispute and of dispute settlement procedures involving a least-developed country Member, particular consideration shall he given to the special situation of least-developed country Members. In this regard, Members shall exercise due restraint in raising matters under these procedures involving a least-developed country Member. If nullification or impairment is found to result from a measure taken by a least-developed country Member, complaining parties shall exercise due restraint in asking for compensation or seeking authorisation to suspend the application of concessions or other obligations pursuant to these procedures.

2   In dispute settlement cases involving a less developed country Member, where a satisfactory solution has not been found in the course of consultations the Director General or the Chairman of the DSB shall, upon request by a least-developed country Member, offer their good of offices, conciliation and mediation with a view to assisting the parties to settle the dispute, before a request for a panel is made. The Director General or the Chairman of the DSB, in providing the above assistance, may consult any source which either deems appropriate.

Article 25 – Arbitration

1   Expeditious arbitration within the WTO as an alternative means of dispute settlement can facilitate the solution of certain disputes that concern issues that are clearly defined by both parties.

2   Except as otherwise provided in this understanding, resort to arbitration shall be subject to mutual agreement of the parties which shall agree on the procedures to be followed. Agreements to resort to arbitration shall be notified to all Members sufficiently in advance of the actual commencement of the arbitration process.

3   Other Members may become party to an arbitration proceeding only upon the agreement of the parties which have agreed to have recourse to arbitration. The parties to the proceeding shall agree to abide by the arbitration award. Arbitration awards shall be notified to the DSB and the Council or Committee of any relevant agreement where any Member may raise any point relating thereto.

4 Articles 21 and 22 of this understanding shall apply *mutatis mutandis* to arbitration awards.

Article 26

1 Non-violation complaints of the type described in para 1(b) of Article XXIII of GATT 1994

Where the provisions of para 1(b) of Article XXIII of GATT 1994 are applicable to a covered agreement, a panel or the Appellate Body may only make rulings and recommendations where a party to the dispute considers that any benefit accruing to it directly or indirectly under the relevant covered agreement is being nullified or impaired or the attainment of any objective of that agreement is being impeded as a result of the application by a Member of any measure, whether or not it conflicts with the provisions of that agreement. Where and to the extent that such party considers and a panel or the Appellate Body determines that a case concerns a measure that does not conflict with the provisions of a covered agreement to which the provisions of para 1(b) of Article XXIII of GATT 1994 are applicable, the procedures in this understanding shall apply, subject to the following:

(a) the complaining party shall present a derailed justification in support of any complaint relating to a measure which does not conflict with the relevant covered agreement;

(b) where a measure has been found to nullify or impair benefits under, or impede the attainment of objectives of, the relevant covered agreement without violation thereof, there is no obligation to withdraw the measure. However, in such cases, the panel or the Appellate Body shall recommend that the Member concerned make a mutually satisfactory adjustment;

(c) notwithstanding the provisions of Article 21, the arbitration provided for in para 3 of Article 21, upon request of either party, may include a determination of the level of benefits which have been nullified or impaired, and may also suggest ways and means of reaching a mutually satisfactory adjustment; such suggestions shall not be binding upon the parties to the dispute;

(d) notwithstanding the provisions of para 1 of Article 22, compensation may be part of a mutually satisfactory adjustment as final settlement of the dispute.

2 Complaints of the type described in para 1(c) of Article XXIII of GATT 1994

Where the provisions of para 1(c) of Article XXIII of GATT 1994 are applicable to a covered agreement, a panel may only make rulings and recommendations where a party considers that any benefit accruing to it directly or indirectly under the relevant covered agreement is being nullified or impaired or the attainment of any objective of that agreement is being impeded as a result of the existence of any situation other than those to which the provisions of paras 1(a) and 1(b) of Article XXIII of GATT 1994 are applicable. Where and to the extent that such party considers and a panel determines that the matter is covered by this paragraph, the procedures of this understanding shall apply only up to and including the point in the proceedings where the panel report has been circulated to the Members. The dispute settlement rules and procedures contained in the decision of 12 April 1989 (BISD 36S/61–67) shall apply to consideration for adoption, and surveillance and implementation of recommendations and rulings. The following shall also apply:

(a) the complaining party shall present a detailed justification in support of any argument made with respect to issues covered under this paragraph;

(b) in cases involving matters covered by this paragraph, if a panel finds that cases also involve dispute settlement matters other than those covered by this paragraph, the panel shall circulate a report to the DSB addressing any such matters and a separate report on matters falling under this paragraph.

Article 27 – Responsibilities of the secretariat

1   The Secretariat shall have the responsibility of assisting panels, especially on the legal, historical and procedural aspects of the matters dealt with, and of providing secretarial and technical support.

2   While the Secretariat assists Members in respect of dispute settlement at their request, there may also be a need to provide additional legal advice and assistance in respect of dispute settlement to developing country Members. To this end, the Secretariat shall make available a qualified legal expert from the WTO technical cooperation services to any developing country Member which so requests. This expert shall assist the developing country Member in a manner ensuring the continued impartiality of the Secretariat.

3   The Secretariat shall conduct special training courses for interested Members concerning these dispute settlement procedures and practices so as to enable Members' experts to be better informed in this regard.

Appendix 1

Agreements covered by the understanding

(A) Agreement Establishing the World Trade Organisation

(B) Multilateral Trade Agreements

Annex 1A

Multilateral Agreements on Trade in Goods

Annex 1B

General Agreement on Trade in Services

Annex 1C

Agreement on Trade-Related Aspects of Intellectual Property Rights

Annex 2

Understanding on Rules and Procedures Governing the Settlement of Disputes

(C) Plurilateral Trade Agreements

Annex 4

Agreement on Trade in Civil Aircraft Agreement on Government Procurement International Dairy Agreement International Bovine Meat Agreement

The applicability of this Understanding to the Plurilateral Trade Agreements shall be subject to the adoption of a decision by the parties to each agreement setting out the terms for the application of the understanding to the individual agreement, including any special or additional rules or procedures for inclusion in Appendix 2, as notified to the DSB.

Appendix 2

Special or additional rules and procedures contained in the covered agreements

Agreement	Rules and Procedures
Agreement on the Application of Sanitary and Phytosanitary Measures	11.2
Agreement on Textiles and Clothing	2.14, 2.21, 4.4, 5.2, 5.4, 5.6, 6.9, 6.10, 6.11, 8.1 through 8.12
Agreement on Technical Barriers to Trade	14.2 through 14.4, Annex 2
Agreement on Implementation of Article VI of GATT 1994	17.4 through 17.7
Agreement on Implementation of Article VII of GATT 1994	19.3 through 19.5, Annex 11.2(f), 3, 9, 21
Agreement on Subsidies and Countervailing Measures	4.2 through 4.12, 6.6. 7.2 through 7.10, 8.5, footnote 35, 24.4, 27.7, Annex V
General Agreement on Trade in Services	XXII:3, XXIII:3
Annex on Financial Services	4
Annex on Air Transport Services	4
Decision on Certain Dispute Settlement procedures for the GATS	1 through 5

The list of rules and procedures in this Appendix includes provisions where only a part of the provision may be relevant in this context.

Any special or additional rules or procedures in the Plurilateral Trade Agreements as determined by the competent bodies of each agreement and as notified to the DSB.

Appendix 3

Working procedures

1   In its proceedings the panel shall follow the relevant provisions of this understanding. In addition, the following working procedures shall apply.

2   The panel shall meet in closed session. The parties to the dispute, and interested parties, shall be present at the meetings only when invited by the panel to appear before it.

3   The deliberations of the panel and the documents submitted to it shall be kept confidential. Nothing in this understanding shall preclude a party to a dispute from disclosing statements of its own positions to the public. Members shall treat as confidential information submitted by another Member to the panel which that Member has designated as confidential. Where a party to a dispute submits a confidential version of its written submissions to the panel, it shall also, upon request of a Member, provide a non-confidential summary of the information contained in its submissions that could be disclosed to the public.

4   Before the first substantive meeting of the panel with the parties, the parties to the dispute shall transmit to the panel written submissions in which they present the facts of the case and their arguments.

5   At its first substantive meeting with the parties, the panel shall ask the party which has brought the complaint to present its case. Subsequently, and still at the same meeting, the party against which the complaint has been brought shall be asked to present its point of view.

6   All third parties which have notified their interest in the dispute to the DSB shall be invited in writing to present their views during a session of the first substantive meeting of the panel set aside for that purpose. All such third parties may be present during the entirety of this session.

7   Formal rebuttals shall be made at a second substantive meeting of the panel. The party complained against shall have the right to take the floor first to be followed by the complaining party. The parties shall submit, prior to that meeting, written rebuttals to the panel.

8   The panel may at any time put questions to the parties and ask them for explanations either in the course of a meeting with the parties or in writing.

9   The parties to the dispute and any third party invited to present its views in accordance with Article 10 shall make available to the panel a written version of their oral statements.

10 In the interest of full transparency, the presentations, rebuttals and statements referred to in paras 5–9 shall be made in the presence of the parties. Moreover, each party's written submissions, including any comments on the descriptive part of the report and responses to questions put by the panel, shall be made available to the other party or parties.

11 Any additional procedures specific to the panel.

12 Proposed timetable for panel work:

   (a) Receipt of first written submissions of the parties:

       (i) complaining party: 3–6 weeks;

       (ii) party complained against: 2–3 weeks.

   (b) Date, time and place of first substantive meeting with the parties; third party session: 1-2 weeks.

   (c) Receipt of written rebuttals of the parties: 2–3 weeks.

   (d) Date, time and place of second substantive meeting with the parties: 1–2 weeks.

   (e) Issuance of descriptive part of the report to the parties: 2–4 weeks.

   (f) Receipt of comments by the parties on the descriptive part of the report: 2 weeks.

   (g) Issuance of the interim report, including the findings and conclusions, to the parties: 2–4 weeks.

   (h) Deadline for party to request review of part(s) of report: 1 week.

   (i) Period of review by panel, including possible additional meeting with parties: 2 weeks.

   (j) Issuance of final report to parties to dispute: 2 weeks.

   (k) Circulation of the final report to the Members: 3 weeks.

The above calendar may be changed in the light of unforeseen developments. Additional meetings with the parties shall be scheduled if required.

Appendix 4
Expert review groups

The following rules and procedures shall apply to expert review groups established in accordance with the provisions of para 2 of Article 13.

1   Expert review groups are under the panel's authority. Their terms of reference and detailed working procedures shall be decided by the panel, and they shall report to the panel.

2   Participation in expert review groups shall be restricted to persons of professional standing and experience in the field in question.

3   Citizens of parties to the dispute shall not serve on an expert review group without the joint agreement of the parties to the dispute, except in exceptional circumstances when the panel considers that the need for specialised scientific expertise cannot be fulfilled otherwise. government of officials of parties to the dispute shall not serve on an expert review group. Members of expert review groups shall serve in their individual capacities and not as government representatives, nor as representatives or any organisation. governments or organisations shall therefore not give them instructions with regard to matters before an expert review group.

4   Expert review groups may consult and seek information and technical advice from any source they deem appropriate. Before an expert review group seeks such information or advice from a source within the jurisdiction of a Member, it shall inform the government of that Member. Any Member shall respond promptly and fully to any request by an expert review group for such information as the expert review group considers necessary and appropriate.

5   The parties to a dispute shall have access to all relevant information provided to an expert review group, unless it is of a confidential nature. Confidential information provided to the expert review group shall not be released without formal authorisation from the government, organisation or person providing the information. Where such information is requested from the expert review group but release of such information by the expert review group is not authorised, a non-confidential summary of the information will be provided by the government organisation or person supplying the information.

6   The expert review group shall submit a draft report to the parties to the dispute with a view to obtaining their comments, and taking them into account, as appropriate, in the final report, which shall also be issued to the parties to the dispute when it is submitted to the panel. The final report of the expert review group shall be advisory only.

GENERAL AGREEMENT ON TRADE IN SERVICES
PART I – SCOPE AND DEFINITION

Article I – Scope and definition

1   This agreement applies to measures by Members affecting trade in services.

2   For the purposes of this agreement, trade in services is defined as the supply of:

   (a)   from the territory of one Member into the territory of any other Member;

   (b)   in the territory of one Member to the service consumer of any other Member;

(c) by a service supplier of one Member, through commercial presence in the territory of any other Member;

(d) by a service supplier of one Member, through presence of natural persons of a Member in the territory of any other Member.

3   For the purposes of this agreement:

(a) 'measures by Members' means measures taken by:

(i) central, regional or local governments and authorities; and

(ii) non-governmental bodies in the exercise of powers delegated by central regional or local governments or authorities;

in fulfilling its obligations and commitments under the agreement, each member shall take such reasonable measures as may be available to it to ensure their observance by regional and local governments and authorities and non-governmental bodies within its territory;

(b) 'services' includes any service in any sector except services supplied in the exercise of governmental authority;

(c) 'a service supplied in the exercise of governmental authority' means any service which is supplied neither on a commercial basis nor in competition with one or more service suppliers.

PART II – GENERAL OBLIGATIONS AND DISCIPLINES

Article II – Most-favoured-nation treatment

1   With respect to any measure covered by this agreement, each Member shall accord immediately and unconditionally to services and service suppliers of any other Member treatment no less favourable than that it accords to like services and service suppliers of any other country.

2   A Member may maintain a measure inconsistent with para 1 provided that such a measure is listed in, and meets the conditions of, the Annex on Article II Exemptions.

3   The provisions of this agreement shall not be so construed as to prevent any Member from conferring or according advantages to adjacent countries in order to facilitate exchanges limited to contiguous frontier zones of services that are both locally produced and consumed.

Article III – Transparency

1   Each Member shall publish promptly and, except in emergency situations, at the latest by the time of their entry into force, all relevant measures of general application which pertain to or affect the operation of this agreement. International agreements pertaining to or affecting trade in services to which a Member is a signatory shall also be published.

2   Where publication as referred to in para 1 is not practicable, such information shall be made otherwise publicly available.

3   Each Member shall promptly and at least annually inform the Council for Trade in Services of the introduction of any new, or any changes to existing, laws, regulations or administrative guidelines which significantly affect trade in services covered by its specific commitments under this agreement.

4   Each Member shall respond promptly to all requests by any other member for specific information on any of its measures of general application or international agreements within the meaning of para 1. Each Member shall also establish one or more enquiry points to provide specific information to other Members, upon request, on all such matters as well as those subject to the notification requirement in para 3. Such enquiry points shall be established within two years from the date of entry into force of the Agreement Establishing the WTO (referred to in this agreement as the 'WTO Agreement'). Appropriate flexibility with respect to the time limit within which such enquiry points are to be established may be agreed upon for individual developing country Members. Enquiry points need not be depositories of laws and regulations.

5   Any Member may notify to the Council for Trade in Services any measure, taken by any other Member, which it considers affects the operation of this agreement.

Article III bis − Disclosure of confidential information

Nothing in this agreement shall require any Member to provide confidential information, the disclosure of which would impede law enforcement, or otherwise be contrary to the public interest, or which would prejudice legitimate commercial interests of particular enterprises, public or private.

Article V − Economic integration

1   This agreement shall not prevent any of its Members from being a party to or entering into an agreement liberalising trade in services between or among the parties to such an agreement, provided that such an agreement:

(a)   has substantial sectoral coverage; and

(b)   provides for the absence or elimination of substantially all discrimination, in the sense of Article XVII, between or among the parties, in the sectors covered under sub-para (a), through:

   (i)   elimination of existing discriminatory measures; and/or

   (ii) prohibition of new or more discriminatory measures, either at the entry into force of that agreement or on the basis of a reasonable time frame, except for measures permitted under Articles XI, XII, XIV and XIV *bis*.

2   In evaluating whether the conditions under para 1(b) are met, consideration may be given to the relationship of the agreement to a wider process of economic integration or trade liberalisation among the countries concerned.

3   (a)   Where developing countries are parties to an agreement of the type referred to in para 1, flexibility shall be provided for regarding the conditions set out in para 1, particularly with reference to sub-para (b) thereof, in accordance with the level of development of the countries concerned, both overall and in individual sectors and sub-sectors.

   (b)   Notwithstanding para 6, in the case of an agreement of the type referred to in para 1 involving only developing countries, more favourable treatment may be granted to juridical persons owned or controlled by natural persons of the parties to such an agreement.

4   Any agreement referred to in para 1 shall be designed to facilitate trade between the parties to the agreement and shall not in respect of any Member outside the agreement raise the overall level of barriers to trade in services within the respective sectors or sub-sectors compared to the level applicable prior to such an agreement.

5   If, in the conclusion, enlargement or any significant modification of any agreement under para 1, a Member intends to withdraw or modify a specific commitment inconsistently with the terms and conditions set out in its Schedule, it shall provide at least 90 days advance notice of such modification or withdrawal and the procedure set forth in paras 2, 3 and 4 of Article XXI shall apply.

6   A service supplier of any other Member that is a juridical person constituted under the laws of a party to an agreement referred to in para 1 shall be entitled to treatment granted under such agreement, provided that it engages in substantive business operations in the territory of the parties to such agreement.

7   (a) Members which are parties to any agreement referred to in para 1 shall promptly notify any such agreement and any enlargement or any significant modification of that agreement to the Council for Trade in Services. They shall also make available to the Council such relevant information as may be requested by it. The Council may establish a working party to examine such an agreement or enlargement or modification of that agreement and to report to the Council on its consistency with this article.

     (b) Members which are parties to any agreement referred to in para 1 which is implemented on the basis of a time frame shall report periodically to the Council for Trade in Services on its implementation. The Council may establish a working party to examine such reports if it deems such a working party necessary.

     (c) Based on the reports of the working parties referred to in sub-paras (a) and (b), the Council may make recommendations to the parties as it deems appropriate.

8   A Member which is a party to any agreement referred to in para 1 may not seek compensation for trade benefits that may accrue to any other Member from such agreement.

Article VI – Domestic regulation

1   In sectors where specific commitments are undertaken, each Member shall ensure that all measures of general application affecting trade in services are administered in a reasonable, objective and impartial manner.

2   (a) Each Member shall maintain or institute as soon as practicable judicial, arbitral or administrative tribunals or procedures which provide, at the request of an affected service supplier, for the prompt review of, and where justified, appropriate remedies for, administrative decisions affecting trade in services. Where such procedures are not independent of the agency entrusted with the administrative decision concerned, the Member shall ensure that the procedures in fact provide for an objective and impartial review.

     (b) The provisions of sub-para (a) shall not be construed to require a Member to institute such tribunals or procedures where this would be inconsistent with its constitutional structure or the nature of its legal system.

3   Where authorisation is required for the supply of a service on which a specific commitment has been made, the competent authorities of a Member shall, within a reasonable period of time after the submission of an application considered complete under domestic laws and regulations, inform the applicant of the decision concerning the application. At the request of the applicant, the competent authorities of the Member shall provide, without undue delay, information concerning the status of the application.

4   With a view to ensuring that measures relating to qualification requirements and procedures, technical standards and licensing requirements do not constitute unnecessary barriers to trade in services, the Council for Trade in Services shall, through appropriate bodies it may establish, develop any necessary disciplines. Such disciplines shall aim to ensure that such requirements are, *inter alia*:

(a) based on objective and transparent criteria, such as competence and the ability to supply the service;

(b) not more burdensome than necessary to ensure the quality at the service;

(c) in the case of licensing procedures, not in themselves a restriction on the supply of the service.

5   (a) In sectors in which a Member has undertaken specific commitments pending the entry into force of disciplines developed in these sectors pursuant to para 4, the Member shall not apply licensing and qualification requirements and technical standards that nullify or impair such specific commitments in a manner which:

(i)   does not comply with the criteria outlined in sub-paras 4(a), (b) or (c); and

(ii) could not reasonably have been expected of that Member at the time the specific commitments in those sectors were made.

(b) In determining whether a Member is in conformity with the obligation under para 5(a), account shall be taken of international standards of relevant international organisations applied by that Member.

6   In sectors where' specific commitments regarding professional services are undertaken, each Member shall provide for adequate procedures to verify the competence of professionals of any other Member.

Article VII – Recognition

1   For the purposes of the fulfilment, in whole or in part, of its standards or criteria for the authorisation, licensing or certification of services suppliers, and subject to the requirements of para 3, a Member may recognise the education or experience obtained, requirements met, or licenses or certifications granted in a particular country. Such recognition, which may be achieved through harmonisation or otherwise, may be based upon an agreement or arrangement with the country concerned or may be accorded autonomously.

2   A Member that is a party to an agreement or arrangement of the type referred to in para 1, whether existing or future, shall afford adequate opportunity for other interested Members to negotiate their accession to such an agreement or arrangement or to negotiate comparable ones with it. Where a Member accords recognition autonomously, it shall afford adequate opportunity for any other Member to demonstrate that education, experience, licenses, or certifications obtained or requirements met in that other Member's territory should be recognised.

3   A Member shall not accord recognition in a manner which would constitute a means of discrimination between countries in the application of its standards or criteria for the authorisation, licensing or certification of services suppliers, or a disguised restriction on trade in services.

4   Each member shall:

(a) within 12 months from the date on which the WTO Agreement takes effect for it, inform the Council for Trade in Services of its existing recognition measures and state whether such measures are based on agreements or arrangements of the type referred to in para 1;

(b) promptly inform the Council for Trade in Services as far in advance as possible of the opening of negotiations on an agreement or arrangement of the type referred to in para 1 in order to provide adequate opportunity to any other Member to indicate their interest in participating in the negotiations before they enter a substantive phase;

(c) promptly inform the Council for Trade in Services when it adopts new recognition measures or significantly modifies existing ones and state whether the measures are based on an agreement or arrangement of the type referred to in para 1.

5   Wherever appropriate, recognition should be based on multilaterally agreed criteria. In appropriate cases, Members shall work in cooperation with relevant intergovernmental and non-governmental organisations towards the establishment and adoption of common international standards and criteria for recognition and common international standards for the practice of relevant services trades and professions.

Article VIII – Monopolies and exclusive service suppliers

1   Each Member shall ensure that any monopoly supplier of a service in its territory does not, in the supply of the monopoly service in the relevant market, act in a manner inconsistent with that Member's obligations under Article II and specific commitments.

2   Where a Member's monopoly supplier competes, either directly or through an affiliated company, in the supply of a service outside the scope of its monopoly rights and which is subject to that Member's specific commitments, the Member shall ensure that such a supplier does not abuse its monopoly position to act in its territory in a manner inconsistent with such commitments.

3   The Council for Trade in Services may, at the request of a Member which has a reason to believe that a monopoly supplier of a service of any other Member is acting in a manner inconsistent with para 1 or 2, request the Member establishing, maintaining or authorising such supplier to provide specific information concerning the relevant operations.

4   If, after the date of entry into force of the WTO Agreement, a Member grants monopoly rights regarding the supply of a service covered by its specific commitments, that Member shall notify the Council for Trade in Services no later than three months before the intended implementation of the grant of monopoly rights and the provisions of paras 2, 3 and 4 of Article XXI shall apply.

5   The provisions of this article shall also apply to cases of exclusive service suppliers, where a Member, formally or in effect, (a) authorises or establishes a small number of service suppliers and (b) substantially prevents competition among those suppliers in its territory.

Article IX – Business practices

1   Members recognise that certain business practices of service suppliers, other than those falling under Article VIII, may restrain competition and thereby restrict trade in services.

2   Each Member shall, at the request of any other Member, enter into consultations with a view to eliminating practices referred to in para 1. The Member addressed shall accord full and sympathetic consideration to such a request and shall cooperate through the supply of publicly available non-confidential information of relevance to the matter in question. The Member addressed shall also provide other information available to the requesting Member, subject to its domestic law and to the conclusion of satisfactory agreement concerning the safeguarding of its confidentiality by the requesting Member.

Article X – Emergency safeguard measures

1   There shall be multilateral negotiations on the question of emergency safeguard measures based on the principle of non-discrimination. The results of such negotiations shall enter into effect on a date not later than three years from the date of entry into force of the WTO Agreement.

2   In the period before the entry into effect of the results of the negotiations referred to in para 1, any Member may, notwithstanding the provisions of para 1 of Article XXI, notify the Council on Trade in Services of its intention to modify or withdraw a specific commitment after a period of one year from the date on which the commitment enters into force; provided that the Member shows cause to the Council that the modification or withdrawal cannot await the lapse of the three year period provided for in para 1 of Article XXI.

3   The provisions of para 2 shall cease to apply three years after the date of entry into force of the WTO Agreement.

Article XI – Payments and transfers

1   Except under the circumstances envisaged in Article XII, a Member shall not apply restrictions on international transfers and payments for current transactions relating to its specific commitments.

2   Nothing in this agreement shall affect the rights and obligations of the members of the International Monetary Fund under the Articles of Agreement of the Fund, including the use of exchange actions which are in conformity with the articles of agreement, provided that a Member shall not impose restrictions on any capital transactions inconsistently with its specific commitments regarding such transactions, except under Article XII or at the request of the Fund.

Article XII – Restrictions to safeguard the balance-of-payments

1   In the event of serious balance-of-payments and external financial difficulties or threat thereof, a Member may adopt or maintain restrictions on trade in services on which it has undertaken specific commitments, including on payments or transfers for transactions related to such commitments. It is recognised that particular pressures on the balance of payments of a Member in the process of economic development or economic transition may necessitate the use of restrictions to ensure, *inter alia*, the maintenance of a level of financial reserves adequate for the implementation of its programme of economic development or economic transition.

2   The restrictions referred to in para 1:

(a)   shall not discriminate among Members;

(b)   shall be consistent with the Articles of Agreement of the International Monetary Fund;

(c) shall avoid unnecessary damage to the commercial, economic and financial interests of any other Member;

(d) shall not exceed those necessary to deal with the circumstances described in para 1;

(e) shall be temporary and be phased out progressively as the situation specified in para 1 improves.

3 In determining the incidence of such restrictions, Members may give priority to the supply of services which are more essential to their economic or development programmes. However, such restrictions shall not be adopted or maintained for the purpose of protecting a particular service sector.

4 Any restrictions adopted or maintained under para 1, or any changes therein, shall be promptly notified to the General Council.

5 (a) Members applying the provisions pf this article shall consult promptly with the Committee on Balance of Payments Restrictions on restrictions adopted under this article.

(b) The Ministerial Conference shall establish procedures for periodic consultations with the objective of enabling such recommendations to be made to the Member concerned as it may deem appropriate.

(c) Such consultations shall assess the balance of payments situation of the Member concerned and the restrictions adopted or maintained under this article, taking into account, *inter alia*, such factors as:

(i) the nature and extent of the balance of payments and the external financial difficulties;

(ii) the external economic and trading environment of the consulting Member;

(iii) alternative corrective measures which may be available.

(d) The consultations shall address the compliance of any restrictions with para 2, in particular the progressive phaseout of restrictions in accordance with para 2(e).

(e) In such consultations, all findings of statistical and other facts presented by the International Monetary Fund relating to foreign exchange, monetary reserves and balance of payments, shall be accepted and conclusions shall be based on the assessment by the Fund of the balance of payments and the external financial situation of the consulting Member.

6 If a Member which is not a member of the International Monetary Fund wishes to apply the provisions of this article, the Ministerial Conference shall establish a review procedure and any other procedures necessary.

Article XIII – Government procurement

1 Articles II, XVI and XVII shall not apply to laws, regulations or requirements governing the procurement by governmental agencies of services purchased for governmental purposes and not with a view to commercial resale or with a view to use in the supply of services for commercial sale.

2 There shall be multilateral negotiations on government procurement in services under this agreement within two years from the date of entry into force of the WTO Agreement.

Article XIV – General exceptions

Subject to the requirement that such measures are not applied in a manner which would constitute a means of arbitrary or unjustifiable discrimination between countries where like conditions prevail, or a disguised restriction on trade in services, nothing in this agreement shall be construed to prevent the adoption or enforcement by any Member of measures:

(a) necessary to protect public morals or to maintain public order;

(b) necessary to protect human, animal or plant life or health;

(c) necessary to secure compliance with laws or regulations which are not inconsistent with the provisions of this agreement including those relating to:

  (i) the prevention of deceptive and fraudulent practices or to deal with the effects or a default on services contracts;

  (ii) the protection of the privacy of individuals in relation to the processing and dissemination of personal data and the protection of confidentiality of individual records and accounts;

  (iii) safety;

(d) inconsistent with Article XVII, provided that the difference in treatment is aimed at ensuring the equitable or effective imposition or collection of direct taxes in respect of services or service suppliers of other Members;

(e) inconsistent with Article II, provided that the difference in treatment is the result of an agreement on the avoidance of double taxation or provisions on the avoidance of double taxation in any other international agreement or arrangement by which the Member is bound.

Article XIV bis – Security exceptions

1 Nothing in this agreement shall be construed:

(a) to require any Member to furnish any information, the disclosure of which it considers contrary to its essential security interests; or

(b) to prevent any Member from taking any action which it considers necessary for the protection of its essential security interests:

  (i) relating to the supply of services as carried our directly or indirectly for the purpose of provisioning a military establishment;

  (ii) relating to fissionable and fusionable materials or the materials from which they are derived;

  (iii) taken in time of war or other emergency in international relations; or

(c) to prevent any Member from taking any action in pursuance of its obligations under the United Nations Charter for the maintenance of international peace and security.

2 The Council for Trade in Services shall be informed to the fullest extent possible of measures taken under paras 1(b) and (c) and of their termination.

Article XV – Subsidies

1 Members recognise that, in certain circumstances, subsidies may have distortive effects on trade in services. Members shall enter into negotiations with a view to developing the necessary multilateral disciplines to avoid such trade-distortive effects.

The negotiations shall also address the appropriateness of countervailing procedures. Such negotiations shall recognise the role of subsidies in relation to the development programmes of developing countries and take into account the needs of Members, particularly developing country Members, for flexibility in this area. For the purpose of such negotiations, Members shall exchange information concerning all subsidies related to trade in services that they provide to their domestic service suppliers.

2   Any Member which considers that it is adversely affected by a subsidy of another Member may request consultations with that Member on such matters. Such requests shall be accorded sympathetic consideration.

PART III – SPECIFIC COMMITMENTS

Article XVI – Market access

1   With respect to market access through the modes of supply identified in Article 1, each member shall accord services and service suppliers of any other Member treatment no less favourable than that provided for under the terms, limitations and conditions agreed and specified in its Schedule.

2   In sectors where market access commitments are undertaken, the measures which a member shall not maintain or adopt either on the basis of a regional subdivision or on the basis of its entire territory, unless otherwise specified in its Schedule, are defined as:

(a)   limitations on the number of service suppliers whether in the form of numerical quotas, monopolies, exclusive service suppliers or the requirements of an economic needs test;

(b)   limitations on the total value of service transactions or assets in the form of numerical quotas or the requirement of an economic needs test;

(c)   limitations on the total number of service operations or on the total quantity of service output expressed in terms at designated numerical units in the form of quotas or the requirement of an economic needs test;

(d)   limitations on the total number of natural persons that may be employed m a particular service sector or that a service supplier may employ and who are necessary for, and directly related to, the supply of a specific service in the form of numerical quotas or the requirement of an economic needs test;

(e)   measures which restrict or require specific types of legal entity or joint venture through which a service supplier may supply a service; and

(f)   limitations on the participation of foreign capital in terms of maximum percentage limit on foreign shareholding or the total value of individual or aggregate foreign investment.

Article XVII – National treatment

1   In the sectors inscribed in its Schedule, and subject to any conditions and qualifications set out therein, each Member shall accord to services and service suppliers of any other Member, in respect of all measures affecting the supply of services, treatment no less favourable than that it accords to its own like services and service suppliers.

2   A Member may meet the requirement of para 1 by according to services and service suppliers of any other Member, either formally identical treatment or formally different treatment to that it accords to its own like services and service suppliers.

3   Formally identical or formally different treatment shall be considered to be less favourable if it modifies the conditions of competition in favour of services or service suppliers of the Member compared to like services or service suppliers of any other Member.

Article XVIII – Additional commitments

Members may negotiate commitments with respect to measures affecting trade in services not subject to scheduling under Articles XVI or XVII, including those regarding qualifications, standards or licensing matters. Such commitments shall be inscribed in a Member's Schedule.

PART IV – PROGRESSIVE LIBERALISATION

Article XIX – Negotiation of specific commitments

1   In pursuance of the objectives of this agreement, Members shall enter into successive rounds of negotiations, beginning not later than five years from the date of entry into force of the WTO Agreement and periodically thereafter, with a view to achieving a progressively higher level of liberalisation. Such negotiations shall be directed to the reduction or elimination of the adverse effects on trade in services of measures as a means of providing effective market access. This process shall take place with a view to promoting the interests of all participants on a mutually advantageous basis and to securing an overall balance of rights and obligations.

2   The process of liberalisation shall take place with due respect for national policy objectives and the level of development of individual Members, both overall and in individual sectors. There shall be appropriate flexibility for individual developing country Members for opening fewer sectors, liberalising fewer types of transactions, progressively extending market access in line with their development situation and, when making access to their markets available to foreign service suppliers, attaching to such access conditions aimed at achieving the objectives referred to in Article IV.

3   For each round, negotiating guidelines and procedures shall be established. For the purposes of establishing such guidelines, the Council for Trade in Services shall carry out an assessment of trade in services in overall terms and on a sectoral basis with reference to the objectives of this agreement, including those set out in para 1 of Article IV. Negotiating guidelines shall establish modalities for the treatment of liberalisation undertaken autonomously by Members since previous negotiations, as well as for the special treatment for least developed country Members under the provisions of para 3 of Article IV.

4   The process of progressive liberalisation shall be advanced in each such round through bilateral, plurilateral or multilateral negotiations directed towards increasing the general level of specific commitments undertaken by Members under this agreement.

Article XX – Schedules of specific c commitments

1   Each Member shall set out in a schedule the specific commitments it undertakes under Part III of this agreement. With respect to sectors where such commitments are undertaken, each Schedule shall specify:

(a) terms, limitations and conditions on market access;

(b) conditions and qualifications on national treatment;

(c) undertakings relating to additional commitments;

(d) where appropriate the time frame for implementation of such commitments; and

(e) the date of entry into force of such commitments.

2 Measures inconsistent with both Articles XVI and XVII shall be inscribed in the column relating to Article XVI. In this case the inscription will be considered to provide a condition or qualification to Article XVII as well.

3 Schedules of specific commitments shall be annexed to this agreement and shall form an integral part thereof.

Article XXI – Modification of Schedules

1 (a) A Member (referred to in this article as the 'modifying Member') may modify or withdraw any commitment in its Schedule, at any time after three years have elapsed from the date on which that commitment entered into force, in accordance with the provisions of this article.

(b) A modifying Member shall notify its intent to modify or withdraw a commitment pursuant to this article to the Council for Trade in Services no later than three months before the intended date of implementation of the modification or withdrawal.

2 (a) At the request of any Member the benefits of which under this agreement may be affected (referred to in this article as an 'affected Member') by a proposed modification or withdrawal notified under sub-para 1(b) the modifying Member shall enter into negotiations with a view to reaching agreement on any necessary compensatory adjustment. In such negotiations and agreement, the Members concerned shall endeavour to maintain a general level of mutually advantageous commitments not less favourable to trade than that provided for in Schedules of specific commitments prior to such negotiations.

(b) Compensatory adjustments shall be made on a most-favoured-nation basis.

3 (a) If agreement is not reached between the modifying Member and any affected Member before the end of the period provided for negotiations such affected Member may refer the matter to arbitration. Any affected Member that wishes to enforce a right that it may have to compensation must participate in the arbitration.

(b) If no affected Member has requested arbitration, the modifying Member shall be free to implement the proposed modification or withdrawal.

4 (a) The modifying Member may not modify or withdraw its commitment until it has made compensatory adjustments in conformity with the findings of the arbitration.

(b) If the modifying Member implements its proposed modification or withdrawal and does not comply with the findings of the arbitration, any affected Member that participated in the arbitration may modify or withdraw substantially equivalent benefits in conformity with those findings. Notwithstanding Article II, such a modification or withdrawal may be implemented solely with respect to the modifying Member.

5 The Council for Trade in Services shall establish procedures for rectification or modification of Schedules. Any Member which has modified or withdrawn

scheduled commitments under this article shall modify its Schedule according to such procedures.

PART V – INSTITUTIONAL PROVISIONS

Article XXII – Consultation

1   Each Member shall accord sympathetic consideration to, and shall afford adequate opportunity for, consultation regarding such representations as may be made by any other Member with respect to any matter affecting the operation of this agreement. The Dispute Settlement Understanding (DSU) shall apply to such consultations.

2   The Council for Trade in Services or the Dispute Settlement Body (DSB) may, at the request of a Member, consult with any Member or Members in respect of any matter for which it has not been possible to find a satisfactory solution through consultation under para 1.

3   A Member may not invoke Article XVII, either under this article or Article XXIII, with respect to a measure of another Member that falls within the scope of an international agreement between them relating to the avoidance of double taxation. In case of disagreement between Members as to whether a measure falls within the scope of such an agreement between them, it shall be open to either Member to bring this matter before the council for Trade in Services. The Council shall refer the matter to arbitration. The decision of the arbitrator shall be final and binding on the Members.

With respect to agreements on the avoidance of double taxation which exist on the date of entry into force of the WTO Agreement, such a matter may be brought before the Council for Trade in services only with the consent of both parties to such an agreement.

Article XXIII – Dispute settlement and enforcement

1   If any Member should consider that any other Member fails to carry out its obligations or specific commitments under this agreement, it may with a view to reaching a mutually satisfactory resolution of the matter have recourse to the DSU.

2   If the DSB considers that the circumstances are serious enough to justify such action, it may authorise a Member or Members to suspend the application to any other Member or Members of obligations and specific commitments in accordance with Article 22 of the DSU.

3   If any Member considers that any benefit it could reasonably have expected to accrue to it under a specific commitment of another Member under Part III of this agreement is being nullified or impaired as a result of the application of any measure which does not conflict with the provisions of this agreement, it may have recourse to the DSU. If the measure is determined by the DSB to have nullified or impaired such a benefit, the Member affected shall be entitled to a mutually satisfactory adjustment on the basis of para 2 of Article XXI, which may include the modification or withdrawal of the measure. In the event an agreement cannot be reached between the Members concerned, Article 22 of the DSU shall apply.

Article XXIV – Council for trade in services

1   The Council for Trade in Services shall carry out such functions as may be assigned to it to facilitate the operation of this agreement and further its objectives. The

Council may establish such subsidiary bodies as it considers appropriate for the effective discharge of its functions.

2   The Council and, unless the Council decides otherwise, its subsidiary bodies shall be open to participation by representatives of all Members.

3   The Chairman of the Council shall be elected by the Members.

PART VI – FINAL PROVISIONS

Article XXVII – Denial of benefits

A Member may deny the benefits of this agreement:

(a) to the supply of a service, if it establishes that the service is supplied from or in the territory of a non-Member or of a Member to which the denying Member does not apply the WTO Agreement;

(b) in the case of the supply of a maritime transport service, if it establishes that the service is supplied:

   (i) by a vessel registered under the laws of a non-Member or of a Member to which the denying Member does not apply the WTO Agreement; and

   (ii) by a person which operates and/or uses the vessel in whole or in part but which is of a non-Member or of a Member to which the denying Member does not apply the WTO Agreement;

(c) to a service supplier that is a juridical person, if it establishes that it is not a service supplier of another Member, or that it is a service supplier of a Member to which the denying Member does not apply the WTO Agreement.

Article XXVIII – Definitions

For the purpose of this agreement:

(a) 'measure' means any measure by a Member, whether in the form of a law regulation, rule, procedure, decision, administrative action, or any other form;

(b) 'supply of a service' includes the production, distribution, marketing, sale and delivery of a service;

(c) 'measures by Members affecting trade in services' include measures in respect of:

   (i) the purchase, payment or use of a service;

   (ii) the access to and use of, in connection with the supply of a service, services which are required by those Members to be offered to the public generally;

   (iii) the presence, including commercial presence, of persons of a Member for the supply of a service in the territory of another Member;

(d) 'commercial presence' means any type of business or professional establishment, including through:

   (i) the constitution, acquisition or maintenance of a juridical person; or

   (ii) the creation or maintenance of a branch or a representative office, within the territory of a Member for the purpose of supplying a service;

(e) 'sector' of a service means:

   (i) with reference to a specific commitment, one or more, or all, sub-sectors of that service, as specified in a Member's Schedule;

(ii) otherwise, the whole of that service sector, including all of its sub-sectors;

(f) 'service of another Member' means a service which is supplied:

(i) from or in the territory of that other Member, or in the case of maritime transport, by a vessel registered under the laws of that other Member, or by a person of that other Member which supplies the service through the operation of a vessel and/or its use in whole or in part; or

(ii) in the case of the supply of a service through commercial presence or through the presence of natural persons, by a service supplier of that other Member;

(g) 'service supplier' means any person that supplies a service;

(h) 'monopoly supplier of a service' means any person, public or private, which in the relevant market of the territory of a Member is authorised or established formally or in effect by that Member as the sole supplier of that service;

(i) 'service consumer' means any person that receives or uses a service;

(j) 'person' means either a natural person or a juridical person;

(k) 'natural person of another Member' means a natural person who resides in the territory of that other Member or any other Member, and who under the law of that other Member:

(i) is a national of that other Member; or

(ii) has the right of permanent residence in that other Member, in the case of a Member which:

1 does not have nationals; or

2 accords substantially the same treatment to its permanent residents as it does to its nationals in respect of measures affecting trade in services, as notified in its acceptance of or accession to the WTO Agreement, provided that no Member is obligated to accord to such permanent residents treatment more favourable than would be accorded by that other member to such permanent residents. Such notification shall include the assurance to assume, with respect to those permanent residents, in accordance with its laws and regulations, the same responsibilities that other Member bears with respect to its nationals;

(l) 'juridical person' means any legal entity duly constituted or otherwise organised under applicable law, whether for profit or otherwise, and whether privately-owned or governmentally-owned, including any corporation, trust, partnership, joint venture, sole proprietorship or association;

(m) 'juridical person of another Member' means a juridical person which is either:

(i) constituted or otherwise organised under the law of that other Member, and is engaged in substantive business operations in the territory of that Member or any other Member; or

(ii) in the case of the supply of a service through commercial presence, owned or controlled by:

1 natural persons of that Member; or

2 juridical persons of that other Member identified under sub-para (i);

(n) a juridical person is:

    (i) 'owned' by persons of a Member if more than 50% of the equity interest in its beneficially owned by persons of that Member;

    (ii) 'controlled' by persons of a Member if such persons have the power to name a majority of its directors or otherwise to legally direct its actions;

    (iii) 'affiliated' with another person when it controls or is controlled by that other person; or when it and the other person are both controlled by the same person;

(o) 'direct taxes' comprise all taxes on total income, on total capital or on elements of income or of capital, including taxes on gains from the alienation of property, taxes on estates, inheritances and gifts, and taxes on the total amounts of wages or salaries paid by enterprises, as well as taxes on capital appreciation.

Article XXIX – Annexes

The Annexes to this agreement are an integral part of this agreement.

Annex on Article II exemptions

Scope

1   This Annex specifies the conditions under which a Member, at the entry into force of this agreement, is exempted from its obligations under para 1 of Article II.

2   Any new exemptions applied for after the date of entry into force of the WTO Agreement shall be dealt with under para 3 of Article IX of that agreement.

Review

3   The Council for Trade in Services shall review all exemptions granted for a period of more than five years. The first such review shall take place no more than five years after the entry into force of the WTO Agreement.

4   The Council for Trade in Services in a review shall:

    (a) examine whether the conditions which created the need for the exemption still prevail; and

    (b) determine the date of any further review.

Termination

5   The exemption of a Member from its obligations under para 1 of Article II of the agreement with respect to a particular measure terminates on the date provided for in the exemption.

6   In principle, such exemptions should not exceed a period of 10 years. In any event, they shall be subject to negotiation in subsequent trade liberalising rounds.

7   A Member shall notify the Council for Trade in Services at the termination of the exemption period that the inconsistent measure has been brought into conformity with para 1 of Article II of the agreement.

Lists of Article II exemptions

[The agreed lists of exemptions under para 2 of Article II will be annexed here in the treaty copy of the WTO Agreement.]

Annex on movement of natural persons supplying services under the agreement

1   This Annex applies to measures affecting natural persons who are service suppliers of a Member, and natural person of a Member who are employed by a service supplier of a Member, in respect of the supply of a service.

2   The agreement shall not apply to measures affecting natural persons seeking access to the employment market of a Member, nor shall it apply to measures regarding citizenship, residence or employment on a permanent basis.

3   In accordance with Parts III and IV of the agreement, Members may negotiate specific commitments applying to the movement of all categories of natural persons supplying services under the agreement. Natural persons covered by a specific commitment shall be allowed to supply the service in accordance with the terms of that commitment.

4   The agreement shall not prevent a Member from applying measures to regulate the entry of natural persons into, or their temporary stay in, its territory, including those measures necessary to protect the integrity of, and to ensure the orderly movement of natural persons across its borders, provided that such measures are not applied in such a manner as to nullify or impair the benefits accruing to any Member under the terms of a specific commitment.

ANTI-DUMPING AND COUNTERVAILING LAWS IN THE UNITED STATES, AUSTRALIA AND NEW ZEALAND

INTRODUCTION

International anti-dumping and countervailing procedures provide a remedy against countries which sell their exports at less than their fair value with the result that material injury is caused to the importing country's domestic industry.

Obtaining a good understanding of the way in which anti-dumping and countervailing actions are taken by governments is dependent on developing a working knowledge of a number of topics. These are:

(a) the international agreements which form the basis for national procedures;

(b) the national legislation which implements those agreements;

(c) the government agencies which put the legislation into practice; and

(d) the judicial review of decisions of those agencies.

In this chapter, the GATT agreements on dumping and countervailing are examined. Their full texts are attached as appendices. The relevant national legislation is introduced briefly – much of it is extremely complex – and comment is made on the various national agencies which are given by their governments the task of administering the law. The appeals systems are identified and a short commentary touches on the way in which the courts deal with appeals from those agencies.

If it is true that the anti-dumping and countervailing statutes are 'the most technically complex and mystifying part of US trade law'[1] or a 'tangled and confusing subject'[2] the same can probably be said of their counterparts in Australia and, to a lesser degree, New Zealand.

DEFINITIONS

Anti-dumping

It is appropriate to define dumping in the words of the GATT Agreement following the Uruguay Round of trade talks in 1994. Article 2.1 of this agreement[3] defines 'dumping' in the following way:

> [A] product is considered as being dumped, ie introduced into the commerce of another country at less than its normal value, if the export price of the product exported from one

---

1   Low, P, *Trading Free*, 1993, p 80, New York: Twentieth Century Fund Press.

2   US Congressional Budget Office Memorandum, 'A Review of US Anti-Dumping and Countervailing Duty Law and Policy', May 1994, p 1.

3   The full title of the anti-dumping agreement is the Agreement on the Implementation of Article VI of GATT 1994.

country to another is less than the comparable price, in the ordinary course of trade, for the like product when destined for consumption in the exporting country.

The details of 'normal value', 'export price' product, etc will be developed later in this chapter.

Countervailing

The GATT 1994 Agreement on Subsidies and Countervailing Measures provides the following definition:

> The term countervailing duty shall be understood to mean a special duty levied for the purpose of offsetting any subsidy bestowed directly or indirectly upon the manufacture, production or export of any merchandise as provided for in para 3 of Article VI of GATT 1994.[4]

The definitions of 'subsidy', 'prohibited subsidies', 'actionable subsidies and 'non-actionable subsidies' are critical to the understanding of this aspect of international and national law. All are contained in the Agreement on Subsidies and Countervailing Measures[5] which, like the Anti-Dumping Agreement, must be read in conjunction with Article VI of GATT 1994. Countervailing action may also be dependent on the Agreement on Agriculture – see the Summary of the GATT 1994 Agreement on Agriculture at the end of this chapter.

Prerequisites for imposition of anti-dumping or countervailing duties

It can be seen from the definitions above that the existence of dumping or subsidy of goods requires a very careful analysis – either of the difference between the 'export price' and the 'normal price' (the dumping margin) or of the existence of an 'actionable subsidy'.

Even if these are found by national authorities to show that the goods in question have been dumped or subsidised, it must also be established that they are responsible for 'material injury to a domestic industry, threat of material injury to a domestic industry or material retardation of the establishment of such an industry'.[6]

An investigation into an industry allegation of dumping or countervailable subsidy must thus establish the existence of the dumping margin or actionable subsidy and the material injury or threat to the domestic industry. Without proof of both, anti-dumping or countervailing duties as appropriate cannot be imposed.

---

4   Footnote 36 to the Agreement on Subsidies and Countervailable Measures.
5   Articles 1, 3, 5–6 and 8 respectively.
6   Footnote 9 to Article 3 of the Anti-Dumping Agreement.

All national legislation on the topic therefore devotes considerable space to the methods to be used for determining 'export price',[7] 'normal value'[8] and 'material injury'.[9]

Legislation on both anti-dumping and countervailing duties was in place prior to GATT 1994 but has now been amended in the laws of the US, Australia and New Zealand. A short glimpse into the history of these legal provisions will set the scene for an examination of the new legislation in each country.

A BACKGROUND TO THE CURRENT INTERNATIONAL ANTI-DUMPING AND COUNTERVAILING AGREEMENTS

An anti-dumping agreement first made its appearance in Article VI of the General Agreement on Tariffs and Trade 1947 having been proposed by the USA, and based on that country's own Emergency Tariff Act of 1921.[10] Article VI was clarified and upgraded by the GATT Anti-Dumping Agreement of 1967 during the Kennedy Round of multinational negotiations[11] which lasted from 1964–67.

The agreement was again replaced after the Tokyo Round of negotiations (which began in 1973 and concluded in 1979) when it was joined by the first GATT Agreement relating to Subsidies and Countervailing Measures.[12]

The Uruguay Round of GATT negotiations commenced at Punta del Este in September 1986 and was completed in December 1993. It was signed by more than 100 countries at Marrakesh in Morocco in April 1994.[13] Among its achievements were the current Agreements on anti-dumping and countervailing.

The full texts of these agreements are included as Appendices.

A BRIEF HISTORY OF NATIONAL ANTI-DUMPING AND COUNTERVAILING LAWS

United States of America

Initial legislation on countervailing measures in the USA were contained in the Tariff Act of 1897 (the Dingley Act). These provisions were incorporated in s 303 of the Tariff Act of 1930 and remained in force until replaced by the Trade Agreements Act of 1979.

---

7   Section 269TAB of the Customs Act 1901 (Australia).

8   Section 269TAC of the Customs Act 1901 (Australia).

9   Section 269TAE of the Customs Act 1901 (Australia).

10 US International Trade Commission (USITC) Report, 'The Economic Effects of Anti-Dumping and Countervailing Duty Orders and Suspension Agreements', 30 June 1995, Chapter 2.

11 *Ibid.*

12 *Ibid.*

13 Australian Customs Service, 'World Trade Organisation – Uruguay Round – Anti-Dumping and Countervailing – An Explanatory Paper', September 1994.

Anti-dumping provisions made their first appearance in the Anti-Dumping Act 1921, which was part of the Emergency Tariffs Act of the same year.[14] The Anti-Dumping Act was allegedly modelled on Canadian laws which were current then, and required Customs officers to inspect all imports for evidence of dumping.[15] As with the countervailing provisions, the Trade Agreements Act of 1979 implemented the Tokyo round repealing the 1921 act and bringing the new Anti-Dumping Agreement into force as Title VII of the Tariff Act 1930.

Amendments were made to the anti-dumping law in 1988 and 1990 with a major update through the provisions of the Uruguay Round Agreements Act[16] which was signed by President Clinton on 8 December 1994.[17] Title II of this Act makes substantial amendments to the anti-dumping provisions of the Tariff Act 1930 which continues to be the vehicle for these provisions.

Australia

Initial provisions for the implementation of anti-dumping and countervailing measures were contained in the Customs Act 1901 (all Australian legislation involved is brought down by the Commonwealth Parliament).

As a consequence of the ministerial agreement in 1973 during the Tokyo Round of GATT negotiations, the Customs Tariff (Anti-dumping) Act 1975, known as the Anti-Dumping Act 1988,[18] was introduced to impose appropriate duties. This was followed in 1988 by the Anti-Dumping Authority Act which established the Authority to deal with the anti-dumping and countervailing measures already in existence.[19]

All three Acts were substantially amended by the Customs Legislation (World Trade Organisation Amendments) Act 1994 (Cth) and the Customs Tariff (Anti-dumping) (World Trade Organisation Amendments) Act 1994 which implemented the new agreements introduced by the GATT Uruguay Round.

New Zealand

Provisions to implement dumping and countervailing procedures, appropriate duties were introduced as Part VA into the Customs Act 1966 by an amendment to that Act in 1983. It received a major update in 1987 and was repealed by the enactment of the Dumping and Countervailing Duties Act 1988[20] in which its amended version is now found. This act came into force in December 1988 and is now the sole piece of

---

14   USITC Report, above, fn 10.

15   *Ibid.*

16   Pub L no 103–465, 1994.

17   Harrison, D and Ott, J, 'Trade Regulation' (3 April 1995) 17 *The National Law Journal* 31 at p B5 (*sic*).

18   See s 3 of the Anti-Dumping Authority Act 1988.

19   No 72 of 1988 – long title 'An Act to establish an Anti-Dumping Authority and for related purposes'.

20   Act no 158 of 1988 – long title 'An Act to provide for the imposition of dumping and countervailing duties'.

legislation dealing with this topic. The legislation was comprehensively updated in late 1994 to reflect the GATT 1994 agreements.

LOCALISED TRADE AGREEMENTS

A number of trade blocs around the world have formed trade agreements covering their members. In some cases these reduce anti-dumping and countervailing liabilities between those members, and in some cases the GATT agreements remain in force. In relation to the three nations which are the subject of the present study, two such agreements are in place.

The North American Free Trade Association

The North American Free Trade Association (NAFTA) reduces tariff barriers between its member States – the US, Mexico and Canada. Chile's future membership was announced at the Western hemisphere summit in Miami in January 1995[21] – but has no provision for the removal of anti-dumping or countervailing provisions from trade with its members as does ANZCERTA. It is, however, likely that this may change in the near future, reflecting the approach of the European Union, when NAFTA trade and tariff barriers are reviewed.

NAFTA does provide a special line of appeal to a bi-national committee in lieu of the usual judicial review of a decision to impose anti-dumping or countervailing duties.[22]

Australia–New Zealand CER Trade Agreement

The Agreement on Closer Economic Relations between Australia and New Zealand has brought about mutual exemptions from anti-dumping duties as shown in the table below.

Australian legislation	*New Zealand legislation*
Customs Act 1901 (Cth) s 269TAAA	Dumping and Countervailing Duties Act 1988 ss 3B and 10(10)
Customs Tariff (Anti-dumping) Act 1975 (Cth) ss 8 and 9	
Anti-Dumping Authority Act 1988 s 3A	

Note: The Australian and the New Zealand Acts grant exemptions for dumping but not for countervailing duties. It is intended under ANZCERTA that countervailing duties could still be levied on subsidised goods from the other country[23] and indeed this has

---

21 A much wider association – the Free Trade Area of the Americas (FTAA) – is currently proposed to be in operation by 2005 – USA Information Agency.

22 NAFTA Article 1904.

23 NZ Ministry of Commerce – 'Trade Remedies Group – Dumping and Countervailing Guide' (undated), p 3.

been done – canned cat food, alloy wheels and aluminium foil from Australia have all been the subject of investigations in New Zealand.[24]

AUTHORITIES INVOLVED IN THE ADMINISTRATION OF ANTI-DUMPING AND COUNTERVAILING MEASURES

This paragraph introduces the various national authorities involved in anti-dumping and countervailing actions. Their specific statutory responsibilities will be identified more specifically later in this chapter when the relevant national legislation is reviewed.

United States of America

Department of Commerce

Functions include approval of export licence applications and promoting export of US made products. It includes the International Trade Administration, which deals with anti-dumping and subsidy matters. The US Foreign and Commercial Service employs commercial officers in foreign countries to promote US trade and gather commercial intelligence.[25]

The Tariff Act of 1930 gives authority to impose anti-dumping and countervailing orders to the Secretary, Department of Commerce. The latter has delegated this authority to the Under Secretary for International Trade, who is head of the International Trade Administration.[26]

US Treasury Department

Administers the US customs service, which classifies and values imports and enforces US export trade laws and collects duties imposed.[27]

US Trade Representative

A cabinet level post which carries out all bilateral and multinational trade agreements on behalf of the USA. USTR is the principal adviser on trade matters to the President.[28]

International Trade Commission

An independent agency comprising six commissioners appointed by the president from both political parties to investigate, along with the International Trade Administration, matters of unfair trade practices.[29] The commission's powers and duties in the area of anti-dumping and countervailing are provided for by the Tariff Act of 1930 (19 US 1654).

---

24 NZ Trade Remedies Group – Reports issued under the Dumping and Countervailing Duties Act 1988 – Internet 1995.

25 *Ibid*, p 235.

26 Otterness, P, McFaul, F and Cutshaw, K, 'The ABCs of American Trade Laws on Foreign Dumping and Subsidies' (8 December 1986) *Business America.*

27 *Ibid.*

28 *Ibid.*

29 *Ibid.*

Court of International Trade

Most anti-dumping and countervailing decisions of the US International Trade Commission (USITC) and Department of Commerce can be appealed to the US Court of International Trade.[30]

This court is the successor to the US Customs Court and was created by the Customs Courts Act of 1980 (28 USC 251) with the powers of a district court. It has a nine member bench with exclusive jurisdiction over all civil actions against the US arising from federal laws governing import transactions.[31]

Appeals

Appeals from the Court of International Court of Trade may be taken to the US Court of Appeals for the Federal Circuit and, in rare cases, to the Supreme Court.[32]

For certain cases involving Canadian or Mexican imports, appeal may be to a bi-national panel established under the terms of the North American Free Trade Association.[33]

Australia

The Minister responsible

The Australian Federal Minister responsible, and referred to in all the three acts mentioned above, is the Minister for Small Business, Construction and Customs. Responsible to this minister is the Australian Customs Service and the Anti-Dumping Authority (ADA).

The Customs Service

The Customs Service is responsible for determining whether a *prima facie* case of dumping or subsidy exists and for imposing provisional duties. Their positive findings are referred to the ADA. In addition to this role, the Customs Service is responsible for the collection of all duties levied under these statutes.

The Anti-Dumping Authority

This authority conducts investigations into positive preliminary findings by Customs, reviews negative preliminary findings and makes final determinations for action as appropriate by the Minister.

Appeals

Decisions of Customs or the ADA can be appealed under the Judicial Decisions (Administrative Review) Act 1977 to the Federal Court. An appeal from that court will

---

30 1995 Trade Policy Agenda and 1994 Annual Report of the President of the United States on the Trade Agreements Program, p 101.

31 US Government Manual 1994–95, p 76.

32 See, for example, *Zenith Radio Corp v United States*, 98 s Ct 2441, 2444, 57 L Ed 2d 337 (1978).

33 See fn 22 above.

be heard by the full court (three judges) of the Federal Court. A final appeal is possible to the High Court by leave, although this has never yet occurred.

New Zealand

The Minister responsible

The responsible Minister is the Minister of Commerce, who is responsible for final determinations of dumping or subsidy and the imposition of duties.

The Secretary of Commerce

The Secretary of Commerce is responsible for the initiation and conduct of all investigations following a application by or on behalf of New Zealand Producers, and for notifying foreign governments accordingly.

The Trade Remedies Group

The Ministry of Commerce contains a section known as the Trade Remedies Group which acts, *inter alia*, in an advisory role for members of the public submitting such applications and as the recipient for completed applications.[34]

The Customs Department

The Customs Department, which is a separate department from the Ministry of Commerce, is responsible for the collection of all such duties.

Appeals

Appeals from administrative decisions of the Secretary or Ministry of Commerce can be appealed as required by Article 13 of the Anti-Dumping Agreement.

Judicial Review Procedures are provided for in Part 1 of the Judicature Act 1908.[35] Review is conducted by the High Court with appeals to the Court of Appeal. They have been used more sparingly than in the US or Australia.[36]

Investigation procedures

The procedures used to handle a petition, investigations and determinations are similar in the US, Australia and New Zealand but differ principally in that the steps in the procedures are dealt with by different authorities. In the US, Commerce and the

---

34   NZ Ministry of Commerce, 'Trade Remedies Information Leaflet', 1995, p 4.

35   Part 1 is entitled 'Single procedure for the judicial review of the exercise of, or failure to exercise a statutory power'.

36   On five occasions only as at January 1996. The other four citations are *Carlton United Breweries Ltd v Minister for Customs* (C.P25/86), *New Zealand Cereal Foods Ltd v Minister for Customs* (C.P423/87), *Kerry New Zealand Ltd v Comptroller of Customs* (C.P1614/88) and a fourth involving transformers not yet finalised.

USITC operate in parallel in working towards preliminary determinations. In Australia and in New Zealand one authority deals with initial investigations and another, at a later stage, with final determinations.

The following summary may be helpful in understanding how those authorities react to their statutory responsibilities.

Procedure	US	Australia	New Zealand
Receipt of industry petition	May be filed simultaneously with Commerce and USITC	Customs	Secretary, Dept of Commerce Trade Remedies Group
Industry poll if needed	Commerce	Customs	Secretary, Dept of Commerce
Notification of foreign governments	Commerce	Customs	Secretary, Dept of Commerce
Initiation of investigation	Commerce	Customs	Secretary, Dept of Commerce
Preliminary determination – dumping or subsidy	Commerce	Customs	No preliminary determinations Secretary, Dept of Commerce passes findings on dumping, subsidy and injury to Minister of Commerce for determination
Preliminary determination – material injury	USITC	Customs	
Imposition of provisional measures if preliminary finding affirmative	Decision: Commerce Implementing: Customs	Customs	Decision: Minister of Commerce Implementing: Customs
Final determination	Dumping or subsidy: Commerce Injury: USITC Final decision: Commerce	Anti-dumping Authority: approval by Minister	Minister of Commerce
Assessment of duties and retrospectivity if final determination affirmative	Commerce	Anti-Dumping Authority	Minister of Commerce

THE GATT 1994 ANTI-DUMPING AGREEMENT

The following commentary summarises the requirements of the Agreement on Implementation of Article VI of the General Agreement on Tariffs and Trade 1994, often referred to as the anti-dumping agreement. The methods by which each country implements these requirements will be discussed later in this chapter.

The full text of this agreement is reproduced in this book.

Who can apply for the imposition of anti-dumping duties?

To be investigated an application must be made 'by or on behalf of the domestic industry' (Article 5.1), being 'domestic producers whose collective output constitutes more than 50% of the total production of the like product produced by that portion of the domestic industry' which supports or opposes the application.

An investigation is precluded where those producers supporting the application 'account for less than 25% of total production of the like product produced by the domestic industry' (Article 5.4).

What constitutes the domestic industry?

The domestic industry is 'the domestic producers as a whole of the like products or to those of them whose collective output constitutes a major proportion of the total domestic production of those products'. This excludes producers who are controlled by the exporters or importers.

What must applicants prove?

They must prove 'material injury to (the) domestic industry, threat of material injury to (the) domestic industry or material retardation of the establishment of such an industry' (footnote 9 to the GATT Agreement).

'A determination of injury ... shall be based on positive evidence of the volume of dumped imports, the effect of those imports on prices in the domestic market for like products and the consequent impact on domestic producers' (Article 3.1).

In any investigation 'the demonstration of a causal relationship between the dumped imports and the injury to the domestic industry shall be based on an examination of all relevant evidence before the authorities' (Article 3.5).

Do all parties in an investigation receive all information?

'All interested parties in an anti-dumping investigation shall be given notice of the information which the authorities require and ample opportunity to present in writing all evidence which they consider relevant in respect of the investigation in question' (Article 6.1). Interested parties include exporters and importers of the product, their trade associations, the government of the exporter and producers of like products in the importing country (Article 6.11).

Evidence presented in writing by one party must be made available to all other parties – subject to confidentiality requirements (Article 6.1.2). Where a party supplies information in confidence they will be required to provide non-confidential summaries (Article 6.5.1).

All parties involved 'shall have a full opportunity for the defence of their interests'.

Are authorities of an applicant country able to carry out investigations in another country?

Authorities may carry out investigations in another country provided they obtain the agreement of the firms concerned and notify the relevant government in question and the government does not object (Article 6.7 and Annex 1).

What if the effect of the dumped imports is very small?

If the volume of the dumped imports is less than 3% of the imports of the like products or, where there are several countries dumping, the total of imports from them is less than 7% of imports of like products, an application must be rejected and any investigation terminated immediately (Article 5.8).

The same principle applies where the dumping margin is less than 2% of the export price (see below).

What if the exporter supplies the challenged goods to the importing country via a third country?

The prices used for comparison will normally be the price for which the goods are sold by the original exporter and the normal price for them in that exporter's country (Article 2.5).

Is an investigation made public?

A detailed public notice advising of the investigation must be made (Article 12.1.1). Provisional anti-dumping measures must not be taken unless such notice has issued (Article 7.1(i)).

Public notices must also be made of the conclusion or suspension of an investigation and of preliminary and final determinations (Articles 12.2.1 and 12.2.2).

Can a dumping exporter avoid an investigation?

Once a 'preliminary affirmative determination of dumping and injury' has been made (Article 8.2), an exporter can make a voluntary undertaking to revise its prices which will eliminate the injury. If this occurs, proceedings will cease (Article 8.1).

What is the time scale for an investigation?

Exporters required to provide information must be given at least 30 days to respond (Article 6.1).

Investigations must be concluded within 18 months, and except in special circumstances, within one year (Article 5.10).

How is an anti-dumping duty calculated?

The duty must not exceed a 'margin of dumping' (Article 9.3), which will be calculated by comparing the 'weighted average normal value (of domestic sales in the country of export) with a weighted average of prices of all comparable export transactions or by a comparison of normal value and export price on a transaction-to-transaction basis' (Article 2.4.2).

A fair comparison must be made between export price and normal value, usually at ex-factory level and in respect of sales made as nearly as possible at the same time (Article 2.4).

Can a determination of dumping be appealed?

An independent national tribunal to review administrative action relating to determinations of dumping is required by Article 13.

Can a third country seek anti-dumping action against an exporter?

If the domestic industry of a country other than the importer of products is injured by dumped imports, the authorities of that country may apply to the importer's country for anti-dumping action against the dumping exporter (Articles 14.1 and 2). The decision as to whether to take such action rests with the importing country (Article 14.4).

Are developing countries given special consideration?

Developed countries must explore 'possibilities of constructive remedies' before applying anti-dumping measures where these would 'affect the essential interests of developing countries' (Article 15).

Are any GATT authorities involved with dumping issues?

A Committee on Anti-Dumping Practices is established by Article 15, and a Dispute Settlement Body by Article 16.

THE GATT 1994 AGREEMENT ON SUBSIDIES AND COUNTERVAILING MEASURES

In the three countries in question similar procedures are followed by the same authorities for countervailing measures as those for anti-dumping procedures. Many of the criteria involved in establishing subsidies and the right to levy countervailing duties are similar to, and indeed are phrased in similar terms to, those for dumping.

For this reason, the student of these topics may find it easier to examine the Agreement on Subsidies and Countervailing Measures before studying the way in which each country implements the two agreements.

It must be noted that this agreement cannot stand alone. It must be matched with the GATT Agreement on Agriculture. The reason for this is found in Article 10 of the former, which states that 'Countervailing duties may only be imposed ... in accordance with ... this agreement and the Agreement on Agriculture'. A short description of the latter and its connection with the former is published as an Appendix to this chapter.

The full text of the Countervailing Agreement is reprinted in this book.

What does the Countervailing Agreement permit?

It allows member nations to take direct action, in the form of levying duties and other measures, against other members which provide prohibited or specific subsidies on products for export which cause adverse effects on the first nation's domestic industry (Articles 5 and 6).

What are specific and prohibited subsidies?

A subsidy is a financial contribution by a government of a type defined in Article 1. It is a specific subsidy if it applies explicitly to certain enterprises (Article 2). It is a prohibited subsidy if it is contingent upon export performance or upon the use of domestic over imported goods (Article 3).

An illustrative list of actionable subsidies is contained in Annex 1 to the agreement .

What can countries do about such subsidised imports?

First, the offended country may request consultations with the subsidising country which must 'enter into such consultations as quickly as possible' (Articles 4.3 and 7.3).

The matter may be referred to a Dispute Settlement Body (Articles 4.4 and 7.4 whose panel may refer the matter to the Permanent Group of Experts (Articles 4.5 and 24.3). The panel will make a recommendation which, unless appealed (Articles 4.9 and 7.7), will allow the injured country to take countervailing action after a certain time (Articles 4.10 and 7.10).

What subsidies are non-actionable?

Subsidies are non-actionable if they are non-specific and fall into a number of categories listed in Article 8.2ff. Such subsidies must be notified to the Committee on Subsidies and Countervailing Measures (Article 24.1) by 30 June annually.

What restrictions are placed on the imposition of countervailing measures?

They may only be imposed in accordance with investigations conducted under this agreement and the Agreement on Agriculture.

What must an application show?

It must supply evidence of (a) an actionable subsidy, (b) injury to the domestic industry, and (c) a causal link between the two (Article 11.2).

Who can apply for an investigation?

Applications must 'be made by or on behalf of the domestic industry' (Article 16.1), namely by producers of like products who collectively account for 50% of the producers supporting or opposing the application, but who must produce at least 25% of domestic production (Article 11.4 – *cf* Anti-Dumping Agreement, Article 5.4).

What if the subsidy or injury is negligible?

Any investigation must be terminated immediately if the injury is *de minimis*, namely where the subsidy is less than 1% *ad valorem* (Article 11.9 – *cf* Anti-Dumping Agreement, Article 5.8).

How is evidence collected and disseminated?

Questionnaires, with a 30 day answer period, are used and all interested parties shall receive all information other than confidential information, of which non-confidential summaries will be required (Articles 12.1.1, 12.1.2 and 12.4.1 – *cf* Anti-Dumping Agreement, Articles 6.1.1, 6.1.2 and 6.5.1).

Authorities may carry out investigations in another country with notice to that country's authorities (Article 12.6 – *cf* Anti-Dumping Agreement, Article 6.7). See also Annex VI for 'on-the-spot' investigations.

How are subsidies calculated?

Methods of calculating subsidies must be provided for in national legislation and be consistent with Article 14.

How is injury determined?

A determination of injury for the purpose of countervailing measures must 'be based on positive evidence and involve an objective examination of both (a) the volume of the subsidised imports and the effect of subsidised imports on the domestic market for like products and (b) the consequent impact of these products on the domestic producers of such products (Article 15.1). The article contains further detailed criteria.

When can countervailing measures be taken?

Countervailing measures can be taken after an investigation has been properly initiated, public notice to that effect has been given, a preliminary affirmative determination has been made and the authorities consider preliminary measures to be justified. (Article 17.1).

The preliminary measures must not be applied sooner than 60 days from the start of the investigation (Article 17.3).

After a final determination has been made that subsidised exports are causing injury, a countervailing duty no greater than the amount of the subsidy may be imposed (Articles 19.1 and 19.4).

Can subsidised exporters avoid the imposition of duties?

Subsidised exporters can avoid the imposition of duties if satisfactory voluntary undertakings are received from the exporting country, such as removal of the subsidy or revision of export prices to reduce injury (Article 18.1).

How long do countervailing measures remain in force?

No longer than is necessary to counteract injurious subsidisation (Article 21.1) and no longer than five years unless a duly substantiated request from the domestic industry shows that expiry of the duty would lead to recurrence of the subsidy and injury (Article 21.3 – *cf* Anti-Dumping Agreement, Article 11).

What public notice of investigations and duty is required?

Public notice is required giving relevant details (Article 22.2) of the initiation, conclusion or suspension of an investigation, preliminary and final determinations, undertakings accepted and the termination of any countervailing duty (Articles 22.3 and 22.5 – *cf* Anti-Dumping Agreement, Article 12).

Can these decisions be reviewed or appealed?

Independent judicial, arbitral or administrative review tribunals must be maintained by countries the legislation of which provides for countervailing measures (Article 23 – *cf* Anti-Dumping Agreement, Article 13).

Note also the dispute resolution provisions in Articles XXII and XXIII of GATT.

Are any countries exempt from these subsidy provisions?

Developing countries are exempt from many of these provisions as defined in this article and Annex VII (Article 27).

Are there any other guidelines for countervailing provisions?

Calculation of *ad valorem* subsidisation (Annex IV), information concerning serious prejudice (Annex V) and procedures for 'on-the-spot' investigations are contained in annexes to the agreement .

NATIONAL LEGISLATION IMPLEMENTING THE GATT ANTI-DUMPING AGREEMENT

In as short a chapter as this, it is neither possible nor desirable to examine all national legislation in detail. Being the working manuals for government agencies dealing with these topics, the principal acts are lengthy, detailed, and complex. A brief summary of their contents is, therefore, all that will be attempted here.

The completion of the Uruguay round of GATT talks produced, among other items, new dumping and countervailing codes and a new agricultural agreement. As a result, all legislation then current on those topics required updating. The USA, Australia and New Zealand have all passed amending acts through their respective Parliaments and Congress to bring these new GATT agreements into their national laws.

Current legislation in these three countries on the subject of dumping and countervailing, is as follows.

United States of America

The Tariff Act 1930

The countervailing and anti-dumping provisions are contained in Title VII of the Act (19 USC 1671–1677j)[37] in the following parts:

Subtitle A: Imposition of countervailing duties

Subtitle B: Imposition of anti-dumping duties

Subtitle C: Reviews; other actions regarding agreements

Subtitle D: General provisions

Throughout the title reference is made to 'the administering authority', which is the Department of Commerce's Import Administration (see diagram), and to 'the commission' which is the US International Trade Commission.

Subtitles A and B mirror each other in their sections implementing the two GATT agreements:

---

37 For readers without a sound understanding of the US method of citation of statutes, Title 19 of the US Code deals exclusively with Customs Duties and includes, *inter alia*, the whole Tariff Act. Thus '19 USC 1671' refers to Article 1671 of Title 19 of the Code. Title 19 includes subtitle IV, which is Title VII of the Tariff Act, 'Countervailing and anti-dumping duties', and its parts – known as subtitles in the Act. Statutes also have sections as they do in Australia and New Zealand. Both section numbers and US Code identifiers are used when quoting from statutes. The correct citation of the first section of Title VII is therefore: 's 701 (19 USC 1671)'.

Content	Countervailing duties	Anti-dumping duties
Imposition of duties	s 701 (19 USC 1671)	s 731 (19 USC 1673)
Procedures for initiating investigation	s 702 (19 USC 1671a)	s 732 (19 USC 1673a)
Preliminary determinations	s 703 (19 USC 1671b)	s 733 (19 USC 1673b)
Termination of investigations	s 704 (19 USC 1671c)	s 734 (19 USC 1673c)
Final determinations	s 705 (19 USC 1671d)	s 735 (19 USC 1673d)
Assessment of duty	s 706 (19 USC 1671e)	s 736 (19 USC 1673e)
Difference between deposit and final assessed duty	s 707 (19 USC 1671f)	s 737 (19 USC 1673f)
Conditional payment of duty	s 709 (19 USC 1671h)	s 738 (19 USC 1673g)

Subtitle C (s 751 (19 USC 1675)) deals with the administrative review of duty imposed.

Subtitle D (ss 771–83 (19 USC 1677–1677k)) deals with (*inter alia*) definitions, upstream subsidies, subsidies on processed agricultural products, foreign market value, currency conversion, access to information (s 777(b)(1) (19) USC 1677f(b)(1)) uses the terminology 'proprietary' and 'non-proprietary' in place of the GATT terms 'confidential ' and 'non-confidential', sampling and average, conduct of investigations and anti-dumping petitions by third countries.

The Uruguay Round Agreements Act of 1994

This act contains in Title II major amendments to the Tariff Act 1930 to bring the latter in line with the GATT 1994 agreements. It must be read in conjunction with the Tariff Act.

One important introduction of the GATT 1994 Agreement (Article 11) is the five year sunset review of anti-dumping and countervailing duties , incorporated as s 751(c)(1) (19) USC 1675 (c)(1). This provides for an automatic review of duties five years after imposition.

Australia

The Anti-Dumping Authority Act 1988

The Anti-Dumping Authority which is created by this act, and whose functions and powers are defined in the act, conducts all inquiries and investigations into alleged dumped or subsidised goods imported into Australia other than preliminary inquiries conducted by Customs. Despite its name it also deals with countervailing matters. A summary of the most significant parts of this act now follows. The Act consists of five parts:

Part I   Preliminary

Part II   Establishment, functions and powers of the Anti-Dumping Authority

Part III   Constitution of the authority

Part IV   Inquiries

Part V   Miscellaneous

Part I: Preliminary

This part contains an interpretation section (s 3) which defines terms used in the Act, many of which are referred to Part XV of the Customs Act 1901, and an exclusion from anti-dumping duties to goods which are the produce or manufacture of New Zealand (s 3A).

Part II: Functions and powers of the ADA

This part contains the meat of the statute. It establishes the Anti-Dumping Authority (s 4) (hereafter 'the ADA') and lists its functions (s 5). These can be summarised as:

• to recommend to the Minister that a dumping or countervailing duty notice should be published;

• to recommend to the Minister whether such a notice should be fully or partly revoked;

• to review a Customs decision to terminate an investigation and to review negative findings;

• to recommend to the Minister whether an anti-dumping measure should be continued;

• to provide the Minister with anti-dumping reports as required.

Time scales for inquiries by the ADA

In its recommendations (s 7) the ADA, when inquiring into a matter, is required to report on the matter within 120 days and is also required to recommend to the Minister the amount of any duties payable under the Customs Tariff (Anti-dumping) Act. Where the ADA is required to review a Customs decision to terminate an inquiry, the matter must be dealt with within 60 days (s 7A).

Negligible dumping margins or subsidisations

In accordance with Article 5.8 of the GATT Agreement, the ADA must terminate any inquiry in which it finds that dumping volumes or margins or countervailable subsidies are negligible or negligible damage is done to local industry (s 7A).

Acceptance of undertakings by governments or exporters

The ADA may, but is not obliged to, recommend to the Minister whether an undertaking (following an anti-dumping application) by an exporter or a government should be accepted (s 7C).

Continuation of dumping measures

Not later than eight months before an anti-dumping measure expires the ADA must publish in the *Gazette* and a newspaper circulating in each state and territory a notice to that effect. The notice must invite interested parties to apply, within 60 days, for continuation of the measure (s 8A(1)).

If such an application is received the ADA must recommend to the Minister within 120 days of its receipt, whether the measure should continue (s 8A(4)).

Where the Minister accepts a recommendation that a dumping or countervailing duty notice should continue after its expiry date, it will continue for five years unless revoked. If the measure is an undertaking, it will continue for the agreed period (s 8A(10)).

ADA policy constraints

The ADA must have regard to Australian government policy on anti-dumping matters, Australia's obligations under GATT and must ensure that anti-dumping measures are not used 'to assist import competing industries in Australia or to protect industries in Australia from the need to adjust to changing economic conditions' (s 10).

Ministerial direction

The Minister may give the ADA directions on general principles for carrying out its powers. If the Minister does so, particulars must be published in the *Gazette* and laid before each House of the Parliament (s 12).

Part III – Constitution of the authority

This Part provides for the appointment of one member to constitute the ADA (s 13), provisions for the appointment of an acting member to fill a vacancy (s 14), and for associate members (s 15).

Part IV – Inquiries

The authority in its inquiries is not bound to act formally nor is it bound by the rules of evidence (s 22). Details of the public notice required before the start of any inquiry are contained in s 23.

The ADA must maintain a public record of the inquiry, including a full record of the preceding Customs investigation. Such record excludes information provided in confidence but must include a summary of such information that does not breach confidentiality (s 23A).

A penalty of $2,000 for a natural person or $10,000 for a body corporate is available for the provision to the ADA of information which is false or misleading in a material particular (s 24).

Section 27 prohibits an employer from prejudicing an employee who has assisted or who proposes to assist the ADA. A penalty of $1000 applies to an individual and $5000 to a corporation.

Part V – Miscellaneous

The ADA must make available to the public all its reports and must publish in the *Gazette* a notice advising of the availability of such reports (s 28). An annual report on the ADA's activities is presented to the Minister and tabled in the Parliament (s 29).

Section 34 in this part deals with the conduct of directors, servants and agents of corporations and the deeming of such conduct to be the conduct of the corporation or principal (s 34).

The Customs Tariff (Anti-Dumping) Act 1975

This act is the authority for the imposition of special duties of customs known as anti-dumping and countervailing duties, and hence is incorporated with the Customs

Act 1901, in which it is known as the 'Anti-Dumping Act'. It prescribes in considerable detail the mechanics of imposing and collecting these duties. It has only one part whose most significant sections are explained below.

Dumping duties

Duties of Customs are imposed in accordance with this act (s 7).

Dumping duties and interim duties, from which New Zealand products are exempt (s 8(1)) are defined in s 8. The quantum of these duties is the sum of two values:

- the difference between the export price and the value of the subject goods; and
- the difference between the export price and that ascertained by the Minister (s 8(4)).

A value known as the 'non-injurious price' is introduced in s 8(5A). This price indicates the price at which no injury is deemed to be suffered by the local industry (See s 269TAC(a) of the Customs Act 1901). The export price plus any dumping duty imposed must not exceed that non-injurious price (s 8(5B)). The Minister may exempt goods from dumping duty if certain conditions are fulfilled (s 8(7)).

Third country dumping duties follow in s 9. As with s 8, it excludes products of New Zealand (s 9(1)). Section 8 does not define 'third country dumping' but see s 269TH of the Customs Act 1901.

Countervailing duties

Countervailing duties (s 10(1)), interim countervailing duties (s 10(3)) and third country countervailing duties (s 11) are next defined and cross-referred to the relevant sections in the Customs Act 1901.

Sections 8, 9, 10 and 11 form a complex and comprehensive code not easy for the inexperienced reader to follow. Sections 9, 10 and 11 follow the same pattern, even following similar subsections with regard to the calculation of the duty, to that in s 8.

The Customs Act 1901

Part XVB of the Act contains procedures for initiating and conducting anti-dumping and countervailing investigations and review of existing measures. It gives powers to and imposes obligations on the Chief Executive Officer of Customs – formerly 'the Comptroller'[38] – and the Minister for Customs in respect of anti-dumping and countervailing actions.

Division 1 of Part XVB

This division defines terms used in the Act, including: countervailable subsidies – s 269TAAC, arms length transactions – s 269TAA – (although the definition is awkward, being by exception), export price – s 269TAB, normal value of goods – s 269TAC, and two new sections on 'Working out whether dumping has occurred' (s 269TACB) and 'Working out whether benefits have occurred and amount of subsidy' (s 269TACC).

---

38 Change effected from 1 July 1995 by the Customs, Excise and Bounty Legislation Amendment Act no 85 of 1995.

Division 2 of Part XVB

This division deals with Consideration of Anti-dumping Matters by Customs. It includes preliminary findings (s 269TD), termination of investigations (s 269TDA) and reviews by the Anti-Dumping Authority (s 269TF).

Division 3 of Part XVB

This division is headed 'Consideration of anti-dumping matters by the Minister' but includes countervailing duties (s 269TJ), third country countervailing duties (s 269TK) as well as dumping duties (s 269TG) and third country dumping duties (s 269TH).

Division 4 of Part XVB

This division deals with the assessment of dumping and countervailing duties.

Division 5 of Part XVB

This division deals with interim duty.

Division 6 of Part XVB

This division deals with accelerated review of dumping and countervailing notices.

Division 7 of Part XVB

This contains lengthy details of the requirements of public notices required by the Act (and the GATT Agreements).

The Customs Act is a detailed, lengthy and complex piece of legislation. A useful handbook containing the sections most relevant to dumping and countervailing matters, the other relevant statutes and the changes to them following GATT 1994 is available from the Australian Customs Service.

The Administrative Decisions (Judicial Review) Act 1977

This Act provides the authority for review by the Federal Court of administrative decisions such as those made on dumping and countervailing issues by Customs and the Anti-Dumping Authority. It complies with the requirements of Article 13 of the Anti-Dumping Agreement and Article 23 of the Agreement on Subsidies and Countervailing Measures.

A comprehensive list of grounds on which review may be granted is contained in s 5(1) and (2). Review may also be sought on the basis of the conduct of the decision-maker (s 6) and in respect of a failure to make a decision (s 7). State courts are precluded from hearing any matter to which this Act applies (s 9) saving those matters in s 9(4). Applications are made in accordance with s 11 and the rules of court. Persons interested in a decision may apply to the court to be made a party to the proceedings (s 12). Information in confidence need not be disclosed to the court (s 13). The federal Attorney-General may certify that other information would be contrary to the public interest (s 14).

Schedule 2 lists classes of decisions to which this section does not apply. The court has powers to quash or set aside decisions, refer them for further consideration, declare the rights of parties or their obligations, or order that a decision be made (s 16). Schedule 1 lists classes of decisions to which the act does not apply. The regulations under the act may do likewise (s 19).

New Zealand

The Anti-Dumping and Countervailing Duties Act 1988

This statute is briefer and simpler than the US and Australian legislation. It authorises the Secretary of Commerce to initiate and conduct investigations into allegations of dumping and countervailing, and the Minister of Commerce to make final determinations and impose duties. Goods of Australian origin are exempt from anti-dumping investigations.

The act was amended substantially in late 1994 to comply with the WTO Agreement.

Meaning of industry

Industry is defined in s 3A. Goods of Australian origin are defined in s 3B (see also s 10(10) – exemption from anti-dumping duties).

Export price and normal value

The Secretary of Commerce has the authority to determine each of these two values in accordance with specific and detailed instructions in ss 4 and 5. The Secretary may determine them in the absence of adequate information (s 6).

Subsidies

The Secretary also has the authority to determine, subject to the criteria in s 7, the amount of any subsidy paid. They may also determine the amount in the absence of adequate information (s 7(5)).

Material injury

The Secretary determines any material injury or the retardation of the establishment of an industry in accordance with criteria in s 8.

Notice

The public notice required in several instances by the act is defined in s 9.

Initiation of investigations

The criteria for a 'properly documented application' are listed comprehensively in s 10. Detail is provided of the nature of evidence required (s 10(2a)) and information to be provided to the Secretary. Investigations will not be initiated unless the producers making the application comprise 25% or more of the NZ industry and more than 50% of NZ producers supporting and opposing the application. (s 10(3)). Confidential information will be respected and non-confidential summaries will be required (s 10(7) and (8)). Goods of Australian origin as defined in s 3B are exempt from anti-dumping investigations (s 10(10)).

Termination of investigations

Investigations will be terminated if there is insufficient evidence of dumping or subsidy (s 11(1)(a)) or material injury to the industry (s 11(1)(b)), where imposition of a duty would be inconsistent with New Zealand's obligations under the WTO (s 11(1)(c)) or where the dumping or subsidy is *de minimis* (s 11(2)). Further investigations may be initiated by the Secretary where information provided proves to be materially defective (s 11(3)).

Final determinations

The Minister of Commerce must make a final determination within 180 days of the initiation of an investigation as to whether dumping or subsidisation has taken place and has caused material injury (s 13).

Price undertakings by exporting countries

The Minister may accept undertakings from exporting countries and terminate investigations initiated by the Secretary where appropriate (s 15).

Preliminary determinations and provisional measures

Preliminary determinations have been deleted from the Act by the 1994 amendments, but provisional measures may still be imposed after 60 days from initiation of an investigation where the Minister is satisfied that they are necessary to prevent material injury during the investigation period (s 16(1)(b)).

Imposition and collection of duties

After making a final determination, the Minister may order appropriate duties to be collected by the collector appointed under s 2 of the Customs Act 1966. Criteria for the imposition of these duties are contained in s 14. These duties may be imposed retrospectively to the date of the imposition of provisional measures (s 17).

Third country anti-dumping and countervailing duties

Section 18 makes provision for the imposition of duties on the request of the government of a third country. Such imposition must follow the provisions for internal investigations.

The Judicature Act 1908

The Judicature Act was amended substantially in 1972 to introduce a new Part 1 – 'Single Procedure for the Judicial Review of the exercise of, or failure to exercise, a statutory power.' This provides for judicial review to be exercised by the High Court (s 4) with appeals from that court to the Court of Appeal (s 11).

SAFEGUARDS – AS OPPOSED TO DUMPING AND COUNTERVAILING ACTION

Article XIX (often referred to as the escape clause) of the GATT allows for emergency action against particular products. This permits a country to take protective action against imported goods when, in unforeseen circumstances and as a result of the obligations incurred under the GATT, those imports have increased in such quantities as to cause or threaten serious injury to the domestic producers of like or directly competitive goods.[39]

These provisions are contained in the Agreement on Safeguards which forms part of Annex 1A to the Agreement establishing the World Trade Organisation.

---

39 New Zealand Ministry of Commerce, 'Trade Remedies and the GATT – The outcome of the Uruguay Round – An Explanatory paper', March 1994, Wellington, p 71.

Such action different from anti-dumping and countervailing action in that:

> ... unlike anti-dumping and countervailing measures, which can apply as long as there is dumping (or subsidy) and injury or threat of injury, safeguard measures are applied on a temporary basis only and provide time for an industry to adjust to unforeseen and increased volumes of imports that cause or threaten to cause injury to an industry, before returning to the standard level of tariff assistance seen as appropriate to that industry.[40]

United States of America

The USA deals with safeguard matters through tariff action or import restriction under s 201 of the 1974 Trade Act.[41] This legislation, which complies with the Safeguards Agreement, empowers the President to grant temporary relief to an industry after the International Trade Commission has found serious injury or threat thereof from increased imports.[42] Section 201 is not used as widely as the anti-dumping and countervailing procedures – indeed one commentator has suggested that even in 1993 it was suffering from atrophy.[43]

Australia

Successive Australian governments have made a deliberate decision not to legislate for safeguards as provided for in the GATT Agreement. They have decided that the anti-dumping and countervailing provisions are adequate to balance the requirements of free trade and competition.

New Zealand

New Zealand has enacted the Temporary Safeguard Authorities Act 1987 which complies with the GATT Agreement. The Act allows the New Zealand Minister for Commerce to establish authorities to investigate possible situations of material injury to domestic industry and recommend action.[44]

THE COURTS AND DUMPING/COUNTERVAILING

United States of America

In a significant majority of cases on appeal the courts have shown reluctance to overturn either the decision of an administrative body or that of the court below. An argument has often developed as to whether an authority has made the correct determination. In

---

40   *Ibid.*

41   1995 Trade Policy Agenda and 1994 Annual report of the President of the United States on the Trade Agreements Program, p 102.

42   *Ibid.*

43   Low, *op cit*, p 80.

44   See fn 1 above.

Smith-Corona Group v United States,[45] the plaintiff argued that a definition made by the International Trade Administration should have been in line with its submission. In his judgment Smith CJ stated: 'The ITA has defined the term differently, however, and our inquiry is at an end if that interpretation is reasonable.'

Again in *American Spring Wire Corp v United States*,[46] the judge in the US Court of International Trade found that though the plaintiffs had adduced considerable evidence to prove that they had suffered material injury, it 'was reasonable for the ITA to find that the loss did not outweigh ... the other indicia of a healthy industry'.[47]

In his judgment in *Maple Leaf Fish Co v United States*[48] Davis J stated: 'In international trade controversies of this highly discretionary kind ... this court and its predecessors have often reiterated the very limited role of reviewing courts. For a court to interpose there has to be a clear misconstruction of the governing statute, a significant procedural violation or action outside delegated authority.'

A good example of the complexity which can typify modern anti-dumping and countervailing actions can be found in the recent *Nippon Steel* case, which finally found its way to the US Court of International Trade in 1995.[49] The initial petitioners to the US International Trade Commission, and who reappeared as defendant/intervenors before the court, comprised nine major US steel manufacturers. They alleged dumping and/or subsidisation by nineteen foreign steelmaking countries including – for the purpose of this chapter – New Zealand and Australia.[50] Eventually, products from six countries, one of which was Australia, were found to have been dumped or subsidised. The report of the USITC was contained in three volumes totalling nearly 1,200 pages. The transcript of the appeal before the Court of International Trade comprised a mere 72 pages. Some 30 attorneys from eight major US law firms represented the 16 defendants.[51]

Of five separate investigations against BHP Australia and BHP Steel (New Zealand) initiated by the USITC, three were discontinued following a finding by the commission that no material injury had resulted. The other two, one each involving BHP Australia and BHP (New Zealand) resulted in a final determination by the Department of Commerce of dumping against the Australian company (24.96%) and against the New Zealand Company of subsidy (36.05%). The final injury determination by the commission was negligible against New Zealand and material injury against BHP Australia. The Department of Commerce therefore issued an anti-dumping notice

---

45   713 F 2d 1568 (1983) US Court of Appeals (Fed Cir) quoted in Schaffer, R, Earle, B and Agusti, F, *International Business Law and its Environment*, 2nd edn, 1993, St Paul, Minneapolis: West Publishing.

46   590 F Supp 1273 (1984) quoted in Schaffer, *op cit*.

47   *Ibid*.

48   762 F 2d 86 (1985) US Court of Appeals (Fed Cir).

49   *Nippon Steel Corp and Others v United States and Others* (US Court of International Trade) Consol Ct no 93-09-00555-INJ, 3 April 1995.

50   *Ibid* at 1–2.

51   *Ibid* at 1–2.

against BHP Australia on 19 August 1993. By right under statute (19 USC s 1516a) BHP (and 16 other foreign steelmakers) appealed to the Court of International Trade.[52]

The court was consistent with its previous stances, requiring major cause before overturning findings of the Department of Commerce or the commission. In answer to the argument by the petitioners/appellants that the commission had erred in its interpretation of the evidence, the court stated that 'Evidence of some dissimilarities is not sufficient to overturn a determination where there is otherwise substantial evidence to support the commission's findings'[53] and later 'the commission is afforded discretion in interpreting the data, and the court does not weigh the evidence'.[54] Faced with an allegation by BHP Australia that the commission had ignored evidence in its favour, the court supported the commission, holding that 'when there is a choice between two fairly conflicting views the court will not substitute its judgment for that of the agency'.[55]

In all, the court dismissed the appeals against the commission in all but one of its findings, remanding that finding (against Mexico) to the USITC for reconsideration.[56]

Australia

Appeals from decisions of Customs and the Anti-Dumping Authority have been numerous. The whole legislative scheme in this area 'has been a fertile field for litigation', according to Lee J in the full court of the Federal Court hearing an appeal from a single judge of that court in *Pilkington (Australia) Ltd v The Anti-Dumping Authority*.[57]

As in the USA, the courts in Australia have been unwilling to overturn previous decisions. The courts have been careful not to exceed the reasons for disturbing prior decisions laid down in s 5 of the Administrative Decisions (Judicial Review Act) 1977 (see comments on that act above).

In *Minister for Aboriginal Affairs v Peko Wallsend Ltd*,[58] a case dealing not with dumping and countervailing but equally concerned with judicial review, Mason J (as he was then), stated that 'in the context of administrative law a court should proceed with caution when reviewing an administrative decision on the grounds that it does not give proper weight to relevant factors, lest it exceed its supervisory role by reviewing the decision on its merits'.

---

52 O'Mulveny and Myers, attorneys, Washington DC, summary of the USITC and USCIT hearings, 17 January 1996 at 4–5.

53 USCIT transcript (see note A) at 19.

54 *Ibid* at 69.

55 *Ibid* at 18.

56 *Ibid* at 72.

57 7 April 1995 Federal Court, unreported. An interesting case in which it was decided that a commission earned by an agent did not arise 'after exportation' but at the time of making the contract which earned it.

58 (1986) 162 CLR 24 at 42.

Although plaintiffs frequently claim that Customs or the ADA should have decided differently on the evidence available to them, that is seldom sufficient for a decision in their favour. As Hill J of the Federal Court put it in *Enichem Anic Srl v Anti-Dumping Authority*: 'Decision-making is a function of the real world. A decision-maker is not bound to investigate each avenue that may be suggested to him by a party interested. Ultimately a decision-maker must do the best on the material available after giving interested parties the right to be heard on the question.'[59]

Where it is clearly demonstrated that a decision maker failed to comply with a section of the legislation, however, the courts have no hesitation in overturning such a decision, especially if the failure falls within the criteria in s 5 of the ADJR Act 1977 – see *Wattmaster Alco Pty Ltd v Button per* Pincus J.[60]

New Zealand

Appeals from decisions of the Department of Commerce have not been as frequent as is the case in the USA and Australia.

In a landmark case, *Auckland Harbour Board v Comptroller of Customs*,[61] the Court of Appeal was presented with a case where Customs had applied an anti-dumping duty on subsidised imports because the time had run out under the legislation for the appropriate countervailing duty. The court found unanimously that this was invalid, being not only beyond the scope of the legislation but also contravening Article VI of GATT which provided that the duties were not interchangeable.

SUMMARY AND COMMENT

While the concept and principle of anti-dumping and countervailing duties are relatively straightforward, the implementation of them is bound up in some of the most convoluted legislation on the statute books of each country considered in this chapter. It is not contended that this complexity is unnecessary given the current circumstances and the need to make highly detailed comparisons and calculations of prices and values, although some of those who work in the area believe it could and should be simplified. Indeed, the New Zealand legislation is far shorter and its procedures less convoluted that those of the USA and Australia.

It is, however, an area difficult to summarise and one where a little knowledge may be a dangerous thing. Certainly the practitioner in this area needs to master a mass of legislation and a large number of precedents on which this chapter has dwelt only briefly.

The whole principle of countervailable subsidies is complicated by the Agreement on Agriculture, itself not known for ease of understanding, and which is made complex by the exemptions for developing countries of varying levels.

---

59   (1992) 39 FCR 458.

60   (1985) 8 FCR 471.

61   (1992) 3 NZLR 392.

More fundamentally, the conception of free trade and eventual dispersion of trade barriers sits uncomfortably with the anti-dumping and countervailing regimes. As the world develops more and more trading blocs, the use of these procedures will probably decrease except between blocs.

On 7 April 1994, the US Under Secretary for International Trade made the statement that 'a strong anti-dumping law, vigorously enforced, is more important than ever in terms of American interests'.[62] There is, however, evidence, at least in the USA, that the number of actions in these areas, which peaked in the mid-80s, are on the decline, especially in the case of countervailing actions.[63] In Australia, the evidence points to a slight increase in actions by the Anti-Dumping Authority over the last five years.[64] There is also concern in some quarters that the whole procedure may well be costing consumers more than any benefit they may gain.[65] It will be interesting to see whether the Under Secretary's view, and that of others with a similar role in other countries, is the same in five years time.

APPENDIX

A SUMMARY OF THE GATT 1994 AGREEMENT ON AGRICULTURE

The long-term objective of negotiations on agriculture under the Uruguay Round of the GATT is 'to establish a fair and market-oriented agricultural trading system' and 'to provide for substantial progressive reductions in agricultural support and protection'.[66]

Under the Agreement on Agriculture Member States are committed to capping and reducing current agricultural support measures including domestic support and export subsidies, in accordance with negotiated timetables.[67] For developed countries there is a six year implementation timetable and for developing countries a 10 year implementation period,[68] both starting in 1995. Member States 'undertake not to provide export subsidies otherwise than in conformity with this agreement'.[69] This means that members cannot introduce new export subsidies. Further, members are not to apply export subsidies 'in a manner which results in, or which threatens to lead to, circumvention of export subsidy commitments, nor shall non–commercial transactions be used to circumvent such transactions'.[70]

---

62 Report of Mr Garten's address to the US Chamber of Commerce International Forum, US Information Agency, Washington DC, Wireless File, 7 April 1995 .

63 Low, P, *op cit*, pp 82–85.

64 Anti-Dumping Authority Annual Report 1994–95, Australian Government Publishing Service, Canberra.

65 Report of the US International Trade Commission, US Information Agency, Wireless File, Washington DC, 5 July 1995.

66 Preamble to the Agreement on Agriculture.

67 Articles 6 and 8.

68 Article 15.2.

69 Article 8.

70 Article 10.1.

The agricultural products to which the agreement relates are listed in Annex 1 and the export subsidies subject to reduction commitments are listed in Article 9.

In accordance with Article 13 of the Agreement, where a member meets its reduction commitments in terms of domestic support and export subsidies, those measures captured by the Agriculture Agreement are exempt from action under the Agreement on Subsidies and Countervailing Measures. More specifically, domestic support measures that conform fully to the provisions of Annex 2 of the Agreement on Agriculture (which allows exemption from reduction to domestic subsidies 'which have no or minimal trade distorting effects') are non-actionable subsidies for the purpose of countervailing measures.[71] In addition, those subsidies which conform with Article 6 of the Agriculture Agreement (domestic support commitments) are exempt from countervailing duties unless a determination of injury or threat thereof is made, and even then 'due restraint' must be shown in imposing such duties.[72] It should be noted, however, that in accordance with the so-called 'peace clause', this exemption is to apply only for nine years commencing in 1995.[73]

A WTO Committee on agriculture is created[74] to review the implementation of commitments under this agreement and to monitor their effect on 'least developed and net food-importing countries'.[75] Member countries agree to consult annually in this committee on 'their participation in the normal growth of world trade in agricultural products within the framework of the commitments on export subsidies under this agreement'.[76]

TUTORIAL QUESTIONS

Answer or discuss as appropriate the following questions from the point of view of your own country. Reference your answers to the relevant clause of the GATT agreement as well as to your own national legislation where appropriate.

1 How does an agreement of the World Trade Organisation become law in your country?

2 What statutes were introduced following the completion of the Uruguay Round of Trade Talks to update national legislation?

3 What is the difference between the regimes of safeguards and anti-dumping or countervailing? How does your country implement the former?

4 Define 'dumping' and 'countervailing' with reference to the GATT Agreements.

---

71 Article 13(a).
72 Article 13(c).
73 Article 1(f).
74 Article 17.
75 Article 16.
76 Article 18(5).

5   If a country exports subsidised agricultural products to your country, those products may not be able to be levied with a countervailing duty. Why?

6   Who can initiate an anti-dumping or countervailing petition? What support must it have from domestic industry?

7   To whom is such a petition addressed? What action is then taken, prior to an investigation, and by whom?

8   Define 'normal value' and 'dumping margin' for the purpose of an anti-dumping investigation.

9   In such an investigation the margin may be found to be *de minimis*. Exactly what is this and what is the effect on the investigation?

10 Who is responsible for preliminary determinations of material injury?

11 What subsidies are countervailable and why?

12 Are developing countries exempt from countervailing action?

13 Are you as an importer required to disclose sensitive or confidential information to an authority in an investigation? If not, what may you be required to do?

14 What public notices must be published in the course of an investigation of dumping or subsidisation?

15 Is a country other than the importer and exporter able to cause anti-dumping or countervailing duties to be levied on imported goods?

16 What time-scale can you expect to be applied between the petition and the final determination in an anti-dumping or countervailing investigation?

17 Who is responsible for collecting the duties finally levied as the result of an investigation?

18 What is meant by the phrase 'to suspend liquidation'?

19 As an importer you believe that anti-dumping duties have been unfairly levied on your goods. What right do you have to appeal that decision?

20 What is the alternative to the levying of duties on goods found to have been dumped or subsidised?

21 As a domestic producer you hear that as a result of your petition the authority has determined that the subject product has not been dumped or that there is no material injury to the domestic industry. What further action can you take?

22 What action can the authority take on a positive preliminary finding of dumping or subsidy?

23 Are the governments of exporters involved in allegations of dumping or subsidy made aware of action against their nationals?

24 If dumping or subsidy is finally determined, to what extent can duties be levied retroactively?

25 'In the perfect free trade world neither anti-dumping nor countervailing action would be necessary.' Discuss.

26 'Given the facility to take anti-dumping or countervailing action, there is no need to have additional provisions for safeguards as provided by Article XIX and the Safeguards Agreement of GATT 1994.' Discuss.

27 'The length of time it takes to make a final determination and impose duties on dumped or subsidised imports is so great as to be of little help to domestic industry.' Discuss.

28 'The decision by the European Union to discontinue dumping and countervailing actions among its members, and the likelihood of the proposed FTAA doing the same, will sound the death knell of all anti-dumping and countervailing measures internationally.' Discuss.

29 Dumping is widely thought to be unfair and injurious to America's domestic industries. But an increasing number of trade commentators argue that dumping is generally beneficial to the importing country and that anti-dumping laws harm the prospects for world trade liberalisation.

Answer the following questions:

(i) What constitutes 'dumping' in USA, Australian, New Zealand and GATT law? In your answer refer to, and discuss, the relevant legal provisions.

(ii) Should the USA dump its anti-dumping laws? Give reasons for your view.

FURTHER READING

Australian Anti-Dumping Authority reports nos 27, 140, 141, 147.

Australian Customs Service, *Australia's Anti-Dumping and Countervailing Legislation Post Uruguay Round – A Description of the Changes*, 1995.

Australian Customs Service, *World Trade Organisation – Uruguay Round – Anti-dumping and Countervailing – An Explanatory Paper*, September 1994.

Australian Customs Service, *Australia's Anti-Dumping and Countervailing Administration*, October 1995.

Australian Customs Service, *Australia's Anti-Dumping and Countervailing Legislation Post Uruguay Round*, 1995 (undated).

Department of Foreign Affairs and Trade, *Marrakesh Agreement Establishing the World Trade Organisation*, Australian Treaty Series, no 8, 1995, Canberra.

Harrison, D and Ott, J, 'Trade regulation' (3 April 1995) *US National Law Review*.

Low, P, *Trading Free – The GATT and US Trade Policy*, 1993, New York: Twentieth Century Fund Press.

Ministry of Commerce, Wellington, NZ, *Trade Remedies and the GATT – The Outcome of the Uruguay Round – An Explanatory Paper*, March 1994.

Otterness P, McFaul, F and Kutshaw, K, 'The ABCs of American Trade Laws on Foreign Dumping and Subsidies' (8 December 1986) *Business America*.

Schaffer R, Earle B and Agusti F, *International Business Law and its Environment*, 2nd edn, 1993, St Paul, Minneapolis: West Publishing.

US Congressional Budget Office, *A Review of US Anti-Dumping and Countervailing Duty Law and Policy,* May 1994.

US Information Agency, *Administration of Anti-Dumping and Countervailing Duty Laws,* USITC study no 6170, July 1995, Washington DC.

1995 Trade Policy Agenda and 1994 Annual Report of the President of the United States on the Trade Agreements Program.

Statutes

United States of America:	Tariff Act 1930 (19 USC 1671–1677)
	The Uruguay Round Agreements Act of 1994
Australia:	Customs Act 1901
	Tariff (Anti-Dumping) Act 1975
	Anti-Dumping Authority Act 1988
	Administrative Decisions (Judicial Review) Act 1977
New Zealand:	Customs Act 1966
	Anti-dumping and Countervailing Duties Act 1988
	Temporary Safeguards Authorities Act 1987
	Judicature Act 1908

ACKNOWLEDGMENTS

I wish to acknowledge the assistance provided to me in researching this chapter by the Orange Agricultural College of the University of Sydney whose research grant funded my travel, purchase of material and telecommunications needs. I also wish to thank a number of people who gave so generously of their time and expertise to help me. These include Nicholas Deane and Peter Gilbert of the US Consulate General, Sydney, Kermit Almstedt of O'Mulvany and Myers, Washington DC, Dr Trevor Mathieson of the New Zealand High Commission, Canberra, Bruce Cullen and Jane Fibbes of the Trade Remedies Group, NZ Ministry of Commerce, John Arndell of the Australian Anti-Dumping Authority, Ken Muldoon and Tom van Sebille of the Australian Customs Service, and Louise Hingee of Department of Foreign Affairs and Trade, Canberra.

AGREEMENT ON IMPLEMENTATION OF ARTICLE VI OF THE GENERAL AGREEMENT ON TARIFFS AND TRADE 1994

Members hereby agree as follows:

PART I

Article 1 – Principles

An anti-dumping measure shall be applied only under the circumstances provided for in Article VI of GATT 1994 and pursuant to investigations initiated and conducted in accordance with the provisions of this agreement. The following provisions govern the application of Article VI of GATT 1994 in so far as actions taken under anti-dumping legislation or regulations.

Article 2 – Determination of dumping

2.1   For the purpose of this agreement a product is to be considered as being dumped, ie introduced into the commerce of another country at less than its normal value, if the export price of the product exported from one country to another is less than the comparable price, in the ordinary course of trade, for the like product when destined for consumption in the exporting country.

2.2   When there are no sales of the like product in the ordinary course of trade in the domestic market of the exporting country or when, because of the particular market situation or the low volume of the sales in the domestic market of the exporting country such sales do not permit a proper comparison, the margin of dumping shall be determined by comparison with a comparable price of the like product when exported to an appropriate third country, provided that this price is representative, or with the cost of production in the country of origin plus a reasonable amount for administrative, selling and general costs and for profits.

2.2.1   Sales of the like product in the domestic market of the exporting country or sales to a third country at prices below per unit (fixed and variable) costs of production plus administrative, selling and general costs may be treated as not being in the ordinary course of trade by reason of price and may be disregarded in determining normal value only if the authorities determine that such sales are made within an extended period of time in substantial quantities and are at prices which do not provide for the recovery of all costs within a reasonable period of time. If prices which are below per unit costs at the time of sale are above weighted average per unit costs for the period of investigation, such prices shall be considered to provide for recovery of costs within a reasonable period of time.

2.2.1.1   For the purpose of para 2, costs shall normally be calculated on the basis of records kept by the exporter or producer under investigation, provided that such records are in accordance with the generally accepted accounting principles of the exporting country and reasonably reflect the costs associated with the production and sale of the product under consideration. Authorities shall consider all available evidence on the proper allocation of costs, including that which is made available by the exporter or producer in the course of the investigation provided that such allocations have been historically utilised by the exporter or producer, in particular in relation to establishing appropriate amortisation and depreciation periods and allowances for capital expenditures and other development costs. Unless already reflected in the cost allocations under this sub-paragraph, costs shall be adjusted appropriately for those non-recurring items of cost which benefit future and/or current production, or for circumstances in which costs during the period of investigation are affected by start-up operations.

2.2.2   For the purpose of para 2, the amounts for administrative, selling and general costs and for profits shall be based on actual data pertaining to production and sales in the ordinary course of trade of the like product by the exporter or producer under investigation When such amounts cannot be determined on this basis, the amounts may be determined on the basis of:

(i)   the actual amounts incurred and realised by the exporter or producer in question in respect of production and sales in the domestic market of the country of origin of the same general category of products;

(ii)   the weighted average of the actual amounts incurred and realised by other exporters or producers subject to investigation in respect of production and sales of the like product in the domestic market of the country of origin;

(iii)   any other reasonable method, provided that the amount for profit so established shall not exceed the profit normally realised by other exporters or producers on sales of products of the same general category in the domestic market of the country of origin.

2.3   In cases where there is no export price or where it appears to the authorities concerned that the export price is unreliable because of association or a compensatory arrangement between the exporter and the importer or a third party, the export price may be constructed on the basis of the price at which the imported products are first resold to an independent buyer, or if the products are not resold to an independent buyer, or not resold in the condition as imported, on such reasonable basis as the authorities may determine.

2.4   A fair comparison shall be made between the export price and the normal value. This comparison shall be made at the same level of trade, normally at the ex-factory level, and in respect of sales made at as nearly as possible the same time. Due allowance shall be made in each case, on its merits, for differences which affect price comparability, including differences in conditions and terms of sale, taxation, levels of trade, quantities, physical characteristics, and any other differences which are also demonstrated to affect price comparability. In the cases referred to in para 3, allowances for costs, including duties and taxes, incurred between importation and resale, and for profits accruing, should also be made. If in these cases price comparability has been affected, the authorities shall establish the normal value at a level of trade equivalent to the level of trade of the constructed export price, or shall make due allowance as warranted under this paragraph. The authorities shall indicate to the parties in question what information is necessary to ensure a fair comparison and shall not impose an unreasonable burden of proof on those parties.

2.4.1   When the comparison under para 4 requires a conversion of currencies, such conversion should be made using the rate of exchange on the date of sale provided that when a sale of foreign currency on forward markets is directly linked to the export sale involved, the rate of exchange in the forward sale shall be used. Fluctuations in exchange rates shall be ignored and in an investigation the authorities shall allow exporters at least 60 days to have adjusted their export prices to reflect sustained movements in exchange rates during the period of investigation.

2.4.2   Subject to the provisions governing fair comparison in para 4, the existence of margins of dumping during the investigation phase shall normally be established on the basis of a comparison of a weighted average normal value with a weighted average of prices of all comparable export transactions or by a comparison of normal value and export prices on a transaction-to-transaction basis. A normal value established on a weighted average basis may be compared to prices of individual export transactions if the authorities find a pattern of export prices which differ significantly among different purchasers, regions or time periods, and if an explanation is provided as to why such differences cannot be taken into account appropriately by the use of a weighted average-to-weighted average or transaction-to-transaction comparison.

2.5   In the case where products are not imported directly from the country of origin but are exported to the importing Member from an intermediate country, the price at which the products are sold from the country of export to the importing Member shall normally be compared with the comparable price in the country of export. However, comparison may be made with the price in the country of origin, if, for example, the products are merely trans-shipped through the country of export, or such products are not produced in the country of export, or there is no comparable price for them in the country of export.

2.6   Throughout this agreement, the term 'like product' ('*produit similaire*') shall be interpreted to mean a product which is identical, ie alike in all respects to the product under consideration, or in the absence of such a product, another product which, although not alike in all respects, has characteristics closely resembling those of the product under consideration.

2.7   This article is without prejudice to the second Supplementary Provision to para 1 of Article VI in Annex I to GATT 1994.

Article 3 – Determination of injury

3.1   A determination of injury for purposes of Article VI of GATT 1994 shall be based on positive evidence and involve an objective examination of both (a) the volume of the dumped imports and the effect of the dumped imports on prices in the domestic market for like products, and (b) the consequent impact of these imports on domestic producers of such products.

3.2   With regard to the volume of the dumped imports, the investigating authorities shall consider whether there has been a significant increase in dumped imports, either in absolute terms or relative to production or consumption in the importing Member. With regard to the effect of the dumped imports on prices, the investigating authorities shall consider whether there has been a significant price undercutting by the dumped imports as compared with the price of a like product of the importing Member, or whether the effect of such imports is otherwise to depress prices to a significant degree or prevent price increases, which otherwise would have occurred, to a significant degree. No one or several of these factors can necessarily give decisive guidance.

3.3   Where imports of a product from more than one country are simultaneously subject to anti-dumping investigations, the investigating authorities may cumulatively assess the effects of such imports only if they determine that (a) the margin of dumping established in relation to the imports from each country is more than *de minimis* as defined in para 8 of Article 5 and the volume of imports from each country is not negligible, and (b) a cumulative assessment of the effects of the imports is appropriate in light of the conditions of competition between the imported products and the conditions of competition between the imported products and the like domestic product.

3.4 The examination of the impact of the dumped imports on the domestic industry concerned shall include an evaluation of all relevant economic factors and indices having a bearing on the state of the industry, including actual and potential decline in sales, profits, output, market share, productivity, return on investments, or utilisation of capacity; factors affecting domestic prices; the magnitude of the margin of dumping; actual and potential negative effects on cash flow, inventories, employment, wages, growth, ability to raise capital or investments. This list is not exhaustive, nor can one or several of these factors necessarily give decisive guidance.

3.5 It must be demonstrated that the dumped imports are, through the effects of dumping, as set forth in paras 2 and 4, causing injury within the meaning of this agreement. The demonstration of a causal relationship between the dumped imports and the injury to the domestic industry shall be based on an examination of all relevant evidence before the authorities. The authorities shall also examine any known factors other than the dumped imports which at the same time are injuring the domestic industry, and the injuries caused by these other factors must not be attributed to the dumped imports. Factors which may be relevant in this respect include, *inter alia*, the volume and prices of imports not sold at dumping prices, contraction in demand or changes in the patterns of consumption, trade restrictive practices of and competition between the foreign and domestic producers, developments in technology and the export performance and productivity of the domestic industry.

3.6 The effect of the dumped imports shall be assessed in relation to the domestic production of the like product when available data permit the separate identification of that production on the basis of such criteria as the production process, producers' sales and profits. If such separate identification of that production is not possible, the effects of the dumped imports shall be assessed by the examination of the production of the narrowest group or range of products, which includes the like product, for which the necessary information can be provided.

3.7 A determination of a threat of material injury shall be based on facts and not merely on allegation, conjecture or remote possibility. The change in circumstances which would create a situation in which the dumping would cause injury must be clearly foreseen and imminent. In making a determination the existence of a threat of material injury, the authorities should consider, *inter alia*, such factors as:

(i) a significant rate of increase of dumped imports into the domestic market indicating the likelihood of substantially increased importation;

(ii) sufficient freely disposable, or an imminent, substantial increase in, capacity of the exporter indicating the likelihood of substantially increased dumped exports to the importing Member's market, taking into account the availability of other export markets to absorb any additional exports;

(iii) whether imports are entering at prices that will have a significant depressing or suppressing effect on domestic prices, and would likely increase demand for further imports; and

(iv) inventories of the product being investigated.

No one of these factors by itself can necessarily give decisive guidance but the totality of the factors considered must lead to the conclusion that further dumped exports are imminent and that, unless protective action is taken, material injury would occur.

3.8   With respect to cases where injury is threatened by dumped imports, the application of anti-dumping measures shall be considered and decided with special care.

Article 4 — Definition of domestic industry

4.1   For the purposes of this agreement, the term 'domestic industry' shall be interpreted as referring to the domestic producers as a whole of the like products or to those of them whose collective output of the products constitutes a major proportion of the total domestic production of those products, except that:

   (i)   when producers are related to the exporters or importers or are themselves importers of the allegedly dumped product, the term 'domestic industry' may be interpreted as referring to the rest of the producers;

   (ii)   in exceptional circumstances the territory of a Member may, for the production in question, be divided into two or more competitive markets and the producers within each market may be regarded as a separate industry if (a) the producers within such market sell all or almost all of their production of the product in question in that market, and (b) the demand in that market is not to any substantial degree supplied by producers of the product in question located elsewhere in the territory. In such circumstances, injury may be found to exist even where a major portion of the total domestic industry is not injured, provided there is a concentration of dumped imports into such an isolated market and provided further that the dumped imports are causing injury to the producers of all or almost all of the production within such market.

4.2   When the domestic industry has been interpreted as referring to the producers in a certain area, ie a market as defined in para 1(ii), anti-dumping duties shall be levied only on the products in question consigned for final consumption to that area. When the constitutional law of the importing Member does not permit the levying of anti-dumping duties on such a basis, the importing Member may levy the anti-dumping duties without limitation only if (a) the exporters shall have been given an opportunity to cease exporting at dumped prices to the area concerned or otherwise give assurances pursuant to Article 8 and adequate assurances in this regard have not been promptly given, and (b) such duties cannot be levied only on products of specific producers which supply the area in question.

4.3   Where two or more countries have reached under the provisions of para 8(a) of Article XXIV of GATT 1994 such a level of integration that they have the characteristics of a single, unified market, the industry in the entire area of integration shall be taken to be the domestic industry referred to in para 1.

4.4   The provisions of para 6 of Article 3 shall be applicable to this article.

Article 5 — Initiation and subsequent investigation

5.1   Except as provided for in para 6, an investigation to determine the existence, degree and effect of any alleged dumping shall be initiated upon a written application by or on behalf of the domestic industry.

5.2   An application under para 1 shall include evidence of (a) dumping, (b) injury within the meaning of Article VI of GATT 1994 as interpreted by this agreement and (c) a causal link between the dumped imports and the alleged injury. Simple assertion, unsubstantiated by relevant evidence, cannot be considered sufficient to meet the requirements of this paragraph. The application shall contain such information as is reasonably available to the applicant on the following:

(i) the identity of the applicant and a description of the volume and value of the domestic production of the like product by the applicant. Where a written application is made on behalf of the domestic industry, the application shall identify the industry on behalf of which the application is made by a list of all known domestic producers of the like product (or associations of domestic producers of the like product) and, to the extent possible, a description of the volume and value of domestic production of the like product accounted for by such producers;

(ii) a complete description of the allegedly dumped product, the names of the country or countries of origin or export in question, the identity of each known exporter or foreign producer and a list of known persons importing the product in question;

(iii) information on prices at which the product in question is sold when destined for consumption in the domestic markets of the country or countries of origin or export (or, where appropriate, information on the prices at which the product is sold from the country or countries of origin or export to a third country or countries, or on the constructed value of the product) and information on export prices or, where appropriate, on the prices at which the product is first resold to an independent buyer in the territory of the importing Member;

(iv) information on the evolution of the volume of the allegedly dumped imports, the effect of these imports on prices of the like product in the domestic market and the consequent impact of the imports on the domestic industry, as demonstrated by relevant factors and indices having a bearing on the state of the domestic industry, such as those listed in paras 2 and 4 of Article 3.

5.3 The authorities shall examine the accuracy and adequacy of the evidence provided in the application to determine whether there is sufficient evidence to justify the initiation of an investigation.

5.4 An investigation shall not be initiated pursuant to para 1 unless the authorities have determined, on the basis of an examination of the degree of support for, or opposition to, the application expressed by domestic producers of the like product, that the application has been made by or on behalf of the domestic industry. The application shall be considered to have been made 'by or on behalf of the domestic industry' if it is supported by those domestic producers whose collective output constitutes more than 50% of the total production of the like product produced by that portion of the domestic industry expressing either support for or opposition to the application. However, no investigation shall be initiated when domestic producers expressly supporting the application account for less than 25% of total production of the like product produced by the domestic industry.

5.5 The authorities shall avoid, unless a decision has been made to initiate an investigation, any publicising of the application for the initiation of an investigation. However, after receipt of a properly documented application and before proceeding to initiate an investigation, the authorities shall notify the government of the exporting Member concerned.

5.6   If, in special circumstances, the authorities concerned decide to initiate an investigation without having received a written application by or on behalf of a domestic industry for the initiation of such investigation, they shall proceed only if they have sufficient evidence of dumping, injury and a causal link, as described in para 2, to justify the initiation of an investigation.

5.7   The evidence of both dumping and injury shall be considered simultaneously (a) in the decision whether or not to initiate an investigation, and (b) thereafter, during the course of the investigation, starting on a date not later than the earliest date on which in accordance with the provisions of this agreement provisional measures may be applied.

5.8   An application under para 1 shall be rejected and an investigation shall be terminated promptly as soon as the authorities concerned are satisfied that there is not sufficient evidence of either dumping or of injury to justify proceeding with the case. There shall be immediate termination in cases where the authorities determine that the margin of dumping is *de minimis*, or that the volume of dumped imports, actual or potential, or the injury, is negligible. The margin of dumping shall he considered to be *de minimis* if this margin is less than 2%, expressed as a percentage of the export price. The volume of dumped imports shall normally be regarded as negligible if the volume of dumped imports from a particular country is found to account for less than 3% of imports of the like product in the importing Member, unless countries which individually account for less than 3% of the imports of the like product in the importing Member collectively account for more than 7% of imports of the like product in the importing Member.

5 9   An anti-dumping proceeding shall not hinder the procedures of customs clearance.

5.10   Investigations shall, except in special circumstances, be concluded within one year, and in no case more than 18 months, after their initiation.

Article 6 – Evidence

6.1   All interested parties in an anti-dumping investigation shall be given notice of the information which the authorities require and ample opportunity to present in writing all evidence which they consider relevant in respect of the investigation in question.

6.1.1   Exporters or foreign producers receiving questionnaires used in an anti-dumping investigation shall be given at least 30 days for reply. Due consideration should be given to any request for an extension of the 30 day period and, upon cause shown, such an extension should be granted whenever practicable.

6.1.2   Subject to the requirement to protect confidential information, evidence presented in writing by one interested party shall be made available promptly to other interested parties participating in the investigation.

6.1.3   As soon as an investigation has been initiated, the authorities shall provide the full text of the written application received under para 1 of Article 5 to the known exporters and to the authorities of the exporting Member and shall make it available, upon request, to other interested parties involved. Due regard shall be paid to the requirement for the protection of confidential information, as provided for in para 5.

6.2   Throughout the anti-dumping investigation all interested parties shall have a full opportunity for the defence of their interests. To this end, the authorities shall, on request, provide opportunities for all interested parties to meet those parties with adverse interests, so that opposing views may be presented and rebuttal arguments offered. Provision of such opportunities must take account of the need to preserve confidentiality and of the convenience to the parties. There shall be no obligation on any party to attend a meeting, and failure to do so shall not be prejudicial to that party's case. Interested parties shall also have the right, on justification, to present other information orally.

6.3   Oral information provided under para 2 shall be taken into account by the authorities only in so far as it is subsequently reproduced in writing and made available to other interested parties, as provided for in sub-para 1.2.

6.4   The authorities shall whenever practicable provide timely opportunities for all interested parties to see all information that is relevant to the presentation of their cases, that is not confidential as defined in para 5, and that is used by the authorities in an anti-dumping investigation, and to prepare presentations on the basis of this information.

6.5   Any information which is by nature confidential (for example, because its disclosure would be of significant competitive advantage to a competitor or because its disclosure would have a significantly adverse effect upon a person supplying the information or upon a person from whom that person acquired the information), or which is provided on a confidential basis by parties to an investigation shall, upon good cause shown, be treated as such by the authorities. Such information shall not be disclosed without specific permission of the party submitting it.

6.5.1   The authorities shall require interested parties providing confidential information to furnish non-confidential summaries thereof. These summaries shall be in sufficient detail to permit a reasonable understanding of the substance of the information submitted in confidence. In exceptional circumstances, such parties may indicate that such information is not susceptible of summary. In such exceptional circumstances, a statement of the reasons why summarisation is not possible must be provided.

6.5.2   If the authorities find that a request for confidentiality is not warranted and if the supplier of the information is either unwilling to make the information public or to authorise its disclosure in generalised or summary form, the authorities may disregard such information unless it can be demonstrated to their satisfaction from appropriate sources that the information is correct.

6.6   Except in circumstances provided for in para 8, the authorities shall during the course of an investigation satisfy themselves as to the accuracy of the information supplied by interested parties upon which their findings are based.

6.7   In order to verify information provided or to obtain further details, the authorities may carry out investigations in the territory of other Members as required, provided they obtain the agreement of the firms concerned and notify the representatives of the government of the Member in question, and unless that Member objects to the investigation. The procedures described in Annex I shall apply to investigations carried out in the territory of other Members. Subject to the requirement to protect confidential information, the authorities shall make the results of any such investigations available, or shall provide disclosure thereof pursuant to para 9, to the firms to which they pertain and may make such results available to the applicants.

6.8   In cases in which any interested party refuses access to, or otherwise does not provide, necessary information within a reasonable period or significantly impedes the investigation, preliminary and final determinations, affirmative or negative, may be made on the basis of the facts available. The provisions of Annex II shall be observed in the application of this paragraph.

6.9 The authorities shall, before a final determination is made, inform all interested parties of the essential facts under consideration which form the basis for the decision whether to apply definitive measures. Such disclosure should take place in sufficient time for the parties to defend their interests.

6.10 The authorities shall, as a rule, determine an individual margin of dumping for each known exporter or producer concerned of the product under investigation. In cases where the number of exporters, producers, importers or types of products involved is so large as to make such a determination impracticable, the authorities may limit their examination either to a reasonable number of interested parties or products by using samples which are statistically valid on the basis of information available to the authorities at the time of the selection, or to the largest percentage of the volume of the exports from the country in question which can reasonably be investigated.

6.10.1 Any selection of exporters, producers, importers or types of products made under this paragraph shall preferably be chosen in consultation with and with the consent of the exporters, producers or importers concerned.

6.10.2 In cases where the authorities have limited their examination, as provided for in this paragraph, they shall nevertheless determine an individual margin of dumping for any exporter or producer not initially selected who submits the necessary information in time for that information to be considered during the course of the investigation, except where the number of exporters or producers is so large that individual examinations would be unduly burdensome to the authorities and prevent the timely completion of the investigation. Voluntary responses shall not be discouraged.

6.11 For the purposes of this agreement, interested parties' shall include:

(i) an exporter or foreign producer or the importer of a product subject to investigation, or a trade or business association a majority of the members of which are producers, exporters or importers of such product;

(ii) the government of the exporting Member; and

(iii) a producer of the like product in the importing Member or a trade and business association a majority of the members of which produce the like product in the territory of the importing Member.

This list shall not preclude Members from allowing domestic or foreign parties other than those mentioned above to be included as interested parties.

6.12 The authorities shall provide opportunities for industrial users of the product under investigation, and for representative consumer organisations in cases where the product is commonly sold at the retail level, to provide information which is relevant to the investigation regarding dumping, injury and causality.

6.13 The authorities shall take due account of any difficulties experienced by interested parties, in particular small companies, in supplying information requested, and shall provide any assistance practicable.

6.14 The procedures set out above are not intended to prevent the authorities of a Member from proceeding expeditiously with regard to initiating an investigation, reaching preliminary or final determinations, whether affirmative or negative, or from applying provisional or final measures, in accordance with relevant provisions of this agreement.

Article 7 – Provisional measures

7.1 Provisional measures may be applied only if:

    (i) an investigation has been initiated in accordance with the provisions of Article 5, a public notice has been given to that effect and interested parties have been given adequate opportunities to submit information and make comments;

    (ii) a preliminary affirmative determination has been made of dumping and consequent injury to a domestic industry; and

    (iii) the authorities concerned judge such measures necessary to prevent injury being caused during the investigation.

7.2 Provisional measures may take the form of a provisional duty or, preferably, a security by cash deposit or bond – equal to the amount of the anti-dumping duty provisionally estimated, being not greater than the provisionally estimated margin of dumping. Withholding appraisement is an appropriate provisional measure, provided that the normal duty and the estimated amount of the anti-dumping duty be indicated and as long as the withholding of appraisement is subject to the same conditions as other provisional measures.

7.3 Provisional measures shall not be applied sooner than 60 days from the date of initiation of the investigation.

7.4 The application of provisional measures shall be limited to as short a period as possible, not exceeding four months or, on decision of the authorities concerned, upon request by exporters representing a significant percentage of the trade involved, to a period not exceeding six months. When authorities, in the course of an investigation, examine whether a duty lower than the margin of dumping would be sufficient to remove injury, these periods may be six and nine months, respectively.

7.5 The relevant provisions of Article 9 shall be followed in the application of provisional measures.

Article 8 – Price undertakings

8.1 Proceedings may suspended or terminated without the imposition of provisional measures or anti-dumping duties upon receipt of satisfactory voluntary undertakings from any exporter to revise its prices or to cease exports to the area in question at dumped prices so that the authorities are satisfied that the injurious effect of the dumping is eliminated. Price increases under such undertakings shall not be higher than necessary to eliminate the margin of dumping. It is desirable that the price increases be less than the margin of dumping if such increases would be adequate to remove the injury to the domestic industry.

8.2 Price undertakings shall not be sought or accepted from exporters unless the authorities of the importing Member have made a preliminary affirmative determination of dumping and injury caused by such dumping.

8.3 Undertakings offered need not be accepted if the authorities consider their acceptance impractical, for example, if the number of actual or potential exporters is too great, or for other reasons, including reasons of general policy. Should the case arise and where practicable, the authorities shall provide to the exporter the reasons which have led them to consider acceptance of an undertaking as inappropriate, and shall, to the extent possible, give the exporter an opportunity to make comments thereon.

8.4   If an undertaking is accepted, the investigation of dumping and injury shall nevertheless be completed if the exporter so desires or the authorities so decide. In such a case, if a negative determination of dumping or injury is made, the undertaking shall automatically lapse, except in cases where such a determination is due in large part to the existence of a price undertaking. In such cases, the authorities may require that an undertaking be maintained for a reasonable period consistent with the provisions of this agreement. In the event that an affirmative determination of dumping and injury is made, the undertaking shall continue consistent with its terms and the provisions of this agreement.

8.5   Price undertakings may be suggested by the authorities of the importing Member: but no exporter shall be forced to enter into such undertakings. The fact that exporters do not offer such undertakings, or do not accept an invitation to do so, shall in no way prejudice the consideration of the case. However, the authorities are free to determine that a threat of injury is more likely to be realised if the dumped imports continue.

8.6   Authorities of an importing Member may require any exporter from whom an undertaking has been accepted to provide periodically information relevant to the fulfilment of such an undertaking and to permit verification of pertinent data. In case of violation of an undertaking, the authorities of the importing Member may take, under this agreement in conformity with its provisions, expeditious actions which may constitute immediate application of provisional measures using the best information available. In such cases, definitive duties may be levied in accordance with this agreement on products entered for consumption not more than 90 days before the application of such provisional measures, except that any such retroactive assessment shall not apply to imports entered before the violation of the undertaking.

Article 9 – Imposition and collection of anti-dumping duties

9.1   The decision whether or not to impose an anti-dumping duty in cases where all requirements for the imposition have been fulfilled, and the decision whether the amount of the anti-dumping duty to be imposed shall be the full margin of dumping or less, are decisions to be made by the authorities of the importing Member. It is desirable that the imposition be permissive in the territory of all Members, and that the duty be less than the margin if such lesser duty would be adequate to remove the injury to the domestic industry.

9.2   When an anti-dumping duty is imposed in respect of any product, such anti-dumping duty shall be collected in the appropriate amounts in each case, on a non-discriminatory basis on imports of such product from all sources found to be dumped and causing injury, except as to imports from those sources from which price undertakings under the terms of this agreement have been accepted. The authorities shall name the supplier or suppliers of the product concerned. If, however, several suppliers from the same country are involved, and it is impracticable to name all these suppliers, the authorities may name the supplying country concerned. If several suppliers from more than one country are involved, the authorities may name either all the suppliers involved, or, if this is impracticable, ail the supplying countries involved.

9.3   The amount of the anti-dumping duty shall not exceed the margin of dumping as established under Article 2.

9.3.1 When the amount of the anti-dumping duty is assessed on a retrospective basis, the determination of the final liability for payment of anti-dumping duties shall take place as soon as possible, normally within 12 months, and in no case more than 18 months, after the date on which a request for a final assessment of the amount of the anti-dumping duty has been made. Any refund shall be made promptly and normally in not more than 90 days following the determination of final liability made pursuant to this sub-paragraph. In any case, where a refund is not made within 90 days, the authorities shall provide an explanation if so requested.

9.3.2 When the amount of the anti-dumping duty is assessed on a prospective basis, provision shall be made for a prompt refund, upon request, of any duty paid in excess of the margin of dumping. A refund of any such duty paid in excess of the actual margin of dumping shall normally take place within 12 months, and in no case more than 18 months, after the date on which a request for a refund, duly supported by evidence, has been made by an importer of the product subject to the anti-dumping duty. The refund authorised should normally be made within 90 days of the above-noted decision.

9.3.3 In determining whether and to what extent a reimbursement should be made when the export price is constructed in accordance with para 3 of Article 2, authorities should take account of any change in normal value, any change in costs incurred between importation and resale, and any movement in the resale price which is duly reflected in subsequent selling prices, and should calculate the export price with no deduction for the amount of anti-dumping duties paid when conclusive evidence of the above is provided.

9.4   When the authorities have limited their examination in accordance with the second sentence of para 10 of Article 6, any anti-dumping duty applied to imports from exporters or producers not included in the examination shall not exceed:

(i)   the weighted average margin of dumping established with respect to the selected exporters or producers; or

(ii)   where the liability for payment of anti-dumping duties is calculated on the basis of a prospective normal value, the difference between the weighted average normal value of the selected exporters or producers and the export prices of exporters or producers not individually examined,

provided that the authorities shall disregard for the purpose of this paragraph any zero and *de minimis* margins and margins established under the circumstances referred to in para 8 of Article 6. The authorities shall apply individual duties or normal values to imports from any exporter or producer not included in the examination who has provided the necessary information during the course of the investigation, as provided for in sub-para 10.2 of Article 6.

9.5   If a product is subject to anti-dumping duties in an importing Member, the authorities shall promptly carry out a review for the purpose of determining individual margins of dumping for any exporters or producers in the exporting country in question who have not exported the product to the importing Member during the period of investigation, provided that these exporters or producers can show that they are not related to any of the exporters or producers in the exporting country who are subject to the anti-dumping duties on the product. Such a review shall be initiated and carried out on an accelerated basis, compared to normal duty assessment and review proceedings in the importing Member. No anti-dumping duties shall be levied on imports from such exporters or producers while the review is being carried out. The authorities may, however, withhold appraisement and/or request guarantees to ensure that, should such a review result in a determination of dumping in respect of such producers or exporters, anti-dumping duties can be levied retroactively to the date of the initiation of the review.

Article 10 – Retroactivity

10.1 Provisional measures and anti-dumping duties shall only be applied to products which enter for consumption after the time when the decision taken under para 1 of Article 7 and para 1 of Article 9, respectively, enters into force, subject to the exceptions set out in this article.

10.2 Where a final determination of injury (but not of a threat thereof or of a material retardation of the establishment of an industry) is made or, in the case of a final determination of a threat of injury, where the effect of the dumped imports would, in the absence of the provisional measures, have led to a determination of injury, anti-dumping duties may be levied retroactively for the period for which provisional measures, if any, have been applied.

10.3 If the definitive anti-dumping duty is higher than the provisional duty paid or payable, or the amount estimated for the purpose of the security, the difference shall not be collected. If the definitive duty is lower than the provisional duty paid or payable, or the amount estimated for the purpose of the security, the difference shall be reimbursed or the duty recalculated, as the case may be.

10.4 Except as provided in para 2, where a determination of threat of injury or material retardation is made (but no injury has yet occurred) a definitive anti-dumping duty may be imposed only from the date of the determination of threat of injury or material retardation, and any cash deposit made during the period of the application of provisional measures shall be refunded and any bonds released in an expeditious manner.

10.5 Where a final determination is negative, any cash deposit made during the period of the application of provisional measures shall be refunded and any bonds released in an expeditious manner.

10.6 A definitive anti-dumping duty may be levied on products which were entered for consumption not more than 90 days prior to the date of application of provisional measures, when the authorities determine for the dumped product in question that:

(i) there is a history of dumping which caused injury or that the importer was, or should have been, aware that the exporter practises dumping and that such dumping would cause injury; and

(ii) the injury is caused by massive dumped imports of a product in a relatively short time which in light of the timing and the volume of the dumped imports and other circumstances (such as a rapid build-up of inventories of the imported product) is likely to seriously undermine the remedial effect of the definitive anti-dumping duty to be applied, provided that the importers concerned have been given an opportunity to comment.

10.7   The authorities may, after initiating an investigation, take such measures as the withholding of appraisement or assessment as may be necessary to collect anti-dumping duties retroactively, as provided for in para 6, once they have sufficient evidence that the conditions set forth in that paragraph are satisfied.

10.8   No duties shall be levied retroactively pursuant to para 6 on products entered for consumption prior to the date of initiation of the investigation.

Article 11 – Duration and review of anti-dumping duties and price undertakings

11.1   An anti-dumping duty shall remain in force only as long as and to the extent necessary to counteract dumping which is causing injury.

11.2   The authorities shall review the need for the continued imposition of the duty, where warranted, on their own initiative or, provided that a reasonable period of time has elapsed since the imposition of the definitive anti-dumping duty, upon request by any interested party which submits positive information substantiating the need for a review. Interested parties shall have the right to request the authorities to examine whether the continued imposition of the duty is necessary to offset dumping, whether the injury would be likely to continue or recur if the duty were removed or varied, or both. If, as a result of the review under this paragraph, the authorities determine that the anti-dumping duty is no longer warranted, it shall be terminated immediately.

11.3   Notwithstanding the provisions of paras 1 and 2, any definitive anti-dumping duty shall be terminated on a date not later than five years from its imposition (or from the date of the most recent review under para 2 if that review has covered both dumping and injury, or under this paragraph), unless the authorities determine, in a review initiated before that date on their own initiative or upon a duly substantiated request made by or on behalf of the domestic industry within a reasonable period of time prior to that date, that the expiry of the duty would be likely to lead to continuation or recurrence of dumping and injury. The duty may remain in force pending the outcome of such a review.

11.4   The provisions of Article 6 regarding evidence and procedure shall apply to any review carried out under this article. Any such review shall be carried out expeditiously and shall normally be concluded within 12 months of the date of initiation of the review.

11.5   The provisions of this article shall apply *mutatis mutandis* to price undertakings accepted under Article 8.

Article 12 – Public notice and explanation of determinations

12.1   When the authorities are satisfied that there is sufficient evidence to justify the initiation of an anti-dumping investigation pursuant to Article 5, the Member or Members the products of which are subject to such investigation and other interested parties known to the investigating authorities to have an interest therein shall be notified and a public notice shall be given.

12.1.1 A public notice of the initiation of an investigation shall contain, or otherwise make available through a separate report, adequate information on the following:

  (i)   the name of the exporting country or countries and the product involved;

  (ii) the date of initiation of the investigation;

  (iii) the basis on which dumping is alleged in the application;

(iv) a summary of the factors on which the allegation of injury is based;

(v) the address to which representations by interested parties should be directed;

(vi) the time limits allowed to interested parties for making their views known.

12.2 Public notice shall tee given of any preliminary or final determination, whether affirmative or negative, of any decision to accept an undertaking pursuant to Article 8, of the termination of such an undertaking, and of the termination of a definitive anti-dumping duty. Each such notice shall set forth, or otherwise make available through a separate report, in sufficient detail the findings and conclusions reached on all issues of fact and law considered material by the investigating authorities. All such notices and reports shall be forwarded to the Member or Members the products of which are subject to such determination or undertaking and to other interested parties known to have an interest therein.

12.2.1 A public notice of the imposition of provisional measures shall set forth, or otherwise make available through a separate report, sufficiently detailed explanations for the preliminary determinations on dumping and injury and shall refer to the matters of fact and law which have led to arguments being accepted or rejected. Such a notice or report shall, due regard being paid to the requirement for the protection of confidential information, contain in particular:

(i) the names of the suppliers, or when this is impracticable, the supplying countries involved;

(ii) a description of the product which is sufficient for customs purposes;

(iii) the margins of dumping established and a full explanation of the reasons for the methodology used in the establishment and comparison of the export price and the normal value under Article 2;

(iv) considerations relevant to the injury determination as set out in Article 3;

(v) the main reasons leading to the determination.

12.2.2 A public notice of conclusion or suspension of an investigation in the case of an affirmative determination providing for the imposition of a definitive duty or the acceptance of a price undertaking shall contain, or otherwise make available through a separate report, all relevant information on the matters of fact and law and reasons which have led to the imposition of final measures or the acceptance of a price undertaking, due regard being paid to the requirement for the protection of confidential information. In particular, the notice or report shall contain the information described in sub-para 2.1, as well as the reasons for the acceptance or rejection of relevant arguments or claims made by the exporters and importers, and the basis for any decision made under sub-para 10.2 of Article 6.

12.2.3 A public notice of the termination or suspension of an investigation following the acceptance of an undertaking pursuant to Article 8 shall include, or otherwise make available through a separate report, the non-confidential part of this undertaking.

12.3 The provisions of this article shall apply *mutatis mutandis* to the initiation and completion of reviews pursuant to Article 11 and to decisions under Article 10 to apply duties retroactively.

Article 13 – Judicial review

Each Member whose national legislation contains provisions on anti-dumping measures shall maintain judicial, arbitral or administrative tribunals or procedures for the purpose, *inter alia*, of the prompt review of administrative actions relating to final determinations and reviews of determinations within the meaning of Article 11. Such tribunals or procedures shall be independent of the authorities responsible for the determination or review in question.

Article 14 – Anti-dumping action on behalf of a third country

14.1   An application for anti-dumping action on behalf of a third country shall be made by the authorities of the third country requesting action.

14.2   Such an application shall be supported by price information to show that the imports are being dumped and by detailed information to show that the alleged dumping is causing injury to the domestic industry concerned in the third country. The government of the third country shall afford all assistance to the authorities of the importing country to obtain any further information which the latter may require.

14.3   In considering such an application, the authorities of the importing country shall consider the effects of the alleged dumping on the industry concerned as a whole in the third country; that is to say, the injury shall not be assessed in relation only to the effect of the alleged dumping on the industry's exports to the importing country or even on the industry's total exports.

14.4   The decision whether or not to proceed with a case shall rest with the importing country. If the importing country decides that it is prepared to take action, the initiation of the approach to the Council for Trade in Goods seeking its approval for such action shall rest with the importing country.

Article 15 – Developing country members

It is recognised that special regard must be given by developed country Members to the special situation of developing country Members when considering the application of anti-dumping measures under this agreement. Possibilities of constructive remedies provided for by this agreement shall be explored before applying anti-dumping duties where they would affect the essential interests of developing country Members.

PART II

Article 16 – Committee on anti-dumping practices

16.1   There is hereby established a Committee on Anti-Dumping Practices (referred to in this agreement as the 'committee') composed of representatives from each of the Members. The committee shall elect its own Chairman and shall meet not less than twice a year and otherwise as envisaged by relevant provisions of this agreement at the request of any Member. The committee shall carry out responsibilities as assigned to it under this agreement or by the Members and it shall afford Members the opportunity of consulting on any matters relating to the operation of the agreement or the furtherance of its objectives. The WTO Secretariat shall act as the secretariat to the committee.

16.2   The committee may set up subsidiary bodies as appropriate.

16.3   In carrying out their functions, the committee and any subsidiary bodies may consult with and seek information from any source they deem appropriate. However, before the committee or a subsidiary body seeks such information from a source within the jurisdiction of a Member, it shall inform the Member involved. It shall obtain the consent of the Member and any firm to be consulted.

16.4 Members shall report without delay to the committee all preliminary or final anti-dumping actions taken. Such reports shall be available in the Secretariat for inspection by other Members. Members shall also submit, on a semi-annual basis, reports of any anti-dumping actions taken within the preceding six months. The semi-annual reports shall be submitted on an agreed standard form.

16.5 Each Member shall notify the committee (a) which of its authorities are competent to initiate and conduct investigations referred to in Article 5, and (b) its domestic procedures governing the initiation and conduct of such investigations.

Article 17 – Consultation and dispute settlement

17.1 Except as otherwise provided herein, the Dispute Settlement Understanding is applicable to consultations and the settlement of disputes under this agreement.

17.2 Each Member shall afford sympathetic consideration to, and shall afford adequate opportunity for consultation regarding, representations made by another Member with respect to any matter affecting the operation of this agreement.

17.3 If any Member considers that any benefit accruing to it, directly or indirectly, under this agreement is being nullified or impaired, or that the achievement of any objective is being impeded, by another Member or Members, it may, with a view to reaching a mutually satisfactory resolution of the matter, request in writing consultations with the Member or Members in question. Each Member shall afford sympathetic consideration to any request From another Member for consultation.

17.4 If the Member that requested consultations considers that the consultations pursuant to para 3 have failed to achieve a mutually agreed solution, and if final action has been taken by the administering authorities of the importing Member to levy definitive anti-dumping duties or to accept price undertakings, it may refer the matter to the Dispute Settlement Body (DSB). When a provisional measure has a significant impact and the Member that requested consultations considers that the measure was taken contrary to the provisions of para 1 of Article 7, that Member may also refer such matter to the DSB.

17.5 The DSB shall, at the request of the complaining party, establish a panel to examine the matter based upon:

(i) a written statement of the Member making the request indicating how a benefit accruing to it, directly or indirectly, under this agreement has been nullified or impaired, or that the achieving of the objectives of the agreement is being impeded; and

(ii) the facts made available in conformity with appropriate domestic procedures to the authorities of the importing Member.

17.6 In examining the matter referred to in para 5:

(i) in its assessment of the facts of the matter, the panel shall determine whether the authorities' establishment of the facts was proper and whether their evaluation of those facts was unbiased and objective. If the establishment of the facts was proper and the evaluation was unbiased and objective, even though the panel might have reached a different conclusion, the evaluation shall not be overturned;

(ii) the panel shall interpret the relevant provisions of the agreement in accordance with customary rules of interpretation of public international law. Where the panel finds that a relevant provision of the agreement admits of more than one permissible interpretation, the panel shall find the authorities' measure to be in conformity with the agreement if it rests upon one of those permissible interpretations.

17.7 Confidential information provided to the panel shall not be disclosed without formal authorisation from the person, body or authority providing such information. Where such information is requested from the panel but release of such information by the panel is not authorised, a non-confidential summary of the information, authorised by the person, body or authority providing the information, shall be provided.

Part III

Article 18 – Final provisions

18.1 No specific action against dumping of exports from another Member can be taken except in accordance with the provisions of GATT 1994, as interpreted by this agreement.

18.2 Reservations may not be entered in respect of any of the provisions of this agreement without the consent of the other Members.

18.3 Subject to sub-para 3.1 and 3.2, the provisions of this agreement shall apply to investigations, and reviews of existing measures, initiated pursuant to applications which have been made on or after the date of entry into force for a Member of the WTO Agreement.

18.3.1 With respect to the calculation of margins of dumping in refund procedures under para 3 of Article 9, the rules used in the most recent determination or review of dumping shall apply.

18.3.2 For the purposes of para 3 of Article 11, existing anti-dumping measures shall be deemed to be imposed on a date not later than the date of entry into force for a Member of the WTO Agreement, except in cases in which the domestic legislation of a Member in force on that date already included a clause of the type provided for in that paragraph.

18.4 Each Member shall take all necessary steps, of a general or particular character, to ensure, not later than the date of entry into force of the WTO Agreement for it, the conformity of its laws, regulations and administrative procedures with the provisions of this agreement as they may apply for the Member in question.

18.5 Each Member shall inform the committee of any changes in its laws and regulations relevant to this agreement and in the administration of such laws and regulations.

18.6 The committee shall review annually the implementation and operation of this agreement taking into account the objectives thereof. The committee shall inform annually the Council for Trade in Goods of developments during the period covered by such reviews.

18.7 The Annexes to this agreement constitute an integral part thereof.

Annex I

Procedures on-the-spot investigations pursuant to para 7 of Article 6

1   Upon initiation of an investigation, the authorities of the exporting Member and the firms known to be concerned should be informed of the intention to carry out on-the-spot investigations.

2   If in exceptional circumstances it is intended to include non-governmental experts in the investigating team, the firms and the authorities of the exporting Member should be so informed. Such non-governmental experts should be subject to effective sanctions for breach of confidentiality requirements.

3   It should be standard practice to obtain explicit agreement of the firms concerned in the exporting Member before the visit is finally scheduled.

4   As soon as the agreement of the firms concerned has been obtained, the investigating authorities should notify the authorities of the exporting Member of the names and addresses of the firms to be visited and the dates agreed.

5   Sufficient advance notice should be given to the firms in question before the visit is made.

6   Visits to explain the questionnaire should only be made at the request of an exporting firm. Such a visit may only be made if (a) the authorities of the importing Member notify the representatives of the Member in question, and (b) the latter do not object to the visit.

7   As the main purpose of the on-the-spot investigation is to verify information provided or to obtain further details, it should be carried out after the response to the questionnaire has been received unless the firm agrees to the contrary and the government of the exporting Member is informed by the investigating authorities of the anticipated visit and does not object to it; further, it should be standard practice prior to the visit to advise the firms concerned of the general nature of the information to be verified and of any further information which needs to be provided, though this should not preclude requests to be made on the spot for further details to be provided in the light of information obtained.

8   Enquiries or questions put by the authorities or firms of the exporting Members and essential to a successful on-the-spot investigation should, whenever possible, be answered before the visit is made.

Annex II

Best information available in terms of para 8 of Article 6

1   As soon as possible after the initiation of the investigation, the investigating authorities should specify in detail the information required from any interested party, and the manner in which that information should be structured by the interested party in its response. The authorities should also ensure that the party is aware that if information is not supplied within a reasonable time, the authorities will be free to make determinations on the basis of the facts available, including those contained in the application for the initiation of the investigation by the domestic industry.

2   The authorities may also request that an interested party provide its response in a particular medium (eg computer tape) or computer language. Where such a request is made, the authorities should consider the reasonable ability of the interested party

to respond in the preferred medium or computer language, and should not request the party to use for its response a computer system other than that used by the party. The authority should not maintain a request for a computerised response if the interested party does not maintain computerised accounts and if presenting the response as requested would result in an unreasonable extra burden on the interested party, eg it would entail unreasonable additional cost and trouble. The authorities should not maintain a request for a response in a particular medium or computer language if the interested party does not maintain its computerised accounts in such medium or computer language and if presenting the response as requested would result in an unreasonable extra burden on the interested party, eg it would entail unreasonable additional cost and trouble.

3   All information which is verifiable, which is appropriately submitted so that it can be used in the investigation without undue difficulties, which is supplied in a timely fashion, and, where applicable, which is supplied in a medium or computer language requested by the authorities, should be taken into account when determinations are made. If a party does not respond in the preferred medium or computer language but the authorities find that the circumstances set out in para 2 have been satisfied, the failure to respond in the preferred medium or computer language should not be considered to significantly impede the investigation.

4   Where the authorities do not have the ability to process information if provided in a particular medium (eg computer tape), the information should be supplied in the form of written material or any other form acceptable to the authorities.

5   Even though the information provided may not be ideal in all respects, this should not justify the authorities from disregarding it, provided the interested party has acted to the best of its ability.

6   If evidence or information is not accepted, the supplying party should be informed forthwith of the reasons therefore, and should have an opportunity to provide further explanations within a reasonable period, due account being taken of the time limits of the investigation. If the explanations are considered by the authorities as not being satisfactory, the reasons for the rejection of such evidence or information should be given in any published determinations.

7   If the authorities have to base their findings, including those with respect to normal value, on information from a secondary source, including the information supplied in the application for the initiation of the investigation, they should do so with special circumspection. In such cases, the authorities should, where practicable, check the information from other independent sources at their disposal, such as published price lists, official import statistics and customs returns, and from the information obtained from other interested parties during the investigation. It is clear, however, that if an interested party does not cooperate and thus relevant information is being withheld from the authorities, this situation could lead to a result which is less favourable to the party than if the party did cooperate.

AGREEMENT ON SUBSIDIES
AND COUNTERVAILING MEASURES

Members hereby agree as follows:

PART I – GENERAL PROVISIONS

Article I – Definition of a subsidy

1.1   For the purpose of this agreement, a subsidy shall be deemed to exist if:

(a)(1) there is a financial contribution by a government or any public body within the territory of a Member (referred to in this agreement as 'government'), ie where:

(i)   a government practice involves a direct transfer of funds (eg grants, loans, and equity infusion), potential direct transfers of funds or liabilities (eg loan guarantees);

(ii)   government revenue that is otherwise due is foregone or not collected (eg fiscal incentives such as tax credits);

(iii) a government provides goods or services other than general infrastructure, or purchases goods;

(iv)   a government makes payments to a funding mechanism, or entrusts or directs a private body to carry out one or more of the type of functions illustrated in (i) to (iii) above which would normally be vested in the government and the practice, in no real sense, differs from practices normally followed by governments; or

(a)(2) there is any form of income or price support in the sense of Article XVI of GATT 1994; and

(b)   a benefit is thereby conferred.

1.2   A subsidy as defined in para 1 shall be subject to the provisions of Part II or shall be subject to the provisions of Part III or V only if such a subsidy is specific in accordance with the provisions of Article 2.

Article 2 – Specificity

2.1   In order to determine whether a subsidy, as defined in para 1 of Article l, is specific to an enterprise or industry or group of enterprises or industries (referred to in this agreement as 'certain enterprises') within the jurisdiction of the granting authority, the following principles shall apply:

(a)   Where the granting authority, or the legislation pursuant to which the granting authority operates, explicitly limits access to a subsidy to certain enterprises, such subsidy shall be specific.

(b)   Where the granting authority, or the legislation pursuant to which the granting authority operates, establishes objective criteria or conditions governing the eligibility for, and the amount of, a subsidy, specificity shall not exist, provided that the eligibility is automatic and that such criteria and conditions are strictly adhered to. The criteria or conditions must be clearly spelled out in law, regulation, or other official document, so as to be capable of verification.

(c)   If, notwithstanding any appearance of non-specificity resulting from the application of the principles laid down in sub-paras (a) and (b), there are reasons to believe that the subsidy may in fact be specific, other factors may be considered. Such factors are: use of a subsidy programme by a limited number of certain enterprises, predominant use by certain enterprises, the granting of disproportionately large amounts of subsidy to certain enterprises, and the manner in which discretion has been exercised by the granting authority in the decision to grant a subsidy. In applying this sub-paragraph, account shall be taken of the extent of diversification of economic activities within the jurisdiction of the granting authority, as well as of the length of time during which the subsidy programme has been in operation.

2.2 A subsidy which is limited to certain enterprises located within a designated geographical region within the jurisdiction of the granting authority shall be specific. It is understood that the setting or change of generally applicable tax rates by all levels of government entitled to do so shall not be deemed to be a specific subsidy for the purposes of this agreement.

2.3 Any subsidy falling under the provisions of Article 3 shall be deemed to be specific.

2.4 Any determination of specificity under the provisions of this article shall be clearly substantiated on the basis of positive evidence.

PART II – PROHIBITED SUBSIDIES

Article 3 – Prohibition

3.1 Except as provided in the Agreement on Agriculture, the following subsidies, within the meaning of Article 1, shall be prohibited:

(a) subsidies contingent, in law or in fact whether solely or as one of several other conditions, upon export performance, including those illustrated in Annex I:

(b) subsidies contingent, whether solely or as one of several other conditions, upon the use of domestic over imported goods.

3.2 A Member shall neither grant nor maintain subsidies referred to in para 1.

Article 4 – Remedies

4.1 Whenever a Member has reason to believe that a prohibited subsidy is being granted or maintained by another Member, such Member may request consultations with such other Member.

4.2 A request for consultations under para 1 shall include a statement of available evidence with regard to the existence and nature of the subsidy in question.

4.3 Upon request for consultations under para 1, the Member believed to be granting or maintaining the subsidy in question shall enter into such consultations as quickly as possible. The purpose of the consultations shall be to clarify the facts of the situation and to arrive at a mutually agreed solution.

4.4 If no mutually agreed solution has been reached within 30 days of the request for consultations, any Member party to such consultations may refer the matter to the Dispute Settlement Body ('DSB') for the immediate establishment of a panel, unless the DSB decides by consensus not to establish a panel.

4.5 Upon its establishment, the panel may request the assistance of the Permanent Group of Experts (referred to in this agreement as the 'PGE') with regard to whether the measure in question is a prohibited subsidy. If so requested, the PGE shall immediately review the evidence with regard to the existence and nature of the measure in question and shall provide an opportunity for the Member applying or maintaining the measure to demonstrate that the measure in question is not a prohibited subsidy. The PGE shall report its conclusions to the panel within a time-limit determined by the panel. The PGE's conclusions on the issue of whether or not the measure in question is a prohibited subsidy shall be accepted by the panel without modification.

4.6 The panel shall submit its final report to the parties to the dispute. The report shall be circulated to all Members within 90 days of the date of the composition and the establishment of the panel's terms of reference.

4.7 If the measure in question is found to be a prohibited subsidy, the panel shall recommend that the subsidising Member withdraw the subsidy without delay. In this regard, the panel shall specify in its recommendation the time period within which the measure must be withdrawn.

4.8 Within 30 days of the issuance of the panel's report to all Members, the report shall be adopted by the DSB unless one of the parties to the dispute formally notifies the DSB of its decision to appeal or the DSB decides by consensus not to adopt the report.

4.9 Where a panel report is appealed, the Appellate Body shall issue its decision within 30 days from the date when the party to the dispute formally notifies its intention to appeal. When the Appellate Body considers that it cannot provide its report within 30 days, it shall inform the DSB in writing of the reasons for the delay together with an estimate of the period within which it will submit its report. In no case shall the proceedings exceed 60 days. The appellate report shall be adopted by the DSB and unconditionally accepted by the parties to the dispute unless the DSB decides by consensus not to adopt the appellate report within 20 days following its issuance to the Members.

4.10 In the event the recommendation of the DSB is not followed within the time period specified by the panel, which shall commence from the date of adoption of the panel's report or the Appellate Body's report, the DSB shall grant authorisation to the complaining Member to take appropriate countermeasures, unless the DSB decides by consensus to reject the request.

4.11 In the event a party to the dispute requests arbitration under para 6 of Article 22 of the Dispute Settlement Understanding (DSU), the arbitrator shall determine whether the countermeasures are appropriate.

4.12 For purposes of disputes conducted pursuant to this article, except for time-periods specifically prescribed in this article, time periods applicable under the DSU for the conduct of such disputes shall be half the time prescribed therein.

PART III – ACTIONABLE SUBSIDIES

Article 5 – Adverse effects

No Member should cause, through the use of any subsidy referred to in paras 1 and 2 of Article 1, adverse effects to the interests of other Members, ie:

(a) injury to the domestic industry of another Member;

(b) nullification or impairment of benefits accruing directly or indirectly to other Members under GATT 1994 in particular the benefits of concessions bound under Article II of GATT 1994;

(c)   serious prejudice to the interests of another Member.

This article does not apply to subsidies maintained on agricultural products as provided in Article 13 of the Agreement on Agriculture.

Article 6 – Serious prejudice

6.1   Serious prejudice in the sense of para (c) of Article 5 shall be deemed to exist in the case of:

    (a)   the total *ad valorem* subsidisation of a product exceeding 5%;

    (b)   subsidies to cover operating losses sustained by an industry;

    (c)   subsidies to cover operating losses sustained by an enterprise, other than one-time measures which are non-recurrent and cannot be repeated for that enterprise and which are given merely to provide time for the development of long term solutions and to avoid acute social problems;

    (d)   direct forgiveness of debt, ie forgiveness of government-held debt, and grants to cover debt repayment.

6.2   Notwithstanding the provisions of para 1, serious prejudice shall not be found if the subsidising Member demonstrates that the subsidy in question has not resulted in any of the effects enumerated in para 3.

6.3   Serious prejudice in the sense of para (c) of Article 5 may arise in any case where one or several of the following apply:

    (a)   the effect of the subsidy is to displace or impede the imports of a like product of another Member into the market of the subsidising Member;

    (b)   the effect of the subsidy is to displace or impede the exports of a like product of another Member from a third country market;

    (c)   the effect of the subsidy is a significant price undercutting by the subsidised product as compared with the price of a like product of another Member in the same market or significant price suppression, price depression or lost sales in the same market;

    (d)   the effect of the subsidy is an increase in the world market share of the subsidising Member in a particular subsidised primary product or commodity as compared to the average share it had during the previous period of three years and this increase follows a consistent trend over a period when subsidies have been granted.

6.4   For the purpose of para 3(b), the displacement or impeding of exports shall include any case in which, subject to the provisions of para 7, it has been demonstrated that there has been a change in relative shares of the market to the disadvantage of the non-subsidised like product (over an appropriately representative period sufficient to demonstrate clear trends in the development of the market for the product concerned, which, in normal circumstances, shall be at least one year). 'Change in relative shares of the market' shall include any of the following situations: (a) there is an increase in the market share of the subsidised product; (b) the market share of the subsidised product remains constant in circumstances in which, in the absence of the subsidy, it would have declined; (c) the market share of the subsidised product declines, but at a slower rate than would have been the case in the absence of the subsidy.

6.5   For the purpose of para 3(c), price undercutting shall include any case in which such price undercutting has been demonstrated through a comparison of prices of the subsidised product with prices of a non-subsidised like product supplied to the same market. The comparison shall be made at the same level of trade and at comparable times, due account being taken of any other factor affecting price comparability. However, if such a direct comparison is not possible, the existence of price undercutting may be demonstrated on the basis of export unit values.

6.6   Each Member in the market of which serious prejudice is alleged to have arisen shall subject to the provisions of para 3 of Annex V, make available to the parties to a dispute arising under Article 7, and to the panel established pursuant to para 4 of Article 7, all relevant information that can be obtained as to the changes in market shares of the parties to the dispute as well as concerning prices of the products involved.

6.7   Displacement or impediment resulting in serious prejudice shall not arise under para 3 where any of the following circumstances exist during the relevant period:

(a)   prohibition or restriction on exports of the like product from the complaining Member or on imports from the complaining Member into the third country market concerned;

(b)   decision by an importing government operating a monopoly of trade or state trading in the product concerned to shift, for non-commercial reasons, imports from the complaining Member to another country or countries;

(c)   natural disasters, strikes, transport disruptions or other *force majeure* substantially affecting production, qualities, quantities or prices of the product available for export from the complaining Member;

(d)   existence of arrangements limiting exports from the complaining Member;

(e)   voluntary decrease in the availability for export of the product concerned from the complaining Member (including, *inter alia*, a situation where firms in the complaining Member have been autonomously reallocating exports of this product to new markets);

(f)   failure to conform to standards and other regulatory requirements in the importing country.

6.8   In the absence of circumstances referred to in para 7, the existence of serious prejudice should be determined on the basis of the information submitted to or obtained by the panel, including information submitted in accordance with the provisions of Annex V.

6.9   This article does not apply to subsidies maintained on agricultural products as provided in Article 13 of the Agreement on Agriculture.

Article 7 – Remedies

7.1   Except as provided in Article 13 of the Agreement on Agriculture, whenever a Member has reason to believe that any subsidy referred to in Article 1, granted or maintained by another Member, results in injury to its domestic industry, nullification or impairment or serious prejudice, such Member may request consultations with such other Member.

7.2   A request for consultations under para 1 shall include a statement of available evidence with regard to (a) the existence and nature of the subsidy in question, and

(b) the injury caused to the domestic industry, or the nullification or impairment, or serious prejudice caused to the interests of the Member requesting consultations.

7.3   Upon request for consultations under para 1, the Member believed to be granting or maintaining the subsidy practice in question shall enter into such consultations as quickly as possible. The purpose of the consultations shall be to clarify the facts of the situation and to arrive at a mutually agreed solution.

7.4   If consultations do not result in a mutually acceptable solution within 60 days, any Member party to such consultations may refer the matter to the DSB for the establishment of a panel, unless the DSB decides by consensus not to establish a panel. The composition of the panel and its terms of reference shall be established within 15 days from the date when it is established.

7.5   The panel shall review the matter and shall submit its final report to the parties to the dispute. The report shall be circulated to all Members within 120 days of the date of the composition and establishment of the panel's terms of reference.

7.6   Within 30 days of the issuance of the panel's report to all Members, the report shall be adopted by the DSB unless one of the parties to the dispute formally notifies the DSB of its decision to appeal or the DSB decides by consensus not to adopt the report.

7.7   Where a panel report is appealed, the Appellate Body shall issue its decision within 60 days from the date when the party to the dispute formally notifies its intention to appeal. When the Appellate Body considers that it cannot provide its report within 60 days, it shall inform the DSB in writing of the reasons for the delay together with an estimate of the period within which it will submit its report. In no case shall the proceedings exceed 90 days. The appellate report shall be adopted by the DSB and unconditionally accepted by the parties to the dispute unless the DSB decides by consensus not to adopt the appellate report within 20 days following its issuance to the Members.

7.8   Where a panel report or an Appellate Body report is adopted in which it is determined that any subsidy has resulted in adverse effects to the interests of another Member within the meaning of Article 5, the Member granting or maintaining such subsidy shall take appropriate steps to remove the adverse effects or shall withdraw the subsidy.

7.9   In the event the Member has not taken appropriate steps to remove the adverse effects of the subsidy or withdraw the subsidy within six months from the date when the DSB adopts the panel report or the Appellate Body report, and in the absence of agreement on compensation, the DSB shall grant authorisation to the complaining Member to take countermeasures, commensurate with the degree and nature of the adverse effects determined to exist, unless the DSB decides by consensus to reject the request.

7.10   In the event that a party to the dispute requests arbitration under para 6 of Article 22 of the DSU, the arbitrator shall determine whether the countermeasures are commensurate with the degree and nature of the adverse effects determined to exist.

PART IV – NON-ACTIONABLE SUBSIDIES

Article 8 – Identification of non-actionable subsidies

8.1   The following subsidies shall be considered as non-actionable:

(a)   subsidies which are not specific within the meaning of Article 2;

(b)   subsidies which are specific within the meaning of Article 2 but which meet all of the conditions provided for in paras 2(a), 2(b) or 2(c) below.

8.2   Notwithstanding the provisions of Parts III and V, the following subsidies shall be non-actionable:

(a)   assistance for research activities conducted by firms or by higher education or research establishments on a contract basis with firms if the assistance covers not more than 75% of the costs of industrial research or 50% of the costs of pre-competitive development activity; and provided that such assistance is limited exclusively to:

(i)   costs of personnel (researchers, technicians and other supporting staff employed exclusively in the research activity);

(ii)   costs of instruments, equipment, land and buildings used exclusively and permanently (except when disposed of on a commercial basis) for the research activity;

(iii) costs of consultancy and equivalent services used exclusively for the research activity, including bought-in research, technical knowledge, patents, etc;

(iv) additional overhead costs incurred directly as a result of the research activity;

(v)   other running costs (such as those of materials, supplies and the like), incurred directly as a result of the research activity;

(b)   assistance to disadvantaged regions within the territory of a Member given pursuant to a general framework of regional development and non-specific (within the meaning of Article 2) within eligible regions provided that:

(i)   each disadvantaged region must be a clearly designated contiguous geographical area with a definable economic and administrative identity;

(ii)   the region is considered as disadvantaged on the basis of neutral and objective criteria, indicating that the region's difficulties arise out of more than temporary circumstances; such criteria must be clearly spelled out in law, regulation, or other official document, so as to be capable of verification;

(iii) the criteria shall include a measurement of economic development which shall be based on at least one of the following factors:

•   one of either income per capita or household income per capita, or GDP per capita, which must not be above 85% of the average for the territory concerned;

•   unemployment rate, which must be at least 110% of the average for the territory concerned;

•   as measured over a three year period; such measurement, however, may be a composite one and may include other factors;

(c) assistance to promote adaptation of existing facilities to new environmental requirements imposed by law and/or regulations which result in greater constraints and financial burden on firms, provided that the assistance:

    (i) is a one time non–recurring measure; and

    (ii) is limited to 20% of the cost of adaptation; and

    (iii) does not cover the cost of replacing and operating the assisted investment, which must be fully borne by firms; and

    (iv) is directly linked to and proportionate to a firm's planned reduction of nuisances and pollution, and does not cover any manufacturing cost savings which may be achieved; and

    (v) is available to all firms which can adopt the new equipment and/or production processes.

8.3   A subsidy programme for which the provisions of para 2 are invoked shall be notified in advance of its implementation to the committee in accordance with the provisions of Part VII. Any such notification shall be sufficiently precise to enable other Members to evaluate the consistency of the programme with the conditions and criteria provided for in the relevant provisions of para 2. Members shall also provide the committee with yearly updates of such notifications, in particular, by supplying information on global expenditure for each programme, and on any modification of the programme. Other Members shall have the right to request information about individual cases of subsidisation under a notified programme.

8.4   Upon request of a Member, the Secretariat shall review a notification made pursuant to para 3 and, where necessary, may require additional information from the subsidising Member concerning the notified programme under review. The Secretariat shall report its findings to the committee. The committee shall, upon request, promptly review the findings of the Secretariat (or, if a review by the Secretariat has not been requested, the notification itself), with a view to determining whether the conditions and criteria laid down in para 2 have not been met. The procedure provided for in this paragraph shall be completed at the latest at the first regular meeting of the committee following the notification of a subsidy programme, provided that at least two months have elapsed between such notification and the regular meeting of the committee. The review procedure described in this paragraph shall also apply, upon request, to substantial modifications of a programme notified in the yearly updates referred to in para 3.

8.5   Upon the request of a Member, the determination by the committee referred to in para 4, or a failure by the committee to make such a determination, as well as the violation, in individual cases, of the conditions set out in a notified programme, shall be submitted to binding arbitration. The arbitration body shall present its conclusions to the Members within 120 days from the date when the matter was referred to the arbitration body. Except as otherwise provided in this paragraph, the DSU shall apply to arbitrations conducted under this paragraph.

Article 9 – Consultations and authorised remedies

9.1   If, in the course of implementation of a programme referred to in para 2 of Article 8, notwithstanding the fact that the programme is consistent with the criteria laid down in that paragraph, a Member has reasons to believe that this programme has resulted in serious adverse effects to the domestic industry of that Member, such as to cause damage which would be difficult to repair, such Member may request consultations with the Member granting or maintaining the subsidy.

9.2   Upon request for consultations under para 1, the Member granting or maintaining the subsidy programme in question shall enter into such consultations as quickly as possible The purpose of the consultations shall be to clarify the facts of the situation and to arrive at a mutually acceptable solution.

9.3   If no mutually acceptable solution has been reached in consultations under para 2 within 60 days of the request for such consultations, the requesting Member may refer the matter to the committee.

9.4   Where a matter is referred to the committee, the committee shall immediately review the facts involved and the evidence of the effects referred to in para 1. If the committee determines that such effects exist, it may recommend to the subsidising Member to modify this programme in such a way as to remove these effects. The committee shall present its conclusions within 120 days from the date when the matter is referred to it under para 3. In the event the recommendation is not followed within six months, the committee shall authorise the requesting Member to take appropriate countermeasures commensurate with the nature and degree of the effects determined to exist.

PART V – COUNTERVAILING MEASURES

Article 10 – Application of Article V7 of GATT 1994

Members shall take all necessary steps to ensure that the imposition of a countervailing duty on any product of the territory of any Member imported into the territory of another Member is in accordance with the provisions of Article VI of GATT 1994 and the terms of this agreement. Countervailing duties may only be imposed pursuant to investigations initiated and conducted in accordance with the provisions of this agreement and the Agreement on Agriculture.

Article 11 – Initiation and subsequent investigation

11.1   Except as provided in para 6, an investigation to determine the existence, degree and effect of any alleged subsidy shall be initiated upon a written application by or on behalf of the domestic industry.

11.2   An application under para 1 shall include sufficient evidence of the existence of (a) a subsidy and, if possible, its amount, (b) injury within the meaning of Article VI of GATT 1994 as interpreted by this agreement, and (c) a causal link between the subsidised imports and the alleged injury. Simple assertion, unsubstantiated by relevant evidence, cannot be considered sufficient to meet the requirements of this paragraph. The application shall contain such information as is reasonably available to the applicant on the following:

(i)   the identity of the applicant and a description of the volume and value of the domestic production of the like product by the applicant. Where a written application is made on behalf of the domestic industry, the application shall identify the industry on behalf of which the application is made by a list of all known domestic producers of the like product (or associations of domestic producers of the like product) and, to the extent possible, a description of the volume and value of domestic production of the like product accounted for by such producers;

(ii) a complete description of the allegedly subsidised product, the names of the country or countries of origin or export in question, the identity of each known exporter or foreign producer and a list of known persons importing the product in question;

(iii) evidence with regard to the existence, amount and nature of the subsidy in question;

(iv) evidence that alleged injury to a domestic industry is caused by subsidised imports through the effects of the subsidies, this evidence includes information on the evolution of the volume of the allegedly subsidised imports, the effect of these imports on prices of the like product in the domestic market and the consequent impact of the imports on the domestic industry, as demonstrated by relevant factors and indices having a bearing on the state of the domestic industry, such as those listed in paras 2 and 4 of Article 15.

11.3 The authorities shall review the accuracy and adequacy of the evidence provided in the application to determine whether the evidence is sufficient justify the initiation of an investigation.

11.4 An investigation shall not be initiated pursuant to para 1 unless the authorities have determined, on the basis of an examination of the degree of support for, or opposition to, the application expressed by domestic producers of the like product, that the application has been made by or on behalf of the domestic industry. The application shall be considered to have been made 'by or on behalf of the domestic industry' if it is supported by those domestic producers whose collective output constitutes more than 50% of the total production of the like product produced by that portion of the domestic industry expressing either support for or opposition to the application. However, no investigation shall be initiated when domestic producers expressly supporting the application account for less than 25% of total production of the like product produced by the domestic industry.

11.5 The authorities shall avoid, unless a decision has been made to initiate an investigation, any publicising of the application for the initiation of an investigation.

11.6 If, in special circumstances, the authorities concerned decide to initiate an investigation without having received a written application by or on behalf of a domestic industry for the initiation of such investigation, they shall proceed only if they have sufficient evidence of the existence of a subsidy, injury and causal link, as described in para 2, to justify the initiation of an investigation.

11.7 The evidence of both subsidy and injury shall be considered simultaneously (a) in the decision whether or not to initiate an investigation and (b) thereafter, during the course of the investigation, starting on a date not later than the earliest date on which in accordance with the provisions of this agreement provisional measures may be applied.

11.8 In cases where products are not imported directly from the country of origin but are exported to the importing Member from an intermediate country, the provisions of this agreement shall be fully applicable and the transaction or transactions shall, for the purposes of this agreement, be regarded as having taken place between the country of origin and the importing Member.

11.9 An application under para 1 shall be rejected and an investigation shall be terminated promptly as soon as the authorities concerned are satisfied that there is not sufficient evidence of either subsidisation or of injury to justify proceeding with the case. There shall be immediate termination in cases where the amount of a subsidy is *de minimis*, or where the volume of subsidised imports, actual or potential, or the injury, is negligible. For the purpose of this paragraph, the amount of the subsidy shall be considered to be *de minimis* if the subsidy is less than 1% *ad valorem*.

11.10   An investigation shall not hinder the procedures of customs clearance.

11.11   Investigations shall, except in special circumstances, be concluded within one year, and in no case more than 18 months, after their initiation.

Article 12 – Evidence

12.1   Interested Members and all interested parties in a countervailing duty investigation shall be given notice of the information which the authorities require and ample opportunity to present in writing all evidence which they consider relevant in respect of the investigation in question.

12.1.1   Exporters, foreign producers or interested Members receiving questionnaires used in a countervailing duty investigation shall be given at least 30 days for reply. Due consideration should be given to any request for an extension of the 30 day period and, upon cause shown, such an extension should be granted whenever practicable.

12.1.2   Subject to the requirement to protect confidential information, evidence presented in writing by one interested Member or interested party shall be made available promptly to other interested Members or interested parties participating in the investigation.

12.1.3   As soon as an investigation has been initiated, the authorities shall provide the full text of the written application received under para 1 of Article 11 to the known exporters and to the authorities of the exporting Member and shall make it available, upon request, to other interested parties involved. Due regard shall be paid to the protection of confidential information, as provided for in para 4.

12.2   Interested Members and interested parties also shall have the right, upon justification, to present information orally. Where information is provided orally, the interested Members and interested parties subsequently shall be required to reduce such submissions to writing. Any decision of the investigating authorities can only be based on such information and arguments as were on the written record of this authority and which were available to interested Members and interested parties participating in the investigation, due account having been given to the need to protect confidential information.

12.3   The authorities shall whenever practicable provide timely opportunities for all interested Members and interested parties to see all information that is relevant to the presentation of their cases, that is not confidential as defined in para 4, and that is used by the authorities in a countervailing duty investigation, and to prepare presentations on the basis of this information.

12.4 Any information which is by nature confidential (eg because its disclosure would be of significant competitive advantage to a competitor or because its disclosure would have a significantly adverse effect upon a person supplying the information or upon a person from whom the supplier acquired the information), or which is provided on a confidential basis by parties to an investigation shall, upon good cause shown, be treated as such by the authorities. Such information shall not be disclosed without specific permission of the party submitting it.

12.4.1 The authorities shall require interested Members or interested parties providing confidential information to furnish non-confidential summaries thereof. These summaries shall be in sufficient detail to permit a reasonable understanding of the substance of the information submitted in confidence. In exceptional circumstances, such Members or parties may indicate that such information is not susceptible of summary. In such exceptional circumstances, a statement of the reasons why summarisation is not possible must be provided.

12.4.2 If the authorities find that a request for confidentiality is not warranted and if the supplier of the information is either unwilling to make the information public or to authorise its disclosure in generalised or summary form, the authorities may disregard such information unless it can be demonstrated to their satisfaction from appropriate sources that the information is correct.

12.5 Except in circumstances provided for in para 7, the authorities shall during the course of an investigation satisfy themselves as to the accuracy of the information supplied by interested Members or interested parties upon which their findings are based.

12.6 The investigating authorities may carry out investigations in the territory of other Members as required, provided that they have notified in good time the Member in question and unless that Member objects to the investigation. Further, the investigating authorities may carry out investigations on the premises of a firm and may examine the records of a firm if (a) the firm so agrees, and (b) the Member in question is notified and does not object. The procedures set forth in Annex VI shall apply to investigations on the premises of a firm. Subject to the requirement to protect confidential information, the authorities shall make the results of any such investigations available, or shall provide disclosure thereof pursuant to para 8, to the firms to which they pertain and may make such results available to the applicants.

12.7 In cases in which any interested Member or interested party refuses access to, or otherwise does not provide, necessary information within a reasonable period or significantly impedes the investigation, preliminary and final determinations, affirmative or negative, may be made on the basis of the facts available.

12.8 The authorities shall, before a final determination is made, inform all interested Members and interested parties of the essential facts under consideration which form the basis for the decision whether to apply definitive measures. Such disclosure should take place in sufficient time for the parties to defend their interests.

12.9 For the purposes of this agreement, 'interested parties' shall include:

(i) an exporter or foreign producer or the importer of a product subject to investigation, or a trade or business association a majority of the members of which are producers, exporters or importers of such product; and

(ii) a producer of the like product in the importing Member or a trade and business association a majority of the members of which produce the like product in the territory of the importing Member.

This list shall not preclude Members from allowing domestic or foreign parties other than those mentioned above to be included as interested parties.

12.10 The authorities shall provide opportunities for industrial users of the product under investigation, and for representative consumer organisations in cases where the product is commonly sold at the retail level, to provide information which is relevant to the investigation regarding subsidisation, injury and causality.

12.11 The authorities shall take due account of any difficulties experienced by interested parties, in particular small companies, in supplying information requested, and shall provide any assistance practicable.

12.12 The procedures set out above are not intended to prevent the authorities of a Member from proceeding expeditiously with regard to initiating an investigation, reaching preliminary or final determinations, whether affirmative or negative, or from applying provisional or final measures, in accordance with relevant provisions of this agreement.

Article 13 – Consultations

13.1 As soon as possible after an application under Article 11 is accepted, and in any event before the initiation of any investigation, Members the products of which may be subject to such investigation shall be invited for consultations with the aim of clarifying the situation as to the matters referred to in para 2 of Article 11 and arriving at a mutually agreed solution.

13.2 Furthermore, throughout the period of investigation, Members the products of which are the subject of the investigation shall be afforded a reasonable opportunity to continue consultations, with a view to clarifying the factual situation and to arriving at a mutually agreed solution.

13.3 Without prejudice to the obligation to afford reasonable opportunity for consultation, these provisions regarding consultations are not intended to prevent the authorities of a Member from proceeding expeditiously with regard to initiating the investigation, reaching preliminary or final determinations, whether affirmative or negative, or from applying provisional or final measures, in accordance with the provisions of this agreement.

13.4 The Member which intends to initiate any investigation or is conducting such an investigation shall permit, upon request, the Member or Members the products of which are subject to such investigation access to non-confidential evidence, including the non-confidential summary of confidential data being used for initiating or conducting the investigation.

Article 14 – Calculation of the amount of a subsidy in terms of the benefit to the recipient

For the purpose of Part V, any method used by the investigating authority to calculate the benefit to the recipient conferred pursuant to para 1 of Article 1 shall be provided for in the national legislation or implementing regulations of the Member concerned and its application to each particular case shall be transparent and adequately explained. Furthermore, any such method shall be consistent with the following guidelines:

(a) government provision of equity capital shall not be considered as conferring a benefit, unless the investment decision can be regarded as inconsistent with the usual investment practice (including for the provision of risk capital) of private investors in the territory of that Member;

(b) a loan by a government shall not be considered as conferring a benefit, unless there is a difference between the amount that the firm receiving the loan pays on the government loan and the amount the firm would pay on a comparable commercial loan which the firm could actually obtain on the market. In this case, the benefit shall be the difference between these two amounts;

(c)   a loan guarantee by a government shall not be considered as conferring a benefit, unless there is a difference between the amount that the firm receiving the guarantee pays on a loan guaranteed by the government and the amount that the firm would pay on a comparable commercial loan absent the government guarantee. In this case, the benefit shall be the difference between these two amounts adjusted for any differences in fees;

(d)   the provision of goods or services or purchase of goods by a government shall not be considered as conferring a benefit unless the provision is made for less than adequate remuneration, or the purchase is made for more than adequate remuneration. The adequacy of remuneration shall be determined in relation to prevailing market conditions for the good or service in question in the country of provision or purchase (including price, quality, availability, marketability, transportation and other conditions of purchase or sale).

Article 15 – Determination of injury

15.1   A determination of injury for purposes of Article VI of GATT 1994 shall be based on positive evidence and involve an objective examination of both (a) the volume of the subsidised imports and the effect of the subsidised imports on prices in the domestic market for like products; and (b) the consequent impact of these imports on the domestic producers of such products.

15.2   With regard to the volume of the subsidised imports, the investigating authorities shall consider whether there has been a significant increase in subsidised imports, either in absolute terms or relative to production or consumption in the importing Member. With regard to the effect of the subsidised imports on prices, the investigating authorities shall consider whether there has been a significant price undercutting by the subsidised imports as compared with the price of a like product of the importing Member, or whether the effect of such imports is otherwise to depress prices to a significant degree or to prevent price increases, which otherwise would have occurred, to a significant degree. No one or several of these factors can necessarily give decisive guidance.

15.3   Where imports of a product from more than one country are simultaneously subject to countervailing duty investigations, the investigating authorities may cumulatively assess the effects of such imports only if they determine that (a) the amount of subsidisation established in relation to the imports from each country is more than *de minimis* as defined in para 9 of Article 11 and the volume of imports from each country is not negligible and (b) a cumulative assessment of the effects of the imports is appropriate in light of the conditions of competition between the imported products and the conditions of competition between the imported products and the like domestic product.

15.4   The examination of the impact of the subsidised imports on the domestic industry shall include an evaluation of all relevant economic factors and indices having a bearing on the state of the industry, including actual and potential decline in output, sales, market share, profits, productivity, return on investments, or utilisation of capacity; factors affecting domestic prices; actual and potential negative effects on cash flow, inventories, employment, wages, growth, ability to raise capital or investments and, in the case of agriculture, whether there has been an increased burden on government support programmes. This list is not exhaustive, nor can one or several of these factors necessarily give decisive guidance.

15.5   It must be demonstrated that the subsidised imports are, through the effects of subsidies causing injury within the meaning of this agreement. The demonstration of a causal relationship between the subsidised imports and the injury to the domestic industry shall be based on an examination of all relevant evidence before the authorities. The authorities shall also examine any known factors other than the subsidised imports which at the same time are injuring the domestic industry, and the injuries caused by these other factors must not be attributed to the subsidised imports. Factors which may be relevant in this respect include, *inter alia*, the volumes and prices of non-subsidised imports of the product in question, contraction in demand or changes in the patterns of consumption, trade restrictive practices of and competition between the foreign and domestic producers, developments in technology and the export performance and productivity of the domestic industry.

15.6   The effect of the subsidised imports shall be assessed in relation to the domestic production of the like product when available data permit the separate identification of that production on the basis of such criteria as the production process, producers' sales and profits. If such separate identification of that production is not possible, the effects of the subsidised imports shall be assessed by the examination of the production of the narrowest group or range of products, which includes the like product, for which the necessary information can be provided.

15.7   A determination of a threat of material injury shall be based on facts and not merely on allegation, conjecture or remote possibility. The change in circumstances which would create a situation in which the subsidy would cause injury must be clearly foreseen and imminent. In making a determination regarding the existence of a threat of material injury, the investigating authorities should consider, *inter alia*, such factors as:

(i)   nature of the subsidy or subsidies in question and the trade effects likely to arise there from;

(ii)   a significant rate of increase of subsidised imports into the domestic market indicating the likelihood of substantially increased importation;

(iii) sufficient freely disposable, or an imminent, substantial increase in, capacity of the exporter indicating the likelihood of substantially increased subsidised exports to the importing Member's market, taking into account the availability of other export markets to absorb any additional exports;

(iv)   whether imports are entering at prices that will have a significant depressing or suppressing effect on domestic prices, and would likely increase demand for further imports; and

(v)   inventories of the product being investigated.

No one of these factors by itself can necessarily give decisive guidance but the totality of the factors considered must lead to the conclusion that further subsidised exports are imminent and that, unless protective action is taken, material injury would occur.

15.8   With respect to cases where injury is threatened by subsidised imports, the application of countervailing measures shall be considered and decided with special care.

Article 16 – Definition of domestic industry

16.1   For the purposes of this agreement, the term 'domestic industry' shall, except as provided in para 2, be interpreted as referring to the domestic producers as a whole of the like products or to those of them whose collective output of the products constitutes a major proportion of the total domestic production of those products, except that when producers are related to the exporters or importers or are themselves importers of the allegedly subsidised product or a like product from other countries, the term 'domestic industry' may be interpreted as referring to the rest of the producers.

16.2   In exceptional circumstances, the territory of a Member may, for the production in question, be divided into two or more competitive markets and the producers within each market may be regarded as a separate industry if (a) the producers within such market sell all or almost all of their production of the product in question in that market, and (b) the demand in that market is not to any substantial degree supplied by producers of the product in question located elsewhere in the territory. In such circumstances, injury may be found to exist even where a major portion of the total domestic industry is not injured, provided there is a concentration of subsidised imports into such an isolated market and provided further that the subsidised imports are causing injury to the producers of all or almost all of the production within such market.

16.3   When the domestic industry has been interpreted as referring to the producers in a certain area, ie a market as defined in para 2, countervailing duties shall be levied only on the products in question consigned for final consumption to that area. When the constitutional law of the importing Member does not permit the levying of countervailing duties on such a basis, the importing Member may levy the countervailing duties without limitation only if (a) the exporters shall have been given an opportunity to cease exporting at subsidised prices to the area concerned or otherwise give assurances pursuant to Article 18, and adequate assurances in this regard have not been promptly given, and (b) such duties cannot be levied only on products of specific producers which supply the area in question.

16.4   Where two or more countries have reached under the provisions of para 8(a) of Article XXIV of GATT 1994 such a level of integration that they have the characteristics of a single, unified market, the industry in the entire area of integration shall be taken to be the domestic industry referred to in paras 1 and 2.

16.5   The provisions of para 6 of Article 15 shall be applicable to this article.

Article 17 – Provisional measures

17.1   Provisional measures may be applied only if:

(a)   an investigation has been initiated in accordance with the provisions of Article 11, a public notice has been given to that effect and interested Members and interested parties have been given adequate opportunities to submit information and make comments;

(b)   a preliminary affirmative determination has been made that a subsidy exists and that there is injury to a domestic industry caused by subsidised imports; and

(c)   the authorities concerned judge such measures necessary to prevent injury being caused during the investigation.

17.2 Provisional measures may take the form of provisional countervailing duties guaranteed by cash deposits or bonds equal to the amount of the provisionally calculated amount of subsidisation.

17.3 Provisional measures shall not be applied sooner than 60 days from the date of initiation of the investigation.

17.4 The application of provisional measures shall be limited to as short a period as possible, not exceeding four months.

17.5 The relevant provisions of Article 19 shall be followed in the application of provisional measures.

Article 18 – Undertakings

18.1 Proceedings may be suspended or terminated without the imposition of provisional measures or countervailing duties upon receipt of satisfactory voluntary undertakings under which:

(a) the government of the exporting Member agrees to eliminate or limit the subsidy or take other measures concerning its effects; or

(b) the exporter agrees to revise its prices so that the investigating authorities are satisfied that the injurious effect of the subsidy is eliminated. Price increases under such undertakings shall not be higher than necessary to eliminate the amount of the subsidy. It is desirable that the price increases be less than the amount of the subsidy if such increases would be adequate to remove the injury to the domestic industry.

18.2 Undertakings shall not be sought or accepted unless the authorities of the importing Member have made a preliminary affirmative determination of subsidisation and injury caused by such subsidisation and, in case of undertakings from exporters, have obtained the consent of the exporting Member.

18.3 Undertakings offered need not be accepted if the authorities of the importing Member consider their acceptance impractical, for example if the number of actual or potential exporters is too great, or for other reasons, including reasons of general policy. Should the case arise and where practicable, the authorities shall provide to the exporter the reasons which have led them to consider acceptance of an undertaking as inappropriate, and shall, to the extent possible, give the exporter an opportunity to make comments thereon.

18.4 If an undertaking is accepted, the investigation of subsidisation and injury shall nevertheless be completed if the exporting Member so desires or the importing Member so decides. In such a case, if a negative determination of subsidisation or injury is made, the undertaking shall automatically lapse, except in cases where such a determination is due in large part to the existence of an undertaking. In such cases, the authorities concerned may require that an undertaking be maintained for a reasonable period consistent with the provisions of this agreement. In the event that an affirmative determination of subsidisation and injury is made, the undertaking shall continue consistent with its terms and the provisions of this agreement.

18.5 Price undertakings may be suggested by the authorities of the importing Member, but no exporter shall be forced to enter into such undertakings. The fact that governments or exporters do not offer such undertakings, or do not accept an invitation to do so, shall in no way prejudice the consideration of the case. However, the authorities are free to determine that a threat of injury is more likely to be realised if the subsidised imports continue.

18.6 Authorities of an importing Member may require any government or exporter from whom an undertaking has been accepted to provide periodically information relevant to the fulfilment of such an undertaking, and to permit verification of pertinent data. In case of violation of an undertaking, the authorities of the importing Members may take, under this agreement in conformity with its provisions, expeditious actions which may constitute immediate application of provisional measures using the best information available. In such cases, definitive duties may be levied in accordance with this agreement on products entered for consumption not more than 90 days before the application of such provisional measures, except that any such retroactive assessment shall not apply to imports entered before the violation of the undertaking.

Article 19 – Imposition and collection of countervailing duties

19.1 If, after reasonable efforts have been made to complete consultations, a Member makes a final determination of the existence and amount of the subsidy and that, through the effects of the subsidy, the subsidised imports are causing injury, it may impose a countervailing duty in accordance with the provisions of this article unless the subsidy or subsidies are withdrawn.

19.2 The decision whether or not to impose a countervailing duty in cases where all requirements for the imposition have been fulfilled, and the decision whether the amount of the countervailing duty to be imposed shall be the full amount of the subsidy or less, are decisions to be made by the authorities of the importing Member. It is desirable that the imposition should be permissive in the territory of all Members, that the duty should be less than the total amount of the subsidy if such lesser duty would be adequate to remove the injury to the domestic industry, and that procedures should be established which would allow the authorities concerned to take due account of representations made by domestic interested parties whose interests might be adversely affected by the imposition of a countervailing duty.

19.3 When a countervailing duty is imposed in respect of any product, such countervailing duty shall be levied, in the appropriate amounts in each case, on a non-discriminatory basis on imports of such product from all sources found to be subsidised and causing injury, except as to imports from those sources which have renounced any subsidies in question or from which undertakings under the terms of this agreement have been accepted. Any exporter whose exports are subject to a definitive countervailing duty but who was not actually investigated for reasons other than a refusal to cooperate, shall be entitled to an expedited review in order that the investigating authorities promptly establish an individual countervailing duty rate for that exporter.

19.4 No countervailing duty shall be levied on any imported product in excess of the amount of the subsidy found to exist, calculated in terms of subsidisation per unit of the subsidised and exported product.

Article 20 – Retroactivity

20.1 Provisional measures and countervailing duties shall only be applied to products which enter for consumption after the time when the decision under para 1 of Article 17 and para 1 of Article 19, respectively, enters into force, subject to the exceptions set out in this article.

20.2   Where a final determination of injury (but not of a threat thereof or of a material retardation of the establishment of an industry) is made or, in the case of a final determination of a threat of injury, where the effect of the subsidised imports would, in the absence of the provisional measures, have led to a determination of injury, countervailing duties may be levied retroactively for the period for which provisional measures, if any, have been applied.

20.3   If the definitive countervailing duty is higher than the amount guaranteed by the cash deposit or bond, the difference shall not be collected. If the definitive duty is less than the amount guaranteed by the cash deposit or bond, the excess amount shall be reimbursed or the bond released in an expeditious manner.

20.4   Except as provided in para 2, where a determination of threat of injury or material retardation is made (but no injury has yet occurred) a definitive countervailing duty may be imposed only from the date of the determination of threat of injury or material retardation, and any cash deposit made during the period of the application of provisional measures shall be refunded and any bonds released in an expeditious manner.

20.5   Where a final determination is negative, any cash deposit made during the period of the application of provisional measures shall be refunded and any bonds released in an expeditious manner.

20.6   In critical circumstances where for the subsidised product in question the authorities find that injury which is difficult to repair is caused by massive imports in a relatively short period of a product benefiting from subsidies paid or bestowed inconsistently with the provisions of GATT 1994 and of this agreement and where it is deemed necessary, in order to preclude the recurrence of such injury, to assess countervailing duties retroactively on those imports, the definitive countervailing duties may be assessed on imports which were entered for consumption not more than 90 days prior to the date of application of provisional measures.

Article 21 – Duration and review of countervailing duties and undertakings

21.1   A countervailing duty shall remain in force only as long as and to the extent necessary to counteract subsidisation which is causing injury.

21.2   The authorities shall review the need for the continued imposition of the duty, where warranted, on their own initiative or, provided that a reasonable period of time has elapsed since the imposition of the definitive countervailing duty, upon request by any interested party which submits positive information substantiating the need for a review. Interested parties shall have the right to request the authorities to examine whether the continued imposition of the duty is necessary to offset subsidisation, whether the injury would be likely to continue or recur if the duty were removed or varied, or both. If, as a result of the review under this paragraph, the authorities determine that the countervailing duty is no longer warranted, it shall be terminated immediately.

21.3   Notwithstanding the provisions of paras 1 and 2, any definitive countervailing duty shall be terminated on a date not later than five years from, its imposition (or from the date of the most recent review under para 2 if that review has covered both subsidisation and injury, or under this paragraph), unless the authorities determine, in a review initiated before that date on their own initiative or upon a duly substantiated request made by or on behalf of the domestic industry within a reasonable period of time prior to that date, that the expiry of the duty would be likely to lead to continuation or recurrence of subsidisation and injury. The duty may remain in force pending the outcome of such a review.

21.4   The provisions of Article 12 regarding evidence and procedure shall apply to any review carried out under this article. Any such review shall be carried out expeditiously and shall normally be concluded within 12 months of the date of initiation of the review.

21.5   The provisions of this article shall apply *mutatis mutandis* to undertakings accepted under Article 18.

Article 22 – Public notice and explanation of determinations

22.1   When the authorities are satisfied that there is sufficient evidence to justify the initiation of an investigation pursuant to Article 11, the Member or Members the products of which are subject to such investigation and other interested parties known to the investigating authorities to have an interest therein shall be notified and a public notice shall be given.

22.2   A public notice of the initiation of an investigation shall contain, or otherwise make available through a separate report, adequate information on the following:

(a)   the name of the exporting country or countries and the product involved;

(b)   the date of initiation of the investigation;

(c)   a description of the subsidy practice or practices to be investigated;

(d)   a summary of the factors on which the allegation of injury is based;

(e)   the address to which representations by interested Members and interested parties should be directed; and

(f)   the time limits allowed to interested Members and interested parties for making their views known.

22.3   Public notice shall be given of any preliminary or final determination, whether affirmative or negative, of any decision to accept an undertaking pursuant to Article 18, of the termination of such an undertaking, and of the termination of a definitive countervailing duty. Each such notice shall set forth, or otherwise make available through a separate report, in sufficient detail the findings and conclusions reached on all issues of fact and law considered material by the investigating authorities. All such notices and reports shall be forwarded to the Member or Members the products of which are subject to such determination or undertaking and to other interested parties known to have an interest therein.

22.4   A public notice of the imposition of provisional measures shall set forth, or otherwise make available through a separate report, sufficiently detailed explanations for the preliminary determinations on the existence of a subsidy and injury and shall refer to the matters of fact and law which have led to arguments being accepted or rejected. Such a notice or report shall, due regard being paid to the requirement for the protection of confidential information, contain in particular:

(i)   the names of the suppliers or, when this is impracticable, the supplying countries involved;

(ii)   a description of the product which is sufficient for customs purposes;

(iii)   the amount of subsidy established and the basis on which the existence of a subsidy has been determined;

(iv) considerations relevant to the injury determination as set out in Article 15;

(v) the main reasons leading to the determination.

22.5　A public notice of conclusion or suspension of an investigation in the case of an affirmative determination providing for the imposition of a definitive duty or the acceptance of an undertaking shall contain, or otherwise make available through a separate report, all relevant information on the matters of fact and law and reasons which have led to the imposition of final measures or the acceptance of an undertaking, due regard being paid to the requirement for the protection of confidential information.

In particular, the notice or report shall contain the information described in para 4, as well as the reasons for the acceptance or rejection of relevant arguments or claims made by interested Members and by the exporters and importers.

22.6　A public notice of the termination or suspension of an investigation following the acceptance of an undertaking pursuant to Article 18 shall include, or otherwise make available through a separate report, the non-confidential part of this undertaking.

22.7　The provisions of this article shall apply *mutatis mutandis* to the initiation and completion of reviews pursuant to Article 21 and to decisions under Article 20 to apply duties retroactively.

Article 23 – Judicial review

Each Member whose national legislation contains provisions on countervailing duty measures shall maintain judicial, arbitral or administrative tribunals or procedures for the purpose, *inter alia*, of the prompt review of administrative actions relating to final determinations and reviews of determinations within the meaning of Article 21. Such tribunals or procedures shall be independent of the authorities responsible for the determination or review in question, and shall provide all interested parties who participated in the administrative proceeding and are directly and individually affected by the administrative actions with access to review.

PART VI – INSTITUTIONS

Article 24 – Committee on subsidies and countervailing measures and subsidiary bodies

24.1　There is hereby established a Committee on Subsidies and Countervailing Measures composed of representatives from each of the Members. The committee shall elect its own Chairman and shall meet not less than twice a year and otherwise as envisaged by relevant provisions of this agreement at the request of any Member. The committee shall carry out responsibilities as assigned to it under this agreement or by the Members and it shall afford Members the opportunity of consulting on any matter relating to the operation of the agreement or the furtherance of its objectives. The WTO Secretariat shall act as the secretariat to the committee.

24.2　The committee may set up subsidiary bodies as appropriate.

24.3　The committee shall establish a Permanent Group of Experts composed of five independent persons, highly qualified in the fields of subsidies and trade relations. The experts will be elected by the committee and one of them will be replaced every year. The PGE may be requested to assist a panel, as provided for in para 5 of Article 4. The committee may also seek an advisory opinion on the existence and nature of any subsidy.

24.4 The PGE may be consulted by any Member and may give advisory opinions on the nature of any subsidy proposed to be introduced or currently maintained by that Member. Such advisory opinions will be confidential and may not be invoked in proceedings under Article 7.

24.5 In carrying out their functions, the committee and any subsidiary bodies may consult with and seek information from any source they deem appropriate. However, before the committee or a subsidiary body seeks such information from a source within the jurisdiction of a Member, it shall inform the Member involved.

PART VII – NOTIFICATION AND SURVEILLANCE

Article 25 – Notifications

25.1 Members agree that, without prejudice to the provisions of para 1 of Article XVI of GATT 1994, their notifications of subsidies shall be submitted not later than 30 June of each year and shall conform to the provisions of paras 2 through 6.

25.2 Members shall notify any subsidy as defined in para 1 of Article 1, which is specific within the meaning of Article 2, granted or maintained within their territories.

25.3 The content of notifications should be sufficiently specific to enable other Members to evaluate the trade effects and to understand the operation of notified subsidy programmes. In this connection, and without prejudice to the contents and form of the questionnaire on subsidies, Members shall ensure that their notifications contain the following information:

(a) form of a subsidy (ie grant, loan, tax concession, etc);

(b) subsidy per unit or, in cases where this is not possible, the total amount or the annual amount budgeted for that subsidy (indicating, if possible, the average subsidy per unit in the previous year);

(c) policy objective and/or purpose of a subsidy;

(d) duration of a subsidy and/or any other time limits attached to it;

(e) statistical data permitting an assessment of the trade effects of a subsidy.

25.4 Where specific points in para 3 have not been addressed in a notification, an explanation shall be provided in the notification itself.

25.5 If subsidies are granted to specific products or sectors, the notifications should be organised by product or sector.

25.6 Members which consider that there are no measures in their territories requiring notification under para 1 of Article XVI of GATT 1994 and this agreement shall so inform the Secretariat in writing.

25.7 Members recognise that notification of a measure does not prejudge either its legal status under GATT 1994 and this agreement, the effects under this agreement, or the nature of the measure itself.

25.8 Any Member may, at any time, make a written request for information on the nature and extent of any subsidy granted or maintained by another Member (including any subsidy referred to in Part IV), or for an explanation of the reasons for which a specific measure has been considered as not subject to the requirement of notification.

25.9 Members so requested shall provide such information as quickly as possible and in a comprehensive manner, and shall be ready, upon request, to provide additional information to the requesting Member. In particular, they shall provide sufficient details to enable the other Member to assess their compliance with the terms of this agreement. Any Member who considers that such information has not been provided may bring the matter to the attention of the committee.

25.10 Any Member who considers that any measure of another Member having the effects of a subsidy has not been notified in accordance with the provisions of para 1 of Article XVI of GATT 1994 and this article may bring the matter to the attention of such other Member. If the alleged subsidy is not thereafter notified promptly, such Member may itself bring the alleged subsidy in question to the notice of the committee.

25.11 Members shall report without delay to the committee all preliminary or final actions taken with respect to countervailing duties. Such reports shall be available in the Secretariat for inspection by other Members. Members shall also submit, on a semi-annual basis, reports on any countervailing duty actions taken within the preceding six months. The semi-annual reports shall be submitted on an agreed standard form.

25.12 Each Member shall notify the committee (a) which of its authorities are competent to initiate and conduct investigations referred to in Article 11, and (b) its domestic procedures governing the initiation and conduct of such investigations.

Article 26 – Surveillance

26.1 The committee shall examine new and full notifications submitted under para 1 of Article XVI of GATT 1994 and para 1 of Article 26 of this agreement at special sessions held every third year. Notifications submitted in the intervening years (updating notifications) shall be examined at each regular meeting of the committee.

26.2 The committee shall examine reports submitted under para 11 of Article 25 at each regular meeting of the committee.

PART VIII – DEVELOPING COUNTRY MEMBERS

Article 27 – Special and differential treatment of developing country members

27.1 Members recognise that subsidies may play an important role in economic development programmes of developing country Members.

27.2 The prohibition of para 1(a) of Article 3 shall not apply to:

(a) developing country Members referred to in Annex VII;

(b) other developing country Members for a period of eight years from the date of entry into force of the WTO Agreement, subject to compliance with the provisions in para 4.

27.3 The prohibition of para 1(b) of Article 3 shall not apply to developing country Members for a period of five years, and shall not apply to least developed country Members for a period of eight years, from the date of entry into force of the WTO Agreement.

27.4 Any developing country Member referred to in para 2(b) shall phase out its export subsidies within the eight year period, preferably in a progressive manner. However, a developing country Member shall not increase the level of its export subsidies and shall eliminate them within a period shorter than that provided for in this paragraph when the use of such export subsidies is inconsistent with its development needs. If a developing country Member deems it necessary to apply such subsidies beyond the eight year period, it shall not later than one year before the expiry of this period enter into consultation with the committee, which will determine whether an extension of this period is justified after examining all the relevant economic, financial and development needs of the developing country Member in question. If the committee determines that the extension is justified, the developing country Member concerned shall hold annual consultations with the committee to determine the necessity of maintaining the subsidies. If no such determination is made by the committee, the developing country Member shall phase out the remaining export subsidies within two years from the end of the last authorised period.

27.5   A developing country Member which has reached export competitiveness in any given product shall phase out its export subsidies for such product(s) over a period of two years. However, for a developing country Member which is referred to in Annex VII and which has reached export competitiveness in one or more products, export subsidies on such products shall be gradually phased out over a period of eight years.

27.6   Export competitiveness in a product exists if a developing country Member's exports of that product have reached a share of at least 3.25% in world trade of that product for two consecutive calendar years. Export competitiveness shall exist either (a) on the basis of notification by the developing country Member having reached export competitiveness, or (b) on the basis of a computation undertaken by the Secretariat at the request of any Member. For the purpose of this paragraph, a product is defined as a section heading of the Harmonised System Nomenclature. The committee shall review the operation of this provision five years from the date of the entry into force of the WTO Agreement.

27.7   The provisions of Article 4 shall not apply to a developing country Member in the case of export subsidies which are in conformity with the provisions of paras 2 through 5. The relevant provisions in such a case shall be those of Article 7.

27.8   There shall be no presumption in terms of para 1 of Article 6 that a subsidy granted by a developing country Member results in serious prejudice, as defined in this agreement. Such serious prejudice, where applicable under the terms of para 9, shall be demonstrated by positive evidence, in accordance with the provisions of paras 3 through 8 of Article 6.

27.9   Regarding actionable subsidies granted or maintained by a developing country Member other than those referred to in para 1 of Article 6, action may not be authorised or taken under Article 7 unless nullification or impairment of tariff concessions or other obligations under GATT 1994 is found to exist as a result of such a subsidy, in such a way as to displace or impede imports of a like product of another Member into the market of the subsidising developing country Member or unless injury to a domestic industry in the market of an importing Member occurs.

27.10 Any countervailing duty investigation of a product originating in a developing country Member shall be terminated as soon as the authorities concerned determine that:

(a) the overall level of subsidies granted upon the product in question does not exceed 2% of its value calculated on a per unit basis; or

(b) the volume of the subsidised imports represents less than 4% of the total imports of the like product in the importing Member, unless imports from developing country Members whose individual shares of total imports represent less than 4% collectively account for more than 9% of the total imports of the like product in the importing Member.

27.11 For those developing country Members within the scope of para 2(b) which have eliminated export subsidies prior to the expiry of the period of eight years from the date of entry into force of the WTO Agreement, and for those developing country members referred to in Annex VII, the number in para 10(a) shall be 3% rather than 2%. This provision shall apply from the date that the elimination of export subsidies is notified to the committee, and for so long as export subsidies are not granted by the notifying developing country Member. This provision shall expire eight years from the date of entry into force of the WTO Agreement.

27.12 The provisions of paras 10 and 11 shall govern any determination of *de minimis* under para 3 of Article 15.

27.13 The provisions of Part III shall not apply to direct forgiveness of debts, subsidies to cover social costs, in whatever form, including relinquishment of government revenue and other transfer of liabilities when such subsidies are granted within and directly linked to a privatisation programme of a developing country Member, provided that both such programme and the subsidies involved are granted for a limited period and notified to the committee and that the programme results in eventual privatisation of the enterprise concerned.

27.14 The committee shall, upon request by an interested Member, undertake a review of a specific export subsidy practice of a developing country Member to examine whether the practice is in conformity with its development needs.

27.15 The committee shall, upon request by an interested developing country Member, undertake a review of a specific countervailing measure to examine whether it is consistent with the provisions of paras 10 and 11 as applicable to the developing country Member in question.

PART IX – TRANSITIONAL ARRANGEMENTS

Article 28 – Existing programmes

28.1 Subsidy programmes which have been established within the territory of any Member before the date on which such a Member signed the WTO Agreement and which are inconsistent with the provisions of this agreement shall be:

(a) notified to the committee not later than 90 days after the date of entry into force of the WTO Agreement for such Member; and

(b) brought into conformity with the provisions of this agreement within three years of the date of entry into force of the WTO Agreement for such Member and until then shall not be subject to Part II.

28.2 No Member shall extend the scope of any such programme, nor shall such a programme be renewed upon its expiry.

Article 29 – Transformation into a market economy

29.1 Members in the process of transformation from a centrally planned into a market, free enterprise economy may apply programmes and measures necessary for such a transformation.

29.2   For such Members, subsidy programmes falling within the scope of Article 3, and notified according to para 3, shall be phased out or brought into conformity with Article 3 within a period of seven years from the date of entry into force of the WTO Agreement. In such a case, Article 4 shall not apply. In addition during the same period:

(a)   Subsidy programmes falling within the scope of para 1(d) of Article 6 shall not be actionable under Article 7;

(b)   With respect to other actionable subsidies, the provisions of para 9 of Article 27 shall apply.

29.3   Subsidy programmes falling within the scope of Article 3 shall be notified to the committee by the earliest practicable date after the date of entry into force of the WTO Agreement. Further notifications of such subsidies may be made up to two years after the date of entry into force of the WTO Agreement.

29.4   In exceptional circumstances, Members referred to in para 1 may be given departures from their notified programmes and measures and their time frame by the committee if such departures are deemed necessary for the process of transformation.

PART X – DISPUTE SETTLEMENT

Article 30

The provisions of Articles XXII and XXIII of GATT 1994 as elaborated and applied by the Dispute Settlement Understanding shall apply to consultations and the settlement of disputes under this agreement, except as otherwise specifically provided herein.

PART XI – FINAL PROVISIONS

Article 31 – Provisional application

The provisions of para 1 of Article 6 and the provisions of Article 8 and Article 9 shall apply for a period of five years; beginning with the date of entry into force of the WTO Agreement. Not later than 180 days before the end of this period, the committee shall review the operation of those provisions, with a view to determining whether to extend their application, either as presently drafted or in a modified form, for a further period.

Article 32 – Other final provisions

32.1   No specific action against a subsidy of another Member can be taken except in accordance with the provisions of GATT 1994, as interpreted by this agreement.

32.2   Reservations may not be entered in respect of any of the provisions of this agreement without the consent of the other Members.

32.3   Subject to para 4, the provisions of this agreement shall apply to investigations and reviews of existing measures, initiated pursuant to applications which have been made on or after the date of entry into force for a Member of the WTO Agreement.

32.4   For the purposes of para 3 of Article 21, existing countervailing measures shall be deemed to be imposed on a date not later than the date of entry into force for a Member of the WTO Agreement, except in cases in which the domestic legislation of a Member in force at that date already included a clause of the type provided for in that paragraph.

32.5   Each Member shall take all necessary steps, of a general or particular character, to ensure, not later than the date of entry into force of the WTO Agreement for it, the conformity of its laws, regulations and administrative procedures with the provisions of this agreement as they may apply to the Member in question.

32.6 Each Member shall inform the committee of any changes in its laws and regulations relevant to this agreement and in the administration of such laws and regulations.

32.7 The committee shall review annually the implementation and operation of this agreement, taking into account the objectives thereof. The committee shall inform annually the Council for Trade in Goods of developments during the period covered by such reviews.

32.8 The Annexes to this agreement constitute an integral part thereof.

Annex I

Illustrative list of export subsidies

(a) The provision by governments of direct subsidies to a firm or an industry contingent upon export performance.

(b) Currency retention schemes or any similar practices which involve a bonus on exports.

(c) Internal transport and freight charges on export shipments, provided or mandated by governments, on terms more favourable than for domestic shipments.

(d) The provision by governments or their agencies either directly or indirectly through government-mandated schemes, of imported or domestic products or services for use in the production of exported goods, on terms or conditions more favourable than for provision of like or directly competitive products or services for use in the production of goods for domestic consumption, if (in the case of products) such terms or conditions are more favourable than those commercially available on world markets to their exporters.

(e) The full or partial exemption remission, or deferral specifically related to exports, of direct taxes or social welfare charges paid or payable by industrial or commercial enterprises.

(f) The allowance of special deductions directly related to exports or export performance, over and above those granted in respect to production for domestic consumption, in the calculation of the base on which direct taxes are charged.

(g) The exemption or remission, in respect of the production and distribution of exported products, of indirect taxes in excess of those levied in respect of the production and distribution of like products when sold for domestic consumption.

(h) The exemption, remission or deferral of prior-stage cumulative indirect taxes on goods or services used in the production of exported products in excess of the exemption, remission or deferral of like prior-stage cumulative indirect taxes on goods or services used in the production of like products when sold for domestic consumption, provided, however, that prior-stage cumulative indirect taxes may be exempted, remitted or deferred on exported products even when not exempted, remitted or deferred on like products when sold for domestic consumption, if the prior-stage cumulative indirect taxes are levied on inputs that are consumed in the production of the exported product (making normal allowance for waste). This item shall be interpreted in accordance with the guidelines on consumption of inputs in the production process contained in Annex II.

(i)   The remission or drawback of import charges in excess of those levied on imported inputs that are consumed in the production of the exported product (making normal allowance for waste); provided, however, that in particular cases a firm may use a quantity of home market inputs equal to, and having the same quality and characteristics as, the imported inputs as a substitute for them in order to benefit from this provision if the import and the corresponding export operations both occur within a reasonable time period, not to exceed two years. This item shall be interpreted in accordance with the guidelines on consumption of inputs in the production process contained in Annex II and the guidelines in the determination of substitution drawback systems as export subsidies contained in Annex III.

(j)   The provision by governments (or special institutions controlled by governments) of export credit guarantee or insurance programmes, of insurance or guarantee programmes against increases in the cost of exported products or of exchange risk programmes, at premium rates which are inadequate to cover the long term operating costs and losses of the programmes.

(k)   The grant by governments (or special institutions controlled by and/or acting under the authority of governments) of export credits at rates below those which they actually have to pay for the funds so employed (or would have to pay if they borrowed on international capital markets in order to obtain funds of the same maturity and other credit terms and denominated in the same currency as the export credit), or the payment by them of all or part of the costs incurred by exporters or financial institutions in obtaining credits, in so far as they are used to secure a material advantage in the field of export credit terms. Provided, however, that if a Member is a party to an international undertaking on official export credits to which at least 12 original Members to this agreement are parties as of 1 January 1979 (or a successor undertaking which has been adopted by those original Members), or if in practice a Member applies the interest rates provisions of the relevant undertaking, an export credit practice which is in conformity with those provisions shall not be considered an export subsidy prohibited by this agreement.

(l)   Any other charge on the public account constituting an export subsidy in the sense of Article XVI of GATT 1994.

Annex II

Guidelines on consumption of inputs in the production process

I

1   Indirect tax rebate schemes can allow for exemption, remission or deferral of prior-stage cumulative indirect taxes levied on inputs that are consumed in the production of the exported product (making normal allowance for waste). Similarly, drawback schemes can allow for the remission or drawback of import charges levied on inputs that are consumed in the production of the exported product (making normal allowance for waste).

2   The Illustrative List of Export Subsidies in Annex I of this agreement makes reference to the term 'inputs that are consumed in the production of the exported product' in paras (h) and (i). Pursuant to para (h), indirect tax rebate schemes can constitute an export subsidy to the extent that they result in exemption, remission or deferral of prior-stage cumulative indirect taxes in excess of the amount of such taxes actually levied on inputs that are consumed in the production of the exported

product. Pursuant to para (i), drawback schemes can constitute an export subsidy to the extent that they result in a remission or drawback of import charges in excess of those actually levied on inputs that are consumed in the production of the exported product. Both paragraphs stipulate that normal allowance for waste must be made in findings regarding consumption of inputs in the production of the exported product. Paragraph (i) also provides for substitution, where appropriate.

II

In examining whether inputs are consumed in the production of the exported product, as part of a countervailing duty investigation pursuant to this agreement, investigating authorities should proceed on the following basis:

1 Where it is alleged that an indirect tax rebate scheme, or a drawback scheme, conveys a subsidy by reason of over-rebate or excess drawback of indirect taxes or import charges on inputs consumed in the production of the exported product, the investigating authorities should first determine whether the government of the exporting Member has in place and applies a system or procedure to confirm which inputs are consumed in the production of the exported product and in what amounts. Where such a system or procedure is determined to be applied, the investigating authorities should then examine the system or procedure to see whether it is reasonable, effective for the purpose intended, and based on generally accepted commercial practices in the country of export. The investigating authorities may deem it necessary to carry out, in accordance with para 6 of Article 12, certain practical tests in order to verify information or to satisfy themselves that the system or procedure is being effectively applied.

2 Where there is no such system or procedure, where it is not reasonable, or where it is instituted and considered reasonable but is found not to be applied or not to be applied effectively, a further examination by the exporting Member based on the actual inputs involved would need to be carried out in the context of determining whether an excess payment occurred. If the investigating authorities deemed it necessary, a further examination would be carried out in accordance with para 1.

3 Investigating authorities should treat inputs as physically incorporated if such inputs are used in the production process and are physically present in the product exported. The Members note that an input need not be present in the final product in the same form in which it entered the production process.

4 In determining the amount of a particular input that is consumed in the production of the exported product, a 'normal allowance for waste' should be taken into account, and such waste should be treated as consumed in the production of the exported product. The term 'waste' refers to that portion of a given input which does not serve an independent function in the production process, is not consumed in the production of the exported product (for reasons such as inefficiencies) and is not recovered, used or sold by the same manufacturer.

5 The investigating authority's determination of whether the claimed allowance for waste is 'normal' should take into account the production process, the average experience of the industry in the country of export, and other technical factors, as appropriate. The investigating authority should bear in mind that an important question is whether the authorities in the exporting Member have reasonably calculated the amount of waste, when such an amount is intended to be included in the tax or duty rebate or remission.

Annex III

**Guidelines in the determination of substitution
drawback systems as export subsidies**

I

Drawback systems can allow for the refund or drawback of import charges on inputs which are consumed in the production process of another product and where the export of this latter product contains domestic inputs having the same quality and characteristics as those substituted for the imported inputs. Pursuant to para (i) of the Illustrative List of Export Subsidies in Annex I, substitution drawback systems can constitute an export subsidy to the extent that they result in an excess drawback of the import charges levied initially on the imported inputs for which drawback is being claimed.

II

In examining any substitution drawback system as part of a countervailing duty investigation pursuant to this agreement, investigating authorities should proceed on the following basis:

1   Paragraph (i) of the Illustrative List stipulates that home market inputs may be substituted for imported inputs in the production of a product for export provided such inputs are equal in quantity to, and have the same quality and characteristics as, the imported inputs being substituted. The existence of a verification system or procedure is important because it enables the government of the exporting Member to ensure and demonstrate that the quantity of inputs for which drawback is claimed does not exceed the quantity of similar products exported, in whatever form, and that there is not drawback of import charges in excess of those originally levied on the imported inputs in question.

2   Where it is alleged that a substitution drawback system conveys a subsidy, the investigating authorities should first proceed to determine whether the government of the exporting Member has in place and applies a verification system or procedure. Where such a system or procedure is determined to be applied, the investigating authorities should then examine the verification procedures to see whether they are reasonable, effective for the purpose intended, and based on generally accepted commercial practices in the country of export. To the extent that the procedures are determined to meet this test and are effectively applied, no subsidy should be presumed to exist. It may be deemed necessary by the investigating authorities to carry out, in accordance with para 6 of Article 12, certain practical tests in order to verify information or to satisfy themselves that the verification procedures are being effectively applied.

3   Where there are no verification procedures, where they are not reasonable, or where such procedures are instituted and considered reasonable but are found not to be actually applied or not applied effectively, there may be a subsidy. In such cases, a further examination by the exporting Member based on the actual transactions involved would need to be carried out to determine whether an excess payment occurred. If the investigating authorities deemed it necessary, a further examination would be carried out in accordance with para 2.

4   The existence of a substitution drawback provision under which exporters are allowed to select particular import shipments on which drawback is claimed should not of itself be considered to convey a subsidy.

5   An excess drawback of import charges in the sense of para (i) would be deemed to exist where governments paid interest on any moneys refunded under their drawback schemes, to the extent of the interest actually paid or payable.

Annex IV

Calculation of the total *ad valorem* subsidisation (para 1(a) of Article 6)

1   Any calculation of the amount of a subsidy for the purpose of para 1(a) of Article 6 shall be done in terms of the cost to the granting government.

2   Except as provided in paras 3 through 5, in determining whether the overall rate of subsidisation exceeds 5% of the value of the product, the value of the product shall be calculated as the total value of the recipient firm's sales in the most recent 12-month period, for which sales data is available, preceding the period in which the subsidy is granted.

3   Where the subsidy is tied to the production or sale of a given product, the value of the product shall be calculated as the total value of the recipient firm's sales of that product in the most recent 12 month period, for which sales data is available, preceding the period in which the subsidy is granted.

4   Where the recipient firm is in a start-up situation, serious prejudice shall be deemed to exist if the overall rate of subsidisation exceeds 15% of the total funds invested. For purposes of this paragraph, a start-up period will not extend beyond the first year of production.

5   Where the recipient firm is located in an inflationary economy country, the value of the product shall be calculated as the recipient firm's total sales (or sales of the relevant product, if the subsidy is tied) in the preceding calendar year indexed by the rate of inflation experienced in the 12 months preceding the month in which the subsidy is to be given.

6   In determining the overall rate of subsidisation in a given year, subsidies given under different programmes and by different authorities in the territory of a Member shall be aggregated.

7   Subsidies granted prior to the date of entry into force of the WTO Agreement, the benefits of which are allocated to future production, shall be included in the overall rate of subsidisation.

8   Subsidies which are non-actionable under relevant provisions of this agreement shall not be included in the calculation of the amount of a subsidy for the purpose of para 1(a) of Article 6.

Annex V

Procedures for developing information concerning serious prejudice

1   Every Member shall cooperate in the development of evidence to be examined by a panel in procedures under paras 4 through 6 of Article 7. The parties to the dispute and any third country Member concerned shall notify to the DSB, as soon as the provisions of para 4 of Article 7 have been invoked, the organisation responsible for administration of this provision within its territory and the procedures to be used to comply with requests for information.

2   In cases where matters are referred to the DSB under para 4 of Article 7, the DSB shall, upon request, initiate the procedure to obtain such information from the

government of the subsidising Member as necessary to establish the existence and amount of subsidisation, the value of total sales of the subsidised firms, as well as information necessary to analyse the adverse effects caused by the subsidised product. This process may include, where appropriate, presentation of questions to the government of the subsidising Member and of the complaining Member to collect information, as well as to clarify and obtain elaboration of information available to the parties to a dispute through the notification procedures set forth in Part VII.

3   In the case of effects in third country markets, a party to a dispute may collect information, including through the use of questions to the government of the third country Member, necessary to analyse adverse effects, which is not otherwise reasonably available from the complaining Member or the subsidising Member. This requirement should be administered in such a way as not to impose an unreasonable burden on the third country Member. In particular, such a Member is not expected to make a market or price analysis specially for that purpose. The information to be supplied is that which is already available or can be readily obtained by this Member (eg most recent statistics which have already been gathered by relevant statistical services but which have not yet been published, customs data concerning imports and declared values of the products concerned, etc). However, if a party to a dispute undertakes a detailed market analysis at its own expense, the task of the person or firm conducting such an analysis shall be facilitated by the authorities of the third country Member and such a person or firm shall be given access to all information which is not normally maintained confidential by the government.

4   The DSB shall designate a representative to serve the function of facilitating the information-gathering process. The sole purpose of the representative shall be to ensure the timely development of the information necessary to facilitate expeditious subsequent multilateral review of the dispute. In particular, the representative may suggest ways to most efficiently solicit necessary information as well as encourage the cooperation of the parties.

5   The information-gathering process outlined in paras 2 through 4 shall be completed within 60 days of the date on which the matter has been referred to the DSB under para 4 of Article 7. The information obtained during this process shall be submitted to the panel established by the DSB in accordance with the provisions of Part X. This information should include, *inter alia*, data concerning the amount of the subsidy in question (and, where appropriate, the value of total sales of the subsidised firms), prices of the subsidised product, prices of the non-subsidised product, prices of other suppliers to the market, changes in the supply of the subsidised product to the market in question and changes in market shares. It should also include rebuttal evidence, as well as such supplemental information as the panel deems relevant in the course of reaching its conclusions.

6   If the subsidising and/or third country Member fails to cooperate in the information-gathering process, the complaining Member will present its case of serious prejudice, based on evidence available to it, together with facts and circumstances of the non-cooperation of the subsidising and/or third country Member. Where information is unavailable due to non-cooperation by the subsidising and/or third country Member, the panel may complete the record as necessary relying on best information otherwise available.

7   In making its determination, the panel should draw adverse inferences from instances of non- cooperation by any party involved in the information-gathering process.

8   In making a determination to use either best information available or adverse inferences, the panel shall consider the advice of the DSB representative nominated under para 4 as to the reasonableness of any requests for information and the efforts made by parties to comply with these requests in a cooperative and timely manner.

9   Nothing in the information-gathering process shall limit the ability of the panel to seek such additional information it deems essential to a proper resolution to the dispute, and which was not adequately sought or developed during that process. However, ordinarily the panel should not request additional information to complete the record where the information would support a particular party's position and the absence of that information in the record is the result of unreasonable non-cooperation by that party in the information-gathering process.

Annex VI

Procedures for on–the–spot investigations pursuant to para 6 of Article 12

1   Upon initiation of an investigation, the authorities of the exporting Member and the firms known to be concerned should be informed of the intention to carry out on-the-spot investigations.

2   If in exceptional circumstances it is intended to include non-governmental experts in the investigating team, the firms and the authorities of the exporting Member should be so informed. Such non-governmental experts should be subject to effective sanctions for breach of confidentiality requirements.

3   It should be standard practice to obtain explicit agreement of the firms concerned in the exporting Member before the visit is finally scheduled.

4   As soon as the agreement of the firms concerned has been obtained, the investigating authorities should notify the authorities of the exporting Member of the names and addresses of the firms to be visited and the dates agreed.

5   Sufficient advance notice should be given to the firms in question before the visit is made

6   Visits to explain the questionnaire should only be made at the request of an exporting firm In case of such a request the investigating authorities may place themselves at the disposal of the firm; such a visit may only be made if (a) the authorities of the importing Member notify the representatives of the government of the Member in question, and (b) the latter do not object to the visit.

7   As the main purpose of the on-the-spot investigation is to verify information provided or to obtain further details, it should be carried out after the response to the questionnaire has been received, unless the firm agrees to the contrary and the government of the exporting Member is informed by the investigating authorities of the anticipated visit and does not object to it; further, it should be standard practice prior to the visit to advise the firms concerned of the general nature of the information to be verified and of any further information which needs to be provided, though this should not preclude requests to be made on-the-spot for further details to be provided in the light of information obtained.

8   Enquires or questions put by the authorities or firms of the exporting Members and essential to a successful on-the-spot investigation should, whenever possible, be answered before the visit is made.

Annex VII

Developing country Members referred to in para 2(a) of Article 27

The developing country Members not subject to the provisions of para 1(a) of Article 3 under the terms of para 2(a) of Article 27 are:

(a) Least-developed countries designated as such by the United Nations which are Members of the WTO.

(b) Each of the following developing countries which are Members of the WTO shall be subject to the provisions which are applicable to other developing country Members according to para 2(b) of Article 27 when GNP per capita has reached $1,000 per annum: Bolivia, Cameroon, Congo, Côte d'Ivoire, Dominican Republic, Egypt, Ghana, Guatemala, Guyana, India, Indonesia, Kenya, Morocco, Nicaragua, Nigeria, Pakistan, Philippines, Senegal, Sri Lanka and Zimbabwe.

CHAPTER 9

TRADING BLOCS: NAFTA

INTRODUCTION

The purpose of this chapter is to introduce readers to the North American Free Trade Agreement 1992 (NAFTA)[1] and to provide an overview and an analysis of its key provisions and to identify the key concepts which animate and inform it.

NAFTA is one of many agreements comprising the scheme of North American Free Trade Agreements entered into between the governments of the USA, Canada and the United Mexican States ('the parties'). NAFTA entered into force on 1 January 1994 (Article 2203) and establishes a Free Trade Area (FTA) in the territories of the parties (Article 101).[2]

The objectives of NAFTA, as elaborated more specifically through its principles and rules, including national treatment, most-favoured-nation treatment and transparency are:

1   to eliminate barriers to trade in, and facilitate the cross-border movement of, goods and services between the territories of the parties;

2   to promote conditions of fair competition in the Free Trade Area;

3   to increase substantially investment opportunities in the territories of the parties;

4   to provide adequate and effective protection and enforcement of intellectual property rights in each party's territory;

5   to create effective procedures for the implementation and application of NAFTA, for its joint administration and for the resolution of disputes;

6   to establish a framework for further trilateral, regional and multilateral cooperation to expand and enhance the benefits of NAFTA (Article 102(1)(a)–(f)).

Under NAFTA, the parties have established a Free Trade Commission (Article 2001(1)) which supervises the implementation of NAFTA (Article 2001(2)(a)–(e)).[3]

NAFTA is a trilateral regional free trade agreement between the parties. It functions in a complementary manner to other bilateral and multilateral trade related international

---

1   North American Free Trade Agreement Washington, Ottawa, Mexico City, 8–17 December 1992; 32 ILM 289 (1993) Preamble ('NAFTA'). NAFTA has been incorporated into US domestic law by the North American Free Trade Implementation Act 1993. NAFTA is part of domestic Canadian law by virtue of the North American Free Trade Implementation Act 1993. References to provisions of international treaties in this Chapter are to provisions of NAFTA, unless the contrary is stated. NAFTA can be accessed on the Internet at the following site:
    http://www.sice.oas.org/trade/nafta/naftatce.stm.

2   The free trade area consists of Canada, the United Mexican States and the USA.

3   27 *Halsbury's Laws of Australia*, Trade and Commerce, para [420–2395].

agreements[4] including the Marrakesh Agreement establishing the World Trade Organisation (Marrakesh – 15 April 1994; Aust TS 1995 no 8; 33 ILM 1125) (the WTO Agreement, considered earlier in Chapter 7). Article 103(1) provides that the parties affirm their existing rights and obligations with respect to each other under the WTO Agreement and other agreements to which they are party.

If we reflect on certain statements of principle enumerated in the Preamble to NAFTA, it is quite clear that some of the forces which provide the impetus for NAFTA is the notion of mercantilism, that is the forces of commerce which are highly influential in shaping and contributing to the formation of national policy and international relations. The following extracts from the Preamble to NAFTA reflect this notion of mercantilism:

> The government of Canada, the government of the United Mexican States and the government of the USA, resolved to:
>
> Contribute to the harmonious development and expansion of world trade and provide a catalyst to broader international cooperation;
>
> Create an expanded and secure market for the goods and services produced in their territories;
>
> Reduce distortions to trade;
>
> Establish clear and mutually advantageous rules governing their trade;
>
> Ensure a predictable commercial framework for business planning and investment;
>
> Build on their respective rights and obligations under the General Agreement on Tariffs and Trade and other multilateral and bilateral instruments of cooperation;
>
> Enhance the competitiveness of their firms in global markets;
>
> Foster creativity and innovation, and promote trade in goods and services that are the subject of intellectual property rights;
>
> Create new employment opportunities and improve working conditions and living standards in their respective territories.

Commentators Snape, Adams and Morgan, writing in 1993 before the consummation of NAFTA, identified the motives behind NAFTA as encompassing both economic and political factors. They write:

> In terms of general economic objectives, each country [Canada, Mexico and the USA] aims to improve resource allocation across North America to increase economic efficiency and competitiveness. Expanding and securing trade with their largest partners is clearly important for each country. More specifically, in the FTA [Free Trade Agreement] with Canada, the USA was particularly interested in achieving reduced barriers and clearer rules for investment and trade in services, and increasing market access for certain products.
>
> The same ambitions (and improved intellectual property protection) apply to Mexico. However, the opportunity to lock in and reinforce recent Mexican economic reforms is probably the single most important economic and political motivation, for both the USA and Mexico. In addition, increased economic growth in Mexico is clearly in the interests

---

4   *Ibid*, para [420–2000].

of the USA for many reasons, including the high proportion of Mexican income spent on imports from the USA.

USA motivations also have a systemic angle. The USA maintained that the FTA would establish a 'building block' for multilateral liberalisation particularly in services and investment and, incidentally, would demonstrate the viability of the American regional option to Europe as the Single Market and the Uruguay Round were proceeding ... Moreover NAFTA is seen by some as a blueprint for further trade agreements in Central and South America, with the stated aim of securing hemisphere-wide 'free' trade. [citation omitted.][5]

Before we consider the key provisions, policies and concepts, we need to note one of the main constructs that is used frequently in NAFTA, namely the concept of 'measure'. 'Measure' is the generic term used to refer to legislative and administrative instruments that impose or create obligations (that is, rights and duties) for persons under the applicable legal system that is referred to. In the context of NAFTA, Article 201(1) defines 'measure' to include any law, regulation, procedure, requirement or practice. Thus the term embraces primary and secondary legislation as well as instruments issued by the executive branch of a government of a party of NAFTA.

NATIONAL TREATMENT AND MARKET ACCESS FOR GOODS

Chapter 3 of NAFTA (Articles 300–18, plus annexes) is devoted to the theme of national treatment and market access for goods. Chapter 3 is one of the pivotal chapters of NAFTA. It deals with two distinct but inter-related topics, namely national treatment and market access for goods. The coverage of Chapter 3 of NAFTA is limited by certain exceptions set out in Annexe 301.3, which constitute a series of exceptions to the operation of Articles 301 and 309. Otherwise, the scope of Chapter 3 of NAFTA is that it extends to trade in goods of a party.

One of the twin pillars of Chapter 3 of NAFTA is the concept of 'national treatment'. Article 301(1) obliges each party to accord national treatment to the goods of another party in accordance with Article III of the General Agreement on Tariffs and Trade 1994.[6] In turn, Article III of the GATT 1994 defines the term 'equality of national treatment' as being the regime where the products of any member of the WTO that are imported into the territory of another member:

1 are not to be subject, directly or indirectly, to internal taxes or other internal charges of any kind in excess of those applied, directly or indirectly, to like domestic products;

2 are to be accorded treatment no less favourable than that accorded to like products of national origin in respect of all laws, regulations and requirements affecting their

---

5   Snape, RH, Adams, J and Morgan, D, *Regional Trade Agreements: Implications and Options for Australia*, 1993, p 25, Canberra: AGPS.

6   NAFTA, Article 301(1) has an ambulatory operation, for it sweeps up and applies successor provisions to GATT 1947 (such as the WTO Agreement, see Chapter 6 above) to the parties.

internal sale, offering for sale, purchase, transportation, distribution or use: see GATT 1994 Articles III(2) and (3). The operation of the principle of equality of national treatment under NAFTA Article 301(1) is extended and applied to states and provinces as well by virtue of Article 301(2).

Complementing the principle of national treatment are a range of measures concerning the liberalisation of market access for goods. These provisions span both tariff measures and non–tariff measures. Under the rubric of tariff measures are a series of provisions, some of which are summarised below:

- Except as provided by NAFTA, no party may increase any existing customs duty, or adopt any customs duty, on an originating good (Article 302(1)).

- Except as provided by NAFTA, each party much progressively eliminate its customs duties on originating goods in accordance with its Schedule to Annexe 302.2 (Article 302(2)).

- No party may refund the amount of customs duties paid, or waive or reduce the amount of customs duties owed, on good imported into its territory on condition that the good is subsequently exported to the territory of another party, or is used as a material in the production of another good that is subsequently exported to the territory of another party or which is substituted by an identical or similar good used as material in the production of another good that is subsequently exported to the territory of another party (Article 303(1)).

- No party may, on condition of export, refund, waive or reduce an anti–dumping or countervailing duty that is applied under a party's domestic law and that is not applied consistently with Chapter 19 of NAFTA, a premium offered or collected on imported goods arising out of any tendering system concerning the administration of quantitative import restrictions, tariff rate quotas or tariff preference levels, or customs duties paid or owed on goods imported into its territory and substituted by an identical or similar good that is subsequently exported to the territory of another party (Article 303(2)).

- No party may adopt any new waiver of customs duties, or expand with respect to existing recipients or extend to any new recipient the application of an existing waiver of customs duty, where the waiver is conditioned explicitly or implicitly, on the fulfilment of a performance requirement (Article 304(1)).

- Each party must grant duty free temporary admission for professional equipment necessary for carrying out business activities, trades or professions of business people who qualify for temporary entry under Chapter 16: see Article 305(1)(a). This provision, in particular, reflects a notion of the free movement of goods associated with the complementary notion of the free movement of persons.

Non-tariff measures contained in Chapter 3 of NAFTA include:

- A prohibition on the adoption or maintenance of any prohibitions or restrictions on the importation of any goods of another party or on the exportation or sale for export of any goods destined for the territory of another party except in accordance with Article XI of GATT 1994 (Article XI of GATT 1994 deals with the general elimination of quantitative restrictions). [7]

- Each party must grant duty free entry to commercial samples of negligible value, and to printed advertising materials, imported from the territory of another party, regardless of their origin: see Article 306.

- Goods which are re-entered after repair or alteration are also free from customs duties (Article 307).

Non-tariff measures falling within the overall principle of market access are as follows. Under Article 309, no party may adopt or maintain any prohibition or restriction on the importation of any goods of another party or on the exportation or sale for export of any goods destined for the territory of another party except in accordance with Article XI of GATT 1994 (see Article 309(1)). There is a complementary understanding that this prohibition extends to measures such as export price requirements and import price requirements (except as permitted in enforcing countervailing and anti-dumping orders and undertakings) (see Article 309(2)). Certain customs user fees described in Annex 310.1 for originating goods may not be adopted by any party: see Article 310(1). In the case of export taxes (except as set out in Annexe 314) under Article 314 no party may adopt or maintain any duty, tax or other charge on the export of any goods to the territory of another party unless that impost is adopted or maintained on the export of any such goods to the territory of all other parties and when any such goods are destined for domestic consumption.

Article 316 of NAFTA establishes a Committee on Trade in Goods, comprising representatives of each party. This committee meets on the request of any party or of the Free Trade Commission (FTC) to consider any matter arising under Chapter 3 of NAFTA. There is also a commitment to at least annual meetings for the purpose of addressing issues relating to the movement of goods through each party's ports of entry.

RULES OF ORIGIN

Rules of origin are covered by Chapter 4 of NAFTA. These rules have a distributive operation across NAFTA. For example, see Article 302(1) which provides that no party may increase any existing customs duty, or adopt any customs duty, on an originating good (except as otherwise provided by NAFTA). Under Article 201(1), 'originating' means qualifying under the rules of origin set out in Chapter 4. The operation of the Chapter 4 rules of origin under NAFTA are significant because they identify those goods which, when traded, enjoy the benefit of the principles of national treatment and market access for goods. Conversely, those goods which do not fall within the scope of the rules of origin do not enjoy the operation of these beneficial rules. The rules of origin differ according to the presence or absence of certain criteria, including whether they are automotive goods, fungible goods and materials, accessories, spare parts and tools, indirect materials, packaging materials and containers for retail sale or for

---

7   See Chapter 6 above and 27 *Halsbury's Laws of Australia,* Trade and Commerce, para [420–2035].

shipment. Specific interpretation and application rules, as well as Chapter 4 definitions, apply to the meaning and operation of some of the key concepts of Chapter 4 by virtue of Articles 413 and 415.

The linchpin of Chapter 4 is whether goods qualify as 'originating goods'. Under Article 401, goods are originating goods in the territory of a party where:

- The good is wholly obtained or produced entirely in the territory of one or more of the parties (see Article 415 for the list of those types of goods that are 'goods wholly obtained or produced entirely in the territory of one or more of the parties').

- Any non-originating materials used in the production of any goods undergo an applicable change in tariff classifications set out in Annex 401 as a result of production occurring entirely in the territory of one or more of the parties.

- The goods are produced entirely in the territories of one or more of the parties exclusively from originating materials.

- Certain goods are produced entirely in the territory of one or more of the parties but one or more of the non-originating materials provided for as parts that are used in the production of the goods do not undergo certain changes in tariff classification, and also that the regional value content of the goods (determined in accordance with Article 402) is not less than 60% where the transaction value method is used, or is not less than 50% where the net cost method is used, and the goods satisfy all other applicable requirements of Chapter 4.

The origin value content rules set out in Article 402 are invoked by Article 401. In essence, there are two methods of calculating regional value content, namely transaction value (see Article 402(2)) or the net cost method (see Article 402(3)). Where the goods are automotive goods, Article 403 contains a separate regime for calculating the regional value content under the net cost method set out in Article 402(3). Accumulation rules contained in Article 404 deal with the situation where one producer accumulates or aggregates his, her or its goods with those of other producers (whether in the same territory or other territories), with the accumulating producer claiming a preferential tariff treatment. The effect of Article 405 is that goods are considered to be originating goods if the value of all non-originating materials used in the production of those goods that do not undergo an applicable change in tariff classification is not more than 7% of the transaction value of the goods, adjusted to a FOB basis, or, if the transaction value of the good is unacceptable under Article 1 of the Customs Valuation Code, the value of all such non-originating materials is not more than 7% of the total cost of the goods (see Article 405(1)). Qualifications to this *de minimis* rule are contained in Articles 405(3)–(6). Where the goods are 'fungible' (defined by Article 415 to mean goods or materials that are interchangeable for commercial purposes and whose properties are essentially identical) then obviously some method is needed to decide the origin of goods where such fungible goods or materials originate within or outside the Free Trade Area (FTA). The rules of origin concerning fungible goods and materials are laid out in Article 406. Basically, where originating and non-originating fungible materials are used in the production of goods, the determination of whether the materials are originating or not need not be made through the identification of any specific fungible material, but may be determined on the basis of any of the inventory management methods set out in the Uniform Regulations (See Article 406(a)). In the case where originating and non-originating fungible goods are commingled and exported in the same form, then again, recourse may be had to any of the inventory management methods set out in Uniform Regulations (see Article 406(b)).

There are some inputs into processes of manufacture which themselves may be classified as consumables or non-consumables, especially where they aid the production of the goods themselves. Under Article 408, these are classified as indirect materials, and indirect materials are considered to be originating materials without regard to where they are produced. Article 415 defines 'indirect materials' to mean goods used in the production, testing or inspection of goods but not physically incorporating the goods, or goods used in the maintenance of buildings or the operation of equipment associated with the production of goods, including matters such as fuel and energy, tools, dies, and moulds and any other goods that are not incorporated into the goods but whose use in the production of the goods can reasonably be demonstrated to be a part of that production process. Related to indirect materials (in the sense of being on the periphery of the production of goods for the purposes of the rules of origin) are packaging materials and containers for retail sale. Under Article 409, packaging materials and containers for retail sale are disregarded for the purpose of determining whether all of the non-originating materials used in the production of the goods undergo an applicable change in tariff classification. A similar result is attributed to packing materials and containers for shipment under Article 410. Certain goods do not qualify as originating goods where they are the subject of trans-shipment. Under Article 401, trans-shipped goods that are produced in the territory of the party lose their originating goods status if they undergo further production or any other operation outside the territories of the parties, other than unloading, reloading or any other operation necessary to preserve them in good condition or to transport the goods to the territory of the party. For the purposes of the administration of the rules of origin under Chapter 4 of NAFTA, under Articles 501–08 a regime for the establishment of a system of certificates of origin exists. In essence, the certificate of origin system aids the operation of the rules of origin under Chapter 4.

ENERGY AND BASIC PETROCHEMICALS

Chapter 6 of NAFTA deals with energy and basic petrochemicals. One of the principles which informs Chapter 6 is that the parties recognise that it is desirable to strengthen the important role that trading energy and basic petrochemical goods plays in the FTA and to enhance this role through sustained and gradual liberalisation (Article 601(2)). In addition, the parties recognise the importance of having viable and internationally competitive energy and petrochemical sectors to further their individual national interests (see Article 601(3)). The kinds of energy and basic petrochemical goods which are covered by Chapter 6 of NAFTA are those referred to in Article 602. Some restrictions on imports and exports of energy and basic petrochemical goods are permitted by Article 603. These restrictions are to be in conformity with Article XI of the GATT which is concerned with the general elimination of quantitative restrictions on the importation of products. Under Article 604, no party may adopt or maintain any duty, tax or other charge on the export of any energy or basic petrochemical goods to the territory of another party, unless that impost is adopted or maintained on exports of any such goods to the territory of all other parties and on any such goods when destined for domestic consumption. Article 604 conforms to Article XI of GATT because Article XI:1 of the GATT does not prohibit or restrict duties, taxes or other charges under the umbrella of the concept concerning the general elimination of quantitative restrictions. Where any of the parties impose energy regulatory measures under their own domestic laws, these are subject to the disciplines of national treatment (see Article 301), import and export restrictions (see Article 603) and export taxes (see Article 604): see Article 606(1). Alongside such energy regulatory measures are those which can be adopted or maintained pursuant to national security measures. Under Article 607, measures relating to national security can be adopted or maintained by any party with respect to the import or export of energy or basic petrochemical goods only to the extent necessary to supply military establishments, to fulfil a critical defence contract, to respond to a situation of armed conflict, to implement national policies or international agreements relating to the non-proliferation of nuclear weapons or to respond to direct threats of disruption to the supply of nuclear materials for defence purposes (see Article 607). The key criterion which informs the ability to adopt or maintain such national security measures is the concept of proportionality, that is, the means must be proportionate to the ends.

Annexes 602.3, 603.6, 605, 607 and 608.2 provide various inroads into the principles outlined above, and should be consulted where the details of the energy regulatory regime of NAFTA are of critical moment.

GOVERNMENT PROCUREMENT

The government procurement regime of NAFTA is contained in Chapter 10. The provisions of Chapter 10 are grouped as follows:

- scope and coverage and national treatment: Articles 1001–07.
- tendering procedures, spanning Articles 1008–16.
- bid challenge – comprising Article 1017.
- general provisions (Articles 1018–25) and Annexes.

Chapter 10 of NAFTA applies to procurement by government entities, being Federal government entities, government enterprises, and State or provincial government entities. The significance of the inclusion of government procurement within the framework of NAFTA is that governments of the parties of NAFTA are some of the biggest individual consumers of goods and services.[8] Therefore access to the government procurement market by enterprises from all the parties of NAFTA on equal terms is an important component of achieving the goals of NAFTA.

---

8   This is an adaptation of a comment made concerning procurement in the context of the Free Trade Area of the Americas (FTAA), with a Working Group to be established to examine procurement standards: see http://www.sice.oas.org/root/FTAA/cartage/overvue.stm.

The scope and coverage of Chapter 10 is delineated by Article 1001. Various annexes to Chapter 10 control the extent to which it applies to various government procurement activities. An 'anti-avoidance' measure of a kind is Article 1001(4) which provides that no party may prepare, design or otherwise structure any procurement contract in order to avoid the obligations of Chapter 10. As well, Chapter 10 delineates the kinds of transactions which fall within the ambit of the procurement regime. Under Article 1001(5), procurement includes procurement by methods such as purchase, lease or rental either with or without an option to buy. Excluded from the ambit of 'procurement' are non-contractual agreements or any form of government assistance (including co-operative agreements, grants, loans, equity infusions, guarantees, fiscal incentives, and government provision of goods and services to persons or State, provincial and regional governments) and the acquisition of fiscal agency or depository services, liquidation and management services for regulated financial institutions and sale and distribution services for government debt. These exceptions leave the procurement regime covering an important residue of commercial activities of a non-institutional kind undertaken by government entities.

Article 1001(1)(c) sets out various monetary thresholds at which or above government procurement activities are captured by the government procurement regime of Chapter 10. To augment and implement the standards which are thus set, Article 1002 contains various valuation rules which apply to value government procurement contracts.

Obviously, principles of national treatment and non-discrimination are necessary to achieve trade liberalisation in the sphere of government procurement. The national treatment principle finds expression in Article 1003(1), which obliges each party to accord to goods of another party, to the suppliers of such goods and services of another party, treatment no less favourable than the most favourable treatment that the party accords to its own goods and suppliers and the goods and suppliers of another party. This rule is supplemented by another rule which prohibits any party from treating a locally established supplier less favourably than another locally established supplier on the basis of the degree of foreign affiliation or ownership, or to discriminate against a locally established supplier on the basis that the goods or services offered by that supplier for the particular procurement are goods or services of another party. Both of the national treatment and the non-discrimination principles just covered are reinforced by the prohibition on any party applying rules of origin to goods imported from another party for the purposes of government procurement that are different from or inconsistent with the rules of origin applied in the normal course of trade (see Article 1004).

It can be said that the national treatment and non-discrimination principles relating to government procurement are fundamental but not absolute. There is machinery available for a party to deny these benefits (and other benefits of Chapter 10) to a service supplier of another party where the party establishes that the services being provided by an enterprise that is owned or controlled by persons of a non-party and that has no substantial business activities in the territory of any party (see Article 1005(1)). This provision has implications for the manner in which non-party investors structure their enterprises if their objective (or one of their objectives) is to engage and compete in the government procurement market. Beyond the immediate activity of supplying services, there can also be denial of benefits to an enterprise of another party to goods as well where the criteria laid down in Article 1005(2) are satisfied. In essence, these concern the satisfaction of criteria in Article 1113(1)(a) and the denying party adopts or maintains measures in respect of the non-party that would be circumvented if the denial of benefits could not take place. The underlying idea is that the denying party is not obliged to extend benefits to a non-party owned or controlled enterprise of that other party that it would not wish to extend to an enterprise of that non-party that is established directly in the territory of the denying party.

The concept that there is to be trade liberalisation in procurement is also reinforced by the prohibition of offsets under Article 1006. Under this article, 'offsets' mean conditions imposed or considered by an entity prior to or in the course of its procurement process that encourage local development or improve its party's balance of payments accounts, by means of requirements of local content, licensing of technology, investment, counter-trade, or similar requirements. This article states that in the prohibition of offsets each party must ensure that its entities do not, in the qualification and selection of suppliers, goods or services, in the evaluation of bids or the award of contracts, consider, seek or impose offsets. Finally, it is to be noted that each party must ensure that its entities do not procure, adopt or apply any technical specification with the purpose or effect of creating unnecessary obstacles to trade (see Article 1007(1)). Article 1025(1) defines a technical specification to mean a specification which lays down goods characteristics or their related processes and production methods, or service characteristics or their related operating methods, including any applicable administrative provisions. They may also include or deal exclusively with terminology, symbols, packaging, marking or labelling requirements as may apply to a good, process, or production or operating method.

The provisions of Chapter 10 clustered under the rubric of 'tendering procedures' deal with the participants, formation and conduct of procurement tendering procedures. We elaborate on these next.

Under Article 1008, each party commits itself to ensuring that the tendering procedures of their entities are applied in a non-discriminatory manner and are consistent with Articles 1008–16. This obligation is reinforced by an obligation that each party must ensure that their entities do not provide to any supplier information with respect to a specific procurement in a manner that would have the effect of precluding competition and provides all suppliers equal access to information with respect to a procurement during the pre-tender process (see Article 1008(2)). Alongside open, non-discriminatory tendering procedures, no entity of a party may, in the process of qualifying suppliers and their tendering procedure, discriminate between suppliers of the other parties or between domestic suppliers and suppliers of the other parties (Article 1009(1)). In effect, this ensures a 'level playing field'. The qualification procedures to be followed by an entity are to be consistent with criteria laid down in Article 1009(2), including advance publication of conditions for participation, participation conditions for suppliers being limited to those that are essential to fulfil the fulfilment of the contract in question and open and transparent qualification procedures. Any invitation to participate in a procurement must comply with the manner and form requirements laid down in Article 1010. The tendering process itself can be subdivided further into two categories, namely open tenders and selective tenders. A selective tender is one where an entity maintains a permanent list of qualified suppliers, and selects suppliers to be invited to tender for a particular procurement from among those listed (see Article 1011(2)). An entity of the party must observe the time limits for tendering and delivery of tenders laid down in Article 1012, and the stipulations or measures concerning tender documentation must be consistent with those laid down in Article 1013. Under Article 1014(3), an entity must treat all tenders in confidence. In particular, no entity may provide to any person information intended to assist any supplier to bring its tender up to the level of any other tender. During the course of any negotiations concerning a tender, no entity may discriminate between suppliers (see Article 1014(4)). It is possible for an entity of a party, by complying with conditions set out in Article 1016(2), to use limited tendering procedures which derogate from Articles 1008–15. This is subject to the proviso that such limited tendering procedures are not used with a view to avoiding maximum possible competition or in a manner that would constitute a means of discrimination between suppliers of the other parties or protection of domestic suppliers. The latter restriction, in particular, reinforces the integrity of the rule of non-discrimination laid down in Article 1003(2). Alongside selective tendering procedures are open tendering procedures. These are, by exhaustion, any other tendering procedure besides a selective tendering procedure.

Complementing tendering procedures machinery is the mechanism for bid challenge under Article 1017. Article 1017 obliges each party to adopt and maintain bid challenge procedures for procurement covered by Chapter 10 of NAFTA in accordance with criteria laid down in Article 1017(1)(a)–(p). Some comments may be made about the bid challenge procedures mandated by Article 1017. First, the extent to which these procedures override or dovetail with judicial review mechanisms depends on the domestic law of each of the parties. An aggrieved and unsuccessful tenderer may well be disposed to initiating judicial review if it considers that the tendering procedures are flawed by some procedural or substantive irregularity. The manner in which any judicial review proceeding will be conducted depends upon the domestic law of the party concerned. This domestic law must now conform with Article 1017. Secondly, the bid challenge procedures imply that even where a tenderer is successful, that tenderer cannot be assured that it will ultimately succeed in securing a contract for procurement because of the possibility under Article 1017(1)(j), in investigating a bid challenge, the competent reviewing authority may delay the rewarding of the proposed contract pending resolution of the challenge, except in cases of urgency or where the delay would be contrary to the public interest. Thirdly, the objective of the bid challenge procedures is to promote fair, open and impartial procurement procedures (see Article 1017(1)).

As might be expected with an important matter such as government procurement, there are exceptions to the principles outlined above. In particular, nothing in Chapter 10 is to be construed to prevent a party from taking any action or not disclosing any information which it considers necessary for the protection of its essential security interests relating to the procurement of arms, ammunition or war materials, or for procurement which is indispensable for national security or for national defence purposes (Article 1018(1)). As well, nothing in Chapter 10 is to be construed to prevent any party from adopting or maintaining measures necessary to protect public morals, order or safety, to protect human, animal or plant life or health, to protect intellectual property, or relating to goods or services of handicapped persons, or philanthropic institutions or of prison labour. The proviso is that such measures are not to be applied in the manner which constitutes a means of arbitrary or unjustifiable discrimination between parties where the same conditions prevail or a disguised restriction on trade between them (see Article 1018(2)).

Access to information is critical if there is to be fair, open and impartial procurement procedures. The way NAFTA deals with this is to impose on each party a duty to promptly publish any law, regulation, precedential judicial decision, administrative ruling of general application and any procedure, including standard contract clauses, regarding government procurement covered by Chapter 10 in the appropriate publications referred to Annex 1010.1. This reflects the important attribute of transparency which is dealt with in more detail at 11 below. Transparency is important because it ensures that all information necessary to ensure fair and open competition in the tendering procedures is made available to all actual or potential competitors.

There is scope under Article 1022(1) for a party to modify, on a unilateral basis, its coverage under Chapter 10, but 'only in exceptional circumstances'. These are not defined (as might be expected). Where a party modifies its coverage under Chapter 10, that party must notify the other parties of the modification and propose to the other parties appropriate compensatory adjustments to its coverage in order to maintain a level of coverage comparable to that existing prior to the modification (Article 1022(2)). The idea behind this duty is that where, for example, a party reduces the level of government procurement in one particular sector, it may compensate for such reduction by enlarging government procurement in other sectors. Reductions in coverage can also be achieved by other methods, including divestiture by a party of ownership or control of an entity under Article 1023. This would include processes such as privatisation (corporatisation of an entity may well be a precursor to privatisation but on its own, corporatisation would not be an act of divestiture because ownership or control of the corporatised entity would still remain with the party). The basic rule here under Article 1023(1) is that nothing in Chapter 10 is to be construed as preventing a party from divesting an entity covered by Chapter 10. An entity can be divested either through the public offering of shares in it (in other words, a 'float'), or through other methods, so that the entity is no longer subject to Federal government control, then that entity may be deleted from its Schedule to Annexe 1001.1(a)–(l). If another party objects to the withdrawal of an entity from Chapter 10 on the grounds that the entity remains subject to Federal government control, that party may have recourse to the dispute settlement procedures under Chapter 20 dealing with institutional arrangements and dispute settlement procedures.

Finally, under Article 1024, the parties commit themselves to commencing further negotiations no later than 31 December 1998 with a view to the further liberalisation of their respective government procurement markets.

INVESTMENT[9]

Chapter 11 of NAFTA deals with investment. Standing alone, and viewed in isolation, this fact might appear unexceptional. When one, however, factors in Mexico's historic prohibition on foreign investment, since reversed by its Foreign Investment Law of 1993, then the significance of the inclusion of an investment regime under NAFTA becomes readily apparent.[10]

The investment chapter of NAFTA spans Articles 1101–139, together with annexes 1120.1, 1137.2, 1137.4 and 1138.2. The breakdown of the investment chapter is between those articles dealing with investment generally (Articles 1101–114) and the settlement of investment disputes between a party and an investor of another party (Articles 1115–139). We will deal with selected aspects of each of these two groups of provisions.

Chapter 11 of NAFTA applies to two key phenomena of international investment law, namely legal subjects (investors) and the legal object (investments). Each is defined in Article 1139. 'Investment' is defined extensively, and the key components are:

- an enterprise (under Article 210, 'enterprise' means any entity constituted or organised under applicable law, whether or not for profit, and whether privately-owned or governmentally-owned, including any corporation, trust, partnership, sole proprietorship, joint venture or other association. This expansive definition spans natural and juristic persons as well as associations of persons who do not comprise a separate juridical person to the members of such an association);

- an equity security of an enterprise;

- a debt security of an enterprise;

- a loan to an enterprise;

- interest in an enterprise that entitles the owner to share an income or profits of the enterprise;

- real estate or other property (tangible or intangible) acquired in the expectation or used for the purpose of economic benefit or for other business purposes; and

- interests arising from the commitment of capital or other resources in the territory of a party to economic activity in such territory, such as under contracts involving the presence of an investor's property in the territory of the party, including turnkey or construction contracts, or concessions, or contracts where remuneration depends substantially on the production, revenues or profits of an enterprise.

---

9   For a comprehensive review of investment under the NAFTA regime, see Rubin, SJ and Alexander, DC (eds), *NAFTA and Investment*, 1995, Boston: Kluwer Law International.

10   See Alexander, DC, 'Mexico's Foreign Investment Law of 1993, Amendments to the Maquita Decree and an Overview of Maquiladoras', in Rubin and Alexander, *ibid*, pp 65–83.

Exclusions from the meaning of investment in Article 1139 are claims to money that arise solely from commercial contracts for the sale of goods or services, the extension of credit in connection with commercial transactions (such as trade financing) and any other claims as to money that do not involve the kind of interests set out above. Turning from the subject matter of investments to the legal actors concerned in investment activities, 'investor of a party' means a party or state enterprise of that party, or a national or an enterprise of that party, that seeks to make, is making or has made an investment. A subsidiary definition of some importance is the definition of 'enterprise'. Article 1139 invokes the general definition of 'enterprise' in Article 201 which is an entity (not separately defined) constituted or organised under applicable law, whether or not for profit, and whether privately-owned or governmentally-owned, including any corporation, trust, partnership, sole proprietorship, joint venture or other association. In other words, 'enterprise' refers to a specific kind of legal actor, whether or not formed for the purpose of deriving profits, and irrespective of the particular legal form or juridical nature it takes. From the definition just cited, it is apparent also that 'enterprise' also embraces natural as well as juridical persons. Having laid down these important preliminary considerations, we turn now to consider the investment rules of Chapter 11.

Article 1101 delineates the scope and coverage of Chapter 11 to those measures adopted or maintained by a party relating to investors of another party, investments of investors of another party in the territory of the party and with respect to Articles 1106 and 1114, all investments in the territory of the party. In effect, the scheme of NAFTA is to regulate 'measures' concerning cross-border investment. Chapter 11 is underpinned by a principle of equality of treatment. This emerges in the principle of national treatment under Article 1102(1), which obliges each party to accord to investors of another party treatment no less favourable than that it accords, in like circumstances, to its own investors with respect to the establishment, acquisition, expansion, management, conduct, operation, and sale or other disposition of investments. This principle of national treatment is extended under Article 1102(2) from investors *simpliciter* to the investments of investors. The national treatment principle is extended from the macro-institutional level of 'parties' themselves to the 'micro-institutional' level, in its application to states or provinces under Article 1102(3). Complementing the notion of equality of national treatment is the most-favoured-nation (MFN) treatment clause in the context of investments, namely Article 1103. Under this article, each party must accord to investors or investments of investors of another party treatment no less favourable than that it accords, in like circumstances, to investors or investments of investors of another party or of a non-party with respect to the establishment, acquisition, expansion, management, conduct, operation, and sale or other disposition of investments (see Articles 1103(1) and (2)). In broad terms, the differences between Articles 1102 and 1103 lie in their respective reach. The national treatment principle uses as the comparator to foreign investments and foreign investors domestic investments and domestic investors. By contrast, under Article 1103, the MFN principle uses as the comparators foreign investments and foreign investors as well as third party foreign investments and third party foreign investors. Given the different bases for these comparisons, it is possible, of course, that there can be different standards of treatment meted out to foreign investments and foreign investors. The way NAFTA deals with this is to oblige each party to accord to investments of another party and investments of investors of another party the better of the standards of treatment required by Articles 1102 and 1103 (see Article 1104). In other words, the referent is the higher common denominator, not the lower common denominator. In order to give some content to the standard of treatment to be accorded by each party to the investments of investors of another party or to the investors of another party, there is invoked the concept of treatment in accordance with international law. More particularly, this finds expression in Article 1105(1) which obliges each party to accord to investments of investors of another party treatment in accordance with international law including fair and equitable treatment and full protection and security.[11]

It is possible to control, if not eliminate, whether wholly or partially, investments or certain forms of investments by the judicious manipulation of performance criteria. To counter this possibility, NAFTA, in Article 1106(1) provides that no party may impose or enforce requirements stated in Articles 1106(1)(a)–(g), or enforce any commitment or undertaking, in connection with the establishment, acquisition, expansion, management, conduct or operation of an investment of an investor of a party or of a non-party in its territory. Among the practices proscribed would be a requirement on the part of a foreign investor to engage in counter-trade.[12]

Various qualifications to these principles are laid out in Articles 1106(2)–(6). As well as controls on foreign investment exerted at the institutional level as well as at the establishment phase of the foreign investment cycle (see Articles 1101–106 discussed above), NAFTA also regulates the *control* of enterprises which comprise investments of an investor of another party. The basic position is that, under Article 1107(1) no party may require that an enterprise of that party that is an investment of an investor of another party appoint to senior management positions individuals of any particular nationality. The freedom given to enterprises under that provision is scaled back by Article 1107(2) which empowers a party to require that a majority of the Board of Directors (or any committee) of an enterprise of that party that is an investment of an investor of another party to be of a particular nationality, or to be resident in the territory of that party, providing that the requirement does not materially impair the ability of the investor to exercise control over its investment. One would think that the determination of the issue whether or not there is a material impairment of the ability of the investor to exercise control over its investment would lie with the investor. However, that conclusion does not necessarily follow because it is not couched in language or text which supports a subjective, as opposed to an objective, determination. If one adheres to general canons of interpretation of legal instruments (including

---

11 See Levy, T, 'NAFTA's Provision for Compensation in the event of Expropriation: a Reassessment of the "Prompt, Adequate and Effective" Standard' (1995) 31 *Stanford Journal of International Law* 423–43. See McDermott, PM, 'Investment Security in Asia and the Pacific', in Wilde, KCDM (ed), *International Transactions: Trade and Investment, Law and Finance*, 1993, pp 373–91, Sydney: Law Book Co for a regional analysis of the application of the law governing securities over property.

12 This follows, by implication, from Articles 1106(1)(c) and (g). On counter-trade generally, see 27 *Halsbury's Law of Australia*, Trade and Commerce, paras [420–3105]–[420–3125].

international treaties), then it would seem that this 'material impairment' test is to be applied objectively, not subjectively. This gives more weight to the intentions of a governmental agency of a party having concerns about the composition (in terms of nationality or residence) of directors and controllers of enterprises consisting of investments than the enterprise or its foreign controllers might wish to yield. There are a series of reservations and exceptions to Articles 1102, 1103, 1106 and 1107. These are set out or are referred to in Article 1108. Obviously, these should be consulted and analysed carefully to determine the extent to which there is any derogation from, in particular, the principle of equality of treatment and the MFN principle.

Without needing to have recourse to empirical evidence, it may be safely presumed that the object of any business enterprise is to provide a dividend or profit for the proprietors of that enterprise or of any proprietary or economic interests in that enterprise. When one factors into this business norm the fact of cross-border investment (or foreign investment), then the difficulties in repatriating dividends or profits (or whatever form the return on investment takes) becomes more difficult. The relative freedom provided by NAFTA to engage in foreign investment for the investors of each of the NAFTA parties is supplemented by relative freedom of repatriation. This appears in the guise of Article 1109 which uses the construct of a 'transfer'. Article 1139 defines transfers to mean 'transfers and international payments'. This definition is not particularly helpful to the uninitiated. It is probably wide enough to encompass transfers of money as well as of value. Article 1109(1) obliges each party to permit all transfers relating to an investment of an investor of another party in the territory of that party to be made freely and without delay. The particular kinds of transfers enumerated include profits, dividends, interest, capital gains, royalty payments, management fees, technical assistance and other fees, returns in kind and other amounts derived from the investment, proceeds from the sale of all or any part of the investment or from the partial or complete liquidation of the investment, payments made under a contract entered into by the investor, or its investment, including payments made under a loan agreement, any payments made following the expropriation of an investment of an investor and compensation paid by the expropriation. If we focus on the forms of transfer, these span a wide range of 'returns' (to use a neutral term) on investment. Obviously, the form of the return will depend upon its correct juridical characterisation and whether the investment is in the form of equity, debt or some form of technology transfer payment (such as a royalty). NAFTA does not operate on the basis of a single common currency between the parties. To overcome the prospect that domestic exchange controls could be used to prohibit or delay the repatriation of returns on investment, Article 1109(2) requires each party to permit transfer to be made in a freely usable currency at the market rate of exchange providing on the date of transfer with respect to spot transactions in the currency to be transferred. The relative freedom of repatriation of returns on investment is scaled back to some extent by Article 1109(4) which empowers a party to prevent a transfer through the equitable, non-discriminatory and good faith applications of its laws relating to bankruptcy, insolvency, issuing, trading or dealing with securities, criminal or penal offences, currency transfer reports or ensuring the satisfaction of judgments in adjudicatory proceedings.

Of critical importance in cross-border investment is the prospect of expropriation by the host state.[13] Investment security for foreign investments can be dealt with on a bilateral basis, and there are in force many bilateral investment treaties (BITs) which deal with the reciprocal encouragement and protection of investments.[14] In NAFTA, investment security is dealt with in a trilateral basis in the context of Article 1110 dealing with expropriation and compensation. Under this provision, no party may directly or indirectly nationalise or expropriate an investment of an investor of another party in its territory or take a measure tantamount to nationalisation or expropriation ('expropriation') except for a public purpose, on a non-discriminatory basis, in accordance with due process of law (including fair and equitable treatment and full protection and security) and on payment of compensation calculated in accordance with Articles 1110(2)–(6) (see Article 1110(1)). The measure of compensation is that it must be equivalent to the fair market value of the expropriated investment immediately before expropriation took place. Such compensation must not reflect any change in value occurring because the intended expropriation had become known earlier. Thus the device of signalling in advance an expropriation in order to drive down its value when the time comes to pay compensation is ineffective in light of this provision. In order to determine fair market value, valuation criteria include going concern value, asset value (including declared tax value of tangible property) and other criteria as appropriate (see Article 1110(2)). Compensation is to be paid without delay and is to be fully realisable (see Article 1110(3)). On payment, compensation must be freely transferable as provided for in Article 1109 (see Article 1110(6)). Thus payments representing a return on investment and the compensation payable on expropriation of investments are treated equally favourably in terms of the ability to repatriate these. The way that the expropriation regime under NAFTA is harmonised with the intellectual property regime (Chapter 17 of NAFTA) is that the expropriation regime does not apply to the issue of compulsory licences granted in relation to intellectual property rights, or to the revocation, limitation or creation of such rights (see Article 1110(7)). On a broader canvass, the relationship between Chapter 11 of NAFTA and other chapters of NAFTA is governed by the provision which provides that other chapters of NAFTA prevail over Chapter 11 to the extent of any inconsistency (see Article 1112(1)).

There is scope under NAFTA for a party to deny the benefits of Chapter 11 to certain investors. Denial of benefits is permitted to an investor of another party that is an enterprise of that party and to investments of that investor if investors of a non-party owned or controlled the enterprise and the denying party does not maintain diplomatic relations with the non-party or adopts or maintains measures with respect to the non-party that prohibit transactions with the enterprise or that would be violated or circumvented if the benefits of Chapter 11 were accorded to the enterprise or to its

13   See Sornarajah, M, 'Nationalisation of Foreign Investment', Chapter 17 in Wilde, KCDM (ed), *International Transactions: Trade and Investment, Law and Finance*, 1993, pp 334–59, Sydney: Law Book Co.

14   See 27 *Halsbury's Laws of Australia*, Trade and Commerce, paras [420–2375]–[420–2385] for a survey of some BITs from an Australian legal perspective.

investments (see Article 1113(1)). A possible application of this provision is illustrated by the following scenario. Suppose that an enterprise of Taiwan (the Republic of China) invests in a Canadian enterprise. Suppose further that that Canadian enterprise acquires a portfolio investment or even a direct investment in a US enterprise. It is open for the USA to deny benefits under Chapter 11 of NAFTA to that non-party (Taiwanese) owned or controlled Canadian enterprise. This is on the basis that the USA no longer accords full diplomatic recognition to Taiwan. Instead, full diplomatic recognition has been accorded to the Peoples Republic of China (PRC).

Before we depart from the general investment regime of NAFTA to consider the settlement of investment disputes regime, one final comment needs to be made. This concerns the fact that Chapter 11 of NAFTA differs from most of the other chapters of NAFTA in that it makes specific reference to persons besides States who have rights and are subject to duties. This is significant because it is usually only States who have any standing and juridical status in public international law (that is, international legal personality). In this sphere, there is a concession made to enterprises because they are most directly affected by expropriation even if a party to NAFTA could claim it has suffered damage personally under the principles of public international law if an investment of an enterprise were to be expropriated.

Section B of Chapter 11 of NAFTA (spanning Articles 1115–139) deals with the settlement of investment disputes between a party and the investor of another party. The comment made above concerning the limited legal personality accorded to enterprises applies here with equal force. The NAFTA settlement of investment disputes regime bears a close affinity to the convention on the Settlement of Investment Disputes between States and Nationals of Other States (ICSID Convention) 1965. (Washington, 18 March 1965; UKTS 1967 no 25 (Cmd 3255); Cmnd 2745; 575 UNTS 150; 4 ILM 532; NZTS 1980 no 17) opened for signature in Washington DC in 1965. The convention is known as the 'ICSID Convention' or the 'Washington Convention'. It is implemented in Australia by International Arbitration Act 1974 (CTH) Pt IV (introduced by the ICSID Implementation Act 1990 (CTH)) where it is called the 'Investment Convention'. The text of the ICSID Convention 1965 is set out in Schedule 3 of the International Arbitration Act 1974 (CTH). Only ICSID Convention 1965 Articles 25–63 have the force of law within Australia (see s 32 of the International Arbitration Act 1974 (CTH)).[15]

In outline form only, the key components of the NAFTA investment dispute settlement regime are as follows.

The rationale for the NAFTA investment dispute settlement regime ('the investment dispute settlement regime') is indicated in Article 1115, which says that it provides a mechanism for the settlement of investment disputes that assures both equal treatment among investors of the parties in accordance with the principle of international reciprocity and due process before an impartial tribunal. The coverage of

---

15 On the ICSID Convention and the International Centre for the Settlement of Investment Disputes ('ICSID'), see 17 *Halsbury's Laws of Australia*, Trade and Commerce, paras [420–2300], [420–2525]–[420–2650].

disputes which are amenable to the investment dispute settlement regime are any breach of an obligation under Articles 1101–114, 1503(2) and 1052(3)(a), being breaches which result in an investor incurring loss or damage by reason of, or arising out of, that breach. This loss-recognition principle invokes the concept of causation. The investment dispute settlement regime under NAFTA, in keeping with the ICSID Convention, gives 'investors' standing to pursue claims for loss or damage caused by, or resulting from, a breach of the investment rules under Section B of Chapter 11 of NAFTA. The reason this is significant is that, as a general rule, the only persons who enjoy legal personality under public international law are States and certain inter-governmental organisations. There is a time bar applicable to the making of a claim by an investor, and that it is not competent if more than three years have elapsed from the date on which the investor first acquired, or should have first acquired, knowledge of the alleged breach and knowledge that the investor has suffered loss or damage (see Article 1116(2)). This provision imports states of knowledge that are functionally equivalent to the common law dichotomy between actual knowledge and constructive knowledge.

Claims under the investment dispute settlement regime cannot be made by an 'investment' (see Article 1117(4)) since in some cases (particularly portfolio investment as opposed to foreign direct investment) an investment is a legal object, *not* a legal subject. An investment can of course be a legal subject (or legal person) when it is an 'enterprise' (see para (a) of the definition of 'investment' in Article 1139). Under Article 1117, an investor of a party, on behalf of an enterprise of another party that is a juridical person that the investor owns or controls (directly or indirectly) may submit to arbitration under the investment dispute settlement regime a claim that the other party (the host state where the enterprise is incorporated or established or has its legal existence recognised) a claim that the host state has breached obligations under Articles 1101–114, 1503(2) or 1502(3)(a), and that the enterprise has incurred loss or damage by reason of, or arising out of, that breach (Article 1117(1)). The difference between this provision and Article 1116 discussed above is that in the former case the investor complaining of a breach is not itself the 'enterprise' that is affected by some act or omission of the host State. In practical terms, that investor is a shareholder in or proprietor of an enterprise. In the case of an Article 1116 claim, the investor is directly and personally affected by the breach on the part of the host State. Claims under Article 1117 are particularly suited to corporate groups operating under the umbrella of a holding company having, say, subsidiaries in a host State, where the subsidiary is incorporated in a different State to the State in which the investor is incorporated. It is for the domestic laws of the parties of NAFTA to determine the circumstances under which an enterprise that is foreign owned by another enterprise or entity located within or established within another party is or is not a subsidiary or some other legal relation to the parent entity. NAFTA provides no rules of recognition to decide such matters.

The dispute settlement machinery under the investment dispute settlement regime is as follows:

- The disputing parties must first attempt to settle a claim through consultation or negotiation (see Article 1118).

- Assuming a claim is not settled through the processes of consultation or negotiation, the next stage is for the disputing investor to deliver to the disputing party written notice of its intention to submit a claim to arbitration at least 90 days before the claim is submitted, with the notice complying with the formal requirements listed in Articles 1119(a)–(d).

- So long as six months have elapsed since the events giving rise to a claim (in practice at least 90 days after notice of intent under Article 1119 is given), a disputing investor may submit the claim to arbitration under one of these three regimes, namely the ICSID Convention, the Additional Facility Rules of ICSID[16] or the UNCITRAL Arbitration Rules (see Article 1120(1)).[17]

- Various procedural steps associated with the submission of claims to arbitration are laid down in Articles 1121–138.

CROSS-BORDER TRADE IN SERVICES

Chapter 12 of NAFTA is concerned with cross-border trade in services. Article 1213(2) defines 'cross-border provision of a service' or 'cross-border trade in services' to mean the provision of a service from the territory of a party into the territory of another party, into the territory of a party by a person of that party to a person of another party or by a national of a party in the territory of another party, but excludes the provision of services in the territory of a party by an investment. In that instance, an 'investment' would be a legal or juridical person, that is a legal subject not a legal object. Thus the investment regime is mutually exclusive of the trade in services regime. An understanding of Chapter 12 of NAFTA is enhanced when we navigate the coverage and exclusions from it. Chapter 12 applies to measures adopted or maintained by a party relating to cross-border trade in services by service providers of another party, including measures respecting:

(a) the production, distribution, marketing, sale and delivery of a service;

(b) the purchase or use of, or payment for, a service;

(c) the access to and use of distribution and transportation systems in connection with the provision of a service;

(d) the presence in its territory of a service provider of another party; and

(e) the provision of a bond or other form of financial security as a condition for the provision of a service (see Article 1201(1)).

The range of services falling outside the ambit of Chapter 12 are these:

(a) financial services, as defined in Chapter 14 (Financial Services);

---

16 See 27 *Halsbury's Laws of Australia*, Trade and Commerce, para [420-2550].

17 See Chapter 11 below 27 *Halsbury's Laws of Australia*, Trade and Commerce, paras [420–2515]–[420–2520].

(b) air services, including domestic and international air transportation services, whether scheduled or non-scheduled, and related services in support of air services, other than:

  (i) aircraft repair and maintenance services during which an aircraft is withdrawn from service; and

  (ii) specialty air services;

(c) procurement by a party or a state enterprise; or

(d) subsidies or grants provided by a party or a state enterprise, including government supported loans, guarantees and insurance (see Article 1201(2)).

The conceptual underpinnings to cross-border trade in services are the twin pillars of national treatment and MFN treatment. Article 1202(1) states, in familiar terms, that each party must accord to service providers of another party treatment no less favourable than that it accords, in like circumstances, to its own service providers. Article 1213(2) defines 'service provider' of a party to mean a person of a party that seeks to provide or provides a service ('service' is not separately defined, either in Chapter 12 or in Chapter 2 of NAFTA). So the word 'service' carries its ordinary meaning as modified to take account of its positioning in a treaty such as NAFTA. The MFN treatment principle assumes the guise of Article 1203, which obliges each party to accord to service providers of another party treatment no less favourable than that it accords, in like circumstances, to service providers of any other party or of a non-party. Chapter 12 of NAFTA operates alongside broader, multilateral trade in service treaties such as the General Agreement on Trade in Services (GATS).[18] Canada, Mexico and the USA are, of course, members of the WTO, so that their obligations under NAFTA Chapter 12 operate in parallel with their obligations under the GATS.[19] To the extent that there is any difference in the standard of treatment under Articles 1202 and 1203, Article 1204 obliges each party to accord to service providers of any other party the better of the standards of treatment mandated under these other provisions. The emphasis of Chapter 12 is the *cross-border* trade in services regime. This emphasis implies a number of things which we touch on briefly. Under Article 1205, no party may require a service provider of another party to establish or maintain a representative office or any form of enterprise, or to be resident, in its territory as a condition for the cross-border provision of a service. Article 1205 does not derogate from the principle of freedom of establishment, nor the concept of freedom of movement.[20] In fact, it consistent with these principles because it reinforces the allied notion of freedom from establishment as it allows service providers to elect whether or not to establish themselves in the territory of another party as a precursor to providing such services. The freedom of establishment principle finds

---

18 See Chapter 6 above, Chapter 10 below and 27 *Halsbury's Laws of Australia*, Trade and Commerce, paras [420–2105]–[420–2140].

19 On the Internet, an unofficial site which can be accessed to find out the status of WTO membership is: http//itl.irv.uitno/tradelaw/documents/freetrade/wta-94/status/wto-status.html.

20 On these freedoms under the European Union (EU), see Chapter 9 below and Moens, GA, 'Freedom of Movement of Goods in the European Community' (1990) 17 *Melbourne University Law Review* 733.

particular voice in the provisions of NAFTA dealing with investment (see Chapter 11 of NAFTA discussed above). There are some reservations to these important foundational principles, and they are referred to in Article 1206. It is competent for a party to maintain quantitative restrictions at a Federal, state or provincial (but not at a local government) level under Article 1207. Under Article 1208, each party commits itself to liberalising quantitative restrictions, licensing requirements, performance requirements or other non-discriminatory measures concerning cross-border trade in services.

In the course of cross-border provision of services, there is always the possibility that the host state can impose disguised barriers to trade in the guise of licensing and certification requirements. To counter this possibility, Article 1210(1) provides that any measure adopted or maintained by a party relating to the licensing or certification of nationals of another party does not constitute an unnecessary barrier to trade, so that any such measure must comply with these criteria:

(a) is based on objective and transparent criteria, such as competence and the ability to provide a service;

(b) is not more burdensome than necessary to ensure the quality of a service; and

(c) does not constitute a disguised restriction on the cross-border provision of a service (see Article 1210(1)).[21]

It is competent for a party to deny the benefits of Chapter 12 to a service provider of another party where the denying party establishes that the services being provided by an enterprise earned or controlled by nationals of a non-party and the denying party does not maintain diplomatic relations with the non-party or the denying party adopts or maintains measures with respect to the non-party that prohibit transactions with the enterprise or that would be violated or circumvented if the benefits of this Chapter were accorded to that enterprise (see Article 1211(1)).

TELECOMMUNICATIONS

The scope and coverage of Chapter 13 of NAFTA, dealing with telecommunications, is delineated by Article 1301. This provision states that Chapter 13 applies to:

---

21 An Australian analogue is the mutual recognition scheme. The mutual recognition scheme evolved out of an inter-governmental agreement dated 11 May 1992 between the Commonwealth, the Australian Capital Territory, the Northern Territory and all other States except Western Australia. Western Australia acceded to the mutual recognition scheme in late 1995. The inter-governmental agreement on mutual recognition resulted in the enactment of virtually identical legislation by the Commonwealth and each State and Territory in order to give effect to the terms of that agreement. The legislative package which emerged consists of the following statutes: Mutual Recognition Act 1992 (CTH); Mutual Recognition (Australian Capital Territory) Act 1992 (ACT); Mutual Recognition (Northern Territory) Act 1992 (NT); Mutual Recognition (New South Wales) Act 1992 (NSW); Mutual Recognition (Queensland) Act 1992 (Qld); Mutual Recognition (South Australia) Act 1993 (SA); Mutual Recognition (Tasmania) Act 1993 (Tas); Mutual Recognition (Victoria) Act 1993 (Vic); Mutual Recognition (Western Australia) Act 1995 (WA).

(a) measures adopted or maintained by a party relating to access to and use of public telecommunications transport networks or services by persons of another party, including access and use by such persons operating private networks;

(b) measures adopted or maintained by a party relating to the provision of enhanced or value-added services by persons of another party in the territory, or across the borders, of a party; and

(c) standards-related measures relating to attachment of terminal or other equipment to public telecommunications transport networks (see Article 1301(1)).

The particular legal instruments which Article 1301 applies to are 'measures' dealing with access to and use of public telecommunications transport networks or services, or to enhanced or value-added services or standards-related measures.

One of the key provisions of the telecommunications regime under NAFTA is that it is concerned with equality of access to public telecommunications, transport networks or services. This appears in the form of Article 1302(1) which provides that each party must ensure that persons of another party have access to and use of any public telecommunications transport network or service, including private leased circuits, offered in its territory or across its borders for the conduct of the business, on reasonable and non-discriminatory terms and conditions, including those set out in Articles 1302(2)–(8). These kinds of networks or services are not the only ones governed by Chapter 13 of NAFTA. Also benefitting from trade liberalisation initiatives under Chapter 13 of NAFTA are enhanced or value-added services. Under Article 1303(1), each party must ensure that any licensing, permit, registration or notification procedure that it adopts or maintains concerning the provision of enhanced or value-added services is transparent and non-discriminatory and that applications filed under such procedures are processed expeditiously (Article 1301(1)(a)). In addition, each party must ensure that information required under such application procedures is limited to that necessary to demonstrate that the applicant has the financial solvency to begin providing services or to access conformity of the applicant's terminal or other equipment with the party's applicable standards of technical regulations. To prevent the prospect that standards-related measures could be used to function as a disguised barrier to trade, each party is under a duty under Article 1304 to ensure that its standards-related measures relating to the attachment of terminal or other equipment to the public telecommunications transport networks are adopted or maintained only to the extent necessary to prevent technical damage to public telecommunications transport networks and to maintain the integrity and rights of access of public telecommunications transport services (see Article 1304(1)).

In the area of telecommunications, the principle of transparency of the publication of measures relating to access to and use of public telecommunication transport networks or services is critical. The particular measures which are burdened by the phenomenon of transparency are those listed in Article 1306.

To sum up: the telecommunications regime under NAFTA has as its basic concern the principle of equality of access to public telecommunications networks and services by persons of other NAFTA parties. Measures (whether legal or executive or other instruments) to control such access must be consistent only with ensuring the technical integrity of such services and networks, and must not function as disguised barriers to trade.

FINANCIAL SERVICES

Chapter 14 of NAFTA is entitled 'Financial Services'. Chapter 14 applies to measures adopted or maintained by a party relating to financial institutions of another party, investors of another party, and investments of such investors, in financial institutions in the party's territory and cross-border trade in financial services (see Article 1404(1)). By Article 1406, 'financial institution' means any financial intermediary or other enterprise that is authorised to do business and regulated or supervised as a financial institution under the law of the party in whose territory it is located. 'Cross-border trade in financial services' (and 'cross-border provision of a financial service') means the provision of a financial service from the territory of a party into the territory of another party, in the territory of a party by a person of that party to a person of another party or by a national of a party in the territory of another party, but does not include the provision of a service in the territory of a party by an investment in that territory (see Article 1416). Thus the financial services regime is mutually exclusive of the investment regime as well as of the services regime. The definitions just cited also underscore the fact that it applies to two-way trade in financial services, that is, trade in each direction between any two parties (one could extrapolate this to cover three-way trade in financial services between each of the three member of NAFTA). Another vital definition is that of 'financial service' which is defined in Article 1416 to mean a service of a financial nature, including insurance, and a service incidental or auxiliary to a service of a financial nature. A person of a party that is engaged in the business of providing a financial service within the territory of that party is known as a 'financial service provider of a party' under Article 1416.

If we stand back from the details of the scope and coverage of Chapter 14 of NAFTA, we see there are three key phenomena which inform and shape this Chapter:

- Freedom of establishment.
- Freedom of participation.
- Trade-liberalisation.

We will see these three phenomena at work as we consider selected aspects of the financial services regime of NAFTA.

The principle of freedom of establishment finds expression in Article 1403. Article 1403(1) provides that each party recognises the principle that an investor of another party is to be permitted to establish a financial institution in the territory of a party in the juridical form chosen by such an investor. Although such an investor has a freedom to select the juridical vehicle to establish a financial institution (that is, freedom of enterprise choice), this will depend upon the rules of recognition for the establishment of financial institutions in the territory of the party in which it is proposed to establish that institution. The principle of freedom of participation underpins Article 1403(2).

This provides that the parties also recognise the principle that an investor of another party should be permitted to participate widely in a party's market through the ability of such investor to provide in that party's territory a range of financial services through separate financial institutions as may be required by that party, and to expand geographically, and to own financial institutions in that party's territory without being subject to ownership requirements that are specific to foreign financial institutions. This principle of freedom of participation extends to the important economic activity of market penetration through diversification and product differentiation. It also extends to permitting vertical integration in the ownership of enterprises providing financial services, although this would take place against the backdrop of competition laws applicable in each of the parties. This principle of freedom of participation is particularly important in the activity of providing financial services because of the way that market share in the retail financial services sector is gained through having suitably geographically dispersed networks and distribution points. Of course, financial service providers can elect not to have such networks if they wish as this is consistent with the corollary of the principle of freedom of establishment, namely the freedom not to establish such networks.

The principle of trade liberalisation is imprinted upon Article 1404. This Article is concerned with cross-border trade in financial services. Article 1404(1) provides that no party may adopt any measure restricting any type of cross-border trade in financial services by cross-border financial service providers of another party that the party permits on the date of entry into force of NAFTA (1 January 1994 (see Article 2203)), except to the extent set out in Section B of the party's schedule to annex VII. Complementing this provision is another which obliges each party to allow persons located in its territory, and its national wherever located, to purchase financial services from cross-border financial service providers of another party located in the territory of that other party or of another party (see Article 1404(2)).

In Chapter 14 of NAFTA, we see the emergence, once more, of the principles of national treatment (or equality of treatment) and MFN treatment. Under Article 1405, each party must accord to investors, to financial institutions and to investments of investors of another party in financial institutions treatment no less favourable than that it accords to its own investors, its own financial institutions and to investments of its own investors in financial institutions, in like circumstances, concerning the establishment, acquisition, expansion, management, conduct, operation, and sale or other disposition of financial institutions and investments (see Articles 1405(1) and (2)). These particular expressions of equality of treatment are augmented by Articles 1405(3)–(7) in the elaboration of further matters and factors pertinent to financial institutions. A construct which features in some of these provisions is the concept of 'equal competitive opportunities'. Under Article 1405(6), a party's treatment affords 'equal competitive opportunities' if it does not disadvantage financial institutions and cross-border financial institution services providers of another party in their ability to provide financial services as compared with the ability of the party's own financial institutions and financial services providers to provide such services, in like circumstances. Complementing the ideal of equality of treatment is the MFN treatment clause in Chapter 14, Article 1406.

In this Chapter, this provision assumes the form of the provision that obliges each party to accord to investors, financial institutions, investments of investors in financial institutions and cross-border financial service providers of another party treatment no less favourable than that it accords to such persons of another party or of a non-party, in like circumstances (Article 1406(1)).

The financial services sector is one in which there is constant product innovation and differentiation. These commercial factors provide the impulse for increased competition, and for financial service participants to increase their market share at the expense of others. These commercial impulses receive recognition and some measure of protection under Article 1407, which provides that each party must permit a financial institution of another party to provide any new financial service of a type similar to those services that the party permits its own financial institutions, in like circumstances, to provide under its domestic law. A party is also empowered to determine the institutional and juridical form through which the service may be provided and may require authorisation for the provision of that service (see Article 1407(1)).

The financial services regime under NAFTA is liberalised but not completely unregulated or unrestricted. Certain forms of reservations and specific commitments are laid down under Article 1409. Under Article 1410, it is competent for a party to adopt or maintain reasonable measures for prudential supervision reasons, such as the protection of investors, depositors, financial market participants, policy holders, policy claimants or persons to whom a fiduciary duty is owed by financial institutions or cross-border financial service provider. In addition, measures may be adopted or maintained for the maintenance of the safety, soundness, integrity or financial responsibility of financial institutions or cross-border financial service providers and ensuring the integrity and stability of a party's financial system (see Article 1410(1)).

Under Chapter 14, there is a specific transparency regime which displaces that under Article 1802(2) (dealt with below). Under Article 1411(1), each party must, to the extent practicable, provide in advance to all interested persons any measure of general application that the party proposes to adopt in order to allow an opportunity for persons to comment on the measure. Such measures must be provided by means of official publication, or in other written form or in such form as permits an interested person to make informed comments on the proposed measure. As well, each party's regulatory authorities must make available to interested persons their requirements for completing applications relating to the provision of financial services (see Article 1411(2)).

In an institutional capacity or sense, the financial services regime of NAFTA also covers:

- the establishment of a Financial Services Committee under Articles 1412;
- machinery for consultations under Article 1413;
- dispute settlement under Article 1414;
- investment disputes and financial services under Article 1415.

INTELLECTUAL PROPERTY

Chapter 17 of NAFTA comprises the intellectual property regime. This regime differs in some respects from the coverage of NAFTA considered earlier in this chapter in that its focal point is the protection of property rather than measures directly associated with the liberalisation of trade and improving market access, although it is arguable that intellectual property rights can be used to achieve or improve market access through their capacity to drive down competition in the trade of goods and services; this collides with the notion that intellectual property rights should not be used to create or maintain barriers to legitimate trade, discussed below in the context of Article 1701(1)). To put Chapter 17 of NAFTA into context, it is helpful to bear in mind that it operates alongside the Agreement on Trade Related Aspects of Intellectual Property Rights ('TRIPS').[22]

The basic obligation expressed in Chapter 17 in NAFTA is the duty each party has to provide in its territory to the nationals of another party adequate and effective protection and enforcement of intellectual property rights, while ensuring that measures to enforce intellectual property rights do not themselves become barriers to legitimate trade (see Article 1701(1)). There are a number of other international treaties which are concerned with the protection of certain forms of intellectual property rights. Under Article 1701(2) of NAFTA, the parties commit themselves to giving effect to Chapter 17 and to the substantial provisions of these conventions:

(a) the Geneva Convention for the Protection of Producers of Phonograms Against Unauthorised Duplication of their Phonograms 1971 (Geneva Convention);

(b) the Berne Convention for the Protection of Literary and Artistic Works 1971 (Berne Convention);

(c) the Paris Convention for the Protection of Industrial Property 1967 (Paris Convention); and

(d) the International Convention for the Protection of New Varieties of Plants 1978 (UPOV Convention), or the International Convention for the Protection of New Varieties of Plants 1991 (UPOV Convention).

The forms of intellectual property rights and media which are accorded protection under Chapter 17 of NAFTA include:

- Copyright – see Article 1705.

- Sound recordings – see Article 1706.

- Encrypted program carrying satellite signals – see Article 1707.

- Trade marks – see Article 1708.

- Patents – see Article 1709.

- Layout designs of semiconductor integrated circuits – see Article 1710.

---

22   TRIPS is annexed to the WTO Agreement (Marrakesh, 15 April 1994; Aust TS 1995 no 8; 33 ILM 1125), Annex IC. See Chapter 6 above and 27 *Halsbury's Laws of Australia*, Trade and Commerce, paras [420–2145]–[420–2170].

- trade secrets – see Article 1711.

- geographical indications – see Article 1712.

- industrial designs – see Article 1713.

In a work of this nature, it is not possible to analyse exhaustively these various subject matters of intellectual property rights. Instead, we will concentrate on the fundamental trade related and trade liberalisation aspects which are more likely to be of interest from a market access viewpoint.

Once again, the theme of national treatment (or equality of treatment) surfaces strongly in Chapter 17 of NAFTA. The basic provision is Article 1703(1) which reads:

> Each party shall accord to nationals of another party treatment no less favourable than that it accords to its own nationals with regard to the protection and enforcement of all intellectual property rights. In respect of sound recordings, each party shall provide such treatment to producers and performers of another party, except that a party may limit rights of performers of another party in respect of secondary uses of sound recordings to those rights its nationals are accorded in the territory of such other party.

This provision is similar to Article 3:1 of TRIPS. One of the continuing tensions in intellectual property law is its interface with competition law.[23] The way this interface is dealt with under NAFTA is by Article 1704. It provides that nothing in Chapter 17 prevents a party from specifying in its domestic law licensing practices or conditions that may in particular cases constitute an abuse of intellectual property rights having an adverse effect on competition in the relevant market. A party may adopt or maintain, consistent with the other provisions of NAFTA, appropriate measures to prevent or control such practices or conditions. Obviously, the extent to which Article 1704 is implemented will depend upon the domestic law of each of the parties to NAFTA.

An important theme in Chapter 17 of NAFTA is the theme of enforcement of intellectual property rights. Provisions in NAFTA are devoted to this theme at a general level (see Article 1714) and at a specific level (see Article 1715). We consider each briefly:

The general regime associated with the enforcement of intellectual property rights under Article 1714 has these features:

- Each party must ensure that their enforcement procedures (as specified in Articles 1714–18) are available under its domestic law so as to permit effective action to be taken against any act of infringement of intellectual property rights covered by Chapter 17. This includes expeditious remedies to prevent infringements and remedies to deter further infringements. These enforcement procedures are to be applied so as to avoid the creation of barriers to legitimate trade and to provide safeguards against abuse of these procedures.

- Each party must ensure that its procedures for the enforcement of intellectual property rights are fair and equitable, are not unnecessarily complicated or costly, and do not entail unreasonable time limits or unwarranted delays.

---

23   For a good treatment of the Australian domestic law position, see Calvert, M, *Technology Contracts: A Handbook for Law and Business in Australia*, 1995, pp 381–426, Sydney: Butterworths.

- Each party must ensure that decisions on the merits of a case in judicial and administrative enforcement proceedings:

  1 are preferably in writing and state the reasons on which the decisions are based (this reflects the notion of principled decision-making);

  2 be made available at least to the parties and proceeding without undue delay;

  3 are based only on evidence in respect of which parties were offered the opportunity to be heard (which is an analogue of the concept of natural justice) (or procedural fairness) where there is a right to be heard and a hearing by a decision-maker whose mind is open to persuasion.[24]

At a lower level of abstraction, specific procedural and remedial aspects associated with the enforcement of intellectual property rights are enshrined in Article 1715. The key features of this regime to note are these:

- Each party must make available to 'right holders' (the holders of intellectual property rights) civil procedures for the enforcement of any intellectual property right provided in Chapter 17.

- Each party must provide that:

  (a) defendants have the right to written notice that is timely and contains sufficient detail, including the basis of the claims;

  (b) parties in a proceeding are allowed to be represented by independent legal counsel;

  (c) the procedures do not include imposition of overly burdensome requirements concerning mandatory personal appearances;

  (d) all parties in a proceeding are duly entitled to substantiate their claims and to present relevant evidence; and

  (e) the procedures include a means to identify and protect confidential information: (see Article 1715(1)).

Under Article 1715(2), each party must ensure that its judicial authorities are empowered to do the things set out in Articles 1715(2)(a)–(f). Complementing this provision is one which deals with provisional (or interim) measures which is the subject of Article 1716. The basic provision here is that each party must provide that its judicial authorities have the authority to order prompt and effective provisional measures to prevent infringement of any intellectual property right, and in particular to prevent the entry into the channels of commerce in the jurisdiction of allegedly infringing goods. In addition, the judicial authorities must be empowered to preserve relevant evidence in regard to the alleged infringement. The first limb intersects with customs laws and laws dealing with commercial practices such as parallel importing, and the second limb deals with matters such as Anton Piller orders (see Article 1716(1)). Other procedural matters associated with the enforcement of intellectual property rights are these:

---

24 Forbes, JRS, *Disciplinary Tribunals*, 2nd edn, 1996, p 84, Sydney: Federation.

- Article 1717 deals with criminal procedures and penalties.
- Article 1718 deals with the enforcement of intellectual property rights at the border.
- Article 1719 commits the parties to cooperation and technical assistance.
- Article 1720 deals with the extent to which Chapter 17 of NAFTA protects existing subject matter and intellectual property rights.

PUBLICATION, NOTIFICATION AND ADMINISTRATION OF LAWS

Chapter 18 of NAFTA deals with the publication, notification and administration of laws. In short, this is the important principle of transparency that is invoked here. Chapter 18 forms part of a continuum of chapters which can be grouped under rubric of 'administrative and constitutional provisions' which comprise Part 7 of NAFTA. Obviously, if the members of NAFTA are to organise their internal domestic laws in accordance with the provisions of NAFTA, and also so that persons affected by the operation of NAFTA (in particular business enterprises and individuals engaging in commerce) can organise their affairs in accordance with the bodies of commercial law as they are impacted by NAFTA, then the idea that laws and other 'measures' must be notified publicly is a step to achieving such goals. Within Chapter 18 of NAFTA, a principle that is given particular expression is the principle of transparency. This is reflected in Articles 1802 and 1803. Article 1802 obliges each party to ensure that its laws, regulations, procedures and administrative rulings of general application respecting any matter covered by NAFTA are promptly published or otherwise made available in such a manner as to enable interested persons and parties to become acquainted with them (see Article 1802(1)).

The benefit of this particular application of the principle of transparency is that it allows both the parties to NAFTA and to persons interested in or affected by its provisions to become acquainted with those provisions so that they can organise their affairs accordingly. Article 1803 builds on this ideal and obliges each party to notify any other party with an interest in the matter of any proposed or actual measure that the party considers might materially affect the operation of NAFTA or otherwise affect another party's interest under NAFTA (see Article 1803(1)). The benefits of this notification obligation might be more illusory than real if the parties to NATFA interpret (and apply) this provision as having too high a threshold that must be activated before a measure is notified. It should be noted that Article 1803(1) is couched in subjective language, and this militates against an application that is consistent with a teleological or purposive approach to NAFTA.

Many matters which are the subject of NAFTA are the subject of administrative proceedings or adjudication. NAFTA, in Article 1804, prescribes certain criteria which such administrative proceedings must adhere to. Under Article 1804, with a view to administering in a consistent, impartial and reasonable manner all measures of general application affecting matters covered by NAFTA, each party must ensure that in its administrative proceedings applying Article 1802 measures to particular persons, goods or services of another party in specific cases that:

- Persons of another party that are directly affected by proceeding are provided reasonable notice, in accordance with domestic procedures, when a proceeding is initiated. Such reasonable notice includes a description of the nature of the proceeding, a statement of the legal authority under which the proceeding is initiated and a general description of any issues in controversy.
- Such persons are afforded a reasonable opportunity to present facts and arguments in support of their positions prior to any final administrative action when time, the nature of the proceeding and the public interest so permits.
- Its procedures are in accordance with domestic law.

Article 1805 builds on the Article 1804 standards and requires each party to establish or maintain judicial, quasi-judicial or administrative tribunal procedures for the purpose of the prompt review and correction of final administrative actions regarding matters covered by NAFTA.

INSTITUTIONAL ARRANGEMENTS AND DISPUTE SETTLEMENT PROCEDURES

Chapter 20 of NAFTA is entitled 'Institutional Arrangements and Dispute Settlement Procedures'. The coverage of Chapter 20 of NAFTA is divided between:

Section A – Institutions (Articles 2001 and 2002).

Section B – Dispute Settlement (Articles 2003 – 2019).

Section C – Domestic Proceedings and Private Commercial Dispute Settlement (Articles 2020–2022).

We consider the key components of each of these sections next.

In an institutional sense, the major organ established by NAFTA is the Free Trade Commission (FTC). The FTC establishes cabinet-level representatives of the parties or their designees (Article 2001(1)). The charter of the FTC is that it must:

(a) supervise the implementation of NAFTA;

(b) oversee the further elaboration of NAFTA;

(c) resolve disputes that may arise regarding NAFTA's interpretation or application;

(d) supervise the work of all committees and working groups established under NAFTA, referred to in Annex 2001.2; and

(e) consider any other matter that may affect the operation of NAFTA.

The FTC is given a broad range of powers to execute its charter under Article 2001(3). Under Article 2001(4), the FTC must establish its own rules and procedures. All decisions of the FTC are to be taken by consensus, except as it may otherwise agree.

Supporting the FTC is the Secretariat which comprises national sections. Under Article 2002(3), the Secretariat must provide assistance to the FTC, and administrative assistance to panels and committees established under Chapter 19 of NAFTA and to panels established under Chapter 20. As well, the Secretariat must, as the FTC directs, support the work of other committees and groups established under NAFTA and to otherwise facilitate the operation of NAFTA. In broad terms, the division of functions between the FTC and the Secretariat is as follows: The FTC is the policy-setting organ within NAFTA. The FTC is also charged with supervision of the implementation of NAFTA. The Secretariat is the organ charged with the implementation of NAFTA, and the execution of its provisions. In short, the distinction is between policy and the administration of policy.

The dispute settlement framework of NAFTA moves through various layers of formality along a spectrum of less formal procedures at the one end and more formal at the other end. At the less formal end of the spectrum, the basic dispute settlement procedure is cooperation. This is reflected in Article 2003, which imposes on each party a duty at all times to endeavour to agree on the interpretation and application of NAFTA, and to make every attempt through cooperation and consultations to arrive at a mutually satisfactory resolution of any matter that might affect the operation of NAFTA. The machinery for consultations, in particular initiating and conducting them, is laid down in Article 2006. The next point along the spectrum are the procedures of good offices, conciliation, mediation or other dispute resolution procedures. These are available under Article 2007 if the consulting parties fail to resolve the matter under Article 2006. There are various time frames laid down in Article 2007(1) which are differentiated according to the subject matter of the consultations and whether or not consultations have been requested or participated in. The next point along the dispute resolution spectrum are arbitral proceedings. These can be activated under Article 2008 if the FTC has convened under Article 2007(4) and the matter in dispute has not been resolved within time frames laid down in Article 2008(1). On delivery of a request by a party to establish an arbitral panel, the FTC must establish it (see Article 2008(2)). The procedures for empanelling an arbitral panel are laid down in Articles 2009–17. Once a panel makes a final report, the disputing parties must agree on the resolution of the dispute, which normally must conform with the determinations and recommendations of the panel, and must notify their sections of the Secretariat of any agreed resolution or of any dispute (see Article 2018(1)). This shows that panel reports are not self-executing and that they do not bind the parties to a dispute, so that it is impossible to say that the panel procedure is other than advisory or hortatory . This must raise serious questions about its efficacy in a general sense.

The third cluster of provisions under Chapter 20 of NAFTA are concerned with domestic proceedings and private commercial dispute settlement. The context which surrounds these provisions of NAFTA (Articles 2020–2022) is that in domestic judicial administrative proceedings of a party to NAFTA, issues of interpretation or application of NAFTA may arise. Where this occurs, and any party considers that it should intervene, or if a court or administrative body solicits the view of a party, that party must notify the other parties and its section of the Secretariat. The usual response to such a notification is that the FTC must endeavour to agree on an appropriate response as expeditiously as possible (see Article 2020(1)). If the FTC has agreed an interpretation, then the party in whose territory the court or administrative body is located must submit it to that court or body in accordance with the rules of that forum (see Article 2020(2)).

Only if the FTC is unable to agree an issue of interpretation or application of NAFTA, then that party may submit its own views to the court or body in accordance with the laws of that forum (see Article 2020(3)). These provisions do not ascribe the effect that the views or opinions submitted to the court or body bind that court or body, otherwise this would infringe principles of judicial independence and autonomy (to the extent that they apply to judicial bodies under the domestic or organic laws of the members of NAFTA).

There is some scaling back or quarantining of private rights under NAFTA. Under Article 2021, no party may provide for a right of action under its domestic law against another party on the ground that a measure of another party is inconsistent with NAFTA. This ensures the supremacy of NAFTA over domestic law. This provision does not affect the operation of the investment dispute settlement regime under NAFTA (see Chapter 11 of NAFTA discussed above) since certain rights of action are provided for under that Chapter of NAFTA.

The phenomenon of Alternative Dispute Resolution (ADR) is important in the domestic law of many developed economies. This same phenomenon is also reflected in NAFTA, Article 2022(1) which provides that each party must, to the maximum extent possible, encourage and facilitate the use of arbitration and other means of ADR with the settlement of international commercial disputes between private parties and the Free Trade Area.[25]

EXCEPTIONS

Chapter 21 of NAFTA provides a range of exceptions which restrict the operation of NAFTA in certain respects. Some of the key exceptions to note are these:

- *National security* – Under Article 2102, nothing in NAFTA is to be construed to require any party to furnish or allow access to any information the disclosure of which it determines to be contrary to its essential security interests, or to prevent any party from taking any actions that it considers necessary for the protection of its essential security interests relating to military hardware or war, or to prevent any party from taking action in pursuance of its obligations under the United Nations Charter for the maintenance of international peace and security.

- *Taxation* – In general, nothing in NAFTA applies to any taxation measure (see Article 2103(1)). Under Article 2103(2), nothing in NAFTA affects the rights and duties of any party under any tax convention.

- *Balance of Payments* – Nothing in NAFTA is to be construed to prevent a party from adopting or maintaining measures that restrict transfers where the party experiences serious balance of payment difficulties, or the threat of these, and such restrictions are consistent with Articles 2104(2)–(4).

---

25   On international commercial arbitration, see Chapter 11 below.

CONCLUSIONS

It has been argued in this chapter that one of the key constructs that informs and animates NAFTA is the notion of mercantilism, that is, the policy of preferring commercial interests to other interests. This is reflected in the principles of trade liberalisation, enhanced market access, freedom of movement, freedom of establishment, freedom of participation, security of investment and the protection of property (particularly intellectual property) that are embedded in specific provisions of NAFTA. Alongside these trade related freedoms and principles are some principles that are generic to many international commercial treaties such as equality of national treatment, most-favoured-nation status (MFN) and transparency. In combination, these principles shore up the policy of enhanced market access via uniform, borderless markets.

TUTORIAL QUESTIONS

1   Identify and explain the relationship between the main underlying principles that inform and shape NAFTA.

2   Ethical issues and interests are not expressly articulated in NAFTA. If this is correct, then consider whether, and if so, on what basis and to what extent, these can be derived. As an example only, is it possible to invoke considerations of, say, commercial morality and 'fair play' in deciding on the interpretation of NAFTA?

3   Consider the Preamble to NAFTA reproduced at p 669 of this chapter. Discuss and evaluate the extent to which the ideals of NAFTA are borne out in the text and likely practice of NAFTA.

4   Explain the extent to which individuals and other juristic persons have standing (or juridical personality) under NAFTA. If you consider that individuals do have standing (or juridical personality), then evaluate how effective this is in meeting the policy objectives of NAFTA?

5   How do individuals and other juristic persons gain access to the trade-liberalisation initiatives of NAFTA. Do you consider that the dispute settlement procedures of NAFTA are suitable vehicles to achieve this goal? What are their strengths and weaknesses and what criteria do you suggest or propose to decide such matters?

6   Identify the points of intersection between NAFTA and the WTO Agreement (see also Chapter 6 above).

7   Is the principle of enhanced market access uniformly applied across all of the sectors of NAFTA? Can you identify any sectors of economic activity where this principle might be diluted, and if so, what are or seem to be the justification(s) for this derogation?

8   With reference to the text of NAFTA, discuss the extent to which the exceptions listed at p 701 of this chapter derogate from the objectives of NAFTA.

9   How does NAFTA deal with disguised barriers in cross-border trade that otherwise function as impediments to trade? If you consider that NAFTA's treatment is

inadequate, then what improvements do you suggest should be made to NAFTA to strengthen the removal of trade barriers?

10 Media reports in Australia and Canada in December 1996 have suggested that Australia should consider acceding to NAFTA. Accepting for the moment that this is not fanciful or remote, why should Australia consider this proposal seriously, and what benefits would accrue to Australia? In any event, how would this affect the Closer Economic Relations Treaty with New Zealand?

FURTHER READING

Besides the works cited above, the following works may be consulted:

Nunez, O, 'Quebec's Perspective on Social Aspects and the Broadening of Free Trade in the Americas' (1996) 11 *Connecticut Journal of International Law* 279–99.

Long, F, 'Getting the Most out of NAFTA' (1995) 41 *The Practical Lawyer* 55.

Naranjo, D, 'Alternative Dispute Resolution of International Private Commercial Disputes Under NAFTA' (1996) 59 *Texas Bar Journal* 116.

Symposium; various authors, 'NAFTA: Reflections on the First Year and Visions for the Future' (1995) 12 *Arizona Journal of International and Comparative Law* 367–652.

Kozolchyk, B, 'NAFTA in the Grand and Small Scheme of Things' (1996) 13 *Arizona Journal of International and Comparative Law* 135.

Bakken, L, 'The North American Free Trade Agreement: the Foundation for a New Trade Alliance' (1995) 18 *Hamline Law Review* 329.

Thomure, J, 'The Uneasy Case for the North American Free Trade Agreement' (1995) 21 *Syracuse Journal of International Law and Commerce* 181.

CHAPTER 10

TRADING BLOC: THE EUROPEAN UNION

INTRODUCTION

The European Union (EU)[1] is a powerful trading bloc which, by the end of 1992, has largely succeeded in establishing a single market where there is free movement of goods, services, persons and capital. This achievement was accentuated with the coming into force of the Union (Maastricht) Treaty on 1 November 1993. This chapter serves as an introduction to the EU. It will concentrate on the EU's political institutions and legal acts. It will also provide an overview of freedom of movement of goods and the trading relationship between the EU and non-member States.

THE THREE EUROPEAN COMMUNITIES AND THE EUROPEAN UNION

The Union Treaty declares that it establishes a European Union 'founded on the European Communities, supplemented by the policies and forms of cooperation established by this Treaty'.[2] The Union (Maastricht) Treaty significantly amended these treaties and placed them within a new structure sometimes described as three pillars, under a common roof. The 'roof' created by the Union Treaty is found in its Title I and sets out common provisions for the three pillars. It creates the European Union which deals with the matters that come under the three 'pillars'. The first pillar consists of the European Communities which already existed at the time of the signing of the Union Treaty on 7 February 1992.

Although most observers refer to the European Community in the singular, there are in effect three European Communities. They are:

- European Coal and Steel Community (ECSC);
- European Community (EC); and
- European Atomic Energy Community (Euratom).

It is interesting to note that these Communities have nothing to do with the European Convention on Human Rights (ECHR). All 15 member States of the EU have signed the ECHR and therefore it is binding on them in international law, but the convention does not create directly effective law in all the member States so as to enable citizens to

---

1   The European Economic Community Treaty, done at Rome on 25 March 1957, which established the EC, originally, by Article 1, entitled the Community as the European Economic Community. Following the 12 October 1993 rejection by the German Constitutional Court of the final challenge to the validity of the adoption of the Union Treaty, done at Maastricht on 7 February 1992, this latter Treaty came into force on 1 November 1993. The Union (Maastricht) Treaty amended the EEC Treaty so that the title of the Community was altered to the EC (Union Treaty Article G(A)).

2   Article A.

rely upon it in national courts. The second pillar creates a Common Foreign and Security Policy which is to be found under Title V, Union Treaty, Article J. The third pillar institutes Cooperation in Justice and Home Affairs. The second and third pillars are based on intergovernmental decision making and are usually taken on a majority basis so that any State may block a proposal.

The ECSC was established by the Treaty of Paris signed on 18 April 1951. The parties to the Treaty were Belgium, The Netherlands, Luxemburg, France, Germany and Italy. The ECSC directs and controls output, markets, supply and demand in the limited area of coal and steel. Euratom and the EEC (later renamed EC) were established by the Treaties of Rome signed on 25 March 1957. The Treaties came into force on 1 January 1958. The Euratom Community controls the development of nuclear energy for peaceful purposes. The general aim of the EC is to establish a common market within which the economic policies of the Member States are harmonised.

The EC achieves its tasks through a number of activities which are outlined in Article 3 of the EC Treaty. In particular, these activities include the elimination of customs duties and quantitative restrictions on the imports and exports between Member States and the establishment of a common external customs tariff and a common commercial policy towards non-member countries. The EC is financed, at least in part, from the levies charged at the Community's frontiers.[3] Article 3a of the Treaty requires the Member States to conduct the activities pertaining to the Community in a spirit of close co-ordination of economic policies conducted 'in accordance with the principle of an open market with free competition' leading to the adoption of one currency and a condition of 'stable prices, sound public finances and monetary conditions and a sustainable balance of payments.'

FUNDAMENTAL FREEDOMS OF THE EC TREATY

The EC Treaty requires the implementation of the EC's four fundamental freedoms, namely abolition as between Member States of obstacles to freedom of movement of goods,[4] persons,[5] services,[6] and capital.[7] It also provides for the adoption of common policies on agriculture[8] and transport.[9] There is also a system for ensuring that competition in the EC is not distorted.[10] The economic policies of the Member States are co-ordinated and, to that end, national laws are approximated, including the wildly diverse national rules on indirect taxation.[11]

---

3   See Council Decision 85/257 of 7 May 1985 on the Communities' system of own resources.
4   EC Treaty Article 3(a).
5   *Ibid*, 3(c).
6   *Ibid*.
7   *Ibid*.
8   *Ibid*, Article 3(e).
9   *Ibid*, Article 3(f).
10 *Ibid*, Article 3(g).
11 *Ibid*, Article 3(h).

CITIZENSHIP OF THE UNION

Article G(C) of the Union Treaty inserts into the EC Treaty a new Part Two entitled 'Citizenship of the Union', consisting of new Articles 8–8e. Article 8(1) establishes that: 'Every person holding nationality of a Member State shall be a citizen of the Union.' Article 8a gives every citizen of the Union the right to move and reside freely within the Union. Article 8b gives a citizen of the Union the right to stand for election in municipal elections in the state of residence. Article 8c confers on citizens a right to diplomatic protection by any legation of any member State. Article 8d confers on every citizen the right to petition the European Parliament or apply to the Ombudsman. Article 8e requires the Commission to report to the Parliament before 31 December 1993 and each three years thereafter on the application of Part Two. Thus, if a citizen of the Union is employed by an exporter, that citizen has a right to reside anywhere in the Union where the best effect for the exporter's business will accrue.

Article G(E) of the Union Treaty inserts into the EC Treaty, *inter alia*, Articles 138d and 138e. Article 138d gives every citizen, natural and legal person residing or having a registered office in any Member State, the right to petition the European Parliament, either by himself or herself, or in conjunction with others, upon any matter which comes within the fields of activity of the Community. Similarly, Article 138e gives every citizen, natural and legal person residing or having a registered office in any member State, the right to complain to the Ombudsman concerning the maladministration of any Community body, except the European Court of Justice or the Court of First Instance when they are acting in their judicial capacity.

The new Article 100c(1) and (3)[12] enables the Council of Ministers, acting by a qualified majority since 1 January 1996, to determine which nationals should be in possession of a visa when they cross the external frontiers of the Union. This article requires that the Council act on a proposal from the Commission and after consulting the European Parliament. However, in an emergency situation the Council, acting by a qualified majority, may impose visa restrictions for a period not exceeding six months.

By Article O of the Union Treaty, any European state may apply to join the Union. This could raise an interesting geographical question if ever Russia should apply to join the Union.

THE COMMUNITY ORGANS

The ECSC, EC and Euratom Treaties each provided for an Assembly (later renamed European Parliament), a Council of Ministers, a Commission and a European Court of Justice.[13] The Union Treaty has added a fifth body to the list of institutions, a Court of Auditors.[14] On 8 April 1965, the Member States adopted the Treaty Establishing a Single Council and a Single Commission of the European Communities.[15] This Treaty,

---

12   Inserted by the Union Treaty Article G(D).

13   EC Treaty, Article 4.

14   *Ibid.*

15   Merger Treaty which came into effect on 1 July 1967.

with effect from 1 July 1967, provided for the merger of the existing Communities Councils and Commissions into a single Commission and Council. The EC was enlarged on 1 January 1973, when the UK, Ireland and Denmark joined; on 1 January 1981, when Greece joined; on 1 January 1986 when Spain and Portugal joined; and on 1 January 1996 when Austria, Sweden and Finland were admitted as full Member States. The EC thus currently consists of 15 Member States.

The European Economic Community as originally conceived was concerned primarily with economic issues, especially the creation of a market in which there is free movement of goods, persons, services and capital. But as a consequence of the adoption of many new laws, the EC has now expanded and the range of issues and matters with which the EC law deals grows steadily. Although economic integration remains at the core of the EC, the EC now deals with such issues as basic human rights, equality between the sexes, education, migrant workers from third countries, social and cultural affairs and protection of the environment.

DECLARATION ON APPROXIMATION

By virtue of Article 100a of the EC Treaty, the:

> Council shall, acting in accordance with the procedure referred to in Article 189b ... adopt the measures for the approximation of the provisions laid down by law, regulation or administrative action in Member States which have as their object the establishment and functioning of the internal market.

Article 189b provides for a co-decision procedure involving the Commission, the Council and the Parliament. It enables the Parliament to veto legislative proposals; it also provides for the establishment of a conciliation committee to be appointed with equal numbers of Council and Parliament representatives in circumstances involving a dispute between the Council and the Parliament. Thus, following the coming into force of the Union Treaty, Article 100a(1) requires that the democratic procedure of Article 189b be followed in regard to the approximation of laws with respect to the establishment and operation of the internal market which is defined in Article 7a as 'an area without internal frontiers in which the free movement of goods, persons, services and capital is ensured in accordance with the provisions of this Treaty'.

The Council sometimes operates through a system of weighted voting. If a measure must be adopted by qualified majority, 62 votes out of 87 are needed. Articles which now require a qualified majority include Article 49 (freedom of movement for workers), approximation of laws for the completion of the internal market (establishment and functioning of the internal market), alteration or suspension of duties in the common customs tariff,[16] freedom to provide cross-frontier services by non-EC nationals established in a Member State,[17] co-ordination of national exchange policies to implement the free movement of capital,[18] and the liberalisation of

---

16 Article 28.
17 Article 59(2).
18 Article 70(1).

intra-community air and sea transport.[19] Article 100, which refers to the issuing of directives for the approximation of laws directed to the establishment and operation of the common market, was amended by the Union Treaty to require the Council to consult the European Parliament and the Economic and Social Committee in all cases and not only when the laws of any Member State would require amendment to comply with a directive. Unanimity has been retained for harmonisation of national laws for the training and admission to the professions,[20] and for the harmonisation of indirect taxation.[21]

ECONOMIC AND POLITICAL UNION

One of the most significant changes introduced by the Union (Maastricht) Treaty is the establishment of an economic and monetary union (EMU). The first stage of EMU commenced in July 1990. This first stage involved a number of initiatives including:

1   procedures to promote co-ordination of economic and monetary policies;

2   the bringing of all member States' currencies into the exchange rate mechanism (ERM) of the European Monetary System (EMS); and

3   the granting to a Committee of Central Bank Governors a role in formulating non-binding opinions upon economic and monetary policies, foreign exchange policy and banking supervision.

With Decision 90/102[22] the responsibilities of the Committee of Central Bank Governors was refined and increased. The tasks of this committee now include:

1   to consult concerning general principles and broad lines of policy of central banking;

2   to exchange information on matters within the competence of the central banks;

3   to promote the co-ordination of monetary policy of the member States;

4   to formulate opinions upon monetary and exchange rate policy; and

5   to express opinions to the governments of member States concerning internal and external monetary position of the Community and in particular the operation of the ERM.

The ERM took a battering in 1993 when the allowable margins in which currencies were allowed to fluctuate were substantially increased and the pound sterling was withdrawn from ERM. The Union Treaty inserted a new Article 3a in the EC Treaty[23] which provides for the irrevocable fixing of exchange rates of the Member States currencies, with a view to the introduction of a single currency, the Euro.

---

19   Article 84(2).

20   Article 57(2).

21   Article 99.

22   OJ 1990 L78/25.

23   Article G(B)(4).

CAPITAL AND PAYMENTS

It was projected by the Union Treaty that from 1 January 1994[24] Articles 67–73 of the EC Treaty would be replaced by Articles 73a–h.[25] Article 73b(1) abolishes all restrictions upon the movement of capital between member States and between member States and third countries. Similarly, Article 73b(2) abolishes all restrictions upon payments between member States and between member States and third countries. Article 73c allows restrictions upon the movement of capital to third countries which are in place on 31 December 1993 to remain. Article 73c(2) allows the Council, by qualified majority, to adopt measures with respect to capital movements between member States and third countries, but should the measure be a derogation from the current status of freedom of movement, unanimity is required. Article 73d allows member States to apply national tax laws which distinguish between taxpayers on the basis of residence; to take measures to prevent infringement of national laws, especially in the fields of taxation and prudential supervision of financial institutions. Article 73e allows member States, who by Community law have a derogation from the free movement of capital to maintain that derogation until 31 December 1995. Article 73f allows safeguard measures to be taken where movements of capital cause or threaten to cause serious difficulties for the operation of economic or monetary union. Article 73h contains transitional provisions to operate until 1 January 1994.

MONETARY POLICY

The new Article 4A[26] of the EC Treaty establishes a European System of Central Banks (ESCB) and a European Central Bank (ECB). The ESCB is composed of the ECB and the central banks of the member States.[27] The primary objective of the ESCB is to maintain price stability.[28] The basic tasks of the ESCB are set out in Article 105(2) as:

- to define and implement the monetary policy of the Community;
- to conduct foreign exchange operations consistent with Article 109;
- to hold and to manage the official foreign reserves of the member States; and
- to promote the smooth operation of the payment systems.

To carry out its tasks the ECB is given legal personality.[29] The ECB has the exclusive right to authorise the issue of bank notes within the community, which notes may be issued by the ECB and the national central banks.[30] The ECB has two decision making

---

24 EC Treaty Article 73A inserted by Union Treaty Article G(D)(15).
25 Union Treaty Article G(D)(15).
26 Inserted by the Union Treaty Article G(B)(7).
27 Article 106(1).
28 Article 105(1).
29 Article 106(2).
30 Article 105a.

bodies, the Governing Council and the Executive Board.[31] The executive Board of the ECB comprises the president, the vice president, and four members (all nationals of the member States) appointed from persons or recognised standing in banking and money matters for an eight year non-renewable term.[32] The Governing Council consists of the Executive Board of the ECB and the Governors of the national central banks.[33] The ECB is made independent of the Community institutions and the governments of the Member States.[34]

EXCHANGE RATE POLICY

The exchange rate policy of the final stage of EMU is to be governed by Article 109.[35] On a recommendation from the ECB or Commission (after consulting the ECB if the latter), the Council may, acting unanimously, conclude agreements on an exchange rate system for the ECU in relation to non-Community currencies.[36] In the absence of such agreements, the Council, acting by qualified majority, acting on a recommendation of either the ECB or the Commission (after consulting the ECB if the latter) the Council 'may formulate general orientations for exchange rate policy'.[37]

COMMUNITY LEGISLATION

Article 189 of the EC Treaty

The legal acts available to the Community are listed in Article 189 of the EC Treaty. This article reveals that the Community legal acts are:

(i)   Regulations,

(ii) Directives,

(iii) Decisions,

(iv) Recommendations, and

(v)   Opinions.

Regulations

Regulations are directly applicable in the sense that they automatically become part of the domestic law of the Member States and, therefore, need not be the subject of further legislative action by the national parliaments. A Member State therefore cannot selectively apply a regulation so as to frustrate aspects of EC legislation which it has

---

31   Article 106(3).
32   Article 109A(2).
33   Article 109A(1).
34   Article 107.
35   Inserted by Union Treaty Article G(D)(25).
36   Article 109(1).
37   Article 109(2).

opposed or which it considers contrary to its national interests.[38] Neither may it be plead 'provisions, practices or circumstances existing in its legal system in order to justify a failure to comply with its obligations under Community law'.[39] Indeed, the Community nature of a regulation is not permitted to be obscured by the re-enactment of a Community measure as a national measure.[40] In *Confédération nationale des producteurs de fruits et légumes v Council*[41] the nature of a regulation was discussed. The court held that a regulation:

> ... being of an essentially normative character, is applicable not to a limited identifiable number of designees but rather to categories of persons envisaged both in the abstract and as a whole.[42]

The court continued and said that:

> One cannot, however, consider that an administrative act constitutes a Decision when that act is applicable to objectively stated situations, which involve immediate juridical consequences, in all the Member States, for categories of persons envisaged in a general and abstract manner.[43]

Regulations prevail over national law pre-dating them,[44] or post-dating them,[45] even if the national measure is a constitutional measure.[46]

Directives

Directives stipulate a result which Member States are to achieve but leave the choice of means to the discretion of the Member States. A example of the usefulness of directives is Council Directive 85/374 of 25 July 1985. This Directive concerned the approximation of laws, regulations and administrative provisions of Member States regarding manufacturers' liability for defective products.[47] It imposes on Member States an obligation to 'bring into force, not later than three years from the date of notification of this Directive, the laws, regulations and administrative provisions necessary to comply with this Directive' (Article 19).

Directives may, however, become directly effective. This may occur when the Directive is unambiguous and unconditional and either it has not been implemented by the Member State concerned within the time limit allowed,[48] or the Directive has been

---

38 *Case 39/72 Commission v Italian Republic* [1973] ECR 101.

39 *Case C217/88 Re Distillation of Table Wine: EC Commission v Germany* [1993] 1 CMLR 18 at 38.

40 *Case 50/76 Amsterdam Bulb BV v Hoofdproduktschap voor Siergewassen* [1977] ECR 137.

41 [1963] CMLR 160.

42 *Ibid*, 173.

43 *Ibid*, 174.

44 *Case 13/68 Spa Salgoil v Ministry of Foreign Trade of Italy* [1969] CMLR 181.

45 *Case 93/71 Orsolina Leonesia v Ministry of Agriculture and Forestry of Italy* [1973] CMLR 343.

46 *R v Secretary of State for Transport; ex p Factortame Ltd (No 2)* [1991] 1 AC 603.

47 See also Council Directive 92/59 of 29 June 1992 on general product safety (OJ 1992 L228/24). Council Directive 85/374 was the model, in Australia, for the Trade Practices Act Amendment Act 1992 which inserted Part VA into the Trade Practices Act 1974.

48 Case 244/78 *Union Laitiere Normandie v French Dairy Farmers Ltd* [1979] ECR 1629.

implemented in a manner incompatible with the Directive.[49] In *Grad v Finanzamt Traunstein*[50] the court held:

> It is true that by virtue of Article 189, regulations are directly applicable and may therefore produce direct effects because of their nature as law. However, it does not follow from this that no other categories of legal measures mentioned in that article could never produce similar effects.[51]

The court was, in *Grad v Finanzamt Traunstein*, concerned with the direct effect of a Directive combined with a Decision. In *SACE SpA v Italian Ministry of Finance*,[52] the direct effect of a Treaty provision combined with a Directive was in issue. In *Van Duyn v Home Office*,[53] and *Bonsignore v Oberstadtdirektor der Stadt Köln*,[54] the court held that Council Directive 64/221[55] standing alone was directly effective.

If a Member State fails its duty to implement a directive the Commission may bring an action before the court under Article 169. The directive must be affirmatively implemented by the Member State. 'As the court has consistently held in judgments concerning the implementation of directives, mere administrative practices, which by their nature are alterable at will by the authorities and are not given the appropriate publicity, cannot be regarded as constituting the proper fulfilment of a Member State's obligations under the Treaty.'[56]

Decisions

Decisions are exclusively directed at individual determinable addressees and they are the usual means whereby the EC institutions deal with individual cases.[57] They are of two types, those which apply EC law and those which make law. Decisions which apply law are those which find facts which raise issues of Community law, for example, Decisions under Article 2 of Regulation 17/62 granting a negative clearance.[58] Decisions which make law are of the type made under Articles 6 and 8 of Regulation 17/62 invoking Article 85(3) of the Treaty granting a declaration of inapplicability of Article 85(1) of the Treaty.[59]

---

49 Case 148/78 *Publico v Ratti* [1971] CMLR 123.

50 [1971] CMLR 1.

51 *Ibid*, 23. See also Case 33/70 *SACE SpA v Italian Ministry of Finance* [1971] CMLR 123.

52 [1971] CMLR 123.

53 [1974] ECR 1337.

54 [1975] ECR 297.

55 Made 24 February 1964. Published in 1964 OJ 850.

56 Case C236/91 *Re the Directive on Animal Semen: EC Commission v Ireland* [1993] 1 CMLR 320 at 324.

57 Joined Cases 16–17/62 *Confederation nationale des producteurs de fruits et légumes v Council* [1963] CMLR 160.

58 See below.

59 See, *Inntrepreneur Estates Ltd v Mason* [1993] CMLR 293.

Recommendations and opinions

Recommendations and opinions are not binding and give rise to no legal obligations on the part of the addressees. Recommendations are generally made on the initiatives of the Community institutions whereas opinions are delivered as a result of outside initiatives. An opinion may contain a general assessment of certain facts and may prepare the ground for subsequent legal proceedings.[60]

Difference of nomenclature: EC and ECSC treaties

It should be pointed out, for reasons of clarity, that the legal acts listed in Article 14 of the ECSC Treaty do not adopt the same names for legal acts as in the EC Treaty discussed above.

Freedom of movement of goods

The principles of free movement of goods in the EU are contained in Articles 9–37 of the EC Treaty and of the relevant decisions of the court. The Treaty provisions deal with the customs union,[61] the common customs tariff and the Elimination of Quantitative Restrictions between Member States. They are very important to non-EC resident nationals who export goods to the European Union. The importance stems from the fact that exporters obviously need information on whether the EU has established a common external customs tariff with regard to their products and whether their products gain free circulation throughout the Community once they have been landed in a Member State.

Article 9 of the EC Treaty provides for the establishment of a customs union. The term 'customs union' is derived from Article XIV of the General Agreement on Tariffs and Trade (GATT). A customs union requires the removal of duties of customs between Members of the Union, the prohibition of charges having an equivalent effect, quantitative restrictions upon the flow of goods and the adoption of a common customs tariff applied to the goods originating in non-Member States. In contrast, a free trade area does not entail the removal of duties of customs or quantitative restrictions on the flow of goods between members of the area, except for goods originating within the Member States of the free trade area. Also there is no requirement for a common external customs tariff.

The EC Customs Union is based on para 1 of Article 9 which states in its relevant part that the 'Community shall be based upon a customs union which shall cover all trade in goods and which shall involve the prohibition between Member States of customs duties on imports and exports and of all charges having equivalent effect'. The term 'goods' in para 1 has been given an extended meaning. The ECJ held in

---

60 See, Article 169 and Article 170 of the EEC Treaty.

61 Articles 9–11.

Commission v Italy[62] that goods are 'products which can be valued in money and which are capable, as such, of forming the subject of commercial transactions'.[63] As the goods themselves benefit from the prohibition of the imposition of customs duties, the nationality of the consignor, the bailee or the consignee is irrelevant.

Treaty provisions for the elimination of internal customs duties

The EC Treaty deals in more detail with the elimination of customs duties between Member States in Articles 12–17. Article 12 stipulates that 'Member States shall refrain from introducing between themselves any new customs duties on imports or exports or any charges having equivalent effect'. The customs union between the Member States thus requires not only the abolition of customs duties but also the abolition of charges having an effect equivalent to customs duties. In *Re Import Duties on Gingerbread: Commission v Grand Duchy of Luxemburg and Kingdom of Belgium*[64] the court held that:

> ... a duty, whatever it is called and whatever its mode of application, which is imposed unilaterally either at the time of importation or subsequently and which, if imposed specifically on an imported product from a Member State to the exclusion of a similar national product, results, by an alteration to its price, in the same effect as a customs duty upon the free movement of products, can be considered as a tax having an equivalent effect within the meaning of Articles 9 and 12.[65]

A charge has an equivalent effect if it is levied, no matter at what rate, because the goods cross a frontier.[66] The court is not concerned whether or not protection is the aim of the charge.[67] In *Re Extraordinary Customs Clearance: EC Commission v Italy*,[68] the court considered an Italian order establishing a system of charges for customs clearances obtained outside the normal customs area or outside the normal office hours. Where a bulk of goods were imported by more than one importer and the goods were cleared in one bulk, the customs officers concerned were remunerated by one payment, but the importers were charged the time in proportion to their goods with a minimum charge of one hour. Therefore if five importers imported a bulk of goods in equal shares and the goods were cleared after hours and the clearance took 50 minutes each importer would by charged one hour, a total charge of five hours for 50 minutes service to all the importers. The court held that the minimum charge of one hour was so remote from the actual service received that the charge was one equivalent to a duty of customs.

---

62 [1968] ECR 423.

63 *Ibid*, 428.

64 [1963] CMLR 199.

65 *Ibid*, 216–17.

66 Case 24/68 *Commission* v *Italy* [1969] ECR 193; [1971] CMLR 611.

67 Joined Cases 2–3/69 *Sociaal Fonds voor de Diamantarbeiders v SA Ch Brachfield and Sons* [1969] CMLR 335.

68 [1993] 1 CMLR 155.

Common customs tariff

Article 9 also provides in para 1 for the adoption of an external common customs tariff. Council Regulation 4151/88 of 21 December 1988[69] lays down the provisions applicable to goods brought into the customs territory of the Community. The Regulation provides in Article 2 that goods are subject to customs supervision upon their entry into the Community. The establishment of the common customs tariff is linked by Article 3 of the EC Treaty to the establishment of a common commercial policy toward third countries. The EC's commercial policy, which is based on Articles 110 and 113 of the Treaty, is discussed in more detail later in this chapter.

Free circulation of goods in the Community

Once imported into the Community, goods are able to circulate freely within any part of the Community.[70] Indeed, para 2 of Article 9 of the EC Treaty stipulates that the Community rules also apply 'to products coming from third countries which are in free circulation in Member States'. In accordance with Article 10, such products are considered 'to be in free circulation in a Member State if the import formalities have been complied with and any customs duties or charges having equivalent effect which are payable have been levied in that Member State'.

Elimination of customs duties and establishment of the common customs tariff

The Council has eliminated customs duties and tariffs as between Member States, and succeeded in establishing the common external customs tariff. Under Article 23(3) of the EC Treaty, the common customs tariff was to have commenced on 1 January 1970 but the original six Member States of the EEC agreed to apply a common customs tariff from 1 July 1968. Customs duties upon goods in trade between Member States were also abolished as from the same date from which the common customs tariff applied. The abolition of customs duties between the member States substantially facilitated free inter-State trade in the EC. In *Simmenthal v Amministrazione delle Finanze dello Stato*,[71] the court accepted that where inspection of goods could legally be conducted in inter-State trade, the member States could charge for the inspection. In inter-State trade, these inspections are lawful if the charge does not exceed the cost of the inspection. The charge for the inspection of goods from non-member States could be greater than the charge for the inspection of Member States' products provided the difference was not excessively disproportionate. In *IFG Intercontinentale Fleischhandels GmbH and Co KG v*

---

69   OJ 1988 L367/1.

70   Case 21/75 *I Schroder KG v Oberstadtdirektor der Stadt Koln* [1975] ECR 905. For the standard rate of duty, see Council Regulation 2658/87 as amended (OJ 1987 L256/1) on the tariff and statistical nomenclature and on the common customs tariff.

71   [1978] ECR 1453.

Freistaat Bayern[72] the court accepted that the lawfulness of the imposition of such a charge was not dependent upon the existence of similar charges in other Member States. Thus, there may be a difference of treatment of imports from non-EC countries depending upon the Member State into which the goods are imported. In 1985, the Council promulgated Directive 85/73. This Directive concerned the financing of inspections and controls of fresh meat and poultry meat and was to set standard rules and criteria. The Directive expressly allows Member States to exceed the charge fixed by the Directive providing the fee charged by the Member State does not exceed the actual cost of the inspection.

Article 30 of the EC Treaty

Article 30 of the EC Treaty stipulates that 'Quantitative restrictions on imports and all measures having equivalent effect ... shall ... be prohibited between Member States'.[73] *EMI Records Ltd v CBS UK Ltd*[74] establishes that the prohibition of Article 30 is directed to trade between Member States and therefore Article 30 is not relevant to trade between a Member State and a non-Member State. On 22 December 1969 the Commission issued Directive 70/50 which listed all types of national measures which have an equivalent effect to quantitative restrictions. Any law, regulation, administrative rule or practice of a public authority that make imports more costly or difficult to market than similar local products is a measure having an equivalent effect to quantitative restrictions.[75] The requirement for import licences, even as a formality, is a measure incompatible with Article 30.[76] In *Freistaat Bayern v Eurim-Pharm GmbH*,[77] a German requirement that pharmaceutical products be not imported without a permit was in question. In order to obtain a permit it had to be shown that the pharmaceutical products, at the time of importation, were marked in the German language. The court held that these requirements were incompatible with Article 30 and were not saved by the public health requirement of Article 36. In *Geddo v Ente Nazionale Risi*,[78] the court indicated that 'measures which amount to a total or partial restraint of, according to the circumstances, imports, exports, or goods in transit'[79] constitute quantitative restrictions. In *International Fruit Co v Produktschap voor Groenten en Fruit*,[80] it was decided that, in intra-Community trade, the national requirement of obtaining an import licence is a measure having an equivalent effect to a quantitative restriction, even where such

---

72 [1984] ECR 349; [1985] 1 CMLR 453.

73 In Case 190/73 *Officier van Justitie v Van Haaster* [1974] ECR 1123; [1974] 2 CMLR 521 the court held that national production quotas amounted to measures having an effect equivalent to quantitative restrictions.

74 [1976] ECR 811; [1976] 2 CMLR 235.

75 Case 8/74 *Procurer du Roi v Dassonville* [1974] ECR 837; [1974] 1 CMLR 436.

76 Case 235/91 *Re Imports of Animal Semen: EC Commission v Ireland* [1993] 1 CMLR 325 at 334.

77 [1993] 1 CMLR 616.

78 [1973] ECR 865.

79 *Ibid*, 879.

80 [1971] ECR 1107.

licences are granted automatically. Also, legislation fixing a maximum retail price for sugar is a measure having an effect equivalent to a quantitative restriction. This was stated by the court in *SADAM v Comitato Interministeriale dei Prezzi*.[81] *Procureur du Roi v Dassonville*[82] involved a Belgian statute which prohibited the importation and sale of spirits that carried an authorised designation of origin, unless the importer or seller possessed a certificate of origin (CO). The product in question was Scotch whisky. The Belgian authorities only accepted as a valid CO a document issued by, and obtainable from, the British customs authorities. The defendant, Dassonville, had imported the Scotch whisky into Belgium from France. The importer could only obtain the CO 'with great difficulty, unlike the importer who imports directly from the producer country'.[83] The court decided that 'All trading rules enacted by Member States which are capable of hindering, directly or indirectly, actually or potentially, intra-Community trade'[84] constituted a measure having an effect equivalent to quantitative restrictions on trade. However, a non-discriminatory national law based on the national or regional socio-cultural characteristics, which law complies with Community law, particularly the measures required to overcome the disruptions to the market concerned, is allowed. Thus measures designed to prevent immediate price fluctuations would come within the purview of Article 103 whereas a measure to develop the market on a long term basis would not. Regulation 974/71[85] concerned the conjunctoral policy following the temporary widening of the margins allowed for the fluctuations of the currencies of some of the Member States, to allow the income of the primary producers to be stabilised. The consultation of Article 103 applies if any problem should arise in the supply of certain products. In *SADAM v Comitato Interministeriale dei Prezzi*,[86] the court held that a Member State, however, could not rely on Article 103 to avoid the implementation of Article 30 of the Treaty.

Article 115 of the EC Treaty

With the exception of Article 36, Article 115 of the EC Treaty is the most important statutory exception to the principle of free movement of goods within the Community. Article 115 applies only to goods originating from outside the Community but are in free circulation within it. However, in the absence of a fully developed EC commercial policy, it is possible for Member States to sustain quantitative restrictions against certain imports of non-EC countries, thereby largely limiting the products in free circulation in the EU to EC-made goods. Restrictions on intra-Community trade imposed by Member States, and authorised by the Commission, does not justify private persons implementing concerted practices intended to restrict competition in those goods.[87]

---

81   [1976] ECR 323; [1977] 2 CMLR 183.

82   [1974] ECR 837; [1974] 2 CMLR 436.

83   *Ibid*, 852; 453.

84   *Ibid*, 852; 453–54.

85   OJ special (English) edn, December 1992 at 257.

86   [1976] ECR 323; [1977] 2 CMLR 183.

87   Joined Cases *100–103/80 Musique Diffusion Francaise SA v Commission* [1983] ECR 1825.

The progressive introduction of a common commercial policy and the execution of measures of a commercial policy taken in accordance with the EC Treaty by a Member State could result in economic difficulties in one or more Member States and has the potential of resulting in a deflection of trade. In accordance with Article 115, the Commission is entitled to authorise Member States to take protective measures. The measures taken under this article by Member States have been numerous and of an *ad hoc* character. In *Bock v Commission*,[88] the court noted that, as it was an exception to the free movement of goods, Article 115 had to be interpreted strictly.[89]

As the Community adopts a common commercial policy relating to products or to imports from non-EC countries, Article 115 will cease to be applicable to those products.[90] Where goods are subject to a commercial policy in accordance with the Treaty, the importer may be required by Member States to declare the actual origin of the goods in question 'even in the case of goods put into free circulation in another Member State'.[91] Penalties for failure to supply the required information must, however, not be disproportionate. Seizure of the goods or the imposition of a pecuniary penalty fixed according to the value of the goods is disproportionate.[92] Unless a derogation has been authorised by the Commission, a requirement for an import licence will be incompatible with Community law.[93]

The rule of reason

In addition to Article 36, there is also a judicial (as opposed to a statutory) exception to Article 30 of the EC Treaty. The judicial exception was developed in a long line of cases in the court. The judicial exception was first elaborated in *Procureur du Roi v Dassonville*.[94] This exception has become known in the relevant literature as the 'rule of reason'. The rule was not clearly stated in *Dassonville* but was elaborated in the leading case of *Rewe-Zentral AG v Bundesmonopolverwalting Für Branntwein*,[95] popularly referred to as the *Cassis de Dijon* case. The elaboration makes the rule of reason clear. First, it lists four mandatory aims which national measures restricting free movement of goods are allowed to achieve. These aims are mandatory in the sense that they are indispensable for the welfare of a Member State. These requirements are the fairness of commercial

---

88   [1971] ECR 897, 909.

89   See also Case 41/76 *Criel v Procureur de la République at the Tribunal de Grand Instance* [1976] ECR 1921.

90   See, for example, Case 29/75 *Kaufhof AG v Commission* [1976] ECR 431 at 448; Case 52/77 *Cayrol v Giovanni Rivoira e Figli* [1977] ECR 2261 at 2289; [1978] 2 CMLR 253 at 263.

91   Case 41/76 *Criel v Procureur de la République* [1976] ECR 1921 at 1938; [1977] 2 CMLR 535 at 552 (goods not covered by the common commercial policy).

92   Case 41/76 *Criel v Procureur de la République* [1976] ECR 1921 at 1938; [1977] 2 CMLR 535 at 552.

93   Joined Cases 51–54/71 *International Fruit Co v Produktschap voor Groenten en Fruit (No 2)* [1971] ECR 1107 at 1116.

94   [1974] ECR 837; [1974] 2 CMLR 436.

95   [1979] ECR 649; [1979] 3 CMLR 494.

transactions, the effectiveness of fiscal supervision, the protection of public health and consumer protection. Secondly, the court stipulates that national laws restricting the free movement of goods, if they are to qualify under the rule of reason, must be necessary in order to satisfy these aims. Thus, not all measures aimed at protecting the consumer or public health will be exempted from the prohibition in Article 30. Indeed, those measures which are not necessary for the achievement of that aim will not be exempted. In other words, the necessity rule involves an application of the familiar principle of proportionality according to which 'a public authority may not impose obligations on a citizen except to the extent to which they are strictly necessary in the public interest to attain the purpose of the measure'.[96]

As is illustrated in the *Cassis de Dijon* case, a right to import goods is of extremely low value if the goods, once imported, cannot be sold. The ECJ has accepted that, subject to the restriction in Article 36, the prohibition on the sale of goods in any Member State infringes Article 30, provided they have been lawfully produced, manufactured and sold in the originating State. In the absence of harmonisation legislation, adopted in accordance with Article 100 of the Treaty, there will be some interests or values which may still justify the introduction, by Member States, of quantitative restrictions on goods from another Member State. This is the effect of the doctrine of the rule of reason. To be justifiable under the doctrine, the prohibition must be applied equally (or indistinctly) to both national and inter-State goods. However even a law of general application may be incompatible with the EC Treaty where the national measure is unnecessary to enable the State to achieve its legitimate objective. For example, the court decided that the Belgian Sunday trading law is compatible with Article 30 of the EC Treaty because the opening hours of retail premises is influenced by certain political and economic choices which may justifiably be made by Member States. Also, the court pointed out that the restrictive effects of such law are not disproportionate to the aims that Member States are allowed to pursue.[97]

Rule of reason not an extension of Article 36

The rule of reason is not an extension of Article 36 of the Treaty and, like Article 36, it is construed strictly. An applicant who wishes to invoke the rule of reason carries the onus of proving that the restriction is justified. When a Member State wishes to invoke the restriction of Article 36 or the rule of reason to prevent the free movement of goods contrary to Article 30 of the EC Treaty, that State is obliged to prove that its legislation applies equally to local and inter-State products.

---

96 Hartley, TC, *The Foundations of European Community Law,* 2nd edn, 1988, p 146.
97 Case C332/89 *Re Marchandise and Others* [1991] ECR 1027; [1992] 2 CEC 411.

The necessity and proportionality principles

The necessity principle must be examined in more detail because it raises a number of interpretation issues. First, as suggested above, the necessity principle and the proportionality principle are closely related. This relation stems from the fact that disproportionate measures are unnecessary to enable the State to achieve its mandatory aims. However, these two principles, while they overlap, are distinct. Indeed, if one says that a particular measure or law is 'necessary', then this statement does not say anything about the specific measure that may legitimately be adopted. The proportionality principle, however, discloses some information about the specific measure: it requires the measure to be proportionate to the evil or problem which the adopting State seeks to combat.

Second, the application of the necessity principle may result in the adoption of the least restrictive and, therefore, the most basic level of product regulation in the EC, thereby potentially affecting the quality and safety of consumer products. The complexities associated with these principles could be clarified by discussing the following fact situation. Assume that Member State A enacts a number of legislative measures prohibiting the use of flavouring additives in beer. These measures, in their totality, are deemed by State A to be necessary to protect the health of its beer drinking citizens. Also assume that Member State B equally wants to protect the health of its beer drinking citizens but decides that, in addition to laws prohibiting the use of flavouring additives, a number of other purity requirements for beer are necessary to achieve the State's aim. Obviously, both States agree that measures prohibiting the use of flavouring additives are necessary to protect the health of their citizens but these measures are not considered sufficient by Member State B. It is equally evident that the totality of measures taken by State B are more likely than the measures taken by State A to inhibit inter-State trade within the Community, as inter-State products which do not satisfy the stringent health standard of State B cannot be imported or, more likely, marketed. In the context of this example, it is fair to say that the court would be tempted to decide that the measures decided upon by State B are disproportionate, in the sense that they are not strictly necessary to attain the State's legitimate interest in protecting the health of its beer drinking citizens. In such a case, the court's decision could not be described as arbitrary since it can reasonably be assumed that State A's health regulations would only have been adopted following a judicious study of all the relevant health factors. Thus, if the court is faced with two sets of health regulations, enacted by two Member States, both acting in the best interests of their people, it may not be unreasonable for the court to give preference to that set of regulations which least impedes inter-State trade. However, if the court were to give preference to national legislative measures which least inhibit (or most promote) inter-State trade, the necessity principle could easily become meaningless. Indeed, taken to its logical extreme, such an application of the necessity principle could lead to the conclusion that, in cases where a State does not consider it necessary at all to legislate for the protection of the health of its citizens, any relevant legislative measure taken by another State could be interpreted as violating Article 30 of the Treaty. On this interpretation of the necessity principle, any product that is legally produced and sold in one Member State, can be legally marketed in another.

Application of the necessity principle

The above analysis is supported by the court's judgment in the celebrated beer case of 1987, *Re Purity Requirements for Beer: EC Commission v Germany*.[98] German food purity laws laid down stringent rules regarding the permitted ingredients for beer and the prohibition of all additives. Inter-State beers which contain other ingredients but have no additives may be imported in Germany but may not be marketed under the designation 'bier'. If these inter-State beverages contain additives, they cannot be marketed in Germany at all. The German government sought to justify its 'Reinheitsgebot' (purity rule) on grounds of the protection of human health. However, at the hearing, the German government conceded that the rule on designation was merely intended to protect consumers. Its counsel explained that in Germany, beer drinkers associated 'bier' with a beverage produced in conformity with German legislation. The Government also pointed out that its purity rule could, presumably, be complied with by inter-State producers of beer wishing to export their product to Germany.

The court decided that the German rule, which prohibited the designation of a beverage as beer if it contained non-approved ingredients, was not necessary in order to protect the consumer. Turning its attention to the absolute prohibition on the marketing of beers containing additives, the court decided that this ban cannot be justified on human health grounds. The court applied the necessity requirement to the statutory exception of Article 36, even though it could as easily have presented its decision as involving an application of the 'rule of reason'. Indeed, both the rule of reason and the statutory exception allow the adoption by Member States of national measures aimed at safeguarding public health. In applying the necessity requirement, the ECJ unequivocally indicated that it preferred that set of State regulations which is least restrictive of inter-State trade.

In *De Peijper*,[99] the court held that Article 36 did not justify the adoption of restrictions that are disproportionate to the interest sought and which were motivated primarily by a concern to facilitate the task of the authorities. In two recent judgments, *Drei Glocken GmbH and Anor v Unita Sanitaria*[100] and *Re Zoni*,[101] the court decided that a complete prohibition on the importation and marketing of pasta products made from common wheat or a mixture of common wheat and durum wheat necessarily containing additives or colourants was contrary to the principle of proportionality and not justified on the ground of the protection of public health.

---

98 [1987] ECR 1227; [1988] 1 CMLR 780.
99 [1976] ECR 613.
100 [1988] ECR 4233; [1990] 1 CEC 540.
101 [1988] ECR 4285; [1990] 1 CEC 570.

The proposition of the rule of reason

The previous analysis indicates that the rule of reason has been reduced to the simple proposition that once products have lawfully been produced and marketed in one Member State, their importation and sale in another Member State cannot be prevented without contravening Article 30 of the EC Treaty. The court in *Schutzverband Gegen Unwesen ID Wirtschaft v Weinvertriebs GmbH*[102] also decided that goods not manufactured in accordance with the rules of the country of origin but in accordance with those of the country of destination are equally entitled to free movement throughout the European Community.

Keck and Mithouard[103] involved the criminal prosecution of two shopkeepers, Keck and Mithouard. In particular, the two men were prosecuted under Article 1 of French Act 63–628, for reselling products below their purchase price. They contested their prosecution invoking Article 30 of the EC Treaty. The case was referred to the ECJ, pursuant to Article 177 of the EC Treaty. Citing the 'increasing tendency of traders to invoke Article 30 as a means of challenging any rules whose effect is to limit their commercial freedom,' the court found that the French legislation did not contravene Article 30. The court found it 'necessary to re-examine and clarify its case law on this matter'. After reiterating the *Cassis de Dijon* rule the court stated that:

> Contrary to what has previously been decided, the application to products from other Member State of national provisions restricting or prohibiting certain selling arrangements is not such as to hinder directly or indirectly, actually or potentially, trade between Member States within the meaning of the *Dassonville* judgment, provided that those provisions apply to all affected traders operating within the national territory and provided that they affect in the same manner, in law and in fact, the marketing of domestic products and of those from other Member States.

The ECJ, by thus holding, narrowed the judicial exception it had created. It is possible that this application has impinged the justice sought by the court in *Dassonville* and *Cassis*, in that it excludes certain selling arrangements from the ambit of the exception. However, the ECJ seems to have maintained the expediency by retaining the notions of reasonability, necessity, and proportionality, articulated in these cases.

Harmonisation

The court's rulings on free movement of goods has had the effect of invalidating many technical barriers to inter-State trade. But the court's contribution to deregulation in this field inevitably proceeded in an *ad hoc* manner since it can only act in cases submitted for decision. Under these circumstances, it is not totally surprising that the EC in the past promoted, and is now actively involved in, the harmonisation of the relevant national rules. In harmonising national rules, the EC not only creates rules which are valid throughout the Community but it also obviates the need for the court to apply the

---

102 [1983] ECR 1217.

103 1 CMLR 101 (1995). *Keck and Mithouard* has been followed in *Netherlands v Tankstation 't Heukske*, 3 CMLR 501 (1995).

necessity principle, both in its judicial and statutory versions. Indeed, the court has, on many occasions, indicated that the judicial and statutory exceptions to Article 30, which involve the application of the necessity principle, only apply in the absence of relevant Community rules.

The earliest Directive on free movement of goods was Commission Directive 70/50 issued by the EC Commission on 22 December 1969. The legislative effort relating to free movement of goods has to be seen as an attempt by the EC to respond to the vacuum which is often created by the court as a consequence of the application of the necessity principle.

Mutual acceptance of goods

The enormous number of Directives needed to harmonise the existing national restrictions on free movement of goods has precipitated the development of the principle of mutual acceptance of goods. This principle involves the recognition by Member States of the different national standards concerned, with the result that goods lawfully manufactured or marketed in one Member State are deemed to comply with the specifications of other Member States. Thus, Member States are able to control the production and manufacturing of products on their own territory, but they may not prevent the importation or sale of inter-State products which have legally been made in another Member State. The principle of mutual acceptance of goods, as a means to achieve free movement of goods, is preferred to the harmonisation technique because it preserves existing and future national legislation, thereby enabling Member States to achieve their national priorities and aims. The implementation of this principle also avoids the single most disadvantageous consequence of the application of the necessity principle, namely the potential erosion of national standards of excellence. Such erosion may occur if the court selects that set of national regulations which are least restrictive of inter-State trade. The principle of mutual acceptance of goods also promotes true competition because the Member States retain the privilege to implement their vision of product excellence, a vision which, however, will be compared by consumers with similar inter-State products made under different conditions using different manufacturing techniques. Thus, the free market would become the true arbiter, and would determine which products were to fail, and which would succeed.

Technical harmonisation and standards

The adoption of EC-wide standards benefits both EC and non-Community companies because their goods can now be produced or manufactured in accordance with a single set of specifications. On 28 March 1983, the Council adopted Directive 83/189 which lays down a procedure for the provision of information in the field of technical standards and regulations.[104] The Directive authorised the Commission to prevent Member States

---

104 OJ 1983 L109/8.

from introducing technical standards which would result in the reduction of trade in the European Community. During the last decade, the EC has adopted a number of acts which set out the essential requirements with regard to safety, health, consumer and environmental protection, with which products must comply. Evidence of compliance is provided by attestation by an appropriate body. The European Committee for Standardisation (CEN), the European Committee for Electrotechnical Standardisation (CENELEC) and the European Telecommunications Institute (ETSI) publish EC-wide standards using as their basis, standards developed by international bodies, such as the International Organisation for Standardisation (ISO) and the International Electrotechnical Association (IEC). European manufacturers in the EC and EFTA usually conform to these European standards. Alternatively, they may through independent testing and attestation establish a product which complies with the essential requirements of EC law.

Directive on product safety

Council adopted Directive 92/59 of 29 June 1992 on general product safety.[105] This Directive, which is a catch all provision in the sense that it fills gaps in existing legislative provisions, imposes an obligation on suppliers and manufacturers to place only safe products on the market. They are also obliged to provide consumers with all the necessary information concerning possible risks involved in the use of these products. Finally, manufacturers and suppliers are required to adopt measures to ensure that consumers are informed whenever any dangers associated with the use of the relevant product come to their attention. This Directive came into effect on 29 June 1994 following its implementation by the Member States.

Council Decision 90/683 of 13 December 1990 concerns the modules for the various phases of the conformity assessment procedures which are intended to be used in the technical harmonisation directives. The Commission has proposed a regulation concerning the affixing and use of the 'CE' mark of conformity.[106] The 'CE' mark will indicate that the product conforms with the essential requirements of the Directive. Australian and other foreign manufacturers could only affix the mark if the conformity of the relevant industrial product is attested to by an EC notifying body. However, the EC is considering procedures for negotiating Mutual Recognition Agreements (MRAs) on assessments in non-EC countries. The EC's interest in the mutual recognition of the standards of non-EC countries and the development of EC standards consistent with international standards is, of course, dictated by the acceptance by the EC of its obligations under the WTO-GATT Agreement on Technical Barriers to Trade.

---

105 OJ 1992 L228/24.
106 See OJ 1992 C195/11.

APPENDIX
THE EC'S TREATY STRUCTURE

25 July 1957	Treaty of Paris (signed 18 April 1951) The European Coal and Steel Community (ECSC)
	Member States: Belgium, The Netherlands, Luxemburg, France, Germany and Italy
1 January 1958	Treaty of Rome (signed 25 March 1957)
	The European Economic Community (EEC) Member States: Belgium, The Netherlands, Luxemburg, France, Germany and Italy
1 January 1958	Treaty of Rome (signed 25 March 1957)
	The European Atomic Energy Community (Euratom)
	Member States: Belgium, The Netherlands, Luxemburg, France, Germany and Italy
1 July 1967	Merger Treaty (signed 8 April 1965)
	Treaty Establishing a Single Council and a Single Commission of the European Communities
1 January 1973	First Treaty of Accession (signed 22 January 1972)
	Accession to the EC by the UK, Ireland and Denmark
1 January 1981	Second Treaty of Accession (signed 28 May 1979)
	Accession to the EC by Greece
1 January 1986	Third Treaty of Accession (signed 12 June 1985)
	Accession to the EC by Spain and Portugal
1 July 1987	Single European Act (SEA) (signed 28 February 1986)
1 January 1993	Establishment of the European Economic Area (EEA) consisting of the EEC and EFTA (signed 2 May 1992)
	1 November 1993 Union (Maastricht) Treaty (signed 7 February 1992)
	Establishment of the European Union
1 January 1996	Fourth Treaty of Accession (signed 1995)
	Accession to the EC by Austria, Sweden and Finland

TUTORIAL QUESTIONS

1   Is a Member State of the EC entitled to rely upon the ground of 'public morality' within the meaning of Article 36 of the EC Treaty in order to prohibit the importation of certain goods on the ground that they are indecent or obscene? Discuss the relevant case law.

2   There has been much theoretical discussion of the problem of the effect to be given by a national judge to a law deliberately promulgated ... subsequent to and in direct

opposition to a Community regulation or, indeed, to the Treaty itself ... If such a case arose I suspect the solution would have to be a political and not a legal one, since deliberately to legislate against Community law would demonstrate a total absence of the political will on which the Community must rest.

(Lord Mackenzie Stuart, *The European Communities and the Rule of Law*, 1977, p 16, London: Stevens.)

Discuss the relationship between Community law and national law in the light of the above statement.

3   In 1998, London and other places in the UK are plagued by riots which are sparked by the spiralling cost of beer. The worst riots occur on New Year's Eve 1998 in Trafalgar Square where more than 50,000 people gather to protest against the high cost of beer. Speakers at the rally denounce the governing Sound Management Party (SMP) for failing to impose a maximum price for beer. The rioters get excited and destroy the statue of Lord Nelson; police officers who try to intervene are thrown by the protesters into the nearby oil-soaked polluted waters of the Thames. At the time of the riots, beer (including beer imported from other EU countries), costs £16.00 sterling a litre in a London pub.

The Beer Promotion Party (BPP) wins the election which is held in February 1999. The new House of Commons, dominated by BPP members, adopts The Beer Relief (Fair Pricing) Act 1999. The legislation treats locally produced beer (ie beer produced in the UK) and imported beer (ie inter-State beer produced in other EU countries) differently. Beer produced in the UK is subject to a price freeze applied as of 1st April 1999. Section 14 of the legislation stipulates that the price of imported (inter-State) beer is to be fixed at the level of the selling price charged by producers in the EU State of production. The legislation, which in effect provides for maximum prices for beer products, is administered by the Beer Prices Surveillance Authority (BPSA). Any future applications by producers of local and imported beers for an increase in the selling prices of their beers, are assessed by the Director of BPSA. The Director, in the exercise of his or her function, is only constrained by s 27 of the legislation which states that 'he shall take into consideration the profitability of breweries established in the UK, and the public's interests'.

The implementation of the legislation places inter-State producers in a situation in which they are compelled either to accept for their exported beers a price which corresponds to the level prevailing in the EU State of origin or to forego the opportunity of selling their products on the market of the UK.

Mr Danny Debiere, who gave up a successful taxation law practice to pursue his interests in beer, imports the highly acclaimed 'Brussels Light' beer which is produced by a small brewery in Brussels, Belgium. 'Brussels Light' beer is sold in Belgian pubs for £12.00 sterling (or the equivalent in Belgian francs) a litre.

Mr Debiere initiates legal proceedings in an English court in order to test the validity of the Beer Relief (Fair Pricing) Act 1999. In particular, he argues that the legislation constitutes a quantitative restriction on imports or is a measure having an equivalent effect since it is no longer profitable for him to import 'Brussels Light' beer from

Belgium. Mr Debiere alleges that the Beer Relief (Fair Pricing) Act 1999 violates Article 30 of the EC Treaty. The English court suspends the application of the Act and refers the question of the compatibility or incompatibility of the UK law with the EC Treaty to the European Court of Justice (ECJ).

During a hearing in the ECJ, legal representatives of the UK contend that the legislation is the only effective way in which inflation can be combated. They also point out that since the implementation of the impugned law, riots have ceased to disrupt law and order in the UK.

Answer the following questions:

1   Is it possible for an English court to suspend the application of the Beer Relief (Fair Pricing) Act 1999 before its incompatibility or compatibility with the EC Treaty has been established? Give reasons.

2   Is the Beer Relief (Fair Pricing) Act 1999 compatible with Article 30 of the EC Treaty? In your answer refer to, and discuss, the relevant jurisprudence of the European Court of Justice.

FURTHER READING

Bellamy, C and Child, GD, *Common Market Law of Competition*, 3rd edn, 1987, London: Sweet and Maxwell.

Bronitt, S, Burns, FR and Kinley, D, *Principles of European Community Law: Commentary and Materials*, 1995, Sydney: Law Book Co.

Burrows, F, *Free Movement in European Community Law*, 1987, Oxford: Clarendon Press.

Hartley, TC, *The Foundations of European Community Law*, 3rd edn, 1994, Oxford: Clarendon Press.

Moens, G and Flint, D, *Business Law of the European Community*, 1993, Brisbane: Data Legal Publications.

Rasmussen, H, *The European Community Constitution: Summaries of Leading EC Court Cases*, 1989, Copenhagen: Nyt Nordisk Forlag Arnold Busck.

Steiner, J, *Textbook on EEC Law*, 2nd edn, 1990, London: Blackstone Press.

Tillotson, J, *European Community Law: Text, Cases and Materials*, 1993, London: Cavendish Publishing.

CHAPTER 11

INTERNATIONAL COMMERCIAL ARBITRATION

ARBITRATION AND INTERNATIONAL TRADE

Arbitration is the most common method of dispute resolution in international trade. It is a private means of dispute resolution based on the agreement of parties to refer their disputes to a private tribunal and to abide by its determination. It is preferred to litigation for a number of reasons. Arbitration tends to be speedier than litigation conducted in national courts. An arbitral tribunal is appointed to hear a particular dispute and will devote its full attention continuously to that dispute. Courts, by contrast, have long and varied lists of cases demanding their attention and sometimes a case may be protracted to the point where it has to be heard by a succession of judges. Although arbitral tribunals must observe the requirements of natural justice and decide according to law, they can adopt flexible and expeditious procedures. Arbitration allows the use of experts as adjudicators. Although arbitration can be more expensive than litigation to conduct, traders stand to gain in the long run because of the time saved in reaching finality. Besides, the costs of arbitration are borne by the parties and not the taxpayer. Traders often prefer the privacy of the arbitral process to the publicity that attends court proceedings.[1]

However, the greatest historical impetus for arbitration in international trade is the fear of parties to litigate in foreign lands. International commercial disputation, by its nature, involves parties of different nationalities, but litigation has to be conducted before the courts of one nation. Litigants have justifiable apprehension of being unequally treated by foreign courts. The parlous state of the rule of law in many countries has not helped. The fear of unfair treatment is heightened when states are parties to disputes or when national interests are involved. Even where courts are unbiased, foreign litigants remain disadvantaged by having to proceed in unfamiliar legal environments using local lawyers. In these circumstances arbitration is a logical alternative.

Of course, arbitration is not without its drawbacks. By its nature, it is available only to resolve disputes between parties to an arbitration agreement. Hence, it is a process that usually occurs among traders. Consumers, for example, rarely have arbitration agreements with retailers. Note though, that it is possible for parties to a dispute to refer a dispute to arbitration after the dispute has arisen if they agree to do so. In other words, an arbitration agreement may concern future disputes or past disputes.[2] However, even where a trading contract contains an arbitration agreement, not all parties to a dispute

---

1 Note however, that confidentiality of documents and information disclosed is not assured following *Esso Australia Resources v Plowman* (1995) 183 CLR 10 at 33 *per* Mason CJ.

2 See definition of 'arbitration agreement' in s 4(1) of the Commercial Arbitration Act 1984 (NSW), Article II(1) of the Convention on the Recognition and Enforcement of Foreign Arbitral Awards (New York Convention) and Article 7(1) of the UNCITRAL Model Law.

may be parties to the agreement, thus creating obstacles to a final resolution. Arbitral tribunals also have no coercive powers and hence, often need the intervention and support of the courts. However, despite its limitations, the practice of arbitration has grown to the point that it has become an integral feature of global trade. Its importance to international trade has been recognised by national legal systems and by the community of nations which have established a global statutory framework to facilitate the arbitral process.

Although the arbitral process is essentially a private mechanism based on contract, like all other contracts, it needs an institutional infrastructure to be effective. In fact, owing to its adjudicative character, it needs more infrastructure than ordinary contracts. There are two types of institutional infrastructure which support international commercial arbitration. One type consists of laws which enable courts to enforce arbitration agreements and arbitral awards and to assist and supervise the arbitral process. The second type of infrastructure consists of services provided by organisations such as the International Chamber of Commerce (ICC), the American Arbitration Association (AAA), the London Court of International Arbitration (LCIA) and the International Centre for Settlement of Investment Disputes (ICSID). These organisations have formulated arbitration rules which can be incorporated easily into contracts by reference and provide the personnel and the facilities to hold arbitration proceedings. This chapter is concerned mainly with the former type of infrastructure.

It is not possible in a short essay to deal comprehensively even with that part of the infrastructure which involves the courts. Hence we propose to limit our discussion to three key aspects of the infrastructure involving the courts which are important for the success of arbitration as a mode of international commercial dispute resolution. They are, in the order of discussion:

- recognition and enforcement by courts of arbitration agreements such that parties are not permitted to litigate in violation of such agreements;

- limited judicial review of arbitral decisions which encourages the finality of arbitral awards while providing recourse against illegal decisions; and

- enforcement of arbitral awards.

The chapter will discuss how each of these conditions is promoted by the statutory regimes applicable to international commercial arbitration in Australia. However, before commencing this inquiry it is useful to gain a clear idea of the nature of arbitration generally and of international commercial arbitration specifically.

TYPES OF ARBITRATION

International commercial arbitration is a species of commercial arbitration. Commercial arbitration is a special kind of arbitration. Hence, we must first consider the nature of arbitration and commercial arbitration generally. It is critical to understand the concept of arbitration because national laws and international treaties on arbitration have no application to other processes. There are also provisions which apply only to international commercial arbitration, hence we need to know when arbitration is 'international'.

Arbitration

Arbitration is a method of private dispute resolution which arises from the agreement of the parties in dispute. Arbitration is conducted in a judicial manner and the decision of the arbitral tribunal is binding upon the parties and is recognised and enforced by courts. In arbitration, the parties are the sole source of the arbitral tribunal's power and they have much more control of the arbitral process than litigants have of judicial proceedings in the courts.

Arbitration is a form of adjudication which has its roots in the ancient world. The lack of permanent formal courts meant that disputes had to be referred to impartial persons on an *ad hoc* basis. The process involved a combination of conciliation and adjudication.

The term arbitration is used loosely today. It is used sometimes to refer to what are actually the processes of assessment, valuation or the inquiry of particular factual issues in civil cases by referees appointed by courts.[3] It also refers to quasi-legislative processes such as the Australian system for making awards in industrial relations disputes which determine wages and other conditions of employment of workers. In determining industrial disputes, the Industrial Relations Commission and its State counterparts can make decisions in disregard of contractual terms. In other words these tribunals can create new rights and obligations in place of existing ones in order to settle an industrial dispute.[4]

In this paper the term 'arbitrator' will also include the situation where the parties have appointed an umpire.

Commercial arbitration

Commercial arbitration is distinguished from these types of arbitration inasmuch as the commercial arbitrators derive their authority solely from contract, they resolve the whole dispute and, generally, do so according to law. There is a major exception to the rule that a commercial arbitrator should decide according to law. Sometimes, merchants insert clauses in arbitration agreements which authorise arbitrators to resolve disputes *ex aequo et bono* or as *amiable compositeurs*. In the former case the arbitrators may depart from strict law and decide the case according to equity and good sense. In the latter case, the arbitrator will use her good offices to engineer an amicable settlement. Strictly speaking, amicable settlement is not a determination but the conclusion of a new contract to settle the dispute. Some national laws expressly recognise this type of arbitration.[5]

---

3   See, for example, Supreme Court Rules (NSW), Part 72, r 2; Rules of the Supreme Court (Vic), O 50.01; Supreme Court Rules (Qld), O 97, r 1; s 65 of the Supreme Court Act 1935 (SA).

4   See, for example, s 100(2) and s 104(1) of the Workplace Relations Act 1996 (Cth).

5   See, for example, s 22 of the Commercial Arbitration Act 1984 (NSW).

International commercial arbitration

What makes commercial arbitration international? This question is important because there are international conventions which establish special rules for facilitating international commercial arbitration and for the recognition and enforcement of international arbitral awards. There are two major conventions which have been implemented in Australia, namely: the Convention on the Recognition and Enforcement of Foreign Arbitral Awards (commonly known as the New York Convention)[6] and the UNCITRAL Model Law on International Commercial Arbitration.[7] The New York Convention is restricted to the imposition of duties on State parties to recognise and enforce foreign arbitral awards. The UNCITRAL Model Law is a more extensive code. The New York Convention does not actually use the term 'international' but applies its provisions to 'arbitral awards made in the territory of a State other than the State where the recognition and enforcement of such awards are sought' and to 'arbitral awards not considered as domestic awards in the State where their recognition and enforcement are sought'.[8] In keeping with this clause, s 3 of the International Arbitration Act states that a 'foreign award' means 'an arbitral award made, in pursuance of an arbitration agreement, in a country other than Australia, being an arbitral award in relation to which the convention applies'.[9] The UNCITRAL Model Law gives a more detailed account of what constitutes 'international' arbitration. Under Article 1(3), an arbitration is international if, at the time of the conclusion of the agreement, the parties have their places of business in different States. Where the parties have their places of business in the same State, the arbitration will yet be international if the designated place of arbitration, the place where a substantial part of the commercial obligations have to be performed or the place with which the subject matter of the dispute is most closely connected is outside such State. Finally, even if all of the above criteria remain unmet, the arbitration will be international if 'the parties have expressly agreed that the subject matter of the arbitration agreement relates to more than one country'.[10]

THE STATUTORY FRAMEWORK OF INTERNATIONAL COMMERCIAL ARBITRATION IN AUSTRALIA

The law applicable to the arbitral process and the law governing the recognition and enforcement of international arbitral awards depend ultimately on the choice of law rules in private international law. It is necessary, therefore, to determine which country's law regulates the matters in question. We will turn to these issues later. But first, let us

---

6   Adopted by the United Nations Conference on International Commercial Arbitration in 1958 at its 24th meeting and implemented in Australia by Part II of the International Arbitration Act 1974 (Cth).

7   Adopted by the United Nations Commission on International Trade Law on 21 June 1985 and implemented in Australia by Part III of the International Arbitration Act 1974 (Cth).

8   Article 1(1).

9   Article 1(1) of the New York Convention.

10   Article 1(3)(c).

assume that the applicable law is Australian law and consider the possible permutations within that law.

The statutory rules governing international commercial arbitration in Australia are found in the New York Convention, the UNCITRAL Model Law and where these are not applicable, the law of the relevant Australian State. The New York Convention and the Model Law are very different in scope. The convention governs only matters concerning the recognition and enforcement of foreign arbitration agreements and foreign arbitral awards. The Model Law is a wide ranging code on the subject which regulates all major aspects of the arbitral process as well as the recognition and enforcement of arbitration agreements and arbitral awards made in Australia or overseas. The commercial arbitration statutes of the several Australian States are also comprehensive documents. The scheme of the Commercial Arbitration Act 1984 (NSW) gives a good idea of the aspects of the arbitral process which may be regulated by statute. Reference in this paper will be to the NSW Act rather than to a 'uniform Commercial Arbitration Act' as used in some other texts. Where the NSW Statute varies from that of other Australian States, this will be indicated.

The NSW Act deals with, *inter alia*, the following aspects:

- Appointment of arbitrators and umpires (Part II) and their removal (s 44).
- The conduct of arbitrations (Part III).
- Awards and costs (Part IV).
- Powers of court to review arbitral awards and processes including powers to hear appeals from awards, determine preliminary questions of law during the course of arbitration, set aside awards, and remit matters to arbitrators (Part V).
- The enforcement of arbitration agreements (as opposed to awards) in the form of the stay of judicial proceedings where parties are obliged to submit to arbitration under an agreement (s 53).
- Enforcement of arbitral awards (s 33)

Analyses of these instruments reveal that there are different statutory regimes which can apply to an international arbitration if the applicable law is the Australian law.

International arbitration agreements without opt-out clauses

Section 16 of the International Arbitration Act 1974 provides that, subject to Part III of that Act, the Model Law has the force of law in Australia. Hence, provisions of the Model Law as modified or supplemented by Part III of the Act will apply to all international commercial arbitrations unless there is an opt-out agreement under s 21. Where parties have not opted out of the Model Law, the resulting position may be summarised as follows:

- The whole of the Model Law will apply if the arbitration is international and if it is held in Australia.
- If the place of arbitration is not within Australia, only Articles 8, 9, 35 and 36 of the Model Law will apply, as provided by Article 1(2). Article 8 deals with the

recognition and enforcement of arbitration agreements, Article 9 preserves the power of courts to make interim orders for the protection of the interests of parties pending arbitration and Articles 35 and 36 are concerned with the recognition and enforcement of arbitral awards.

- If Part II of the International Arbitration Act 1974 implementing the enforcement provisions of the New York Convention applies to the award, Articles 35 and 36 (Ch VIII) of the Model Law will not apply. As regards the enforcement of arbitral awards, the intention of UNCITRAL was to make the Model Law uniform with the widely accepted and highly successful New York Convention provisions.[11] In order to ensure that the New York Convention continues to govern the recognition and enforcement of foreign arbitral awards, s 20 of the International Arbitration Act 1974 provides that where Part II of the Act applies to an award, Chapter VIII of the Model Law does not apply.

- Section 22 of the International Arbitration Act 1974 also allows parties to 'opt in' to the facilitative provisions contained in Part III, Division 3 of the Act. These provisions concerning matters such as the consolidation of arbitrations, interest payable up to and upon making of the award, and costs have no automatic application but must be adopted by the parties. Thus, there is a further category of arbitration agreements, namely: those governed by the Model Law as supplemented by the facilitative provisions of Part III, Division 3.

International arbitration agreements with opt-out clauses

Section 21 of the International Arbitration Act 1974 provides:

> If the parties to an arbitration agreement have (whether in the agreement or in any other document in writing) agreed that any dispute that has arisen or may arise between them is to be settled otherwise than in accordance with the Model Law, the Model Law does not apply in relation to the settlement of that dispute.

This provision allows parties to a dispute by agreement to opt out of the Model Law at any time, whether before or after the dispute has arisen. There is some doubt as to the precise effect of an 'opt-out' clause. Do the words 'settled otherwise than in accordance with the Model Law' and 'does not apply in relation to the settlement of that dispute' mean that the whole of the Model Law including the enforcement provisions ceases to apply? The Attorney General's Explanatory Memorandum accompanying the Bill made it clear that the Model Law will apply 'unless the parties agree otherwise'.[12] The words 'in relation to the settlement of the dispute' read in the light of the Attorney General's comment strongly suggest the non-applicability of the whole of the Model Law. If the Model Law does not apply, which Australian statutory regime would apply to an international commercial arbitration? The position could be summarised as follows:

---

11 For the legislative history of Articles 35 and 36, see Holtzmann, HM and Neuhaus, JE, *A Guide to the UNCITRAL Model Law on International Commercial Arbitration: Legislative History and Commentary*, 1989, pp 1054–63, Deventer: Kluwer.

12 Cited by Jacobs, MS, *International Commercial Arbitration in Australia: Law and Practice*, 1992, p 5910, Sydney: Law Book Co.

- If, under the arbitration agreement, the arbitration is to be held in Australia, all matters concerning the arbitration and the enforcement of the arbitral award would be governed by the commercial arbitration statute of the Australian State within which the arbitration is to be held. Note that s 8 of the International Arbitration Act 1974 which implements the enforcement provisions of the New York Convention applies only to 'foreign awards' which means awards made in a country other than Australia'.[13] However, the recognition of the agreement for the purpose of stay of judicial proceedings in Australia would be governed by Part II of the International Arbitration Act 1974 as s 7, which deals with the subject, applies to arbitration agreements which are connected to a Convention country in any of the ways set out in sub-s (1) of that section. Note that an opt-out agreement under s 21 of the Act only makes the Model Law inapplicable. The provisions of the Act itself continue to apply.

- If the arbitration is being conducted in a country other than Australia, the recognition and enforcement of the arbitration agreement by stay of judicial proceedings in Australia and the enforcement of the arbitral award in Australia would be governed by Part II of the International Arbitration Act 1974.

The requirement of written agreement

It must be noted that the several statutory regimes referred to have no application to an arbitration unless the arbitration agreement is in writing. The UNCITRAL Secretariat in its preparatory study for the Model Law found this to be an almost universal requirement of domestic laws.[14] The position is confirmed by s 3(2)(a) read with s 4(1) of the Commercial Arbitration Act 1984 (NSW), s 3(1) of the International Arbitration Act 1974 and Article 7(2) of the Model Law. According to the latter provision, apart from the usual forms of written agreement, the requirement can be satisfied, *inter alia*, by an exchange of statements of claim and defence in which the existence of an agreement is alleged by one party and is not denied by another. Note, however, that where no written agreement exists, a party may, in exceptional circumstances, be able to invoke the court's inherent jurisdiction.[15]

RECOGNITION AND ENFORCEMENT OF INTERNATIONAL ARBITRATION AGREEMENTS

Perhaps the most important requirement of an effective system of arbitration is a means of enforcing arbitration agreements. Arguably, this is even more important than the means of enforcing arbitral awards. If parties are free to walk away from arbitration agreements and commence litigation whenever they fear arbitral outcomes, the efficacy of the arbitration system is undermined. The traditional means of enforcing an

---

13   Section 3 of the International Arbitration Act 1974 (Cth), definition of 'foreign award'.
14   Holtzmann and Neuhaus, *op cit*, p 260.
15   *Etrie Fans Ltd v NMB (UK) Ltd* [1987] 2 Lloyd's Rep 565 at 568 *per* Woolf LJ.

arbitration agreement in the English law was through the power of the courts to stay judicial proceedings for the purpose of compelling parties to resort to arbitration where the dispute in question was one which was arbitrable under a subsisting arbitration agreement. The courts have historically asserted an inherent power to grant a stay in these circumstances, in order to prevent an abuse of process.[16] This inherent power is supplemented by statutory powers. With regard to domestic arbitrations, the courts have a substantial discretion to refuse the stay of judicial proceedings. Thus, under s 53 of the Commercial Arbitration Act 1984 (NSW) (which duplicates s 4(1) of the UK Arbitration Act 1950), the court *may* stay proceedings if satisfied that there is no sufficient reason why the matter should not be referred to arbitration'. This discretion has allowed courts to refuse the stay of judicial proceedings where the dispute involved constitutional questions[17] or 'serious and difficult questions of law',[18] where the arbitrator's conduct was in question,[19] and where the application for stay was unduly delayed.[20]

Enforcement of agreement under the New York Convention

The discretion to refuse a stay of judicial proceedings has been drastically curtailed in relation to international arbitration agreements. In implementing the New York Convention, s 7(2) of the International Arbitration Act 1974 provides:

> Subject to this Part, where:
>
> (a) proceedings instituted by a party to an arbitration agreement to which this section applies against another party to the agreement are pending in a court; and
>
> (b) the proceedings involve the determination of a matter that, in pursuance of the agreement, is capable of settlement by arbitration;
>
> on the application of a party to the agreement, the court *shall*, by order, upon such conditions (if any) as it thinks fit, stay the proceedings or so much of the proceedings as involves the determination of that matter, as the case may be, and refer the parties to arbitration in respect of that matter. [emphasis added]

Where the conditions specified in the section are present, the court's discretion is removed by the words 'shall ... stay the proceedings'. The only grounds upon which the court can refuse a stay are set out in s 7(5) in non-discretionary terms.

> A court shall not make an order under sub-s (2) if the court finds that the arbitration agreement is null and void, inoperative or incapable of being performed.

Accordingly, the decision whether or not to stay proceedings depends on the answers to two questions of law, namely:

---

16 For a recent instance of the use of inherent powers to stay judicial proceedings, see *Channel Tunnel Group Ltd v Balfour Beatty Construction Ltd* [1993] 2 WLR 262.

17 *Carrington Steamship v Commonwealth* (1921) 29 CLR 596.

18 *Dillingham Constructions v Downs* (1969) 90 WN (Part 1) NSW 258.

19 *Blackwell v Derby Corp* (1911) 75 JP 129.

20 *The Elizabeth* [1962] 1 Lloyd's Reps 172.

1   whether the agreement itself 'is null and void, inoperative or incapable of being performed'; and

2   whether the matter 'in pursuance of the agreement, is capable of settlement by arbitration'.

Question 1 is concerned with the validity or the effectiveness of the arbitration agreement whereas question 2 is concerned with the validity or the effectiveness of the particular reference to arbitration under a valid agreement.

The question whether a matter is capable of settlement by arbitration raises two distinct issues. The first is whether the particular matter is one which the parties agreed to refer to arbitration. The second is whether, as a matter of law, the dispute is capable of settlement by arbitration. To answer the first question, the terms of the arbitration agreement need to be interpreted, the question being, whether the parties intended an arbitrator to deal with the matter in dispute or whether that power has been left to the court. Even if the parties have used such comprehensive terms as 'all disputes under this contract shall be referred to arbitration', serious questions may remain. For instance, under these terms, would a dispute concerning pre-contractual statements which may vitiate the very existence of the contract be referrable to arbitration? Can a dispute as to liability in tort be referred to the arbitrator? Judicial attitudes on this question have changed over the years. As Pryles notes, 'initially the courts tended to adopt a fairly strict construction of arbitration agreements but have evinced a more liberal attitude in recent years'.[21]

In *Francis Travel Marketing Pty Ltd v Virgin Atlantic Airways Ltd*,[22] Gleeson CJ articulated the current judicial approach to these questions.

> When the parties to a commercial contract agree, at the time of making the contract, and before any disputes have yet arisen, to refer to arbitration any dispute or difference arising out of the agreement, their agreement should not be construed narrowly. They are unlikely to have intended that different disputes should be resolved before different tribunals, or that the appropriate tribunal should be determined by fine shades of difference in the legal character of individual issues, or by the ingenuity of lawyers in developing points of argument.[23]

Gleeson CJ went on to say:

> It is consistent with the modern policy of encouragement of various forms of alternative dispute resolution, including arbitration, mediation and conciliation, that courts should facilitate, rather than impede, agreements for the private resolution of all forms of dispute, including disputes involving claims under statutes such as the Trade Practices Act 1974 (Cth).[24]

The question whether a matter which the parties clearly agreed to refer to arbitration, is capable of settlement by arbitration raises a distinct set of issues. National laws may

---

21   Pryles, M, 'Drafting Arbitration Agreements' (1993) 67 *Australian Law Journal* 503 at 507.

22   (1996) 39 NSWLR 160.

23   (1996) 39 NSWLR 160 at 165 (CA).

24   (1996) 39 NSWLR 160 at 166.

exclude from arbitration, categories of disputes on grounds of public policy. In Australia, for example, disputes concerning insurance contracts[25] and carriage of goods by sea[26] have limited arbitrability by express legislative provision.

Apart from those excluded by statute, there are matters which courts have treated as non-arbitrable as a matter of judicially determined public policy. Some obvious examples are disputes relating to family law or criminal law or disputes which may raise issues of public concern which go beyond the resolution of the immediate dispute, such as those arising under the Constitution. Trade practices disputes have been a contentious area. The courts of the USA and New Zealand have held that trade practice disputes are fully arbitrable.[27] The Australian courts have been more cautious in their approach, but in the recent case of *IBM Australia Ltd v National Distribution Services Ltd*,[28] the New South Wales Court of Appeal held that the arbitration clause was wide enough and could encompass trade practices disputes. A similar finding was made in *QH Tours Ltd v Ship Design and Management (Aust) Pty Ltd*.[29] It should also be noted that the question of arbitrability can arise at the stage of application for judicial enforcement of an arbitral award. This aspect of the law will be discussed presently, but for the moment it is important to note that courts may sometimes allow a dispute to go to arbitration in the knowledge that its arbitrability can be tested at the stage of the enforcement of the award. Thus, in the *Mitsubishi* case, Blackmun J noted that, whilst he was allowing the matter to proceed to arbitration:

> The national courts of the USA will have the opportunity at the award enforcement stage to ensure that the legitimate interest in the enforcement of the anti-trust laws is addressed.[30]

This is now referred to as the 'second look doctrine' and suggests that 'judicial review of the contents of awards, at least for their conformity with public policy, is the cost for letting the dispute go to arbitration'.[31]

Enforcement of arbitration agreement under the Model Law

In the preparation of the Model Law, UNCITRAL aimed to achieve uniformity with the New York Convention with regard to the recognition and enforcement of international arbitration agreements and international arbitral awards. Consequently, it

---

25 Section 43 of the Insurance Contracts Act 1984 (Cth), although parties are free to agree after a dispute has arisen to refer that dispute to arbitration (s 43(2)).

26 Section 2C of the International Arbitration Act saving the continued operation of s 9 of the Sea Carriage of Goods Act 1924 (Cth) and the operation of ss 11 and 16 of the Carriage of Goods by Sea Act 1991 (Cth).

27 For the US, see *Mitsubishi Motors v Soler Chrysler-Plymouth* 473 US 614 (1984); and for New Zealand, see *AG v Mobil Oil New Zealand* [1989] 2 NZLR 649.

28 (1991) NSWLR 466.

29 (1991) 33 FCR 227.

30 473 US 614 at 638.

31 Park, WW, 'National Law and Commercial Justice: Safeguarding Procedural Integrity in International Arbitration' (1989) 63 *Tulane Law Review* 647 at 669.

adopted the convention's substantive provisions concerning stay of judicial proceedings while making two procedural improvements. Article 8 of the Model Law reads:

1   A court before which an action is brought in a matter which is the subject of an arbitration agreement shall, if a party so requests not later than when submitting his first statement on the substance of the dispute, refer the parties to arbitration unless it finds that the agreement is null and void, inoperative or incapable of being performed.

2   Where an action referred to in para (1) of this article has been brought, arbitral proceedings may nevertheless be commenced or continued, and an award may be made, while the issue is pending before the court.

As mentioned, the Model Law represents two advances on the New York Convention. First, it fixes a time before which the application for enforcement must be made, namely before submission of the first statement on the substance of the dispute. Secondly, it allows the arbitration to continue pending the determination by the court of the application to refer the matter to arbitration.

'Null and void, inoperative or incapable of being performed'

Both the New York Convention and the Model Law permit the courts to refuse a stay of judicial proceedings or an application to refer a dispute to arbitration where the arbitration agreement is 'null and void, inoperative or incapable of being performed'. The term 'null and void' refers to voidness *ab initio* and not mere voidability.[32] Mustill and Boyd speculate that the word 'inoperative' which has no accepted meaning in English law, may be construed as applying to situations where a court has ordered that an arbitration agreement shall cease to have effect, where an agreement is frustrated or discharged by breach or where the agreement ceases to have effect by reason of some further agreement of the parties.[33] It may also be construed as referring to one or both of the following kinds of situations. The first is where the agreement is made but its operation depends on the fulfilment of a condition or the happening of an event which has not yet occurred. For example, if the agreement is to commence on a particular date, it would have no application to disputes which occur before that date. The second type of situation is where the agreement is valid but it has no operation in relation to the dispute in question as it is not within the specified class of referrable disputes. It should be noted that the latter class of cases is also covered by the words 'capable of settlement by arbitration' used in Article II(1) of the New York Convention and s 7(2) of the International Arbitration Act 1974 which implements that article in Australia. The words 'incapable of being performed' appear to refer to a condition that makes a valid and operative agreement incapable of being performed due to a supervening cause. There has been no authoritative judicial exposition of this term by the courts. However,

---

32   *The Tradesman, SA Hersent v United Towing Co Ltd* [1961] 1 WLR 61, following *Heyman v Darwins Ltd* [1942] AC 356.

33   Mustill, MJ and Boyd, SC, *The Law and Practice of Commercial Arbitration* 2nd edn, 1989, p 464, London and Edinburgh: Butterworths. See *H Kruiddenier (London) Ltd v Egyptian Navigation Co, The El Amria (No 2)* [1980] 2 Lloyd's Rep 166.

in *Paczy v Haendler and Naterman*,[34] the term was construed as not including the case of a party's non performance of the agreement due to impecuniosity. Buckley LJ explained that 'the agreement only becomes incapable of performance ... if the circumstances are such that it could no longer be performed, even if both parties were ready, able and willing to perform it'.[35]

The question of severability

The question whether an arbitration agreement is null and void is frequently tied up with the question of the validity of the substantive contract. The agreement to arbitrate is often a part of the substantive contract. Where a party alleges that the contract is void, can an arbitral tribunal decide that question? The conceptual difficulty here is that if the arbitral tribunal decides that the contract is void, it may be contended that the arbitral tribunal lacked the power to make the decision as it derives its authority from the contract. The practical problem is that if the voidness of the main contract deprives the arbitrator of her authority, a party to an arbitration agreement could subvert or delay the arbitration process simply by calling into question the validity of the main contract. The solution adopted by many legal systems is to treat the arbitration clause of a contract as a separate agreement although it is included in the larger contract. This approach is known as the doctrine of severability or separability. Under the doctrine, the arbitration clause is regarded as having an autonomous existence which can survive the demise of the main contract.[36]

The doctrine of severability, however, supplies only a partial solution as it is open to a party to deny the jurisdiction of the arbitrator by challenging the validity of the arbitration agreement itself. The traditional means of dealing with this problem has been through the provisions enabling courts to stay judicial proceedings unless the agreement is found to be null and void or inoperative or incapable of being performed. Thus jurisdictional questions are determined expeditiously as preliminary issues before court. In the rare case of an international arbitration where the Model Law has been excluded by agreement and the New York Convention does not apply, the domestic State law will govern the question. Section 53(1) of the Commercial Arbitration Act 1984 (NSW), which empowers the court to stay judicial proceedings in order to enforce an arbitration agreement, presupposes the validity of the agreement. The court will determine the question of validity in an interlocutory manner,[37] upon an application

---

34   [1981] 1 Lloyd's Rep 302.

35   [1981] 1 Lloyd's Rep 302 at 307.

36   *Bremer Vulkan Schiffbau und Maschinenfabrik v South India Shipping Corp* [1981] 2 WLR 141; *Codelfa Construction Pty Ltd v State Rail Authority (NSW)* (1982) 150 CLR 29; *Ferris v Plaister* (1994) 34 NSWLR 474 (CA); *Harbour Assurance Co (UK) Ltd v Kansa General International Assurance Co Ltd* [1993] QB 701.

37   See *Modern Buildings Wales Ltd v Limmer and Trinidad* [1975] 2 All ER 549 at 554, interpreting the identical s 4(1) of the Arbitration Act 1950 (UK).

made before the applicant has delivered pleadings or taken any other step other than the entry of an appearance.[38]

The Model Law, however, has gone further in addressing the problem of jurisdictional questions. Following the domestic laws of many countries, it explicitly recognises the competence of the arbitral tribunal to determine in the first instance challenges to its own jurisdiction (*compétence de la compétence*). Article 16(1) provides:

> The arbitral tribunal may rule on its own jurisdiction, including any objections with respect to the existence or validity of the arbitration agreement. For that purpose, an arbitration clause which forms part of a contract shall be treated as an agreement independent of the other terms of the contract. A decision by the arbitral tribunal that the contract is null and void shall not entail *ipso jure* the invalidity of the arbitration clause.

According to Article 16(3), the decision of the arbitral tribunal on a jurisdictional question is reviewable by the court upon the request of a party made within 30 days of receiving notice of the decision. The sub-article also provides that the decision of the court, (which, in Australia, is the Supreme Court of the State or Territory within which the arbitration takes place)[39] 'shall be subject to no appeal'. This stipulation is clearly unconstitutional in Australia where the High Court has held that Parliament cannot remove from the High Court its jurisdiction under s 73 to hear appeals from all 'judgments, decrees, orders and sentences' of State Supreme Courts.[40] Although, in terms of Australian constitutional law, a further appeal may lie to the High Court with its leave, Article 16(3) enables the arbitral tribunal to continue the arbitral proceeding and to make an award pending the judicial review.

It should be not be overlooked that the validity of the arbitration agreement may be questioned at later stages by recourse to the general statutory rights of appeal against arbitral decisions and by resisting applications for enforcement of the award. These options will be discussed later in this chapter.

The applicable law

In the case of an international arbitration agreement, it is invariably necessary to determine which nation's laws will govern the questions whether a dispute is arbitrable and whether the agreement is 'null and void, inoperative or incapable of being performed'. These concern both the validity of the agreement and the interpretation of its terms. The basic principle is that the applicable law is the law which the parties intended should apply. In the absence of express agreement, the intention of the parties must be gathered from factors such as implied terms and the general tenor of the agreement, the place where the agreement was drawn up and executed and the place to which the transaction has the closest and most real connection.[41] Two points may be noted.

---

38   Section 53(2), according to which, a late application requires leave of the court.
39   Section 18 of the International Arbitration Act 1974 (Cth).
40   *Cockle v Isaksen* (1957) 99 CLR 155 at 165–66.
41   *Norske Atlas Insurance v London General Insurance* [1927] 28 Lloyd's Rep 104.

First, as already observed, the arbitration agreement is treated by courts as an autonomous agreement separate from the main contract. Hence, it is possible that different systems of law will govern the main contract and the arbitration agreement.[42] Second, in some circumstances, the individual reference of a dispute to arbitration may be regarded as an agreement separate from and independent of the arbitration agreement. In such cases different national laws may apply to the arbitration agreement and the individual reference.[43]

JUDICIAL REVIEW OF ARBITRAL AWARDS: THE BALANCE BETWEEN FINALITY AND LEGALITY

As we observed at the outset, one of the great incentives for choosing arbitration over litigation as a means of resolving international trade disputes is the system's independence from national courts. This independence is achieved through the finality of arbitral decisions. So long as the consensual relationship between parties persists and they have no need to call on the courts for assistance, the legality of the arbitration procedure or the arbitral award would not be in issue. When the consensus breaks down and a party wishes to walk away from the agreement, there is a need to provide some recourse to the courts. However, the nature of arbitration as a contractual arrangement means that the courts will review arbitral decisions on very limited grounds.

In Australia, the powers of courts to review decisions made in the course of international commercial arbitrations depend on whether the international arbitration agreement contains an opt-out clause excluding the application of the UNCITRAL Model Law. It is important to remember that the New York Convention has nothing to say on the subject of appeals from or review of arbitral decisions. If there is no opt-out clause, this subject will be governed by the Model Law. If the parties have opted out of the Model Law, the issue will be determined by the law of the relevant Australian State.

Arbitral tribunals must not only make final decisions concerning the rights and liabilities of parties, but are often required to make decisions on questions of law arising in the course of the proceedings. Hence judicial review must be considered in relation to both preliminary and final decisions of arbitral tribunals.

Judicial review under the Model Law – preliminary orders

Article 5 of the Model Law enacts that 'in matters governed by this law, no court shall intervene except where so provided in this law'. There is no provision under the Model Law for an arbitral tribunal to refer questions of law to a court during the course of an arbitration. However, Article 16 of the Model Law provides an avenue of judicial review of preliminary decisions on jurisdictional questions. Under Article 16(1), the arbitral tribunal 'may rule on its own jurisdiction, including any objections with respect to the existence or the validity of the arbitration agreement'. According to Article 16(3),

---

42   See, for example, *DST v Raknoc* [1987] 2 All ER 769.
43   See, for example, *The Amazonia* [1989] 1 Lloyd's Rep 403.

the arbitral tribunal may dispose of an objection to jurisdiction in the final award or by ruling on a preliminary question. Where the tribunal decides as a preliminary issue that it has jurisdiction, its decision may be reviewed by a court upon the request of a party made within 30 days of receiving notice of the decision.

It is important to note that the Model Law makes no provision for judicial review where the tribunal decides that it lacks jurisdiction. The only practical remedy then is to ask for a stay of judicial proceedings if and when a party sues in respect of the dispute. The court will then have an opportunity to determine whether the arbitration agreement is valid and whether the dispute is arbitrable. Where no action is brought, the party who wishes to arbitrate has no effective remedy as specific performance cannot in practice be enforced and damages are hard to prove.[44]

Judicial review under the Model Law – final awards

Article 34(1) of the Model Law provides: 'Recourse to a court against an arbitral award may be made only by an application for setting aside in accordance with paras (2) and (3) of this article.' Paragraph (2) sets out the grounds for setting aside an award and para (3) lays down the period of three months for making an application for setting aside. Before discussing the specific grounds, three preliminary points must be noted. The first is that the grounds for setting aside in Article 34 are, in material respects, exactly the same as the grounds upon which an application for enforcement of the award may be refused under Article 36. The only differences arise from the fact that Article 36 is intended to apply to any international arbitral award irrespective of the country in which it was made, whereas, Article 34 applies only to awards made within the country in which the application for setting aside is made. The second point to note is that the grounds are also materially identical to the grounds for refusing enforcement of an arbitral award under the New York Convention. Thus, we observe a deliberate alignment of the recourse available against awards under the Model Law with the enforcement provisions of the New York Convention. The third point is that as a consequence of this alignment, the Model Law does not permit an arbitral award to be set aside on the ground of error committed within jurisdiction whether such error relates to a question of fact or of law. We may now consider briefly each of the grounds for setting aside specified in Article 34(1).

A court which is called upon to set aside an award, may on request of a party suspend the setting aside proceedings in order to enable the arbitral tribunal to eliminate the grounds which make the award susceptible to be set aside. This power conferred by Article 34(4) is akin to the common law courts' power of remission. This provision gives parties the option of saving the sound parts of the award and thereby avoiding the costs of another arbitration or litigation in the courts.

---

44 Mustill, MJ and Boyd, SC, *The Law and Practice of Commercial Arbitration*, 2nd edn, 1989, p 7, London and Edinburgh: Butterworths.

Invalidity of arbitration agreement by reason of applicable law — Article 34(2)(i)

The applicable law is stipulated to be the 'law to which the parties have subjected it or, failing any indication thereon, under the law of this State'. This provision marks a departure from the general position in private international law. According to established principles, in the absence of an express choice of law, the matter will be governed by the proper law. Although the most important factor in determining the proper law is the place of arbitration, it is by no means conclusive. Thus, in *Compagnie d'Armement Maritime SA v Compagnie Tunisienne de Navigation SA*, the French law was held to apply to the agreement although the place of arbitration was London, the reason being that the main contract appertained to France and Tunisia which shared a common system of law.[45] However, under Article 34(1) of the Model Law, in the absence of an express choice of law, the place of arbitration is decisive. The reason is that the words 'this State' must refer to the place of arbitration as Article 34 applies only if the arbitration is held within that State.[46]

Lack of notice of the appointment of the arbitrator or lack of proper hearing — Article 34(2)(ii)

This ground is concerned with one of the two great common law rules of natural justice encapsulated in the maxim *audi alteram partem*. This rule ensures that decisions which adversely affect a party's legal status shall not be taken without affording that party a fair hearing. The violation of the other great rule, that against actual or apparent bias, captured by the maxim *nemo judex in sua causa*, is not expressly recognised as a ground for set aside in the Model Law. However, s 19(b) of the International Arbitration Act 1974 clarifies that an award would be in conflict with public policy in Australia if made in breach of the rules of natural justice. Hence, in the case of bias, the award could be set aside under Article 34(2)(b)(ii).

The dispute was not contemplated by or does not fall within the terms of the submission to arbitration — Article 34(2)(a)(iii)

This ground is concerned with the situation where the award goes beyond the scope of the terms by which the dispute or disputes were referred to arbitration. It is important here to note the difference between the terms of the arbitration agreement and the terms of the submission. If one party seeks to refer to arbitration a dispute which does not fall within the terms of the arbitration agreement, the jurisdiction of the arbitral tribunal may be challenged by the other parties as being *ultra vires* the arbitration agreement. In such cases there will be no valid submission. However, it is possible for parties to agree to submit a dispute to arbitration even if the matter is not envisaged as arbitrable by the original arbitration agreement. This is because an arbitration agreement can provide for the reference of existing disputes to arbitration. Thus, the agreement to submit is in fact a new arbitration agreement which becomes the source of the arbitrator's competence.

---

45 [1971] AC 572.
46 Article 1(2).

Article 34(2)(a)(iii) refers to awards which exceed the terms of submission agreements as distinguished from awards which go beyond the original arbitration agreement. The reason for not including the latter ground in Article 34 and Article 36 is clear enough. If a party wishes to halt an arbitration of a dispute which is sought to be referred to arbitration by another party on the ground that it is not within the arbitration agreement, all she has to do is to refuse to participate in the arbitration and litigate if necessary. If, in fact, the dispute is not referrable under the arbitration agreement, an application for a stay of judicial proceedings under Article 8 of the Model Law can be resisted on the ground that the agreement is inoperative in relation to the dispute.

Where an award contains decisions on matters within the submission agreement as well as matters outside it, Article 34(2)(a)(iii) allows the court to strike out only the *ultra vires* parts of the award leaving the *intra vires* parts intact, provided that they can be separated.

The composition of the arbitral tribunal or the arbitral procedure was not in accordance with the agreement or failing such agreement was not in accordance with the Model Law – Article 34(2)(a)(iv)

Where the parties have agreed on a specific procedure, it must be observed in addition to the general requirements of natural justice. Clearly, however, the terms cannot derogate from the rules of natural justice as this would offend the public policy of Australia. Where the arbitration agreement is silent as regards the composition of the tribunal or the procedure, the provisions of the Model Law will apply if the arbitration is held in Australia.[47]

The subject matter of the dispute is not capable of arbitration under Australian law – Article 34(2)(b)(i)

This raises the question of arbitrability which has already been discussed in relation to the enforcement of arbitration agreements.

The award is in conflict with the public policy of Australia – Article 34(2)(b)

Section 19 of the International Arbitration Act 1974 declares for the avoidance of any doubt, that an award is in conflict with the public policy of Australia if:

(a) the making of the award was induced or affected by fraud or corruption; or

(b) a breach of the rules of natural justice occurred in connection with the making of the award.

This provision is clearly non-exhaustive and there are many other ways in which an award can offend the public policy of Australia. Public policy is an ill-defined legal concept which has been judicially compared to 'an unruly horse [which] once you get

---

47 Assuming of course that the parties have not opted out of the Model Law under s 21.

745

astride it you never know where it will carry you'.[48] The concept has been considered mainly in relation to enforcement provisions. In the US, in *Parsons and Whitmore Overseas Co v Société General de L'Industrie du Papier*, public policy was explained as 'those mandatory norms that comprise a State's most basic notions of morality and justice'.[49] The Court of Appeals, Second Circuit, held that the concept of public policy employed in Article V(2)(b) is narrower than the notion of national policy. Accordingly, the court rejected an objection to the enforcement of an arbitration award in favour of an Egyptian defendant on the ground that it violated current US foreign policy towards Egypt.

Although in private international law, parties to a contract are free to choose the place of arbitration as well as the applicable law, early cases held that certain types of disputes, for example, those involving breaches of securities laws and anti-trust laws were not arbitrable on grounds of public policy. However, more recent cases in the US courts have resiled from that position. In the leading case of *Mitsubishi Motors Corporation v Soler-Chrysler-Plymouth Inc*, the US Supreme Court rejected the argument that anti-trust claims were inappropriate for arbitration owing to the 'pervasive public interest' in enforcing anti-trust law. The court stated:

> [C]oncerns of international comity, respect for the capacities of foreign and transnational tribunals, and sensitivity to the need of the international system for predictability in the resolution of disputes require that we enforce the parties' agreement, even assuming that a contrary result would be forthcoming in a domestic context.[50]

Many of the decisions refusing enforcement of arbitral awards on grounds of public policy concern fraud or the breach of natural justice. Errors of law do not *per se* conflict with public policy. However decisions in deliberate and manifest disregard of the law may be liable to set aside.[51] Some writers claim that there is a category of 'transnational public policy' representing globally accepted norms of conduct with respect to international transactions. However, there is scarce judicial support for the proposition.[52]

Judicial review under the Commercial Arbitration Act 1984 (NSW)

As we have noted, if the parties to an arbitration agreement governed by Australian law have opted out of the Model Law, the local State law applies to the arbitral process unless, of course, it is a matter governed by the New York Convention. Since the convention is silent on the judicial review of arbitral awards, the local law will apply. Hence the need to consider the grounds for review under the Commercial Arbitration Act 1984 (NSW).

---

48 *Richardson v Mellish* (1824) 2 Bing 228 at 252.

49 508 F 2d 969, 974 (2d Cir 1974).

50 473 US 614 at 629.

51 See *Sidarma Societa Italiana, etc v Holt Marine*, 515 F Supp 1362 (1981).

52 See Buchanan, MA, 'Public Policy and International Commercial Arbitration' (1988) 26 *American Business Law Journal* 511 at 514–15 and opinions cited therein.

The commercial arbitration legislation of Australian States has been modelled on the successive Arbitration Acts of the UK. In the old law of England, the only means of reviewing arbitral awards was by way of the writ of *certiorari* issued on the ground of error on the face of the record. Under this procedure, the court could quash but not change the award. The Common Law Procedure Act 1854 introduced the special case procedure which was incorporated later in the successive Arbitration Acts of the UK. Under this procedure, the arbitrator could refer questions of law to the High Court and where the arbitral tribunal declined to do so, the parties could obtain orders from the High Court directing it to state a case.[53] In addition, the High Court had almost unlimited power to remit matters to the arbitrators for reconsideration.[54] In 1979, following demands by the commercial community, the Commercial Court Committee recommended far reaching reforms which were implemented by the Arbitration Act 1979 (UK). The provisions of this Act were copied into the Australian statutes and were to be found in ss 38 and 39 of the Commercial Arbitration Act 1984 (NSW) until that Act was amended in 1990.

The 1979 UK Act replaced all pre-existing remedies against arbitral awards with two means of recourse, namely: an appeal to the High Court from an award and an application to the High Court with respect to questions arising in the course of arbitral proceedings. This reform was meant to curb drastically the number of arbitrations which end up in court, a factor which traders feared was making London arbitration less attractive. However, the Commercial Arbitration Act 1984 (NSW) retains the remedy of set aside limited to the grounds of misconduct of the arbitral tribunal, misconduct of the arbitral proceedings or the improper procurement of the arbitration agreement or the award.[55] The court's power to remit matters also survives in a very restricted form in s 43, the power being subject to s 38(1) which provides that apart from the right of appeal given in sub-s (2), the court shall not have jurisdiction to set aside or remit an award on the ground of error of fact or law on the face of the award. The 1979 UK Act was later superseded by the Arbitration Act 1996, which further limited the powers of courts to intervene in arbitral proceedings or outcomes. The 1996 Act consolidates all the previous UK Acts and is meant to simplify the law of arbitration in the UK.

Appeal from award – s 38 of the Commercial Arbitration Act 1984 (NSW)

The appeal from the award as provided for by s 38 has the following features:

- The appeal lies only from a question of law arising out of an award.
- An appeal may be brought only:

  with consent of all the parties to the agreement; or

  with the leave of the Supreme Court obtainable only in the absence of an agreement excluding appeals under s 40.

- Sub-section 38(5), as amended in 1990, provides:

  The Supreme Court shall not grant leave under sub-s 4(b) unless it considers that:

---

53 Section 21 of the Arbitration Act 1950 (UK).
54 Section 22.
55 Section 42.

(a) having regard to all the circumstances, the determination of the question of law concerned could substantially affect the rights of one or more parties to the arbitration agreement; and

(b) there is:

    (i) a manifest error of law on the face of the award; or

    (ii) strong evidence that the arbitrator or umpire made an error of law and that the determination of the question may add, or may be likely to add, substantially to the certainty of commercial law.

- Leave may be granted subject to conditions.

- On the determination of the appeal, the court may confirm, vary or set aide the award or remit the award for reconsideration in the light of the court's opinion on the question of law.

Exclusion of appeals by agreement

The statutory right of appeal to the Supreme Court granted by s 38 can be extinguished by an exclusion agreement made under s 40. With respect to international arbitrations, an exclusion agreement can be made before or after the commencement of the arbitration whereas in the case of domestic arbitrations, the agreement, to be effective, must be concluded after the commencement of the arbitration.[56] An exclusion agreement must be in writing. In *The Rio Sun*,[57] Denning LJ assumed that a clause in a charter party arbitration agreement which stated that the award 'shall be final' amounted to an exclusion agreement.[58] This proposition is not free of doubt as these words were part of the traditional charter party terminology long before the UK Act was passed. Denning LJ also proposed that an exclusion agreement is concluded where all parties inform the arbitral tribunal that they accept its decision as final and that a request by a party to the arbitrator to give reasons thereby waives any exclusion.[59]

When is leave granted?

The two key conditions for an appeal are:

(a) the existence of a question of law; and

(b) leave of the Supreme Court where the consent of all other parties to the agreement is not forthcoming.

It seems that under s 38(5), the court has a residual discretion to refuse leave. Hence the need for consistency in granting or refusing leave is clear. With regard to the question, 'what is a question of law?', the civil law and common law approaches diverge. In civil law countries, questions concerning the interpretation of contractual terms and the frustration of contracts are treated as questions of fact. In English law, construction of

---

56 Section 40(6). For definition of domestic arbitration, see sub-s (7).

57 [1982] 1 WLR 158.

58 [1982] 1 WLR 158 at 162.

59 [1982] 1 WLR 158 at 162.

documents is generally a question of law. An exception to this rule is where a special meaning has been established by custom. In such instances, an explicit finding of fact will be binding on the court.[60] With regard to frustration of the contract the common law approach is to regard it as a matter of inference of law to be drawn by the court from the facts found to exist.

In *Pioneer Shipping v BTP Tioxide; The 'Nema'*,[61] the House of Lords addressed the need for guidelines in granting leave under the UK provisions. Lord Diplock considered two types of cases: those involving questions of interpretation of the contract and those raising questions concerning the frustration of the contract.

In relation to the interpretation of contracts, His Lordship distinguished between 'one-off' clauses (those peculiar to the contract) and 'standard form clauses'. In the case of one-off clauses, His Lordship stated that normally, leave would not be given unless it was apparent to the judge on a mere perusal of the reasoned award without the benefit of adversarial argument that the arbitrator is wrong. If on perusal of the award, it appears that despite first impressions, the court may be persuaded by argument that the arbitrator might be wrong, no leave will be given.[62] With respect to standard form contracts, Lord Diplock foreshadowed less stringent criteria. In these cases, the court should grant leave if in the circumstances of the case, resolving the question of construction would add significantly to the clarity and certainty of English commercial law and a strong *prima facie* case is made out that the arbitrator is wrong. If the construction of the standard form clause relates to a 'one-off' event, the stricter criteria applicable to one off clauses should be applied.[63]

In relation to questions of frustration, Lord Diplock again distinguished between one-off situations and non one-off situations. Non-one-off situations are those where a large number of contracts are similarly affected by the same set of circumstances. Examples of such mass affectation include the effects of the closure of the Suez Canal, the US soya bean embargo and the Iran-Iraq war. His Lordship stated that in the case of a one-off event, leave should be given only if, upon perusal of the award, it is evident that the arbitrator had misdirected himself or that no reasonable arbitrator could have reached such a conclusion. In non-one-off situations, leave would be given if in the judge's view the decision was 'not right'.[64]

Lord Diplock's guidelines were approved in *Promenade Investments Pty Ltd v State of New South Wales*[65] where Sheller LJ noted that the 1990 amendments to s 38 of the Commercial Arbitration Act 1984 (NSW) sought to 'constrain the exercise of court control over arbitral awards in the manner described by the House of Lords in *The*

---

60   *The Atlantic Sun* [1972] 1 Lloyd's Rep 509.
61   [1982] AC 724.
62   [1982] AC 724 at 742.
63   [1982] AC 724 at 743.
64   [1982] AC 724 at 744.
65   (1991) 26 NSWLR 203.

Nema.[66] Thus, the requirement under s 38(5)(b)(ii) that 'the determination of the question may add, or may be likely to add, substantially to the certainty of commercial law' will be satisfied in the case of standard form clauses in common use and thus therefore justifies the less stringent criteria of 'strong evidence'. Whilst the more stringent provisions of s 38(5)(b)(i), more applicable to a 'one-off' clause, require that the error of law on the face of the award be manifest, counsel may still be heard 'to point out the error or to remind the court of the relevant principles and authorities'.[67]

Application to determine questions of law arising in the course of proceedings – s 39 of the Commercial Arbitration Act 1984 (NSW)

An application for a determination of a question of law arising in the course of the arbitral proceedings can be made only with the consent of the arbitrator or umpire or the consent of all the other parties. Even where an application is made with such consent, the Supreme Court is asked not to entertain it unless it is satisfied that the determination of the application might produce substantial savings in costs to the parties and the question of law is one in respect of which leave would be likely to be granted under s 38(4)(b).

ENFORCEMENT OF INTERNATIONAL ARBITRATION AWARDS

An arbitral award is intrinsically enforceable as its observance is a matter of contractual obligation. As Holt CJ stated in *Purslow v Baily*, 'the submission is an actual mutual promise to perform the award of the arbitrators'.[68] The basis of the action being breach of contract, the following forms of relief are available to the plaintiff where appropriate:

(a) judgment for the amount awarded;

(b) specific performance to pay the sum;[69]

(c) damages for breach of contract;[70]

(d) injunction; and

(e) declaration that the award is binding.

In a common law action on the award, the plaintiff has to prove the existence of a valid arbitration agreement, the submission of the dispute, the appointment of the arbitrators in accordance with the agreement, the making of the award and the non-performance of the award. The position is no different with respect to foreign arbitral awards provided that the award is valid according to the *lex fori*.

---

66 (1991) 26 NSWLR 203 at 222. See also *Natoli v Walker*, unreported, BC9402554, 26 May 1994, Kirby P and Mahoney and Meagher JJA.

67 *Commonwealth v Rian Financial Services and Developments Pty Ltd* (1992) 36 FCR 101 at 108 *per* Davies and Neaves JJ.

68 (1705) 2 Ld Raym 1039 at 1040.

69 *Beswick v Beswick* [1968] AC 58.

70 *Birtly v Windy Nook (no 2)* [1960] 2 QB 1.

Sections 8(1) and (2) of the International Arbitration Act 1974 (Cth) which implement the New York Convention, provide that a foreign award is binding for all purposes on the parties to the agreement and that it may be enforced in a court of a State or Territory as if the award had been made in that State or Territory in accordance with the law of that State or Territory. A foreign award is defined by s 3 as an arbitral award made in a country other than Australia, being an arbitral award to which the convention applies. If the award is made in a country which is not a convention country, the enforcement provisions do not apply unless the person seeking enforcement is domiciled or ordinarily resident in Australia or a convention country.

Section 8(5) of the International Arbitration Act 1974 sets out the defences to an action for enforcement. They are for the most part materially identical to the grounds for setting aside an award provided in Article 34 of the UNCITRAL Model Law which we discussed previously. The only additional ground is that the award has not yet become binding on the parties to the arbitration agreement or has been set aside or suspended by a competent authority of the country in which, or under the law of which, the award was made.[71] This ground states the obvious precondition for enforcement, namely that there must be a valid and operative award.

Since s 8(2) states that a foreign award may be enforced as if made in the State or Territory, the procedure for enforcement is governed by the relevant local law. The relevant provision in New South Wales is s 33(1) of the Commercial Arbitration Act 1984 which provides that an award made under an arbitration agreement may, by leave of the court, be enforced in the same manner as a judgment or order of the court to the same effect, and where leave is so given, judgment may be entered in terms of the award. It is not necessary to obtain a judgment on the award, but it is prudent when leave to enforce is granted, to have judgment entered in terms of the award because a formal judgment is necessary for certain statutory purposes such as the obtaining of a bankruptcy notice[72] or the subsequent enforcement of the award in another State or Territory under the Service and Execution of Process Act 1901 (Cth). Under s 9 of the International Arbitration Act 1974, a person seeking enforcement has to produce to the court a duly authenticated original award or a duly certified copy and the original arbitration agreement or a duly certified copy.

The court has a discretion to grant leave to enforce an award, although as a matter of practice, leave is given 'unless there is a real ground for doubting the validity of the award'.[73] Where leave is not granted, the party seeking enforcement has to resort to the more expensive and time consuming method of bringing an action upon the award and obtaining a local judgment.

It should be remembered that the New York Convention provisions regarding enforcement apply only to foreign awards which means awards made outside Australia. If an award is made in Australia in pursuance of an international arbitration agreement,

---

71 Section 8(5)(f).

72 *Re Hayek* (1957) 19 ABC 1.

73 *Middlemiss and Gould v Hartlepool Corp* [1972] 1 WLR 1643 at 1645 *per* Lord Denning MR.

its enforcement in Australia will be governed by Articles 35 and 36 of the UNCITRAL Model Law unless the parties have opted out of the Model Law. The grounds for refusing enforcement are virtually identical to the grounds set out in the New York Convention.

Where neither the New York Convention nor the Model Law applies, the party seeking enforcement has to bring an action upon the award. In the leading case of *Norske Atlas Insurance Co Ltd v London General Insurance Co Ltd*, MacKinnon J set out the matters which need to be proved in an action on the award:

> In order to sue on an award, it is, I think, necessary for the plaintiffs to prove first, that there was a submission; secondly, that the arbitration was conducted in pursuance of the submission; and, thirdly, that the award is a valid award made pursuant to the provisions of the submission, and valid according to the *lex fori* of the place where the arbitration was carried out and where the award was made.[74]

Following this case, Dicey and Morris infer that at common law, a foreign award will be recognised and enforced if the award is:

(a) in accordance with an agreement to arbitrate which is valid by its proper law; and

(b) valid and final according to the law governing the arbitration proceedings.[75]

The two requirements recognise the fact that the applicable law concerning the validity and construction of the arbitration agreement may be different to the law applicable to the arbitration procedure. However, it should be noted that the proper law of the arbitration agreement is most often also the law applicable to the arbitral procedure inasmuch as a clause specifying arbitration in a particular country is a very strong indication that the proper law of the agreement is the law of the country where the arbitration is to be held.[76]

TUTORIAL QUESTIONS

1 Why cannot parties to an arbitration agreement absolutely exclude judicial review?

2 Describe the various roles of the International Arbitration Act 1974 (Cth), the New York Convention and the UNCITRAL Model Law.

3 Does the legislative framework in Australia now adequately deal with international commercial arbitration?

4 What issues do the parties need to address when drafting an international arbitration agreement?

5 Identify some advantages and some disadvantages in using arbitration rather than the judicial system to resolve an international commercial dispute.

---

74 (1927) 28 Lloyd's Rep 104 at 106–07.

75 Dicey, AV and Morris, JHC, *Dicey and Morris on the Conflict of Law*, 12th edn, 1993, p 601, London: Sweet & Maxwell.

76 *Tzoritz v Monarch Line A/B* [1968] 1 WLR 406 at 41.

FURTHER READING

Broches, A, *Commentary on the UNCITRAL Model Law on International Commercial Arbitration*, 1990, Deventer: Kluwer.

Buchanan, MA, 'Public Policy and International Commercial Arbitration' (1988) 26 *American Business Law Journal* 511.

Dicey, AV and Morris, JHC, *Dicey and Morris on the Conflict of Laws*, 12th edn, 1993, London: Sweet & Maxwell.

Holtzmann, HM and Neuhaus, JE, *A Guide to the UNCITRAL Model Law on International Commercial Arbitration: Legislative History and Commentary*, 1989, Deventer: Kluwer.

Jacobs, MS, *International Commercial Arbitration in Australia: Law and Practice*, 1992, Sydney: Law Book Co.

Mustill, MJ and Boyd, SC, *The Law and Practice of Commercial Arbitration*, 2nd edn, 1989, London and Edinburgh: Butterworths.

Park, WW, 'National Law and Commercial Justice: Safeguarding Procedural Integrity in International Arbitration' (1989) 63 *Tulane Law Review* 647.

Pryles, M, 'Drafting Arbitration Agreements' (1993) 67 *Australian Law Journal* 503.

Redfern, A, and Hunter, M, *Law and Practice of International Commercial Arbitration*, 2nd edn, 1991, London: Sweet & Maxwell.

UNCITRAL MODEL LAW ON INTERNATIONAL COMMERCIAL ARBITRATION

(as adopted by the United Nations Commission on International Trade Law on 21 June 1985)

Chapter 1 – General provisions

Article 1 – Scope of application

1   This law applies to international commercial arbitration, subject to any agreement in force between this State and any other State or States.

2   The provisions of this law, except Articles 8, 9, 35 and 36, apply only if the place of arbitration is in the territory of this State.

3   An arbitration is international if:

(a)   the parties to an arbitration agreement have, at the time of the conclusion of that agreement, their places of business in different States; or

(b)   one of the following places is situated outside the State in which the parties have their places of business:

(i)   the place of arbitration if determined in, or pursuant to, the arbitration agreement;

(ii)   any place where a substantial part of the obligations of the commercial relationship is to be performed or the place with which the subject matter of the dispute is most closely connected; or

(c)   the parties have expressly agreed that the subject matter of the arbitration agreement relates to more than one country.

4   For the purposes of para (3) of this article:

(a)   if a party has more than one place of business, the place of business is that which has the closest relationship to the arbitration agreement;

(b)   if a party does not have a place of business, reference is to be made to his habitual residence.

5   This law shall not affect any other law of this State by virtue of which certain disputes may not be submitted to arbitration or may be submitted to arbitration only according to provisions other than those of this law.

Article 2 – Definitions and rules of interpretation

For the purposes of this law:

(a)   'arbitration' means any arbitration whether or not administered by a permanent arbitral institution;

(b)   'arbitral tribunal' means a sole arbitrator or a panel of arbitrators;

(c)   'court' means a body or organ of the judicial system of a State;

(d)   where a provision of this law, except Article 28, leaves the parties free to determine a certain issue, such freedom includes the right of the parties to authorise a third party, including an institution, to make that determination;

(e)   where a provision of this law refers to the fact that the parties have agreed or that they may agree or in any other way refers to an agreement of the parties; such agreement includes any arbitration rules referred to in that agreement;

(f) where a provision of this law, other than in Articles 25(a) and 32(2)(a), refers to a claim, it also applies to a counter claim, and where it refers to a defence, it also applies to a defence to such counter claim.

Article 3 – Receipt of written communications

1 Unless otherwise agreed by the parties:

   (a) any written communication is deemed to have been received if it is delivered to the addressee personally or if it is delivered at his place of business, habitual residence or mailing address; if none of these can be found after making a reasonable inquiry, a written communication is deemed to have been received if it is sent to the addressee's last known place of business, habitual residence or mailing address by registered letter or any other means which provides a record of the attempt to deliver it;

   (b) the communication is deemed to have been received on the day it is so delivered.

2 The provisions of this article do not apply to communications in court proceedings.

Article 4 – Waiver of right to object

A party who knows that any provision of this law from which the parties may derogate or any requirement under the arbitration agreement has not been complied with and yet proceeds with the arbitration without stating his objection to such non-compliance without undue delay or, if a time limit is provided therefor within such period of time, shall be deemed to have waived his right to object.

Article 5 – Extent of court intervention

In matters governed by this law, no court shall intervene except where so provided in this law.

Article 6 – Court or other authority for certain functions of arbitration assistance and supervision

The functions referred to in Articles 11(3), 11(4), 13(3), 14, 16(3) and 34(2) shall be performed by … [Each State enacting this Model Law specifies the court, courts or. where referred to therein, other authority competent to perform these functions.]

Chapter II – Arbitration agreement

Article 7 – Definition and form of arbitration agreement

1 'Arbitration agreement' is an agreement by the parties to submit to arbitration all or certain disputes which have arisen or which may arise between them in respect of a defined legal relationship whether contractual or not. An arbitration agreement may be in the form of an arbitration clause in a contract or in the form of a separate agreement.

2 The arbitration agreement shall be in writing. An agreement is in writing if it is contained in a document signed by the parties or in an exchange of letters, telex, telegrams or other means of telecommunication which provide a record of the agreement or in an exchange of statements of claim and defence in which the existence of an agreement is alleged by one party and not denied by another. The reference in a contract to a document containing an arbitration clause constitutes an arbitration agreement provided that the contract is in writing and the reference is such as to make that clause part of the contract.

Article 8 – Arbitration agreement and substantive claim before court

1   A court before which an action is brought in a matter which is the subject of an arbitration agreement shall, if a party so requests not later than when submitting his first statement on the substance of the dispute, refer the parties to arbitration unless it finds that the agreement is null and void, inoperative or incapable of being performed.

2   Where an action referred to in para (1) of this article has been brought, arbitral proceedings may nevertheless be commenced or continued, and an award may be made, while the issue is pending before the court.

Article 9 – Arbitration agreement and interim measures by court

It is not incompatible with an arbitration agreement for a party to request, before or during arbitral proceedings, from a court, an interim measure of protection and for a court to grant such measure.

Chapter III – Composition of arbitral tribunal

Article 10 – Number of arbitrators

1   The parties are free to determine the number of arbitrators.

2   Failing such determination the number of arbitrators shall be three.

Article 11 – Appointment of arbitrators

1   No person shall be precluded by reason of his nationality from acting as an arbitrator, unless otherwise agreed by the parties.

2   The parties are free to agree on a procedure of appointing the arbitrator or arbitrators, subject to the provisions of paras (4) and (5) of this article.

3   Failing such agreement:

 (a)   in an arbitration with three arbitrators, each party shall appoint one arbitrator, and the two arbitrators thus appointed shall appoint the third arbitrator; if a party fails to appoint the arbitrator within 30 days of receipt of a request to do so from the other party, or if the two arbitrators fail to agree on the third arbitrator within 30 days of their appointment, the appointment shall be made, upon request of a party, by the court or other authority specified in Article 6;

 (b)   in an arbitration with a sole arbitrator, if the parties are unable to agree on the arbitrator, he shall be appointed, upon request of a party, by the court or other authority specified in Article 6.

4   Where, under an appointment procedure agreed upon by the parties:

 (a)   a party fails to act as required under such procedure; or

 (b)   the parties, or two arbitrators, are unable to reach an agreement expected of them under such procedure; or

 (c)   a third party including an institution, fails to perform any function entrusted to it under such procedure,

any party may request the court or other authority specified in Article 6 to take the necessary measure, unless the agreement on the appointment procedure provides other means for securing the appointment.

5   A decision on a matter entrusted by paras (3) and (4) of this article to the court or other authority specified in Article 6 shall be subject to no appeal. The court or other

authority, in appointing an arbitrator, shall have due regard to any qualifications required of the arbitrator by the agreement of the parties and to such considerations as are likely to secure the appointment of an independent and impartial arbitrator and, in the case of a sole or third arbitrator, shall take into account as well the advisability of appointing an arbitrator of a nationality other than those of the parties.

Article 12 – Grounds for challenge

1   When a person is approached in connection with his possible appointment as an arbitrator, he shall disclose any circumstances likely to give rise to justifiable doubts as to his impartiality or independence. An arbitrator, from the time of his appointment and throughout the arbitral proceedings, shall without delay disclose any such circumstances to the parties unless they have already been informed of them by him.

2   An arbitrator may be challenged only if circumstances exist that give rise to justifiable doubts as to his impartiality or independence, or if he does not possess qualifications agreed to by the parties. A party may challenge an arbitrator appointed by him, or in whose appointment he has participated, only for reasons of which he becomes aware after the appointment has been made.

Article 13 – Challenge procedure

1   The parties are free to agree on a procedure for challenging an arbitrator, subject to the provisions of para (3) of this article.

2   Failing such agreement, a party who intends to challenge an arbitrator shall, within fifteen days after becoming aware of the constitution of the arbitral tribunal or after becoming aware of any circumstance referred to in Article 12(2), send a written statement of the reasons for the challenge to the arbitral tribunal. Unless the challenged arbitrator withdraws from his office or the other party agrees to the challenge, the arbitral tribunal shall decide on the challenge.

3   If a challenge under any procedure agreed upon by the parties or under the procedure of para (2) of this article is not successful, the challenging party may request, within 30 days after having received notice of the decision rejecting the challenge, the court or other authority specified in Article 6 to decide on the challenge, which decision shall be subject to no appeal; while such a request is pending, the arbitral tribunal, including the challenged arbitrator, may continue the arbitral proceedings and make an award.

Article 14 – Failure or impossibility to act

1   If an arbitrator becomes *de jure* or *de facto* unable to perform his functions or for other reasons fails to act without undue delay, his mandate terminates if he withdraws from his office or if the parties agree on the termination. Otherwise, if a controversy remains concerning any of these grounds, any party may request the court or other authority specified in Article 6 to decide on the termination of the mandate, which decision shall be subject to no appeal.

2   If, under this article or Article 13(2), an arbitrator withdraws from his office or a party agrees to the termination of the mandate of an arbitrator this does not imply acceptance of the validity of any ground referred to in this article or Article 12(2).

Article 15 – Appointment of substitute arbitrator

Where the mandate of an arbitrator terminates under Article 13 or 14 or because of his withdrawal from office for any other reason or because of the revocation of his mandate by agreement of the parties or in any other case of termination of his mandate, a substitute arbitrator shall be appointed according to the rules that were applicable to the appointment of the arbitrator being replaced.

Chapter IV – Jurisdiction of arbitral tribunal

Article 16 – Competence of arbitral tribunal to rule on its jurisdiction

1   The arbitral tribunal may rule on its own jurisdiction, including any objections with respect to the existence or validity of the arbitration agreement. For that purpose, an arbitration clause which forms part of a contract shall be treated as an agreement independent of the other terms of the contract. A decision by the arbitral tribunal that the contract is null and void shall not entail *ipso jure* the invalidity of the arbitration clause.

2   A plea that the arbitral tribunal does not have jurisdiction shall be raised not later than the submission of the statement of defence. A party is not precluded from raising such a plea by the fact that he has appointed, or participated in the appointment of, an arbitrator. A plea that the arbitral tribunal is exceeding the scope of its authority shall be raised as soon as the matter alleged to be beyond the scope of its authority is raised during the arbitral proceedings. The arbitral tribunal may, in either case, admit a later plea if it considers the delay justified.

3   The arbitral tribunal may rule on a plea referred to in para (2) of this article either as a preliminary question or in an award on the merits. If the arbitral tribunal rules as a preliminary question that it has jurisdiction, any party may request, within 30 days after having received notice of that ruling, the court specified in Article 6 to decide the matter, which decision shall be subject to no appeal: while such a request is pending, the arbitral tribunal may continue the arbitral proceedings and make an award.

Article 17 – Power of arbitral tribunal to order interim measures

Unless otherwise agreed by the parties, the arbitral tribunal may, at the request of a party, order any party to take such interim measure of protection as the arbitral tribunal may consider necessary in respect of the subject matter of the dispute. The arbitral tribunal may require any party to provide appropriate security in connection with such measure.

Chapter V – Conduct of arbitral proceedings

Article 18 – Equal treatment of parties

The parties shall be treated with equality and each party shall be given a full opportunity of presenting his case.

Article 19 – Determination of rules of procedure

1   Subject to the provisions of this law, the parties are free to agree on the procedure to be followed by the arbitral tribunal in conducting the proceedings.

2   Failing such agreement, the arbitral tribunal may, subject to the provisions of this law, conduct the arbitration in such manner as it considers appropriate. The power conferred upon the arbitral tribunal includes the power to determine the admissibility, relevance, materiality and weight of any evidence.

Article 20 – Place of arbitration

1   The parties are free to agree on the place of arbitration. Failing such agreement, the place of arbitration shall be determined by the arbitral tribunal having regard to the circumstances of the case, including the convenience of the parties.

2 Notwithstanding the provisions of para (1) of this article, the arbitral tribunal may, unless otherwise agreed by the parties, meet at any place it considers appropriate for consultation among its members, for hearing witnesses, experts or the parties, or for inspection of goods, other property or documents.

Article 21 – Commencement of arbitral proceedings

Unless otherwise agreed by the parties, the arbitral proceedings in respect of a particular dispute commence on the date on which a request for that dispute to be referred to arbitration is received by the respondent.

Article 22 – Language

1 The parties are free to agree on the language or languages to be used in the arbitral proceedings. Failing such agreement, the arbitral tribunal shall determine the language or languages to be used in the proceedings. This agreement or determination, unless otherwise specified therein, shall apply to any written statement by a party, any hearing and any award, decision or other communication by the arbitral tribunal.

2 The arbitral tribunal may order that any documentary evidence shall be accompanied by a translation into the language or languages agreed upon by the parties or determined by the arbitral tribunal.

Article 23 – Statements of claim and defence

1 Within the period of time agreed by the parties or determined by the arbitral tribunal, the claimant shall state the facts supporting his claim, the points at issue and the relief or remedy sought, and the respondent shall state his defence in respect of these particulars, unless the parties have otherwise agreed as to the required elements of such statements. The parties may submit with their statements all documents they consider to be relevant or may add a reference to the documents or other evidence they will submit.

2 Unless otherwise agreed by the parties either party may amend or supplement his claim or defence during the course of the arbitral proceedings, unless the arbitral tribunal considers it inappropriate to allow such amendment having regard to the delay in making it.

Article 24 – Hearings and written proceedings

1 Subject to any contrary agreement by the parties, the arbitral tribunal shall decide whether to hold oral hearings for the presentation of evidence or for oral argument or whether the proceedings shall be conducted on the basis of documents and other materials. However, unless the parties have agreed that no hearings shall be held, the arbitral tribunal shall hold such hearings at an appropriate stage of the proceedings if so requested by a party.

2 The parties shall be given sufficient advance notice of any hearing and of any meeting of the arbitral tribunal for the purposes of inspection of goods, other property or documents.

3 All statements, documents or other information supplied to the arbitral tribunal by one party shall be communicated to the other party. Also, any expert report or evidentiary document on which the arbitral tribunal may rely in making its decision shall be communicated to the parties.

Article 25 – Default of a party

Unless otherwise agreed by the parties, if, without showing sufficient cause:

(a) the claimant fails to communicate his statement of claim in accordance with Article 23(1), the arbitral tribunal shall terminate the proceedings;

(b) the respondent fails to communicate his statement of defence in accordance with Article 23(1), the arbitral tribunal shall continue the proceedings without treating such failure in itself as an admission of the claimant's allegations.

(c) any party fails to appear at a hearing or to produce documentary evidence, the arbitral tribunal may continue the proceedings and make the award on the evidence before it.

Article 26 – Expert appointed by arbitral tribunal

1   Unless otherwise agreed by the parties the arbitral tribunal:

(a) may appoint one or more experts to report to it on specific issues to be determined by the arbitral tribunal;

(b) may require a party to give the expert any relevant information or to produce, or to provide access to, any relevant documents, goods or other property for his inspection.

2   Unless otherwise agreed by the parties, if a party so requests or if the arbitral tribunal considers it necessary, the expert shall, after delivery of his written or oral report, participate in a hearing where the parties have the opportunity to put questions to him and to present expert witnesses in order to testify on the points at issue.

Article 27 – Court assistance in taking evidence

The arbitral tribunal or a party with the approval of the arbitral tribunal may request from a competent court of this State assistance in taking evidence. The court may execute the request within its competence and according to its rules on taking evidence.

Chapter VI – Making of award and termination of proceedings

Article 28 – Rules applicable to substance of dispute

1   The arbitral tribunal shall decide the dispute in accordance with such rules of law as are chosen by the parties as applicable to the substance of the dispute. Any designation of the law or legal system of a given State shall be construed, unless otherwise expressed, as directly referring to the substantive law of that State and not to its conflict of laws rules.

2   Failing any designation by the parties the arbitral tribunal shall apply the law determined by the conflict of laws rules which it considers applicable.

3   The arbitral tribunal shall decide *ex aequo et bono* or as *amiable compositeur* only if the parties have expressly authorised it to do so.

4   In all cases, the arbitral tribunal shall decide in accordance with the terms of the contract and shall take into account the usages of the trade applicable to the transaction.

Article 29 – Decision-making by panel of arbitrators

In arbitral proceedings with more than one arbitrator, any decision of the arbitral tribunal shall be made, unless otherwise agreed by the parties by a majority of all its members. However, questions of procedure may be decided by a presiding arbitrator, if so authorised by the parties or all members of the arbitral tribunal.

Article 30 – Settlement

1   If, during arbitral proceedings, the parties settle the dispute, the arbitral tribunal shall terminate the proceedings and, if requested by the parties and not objected to by the arbitral tribunal, record the settlement in the form of an arbitral award on agreed terms.

2   An award on agreed terms shall be made in accordance with the provisions of Article 31 and shall state that it is an award. Such an award has the same status and effect as any other award on the merits of the case.

Article 31 – Form and contents of award

1   The award shall be made in writing and shall be signed by the arbitrator or arbitrators. In arbitral proceedings with more than one arbitrator, the signatures of the majority of all members of the arbitral tribunal shall suffice, provided that the reason for any omitted signature is stated.

2   The award shall state the reasons upon which it is based, unless the parties have agreed that no reasons are to be given or the award is an award on agreed terms under Article 30.

3   The award shall state its date and the place of arbitration as determined in accordance with Article 20(1). The award shall be deemed to have been made at that place.

4   After the award is made, a copy signed by the arbitrators in accordance with para (1) of this article shall be delivered to each party.

Article 32 – Termination of proceedings

1   The arbitral proceedings are terminated by the final award or by an order of the arbitral tribunal in accordance with para (2) of this article.

2   The arbitral tribunal shall issue an order for the termination of the arbitral proceedings when:

(a)   the claimant withdraws his claim. unless the respondent objects thereto and the arbitral tribunal recognises a legitimate interest on his part in obtaining a final settlement of the dispute;

(b)   the parties agree on the termination of the proceedings;

(c)   the arbitral tribunal finds that the continuation of the proceedings has for any other reason become unnecessary or impossible.

3   The mandate of the arbitral tribunal terminates with the termination of the arbitral proceedings, subject to the provisions of Articles 33 and 34(4).

Article 33 – Correction of interpretation of award; additional award

1   Within 30 days of receipt of the award unless another period of time has been agreed upon by the parties:

(a)   a party, with notice to the other party may request the arbitral tribunal to correct in the award and any errors in computation, any clerical or typographical errors or any errors of similar nature;

(b)   if so agreed by the parties, a party, with notice to the other party, may request the arbitral tribunal to give an interpretation of a specific point or part of the award.

If the arbitral tribunal considers the request to be justified, it shall make the correction or give the interpretation within 30 days of receipt of the request. The interpretation shall form part of the award.

2   The arbitral tribunal may correct any error of the type referred to in para (1)(a) of this article on its own initiative within 30 days of the day of the award.

3   Unless otherwise agreed by the parties, a party with notice to the other party, may request, within 30 days of receipt of the award, the arbitral tribunal to make an additional award as to claims presented in the arbitral proceedings but omitted from the award. If the arbitral tribunal considers the request to be justified, it shall make the additional award within 60 days.

4   The arbitral tribunal may extend, if necessary, the period of time within which it shall make a correction, interpretation or an additional award under para (1) or (3) of this article.

5   The provisions of Article 31 shall apply to a correction or interpretation of the award or to an additional award.

Chapter VII – Recourse against Award

Article 34 – Application for setting aside as exclusive recourse against arbitral award

1   Recourse to a court against an arbitral award may be made only by an application for setting aside in accordance with paras (2) and (3) of this article.

2   An arbitral award may be set aside by the court specified in Article 6 only if:

(a) the party making the application furnishes proof that:

(i)   a party to the arbitration agreement referred to in Article 7 was under some incapacity; or the said agreement is not valid under the law to which the parties have subjected it or, failing any indication thereon, under the law of the State; or

(ii) the party making the application was not given proper notice of the appointment of an arbitrator or of the arbitral proceedings or was otherwise unable to present his case; or

(iii) the award deals with a dispute not contemplated by or not falling within the terms of the submission to arbitration, or contains decisions on matters beyond the scope of the submission to arbitration, provided that, if the decisions on matters submitted to arbitration can be separated from those not so submitted, only that part of the award which contains decisions on matters not submitted to arbitration may be set aside; or

(iv) the composition of the arbitral tribunal or the arbitral procedure was not in accordance with the agreement of the parties, unless such agreement was in conflict with a provision of the law from which the parties cannot derogate or, failing such agreement, was not in accordance with this law;

(b) the court finds that:

(i)   the subject matter of the dispute is not capable of settlement by arbitration under the law of this State; or

(ii) the award is in conflict with the public policy of this State.

3   An application for setting aside may not be made after three months have elapsed from the date on which the party making that application had received the award or,

if a request had been made under Article 33, from the date on which that request had been disposed of by the arbitral tribunal.

4   The court, when asked to set aside an award, may, where appropriate and so requested by a party, suspend the setting aside proceedings for a period of time determined by it in order to give the arbitral tribunal an opportunity to resume the arbitral proceedings or to take such other action as in the arbitral tribunal's opinion will eliminate the grounds for setting aside.

Chapter VIII – Recognition and Enforcement of Awards

Article 35 – Recognition and enforcement

1   An arbitral award, irrespective of the country in which it was made, shall be recognised as binding and, upon application in writing to the competent court, shall be enforced subject to the provisions of this article and of Article 36.

2   The party relying on an award or applying for its enforcement shall supply the duly authenticated original award or a duly certified copy thereof, and the original arbitration agreement referred to in Article 7 or a duly certified copy thereof. If the award or agreement is not made in an official language of this State, the party shall supply a duly certified translation thereof into each language.

Article 36 – Grounds for refusing recognition or enforcement

1   Recognition or enforcement of an arbitral award, irrespective of the country in which it was made, may be refused only:

(a)   at the request of the party against whom it is invoked, if that party furnishes to the competent court where recognition or enforcement is sought proof that:

    (i)   a party to the arbitration agreement referred to in Article 7 was under some incapacity; or the said agreement is not valid under the law to which the parties have subjected it or, failing any indication thereon, under the law of the country where the award was made; or

    (ii)   the party against whom the award is invoked was not given proper notice of the appointment of an arbitrator or of the arbitral proceedings or was otherwise unable to present his case; or

    (iii) the award deals with a dispute not contemplated by or not falling within the terms of the submission to arbitration, or it contains decisions on matters beyond the scope of the submission to arbitration, provided that, if the decisions on matters submitted to arbitration can be separated from those not so submitted, that part of the award which contains decisions on matters submitted to arbitration may be recognised and enforced; or

    (iv)   the composition of the arbitral tribunal or the arbitral procedure was not in accordance with the agreement of the parties or, failing such agreement, was not in accordance with the law of the country where the arbitration took place; or

    (v)   the award has not yet become binding on the parties or has been set aside or suspended by a court of the country in which, or under the law of which that award was made; or

(b)   if the court finds that:

    (i)   the subject matter of the dispute is not capable of settlement by arbitration under the law of this State; or

(ii) the recognition or enforcement of the award would be contrary to the public policy of this State.

2   If an application for setting aside or suspension of an award has been made to a court referred to in para (1)(a)(v) of this article, the court where recognition or enforcement is sought may, if it considers it proper, adjourn its decision and may also, on the application of the party claiming recognition or enforcement of the award, order the other party to provide appropriate security.

CONVENTION ON THE RECOGNITION AND ENFORCEMENT OF FOREIGN ARBITRAL AWARDS

New York, 10 June 1958

Status of this Convention

Article I

1   This Convention shall apply to the recognition and enforcement of arbitral awards made in the territory of a State other than the State where the recognition and enforcement of such awards are sought, and arising out of differences between persons, whether physical or legal. It shall also apply to arbitral awards not considered as domestic awards in the State where their recognition and enforcement are sought.

2   The term 'arbitral awards' shall include not only awards made by arbitrators appointed for each case but also those made by permanent arbitral bodies to which the parties have submitted.

3   When signing, ratifying or acceding to this convention, or notifying extension under Article X thereof, any State may on the basis of reciprocity declare that it will apply the Convention to the recognition and enforcement of awards made only in the territory of another Contracting State. It may also declare that it will apply the Convention only to differences arising out of legal relationships, whether contractual or not, which are considered as commercial under the national law of the State making such declaration.

Article II

1   Each Contracting State shall recognise an agreement in writing under which the parties undertake to submit to arbitration all or any differences which have arisen or which may arise between them in respect of a defined legal relationship, whether contractual or not, concerning a subject matter capable of settlement by arbitration.

2   The term 'agreement in writing' shall include an arbitral clause in a contract or an arbitration agreement, signed by the parties or contained in an exchange of letters or telegrams.

3   The court of a Contracting State, when seized of an action in a matter in respect of which the parties have made an agreement within the meaning of this article, at the request of one of the parties, refer the parties to arbitration, unless it finds that the said agreement is null and void, inoperative or incapable of being performed.

Article III

Each Contracting State shall recognise arbitral awards as binding and enforce them in accordance with the rules of procedure of the territory where the award is relied upon, under the conditions laid down in the following articles. There shall not be imposed substantially more onerous conditions or higher fees or charges on the recognition or enforcement of arbitral awards to which this convention applies than are imposed on the recognition or enforcement of domestic arbitral awards.

Article IV

1 To obtain the recognition and enforcement mentioned in the preceding article, the party applying for recognition and enforcement shall, at the time of the application, supply:

 (a) the duly authenticated original award or a duly certified copy thereof;

 (b) the original agreement referred to in Article II or a duly certified copy thereof.

2 If the said award or agreement is not made in an official language of the country in which the award is relied upon, the part applying for recognition and enforcement of the award shall produce a translation of these documents into such language. The translation shall be certified by an official or sworn translator or by a diplomatic or consular agent.

Article V

1 Recognition and enforcement of the award may be refused, at the request of the party against whom it is invoked, only if that party furnishes to the competent authority where the recognition and enforcement is sought, proof that:

 (a) the parties to the agreement referred to in Article II were, under the law applicable to them under some incapacity or the said agreement is not valid under the law to which the parties have subjected it or, failing any indication thereon, under the law of the country where the award was made; or

 (b) the party against whom the award is invoked was not given proper notice of the appointment of the arbitrator or of the arbitration proceedings or was otherwise unable to present his case; or

 (c) the award deals with a difference not contemplated by or not falling within the terms of the submission to arbitration or it contains decisions on matters beyond the scope of the submission to arbitration, provided that, if the decisions on matters submitted to arbitration can be separated from those not so submitted, that part of the award which contains decisions on matters submitted to arbitration may be recognised and enforced; or

 (d) the composition of the arbitral authority or the arbitral procedure was not in accordance with the agreement of the parties, or failing such agreement, was not in accordance with the law of the country where the arbitration took place; or

 (e) the award has not yet become binding on the parties, or has been set aside or suspended by a competent authority of the country in which, or under the law of which, that award was made.

2 Recognition and enforcement of an arbitral award may also be refused if the competent authority in the country where recognition and enforcement is sought finds that:

 (a) the subject matter of the difference is not capable of settlement by arbitration under the law of that country; or

 (b) the recognition or enforcement of the award would be contrary to the public policy of that country.

Article VI

If an application for the setting aside or suspension of the award has been made to a competent authority referred to in Article V(1)(e), the authority before which the award is sought to be relied upon may, if it considers it proper, adjourn the decision on the enforcement of the award and may also on the application of the party claiming enforcement of the award, order the other party to give suitable security.

Article VII

1   The provisions of the present Convention shall not affect the validity of multilateral or bilateral agreements concerning the recognition and enforcement of arbitral awards entered into by the contracting States nor deprive any interested party of any right he may have to avail himself of an arbitral award in the manner and to the extent allowed by the law or the treaties of the country where such award is sought to be relied upon.

2   The Geneva Protocol on Arbitration Clauses of 1923 and the Geneva Convention on the Execution of Foreign Arbitral Awards of 1927 shall cease to have effect between Contracting States on their becoming bound and to the extent that they become bound, by this convention.

Article VIII

1   This Convention shall be open until 31 December 1958 for signature on behalf of any Member of the United Nations and also on behalf of any other State which is or hereafter becomes a member of any specialised agency of the United Nations or which is or hereafter becomes a party to the Statute of the International Court of Justice, or any other State to which an invitation has been addressed by the General Assembly of the United Nations.

2   This Convention shall be ratified and the instrument of ratification shall be deposited with the Secretary General of the United Nations.

Article IX

1   This Convention shall be open for accession to all States referred to in Article VIII.

2   Accession shall be effected by the deposit of an instrument of accession with the Secretary General of the United Nations.

Article X

1   Any State may, at the time of signature, ratification or accession, declare that this convention shall extend to all or any of the territories for the international relations of which it is responsible. Such a declaration shall take effect when the convention enters into force for the State concerned.

2   At any time thereafter any such extension shall be made be notification addressed to the Secretary General of the United Nations and shall take effect as from the ninetieth day after the day of receipt by the Secretary General of the United Nations of this notification, or as from the date of entry into force of the convention for the State concerned, whichever is the later.

3   With respect to those territories to which this convention is not extended at the time of signature ratification or accession, each State concerned shall consider the possibility of taking the necessary steps in order to extend the application of this convention to such territories, subject, where necessary for constitutional reasons, to the consent of the governments of such territories.

Article XI

In the case of a federal or non-unitary State, the following provisions shall apply:

(a) With respect to those articles of this convention that come within the legislative jurisdiction of the federal authority, the obligations of the Federal Government shall to this extent be the same as those of Contracting States which are not Federal States;

(b) With respect to those articles of this convention that come within the legislative jurisdiction of constituent states or provinces which are not, under the constitutional system of the federation, bound to take legislative action, the Federal Government shall bring such articles with a favourable recommendation to the notice of the appropriate authorities of constituent states or provinces at the earliest possible moment;

(c) A Federal State Party to this convention shall, at the request of any other Contracting State transmitted through the Secretary General of the United Nations, supply a statement of the law and practice of the federation and its constituent units in regard to any particular provision of this convention, showing the extent to which effect has been given to that provision by legislative or other action.

Article XII

1 This convention shall come into force on the 90th day following the date of deposit of the third instrument of ratification or accession.

2 For each State ratifying or acceding to this Convention after the deposit of the third instrument of ratification or accession, this Convention shall enter into force on the 90th day after deposit by such State of its instrument of ratification or accession.

Article XIII

1 Any Contracting State may denounce this Convention by a written notification to the Secretary General of the United Nations. Denunciation shall take effect one year after the date of receipt of the notification by the Secretary General.

2 Any State which has made a declaration or notification under Article X may, at any time thereafter by notification to the Secretary General of the United Nations, declare that this Convention shall cease to extend to the territory concerned one year after the date of the receipt of the notification by the Secretary General.

3 This Convention shall continue to be applicable to arbitral awards in respect of which recognition and enforcement proceedings have been instituted before the denunciation takes effect.

Article XIV

A Contracting State shall not be entitled to avail itself of the present convention against other Contracting States except to the extent that it is itself bound to apply the convention.

Article XV

The Secretary General of the United Nations shall notify the States contemplated in Article VIII of the following:

(a) Signatures and ratifications in accordance with Article VIII.

(b) Accessions in accordance with Article IX.

(c) Declarations and notifications under Articles I, X and XI.

(d) The date upon which this convention enters into force in accordance with Article XII.

(e) Denunciations and notifications in accordance with Article XIII.

Article XVI

1   This Convention, of which the Chinese, English, French, Russian and Spanish texts shall be equally authentic, shall be deposited in the archives of the United Nations.

2   The Secretary General of the United Nations shall transmit a certified copy of this convention to the States contemplated in Article VIII.

CHAPTER 12

EXTRATERRITORIAL CONTROL OF BUSINESS

INTRODUCTION

Many nations or trading blocks attempt to preserve competition by enacting legislation designed to prevent artificial distortions or restrictions occurring in the market place. This legislation usually aims at preventing trading entities monopolising the market by entering into arrangements which have the effect of reducing competition. A great problem arises when the nation or trading block attempts to apply its competition law extraterritorially. This chapter will discuss the manner by which the European Community (EC) applies its competition law and its anti-dumping law and how that law interacts with non resident trading entities and then make a brief comparison with how the USA attempts to control certain aspects of extraterritorial business activity.

As the EC is established by the Treaty of Rome[1] it will be first necessary to outline the competition law of the EC.

The EC was established as a common market, with a single external tariff and no tariff barriers between Member States. This has the result that when goods are landed in any Member State and are cleared for home consumption, those goods are free to circulate in any of the Member States.

If goods are exported to the EC and sold at lower prices than are charged for those goods in the home market of the goods (dumping) the EC is able, in some circumstances to apply an anti-dumping duty to offset the effects of the dumping. If the goods have been subsidised by the home government, the EC may be able to apply a countervailing duty to remove the effects of the subsidy. Both the anti-dumping duty and the countervailing duty apply to goods imported into the EC and so are both methods which the EC has to counter what it sees as unfair trading practices of non-EC businesses.

COMPETITION LAW OF THE EC

The EC has as one of its fundamental freedoms the freedom of movement of goods[2] and this fundamental freedom is reinforced by 'a system of ensuring that competition in the internal market is not distorted.'[3] Articles 85–94[4] implement the EC competition law.

---

1   Signed 25 March 1957 at Rome and came into effect 1 January 1958.

2   EC Treaty Article 3(c). Unless otherwise specified all references to an Article will be a reference to the EC Treaty. The Treaty provisions which ensure governments do not restrict free movement of goods are contained in Articles 30–36. These measures will not be dealt with in this chapter.

3   Article 3(g).

4   Title V: Common Rules on Competition, Taxation and Approximation of Laws. Chapter 1 (Rules on Competition) has three sections: s 1 Rules applying to undertakings (Articles 85–90), is the section with which this chapter will be involved.

The Council and Commission, acting under the powers granted by Articles 87 and 90, have made and promulgated a number of regulations concerning competition law. The most important of these is Regulation 17/62 which implements Articles 85 and 86.

Article 3(g) is the basis of EC competition law. Articles 85 and 86 implement this basic principle. Article 85(1) states:

> The following shall be prohibited as incompatible with the common market: all agreements between undertakings, decisions by associations of undertakings and concerted practices which may affect trade between Member States and which have as their object or effect the prevention restriction or distortion of competition within the common market ...

Agreements, within the meaning of Article 85(1) include both horizontal and vertical agreements. Horizontal agreements are those made between undertakings competing at the same level of commercial activity, for example at the retail level, whilst vertical agreements involve those made between undertakings at varying levels of commercial activity such as a manufacturer and retailer. Article 85(1) applies to all undertakings whether the undertaking supplies goods or services. Any agreement incompatible with Article 85(1) is rendered 'automatically void' by Article 85(2).

Articles 85 and 86 are directly effective. As the European Court of Justice (ECJ) stated in case 127/73 *Belgische Radio en Televisie v Sabam*:[5]

> ... as the prohibitions of Articles 85(1) and 86 tend by their very nature to produce direct effects in relations between individuals, these articles create direct rights in respect of the individuals concerned which the national courts must safeguard.[6]

Article 85(2), however, only operates to render the particular stipulations or decisions which are incompatible with Article 85(1) void. Where the void stipulations can not be severed then the whole agreement will be void.[7] Where only some of the terms of an agreement are void the validity of the remaining terms of the agreement is considered under the relevant national law.[8] This was considered by the High Court of England and Wales in *Inntrepreneur Estates Ltd v Mason*.[9] The brewery had leased a hotel to a publican, which lease contained two clauses which were in dispute. The first disputed clause required the publican to purchase beer from the lessor brewery (a tied house agreement). The second disputed clause was a forfeiture clause. The tie clause was held to be incompatible with Article 85 and therefore, in terms of Article 85(2), void. The defendant argued that as the tie clause was void the whole lease agreement was void as a

---

5   [1974] ECR 51; [1974] 2 CMLR 238.

6   *Ibid* at 62; 271.

7   Case 319/82 *Société de Vente de Ciments et Bétons de l'Est SA v Kerpen and Kerpen* [1983] ECR 4173; [1985] 1 CMLR 511.

8   Case 56/65 *Société Technique Minière v Mashinenbau Ulm GmbH* [1966] ECR 235; *Chemidus Wavin Ltd v Société pour la Transformation et l'Exploitation des Résiners Industrielles SA* [1987] 2 CMLR 387 *per* Walton J, Chancery Division High Court of Justice of England and Wales; affirmed [1977] FSR 181; [1978] 3 CMLR 514, Court of Appeal of England and Wales; *Inntrepreneur Estates Ltd v Mason* [1993] 2 CMLR 293.

9   [1993] 2 CMLR 293.

result. Therefore, the publican argued, he was not subject to the forfeiture clause of the lease. The court held that although the tie clause and related matters were void under community law, under English law the parties were in receipt of substantially that for which they had bargained and thus the defendant was bound by the valid remainder of the lease, which included the forfeiture clause.

Article 85(1) is restricted to arrangements that affect trade between Member States. Therefore, there must be a perceptible effect, actual or potential, on interstate trade before Article 85(1) is infringed.[10] However, arrangements confined in their operation to one Member State may be subject to EC competition law if those agreements impede the importation of goods from other Member States.[11] The types of agreements likely to distort competition in the EC is given by a non-comprehensive list in Article 85(1). The rules of competition may apply to agreements prescribed by the EC Treaty which affect both imports and exports of the Community, provided the other conditions of Articles 85 and 86 are met.

Not all agreements which are incompatible with Article 85 are prohibited. Article 85(3) allows for exemption from Article 85(1). To satisfy Article 85(3) the agreement must be one:

> ... which contributes to improving the production or distribution of goods or to promoting technical or economic progress, while allowing consumers a fair share of the resulting benefit, and which does not:
>
> (a) impose on the undertaking concerned restrictions which are not indispensable to the attainment of these objectives;
>
> (b) afford such undertakings the possibility of eliminating competition in respect of a substantial part of the products in question.[12]

Four conditions are set out in Article 85(3) and each one must be satisfied otherwise an exemption will be refused. Thus, any harmful effects arising from an agreement must be offset by two beneficial effects without being incompatible with Article 85(3)(a) or (b) if the agreement is to be exempted from the requirements of Article 85(1). Individual exemptions are of two types, negative clearance and declaration of inapplicability.

A negative clearance is sought under the terms of Regulation 17/62. Undertakings notify an agreement thought to be incompatible with the Treaty to the Commission and apply for a negative clearance. The Commission:

> ... may certify that, on the basis of the facts in its possession, there are no grounds under Article 85(1) or Article 86 of the Treaty for action on its part in respect of an agreement, decision or practice.[13]

Thus, if the Commission is of the opinion that the agreement notified to it is not incompatible with the Treaty it may so certify.

---

10 Case 28/77 *Tepa BV v Commission* [1978] ECR 1391.

11 Case 51/75 *EMI Records Ltd v CBS (UK) Ltd* [1976] ECR 811.

12 EC Treaty, Article 85(3).

13 Regulation 17/62, Article 2.

The Commission also has power given in Article 85(3) to declare that the provisions of Article 85(1) are inapplicable to an agreement. Article 85(1) prohibits agreements between undertakings which restrict or distort competition. Fines up to 10% of the gross annual turnover in the relevant goods in the previous year may be imposed for behaviour incompatible with Article 85.[14] Agreements which may be incompatible with Article 85(1) and for which the parties wish an exemption must be notified to the Commission.[15] The Commission then forms an opinion whether the agreements are incompatible with Article 85(1) and whether Article 85(3) is satisfied so as to allow an exemption to be granted. If the Commission refuses an exemption, the undertakings are liable to be fined.[16] The notification of an agreement which may infringe Article 85(1) gives the undertaking an immunity from fines from the notification until the Commission makes a decision.[17] This immunity is provided as the Commission may take significant time deciding whether to grant the exemption and if, during that time, the agreement was not given effect, the undertakings concerned might suffer considerable losses. But, after a preliminary investigation, the Commission may determine that the agreement appears to be incompatible with Article 85(1) and there does not appear to be grounds to justify an exemption then, upon the Commission so notifying the undertakings, the immunity ceases.[18]

If the Commission is of the opinion that the agreement as notified to it does not infringe Article 85, the Commission may not conduct a full investigation but may wish to close its file. When the investigation is so abbreviated by the Commission a letter, known as a comfort letter, is sent to the applicant undertakings. The relevance of a comfort letter was commented upon by the ECJ in joined cases 253/78 and 1–3/79 *Procureur de la République v Giry and Guerlain*:[19]

> It is plain that letters such as those sent to the companies in question by the Directorate-General for Competition, which were dispatched without publication as laid down in Article 19(3) of Regulation no 17 and which were not published pursuant to Article 21(1) of that regulation, constitute neither decisions granting negative clearance nor decisions in application of Article 85(3) within the meaning of Articles 2 and 6 of Regulation no 17. As is stressed by the Commission itself, they are merely administrative letters informing the undertaking concerned of the Commission's opinion that there is no need for it to take action in respect of the contracts in question under the provisions of Article 85(1) of the Treaty and that the file on the case may therefore be closed.

Such letters, which are based only upon the facts in the Commission's possession, and which reflect the Commission's assessment and bring to an end the procedure of examination by the department of the Commission responsible for this, do not have the effect of preventing national courts, before which the agreements in question are alleged

---

14 Regulation 17/62, Article 15.
15 Regulation 17/62, Article 4.
16 Regulation 17/62, Article 15(2).
17 Regulation 17/62, Article 15(5).
18 Regulation 17/62, Article 15(6).
19 [1980] ECR 2327; [1981] 2 CMLR 99.

to be incompatible with Article 85, from reaching a different finding as regards the agreements concerned on the basis of the information available to them.[20]

As is stated by the ECJ, the Commission makes its decision as to whether a comfort letter will be dispatched on the materials before it. The letter does not prevent a national court determining the compatibility of the impugned agreement with Article 85, and to decide the matter upon the material before the court. That is, an applicant for a negative clearance or a declaration of inapplicability should always make full and true disclosure of all material facts.

Due to the large number of undertakings within the EC, which have made agreements potentially incompatible with Article 85(1), the Commission has promulgated a number of block exemptions as regulations. If the agreements made by the undertakings remain within the specific terms of the relevant regulations, the agreements do not require to be notified to the Commission.[21]

US COMPETITION LAW

In the USA, the Sherman Act was enacted by Congress in 1890.[22] The Act, in its Article 1, declares any 'contract, combination ... or conspiracy, in restraint of trade or commerce among the several States, or with foreign nations' to be illegal. Congress promulgated this statute pursuant to its constitutional power to regulate interstate and foreign commerce. Marshall J decided in 1824 in *Gibbons v Ogden*[23] that the Commerce clause conceivably reaches 'every species of commercial intercourse between the US and foreign nations'.

OBJECTIVES OF EC COMPETITION RULES

The objective of the rules of competition is to give effect to Article 3(g) by ensuring that the trading patterns of the market are not distorted.

Article 85(1) is aimed at 'undertakings' but the Treaty does not define undertaking. The court has found that 'undertaking' is a wider and looser concept than is the concept of person.[24] The concept of undertaking does not depend upon the form of the legal character of the entity.[25] An essential characteristic is that the entity should pursue a commercial or economic activity.[26] Economic activity is widely construed and will

---

20 *Ibid* at 2,373–74; 135.

21 For examples of areas where block exemptions have been granted see Moens, G and Flint, D, *Business Law of the European Community,* 1993, para 4.1.4, Brisbane: DataLegal.

22 15 USC s 1, 1890.

23 22 US (9 Wheat) 1, 7, 6 L Ed 23, 69 (1824).

24 Joined cases 6–7/73 *Instituto Chemioterapico Italiano SpA and Commercial Solvents Corporation v Commission* [1974] ECR 223; [1974] 1 CMLR 309 *per* Advocate General Warner at 263; 319.

25 Case 32/65 *Republic of Italy v Council and Commission* [1966] ECR 389 at 418–19; [1969] CMLR 39 at 52 *per* Advocate General Roemer.

26 Case 155/73 *Guiseppi Sachi* [1974] ECR 409 at 430; [1974] 2 CMLR 177 at 183.

include cultural matters.[27] The Commission endorsed this wide view in its 9th Report on Competition Policy[28] where the rules were applied to professional sport. The absence of either a profit motive or a profit is irrelevant provided the objective of the entity is commercial or economic. This was summarised in case 41/90 *Hofner and Elser v Macrotron*[29] where the ECJ held 'in the context of competition law, the concept of an undertaking encompasses every entity engaged in economic activity, regardless of the legal status of the entity and the way it is financed'. Following the formulation in the *Hofner* case, it is not relevant if the entity is public or private for the competition rules to apply. An undertaking will thus not only include a company but also partnerships, mutual associations, agricultural co-operatives, performing rights societies, and even individuals, providing the entity is engaged in an economic activity.

The undertaking having a domicile outside the Community does not affect its existence as an undertaking for the purposes of the Community competition rules. A non-resident undertaking which is able to direct a subsidiary resident in a Member State is regarded as being resident in the European Community.[30] Such an undertaking is subject to EC competition law because it and its subsidiary are treated as one economic entity.[31] Being one economic entity means agreements between the subsidiary and its parent company are not agreements to which Article 85(1) applies.

If the undertaking does not conduct an economic activity it will not be caught by the competition rules. In joined cases 159 and 160/91 *Christian Poucet v Générales de France*[32] organisations were set up for the social function of administering a national social security system. The administration was not conducted as an economic activity and therefore the bodies were not undertakings for the purposes of Articles 85 and 86.

AGREEMENT FOR THE COMPETITION RULES

Essentially, for an agreement to come under Article 85, an undertaking must voluntarily reach a consensus or plan with another undertaking which limits its freedom of commercial action in relation to that other undertaking.[33] Thus, unilateral action will not create an agreement within the meaning of Article 85. Passive acceptance of an action may amount to an agreement for the purposes of Article 85. In case 107/82 *AEG v Commission*[34] AEG used standard terms and conditions of doing business and the passive acceptance of those standard terms and conditions amounted to an agreement

---

27 Joined cases 43 and 63/82 *Vereniging ter Bevordering van het Vlaamse Boekwezen (VBVB) and Vereniging ter Bevordering van de Belangen des Boekhandels (VBBBV) v Commission* [1984] ECR 19; [1985] 1 CMLR 27; CMR 14,042.

28 Point 116 concerning the English Football League. *Cf* professional football in Australia: *Adamson v Western Australian Football League* (1979) 143 CLR 190.

29 [1991] ECR 179.

30 Case 48/69 *ICI v Commission* [1972] ECR 619.

31 Case T102/92 *Viho Europe BV v Commission* [1995] ECR II 17.

32 [1993] ECR I 637.

33 Decision 74/634 *Re Franco-Japanese Ballbearings Agreement* [1975] 1 CMLR D 8.

34 [1983] ECR 3151; [1984] 3 CMLR 325.

which infringed Article 85. In case 277/87 *Sandoz Prodotti Farmacceutici Spa v Commission*[35] Sandoz had stamped its invoices 'export prohibited'. The Commission had fined Sandoz for behaviour incompatible with Article 85 and the ECJ dismissed an appeal against the fine. The course of business had created an agreement as the prohibition imposed by Sandoz had been agreed to by the customers. Even where there is no written agreement, the behaviour of the parties may evidence the existence of an agreement.[36] The characterisation of the 'agreement' in national law is irrelevant for the purposes of Article 85, as Article 85 applies throughout the EC.[37] As there is not a requirement for formality in the making of an agreement[38] the behaviour of undertakings may amount to an agreement.[39]

Concerted practices

Similar or even identical behaviour is not necessarily concerted practice unless the only reasonable explanation of the behaviour is implied agreement.[40] There must be an agreement for there to be a concerted practice. Therefore, if the similar or identical behaviour is the result of independent judgment the behaviour will not be incompatible with the Treaty. However, if there is not independent assessment, eg representatives of undertakings meeting with the aim of influencing the commercial behaviour of the other, that is sufficient to be a concerted action whether or not the undertakings formally adopt a plan.[41] A mutual understanding between two or more undertakings that a practice adopted by one will be adopted by the others will amount to concerted behaviour.[42]

The object of the agreement

Agreements 'which have as their object or effect the prevention, restriction, or distortion of competition within the common market' are incompatible with Article 85(1). Competition for Article 85(1) means the competition which would exist but for the agreement.[43] Therefore, an agreement may be incompatible with Article 85(1) even though the agreement has not entered into force. If the form of the agreement is not

---

35   [1990] ECR 45.

36   Case 107/82 *AEG-Telefunken AG v Commission* [1983] ECR 3151; [1984] 3 CMLR 325.

37   Case 8/72 *Vereniging van Cementhandelaren v Commission* [1972] ECR 977; [1973] CMLR 7.

38   For examples of what has been held to be an agreement see Moens, G and Flint, D, *Business Law of the European Community*, 1993, para 4.4.5, Brisbane: Data Legal.

39   Decision 80/257 *Re Rolled Steel* [1980] 3 CMLR 193.

40   *Ahlstrom Osakeyhito and Others v Commission* (*Wood Pulp* case) [1993] ECR 1307; [1993] 4 CMLR 407.

41   Case 48/69 *ICI v Commission* [1972] ECR 619.

42   See case 28/77 *Tepea BV v Commission* [1978] ECR 1391 at 1416; [1978] 3 CMLR 392 at 415; CMR 8467 where manufacturers and their distributors cooperated to identify parallel importers, a finding of a concerted practice incompatible with Article 85 was found. See also case 86/82 *Hasselblad (GB) Ltd v Commission* [1984] ECR 883; [1984] 1 CMLR 559; CMR 14,014.

43   Case 56/65 *Société Technique Miniére v Maschinenbau Ulm GmbH* [1966] ECR 235; [1966] CMLR 357; CMR 8047.

expressed in a manner which makes the agreement incompatible with Article 85(1), then the actual operation of the agreement is examined to decide whether Article 85 is infringed.

In Article 85(1), the terms 'prevention, restriction or distortion' are not mutually exclusive so it is not necessary to inquire which term most accurately describes the challenged agreement or practice.

Effect on trade between Member States

Article 85(1) only applies to an agreement or practice that affects trade between Member States.[44] This requirement sets the boundary between Community and national law. However, anti-competitive behaviour within a Member State may effect trade between Member States and so be incompatible with the Treaty.[45] Anti-competitive conduct which only affects trade within a single Member State is governed by the law of the Member State concerned.[46] The Commission has given trade a wide definition in EC competition law. In Decision 81/103 *Re GVL*,[47] the Commission asserted that trade encompassed all commercial and business transactions, including the provision of services. In its case law the ECJ has found that trade includes banking,[48] insurance[49] and telecommunications.[50] The key point:

> ... is whether the agreement is capable of constituting a threat, either direct or indirect, actual or potential, to freedom of trade between Member States in a manner which might harm the attainment of the objectives of a single market between States.[51]

So, if an agreement or practice makes such a threat it will be incompatible with Article 85(1).[52]

The *Wood Pulp* case

In joined cases 89, 104, 116–17 and 125–129/85 *Ahlstrom Osakeyhtio and Others v Commission* (*Wood Pulp* case)[53] the ECJ had to consider these principles. Wood pulp

---

44 Case 28/77 *Tepa BV v Commission* [1978] ECR 1391.

45 Case 51/75 *EMI Records Ltd v CBS (UK) Ltd* [1976] ECR 811.

46 Case 22/78 *Hugin Kassaregister AB v Commission* [1979] ECR 1869; [1979] 3 CMLR 345; CMR 8524.

47 [1982] 1 CMLR 221.

48 Case 172/80 *Züchner v Bayerische Vereinsbank AG* [1981] ECR 2021; [1982] 1 CMLR 313; CMR 8706.

49 Decision 85/75 *Re Fire Insurance* [1985] 3 CMLR 246.

50 Decision 82/861 *Re British Telecommunications* [1983] 1 CMLR 457 affirmed by the court in case 41/83 *Republic of Italy v Commission* [1985] ECR 873; [1985] 2 CMLR 368; CMR 8135.

51 Joined cases 56 and 58/64 *Consten and Grundig v Commission* [1966] ECR 299 at 341. See also case 5/69 *Volk v Vervaecke* [1969] ECR 295; [1969] CMLR 273; CMR 8074; case 1/71 *Cadillon SA v Hoss Maschinenbau KG* [1971] ECR 351; [1971] CMLR 420; CMR 8135.

52 Case 19/77 *Miller International Schallplatten GmbH v Commission* [1978] ECR 131; [1978] 2 CMLR 334; CMR 8439.

53 [1988] ECR 5193; [1988] 4 CMLR 901.

producers, who had their registered offices outside the EC, had formed a trade association which assisted the producers to sell their pulp to paper manufacturers inside the EC. The wood pulp was mainly produced in Canada, USA, Sweden and Finland. The Commission investigated the agreement made by the producers and concluded that Article 85(1) had been infringed particularly with respect to price fixing, recommendations as to prices to be charged for pulp and the exchange of information between Members of the Association. The Commission fined the Association and its Members. Actions were brought by several of the fined entities under Article 173 to annul the decision of the Commission, on the grounds that the Commission had no jurisdiction to make a decision against foreign undertakings.

The ECJ held that where pulp was produced outside the EC and the producers engage in price competition to sell the pulp to manufacturers within the EC then that constituted competition within the EC. It therefore followed that where the producers had coordinated the prices at which they would sell within the EC, that was concerted action to restrict competition within the EC and so was incompatible with Article 85(1), that is the ECJ held that where the effect of the concerted action was effective within the EC that behaviour was incompatible with Article 85(1). The applicants for annulment specifically argued that the decision of the Commission was incompatible with public international law in that the Commission had made an error in the territorial scope of Article 85(1) as the decision was based exclusively on the economic effects of an agreement made outside the EC and having its effect within the EC, that is both the formation and effect of the agreement should take place within the EC. The ECJ answered this argument by holding that an infringement of Article 85 has two elements, the formation of an incompatible agreement and then the implementation of that agreement. If the place of the formation of the agreement was to be the critical feature EC competition law would be easily evaded and therefore the decisive factor was where the agreement was implemented. As the agreement was implemented within the EC; whether or not the undertakings used agents, branches or subsidiaries; and the applicants had been involved in the making of the agreement, the behaviour incompatible with Article 85(1) took place within the EC and thus was within the jurisdiction of the Commission to apply EC law within the EC.

Abuse of a dominant position

While Article 85 deals with concerted action, Article 86 deals with unilateral action. Article 86 prohibits the abuse of a dominant position and ascribes abuse to four types of behaviour:

1   imposition of unfair trading conditions, especially regarding price;[54]

2   the limiting of production, markets or technical development to the prejudice of consumers;[55]

---

54   Case 27/76 *United Brands Co v Commission* [1978] ECR 207: joined cases 40–48, 50, 54–56, 111 and 113–14/73 *Coöperatieve Vereniging 'Suiker Unie' (CSM) v EC Commission* [1975] ECR 1663; [1976] 1 CMLR 295; CMR 8334.

55   Joined cases 40–48, 50, 54–56, 111 and 113–14/73 *Coöperatieve Vereniging 'Suiker Unie' (CSM) v EC Commission* [1975] ECR 1663; [1976] 1 CMLR 295; CMR 8334.

3   applying dissimilar conditions to equivalent transactions so that competitors are placed at a disadvantage in the market;[56] and

4   arrangements where a trading partner is obliged to enter upon supplementary obligations to take goods or services not related to the fundamental terms of the transaction.[57]

A dominant position, *per se*, is not incompatible with Article 86, as the dominant position may be the result of the undertaking's efficiency or ability to correctly anticipate the requirements of the market. Compare the US decision in *United States v Aluminium Co of America (ALCOA)*[58] where the Supreme Court of the USA held that ALCOA had breached the Sherman Act by anticipating the needs of the market and had thus established an illegal monopoly. It is the abuse of the dominant position which is incompatible with Article 86. A dominant position most usually is a position of economic strength which insulates an undertaking from effective competition. If an undertaking is in a dominant position it may be an abuse of that position if an attempt is made by the undertaking to lessen its competition by launching a takeover bid for a competitor.[59] In common with Article 85(1), Article 86 is a detailed implementation of Article 3(g) of the Treaty. Behaviour is incompatible with Article 86 if:

1   there is an undertaking in a dominant position;

2   there is an abuse of that position; and

3   the abuse is prejudicial to trade between the Member States.

Article 86 of the Treaty applies to all undertakings whether private or public institutions. It also applies to statutory authorities and non–profit organisations.

Article 86 not only has direct effect[60] which gives individuals rights which the national courts have a duty to uphold, but also is an independent legal right not subject to Article 85. This was decided in case T51/89 *Tetra Pak Rausing v Commission*[61] where the applicant argued that it could not be fined for infringement of Article 86 where an exemption was in force under Article 85(3). The court found that the two articles were independent legal powers and so it was possible for an undertaking to abuse a dominant position notwithstanding that the agreement giving rise to the abuse was exempted from the operation of Article 85.

Abuse is defined in an objective manner as shown in case 85/76 *Hoffmann-La Roche and Co AG v Commission*[62] where the court held:

---

56   Case 27/76 *United Brands Co v Commission* [1978] ECR 207.

57   Case 26/75 *General Motors Continental BV v Commission* [1975] ECR 1367: *Inntrepreneur Estates Ltd v Mason* [1993] 2 CMLR 293.

58   148 F 2d 416 (1945).

59   Case 6/72 *Europemballage and Continental Can Co Inc v Commission* [1973] ECR 215.

60   Case 127/73 *BRT v SABAM* [1974] ECR 51 at 62.

61   [1990] ECR II 309.

62   [1979] ECR 461; [1979] 3 CMLR 211; CMR 8527: see also case 31/80 *L'Oréal v De Nieuwe AMCK* [1980] ECR 3775; [1981] 2 CMLR 235; CMR 8715: case 322/81 *Nederlandsche Banden-industrie Michelin NV v Commission* [1983] ECR 3461; [1985] 1 CMLR 282; CMR 14,031.

Article 86 prohibits any abuse by an undertaking of a dominant position in a substantial part of the Common Market in so far as it may affect trade between Member States. The dominant position thus referred to relates to a position of economic strength enjoyed by an undertaking which enables it to prevent effective competition being maintained on the relevant market by affording it the power to behave to an appreciable extent independently of its competitors, its customers and ultimately of the consumers ... An undertaking which has a very large market share and holds it for some time, by means of the volume of production and the scale of the supply which it stands for ... is by virtue of that share in a position of strength which makes it an unavoidable trading partner and which, already because of this, secures for it, at the very least during a relatively long period, that freedom of action which is the special feature of a dominant position.[63]

Location of the abuse

Article 86 applies to abuse of a dominant position 'within the common market or in a substantial part of it'. The area in which the abuse takes place is therefore the 'relevant product market'. In case 27/76 *United Brands Co and United Brands Continental BV v Commission*[64] the ECJ held, in relation to the relevant product market for bananas:

For the banana to be regarded as forming a market which is sufficiently differentiated from other fruit markets it must be possible for it to be singled out by such special features distinguishing it from other fruits that it is only to a limited extent interchangeable with them and is only exposed to their competition in a way that is hardly perceptible.

This means that the market for bananas must be sufficiently differentiated from the market for other goods so that if bananas are not available in the accepted price range there is only a limited substitution of other goods for bananas and therefore bananas are either not exposed to competition from other products or only exposed to competition in a way which is hardly perceptible. Obviously, what holds good for bananas holds good for any product. If two or more products are readily substituted, the relevant product market will contain all those products although they may not be exactly the same.[65]

The degree to which goods would be substituted may assist in defining the relevant product market. If small price rises of goods A would lead to a large substitution of goods B for goods A, goods B are part of the relevant product market of goods A. But where large price rises of goods A would lead to only a minimal small amount of substitution by goods B, goods B are not part of the relevant product market of goods A.

The dominant position of the undertaking need not encompass the whole of the EC. The geographic extent of the market for which a dominant position is considered 'is an area where the objective conditions of competition applying to the product in

---

63   *Ibid* at 520–21; 275.

64   [1978] ECR 207, 272; [1978] 1 CMLR 429 at 482–83; CMR 8429.

65   Joined cases 19 and 20/74 *Kali und Salz und Kali-Chemie v Commission* [1975] ECR 499; [1975] 2 CMLR 154 where potash fertiliser and compound potash fertiliser were in the one relevant product market.

question must be the same for all traders',[66] that is, the geographic extent of the market is the geographic area in which the product is marketed under similar conditions. The sales of the undertaking as a proportion of total sales in that district also is used in determining the relevant market. The volume and consumption of goods within the relevant geographical area is also used to test whether the district is a substantial portion of the EC. If the whole of the EC is not the relevant market then the relevant market will, naturally, be portion of the EC. However, to determine whether an undertaking within the Community has achieved a dominant position, an examination of the activities of the undertaking outside the Community may be required. The relationship of an undertaking to a multinational group may also be relevant to the determination of dominance. Portions of the EC which have been found to be a 'substantial part' of the EC include Belgium and Luxemburg, Belgium, the southern part of Germany, Germany, and The Netherlands.

Derogation from free movement of goods

Article 36 allows a derogation from the free movement of goods and services on the grounds of the 'protection of industrial and commercial property'. When the intellectual property rights, given by the law of the Member States, are exercised in conformity with Article 36, Article 86 is not infringed on the ground that the undertaking is in a dominant position.[67] If goods protected by a patent are exorbitantly priced, if the price is not justifiable by objective criteria, this may be evidence of an abuse of dominant position.

Where the combined operations of several undertakings amounts to a dominant position and the undertakings engage in concerted practices incompatible with Article 85(1) the undertakings may be regarded as an economic unit with the members of that unit being jointly and severally liable for the damage caused. However, it is likely that the behaviour would be dealt with under Article 85 rather than Article 86.

To establish an abuse of a dominant position, the court does not have to find an intention on the part of the undertaking to act in a manner incompatible with Article 86. However, if an undertaking, which is in a dominant position, acts in a objectionable manner towards competitors, the objectionable behaviour may convert otherwise acceptable behaviour into behaviour incompatible with Article 86.

As with Article 85, the scope of Article 86 is restricted by the requirement that the abuse of a dominant position should affect trade between Member States, leaving trade within Member States to be regulated by the law of the Member States. As in Article 85, the meaning of trade in Article 86 has been given a wide meaning. Article 86 has been applied to prevent abuse of a dominant position in telecommunication services, insurance, banking, copyright collecting societies, television advertising, type approvals for motor cars and film distribution.

---

66 Case 27/76 *United Brands Co and United Brands Continental BV v Commission* [1978] ECR 207 at 274.

67 Case 102/77 *Hoffmann-La Roche and Co AG v Centrafarm Pharmazeutischer Erzeugnisse GmbH* [1978] ECR 1139; [1978] 3 CMLR 217; CMR 8466.

The allegation of abuse of a dominant position would be raised in national courts and those courts have the duty to give effect to the rights created by Article 86.[68] The court would assess the effect of an abuse of a dominant position to decide the matters being litigated.[69]

COMMERCIAL LAW OF THE EC

The common commercial policy of the European Community is based on Articles 110–15 of the EC Treaty. Article 110 reads as follows:

> By establishing a customs union between themselves Member States aim to contribute, in the common interest, to the harmonious development of world trade, the progressive abolition of restrictions on international trade and the lowering of customs barriers.
>
> The common commercial policy shall take into account the favourable effect which the abolition of customs duties between Member States may have on the increase in the competitive strength of undertakings in those States.

Article 110 of the Treaty apparently indicates that the main thrust of the commercial policy of the EC is basically concerned with the import and export of goods. However, Article 113 indicates that the commercial policy is not so restricted.

Article 113 states:

1   The common commercial policy shall be based on uniform principles, particularly in regard to changes in tariff rates, the conclusion of tariff and trade agreements, the achievement of uniformity in measures of liberalisation, export policy and measures to protect trade such as those to be taken in case of dumping or subsidies.

2   The Commission shall submit proposals to the Council for implementing the common commercial policy.

3   Where agreements with one or more States or international organisations need to be negotiated, the Commission shall make recommendations to the Council, which shall authorise the Commission to open the necessary negotiations.

   The Commission shall conduct these negotiations in consultation with a special committee appointed by the Council to assist the Commission in this task and within the framework of such directives as the Council may issue to it.

   The relevant provisions of Article 228 shall apply.

4   In exercising the powers conferred upon it by this article, the Council shall act by a qualified majority.

In *Re International Agreement on Natural Rubber*,[70] the court gave Article 113 a wide meaning. The court said:[71]

---

68   Case 127/73 *Belgische Radio en Televisie and Société Belge des Auteurs, Compositeurs et Editeurs v SV SABAM and NV Fonier* [1974] ECR 51 and [1974] ECR 313; [1974] 2 CMLR 238; CMR 8268: case 37/79 *Anne Marty SA v Estée Lauder SA* [1980] ECR 2481; [1981] 2 CMLR 143; CMR 8713.

69   Case 22/79 *Greenwich Film Production v Société des Auteurs, Compositeurs et Editeurs de Musique (SCAEM) and Société des Editions Labrador* [1979] ECR 3275; [1980] 1 CMLR 629.

70   [1979] ECR 2871; [1979] 3 CMLR 639.

71   At 2913; 677.

Article 113 empowers the Community to formulate a commercial 'policy', based on 'uniform principles' thus showing that the question of external trade must be governed from a wide point of view and not only having regard to the administration of precise systems such as customs and quantitative restrictions. The same conclusion may be deduced from the fact that the enumeration in Article 113 of the subjects covered by commercial policy (changes in tariff rates, the conclusion of tariff and trade agreements, the achievement of uniformity in measures of liberalisation, export policy and measures to protect trade) is conceived as a non-exhaustive enumeration which must not, as such, close the door to the application in a Community context of any other process intended to regulate external trade. A restrictive interpretation of the concept of common commercial policy would risk causing disturbances in intra-Community trade by reason of the disparities which would then exist in certain sectors of economic relations with non-Member countries.

Thus, the EC common commercial policy goes further than import and export of goods. Indeed, Article 113 specifically provides for the EC itself to become a party to tariff and trade agreements with third countries.[72] Under the powers to implement the common commercial policy, the EC has established a common external tariff. Another feature of the common commercial policy is the measures which may be taken by the EC to protect trade, including the introduction of anti-dumping and countervailing duties. It is largely by this feature of the common commercial policy that the EC attempts to control extraterritorial business.

Anti-dumping and subsidies

Article 113 allows the EC, *inter alia*, to enter into agreements to liberalise world trade, to hold membership of the World Trade Organisation (WTO) (formerly General Agreement on Tariffs and Trade (GATT)) or to enter into agreements which allow for access, by third countries, to markets in the Community. An example where the EC has provided for access by other nations to the common internal market of the EC is provided by the successive Lomé Conventions. These Conventions have allowed a number of products originating in African, Carribean and Pacific countries to enjoy free access to the EC market.

As there is not a *laissez-faire* system of world trade and some world traders may subscribe to the theory that greed is good, the EC will monitor unfair trade practices of third countries or foreign producers or manufacturers of goods. Article 113 lists dumping and subsidies as measures to be countered to protect trade.

As part of the common commercial policy, anti-dumping provisions were first adopted by the Council in Regulation 459/68.[73] The current anti-dumping regulation is Regulation 2423/88[74] on protection against dumped or subsidised imports from countries not Members of the European Community. The current regulation was adopted on 11 July 1988. Article 5(3) of Regulation 2423/88 makes the Commission

---

72   See also Council Regulation 288/82 on Common Rules for Imports.

73   1968 OJ L256/1. See also Council Regulation 2641/84, 1984 OJ L252/1.

74   1988 OJ L209/1.

responsible for the investigation of complaints lodged under the anti-dumping law. These complaints are investigated by the Anti-dumping Unit of the Commission. Article 12 of Regulation 2423/88 gives the Council power to impose anti-dumping duties or countervailing duties.

Article 1 of Regulation 2423/88 states that it 'lays down provisions for protection against dumped or subsidised imports from countries not Members of the European Economic Community'. Articles 85 and 86 are used to counter dumping by a Member State into another Member State.

Article VI of GATT grants the justification of the EC law regarding anti-dumping and countervailing duties. It reads, in its relevant part, as follows:

1   The contracting parties recognise that dumping, by which products of one country are introduced into the commerce of another country at less than the normal value of the products, is to be condemned if it causes or threatens material injury to an established industry in the territory of a contracting party or materially retards the establishment of a domestic industry. For the purposes of this article, a product is to be considered as being introduced into the commerce of an importing country at less than its normal value, if the price of the product exported from one country to another:

   (a) is less than the comparable price, in the ordinary course of trade, for the like product when destined for consumption in the exporting country ...

3   No countervailing duty shall be levied on any product of the territory of any contracting party imported into the territory of another contracting party in excess of an amount equal to the estimated bounty or subsidy determined to have been granted, directly or indirectly, on the manufacture, production or export of such product in the country of origin or exportation, including any special subsidy to the transportation of a particular product.

Article VI of GATT reveals that dumping involves the practice of selling products in an external market at a lower price than that charged in the home market. In other words, dumping in the EC involves an exporter of goods to the EC selling those goods at a price lower than that commonplace in the home market of the exporter. The mere selling of products at a lower price than that charged for similar products in the importing State does not, of itself, constitute dumping.

To ascertain if dumping has occurred the domestic price of the goods (the normal value) is compared to the price charged in the EC (the export price). Any investigation of an alleged incident of dumping requires the normal price and the export price to be established. Once established, the two prices are compared at a like level of trade. Dumping is typified by the export price being less than the normal price.[75]

The amount by which the normal value exceeds the export price is the dumping margin.[76] Where injury to EC manufacturers is caused or is threatened by the dumping, the Council may impose an anti-dumping duty on the dumped goods.[77] The

---

75 Article 2(2) of Regulation 2423/88.

76 Article 2(14) of Regulation 2423/88.

77 Article 2(1) of Regulation 2423/88.

Commission will usually investigate the six months immediately preceding the lodgement of the complaint.[78] However, the time span investigated is indeterminate as the Commission has a wide discretion as to the period to be considered in determining whether an injury has occurred to Community industry.[79] For example, in *Epicheiriseon Metalleftikon Viomichanikon Kai Naftiliakon and Others v Council*,[80] the court found that sales over a period of four years could be taken into account in the circumstances of that case under the terms of Article 4(1) of Regulation 2176/84.[81]

The normal value of goods is the price paid for the product on the domestic or home market of the exporter.[82] The normal value can only be calculated this way when the product concerned or like products are on sale in the domestic market of the exporter. Like products are products which have features approximating the features of the goods being investigated.[83] As the sales on the domestic market must be in the ordinary course of trade, sales to related companies are not accepted as being in the normal course of trade.[84] Where the goods are solely produced for the export market, the normal value will be the price of the goods in a third market[85] or the constructed price.

The constructed price is the price calculated by adding the costs of production and a reasonable profit margin.[86] As the constructed price is calculated to represent the price charged in the domestic market of the producer all costs of sales on the domestic market are included in the constructed price.[87] In *NTN Toyo Bearing Co Ltd v Council*,[88] the applicant challenged the regulation which imposed the definitive anti-dumping duty because, in calculating the dumping margin the normal value had been calculated as the weighted average of the prices charged in the domestic market and the export price had been ascertained from each transaction. The court held Article 2(13)(b) of Regulation 2176/84[89] gave the Commission a discretion to employ the most appropriate method in calculating the constructed price to prevent damage to EC industry caused by the dumping of goods on the EC Market. Where an attempt to disguise the dumping is made by charging different prices for each consignment of goods, with these prices fluctuating about the normal value, taking the price of each transaction is an appropriate means to deal with the procedure. By using the weighted average method to determine

---

78 Regulation 2423/88, Article 7(1)(c).
79 Regulation 2423/88, Article 4.
80 [1989] ECR 3919.
81 Now Regulation 2423/88, Article 4(1).
82 Regulation 2423/88, Article 2(3)(a).
83 Regulation 2423/88, Article 2(12).
84 Regulation 2423/88, Article 2(7).
85 Regulation 2423/88, Article 2(3)(b)(i).
86 Regulation 2423/88, Article 2(3)(b)(ii).
87 *Brother Industries Ltd and Others v Commission* [1988] ECR 5655; [1990] 1 CMLR 792; [1990] 1 CEC 594.
88 [1987] ECR 1809; [1989] 2 CMLR 76; CMR 14,386.
89 Now Regulation 2423/88, Article 2(13).

the export price in this case would have disguised the dumping and so prevented the application of an anti-dumping duty to the injury suffered by the Community industry. This principle has been applied in numerous cases, for example, *Nippon Seiko KK v Council*,[90] *Mineba Co Ltd v Council*,[91] *Nachi Fujikoshi Corp v Council*,[92] *Canon Inc v Council*,[93] *Tokyo Electric Co Ltd v Council*[94] and *Silver Seiko Ltd v Council*.[95]

Constructed value includes sales costs

Where sales are made by a subsidiary company, the costs of this company may be included in the construction of the normal value as occurred in *Tokyo Electric Co Ltd v Council*.[96] Tokyo Electric made its domestic sales through a subsidiary rather than its own sales department. The goods in question, electronic typewriters, were not sold on the domestic market, but in constructing the normal value, the costs of the subsidiary were taken into account. These costs of sales were thereby included in the normal price of the goods.

Constructed value includes profit

The constructed normal value will include a reasonable amount for the profit margin.[97] When assessing the profit margin, the Commission is under no obligation to select the profit margin of the parent or the subsidiary but may add the two profit margins. This information may not be available from the undertaking, and so may be an estimate based upon confidential information of competitors of the impugned undertaking. In *Tokyo Electric Co Ltd v Council*,[98] the court held that a profit margin had to be included in the normal price or there would be a miscalculation of the dumping margin and therefore when a definitive anti-dumping duty was imposed the damage done by the dumping would not be fully remedied. In *Canon Inc v Council*,[99] it was argued that Article 2(3)(b) of Regulation 2176/84[100] required that the Commission should adopt the price of the product when it was exported to a third country as the normal value, when there was no domestic price. The court held that Article 2(3)(b) 'does not indicate that use of the price for exportation to a third country is to take precedence over construction of the

---

90   [1987] ECR 1923; [1989] 2 CMLR 76; CMR 14,369.

91   [1987] ECR 1975; [1989] 2 CMLR 76; CMR 14,370.

92   [1987] ECR 1861; [1989] 2 CMLR 76; CMR 14,486.

93   [1988] ECR 5731; [1989] 1 CMLR 915; CMR 14,514.

94   [1988] ECR 5855; [1989] 1 CMLR 169; CMR 14,512.

95   [1988] ECR 5927; [1989] 1 CMLR 249; CMR 14,513.

96   [1988] ECR 5855; [1989] 1 CMLR 169; CMR 14,512. See also *Sharp Corp v Council* [1988] ECR 5813; CMR 14515.

97   Regulation 2423/88, Article 2(3)(b)(ii).

98   [1988] ECR 5855; [1989] 1 CMLR 169; CMR 14,512.

99   [1988] ECR 5731; [1989] 1 CMLR 915; CMR 14,514.

100 Now Regulation 2423/88, Article 2(3)(b).

normal value'.[101] The Commission has a discretion in constructing the normal price where figures are not available from the undertaking concerned. If the constructed price is challenged the onus is on the applicant to show that the discretion has been abused.

Export price

The export price is usually the price paid by the EC importer.[102] Regulation 2423/88 allows the export price to be constructed where there is no export price, eg in situations involving barter; where there appears to be an association between the exporter and importer,[103] eg where the importer is a subsidiary of the exporter; and where the price charged by the exporter is unreliable for other reasons.[104]

Calculation of the constructed export price

The constructed export price is calculated by adding to the price of the goods when they are first sold to an independent reseller the costs incurred between importation and resale and a reasonable profit margin.[105] Where the goods are not sold to an independent reseller, or the goods are inputs for further manufacture, the constructed export price is calculated on a reasonable basis.[106] In *Silver Seiko v Council*,[107] the court held that the Commission, under Article 2(8)(b) of Regulation 2176/84,[108] could disregard the invoice price paid by a subsidiary located within the EC to its parent and rely upon a price paid by an independent importer. The comparison of the normal price and export price is made at the same level of trade, usually at the factory gate.

Differences in exchange rate considered

As the normal value is the domestic price of the goods and the export price is the price paid in the EC there must be a attention given to exchange rates. In *Nachi Fujikoshi Corp v Council*,[109] the Council had used an average over a period of twelve months in order to take account of a fluctuating exchange rate. This method of calculation was upheld.

---

101 *Canon Inc v Council* [1988] ECR 5731 at 5800; [1989] 1 CMLR 915 at 947–48.

102 Regulation 2423/88, Article 2(8)(a).

103 Regulation 2423/88, Article 2(8)(b).

104 *Ibid.*

105 Regulation 2423/88, Article 2(8)(b)(i)–(iii). See also *Nachi Fujikoshi Corp v Council* [1987] ECR 1861; [1989] 2 CMLR 76; CMR 14,486; *Nippon Seiko KK v Council* [1987] ECR 1923; [1989] 2 CMLR 76; CMR 14369 and *Mineba Co Ltd v Council* [1987] ECR 1975; [1989] 2 CMLR 76; CMR 14370.

106 Regulation 2423/88, Article 2(8)(b).

107 [1988] ECR 5927; [1989] 1 CMLR 249; CMR 14,513

108 Now Regulation 2423/88, Article 2(8)(b).

109 [1987] ECR 1861; [1989] 2 CMLR 76; CMR 14,486.

Dumping margin

Usually, the dumping margin is the amount by which the normal value exceeds the export price.[110] However, where, dumping margins vary in each transaction the Commission may establish the dumping margin of each transaction, or by reference to the most frequently recurring transaction or on a weighted average price basis.[111] The calculation of the dumping margin is to permit the application of an anti-dumping duty to remove the damage to EC industry caused by goods being dumped.

Subsidies

If a subsidy is paid on goods exported to the EC a countervailing duty may be imposed to offset the effect of the subsidy, if the payment of the subsidy allows the goods to be sold at a price which causes injury in the EC.[112] In the Annex to Regulation 2423/88 is an illustrative, non-exhaustive, list of export subsidies.[113] Where exports are exempted from taxes assessed upon domestically sold goods, that exemption is not a subsidy. Article VI(4) of GATT states that:

> No product of the territory of any contracting party imported into the territory of any
> other contracting party shall be subject to anti-dumping or countervailing duty by reason
> of the exemption of such product from duties or taxes borne by the like product when
> destined for consumption in the country of origin or exportation, or by reason of the
> refund of such duties or taxes.

Article VI of GATT is given effect to by Article 3(3) of Regulation 2423/88. Article VI of Gatt was applied by the US Supreme Court in *Zenith Radio Corp v United States*.[114] The court considered a Japanese law which exempted exports from taxes imposed upon the manufacture of electronic goods. The taxes were remitted to the manufacturer upon proof of export of the goods. The court decided that the tax exemption was not subject to countervailing duty because the amount remitted did not exceed the tax payable.

Types of subsidy

The subsidy is usually paid on the basis per unit of the goods exported.[115] Fees and costs necessarily incurred to obtain the subsidy are subtracted from the subsidy.[116] If the subsidy is not paid on a unit basis, the amount per unit of the subsidy is determined by allocating the subsidy over a period, usually the accounting year of the recipient of the

---

110 Regulation 2423/88, Article 2(14)(a).
111 Regulation 2423/88, Article 2(14)(b).
112 Regulation 2423/88, Article 3(1).
113 Regulation 2423/88, Article 3(2).
114 437 US 443 (1978).
115 Regulation 2423/88, Article 3(4)(a).
116 Regulation 2423/88, Article 3(4).

subsidy thus arriving at a nominal unit amount.[117] Where the subsidy is paid for the purchase of fixed assets, the subsidy is spread over a period which reflects the life of the assets in that industry. Where the assets do not depreciate, the subsidy is treated as an interest-free loan.[118] 'Where the amount of subsidisation varies, weighted averages may be established.'[119]

Injury

The Commission is only empowered to make a finding of injury when the dumping or subsidisation of goods causes injury to an established Community industry or substantially impedes the establishment of an industry.[120] The alleged injury is tested by the effect upon similar products produced in the EC.[121] If the difficulties of EC producers are caused by an increase of imports or a decrease in the price of imports when those imports are not dumped or subsidised, it is not open to the Commission to make a finding that the imports are causing injury.[122] This was stated in *Epicheiriseon Metalleftikon Viomichanikon Kai Naftiliakon v Council*[123] where the court held that Article 4(1) of Regulation 2176/84[124] does not prevent:

> ... the existence of injury allegedly suffered by Community industries from being ascertained independently of the two other conditions required for the imposition of anti-dumping duties, namely a definitive finding of dumping and the need to act in the interests of the Community.[125]

The court found that the wording of Articles 2 and 4 of Regulation 2176/84[126] indicated that a finding of dumping or injury was established on different requirements, therefore they were to be established independently. This means that once there was a finding of no injury the investigation could be terminated.

Factors of injury

The factors which are considered in a finding of injury are:

> An examination of injury shall involve the following factors, no one or several of which can necessarily give decisive guidance:
>
> (a) volume of dumped or subsidised imports, in particular whether there has been a significant increase, either in absolute terms or relative to production or consumption in the Community;

---

117 Regulation 2423/88, Article 3(4)(c).
118 *Ibid.*
119 Regulation 2423/88, Article 3(4)(e).
120 Regulation 2423/88, Article 4(1).
121 Regulation 2423/88, Article 4(4).
122 Regulation 2423/88, Article 4(4).
123 [1989] ECR 3919.
124 Now Regulation 2423/88, Article 4(1).
125 *Epicheiriseon Metalleftikon Viomichanikon Kai Naftiliakon v Council* [1989] ECR 3919 at 3951.
126 Now Regulation 2423/88, Articles 2 and 4.

(b) the prices of dumped or subsidised imports, in particular whether there has been a significant price undercutting as compared with the price of a like product in the Community;

(c) the consequent impact on the industry concerned as indicated by actual or potential trends in the relevant economic factors such as: production, utilisation of capacity, stocks, sales, market share, prices (ie depression of prices or prevention of price increases which otherwise would have occurred), profits, return on investment, cash flow, employment.[127]

In *Silver Seiko Ltd v Council*[128] the court considered the factors listed in Article 4(2) of Regulation 2176/84.[129] It held that the list is merely representative and therefore the Commission has a discretion as to the weight to be given to each factor and even if a factor is given no weight that does not render a finding *ultra vires*. Further, the Commission is able to aggregate the dumping of numerous undertakings, even when the undertakings are located in different non-Member States, to consider the overall effect upon the Community industry, even where the exports from each non-Member State are small.[130] In *Canon Inc v Council*,[131] the court held that it was possible to establish injury to EC industry notwithstanding that the sales of the Community industry actually increased during the period of the injury. The evidence in this case indicated that the EC producers had an increasing volume of sales but a declining market share of an expanding market. The court upheld the finding of the Commission that the market share was declining because of dumping. Should there be factors additional to the dumping causing the injury the anti-dumping duty is set at a level to remove the injury directly attributable to the dumping.[132]

Where dumping and injury have been established

Where dumping and injury had been established, the Council and the Commission have a discretion to decide whether an anti-dumping duty is in the interests of the Community.[133] The fact 'that a Community producer is facing difficulties attributable in part to causes other than dumping is not a reason for depriving that producer of all protection against the injury caused by the dumping'.[134] Where an exporter was found to have dumped products in the EC, and some EC undertakings had imported a small quantity some of the lower priced models manufactured by the exporter, which models were sold under the importers' brand the court found that importers had been injured by the dumping.[135]

---

127 Regulation 2423/88, Article 4(2).

128 [1988] ECR 5927; [1989] 1 CMLR 249; CMR 14,513.

129 Now Regulation 2423/88, Article 4(2).

130 *Technointorg v Council and Commission* [1988] ECR 6077; [1989] 1 CMLR 281; [1989] CEC 160.

131 [1988] ECR 5731; [1989] 1 CMLR 915; CMR 14,514.

132 *Canon Inc v Council* [1988] ECR 5731; [1989] 1 CMLR 915; CMR 14,514.

133 *Brother Industries Ltd v Council* [1988] ECR 5683; [1990] 1 CMLR 792; [1990] 1 CEC 594.

134 *Brother Industries Ltd v Council* [1988] ECR 5683 at 5728; [1990] 1 CMLR 792 at 811; [1990] 1 CEC 594 at 625.

135 *Tokyo Electric Co Ltd v Council* [1988] ECR 5855; [1989] 1 CMLR 169; CMR 14,512.

Threat of injury

Article 4(3) of Regulation 2423/88 states a 'determination of threat of injury may only be made where a particular situation is likely to develop into actual injury'. The factors taken into account to determine whether a situation will produce actual injury are:

1　the rate of increase in the import of the dumped or subsidised goods into the Community;[136]

2　the export capacity of the country of origin of the goods or the exporting country, which currently exists or which is planned to come into existence, and the likelihood that that capacity will be used to export to the Community;[137] and

3　the nature of any subsidy and the likely effects of that subsidy upon trade in those goods.[138]

In dealing with a threat of injury the nature of the subsidy is examined in detail. If the subsidy is aimed at the domestic market only it will not pose a threat to the EC as would a subsidy payable upon exports. However, if a domestic subsidy designed to stimulate local production continues in spite of local consumption being fully met, it may be considered as a threat of injury as any surplus production may be exported to the EC.

Community industry

The community industry concerned with dumping or a subsidy includes producers within the EC who manufacture similar products.[139] However, if a producer is a related undertaking of the exporter or importer of dumped or subsidised goods, the Community industry may exclude the related undertaking.[140] This discretion is exercised by the Council or Commission.[141] This discretion is given to prevent the associated undertaking hindering the balance of the industry making a complaint to the Commission pertaining to the alleged dumping or subsidy. If the related undertaking was in a dominant position and had to be considered as part of the Community industry during the investigation, the remaining undertakings may have problems showing the necessary interest to lodge a complaint. Further, the discretion may prevent the undertaking from gaining an advantage from the questioned behaviour because upon its exercise the dominant position of the undertaking is ignored when the Commission makes a finding of injury to the Community industry.

136　Regulation 2423/88, Article 4(3)(a).

137　Regulation 2423/88, Article 4(3)(b).

138　Regulation 2423/88, Article 4(3)(c).

139　Regulation 2423/88, Article 4(5).

140　*Ibid.*

141　*Gestetner Holdings plc v Council and Commission* [1990] 1 CMLR 820.

Division of market within the EC

In circumstances where undertakings within a particular region sell all or almost all the goods produced in that region within that region and importation into the region of those goods is minimal the region may be designated as a regional market.[142] When a regional market is found to exist, the Commission may find that injury is caused within the regional market by dumped or subsidised goods even if the whole of the Community industry is not injured.[143]

Community interest

The Commission, even after finding that dumping has occurred or that a subsidy has been paid and that dumping or subsidy is causing or may cause injury, cannot proceed directly to the imposition of an anti-dumping duty or countervailing duty, but first must consider the overall Community interest.[144] The processing industry, for example, has an interest in purchasing its manufacturing inputs cheaply and if this interest outweighs the interest of other undertakings penalty duties will not be imposed.

The investigation

The investigation is launched by a complaint in writing forwarded to the Commission at the request of a Community industry.[145] The Commission considers the complaint and if it is of opinion that an inquiry is warranted, it will publish its intent to examine the complaint. The intention is published in the *Official Journal of the European Communities*.[146] The Commission will also advise the exporters and importers of that product, the exporting country and the complainant.[147] Although an investigation is to be held or is being held the customs service may still clear the goods for Community consumption.[148] Any confidential information supplied to the Commission to allow the investigation to progress remains confidential and may not be used for any other purpose.[149] To have the information classified as confidential, the provider of the information must supply cogent reasons. If the Commission is of opinion that the reasons are not cogent, the undertaking providing the information has the option to publish the information or having the Commission disregarding the information.[150] The undertaking against whom a penalty duty is to be imposed is entitled to be given the

---

142 Regulation 2423/88, Article 4(5).
143 *Ibid.*
144 Regulation 2423/88, Article 12(1).
145 Regulation 2423/88, Article 5(1).
146 Regulation 2423/88, Article 7(1)(a).
147 Regulation 2423/88, Article 7(1)(b).
148 Regulation 2423/88, Article 7(8).
149 Regulation 2423/88, Article 8(1).
150 Regulation 2423/88, Article 8(4).

facts upon which the decision is based and the reasons for the decision. In *Timex Corporation v Council and Commission*,[151] this right to know the facts and reasons for the decision had to be balanced against the right of the owners of the information to keep that information confidential. The court held that the Commission should, while maintaining business secrets, provide Timex information applicable to the protection of the Timex interests. The divulging of the items which had been included within the construction of the normal value, without providing values assigned to each item, was an inadequate disclosure.

Termination of the investigation and the proceedings

The investigation is usually concluded by termination or by definitive action. The investigation should be concluded within a year of its commencement.[152] When Regulation 3017/79 was in force, Article 7(9)[153] designated a duration of one year for the investigation. The court held that this duration was a guide to the Commission as an example of a reasonable period which reasonable period should not ordinarily be exceeded.[154] Article 7(9) of Regulation 2176/84,[155] which stated that an investigation should normally be completed within one year of the commencement of the investigation was also found to give a discretion as to the length of an investigation.[156] Article 4 of Regulation 2176/84[157] required the Commission to ascertain the magnitude of injury to a Community industry. In *Hellenic Republic v Council*,[158] the duration of the investigation was four years. Even though the investigation lasted four years, the inquiry was required to investigate six months before the lodging of the complaint and to establish the extent of the injury so that appropriate protective measures could be adopted. Regulation 2423/88 does not specify a time limit for an investigation.[159] Anti-dumping or countervailing duties and a decision by the Commission to accept an undertaking may be reviewed after a year.[160] The investigation may be completed without definitive action by the Commission terminating it without imposing anti-dumping or countervailing duties or the acceptance of undertakings,[161] or by terminating the proceedings with acceptance of undertakings which the Commission, after consultation with the Advisory

---

151 [1985] ECR 849; [1985] 3 CMLR 550.

152 Regulation 2423/88, Article 7(9)(a).

153 Since repealed and ultimately replaced by Regulation 2423/88.

154 *Continentale Produkten-Gesellschaft Erhard-Renken GmbH und Co v Hauptzollamt München-West* [1989] ECR 1151; [1991] 1 CMLR 761.

155 Since repealed and replaced by Regulation 2423/88.

156 *Epicheiriseon Metalleftikon Viomichanikon Kai Naftiliakon AE and Others v Council* [1989] ECR 3919; *Epicheiriseon Metalleftikon Viomichanikon Kai Naftiliakon AE and Others v Council* [1989] ECR 3959.

157 Now Regulation 2423/88, Article 4.

158 [1989] ECR 3963.

159 Regulation 2423/88, Article 7(9).

160 Regulation 2423/88, Article 14(1).

161 Regulation 2423/88, Article 7(9)(b).

Committee.[162] considers sufficient, either with or without the definitive collection of amounts secured[163] by way of provisional duties.[164]

A proceeding is completed by terminating the investigation without the imposition of duties and without requiring undertakings,[165] by the expiry or repeal of imposed duties,[166] or by the termination of the undertakings which were given.[167] If the Commission is of opinion that protective measures are unnecessary, it consults the Advisory Committee. If the Committee agrees, the investigation will cease.[168] If the Committee disagrees, the Commission reports its opinion to the Council. If the Council requires the investigation to continue, it determines by a qualified majority within a month, that the proceeding is to continue. If the Council does not so determine the investigation is automatically terminated.[169] When a matter is terminated, the Commission publishes the termination in the same way as it publishes the commencement, with the addition of giving reasons for the termination.[170]

Undertakings accepted by the Commission

The acceptance of undertakings allow a proceeding to be terminated by producers or exporters voluntarily ceasing the behaviour which is causing injury to EC industry. The undertaking must have the consequence of eliminating the injurious effect of the subsidy or to revise the export price to eliminate the injury.[171] The undertakings acceptable to the Commission usually contain a clause requiring the supply of periodical information to the Commission and permission for the Commission to confirm that information.[172] A breach of the undertaking will occur if the conditions are not observed.[173] The Commission has a discretion to invite the offer of undertakings. A refusal of such an invitation, or its non issue, does not prejudice the investigation. If the challenged behaviour continues after the investigation has commenced, this may be accepted as evidence that a threat of injury is likely to become injury.[174] An undertaking normally lapses after a term of five years.[175]

---

162 Regulation 2423/88, Article 6(1).
163 Regulation 2423/88, Article 12(2).
164 Regulation 2423/88, Article 10(1).
165 *Ibid.*
166 Under the EC Treaty countervailing duties are applied by regulation: Regulation 2423/88, Article 13(1).
167 Regulation 2423/88, Article 7(9)(b).
168 Regulation 2423/88, Article 9(1).
169 *Ibid.*
170 Regulation 2423/88, Article 9(2).
171 Regulation 2423/88, Article 10(2).
172 Regulation 2423/88, Article 10(5).
173 *Ibid.*
174 Regulation 2423/88, Article 10(3).
175 Regulation 2423/88, Article 15(1).

Breach of undertaking

Where the Commission is of opinion that there has been a breach of an undertaking given to prevent dumping and it is in the interests of the EC, after consulting the Advisory Committee and giving the challenged party a hearing, the Commission may straight away impose provisional anti-dumping or countervailing duties using the information to hand when the undertaking was accepted.[176] Undertakings, once given, may be subject to review.[177] Following the review, the undertakings may be amended, repealed or annulled. In *Koyo Seiko Co Ltd v Council*,[178] the court held that a review of the undertakings accepted under Article 14 of Regulation 3017/79[179] could commence on the motion of the Commission. The review need not be initiated by a complaint and the review and subsequent investigation could include matters outside the original complaint.

Anti-dumping and countervailing duties

After a finding of injury and that it is in the interests of the EC so to do, an anti-dumping duty to the extent of the dumping margin may be applied.[180] Similarly, a countervailing duty to the extent of the subsidy granted in the country of origin or export may be applied.[181] These duties are imposed by regulation.[182] The regulation imposing the duty must state the type and amount of the duty, the product covered, the country of origin or export, the name of the supplier and the material questions of fact upon which the measure is based.[183] The duty is to remove the injury to EC industry attributable to the dumping or subsidy and therefore must not exceed the dumping margin or the subsidy granted but may be a lesser amount if this lesser amount is adequate to remove the injury.[184]

Duty applied prospectively

The duty is normally imposed or increased with effect from the date of the regulation.[185] The court in *Continentale Produkten-Gesellschaft Erhard-Renken GmbH & Co v Hauptzollamt München-West*[186] held that the wording of Article 13(4)(a) of

---

176 Regulation 2423/88, Article 10(6).

177 Regulation 2423/88, Article 14.

178 [1987] ECR 1899; [1989] 2 CMLR 76; CMR 14,487.

179 Now Regulation 2423/88, Article 14.

180 Regulation 2423/88, Article 2(1).

181 Regulation 2423/88, Article 3(1).

182 Regulation 2423/88, Article 13(1).

183 Regulation 2423/88, Article 13(2).

184 Regulation 2423/88, Article 13(3). *Allied Corporation v Commission* [1985] ECR 1621; [1986] 3 CMLR 605; CMR 14,200.

185 Regulation 2423/88, Article 13(4)(a).

186 [1989] ECR 1151; [1991] 1 CMLR 761.

Regulation 3017/79[187] states a rule that the application of retrospective, definitive anti-dumping duties is not permitted. Such a retrospective definitive duty is allowed where a provisional duty has been imposed by an earlier regulation, for the period of the provisional duty, where the definitive duty does not exceed the provisional duty. The duty is collected by the Member States and accounted for separately to customs duties, taxes and other charges imposed on imports.[188] The duty is imposed by Directive 79/623 on the harmonisation of provisions relating to customs.[189]

Definitive duty under Article 12

Article 12 of Regulation 2423/88 states that when dumping and injury have been found and the interests of the Community so requires, the Council must apply a definitive duty based on a proposal from the Commission. In *Epicheiriseon Metalleftikon Viomichanikon Kai Naftiliakon v Council*,[190] the court held that the wording of Article 12 of Regulation 2176/84[191] empowered the Council to decide the conditions to be imposed in an anti-dumping duty without being required to adopt every proposal of the Commission.[192]

Provisional duty

Where a preliminary investigation reveals dumping or a subsidy and there is sufficient evidence of injury so caused and the interests of the Community require the removal of the injury during the investigation, the Commission may, after consulting the Advisory Committee, impose a provisional anti-dumping or countervailing duty.[193] In intense emergency, the Commission may, after informing Member States, impose such a duty, but must consult the Advisory Committee within 10 days.[194] When a Member State requests the immediate imposition of a provisional anti-dumping or countervailing duty, the Commission has five working days to decide whether to impose the duty as requested.[195] If the Commission decline to impose a provisional duty that decision does not preclude a later decision to impose such a duty if requested by another Member State or even on the motion of the Commission.[196] Imposition of provisional duty does not involve payment of the duty, but rather the provision of security for the provisional duty before the clearance of the goods for entry into the EC market.[197] The provisional duty is levied for four months but the duty may be extended for a further period of two

---

187 Now Regulation 2423/88, Article 13(4)(a).
188 Regulation 2423/88, Article 13(8).
189 Regulation 2423/88, Article 13(4)(a).
190 [1989] ECR 3919.
191 Now Regulation 2423/88, Article 12.
192 See also *Epicheiriseon Metalleftikon Viomichanikon Kai Naftiliakon v Council* [1989] ECR 3919.
193 Regulation 2423/88, Article 11(1).
194 Regulation 2423/88, Article 11(2).
195 Regulation 2423/88, Article 11(3).
196 Regulation 2423/88, Article 11(4).
197 Regulation 2423/88, Article 11(1).

months.[198] One month before the expiry of a provisional duty, the Commission must notify the Council of its intention to apply a definitive duty under Article 11 of Regulation 2423/88. The Council may, by qualified majority, amend the Commission's proposal.[199] When a provisional duty expires the security is released except the amount which has been applied as a definitive duty.[200] It is the obligation of the Council to decide how much of the provisional duty is to be applied as a definitive duty.[201]

Definitive duty

A definitive duty may only be levied where the Commission has found dumping or a subsidy have caused injury in the EC and the Community interest requires the cessation of the injury.[202] Regulation 2423/88 requires the Commission to consult the Advisory Committee with its proposal. The Council, acting by qualified majority, then may impose a duty.[203] Where a regulation to impose a provisional duty is challenged in the court and a regulation imposing a definitive duty supersedes the earlier regulation before the proceedings are brought to a conclusion and the definitive duty is challenged by the same applicant, the court will not decide on the earlier application as it has been superseded by the latter.[204]

Review of definitive duties

The imposition of definitive duty may be reviewed either by the request of an official organ of the EC (a Member State or on the Commission's own motion); or at the request of a party interested in the outcome of the inquiry. An interested party must wait one year after the initial inquiry and must submit evidence of changed circumstances to justify the review.[205] If the review is justified, the investigation is reopened in accordance with Article 7 of Regulation 2423/88.[206] Where a review determines that the circumstances upon which the regulation imposing the definitive duty was levied has substantially altered the regulation imposing the definitive duty is amended, replaced or repealed as required.[207] Six months prior to the expiry of a regulation imposing a definitive duty or accepted undertakings, the Commission publishes a notice of the

---

198 Regulation 2423/88, Article 11(5).

199 Regulation 2423/88, Article 11(6).

200 Regulation 2423/88, Article 11(7).

201 Regulation 2423/88, Article 12(2)(a).

202 Regulation 2423/88, Article 12(1).

203 Regulation 2423/88, Article 12(1).

204 *Brother Industries Ltd v Commission* [1988] ECR 5655; [1990] 1 CMLR 792; [1990] 1 CEC 586; *Technointorg v Council and Commission* [1988] ECR 6077; [1989] 1 CMLR 281; [1989] 1 CEC 160.

205 Regulation 2423/88, Article 14(1).

206 Regulation 2423/88, Article 14(2).

207 Regulation 2423/88, Article 14(3).

impending expiry.[208] The publication must state by when persons may object to the lapse of the regulation or undertakings.[209] Where it is shown that the injury would re-occur on the lapse of the regulation or undertakings the Commission will conduct a review.[210]

The court in the review process

Any Act of an EC authority which is of direct and individual concern to an undertaking may be challenged under Article 173 of the EC Treaty.[211] In *Timex Corporation v Council and Commission*,[212] the court held that a regulation imposing an anti-dumping duty was such a measure. Therefore, the undertaking is entitled to put before the court any matters which would assist the court to review whether the Commission has observed the procedural matters contained in Regulation 3017/79,[213] whether the Commission has exceeded its powers, whether the Commission has failed to take any relevant consideration into account, or whether the Commission has based its decision on matters which amount to an abuse of power. The court, in *EEC Seed Crushers' and Oil Processors' Federation (FEDIOL) v Commission*[214] expressed these rights in saying:

> It seems clear ... that complainants must be acknowledged to have a right to bring an action where it is alleged that the Community authorities have disregarded rights which have been recognised specifically in the regulation, namely the right to lodge a complaint, the right, which is inherent in the aforementioned right, to have that complaint considered by the Commission with proper care and according to the procedure provided for, the right to receive information within the limits set by the regulation and finally, if the Commission decides not to proceed with the complaint, the right to receive information comprising at the least the explanations guaranteed by Article 9(2) of the regulation.

> Furthermore, it must be acknowledged that, in the spirit of the principles which lie behind Articles 164 and 173 of the Treaty, complainants have the right to avail themselves, with regard both to the assessment of the facts and to the adoption of the protective measures provided for by the regulation, of a review by the court appropriate to the nature of the powers reserved to the Community institutions on the subject.

> ... the court is required to exercise its normal powers of review over a discretion granted to a public authority, even though it has no jurisdiction to intervene in the exercise of the discretion reserved to the Community authorities by the ... regulation.[215]

The rejection by the Commission of undertakings offered by an exporter is not a measure which will attract the protection of Article 173 as the rejection of tendered

---

208 Regulation 2423/88, Article 15(2).

209 *Ibid.*

210 Regulation 2423/88, Article 15(3).

211 *Allied Corporation and Others v Commission* [1984] ECR 1005; CMR 14084.

212 [1985] ECR 849; [1985] 3 CMLR 550.

213 Now Regulation 2423/88.

214 [1983] ECR 2913.

215 *Ibid* at 2935–936.

undertakings is a step leading to a reviewable decision and therefore is not a reviewable act.[216]

THE US APPLICATION OF ITS LAW

The USA has applied its competition law to conduct that occurs exclusively outside their borders in a number of cases which favour the application of the extraterritorial principle. The first case is *American Banana Co v United Fruit Co*.[217] American Banana asserted that United Fruit had unlawfully monopolised the banana trade between the US and Central America, namely Panama and Costa Rica. Oliver Wendell Holmes J, writing for an unanimous court found it a startling proposition that the Sherman Act might be applied to conduct, regardless of its effect, taken entirely outside the US. The leading case is undoubtedly the case *United States v Aluminium Co of America (ALCOA)*.[218] In this case, the US government alleged that a subsidiary of ALCOA had illegally conspired with British, Swiss, German and French companies to fix production quotas of ingots due to be imported into the US. Hand JL argued that the most dispositive factor in determining Congressional intent to apply the Sherman Act to extraterritorial conduct is whether the illegal restraint had actually affected US commerce. His Honour held: 'it is settled law ... that any State may impose liabilities, even upon persons not within its allegiance, for conduct outside its borders which has consequences within its borders which the State reprehends; and these liabilities other States will ordinarily recognise.'[219] He thought that this was consistent with international law because it governed 'liabilities other States will ordinarily recognise'. This is the effects doctrine, according to which foreign based defendants that had caused an intended and actual effect on US commerce could be sued under the Sherman Act, even if they had no territorial connection with or to the US. Further cases have limited themselves to a consideration of the degree of intent and actual effect that must be shown. For example, is the effect foreseeable, and is the effect both direct and substantial.[220]

The effects of ALCOA were swift. America's trading partners strongly disagreed with the use of the Sherman Act for the purpose of controlling anti-competitive conduct outside US borders. They believed that jurisdiction based solely on effects unreasonably infringed on their sovereignty and violated international customary law. As a consequence, many States enacted blocking legislation which attempts to thwart US enforcement jurisdiction by forbidding compliance with US discovery demands, or refusing to recognise a judgment rendered by a US court. For example, Australia enacted a blocking statute in 1984.[221]

---

216 *Nashua Corporation v Council and Commission* [1990] ECR 719; [1990] 2 CMLR 6; *Gestetner Holdings plc v Council and Commission* [1990] 1 CMLR 820.

217 213 US 347 (1909).

218 148 F 2d 416 (1945).

219 *Ibid* at 443.

220 See *Rivendell Forest Products Ltd v Canadian Forest Products Ltd* 810 F Supp 1116 (1993).

221 Foreign Proceedings (Excess of Jurisdiction) Act 1984. See also Griffin, EC and US Extraterritoriality: Activism and Cooperation (1994) 17 Fordham International LJ 353.

Following this strong reaction, the effects doctrine has been moderated by reference to the principle of international comity. Comity requires an investigation as to 'whether the interests of, and links to, the United States – including the magnitude of the effect on American foreign commerce – are sufficiently strong, vis à vis those of other nations, to justify an assertion of extraterritorial authority'.[222] These principles were incorporated into anti–trust law in the seminal case of *Timberlane Lumber Co v Bank of America*.[223] In *Timberlane*, Choy J held that the ALCOA intended and actual effects test was incomplete because it fails to consider other nations' interests.[224] He felt that overly broad application of ALCOA would be inappropriate in situations in which 'comity considerations would indicate dismissal'. He developed a 'balancing test' (also known as the 'jurisdictional rule of reason') in order to protect the regulatory and sovereignty interests of other nations. Under *Timberlane's* analysis, the decision whether to exercise jurisdiction – assuming the requisite intent and actual effect on US commerce have already been shown – is based on a balancing of the following factors:

- the degree of conflict with foreign law and policy;
- the nationality of the parties and the location of the principal places of business of corporations;
- the extent to which enforcement by either state can be expected to achieve compliance;
- the relative significance of effect in the US as compared with those elsewhere;
- the extent to which there is explicit purpose to harm or affect US commerce;
- the foreseeability of such effect; and
- with respect to the violation charged, the relative importance of conduct within the US as compared with conduct abroad.

This analysis was complemented by another case, *Mannington Mills Inc v Congoleum Corporation*[225] in which Weis J enlarged the *Timberlane* factors:

- possible effect upon foreign relations, if the court exercises jurisdiction and grants relief;
- if relief is granted, whether a party will be placed in the position of being forced to perform an act illegal in either country or be under conflicting requirements by both countries;
- whether an order for relief would be acceptable in this country if made by a foreign nation under similar circumstances; and
- whether a treaty with the affected nations has addressed the issue.

The comity doctrine is reminiscent of Marshall CJ's point in *Murray v The Charming Betsy*[226] that 'an act of Congress ought never to be construed to violate the law of

---

222 *Timberlane Lumber Co v Bank of America* 549 F 2d 597 (1996) at 613.
223 549 F 2d 597 (1976).
224 *Ibid* at p 611–12.
225 595 F 2d 1287 (1979) at 1297–298.
226 2 Cranch 64, 118, 2 L Ed 208 (1804).

nations if any other possible construction remains'. The comity doctrine acts as a basis for declining to exercise jurisdiction as decided recently by the Supreme Court in *Hartford Fire Insurance Co v California*.[227] Thus the doctrine comes into being once the Sherman Act's jurisdiction has already been established and therefore acts as an abstention. Souter J said that:

> The only substantial question in this case is whether there is in fact a true conflict between domestic and foreign law ... no conflict exists, for these purposes, where a person subject to regulation by two States can comply with the laws of both.

However, he leaves open what has to be done when there is a true conflict.

Now American courts interpret antitrust laws as effectively displacing foreign treaties and laws on the basis of the most minimal American connection. In the Foreign Trade Antitrust Improvements Act 1982, American anti-trust law applies to conduct that has a 'direct, substantial, and reasonably foreseeable effect on US commerce or on the business of a person engaged in exporting goods from the US to foreign nations'. However, many nations may wish to adopt so-called 'blocking legislation' in order to prevent the US to enforce its economic policies abroad by seeking discovery of documents.

CONCLUSION

With the decision in the *Wood Pulp* case,[228] it is clear that the Commission has jurisdiction to combat anti-competitive behaviour within the EC, even if the undertakings concerned have their domicile outside the EC as long as the behaviour takes place within the EC. When foreign entities dump products within the EC and that dumping causes injury to EC entities then the Commission may take action to apply an anti-dumping duty to remove the injury to EC trade. Similarly, if origin goods are subsidised in the country of origin and that subsidy causes injury to EC business, a countervailing duty may be applied to remove the injury caused by the subsidy. These anti-dumping duties or countervailing duties are imposed to undo the injury caused to EC industry by the impugned behaviour of the undertaking concerned. This is to be contrasted with the position in the USA where the *Foreign Trade Anti-trust Improvements Act* 1982 applies American anti-trust law to conduct that has a 'direct, substantial, and reasonably foreseeable effect on US commerce or on the business of a person engaged in exporting goods from the US to foreign nations'. The EC position requires the injury to take place in the EC whereas the USA looks to injury wherever it happens.

---

227 113 St Ct 2891, 125 L Ed 2d 612 (1993).

228 Joined Cases 89, 104, 117 and 125–29/85 *Ahlstrom Osakeyhtio and Others v Commission* [1988] ECR 5193; [1988] 4 CMLR 901.

TUTORIAL QUESTIONS

In these questions Manufacturer is a partnership in the British Virgin Islands and is the sole shareholder in, and provide all the directors of, Distributor, a company incorporated in France. Manufacturer hold worldwide patents for Machine. Machine is manufactured in the Virgin Islands (VI) at a cost of 100 ECU. Distributor imports Machine into the EC and distribute it in all Member States. Small Trader is a cooperative in Belgium.

1   Manufacturer come to an agreement with Distributor that the Machine will be landed in the EC at a cost of 10,000 ECU and sold to retailers at 11,000 ECU. Small Trader, a cooperative in Belgium, wishes to import Machine from Manufacturer but is referred to Distributor.

Advise Small Trader.

2   Small Trader purchases Machine from Distributor and finds, stamped on the invoice, 'Machine is to be sold by Small Trader in Belgium at a cost of 12,500 ECU.'

Advise:

(a) Small Trader if it accepts the condition imposed by Distributor; and

(b) Small Trader of its rights if it proposes to sell Machine to a Netherlands purchaser for 12,000 ECU.

3   Small Trader builds up a substantial trade in Machine and Manufacturer proposes to cease operating Distributor. Manufacturer proposes to Small Trader that it should take up the sole distribution of Machine on the same terms as Distributor except that Machine would be invoiced to Small Trader at 9,500 ECU.

Advise Small Trader.

4   Small Trader accepts the distributorship of Machine. It decides that it would charge 15,000 ECU per Machine but would give a discount of 1% for the purchase of 10 or more Machines and 1% for payment within 30 days. Manufacturer agrees that Small Trader may adopt the new pricing policy.

Advise.

5   A general price rise occurred in the VI and the cost of production has risen to 15,000 ECU. Manufacture does not wish to lose market share and continues its agreement with its distributor, Small Trader. Medium Trader, an Austrian undertaking making a machine which would compete with Machine, complains to the Commission that it cannot sell its machine, as its machine costs 14,500 ECU to manufacture and Medium Trader is being undercut by Small Trader.

Discuss.

6   When the patent on Machine was about to expire Manufacturer calls a conference of itself, Small Trader and Medium Trader (the Austrian manufacturer of a competing machine). The conference is held in Geneva. At that conference it is agreed that Manufacturer would share its trade secrets with Medium Trader and they would both manufacture Machine. Medium Trader would pay Manufacturer a royalty of 2,000 ECU per Machine built and Small Trader would source its

Machine from Medium Trader. Medium Trader would distribute Machine in Austria, Germany, The Netherlands and Belgium. Small Trader would distribute Machine to the remainder of the EC. Manufacturer would cease exporting Machine to the EC and neither Small Trader nor Medium Trader would export Machine from the EC. Small Trader and Medium Trader further agreed to follow the pricing policy of Manufacturer. The Commission decides to investigate.

Discuss.

7   The Commission conducts an investigation into the activities of Manufacturer and find that the normal price of Machine is 12,000 ECU and the export price in the last six transactions is 14,000, 10,000, 13,000, 11,000, 15,000 and 9,000 ECU respectively. When the export price has been below the normal price Manufacturer has had almost three times the quantity of Machines in each consignment. The Commission contends that dumping has occurred on each occasion when the export price has been lower than the normal price.

Discuss.

8   If dumping has occurred but the EC industry cannot show damage the Commission will not impose an anti-dumping duty.

Discuss.

9   If Manufacturer only exports Machine to Austria, and Machine is not used anywhere else in the EC, Medium Trader will not have any cause for complaint, even if Medium Trader suffers injury, as Medium Trader only operates in Austria.

Discuss.

10 After the patent for Machine has expired, even if the manufacture of Machine in VI is subsidised to 50% of the normal price, a countervailing duty will not be imposed if the machine sold by Medium Trader is freely interchangeable with Machine.

Discuss.

11 Manufacturer wishes to argue in the ECJ that even if Manufacturer has dumped Machine in the EC market, an anti-dumping duty should not be applied because Medium Trader is not injured as its machine infringes Manufacturer's patent, and Medium Trader is thus unable to lawfully manufacture its machine (Manufacturer has a judgment of the appropriate Austrian court to that effect).

Discuss.

12 During an investigation into the activities of Manufacturer, Manufacturer refuses to disclose its manufacturing records to the Commission. The Commission requests your advice whether it may use Medium Trader's records to construct a normal value.

13 After the patent on Machine had expired Manufacturer found it could land Machine in the EC for 10,000 ECU and, allowing itself a profit margin of 20%, could sell Machine to the distributor for 12,000 ECU. Without any contact with Manufacturer, Medium Trader decide to sell its machine to Distributor for 12,000 ECU. The Spanish government complains to the Commission that Manufacturer

and Medium Trader are acting in a manner incompatible with Article 85(1) of the Treaty.

Advise the Commission.

14 After an investigation by the Commission, a finding is made that the price of 7,000 ECU charged by Manufacturer to land Machine in the EC is because the VI government has subsidised each Machine by 5,000 ECU. The Commission imposes a countervailing duty of 7,000 ECU per Machine because Medium Trader is only able to manufacture its machine at a cost of 14,000 ECU.

Discuss.

15 When the patent on Machine is about to expire Manufacturer calls a conference of itself, Small Trader and Medium Trader (the Austrian manufacturer of a competing machine). The conference is held in Geneva. At that conference it is agreed that Manufacturer would share its trade secrets with Medium Trader and they would both manufacture Machine. Medium Trader would pay Manufacturer a royalty of 2,000 ECU per Machine built and Small Traders would source its Machine from Medium Trader. Medium Trader would distribute Machine in Austria, Germany, the Netherlands and Belgium. Small Trader would distribute Machine to the remainder of the EC. Manufacturer would cease exporting Machine to the EC and neither Small Trader nor Medium Trader would export Machine from the EC. Small Trader and Medium Trader further agreed to follow the pricing policy of Manufacturer. The parties notify the Commission of the agreement and the Commission are of opinion that the agreement is not incompatible with the Treaty.

Discuss what action the Commission may take and what would be the result of any action taken by the Commission if the agreement was challenged in a national court.

FURTHER READING

Christoforou, T and Rockwell, DB, 'EEC Law: The Territorial Scope of Application of EEC Antitrust Law: The Wood Pulp Judgement' (1989) *Harvard International Law Journal* 195.

Lange, D and Born, G (eds), *The Extraterritorial Application of National Laws*, 1987, Boston: Kluwer.

Lowe, V, 'International Law and the Effects Doctrine in the European Court of Justice' (1989) 48 *Cambridge Law Journal* 9.

Moens, G and Flint, D, *Business Law of the European Community*, 1993, Brisbane: DataLegal.

Williams, MD, 'European Antitrust Law and its Application to American Corporations and their Subsidiaries' (1987) *Whittier L Rev* 517–35.

SELECT BIBLIOGRAPHY

Schaffer, R, Earle, B and Agusti, P, *International Business Law and Its Environment*, 1990, St Paul: West Publishing.

Moens, G and Flint, D, *Business Law of the European Community*, 1993, Brisbane: DataLegal.

Schmitthoff, CM, *Export Trade: The Law and Practice of International Trade*, 9th edn, 1990, London: Stevens.

Burnett, R, *The Law of International Business Transactions*, 1994, Sydney: Federation.

Honnold, JO, *Uniform Law for International Sales Under the 1980 United Nations Convention,* 2nd edn, 1991, Deventer: Kluwer Law and Taxation.

Wilde, KCDM and Rafiqul Islam, M (eds), *International Transactions: Trade and Investment, Law and Finance*, 1993, Sydney: Law Book Co.

INDEX

Abuse of dominant position, 777–81

Acceptance
  of contracts, 14–17, 85–87
  of delivery of goods, 29
  of tender of documents, 399

Acceptance credits, 392

Administration
  See also State regulation
  of anti-dumping and
    countervailing procedures, 588–91
  of NAFTA, 698–99
  of trade regulations, 500–01

Agreement on Trade-Related
Aspects of Intellectual
Property Rights (TRIPS), 444, 473, 695

Agreements
  between undertakings,
    competition policies and, 769–81,
      798–800
  exclusion agreements, 748
  free trade
    See Free trade agreements
  to usages, 13

Agriculture, GATT and, 594, 608, 609–10

Air transport, 249, 298–327,
    332–38, 384–86
  Australian federal regulation of, 298–301
  deregulation of, 324–25
  Incoterms and, 123
  international conventions
    on, 302–22, 325, 326
  texts of, 332–38, 384–86
  liability in, 305–20, 322–27
  passenger, 303, 319–20, 322–27

Air waybills, 304–05

Aircraft, 7

Ambiguity, interpretation of, 400–02

Animals, carriage of, 187–88

Anti-dumping and countervailing
procedures
  authorities involved in
    administration of, 588–91
  EU and, 769, 781–98
  GATT and, 471, 496–97,
    583–85, 592–605,
    609–10, 614–67

localised trade agreements and, 587–88
national, 585–87, 597–605, 613
  courts and, 589–90, 605–08
  tutorial questions on, 610–12
  in USA, 585–86, 588–89,
    590–91, 597–98,
    605–07, 613

Anticipatory breach of contract, 33–34

Appearance of documents, 399–400

Approximation principle, 708–09

Arbitration, 729–52
  Australian statutory
    framework of, 732–35
  carriage of goods by sea and, 195
  GATT and, 560–61
  international
    conventions on, 732,
      736–38, 764–68
  international trade and, 729–30
  judicial review of arbitral
    awards, 742–50
  model law on, 732, 738–39,
    742–46, 754–64
  recognition and
    enforcement of, 735–42,
      750–52, 763–64
  tutorial questions on, 752
  types of, 730–32
  UNIDROIT principles and, 83–84, 92

Assignment of proceeds under
a documentary credit, 396–97

Auctions, 7

Australia-New Zealand CER
Trade Agreement, 587–88

Australian Capital Territory,
  regulation of road transport in, 282

Australian federal regulation
  of air transport, 298–301
  anti-dumping and
    countervailing procedures, 586,
      587–88,
      589–90, 591,
      598–602, 605,
      607–08, 613
  of international
    commercial arbitration, 732–35,
      745–46

of rail transport, 284–90
of road transport, 250, 257–69
compliance and enforcement
 module, 264
dangerous goods module, 264–65
Heavy Vehicles Agreement, 259, 261, 262
Interstate Commission, 268–69
Light Vehicles Agreement, 259–62
Ministerial Council, 268
National Road Transport
 Commission, 267–68
scope of uniform road
 transport legislation, 265–67
vehicle operations module, 262–64
Australian state/territory
regulation of international
commercial arbitration, 733, 746–50
of rail transport, 290–92
of road transport, 250, 269–84
Australian Capital Territory, 282
 New South Wales, 269–72
 Northern Territory, 283–84
 Queensland, 275–77
 South Australia, 277
 Tasmania, 279–82
 Victoria, 273–75
 Western Australia, 277–79
Autonomy principle of
letters of credit, 409–17
Avoidance of contract, 19, 26–27,
 30, 87–88
 effects of, 38–40

Back-to-back credits, 396
Bad faith, 84
Baggage check, 303
Balance of payments problems
 GATT and, 456–57, 459,
 460–61, 464,
 502–04, 571–72
 NAFTA and, 701
Banks
 free trade in financial
 services and, 692–94
 letters of credit and, 387–419, 421–42

Barter, 7
Battle of the forms, 86
Bills of exchange, 389, 392, 410
Bills of lading, 124–25
 Hague Rules on, 175–77, 180–200,
 210–13, 215, 216–35
Blocs
 See Trading blocs
Breach of contract, 18–19
 anticipatory, 33–34
 damages for, 35–37, 95–97
 passing of risk and, 33
 remedies for, 24–28, 29–31
Businesses, extraterritorial
 control of, 769–803

C category Incoterms, 126–27,
 137–44, 162–67
Capital movements within EU, 710
Carriage of goods, 21
 air transport, 123, 249,
 298–327,
 332–38, 384–86
 beginning and end of, 190–91
 dangerous goods, 264–65, 289,
 291–92, 301, 313
 delay in, 191–92,
 253–54, 311–13
 goods sold in transit, 32
 Incoterms used in, 121–53, 155–73
 C category, 126–27,
 137–44, 162–67
 D category, 127,
 145–52, 167–73
 E category, 126,
 128–30, 155–57
 F category, 126,
 130–37, 157–62
 by land/air, 123,
 249–329, 332–86
 liability in, 185–86, 196–200,
 251, 253, 288–90,
 305–20, 322–27
 passing of risk and, 31–32
 rail transport, 284–84, 339–71

road transport, 250–84, 295–97, 371–83

by sea, 123, 124–25, 175–207, 210–48

transport developments, 123–24

tutorial questions on, 206–07, 327–29

Carriage and insurance paid to (CIP), 142, 144, 164–67

Carriage paid to (CPT), 142, 143–44

Carriers

common, 249, 250

private, 251–56

Cash credits, 389

CE mark, 725

Charges, import and export, 499

Choses in action, assignment of, 396–97

Cinema films, 495

Citizenship of European Union, 707

Commercial arbitration

See Arbitration

Commercial law, EU, 781–98

Common carriers, 249, 250

Communication

miscarriage in, 19–20

of offers, 17

Competition policy

EU, 769–81

US, 773, 798–800

Conditions

See Terms and conditions in contracts

Confidentiality, 84–85

Confirmed irrevocable credits, 391

Conformity of goods, 22–24

early delivery and, 23

examination by buyer, 23

liability for non-conformity, 23

notice period, 23–24

quality, 22–23

Consideration in contracts, 17–18, 85

Constructed prices, 784–86

Consumer goods, 7

Containerisation, 180

Incoterms and, 124

Contracting out

in rail transport, 289–90

in road transport, 251–53

Contracts

acceptance of, 14–17, 85–87

avoidance of, 19, 26–27, 30, 38–40, 87–88

breach of, 18–19, 33–34

damages for, 35–37, 95–97

remedies for, 24–28, 29–31

carriage of goods by land/air, 249–329, 332–86

carriage of goods by sea, 124–25, 175–207, 210–48

conformity of goods in, 22–24

consideration in, 17–18, 85

content of, 19, 22–23, 86, 89, 109–10

contract law, 82–84

force majeure and, 37, 38, 91, 92–93

formation of, 14–17, 85–87, 102–05

frustration of, 37–38, 93

hardship in, 91–92, 113

Incoterms in, 121–53, 155–73

instalment, 34–35

intention to create legal relations, 18

interpretation of, 88–89, 108–09

letters of credit, 387–419, 421–42

modification of, 20

non-performance of, 93–94, 113–19

obligations in, 33–41

buyer's, 28–29

seller's, 20–22

passing of risk in, 31–33

performance of, 89–91, 110–13

facilitation of, 38

frustration of, 37–38, 93

specific, 20, 25, 29–30, 94

pre-contractual negotiations, 84–85

remedies in, 24–28, 29–31, 94–97

termination of, 20, 95

UN Convention on Contracts for
the International Sale of
Goods and,   7, 8–10,
14–18, 52–54
UNIDROIT Principles of
International Commercial
Contracts and,   80–99, 100–19
validity of,   87–88, 105–08
Convention Concerning
International Carriage by Rail,   292–94
text of,   339–71
Convention on the Contract of
International Carriage of
Goods by Road,   295–97
text of,   371–83
Convention on the Law Applicable
to Contracts for the International
Sale of Goods,   70, 83
text of,   71–77
Convention on the Recognition and
Enforcement of Foreign
Arbitral Awards,   732, 736–38
text of,   764–68
Convention for the Unification
of Certain Rules Relating to
International Carriage by Air
(Warsaw Convention),   298, 301,
302–20
text of,   332–38
Copyright
See Intellectual property rights
Cost and freight (CFR),   137, 142
Cost, insurance and
freight (CIF),   137–41, 162–64
Counter-offers,   15
Counter-trade,   7
Countervailing procedures
See Anti-dumping and
countervailing procedures
Courts
anti-dumping and countervailing
procedures and,   589–90,
605–08, 797–98
enforcement of arbitration
and,   736, 738, 739
judicial review of arbitral
awards,   742–50

Cumulative revolving credits,   393
Currency of payments,   90–91
Customs, valuation for,   497–99
Customs duties, EU,   715–17
Customs unions,   519

D category Incoterms,   127, 145–52,
167–73
Damages
in air transport,   318
for breach of contract,   35–37, 95–97
in road transport,   255
Dangerous goods
air transport and,   301, 313
rail transport and,   289, 291–92
road transport and,   264–65
Data transmission, electronic,   124–26
Death, liability for,   10, 322–23
Decisions, EU,   713
Deck cargo,
Hague Rules and,   186–87
Deferred payment credits,   391–92
Delay in carriage of goods,   191–92, 253–54
Delivered at frontier (DAF),   145–46, 167–70
Delivered duty paid (DDP),   151–52
Delivered duty unpaid
(DDU),   150–51, 170–73
Delivered ex-quay
(duty paid) (DEQ),   148–49
Delivered ex-ship (DES),   146–48
Delivery of goods,   21
acceptance of,   29
excess,   28
Incoterms and,   128–52
insurance,   21, 137–41,
142, 144, 162–67
misdelivery,   254
partial,   27–28
passing of risk and,   31–32
place of,   21
time of,   22
early,   23, 28

Deregulation of air transport, 324–25

Developing countries
preferential treatment in
GATT for, 456–71, 656–58
development assistance, 465–71,
509–15, 526–29
import restrictions, 456–65

Deviation from route in road
transport, 254

Directives, EU, 712–13

Dispute settlement
in GATS, 577
in GATT, 452–56, 659
in NAFTA, 687–88, 700–01
in WTO, 474, 544–65

Documentary credits
See Letters of credit

Documents
See also Bills of exchange; Bills
of lading; Letters of credit
acceptance of tender of, 399
appearance of, 399–400
battle of the forms, 86
linkage of, 404–06
for sale of goods, 22
written, 13, 735

Dominant position, abuse of, 777–81

Drawback systems, 663–64

Dumping
See Anti-dumping and
countervailing procedures

Duties
countervailing
See Anti-dumping and
countervailing procedures
customs, 715–17

E category Incoterms, 126,
128–30, 155–57

Early delivery, 23, 28

Economic and political
union in EU, 709

Electricity, 7

Electronic data transmission, 124–26

Emergency anti-dumping measures, 604–05

Emergency import restrictions, 515–16

Energy/petrochemical sector,
NAFTA and, 675–76

Enforcement of arbitration, 735–42,
750–52, 763–64
international
convention on, 732,
736–38, 764–68

European Atomic Energy
Community (Euratom), 705, 706

European Central Bank (ECB), 710–11

European Coal and Steel
Community (ECSC), 705, 706

European Community (EC), 705, 706, 708

European Convention on
Human Rights, 705–06

European System of Central
Banks (ECSB), 710

European Union (EU), 705–28
anti-dumping and countervailing
procedures and, 769, 781–98
approximation principle in, 708–09
capital movements within, 710
citizenship of, 707
commercial law of, 781–98
competition policy in, 769–73, 774–81
objectives of, 773–74
components of, 705–06
economic and political union in, 709
exchange rate policy in, 711
fundamental freedoms in, 706
institutions of, 707–08
legislation in, 711–25
monetary policy in, 710–11
treaties of, 705,
706, 707–10,
711–14, 715,
716, 717–19, 720,
726, 769–73, 777–82
tutorial questions on, 726–28

Evergreen clauses, 393

Ex-Works (ExW), 126, 127,
128–30, 155–57

Examination of goods by buyer, 23

Excess delivery, 28

Exchange rate
  exchange rate policy in
    European Union,   711
  valuation of goods and,   786

Exclusion agreements,   748

Exclusive service providers,   570

Export finance
  See Letters of credit

Extraterritorial control of business,   769–803

EU commercial law and,   781–98

EU competition policy and,   769–81
  tutorial questions on,   801–803
  US competition policy and,   773, 798–800

F category Incoterms,   126, 130–37, 157–62

Facilitation of performance,   38

Fees, import and export,   499

Films,   495

Financial services, NAFTA and,   692–94

Fire, carriage by sea and,   189–90

Force majeure,   37, 38, 91, 92–93

Foreign investment, NAFTA and,   681–88

Form, requirements of,   13

Formalities, import and export,   499

Formation of contracts,   14–17, 85–87, 102–05

Fraud, letters of credit and,   412–16

Free alongside ship (FAS),   132–34, 157–60

Free on board (FOB),   134–37, 160–62

Free carrier (FCA),   130–32

Free movement of goods in EU,   714–15, 716, 718–19
  derogation from,   780–81

Free trade agreements,   519
  anti-dumping and countervailing
    procedures and,   587–88
  NAFTA,   587, 669–703

Freedom of transit,   495–96

Frustration of contracts,   37–38, 93

Functional package test,   193–94

Fundamental breach of contract,   18–19, 27, 33

General Agreement on Tariffs
  and trade (GATT),   443, 444–73
  agriculture and,   594, 608, 609–10
  developing
    countries and,   456–71, 509–15, 526–29, 656–58
  dispute settlement in,   452–56, 659
  dumping and,   471, 496–97, 583–85, 592–605, 609–10, 614–67
  economic
    development and,   465–71, 509–15, 526–29
  framework of,   446
  legal principles of,   447–56
  most-favoured-nation
    principle,   448–49, 491–93
  national treatment
    principle,   449–51, 493–94
    reciprocity principle,   451–52
  membership of,   447, 530–32
  panel system,   454–56
  preferential treatment and,   456–71
  rounds,   444
  subsidies and,   471–73, 508, 594–97, 634–42
  text of,   490–544, 614–67
  tutorial questions on,   480–81

General Agreement on Trade in
  Services (GATS),   444, 473, 475–80, 689
  text of,   565–81

Good faith,   84

Government
  See State; State regulation

Guadalajara Convention,   320–22

Guarantees,   393–94

Hague Conference on Private
International Law, 79

Hague Rules
See International Convention for
the Unification of Certain Rules
of Law Relating to Bills of Lading

Hague Uniform Laws on
International Laws, 1

Hamburg Rules, 177–79, 180–200,
210–13, 215

arguments against
introduction of, 201–05
text of, 235–48

Hardship, 91–92, 113

Harmonisation of technical
standards, 723–25

Hazardous goods
See Dangerous goods

Heavy Vehicles Agreement, 259, 261, 262

Horizontal agreements, 770

IATA Intercarrier Agreement
of Passenger Liability, 326–27, 384–86
text of, 384–86

Implied terms, 22–23

Import permits, 717–18

Impossibility of contracts, 37, 91

Incoterms, 121–53, 155–73
categories of, 126–28
C category, 126–27,
137–44, 162–67
D category, 127,
145–52, 167–73
E category, 126,
128–30, 155–57
F category, 126,
130–37, 157–62
electronic data
transmission and, 124–26
functions of, 122–23
incorporation into
contracts of, 123
legal status of, 123
transport developments and, 123–24

tutorial questions on, 152–53
use of intermediaries and, 124

Industrial property rights, 24

Infant industry protection, 457, 458,
461, 463–65

Injury, liability for, 322–23

Instalment contracts, 34–35

Insurance of goods, 21, 137–41,
142, 144, 162–67

Intellectual property rights, 24, 444
NAFTA and, 695–98

Intent, determination of, 12–13

Intention to create legal relations, 18

Interest, entitlement to, 37, 96

International Chamber of
Commerce, 79, 121
uniform customs and practice
for letters of credit, 389, 390, 392,
394, 395–96, 398,
399, 400, 402,
403, 406, 409–10,
417–18, 421–42

International commercial arbitration
See Arbitration

International Commercial Trade Terms
See Incoterms

International Convention for the
Unification of Certain Rules of
Law Relating to Bills of Lading
amended (Hague-Visby Rules), 175, 177,
180–200,
210–13, 215
text of, 229–35
Hague Rules, 175–77, 180–200,
210–13, 215
signatories to, 216–18
text of, 218–35
Hamburg Rules, 177–79, 180–200,
210–13, 215
arguments against
introduction of, 201–05
text of, 235–48

International Monetary Fund (IMF), 474, 506

International Trade
  Organisation (ITO),   443, 444

Interpretation
  of ambiguity,   400–02
  of contracts,   88–89, 108–09
  of UN Convention on Contracts
    for the International Sale
    of Goods,   11–12
  of UNIDROIT Principles of
    International Commercial
    Contracts,   82

Interstate Commission,   268–69

Investment,   7
  NAFTA and,   681–88

Invitation to make offers,   15

Irrevocable credits,   390, 391

Judicial review of arbitral awards,   742–50

Jurisdiction
  in carriage of goods by sea,   195–96
  enforcement of arbitration and,   740–41

Knockout rule,   86

Law, sale of goods by
  authority of,   7

Legal relations,
  intention to create,   18

Letters of credit,   387–419, 421–42
  fraud and,   412–16
  ICC uniform customs and
    practice for,   389, 390, 392,
         394, 395–96, 398,
         399, 400, 402,
         403, 406, 409–10,
         417–18, 421–42
  principles of,   397–17
    autonomy principle,   409–17
    strict compliance doctrine,   397–409
    tutorial questions on,   418–19
    types of,   390–97

Lex mercatoria,   79, 82

Licences, import,   717–18

Lien in road transport,   255

Light Vehicles Agreement,   259–62

Linkage of documents,   404–06

Live animals, carriage of,   187–88

Lomé Conventions,   782

Mareva injunctions,   416–17

Market access principle,   574
  NAFTA and,   671–73

Marks of origin,   499–500, 718

Mercantilism,   670

Ministerial Council,   268

Miscarriage in communication,   19–20

Misconduct,   188–89, 309–11

Misdelivery in road transport,   254

Mitigation,   97

Model law on arbitration,   732, 738–39,
         742–46, 754–64

Monetary policy in European
  Union,   710–11

Monopolies,   570

Most-favoured-nation principle
  in GATT,   448–49,
         491–93, 566
  in NAFTA,   689

Multi-modal transport,
  Incoterms and,   123

Mutual recognition principle,   724, 725

Nachfrist,   26, 29, 30

National Road Transport
  Commission,   267–68

National security, NAFTA and,   701

National treatment principle
  in GATT,   449–51,
         493–94, 574–75
  in NAFTA,   671–73, 689

Nautical fault,   188–89

Necessity principle,   721–22

Negligent management, 188–89

Negotiation credits, 392

Negotiations
GATT rounds, 444
pre-contractual, 84–85

New South Wales
regulation of international
commercial arbitration, 733, 746–50
regulation of rail transport in, 290
regulation of road transport in, 269–72

New Zealand
anti-dumping and countervailing
procedures in, 586–88, 590,
591, 603–04,
605, 608, 613
Australia-New Zealand CER
Trade Agreement and, 587–88

Non-contractual liability, Hague
rules and, 185–86

Non-cumulative revolving
credits, 393

Non-performance of contracts, 93–94, 113–19

North American Free Trade
Agreement (NAFTA), 669–703
administration of, 698–99
anti-dumping and countervailing
procedures in, 587
dispute settlement in, 687–88, 700–01
energy/petrochemical
sector in, 675–76
exceptions from, 701
financial services in, 692–94
government procurement
policies in, 676–81
institutional arrangements, 699–700
intellectual property rights in, 695–98
investment in, 681–88
market access for goods in, 671–73
national treatment in, 671–73, 689
rules of origin in, 673–75
service sector trade in, 688–90
telecommunications sector in, 690–92
tutorial questions on, 702–03

Northern Territory, regulation
of road transport in, 283–84

Offer in contracts, 14–17, 85–87

Opinions, EU, 714

Origin
marks of, 499–500, 718
NAFTA and rules of, 673–75

Overriding credits, 396

Package, definition of, 193–94

Parallel negotiations, 84

Partial delivery, 27–28

Passenger tickets, 319–20

Passenger transport
air, 303, 319–20, 322–27
rail, 290, 292–93
road, 255–56, 271–72,
273–74, 276–77,
278–79, 281–82, 283–84

Payments, 28–29, 89–91
of damages, 96
under reserve, 406–08

Penalty clauses, 97

Performance of contracts, 89–91, 110–13
facilitation of, 38
frustration of, 37–38, 93
right to, 94
specific, 20, 25, 29–30, 94

Permits, import, 717–18

Personal injury, liability for, 10

Petrochemical sector,
NAFTA and, 675–76

Place of delivery of goods, 21

Power of sale, 40–41

Pre-contractual negotiations, 84–85

Preferential treatment, GATT and, 456–71

Preservation of goods, duty of, 40–41

Price
anti-dumping and countervailing
procedures and, 782–86
determination of, 89
payment of, 28–29, 89–91
reductions in, 27
retail, 718

Private carriers in road transport, 251–56

Private Key system, 125

Product safety, EU and, 725

Profit margins, 785–86

Property rights
See Intellectual property rights

Property transfer rules, 21, 41

Proportionality principle, 721

Public sector enterprises, 508–09

Public sector procurement, 572
NAFTA and, 676–81

Publication
of NAFTA laws, 698–99
of trade regulations, 500–01

Quality of goods, 22–23

Quantitative restrictions
EU and, 717–18
GATT and, 456,
457–58, 459–63,
501–02, 504–06

Queensland
regulation of rail transport in, 290–91
regulation of road transport in, 275–77

Questions
See Tutorial questions

Rail transport, 284–94, 339–71
Australian federal
regulation of, 284–90
Australian state regulation of, 290–92
international conventions on, 292–94
text of, 339–71
passenger, 290, 292–93

Reason, rule of, 719–20, 723

Reciprocity principle, 451–52

Recognition and enforcement
of arbitration, 735–42,
750–52, 763–64
international convention on, 732,
736–38, 764–68

Recommendations, EU, 714

Red clause credits, 392–93

Regional trading blocs
See Trading blocs

Regulation
See State regulation

Regulations, EU, 711–12

Rejection of offers, 15

Remedies
for breach of contract, 24–28, 29–31
UNIDROIT Principles of
International Commercial
Contracts and, 94–97

Repair of goods, 25

Reserve, payments under, 406–08

Revocable credits, 390

Revolving credits, 393

Risk, passing of, 31–33

Road transport, 250–84,
295–97, 371–83
Australian federal
regulation of, 250, 257–69
Australian state/territory
regulation of, 250, 269–84
common carriers in, 250
contracting out of, 251–53
damages in, 255
delay in, 253–54
deviation from route in, 254
international conventions on, 295–97
text of, 371–83
liability in, 251, 253
lien in, 255
misdelivery in, 254
passenger, 255–56,
271–72, 273–74,
276–77, 278–79,
281–82, 283–84
private carriers in, 251–56
transit and stoppage in, 254

Route, deviation from, 254

Rules of origin, 673–75

Safeguard measures, 604–05

Safety of products, EU and, 725

Sale of goods
breach of contract in, 18–19, 33–34
damages for, 35–37, 95–97
remedies for, 24–28, 29–31
conformity of goods in, 22–24
Incoterms and, 121–53, 155–73
obligations in, 33–41
buyer's, 28–29
seller's, 20–22
passing of risk in, 31–33
UN Convention on Contracts
for the International Sale
of Goods and, 7, 18–41, 54–67

Sea transport, 175–207, 210–48
application of rules on, 182–85
beginning and end of, 190–91
bill of lading and, 124–25
deck cargo, 186–87
definition of package in, 193–94
delay in, 191–92
effect of rules on, 181–82
fire in, 189–90
Hague Rules, 175–77, 180–200,
210–13, 215
signatories to, 216–18
text of, 218–35
Hamburg Rules, 177–79, 180–200,
210–13, 215
arguments against
introduction of, 201–05
text of, 235–48
Incoterms and, 123, 124
jurisdiction/arbitration in, 195–96
liability in, 185–86, 196–200
live animals in, 187–88
nautical fault/negligent
management in, 188–89
time bars to actions in, 193
tutorial questions on, 206–07

Service providers, exclusive, 570

Service sector
financial services, 692–94
NAFTA and, 688–90, 692–94
trade agreement on, 444, 473,
475–80, 565–81

Severability doctrine, 740–41

Ships, 7

Sight credits, 391

South Australia, regulation of
road transport in, 277

Specific performance of contracts, 20, 25,
29–30, 94

Specifications, failure to supply, 30–31

Standards, harmonisation of, 723–25

Standby credits, 393–94

State
assistance to economic
development from, 509–15
government procurement
policies, 572
NAFTA and, 676–81
state trading enterprises, 508–09

State regulation
of air transport, 298–301, 324–25
anti-dumping and
countervailing
procedures, 585–87, 589–90,
597–608, 613
deregulation, 324–25
of international commercial
arbitration, 732–35, 746–50
of rail transport, 284–92
of road transport, 250, 257–84

Stoppage in transit in road transport, 254

Stowaways, 301

Strict compliance doctrine of
letters of credit, 397–409

Subsidies
See also Anti-dumping and
countervailing procedures
EU and, 782–85
GATS and, 573–74
GATT and, 471–73, 508,
594–97, 634–42

Substitute goods, supply of, 25

Substitution drawback systems, 663–64

Tasmania, regulation of road
transport in, 279–82

Taxation, NAFTA and, 701

Technical standards,
harmonisation of, 723–25

Telecommunications sector,
NAFTA and, 690–92

Tender of documents,
acceptance of, 399

Tendering procedures, 678–79

Termination of contracts, 20, 95

Terms and conditions in contracts, 19, 86,
89, 109–10
implied, 22–23
interpretation of, 88–89, 108–09

Third parties
Hague Rules and, 184–85
pre-contractual negotiations and, 84
sale of goods and, 24
use of Incoterms and, 124

Third World
See Developing countries

Time
acceptance/rejection of tender
of documents and, 399
conformity of goods and, 23–24
of delivery, 22, 23, 28
extra time as remedy for
breach of contract, 26, 29, 30
time bars for actions, 193, 289, 318

Trade usages, 13

Trading blocs
EU, 705–28
NAFTA, 587, 669–703

Transferable credits, 394–96

Transit, freedom of, 495–96

Transit and stoppage in transit
in road transport, 254

Transport
See Carriage of goods

Tutorial questions
anti-dumping and countervailing
procedures, 610–12

arbitration, 752
carriage of goods by land/air, 327–29
carriage of goods by sea, 206–07
EU, 726–28
extraterritorial control of
business, 801–03
GATT/WTO, 480–81
Incoterms, 152–53
letters of credit, 418–19
NAFTA, 702–03
UN Convention on Contracts
for the International Sale
of Goods, 41–44
UNIDROIT Principles of
International Commercial
Contracts, 98–99

Unconfirmed credits, 390

UNIDROIT Principles of
International Commercial
Contracts, 79, 80–99
content of contracts and, 89, 109–10
contract law and, 82–84
force majeure and, 91, 92–93
formation of contracts and, 85–87, 102–05
hardship and, 91–92, 113
interpretation of contracts and, 88–89,
108–09
non-performance of contracts
and, 93–94, 113–19
performance of contracts and, 89–91,
110–13
pre-contractual
negotiations and, 84–85
remedies and, 94–97
text of, 100–19
tutorial questions on, 98–99
validity of contracts and, 87–88, 105–08

Uniform Customs and Practice
for Letters of Credit, 389, 390,
392, 394,
395–96, 398,
399, 400, 402,
403, 406, 409–10,
417–18, 421–42

Uniform Law on International
Sale of Goods,   1

Unit, definition of,   193–94

United Nations Commission on
International Trade Law
(UNCITRAL),   1, 79
    model law on arbitration,   732, 738–39,
       742–46, 754–64

United Nations Convention on
Contracts for the International
Sale of Goods,   1-44, 79–80
    contract provisions in,   7, 8–10,
       14–18, 52–54
    exclusions from,   7-11
    general provisions of,   11–13, 50–52
    sale of goods provisions in,   7, 18–41, 54–67
    signatories to,   1, 46–47
    sphere of application on,   3-11, 50–52
    text of,   48–70
    tutorial questions on,   41–44

United Nations Economic and
Social Council (ECOSOC),   443

United States of America
    See also North American Free
    Trade Agreement
    anti-dumping and
       countervailing
       procedures in,   585–86,
       588–89,
       590–91, 597–98,
       605–07, 613
    competition policy in,   773, 798–800

Usages
    See also Incoterms
    agreement to,   13

Validity of contracts,   87–88, 105–08

Valuation
    anti-dumping and countervailing
       procedures and,   782–86
    for customs purposes,   497–99

Vehicle operations, regulation of,   262–64

Vertical agreements,   770

Victoria
    regulation of rail transport in,   291–92
    regulation of road transport in,   273–75

Vienna Convention
    See United Nations Convention
    on Contracts for the International
    Sale of Goods

Warsaw Convention
    See Convention for the Unification
    of Certain Rules Relating to
    International Carriage by Air

Western Australia
    regulation of rail transport in,   292
    regulation of road transport in,   277–79

World Bank,   474

World Trade Organisation (WTO),   444, 445,
       473–80
    Agreement Establishing,   473–74,
       484–90, 670
    dispute settlement
       understanding in,   474, 544–65
    General Agreement on Trade
       in Services (GATS) and,   444,
       473, 475–80,
       565–81, 689
    significance of,   474–75

Writing, requirements of,   13, 735